ISBN 978-1-5277-6947-2
PIBN 10889731

English
Français
Deutsche
Italiano
Español
Português

www.forgottenbooks.com

Mythology Photography **Fiction**
Fishing Christianity **Art** Cooking
Essays Buddhism Freemasonry
Medicine **Biology** Music **Ancient**
Egypt Evolution Carpentry Physics
Dance Geology **Mathematics** Fitness
Shakespeare **Folklore** Yoga Marketing
Confidence Immortality Biographies
Poetry **Psychology** Witchcraft
Electronics Chemistry History **Law**
Accounting **Philosophy** Anthropology
Alchemy Drama Quantum Mechanics
Atheism Sexual Health **Ancient History**
Entrepreneurship Languages Sport
Paleontology Needlework Islam
Metaphysics Investment Archaeology
Parenting Statistics Criminology
Motivational

THE

ANGLER'S DIARY

AND

Tourist Fisherman's Gazetteer

OF THE

RIVERS AND LAKES OF THE WORLD.

By J. E. B. C.,

EDITOR OF "FACTS AND USEFUL HINTS RELATING TO FISHING AND SHOOTING,"
AND AUTHOR OF "THE GAMEKEEPER'S AND GAME PRESERVER'S
ACCOUNT BOOK AND DIARY," ETC.

PRICE EIGHTEENPENCE.

LONDON:
HORACE COX,
"THE FIELD" OFFICE, WINDSOR HOUSE, BREAM'S BUILDINGS, E.C.

1907.

ENRIGHT'S
"GREENHEART" RODS
Fly-Casting.

Mr. John Enright, using the above rods, won the **CHAMPIONSHIP OF THE WORLD** open to all-comers on Harlem Lake, New York City, U.S.A., October 12 and 13, 1906, making Three World Records.

English Tournament, 1904.

The "Professional" & "Amateur" Championships were won with "Enright's" Rods. N.B.— The ONLY two double-handed events in programme.

American Tournament, 1906.

Mr. John Enright's World Record with an "Enright" 14ft. Rod is

42 yds.

Mr. Enright is also Holder of the BRITISH RECORD CAST with Single-handed Rod, distance 34yds. 2ft., and is the only man in the world who has ever thrown over 50yds. at a Tournament (British or American) in an Exhibition Cast.

Catalogue, "Best in the World" Rods, from

JOHN ENRIGHT & SON, CASTLECONNELL, IRELAND.

BALA LAKE.

WHITE LION ROYAL HOTEL,

BALA, NORTH WALES.

THIS Hotel has been RE-FURNISHED throughout, and no expense has been spared to provide every comfort and convenience to visitors.

Boarding terms from October to May, except Easter week, 49*s.* per week. Easter week, and the remaining months, 63*s.* per week.

The fishing has much improved from the rigid observance of the close time, and the preservation insisted upon by the landed proprietors. (See page 171.)

Free Trout Fishing on the Treweryn river, which is strictly preserved for Visitors staying in the Hotel.

Pleasure boats are kept for the use of visitors to this hotel.

Bala, from its elevation above sea level (about 700 feet), and its lake four and a half miles long, affords a beneficial change of air not to be found elsewhere in the kingdom. Epidemics are unknown.

Bala is the Nearest Station to the Vyrnwy Lake, which is well worthy of a visit. The scenery in the neighbourhood is both beautiful and grand.

Any inquiries respecting the neighbourhood, private lodging accommodation, &c., will receive prompt attention from the Proprietor, if stamp is inclosed.　　　　　　　　　　　　　　WILLIAM OWEN.

The **PLASCOCH HOTEL** is also under the same management at a lower tariff.

THE

ANGLER'S DIARY

AND

TOURIST FISHERMAN'S GAZETTEER

OF THE

RIVERS AND LAKES OF THE WORLD;

TO WHICH ARE ADDED

FORMS FOR REGISTERING THE FISH TAKEN DURING THE YEAR.

By J. E. B. C.,

EDITOR OF "FACTS AND USEFUL HINTS RELATING TO FISHING AND SHOOTING."

LONDON:

HORACE COX,

THE "FIELD" OFFICE, WINDSOR HOUSE,

BREAM'S BUILDINGS, E.C.

1907.

HOWIETOUN FISHERY.

THE

HISTORY OF HOWIETOUN.

CONTAINING A

FULL DESCRIPTION

OF THE VARIOUS

HATCHING-HOUSES AND PONDS, AND OF THE EXPERIMENTS UNDERTAKEN FROM 1873 TO 1886.

AND ALSO OF

THE FISH CULTURAL WORK

AND THE

MAGNIFICENT RESULTS OBTAINED.

BY THE LATE

Sir J. RAMSAY-GIBSON-MAITLAND, Bart.,

F.L.S., F.G.S., F.Z.S., &c., &c., the Founder of the Howietoun Fishery.

HOWIETOUN FISHERY,

STIRLING, N.B.,

Is now the largest piscicultural establishment in the world, producing over twenty millions trout ova yearly. Stocking water by means of artificial redds sown with eyed ova has been most successful. For Price List of two-year-old and yearling trout, and of ova, apply to

HOWIETOUN FISHERY CO., STIRLING.

PAMPHLET ON STOCKING, 5th Edition, price 6d.

CONTENTS.

RIVERS AND THEIR STATIONS.

ENGLAND.

Rivers and their Tributaries.			Stations.
ADUR (Sussex)	... ...		Burgess Hill, Hassock Gate, Henfield, Billinghurst, Grinstead. Partridge Green Steyning, Bramber, New Shoreham
AIRE	*Malham Tarn..*	....	Settle or Bellbusk.
	Gardale Beck ..	....	Bellbusk.
	Kirk Gill Beck	....	Bellbusk.
	Eshton Tarn ..	....	Bellbusk.
	Otterburn Beck	....	Long Preston.
....		*Inglebeck*	Bellbusk.
		....	Bellbusk.
	Conniston House Lake	....	Bellbusk.
.. . .		....	Gargrave.
	Eshton Beck ..	*Mill Beck ...*	Gargrave.
	Butler How Pond	....	Gargrave.
	Elslack Brook..	....	Barnoldswicke Junction, Earby, Thornton, Elslack.
....		....	Skipton.
	Ellerbeck	....	Skipton.
....		....	Cononley, Kildwick
	Eastbourne Brk.	*Cowcloughton Dam*	Kildwick.
....	....		Steeton.
	Silsden Beck ..	....	Steeton.
....		....	Keighley.
	Worth	....	Oakworth.
		Oxenhope Beck	Oakworth.
....			Ingrow, Keighley.
		Keighley Moor Pond	Keighley.
	Moulton Beck..	....	Bingley.
. ...	....	....	Bingley.
	Harden Beck ..	*Denholme Resr.*	Denholme.
	....	....	Cullingworth, Bingley.
. ...	....	....	Shipley.
	Bradford Beck	....	Thornton.
		Clayton Beck..	Thornton.
		Denby Pond ..	Thornton.
	....	....	Bradford, Shipley.
....		....	Baildon.
	Gill Beck	....	Baildon.
....		....	Esholt.
	Yeadon Beck ..	*Yeadon Moor Pond*	Guiseley, Esholt.
....		....	Calverley, Newlay.
	Oldmill Brook .	....	Newlay.
....		....	Bickstall, Leeds.
	Farmley Brook	....	Bramley, Leeds.

The Angler's Diary.

ENGLAND—*continued.*

RIVERS AND THEIR TRIBUTARIES.			STATIONS.
AIRE (cont.) ..	Addle Beck ..	Bushes Farm Pond	Arthington.
	Black Hill Dam	....	Arthington.
	Addle Dam ..	....	Arthington.
	Addle Beck....	....	Leeds.
....	....	....	Hunslet.
	Killing Beck ..	Roundhay Park Lake	Leeds.
	....	....	Hunslet.
....	....	....	Woodlesford.
	Rothwell Beck..	....	Woodlesford.
....	....	....	Methley.
	Hollin Beck ..	....	Methley.
	....	....	Castleford.
	Calder..........	....	Hulme, Portsmouth.
		Redmires Dam	Todmorden.
	....	....	Todmorden, Eastwood, Hebden
		{ Calderclough Beck	
		{ Nodale Dam ..	Hebden.
		{ Hebden	
		Widdop Water	Hebden.
		Gorple Water..	Hebden.
		Wadsworth Beck	Hebden.
		Horsebridge Beck	Hebden.
		{ Hebden	Hebden.
	....	....	Luddenden Foot.
		{ Luddenden Beck	
		{ Cold Edge Dam	Luddenden.
	....	....	Sowerby Bridge.
		Ribourne ...	Rishworth, Sowerby Bridge.
	....	....	Elland.
		Dean	Rishworth, Stainland, Elland.
	....	....	Brighouse, Cooper Bridge.
		{ Colne	
		Wissenden Res.	Marsden.
		March Hill Res.	Marsden.
		Colne	Slaithwaite.
		Slaithwaite Common Pond	Slaithwaite.
		{ Colne	Longwood, Huddersfield.
		{ Holme	
		{ Bilbury Res.	Holmfirth.
		{ Holmesley Res.	Holmfirth.
		{ Holme Res...	Hurley, Meltham.
		{ Holme	Huddersfield.
		Colne	Deighton.
		Burton Beck ..	Kirkburton, Deighton.
		Colne	Cooper Bridge.
	....	....	Mirfield, Dewsbury, Horbury.
		Chevel Pk. Lake	Sandal.
	....	....	Wakefield.
		{ Walton Beck	
		{ Cold Hindley Reservoir	Ryhill.
		{ Walton Park Lake	Sandal.
		{ Walton	Sandal, Wakefield.
	....	....	Stanley, Castleford.
	....	....	Knottingley, Temple Hurst, Snaith, Rawcliffe.
ALDE	....	....	Saxmundham.
	Ore	Framlingham Pond	Framlingham.
	....	....	Parham, Marlesford.
....	....	....	Snape.
	Saxmundham Brk.	....	Saxmundham, Snape.
....	....	....	Aldborough, Orford.
ALLER	....	....	Porlock.
ALNE	....	....	Alnwick.

ENGLAND—*continued.*

RIVERS AND THEIR TRIBUTARIES.			STATIONS.
ALPHINGTON ..	.. ..	.. ..	Exeter.
	Adder Water ..	.. ..	Exeter.
ALT	*Knowsley Park Lake*	.. ..	Prescot, West Derby.
	Flukers Brook ..	.. ..	Kirkby.
	Simonswood Bk.	.. ..	Kirkby.
.. ..	.. ..	.. ..	Kirkby.
	Lydiate Brook ..	.. ..	Aintree, Sefton, Lydiate.
.. ..	.. ..	.. ..	Altcar.
	Downholland Bk.	.. ..	Barton, Altcar.
.. ..	.. ..	.. ..	Hightown.
ANCHOLME	*Ancholme Head*	.. ..	Lincoln, Market Rasen.
	Rase	.. ..	Market Rasen.
	Owersby Drain	.. ..	Holton Moor.
.. ..	.. ..	.. ..	Scawby.
	North Kelsey Beck	.. ..	Howsham, Scawby.
.. ..	.. ..	.. ..	Brigg, Appleby.
	Broughton Decoy	.. ..	Appleby.
ANNASIDE BK.	*Bootle Beck* ..	.. ..	Bootle.
ARUN (Sussex)	.. ..	.. ..	Horsham.
	Channel Brook.	.. ..	Horsham.
.. ..	.. ..	.. ..	Itheringfield, Slynfold, Rudgwick, Billinghurst, Haslemere, Pulborough.
	Rother	.. ..	Liss, Petersfield, Rogate, Elstead, Liphook, Midhurst, Petworth, Pulborough.
.. ..	.. ..	.. ..	Amberley, Arundel, Ford, Goring, Angmering, Littlehampton.
AVON (Devon).	.. ..	.. ..	Brent, Loddiswell.
AVON (Hants).	.. ..	.. ..	Devizes, Woodborough, Porton, Salisbury.
	Wylye	.. ..	Warminster, Heytesbury, Codford, Wylye, Wishford, Wilton.
		Nadder	Shaftesbury, Tisbury, Dinton, Wilton.
	.. ..	.. ..	Salisbury.
	Winterbourne ...	.. ..	Grateley, Porton, Salisbury.
	Chalk Stream ...	.. ..	Tisbury.
.. ..	.. ..	.. ..	Downton, Braemore, Fordingbridge, Ringwood, Christchurch.
AVON (Somrst.)	.. ..	.. ..	Tetbury, Minety. [wood, Christchurch.
	Dauntsey Brook	.. ..	Dauntsey.
	Thunder Brook	.. ..	Wootton Bassett, Dauntsey.
.. ..	.. ..	.. ..	Chippenham.
	Marden	.. ..	Calne, Chippenham.
	Corsham Lake.	.. ..	Corsham.
.. ..	.. ..	.. ..	Melksham, Holt.
	Seende Brook ..	.. ..	Devizes, Seende, Westbury, Melksham.
	Biss	.. ..	Westbury, Frome, Trowbridge.
.. ..	.. ..	.. ..	Bradford, Freshford.
	Frome	.. ..	Witham, Frome.
		Lechmere Water	Binegar.
	Freshford Brook	.. ..	Freshford.
.. ..	.. ..	.. ..	Limpley.
	Norton Brook ..	.. ..	Hallatrow, Midsomer Norton.
		Chilcompton Brook	Chilcompton, Midsomer Norton.
	.. ..	.. ..	Radstock, Wellow, Midford.
		Wellow Brook ..	Hallatrow, Wellow, Midford.
	.. ..	.. ..	Limpley.
.. ..	.. ..	.. ..	Bathampton.
	Box Brook	.. ..	Box, Bathampton.
	.. ..	.. ..	Bathampton.
.. ..	.. ..	.. ..	Bath, Weston, Twiverton, Kelston, Saltford
	Boyd	.. ..	Yate.
		Feltham Brook	Mangotsfield.
	.. ..	.. ..	Warmley, Britton.
.. ..	.. ..	.. ..	Keynsham.
	Chew	.. ..	Hallatrow, Clutton.
		Clutton Brook ..	Clutton.
	.. ..	.. ..	Pensford, Keynsham.

ENGLAND—*continued.*

RIVERS AND THEIR TRIBUTARIES.			STATIONS.
Avon (Somrst.)	*Siston Brook* ..	....	Mangotsfield, Warmley, Britton.
(*cont.*)	....	....	Brislington.
....	....	....	Bristol.
Ax	....	....	Wookey, Lodge Hill.
	Stoke Lakes ..	....	Draycot.
	Chedder Water	....	Chedder.
	....	....	Axbridge.
	Loxton Brook .	....	Winscombe.
Axe	....	....	Misterton, Crewkerne.
	Chard Brook ..	....	Chard.
....	....	....	Chard Junction, Axminster.
....	*Yarty*	....	Ilminster, Axminster.
.. ..	....	....	Colyton, Colyford.
	Coly	....	Honiton, Seaton Junction, Colyton.
		Offwell Brook ..	Honiton, Colyton.
.. ..	....	....	Colyford.
.. ..	....	....	Seaton.
BAIN	....	....	Horncastle.
BALINGLEY	....	*Hillington Hall Lake*	Castle Rising.
BASSEN- THWAITELAKE	. ...	.. ..	Peel Wyke.
BEAME (Essex).	....	....	Romford, Rainham.
	Dagenham Lake	....	Rainham.
BEAULIEU	....	.. ..	Beaulieu.
BELA	*Sunday Beck* ..	....	Oxenholme.
	Beehive Beck ..	*Hayfell Tarn* ...	Kendal.
	....	....	Oxenholme.
	....	....	Milnthorpe.
	Peasey or Hutton Beck ..	*Lily Mere*	Sedbergh.
		Killington Res.	Sedbergh.
		....	Oxenholme.
		{ *Lupton Beck* ..	
		{ *Tarnhouse Tarn*	Kirkby Lonsdale.
		{ *Terrybank Tarn*	Kirkby Lonsdale.
		{ *Lupton Beck* ..	Kirkby Lonsdale.
		....	Milnthorpe.
	.. ..	....	Milnthorpe.
BENACRE BROAD	....	....	Southwold.
BERRY WATER	....	.. ..	Ilfracombe.
BIDEFORD BRK.	.. ..	....	Aure.
	Blackpool Brk.	....	Speechhouse, Aure.
BILLOW BROOK	....	.. ..	Berkeley.
BLACKANTON ..	.. ..	....	Slapton Ley.
	Slapton Ley ..	....	Slapton Ley.
BLACK BECK	....	....	Green Road.
BLACKPOOL ..	.. ..	....	Stoke Flemming.
BLACKWATER (Essex).	....	.. ..	Saffron Walden, Braintree, Kelvedon, Witham.
	Pod's Brook ..	....	Braintree, Bulford, Witham.
....	....	....	Wickham, Langford, Malden.
	Chelmer	....	Dunmow, Felsted, Chelmsford.
		Cann	Chipping Ongar, Ingatestone, Chelmsford, Langford, Malden.
BLAKENEY	....	....	New Walsingham.
BLYTH	*Haveringham Park Lake* ..	....	Halesworth.
	Wisset Brook ..	....	Halesworth.
....	....	....	Wenhaston.
	Stoven Brook ..	....	Southwold.
....	....	....	Southwold.
BOLDRE (Hants).	....	.. ..	Holmsley, Lyndhurst, Brockenhurst, Lymington.
BOSCASTLE BRK.	.. ..	....	Forraburry.

ENGLAND.—*continued.*

RIVERS AND THEIR TRIBUTARIES.			STATIONS
BRADING (I. of W.).	....	....	Wroxhall, Horringford, Newchurch, Brading, Alverstone, Sandown.
BRANSCOMBE ..	....	....	Beer.
BRAUNTON	....	....	Mortehoe Station, Braunton.
	Knowle Water..	....	Braunton.
BREAM	....	....	Victoria, Bridges.
	Luxulion Water	....	Bridges.
....	....	....	St. Blazey, Par.
BREEDY	....	....	Burton Bradstock.
BRITT	....	....	Toller, Bridport.
	Asker	....	Porstock, Bridport.
BRIXHAM	....	....	Brixham.
BRUE	*Combe*	....	Bruton.
	Cambe	....	Bruton.
....	....	....	Cole.
	Shepton Brook .	....	Cole.
....	....	....	Castle Carey.
	Evercreech Brk.	....	Evercreech, Evercreech Junction, Castle Carey.
....	....	....	Glastonbury.
	Wootton Brook	....	Pennard, Glastonbury.
....	....	....	Meare.
	Godney Brook	....	Shepton Mallet, Wells, Polsham, Meare.
....	....	....	Shapwick, Edington, Woolavington, Highbridge.
BUDE	....	....	Holsworthy, Bude.
BUDOAK WTR.	....	....	Falmouth.
BURE	*Melton Pk. Lake*	....	Hindolvestone.
....	*Thurning Hall Lake*........	....	Corpusty.
....	....	....	Corpusty.
	Appletree Plantation Ponds	....	Aylsham.
	{ *Aldborough Beck*	....	Cromer.
	{ *Aldborough Mill Pond*........	....	Aylsham.
		Barningham Park Lake ..	Corpusty.
	....	....	Corpusty.
	Blickling Lake..	....	Aylsham.
....	....	....	Aylsham.
	{ *Gunton Beck*		
	{ *Gunton Pk. Lake*	....	Gunton.
	{ *Gunton*	....	Felmingham, Buxton.
	{ *Stoke Beck*		
	Perch Pond and Mill Pond Heath Plantation ..	....	North Walsham.
	Scotton Pond ..	....	Worstead.
	{ *Stoke*	....	Buxton.
....	*Spixworth Beck*	....	Coltishall, Wroxham.
	Brickfield Broad	....	Drayton.
	Belaugh Broad .	....	Wroxham.
	Little Belaugh Broad	....	Wroxham.
	Bridge Broad..	....	Wroxham.
	Knapes Water..	....	Wroxham.
	Wroxham Brd.	....	Wroxham.
	Hoveton Gt. Brd.	....	Wroxham.
	Salhouse Broad	....	Salhouse.
	Decoy or Woodbastwick Brd.	....	Salhouse.
	Little Hoveton Broad	....	Wroxham.

ENGLAND—*continued.*

Rivers and their Tributaries.			Stations.
BURE (*cont.*) ..	*Hoveton Brook.*	....	Wroxham.
	Hoveton Hall Lake		
	Burnt Fen Brd.	....	Wroxham.
	King's Water ..	....	Wroxham.
	Hoveton Broad	....	Wroxham.
	Little Broad ..	....	Salhouse.
	Ranworth Brd.	....	Salhouse.
	Ant	*Antingham Ponds*	North Walsham.
		Dilham Lake ..	Horning.
		Worstead House Lake........	Worstead.
		Stalham Broad	Stalham.
		Barton Broad..	Catfield.
		Beeston Hall Lake	Wroxham.
		Oliver Broad ..	Wroxham.
	Fleet Dyke	*Peaty Mill Dam*	Salhouse.
		Walsham Broad	Salhouse.
	Hundred Stream or Thurne ..	*Martham Broad*	Martham.
		Horsey Mere ..	Martham.
		Hickling, Chapman, & Whitesley Broads ..	Potter Higham.
		Wormack Broad	Catfield.
....	....	....	Acle.
	Muck Fleet	*Ormsby, Rollesby, & Filby Broads*	Ormsby.
	Turnstall Dyke	*Acle Decoy*	Acle.
....	....	....	Yarmouth.
BURY BROOK ..	....	....	Cheriton.
CAERLEON	....	.. ..	Ruan Minor.
	Croft Pascoe Pool	....	Ruan Minor.
	Leech Pool	....	Ruan Minor.
CAM BROOK	....	.. ..	Dursley, Cam, Dursley Junction.
	Ham Brook ..	....	Dursley Junction.
	Slimbridge Brk.	....	Frocester.
CAMEL	.. ..	....	Bodmin.
	Kirland Water	.. ..	Bodmin.
	Lanivet Water	....	Bodmin.
	Withiel Water ..	....	Victoria, Bodmin.
	Kestle Water ..	.. ..	Wades Bridge.
	.. ..	.. ..	Wades Bridge.
	Manscowe Brk.	....	Wades Bridge.
	Combe Water ..	....	Wades Bridge.
CAPEL BROOK ..	....	....	Capel, Bentley.
	Stutton Mill Pond	....	Manningtree.
CARRY	.. ..	....	Castle Carey, Sparkford, Langport, Bridgwater.
CHAR	.. ..	....	Charmouth.
CLIST	.. ..	....	Hele, Broad Clist.
	South Brook ..	.. ..	Whimple, Broad Clist.
	Halbrook	....	Broad Clist.
.. ..	....	.. ..	Topsham.
	Greendale Brook	....	Topsham.
COCKER	....	....	Bay Horses, Cockerham.
COLNE	....	....	Yeldham, Hedingham, Halstead.
	Gosfield Brook.	*Gosfield Hall Lake*	Halstead.
....	....	....	Colne.
	Pebmarsh Brook	....	Colne.
....	....	....	Chapple, Colchester.

ENGLAND—*continued.*

RIVERS AND THEIR TRIBUTARIES.			STATIONS.
CONDOR	....	....	Lancaster.
	Rowton Brook ..	....	Lancaster.
....	....	....	Galgate, Condor Green.
CONE BROOK	....	.. ..	Woolaston.
COQUET	....	....	Acklington, Felton, Harbottle, Holystone Rothbury. Weldon Bridge, Warkworth.
CORFE	.. ..	....	Wareham.
	Byle Brook	....	Wareham.
... .	.. ..	Poole.
CORYINACK ..	.. ..	....	St. Mawes.
COSTAR	.. ..	.. ..	Costar.
CROUCH AND ROACH (Essex)	....	.. ..	Burnham, Southend.
CRUGSIBLACK	.. ..	.. ..	Veryan.
CUCKMARE	.. ..	.. ..	Hailsham, Berwick.
DARENTH .... (Kent).	....	.. ..	Dunton Green, Sevenoaks, Otford, Shoreham, Eynesford, Dartford.
	Cray	.. ..	Orpington, St. Mary's Cray, Bexley, Crayford, Dartford.
DARK WATER	.. ..	.. ..	Fawley.
DART (Devon)	.. ..	.. ..	Princetown, Ashburton, Buckfastleigh Staverton, Totnes, Dartmouth.
DARWEN	....	.. ..	Over Darwen, Lower Darwen, Mill Hill, Cherrytree, Fenniscowles.
	Roddlesworth ..	*Rivington Res.*	Chorley, Brinscall, Withnell, Fenniscowles.
.. ..	.. ..	.. ..	Houghton, Preston.
DAWLISH	.. ..	....	Dawlish.
DEBEN	....	....	Debenham.
	Potford Brook	....	Wickham Market.
....	....	....	Wickham Market.
	Ash Abbey Decoy	....	Wickham Market.
....	....	....	Melton, Woodbridge.
	Fyn	....	Bealings.
		Playford Mere	Bealings.
		Otley Brook ..	Bealings.
	....	....	Woodbridge.
DEE	*Afon-yr-Wynt* ..	....	Llannwchllyn.
	Dwfrdwy	....	Llannwchllyn.
	Twrch	*Llyn Uiwobran* ..	Llannwchllyn.
	{ *Bala Lake* ..	....	Llannwchllyn.
	{ *Llafar*	....	Llannwchllyn.
	{ *Rhydwen* ..	.. ..	Llannwchllyn.
	(*Bala Lake*	....	Bala.
	....	....	Bala.
	Tryweryn	*Llyn Trywerryn*	Arenig.
		Llyn Arenig ..	Arenig.
		{ *Gelyn*	
		{ *Llyn Arenigbach*	Arenig.
		{ *Hescyn*	Arenig, Frongoch.
		(*Llyn Hescyn* ..	
	....	....	Frongoch, Bala.
	Corgnaut	....	Bala.
	Meloch	.. ..	Bala.
	Hirnant	....	Bala.
		Cymmerig	Bala.
	Caletwr	....	Llanderfel.
	....	....	Llanderfel, Llandicillo.
	Cendiog	....	Llandicillo.
	Llyn Mynyllod.	....	Llandicillo.
	Llynor	....	Llandicillo.
	....	....	Cynwyd.
	Trystion	....	Cynwyd.
	Alwen	*Llyn Alwen*	Bettws-y-Coed.

ENGLAND—*continued.*

RIVERS AND THEIR TRIBUTARIES.			STATIONS.
DEE *(cont.)*..		Llyn-dau-Ychen	Cerrig-y-Druidion.
		{ Brenig:	
		{ Llyn Llymbran .	Denbigh.
		....	Llanfihangel Glyn-Myfyr.
		Derwcyd	Llanfihangel Glyn-Myfyr.
		....	Maerdy.
		Geirw	Cerrig-y-Druidion.
		{ Merddwr	
		{ Llyn Grwyni ..	Llanderfel.
		{ Geirw	Maerdy.
		Ffranan	Maerdy.
	Dwr	....	Gwyddelwern.
....	....	....	Corwen.
	Trewyn	....	Corwen.
	Camladd......	....	Corwen.
	Alechog	....	Corwen.
....	....	....	Carrog.
	Merwynion....	....	Carrog.
....	....	....	Glyndyfrdwy, Berwyn.
	Berwyn	....	Berwyn.
....	....	....	Llangollen, Trevor, Cefn
	Wynnstay Park Lakes	....	Ruabon, Cefn.
	Ceiriog	....	Carrog.
		Chirk Pk. Lake	Chirk.
	....	....	Chirk.
		Morlas	Prysgwaen.
	....	....	Cefn.
	Shell Brook ..	....	Ellesmere.
	Clywedog	Llyn-Mawr-y-Mynydd ...。	Brymbo.
	....	....	Wrexham.
		Saddle Brook..	Wrexham.
		Wrexham Brook	Wrexham.
	Worthenbury Bk.	Llyn Bedydd ..	Bettisfield.
		Hanmer Hall Lake	Bettisfield.
		Hanmere Mere	Bettisfield.
		Bettisfield Park Lakes	Bettisfield.
	Halghton Mill Ponds	....	Fenns Bank.
		Halghton Brook	Ellesmere.
		{ Sarn	
		{ Wolversacre	
		{ Mill Pond	Whitchurch.
		{ Dirtwich Mill	
		{ Pond	Whitchurch.
....	....	....	Holt.
	Alyn	....	Eyearth.
		Rhys	Eyearth.
		Llyn Cyffynny	Eyearth.
	....	....	Rhyd-y-Mwyn.
		Fechlas Brook	Rhyd-y-Mwyn.
	....	....	Mold, Llong.
		{ Ferrig........	
		{ Llyn-y-Mynydd-	
		{ du	Llong.
		{ Llyn Neym	Llong.
		{ Ferrig........	Llong.
	....	....	Hope
		Eadyn	Brymbo, Hope.
....	....	....	Gresford, Rosset, Holt.
	Pulford Brook	....	Rosset.
	Holywell Edge Mill Pond ..	....	Malpas.
	Holywell	....	Broxton.
		Keys Brook ..	Tattenhall.

ENGLAND—*continued.*

RIVERS AND THEIR TRIBUTARIES.			STATIONS.
DEE (*cont.*) ..	*Eaton Hall Lakes*	....	Chester.
....	....	....	Chester.
DERWENT	*Sprinkling Tarn*	....	Wastdale Head Hotel.
(Cumb.)	*Styhead Tarn..*	....	Wastdale Head Hotel.
	....	....	Rosthwaite.
.. ..	*Stonethwaite Bk.*	*Angle Tarn* ..	Wastdale Head Hotel.
			Rosthwaite.
....	....	....	Borrowdale.
	Derwent Water	....	Borrowdale.
		Watendlath Bk.	
		Blea Tarn	
		Watendlath Tn.	Borrowdale.
		Brockle Beck ..	Keswick.
....	....	....	Keswick.
	Greta or Glen-	*Troutbeck*	Troutbeck.
	dermakin ..	*Mosedale Beck*	Threlkeld.
		....	Threlkeld.
		St. John's or	
		Wyth Beck ..	
		Dale Head Tn.	
		Harrop Tarn..	Threlkeld.
		Thirlmere	
		Naddle Beck ..	Threlkeld.
		Glenderaterra	
		Beck......	Threlkeld.
....	....	....	Keswick.
	Bassenthwaite		
	Lake		Keswick.
		Newlands Beck	Borrowdale.
		Little Dale Bk.	
		Rigg Beck	
		Coledale Beck	Braithwaite.
....	....	....	Bassenthwaite.
		Dash Beck....	Bassenthwaite.
	Isell Beck	....	Cockermouth.
....	....	....	Cockermouth.
	Cocker........	*Buttermere Lk.*	Buttermere.
		Bleaberry Tarn	Buttermere.
....	....	*Crummock Wtr.*	Buttermere, Scale Hill.
		Mosedale Beck	Scale Hill.
		Floutern Tarn	
		Lowes Water ..	
....	*Whit Beck*	....	Scale Hill.
.. ..	....	....	Scale Hill.
.. . .	*Doverby Beck* ..	....	Cockermouth.
	Ellerbeck	....	Brigham.
		....	Brigham.
....	*Marron*	....	Brigham.
		....	Marron Junction.
		Scallow Beck ..	Rowrah.
		Woodbeck	Rowrah.
....	....	....	Rowrah.
		Mockerkin Trn.	Wright Green, Ullock.
.. ..	....	....	Ullock.
	Lostrigg Beck ..	....	Branthwaite, Marron Junction.
....	....	....	Branthwaite, Marron Junction.
			Camerton, Workington.
	....		Hackness.
(York)	*Jugger Howe Beck*	....	Fyling Hall.
		Helwath Beck ..	Peak.
		Bloody Beck ..	Hackness.
	Black Beck....	....	Hackness.
		Stockland Beck	Hackness.
		Hipper Beck ..	Hackness.
		Deep Dale Beck	Hackness.
	Troutsdale Beck	....	Hackness.
	Lowdales Beck .	....	Hackness.

ENGLAND—*continued.*

RIVERS AND THEIR TRIBUTARIES.			STATIONS
DERWENT (*cont.*)	....	....	Ayton, Ganton.
	Helford River.	....	Gristhorpe, Filey, Cayton, Ganton.
....	*Rustin or Beedale Beck*	....	Wykeham.
		Sawdon Beck..	Sawdon, Wykeham.
	....	....	Ganton.
	Brompton Beck	....	Wykeham.
....	....	....	Yedingham.
	Scampston Beck	*Winteringham Pond*	Rillington, Yedingham.
	Scampston Pk.Lake		[Yedingham.
	Thornton Beck	....	Levisham, Wilton, Thornton Dale,
....	....	....	Rillington.
....	*Rye*	....	Helmsley.
	Prodale Beck..		Helmsley.
	Wheat Beck ..		Helmsley.
	Blow Gill Beck		Helmsley.
	Ladhill Beck..		Helmsley.
	{ *Seph* *Raisdale Beck.*		Stokesley.
	Billsdale Beck..		Stokesley.
	} *Seph* *Ledge Beck....*		Helmsley.
	Seph		Helmsley.
	....	....	Helmsley, Nunnington.
	Riccal		Helmsley.
	{ *Dove*		Kirkby Moorside.
	Hodge Beck ..		Kirkby Moorside.
	Dore		Helmsley.
	Hole Beck		Gilling, Hovingham.
	ColtonMill' Pond		
	Marrs Beck ..		Hovingham.
	Wath Beck....		Hovingham.
	Park Lakes ..		Slingsby.
	Seven		Sinnington.
	Northdale Beck		Sinnington.
	Harloft Beck..		Sinnington.
	Sutherland Beck		Sinnington.
	Catter or Rudland Beck ..		Kirkby Moorside
	Seven		Sinnington.
	....	....	Malton.
	{ *Costa Beck....*		Pickering.
	Kirkby Misperton Pond....		Pickering.
	{ *Pickering Bk.*		Levisham.
	Levisham Bk.		Levisham.
	Pickering ..		Pickering.
	Costa		Pickering.
	....	....	Rillington
	Settington Brk	*Settington Lake*	Malton.
	....	....	Malton.
	Welham Pond..	....	Malton.
....	....	....	Huttons Ambo.
	Menethorpe Beck.	*Birdsall Ings Pnd*	Wharram, Huttons Ambo.
	Howl Beck....	....	Huttons Ambo.
	Mill Beck	....	Huttons Ambo.
....	....	....	Castle Howard.
	Cram Beck	*Cas. Howard Lake*	Castle Howard.
	Spittle Beck ..	....	Hovingham, Barton Mill. Castle Howard.
	Bulmer Beck..	....	
	White Carr Beck	....	Castle Howard.
	Leppington Beck	....	Castle Howard.
	Swallowpits Beck	....	Castle Howard.
	Skirpen Beck..	....	Stamford Bridge
....	....	....	Stamford Bridge.

ENGLAND—*continued.*

RIVERS AND THEIR TRIBUTARIES.			STATIONS.
DERWENT (cont.).	Buttercrambe Moor Ponds	....	Stamford Bridge.
....	....	....	Kexby, Sutton-on-Derwent.
....	Foss Beck	....	Fangfoss, Sutton-on-Derwent.
....	....	....	East Cottingwith, Bubwith, Breighton, Menthorpe, Wressel.
DITTON BROOK or TORBOCK	Missy Dam ..	....	Prescot, Huyton Quarry.
	Logwood Mill Dam	....	Huyton Quarry.
	Childwall Brook	....	Childwall.
....	....	....	Halewood.
DON	Dunford Bridge Reservoir....	....	Dunford Bridge, Hazlehead Bridge, Penistone.
	Scout Dyke....	....	Penistone.
....	....	....	Deep Car.
....	Little Don	....	Dunford Bridge, Hazlehead Bridge, Deep Car.
	Ewden........	....	Deep Car.
....	....	....	Oughtibridge.
	Tinkers Brook	....	Oughtibridge.
	....	....	Wadesley Bridge.
	Rowel	Reservoir	Wadesley Bridge.
		Agden Reser...	Wadesley Bridge.
		Uphill Brook..	Wadesley Bridge.
		Storr Brook ..	Wadesley Bridge.
		{ Rivelin Reser.	Sheffield.
		{ Rivelin	Wadesley Bridge.
....		....	Sheffield.
	Porter Brook..	....	Sheffield.
	Sheaf		Beauchief.
		Fenny Brook ..	Beauchief.
	....	....	Mill Houses.
		Norton Hall Lake	Mill Houses.
	....	....	Heeley.
		Moors Brook ..	Heeley.
	....	....	Sheffield.
....	....	....	Brightside, Blackburn Junction.
	Car Brook	....	Blackburn Junction.
	Blackburn Brk.	....	Chapeltown, Ecclesfield, Grange Lane, Blackburn Junction.
....	....	....	Rotherham.
	Rother		Clay Cross.
		Hockley Brook	Chesterfield.
		Great Dam....	Chesterfield.
		Hockley Brook Wingerworth	
		Hall Lakes	Clay Cross.
		Hockley	Clay Cross.
....		....	Chesterfield.
		Hipper	Rowsley.
		Swiss Cottage	
		Ponds	Rowsley.
		{ Linacre Brk.	Chesterfield.
		{ Birley Pond	Chesterfield.
		Hipper	Chesterfield.
		Muster Brook..	
		Williamthorpe	
		Ponds	Clay Cross
		Muster Brook..	Chesterfield.
....		....	Whittington.
		{ Drone	Dronfield, Unston, Sheepsbridge.
		{ Millthorpe Brk.	Sheepsbridge.
		{ Drone	Whittington.

ENGLAND—*continued.*

RIVERS AND THEIR TRIBUTARIES.			STATIONS.
DON (*cont.*)	....	....	Staveley.
		All Pits Pond..	Chesterfield.
	....		Eckington.
		{ *Doe Lea*	
		Great Pond and Millers Pond	Seversall.
		Stainsby Pond	Seversall.
		Stockley Brook	Seversall.
		Sutton Scarsdale Park Lake ..	Chesterfield.
		Woodthorpe Mill Dam	Staveley.
		Doe Lea..	Eckington.
		Quarry Dam ..	Eckington.
		Moss Brook ..	Killamarsh.
	....	....	Killamarsh.
		{ *Short Brook* ..	Killamarsh.
		Pebley Brook ..	
		Barlborough Hall Lake	Killamarsh.
		Pebley Dam ..	Killamarsh.
		Harthill Reser.	Killamarsh.
		Woodhall Pond	Killamarsh.
		Woodhall Moor Dams	Killamarsh
		Pebley Brook..	Killamarsh.
		{ *Pigeon Bridge Brook*	
		Sickers Wood Pond	Woodhouse Mill.
		Pigeon Bridge Brook	Woodhouse.
		Shire Brook ..	Woodhouse.
	....	....	Woodhouse, Treeton, Rotherham.
.. ..	....	....	Park Gate.
	Dalton Brook..	....	Park Gate.
	Morley Brook	*Morley Ponds*..	Park Gate.
.. ..	....	....	Kilnhurst, Swinton, Mexborough.
	Dearne	....	Denby Dale, West Clayton.
	Bretton Pk. Lake	....	Haigh.
	....	....	Haigh, Darton.
		{ *Darton Brook* *Gamsthwaite Pond*	Penistone.
		Darton Brook	Darton.
	....	....	Barnsley, Cudworth, Darfield.
		{ *Dove*	
		Lowe Mill Reservoir	Dodworth.
		Reservoir	Dove Cliff.
		Rockley Dam ..	Birdwell.
		Dove	Dove Cliff, Wombwell, Darfield.
		{ *New Beck Reservoir*......	Chapeltown.
		New Beck	Darfield.
		Ings Dyke	Darfield.
	....	....	Bolton-on-Dearne, Conisborough.
....	....	... .	Conisborough, Doncaster, Barnby, Stainforth, Thorne.
	West	*Sharlestone Mill Pond*	Sharleston.
		Nostell Priory Lakes	Nostell.
	....	....	Ackworth, Kirk Smeaton, Norton.
		{ *Lake Drain* ..	
		Stapleton Park Lake	Wormesley.

ENGLAND—*continued.*

RIVERS AND THEIR TRIBUTARIES.			STATIONS.
DON (*cont.*)..	....	....	Balne, Thorne.
....	....	....	Goole.
DOUGLAS	*Horwich Brook*	*Wallsuches Pnd.*	Blackrod.
	Blackrod Ponds	....	Blackrod.
....	....	....	Adlington.
	Barsden Brook	....	Hindley, Dicconson, Hilton, Adlington. Standish.
	Idlinyton Brook	....	Standish.
....	....	....	Standish, Boar's Head, Wigan.
	Clarenden Brk.	....	Wigan.
	Standish Mill Pond	....	Gathurst.
....	....	....	Gathurst.
	Ruby Mill Pond	....	Gathurst.
....	....	....	Apply Bridge.
	Wrighton Hall Lake........	....	Apply Bridge.
....	....	....	Parbold, Hoscar Moss.
	Fawd	....	Pimbo Lane, Skelmersdale, Hoscar Moss.
	Henley Brook ..	....	Hoscar Moss.
....	....	....	Rufford.
	Eller Brook ..	....	Ormskirk, Burscough, Rufford.
	Yarrow	....	Chorley.
		Liverpool Waterworks Reserroirs ..	Chorley.
		Black Brook ..	Heapy.
		Heapy Pond .	Heapy.
		Black Brook ..	Chorley.
....	....	....	Coppull.
	Coppull Mill Ponds	....	Coppull.
....	....	....	Euxton, Croston.
		Lostock	Leyland.
		Leyland Pond..	Leyland.
		Lostock	Bamber Bridge.
		Bamber Bridge Lake	Bamber Bridge.
		Lostock	Lostock Hall, Farrington, Midge Hall, Croston.
		Wyncott Brook	Croston.
		Lostock	Croston.
....	....	....	Hesketh Bank.
DOUE	....	....	Kearsney, Dover.
DUDDEN	....	....	Broughton-in-Furness, Green Road, Silecroft.
DUNSTER BROOK	....	....	Dunster.
EDEN	....	....	Hawes.
	Hell Gill Beck	....	Hawes.
	....	....	Kirkby Stephen.
	Rigg Beck	....	Kirkby Stephen.
	Birkett Beck ..	....	Kirkby Stephen.
	Scandal Beck..	{*Artlegarth Bk.* {*Greenside Tarn*	Ravenstonedale.
		....	Smardale, Crossby Garrett.
			Kirkby Stephen.
	Belah	....	Kirkby Stephen.
		Greenfell Beck	Kirkby Stephen.
		Argill Beck ..	Kirkby Stephen.
	....	....	Musgrave.
	Stainmore Beck	*Hell Gill Beck*	Musgrave.
	....	....	Warcop, Ormside.
	Helm Beck....	....	Crossby Garrett.
	Hilton Beck ..	*Gaskill Tarn* ..	Appleby, Ormside.
	....	....	Appleby.

RIVERS AND THEIR TRIBUTARIES.			STATIONS.
EDEN (*cont.*)....*Hoff Beck*	....		Ormside, Appleby.
....	....		Kirkby Thore.
Trout Beck....	....		Long Marton, Kirkby Thore.
....	....		Temple Sowerby.
Lyvennett	*Leith*		Shap, Clifton, Cliburn.
	....		Temple Sowerby.
Eller Beck	....		Newbiggin.
	Milburn Beck..		Newbiggin.
	....		Temple Sowerby.
....	....		Culgaith.
Eamont	{ *Goldrill Beck* ..		Patterdale.
	Hayes Tarn ..		
	Brothers Water		
	Angle Tarn ..		
	Bendale Beck ..		
	Ullswater Lake		
	Griesdale Beck		Patterdale.
	Griesdale Tarn		
	Glenridding Bk.		Patterdale.
	Red Tarn		
	Keppel Cove		
	Tarn		
	Greenside Res.		
	Ara Beck		Patterdale.
	Dane Beck		Penruddock, Penrith.
	....		Penrith.
	{ *Lowther*		Shap.
	Swindale Beck		Shap.
	{ *Hawes Beck*		
	Blea Tarn ..		
	Small Water		
	Tarn		
	Rigindale Bk.		
	Hawes Water		
	Lake		
	Measand Beck		
	Howes Beck ..		
	Ghyll Beck		
	Heltondale Beck		
	Lowther		Clifton.
	....		Penrith.
....	....		Longwathby, Little Salkeld.
{ *Briggle Beck*..	....		Longwathby.
Blencarn Beck			
Hunsonby Beck	....		Little Salkeld.
....	....		Lazonby.
Glassonby Beck	....		Lazonby.
Raven Beck ..	....		Lazonby.
Croglin Water	....		Lazonby.
....	....		Armathwait, Coathill.
			Cumwhinton, Wetheral.
Trout Beck....	....		How Mill, Wetheral.
Irthing	*Butterburn*....		
•	....		Gilsland.
			Low Row, Brampton.
	{ *King's Water*		Gilsland.
	{ *Mill Beck*		Gilsland, Brampton.
	{ *Cam Beck*		Brampton.
	{ *Knossen Beck*..		
	{ *Gelt*		How Mill.
	{ *Talkin Tarn* ..		Brampton.
	....		Wetheral.
Scotby Beck....	....		Coathill, Cumwhinton.
			Scotby, Wetheral.
	....		Carlisle.
Petterill	....		Blencow, Penrith.
			Plumpton, Calthwaite.
			Southwaite, Wreay.
			Cumwhinton, Carlisle

ENGLAND—*continued.*

RIVERS AND THEIR TRIBUTARIES.			STATIONS.
EDEN (*cont.*)....	Brunstock Beck	....	Carlisle.
	Caldew	....	Keswick, Trout Beck.
		Gilcambon Bk.	
		{ Cald Beck	
		{ Parkend Beck	
		{ Roe Beck......	
		{ Ive	Calthwaite, Southwaite.
		....	Dalston.
		....	Dalston.
		Pow Beck	Dalston.
		....	Cummersdale, Carlisle.
		....	Kirkandrew.
	Powburgh Beck	....	Carlisle, Kirkandrew.
EHEW	Liza		Boathouse Inn.
	Ennerdale Lk.		Boathouse Inn.
	Crossdale Beck		Frizington.
	Wyndergill Bs.		Bowrah, Frizington.
	Singla Beck ..		Frizington.
....		....	Woodend.
	Keekle........	....	Moorsby Park.
		Dub Beck	Moorsby Park.
....		....	Moreton Junction, Woodend.
....		....	Egremont, Beckermet.
			Braystones.
	Kirkbeck......	....	Egremont, Beckermet.
	Black Beck....	....	Beckermet.
....		....	Sellafield.
	Calder	Worm Beck ..	Beckermet, Sellafield.
	New Mill Beck	....	Sellafield.
EMS..	....	.. ..	Emsworth.
ERME	.. ..	.. ..	Ivy Bridge.
	Ugborough Brk.	....	Kingsbridge Road
ESK (Cumb)..	Lingrove Beck	....	Esk Bridge.
	Cowcove Beck..	....	Esk Bridge.
	Stony Tarn ..	....	Esk Bridge.
....			Boot.
	Whillan Beck	Burnmore Trn.	Boot.
		Eel Tarn	Boot.
	Stanley Gill ..	....	Boot.
....		....	Beckfoot.
	Blea Tarn	....	Beckfoot.
....		....	Eskdale Green.
	Linbeck Gill ..	Devoke Water	Eskdale Green.
	Sangarth Beck	....	Eskmeals.
....		....	Eskmeals.
			Ravenglass.
	Mite		Irton Road, Muncaster.
			Ravenglass.
	Irt		Wasdale Head.
	Wastwater	....	Wasdale Head.
		{ Overbeck......	Wasdale Head.
		{ Low Tarn	
		{ Nether Beck ..	Wasdale Head.
		{ Scoat Tarn....	Wasdale Head.
		{ Greendale Beck	Wasdale Head.
		{ Greendale Tarn	Wasdale Head.
		Bleng	Drigg.
....		....	Drigg, Ravenglass.
ESK (Yorkshire)	... ...	.. ..	Castleton.
	Stockdale Beck	....	Castleton.
	Tower Beck ..	....	Castleton.
	Basedale Beck	....	Castleton.
	Danby Beck ..	....	Castleton.
	Commondale Bk.	....	Commondale, Castleton.
	....	....	Danby, Lealholme.

ENGLAND—*continued.*

RIVERS AND THEIR TRIBUTARIES			STATIONS.
Esk (*cont.*)..	Gt. Fryup Beck	....	Lealholme.
....	....	....	Glaisdale.
	Glaisdale Beck	....	Glaisdale.
....	....	....	Egton, Grosmont.
	Murk Esk.. ..	....	Grosmont.
		Rutmoor Beck	Grosmont.
....	....	....	Goathland.
		Eller Beck.... ⎫	
		Little Eller Bk. ⎬ Goathland	
		Brocka Beck .. ⎪	
		Little Beck.... ⎭	
....	....	....	Sleights.
	Little Beck	....	Sleights.
....	....	....	Ruswarp.
	Wash Beck....	....	Ruswarp.
	Rigg Mill Beck	....	Ruswarp.
....	....	....	Whitby.
Ewe	....	....	Burngullow
Exe (Devon)..	....	....	Dulverton.
	Quarum	....	Dulverton.
	Hadeo........	....	Dulverton.
	Barle	....	Dulverton.
		Danes Brook ..	Dulverton.
	Brushford Brk.	....	Dulverton.
	Belbrook.....	....	Bampton.
	Bampton Brook	....	Venn Cross, Morebath, Bampton.
....	....	....	Tiverton.
	Loman	....	Tiverton.
....	....	....	Bickleigh.
	Dart	....	Bickleigh.
	Butterleigh Brk.	....	Thorverton.
....	....	....	Silverton, Thorverton, Brampford Speke.
	Culm	....	Hemyock, Culmstock.
		Sheldon Brook	Ufculme.
	....	....	Ufculme, Tiverton Junction, Collumpton
		Kentisbere Brk	Collumpton.
		Ashford Brook	Tiverton Junction, Collumpton.
		Langford Brook	Collumpton.
	....	....	Brampford Speke.
	Creedy	....	Crediton.
		Yeo Brook ..	Crediton.
		Sandford Brook	Crediton.
		Spreyton Water	Bow, Crediton.
	....	....	St. Cyres.
		Shobrook Brook	St. Cyres.
....	....	....	Exeter.
Fal	....	....	St. Columb, Grampound.
	Gwendra Water	....	Grampound.
Foulness	....	....	Holme.
	Foss Dyke	....	Holme.
....	....	....	Staddlethorpe.
Fowey	....	....	Bodmin, Doublebois.
	St. Neot	....	Liskeard, Doublebois.
	Temple Brook..	....	Bodmin Road.
	....	....	Bodmin Road.
	Milton Brook ..	....	Bodmin Road.
....	....	....	Lostwithiel.
	Red Brook	....	Lostwithiel.
	Leign	....	Lostwithiel.
	Trebant Water..	....	Fowey.
	Pont Brook....	....	Fowey.
....	....	....	Fowey.
Frome (Dorset)	....	....	Toller, Malden Newton Grimston, Dorchester.
	Cerne	....	Evershot, Dorchester.
....	....	....	Moreton, Wool, Wareham.
Frome (Bristol).	....	....	Yate, Iron Acton.
	Laden	....	Wickwar, Tytherington.

ENGLAND—*continued.*

RIVERS AND THEIR TRIBUTARIES.			STATIONS.
FROME (Bristol) (*cont.*)	... ...	... ...	Filton.
	Bradley Brook ..	... ...	Thornbury, Filton.
....	... ...	... ...	Fishponds.
	Stoke Park Lake	... ...	Fishponds.
... ...	... ...	... ...	Stapleton Road, Bristol.
FROME (Glo'ster)	....	... ...	Stroud, Brimscombe.
	Slean Brook ..	....	Stroud.
	Painswick Brk.	....	Wooton, Stroud.
	Nailsworth Brk.	....	Nailsworth, Woodchester, Stroud.
....	... ...	....	Stonehouse.
GIPPING	*Wetherden Lake*	....	Haughley, Stowmarket.
	Rattlesdon Brk.	... ...	Stowmarket.
....	....	....	Needham Market.
	Bos Mere	....	Needham Market.
....	....	....	Claydon, Bramford, Ipswich.
	Flowton Brook.	....	Ipswich.
GLAVEN	*Selbrigg Pond* ..	....	Holt.
	Holt Mill Pond	....	Holt.
	Pond Hills	....	Holt.
	Thornage		
	Brook	... ...	Holt, Gunthorpe, Thursford, Hull.
... ...	... ...	... ...	Holt.
GLEN AND TILL	... ...	... ...	Kirknewton, Wooler. (See Till, Scotland
GULVALE BRK.	....	....	Penzance.
GWYTHIAN	....	....	Cambourne.
	Gwinear Brook	....	Gwinear.
HAMBLE	... ...	....	Bishops Waltham, Botley.
HARTLAND AB-BEY STREAM.	....	....	Hartland.
HAYBURN BECK	....	....	Hayburn Wyke
HAYLE	... ...	....	Gwinear.
	Germoe Brook ..	....	St. Earth.
....	... ...	....	St. Earth, Hayle.
	Gwinear Water	....	Hayle.
HELFORD	....	....	Constantine.
	Trecoos Brook ..	....	Constantine.
	Gweek Water ..	....	Helston, Constantine.
HELSTON	....	....	Pool, Helston.
HOLBROOK BRK.	....	....	Bentley.
	Tottingstone *Place Lakes* ..	....	Bentley.
HOLLAND BRK.	....	... ...	Thorpe.
HOLYWELL BRK.	....	....	New Quay.
HOPE BROOK ..	... ...	... ...	Longhope, Westbury.
HULL	....	....	Southburn, Driffield.
	Driffield Beck ..	....	Driffield.
....	....	....	Nafferton.
	Skerne Beck ..	....	Hutton, Nafferton.
	Kelk or Froding-ham Beck ..	... .	Lowthorpe.
	Watton Beck ..	....	Lockington.
	Pike Beck	....	Lockington.
		Scorboro' Beck	Lockington.
....	....	....	Arram, Beverley, Cottingham, Sutton, Hull.
IDLE	*Poulter*	*Whaley Mill* ..	Langwith.
	Langwith *Lodge Lake* ..	....	Langwith.
		Welbeck Park Lakes	Whitwell.
	Carburton Forge Lake	....	Worksop.
	Clumber Park Lake	....	Checker House.
	Poulter	....	Tuxford.
	Meden	....	Teversall.
		Car Ponds	Teversall.

b

ENGLAND—*continued.*

RIVERS AND THEIR TRIBUTARIES.			STATIONS.
IDLE *(cont.)* ..	....	....	Shirebrook.
		Park Hall Lake	Mansfield Woodhouse.
	Thoresby Park Lake........	....	Ollerton.
	Meden	....	Tuxford.
	Maun	Bath Wood Lake	Sutton.
	King's Mill Res.		Sutton.
	Maun	....	Mansfield.
		Coldwell Brook .	Mansfield.
	....	....	Mansfield Woodhouse.
		Vicay Water ..	Mansfield Woodhouse.
	....	....	Ollerton.
		Rainsworth Brk Rainsworth Pnd	Mansfield.
		Foul Evil Brook	Mansfield.
		Inkersal Dam..	Farnsfield.
		Rufford Dam..	Ollerton.
		Bevercotes Brook	Tuxford.
	....	....	Tuxford.
	....	....	Retford.
....	Babsworth Hall Lake	....	Retford.
....	....	....	Ramskill, Scrooby, Bawtry.
	Ryton	....	Worksop.
		Manor Pk. Lake	Worksop.
	....	....	Chequer House, Ramskill
		Old Coates Dyke	Rotheram.
		Laughton Pond.	Kiveton Park.
		Spont Dyke.. Moor Mill Dam......	Shireoak.
		Carlton Lake.	Worksop.
		Langold Lake	Worksop.
		Spont	Ramskill.
		Oldcoates......	Ramskill.
	....	....	Scrooby.
		Serlby Pk. Lake	Ramskill.
	....	....	Bawtry.
	Torne	Sandbeck Park Lake........	Tickhill, Rossington
		St. Catharine's Well Stream.. Crookhill Hall Lake........	Conisborough.
	....	....	Firmingley.
....	....	....	Crowle, Althorpe.
INGREBURN	....	....	Brentwood, Rainham
ITCHEN (Hants)	....	.. ..	Alresford, Itchen Abbas, Winchester Bishopstoke, Southampton.
KEER	....	....	Borwick, Carnforth.
KENN (Devon)	.. ..	.. ..	Exminster, Starcross.
KENN (Somst.)	....	.. ..	Bourton, Nailsea, Clevedon.
KENT	Kentmere Res.	....	Staveley.
	Skeggles Water		Staveley.
	Gowan........	....	Windermere, Staveley.
	Gurnal Dubs ..	....	Staveley.
	....		Burnside.
	Sprint........	....	Burnside.
	Skelsmergh Tn.		Burnside.
	Mint	....	Grayrigg.
		Grayrigg Tn...	Grayrigg.
	....		Kendal.
	....		Kendal.
	Gilpin........		Kendal.
		Underbarrow Bk.	Keswick, Kendal.
KESTLE	....	....	St. Columb.
	Tredinick Water	....	Grampound.
....	....	....	New Quay.

ENGLAND—*continued.*

RIVERS AND THEIR TRIBUTARIES.			STATIONS.
KIRTON BROOK	Bixley Decoy Ponds	....	Ipswich.
....	....	....	Woodbridge.
KITTLE BROOK	.. ..	.. ..	Bishopston.
LACKEY BECK.	....	....	Grimsby.
LEA (Essex) ..	.. ..	.. ..	Luton, New Mill End, Harpenden, Wheathampstead, Hatfield, Hertford.
	Mimram	....	Welwyn, Hertford.
	Beame	.. ..	Stevenage, Hertford.
	Rib	.. ..	Buntingford, Westmill, Braughing.
		Quin	Braughing.
	.. ..	.. ..	How Street, Hertford.
.. ..	.. ..	....	Ware.
	Ash	....	Hadham Cross, Widford, Ware.
....	.. ..	.. ..	St. Margaret's, Hoddesdon.
	Stort	.. ..	Stanstead, Bishop Stortford, Sawbridgeworth, Harlow.
		Pincey Brook..	Takeley, Harlow.
	....	.. ..	Burnt Mill, Roydon, Hoddesdon.
.. ..	.. ..	.. ..	Broxbourne, Cheshunt, Waltham.
	Cobbin's Brook	.. ..	Waltham.
....	.. ..	.. ..	Enfield, Angel-road, Park Station. Tottenham, Lea Bridge, Stratford.
LEVEN	Rothay	{ Easdale Beck .. { Codale Tarn .. { Easdale Tarn..	Grasmere.
	.. ..	....	Grasmere.
	Rydal Water..	Rydal Beck ..	Ambleside.
	....	Scandal Beck..	Ambleside.
	Brathay	....	Skelwith Bridge.
	.. ..	Blea Tarn	Skelwith Bridge.
	Little Langdale Tarn	....	Skelwith Bridge.
	Elter Water ..	....	Skelwith Bridge.
	....	{ Gt. Langdale Bk.	Skelwith Bridge.
	....	{ Stickle Tarn ..	Skelwith Bridge.
	....	{ Loughrigg Tarn	Skelwith Bridge.
	....	....	Ambleside.
	Windermere ..	.. ..	Ambleside.
	....	Trout Beck....	Windermere.
	....	....	Bowness, Lake Side Station.
	....	Blelham Tarn	Ambleside.
	.. .. ;	....	Ferry Hotel.
	....	{ Cunsey Beck ..	Hawkshead.
	....	{ Esthwaite Wtr.	Hawkshead.
	....	{ Cunsey Beck ..	Ferry Hotel.
	....	High Tarn....	Lake Side.
.. ..	.. ..	....	Newby Bridge.
	Bortree Tarn..	....	Newby Bridge.
.. ..	....	....	Haverthwaite.
	Bigland Tarn..	....	Haverthwaite.
.	Rusland Pool..	....	Hawkshead.
.. ..	....	....	Greenodd.
	Colton Beck ..	....	Greenodd.
	Crake	....	Coniston.
	....	Low Tarn	Coniston.
	....	{ Church Beck..	Coniston.
	....	{ Lever Water ..	
	Coniston Lake..	....	Coniston, Torver.
	....	{ Torver Beck ..	Torver.
	....	{ Goats Water ..	
	....	....	Lake Bank Hotel.
	....	Beacon Tarn ..	Lake Bank Hotel.
	Crake	....	Greenodd.
.. ..	Newland Beck..	....	Greenodd, Ulverston.
.. ..	....	....	Ulverston.
LITTLE AVON	....	.. ..	Wickwar, Charfield
	Ozleworth Brook	.. ..	Charfield.

ENGLAND—*continued.*

RIVERS AND THEIR TRIBUTARIES.			STATIONS.
LIT. AVON (*cont.*)	Tortworth Brk.	.. ..	Wickwar.
.. ..	....	.. ..	Berkeley.
	Waterley Brook	....	Dursley, Berkeley.
LOOE	....	....	Liskeard, Menheniot.
LUDD	....	....	Hallington, Louth
LUNE	Greenside Beck } Sanwath Beck.. }	.. ..	Ravenstonedale.
	Weasdale Beck	....	Ravenstonedale.
	Bowderdale Beck	....	Ravenstonedale.
....	....	....	Gaisgill.
	Langdale Beck	....	Gaisgill.
	Ellergill Beck..	....	Gaisgill.
	Rais Beck	Sunbiggin Tarn	Ravenstonedale.
....	....	....	Gaisgill.
	Tebay Gill....	....	Tebay.
	Chapel Beck ..	....	Gaisgill.
	Blind Beck ..	....	Tebay.
	Birk Beck	Wasdale Beck..	Tebay.
		Bretherdale Bck	Tebay.
....	....	....	Tebay.
	Barrow Beck..	....	Tebay.
....	....	....	Howgill.
	Blands Gill ..	....	Howgill.
	Crossdale Beck	....	Sedbergh.
....	....	....	Sedbergh.
	Rawthey River	West Baugh .. } Fell Tarns .... }	Hawes Junction.
	....	Red Gill ...... } East Tarns.... }	Hawes Junction.
	....	Sally Beck	Hawes Junction.
	....	Wandale Beck..	Hawes Junction.
	....	Backs Beck....	Hawes Junction.
	....	Crosshow Beck ..	Hawes Junction.
	....	Vor Gill	Hawes Junction.
	....	Clough River.. } Gresdale Beck.. } East Haugh Fell } Tarn ......}	Hawes Junction.
....	....	....	Sedbergh.
		Dee	Dent.
		Deepdale Beck	Dent.
		Dee	Sedbergh.
....	....	....	Middleton, Barbon.
	Barbon Beck ..	....	Barbon.
....	....	....	Kirkby Lonsdale.
	Leek Beck	....	Kirkby Lonsdale.
....	....	....	Arkholme.
	Greeta........	....	Ingleton.
		Doe or Dale Beck	Ingleton.
....	....	....	Arkholme.
	Caut Beck	....	Arkholme.
	Beckthwaite Beck	....	Arkholme.
....	....	....	Melling, Hornby.
	Wenning......	Kettles Beck.... } Fen Beck...... } Austwick Beck.. } Clapham Beck. } Newby Beck .. }	Clapham.
		Reasden Beck..	Clapham.
	....		Bentham, Hornby.
		Hindburn ....} Whitcray Beck	Clapham.
		Tatham Beck..	Clapham.
		Roeburndale River	Hornby.
		Hindburn	Hornby.
....	....	....	Caton.
	Farn Brook ..	....	Caton.
	Artle	Foxdale Beck.. } Udale Beck.... }	Caton.

ENGLAND—*continued.*

RIVERS AND THEIR TRIBUTARIES.			STATIONS.
LUNE (*cont.*) ..	....	....	Caton.
....	....	....	Halton.
	Cote Beck	....	Halton.
....	....	....	Lancaster.
LYDNEY BROOK	....	....	Lydney.
LYN	.. ..	....	Lynmonth.
	Oare Water ..	....	Lynmouth.
		Badgworthy Wtr.	Lynmouth.
LYNE	.. ..	....	Bewcastle, Bolton.
LYVENNET	....	.. ..	Crosby Ravensworth.
MADRON BROOK	....	.. ..	Penzance.
MANACCAN BRK.	....	....	Manaccan.
MARAZION WTR.	....	....	Marazion.
MARDYKE	.. ..	....	Purfleet.
MARSHLAND ..	....	....	Hartland.
MAWGAN	....	....	St. Columb.
	Whitewater	....	St. Columb.
MEDINA(I.ofW.)	.. ..	....	Blackwater, Shide, Newport, Cowes.
MEDWAY(Kent)	....	.. ..	East Grinstead, Hartfield, Withyham, Tunbridge Wells, Groombridge, Tonbridge.
	Eden	....	Edenbridge, Chiddingstone, Tonbridge.
.. ..	.. ..	....	Yalding.
	Teise	....	Tunbridge Wells, Yalding.
	Beult	.. ..	Headcorn, Staplehurst, Yalding.
....	.. ..	....	Wateringbury, East Farleigh, Maidstone Aylsford, Snodland, Rochester.
MELLINCORE ..	....	....	St. Columb, New Quay.
MEON (Hants)	.. ..	....	Petersfield, Fareham.
MERSEY OF GOYT	....	....	Buxton.
	Moorstone Brk.	....	Buxton.
....	....	....	Wale.
	Tunstead Reservoir	....	Chapel-en-le-Frith.
	Wale Reservoir	....	Wale.
	Black Brook ..	....	Chapel-en-le-Frith, Bigsworth.
....	....	....	New Mills.
	Sett Brook	....	Hayfield.
		Lady Gate Brk.	New Mills.
....	....	....	Strines, Marple.
	Etherow	Woodhead Res.	Woodhead.
		Witherow Brk.	Woodhead.
	Torside Reservoir	....	Woodhead.
		Great Cowdon Brook ...... Little Cowdon Brook	Woodhead.
	Etherow		Hadfield.
		Hollingworth Brook	Hadfield.
		Armfield Brook	Hadfield.
		Shelf Brook ..	Glossop, Hadfield.
	....	....	Broadbottom, Marple.
.. ..	.. ..	....	Stockport.
	Tame	....	Saddleworth.
		Diggle Brook..	Saddleworth.
	....	....	Greenfield.
		Greenfield Brk. Chew Brook ..	Greenfield. Greenfield.
	....	....	Mossley.
		Car Brook	Mossley.
		Swinaeshaw Bk.	Stalybridge.
	....	....	Stalybridge, Ashton.
		Gorton Reser.	Fairfield.
	....	....	Denton.
		Godley Reser.	Newton.
	....	....	Reddish, Stockport.
....	....	....	Heaton Mersey, Didsbury.
	Poynton Brook Poynton Park Lake	....	Poynton. Poynton.

ENGLAND—*continued.*

RIVERS AND THEIR TRIBUTARIES.			STATIONS.
MERSEY (*cont.*)	Poynton Brook	....	Cheadle Hulme, Cheadle.
....	....	....	Northenden, Stretford.
....	Gore Brook ..	....	Stretford.
....	....	....	Urmiston, Flixton, Irlam.
	Irwell	....	Bacup, Stackstead, Waterfoot, Rawten-
	Lamy Water ..	....	Rawtenstall. [stall.
	....	....	Ewood Bridge.
	Swinnell Brook		Baxenden, Haslingden, Hulm Shore,
			Ewood Bridge.
	....		Stubbins.
	Hare Hill Pond		Waterfoot.
	....		Ramsbottom, Summerseat, Bury.
	Tottington Brk.		Bury.
	Elton Ponds ..		Bury.
	Reservoir		Bury.
	....		Radcliffe.
	Roch		Walsden.
	Gadden Reservoir		Walsden.
	Upper White Holme Res.		
	Tunnel End Reservoir ..		
	Lower White Holme Res.		
	Blackstone Res.		
	Spoddle Hill Reservoir ..		
....	Roch		Littleborough.
	Hollingworth Reservoir ..		Littleborough.
	Beal		Hey.
	Roch		Rochdale.
	Dod		Shawforth, Facit, Whitworth, Shaw-
			clough, Rochdale.
	Roch		Castleton.
	Saddon Brook		Castleton.
	Bolderstone Pond		Castleton.
	Roch		Heywood.
	Naden Water..		Heywood.
	Roch		Bury.
	Black Brook ..		Bury.
	Roch		Radcliffe.
....	....		Farnworth.
	Tange or Eagle		Bolton le-Moors.
	Longworth Res.		Bolton-le-Moors.
	Springwater Reservoir		Bolton-le-Moors.
	Tange		Oaks.
	Dean Brook ..		
	Rivington Moor Reservoir ..		Bolton.
	Tange		Bolton.
	Croal		
	Hulton Park Lake		Atherton.
	Croal		Chequerbent, Lostock, Bolton.
	Bradshaw Brk.		
	Entwistle Res.		Entwistle.
	Bradshaw Brk.		Turton, Bromley Cross
	Tange		Farnworth.
.. ..	....		Clifton, Manchester.
	Irk		Rowton, Middleton.
	Three Pits Pnds.		Middleton.
	Heaton Lake..		Middleton.
	Medlock		Parkbridge.
	Knoll Hill Lake		Mossley.
	Medlock		Clayton Bridge, Manchester.
....	....		Eccles, Patricroft.

ENGLAND—*continued.*

RIVERS AND THEIR TRIBUTARIES.			STATIONS.
MERSEY (*cont.*)	Worsley Brook		
	Black Leech		
		Pond	Worsley.
	Linnyshaw		
		Dam	Worsley.
	Worsley		Worsley, Patricroft.
	Longford Brook		Urmiston, Patricroft.
....	....		Irlam.
....	....		Partington.
Glaze Brook ..	Atherton Hall		
		Lake	Leigh, Partington.
Wych Brook ..	....		Timperley, Partington.
....	....		Warburton.
Bollin	....		Macclesfield, Presbury, Wilmslow.
	Dean		Bollington, Adlington.
	Stypherson		
		Park Lake	Bollington.
	Dean		Handforth, Kilmslow.
	....		Ashley.
	Birkin		Chelford, Knutsford, Mobberley, Ashley
	Mobberley Brk.		Mobberley, Ashley.
	Ashley Brook..		Ashley.
	Tatton Park		
		Lakes	Knutsford.
	MereHall Lakes		Knutsford.
	Rothern Mere..		Ashley.
	Arden Brook ..		Heatley.
	....		Heatley, Warburton.
....	....		Lymm.
Sow Brook	Lymm Lake		Lymm.
....	....		Thelwall, Warrington.
	Black Brook ..		Warrington.
	Sankey Brook..		Rainford, Mossbank, St. Helen's.
	Eccleston Hall		
		Lake	St. Helen's.
	....		Collin Green.
	Newton Brook..		Mossbank.
	Carr Mill Dam		Mossbank.
	Stanley Mill		
		Pool	St. Helen's.
	Garwood Lake		St. Helen's.
	Newton Brook.		Collin Green.
	....		Warrington.
	Kekwick Brook		Norton, Warrington.
....	....		Runcorn.
MILL BECK ..	....		Fyling Hall.
MOULTRIE	....		Guardbridge.
MOUNTON Bk.	....		Chepstow, Portskewet.
MULLION Brk.	....		Mullion.
NEDDEN Brook	....		Portskewet.
NENE	....		Weedon.
	Fawsley Brook	Fawsley Park	
		Lake	Weedon.
	Streck	Dunsland Res.	Daventry.
		Middlemore Re-	
		servoir	Daventry.
	....		Crick, Weedon.
	Horsestone Brk.		Weedon
	Wootton Brook		Piddington, Northampton.
....	....		Northampton.
....	Maidwell Dale		
	and Maidwell		
	Hall Lakes ..	Lamport Hall	
		Lake	Lamport.
	....		Brixworth.
	Calendar Brook		Brixworth.
....	....		Spratton.
	Stowe Brook ..		Spratton.
	Pittsford Brook	Faxton Hall	
		Ponds	Lamport, Spratton.

ENGLAND—*continued.*

RIVERS AND THEIR TRIBUTARIES.			STATIONS.
NEN (*cont.*) ..	....	....	Brampton.
	Moulton Brook	....	Brampton.
	Althorp Brook	*Althorp Park Lakes*	Althorp Park, Brampton.
	Dallington Hall Lake	....	Northampton.
	Abington Park Lake	....	Northampton.
	Billing Brook ..	*Overstone Park Lake*	Northampton, Billing.
....	....	....	Billing.
	Sywell Brook ..	*Sywell Pk. Pond} Sywell Mill Pnd}*	Wellingborough, Castle Ashby.
		....	Castle Ashby.
	Ashby Brook ..	*Castle Ashby Park Lakes.*	Castle Ashby.
			Wellingborough.
....	*Ise*	*Kilmarsh Lake*	Kilmarsh, Desborough, Rushton, Geddington, Kettering, Burton, Finedorn.
		Finedorn Hall Lake	Finedorn.
		Dickens Mill Pond	Wellingborough.
....	*Harpers Brook*	....	Ditchford, Higham Ferrers, Ringstead, Weldon, Thrapston. [Thrapston.
....	*Southwick Pond*	....	Thorpe, Oundle.
....	*Elton Prk. Lake*	....	Oundle.
	Willow Brook	*Dene Park Lake*	Elton.
		Blatherwycke Park Lake ..	Weldon.
	....	....	King's Cliff.
....	*Withering Brk.*	*Easton Lake* ..	King's Cliff.
			Nassington, Wansford.
	....	....	Stamford.
....	....	....	Wansford.
	Billing Brook ..	....	Castor.
....	....	....	Castor.
	Milton Park Lakes	....	Overton.
....	*Old River*	....	Peterborough.
			Peterborough, Guyhirne, Wisbeach.
		{Holme Brook {Caldecot Pond.	Ramsey.
		Wiston Brook.	Holme, Ramsey.
		Ramsey Mere.	Huntingdon, Ramsey.
	....	....	Ramsey.
....	*Muscal River or Cats Water* ..	....	March, Wisbeach. [Tydd St. Mary's.
....	....	....	Peterborough, Eye Green, French Drove, Ferry, Tydd St. Mary's, Sutton Bridge.
NEWBIGGIN BECK	*Urswick Tarn*	....	Ulverston.
	Mere Tarn	....	Ulverston.
....	....	....	Newbiggin.
NEW RIVER ..	....	....	Hertford, Hoddesdon, Broxbourne, Cheshunt. Waltham, Enfield, Winchmore Hill, Wood Green, Hornsey, Torrington Park, London.
NEWTOWN	....	....	Newtown.
NORTH TYNE ..	....	....	Tarsett.
OLD DON RIVER	....	....	Crowle.
OLVERTON	....	....	New Passage.
OTTER..........	....	....	Taunton, Honiton.
	Pennythorn Brk.	....	Honiton.
	Blanacombe Brk.	....	Honiton.
	Awlescombe Brook	....	Honiton.
....	....	....	Ottery Road, Ottery St. Mary
....	*Saltwater Brook* ..	....	Ottery St. Mary.
....	....	....	Tipton.

ENGLAND—*continued.*

RIVERS AND THEIR TRIBUTARIES.			STATIONS.
OUSE (Great)..	*Biddlesdon Park Lakes*	....	Brackley.
.. ..	....	.. ..	Brackley.
	Stow Lakes. ..	....	Buckingham.
....		....	Buckingham.
	Claydon	*Cottisford Pond*	Brackley.
	.. ..	....	Claydon.
		Claydon Farm Pond. Middle Claydon Pond	Claydon.
	....	....	Buckingham.
	Whaddon Lake	....	Swanbourn.
.. ..		....	Stoney Stratford.
	Whittlewood Forest Lakes		Stoney Stratford.
....	....	....	Wolverton.
	Tove..........	....	Helmedon, Wappenham.
		Blakesley Brook	Blakesley.
	....	....	Towcester, Wolverton.
....		....	Newport Pagnell.
	Ousel	....	Dunstable, Leighton Buzzard.
		{ *Battlesden Brk. Woburn Abbey Lakes* ...... *Battlesden Park Lakes*	Woburn, Leighton Buzzard.
		Rushmore Pond	Leighton Buzzard.
	....	....	Fenny Stratford.
		Crawley Brook	Woburn.
	....	....	Newport Pagnell.
....	....	....	Olney, Turvey, Harrold, Sharnbrook Oakley, Bedford, Tempsford.
	Ivel	....	Baldock, Arlesey.
		Hir	Hitchin, Arlesey.
		{ *Tod* .. .. *Tingrith House Lakes*	Harlington.
		Flitwick Park Lakes	Ampthill.
		Tod	Shefford.
		Gull Brook....	Shefford.
		{ *Compton Brk* *Wrest Park Lakes*	Shefford. / Ampthill.
		Tod	Arlesey.
	....	....	Biggleswade.
		{ *Sutton Brook.. Gamlingay Prk. Lake*	Gamlingay.
	....	....	Sandy.
		{ *Southill Brook Southill Park Lake* ...... *Old Warden Prk Lake*	Southill.
	....	....	Blunham.
....	.. .... :..	....	St. Neots.
	Kym	....	Kimbolton.
		Warren Fishpond	Kimbolton.
	Gallow Brook ..	....	St. Neots.
.. ..	....	....	Huntingdon.
	Alconbury Brk.	....	Huntingdon.
....	....	....	St. Ives, Swavesey, Earith, Stretham Thetford.
	Cam	*Debden Hall Lakes*	Newport.
	....	....	Newport, Saffron Walden, Great Chesterford, Whittlesford, Shelford.
		Bourn	Linton, Pampisford, Shelford.

ENGLAND—*continued.*

RIVERS AND THEIR TRIBUTARIES.			STATIONS.
Ouse (Gt.)(*cont.*)		*Rhee*	Ashwell, Meldreth.
		Wimvole Park Lake	Old North Road Station.
		Rhee	Harston.
		Bourn	Lords Bridge.
	....		Cambridge, Waterbeach.
		Bottisham Load	Fulbourn, Waterbeach.
		Swaffham Load	Waterbeach.
....	....	....	Ely.
	Lark	....	Bury St. Edmunds.
		Livermere Park Lakes	
		Ampton Park Lake	Ingham.
		Culford Park Lake	
		Linnet	Bury St. Edmunds
		Ickworth Park Lake	Saxham.
		Cavenham Brk.	Saxham.
		....	Mildenhall.
		Kent	Kennet.
....		....	Littleport.
	Mildenhall Drain	....	Littleport.
	Old Croft River	....	Littleport.
	Little Ouse....	*Redgrave Park Lake*	Bottisdale.
		Ixworth	
		Drinkstone Prk. Lake	Shurston.
		Stowlangtoft Hall Lake	Ixworth.
		Euston Pk. Lake	Ixworth.
		....	Thetford.
		Thet	Harling, Thetford.
	....	....	Brandon, Lakenheath.
....	....	....	Hilgay.
	Sams Cut Drain	....	Hilgay.
	Wissey or Stoke River	*Heath Mere* ..	Watton
	....	....	Watton
		Saham Mere ..	Watton
		Erneford Brook	Holm Hale.
		Buckenham House Pk. Lake	Brandon.
		Toffs Mere	Brandon.
		Didlington Hall Lake	Stoke Ferry.
	....	....	Stoke Ferry.
		Barton Brook..	Stoke Ferry.
		Stradset Hall Lake	Downham Market.
	....	....	Hilgay.
....	....	....	Downham Market, Magdalen, King's Lynn.
	Nar or Letchy	....	Litcham, Swaffham, Narborough, King's
	Gawood River..	....	King's Lynn. [Lynn.
Ouse (Sussex)	....	....	Buxted, Isfield, Uckfield, Lewes, Glynd Newhaven.
Ouse (York)..	*Swale*	....	Kirkby Stephen.
		Birkdale Tarn	Keld.
		Gt. Sleddale Beck	Keld.
		Whitsundale Bk.	Keld.
	....	....	Keld.
		Stonesdale Beck	Keld.
	....	....	Muker.
		Muker Beck ..	Muker.
		Thwaite Beck ..	Muker.
		Oxnop Beck ..	Muker.
		Gunnerside Beck	Reeth.

ENGLAND—*continued.*

RIVERS AND THEIR TRIBUTARIES.		STATIONS.
OUSE (*cont.*) ..	Crackpot Beck..	Reeth.
	Summerlodge	
	Tarn	Askrigg.
	Healaugh Beck	Reeth.
....	....	Reeth.
	Arkle Beck....	Reeth.
	Roe Beck......	Reeth.
	Straw Beck....	Reeth.
	Gill Beck......	Leyburn.
	Stainton Moor	
	Beck........	Reeth.
	Gill Beck......	Reeth.
	Maske Beck....	Reeth.
	Moorsdale Beck	Reeth.
	Throstle Beck..	Reeth.
	Clapgate Beck .	Richmond.
....	....	Richmond.
	Sand Beck	Richmond.
	Colburn Beck ..	Catterick Bridge.
....	....	Catterick.
	Skeeby Beck ..	Richmond.
	Smelt Mill Beck	Richmond.
	Aske Beck ..	Richmond.
	Aske Hall	
	Lake	Richmond.
	Skeeby........	Catterick.
	Brough Beck ..	Spennithorne.
	Calfhole Tarn..	Spennithorne.
	Tunstall Beck..	Catterick.
	Brough Beck ..	Catterick.
	Scorton Beck ..	Scorton.
	Howl Beck	Scorton.
	Stell	Scruton.
....	....	Scruton and Ainderby.
	Bedale Beck ..	Spennithorne.
	Barden Moor	
	High and Low	
	Ponds	Spennithorne.
	Bedale Beck ..	Constable Burton, Fingall.
	Newton Beck	Wensley, Leyburn, Constable Burton.
	Bellerby Beck	Hellerby, Constable Burton.
	Newton Beck	Fingall.
	Bedale Beck ..	Crakehall, Bedale, Leeming, Scruton.
....	....	Newby Wiske, Pickhill.
	Wiske	West Rounton, Cowton, Danby Wiske,
	Brompton Bk.	Brompton. Northallerton.
	Winton Beck	Brompton.
	Brompton Bk	Northallerton.
	Wiske	Newby Wiske, Pickhill.
....	....	Skipton Bridge, Topcliffe.
	Cod Beck......	Brompton.
	Howl Beck	Brompton.
	Cod Beck......	Otterington.
	Broad Beck..	Otterington.
	Sorrow Beck	Otterington.
	Cod Beck......	N. Kilvington.
	Spittle Beck ..	N. Kilvington.
	Cod..	Thirsk, Sessay.
	Fisher Beck ..	Sessay.
	Willow Beck	Thirsk.
	Hood Beck ..	Thirsk.
	Willow......	Sessay.
	Cod	Topcliffe.
....	....	Brafferton.
	Sun Beck	Gilling, Ampleforth.
	Gilling Pk. Lake	Ampleforth.
	Park House	
	Lakes	Ampleforth. ton.
	Sun Beck	Coxwold, Husthwaite, Pillmore, Braffer-
Ure	....	Hawes.

ENGLAND—*continued.*

RIVERS AND THEIR TRIBUTARIES.			STATIONS.
OUSE (*cont.*) ..		*Cottexdale Beck*	Hawes.
	{	*Widdale Beck*..	Ribble Head
		Tarn Beck	Hawes.
		{ *Widdale Tarn*	Hawes.
		{ *Snaixeholme*	
		Beck	Hawes.
	{	*Widdale Beck*..	Hawes.
		Hearne Beck ..	Hawes.
		Duerley Beck..	Hawes.
	....	....	Askrigg.
	{	*Baine*	
		Middlelonge	
		Tarn	Askrigg.
		Cray Tarn....	Askrigg.
		{ *Roydale Beck*	Askrigg.
		{ *Outershaw*	
		Tarn	Askrigg.
		Bardale Beck ..	Askrigg.
		Semmer Water	Askrigg.
		Baine	Askrigg.
		Sargill Beck ..	Askrigg.
		Coghill Beck ..	Askrigg.
	....	....	Aysgarth.
	{	*Bishopdale Beck*	Redmire.
	{	*Walden Beck*..	Redmire.
	....	....	Redmire.
	{	*Beldon Beck* ..	Aysgarth.
	{	*Locker Tarn* ..	Aysgarth.
	{	*Beldon*......	Redmire.
		Apedale Beck ..	Redmire.
	....	....	Wensley, Leyburn, Middleham, Coverbridge.
		Cover	Kettlewell, Coverbridge.
		Sowden Beck ..	Coverbridge.
	....	....	Masham.
	{	*Burn*	
		Birkgull Beck..	Masham.
		Spucegill Beck	Masham.
		Grimesgill Bk.	Masham.
	{	*Sale Beck*	Masham.
		Swinton Park	
		Lakes	Masham.
		Burn	Masham.
	{	*Swinney Beck*..	Masham.
	....	....	W. Stanfield, Ripon.
	{	*Laver*	Pateley Bridge.
		Stock Beck	Kirby Malzeard.
		Laver	Kirby Malzeard.
		Kexbec	Kirby Malzeard.
		Laver	Ripon.
		{ *Skell*	Pateley Bridge.
		{ *Eavestone*	
		Lake	Pateley Bridge.
		{ *Studley*	
		{ *Park Lakes*	Ripon.
		{ *Hill House*	
		Lake	Ripon.
		{ *Skell*	Ripon.
		Robert Beck ..	Wormold Green, Copgrove.
	....	....	Boroughbridge.
		Tutt..........	Copgrove, Boroughbridge
....	....	....	Aldwark, Tollerton.
	Kyle	....	Alne.
		Hawkhill Beck	Alne.
		Derings Beck..	Alne.
	....	....	To lerton.
	....	....	Nunmonkton.
....	*Nidd*	....	Ramsgill.
		How Stone Beck	Ramsgill.
		Ramsgill Beck	Ramsgill.

ENGLAND—*continued.*

RIVERS AND THEIR TRIBUTARIES.			STATIONS.
OUSE (*cont.*) ..		*Lat Beck*	Ramsgill.
		Burn Gill	Ramsgill.
		Ashfordside Beck	Pateley Bridge.
		....	Pateley Bridge.
		Greenhow Beck	Pateley Bridge.
		Ear Beck	Pateley Bridge.
		....	Dacre, Darley.
		Darley Beck ..	Darley.
		....	Hampsthwaite.
		Kettlesing Beck	Hampsthwaite.
		Rowden Beck ..	Hampsthwaite.
		....	Ripley.
		{ *Thornton Beck*	
		{ *Ripley Park*	
		{ *Lakes*	Ripley.
		{ *Oak Beck*	Darley.
		{ *Salergate Beck*	Ripley.
		{ *Oak Beck*	Ripley.
		....	Knaresborough, Goldsborough, Little
		{ *Crimple Beck* ..	Harrogate, Pannal. [Ribston.
		{ *Nor Beck*	Pannal.
		{ *Crimple*	Spofforth.
		{ *Allerton Beck* .	Allerton.
		{ *Allerton Park*	
		{ *Lakes*	Allerton.
		{ *Allerton Beck* .	Little Ribston.
		....	Cattal, Hammerton, Nunmonkton.
....	....	....	Poppleton, York.
	Foss	*Moss Tarn*	
		Reservoirs	Coxwold.
		White Car Beck	Strensall.
		....	Strensall, Haxby, York.
		{ *Tang Hall Beck*	Earswick.
		{ *Osbaldwick Bk.*	York.
		{ *Tang Hall Beck*	York.
....	....	....	Naburn.
	Stillingfleet Bk.	....	Escrick.
....	....	....	Cawood.
	Wharfe	*Outershaw Beck*	Ribble Head.
		Greenfield Beck	Ribble Head.
		....	Buckden, Starbolton, Kettlewell.
		{ *Skirfare*	Horton.
		{ *Foxup Beck* ..	Kettlewell.
		{ *Hesleden Beck* .	Horton, Kettlewell.
		{ *Cowside Beck* ..	Kettlewell.
		{ *Skirfare*	Kettlewell.
		....	Grassington.
		Eller Beck	Grassington.
		Hebden Beck ..	Burnsall.
		....	Burnsall.
		{ *Dibb*	Grassington.
		{ *Priest Tarn* ..	Grassington.
		{ *Blea Beck Dams*	Grassington.
		{ *Gate Up Gill* ..	Grassington.
		{ *Guinaith Beck*	Burnsall.
		{ *Dibb*	Burnsall.
		{ *Skyreholm Beck*	Burnsall.
		{ *New Dam*	Burnsall.
		Gill Beck	Burnsall.
		Barden Beck ..	Bolton Abbey.
		....	Bolton Abbey.
		Kex Beck	Bolton Abbey.
		....	Addingham, Ilkley, Ben Rhydding,
		Hollin Beck ..	Otley. [Burley, Otley.
		Mire Beck	Guiseley, Otley.
		{ *Washburn*	
		{ *Tarn Gill*	Burnsall.
		{ *Harden Beck* ..	Bolton Abbey.
		{ { *Akeds Beck*	
		{ { *Akeds Dam* ..	Bolton Abbey.

ENGLAND—*continued.*

RIVERS AND THEIR TRIBUTARIES.			STATIONS.
OUSE (*cont.*) ..		*Washburn*	Darley.
		Gill Beck	Darley.
		Spinksburn Bk.	Darley.
		Washburn	Poole.
		....	Poole
		Riffa Beck	Poole.
		....	Arthington, Weeton
		Harewood Beck	Bardsey.
		Eccup Beck	
		Alwordley	
		Reservoir	Arthington.
		Harewood	
		Park Lakes	Weeton.
		Harewood	Weeton.
		....	Collingham.
		Collingham Bk.	Bardsey, Collingham.
		....	Wetherby, Thorpe Arch, **Newton Kyme** Tadcaster.
		Cock Beck	Scholes.
		Carr Beck	Scholes.
		Parlington	
		Hollins Lake ..	Garforth.
		Cock Beck	Stutton.
		....	Ulleskell.
		Foss	Tadcaster.
		Catterton Bk.	Tadcaster.
		Angram Dam	Copmanthorpe.
		Foss	Bolton Percy, Ulleskell.
		....	Byther.
		....	Cawood.
PARACOMBE	....	....	Linton.
PARRET	....	....	Crewkerne.
	Hinton Brook ..	....	Crewkerne.
....	....	....	Martock.
	Isle	....	Ilminster.
....	.. ..	....	Langport.
	Yeo	....	Sherborne.
		Milbourne Brk.	Milborne Port, Sherborne.
		Yet	Yetminster.
		.. ..	Yeovil Junction.
		Evershott Brook	Sutton Bingham, **Evershott, Yeovil** Junction.
		.. ..	Yeovil.
		Sparkford Brk.	Sparkford, Marston Magna.
		.. ..	Martock, Langport.
	Hatch Brook ..	.. ..	Hatch.
.. ..	.. ..	.. ..	Athelney.
	Tone	.. ..	Wiveliscombe, Wellington.
		Milverton Brook	Wiveliscombe, Milverton.
		Norton Brook ..	Wiveliscombe, Bishops Lydiard, Milverton, Norton Fitzwarren.
		Kingston Brook	Bishops Lydiard, Taunton.
		.. ..	Taunton.
		Black Brook ..	Taunton.
		Durston Brook	Durston.
		.. ..	Athelney.
		....	Bridgwater.
PENRYN	....	....	Penryn.
PERRAN	....	....	Scorrier Gate.
	Gwenna Brook	....	Perran.
....	....	....	Perran.
	Trewedfra Brk.	....	Perran.
	Stithians Water	....	Perran.
PETHERICK	....	....	St. Columb, Padstow.
PEVENSEY	.. ..	.. ..	Pevensey.
PIDDLE	.. ..	....	Grimston, Moreton, Woo.
	Milton Park Lakes	.. ..	Blandford.
.. ..	....	....	Wareham.
	Decoy Pond ..	.. ..	Wareham.
PILLING WATER	....	....	Cogie Hill, Pilling.

ENGLAND—*continued.*

RIVERS AND THEIR TRIBUTARIES.			STATIONS.
PILNING BROOK	.. ..	.. ..	Pilning, New Passage.
PLYM		.. ..	Bickley.
	Meavy	.. ..	Horrowbridge, Bickley
.. ..	.. ..	.. ..	Marsh Mills.
	Tory Brook ..	.. ..	Bickley, Plymton, Marsh Mills.
.. ..	.. ..	.. ..	Plymouth.
POLGLAZE BRK.	.. ..		Tregony.
POLPERRO BRK.	.. ..		Polperro.
POLWHEVERILL	.. ..		Constantine.
PORTHCOTHAN	.. ..		St. Columb.
RAVENSBOURNE	.. ..	.. ..	Bromley, Catford Bridge, Lee, Lewisham
RIBBLE	.. ..		Ribble Head.
	Gale Water ..	.. ..	Ribble Head.
	Cam Beck	.. ..	Ribble Head.
	Tarn	.. ..	Horton.
.. ..	.. ..	.. ..	Horton.
	Horton Berk ..	.. ..	Horton.
	Cowside or Stainforth Beck ..	.. ..	Settle.
	.. ..	.. ..	Settle, Gigglewisck.
	Rathmell Brook	.. ..	Long Preston.
.. ..	.. ..	.. ..	Long Preston.
	Long Preston Bk.	.. ..	Settle, Long Preston.
	Wigglesworth Brook	*Tappa Tarn* ..	
		.. ..	Long Preston.
	Hellifield Brook	.. ..	Hellifield, Newsholme.
.. ..	.. ..	.. ..	Newsholme, Gisburn.
	Stock Beck	.. ..	Barnoldswick, Gisburn.
.. ..	.. ..	.. ..	Rimington.
	Tosside Beck ..	.. ..	Newsholme.
.. ..		*Bond Beck*	Newsholme.
.. ..		*Forest Beck* ..	Newsholme.
.. ..		*Cuddy Beck* ..	Gisburn.
.. ..		*Fell Beck*	Rimington.
	Tosside Beck ..	.. ..	Rimington.
	Swanside Beck	.. ..	Rimington.
		Ings Beck	Rimington.
	Grindleton Beck	.. ..	Chatburn.
.. ..	.. ..	.. ..	Chatburn.
	Bradford Beck	.. ..	Clitheroe.
	Waddington Brk.	.. ..	Clitheroe
.. ..	.. ..	.. ..	Clitheroe.
	Bashall Brook ..	*Bashall Moor Pond*	Clitheroe.
	Clitheroe Beck	.. ..	Clitheroe.
.. ..	.. ..	.. ..	Mitton.
	Hodder	*Hasgill Beck* ..	Slaidburn.
		Bridge House Beck	Slaidburn.
		Barm Gill	Slaidburn.
	.. ..	.. ..	Slaidburn.
		{ *Dunsop*	Slaidburn.
		{ *Croasdale Beck*	Slaidburn.
		{ *Eller Beck*	Slaidburn.
	.. ..	.. ..	Newton.
		Easington Brk.	Newton.
		{ *Whitendale Riv.*	Newton.
		{ *Brennand River*	Newton.
		Langden River	Whitewell.
	.. ..	.. ..	Whitewell.
		Greystoneley Brk.	Whitewell.
		{ *Loud*	Longridge.
		{ *Chipping Beck*	Longridge.
		{ *Lees Beck*	Longridge.
		{ *Loud*	Whitewell.
		Mill Beck	Whitewell.
	.. ..	.. ..	Mitton.
	West Calder ..	.. ..	Holme.
		Castle Hill Pond	Burnley.
	.. ..	.. ..	Burnley.

ENGLAND—*continued.*

RIVERS AND THEIR TRIBUTARIES.			STATIONS.
RIBBLE (*cont.*)	*Don*		Burnley.
	Swinden Water		Burnley.
	Bran River ..		Burnley.
	Laneshaw		Colne.
	Wycoller Water		Colne.
	Trawden Brook		Colne.
	3 Foulridge Re-		
	servoirs		Foulridge.
	Catlow Brook..		Colne.
	Laneshaw		Burnley.
	Roughlee Water		Colne, Burnley.
	....		Padiham.
	Lodge		Rose Grove.
	Tower Beck ..		Rose Grove.
	Shaw Brook ..		Padiham.
	Lodge		Padiham.
	Hyndburn Brk.		Accrington.
	Church Brook..		Accrington.
	Rishton Reserv.		Rishton.
	Sabden Brook..		Whalley.
	....		Whalley.
	Park Brook ..	....	Wilpshire, Whalley.
	Dean Brook ..	*Moor Game*	
		Hall Pond	Whalley.
		Crowshaw Res.	Ribchester.
	Starting Brook	....	Ribchester.
	....		Ribchester.
....	*Boyce's Brook*	*Dutton Brook..*	Ribchester.
....		....	Fulwood.
	Tun Brook....	....	Grimsargh, Fulwood.
	Mellor Brook..	....	Fulwood.
....	....	....	Preston.
ROCKLE	....	....	Wareham, Poole.
RODING (Essex)	....	....	Dunmow, Takeley, Chipping Ongar.
	Cripsy Brook..	....	Chipping Ongar.
....	....	....	Chigwell Lane, Loughton, Buckhurst Hill, Woodford, George Lane, Leytonstone, Ilford.
ROMAN RIVER..	....	....	Marks.
	Birch Hall Lake	....	Marks.
	Layer Brook ..	....	Wyvenhoe.
....	....	....	Wyvenhoe.
ROTHER (Kent)	....	....	Ticehurst, Etchingham, Robert's Bridge, Rye.
	Tillingham Water	....	Rye.
	Brede	....	Battle, Winchelsea, Rye.
SCALBY BECK ..	....	....	Hackness, Scalby.
	Burniston Beck	....	Cloughton.
		Lindhead Beck	Cloughton.
	....	....	Scalby.
SEATON	....	....	Liskeard, Menheniot.
SEVERN	....	....	Llanidloes.
	Brochan......	....	Llangurig.
		Dulas Brook ..	Llangurig.
		Tylwch	Tylwch.
	....	....	Llanidloes.
	Clywedog......	....	Llanidloes.
		Llwyd	Llanidloes.
		Biga	Llanidloes.
		Llyn Derw-	
		llydion....	Llanidloes.
....	....	....	Dolwen.
	Ebyr	*Llyn Ebyr*	Dolwen.
	Berthin	....	Dolwen.
	....	....	Llandinam, Caersws.
	Tarannon	*Llyn Gloyw....*	Carno.
		Relaf	Caersws.
		Ceryst	Llanidloes.
	....	....	Caersws.

ENGLAND—*continued.*

RIVERS AND THEIR TRIBUTARIES.			STATIONS.
SEVERN (*cont.*)	*Garno*	....	Carno.
		Pwll-llydan ..	Carno.
		Cledau	Carno.
		Cerniog	Carno.
		Llyn-Du	Pont-y-ddolgoch.
	... ...	....	Pont-y-ddolgoch.
	Tarw	*Llyn-Tarw*	Pont-y-ddolgoch.
	....	....	Scafell.
		Fachwen Pool...	Scafell.
	Hafren	....	Newtown.
....	....	....	Newtown, Abermule.
	Mule	....	Kerry, Abermule.
....	....	....	Montgomery.
	Rhiw	*Llyn-y-bugail*...	Carno.
		{ *Mawr*	
		{ *Llyn Mawr*	Pont-y-ddolgoch.
	....	....	Montgomery.
....	....	....	Forden.
	Camlad	....	Lydham.
		Caerbitra	Kerry.
		Locks Brook ..	Kerry.
		{ *Hailesford Brk.*	
		{ *Martin Pool* ..	Forden.
	....	....	Forden.
	....	....	Welshpool.
	Sylvan Brook..	....	Welshpool.
....	....	....	Buttington.
	Trewern	....	Middletown.
....	....	....	Criggion.
	Bele Brook....	....	Pool Quay, Criggion.
	Maerdy Brook..	....	Arleen. Criggion.
....	....	....	Llandrinio, Ferry,
	Vyrnwy	....	Bala.
	Lake Vyrnwy ..	*Ennant*	Lake Vyrnwy Hotel.
		Hirddu	Lake Vyrnwy Hotel.
		Cedig	Lake Vyrnwy Hotel.
		Marchnant....	Lake Vyrnwy Hotel.
		Cwny	Lake Vyrnwy Hotel.
		Dyfnant	Lake Vyrnwy Hotel.
		Llwydiarth....	Llanfyllin.
		Cringae	
		{ *Einion*	
		{ *Llyn-hir*	Carno.
		Grahwyddau ..	Carno.
		{ *Banw*	Dinas Mawddwy.
		{ *Ysguthan*	Dinas Mawddwy.
		{ { *Twrch*	Dinas Mawddwy.
		{ { *Llechog*	Dinas Mawddwy.
		{ { *Cathan*	Dinas Mawddwy.
		{ { *Llyn-y-bu-*	
		{ { *gail*	Dinas Mawddwy.
		{ *Banw*	Can-office.
		{ { *Eira*	Llanbrynmair.
		{ { *Cannon*	Llanbrynmair.
		{ { *Llyn Gwyd-*	
		{ { *dior*......	Llanbrynmair.
		{ { *Cledau*	Cerno.
		{ { *Nydwydd*....	Can-office.
		{ { *Gwylferyn*...	Can-office.
		{ { *Llyn Gwyl-*	
		{ { *feryn*	Can-office.
		{ { *Einion*	Can-office.
		{ { *Llyn-hir*	Can-office.
		{ { *Llyn-Gran-*	
		{ { *wyddau* ..	Can-office.
		{ *Banw*	Llanfair.
		Llyn-du	Llansantffraid.
....		....	Llansantffraid.
		{ *Cain*	Llanfyllin.
		{ *Llechwedd* ..	Llanfyllin.

c

ENGLAND—*continued.*

RIVERS AND THEIR TRIBUTARIES.			STATIONS.
SEVERN (*cont.*)		Cain	Llanfechan.
		Bwgan........	Llanfechan.
		Cain	Llansantffraid
		Tanat	Llangynnog.
	{	Goch	Llangynnog.
	{	Llyn-Pennan	Llangynnog.
		Eiarth	Llangynnog.
		Hirnant	Llangynnog.
	(	Moch	Llanrhaiadr-yn-Mochnant.
	)	Llyn - llyn - caws	Llanrhaiadr-yn-Mochnant.
	)	Disgynfa....	Llanrhaiadr-yn-Mochnant.
		Twrch	Llanrhaiadr-yn-Mochnant.
	(	Cynllaith	Oswestry.
	)	Llyn Rhyddwyn	Oswestry.
	(	Llyn Moelin	Llangedwyn.
		Tanat	Llan-y-blodwell.
	....	....	Llanymynech.
		{ Morda	Oswestry.
		{ Aston Lake....	Oswestry.
	Wear Brook ..	Sandford Hall Pond	Kinnerley.
		Onslow Hall Lake	Hanwood.
	Perry	....	Gobowen, Whittington.
		Halston Hall Lakes	Whittington.
	....	....	Rednall.
		Shelyocke Lake	Rednall.
	....	....	Basechurch.
		(Warbrook	Basechurch.
		| Berth Pool	Basechurch.
		| Birch Grove Pool........	Basechurch.
		| Marton Pool..	Basechurch.
		(Fennymere Pool	Basechurch.
	....	....	Leaton, Shrewsbury.
	Raddle	Onslow Hall Lake	Hanwood, Shrewsbury.
	Rea	....	Minsterley.
		Minsterley Brk.	Minsterley.
	....	....	Pontesbury.
		Habberley Brk.	Pontesbury.
	....	....	Hanwood.
		Yockleton Brook	Westbury, Yockleton, Hanwood
		Longdean Brook	Yockleton.
		{ Meole Brook ..	Yockleton.
		{ Bomer Pool ..	Yockleton.
	....	....	Shrewsbury.
		Almond Pool..	Shrewsbury.
		Black Pool....	Shrewsbury.
		Hencott Pool..	Shrewsbury.
	Sundown Brook	....	Yarton, Hadnall.
		Sundorn Castle Lakes	Shrewsbury.
	Tern	Maer Hall Lake	Whitmore.
	....	....	Norton.
		{ Hemp Mill Bk.	Market Drayton.
		{ Daisy Lake....	Market Drayton.
	....	....	Market Drayton.
		Coal Brook....	Market Drayton.
		Buntingsdale Hall Lake ..	Market Drayton.
		(Basle Brook ..	
		| Sandford Hall Pool........	Prees.
		| Big Pool......	Adderley.
		) Old Pool......	Market Drayton.
		| Stych Pool	Market Drayton.
		| Cleverley Pond	Market Drayton.
		| Morden Mill	
		(Pond	Market Drayton.

ENGLAND—*continued.*

RIVERS AND THEIR TRIBUTARIES.			STATIONS
SEVERN (*cont.*)	....	....	Hodnet.
		Salter's Brook..	Hodnet.
	....		Peplow.
		Allford Brook..	Peplow.
		Polford Brook..	Peplow.
		Meess	
		White Sitch Lake	Shifnal.
		Aquadale Mere	Newport.
		Chetwynd Park	
		Pond	Newport.
		Lomeo Brook..	Newport
		Elerton Bk...	
		Heywood	
		Ponds	Market Drayton.
		Canal Re-	
		servoir....	Market Drayton.
		Showed Pond	Newport.
		Meess	Peplow.
	....		Crudgington.
		Strine	Newport.
		Brockton Brk.	Newport.
		Wildmore	
		Pool......	Newport.
		Minton's Pool	Newport.
		LimekilnPool	Newport.
		Preston Brk...	Hadley.
		Strine	Crudgington.
		Beanhill Brook	Crudgington.
	....		Walcott.
		Roden	
		White Meer ..	Ellesmere.
		Black Meer....	Ellesmere.
		Colemere......	Ellesmere.
		Cross Meer ..	Ellesmere.
		Roden	Wem.
		Prees Brook ..	Wem.
		Hawkstone	
		Park Lake..	Wem.
		Roden	Walcott.
	....	....	Shrewsbury.
....	....	....	Berrington.
	Bell Brook	....	Berrington.
	Cound Brook..	....	Church Stretton, Le Botwood, Dorrington,
		Row Brook....	Berrington. [Condover, Berrington.
		Aston Brook ..	Berrington.
		Langley Brook	
		Langley Pond..	Le Botwood.
		Aston Burnell	
		Park Lakes..	Cressage.
		Harnage	
		Grange Pond	Cressage.
....	....	....	Cressage.
	Hughley Brook	....	Presthorpe, Much Wenlock.
	Leighton Brook	....	Cressage.
....	....	....	Buildwas.
	Farley Brook..	....	Much Wenlock, Buildwas.
....	....	....	Ironbridge, Coalport, Linley.
	Linley Brook ..	....	Linley.
	Willey Pk.Lakes	....	Linley.
	Worf	....	Shifnal.
	Buritngton Pool	....	Shifnal.
	New Pool	....	Shifnal.
	Forge Pool....	....	Shifnal.
		Norning Brook	Shifnal
		Weston Park	
		Lakes	Shifnal.
		Tong Brook..	Shifnal.
		Cowley Wood	
		Pond	Shifnal.
		Norton Meer	Shifnal.
		Badger Brook..	Albrighton.
		Snowdon Pool..	Albrighton.

c 2

ENGLAND—*continued.*

RIVERS AND THEIR TRIBUTARIES.			STATIONS.
SEVERN (*cont.*)		Stratford Brook	Albrighton, Linley.
		Claverley Brk.	Linley.
....	....	....	Linley.
....	....	....	Bridgnorth.
	Mor Brook....	....	Much Wenlock.
		Beggar Hill Brk.	Much Wenlock.
....	....	....	Hampton.
	....	....	Hampton, Alverley.
	Borle Brook ..	....	Bridgnorth, Alverley.
....	....	....	Upper Arley, Bewdley.
	Dowles Brook..	....	Alverley, Wyre, Bewdley.
....	....	....	Stourport.
	Gladder Brook	....	Stourport.
	Stour	....	Halesowen, Cradley.
		Gades Green Res.	Dudley.
		New Pool	Cradley.
	....	....	Stourbridge.
		Pensnett Chase Reservoirs ..	Brierley Hill.
		Smestow	Wolverhampton.
		Wombourne....	Wolverhampton.
		Himley Park Ponds	Stourbridge.
		Common Pool..	Stourbridge.
		Philley Brook..	Stourbridge.
	....	....	Kidderminster.
		Hoo Brook	Churchill, Kidderminster.
	....	....	Stourport.
	Dick Brook....	....	Stourport.
		Sharpley Pool	Stourport.
	Frog Pool	....	Stourport.
	Shrawley Brook	....	Stourport.
	Witley Court Ponds	....	Stourport.
	Salwarp	....	Bromsgrove.
		Spadsbourne Bk.	Bromsgrove.
		Hen Brook	Droitwich.
	....	....	Droitwich.
		Body Brook ..	Droitwich.
		Hampton Brk.	Droitwich.
		Dovedale Brook	Thurtlebury.
	....	....	Worcester.
	Teme	....	Knucklas, Knighton, Bucknall, Leintwar- [dine.
		Clun	Clun.
		Lower	Clun.
		Clun	Broome.
		Kempton Brk.	Broome.
		Acton Pool..	Clun.
		Clun	Hopton Heath.
		Redlake Brook	Bucknall, Hopton Heath.
		Clun	Leintwardine.
		Allcox Brook..	Leintwardine.
		Burrington Pool	Leintwardine.
	....	....	Broomfield.
		Onny	
		Marsh Pool....	Lydham.
		Shelve Pool.....	Lydham.
		Black Brook....	Lydham.
		Onny	Lydham, Eaton.
		Eaton Brook..	Le Botwood, Eaton.
		Onny	Plowden.
		Quenny Brk.	Marsh Brook.
		Eaton Brook.	Longville, Harton Road.
		Onny	Craven Arms, Onibury, Bromfield.
		Decoy Pools ..	Bromfield.
	....	....	Ludlow.
		Corve	Presthorpe.
		Thonglands ..	
		Brook	Ludlow.
		Tugford Brook	Ludlow.
		Pye Brook....	Ludlow.

ENGLAND—*continued.*

RIVERS AND THEIR TRIBUTARIES.		STATIONS.
SEVERN (*cont.*)	*Ludford Park Lakes*	Ludlow.
....	....	Wooferton.
	Brimfield Brk.	Wooferton.
....	....	Easton Court.
	West Brook ..	
	Cadmore Brook	Easton Court.
	Ledwych	Ludlow.
	Downton Hall Lakes	Ludlow.
	Dogditch Brook	Ludlow.
	Cay Brook	Ludlow.
	Wooten Pool ..	Ludlow.
	Ledwych	Tenbury.
....	....	Tenbury.
	Kyre	
	Kyre Pool	Tenbury.
	Corn Brook ..	Tenbury.
....	....	Newnham Bridge.
	Rea	Cleobury Mortimer.
	Cleobury Brook	Cleobury Mortimer.
	Rea	Neen Sollers.
	Ranhall Brook	Neen Sollers.
	Hepton Brook	Neen Sollers.
	Rea	Newnham Bridge.
	Bickley Pools ..	Newnham Bridge.
	Piper's Brook ..	Newnham Bridge.
	Stanford Park Lake	Newnham Bridge.
....	....	Knightswick.
	Sapey Brook ..	Knightswick.
....	....	Leigh Court.
	Leigh Brook ..	Colwall, Malvern, Leigh Court.
....	....	Bransford.
	Laughern Brk.	Worcester, Bransford.
....	....	Worcester.
....	....	Upton-on-Severn, Ripple, Tewkesbury.
	Ripple Brook ..	Tewkesbury.
	Croome Park Lakes	Defford.
	Avon	Naseby, Kilworth, Stamford, Lilbourne.
	Naseby Reserv.	
	Yelvertoft Brk.	Lilbourne.
....	....	Clifton, Rugby.
	Swift	Kilworth, Lutterworth, Rugby.
....	....	Brandon, Stoneleigh.
	Sow	Bedworth, Exhall.
	Breach Brook ..	Exhall.
	Sow	Foleshill.
	Marches Brook.	Foleshill.
	Sow	Coventry.
	Withy Brook ..	Coventry.
	Coombe Brk.	Brinklow.
	Burdon Pool	Brinklow.
	Coombe Park. Lake	Brinklow.
	Sherbourne	Coventry.
	Sow	Stoneleigh.
....	....	Leamington.
	Leam	Braunston.
	Rains Brook ..	Rugby.
	Leam	Birdingbury
	Itchene	
	Stoveton House Lake	Fenny Compton.
	Ham Brook.	Fenny Compton.
	Itchene	Harbury, Southam.
	Leam	Leamington.
....	....	Warwick.
	Warwick Park Lake	Warwick.
	Thelesford Brk.	Stratford-on-Avon.

ENGLAND—*continued.*

RIVERS AND THEIR TRIBUTARIES.		STATIONS.
SEVERN (*cont.*)	*Dene*	Kington.
	Coombe Brook	
	Lakes	Kington.
	....	Stratford-on-Avon.
	Stour	Shipston.
	Compton Brook	Shipston.
	Knee Brook ..	Campden, Blockley, Shipston.
	Ealington Park	
	Lake	Shipston.
	Stour	Stratford-on-Avon.
	....	Millcote, Salford Priors.
	Arrow	Alvechurch, Redditch.
	Hewell Grange	
	Lake	Redditch.
	Ipsley Lodge	
	Pond	Redditch.
	Arrow	Studley, Congleton, Alcester.
	Alne........	Henley-in-Arden.
	Edstone Brk.	Hatton, Bearley Cross.
	Alne........	Alcester.
	Rugley Park	
	Lake	Wixford.
	Arrow	Wixford. Salford Priors.
	Ban Brook....	Salford Priors.
	....	Harvington.
	Wickham Brook	Harvington.
	....	Evesham.
	Isborne	Hinton, Evesham.
	....	Pershore.
	Wyre	Inkberrow.
	Whitsun Brook	Pershore.
	Wyre	Pershore.
	....	Defford.
	Bow Brook....	Alcester.
	Dean Brook ..	Alcester.
	Bow Brook	Spetchley, Pershore.
	Stoulton Brook	Spetchley.
	Spetchley Park	
	Lake	Spetchley, Pershore.
	Bow Brook....	Defford.
	....	Bredon, Tewkesbury.
	Carant Brook ..	Tewkesbury.
	Swilgare......	....	Prestbury, Cleve, Tewkesbury.
	Tirle Brook ..	Tewkesbury.
	Chelt	Cheltenham, Gloucester.
	....	Gloucester.
	Longford Brook	Gloucester.
	Broadboard Bk.	Gloucester.
	Leadon	Ledbury.
	Dogberry Pools	Ledbury.
	Canal Reservoir	Ledbury.
	....	Dymock.
	Preston	Dymock.
	....	Upleadon.
	Clynch Brook..	Upleadon.
	Eastnor Castle	
	Lakes	Ledbury.
	Newent Brook ..	Newent, Upleadon.
	....	Gloucester.
	Twiver......	Gloucester.
SHEEPHILL BRK.	....	Bude.
SID	....	Sidmouth.
SPOKES MILL	....	Hartland.
STACKPOLE BK.	....	Cheriton.
ST. ALLEN	....	Truro.
	Boswallock Wtr.	Truro.
	Tregarethan Wtr.	Truro.
	Sevecock Water	Chancewater, Truro.
	Tresillian Water	Grampound Road.
	Trelassick Brook	Grampound Road.
	Kestle Water ..	Grampound Road.

ENGLAND—*continued.*

RIVERS AND THEIR TRIBUTARIES.			STATIONS.
St. Allen (*cont.*)		Woodland Brk.	Truro.
St. Austell ..	....	....	St. Austell.
	Clissy	....	Burngullow, St. Austell.
STAINSBY BK.	....	....	Stockton.
STEEPING RIVER	....	....	Spilsby, Halton Holegate, Thorpe, Wain- [fleet.
STEERS POOL	....	....	Woodland, Broughton, Sandside.
St. GERMANS ..	....	....	Liskeard, Menheniot, St. Germans.
	Cad	....	Launceston.
		Trewartha Wtr.	Launceston.
....	....	....	St. Germans.
STOUPE BECK ..	....	....	Fyling Hall.
STOUR (Kent).	....	....	Ashford, Westonhanger, Wye, Chilham, Chartham, Canterbury, Sturry, Grove Ferry
	Little Stour ..	....	Bekesbourne, Grove Ferry.
	....	....	Minster, Sandwich.
STOUR (Dorset)	....	....	Witham, Gillingham.
	Shreen..........	....	Gillingham.
	Ledden	....	Gillingham.
		Fern Brook ..	Shaftsbury.
	....	....	Gillingham.
	Cale	....	Wincanton, Temple Combe.
.		Bow Brook....	Temple Combe.
	....	....	Stalbridge.
....	Lidden ..	....	Sturminster Newton, Stalbridge.
	Divelish	....	Sturminster.
	Iwerne..........	....	Blandford.
	....	....	Sturminster, Shillingston, Blandford Spettisbury.
	Tarrant	....	Spettisbury.
....	....	....	Bailey Gate, Wimborne.
	Allen	....	Verwood, Wimborne.
	Blackwater....	....	Wimborne.
....	....	....	Hern Bridge.
	Moors........	....	Verwood, Hern Bridge.
....	....	....	Christchurch.
STOUR (Suffolk)	....	....	Haverhill, Sturmer.
	Albery Brook..	....	Haverhill, Sturmer.
	Birdbrook	....	Sturmer.
....	....	....	Stoke, Clare, Cavendish.
	Glemsford Brk.	....	Melford.
....	....	....	Melford.
	Melford Brook	....	Melford.
	Bardfield Brook	....	Sudbury.
	....	....	Sudbury, Bures.
	Assington Mill Pond	....	Bures.
....	....	....	Nayland.
	Boxford	....	Sudbury, Nayland.
	Brett	Brettenham Pk. Lake	Lavenham.
		Lavenham Brk.	Cockfield, Lavenham.
	....	....	Hadleigh.
	....	....	Manningtree.
TAMER	....	....	Plymouth.
	Bude Reservoir	....	Holsworthy.
	Fox Water ..	....	Holsworthy.
	Holsworthy Wtr.	....	Holsworthy.
	Claw	....	Holsworthy.
	Bear Water ..	....	Launceston.
....	....	....	Launceston.
	Yeolm	....	Launceston.
		Cancer Water .	Launceston.
		Wilsey Brook..	Launceston.
		Cowdery Water	Launceston.
	Carey	Kingsford Wtr.	Launceston.
		....	Launceston.
	Attery........	....	Launceston.
	Lyd	....	Lidford, Coryton.
		Lew	Bridestow, Lidford.
		Mary Stow....	Coryton.
	....	....	Lifton.

ENGLAND—*continued.*

RIVERS AND THEIR TRIBUTARIES.			STATIONS.
TAMAR (cont.)..		*Thistle*	Bridestow, Lifton.
	Laudne Water	....	Launceston.
	Inny	....	Launceston.
		Penpont Water	Launceston.
....	....	....	Tavistock.
	Tavy	....	Lidford.
		Rattle	Lidford.
	....	....	Mary Tavy
		Wolmer	Mary Tavy.
	....		Tavistock.
		Lamerton ...	Tavistock.
		Walcombe ...	Mary Tavy, Tavistock, Horrabridge.
	....	....	Bickley.
	....	....	Plymouth.
TAW	....	....	Okehampton.
	Teal Water....	....	Okehampton.
.. ..		....	North Tawton, Lapford.
	Lapford Water	.. ..	Bow.
		Braddiford Brl.	Morchard Road.
	....		Lapford.
		Washford Brl.	Lapford.
.. ..	....	....	Eggesford.
	Hollowcombe Wtr.	... .	Eggesford.
	Little Dart	.. ..	East Anstey
		Sturcombe ...	East Anstey
		.. ..	Eggesford.
	Tiddywater ..	....	Eggesford.
.. ..	.. ..	.. ..	South Molton Road.
	Yeo	.. ..	East Anstey, Molland.
		Molland Water	Molland.
		Mole	South Molton.
		Knowstone Wtr.	East Anstey, Molland, South Molton
		Littlecot Brook..	South Molton.
		Bray	Castlehill, South Molton.
.. ..		.. ..	Portsmouth Arms, Umberleigh.
	Chittlehampton	....	Chapelton.
....	.. ..	....	Chapelton.
	Yarnscombe Bk.	....	Portsmouth Arms, Chapelton.
	Swinbridge Wtr.	....	Swinbridge, Chapelton.
....	.. ..		Barnstaple
	Kentisbury Wtr.	....	Barnstaple.
	Muddiford Bl.	.. ..	Barnstaple
TEES	*Trout Beck*....	....	Culgaith.
	Maize Beck ..	*Gt. Rundale Tarn*	Long Marton.
			Langdon Beck Hotel.
	Harwood Beck.	*Langdon Beck*..	Langdon Beck Hotel.
	....	....	High Force Hotel.
	Skyer Beck....	....	High Force Hotel.
	Blea Beck	....	High Force Hotel.
	Rowton Beck ..	....	Middleton-in-Teesdale.
	....		Middleton-in-Teesdale.
	Lune	*Close Beck*	Mickleton.
		{ *Long Grain Bk.*	Mickleton.
		Arngill Beck ..	
		Arngill Fish Pond	
		Howgill Beck ..	Mickleton.
		Wemmergill Beck	Mickleton.
		{ *Soulgill Beck*..	Mickleton.
		Rowantree Bk.	
	....	....	Mickleton, Middleton.
	East Sikcar Bk.	....	Romaldkirk.
		White Hill Pd.	Romaldkirk.
	....	....	Romaldkirk.
	Reer Beck	....	Romaldkirk.
	Wilden Beck ..	....	Romaldkirk.
	Balder	*Hunder Beck*..	Cotherstone.
	....	....	Cotherstone.

ENGLAND—*continued.*

RIVERS AND THEIR TRIBUTARIES.			STATIONS.
Tees (cont.) ..	Crook Beck....	....	Cotherstone.
	....	....	Lartington.
	Scur Beck	....	Lartington.
	....	....	Barnard Castle.
	Harmire Beck..	....	Barnard Castle.
	Deepdale Beck..	....	Barnard Castle.
	Thorsgill Beck..	....	Barnard Castle.
	Greta	....	Bowes.
		Eller Beck	Bowes.
		Garnathwaite Beck	Bowes.
		Gill Beck	Bowes.
		Tutta Beck....	Bowes, Winston.
	Whorlton Beck	....	Winston.
	....	....	Winston.
	Alwent Beck ..	....	Barnard Castle.
		Raby Pk. Lakes	Barnard Castle.
		Sudburn Beck..	Barnard Castle.
	....	....	Winston.
	....	....	Gainsford, Piercebridge.
	Dyance Beck ..	....	Gainsford.
		Summerhouse Beck	Gainsford.
		....	Piercebridge.
	Ulnaby Beck ..	....	Piercebridge.
	....	....	Croft.
	Clow Beck	....	Barnard Castle, Winston.
			Piercebridge.
		Forcell Park Lake	Piercebridge.
		Waterfall Beck	Croft.
	Skerne	....	Trimdon, Hurworth.
			Sedgefield.
		Hardwicke Hall Lake	Sedgefield.
		....	Bradbury.
		Woodham Burn	Shildon.
		....	Aycliffe, Darlington.
		Crocker Beck..	Piercebridge, Darlington.
		....	Croft.
	....	....	Dalton, Dinsdale.
	Saltergill Beck.	....	Egglescliffe.
	....	....	Egglescliffe.
	Nelly Burdens Beck	....	Egglescliffe.
	Leven	....	Kildale.
		Otters Hill Bk.	Battersby.
		....	Ayton, Stokesley
		Broughton Bridge Beck	Ingleby, Stokesley.
		Broughton Beck	Stokesley.
		West Beck	Stokesley.
		Tame	Stokesley.
		Faceby Beck ..	Sexhow.
		Carlton Beck..	Sexhow.
		....	Sexhow.
		Potto Beck	Sexhow.
		....	Picton, Egglescliffe.
	Bassleton Beck.	....	Egglescliffe.
	....	....	Stockton.
Teign (Devon)	....	....	Moreton Hampstead, Lustleigh.
	Bovey	....	Lustleigh, Bovey.
	....	....	Teigngrace, Newton, Teignmouth.
Test (Hants).	....	....	Overton, Whitchurch, Itchen Abbas, Fullerton Bridge.
	Anton	....	Andover, Goodworth Clatford, Fullerton Bridge.
	....	....	Stockbridge, King Somborne, Mottisfont, Romsey, Redbridge.
	Lyndhurst Brk.	....	Lyndhurst, Redbridge
	....	....	Southampton

ENGLAND—*continued.*

RIVERS AND THEIR TRIBUTARIES.			STATIONS.
TETNEY DRAIN	....	....	Market Rasen.
	Croxby Pond..	....	Moortown.
....			Holton-le-Clay.
THAMES	....	....	Tetbury-road.
	Churn	....	Cirencester.
	Ray	....	Swindon, Purton.
	Byde Mill Brook	....	Shrivenham.
	Cole........ ..	....	Swindon, Shrivenham.
	....	....	Lechlade.
	Colne	....	Shipton, Fairford, Lechlade.
	Leach	....	Lechlade.
....	....	....	Bampton.
	Charney Brook	....	Bampton.
	Windrush	....	Bourton-on-the-Water.
		Dickler	Stow, Bourton-on-the-Water.
	....	....	Witney.
....	....	....	Yarnton.
	Evenlode.....	....	Adlestrop, Chipping Norton, Shipton, Ascott, Charlbury, Handbrough.
		Glyme	Handbrough.
	....	....	Oxford.
	Cherwell	....	Byfield, Copredy, Fenny Compton, Banbury, Aynho, Somerton, Heyford, Kirtlington, Woodstock-road, Islip.
		Ray	Bicester, Islip.
	....	....	Oxford.
....	....	....	Abingdon.
	Ock	....	Abingdon.
....	....	....	Culham, Appleford.
	Thame	....	Aylesbury, Liddington. [ing.
....	....	....	Wallingford, Goring, Pangbourne, Read-
	Kennet	....	Marlborough, Hungerford, Kintbury, Newbury, Thatcham, Midgham, Aldermaston.
		Embourne	Newbury, Midgham, Aldermaston.
	....	....	Theale, Reading.
....	....	....	Shiplake, Twyford.
	Loddon	....	Basingstoke, Mortimer.
		Blackwater....	Farnborough, Blackwater, Sandhurst.
		Whitewater.. ..	Winchfield.
	....	....	Twyford.
		Bull Brook	Bracknell, Twyford.
....	....	....	Henley, Marlow, Bourne End, Cookham.
	Wye	....	West Wycombe, High Wycombe, Loudwater, Woburn, Cookham.
....	....	....	Maidenhead, Windsor, Datchet, Wraysbury.
	Colne	....	Harpenden, St. Alban's, Park Street, Elstree, Radlett, Watford Junction, Watford, Rickmansworth.
		Gade	Hemel Hempstead, Box Moor, Berkhampstead, King's Langley, Rickmansworth.
		Chess	Rickmansworth.
	.. ..	....	Uxbridge, West Drayton, Wraysbury.
.. ..	....	....	Staines, Chertsey, Weybridge.
	Bourne Brook	....	Ascot, Virginia Water, Woking, Weybridge.
	Wey..	....	Alton, Farnham, Liphook, Haslemere, Tongham, Milford, Godalming, Witley, Cranley, Bramley, Shelford.
		Tillingbourne..	Gomshall, Shelford.
	....	....	Guildford, Woking, Pirbright, Weybridge.
.. ..	.. ..	....	Shepperton, Sunbury, Hampton, Hampton Court.
	Mole	.. ..	Crawley, Three Bridges, Horley, Rowfant, Merstham, Red Hill, Holmewood, Betchworth, Dorking, Box Hill, Leatherhead, Esher, Moulsey, Hampton Court.
....	....	....	Thames Ditton, Kingston.
	Hog's Mill River	....	Ewell, Epsom, Malden, Kingston.
.. ..	.. ..	....	Teddington.
	Colne	....	Ashford, Feltham, Teddington.
....	.. ..	....	Twickenham, Richmond, Isleworth.

ENGLAND—*continued.*

RIVERS AND THEIR TRIBUTARIES.			STATIONS.
THAMES (*cont.*)	*Yedding Brook*	....	Southall, Twickenham, Isleworth.
... .	... .	.. ..	Brentford. [Brentford.
	Brent	.. ..	Hendon, Welsh Harp, Willesden, Hanwell,
	....	.. ..	Kew, Mortlake, Barnes, Chiswick, Hammersmith, Putney, Wandsworth.
	Wandle	.. ..	Croydon, Carshalton, Mitcham, Merton,
.. ..	... .	....	London. [Wandsworth.
THORPE BECK	....	....	Carlton, Thorpe Thewles.
			Billingham, Newport.
TORRIDGE	.. ..	.. ..	Bideford.
	Sockington Wtr.	. .. .	Bideford.
	Floodmead Wtr.	....	Bideford.
	Waldon	.. ..	Torrington.
	Whiteleigh Brk.	.. ..	Torrington.
	Buckland Brook	.. ..	Torrington.
	Lew	.. ..	Oakhampton.
		Ashbury Brook.	Oakhampton.
		Wagaford Brk.	Oakhampton.
		Marshford Brk.	Oakhampton.
	.. ..	.. ..	Oakhampton.
		Venton Brook ..	Oakhampton.
	Oakment	.. ..	Bridestow, Oakhampton.
	Exbourne Wtr.	.. ..	Sampford Courtney, Tawton.
	Merton Brook .	....	Torrington.
	Woolley Brook .	.. ..	Torrington
.. ..	.. ..	.. ..	Torrington
	Langtree Brook	.. ..	Torrington.
	Hunshaw Water	.. ..	Torrington.
	Laidland Water	.. ..	Torrington
		Alvington Brk.	Bideford.
	.. ..	.. ..	Bideford.
	Wear Water ..	.. ..	Bideford.
TOWAN	....	....	Perranzabuloe.
	Golla Water ..	....	Perranzabuloe.
TOWSINGTON .	....	....	Exminster.
TREDAWL WTR.	....	....	Ferrabnrry.
TRENT	*Black Bull Res.*	....	Black Bull.
....	....	....	Milton.
	Foxley Brook ..	....	Black Bull, Ford Green, Milton.
....	....	....	Bucknall, Stoke.
	Fowler Brook ..	*Bath Pool*	Tunstall, Burslem, Hanley, Stoke
....	....	....	Fenton, Trentham.
	Lyme	*Racecourse Pond*	Newcastle, Trentham.
	Northwood Brk.	*Keel Hall Park Lakes*	Newcastle.
		Trentham Park Lakes	Trentham.
		Hanchurch Farm Ponds	Trentham.
	Longton Brook .	*Park Hall Lake*	Longton, Trentham.
....	*Trentham Park Lake*	....	Trentham.
....	....	....	Barlaston.
	Barlaston Park Lake........	....	Barlaston.
....	....	....	Stone.
	Filly Brook ..	....	Stone.
	Moddershall Bk	*Moddershall Mill Ponds* ..	Stone.
....	....	....	Weston.
	Gayton Brook ..	....	Weston.
....	....	....	Great Haywood.
	Sow	....	Eccleshall.
	{ *Offley Brook* ..	....	Eccleshall.
	{ *Oatland Lake*..		
	(*Cop Mere*		
	{ *Mease*		Whitmore.
	| *Whitmore Park Lake*		Whitmore.
	| *Hatton Mill* ..		Standon.

ENGLAND—*continued.*

Rivers and their Tributaries.			Stations.
TRENT (*cont.*)		Bromley Brk.	Standon.
		Bromley Mill	Standon.
		Podmore Pool	Standon.
	Mease		
		Mease House Ponds	Standon.
		Swinnerton Park Lake ..	Stone.
	Mease		Norton Bridge.
	....	....	Great Bridgeford, Stafford.
		Chamford Brk.	Stafford.
	Penk		
		Chillington Pk. Pool........	Codsall.
		Penk	Codsall.
		Moseley Mill ..	Bushbury.
		Penk	Four Ashes.
		Saredon Brk.	
		Up. & Lower Brindley Pool......	Hednesford.
		Furnace Pool	
		Hendesford Pool......	
		Saredon	Cannock.
		Hatherton Hall Lake..	Cannock.
		Saredon	Four Ashes
	Penk		Brewood, Penkridge.
		Whiston Brk.	
		Eaton Water.	Gnossall
		Whiston	Penkridge.
		Galey Brook..	Penkridge.
		Galey Reservoir	Galey.
		Pillaton Brk.	
		Pottall Reservoir ..	Cannock.
		Pottal Pools..	Cannock.
		Manstey Wood Pnds	Penkridge.
		Pillaton	Penkridge.
		Keeper's Pls. & Park Pool ..	Penkridge.
		Penk	Stafford.
		Kingston Brook	
		Ingestre Park Pool........	Ingestre or Weston.
		Kingston Pool .	Stafford.
		Tixhall Pk. Pool	Stafford.
		Sherbrook Brk.	
		Upper, Middle, and Lower Sherbrook Pls.	Rugeley.
	....	....	Great Haywood.
	....	....	Colwich.
	Oakedge Park Ponds	....	Colwich.
	....	....	Rugeley.
	Colton Brook ..	....	Rugeley.
	Rising Brook ..	Bolands Pool..	Hednesford.
		New Coppice Pool	Rugeley.
	....	....	Rugeley.
	....	....	Armitage.
	How Brook....	Beaudesert Lake	Armitage.
	Blythe	....	Blythe, Creswell, Leigh.
		Birchwood Park Lake........	Leigh.
	....	....	Grindley, Abbots Bromley.
		Tad Brook....	Abbots Bromley.

ENGLAND—*continued.*

RIVERS AND THEIR TRIBUTARIES.		STATIONS
TRENT (*cont.*)		
	Bromley Brook	
	Bagots Park	
	Lakes	Abbots Bromley.
	Part Brook....	Armitage.
Bourne Brook..	*Coneyhill Pond*	Hammerwich.
	Ashmore Brook	Lichfield.
	Ben Brook	Armitage.
....	....	Alrewas.
Swarbourne Bk.	*Newbore' Lake*	Abbots Bromley.
	Lin Brook	
	Byrkley Park	
	Lake	Burton.
	Snee Pool	Walton.
....	....	Alrewas.
Alrewas Brook.	....	Lichfield.
....	....	Wichnor.
Tame	*Titford Reservoir*	Langley Green.
	Oldbury Pond..	Oldbury.
....		Wednesbury, Bescott Junction.
	Sneyd Brook ..	
	Sneyd Pool	Bloxwich.
	Sneyd Brook ..	Walsall, Bescott Junction.
	Ford Brook....	Pelsall, Walsall, Bescott Junction.
....	....	Newton Road.
	Red House Hall Pond	Newton Road.
	Forge Pond ..	Newton Road.
....	....	Perry Barr.
	Barr Pk. Lakes	Newton Road.
....	....	Aston.
	Aston Pk. Lake	Aston.
	Lodge Pool....	Perry Barr.
	Upper Witton Pool........	Aston.
	Lower Witton Pl.	Aston.
	Rea	Lifford.
	Bourne Brook	
	Frankley Pond	Halesowen.
	Bourne	
	Harborne Mill	Lifford.
	Rea	Birmingham.
	Cannon Hill Lake	Birmingham.
	Edgbaston Reservoir......	Birmingham.
	Thimble Mill	Birmingham.
	Smethwick Reservoir	Birmingham.
	Rotten Park Reservoir..	Birmingham.
	Rea	Aston.
....	....	Castle Bromwich.
	East Brook....	
	Bracebridge Pl.	Sutton Coldfield.
	Blackroot Pool.	Sutton Coldfield.
	Longmore Mill	Sutton Coldfield.
	Powell's Pool	Sutton Coldfield.
	Windley Pool	Sutton Coldfield.
	East Brook....	Castle Bromwich.
....	....	Whitacre Junction.
	Blythe	
	Earlswood Res.	Knowle.
	Blythe	Solihull, Knowle, Hampton.
	Packington Pk.	
	Lakes	Hampton.
	Coleshill Pool..	Coleshill.
	Blythe	Coleshill.
	Cole	Lifford.
	Tillerford Mill	Solihull.

ENGLAND—*continued.*

RIVERS AND THEIR TRIBUTARIES.	STATIONS.
TRENT (*cont.*)	
Inkford Brk.	Solihull.
Cole	Stichford.
Ulverly Bk.	
Kineton Reservoir..	Solihull.
Ulverly ..	Marston Green.
Chelmsley Wood Pds.	Coleshill.
Cole	Coleshill.
Blythe	Whitacre Junction.
Arley Brook ..	Arley, Shustoke, Whitacre.
....	Kingsbury.
Langley Brook.	
Langley Hall Ponds	Sutton Coldfield.
Middleton Hall Lake	Sutton Coldfield.
Gallows Brook..	
Canwell Hall Pd.	Sutton Coldfield.
....	Wilnescote.
Bourne Brook..	
Bourne Pool ..	Sutton Coldfield.
Crane Brook.	
Biddulph's Pl.	Cannock.
Brownhill's Reservoir ..	Brownhills.
Drayton Manor Lakes	Wilnescote.
Bourne	Wilnescote.
....	Tamworth.
Anker	Nuneaton.
Griff Brook..	Bedworth.
Sedswood Pl. and Arbury Park Lake.	Stockingford.
Griff	Nuneaton.
Anker	Atherstone.
Sence	Hugglescote, Heather.
Blower's Brk.	Heather.
Sence	Shakerstone.
Bosworth Bk.	Market Bosworth.
Tweed	Shenton.
Duckery in Bosworth Park ..	Shenton.
Anker	Polesworth, Tamworth.
Freeford Brook	
Swinfin Hall Lakes	Lichfield.
Freeford Hall Lakes	Lichfield.
....	Wichnor.
Mease	Ashby-de-la-Zouch, Snarston, Measham
Willesley Park Lake	Ashby-de-la-Zouch.
Seal Brook	
Over Seal Res.	Over Seal.
Barrat Pool ..	Over Seal.
....	Croxhall, Wichnor.
....	Walton.
Tatenhill Lake	Burton.
....	Burton.
Dove	Longnor, Hartington.
Mannyfold	Longnor.
Blackbrook	Longnor.
Elkstone Brook	Longnor.
Hamps	Leek.
Lower Acre Ponds	Leek.
Mannyfold	Ilam.

ENGLAND—*continued.*

RIVERS AND THEIR TRIBUTARIES.			STATIONS.
TRENT (*cont.*)	....	....	Ashbourne.
		Bradbourne Bk.	Ashbourne.
	.. ..	....	Clifton.
		{ *Henmore*	
		{ *Hopton Hall*	
		{ *Lakes*	Wirksworth, Ashbourne, Clifton.
	....	....	Norbury.
		Calwick Brook	Norbury.
	....	....	Rocester.
		{ *Churnet*	Leek.
		{ *Rudyerd Reserv.*	Leek.
		{ { *Endon Brook*	
		{ { *Stanley Mill*	Endon.
		{ { *Wetley Pond*	Cheddleton.
		{ *Churnet*	Cheddleton.
		{ *West Brook*	Cheddleton.
		{ *Consall Hall*	
		{ *Lake*	Froghall.
		{ *Ipstone Lake* ..	Froghall.
		{ *Churnet*	Froghall.
		{ *Dark Mill*	Froghall.
		{ *Churnet*	Oakamoor, Alton.
		{ { *Halford Brk.*	
		{ { *Woolton*	
		{ { *Grange Lake*	Norbury.
		{ *Churnet*	Denston, Rocester.
		Tean Brook ..	Cheadle, Uttoxeter.
	....	....	Uttoxeter.
		Stoneyford Brk.	Uttoxeter.
	....	....	Marchington.
		Somershall Brk.	Marchington.
	....	....	Sudbury.
		Sudbury Brook	Sudbury.
		Cubley Brook ..	Tutbury.
	....	....	Tutbury.
		{ *Fleam or Little*	
		{ *Dove*	Tutbury.
		} *Rolleston Hall*	
		{ *Lake*	Tutbury.
	....	....	Egginton.
		{ *Longford Brook*	
		{ *Yeldersley Pond*	Ashbourn.
		{ *Shirley Park* ..	Ashbourn.
		{ { *Bradley Brk.*	
		{ { *Bradley Lakes*	Ashbourn.
		{ *Limbersitch Bk.*	Tutbury.
		{ *Longford*	
		{ *Egginaton Hall*	
		{ *Lakes*	Eggington.
... .	....	....	Willington.
	Etwall Brook ..	*Radburn Pond*	Mickleover.
	....	....	Etwall, Egginton, Willington.
	Repton Brook ..	*Hartshorn Pnds.*	Swadlincote.
		Screw Mill	Swadlincote.
		Glover's Mill ..	Swadlincote.
		Repton Mill ..	Swadlincote.
		Bretby Pk. Lakes	Swadlincote.
		Repton Pk. Lake	Willington.
	Foremark Brk. ..	*Repton Rocks*	
		Pond	Swadlincote.
		Foremark Pnds.	Willington.
	Foremark Hall		
	Pond	....	Willington.
... .	....	....	Chellaston.
	Breedon Brook.	*Coleorton Pnds.*..	Ashby-de-la-Zouch, Worthington, Tong, [Melbourne
		{ *Carr Brook* ..	
		{ *Dogkennel Pool.*	Worthington.
		{ *Stanton Hall*	
		{ *Ponds*	Worthington.
		{ *Calke Park Pds.*	Worthington.
		{ *Carr*	Melbourne.

ENGLAND—*continued.*

RIVERS AND THEIR TRIBUTARIES.			STATIONS.
TRENT (*cont.*)	....	....	Weston.
	Donnington Park Lake	....	Weston.
....	....	....	Castle Donnington
	Derwent	....	Ashopton.
		Little Howden Brook	Ashopton.
		Westend	Ashopton.
		Abbey Brook ..	Ashopton.
		Mill Brook	Ashopton.
		Ashop	
		LadyClough Brk.	Glossop.
		Fair Brook	Ashopton.
		Alport	Glossop.
		Ashop	Ashopton.
		Lady Burk	Ashopton.
		Now	Hayfield, Chapel-en-le Frith, Castleton.
		Peaks Hole Wtr	Castleton.
		Bradwell Brook	Castleton.
		....	Hathersage.
		Hood Brook ..	Hathersage.
		Highlow Brook	Hathersage.
		Benbage Brook	Dronfield, Hathersage.
		....	Baslow
		Bar Brook	Baslow.
		Black Leach Bk.	Baslow.
		....	Edensor Rowsley.
		Wye	Buxton, Millers Dale, Monsal Dale, Ashford, Bakewell, Rowsley.
		....	Darley.
		Sydnope Brook	
		Flash Dam	Darley.
		....	Matlock.
		Bentley Brook ..	Matlock.
		....	Cromford, Whatstandwell.
		Alderwasley Ponds	Whatstandwell.
		....	Ambergate.
		Amber	Matlock, Stretton.
		Stretton Brook .	Stretton.
		Amber	Wingfield.
		Normanton Brook	Alfreton.
		Westwood Bk.	Westhouse, Alfreton.
		Birches Brook .	Alfreton.
		Batterley Reser.	Ripley.
		Amber	Ambergate.
		....	Belper.
		Black Brook ..	Belper.
		....	Duffield.
		Ecclesbourne ..	Wicksworth, Idridgehay, Hazzlewood. Duffield.
		....	Little Eaton.
		Holbrook Brook	Kilburn, Coxbench,
		Smalley Mill ..	Coxbench.
		Holbrook	Little Eaton.
		Allastry Hall Pond	Little Eaton.
		Ferryby Brook ..	Breadsall, Derby
		....	Derby.
		Cutler Brook ..	
		Kedleston Park Lake	Duffield, Derby
		Chaddesden Brk	Derby.
		Locko Pk. Lake	Spondon.
		....	Spondon, Borrowash Draycott.
		Elvaston Park Lake	Draycott.
		....	Sawley.
....	....	....	Sawley, Trent

ENGLAND—*continued.*

RIVERS AND THEIR TRIBUTARIES.		STATIONS.
TRENT (*cont.*) Soar	*Leicester Grange*	
	Lake........	Hinckley.
	Claybrook Mill.	Ullsthorpe.
	{ *Normanton Brk*	
	{ *Kirkby Hall*	
	{ *Lake*	Desford.
	{ *Normanton Hall*	
	{ *Lake*	Narborough.
	{ *Normanton Brk*	Narborough.
....	....	Narborough.
	Whetstone Brk.	Narborough.
	{ *Billesdon Brook*	Glen Magna.
	{ *Wiston Hall* ·	
	{ *Lake*	Glen Magna.
	{ *Billesdon*......	Blaby, Narborough.
·· ··	....	Leicester.
	Braunstone Hall	
	Lake........	Leicester.
	Willow Brook..	Leicester.
	Ingersby Brook	Leicester.
	{ *Wreake or Eye*	Wissendine.
	{ *Edmondthorpe*	
	{ *Hall Pond*	Wissendine.
	{ *Leesthorpe Pnd.*	Wissendine.
	{ *Stapleford Pk.*	
	{ *Lake*........	Saxby.
	{ *Wreake*	Saxby.
	{ *Saxby Brook* ..	Saxby.
	{ *Wreake*	Melton Mowbray.
	{ *Melton Brook*	
	{ *Goadby Mar-*	
	{ *wood Lake*	Scalford.
	{ *Melton*......	Melton Mowbray
	{ *Wreake*	Ashfordby.
	{ *Welby Pond* ..	Ashfordby.
	{ *Wreake*	Frisby.
	{ *Saxelby Pond*..	Grimstone.
	{ *Wreake*	Brooksby, Rearsby
	{ *Ox Brook* ..	Rearsby.
	{ *Ragdale Hall*	
	{ *Pond*	Rearsby.
	{ *Queniboro' Bk.*	Syston.
	{ *Ashby Brook.*	Syston.
	{ *Wreake*	Syston.
	{ *Barkby Brook*	Syston.
	{ *Hungerton*	
	{ *Pond*	Syston.
·· ··	....	Syston.
	{ *Rothley Brook*..	Desford.
	{ *Gabriel Pool* ..	Desford.
	{ *Rothley*	Ratby, Glenfield.
....	....	Mount Sorrel, Barrow-on-Soar.
	Quorndon Brook	Glenfield, Barrow-on-Soar
....	....	Loughborough.
	Walton Brk. ..	Loughborough.
	Stanford Hall	
	Lake	Loughborough.
	{ *Dishley Brook* ..	Coalville.
	{ *Carr Brook* ..	
	{ *Old Reservoir*	Swannington
	{ *Garendon Park*	
	{ *Lake*........	Loughborough.
	{ *Dishley*	Loughborough.
······ ...	....	Hathern.
	{ *Osgathorpe Brk.*	
	{ *Coleorton Ponds*	Ashby-de-la-Zouch.
	{ *Dixworth Brk.*	
	{ *Langley Priory*	
	{ *Pond*	Tong.
	{ *Osgathorpe*	Hathern.

ENGLAND—*continued.*

RIVERS AND THEIR TRIBUTARIES.			STATIONS.
TRENT *(cont.)*	....	....	Kegworth.
		Kington Brook.	Kegworth.
	....	....	Trent.
....	....	....	Eaton Junction
	Erwash	....	Pinxton.
		Brookshill Hall Lakes	Pinxton.
	....	....	Pye Bridge, Codnor Park.
		Golden Valley Reservoir ..	Codnor Park.
	....	....	Eastwood.
		Aldercar Hall Lakes	Eastwood.
		Loscoe Dam ..	Eastwood.
	....	....	Newthorpe.
		Gilt Brook	Ilkestone.
	....	....	Ilkestone, Stanton.
		Nut Brook	West Hallam, Stanton.
	....	....	Sandiacre, Eaton Junction.
....	....	....	Attenborough, Beeston.
	Tottle Brook ..	*Bilborough Cut.*	Radford, Beeston.
	Fairham Brk...	....	Widmerpool, Beeston.
....	....	....	Nottingham.
	Leen	*Upper & Lower Lakes, New-stead Abbey* ..	Linby.
		Papplewick Mill	Linby.
		Forge Mill .. .	Bulwell.
		....	Bulwell, Basford.
		Nuthall Lake..	Kimberley.
		Day Brook	Basford.
	....	....	Radford, Nottingham
	....	....	Colwick, Radcliffe.
....	*Thurbeck*	....	Plumtree.
		Roclaveston Manor Lake	Edwalton.
	....	....	Radcliffe.
....	....	....	Burton Joyce.
	Cocker Beck ..	....	Lowdham, Burton Joyce.
	Dover Beck....	....	Lowdham, Burton Joyce
... .	....	....	Bleasby, Fiskerton.
	Greet	*Kirklington Moor Ponds*	Southwell.
		Edingly Cotton Mill Pond ..	Farnsfield.
		Kirklington Hall Lake	Southwell.
		Halam Beck ..	Southwell.
	....	....	Southwell, Rolleston, Fiskerton
....	....	....	Newark.
	Pingley Dyke..	....	Newark.
	Devon	*Kimpton Res.*	Redmile.
		Croxton Park Lake	Scalford.
		Woolsthorpe Lake	Redmile.
	....	....	Bottesford.
		{ *Smite*	Upper Broughton.
		Dalby Brook ..	Upper Broughton.
		Smite	Barnston, Aslacton
		Whipling......	Barnston.
		Smite	Bottesford.
	....	....	Cotham.
		Car Dyke	Bingham, Cotham.
	....	....	Newark.
	....	....	Carlton.
....	*Crosby Dyke* ..	....	Carlton.
	Cowarth Pool & Mons Pool & Collingham Pond	....	Carlton

ENGLAND—*continued.*

RIVERS AND THEIR TRIBUTARIES.			STATIONS.
TRENT (*cont.*)	....	....	Sutton.
	Girton Brook..	*Skelmires Pond*	Swinderby.
	Fleet and Black Pool........	....	Sutton.
	Grassthorpe Brk.	....	Crow Park, Sutton.
....	....	....	Torksey.
	Foss Dyke Navigation	....	Torksey.
....	....	....	Marton, Gainsborough.
TRASILLIEN ..	....	....	Redruth.
TREVOWA	....	....	New Quay.
TRIM	....	....	Felton, Lea Mills.
TWANTER	....	....	Saffron Walden.
TWEED	....	.. ..	Berwick.
TYNE	....	....	Hexham, Riding Mill, Tarsett.
ULCEBY BECK..	*Newsham Abbey Lakes*	....	Brocklesby, Ulceby, Thornton.
USK	....	....	Devynock.
	Hydfer	....	Devynock.
	Clydack	....	Devynock.
	Cray	....	Cray. Devynock.
	Senni	*Treweren*	Devynock.
	Cilieni	....	Devynock.
		Llandeilor Brk.	Devynock.
. . ..	....	....	Aberbran.
	Bran	....	Aberbran.
	Yscir	....	Aberbran.
....	....	....	Brecknock.
	Honddu	....	Brecknock.
	Tarell	*Llyn-cwm-Lliwch*	Brecknock.
	Cynrig	....	Brecknock.
....	....	....	Tal-y-Llyn Junction.
	Mehascia	....	Tal-y-Llyn Junction.
....	....	....	Tal-y-Bont.
	Alwynd	....	Torpanian, Tal-y-Bont.
	Dyfferyn	....	Tal-y-Bont.
	Hogwy	....	Tal-y-Bont.
	Rhiangoll	....	Tolgarth, Gilwern.
....	....	....	Gilwern.
	Grwyne	....	Tolgarth, Gilwern.
	Clydach	....	Gilwern.
....	....	....	Govilon.
	Wenarth......	....	Govilon.
		Forge Pond ..	Govilon.
....	....	....	Abergavenny.
	Gavenny	....	Llanfihangel, Abergavenny.
....	....	....	Penpergum.
	Llanover Brook	....	Penpergum.
	Llangattock Brook	....	Penpergum.
	Llanarth Brook	....	Nantyderry.
....	....	....	Nantyderry, Usk.
	Olway	....	Bigswear, Llandenny.
		Raglan Brook..	Raglan, Llandenny.
		Pill Brook	Llandenny.
	....	....	Usk.
	....	....	Caerleon.
	Llwyd	....	Blaen Afon, Cwm Afon, Abersychan, Pontypool, Panteg, Pontrhydyran, Pontnewydd, Cwmbran, Caerleon.
		Doulas Brook	Llanternan, Cwmbran.
....	....	....	Newport.
VEWLYN BROOK	....	....	Penzance.
WANSBECK ..	.. ..	....	Morpeth.
WARBURN	.. ..	....	Holmsley.
WASHFORD.. .	....	.. ..	Roadwater, Combe Row, Washford, Watchet

The Angler's Diary.

ENGLAND—*continued.*

RIVERS AND THEIR TRIBUTARIES.			STATIONS.
WAVENEY	Diss Mere	.. ..	Diss.
	Eye Brook	.. ..	Eye.
....	.. ..	....	Haileston, Homersfield, Bungay
	Ditchingham		
	Hall Lakes..	....	Bungay.
....	....	....	Geldeston, Beccles.
	Oulton Brook..	....	Mutford, Lowestoft.
	Flixton Decoy.	....	Mutford.
.. ..	Lake at Villa..	....	Mutford.
....	....	....	Somerleyton, Haddiscoe.
	Flitton Decoy..	....	Haddiscoe.
	New Cut	....	Haddiscoe.
....	....	....	Belton.
	Breydon Water	....	Belton.
....	....	....	Yarmouth.
WEAVER	Moss Mere	....	Malpas.
	Capel Mere	....	Malpas.
	Cholmondeley Mere	....	Wrenbury.
....	....	....	Wrenbury.
	Marbury Brook	Brets Mere....	Malpas.
		Bickley Mill ..	Malpas.
		Bar Mere	Malpas.
		Oss Brook	Whitchurch.
		Oss Mere	Whitchurch.
		Marbury Mere.	Whitchurch.
		Marbury Mill..	Whitchurch.
	Sales Brook ..	Combermere	
		Mere	Wrenbury
	....	....	Audlem.
	Adderley Brook	New Pool	Adderley.
		Adderley Hall	
		Lakes	Adderley.
		The Mere	Adderley.
	....	....	Audlem.
	Birch Hall Brk.	Woodfall Pool	Audlem.
	Artle Brook ..	Madeley Manor	
		Park Lakes...	Keel.
	Bowsey Mill Pond	....	Madeley.
		Madeley Brook	
		Madeley Mill	
		Pond	Madeley.
		Wrinehill Mill	
		Pond	Madeley.
	....	....	Nantwich.
		How Beck	
		Doddington Pk.	
		Lakes	Nantwich.
	Baddiley Brook	Baddiley Mere	Wrenbury
....	....	....	Nantwich.
	Cheer Brook ..	....	Nantwich.
....	....	....	Worleston.
	Pool Brook	Harleston Lake	Nantwich.
	Wistaston Brook	Betley Mere ..	Madeley.
	Little Mere ..	....	Madeley.
		Betley Hall Lake	Basford.
	....	....	Basford, Crewe.
		Swill Brook ..	Basford, Crewe.
		Inglesway Brk.	
		Balterley Mere	Basford.
		Monneley Mere	Crewe.
		Crewe House	
		Lakes	Crewe.
		Inglesway Brk.	Crewe.
	....	....	Worleston.
	....	....	Minshull Vernon.
....	Ash Brook	Oak Mere	Delamere.
		Oulton Brook..	
		Fish Pool	Delamere.
		Oulton Mill	
		Pond	Beeston

ENGLAND—*continued.*

RIVERS AND THEIR TRIBUTARIES.			STATIONS.
WEAVER(*cont.*)		*Bedsworth Mill*	
		Pond	Winsford.
		{ *Wettenhall Brk.*	
		{ *Tilston Hall*	
		{ *Lake*	Beeston.
	....	....	Minshull Vernon.
	Storks Hill		
	Lake	....	Winsford.
....	....	....	Winsford.
	Whitgate Brook	*New Church*	
		Common Pnds.	Ouddington.
		Petty Pool	Ouddington.
	....	....	Winsford.
....	....	....	Northwich.
	Dane	....	Buxton.
		Folly Brook ..	Bosley.
		Bosley Reservoir	Bosley.
	....	....	Rushton, Bosley.
		{ *Cow Brook*....	
		{ *Great Oak Res.*	Rode.
		{ *Rode Reservoir*	Rode.
		{ *Cow Brook*....	Bosley.
	....	....	Congleton.
		Biddulph Brook	Congleton.
		Dairy Brook ..	Congleton.
	....	....	Holmes Chapel.
		Bag Mere	Congleton, Holmes Chapel.
		Midge Brook ..	Congleton, Holmes Chapel.
	....	....	Middlewich.
		{ *Wheelock*	
		{ *Moreton Hall*	
		{ *Lake*	Congleton.
		{ *Wheelock*	Sandbach.
		{ *Betchton Brook*	Sandbach.
		{ *Hassall Brk.*	
		{ *Alsager Pond*	Alsager.
		{ { *Lawton Bk.*	
		{ { *Lawton*	
		{ { *Hall Lake*	Alsager.
		{ { *Lawton*	
		{ { *Mere*	Alsager.
		{ { *Rode Hall*	
		{ { *Lake*	Alsager.
		{ { *Lawton Bk.*	Alsager.
		{ *Hassall Brk.*	Sandbach.
		{ *Foul Brook* ..	
		{ *Winterley*	
		{ *Mill Pond*	Crewe.
		{ *Foul Brook* ..	Sandbach.
		Wheelock	Minshull Vernon, Middlewich.
		{ *Croco*	Holmes Chapel, Middlewich.
		{ *Sanderson's*	
		{ *Brook*	Middlewich.
	....	....	Northwich.
	Norcot Brook ..	*Cogshall Lake* ..	Northwich.
	Rudworth Brk.	*Pickmere Mere*	Northwich.
		Rudworth Mere	Northwich.
	Kincham Brk.	*Toft Hall Lake*	Plumley.
		Nether Tabley	
		Lake	Plumley.
		{ *Waterless Brk.*	Northwich.
		{ *Birch Brook*	Northwich.
		{ *Arley Hall*	
		{ *Lake*	Northwich.
		{ *Peover Brook* ..	
		{ *Gawsworth Mill*	
		{ *Pond*	Macclesfield.
		{ *Thorneycroft*	
		{ *Hall Lakes* ..	Macclesfield.
		{ *Chelford Mere*	Chelford.

ENGLAND—*continued.*

RIVERS AND THEIR TRIBUTARIES.			STATIONS.
WEAVER (*cont.*)		Reed's Mere.	Macclesfield.
		Capesthorne	
		Hall Lake	Macclesfield.
		Peover........	Chelford.
		Astle Hall Lake	Chelford
		Bug Brook ..	
		Henbury Hall	
		Lake	Macclesfield.
		Old Hall Lake	Macclesfield.
		Bug	Chelford.
		Over Peover	
		Hall Lake	Chelford.
		Peover........	Plumley.
	....	....	Lostock Chapel.
		Crow Brook ..	Holmes Chapel.
	....	....	Northwich.
	....		Acton.
	Bent Brook....	Flax Mere	Delamere.
		Cuddington Bk.	
		Cuddington Mill	
		Ponds......	Delamere.
	....	....	Acton.
	....	....	Frodsham.
WEAR	Gaunless	....	Bishop Auckland.
	Browney	....	Bishop Auckland.
	Bedburn	....	Bishop Auckland.
WELCOMBE ..	....	....	Hartland.
WELLAND	....	....	Market Harborough.
	Saddington Brk.	Saddington Re-	
		servoir	Kibworth.
	....	....	Market Harborough.
		Gumley Pond..	
		Gumley Hall	} Kibworth or Lubenham.
		Ponds	
	Hardwick Brook	....	Kibworth.
	....	....	Ashley.
	Medbourne Brk.	....	Ashley.
	....	....	Rockingham.
	Eye Brook	....	East Norton, Rockingham.
	....	....	Seaton, Wakerley, Ketton.
	Chater	Withcote Hall	
		Lake........	E. Morton, Manton, Luffenham, Ketton
	....	....	Stamford.
	Gwash	....	Manton.
		Burley Pk. Lake	Oakham.
		Exton Pk. Lake	Stamford.
	....	....	Ryhall, Stamford.
	....	....	Uffington, Tallington, Market Deeping, St. James Deeping, Crowland, Cowbit, Spalding, Surfleet.
	Glen	....	Corby, Little Bytham, Essendine.
		Edenham Brook	Bourn.
		Grimsthorpe	
		Brook	Corby.
		Edenham......	Braceborough Spa.
	....	....	Bourne, Counter Drain, Pinchbeck, Sur- [fleet.
WENNING....	....	....	Clapham.
WHAPLODE			
RIVER	....	....	Whaplode.
WHICHAM BK.	....	....	Silecroft.
WILLITON ...	....	....	Williton.
WINSTER	....	....	Bowness, Grange.
WITHAM......	....	....	Ponton.
	Cringle Brook..	....	Ponton.
	Stoke Brook....	....	Ponton.
		Stoke Mill Pond	Ponton.
	....	....	Grantham.
	Belton Pk. Lakes	....	Grantham.
	....	....	Barkston.
	Syston Pk. Lake	....	Barkston.
	Hornington Beck	....	Barkston.

ENGLAND—*continued.*

RIVERS AND THEIR TRIBUTARIES.				STATIONS.
WITHAM (*cont.*)	....			Hougham.
	Foston Beck....	*Denton House Lake*.......		Grantham.
	Canal Reservoir	....		Grantham, Sedgbrook.
....		....		Claypole, Harmston.
	Brant	....		Caythorpe.
		Leadenham Hall Ponds		Leadenham.
	....	....		Leadenham.
		Sand Beck		Leadenham.
	....	....		Navenby, Harmston.
....		....		Hykeham, Lincoln.
	Foss Dyke Navigation	....		Lincoln.
		Tilt		Lea, Stow Park.
		FillinghamLake		Lea.
		Tilt		Saxelby.
	....			Washingbrough.
	Washingbrough Brook	*Branston Hall Lake*		Branston, Washingbrough.
....		....		Five Mile House.
	Langworth	*HackthorneHall Pond*.......		Langworth, Snelland.
		Fristhorpe Brook		Snelland.
		Snelland Brook		Snelland.
	....	....		Langworth.
		Clay Brook....		Langworth.
		Stainfield Brook		Five Mile House.
	....	....		Five Mile House.
	Tile House Beck	....		Bardney.
....		....		Bardney, Southry.
	Tupholme Brook	*Stourton Hall Ponds*		Horncastle.
	Gaunby Hall Lake........	....		Horncastle.
	....	....		Southry.
....		....		Stixwould, Kirkstead, Tattenhall, Dog dyke.
	Bain..........	....		Louth.
		Benniworth Pool		Horncastle.
	....	....		Horncastle.
		Haltham Beck..		Woodhall Spa.
	....	....		Tattenhall, Dogdyke.
....		....		Langrick, Boston.
	Hammond Beck	....		Donington, Swinehead, Boston
WITHERN....	....	....		Aby.
	Calceby Beck..	*Ormsby Park Lake*		Aby.
....		....		Theddlethorpe, Saltfleet.
	Grayfleet	....		Louth, Grimoldby, Saltfleet.
	Southditch	....		Saltfleet.
WOODBURY ..	....	....		Woodbury Road.
WRENTHAM BK.	....	....		Southwold.
	Easton Broad..	....		Southwold.
WYE	....	....		Llangurig.
	Tavenig	....		Llangurig.
	Bidno	....		Llangurig.
	Marteg	....		Pant-y-dwr, St. Harmon.
....	....	....		Rhayader.
	Glan Llyn	....		Rhayader.
	Elan	*Llyn Helygen*..		Llangurig.
		Gwngy.........		Llangurig.
		Llyn Gwngy ..		Llangurig.
		Hirin		Rhayader.
		Llyn Cerrig =		
		Llwydion-uchaf		Rhayader.
		Llyn Cerrig =		
		Llwydion-isaf		Rhayader.

ENGLAND—*continued.*

RIVERS AND THEIR TRIBUTARIES.				STATIONS
Wye cont.) ..		Clearwen		Strata Florida.
		Figen		Strata Florida.
		Llyn Fryddyn-fach........		Strata Florida.
		Llyn Fryddyn-fawr		Strata Florida.
		Llyn-du		Strata Florida.
		Llyn-figen-felan		Strata Florida.
		Brwynog		Strata Florida.
		Llyn Gynon ..		Strata Florida.
		Arban		Doldowlod.
		Garw		Doldowlod.
		Llyn Garw....		Doldowlod.
		....		Rhayader.
		....		Doldowlod, New Bridge.
	Hirnant	....		Newbridge.
	Ithon	Llyn Dwr		Newtown.
		Cam-ddwr		Llangynllo.
		....		Pen-y-bont.
		Arau		Llangynllo, Dobau, Pen-y-bont.
		Llandegley Brk.		Pen-y-bont.
			Clywedog	Pen-y-bont.
			Fishpool	St. Harmon.
			Crych Brook ..	St. Harmon.
		Camllo		Pen-y-bont.
			Dulas	St. Hermon, Pen-y-bont.
			Llyn Gwyn....	Doldowlod.
		....		Llandrindod.
		Hawddwy		Llandrindod.
		....		New Bridge.
	....	....		Builth Road.
	Dulas	....		Builth Road.
	....	....		Builth.
	Irfon	Gwessin		Llanwrtyd.
		Calant........		Llanwrtyd.
		....		Llanwrtyd.
		Cerdin........		Llanwrtyd.
		Cledau........		Llanwrtyd.
		....		Llangammarch.
		Dulas		Llangammarch.
		Annell		Llangammarch.
		Camddwr		Llangammarch.
			Cammarch	Llangammarch.
			Onyffiad	Llangammarch.
			Einon	Llangammarch.
		....		Garth.
			Dulas	Garth.
			Gwenwest	Garth.
		....		Cilmeri.
		Cneiddon		Builth.
		Chwefru		Doldowlod, Builth.
	Dihonw	....		Garth, Builth.
	....	....		Aberedw.
	Edw..........	....		Pen-y-Bont.
		Llyn Melan ..		New Radnor.
		Camnant		Builth.
			Rhulan	Aberedw.
			Llyn Pools	Aberedw.
		Bailt Brook ..		Builth.
		Llyn Cawr		Aberedw.
		....		Aberedw.
	....	....		Erwood.
	Llogin........	Llyn Llogin ..		Erwood.
	Bach-howey Brook	....		Aberedw.
		Llyn Llanbychllyn		Aberedw.
		....		Erwood.
	Cunrig	....		Erwood.
	....	....		Boughrood, Glasbury.
	Llyfni........	....		Tal-y-Bont.

RIVERS AND THEIR TRIBUTARIES.			STATIONS.
WYE (*cont.*) ..	*Llangorse Lake*	....	Tal-y-Llyn.
		Cwm Brook ..	Trefeinon.
	Llyfni	....	Trefeinon, Talgarth.
		Enig	Talgarth.
		{ *Dulais*	Talgarth.
		{ *Treffrwd Brook*	Talgarth.
....	....	....	Three Cocks Junction, Glasbury
....	....	....	Hay.
	Dulas Brook ..	....	Hay.
....	....	....	Whitney, Eardisley.
	Upcot Brook ..	....	Almeley.
		Holywell Brook	Eardisley.
	Letton Lake ..	....	Almeley, Kinnersley
....	....	....	Credenhill.
	Gage	....	Tram Inn.
....	....	....	Hereford.
	Withy Brook ..	....	Hereford.
	Lugwas Brook .	....	Moorhampton, Credenhill, Hereford.
	Redbrook	....	Holme Lacey.
	Lug	....	Llangynllo.
		{ *Graig Brook* ..	Dolau.
		{ *Graig Pool*	Dolau.
		{ *Bleddfa Brook* .	Llangynllo.
....	....	....	Presteign.
		Boulli Brook ..	Presteign.
		{ *Sumnergill*	
		Brook	New Radnor, Presteign.
		{ *Black Brook* ..	New Radnor, Presteign.
....	....	....	Kingsland, Leominster.
		{ *Pinsley Brook* .	
		{ *Lady Pools* ..	Pembridge, Kingsland Leominster
		{ *Ridgemore*	
		{ *Croft Castle*	
		{ *Ponds*	Eye, Leominster.
		{ *Stretford Brook*	
		{ *Puddleston Brk.*	
		{ *Puddleston Lakes*	
		{ *Cogwell Brook* .	Leominster.
		{ *Arrow*	
		{ *Maun Pools* ..	Aberedw.
		{ *Cwm Illa Brook*	Whitney.
		{ *Arrow*	Kington.
		{ *Gilwern Brook*	Dolhier.
		{ *Cynon Brook* ..	Dolhier.
		{ *Hales Brook* ..	Dolhier.
		{ *Gilwern*	Stanner, Kington.
		{ *Arrow*	Titley, Pembridge, Leominster.
		{ *Stretford Brook*	Moorhampton.
		{ *Tippets Brook* .	Pembridge.
		{ *Stretford*	Leominster.
....	....	....	Ford.
		{ *Humber Brook*	Leominster.
		{ *Hampton Park*	
		{ *Lake*	Ford.
		{ *Humber*	Ford.
		Marston Brook	Ford.
....	....	....	Dinmore.
		Derndale Brook	Moreton.
....	....	....	Moreton, Hereford.
		Sutton Brook ..	Moreton, Hereford.
....	....	....	Holme Lacey.
		{ *Frome*	Bromyard.
		{ *Inkstone Brook*	Bromyard.
		{ *Linton Brook* ..	Bromyard.
		{ *Frome*	Ashperton.
		{ *Leddon*	Bromyard, Ashperton.
		{ *Frome*	Stoke Edith, Holme Lacey.
		{ *Pentelow Brook*	Ashperton, Holme Lacey.
		{ *Devereux Park*	
		{ *Lakes*	

ENGLAND—*continued.*

RIVERS AND THEIR TRIBUTARIES.			STATIONS.
WYE (*cont.*) ..	....	....	Fawley.
	Wriggle Brook	....	Fawley.
	Sollers Brook..	....	Fawley.
....	....	....	Ross.
	Rudhall Brook	....	Mitcheldean Road, Ross.
....	....	....	Kerne Bridge.
	Castle Brook ..	....	Mitcheldean Road.
....	....	....	Simmonds Gate.
	Garran	....	Pontrilas.
		Llanwarne Brook	Fawley.
		Trewarthen Pool	Ross.
		Lammarch Brk.	Ross.
		Luke Brook ..	Kerne Bridge.
....	....	....	Kerne Bridge.
....	....	....	Monmouth.
	Monnow	....	Hay, Pandy.
		Eseley Brook ..	Hay, Pandy.
		Olchon Brook..	Hay, Pandy
....	....	....	Pandy.
		Honddu	Glasbury, Lianfihangel, Pandy.
....	....	....	Pontrilas.
		Rowlston Brook	Pontrilas.
		Dore	Hay, Pontrilas.
		{ Worm Brook .. Allenmore	
		House Ponds	Tram Inn.
		{ Worm Brook ..	Devereux, Pontrilas.
		Dulas Brook ..	Pontrilas.
		{ Blackbrook Blackbrook	
		{ House Ponds	Pontrilas.
		....	Monmouth.
	Trothy........	....	Abergavenny.
		Full Brook....	Pandy, Abergavenny.
		Mynachdy Brk.	Abergavenny.
		....	Dingestow.
		Llumon	Dingestow.
		Nant-y-fuchan.	Dingestow.
	....	....	Monmouth.
....	....	....	Redbrook, Bigsweir, Tintern, Chepstow
WYRE	Grizedale River	....	Bay Horses.
	Marshaw Wyre	....	Bay Horses.
	Catshaw Brook	....	Bay Horses.
	Damas Stream	....	Galgate, Bay Horses.
....	....	....	Scorton, Garstang.
	Grizedale Brk.	....	Garstang.
	Calder River..	....	Garstang.
	Brock River ..	....	Brock.
		{ Blay Brook ..	Brock.
		{ Woodplumpton Brook	Broughton.
		{ Barton Brook..	Barton.
....	....	....	Poulton.
	Marton Brook..	Marton Mere..	Poulton.
....	....	....	Fleetwood.
YAR (I. of W.).	....	....	Yarmouth.
YARE	....	....	Hardingham.
	Blackwater	....	Hardingham.
	Bass..........	....	Wymondham.
		Tiffey	Wymondham.
		Dyke Beck	Wymondham.
	....	....	Kimberley.
		Kimberley Park Lake	Kimberley.
		{ Hackford Brook	Kimberley.
		{ Sea Mere	Hingham.
		{ Wicklewood Mere	Kimberley.

ENGLAND—*continued.*

RIVERS AND THEIR TRIBUTARIES.			STATIONS.
YARE (*cont.*)	*Kettering Hall*		
	Lakes	....	Hetherset.
	Beacon Hall		
	Lakes	....	Swainthorpe.
	Carlton Lodge		
	Lakes	....	Swainthorpe.
....	....	....	Norwich.
	Lese	....	Forncett, Florden, Swainthorpe, Norwich.
	Wensum	....	Fakenham, Ryburgh, North Elmham Lenwade.
	{ *Blackwater*		
	{ *Black Lake*....		Cawston.
	{ *Blackwater*....		Reepham, Lenwade.
	Haveringland		
	Lake		Cawston.
	....		Attlebridge, Drayton, Hellesdon.
	{ *Costessey Brook*		Yaxham.
	{ *Honingham*		
	{ *Pond*		Attlebridge.
	(*Costessey*		Hellesdon.
	....		Norwich.
....	....	....	Withingham, Brundall.
	Surlingham Brd.	....	Brundall.
	Plumpstead Hall		
	Lakes	....	Brundall.
	Strumpshaw Brd.	....	Buckenham.
	Rockland Broad	....	Buckenham.
....	....	....	Buckenham.
	Buckenham Brd.	....	Buckenham.
	Hasingham Brd.	....	Buckenham.
....	....	....	Cantley.
	Chet	*Brook Hall Lake*	Norwich.
	....	....	Loddon, Cantley.
	....	....	Reedham, Yarmouth.
YEALM	....	....	Cornwood.
YEO	....	....	Congresbury.

IRELAND.

RIVER.	STATIONS.
Ballinahinch	Recess, Ballynahinch.
Bandon	Bandon, Ballineen.
Bann	Coleraine.
Barrow	Goresbridge.
Blackwater .	Dromore, Fermoy, Lismore, Kenmare. [Mallow.
Blackwater (Lesser).	
Blarney	Blarney.
Bundrows ..	Bundoran.
Bush	Bushmills.
Cara	Cahirciveen, Glencar, Killorglin, Rossbeigh.
Clady	Gweedore.
Einagh......	Cahirciveen.
Erne	Ballyshannon, Belleek.
Errive.......	Leenan.
Feale	Abbey Feale.
Peartagh ..	Cahirciveen.
Flesk	Killarney.
Glengariffe..	Glengariffe.
Ilen............	Baltimore, Skibbereen.
Kearan	Cahirciveen.

RIVER.	STATIONS.
Launa	Cara Lake, Killarney, Killorglin. Rossbeigh.
Lee	Cork, Macroom.
Liffy	Naas.
Maine	Killorglin.
Mannion....	Kilmurry.
Moy...... .	Ballina.
Owenduff ..	Bangor.
Owena	Ardara, Glenties.
Owenmore ..	Bangor.
Owvane	Inchageelah.
Roughty	Kenmare.
Shannon....	Carrick, Castle Connell, Donass, Killaloe, Limerick, Longford, Meelick, Shannon Bridge.
S. Bride (Cork).	Crookstown.
Suir	Cahir, Carrick, Kilsheelan.
Westmeath Lakes.	Mullingar.

SCOTLAND.

River.	Stations.	River.	Stations.
Ainoig	Oykel Bridge.	Isla	Meikleour.
Annan	Ecclesfechan, Lochmaben, Moffat.	Lochy	Banavie.
Awe	Dalmally, Inveroran, Loch Awe, Taynuilt.	Loch Lomond.	Inverarnan, Tarbet
Blackwater	Strathpeffer.	Moffat	Moffat.
Bogie	Huntley.	Ness	Inverness.
Carron	Ardgay.	Orchy	Dalmally, Inveroran.
Cassley	Oykel Bridge.	Rannoch	Kinloch Rannoch.
Dee (Aberdeen).	Aboyne, Balater, Braemar.	Shin	Lairg, Overskeck.
Deveron	Huntley.	Shiel	Shiel House.
Dionard	Durine Inn	Spean	Banavie, Loch Laggan.
Don	Alford Bridge, Inverurie.	Spey	Craigellachie, Fochabers, Kingussie.
Earn	St. Fillans.	Tay	Aberfeldy, Birnam, Crianlarich, Dalguise, Dunkeld, Grandtully, Kenmore, Killin, Logierait, Luib, Meikleonr, Perth, Stanley, Weem.
Echaig	Kilmun.		
Ericht	Blairgowrie, Dalwhinnie.		
Esk (Dumfries).	Canonby, Langholm.		
Evan	Moffat.	Teith	Callender.
Ewe	Gairloch	Thurso	Brawl Castle, Thurso.
Fleet	Kirkcudbright, Mound, Dromore.	Till	Etal. (See England.)
		Tummel	Kinloch Rannoch, Pitlochrie. Tummel Bridge.
Forth	Tarbet.	Tweed	Clovenford, Inverleithen, Kelso, Peebles, Sprouston, (See England.)
Gala	Stow.		
Garry	Invergarry, Kinloch Rannoch.		
Grudie	Durine Inn.	Yarrow	St. Mary's Loch.
Helmsdale	Helmsdale.	Ythan	Newburg, Ellon.

WALES.

Rivers and their Tributaries.			Stations.
ABER	Llyn-an-Afon		Aber.
	Aber-fawr		Aber.
AERON	Llyn Eiddwen		Tregaron.
	Llyn Fauod		Tregaron.
	Telyn		Tregaron.
	Gwenffrwd		Pont Llanio.
	Meurig		Derry Ormond.
	Rhewfallen		Derry Ormond.
	Nant-y-fergy		Derry Ormond.
	Gelli		Lampeter.
	Gerwen		Lampeter.
	Cilcennin Brook		Aberaeron.
	Mudr		Aberaeron.
			Aberaeron.
AFON (Glamorg.)			Cymmer.
	Cerwg		Cymmer.
			Aberafon.
	Gwinau		Aberafon.
AFON-Y-GARTH			Mostyn.
ALAW			Llanerchymedd.
	Llyn Llywean		Valley Station.
			Valley Station.
ALLAN			St. David's.
ARTH	Llyn March		Llanrhystyd.
	Bran		Aberaeron.
			Aberaeron.
ARTRO	Llyn Dywarchen		Talarnau.
	Llyn Ciddew fach		Talarnau.
	Ciddew	Llyn Du	Talarnau.
	Llyn Ciddewmawr		Talarnau

RIVERS AND THEIR TRIBUTARIES.			STATIONS
ARTRO (cont.)	Bychan	Llyn y-Mor-wynion	Llanbedr.
	Llyn-cwm bychan	.. ..	Llanbedr
		Llyn Gloywlyn..	Llanbedr.
	Nautcol	Llyn Howel ..	Llanbedr.
		Llyn-cwm-hosau	Llanbedr.
		Llyn-y-fer fedden	Llanbedr.
....	....	....	Llanbedr.
	Hafod y-Llyn..	....	Llanbedr.
BRAINT	Llyn Llwydiarth	....	Beaumaris.
....		....	Llanfair, Llangeinwen.
	Llyn Gorsddu .	....	Llangeinwen.
BRAWDY BRK.	....	....	Brawdy.
CADOXTON RIV.	....	....	Cadoxton.
CAERWYCH ...	....	....	Talarnau.
CAREW BROOK	....	....	Saundersfoot, Carew.
CARN	....	....	Templeton, Loveston.
	Langdon Brook	....	Bogelly, Loveston.
CASTLE MARTIN BROOK.	....	....	Pembroke.
	Orielton Lakes	....	Pembroke.
....	....	....	Castle Martin.
CEFNI	....	....	Llangwyllog, Llangefni
	Llanffinan Brk.	....	Llangefni.
CEMMAES	Llyn Felin nant	....	Rhos-Goch.
	Llanfllwin Lakes	....	Llanfechell.
.. ..	....	....	Llanfechell.
CLEDDAU	....	....	Rosebush.
	Marlet Brook..	....	Rosebush.
	Wallis Brook..	....	Haverfordwest.
	Pelcombe Brook	....	Haverfordwest.
....	....	....	Haverfordwest.
	Captlett Brook	....	Haverfordwest.
	Denant Brook..	....	Haverfordwest.
	Milling Brook	....	Haverfordwest.
	Eastern Cleddau	Cortwyn	Crynanich.
			Maenelochog.
CLWYD	....	....	Derwen, Nantclwyd, Eyearth.
	Llanfan Brook	....	Eyearth.
....	....	....	Ruthin, Rhewl, Llanrhaiadr
	Clywedog		Nantclwyd, Ruthin.
		Cyffylliog Brk.	Ruthin.
		Myslyg	Ruthin.
		Ladur........	Ruthin.
	....	.. ..	Rhewl.
		Llewcesog....	Llanrhaiadr.
	....	....	Llanrhaidar.
....	....	....	Denbigh.
	Lliwen	....	Denbigh.
	....	....	Bodfari.
	Wheeler	....	Caerwys, Bodfari.
....	....	....	Trefnant.
	Bach	....	Trefnant.
....	....	....	St. Asaph.
	Elwy	....	Llanrwst.
		Dyffryn-gallt..	Llanrwst.
		Llyn Chwyth ..	Llanrwst.
		Dyffryn-gallt..	
		Derfyn	Llanrwst.
		Fawnog	Tal-y-Cafn.
		Llyn Fawnog	
		Melan	Llanfair Talhaiarn.
	....	....	Llanfair Talhaiarn.
		Aled	
		Llyn Aled	Llanrwst.
		Llyn Nivel frech	Llanrwst.
		Hyrdd	Denbigh.
		Llyn Creiniog..	Llanfair Talhaiarn.
		Dennant	Llanfair Talhaiarn.
		Aled	L'anfair Talhaiarn.

WALES—*continued.*

RIVERS AND THEIR TRIBUTARIES.			STATIONS.
CLWYD (cont.)		Merchion	Trefnant.
....	....	....	Trefnant, St. Asaph.
....	....	....	Rhyddlan.
	Helyg	Llyn Helyg....	St. Asaph, Rhyddlan.
	Gele..........	....	Abergele, Rhyl.
....	....	....	Rhyl.
CONWAY	Llyn Conway ..	....	Ffestiniog.
	Lliw	Llyn Lliw	Ffestiniog.
....	....	....	Arenig or Bettws-y-Coed.
	Clettwr	....	Arenig or Bettws.
	Merddwyr	....	Bettws-y-Coed.
		Laethog	Bettws.
		Llyn-y-Cwrt ..	Bettws.
		Cadnant	Bettws.
	Eidda	....	Bettws.
	Hwch	....	Bettws.
	Machno	Llyn-y-firth-graig	Manod, Bettws.
	Ledr	....	Dolwyddelan
		Llyn Dannogen	Grisian.
		Llynian	
		Duwainnedd ..	Dolwyddelan or Pen-y-Gwryd.
		Ystumian .... }	Dolwyddelan.
		Llyn-y-rebel .. }	
	....	....	Dolwyddelan, Pant-y-Pan
....	....	....	Bettws-y-Coed.
	Lliugwy	Llyn Lliugwy ..	Capel Curig.
		Gwryd........ }	
		Llyn-y-Cwm- }	
		Ffynnon .... }	Pen-y-Gwryd.
		Mymbyr Lakes }	Capel Curig
		Llyn Goddion-	
		duon	Capel Curig.
		Llyn Pen Craig	Llanrwst or Bettws.
		Llyn Helst....	Bettws-y-Coed.
	....	....	Bettws-y-Coed.
	Llyn-y-Parc ..		Llanrwst or Bettws.
....	....	....	Llanrwst, Trefriw.
	Crafnant	Llyn Crafnant	Capel Curig or Trefriw.
		LlynBodgynwydd	Capel Curig or Llanrwst.
		Llyn Bychan ..	Capel Curig or Llanrwst.
		Llyn Geirionydd	Trefriw.
	....	....	Trefriw.
	Ddu..........	Llyn Cwlyd ..	Capel Curig.
	Porth-lwyd....	Ffynnon Llyffain	Bethesda or Capel Curig.
		Llyn Eigian ..	Capel Curig.
	Tal-y-Bont....	Llyn Melynllyn	Bethesda.
		Llyn Dulyn ..	Bethesda or Capel Curig.
	Llyn Sybert ..	....	Tal-y-Cafn.
	Ro	....	Tal-y-Cafn.
	......	....	Tal-y-Cafn.
	Hiraethlyn....	....	Tal-y-Cafn.
....	....	....	Glan Conway.
COWBRIDGE RIV.	....	....	Ystrad, Cowbridge.
CRIGYLL	Gwalchmai Lake	....	Ty-Croes.
	Llyn Strydan..	....	Ty-Croes.
....	....	....	Ty-Croes.
	Llyn Maelog ..	....	Ty-Croes.
	Caradog	....	Ty-Croes.
CYMERAN	....	....	Glan Conway.
DARON	....	....	Aberdaron.
DISSILIO	....	....	Llandissilio Gogo
DOVEY	Llyn Dyfi	....	Dews-y-Nant.
	Parnrhyd	....	Dinas Mowddwy.
	Cowarch	....	Dinas Mowddwy.
....	....	....	Dinas Mowddwy.
	Geryst........	Lyn Figan and	
		Lyn Fach ..	Dinas Mowddwy.
	Cleivion	Clywedog	Dinas Mowddwy.
		{ Tafolog	
		} Llyn Coch-hywad	Dinas Mowddwy.

WALES—*continued.*

RIVERS AND THEIR TRIBUTARIES.			STATIONS.
DOVEY (*cont.*)	....	....	Aber Angell.
	Angell	Her	Aber Angell.
		Llyn Llecoediog	Aber Angell.
		Mynach	Aber Angell.
	....	....	Cemmaes, Cemmaes Junction.
	Twymyn	....	Llanbrynmair.
		Tal	Llanbrynmair.
	....	....	Cemmaes Junction.
	Gwidol	....	Cemmaes Junction.
	Diflas	Llyn Bugeilyn ..	Machynlleth.
		Glaslyn	Machynlleth.
		Crial	Machynlleth.
	Dulas	....	Aber Angell.
		Llefeni	Aber Angell.
		Corys	Tal-y-Llyn.
	....	....	Machynlleth, Gilan Dyfl.
	Llymant	Llyn pen Rhaidr	Machynlleth, Gilan Dyfl.
	Einon	....	Gilan Dyfl.
DROWY	....	....	Llanarth.
DU	....	....	Llanfairfechan.
DULAS	Paint Pools ..	....	Amlwch.
	Llyn Meilw ..	....	Amlwch.
	....	....	Llanerchymedd, Penrhosllligwy.
DWYFAUR	....	....	Beddgellert, Brynkir.
	Istrallyn	Llyn Cwm	
		Istrallyn	Portmadoc.
		Llyn Du	Portmadoc.
	....	....	Brynkir.
	Dwyfach	....	Pontglass, Brynkir, Ynys, Llangybi
	....	....	Criccieth.
DWYBYD	....	•	Tan-y-Grisiau.
	Reservoir	....	Tan-y-Grisiau.
	Orthan	Llyn Cech	Tan-y-Grisiau.
		Llyn Conglog ..	Tan-y-Grisiau.
	Llyn Cwm-orthan	....	Tan-y-Grisiau.
	Ddu	Reservoir	Tan-y-Grisiau.
		Llyn Trwstyllon	Tan-y-Grisiau.
	Bywydd	Llyn Bywydd ..	Diffwys, Manod.
		Llyn Dubach ..	Diffwys.
	Yspytty	Llyn-y-Bryn-du	Ffestiniog.
		Llynian-y-gamellt	,,
		Llyn-y-Morwynion	,,
		{Manod	
		{Llyn Manod ..	Manod.
		{Manod........	Ffestiniog.
	Rhaiadr	Llyn Dywarchen	Ffestiniog.
		Llyn Dubach ..	Ffestiniog.
		Llyn Oraig-y-tan	Ffestiniog.
	....	....	Ffestiniog.
	Llyn-y-oerfa ..	....	Maentwrog Road.
	....	....	Maentwrog.
	Llynen Garnedd	Llyn Hafod-y-Llyn	,,
	Prysor	Llyn Cors-y-	
		barcut	Ffestiniog.
		Llynnen Conglog	
		fach and fawr ..	Trawsfynydd.
		Llyn Dubach ..	Trawsfynydd.
		Llyn-y-garn ..	Trawsfynydd.
		Llyn Rhythlyn..	Trawsfynydd.
		{Harfar	
		{Llyn-y-graig-wen	Trawsfynydd.
	....	....	Trawsfynydd.
		Llyn Llenyrch..	Maentwrog.
	....	....	Penrhyndeudraeth.
DYSYNNI	Llyn Cau	....	Tal-y-Llyn.
	Llyn Trigraienyn	....	Tal-y-Llyn.
	Llyn Tal-y-Llyn	....	Tal-y-Llyn.
	....	....	Abergwynolwyn.
	Gwynolwyn....	....	Abergwynolwyn.
	....	....	Dolgoch, Rhyd-yr-ounen.

WALES—*continued.*

RIVERS AND THEIR TRIBUTARIES.			STATIONS.
DYSYNNI (*cont.*)	*Fefnder*	....	Dolgoch, Brynglas, Rhyd-yr-onnen.
	....	....	Towyn.
EBWY	....	....	Beaufort, Ebbw Vale, Victoria, Cwm, Aberbeeg.
	Ebwy-fach	....	Blaina, Aberfillery, Aberbeeg.
	....	....	Crumlin.
	Pound-y-Coed Cae	....	Aberbeeg, Crumlin.
	....	....	Newbridge, Abercarne, Cross Keys.
	Sirhowey	*Llyn-garn-fawr*	Trefil.
	....	....	Tredegar, Hollybush, Argoed, Blackwood Tredegar Junction, Ynysddu, Cross Keys.
	....	....	Risca, Tydee, Bassalleg, Newport.
ELY	....	....	Llantrissant.
	Dowlas Brook ..	....	Llantrissant.
	....	....	Peterston, St. Fagan's, Ely Bridge, Llandaff Cardiff.
ERCH	....	....	Pwllheli.
	Ceilog	....	Pwllheli.
	....	....	Pwllheli.
		Gerich	Pwllheli.
	....	....	Pwllheli.
FFRAW or GWNA	....	....	Bodorgan.
	Llyn Coron	....	Bodorgan.
	Fraich-wen ..	....	Bodorgan.
	Llyn Bodric ..	....	Tye-Croes.
	....	....	Aberffraw.
FLINT BROOK..	....	....	Flint.
GARNAS......	....	....	Cronware.
GILFACH	....	....	Llanarth.
GLAN-E'-AFON	....	....	Llandulas.
	Llyn Coed Coch	....	Llandulas.
GLASLYN	*Llyn Glaslyn* ..	....	Pen-y-gwryd.
	Llyn Llydaw ..	....	Pen-y-gwryd.
		Llyn Teyrn	Pen-y-gwryd.
	Llyn Gwynant..	....	Pen-y-gwryd.
		{ *Llyn Edno*	Beddgellert.
		{ *Llynian Cwm*..	Beddgellert.
	Llyn-y-Ddinas .	....	Beddgellert.
	....	....	Beddgellert.
	Colwyn........	....	Beddgellert.
	Nant-y-Mor ..	*Llyn-y-adar* ..	Beddgellert.
	Llyn Llagi	....	Beddgellert.
		Llyn Biswail ..	Beddgellert.
		Llyn-y-Arddu..	Beddgellert.
		Hafod-y-Llyn..	Beddgellert.
	Croesor	*Llyn Diffwys* ..	Tan-y-Grisiau.
	Llyn-cwm-y-foel	...●●...	Tan-y-Grisiau.
		Dulif	Portmadoc.
	....	....	Portmadoc.
GLYNPHAW ..	....	....	Carnarvon.
GWAEN	....	....	Rosebush.
	Walen	....	Rosebush.
	....	....	Fishguard.
GWENDRAETH-FACH.	....	....	Nantgaredig, Kidwelly
GWENDRAETH-FAWR.	....	....	Llandybie.
	LlynLlerh-wen.	....	Llandybie.
	....	....	Kidwelly.
GWBFAI	*Llyn-y Gadr* ..	....	Rhyddu.
		Llyn Glas	
		Llyn Goch	
		Llyn-y-Nadroedd	Snowdon Ranger
		Llyn-ffynnon-y-Gwas	
	Llyn Cwellyn..	....	Snowdon Ranger
	....	....	Bettws Garnon, Llanwndla.
	Venno	....	Llanwndla.

WALES—*continued.*

RIVERS AND THEIR TRIBUTARIES.			STATIONS.
HYGEISIAN ..	....	....	Llanfairynghornnwy.
KENFIG	....	....	Cefn, Pyle.
KILVELGY BRK.	....	....	Begelly.
LLANON	....	....	Llansantffraid.
LLIFON	....	....	Groes-lon.
LLIEWY	Llyn Llwyn-crwn	....	Penrhoslligwy.
LLIEEDI	....	....	Llanelley.
LLIW	....	....	Gora, Llwchwr.
	Lesser Lliw ..	....	Llwchwr.
LLWYD	....	....	Llwyngwril.
LLWYNOG	....	....	Conway.
LLYFNI	Llyn-y-dywar-ehen	....	Rhyddu.
	Llynnen Nantlle	....	Nantlle.
	Llyn Ffynnonaw	....	Nantlle.
	Llynian-cwm-silyn	....	Nantlle.
....		....	Pen-y-groes.
	Dulyn	Llyn-cwm-dulyn	Pen-y-groes.
LLWCHWR	....	....	Llandybie. Cross Inn.
	Llandybie Brook	....	Derwydd Road, Llandybie, Cross Inn.
	Lash	....	Cross Inn.
....	....	....	Pantyffynon Junction.
	Alwyd	....	Pantyffynon Junction.
	Amman	....	Bryn-amman, Garnant.
		Garnant	Garnant.
		Pedol	Garnant.
	....	....	Cross Inn, Pantyffnon.
....	....	....	Pont-ar-dulais.
	Dulas	....	Pont-ar-dulais.
	Gwili	....	Pantyffynon, Pont-ar-iulais.
....	....	....	Llangenych.
	Trasarch	....	Llangenych.
....		....	Llwchwr.
MAWDDACH ..	Llyn Crych-y-wayen	....	Drws-y-nant.
	Geirw	....	Tyn-y-groes.
	Gain..........	....	Tyn-y-groes.
		Llyn Gelli-gain.	Tyn-y-groes.
	Eden	Llyn Pryvyd ..	Tyn-y-groes
	Llyn Twrgla ..	....	Tyn-y-groes.
		Llyn Graig-ddrwg	Talsarnau.
		Ddu ....}	Tyn-y-groes.
		Llyn ddu ....}	
	Camlan	Llyn-y-bi......	Tyn-y-groes.
		Llyn-y-frau ..	Tyn-y-groes.
		Llyn Pen-y-gaullwyd	Tyn-y-groes.
	....	....	Tyn-y-groes.
	Wnion	....	Drws-y-nant.
		Harnog	Drws-y-nant.
		Cwm-ochr	Drws-y-nant.
		Ciddow	Drws-y nant.
		Fidw	Drws-y-nant.
....	....	....	Pont Newydd.
....	....	Ddybin	Dolgelly.
....	....	....	Dolgelly.
		Llyn Aras	Dolgelly.
....	....	....	Penmaenpool.
	Mynach	Llyn Cwm Mynach	Penmaenpool.
	Gadr	Llyn Gadr	Dolgelly.
	Llyn Gafr	....	Dolgelly.
		Llyn Gwernan	Dolgelly.
	Llecham	....	Penmaenpool.
	Llyn-y-wylfa ..	....	Arthog.
	Goetref	....	Barmouth.
	Creigennan....	Llyn Gri	Arthog.
		Llyn Creigennan	Arthog.
....	....	....	Barmouth

WALES—*continued.*

RIVERS AND THEIR TRIBUTARIES.			STATIONS.
MULLOCH BRK.	....	....	St. Ishmael's.
NANT-FFYNNON	....	....	Colwyn.
NANT-Y-GRORS	....	....	Colwyn.
NEATH	....	....	Glyn Neath.
	Llia	....	Glyn Neath.
	Hepste	....	Hirwann.
	Nedd	....	Glyn Neath.
....	....	....	Resolyen, Aberdyllas.
	Dylias	....	Crinant, Aberdylias.
....	....	....	Neath.
	Clydach	....	Pont-ar-dawe, Neath
NEAVE	....	....	Crymmych Arms.
	Biron	....	Crymmych Arms.
	Duad	....	Newport.
....	....	....	Newport.
	Clydach	....	Newport.
NORTHOP BRK.	....	....	Flint.
OGMORE	....	....	Blackmill, Tondu.
	Llynvi	....	Cimmer, Maestog, Llangonoyd, Tondu.
....	....	....	Bridgend.
	Evenny	....	Pencoed, Bridgend.
OGWEN	Llyn Llover	....	Capel Curig.
	Llyn Ogwen	....	Capel Curig or Bethesda.
		Llyn Bochlwyd	Capel Curig.
		Llyn-y-Cwm	Capel Curig or Bethesda.
		Llyn Idwell	Capel Curig or Bethesda.
	Berthan	....	Bethesda.
	Caseg	Llyn Caseg	Bethesda.
		Llafer	Bethesda.
....	....	....	Bethesda.
	Ffridd-las	....	Bethesda.
	March	March-llyn-mawr	Llanberris.
		March-llyn-bach	Llanberris.
....	....	....	Bethesda.
....	....	....	Bangor.
PENMAEN BRK.	....	....	Killay, Penmaen.
PENMAR	....	....	Manorbeer, Lamphey, Pembroke.
PERIS	....	....	Llansantffraid
RHEIDOL	....	....	Machynlleth.
	Llyn Llygad	....	Devil's Bridge.
	Llygnant	....	Devil's Bridge.
	Llechweddmawr	....	Devil's Bridge.
	Rhyddlau	....	Devil's Bridge.
	Castell	....	Devil's Bridge.
....	....	....	Devil's Bridge.
	Myherin	Llynnen Jenan	Devil's Bridge
		{ Rhyddnant	
		{ Llyn Rhyddnant	Devil's Bridge.
	Llyn Lon	....	Devil's Bridge.
	Melynddwr	....	Aberystwyth.
	Glan Rheidol Lake	....	Aberystwyth.
....	....	....	Aberystwyth.
RHIW	....	....	Conway.
RICKESTON BK.	....	....	Walwyns Castle.
ROSEMARKET BK.	....	....	Johnston, Rosemarket, New Milford.
RUMNEY	....	....	Rhymney, Pontlottyn, Tyr-Phil, Bargoed.
	Crinlach	....	Ffoe-rhin, Darrau, Bargoed.
	....	....	Pengarn, Hengoed, Bedwas.
	Caffyl	....	Caerphilly, Bedwas.
	Glydyr	....	Caerphilly, Bedwas.
....	....	....	Church Road, Rhywderin, Cardiff.
SEIONT	Cwm-llas Lakes	....	Llanberris.
....	....	....	Llanberris.
	Llyn Peris .... }	....	Llanberris.
	Llyn Padarn.. }		
	Lluch	Llyn-dur Arddu	Llanberris.
		Llyn Dwythwch	Llanberris.
....	....	....	Carnarvon.

WALES—*continued.*

RIVERS AND THEIR TRIBUTARIES.			STATIONS.
SOCH	Coran		Llangian.
	Bodlas		Llangian.
SOLVA BROOK			Solva.
TAF			Crymmych Arms, Clogue, Llanfirnach, [Rhydowen
	Gravil		Rhydowen.
			Llanglydwen, Login.
	Marlas		Narberth.
		Gwaithnoak	Narberth.
	Lease		Whitland.
			Whitland.
	Whitland		Login, Whitland.
	Feni		Whitland.
	Cojer		St. Clare.
			St. Clare.
	Gynin		Llanfirnach.
		{ Llechwydd	Llanfirnach.
		{ Asen	Llanfirnach.
			St. Clare.
		Dewi	St. Clare.
	Cywyn		Cynwil.
		Cynnen	Brauwydd Arms.
			Laugharne.
TAFF			Dolygaer, Pontesticcill, Pant, Cefn.
	Taff-fawr	Llyn-y-Gader	Cefn.
			Merthyr, Traed-y-rhiw, Quakers' Yard.
	Bargawd Taf		Quakers' Yard.
			Aberdare Junction.
	Cynon		Hirwann, Llyndeged, Aberdare, Aberaman.
		Aman	Aberaman.
			Mountain Ash, Aberdare Junction.
	Gelli		Aberdare Junction.
			Pont-y-Prydd.
	Rhondda		Treherbert, Istrad-y-Fodwo, Pont.
		Rhondda Fychan	Aberdare, Pont.
			Pont-y-Prydd.
			Trefforest, Walnut Tree, Llandaff, Cardiff.
TAWE	Llyn Fan-fawr		Penwyllt.
	Byfre		Penwyllt.
	Haffys		Penwyllt.
	Llech		Colbren.
	Giaidd		Penwyllt.
		Cyw	Ystal-y-fera.
			Ystal-y-fera.
	Twrch		Gwys.
		Gwysg	Gwys.
			Ynys-y-geinon, Pont-ar-dawe, Glais.
	Clydach		Glais.
			Morriston, Landore.
	Ffyndrod		Landore.
			Swansea.
TEIFI	Llyn Teifi		Strata Florida.
	Llyn Ifer		Strata Florida.
	Llyn Egnant		Strata Florida.
		Llyn Gron	Strata Florida.
		Llyn-y-Gorlan	Strata Florida.
	Egnant		Strata Florida.
		Mwyro	Strata Florida.
			Strata Florida.
	Glasffrwd		Strata Florida.
	Rhuest		Strata Florida.
	Marchnant		Strata Florida.
		Gwyddyl	Strata Florida.
	Isur		Strata Florida.
	Llyn Maer		Tregaron.
	Camddwr		Tregaron.
		Fulbrook	Tregaron.
			Tregaron.
	Nant-y-Groes		Tregaron.
		Llyn Crugnant	Strata Florida.
		Berwyn	Tregaron.

WALES—*continued.*

RIVERS AND THEIR TRIBUTARIES.			STATIONS.
TEIFI (*cont.*)	....	....	Pont Llanio.
	Carfan	....	Pont Llanio.
	Brenig	....	Pont Llanio.
....	....	....	Derry Ormond.
	Clywedog	....	Derry Ormond.
	Cynon	....	Lampeter.
	Goy	....	Lampeter.
....	....	....	Lampeter.
	Dulas	....	Derry Ormond, Lampeter.
	Granell	....	Llan-y-Byther.
	Llyn Pencarreg	....	Llan-y-Byther.
....	....	....	Llan-y-Byther.
	Ceiliog	....	Maes-y-Crugian.
	Cathal	....	Llan-y-Byther.
....	....	....	Maes-y-Crugian.
	Cletwr	....	Maes-y-Crugian.
		Cletwr-fach	Maes-y-Crugian.
		Geyron	Maes-y-Crugian.
		Cinen	Maes-y-Crugian.
	Cerdin	....	Llandyssil.
		Ythan	Llandyssil.
....	....	....	Llandyssil.
	Twelli	....	Pen-Caber.
		Gweddel	Llandyssil.
....	....	....	Llandyssil.
	Bydrel	....	Llandyssil.
	Gernos	....	Newcastle Emlyn.
....	....	....	Newcastle Emlyn.
	Cert	....	Newcastle Emlyn.
		Bedw	Newcastle Emlyn.
		Dulas	Newcastle Emlyn.
	Cych	....	Newcastle Emlyn.
		Bowy	Newcastle Emlyn.
		Mamog	Newcastle Emlyn.
		Connud	Cardigan.
	Irfed	....	Cardigan.
....	....	....	Cardigan.
	Ffrwydd	....	Cardigan
	Llwyn Llwyd	....	Cardigan.
TOWEY	Llyn Ddu	....	Strata Florida
	Llyn Gorast	....	Strata Florida.
	Camddwr	....	Tregaron.
	Doethiam	Llyn Berwyn	Tregaron.
		Doethiam-fach.	
		{Pysgotwr	Pontllanio.
		{Pysgotwr-fach.	
	Gwenffrwd	....	Cynghordy.
	Rhaiadr	....	Cynghordy.
	Gwenlas	....	Llandovery.
	Dernant	....	Llandovery.
	....	....	Llandovery.
	Bran	....	Cynghordy.
		Crychan	Cynghordy.
		{Gwdderig	Llandovery.
		{Gwenst	Llandovery.
	....	....	Llandovery
....	....	....	Llanwrda.
	Ynys	....	Llanwrda.
	Dulas	....	Llanwrda.
....	....	....	Llangadock.
	Marles	....	Llangadock.
	Sefin	....	Llangadock.
		Llechdawdd	Llangadock.
		Sefin Isaf	Llangadock.
	Sawdde	Llyn-y-fan fach	Pen-y-wyllt.
		Buartharrh	Llangadock.
		Dyfnant	Llangadock.
		{Sawdde fechan	Llangadock.
		{Clydach	Llangadock.
	....	....	Llangadock.

WALES—*continued.*

RIVERS AND THEIR TRIBUTARIES.			STATIONS.
TOWEY (*cont.*)..	....	....	Glanrhyd, Talley Road.
	Dulas	....	Talley Road.
		Taliaris	Talley Road.
		Llyn Taliaris..	Talley Road.
....	....	....	Llandilo.
	Cennen	....	Derwydd Road, Llandilo.
....	....	....	Golden Grove.
	Cyfing	....	Golden Grove.
....	....	....	Llanarthney.
	Dulas	*Sannan*	Llanarthney.
....	....	....	Nantgaredig.
	Cothi	....	Pont Llanio.
		Mancoed	Pont Llanio.
		{*Twrch*	Pont Llanio.
		{*Crompedol*	Lampeter.
		Rannell	Llanwrda.
		Vellindwr	Llanwrda.
		Talley Lakes ..	Talley Road.
		Gorlech	Talley Road.
		Marles	Nantgaredig.
	....	....	Nantgaredig.
....	....	....	Abergwili.
	Gwili	....	Llanpumpsaint, Cynwy.
		Duad	Cynwyl.
	....	....	Branwydd Arms Abergwilli.
....	....	....	Caermarthen.
	Pibwr	....	Nantgaredig, Caermarthen.
TYDI	....	....	Llandissilio Gogo.
WEN	....	....	Llangybi, Chwilog, Afon Wen.
WEPRE BROOK	....	....	St. Mark's.
WYRAI	....	....	Traws-Coed, Llanrhystyd.
	Mabus	*Tryal*	Llanrhystyd.
	Carrog	....	Llanrhystyd.
YSGETHIN	*Llyn*	....	Dyffryn.
	Llyn Bodlyn ..	....	Dyffryn.
	Llyn Irddyn ..	....	Dyffryn.

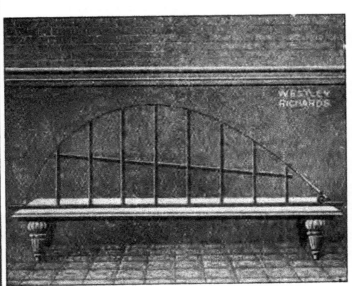

P. D. MALLOCH
Fishing Tackle Manufacturer,
SCOTT STREET, PERTH.

MANUFACTURER OF EVERY DESCRIPTION OF SUPERIOR FISHING TACKLE SUITABLE FOR ALL PARTS OF THE WORLD.

MALLOCH'S NEW PATENT CASTING REEL, Improved Pattern in Gun Metal or Aluminium; the greatest boon to Anglers yet invented for Salmon, Mahseer, and Trout, and all kinds of Coarse Fishing. Unsurpassed for Long-distance Casting; simple, and easy to learn.

Rods and Lines specially suitable for these Reels.

MALLOCH'S PATENT FLY CASE for Salmon, Grilse, Sea Trout, and Eyed Flies of all sizes. Handy and compact. Each Fly secured by neat and effective arrangement.

MALLOCH'S NEW KINGFISHER LINE is absolutely the best line ever offered to anglers. It is thoroughly waterproof, and has a perfectly smooth surface which never cracks or knuckles.

Sample Cards Free on Application.

MALLOCH'S NEW PATENT INVISIBLE SPINNER.

MALLOCH'S NEW PATENT BOAT ANGLER.

MALLOCH'S GOLD MEDAL SALMON AND TROUT REELS IN GUN METAL AND ALUMINIUM.

Illustrated List Free. Telegraphic Address, "MALLOCH, PERTH."

Prize Medals Awarded National Fisheries' Exhibition, Norwich, 1881; International Fisheries' Exhibition, Edinburgh, 1882. The Highest Awards at the Great International Fisheries' Exhibition, London, 1883; Gold Medal for General Collection of Rods and Tackle; Gold Medal for Flies; Gold Medal for Salmon Reels; Gold Medal for Trout Reels; Medal for Trout Rods; Medal for Salmon Rods; Special Money Prizes for Salmon and Trout Reels; Special Money Prize for Salmon Flies; Six Diplomas of Honour; Silver Medal, Bolton, 1889, for Casts of Fish.

ANGLING CLOSE SEASONS AND LICENCES.

NOTE.—S, salmon; T, trout; C F, coarse fish; m, month; w, week; d, day; f, fortnight.

ENGLAND AND WALES.

For all English rivers (except as below) and for Scotch Esk the close time for salmon is from Nov. 2 to Feb. 1, and for trout Oct. 2 to Feb. 1; coarse fish from March 15 to June 15.

NOTE.—The word Salmon includes all migratory Salmonidæ.

ADUR. *Close time*: S, Oct. 1 to Feb. 2; T, Oct. 1 to March 31; C F, March 15 to June 15. *Licences*: S, 5s.; T, 1s.

AVON (DEVON), including Erme. *Close time*: S, Erme, Nov. 30 to April 4; rest of district, Nov. 30 to May 1; T, Oct. 1 to last day of Feb.; C F, none. *Licences*: S, 20s.; T. 10s.; w, 5s.; d, 2s.

AVON AND STOUR (HANTS), including Wily, Lidden, and other tributaries, except in Somerset. *Close time*: S, Oct. 2 to Feb. 1; T, above Amesbury Bridge, Oct. 15 to March 31: between Bickton Mill and Amesbury Bridge, Oct. 1 to March 31; C F, none. *Licences*: S, 30s., m. 20s.; T, 5s.; w, 2s. 6d.; d, 1s. (above Bickton Mill). In Allen and Tarrant, 2s. 6d.; d, 1s.; rest of district, 1s.

AVON (SOMERSET), includes Chew, Frome, Ax, Brue, Parret, Isle, Tone, Yeo, Wilts and Berks Canal (west of Swindon), Taunton and Bridgwater Canal. *Close time*: S, Nov. 2 to Feb. 1; T, Oct. 2 to Feb. 1; C F, March 15 to June 15. *Licences*: S, 15s.; T, Avon and tributaries, 2s. 6d.: m, 1s.: d, 6d.: remainder of district, 5s.; m, 2s. 6d.: d, 1s.

AXE, including Yarty, Bredy, Brit, and Char. *Close time*: S. Nov. 20 to April 30; T, Oct. 2 to Feb. 1; C F, none. *Licences*: S. 10s.; T. 2s. 6d.

AYRON. *Close time*: S, Nov. 15 to Feb. 14; T, Oct. 1 to March 15; C F, March 15 to June 15. *Licences*: S, 10s.: fortnight, 5s.; T, 2s. 6d.: m, 1s.

CAMEL, including Heyl and all rivers on north coast of Cornwall. *Close time*: S, Dec. 1 to April 30; T, Oct. 1 to March 15; C F, March 15 to June 15. *Licences*: S, 12s.; f, 5s.; d, 1s. T, 4s.; f, 2s. 6d.; d, 1s.

CLEDDY, including East and West Cleddy, Gwaen. *Close time*: S, Nov. 1 to Feb. 1; T, Sept. 29 to March 1; C F, March 15 to June 15. *Licences*: S, 10s. 6d.; T, 3s. 6d.; w, 2s. 6d.; d. 1s.

CLWYD AND ELWY, including Aled. *Close time*: S. Nov. 15 to May 15; T, Oct. 2 to Feb. 28; C F, March 15 to June 15. *Licences*: S, 20s.; T, 4s. 6d.; w, 2s.

CONWAY, including Lledr, Llwgwy, Llyn Conway. *Close time*: S, Nov. 1 to April 30: gaff, Nov. 1 to April 30; T, Oct. 1 to last day of Feb.; C F, March 15 to June 15. *Licences*: S, 20s.; m, 10s.; w, 3s.; d, 1s.; T, 2s.; d, 6d.

COQUET. *Close time*: S, Nov. 1 to Jan. 31; gaff, Oct. 1 to Jan. 31; T, Nov. 1 to March 3; C F, March 15 to June 15. *Licences*: S, 5s.; T, 2s. 6d.

CUCKMERE. *Close time*: S, Nov. 2 to Feb. 1; T, Oct. 1 to March 31; C F, March 15 to June 15; *Licences*: S, 5s.; T, 1s.

CUMBERLAND (WEST), including Calder. Eden (below Ennerdale Lake), Esk, Irt, Wastwater. Bleng, Mite. *Close time*: S, Nov. 14 to March 10; gaff, Nov. 14 to June 30; T, Sept. 2 to March 10; C F, March 15 to June 15. *Licences*: S, 10s. 6d.; w, 5s.; d, 2s.; T, 2s. 6d.; w, 1s.

DART, including East Dart, Webbern, Slapton Lea. *Close time*: S, Oct. 1 to last day of Feb.; gaff, Oct. 1 to March 31; T, Oct. 1 to last day of Feb.; C F, March 15 to June 15. *Licences*: S, 20s.; w, 7s. 6d.; d, 2s. 6d.; T, 10s.; m, 5s.; d, 2s.

DEE, including Alwen, Alyn, Ceriog, Gairw, Lliw, Treverryn, Twrch, Bala Lake. *Close time*: S, Nov. 2 to March 31; T, Oct. 14 to Feb. 14; C F, March 15 to June 15. *Licences*: S, 20s.; w, 10s.; d, 5s.; T, none.

England and Wales—*continued.*

DERWENT (CUMBERLAND), including Bassenthwaite, Derwentwater and Loweswater. Crummockwater, Buttermere, St. John's Beck (below Millgill), Naddle Beck (below Roughhow Bridge). Greta, Cocker, Marron. *Close time*: S, Nov. 15 to March 10 ; gaff, Nov. 15 to June 30 ; T, Sept. 15 to March 10. Crummock and Buttermere. for char only, Nov. 1 to June 30. C F, March 15 to June 15. *Licences*: S, 30s.; m,20s.; any part of district, except River Derwent, between Ouse Bridge and sea, 15s.; m. 10s.; T, above Derwent Bridge, 5s.; m, 2s. 6d.; below Derwent Bridge up to June 30, 5s.; m, 2s. 6d.; above Ouse Bridge, d, 1s.

DOVEY, including Artro, Dulas, Dysynni. Mawddach, Glaslyn, Lery, Prysor, Bychan, Llyn Glyn. *Close time* : S, Nov. 1 to April 30 ; gaff, Oct. 21 to May 30 ; T, Oct. 2 to Feb. 1 ; C F, March 15 to June 15. *Licences*: S, 20s.; m, 10s.; w. 5s.; d. 1s. T. 1s.

DWYFACH, including Dwyfawr, Erch. Soch. *Close time*: S, Nov. 15 to March 1 ; T. Oct. 2 to Feb. 1 ; C F, March 15 to June 15. *Licences* : S. 21s.; m. 10s.; w, 5s. ; d, 2s. T, 7s.; m, 5s.; w, 2s.

EDEN, including Eden (below Kirkby Stephen), Petterill (below Wreay Bridge), Caldew (below Hawksdale Bridge), Eamont (below junction with Lowther), Irthing (below boundary of Cumberland), Crodundle, Wampool, Waver. *Close time*: S.; Nov. 16 to Feb. 15; gaff, Nov. 16 to June 30 ; T, Oct. 2 to last day of Feb.; C F, none. *Licences*: S, for whole district, 21s.; above Armathwaite Weir. 15s.; in Irthing, Wampool, and Waver, 7s. 6d., w, 5s.; d, 2s. 6d ; single-handed rods in Duke of Devonshire's socage water 5s.; T. 3s. 6d.; w, 1s.

ESK (YORKS), including Glaisdale. *Close time*: S, Nov. 2 to Feb. 1 ; T, Oct. 1 to March 15 ; C F, March 15 to June 15. *Licences* : S. 10s.; m, 5s.; d, 2s. 6d. (monthly and day licences not to extend beyond June 30); T, 1s. 6d.

EXE (DEVON), including Barle, Culm, Fordton, Clist. *Close time*: S, Oct. 20 to March 1 ; gaff, Oct. 1 to March 14; T, Sept. 15 to last day of Feb.; C F, March 15 to June 15. *Licences*: S, 30s., w, 7s. 6d.; T, 5s.; w, 2s. 6d; d, 1s.

FOWEY. *Close time* : S, between Lostwithiel Bridge and St. Winnow Point, Dec. 1 to April 30; rest of district, Dec. 1 to April 4 ; T, between Lostwithiel Bridge and St. Winnow Point, Oct. 1 to April 30; rest of district, Oct. 1 to March 15; C F, March 15 to June 15. *Licences*: S, 15s.; f (in Fowey and tributaries only), 6s.; T, 5s.

FROME, including Piddle, Corfe, Fleet. *Close time*: S, Nov. 2 to Feb. 1; T, Oct. 2 to Feb. 1 ; C F, March 15 to June 15. *Licences*: S, 20s.; T, none.

KENT AND BELA, including Crake, Coniston Water, Duddon, Kent, Mint, Sleddale, Leven, Esthwaite, Grasmere, Windermere, Troutbeck, Winster. *Close time* : S, Nov. 1 to March 31; gaff, Nov. 1 to June 1; T, in Duddon and tributaries above Foxfield Viaduct, Oct. 2 to April 1; in Bela and tributaries, Sept. 16 to Feb. 15; rest of district, Oct. 2 to March 3 ; C F, March 15 to June 15, except for pike. *Licences* : S, 10s.; w, 5s.; T, Lake Windermere, 5s. ; rest of district, 2s. 6d.; Lake Windermere, from midnight Friday to midnight Monday, 2s. 6d.

LEA, including tributaries. *Close time*: S and T, Sept. 29 to April 30; pike and perch, March 15 to August 1 ; dace and gudgeon, March 31 to June 15 ; other C F, March 31 to July 1.

LUNE, including Cocker, Conder, Keer, Wenning, Hindburn, Greta, Rother, Wyre. *Close time*: S, Nov. 2 to March 1; T, Oct. 2 to March 1; C F, March 15 to June 15. *Licences*: S, 20s.; Lune and tributaries above Lonsdale Bridge, 10s.; for Wyre and tributaries, Keer, Cocker, Conder, Wenning, Greta, 5s.; T, 2s. 6d.

NORFOLK AND SUFFOLK, including Ormesby Broad, River Thurne, Hickling Broad, Horsey Mere, Martham Broad, South Walsham Broad, Upton Broad, Whittleseamere Broad, Heigham Broad, North Walsham and Dilham Canal, Ranworth Broad, Hoven Broad, Wroxham Broad, River Ouse, Wissey and Nar, River Waveney, Fritton Broad, Lake Lothing, River Yare, River Wensum. Breydon Water, Surlingham Broad, Rockland Broad. *Close time*: S, Nov. 2 to Feb. 1; T, Oct. 2 to Feb. 1; C F, None. *Licences*: None.

OGMORE, including Llynvi, Ewenny. *Close time*: S, Nov. 15 to April 30; T, Sept. 30 to last day of Feb.; C F, March 15 to June 15. *Licences*: S, 10s. 6d.; T, 2s.

OTTER. *Close time*: S, Nov. 2 to Feb. 1; T, Oct. 2 to Feb. 1; C F, March 15 to June 15. *Licences*: none.

OUSE AND NENE. *Close Time*: S, Nov. 2 to Feb. 1; T, Oct. 2 to March 31; C F, March 15 to June 15. *Licences*, none.

OUSE (SUSSEX). *Close time*: S, Nov. 1 to April 1; T, Oct. 2 to Feb. 1; C F, March 15 to June 15. *Licences*: S, 5s; T, none.

RHYMNEY. *Close time*: S, Nov. 2 to April 1; gaff, Nov. 2 to April 30; T, Oct. 2 to March 1; C F, March 15 to June 15. *Licences*: S, 10s.; T, 1s.

RIBBLE AND HODDER, including Calder, Douglas. *Close time*: S, Nov. 2 to March 1; gaff, Nov. 2 to April 30; T, Oct. 2 to March 1; C F, March 15 to June 15. *Licences*: S, 20s., month (after June 30), 10s.; d, 5s.; T, 5s.; w,2s. 6d.; d, 1s.

ROTHER (SUSSEX), including Tillingham, Brede. *Close time*: S, Nov. 2 to Feb. 1; T, Oct. 1 to March 31; C F, March 15 to June 15. *Licences*: S. 5s.; T. 1s.

SEIONT, including Braint, Cefni, Gwrfai, Cwm Llyn, Llyfni, Llyn-y-Nantle, Llanberis Lakes. *Close time*: S, Nov. 1 to March 1; gaff, Nov. 2 to March 1; T, in Co. Carnarvon, Sept. 15 to March 1; rest of district, Sept. 15 to Feb. 13; char, Oct. 22 to

England and Wales—*continued.*

March 1; C F, March 15 to June 15. *Licences:* S, 21s.; m, 10s. 6d.; w, 5s.; d, 2s. 6d.: Cefni, Braint, and Llyfni, 10s. 6d.; T, 5s.; w, 2s. 6d.; d, 1s.

SEVERN, including Avon (except in Warwickshire), Little Avon, Frome, Leadon, Teme, Rea, Corve, Clun, Onny, Stour, Worf, Roden, Tern, Mees, Perry, Verniew, Tanat, Banw, Einion, Rhiw, Taranon, Garno, Clwydog, Tylwch, Glo'ster and Berkeley Canal, Birmingham and Worcester Canal (west of Alvechurch). *Close time:* S, Oct. 2 to Feb. 1: T, Oct. 2 to March 1; C F, whole district *below* Verniew mouth, in the counties of Salop, Stafford, Worcester, and Gloucester, and the Avon, where it flows through Worcester and Gloucester. All C F March 15 to June 15. Above Verniew mouth grayling only are preserved. Pike may be killed anywhere, and at all times. *Licences:* S, 10s.; T, Salop, Montgm., and Denbigh, 2s.; rest of district, 1s.

STOUR (KENT), including Lesser Stour. *Close time:* S, Nov. 2 to May 1; T, Oct. 2 to Feb. 1; C F, March 15 to June 15. *Licences:* S, 20s.; T, none.

SUFFOLK AND ESSEX. *Close Time:* S, Nov. 2 to Feb. 1; T, Oct. 2 to April 10; C F, March 15 to June 15. *Licences:* none.

TAFF AND ELY, including Rhondda. *Close time:* S, Nov. 15 to April 30; gaff, Nov. 2 to May 31; T, Sept. 20 to Feb. 1; C F, March 15 to June 15. *Licences:* S, 10s. 6d.; T, 2s. 6d.

TAMAR AND PLYM, including Inney, Attery, Carey, Tavy, Lynher, Yealm, Bude Canal. *Close time:* S, Nov. 2 to March 1; T, Oct. 2 to March 1; C F, March 15 to June 15. *Licences:* S, 10s.; T. 2s. 6d.; d, 1s.

TAW AND TORRIDGE, including Yeo, Bray, Little Dart, Okement. *Close time:* S, Nov. 1 to March 31; gaff, Nov. 1 to May 31; T, Oct. 1 to last day of Feb.; C F, March 15 to June 15. *Licences:* S, 24s.; T, 5s.

TEES, including (Tees below Maize Brook) Leven, Skerne, Greta, Lune. *Close time:* S, Nov. 2 to Feb. 1; T, Oct. 1 to March 15; C F, March 15 to June 15. *Licences:* S, 20s.; T, 2s. 6d.

TEIFI, including Cych, Cery, Nevern, Wirrai. *Close time:* S, Nov. 1 to Feb. 28; T, Oct. 1 to Feb. 28; C F, March 15 to June 15. *Licences:* S, 20s.; m, 10s. 6d.; T, 2s. 6d.

TEIGN (DEVON), including Wrey. *Close time:* S, Nov. 2 to Feb. 1; gaff, Sept. 2 to April 30; T, Oct. 1 to March 2; C F, March 15 to June 15. *Licences:* S, 20s.; d, 2s. T, 5s.

THAMES. *Close time:* Salmon, Sept. 1 to March 31; trout and char, Sept. 11 to March 31, smelts, March 25 to July 25; lamperns, April 1 to Aug. 24; eels, March 15 to June 15, other freshwater fish, March 15 to June 15. *Licences:* none.

TOWY, including Gwili, Cothi, Cennen, Taf, Loughor, Ammon, Gwendraeth Fach, Gwendraeth Fawr. *Close time:* S, Oct. 15 to April 1; gaff, Oct. 1 to April 1; T, between G. W. Ry. Bridge below Carmarthen and confluence of rivers Gwili and Towy, Oct. 2 to June 30; rest of district, Oct. 2 to March 1; C F, none. *Licences:* S, 21s.; T, 2s. 6d.

TRENT, including Ancholm, Idle, Soar, Wreak, Derwent, Wye. Churnet, Dove, Meaue, Anker, Blyth, Tame, Ludd, Witherneau, Birmingham and Fazely, Ashby-de-la-Zouch, and Essington and Wynley canals. *Close time:* S, Nov. 2 to Feb. 1; T, Oct. 2 to Feb. 1: C F, March 15 to June 15. *Licences:* S, 10s.; T, 2s. 6d.; w. 1s.

TYNE, including Derwent, Devil's Water, Allen Water, South Tyne, North Tyne, Redewater. *Close time:* S, Nov. 2 to Feb. 1; T, Oct. 1 to March 21; C F, March 15 to June 15. *Licences:* S, 20s.; w, 10s.; d, 5s.; South Tyne, above Warden Dam, or in Rede only above Old Bridge, 5s.; w, 2s. 6d.; d, 1s.; Rede and North Tyne, above Redemouth, 10s.; w, 5s ; d, 2s. 6d.; T, 2s. 6d.; m, 1s.

USK AND EBBW, including Afon Llwyd. Honddu, Yscir, Bran, Tarrall, Cynrig. *Close time:* S. Nov. 2 to March 1; gaff, Oct. 2 to April 30; T, Sept. 2 to Feb. 14; C F (except eels). March 15 to June 15. *Licences:* S, 30s., f, 10s.; T, 2s. 6d.

WEAR, including Bedburn, Browney. *Close time:* S, Wear and tributaries above South Biddick, Nov. 2 to March 1: rest of district. Nov. 2 to Feb. 1; T, Oct. 2 to March 1; C F, March 15 to June 15. *Licences:* S, 5s.; T, 2s.

WITHAM. *Close time:* S, Nov. 2 to Feb. 1; T, Oct. 2 to Feb. 1; C F, March 15 to June 15. *Licences:* T, 2s. 6d.; w, 1s.

WYE, including Monnow, Trothy, Lugg, Arrow, Ithon. *Close time:* S, Oct. 16 to Feb. 1; gaff, Oct. 2 to April 1; T, Oct. 2 to Feb. 14; C F, none. *Licences:* S, whole district, 30s.; f, 10s.; in Wye above Llanwrthwl Bridge or tributaries above Builth Bridge, 15s.; T, 2s. 6d.; 28 days, 1s.

YORKSHIRE (rivers flowing into Humber), including Aire, Calder, Derwent, Don, Hull, Ouse, Wharfe, Nidd, Ure, Swale, Wiske. Barnsley Canal. *Close time:* S, Nov. 16 to last day of Feb.; gaff, Nov. 2 to April 30; T, Oct. 2 to March 15; C F (except pike, which may be killed at any time), March 15 to June 15. *Licences:* S, 20s.; T, 1s.

IRELAND.

CLOSE TIME FOR SALMON AND TROUT.
All dates inclusive.

The universal charge for a Salmon licence in Ireland is 20s., available for the whole country.

BALLINA—Sept. 16 to Jan. 31. *Exceptions:* River CLOONAGHMORE or PALMERSTON tidal, Nov. 1 to Jan. 31; fresh, Nov. 1 to May 31; River EASKEY, Nov. 1 to Jan. 31.

Ireland—*continued.*

BALLINAKILL—Nov. 1 to Jan. 31. *Exceptions*: Rivers LOUISBURGH, Nov. 1 to May 31 ; CARROWNISKY, Nov. 1 to June 30.

BALLYCASTLE—Nov. 1 to Jan. 31. *Exception*: River BUSH. Oct. 1 to Jan. 31

BALLYSHANNON—Oct. 10 to Feb. 28. *Exceptions*: River BUNDUFF, Oct. 1 to Jan. 31 ; River BUNDROWES, Oct. 1 to Jan. 31; River ERNE, Oct. 1 to last day of Feb.

BANGOR—Oct. 1 to April 30. *Exceptions*: Rivers GLENAMOY and OWENGARVE, Nov. 1 to April 30. Rivers BURRISHOOLE, OWENDUFF, BALLYVEENY, and BALLYCROY, and in ACHIL ISLAND, Nov. 1 to Jan. 31; Rivers OWENMORE and MUNHIM, Oct. 1 to Jan. 31.

BANTRY—Nov. 1 to March 16.

COLERAINE—Oct. 1 to Feb. 28. *Exceptions*: Rivers MAINE and BLACKWATER, Nov. 1 to last day of Feb.

CONNEMARA—Oct. 16 to Jan. 31. *Exceptions*: Rivers CASHLA, DOOHULLA , BALLINA-HINCH, SCREEB and INVER, Nov. 1 to Jan. 31.

CORK—From Ballycotton to Barry's Head, Oct. 18 to Jan. 31: and from Barry's Head to Galley Head, Oct. 13 to Feb. 14. *Exception*: River ARGIDEEN, Nov. 1 to Feb. 14.

DUBLIN—Nov. 1 to Jan. 31. *Exceptions*: BROADMEADOW WATER and WARD Rivers, Oct. 15 to Jan. 31.

DROGHEDA.—Sept. 16 to Feb. 11.

DUNDALK—Nov. 1 to last day of Feb. *Exceptions*: Between Clogher Head and N. boundary of River Annagassan, angling in fresh waters, Oct. 1 to Jan. 31; in tidal waters, Aug. 20 to Feb. 11; between N. boundary of River Annagassan and Ballaghan Point. Oct. 1 to April 30.

GALWAY—Oct. 16 to Jan. 31. *Exceptions*: Rivers SPIDDAL (or SPIDDLE) and CRUMLIN, Nov. 1 to Jan. 31. River OUGHTERARD, Oct. 1 to Jan. 31.

KENMARE—Nov. 1 to March 31.

KILLARNEY—Nov. 1 to March 31. *Exceptions*: Between Inch Point and most W. point of Kells Bay, Oct. 16 to Jan. 31. Rivers LAUNE and MAINE, and their lakes and tributaries. Nov. 1 to Jan. 31.

LETTERKENNY—Nov. 2 to Jan. 31. *Exceptions*: River CRANA (or BUNCRANA), Nov. 1 to last day of Feb. Rivers OWENEA and OWENTOOKER, Oct. 1 to March 31

LIMERICK—Oct. 1 to Jan. 31. *Exceptions*: Rivers FEALE, GEALE, and CASHEN, Nov. 1 to April 30; Dunmore Head to Kerry Head, save rivers OWENMORE and FEOHANAGH, Oct. 1 to March 31; Loop Head to Hag's Head, Oct. 1 to last day of Feb.; Rivers SHANNON and MULCAIR, Nov. 1 to Jan. 31; Rivers OWENMORE and FEOHANAGH, Nov. 1 to April 30. For that part of district situated in Co. Westmeath, the waters of which flow into Lough Ree and the River Shannon, and for Lough Sheelin, Oct. 1 to last day of Feb.

LISMORE—Oct. 1 to Jan. 31.

LONDONDERRY—Oct. 11 to March 31 *Exception*: River CULDAFF, Oct. 16 to Feb. 28.

SKIBBEREEN—Nov. 1 to Jan. 31.

SLIGO—Oct. 1 to Jan. 31. *Exception*: River DRUMCLIFFE and Lake GLENCAR, Oct. 20 to Jan. 31. GRANGE RIVER, Nov. 1 to Jan. 31. SLIGO or GARVOGUE River (tidal), July 16 to Dec. 31.

WATERFORD—Oct. 1 to Jan. 31. *Exception*: River SUIR, Oct. 16 to Jan. 31.

WEXFORD—Oct. 1 to March 14. *Exception*: River SLANEY, Sept. 1 to Feb. 25.

SCOTLAND.

CLOSE TIME FOR SALMON.

All dates inclusive.

For all rivers (except as below)—Nov. 1 to Feb. 10.

ADD, ARAY, ECKAIG, N. ESK, S. ESK, FYNE, RUEL, SHIRA—Nov. 1 to Feb. 15.

ANNAN—Nov. 16 to Feb. 24.

BEAULY, DUNBEATH, LOSSIE, NESS, SPEY and KYLE of SUTHERLAND—Oct. 16 to Feb. 10.

BERVIE, CARRADALE, FLEET (SUTHERLAND), FLEET (KIRKCUDBRIGHT), GARNOCK, GIRVAN, IORSA, INNER (I. OF JURA). IRVINE, LAGGAN, LUCE, SORN. UGIE, YTHAN, and all rivers in HARRIS, N. and S. UIST and of ORKNEY—Nov. 1 to Feb. 24.

BORGIE, HALLADALE, NAVER, STRATHY—Oct. 1 to Jan. 11

DRUMMACHLOY or GLENMORE (BUTE)—Oct. 16 to Feb. 15.

EARN—Nov. 1 to Jan. 31.

ESK (DUMFRIES)—Nov. 2 to Feb. 1; T, Oct. 2 to Feb. 1.

FINDHORN—Oct. 11 to Feb. 10.

HOPE AND POLLA OR STRATHBEG—Sept. 11 to Jan. 11.

NITH—Nov. 15 to Feb. 24.

SHETLAND ISLANDS—Nov. 16 to Jan. 31.

STINCHAR—Nov. 15 to Feb. 24.

TAY (except Earn) and FORTH—Oct. 16 to Jan. 14.

THURSO—Oct. 6 to Jan. 10.

TWEED—Dec. 1 to Jan. 31 ; T, Oct. 15 to Feb. 28.

URR—Nov. 30 to Feb. 24.

LIST OF CONTRACTIONS.

c s.)	Close seasons.	n.s.	Nearest railway station.
E.	East.	N.W.	North-West.
London, L.T.	London, Lower Thames.	S.	South.
,, *M.T.*	,, Middle ,,	S.E.	South-East.
,, *U.T.*	,, Upper ,,	s.t.	Season ticket.
m.	Miles.	S.W.	South-West.
m.t.	Monthly ticket.	W.	West.
N.	North.	w.t.	Weekly ticket.
N.E.	North-East.		

RAILWAYS.

By.R.	Barry Ry.	L.T. & S.R.	London, Tilbury, and South-end Ry.
B.C.R.	Bishops Castle Ry.	M. & M.R.	Manchester and Milford Ry.
B. & M.R.	Brecon and Merthyr Ry.	M.S.J. & A.R.	Manchester South Junction and Altrincham Ry.
C.R.	Cambrian Ry.	M. & C.R.	Maryport and Carlisle Ry
C.L.R.	Cheshire Lines Ry.	Met.R.	Metropolitan Ry.
C. & W.J.R.	Cleator and Workington Junction Ry.	M.R.	Midland Ry.
Cs.R.	Corris Ry.	M. & G.N.J.R.	Midland and Great Northern Joint Ry.
D.N. & S.R.	Didcot, Newbury, and Southampton Ry.	M. & G.W.J.R.	Midland and Great Western Joint Ry.
E. & W.J.R.	East and West Junction Ry.	M. & S.W.J.R.	Midland and South-Western Junction Ry.
F.R.	Festiniog Ry.	N. & B.R.	Neath and Brecon Ry.
Fs.R.	Furness Ry.	N. & B.J.R	Northampton and Banbury Junction Ry.
G. & K.R.	Garstang and Knot End Ry.	N.E.R.	North-Eastern Ry.
G.C.R.	Great Central Ry.	N.S.R.	North Staffordshire R.
G.E.R.	Great Eastern Ry.	N.W.N.G.R.	North Wales Narrow Gauge Ry.
G.E.M. & G.N. J.R.	Great Eastern, Midland, and Great Northern Joint Ry.	O. & A.R.	Oxford and Aylesbury Ry.
N.R.	Great Northern Ry.	R. & E.R.	Ravenglass and Eskdale Ry.
G N. of S.R.	Great North of Scotland Ry.	R. & S.B.R.	Rhondda and Swansea Bay Ry.
G.N. & L. & N.W.J.R.	Great Northern and London and North-Western Joint Ry.	R.R.	Rhymney Ry.
G.W.R.	Great Western Ry.	S. & M.R.	Sheffield and Midland Ry.
G.W. & R.J.R.	Great Western and Rhymney Joint Ry.	S. & D.R.	Somerset and Dorset Ry.
H. & B.R.	Hull and Barnsley Ry.	S.E. & C.R.	South-Eastern and Chatham Ry.
L. & Y.R.	Lancashire and Yorkshire Ry.	S. & C.L.E.R.	Southport and Cheshire Lines Extension Ry.
L.D. & E.C.R.	Lancashire, Derbyshire, and East Coast Ry.	S.R.	Southwold Ry.
L. & N.W.R.	London and North-Western Ry.	T.V.R.	Taff Vale Ry
L. & S.W.R.	London and South-Western Ry.	T.R.	Tal-y-llyn Ry.
L.B. & S.C.R.	London, Brighton, and South Coast Ry.	W.R.	Wirral Ry.

ISLE OF MAN.

I. of M.R .... Isle of Man Ry.

ISLE OF WIGHT.

I. of W.R .... Isle of Wight Ry.

SCOTLAND.

C.R. .... Caledonian Ry.
D. & A.J.R....... Dundee and Arbroath Joint Ry.
G. & K.J.R....... Glasgow and Kilmarnock Joint Ry.
G. & S.W.R. ... Glasgow and South-Western Ry.

G.N. of S R....... Great North of Scotland Ry.
H.R. .... Highland Ry.
L. & A.R.......... Lanarkshire and Ayrshire Ry.
N.B.R. .... North British Ry.
P. & W.J.R. ..... Portpatrick and Wigtownshire Joint Ry.

IRELAND.

B.R. .... Ballycastle Ry.
B. & C.D.R....... Belfast and County Down Ry.
C. & V.B.R....... Castlederg and Victoria Bridge Ry.
C. & L.R.......... Cavan and Leitrim Ry.
C.V.R. .... Clogher Valley Ry.
C. & M.R.... ..... Cork and Muskerry Ry.
C.B. & S.C.R. ... Cork, Bandon, and South Coast Ry.
C. & M.D.R. ... Cork and Macroom Direct Ry.
D.R. .... Donegal Ry.
D.W. & W.R. ... Dublin, Wicklow, and Wexford Ry.

G.N.R. .... Great Northern Ry.
G.S. & W.R....... Great Southern and Western Ry.
L.R. .... Letterkenny Ry.
L. & L.S.R. ...... Londonderry and Lough Swilly Ry.
M. & N.C.R. ... Midland and Northern Counties Ry.
M.G.W.R.......... Midland Great Western Ry.
S. & S.R. .... Schull and Skibbereen Ry.
S.L. & N.C.R. ... Sligo, Leitrim, and Northern Counties Ry.
T. & D.R .... Tralee and Dingle Ry.
W. & T.R.......... Waterford and Tramore Ry.
W.C.R .... West Clare Ry

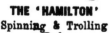

THE
ANGLER'S DIARY

AND

TOURIST FISHERMAN'S GAZETTEER.

A LIST OF FISHING STATIONS IN THE UNITED KINGDOM.

ENGLAND.

Abbots Bromley, n.s. **Rugeley**, 4 m. (Stafford).—L. & N.W.R. Bromley brook. Blythe, 1 m. S.W. (c.s. *Trent*.) Tad brook, 2 m. W. Purt brook, 2 m. S.E. Swarbourne brook, 4 m. S.E. Lin brook, 5 m. S.E. *Lakes*: Bagots Park, 2 m. N. Lake by Newborough 4 m. N.E. (*See Gainsborough*.)

Aberbeeg (Monmouth).—G.W.R. Ebbw; polluted. (c.s. *Usk*.) Ebwyfach; trout. (c.s. *Usk*.) *Lakes*: Pound-y-Coed-Coe (2 m.) (*See Newport*.)

Abercarne (Monmouth).—G.W.R. Ebbw; polluted. (c.s. *Usk*.) (*See Newport*.)

Abertillery (Monmouth).—G.W.R.; L. & N.W.R. Ebwyfach; trout. (c.s. *Usk*.) (*See Newport*)

Aberford (York), n.s. **Garforth** or **Mickfield**, 3 m.—Cock beck. (*See York*.)

Abergavenny (Monmouth).— G.W.R. Usk; salmon, trout; preserved by the Usk and Ebbw Conservators, the United Usk Fishing Association (*see Usk*), and the Abergavenny Town Council. This latter preserves the river for 1 m. Salmon and trout rod licences 30s. and 2s. 6d., of Mr. W. H. Smith, Cross-street, or the Angel Hotel. There are salmon and trout tickets issued—salmon, d.t. 20s.,; trout, w.t. 10s., d.t. 2s. 6d., of Mr. Smith; artizans' ticket, 5s.; boys under 15 half price. *Salmon* fishing begins March 2, ending Nov. 1; *trouting* Feb. 15, and ending Sept. 1. The gaff must not be used before May 1, or after Oct. 1. Minnow fishing for trout begins April 15, and no artificial minnow must exceed 1¼in. in length. Trout fishermen must have a bag or basket for their fish; no dogs. (See *Usk*; *Brecon*). (c.s.) Gavenny; trout. (*See Newport*.) (c.s. *Usk*.) Myuachdy brook, 3 m. Trothey, 4 m.; trout (c.s. *Wye*). Full brook, 5 m. Honddu, 5 m.; trout. Monnow 6, m. trout; both reached by rail. (*See Chepstow*.) Grwyne, 6 m.; plenty of small trout. (*See Newport*.) *Hotels*: Angel, Greyhound. The proprietor of Angel has 3 m. of private water.

Abersychan (Monmouth).—G.W.R.; L. & N.W.R. Llwyd; trout, salmon. (*See Newport*.) (c.s. *Usk*.)

Abingdon (Berks).—G.W.R. Thames and Ock; pike, perch, tench, chub, and roach. *Hotels*: Queen's, Crown and Thistle, Lion. *Fishermen*: Hyde and Trinder. (c.s.) (*See London, M.T.*)

Aby (Lincoln).—G.N.R. Withern. Calceby beck, 2 m. *Lakes*: Ormsby Park, 5 m. (*See Saltfleet*.)

Accrington (Lanca.).—Lanc. & York R. Hynilburn brook. (*See Preston*.)

Acklington (Northland).—N.E.R. Coquet; trout (sea trout and salmon, autumn). The whole of the Duke of Northumberland's water on Coquet is now leased to the Coquet Committee of the Northumbrian Anglers' Federation; Clerk to the committee, John A. Williamson, solicitor, Newcastle-on-Tyne. s.t. 21s., m.t. 10s., w.t. 7s. 6d., d.t. 2s. 6d. The owner of Felton Park will sometimes grant leave for a day. (*See Rothbury, Brinkburn, Weldon Bridge*, and *Felton*.) The committee's permits are available for Lord Armstrong's water at Rothbury. *Hotel*: Railway. (c.s.)

Ackworth (Yorks).—G.N.R.; M.R. Went. *Lakes*: Nostell Priory lake, 3 m W (*See Goole*.)

Acle (Norfolk).—G.E.R. Bure; bream, roach, pike, perch; the half tides are so numerous that a good day's sport is doubtful. Muck Fleet. *Lakes*: Acle Decoy, 1 *m.* S. Walsham Broad, 4 *m.* N.W. *Inns:* Queen's Head and King's Head. (*c.s. Norfolk.*) (*See Yarmouth.*)

Acton (Cheshire).—L. & N.W.R. Weaver. Cuddington brook. Bent brook, 1 *m.* W. (*See Frodsham.*)

Adderley (Cheshire).—G.W.R.; L. & N.W.R. Adderley brook. *Lakes:* Adderley Hall lake. The Mere. New pool at Shavington, 1 *m.* S.W. New pool, Old pool, and Big pool (3 *m.* S.W.) (*See Frodsham; Gloucester.*)

Addingham (York).—M.R. Wharfe (*c.s. York.*) (*See York.*)

Addlestrop (Gloucester).—G.W.R. Evenlode here rises in a lake (*See London, U.T.*)

Addlington (Lancs.)—L. & Y.R.; L. & N.W.R. Douglas. (*c.s. Ribble.*) Barsden brook, 2*m.* S. *Lakes:* Rivington reservoir. (*See Liverpool, Hesketh Bank.*)

Adlington (Lancs.)—L. & N.W.R. Dean. (*See Runcorn.*)

Ainderby (York).—N.E.R. Swale, 1 *m.* W. (*c.s. York.*) Stelt, 3 *m.* N.W., at Langton. (*See York.*)

Aintree (Lancs.)—L. & Y.R.; S. & C.L.R. Alt. (*See Altcar.*)

Albrighton (Salop).—G.W.R. Woof (3 *m.* W.) *Lakes:* Patshull Lake (3 *m.* S.) Chillingham pool (3 *m.*; good fishing.) Snowdon pool (3½ *m.* S.W,) (*See Gloucester.*) (*c.s. Severn.*)

Alcester (Warwick).—M.R.; G.W.R. Arrow; pike, perch, chub, dace, roach, bream, few trout; 3 *m.* good fishing below, belonging to Mr. Twist; s.t. 5s., d.t., 6d., from the Fish Hotel, Wixford. Alne. Bow brook (7 *m.* N.W.) *Lakes:* Ragley Park lake (2 *m.* S.); strictly preserved. (*See Inkberrow; Gloucester.*) *Hotel :* Swan.

Aldeburgh (Suffolk). — G.E.R. Alde. Bass can be taken from the jetty; cod and whiting from the beach; October and November best months. (*See Orford.*) *Hotels :* Brudenall, White Lion.

Aldermaston (Berks).—G.W.R. Kennett; roach, dace, perch, pike, trout; preserved by C. Keyser, Esq., of Aldermaston Park. Emburne; trout. (*See London, M.T.*)

Alderney.—Sea fish of all kinds may be taken from any steep rock. Excellent pollack and other fishing outside the harbour. Strangers should not venture outside alone. Corbet is an excellent fisherman. With the rod, from the breakwater, may be taken whiting, pollack, mackerel, gar fish, occasionally bass and sea bream; this latter also from the steep rocks under the fort. The pollack and pout are the chief fish caught from the rocks or pier in the winter, and they are to be taken, more or less, all the year round, the pout more particularly, by throwing out a ground line; the pollack with a lightly-leaded line, with or without a float, according to local circumstances. The breakwater runs out into water 100ft. deep or more. The other fish to be taken is the atherine or sand smelt which may be caught with a paternoster and a ½oz. or ⅜oz. lead, hooks No. 8 and 9, and a piece of rag worm for bait, ½in. long, on each hook. It is especially a winter-feeding fish, but takes best after dark, under a lamp. Under the fort during a fine summer evening, towing a casting line with three or four flies, and 20yds of line out; or a line with rock or lug worm bait, with a ¼lb. lead, or even without any lead at all, will be successful in taking pollack. You would also catch congers by throwing out a ground line, baited with a piece of a sucker (*Octopus vulgaris*), or a small pout, piece of pollack, or other fresh fish. On sandy bottoms, in the bays, in rough weather in summer and autumn, when there is a good surf, a throw-out or ledger line baited with sucker (here called *pieuvre*), with squid (termed *conée*), or cuttle fish (*seche*), will occasionally take large ground bass, from 6lb. to 14lb. Bass are sometimes plentiful, and are found in the strong tides of the Singe passage, where they are whiffed or trailed for with a small eel or other fish bait. There is a good hotel here.

Aldwark (York), n.s. **Tollerton,** 4 *m.*—Ouse. (*c.s. York.*) (*See York.*)

Alfreton (Derby).—M.R. Normanton brook. Westwood brook, 1 *m.* N.E. Amber, 2 *m.* W.; trout, grayling. Erewash, 3 *m.* S.E. at **Pye Bridge.** *Lakes:* Butterley reservoir, 3 *m.* S. (*See Gainsborough.*)

Allerton (York).—N.E.R. Allerton beck, 1 *m.* W. Nield, 2 *m.* S. (*c.s. York.*) *Lakes :* Allerton Park lakes, 2 *m.* W. (*See York.*)

Almeley (Hereford). — G.W.R. Upcott brook. Letton lake brook. *Lakes :* Newport Park. Upcott. (*See Chepstow.*)

Alne (York).—N.E.R. Kyle Hawkhill beck. Derings beck. (*See York.*)

Alnwick (Northland.).—N.E.R. On Aln; trout and sea trout; season for sea trout, Feb. 2 to Oct. 31; trout, March 1 to Oct. 1 The Duke of Northumberland preserves the water running through Hulne Park, Dairy Grounds, and the pastures to Denwick Bridge. Leave may sometimes be obtained. From Denwick Bridge to Ainmouth Bridge, about 5 *m.* of water, is in the hands of the River Aln Angling Association, except a small portion on the south side of Denwick Bridge, and that part running through the grounds at Lesbury House. Visitors staying within the Association radius are charged 2s. 6d. per day and 10s. per week; tickets may be obtained from the hon. sec., John de C. Paynter, Esq., Alnwick. The rivers Coquet, Breamish, Till, and Glen are within easy distance of Alnwick—a charming spot for an angling holiday. *Hotels :* Northumberland Arms and White Swan Hotel, Queen's Head, and Star. Good accommodation for Coquet anglers can be had at the Angler's Arms, Weldon Bridge, Morpeth, at the Sun Hotel, Warkworth, Railway Hotel, Rothbury, and the Stag's Head, Felton, about 4 *m.* from Acklington station. The upper reaches of the Aln abound with trout, but the water is strictly preserved *Tackleists* : Messrs. Hardy Brothers (*see Advt.*), who are glad to afford visitors all information ; Nettleship & Co. (*see Advt.*)

Alresford (Hants*)*.—L. & S.W.R. Itchen; trout; preserved. (*See Southampton.*) The fishing belongs to Lord Ashburton and Lady Rodney of the Grange; close to the town, Mr. Dunn, below to Mr. Marks, the Baroness Von Zant, and the Tichborne family. *Lakes* : Alresford pond ; pike perch; preserved by the Gresham Angling Society; pike fishing very good and an unmitigated curse to the Itchen, into which the pond drains.

Alrewas (Stafford).—L. & N.W.R. Trent; perch, bream, chub, dace, roach, pike. (*c.s.*) Alrewas brook. Swarbourne brook, 2 *m.* N.W. Tame, 2 *m.* S.E.; chub, dace. (*c.s. Trent.*) Mease, 3 *m.* S.E. (*c.s. Trent.*) Pessal brook, 4 *m.* S.E. (*See Gainsborough.*)

Alsager (Cheshire).—L. & N.W.R. Hassall brook. Lawton brook, 1 *m.* N.E. *Lakes*: Alsager pond. Lawton Hall, 2 *m.* E. Lawton mere, 2 *m.* N.E. Rode Hall, 2 *m.* N.E. (*See Frodsham.*) *Hotel:* Lawton Hall, where fishing can be had in Lawton mere.

Altcar (Lancs.). — W.L. & L.S & P.J.R. Alt; roach, pike, few trout. Downholland brook. Alt rises in the large lake in Knowsley Park, 2 *m.* N.W. of **Prescot**, and, running through a smaller pond in the Park, runs 4 *m.*, to 1 *m.* N.E. of **West Derby**. 4 *m.* down, 1 *m.* S. of **Kirkby**, Flukers brook, 3 *m.* long, joins on right bank, and at the same place and on the same side Simonswood brook joins Alt. This brook is 8 *m.* long, and runs close to **Kirkby**, 2 *m.* up from its junction with Alt. Alt runs 2 *m.* to **Aintree**, **Sefton** 3 *m.*, and 3 *m.* below is joined on right bank by Lydiate brook. Lydiate rises 6 *m.* above **Lydiate**, and joins Alt 3 *m.* below. Alt runs to **Altcar** 2 *m.*, and here Downholland brook joins on right bank. Downholland rises 2 *m.* above **Barton**, and joins Alt at **Altcar**, 6 *m.* below. Alt runs 2 *m.* to the sea at **Hightown**. Lord Sefton preserves parts; elsewhere leave must be obtained.

Althorpe (Lincoln).—G.C.R. Idle ; Idle is formed by the confluence, at Twyford Bridge by Elkesley, 4 *m.* N.W. from **Tuxford** or 4 *m.* S. from **Retford**, of Poulter, Meden, and Maun. Poulter rises in Whaley Mill, 2 *m.* N. from **Langwith**, and, 2 *m.* down, waters the lake at Langwith Lodge. 4 *m.* down Poulter the outflow of the lakes in Welbeck Park, ½ up and 3 *m.* S.E. from **Whitwell**, joins on left bank. 1 *m.* below, Poulter waters a large lake at Carburton Forge, 5 *m.* S. of **Worksop**, and 2 *m.* down it waters the large lake in Clumber Park, 3 *m.* S.W. from **Checker House** Station. Poulter runs to Twyford Bridge in 5 *m.* Meden rises above **Teversall**, and, 1 *m.* down, is joined on left bank by a brook draining the Oar Ponds by Ault Hucknall, 3 *m.* N.W. from **Teversall**. Meden runs 1 *m.* to Pleasley and 4 *m.* to Sookham Chapel, 1 *m* S.E. from **Shirebrook**. Here a brook joins on right bank, draining the lake at Park Hall, 2 *m.* N.E. from **Mansfield Woodhouse**. Meden runs 2 *m.* to Warsop, and, 5 *m.* down, waters the large lake at Thoresby Park, 3 *m.* N.W. of **Ollerton**. Meden runs to Bottomsall, 3 *m.*, and Twyford Bridge, 3 *m.* Maun rises in a lake by Bath Wood at **Sutton**, runs 1 *m.* to the King's Mill resevoir, 1 *m.* N.E. from **Sutton**, and thence to **Mansfield**, 2 *m.* Here Coldwell brook, 3 *m.* long, joins on right bank. Maun, in 2 *m.* runs 1 *m.* E. of **Mansfield Woodhouse**, and, 4 *m.* down, 3 *m.* E. from **Mansfield Woodhouse**, is joined on right bank by Vicay water, 4 *m.* long. Maun runs 3 *m.* to **Ollerton**, and here Rainworth brook joins on right bank. Rainworth rises in a pond 1 *m.* above Rainworth, 4 *m.* S.E. from **Mansfield**, and here, by the railway, it is joined on right bank by Foul Evil brook, 2 *m.* long, and which drains two ponds. Rainworth runs 3 *m.* to Inkersall dam, 3 *m.* N.W. of **Farnsfield** Station, and, 4 *m.* down, waters Rufford dam, 1 *m.* S. from **Ollerton**. Thence to Maun is 1 *m.* Maun runs 6 *m.* to Haughton, 3 *m.* N.W. of **Tuxford**, and here Bevercotes beck, 5 *m.* long, joins on right bank. Close to the junction on left bank are Haughton Decoy and the lower ponds. Maun runs to Twyford Bridge, 2 *m.* The united streams, taking the name of Idle, runs 5 *m.* to **Retford**, and, 2 *m.* down, is joined on left bank by a beck, 5 *m.* long, which waters Babworth Hall lake, 1 *m.* W. of **Retford**. Idle runs 7 *m.* to Mattersey, 2 *m.* E. of **Ranskill**, **Scrooby** 4 *m.*, and **Bawtry** 2 *m.* Here Ryton joins on left bank. Ryton rises above **Worksop**, where the outflow of the lake at Manor Park, 2 *m.* S.W., joins on right bank. Ryton runs 5 *m.* to **Chequer House**, and Blyth, 3 *m.* W. of **Ranskill**, 5 *m.* Here Oldcoates dyke joins on left bank. Oldcoates rises above Maltby, 8 *m.* E. of **Rotherham**, and 2 *m.* down, at Roche Abbey, receives the draining of Laughton pond, 6 *m.* N.E. of **Kiveton Park**. Oldcoates runs 7 *m.* to Blyth. Here Spont dyke joins Oldcoates on right bank. Spont rises in Moor Mill dam, 2 *m.* S.W. of **Shireoaks**, runs by that station, and, 3 *m.* down, waters the lake at Carlton, 3 *m.* N.W. of **Worksop**. 3 *m.* down Spont, the outflow, 2 *m.* long. of the lake at Langold. 5 *m.* N. of **Worksop**, joins Spont on left bank. Spont joins Oldcoates just below, and Oldcoates joins Ryton, 1 *m.* down, at Blyth. Ryton runs to **Scrooby** 7 *m.* and Idle and **Bawtry** 1 *m.*, receiving the outflow of the lake in Serlby Park, 2 *m.* N.W. of **Ranskill** midway. 4 *m.* below **Bawtry** Idle looses some of its waters in the Marther drain, 6 *m* long, connecting Idle with Trent at **Misterton**. 2 *m.* down Idle, at Idle step, the bulk of the river is diverted into an artificial cut, called New Idle drain. 5 *m.* down Idle, Torne river joins on left bank. Torne rises in the lakes in Sandbeck Park, 2 *m.* S. of **Tickhill**, runs in 3 *m.*, 1 *m.* E. of **Tickhill**, and 5 *m.* down, **Rossington**, being 1 *m.* off on right bank. St. Catharine's Well stream, or Warmsworth beck, joins on left bank. St. Catharine rises in the pond at Crookhill Hall, by Edlington, 1 *m.* S.W. of **Conisborough**, and is 7 *m.*

long. Torne runs to **Rossington** 2 m., 3 m. to Auckley (n.s. **Finningley**, 2 m.), and joins Idle 7 m. down. At this point Idle is divided into three streams. Idle north drain, an artificial cut, runs 4 m. to Durtness Bridge. **Crowle** station 2 m., and joins Trent 4 m. below, 1 m. below **Althorpe**. The new Idle river, another artificial cut, takes a similar course, joining the north drain at Newbridge. The original stream of the Idle, after a winding course, joins the North Idle drain at Durtness Bridge. (*c s. Trent.*)

Althorp Park (Northton).—L. & N.W.R. Althorp brook. *Lakes*: Althorp Park. (*See Wisbeach.*)

Alton (Hants).—L. & S.W.R. Wey; trout. (*See London, L.T.*) Hotel, Swan.

Alton (Stafford).—M.R.; L. & N.W.R., and G.N.R. Churnet; trout, grayling; fishing spoilt by Leek drainage. (*c.s. Trent.*) *Lakes*: Alton Park lakes, 1 m. N. (*See Gainsborough.*)

Altrincham (Cheshire).—G.N.R.; M.R., and L. & N.W.R. Close to the station is Nicolls Pool, preserved by a club at Manchester.

Alvechurch (Worcester).—M.R. Arrow. *Lakes*: Great Bittle Reservoir (1½ m. N.W.). (*See Gloucester.*)

Ambergate (Derby).—M.R. Derwent; grayling, trout, pike, coarse fish. (*c.s. Trent.*) Amber; same fish. *Lakes*: Alderwasley ponds, 2 m. N.W. Butterley reservoir, 4 m. E. *Hotel*: Hurt Arms, where fishing can be had. (*See Gainsborough.*)

Amberley (Sussex).—L.B. & S.C.R. Arun; pike, bream, roach, carp, &c. (*See Littlehampton.*) Fishing good.

Ambleside (Westland), n.s. **Windermere**, 6m.—Rothay; trout; preserved by a society, who issue tickets. Brathay; trout; preserved as Rothay. Scandal beck; trout; preserved as Rothay. Rydal beck. 2 m. N. *Lakes*: Windermere; pike, perch, char, trout. (*c.s. Kent.*) Rydal Water; pike, perch, few trout. Bielham tarn, 3m. S. *Hotels*: Salutation, Queen, White Lion, and Waterhead, facing Windermere Lake. (*See Ulverston.*)

Ampleforth (York).—N.E.R. Hole beck. *Lakes*: Gilling Park lake. Pack Horse lakes, 2 m. S.W. (*See York.*)

Ampthill (Beds).—M.R. and L. & N.W.R. Tod (3 m. S.) *Lakes*: Flitwick Park Lakes. (3 m. S.) Wrest Park Lakes (5 m. S.E.) (*See King's Lynn*). Tackleist, E. White, Market-place.

Andover (Hants).—L. & S.W.R. On the Anton; trout and grayling. (*See Southampton.*) *Hotels*: Star and Garter, White Hart. Junction. The river below the town for over a mile is preserved by the Anton Fishing Club of five members. Fishing begins April 1, and ends Oct. 1. Fly only. No dogs. Below the Anton Fishing Club's water comes Mr. E. Lywood's, then Mr. T. Footer's, the Vicar of Goodworth Clatford. Mr. J. Symonds, and Mr. Ironmonger. At Testcombe Bridge the Anton joins the Test. *Tackleist*, E. Chamberlain.

Angel Road (Middx.).—G.E.R. (*See Park.*) On Lea; dace, roach, chub, perch, jack, barbel, bream, carp. (*See Stratford.*) The next fishing station above is at **Ponder's End** and **Enfield** (G.E.R.).

Angmering (Sussex).—L.B. & S.C.R. On tributary of Arun and Patching pond. (*See Littlehampton.*)

Appleby (Lincoln).—G.C.R. Ancholme, 3 m. S.E. *Lakes*: Broughton Decoy, 3 m. S.E. (*See Brigg.*)

Appleby (Westland).—M.R.; N.E.R. Eden; salmon, trout; some free fishing. The King's Head has rights over some good water, and the Tufton Arms has some 9 m. of private water free to visitors. (*c.s.*) Hoff beck, 1 ½m. N.E. Hilton beck, 5 m. N.E. *Hotels*: King's Head, Tufton Arms. (*See Carlisle.*)

Appledore (N. Devon).—Very good bass fishing at times in summer, on flowing tide. Station, Instow. Although there is excellent sea fishing in Bideford Bay, outside Appledore Bar, the tides are so strong, and the bar often so dangerous, that it is much better to fish the bay from Clovelly. (*See Hartland.*)

Apply Bridge (Lancs.).—L. & Y.R. Douglas. (*c.s. Ribble.*) *Lakes*: Wrightington Hall lake, 1 m. N.E. (*See Hesketh Bank.*)

Argoed (Monmouth).—B.R. Sirhowey; polluted. (*See Newport.*)

Arkholme (Lancs.).—M.R. Lune. (*c.s.*) Greeta. (*c.s. Lune.*) Cant beck. Beckthwaite beck. (*See Lancaster.*)

Arlesey (Beds).—G.N.R. Ivel. Hir; trout. (*See King's Lynn*).

Arley (Warwick).—M.R. Arley brook. (*See Gainsborough.*)

Armathwaite (Cumland).—M.R. Eden; salmon, trout; preserved. (*c.s.*) Croglin water, 3 m. E. *Hotels*: Red Lion, Duke's Head. (*See Carlisle.*)

Armitage (Stafford).—L. & N.W.R. Trent; roach, chub, pike. trout. (*c.s.*) How brook, Bourne brook, 2 m. S.E. Ben brook, 2 m. S.E. Blythe, 3 m. N.E. (*c.s. Trent.*) Swarbourne brook. 5 m. N.E. at Yoxall. *Lakes*: Beandesert Park lake, 4 m. S.W. (*See Gainsborough.*)

Arram (York).—N.E.R. Hull. (*See Hull.*) (*c.s. York.*)

Arthington (York).—N.E.R. Wharfe; trout, grayling preserved by F. H. Fowkes, Esq., E. A. Brotherton, Esq., Leeds and District A.S.A. (*See Otley.*) (*c.s. York.*) Addle beck, 2½ m. S.W. *Lakes*: Bushes Farm pond, 2½ m. S.W. Alwoodly reservoir, 2 m. S.E. Blackhill dam, 3½ m. S.W. Addle dam, 4 m. S.W. (*See Rawcliffe, York.*)

Arundel (Sussex).—L.B. & S.C.R. Arun. (*See Littlehampton.*) For fishing go to Amberley or Pulborough.

Ascot (Berks).—L. & S.W.R. (*See London, L.T.*) In 3 m. are Bull brook, Harmans,

Englemore, Sunninghill Park, Sillwood Park, Virginia Water. Broomhill, Charters, Hall Grove, Bagshot Park, Swinley Lodge, ponds.

Ascott (Oxford).—G.W.R. On Evenlode. (*See London, U.T.*)

Asfordby (Leicester).—M.R. Wreak; roach, bream. (*c.s. Trent.*) *Lakes*: Welby pond, 2 m. N. Saxelby pond, 3 m. N. (*See Gainsborough.*)

Ashbourne (Derby).—L. & N.W.R.; N.S.R. Henmoor; trout, grayling. Bradbourne brook. Bentley brook. Dove, 1 m. W.; trout, grayling; preserved for 3½ m. by the Birdsgrove Fishing Club of 30 members ; entrance 4l. 4s.; s.t. 4l. 4s ; Proprietor, G. M. Bond. Esq., Alrewas House, Ashbourne. (*c.s. Trent.*) Manifold, 5 m. N.W. at Ilam. Longford brook, 4 m. S.E. Brailsford brook, 7 m. S. Hamps, 6 m. N.W. at Calton. *Lakes*: The dam and another pond at Bradley, 3 m. E. Yeldersley pond and Shirley Park lakes. Osmaston lakes (stocked with rainbow trout), 3 m. S.E. *Hotels*: for the Dovedale length (3½ m.; d.t. (hotel visitors only) 2s., w.t. 7s. 6d.), Izaak Walton, Peveril, and Dovedale. The waters between the Birdsgrove Club and the Izaak Walton lengths are strictly preserved by the Okeover Club of 5 members. (*See Gainsborough.*) *Tackleists,* Messrs. Foster.

Ashburton (Devon).—G.W.R. On Dart; trout and salmon. *Hotels* : Golden Lion and London. (*See Dartmouth*). Fishing for a small fee. Apply to landlords of hotels. Fishing extends from Dart Bridge *down* to Totnes, and from New Bridge *up* to Dartmeet. Fishing private between Holne Bridge and New Bridge. (*c.s.*)

Ashby-de-la-Zouch (Leicester).—M.R.; L. & N.W.R. Mease. (*c.s. Trent.*) *Lakes* : Willesley Park lake, 1 m. S.W. Asby Wolds reservoir, 4 m. W. Barrat pool, 4 m. S.W. Colcordon ponds. 3 m. E. (*See Gainsborough.*)

Ashford Bakewell (Derby), n.s. **Longstone,** 1 m.—M.R. Wye; trout, grayling ; preserved by the Duke of Devonshire. (*c.s. Trent.*) *Hotel* : Devonshire Arms. (*See Gainsborough.*)

Ashford (Kent).—S.E. & C.R. On Stour; pike, roach, &c. To fish the Stour above Ashford apply to the millowners. A short distance below Wye is a portion of the old river, cut off by the railway. Here are some jack, &c.; but it is much fished. In Eastwell Park (Lord Gerard) there is a large lake ; pike, tench, roach, perch. Leave may sometimes be obtained. Good fishing at Hothfield-place (Lord Hothfield), but permission is rarely given. (*See Sandwich.*) (*c.s.*) *Hotel*: Saracen's Head.

Ashford (Middx.).—L. & S.W.R. On branch of Colne. Thames (2 m.) (*See London, L.T.*)

Ashley (Cheshire).—C. Lines R. Bollin, 1 m. N. ; trout, roach, dace, pike. Ashley brook. 1 m. S. Mobberley brook, 1 m. S. *Lakes* : Rosthern mere. 2 m. W. (*See Runcorn.*)

Ashley (Northamp.).—L. & N.W.R. Medbourne brook. Welland. 1 m. S. (*See Spalding.*)

Ashopton (Derby). n.s. **Bamford,** 3 m.—M.R. Derwent; trout, grayling; preserved below Yorkshire bridge, where the Derwent Fly-fishing Club water (sec., H. Barber, Esq., The Firs, Dore, Sheffield) begins (*see Hathersage*). Ashopton Inn lets above for some distance, thence to its source preserved by the Duke of Norfolk. (*c.s. Trent.*) Ashop; trout. Ladybower brook. Mill brook, 2 m N. Now, 2 m. S. Alport. 5 m. N.W. Abbey brook, 5 m. N. Little Howden brook, 6 m N. Westend, 7 m. N.W. *Hotel* : Ashopton Inn, where accommodation and fishing can be had in Derwent : s.t. 21s., d.t. 2s. 6d. (*See Gainsborough.*)

Ashperton (Hereford).—G.W.R. Frome (2½ m.). Leddon (2½ m.). *Lakes* : Devereux Park lakes (4 m.) (*See Chepstow.*)

Ashton (Lancs.).—L. & N.W.R.; G.C.R.; L. & Y.R.; M.R. Tame. *Lakes* : Knoll Hill, 2 m. N.E. (*See Runcorn.*)

Ashwell (Herts).—G.N.R. Rhee. (*See King's Lynn.*)

Askrigg (York)—N.E.R. Ure ; trout, grayling; preserved by Wensleydale Angling Association for about 5 m. ; s.t. 10s., w.t. 5s.; d.t. 2s. 6d. (*c.s. York.*) Bain ; trout, rudd, bream ; preserved as Ure up to Lake Semmerwater, 3m. S. *Lake* : Semmerwater tarn, trout, rudd, bream : preserved by Mr. Riley, Raydale Grange, Askrigg. *Hotels* : Rose and Crown, Bambridge (tickets for Lake Semmerwater) ; King's Head, Askrigg. (*See York.*)

Aslocton (Notts).—G.N.R. Smite. Whipling river. Car dyke, 2 m. N.W. Devon, 4 m. E. at Bottlford. (*See Gainsborough.*)

Aston (Warwick).—L. & N.W.R. Tame (*c.s. Trent.*) Rea, 1 m. S.E. *Lakes*: Aston Park, Lower Witton pool, 1 m. N. Upper Witton pool, 2 m. N. (*See Gainsborough.*)

Athelney (Somerset).—G.W.R. Parret. Tone. (*See Bridgwater.*) (*c.s. Avon.*)

Atherstone (Warwick).—L. & N.W.R. Anker (*c.s. Trent.*) Sence, 1 m. N.E. Tweed. 2 m. N.E. *Lakes* : Abbey pond and Black pool, 1 m. W. The reservoir, 2 m. S. (*See Gainsborough.*)

Atherton (Lancs.).—L. & N.W.R. Croal. *Lakes* : Hulton Park lake, 4 m. N. (*See Runcorn.*)

Attenborough (Notts).—M.R. Trent; salmon, chub, roach, pike, perch, bream, barbel. (*c.s.*) Erewash, 1 m. W. (*See Gainsborough.*)

Attlebridge (Norfolk).—G.E.R. Wensum. (*c.s. N. and S.*) Costessey brook. 4 m. S. *Lakes* : Haveringland, 3½ m. N. Hopground lake, Horningham, 4 m. S. (*See Yarmouth.*) (*c.s. Norfolk.*)

Audlem (Cheshire).—G.W.R. Weaver. Adderley brook. Birchall brook, 2 m. N.E. *Lakes* : Woodfall pool, 2 m. N.E. (*See Frodsham.*)

Awre (Gloucester).—G.W.R. Bideford brook, which rises in Abbot's Wood, runs 4 m. to Blakeney (n.s. **Awre,** 1½ m.), where Blackpool brook joins on right bank. Blackpool rises 1 m. E. of **Speechhouse**, and is 6 m. long. Bideford brook runs 2 m. to **Awre**, and joins Severn estuary 1 m. down.

Axbridge (Somerset). — G.W.R. Ax; trout and coarse fish. Ax rises N. of **Wookey** (G.W.R.), 1¼ m. from **Wells** (G.W.R.), runs to **Lodge Hill** (G.W.R.) and Westbury 4 m. 1½ m. down, a stream joins on right bank, which drains the decoy lakes at Stoke (n.s. **Draycot**, 1¼ m.). 2 m. down, at Bartlett's Bridge, a road leads to a decoy on right bank 1 m. away. 3 m. down Ax, Chedder Water joins on right bank. Chedder rises by **Chedder**, and 2 m. down waters a decoy on left bank standing almost on the banks of Ax. 1 m. down Ax is Cradle Bridge, and **Axbridge** 1¼ m. off on right bank. Ax runs in 1¼ m. to Lower Weare Bridge, and 2 m. down is joined on right bank by Loxton Brook, which rises above Max Mill near **Winscombe**, and is 3 m. long. To 2 m. down Ax the tide flows. Bleadon is 3 m. down on right bank, Uphill (n.s. **Bleadon** and **Uphill**) 4 m., and the sea 2 m. (*See c.s. Avon.*)

Axminster (Devon). — L. & S.W.R. On Axe and Yarty; trout and salmon, mostly preserved. Above and below Axminster trouting is good, below especially in April and May; strictly preserved by C. Langdon, Esq. Below Axminster salmon fishing is fair; m.t., 15s.; s.t., 30s.; can be had for a portion of the water from Mr. G. Harris. The trout fishing in the Axe Fishery district commences on Feb. 2, and expires on Oct. 1, and rod and line salmon fishing begins on May 1 and ends on Nov. 19. The district is under a body of conservators, who have passed certain by-laws for the better preservation of the trout and salmon fisheries, which have been confirmed by the Board of Trade. Wm. Forward, Esq., of Axminster, is clerk. In addition to obtaining the permission of the riparian owners, conservators' licences for the season are absolutely necessary; rod and line; trout licence, 2s. 6d.; rod and line salmon licence (including trout), 10s. Good accommodation, both public and private, can be obtained in the town. The best flies are the blue and red uprights, blue and red Maxwell, red palmers, blue duns, iron blues, and March brown. (*See Seaton.*) (c.s.)

Ayoliffe (Durham).—N.E.R. Skerne; trout, pike, chub, roach; preserved by Darlington Anglers' Club of 50; entrance 10s.; s.t. 25s. Sec., Mr. A. Lascelles, Northgate, Darlington. Licenses of J. F. Smythe, Fishtackleist, Horsemarket, Darlington. (*c.s. Tees.*) Woodham beck, 2 m. N.W. (*See Stockton.*)

Aylesbury (Bucks).—Met. R.; L. & N.W.R. Thame; coarse fish. (*See London, M.T.*) There is some fair coarse fishing in the Aylesbury Branch Canal.

Aylesford (Kent).—S.E. & C.R. (*See Rochester.*) On Medway.

Aylsham (Norfolk).—G.E.R. and G.N.R. Bure; trout; coarse fish; preserved above, leave from the farmers below. Aldborough beck, 3 m. N.; private. Gunton beck, 3 m. E., at **Felmingham**. *Lakes*: Apple Tree Plantation ponds, 4 m. N.W. Aldborough Mill pond, 5 m. N. Blickling lake, 2 m. N.W. (*See Yarmouth.*)

Aynho (Oxford). — G.W.R. Cherwell; trout. Swere. *Lakes*: Astrop House. (*See London, M.T.*)

Aysgarth (York).—N.E.R. Ure; trout, grayling. Ure is partly preserved by Wensleydale Angling Association; s.t. 1s. Below Aysgarth Falls are a few salmon, roach, pike, and chub. Best trout stretch is from Aysgarth Stepping Stones to Old Mill. (*c.s. York.*) Bishopsdale beck, 1 m. S.E.; mostly reserved. Walden beck, 2 m. S.E. *Lakes*: Locker tarn, 2 m. N. (*See York.*) Fishing from boat in Lake Semmerwater, 4 m. distant, is good. The lake is in private hands, but leave may sometimes be obtained on application to Mr. Riley, Raydale Grange, Askrigg.

Ayton (York), n.s. **Scarborough**, 5 m.—N.E.R.; G.N.R.; L. & N.W.R.; S. & K.J.R.; L. &Y.R. Derwent; trout, grayling above, pike and coarse fish below. Leven; trout; private. (*c.s. Tees.*) The Derwent is preserved by the Derwent Anglers' Club of 40 members, at 50s. a year ; entrance fee, 63s.; also to strangers day tickets are issued at 5s. and 2s. 6d. Trouting begins on 15th April and ends September 30th ; grayling, June 16th and ends March 14th. No fish to be killed under 8in., or more than ten brace in one day. No wading or dogs allowed. There are many perch, grayling, and chub below Ayton. The upper part of the preserve is used for fly only, the lower for minnow and worm. (*c.s. York.*) (*See Forge Valley; Wressel; see Stockton.*)

Bacup (Lancs).—G.N.R.; L. & N.W.R.; M.R. Irwell. (*See Runcorn.*)

Baildon (Yorks).—M.R. Aire. (*c.s. York*). Gill beck, 1 m. N.E. (*See Rawcliffe.*)

Bailey Gate (Dorset).—S. & D.R. Stour; pike, perch; good fishing, preserved by Stour Fishery Association. *Hotel*: Churchill Arms, the landlord of which can sometimes obtain a day's fishing by giving three or four days' notice. (*See Christchurch.*) (*c.s. Avon.*)

Bakewell (Derby).—M.R. Wye; trout, grayling; preserved *above* Bakewell Bridge by the Duke of Devonshire, *below* to **Rowsley**; the landlord of the Rutland Arms has the privilege of 6 tickets per day, free to hotel visitors; no bottom fishing or wading. (*c.s. Trent.*) Derwent, 2 m. N.E. at **Edensor**. (*c.s. Trent.*) (*See Baslow; Gainsborough.*)

Baldersby (York).—N.E.R. Swale, 1 m. E. (*c.s. York.*) (*See Skipton Bridge, York.*)

Baldock (Herts).—G.N.R. Ivel. (*See Kings Lynn.*)

Balne (Yorks).—G.N.R. Went. Lake Drain, 1 m. W. (*See Goole.*)

Bampton (Oxon).—G.W.R. On Thames and Charney brook. (*See London, U.T.*)

Bampton (Devon).—G.W.R. Exe; trout and salmon; free to visitors staying at the hotel. Belbrook; preserved. Batherm; trout; free. *Hotel*: White Horse. (*See Tiverton and Exeter.*)

Banbury (Oxon).—G.W.R.; L. & N.W.R.; N. & B.J.R. Cherwell. *Lakes*: Wroxton Abbey, 3 m. (*See London, M.T.*)

Barbon (Westland.).—M.R. and L. & N.W.R. Lune, 1 m. W. (*c.s.*) Barbon beck. (*See Lancaster.*)

Barcoombe (Sussex).—L.B. & S.C.R. Ouse; trout, pike, perch; d.t. 1s. from J. S. Reed, Station Inn. (*See Newhaven.*) (*c.s.*)

Bardney (Lincoln).—G.N.R. Witham. Tile House beck, 1 m. N. Stainfield brook, 3 m. N. (*See Boston.*)

Bardsey (York).—N.E.R. Collingham beck. Wharfe, 3 m. N. (*c.s. York*) Harewood beck, 4 m. S.W. Eccup beck, 4 m. S. *Lakes*: Alwoodley reservoir, 4 m. S. Harewood Park lakes, 2 m. S.E. (*See York.*)

Barking (Essex).—G.E.R. On Roding. This stream rises 4 m. N.W. of **Dunmow**, and in 3 m. crosses the railway, 1½ m. west of **Takeley**, and runs 15 m. to **Chipping Ongar**. Cripsey brook, 18 m. long, here joins Roding on the right bank. The Roding next runs in 11 m. to **Chigwell Lane, Loughton** 1¼ m., **Buckhurst Hill** 1 m., **Woodford** 1½ m., **George Lane** Station 1¼ m., **Wanstead** 1½ m., **Ilford** 2 m., and Barking is 2 m. The Roding here runs into Barking Creek.

Barkston (Lincoln).—G.N.R. Witham. Honnington beck, 1 m. N. *Lakes*: Syston Park. (*See Boston.*)

Barlaston (Stafford).—L. & N.W.R. Trent, 1 m. W. (*c.s*) *Lakes*: Barlaston Park, 1 m. N. (*See Gainsborough.*)

Barnard Castle (Durham).—N.E.R. Trout, salmon, bull trout, ; tickets (limited) per Earl of Strathmore's agent, W. H. Ralston. Esq., J.P., Streatlam Castle, Darlington. (*c.s.*) Harmire beck. Deepdale beck; trout; private. Scur beck, 1 m. N.W. Thorgill beck, 1 m. S. Tutta beck, 2 m. S. Greta, 3 m. S.E.; trout; private; (*c.s. Tees.*) Whorlton beck, 3 m. E. Sudburn beck, 4 m. N. Langley beck, 5 m. N. Clow beck, 8 m. S.E. *Tackleist*, Mr. Richardson, Teesdale Sporting Depot. *Hotel:* Morrit's Arms. (*See Stockton.*)

Barnby (Yorks).—G.C.R. ; N.E.R. Don. (*c.s. Yorkshire.*) (*See Goole.*)

Barnes (Middx.).—L. & S.W.R. Thames, and lakes in Richmond and Wimbledon Parks, 3 m. (*See London, L.T.*)

Barnetby Junction (Lincs.).—G.C.R. In the large ponds near here is some good perching. The sides are very shallow, so it is necessary to throw out a long line.

Barnoldswick Junction (Yorks).—M.R. Elslack. Stock beck. (*See Rawcliffe* and *Preston.*)

Barnsley (Yorks).—M.R.; G.C.R.; L. & Y.R.; H. & B.W.J.R. Dearne. (*See Goole.*)

Barnstaple (Devon).—G.W.R. and L. & S.W.R. Taw ; salmon, trout, peal, perch, and dace. (*c.s.*) Taw rises close by Okement, on the slopes of Okement Hill (n.s. **Okehampton**, 6 m.), runs 7 m. to South Tawton (n.s. **Okehampton**, 3 m.). 2 m. down, Teal water, 3 m. long, joins on right bank. Taw runs 4 m. to **North Tawton** (tickets, Gostwick Arms Hotel), and 8 m. down (n.s. **Lapford**, 3 m. off) is joined on right bank by Lapford water. Yeo rises S. of **Bow** (L. & S.W.R.), runs 2 m. to Zeal Monachorum, and 3 m. down is joined on right bank by Braddiford brook, which rises E. of **Morchard Road**, and is 3 m. long. 1 m. down, at **Lapford** Washford brook, 10 m. long, joins Lapford on right bank. Lapford runs 3 m. to Taw. Taw runs to **Eggesford** 3 m. (tickets, Fox and Hounds Hotel), and 2 m. down, near Chulmleigh, is joined by Hollowcombe water, 5 m. long, on left bank, and Little Dart on right bank. Little Dart rises 5 m. S. of **East Anstey** on Rackenford Moor, runs 2 m. to Rackenford, and 3 m. down is joined on right bank by Sturcomb river, which rises 4 m. S. of **East Anstey**, near the Little Dart, and is 5 m. long. Little Dart runs 1 m. to Witheridge, Chulmleigh 9 m. (n.s. **Eggesford**, 2 m.), and Taw 2 m. 2 m. down Taw. Little Tiddywater, 4 m. long, joins on left bank. 2 m. down Taw, at **South Molton Road Station** (tickets), Yeo river joins on right bank. Yeo rises by **East Anstey**, and 6 m. down, at **Molland** (s.t. 1s.) is joined on right bank by Molland water, 3 m. long. 5 m. down Yeo, Mole joins on right bank. Mole rises 3 m. N. of North Molton, and 3 m. below that place, at the **South Molton Station** is joined on right bank by Flitton water, 4 m. long. Mole runs to **South Molton** 1 m., and Yeo 1 m. 2 m. down Yeo is Knowstone water. which rises 4 m. S.W. of **East Anstey**. runs 7 m. to Bishops Nympton (n.s. **Molland**, 3 m.), and 3 m. down joins Yeo. ½ m. down Yeo, Littlecot brook, 7 m. long, joins on left bank. 4 m. down Bray river joins on right bank. Bray rises at Challacombe close to Exmoor, runs 6 m., and is joined on left bank by a stream 4 m. long. 2 m. down Bray, a stream 3 m. long joins on right bank. 1 m. down Bray is **Castlehill**. 5 m. down Bray, Nadder water, which rises by **South Molton** and is 4 m. long, joins on left bank. Yeo is 1 m. on, and runs to Taw in 5 m. Taw (private to Barnstaple) runs to **Portsmouth Arms** 3 m., **Umberleigh** 6 m. 2 m. on, Chittlehampton brook, which rises by Chittlehampton and is 4 m. long, joins on right bank. 1 m. down Taw is **Chapelton**, and here Yarnscombe brook joins on left bank. Yarnscombe rises by High Bickington (n.s. **Portsmouth Arms**, 4 m.), and is 6 m. long. Taw runs 3 m. to Tawton, where Swimbridge water joins on right bank. Swimbridge rises by **Swimbridge** , and is 6 m. long. Taw runs 2 m. to **Barnstaple**. Yeo flows through the lake at Arlington, which is the property of Lady B. Chichester, who gives a few permits, and, running down the valley, is fed by many small brooks, and enters at Sherwill, the property of Sir E. Chichester, Bart. Running on in line with the Lynton Railway, Yeo enters the properties of some gentlemen, who sell tickets, and is fishable up to the tidal water of the Taw. At Bittadon a river runs close to the old Ilfracombe coach road, and, passing the Half-way House, runs down the valley 4 m., where, at Muddeford, it is joined by a stream rising at Viviam, about 1 m.; it then runs 3 m., and joins the Taw 1 m. below Barnstaple. At Tawton. close to Barnstaple, is a little river which rises beyond Swimbridge, and runs to Swimbridge; 2 m. below it is Landkey, and 3 m. further on it reaches Bishops Taw-ton, where it joins the Taw. On the Ilfracombe railway, Morthoe S. Railway, is a rapid running stream, and which 3 m. below is joined by two little rivers, one from West Down and Spreacombe. Running on to the railway, it passes Braunton, where Mr. Richmond has a fishery 1 m. below. The estuary is now reached. Good fishing for bass and grey mullet. Trout fishing in most of the rivers commences on March 1, salmon and peal April 1, but they are not taken in quantities until August and September, when the nets are off. and finish Oct. 31. Licences (which include the Lynn rivers) are required on the Taw and Torridge boundaries. trout, s.t. 5s., w.t. 1s.; salmon, 24s. The Lynn rivers at Lynmouth are open earlier than in years past, and permission is not granted. Tickets by the day, week, and year are issued on the rivers. The Badgery water on the Exmoor is a tributary of the Lynn, and extra tickets are issued; the season opens late, and closes the end of October. The stream called Heddon, which rises up the valley towards Exmoor, runs to Parracombe down the valley, and empties itself between two high rocks into the sea. An association now preserves the lower waters of the Taw for 5 m.; s.t. 3l. 3s. *Hotels*: Imperial, King's Arms (which has some fishing for visitors), Fortescue. *Tackleist*, J. Rowe, 62, High-street.

Barnston (Notts).—L. & N.W.R.; G.N.R. Whipling river. Smite 1 m. W. (*See Gains-borough.*)

Barrow-on-Soar (Leicester).—M.R. Soar; chub, dace, roach, pike, perch, bream, carp. tench. (*c.s. Trent.*) Quorndon brook; trout; strictly preserved by the owners of Bradgate Park. Walton brook, 2 m. N. (*See Gainsborough.*)

Barras (Westland.)—N.E.R. Angell Beck; trout.

Barton (Lancs.)—L. & N.W.R. Barton brook. Blundel brook, 1 m. S. (*See Fleetwood.*) Downholland brook. (*See Altcar.*)

Barton Hill (York).—N.E.R. Spittle beck. Derwent, 2 m. E. Whitecarr beck, 4 m. S.E. Loppington beck, 4 m. S.E. Swallowpits beck, 5 m. S.E. at Serayingham. (*See Wressel.*)

Baschurch (Salop).—G.W.R. Perry (1 m. W.). Severn (5 m. S.); chub, dace, pike, trout, salmon. *Lakes*: Birch Grove pool (1½ m. N.E.). Berth pool (2 m. N.E.). Fennymere pool (2 m. N.E.). Marston pool (3 m. N.E.) Leave sometimes given. (*See Gloucester.*) (*c.s. Severn.*)

Basford (Notts).—M.R.; G.N.R. Leen. Day brook. Wistaston brook. Swill brook, 1 m. W. Ingleway brook, 2 m. E. *Lakes*: Balterley mere. 1½ m. E. Doddington Park, 2 m. S.W. Betley Hall, 3 m. S.E. Nuthall lake, 3 m. N.W. Monneley mere, 3 m. N.E. (*See Frodsham; Gainsborough.*)

Basingstoke (Hants).—L. & S.W.R. Newram springs, a series of ponds, the source of Lodden, are near here. Pike. trout. Strictly preserved.

Baslow (Derby), n.s. **Bakewell**, 3 m.—M.R. Derwent; trout, grayling; preserved by the Chatsworth Fishery from Calver weir to Rowsley bridge. Trout fishing begins April 1, and ends Sept. 30; grayling fishing begins June 15, and ends March 15. Anglers are expected to patronise one of the following hotels, where day tickets, 3s. (fly only), may be obtained: **Baslow**—Peacock, Wheatsheaf, Rutland Arms, and the Hydropathic; and **Edensor**—Chatsworth Hotel. (*c.s. Trent.*) Wye at Bakewell. 3 m. S.W. (*c.s. Trent.*) (*See Gainsborough.*)

Bassalleg (Monmouth).—P.C. & N.R.; L. & N.W.R.; G.W.R.; B. & M.R. Ebbw, polluted. (*c.s. Usk.*) (*See Newport.*)

Bassenthwaite (Cumland).—L. & N.W.R. Derwent, 1 m. N.; trout, salmon. (*c.s.*) *Lakes*: Bassenthwaite. (*c.s. Derwent.*) Boats, 8; pike, perch. trout, salmon. *Inn*: Pheasant. (*See Cockermouth, Keswick.*)

Bath (Somerset).—G.W.R. On Avon; roach, pike, perch, chub, very large gudgeon; fishing free. Some fine trout may be taken at Shawford, between Bath and Frome, and also in a brook which joins the river here; the fishing is, we believe, free. Fair trouting in Woolley brook. Leave can be had sometimes from Mr. Shackell, Manor Farm, Swainswick, and from the millers. *Lake*: Batheaston reservoir; trout; leave from the Bath Corpora-tion. (*See Bristol.*) (*c.s.*) *Hotels*: Royal, York House, Empire.

Bathampton (Somerset).—G.W.R. (*See Bristol.*) Avon; good all-round fishing; preserved by Col. Skrine. Bathford brook; fishing completely destroyed by paper mills. St. Catharine's brook; trout; strictly preserved.

Battersby (Yorks).—N.E.R. Leven; trout; private. *c.s. Tees.* Otters Hill beck. (*See Stockton.*)

Battle (Sussex).—S.E. & C.R. On Brede and *lakes* at Beech Mill, Battle Abbey, Catsfield Green, Peppering Powder Mills. (*See Rye; St. Leonards.*) At Mountfield, 4 m. off, is a large lake belonging to Rev. W. Margesson. (*c.s. Rother.*)

Bawtry (York).—G.N.R. Idle; preserved by the River Idle Fly Fishing Club. (*See Retford.*) (*c.s. Trent.*) Ryton. (*See Althorpe.*)

Baxenden (Lancs.)—L. & Y.R. Swinnell brook. (*See Runcorn.*)

Bay Horses (Lancs.)—L. & N.W.R. Wyre, 2 m. E. Cocker. (*c.s. Lune.*) Damas stream, 2 m. N.E. Catshaw brook. 5 m. E. Marshaw Wyre, 7 m. E. Grisedale brook, 7 m. N.E. (*See Fleetwood* and *Cockerham.*)

Bealings (Suffolk).—G.E.R. Fyn. Otley brook; trout; preserved. (*c.s. Suffolk and Essex.*) (*See Woodbridge.*)

Bearley Cross (Warwick).—G.W.R. (*See Henley in Arden, Gloucester.*) Edstone brook. *Lakes:* Large lake at Wootten Warwen (2½ m. N.).

Beauchief (Derby).—G.C.R. Chief. Penny brook, 1 m. S. (*See Goole.*)

Beaufort (Monmouth).—L. & N.W.R. Ebbw; polluted. (*c.s. Usk.*) (*See Newport.*)

Beaulieu (Hants.).—S. & D.R. On Beaulieu. This stream rises in a pond 1 m. N. of old Beaulieu-road Station, now abandoned. In 4½ m. it is joined on right bank by a stream draining a pond 2 m. up. and which is 1½ m. S. of Beaulieu-road Station. These streams hold small trout. Beaulieu runs in 2 m. to Beaulieu; 5 m. down, a stream 4 m. long joins on right bank, which drains Hatchet Mill pond, 1½ m. from Beaulieu. The river joins the sea 3 m. on.

Beccles (Suffolk).—G.E.R. Waveney. (*See Yarmouth.*) (*c.s. Norfolk.*) R. Tilney.

Beckermet (Cumland).—L. & N.W.R. and Fs. R. Ehen. (*c.s. West Cumberland.*) Kirk beck; Black beck. Calder, 2 m. S.W. (*c.s. West Cumberland.*) (At Calderbridge, *Hotel:* Stanley Arms.) (*See Egremont.*)

Beckfoot (Cumland).—R. & E.R. Esk; trout. (*c.s. West Cumberland.*) *Lakes:* Blea tarn, 1 m. N.W. *Hotel:* Beckfoot Temperance. (*See Ravenglass.*)

Bedale (York).—N.E.R. Bedale beck. (*See York.*)

Bedford.—M.R. and L. & N.W.R. Ouse; coarse fish; preserved by Bedford Angling Club (hon. sec., A. R. Thompson, Esq., 163, Tavistock-street) from Kempston 2 m. *above,* to Willington 5 m. *below,* except some free water about the town; a.t. 5s., except for jack and perch; full a.t. 21s.; residents outside the county, minimum ticket 21s. (*c.s. N. and S.*) *Hotels:* Embankment Hole, Swan, George, Lion. (*See King's Lynn.*)

Bedwas (Monmouth).—B. & M.R. Rumney; trout, salmon; preserved. (*c.s.*) Ceffyl-Glydyr. (*See Cardiff, Wales.*)

Bedworth (Leicester).—L. & N.W.R. Sow. (*See Gloucester.*)

Bedworth (Warwick).—L. & N.W.R. Griff brook. (*See Gainsborough.*)

Beer (Devon) (n.s. **Seaton**, 2 m.).—2½ m. W. from here runs Branscombe brook, 3 m. long, joining the sea near the village.

Beeston (Cheshire).—L. & N.W.R. Wettenhall brook, 1 m. N.E. Oulton brook, 4 m. N.E. *Lakes:* Tilston Hall. 1 m. N.E. Oulton Mill and Oulton Hall lake. 4 m. N.E. (*See Frodsham.*)

Beeston (Notts).—M.R. Trent; salmon, chub. roach, pike, perch, bream, barbel; preserved; s.t. 10s. (*c.s.*) Tottle brook. Leen, 2 m. N.E. (*See Gainsborough.*)

Bekesbourne (Kent).—S.E. & C.R. On Little Stour; roach, trout; preserved by a club. (*See Sandwich.*) (*c.s. Stour.*)

Bellbusk (York).—M.R. Aire; trout, grayling; preserved up to Airton Bridge by the Yorkshire Anglers' Club, elsewhere by private owners. (*c.s. York.*) Otterburn beck. Ingle beck, 3 m. N.W. Kirkgill beck, 4 m. N. Gardale beck, 5 m. N. *Lakes:* Coniston House lake. Eshton Farm pond, 2 m. N.E. Malham tarn, 8 m. N.; trout; preserved by W. Morrison, Esq. (*See Rawcliffe.*)

Bellingham (Northland.).—N.B.R. North Tyne; trout, salmon. *Hotel:* Railway, where fishing can be had.

Belper (Derby).—M.R. Derwent; grayling, pike, trout, coarse fish. (*c.s. Trent.*) Black brook. Holbrook brook, 2 m. S.E. Ecclesbourn. 3 m. W (*See Gainsborough.*)

Belton (Suffolk).—G.E.R. Waveney, 1 m. Yare. 2 m. *Lakes:* Breydon Water. Fritton Decoy, 2 m. S.; leave required; boats at Fritton Hall. (*See Yarmouth.*) (*c.s. Norfolk.*)

Ben Rhydding (York).—M.R. Wharfe. (*c.s. York.*) (*See Ilkley, York.*)

Bentham (Yorks.)—M.R. Wenning. (*c.s. Lune.*) Tatham beck, 4 m. S. (*See Lancaster.*)

Bentley (Suffolk).—G.E.R. Holbrook brook. Capel brook, 2 m. S. Holbrook rises 4 m. above **Bentley,** where it waters the lakes in Tattingstone Place, running thence 4 m. to Stour estuary; trout; preserved. (*c.s. Suffolk and Essex*)

Berkeley (Gloucester).—M.R. Little Avon; coarse fish, trout. Waterley brook. Little Avon rises S.E. of **Wickwar,** runs 3 m. to that town, and 3 m. to **Charfield.** Here Ozleworth brook joins on right bank. Ozleworth (trout; preserved for most part by Mr. Rolt, of Ozleworth Park), rises in a lake by Boxwell, and 4 m. down, at Alderley, is joined by Alderley brook on left bank. 1 m. down, the outflow of 3 lakes by Wotton-under-Edge (n.s. **Charfield,** 2 m.) joins on right bank. 3 m. down, Ozleworth joins Little Avon. 3 m. down Avon, Tortworth brook joins on left bank. Tortworth rises 2½ m. W. of **Wickwar** by Cromhall, and 2 m. down waters the lake in Tortworth Park (pike, perch, carp, tench, bream; leave from Earl Ducie in the absence of the family); thence to the Avon is 3 m. Avon runs 4 m. to **Berkeley,** where Waterley brook joins on right bank. Waterley rises 2 m. S.E. of **Dursley,** and is 9 m. long. 2 m. below **Berkeley** is the Severn estuary. The fishing below Charfield is preserved by Lords Ducie and Fitzhardinge. (*c.s. Severn.*) Close by the station rises Billow brook. which runs thence 3 m. to the estuary.

Berkhampstead (Herts).—L. & N.W.R. (*See London. M.T.*) In the Grand Junction Canal are a few trout, and plenty of perch, dace, roach, jack, and tench.

Berney Arms (Norfolk).—G.E.R. Yare. *(See Yarmouth.)*

Berrington (Salop).—G.W.R. Severn (1 *m.* Faveney, 1 *m* S.E. *(See Yarmouth.)* Cound's brook (1¼ *m.* S.W.); trout; private. Tern (2½ *s*); chub, dace, pike, trout, salmon. Cound's (3 *m.* S.). Acton brook (3 *m.* S.). *(See Gloucester N.).* Bell brook (3 *m.* N.E.). Row brook

Berwick (Sussex).—L.B. & S.C.R. On Cuckmark *(c.s. Severn.)* &c. This stream rises in a series of ponds in Heathfield Park and neighbourhood. Carp, &c. This stream rises in at Nettlesworth, close to Warbleton village, where it is R. and in 1 *m.* runs into a large lake some ponds in Backington Wood, close to Heathfield; 2½ *m.* by a small brook, which drains on left bank, which drains some mill ponds 1 *m.* to the east of Warbleton. 4 *m.* on, at Hellingly, a stream joins on right bank, which rises 1 *m.* east of Waldron in a series of ponds, and in 3 *m.* is joined by a small brook on left bank, which drains a pond 1 *m.* up at Horeham. 1½ *m.* down, a stream joins on right bank, which rises in a large pond on Hawkhurst Common, 1¼ *m.* W. of Waldron, and is 3 *m.* long; 4 *m.* brings this brook to Cuckmare. Cuckmare now runs in 7 *m.* to Berwick, and in 8 *m.* to the sea, passing Aldfriston, Litlington, and West Dean.

Berwick-on-Tweed.—N.B.R. Whitadder joins Tweed 1½ *m.* from here. Trout, sea and brown. *Hotel :* Red Lion, King's Arms; very comfortable. The Whitadder from Edington Mill, 1½ *m.* from the Tweed, up to **Chirnside Bridge** railway station, or Allanton Bridge (called indifferently), is good. The lower waters of the Whitadder may be fished from the following stations : Hutton, 7 *m.* from Berwick, small inn and lodgings in the village ; Allanton, 2 *m.* further on ; Chirnside, opposite side of the bridge. The upper waters, from Abbey St. Batham's, 4 *m.* from **Grant's House** Station, and 7 *m.* from Preston Bridge, and the Cottage, 6 *m.* from Dunse. There are several burns containing trout. Very little of the water is preserved, and none of the lower water. Till enters Tweed 2½ *m.* above **Norham** (B. & K.R.), 9 *m.* from Berwick. *Hotel :* Victoria. Trout fishing on Tweed is free, and a day or two's salmon fishing can sometimes be had from the lessees of the fisheries, on payment. The Collingwood Arms, **Cornhill** (B. & K.R.), 5¼ *m.* farther up the line, is very comfortable. There is a good inn at Yetholm, on Bowmont. The fishing for the first 6 *m.* above Tilmouth is very good. There are several good salmon casts. The lower portion of the water belongs to F. Blake, Esq., Tilmouth House, and the Earl of Tankerville has a portion at Heaton ; Mr. Tait, of Shellacres, ½ *m.* on the opposite side, and the Earl of Erroll, 4 *m.* of the upper part. The whole is strictly preserved, but a day's fishing may sometimes be obtained. Just below the village of Etal is The Pool, good for salmon and whiting. Mr. Laing preserves the water at Etal. There is very good pike fishing in the lower part of Till at Ford. The best flies are—sea trout, wing, grey mallard; hackle and body, black; red shoulders and orange tip. Again, dun turkey wing, red and black body, orange tip; in a black water, white wing, black or blue body, and orange tag. Trout flies must be large in spring, woodcock wing; red hackle; large March brown; black wing and hackle; black gnat; hare's ear; a red spinner with partridge wing (good in the end of April). In May, Hoffland's fancy; black and red hackle; landrail and black gnat. In autumn use yellow Sally; coachman; alder fly; landrail.

Bescott Junction (Stafford).—L. & N.W.R. Tame. *(c.s. Trent.)* Sneyd brook. Ford brook. *Lakes :* Pond by railway. *(See Gainsborough.)*

Betchworth (Surrey).—S.E.R. Mole. and *lakes* at Tranquil Dale and Fanchford Place. *(See London, L.T.)*

Bettisfield (Salop).—L. & N.W.R. *Lakes :* Bettisfield Park, 1½ *m.* N. Llyn Bedydd, 2 *m.* N.E. Hanmer mere. 2½ *m.* N. Hanmer Hall lake, 3 *m.* N. *(See Chester.)*

Beverley (York).—N.E.R. Hull. *(See Hull.)* *(c.s. York.)*

Bewcastle (Cumland.).—On the Lyne. Sea trout, whiting, &c.

Bewdley (Worcester).—T.V.R. Severn ; salmon, trout, grayling, chub, dace, pike, &c.; fishing free. Dowles brook (1 *m.* N.); trout. *(See Gloucester.)* *(c.s.)*

Bexley (Kent).—S.E. & C.R. *(See Dartford.)* Cray ; trout; private. Darenth (3 *m.*) ; trout. *Lakes :* Dartford Powder Mills, 3 *m.* Lamb Abbey, 1½ *m.* Preserved by the landowners.

Bibury (Gloucester).—*Stations :* **Foss Cross**, 4 *m.* and **Fairford**, 6 *m.*—Colne ; trout; preserved for 2 *m.* by the Swan Hotel ; d.t. 2s. 6d. ; rods limited. *(See London, U.T.)*

Bicester (Oxford).—L. & N.W.R. Ray. *Lake*, Middleton Park, 3 *m.* *(See London, M.T.)*

Bickleigh (Devon).—G.W.R. Exe ; trout, salmon, dace, &c. ; preserved *above* by the Tiverton Angling Assoc., *below* for 1¼ *m.* privately; thence to **Thorverton**, by the Up. Exe Fish. Assoc. (Sec., J. R. Cummings, Esq., Thorverton); salmon and trout s.t. 63s.; trout (fly only), March 1 to Aug. 31; s.t. 31s. 6d., from May 2, 21s., m.t. 15s., w.t. 7s. 6d. *(c.s.)* *(See Thorverton, Tiverton.)* Dart; trout. *Hotel :* Bickleigh Bridge. *(See Exeter.)*

Bideford (Devon)—L. & S.W.R. Torridge; trout, salmon. *(c.s. Taw.)* Torridge rises on the Ditchin Hills 3 *m.* from Hartland (n.s. **Bideford**, 13 *m.*), runs 3 *m.*, and is joined on right bank by Sockington water, 3 *m.* long. 6 *m.* down Torridge, Floodmead water. which rises by Woodfardisworthy and is 4 *m.* long, joins on left bank. Torridge runs to Putford 2 *m.*, Bulkworthy 2 *m.*. Newton Petrock 3 *m.* 3 *m.* down, at Bradford, Waldon river joins on right bank. Waldon rises by Bradworthy, runs 4 *m.* to Sutcombe, Milton Damerel 2 *m.*, and Torridge 5 *m.* Torridge runs 2 *m.*, and is joined on right bank by Whiteleigh brook, 4 *m.* long. Torridge runs 4 *m.* to Sheepwash, where Buckland brook, 3 *m.* long, joins on left bank. Torridge runs 7 *m.*, and is joined on the right bank by Lew river. Lew rises by Beaworthy, runs 2 *m.*, and is joined on right bank by a stream 2 *m.* long. 2 *m.* down

Bay Horses (Lancs.)—L. & Y.R. Wyorook, 4 m. long, joins on right bank, and Waggaford water 5 m. long. joins in N.E. Chirham brook 3 m. E. May 3 m. down Lew, Marshford brook joins on right bank. Marshford rises 3 m.
(See Fleetwood and Cockerham.) ....ampton (D. & C.R.), runs 2 m. to Inwardleigh, and Lew 3 m. Lew runs
Beatings (Suffolk)—G.E.R. Fyn. Okerleigh (n.s. **Okehampton**, 9 m.), and 1 m. down is joined on left bank by
Essex.) (See Woodbridge.) ....ok, 4 m. long. 1 m. down, Lew joins Torridge, Hatherleigh being 2 m. distant,
Beazley Cross (Warwick)—G.W. Torridge, Okement river joins on right bank. Okement rises close to the Dart,
Lakes: Large lake at Western ...tre of Dartmoor (n.s. **Bridestow**, D. & C.R., 4 m.), runs 9 m. to **Okehampton**
Bosschael (Derby)—G.C.R. ..ast Okement joins on right bank. East Okement rises close to the parent stream,
Bosschurt (Monmouth)—..? m., and is joined by a branch on left bank 4 m. long. 5 m. down is **Okehampton**
Boxaltion (Hants)—....ment runs 6 m. to Exbourne on right bank, and Jacobstow on left bank, and 4 m. down
Beaulion-road Station ...onks Okehampton (n.s. **Tawton**, D. & C.R., 6 m.), Hatherleigh being 3 m. off on left
draining a pool 1½ K., Exbourne water joins on right bank. Exbourne rises near **Sampford Courtney**
hold small trout. ....ation (N.D.R.), runs 3 m. to Exbourne, and 1 m. down is joined on right bank by a
on right bank, ...ook which runs through **Sampford Courtney** and is 4 m. long. Exbourne runs in
etc. a m. ..m. to Okement. 3 m. down, Okement joins Torridge. 5 m. down Torridge, at Merton
Beccles (Suffolk) ....½ m. off the river), Merton brook joins on left bank. Merton rises on Merton Moors, runs
Bechraad (Derby) ...j m., and is joined by a branch 2 m. long, which rises in Berry Moor. Merton is 1 m. down,
Kirk bank; and Torridge 2 m. 7 m. down Torridge, Woolley water joins on right bank. Woolley rises
Bield; Stir by St. Giles's, runs 2 m., and is joined on left bank by a brook 4 m. long, rising by
Beckfoot Roborough. 2 m. down is Torridge. **Torrington** (N.D.R.) is 3 m. on. Here Langtree
townJ brook, 4 m. long, and which rises by Langtree, joins on left bank. Torridge runs 3 m. to
Bedale Wear Giffard, where Hunshaw water, 4 m. long, joins on right bank. 4 m. down, Laidland
Bedf water joins on left bank. Laidland rises 6 m. W. of **Torrington**, runs 6 m., and is
Stow joined on left bank by Alwingtou brook, 5 m. long. Laidland runs 3 m. to Torridge, which
F runs to **Bideford** 2 m. Here two streams join Torridge—one on left bank, 3 m. long,
s and one on right bank, Wear water, 5 m. long. Torridge is mostly private,; Hon. Mark
Rolle and Lord Clinton grant permission, but tickets must be applied for before the end of
April. Bass may be caught in the tidal part of the river and in the estuary by a large
red palmer and brit, affording good sport. *Hotel:* Royal. *(See Hartland.)*

Biggleswade (Beds).—G.N.R. Ivel: coarse fish except barbel; a good centre for fishing.
Sutton brook (2 m.). *(See King's Lynn.)*

Bigsweir (Monmouth). — G.W.R. Wye; chub, dace, pike, perch, salmon. Olway
(2 m.); trout; preserved. *(See Chepstow, Newport.)* *(c.s.)*

Billing (Northton.).—L. & N.W.R. Nen; pike, perch, bream, tench, &c.; preserved by
Nen Angling Society. *(See Northampton; Wisbeach.)*

Billinghurst (Sussex).—L.B. & S.C.R. Arun and Adur. *(See Littlehampton; New
Shoreham.)*

Binegar (Somerset).—S. & D.R. *(See Bristol.)* *Lakes:* Lechmere water; pike, carp,
perch, roach; preserved.

Bingham (Notts).—G.N.R. Car dyke. Smite, 3 m. E. Trent, 3 m. N.W.; chub, roach,
pike, perch, barbel. *(c.s.)* Whipling river, 4 m. E. *(See Gainsborough.)*

Bingley (York).—M.R. Aire; trout, grayling, pike, perch, chub, roach; the river
is preserved *(c.s. York.)* *(See Rawcliffe.)*

Birdingbury (Warwick).—L. & N.W.R. Leam. Itchene (2 m. W.) *(See Gloucester.)*

Birdwell (Yorks).—G.C.R. *Lakes:* Rockley dam, 1 m. N.W. *(See Goole.)*

Birmingham (Warwick).—L. & N.W.R.; M.R.; G.W.R. Rea. *Lakes:* Cannon Hill lake.
Edgbaston reservoir. Thimble Mill pond. Smethwick reservoir. Rotten Park reservoir.
(See Gainsborough.)

Bishop Auckland (Durham).—N.E.R. Wear; salmon, trout. Bedburn also within easy
distance, but the greater part is preserved; leave however may sometimes be procured.
The principal part of the Wear in the neighbourhood is preserved by an Association,
s.t. 5s. *Tackleist*, W. J. Cummins. *(See Advt.)*

Bishops Castle (Salop). — B.C.R. Onny (5 m. N.); trout, chub; preserved by the
Plowden Fishing Club of nineteen members from **Eaton** *above* to **Horderly** *below*
Camlad (3 m. N.W.); trout, grayling. *(See Plowden, Gloucester.)* *(c.s. Severn.)*

Bishops Lydeard (Somerset).—G.W.R. *(See Bridgwater.)* Norton brook; trout.

Bishops Stortford (Herts).—G.E.R. *(See Stratford.)* On Stort; pike; preserved from a
short distance below Stanstead to Stortford by Sir J. Blyth. *Hotel:* Railway.

Bishopstoke (Hants).—L. & S.W.R. Itchen; trout, grayling; Mr. Tankerville Chamberlayne, M.P., of Cranbury Park, preserves 3½ m. of the river; trout fishing from April 10 to
Sept. 10; grayling Sept. 10 to Feb. 10. *(See Southampton and Winchester.)*

Bishops Waltham (Hants).—L. & S.W.R. Hamble; trout. Fishing good. *(See Botley.)*
Hotel: Crown.

Bitton (Glo'ster.)—L. & S.W.R. Boyd; trout; preserved by land and mill owners.
Siston brook; trout, perch; leave from landowners. *Lakes:* Golden Valley pond; reserved.
(See Bristol.)

Blaby (Leicester).—L. & N.W.R. Billesden brook. Soar, 1 m. W. *(c.s. Trent.)* *(See
Gainsborough.)*

Blackbull (Stafford).—L. & N.W.R. Foxley brook. Trent, 1 m. E. *(c.s.)* *Lakes:*
Reservoir, 1 m. N. Reservoir, 1 m. E. *(See Gainsborough.)*

Blackburn (Lancs.).—L. & Y.R.; L. & N.W.R.; M.R. Ribble, Hodder; salmon and trout.
Tackleist. J. Gregson, Penny-street. *(See Mill Hill, Preston.)* Darwen, 1 m. S

Blackburn Junction (Lancs.)—M.R. Don. (*c.s. Yorkshire.*) Carr brook. Blackburn brook. (*See Goole.*)

Blackrod (Lancs.).—L. & Y.R.; L. & N.W.R. Douglas. (*c.s. Ribble.*) Horwich brook. *Lakes*: Blackrod ponds. Rivington reservoir, 1 m. N. (*See Liverpool.*) Wallsuches ponds, 2 m. E. (*See Hesketh Bank.*)

Blackwood (Monmouth).—L. & N.W.R. Sirhowey; all fish have been destroyed by the minerals. (*See Newport.*) (*c.s. Usk.*)

Blaen Afon (Monmouth).—G.W.R. Llwyd; trout. (*c.s. Usk.*) (*See Newport.*)

Blagdon (Somerset).—There is a large reservoir here preserved by the Bristol Waterworks Company, Telephone Avenue, Baldwin Street, Bristol. D.t. (limited to ten), 10s. (use of Company's boat for fly-fishing, 10s. extra), to be obtained of the Company's General Manager.

Blaina (Monmouth).—G.W.R.; L. & N.W.R. Ebwyfach; trout. (*c.s. Usk.*) (*See Newport.*)

Blakesley (Northamp.)—L. & N.W.R. Blakesley brook. (*See King's Lynn.*)

Blandford (Dorset).—L. & S.W.R.; M.R. Stour and Iwerne; pike, perch, &c. Fishing good. (*c.s. Avon.*) (*See Christchurch and Wareham.*)

Bleasby (Notts.).—M.R. Trent, 1 m. S.E. at Hazleford Ferry; perch, roach, dace, barbel, chub, pike; free on both sides, but Mr. Coxon, the landlord of the inn, charges 6d. for fishing from the island, whence there is good barbeling. (*c.s.*) (*See Gainsborough.*)

Blencow (Cumland).—L. & N.W.R. Petterill, 1 m. W.; trout. (*c.s. Eden.*) (*See Carlisle.*)

Bloxwich (Stafford).—L. & N.W.R. Sneyd brook. *Lakes*: Sneyd pool. (*See Gainsborough.*)

Blockley (Worcester).—G.W.R. Knee brook. (*See Gloucester.*)

Blunham (Beds.).—L. & N.W.R. Ouse (1 m. W.); coarse fish except barbel; good jucking; Mr. King, of Roxton, owns the west side, and Mr. J. Gilbert, of Blunham, the south. Ivel; coarse fish except barbel; preserved by Mr. J. Gilbert. (*See King's Lynn.*)

Blythe (Stafford).—L. & N.W.R.; G.N.R.; M.R. Blythe. (*c.s. Trent.*) Tean brook, 4 m. S.E. at Upper Tean. *Lakes*: Whympney wood ponds, 2 m. N.E. by Dilhorne. (*See Gainsboro'.*)

Boar's Head (Lancs.)—L. & N.W.R. Douglas. (*c.s. Ribble.*) (*See Hesketh Bank.*)

Boathouse Inn (Cumland).—Ehen. (*c.s. West Cumberland*). Crossdale beck, 1 m. W. Liza, 3 m. E. *Lake*: Ennerdale; trout, char. (*See Egremont.*)

Bodmin (Cornwall).—G.W.R.; L. & S.W.R. Camel, 1½ m.; trout, sea trout, salmon, peal; fishing mostly preserved, but occasional leave may be obtained. Kirland water. Lanivet water. (*See Wadebridge.*) Fowey (3 m.); sea trout, brown trout, salmon; fish small, banks wooded; wading advisable. (*c.s.*) The fishing is mostly open moor fishing; fish small, but plentiful. Hotel: Royal.

Bodmin Road (Cornwall).—G.W.R. Fowey; trout; fishing preserved hence *up* to **Doublebois** by B. Fortescue, Esq., who grants leave; fishing hence *down* to Fowey free. (*c.s.*) (*See Fowey.*)

Bognor (Sussex).—L.B. & S.C.R. There is good sea-fishing about a mile out; bass, pollack, mackerel, &c. From May to July bream are plentiful. The conger fishing is very good. Grey mullet abound in the shallow water between Felpham and Littlehampton Harbour. The fishing westward is not so good for an amateur. Coarse fishing in the Arun and Chichester canal. The Bognor Amateur Angling Society has its headquarters at the Bedford Hotel; hon. sec., C. C. Hodges, Esq. Hotels: Royal Norfolk, Bedford, Royal Pier.

Bollington (Cheshire).—L. & N.W.R. Dean. *Lakes*: Stypherson Park lake, 1 m. N. (*See Runcorn.*)

Bolton Abbey (York).—M.R. Wharfe; trout, grayling; by staying at the Devonshire Arms, Bolton Bridge, Skipton, free fishing can be had from Bolton Bridge up the river for 6 m., both banks; also minnow, worm, or fly in three large reservoirs. The very finest tackle must be used. (*See Kilnsey and Ilkly.*) Fly fishing only permitted from April 1 to Oct. 1. (*c.s. York.*) Barden beck, 2 m. N.W. Ker beck. 2 m. S.E. Washburn, 6 m. E. *Lakes*: Aked dams, 6 m. N.E. (*See Kilnsey, Grassington, Burnsall, York.*)

Bolton-le-Moors (Lancs.).—L. & N.W.R.; G.N.R.; M.R. Tange. Croal. Bradshaw brook, 1 m. E. Dean brook, 2 m. N.W. *Lakes*: Springwater reservoir. 4 m. N.W. Two reservoirs on Rivington Moor, 4 m. N.W. Longworth reservoir, 6 m. N.W. (*See Runcorn.*)

Bolton-on-Dearne (Yorks).—M.R.; G.C.R. Dearne. Don, 2 m. S.E. (*c.s. Yorkshire.*) (*See Goole.*)

Bolton Percy (York).—G.N.R.; S. & K.J.B.; N.E.R. Foss. Wharfe, 1 m. S. (*c.s. York.*) Ouse. 3 m. E. (*c.s. York.*) (*See York.*)

Boot (Cumland).—R. & E.R. Esk; trout. (*c.s. West Cumberland.*) Whillan beck; Stanley Gill. *Lakes*: Burnmore tarn, 2 m. N.; trout, apply to landlord King of Prussia. Eel tarn, 2 m. N.E. *Inn*: King of Prussia, Eskdale Green. (R. & E.R.) (*See Ravenglass.*)

Bootle (Cumland). — Fs.R. Annaside beck. This stream, under the name of Kinmont, rises 4 m. above **Bootle**, where it is joined by Bootle beck, 3 m. long; the united streams join the sea 3 m. down.

Borroughbridge (York).—N.E.R. Ure; pike, perch, few trout and grayling; mostly free. (*c.s. York.*) Tutt or Innskip beck. Ouse, 2 m. E.; pike, coarse fish. (*c.s. York.*) (*See York.*)

Borrowash (Derby).—M.R. Derwent; pike, coarse fish, grayling, trout (*See Derby.*) (*c.s. Trent.*) *Lakes*: Elvaston Castle lake, 1 m. S. (*See Gainsborough.*)

Borrowdale (Cumland). — Derwent; trout, salmon. (*c.s.*) Watendlath beck; Newlands beck, 3 m. S.W.; trout. *Lakes*: Derwentwater; trout, salmon. (*c.s.*

Derwent). Watendlath tarn, 2 m. S.; Blea tarn, 4 m. S.; trout. (*See Cockermouth, Keswick.*), *Hotels*: Borrowdale, Lowdore.

Borwick (Lancs.).—Fs. & M.R. Keer. (*See Carnforth.*)

Boscastle (Cornwall).—Valency, 4 m. long, and Tredawl Water (2 m. off) 3 m. long. Ottery and Inney, 5 m.; trout, peel. *Hotel*: Wellington; tickets at hotel. Sea fishing very good in calm weather; mackerel, pollack, whiting and cod.

Bosley (Cheshire).—M.R. Dane; trout, dace, roach, chub; private. Folly brook, 5 m. N.E. *Lakes*: Bosley reservoir. (*See Frodsham.*)

Boston (Lincoln).—G.N.R. Witham; pike, perch, chub, tench, rudd, and' bream. Witham rises some 10 m. above **Great Ponton**, and 2 m. above that place is joined on left bank by Cringle brook, 5 m. long. At **Ponton**, Stoke brook, which rises in some ponds above Wyvill, runs 4 m. to Stoke Mill pond, and joins Witham 2 m. below, on left bank. Witham runs to **Grantham** 5 m. 2 m. below, the drainage of the lakes in Belton Park, 1 m. up, joins on right bank. Witham runs to **Barkston** 2 m., and here is Syston Park lake on the right bank. 1 m. below, Honington beck, 5 m. long, joins on right bank. Witham runs 2 m. to **Hougham**, and 2 m. below is joined on left bank by Foston beck. Foston, under the name of Old Beck, rises in the lakes at Denton House, 4 m. S.W. from **Grantham**, runs 1 m. to the Canal reservoir, and reaches **Sedgbrook** in 3 m., joining Witham 6 m. below. Witham runs 6 m. to **Claypole**, Beckingham 6 m., Bassingham 6 m., and 6 m. down at Fishhouse, **Harmston** being 2 m. off on right bank, Brant joins on right bank. Brant rises by Brandon, 2 m. W. of **Claythorpe**, and 3 m. down, at Stragglethorpe, is joined on the right bank by a brook draining some ponds at Leadenham Hall by **Leadenham**, 3 m. up 1 m. down Brant, by Broughton on Brant, 2 m. W. of **Leadenham**, Sand beck, 6 m. long, joins on left bank. Brant runs to Skinnand, 2 m. W. of **Navenby**, 3 m., Blackmoor Causeway 3 m., where **Harmston** is 1 m. off on right bank, and 1 m. below joins Witham. Witham runs to **Hykeham** 2 m., and **Lincoln** 4 m. Here Foss Dyke navigation, joining Trent with Witham, joins on left bank. A railway runs alongside this waterway, and 2 m. E. of **Saxelby** Till joins it on the N. bank. Till rises above Upton 3 m. S.E. of **Lea**, and 4 m. down, 3 m. N.E. from **Stow Park**, is joined on left bank by a brook 5 m. long draining Fillingham lake 8 m. W. of **Lea**. Till runs to Till Bridge 3 m., 4 m. S.E. of **Stow Park**, and 4 m. down joins Foss Dyke. Witham runs to **Washingbrough** 3 m., and 1 m. below is joined on right bank by Washingbrough brook, which rises by **Branston** in Branston Hall ponds, and is 5 m. long. Witham runs to Fiskerton or **Five Mile House** 1 m., and 3 m. down, at Barling's Lock, is joined on left bank by Langworth. Langworth rises in Hackthorne Hall pond, 7 m. N.W. of **Langworth**, and 5 m. down, just below Snarford Bridge, 2 m. N.W. of **Snelland**, is joined on left bank by Fristhorpe brook, 5 m. long. Langworth runs 2 m. to Stainton, where Snelland brook, which rises 5 m. above **Snelland** and is 8 m. long, joins on left bank. 1 m. down Langworth, at **Langworth**, Clay brook, 10 m. long, joins on left bank. Langworth runs 4 m. to Barlings Abbey, just below which, on left bank, Stainfield brook, 6 m. long. joins on left bank. Langworth joins Witham 1 m. down. 1 m. down, Tile House beck, 5 m. long, joins on left bank. Witham runs to **Bardney** 1 m., and **Southry** 3 m. Here Tupholme brook joins on left bank. Tupholme rises in Stourton Hall ponds 5 m. N.W. from **Horncastle**, runs 3 m. to Gauntby Hall lakes, 5 m. N.W. of **Horncastle**, and joins Witham 5 m. down. Witham runs to **Stixwould** 1 m., **Kirkstead** 2 m., **Tattershall** (1 m. E.) 3 m., **Dogdyke** 2 m. Here Bain joins on left bank. Bain rises above Brough on Bain 7 m. W. of **Louth**, and 3 m. below, by Donnington, is joined on right bank by the drainings of Benniworth pool and another pond ½ m. up. These ponds are 8 m. N. of **Horncastle**. Bain runs to Goulsby 2 m., Hemingby 3 m., **Horncastle** 3 m. 5 m. down, at Haltham, 3 m. E. of **Woodhall Spa**, Haltham beck, 6 m. long, joins on left bank. Bain runs to **Tattershall** 4 m., and **Dogdyke** and Witham 2 m. Witham runs to **Langrick** 6 m., and **Boston** 5 m. Here Hammond beck joins on right bank. Hammond rises 4 m. above **Donington**, runs 4 m. to **Swinehead**, and 2 m. below divides into two parts, Old and New Hammond beck, which runs to **Boston** and Witham in 5 m. Witham joins the sea 3 m. below. The Boston Angling Association (sec., B. Whyers, 47, Witham-green, Boston), preserves Witham from Tattershall Bridge to **Boston**; subscriptions voluntary; and the Lincoln Angling Association from Lincoln to Tattershall Bridge. At Cowbridge, 2 m. from Boston, is some good coarse fishing *Hotels*: Peacock and Royal.

Botesdale (Suffolk), n.s. **Mellis**, 4 m.—Little Ouse. *Lakes*: Redgrave Park Lake. (*See King's Lynn.*)

Botley (Hants).—L. & S.W.R. Hamble; sea trout and trout. Hamble rises in a large pond (good piking) by **Bishops Waltham** Station (S.W.R.), and in 1 m. is joined on left bank by the mill-stream from the corn mill at that town. 2¼ m. on is **Botley**. Here are some ponds holding pike in Botley Grange. 6 m. below is Southampton Water. The fishing is mostly private, but leave may sometimes be obtained.

Bottisford (Leicester.)—G.N.R. Devon. Smite, 3 m. N.W. at Orston. Carr dyke, 5 m. N.W. (*See Gainsborough.*)

Bourn (Lincoln).—G.N.R. Edenham brook, 2 m. N.W. Glen, 3 m. S. (*See Spalding.*)

Bourne End (Bucks).—G.W.R. Thames; roach, pike, perch. Wye; polluted. (*See London, M.T.*) *Fisherman*: E. Shaw. *Hotel*: Railway.

Bournemouth (Hants).—L. & S.W.R. Stour; salmon, trout, grayling, pike, perch, barbel, bream, chub, roach, tench, carp. The river is strictly preserved from **Wimborne**,

Dorset, to the Ferry at Wick. Good fishing half hour by rail in Avon at **Ringwood.** (*See Ringwood.*) Some fishing from the pier and in the bay.

Bourton (Somerset).—G.W.R. Kenn. (*See Clevedon.*)

Bourton-on-the-Water (Glo'ster).—G.W.R. On Windrush and Dickler. (*See London, U.T.*) Trout.

Bovey (Devon).—G.W.R. (*See Teignmouth.*) Bovey and Teign. The fishing above Bovey is preserved by the landowners; below Bovey by the Lower Teign Fishing Association; tickets at the hotels and post office. Teign preserved by the same association; s.t. 21s.; m.t. 10s.; w.t. 7s. 6d., ; from the hon. treasurer, H. G. Michelmore, Newton Abbot. Conservators' licences necessary. (*c.s. Teign.*) *Lakes*: Tottiford and Kennick reservoirs, 3 m. trout; preserved by the Corporation of Torquay, who issue a limited number of tickets; apply to F. S. Hex, Esq., Town Clerk, Torquay. *Hotels*: Union, Dolphin, and Railway.

Bow (Devon).—L. & S.W.R. Spreyton water; trout. (*See Exeter.*) Lapford water. (*See Barnstaple.*)

Bowes (Yorks).—N.E.R. Greta; trout; mostly private, but a.t. 5s. for a length can be had from Mr. Dent Meliwaters, Darlington. (*c.s. Tees.*) Eller beck, 2 m. S. Garnathwaite beck, 3 m. S.E. Gill beck, 4 m. S.E. (*See Stockton.*)

Bowness (Westland), n.s. **Windermere**, 1½m.—Winster, 2m. S; trout. (*c.s. Kent.*) (*See Grange.*) *Lakes*: Windermere; pike, perch, char. large trout; s.t. 5s. (*c.s. Kent.*) *Hotels*: Old England, Royal, Crown, Belsfield. (*See Ulverston.*)

Box (Wilts).—G.W.R. (*See Bristol.*) Box brook; trout; preserved by Col. Northey, Bath.

Box Hill (Surrey).—L. & S.W.R and L.B. & S.C.R. Mole. (*See London, L.T.*) *Hotel*: Burford Bridge Hotel. The river runs through the hotel orchard and garden (where visitors only can fish) through private grounds to Leatherhead, 1 m. off; fishing to be had at the mill; d.t. 1s.; also at Castle Mill, Betchworth-road, 1½ m.; d.t. 1s.

Boxmoor (Herts).—L. & N.W.R. On Gade; trout, pike; preserved by Sir A. Cooper, Mr. Halsey, and Earl Brownlow. *Hotel*: Bell, at Two Waters. (*See London, M.T.*)

Braceboro' Spa (Lincoln).—G.N.R. Edenham brook. Glen, 2 m. S.E. Welland, 4 m. S. at **Stamford.** (*See Spalding.*)

Brackley (Northton.).—L. & N.W.R. Ouse. (*c.s. N. and S.*) *Lakes*: Biddlesdon Park (4 m. N.W.) Cottisford pond (5 m. S.) (*See King's Lynn.*)

Bracknell (Berks).—L.& S.W.R. There is a large mill pond at East Hampstead. (*See London, M.T.*) Harman's pond is near.

Bradbury (Durham).—N.E.R. Skerne; trout, pike, chub, roach; partly free, elsewhere preserved by Darlington Anglers' Club of 50; entrance, 10s.; s.t. 25s. Sec., Mr. Lascelles, Northgate, Darlington. Licences of J. F. Smythe, Fishtackleist, Horse Market, Darlington. (*c.s. Tees.*) (*See Stockton.*)

Bradford-on-Avon (Wilts).—G.W.R. (*See Bristol.*) On Avon; perch, roach, dace, chub, trout, &c.; preserved by Bradford-on-Avon Angling Association for 3 m.; s.t., 1l.; m.t., 2s. 6d.; w.t., 1s. 6d.; d.t., 6d. There is a stretch of 5 m. of free fishing, with very few exceptions of trespass on land; half a mile from canal for pike and perch. *Hotel*: The Swan; James Rose, proprietor. (*c.s.*)

Bradford (York).—G.N.R.; M.R.; N.B.R.; L. & Y.R.; L. & N.W.R.; N.E.R. Bradford brook. Aire, 4 m. N. (*c.s. York.*) (*See Rawcliffe.*)

Braemore (Hants).—L. & S.W.R. Avon. (*See Christchurch.*) Sir E. Halse preserves the trout fishing; good. He sometimes gives leave for a day, on a proper introduction. (*c.s.*)

Brafferton (York).—N.E.R. Swale. (*c.s. York.*) Sun beck. (*See York.*)

Braintree (Essex). — G.E.R. (*See Maldon.*) On Brain and Blackwater. The Brain is strictly preserved; pike, perch, dace, roach, tench, in both rivers. 4 m. off is Stisted Hall pond; pike, carp, and tench. Leave from the owner of Stisted Hall, Braintree. Gosfield lake, 5 m.; leave from Mrs. Taylor Lowe, Gosfield Hall. Gosfield Place pond; leave from Rev. B. Sparrow, Gosfield Place. *Hotel*: Horn.

Braithwaite (Cumberland).—L. & N.W.R. (36).—Newlands beck; trout. Coledale beck, marron. (*c.s. Derwent.*) Derwent, 1 m. E.; trout, salmon. (*c.s.*) Lostrigg beck, 2 m. W. *Lakes*: Derwentwater, 2 m. S.E.; pike, perch, salmon, trout, vendace; (*c.s. Derwent*). Bassenthwaite, 2 m. N.W.; pike, perch, trout, salmon. (*c.s. Derwent.*) (*See Cockermouth, Keswick.*)

Bramber (Sussex).—L.B. & S.C.R. On Adur. (*See New Shoreham.*)

Bramford (Suffolk).—G.E.R. Gipping; roach, perch, pike, tench, chub, bream; preserved from Blakenham 3 m. above to Bos Hall 2 m. below by Gipping Angling Preservation Society; s.t. 21s.; d.t., pike 2s. 6d., roach 1s., of the hon. sec., Mr. Charles Prentice, 19, Tower Street, Ipswich. (*See Ipswich.*)

Bramley (Surrey).—L.B. & S.C.R. Wey. Bream, roach, dace. (*See London, L.T.*)

Bramley (York).—G.N.R.; L. & Y.R. Farmley beck. (*See Rawcliffe.*)

Brampford Speke (Devon).—G.W.R. Exe; trout, salmon, dace; preserved below to Cowley Bridge by Lord Iddesleigh Limited number of salmon tickets at 6l. 6s.; s.t. 21s.; after June 1, 10s. 6d.; d.t. 5s. Wading allowed. (*c.s.*) Culm, 1 m. W.; trout. (*See Exeter.*)

Brampton (Cumland).—N.E.R. Irthling, 1 m. N.; trout; preserved by Brampton Angling Association; s.t., 6s.; sec., C. Cheesbrough. (*c.s. Eden.*) Gelt, 1 m. S.; trout; preserved as

Irthing. King's water, 1 m. N. Cam beck, 1 m. N. Eden, 5 m. W.; salmon, trout; preserved. *Lakes:* Talkin Tarn, 3 m. S.E.; pike, perch, trout. Tindale Tarn, 6 m.; pike, perch, trout. *Hotels:* Howard's Arms, White Lion. (*See Carlisle.*)

Brampton (Northton).—L. & N.W.R. Nen. Moulton brook. Althorp brook, 2 m. S.W. (*See Wisbeach.*)

Brandon (Suffolk).—G.E.R. Little Ouse; pike and coarse fish; there is a stretch of free water, and elsewhere permission easily obtained, but the fishing is very poor. *Lakes:* Toffs mere (5 m. N.E.). Buckenham House Park pond (6 m. N.E.). (*See King's Lynn*). (*c.s. Norfolk.*) *Hotel:* Ram.

Brandon (Warwick).—L. & N.W.R. Avon; chub, dace, roach, pike, perch, bream; preserved by R. J. Beech, Esq., on right bank for 4 m.; let to the Coventry Angling Club. (*See Gloucester.*) (*c.s. Severn.*) *Inn:* Royal Oak.

Bransford (Worcester).—G.W.R. Teme; chub, dace, roach, pike, perch, grayling, trout; preserved hence up to Broadwas Church by Bransford Angling Society, s.t. 10s., d.t. 2s. 6d. (*See Gloucester.*) (*c s. Severn.*)

Branston (Lincoln).—G.N.R. Washingbrough brook. Witham, 1 m. N. *Lakes:* Branston Hall. (*See Boston.*)

Braughing (Herts). — G.E.R. (*See Stratford.*) On Rib and Quin; trout, coarse fish. Preserved.

Braunston (Northton).—L. & N.W.R. Leam. Rain's brook (4 m. N.W.) (*See Gloucester.*)

Braunton (Devon).—L. & S.W.R. Braunton water. Braunton rises 1 m. S. of **Morthoe Station** (N.D.R.), runs 1 m. to West Down, and 2 m. down is joined on left bank by Fullabrook, 3 m. long. **Braunton** is 3 m. on. 1 m. below, Knowle water, 6 m. long, joins on left bank.

Braystones (Cumberland).—Fs.R. Ehen. (*c.s. West Cumberland.*) Kirkbeck; Black-beck. (*See Egremont.*)

Breadsall (Derby).—G.N.R. Ferryby brook. Derwent, 1 m. W. (*c.s. Trent.*) *Lakes:* Allestry Hall lake, 1 m. N.W. Kedleston Park lake, 3 m. W. (*See Gainsborough.*)

Bredon (Worcester).—M.R. Avon; chub, dace, roach, pike, perch, bream. Severn, 4 m.); roach, pike, perch, bream, &c. (*See Gloucester.*) (*c.s. Severn.*)

Breighton (York), n.s. **Menthorpe Gate**, 1 m.—Derwent; chub, dace, pike, &c.; fishing free. (*c.s. York.*) (*See Wressel.*)

Brent (Devon).—G.W.R. Avon; salmon, trout; preserved by Avon Fishing Association from beyond Shipley Bridge *above* to Aveton Gifford *below*; s.t. 40s. (limited to 30), m.t. 20s., w.t. 10s. Conservators' licenses—salmon (including trout) s.t. 20s., trout s.t. 10s. w.t. 5s., d.t 2s. (*c.s.*) Tickets from sec., C. E. Turner, Esq., solicitor, Salcombe. Red brook, 2 m. N.; trout. Black brook, 2 m. S.; trout. *Hotel:* Anchor. (*See Loddiswell.*)

Brentford (Middx.).—L. & S.W.R.; G.W.R. Thames and Brent. (*See London, L.T.*)

Brent Knoll (Somerset).—G.W.R. *Lakes:* East Brent ponds, a series of ponds holding pike, perch, carp, tench, rudd; permission from the station master.

Brentwood (Essex).—G.E.R. There are some ponds in Thorndon Hall Park, belonging to Lord Petre. Pike, perch, &c. in Weald Hall. The large lake of Fitzwater is some 2½ m. off.

Brewood (Stafford), n.s. **Four Ashes**, 2 m.—L. & N.W.R. Penk Saredon brook, 3 m. S.E. Whiston brook, 4 m. N.W. *Lakes:* Chillington Park pool, 3 m. S.W. Galey reservoir, 4 m. N.E. Calf Heath ponds. 4 m. E. (*See Gainsborough.*)

Bridestow (Devon).—G.W.R. Lew. (*See Plymouth.*) Okement; trout. Thistle brook (2 m.); trout. (*See Bideford.*) (*c.s. Taw.*)

Bridges (Cornwall).—G.W.R. Bream. Luxulion brook. (*See Par.*) (*c.s. Fowey.*)

Bridgnorth (Shrops.).—G.W.R. Severn; dace, trout, chub, pike, perch, salmon; fishing free. Worf (1 m. W.). Mor brook (2 m. S.W.). Claverley brook (4 m. E.). Borle brook (4 m. S.). Stratford brook (5 m. N.E.) (*See Gloucester.*) (*c.s.*)

Bridgwater (Somerset).—G.W.R. Parret; roach, salmon, few trout. Carey. Parret rises by **Crewkerne**, runs to West Chinnock, where a stream 3 m. long joins on right bank; 1 m. on Hinton Brook joins on left bank. Hinton rises in a pond in Hinton House Park (Lord Paulet), by Hinton St. George (n.s. **Crewkerne**, 3 m.), and 2 m. down, at Merriot, is joined on right bank by a stream working a mill 1 m. up. Hence to Parret is 3 m. 1 m. down Parret, a stream 4 m. long joins on left bank, which rises in some ponds in Hinton House Park, and works two mills. Parret runs in 2 m. to South Petherton (n.s. **Martock;** 3 m. down a stream joins on right bank which rises 1 m. E. of **Martock,** and is 4 m. long, working two mills. Parret runs to Kingsbury 1 m.; 2½ m. below, Isle joins on left bank. Isle rises S. of **Ilminster** (G.W.R.), and after working two mills passes by that town, and working three mills in 4½ m., is joined at Puckington, on left bank, by a stream which rises 3 m. W. of **Ilminster**, and is 5 m. long. Isle runs in 2 m. to Isle Abbot, and 2 m. down is joined on left bank by a stream which rises S.W. of **Hatch** (G.W.R.), and is 6 m. long. 4 m. on Isle joins Parret. Parret runs in 2 m. to **Langport** (G.W.R.). Here Yeo joins on right bank. Yeo rises 3 or 4 m. N. of **Sherborne** (S.W.R.), and is joined at that place by Milborne brook which rises by **Milborne Port** (S.W.R.), and in 3 m. waters the large lake in Sherborne Park. Yeo runs in 4 m. to Bradford Abbas, where Yet joins on left bank. Yet rises 4 m. S. of **Yetminster**, where a stream joins on right bank 3 m. long. Yeo is 2 m. down. Yeo now runs in 1½ m. to **Yeovil Junction** (S.W.R.). Here Evershot brook joins on left bank. Evershot rises 4 m. S. of **Sutton Bingham** (S.W.R.), 1 m. below which a stream joins on right bank which rises in a lake at Melbury Sampford (n.s. **Evershot**), and is 6 m. long. 1½ m. on, a stream joins on left bank, which works a mill 1 *m.* up. Yeo is ¼ *m.* on. Yeo runs in 1 *m.* to **Yeovil** (G.W.R.), 2 *m.* below, a stream joins on right bank working a mill 1 *m.* up; 4 *m.* down Yeo, Sparkford brook joins on right bank. Sparkford rises in a mill pond 4 *m.* N.E. of **Sparkford** (G.W.R.), near North Cadbury, and in 3 *m.* is joined by a small brook working a mill. **Sparkford** is 1 *m.* on. Sparkford runs to Queen's Canal, 1 *m.*, and 3 *m.* down is joined on the left bank by a stream which rises by **Marston Magna** G.W.R.) and is 5 *m.* long. ½ *m.* on Sparkford joins Yeo. Yeo now runs to Ilchester (n.s. **Martock**, G.W.R., 5 *m.*), Long Sutton 4 *m.*, **Langport** and Parret 4 *m.* Here a small stream joins Yeo on right bank rising in Paradise mill pond 1½ *m.* up. Parret now runs through the moors, and 2¼ *m.* down is joined on left bank by a stream which drains seven or eight large ponds in West Sedge Moor. 1 *m.* down Parret, Hatch brook joins on left bank. Hatch rises ¼ *m.* N. of **Hatch Station** (G.W.R.), runs 4 *m.* when it passes 1 *m.* S. of North Curry. 1 *m.* down, a stream joins on right bank, draining a large pond ¼ *m.* up on Sedge Moor, and joins Parret 4 *m.* on. Parret runs in 2 *m.* to Chapel and Borough Bridge (n.s. **Athelney**, G.W.R., 1¼ *m.*). Here Tone joins on left bank. Tone rises above Clatworthy 3 *m.* from **Wiveliscoombe** (G.W.R.), and 3 *m.* down passes 2 *m.* W. of **Wiveliscoombe**, runs to **Wellington** (G.W.R.) 1½ *m.* Here a stream joins on right bank, which works a mill 1 *m.* up. 3 *m.* down, at Bradford, a small stream holding trout joins on right bank. 1 *m.* down, Milverton brook joins on left bank. This stream rises 1 *m.* N.E. of **Wiveliscoombe**. and in 1½ *m.* is joined on right bank by a stream, which rises in Wimorleigh Mill 1½ *m.* S. of **Wiveliscoombe** and is 2 *m.* long. Milverton brook runs in 1½ *m.* to **Milverton** (G.W.R.), and Tone 4 *m.* ¼ mile down Tone, a stream, which rises at West Buckland 3 *m.* up, joins on right bank. 1 *m.* down Tone, Norton brook joins on left bank. Norton rises in Tolland Mill 3 *m.* N.E. of **Wiveliscoombe**, runs 3¼ *m.* to Halse (n.s. **Bishops Lydeard**, G.W.R., 1½ *m.*, or **Milverton** 2 *m.*), **Norton Fitz-warren** (G.W.R.) 4 *m.*, and Tone ¼ *m.* 1 *m.* down Tone, at Bishops Hull, Kingston brook joins on left bank. Kingston brook rises 3 *m.* N. of Kingston (n.s. **Taunton**, G.W.R, 2¼ *m.*); 2 *m.* below Kingston a stream joins on right bank, which rises by **Bishops Lydeard** and is 4 *m.* long. Tone is 1½ *m.* below the junction. Tone runs in 2 *m.* to **Taunton**. 2¼ *m.* below, Black brook joins on right bank. Black brook rises by Trull (n.s. **Taunton** 2 *m.*), and is 6 *m.* long. 2 *m.* down Tone, at Creech St. Michael, a stream joins on left bank, which rises by West Monkton (n.s. **Durston**, G.W.R., 2 *m.*) and is 3 *m.* long. Tone runs in 6 *m.* to **Athelney** (G.W.R.) and Parret 1½ *m.* Parret runs in 6 *m.* to **Bridgwater**. Here a stream joins on left bank, which rises in the lake in Enmore Castle Park 4 *m.* from **Bridgwater**, and 2 *m.* down is joined by a stream on the right bank, which works a mill 1½ *m.* up. The main stream runs to Durleigh and its mill 2 *m.* and Bridgwater 2 *m.* At Cannington, 3 *m.* from **Bridgwater**, runs a stream which rises 5 *m.* S.W. of Cannington, working several mills, and joins the Parret estuary 3 *m.* below. At Otterhampton, 4½ *m.* from **Bridgwater**, a stream joins the Parret estuary, which rises in a mill pond at Fiddington and is 3 or 4 *m.* long. (*c.s. Avon.*)

CAREY River rises at **Castle Carey** (G.W.R.) runs to Babenty 6 *m.* (n.s. **Sparkford** 4 *m.*). 3 *m.* below a stream joins on left bank, which rises at South Barrow 1 *m.* from **Sparkford** and is 5 *m.* long. Carey passes in 1 *m.* within 2 *m.* N. of Ilchester, and runs in 4 *m.* to Somerton (n.s. **Langport** 4 *m.*), and in 5 *m.* enters Sedge Moor, where it joins King's Sedge drain, and after a run of 12 *m.* joins Parret on right bank 3 *m.* below **Bridgwater.**

Bridlington (York).—N.E.R. Angling for billet from the pier, many pollack at Flamborough Head, and a variety of sea fish in the offing.

Bridport (Dorset).—G.W.R. (*See Burton Bradstock.*) On Brit and Asker. Trout. (*c.s. Axe.*) Brit rises near Beaminster (n.s. **Toller**, G.W.R., 6 *m.*) One *m.* down, a stream joins on right bank, working a mill or two by Stoke Abbot, 1½ *m.* up. Six *m.* down is **Bridport**. Here Asker joins on left bank. Asker rises by **Poorstock**, and is 6 *m.* long. Britt joins the sea 2 *m.* below Bridport. Britt is preserved by the landowners and farmers, who frequently give leave. Asker is preserved by a club. Fishing good. Bass fishing from the pier head with squid or cuttle bait. A rod and floated line might be used sometimes with success in rather rough weather. Mackerel, pollack, and pout are caught near the Pollack-stone. *Hotel*: Bull. *Makers of Nets, &c.*, Joseph Gundry and Co.

Brierley Hill (Stafford).—G.W.R. Stour (3 *m.* S.). Smestow (5 *m.* W.). *Lakes*: Pensnet Chase Reservoir, Old Pit Ponds (2 *m.* W.). Askew Bridge Pond (3 *m.* N.W.). Himley Park lakes and Common Pool (4 *m.* N.W.) (*See Gloucester.*) (*c.s. Severn.*)

Brigg (Lincoln).—G.C.R. Ancholme. This river, in North Lincolnshire, with its numerous tributaries, drains about 240 square miles of country. It falls into the Humber at South Ferriby, where is a sluice and tidal lock. The lower part has been canalised for about 21 miles, and in this portion fishing is permitted by the Ancholme Commissioners. The tributary streams, in which fishing is not allowed, form splendid spawning grounds, and the river is abundantly stocked with coarse fish (pike, perch, roach, dace, bream, bleak, tench, gudgeon, eels, and a few burbot). There are also a few trout, and king-carp and rudd have recently been introduced. *Fishing stations*—Ferriby Sluice, 4 *m.* from **Barton-on-Humber** (G.C.R.); Saxeby Bridge, 6 *m.* from Barton-on-Humber; Worlaby Bridge, 2 *m.* from **Appleby Station** (G.C.R.); Brougton, Castlethorpe, and Cadney Bridges, near **Brigg** (G.C.R.), through which town the river passes; Hibaldstow Bridge, 3 *m.* from **Scawby Station** (G.C.R.); Brandywath; Bishopsbridge, 6 *m.* from Market Rasen

(G.C.R.). The Ancholme is preserved by the Commissioners, who make a small charge to anglers, viz., for residents within 3 m., s.t. 1s.; non-resident, s.t. 3s., w.t. 1s., d.t. 4d. Trout—s.t. 2s. 6d., w.t. 1s. A licence issued by the Trent Fishery Board is also necessary.

Brigham (Cumberland).—L. & N.W.R. Derwent; trout, salmon. (c.s.) Doverbeck. Ellerbeck. (*See Cockermouth.*)

Brighouse (York).—L. & Y.R. Calder. (c.s. *York.*) (*See Rawcliffe.*)

Brighton (Sussex).—L.B. & S.C.R. Sea bream and other fish may be caught off here, and bass sometimes from the pier. In the Ouse, not far from Barcombe, for several miles up, there is fair fishing for roach, chub, perch, and eels. and good pike fishing.

Brightside (Yorks).—M.R.; G.C.R. Don. (*See Goole.*)

Brimscombe (Gloucester).—G.W.R. Frome; coarse fish. (*See Stonehouse.*)

Brinkburn (Northland.). — N.B.R. Coquet; trout (sea trout and salmon in the autumn.) The whole of the Duke of Northumberland's water on the Coquet is now leased to the Coquet Committee of the Northumbrian Anglers' Federation (clerk to committee, John A. Williamson, solicitor, Newcastle-on-Tyne); s.t. (also available to fish Lord Armstrong's water at Rothbury), 21s., m.t. 10s., w.t. 7s. 6d., d.t. 2s. 6d. (*See Rothbury.*)

Brinklow (Warwick).—L. & N.W.R. Combe brook. *Lakes:* Burdon Pool (5 m.). (*See Gloucester.*)

Brinscall (Lancs.)—L. & Y.R.; L. & N.W.R. Roddlesworth. (*See Preston.*)

Brislington (Somerset).—G.W.R. (*See Bristol.*) On Avon. (c.s.)

Bristol.—G.W.R.; M.R. On Avon. Avon rises in Shipton Mill Head 1 m. S. of **Tetbury** (G.W.R.), runs 5 m. to Malmesbury (n.s. **Minety**, 8 m.; jack, perch, roach; preserved). Here a stream joins on right bank, which rises in a mill pool by Great Sherston, is 8 m. long, and works six mills. 1 m. below Malmesbury a stream joins Avon on left bank, which rises in Seven Island Pond 5 m. from **Minety**, and is 9 m. long. 1 m. up from its junction with Avon a stream joins it on right bank, which rises in Bredon pond, 3 m. from **Minety**, runs 4 m., where the outflow from the ponds in Charlton Park (pike, perch, carp; leave from Lord Estcourt), 2 m. from Malmesbury, joins on right bank, and 1 m. on joins the main stream. Avon now flows to **Dauntsey** 4 m. Here Thunder brook joins on left bank. Thunder rises in a mill pool 4 m. S. of **Wootton Bassett**, passes by that town, and in 1½ m. is joined by a stream on left bank 1 m. long, rising in a pond at Tockenham Wick, 1 m. from **Dauntsey Station**. 1 m. on a stream joins on right bank, rising in a pond 1½ m. up. From hence to Avon is 6 m. Avon runs to **Chippenham** 10 m., passing Christian Malford midway (good fishing; preserved by Sir H. Meux). At **Chippenham**, Marden river joins Avon. Marden rises at Calstone Willington, 3 m. S.E. of **Calne**, and in 1½ m. is joined on right bank by Elver brook, which works a mill 1 m. up. 1 m. down Marden, a stream 1½ m. long joins on left bank, working a mill. 1 m. below **Calne** is the outflow on left bank of the large lake in Bowood Park (pike, perch, carp, tench, roach; leave from Lord Lansdowne). 1 m. below, Fisher's brook joins on right bank, which rises 2 m. N. from **Calne**, and 3 m. down is joined on right bank by a stream 4 m. long, rising in Whitcombe Mill 4 m. N. of **Calne**. 1 m. down, Marden is reached, and Marden runs in 4 m. to Avon. 5 m. below **Chippenham** Avon receives on right bank the outflow of Corsham Park Lake, 3 m. up (n.s. **Corsham**). 1 m. on, at Lacock (pike, perch, roach; preserved; leave may sometimes be had from C. H. Talbot, Esq., Lacock Abbey), a stream joins on right bank, 2 m. long, which works three or four mills; 2½ m. on, a stream joins on left bank 4 m. long, which drains the lakes in Spy Park (n.s. **Calne**). 1 m. on is **Melksham**, 1 m. below which a stream joins on right bank, draining a pond 1 m. up. At **Holt** a stream joins on left bank, which rises by Urchfont (n.s. **Devizes**, 4 m.). In 1 m. a stream 1 m. long joins on right bank, which rises in a mill pond at Mustead, 2 m. E. from **Devizes**. The main stream now runs in 5 m. to Worten, where a stream 5 m. long joins, which rises in Knowlum's Pond, 1 m. S. of West Lavington (n.s. **Devizes**, 6 m.), and works several mills. The main stream now runs in 3 m. to Bullington (n.s. **Seend**, 3 m.), where a stream 4 m. long joins on left bank, and which rises in a mill pool by Edington (capital tench fishing) (n.s. **Westbury**, 4 m.). 1 m. down the main stream, a stream joins on right bank, which rises in Snake Mead Mill by **Devizes**, and in 2 m. is joined on right bank by a stream which rises in Roundaway Mill, 1 m. from **Devizes**. 3½ m. down, at Bide Mill, 1 m. from **Seend**, a stream joins on left bank, which rises in Drew's pond, 1 m. S. of **Devizes**, and is 5 m. long. 1 m. on, the main stream is reached, which runs to Sennington (n.s. **Melksham**, 3 m.) 3 m., and Avon 2 m. 3 m. below **Holt**, Biss joins Avon on left bank. Biss rises in a mill pond S. of **Westbury**, and in 3 m. is joined on left bank by a stream which rises in Berkley House Park lake (n.s. **Frome**), and is 5 m. long. At the junction of the above with the parent brook a stream 1 m. long joins on left bank, which drains a pond by North Bradley. Half a mile down, a brook joins on right bank, which runs from **Westbury**, working two or three mills, and is 3 m. long. Hence to **Trowbridge** is 3 m. Here a stream joins on left bank, which rises in a pond 3 m. up. Avon is 1½ m. down from **Trowbridge**. Avon runs in 2 m. to **Bradford**, **Freshford** 2 m. Here Frome river (trout and coarse fish) joins on left bank. Frome rises in the lake at New Hitchling, 1½ m. S. of **Witham**, and is joined at that place on right bank by the outflow of the lake in Witham Park, 1½ m. up. 3½ m. down Frome, a stream joins on right bank, which rises in Bradley Mill Pool 1 m. N. of Maiden Bradley, and is 3 m. long. Frome runs in 2 m. to **Frome**, and is here joined on right bank by the brook which drains the lake in Longleat Park (trout, roach, dace, perch, pike; Lord Bath), 5 m. from **Frome**, and also the mill pool at Corsley, 3 m. from

Frome. 1 *m.* below **Frome** Cale joins Frome on left bank. This stream rises in Lechmere water (n.s. **Binegar,** 1½ *m.*), and in 4 *m.* is joined on right bank by a stream which works a mill 1 *m.* up. 1 *m.* on, at Caleford, a stream, working a mill 1 *m.* up, joins on left bank. Cale in 2 *m.* waters the lakes in Mell's Park, and 2 *m.* below, at Elm, a stream 2½ *m.* long joins on right bank, which rises in a pond by Little Elm. 2 *m.* on is the Frome. 1 *m.* down Frome the outflow of the large lake at Orchardleigh, 2 *m.* from Frome, joins on left bank. Frome runs to Beckington 1½ *m.*, Road 2 *m.* (preserved by Avon and Tributaries Angling Association, and then by the owner of Farleigh Castle), Farleigh 3 *m.* (preserved hence to Avon by Avon and Trib. A.A.). **Freshford** and Avon 3 *m.* Avon now runs to **Limpley** 1 *m.*, 1 *m.* below which Midford brook joins on left bank, which rises in the lake in Stone Easton Park (n.s. **Hallatrow**), runs 2½ *m.* to **Midsomer Norton,** where a stream joins on right bank, which rises in a mill pond by **Chilcompton** 2 *m.* up. The main stream flows to **Radstock** 1 *m.*, **Wellow** 4 *m.*, 1 *m.* below which a stream joins on right bank, which rises in the mill pool at Norton St. Philip, and is 2 *m.* long. The main stream flows to **Midford** 2 *m.*, where a stream joins on left bank, which rises by **Hallatrow,** runs 6 *m.* to Combe Hay (n.s. **Wellow,** 1½ *m.*), and **Midford** 2½ *m.* Avon is 1½ *m.* down. Avon runs in 3½ *m.* to **Bathampton.** Here Box brook and St. Catharine's brook join on right bank. Box is some 7 or 8 *m.* long, and works several mills. **Box** is midway. St. Catharine's (trout) works some mills, and is 5 or 6 *m.* long. Avon runs in 2½*m.* to **Bath, Weston,** and **Twerton** 1 *m.* Just above the city Woolley brook joins on right bank. Woolley rises above Langridge (trout), runs to Swanswick (trout, leave from H. G. Bush, Esq., solicitor, Bath), Woolley (trout, leave from Mr. Shackell, Manor Farm), Larkhall, and Lambridge (leave from the millers). 1 *m.* below Bath, Newton brook joins Avon on left bank, which rises in Priston mill, and is 4 *m.* long. 2 *m.* down Avon the outflow of the lakes in Newton Park, 1 *m.* up, joins on left bank. Avon runs in 1 *m.* to **Kelston** and **Saltford.** 3 *m.* down, Boyd river joins on right bank. Boyd rises by Dodington (n.s. **Yate,** 7 *m.*), and in 4 *m.*, at Doynton (trout; private), is joined on right bank by Feltham brook, which rises above Pucklechurch (n.s. **Mangotsfield,** 2 *m.*), and is 3 *m.* long. Boyd, in 1½ *m.*, waters the lake in Wick Court (n.s. **Warmley,** 2 *m.*), and flows to **Bitton,** 3 *m.*, and Avon, 1 *m.* Avon runs to **Keynsham,** 2 *m.* Here Chew river joins on left bank. Chew rises at Chewton Mendip (n.s. **Hallatrow,** 4½ *m.*), runs to West Harptree 4 m. (n.s. **Clutton,** 5 *m.*) (fair trouting; preserved), Chew Stoke 4 *m.* (good trouting; preserved). Here a stream joins on right bank, which rises by Stowey Mill, 3 *m.* off (n.s. **Clutton,** 2½ *m.*). Chew runs to Chewton Magna 2 *m.* (roach, trout, perch; private; the Bristol Waterworks Co. here own a reservoir holding perch, roach, trout; and here a stream joins on left bank, which works the powder mills at Winford 2 *m.* up. Chew 2 *m.* down is joined on left bank by a stream working a mill 2 *m.* up. 1 *m.* down Chew is **Pensford.** 1 *m.* down, the outflow of the lakes in Hounstrete Park, 1½ *m.* up, joins on right bank. Hence to **Keynsham** and Avon is 5 *m.* 1 *m.* down Avon, Siston brook joins on right bank. Siston rises by **Mangotsfield,** runs to **Warmley** 2 *m.*, **Bitton** 2½ *m.*, and Avon 1 *m.* Avon in 4 *m.* is joined on left bank by a brook rising above **Brislington** 2 *m.* up. Avon reaches **Bristol** in 2 *m.* (*c.s.*) Ashton brook, 5 *m.* long, joins Avon at **Long Ashton Station** on left bank.

FROME river here joins Avon on right bank. Frome rises by Chipping Sodbury (n.s. **Yate,** 2 *m.*), runs 5 *m.* to **Yate,** 3 *m.* to **Iron Acton** (preserved below by Clifton Angling Society). 1 *m.* down, Laden river joins on right bank. Laden rises by **Wickwar,** and in 4 *m.* passes 1 *m.* E. of **Tytherington,** and 4 *m.* down joins Frome. 4 *m.* down, Frome (n.s. **Filton,** 3 *m.*) Bradley brook joins on right bank. Bradley (trout and coarse fish) rises by Alveston (n.s. **Thornbury,** 3 *m.*), runs 4 *m.*, and is joined on right bank by Stoke brook, 3 *m.* long. Bradley joins Frome 4 *m.* down. 3 *m.* down Frome the drainings of the Duchess pond in Stoke Park, ½ *m.* up, joins on right bank (n.s. **Fish Ponds,** 1½ *m.*). 2 *m.* down Frome is **Stapleton Road Station,** and 2 *m.* down is **Bristol.** *Tackleists:* O'Handlen & Co. (*See Advt.*) In Grosvenor pond is good jacking; leave from T. E. M. Marsh, Esq., Grosvenor.

Brixham (Devon).—G.W.R. Brixham brook. This stream runs by Churston Ferrers, and is 3 *m.* long. Many large bass are caught at the trawlers' moorings. Dabs and mackerel in the bay, pollack along the rocky shore to Bury Head, and beyond, especially at and around the Cod Rock; enormous shoals of bass are often seen here, from high water and during the ebb. Bream and conger also round this rock. (*See* also *Paignton* and *Torquay.*)

Brixworth (Northton).—L. & N.W.R. Nen. Calender brook. (*See Wisbeach.*)

Broadbottom (Cheshire).—G.C.R. Etherow. (*See Runcorn.*)

Broad Clist (Devon).—L. & S.W.R. Clist. South brook. Halbrook brook. (*See Topsham.*)

Brock (Lancs.)—L. & N.W.R. Brock river. Calder river, 2 *m.* N. Blay brook, 2 *m.* W. Woodhampton brook, 2 *m.* W. Barton brook, 3 *m.* S.E. Wyre, 3 *m.* N.W. (*c s, Lune.*) (*See Fleetwood.*)

Brockenhurst (Hants).—L. & S.W.R. (*See Lymington.*)

Brocklesby (Lincoln).—G.C.R. Ulceby beck. *Lakes*: Newsham Abbey. (*See Ulceby.*)

Bromfield (Salop).—S. & H.R. Teme; grayling, trout, chub, pike; permission from Lord Windsor, of Oakley Park. Onny; trout, grayling, chub, pike; strictly preserved. Corve (1½ *m.* E.); trout, grayling. Pyr brook (4 *m.* N.). *Lakes*: Decoy Pool (1½ *m.* S.W.) (*See Gloucester.*) (*c.s. Severn.*).

Bromley (Kent).—L.C. & D.R. On Ravensbourne. (*See Lewisham.*)

Bromley Cross (Lancs.)—L. & Y.R. Bradshaw brook. Tange, 1 *m.* W. (*See Runcorn.*)

Brompton (York).—N.E.R. Brompton beck. Winton beck. od beck, 4 *m.* E., at Foxton. Howell beck. 4 *m.* E. at Foxton. (*See York.*)

Bromsgrove (Worcester).—M.R. Salwarp: tront. Spadsbourne brook. *Lakes*: Tardibegge reservoir (pike, perch); preserved (*See Gloucester.*)

Bromyard (Hereford).—G.W.R. Frome. Inkstone brook. Linton brook (3 *m.*). Leddon (4 *m.*). (*See Chepstow.*)

Brooksby (Leicester).—M.R. Wreak; roach, bream, chub; preserved by the owner of Brooksby Hall. (*c.s. Trent.*) *Lakes*: Ragdale Hall lake, 3 *m.* N. (*See Gainsborough.*)

Broome (Salop).—L. & N.W.R. Clun; trout, grayling. Kempton brook. (*See Clun. Gloucester.*) (*c.s. Severn.*)

Broughton (Lancs.).—L. & N.W.R. Barton brook. Blundel or Woodplumpton brook. (*See Fleetwood.*)

Broughton-in-Furness (Lancs.).—L. & N.W.R. and M.R. On Duddon. Trout, salmon. This stream rises on the Westmorland border. After 2 *m.*, Gaitscale Gill joins on the right bank. 1 *m.* on a small stream runs in on the left bank which flows out of a small hill tarn. Mossdale Beck, ½ *m.* on, joins on the right bank. Cockley Beck, ½ *m.* further on, joins on the left bank. Some 4 *m.* on a considerable burn joins on the right bank, and 1½ *m.* beyond that Tarn Beck joins on the left bank. Tarn Beck rises on the side of Seathwaite Fells. and, after a short course, runs into Seathwaite tarn. 2½ *m.* from the lake, Long House Gill joins Tarn Beck on the left bank, and on the same side, but 1 *m.* on, a beck joins, which runs out of a hill loch. ½ *m.* beyond this, Tarn Beck joins Duddon. From this point some 3 *m.* down, Crosby Gill, some 5 *m.* in length, joins Duddon on the right bank. On the same side about 1 *m.* on, Hole House Gill joins Duddon. This stream rises in a hill loch near Fox Crags, and has a course of about 4 *m.* From the junction of Hole House Gill and Duddon to the junction of Logan Beck with Duddon on its right bank, is some 2½ *m.* 2 *m.* beyond this point, and close to the town of Broughton-in-Furness, the river Lickle joins Duddon on the left bank. This river rises in the slopes of Dunnerdale, and, after passing through a small tarn in a course of 2½ *m.*, is joined on the left bank by Apple Tree Worth Beck; 1 *m.* beyond this junction a fair beck joins on the right bank. This beck, some 1½ *m.* from its junction, on the left side going up stream, is joined by a small streamlet, which drains a small tarn lying under Stickle Pike. From the junction of this stream with Lickle to the junction of Stickle with Duddon at Broughton-in-Furness is some 3½ *m.* Leave may be sometimes had for the lower portion of the river. At Ulpha, 4 *m.* off, is a comfortable inn, The Traveller's Rest. Leave to fish is freely granted on application to the landowners. Seathwaite tarn (trout and char) and Devoke water (large trout) can also be fished from here. Below this point the Duddon runs into the estuary. Roads run by the banks of all the streams. Steers pool, 2 *m.* E. This stream rises 3 *m.* above **Woodland**, runs 3 *m.* to 2 *m.* E. of **Broughton**, and joins the estuary at **Sandside** 4 *m.* below. *Hotel*: Old King's Head.

Brownhills (Stafford).—L. & N.W.R.; M.R. Crane, 1 *m.* N.E. *Lakes*: Cannock Chase reservoir, 1 *m.* N. (*See Gainsborough.*)

Broxbourne (Herts). — G.E.R. (*See Stratford*; *Cheshunt*; *London.*) New River. Lea; trout pike, barbel, perch, dace, chub, roach, tench, carp; preserved from Currant Tree Island. *Hotel*: Crown. where tickets can be had; s.t., 42s.; bottom and jack fishing; trouting 21s. extra. D.t., bottom, 1s.; jack, 2s.; trout, 5s.; trout fishing commences on April 1st, ends August 31st. No person may fish with more than one rod and line. From the 1st of March to the 1st of August no ledger fishing with worms is allowed, nor must any lobworm or fish bait be used except by trout subscribers during that time. No fishing for jack allowed from March 15th to August 1st. No gorge fishing. No roach or dace to be taken between May 1st and June 15th. No perch to be killed between March 31st and June 15th. Some large roach have recently been taken. The fishing from Currant Tree Hole to the Aqueduct Lock at Broxbourne is private.

Broxton (Cheshire).—L. & N.W.R. Holywell brook, 1 *m.* W. (*See Chester.*)

Brundall (Norfolk).—G.E.R. Yare; roach, bream, perch; preserved by a society at Norwich. (*c.s. N. and S.*) At Coldham Hall, ½ *m.* from Brundall, is a good hotel and good fishing. *Lakes*: Surlingham Broad, leave from Mr. Pratt. (*c.s. N. and S.*) Plumpstead Hall lakes, 2 *m.* N. (*See Yarmouth.*) (*c.s. Norfolk.*)

Bruton (Somerset).—G.W.R. Brue; trout; preserved. (*c.s. Avon*) Cambe. (*See Highbridge.*)

Bubwith (York).—N.E.R. Derwent. (*c.s. York.*) (*See Wressel.*)

Buckden (York), n.s. **Bolton Abbey**, 10 *m.*—Wharfe. (*c.s. York.*) (*See York.*)

Buckenham (Norfolk).—G.E.R. Yare; bream, roach, perch, pike; boats at the inn, fishing free. The mouth of Hassingham Dyke is a good spot. (*c.s. N. and S.*) *Lakes*: Stumpshaw Broad, 1 *m.* N.W. Buckenham Broad and Hassingham Broad, 1 *m.* S.E., preserved by T. Tuck, Esq., and Sir R. Beauchamp. Rockland Broad, 1½ *m.* S.W. on other bank of river, free. (*c.s. N. and S.*) (*See Yarmouth.*)

Buckfastleigh (Devon).—G.W.R. Dart; trout, salmon; fishing preserved from Totnes (7 *m.* one bank and 4 *m.* the other) by Dart Angling Association from one field below the weir, s.t. salmon and trout 20s., w.t. 7s. 6d., d.t. 2s. 6d.; trout s.t. 10s., m.t. (after May 1) 5s., d.t. 2s.; licence from Dart Conservators also necessary. Mr. Nicholls, of Furzeleigh, has 3 *m.* of fishing for visitors staying at the house; he also issues a limited number of s.t. 2l. The sewage farm field next to Austin's Bridge is free. (*c.s.*) (*See Dartmouth.*)

Buckhurst Hill (Essex).—G.E.R. On Roding. (*See Barking.*) Fishing very poor.

Buckingham.—L. & N.W.R. Ouse; preserved by the farmers; leave readily obtained apply, previously by letter, at hotel. (*c.s. N. and S.*) Claydon, 6 *m*. *Lakes*: At Stowe (4 *m*. N.W.); leave, with sufficient notice, can usually be obtained. *Hotel*: White Hart. (*See King's Lynn*).

Bucknell (Salop).—L. & N.W.R. Teme; trout, grayling, chub; preserved by the land-owners. Redlake brook; trout. (*See Gloucester.*) (*c.s. Severn.*)

Bucknall (Stafford).—N.S.R. Trent. (*c.s.*) *Lakes*: Brookhouse mill pool. (*See Gainsborough.*)

Bude (Cornwall).—L. & S.W.R. *Hotels*: Falcon, and others. On Bude. Bude rises by Week St. Mary, runs 3 *m.*, and is joined by Langford brook on right bank, 3 *m.* long. Bude runs 3 *m.* to Marhamchurch (n.s. **Bude**), and 1 *m.* down, Stratton brook joins on right bank. Stratton rises a mile above Stratton (n.s. **Bude**, 1 *m.*), and is 5 *m.* long. Bude runs to **Bude** 2 *m.*, and joins the sea 1 *m.* down. 4 *m.* N. of **Bude** runs Sheephill brook, 5 *m.* long. There is sea fishing from the rocks. Seven miles from **Bude**, near the village of Kilkhampton, is the Tamar Lake or Reservoir, over 70 acres in extent; brown, Loch Leven, and rainbow trout; no coarse fish. Fishing excellent. Season begins March 15th, ends Sept. 30th. Fly only permitted; fish under 8 inches to be returned. Angling from bank and by wading; boat (3s. per diem) needed for deep water. The trout average ½lb., and run up to 2 or 3lb. Tickets issued by the Clerk, Urban District Council, Bude. Season, 10*l*; month, 5*l*; fortnight, 3*l*; week. 2*l*; day, 10s. The lake has been strictly preserved for private fishing for many years; this is the fourth season that angling permits have been issued. Good accommodation can be obtained in either **Bude** or Stratton (Tree Hotel); the latter is two miles nearer the water. Good dace fishing in the Bude Canal.

Budleigh Salterton (Devon).—L. & S.W.R. Good sea-fishing. Whiting, pollack, mackerel, and pout, locally known as "blains," are caught within from five minutes' to half an hour's distance from the beach. Shoals of bass are often found off the harbour's mouth at Otterton Ledge and at the Foot Clout Rock, and, if not too rough, in breezy weather, will take a fly. Mussel bait is fetched from Lympstone, on the Exe, and small fresh-water eels for pollack fishing are procurable with a finely-meshed shrimp net under stones inside the Otter mouth. Many whiting are caught late in autumn in Ladram Bay towards Sidmouth. There is 1 *m.* of free trouting in the Otter, and several miles of preserved fishing can be had by staying at the Rolle Hotel, which has one transferable ticket. (*See Ottery*).

Bugsworth (Derby).)—M.R. Black brook. Goyt or Mersey, 1 *m.* W. (*See Runcorn.*)

Buildwas (Salop).—G.W.R. Severn; pike, perch, chub, trout, grayling, dace, salmon; fishing free. Farley brook. Leighton brook (2¼ *m.* W.). *Hotel*: Abbey. (*See Gloucester.*) (*c.s.*)

Bulford (Essex).—G.E.R. On Pod's brook. (*See Maldon.*)

Bulwell (Notts).—M.R. Leen. *Lakes*: Forge Mill pond, 2 *m.* N. (*See Gainsborough.*)

Bungay (Suffolk).—G.E.R. Waveney. (*c.s. N. and S.*) *Lakes*: Ditchington Hall, 2¼ *m.* N. (*See Yarmouth.*)

Buntingford (Herts). — G.E.R. (*See Stratford.*) On Rib; trout fishing very good, mostly preserved by — Somes, Esq., of Aspeden.

Bures (Suffolk).—G.E.R. Stour; pike, perch, roach, carp, dace, bream, tench. The Stour is under the control of the Suffolk and Essex Fishery Board (A. Townshend Cobbold, Esq., hon. clerk). (*c.s.*) (*See Manningtree.*)

Burgess Hill (Sussex).—L.B. & S.C.R. On Adur; trout. (*See New Shoreham.*)

Burley (York).—G.N.R. and N.E.R. Wharfe. (*c.s. York.*) (*See York.*)

Burngullow (Cornwall).—G.W.R. Clissy. (*See St. Austell; St. Ewe*)

Burnham (Essex).—G.E.R. On Crouch. This stream rises near the village of Great Burstead. 14 *m.* down, a stream joins on the left bank, which rises near Woodham Ferris, and has a course of 4 *m.* Hence to Burnham is 12 *m.* 2 *m.* below Burnham, Roach joins Crouch. Roach rises near Rayleigh, and in 4 *m.* reaches Rochford (n.s. **Southend**, 5 *m.*), where a small brook joins on the right bank. 10 *m.* down, Roach joins Crouch, and 3 *m.* on, the sea.

Burnley (Lancs.).—Lanc. & York R. West Calder; polluted. Don. Laneshaw. Swinden. water, 1 *m.* N.E. Bran, 1 *m.* N.E. Roughlee water, 3 *m.* N.W. *Lakes*: Castle Hill lake, 3 *m.* S. (*See Padiham, Preston.*)

Burnley (York).—L. & Y.R. East Calder, 4 *m.* S.E. (*c.s. York.*) (*See Rawcliffe.*)

Burnsall (York), n.s. **Grassington**, ¾ *m.*—Wharfe; trout, grayling; preserved by Appletreewick, Barden, and Burnsall Angling Club, of 50 members, from Grassington to Barden Bridge, 9 *m.*; hon. sec., Geo. Morrell, 12, Albert-road, Saltaire; d.t. 5s., at Red Lion, Burnsall; New Inn, Appletreewick; and Barden Tower. *Hotels*: Red Lion and Fell House, Burnsall, and New Inn, Appletreewick. Conveyances from Grassington and Bolton Abbey stations. (*c.s. York.*)

Burnside (Westland).—Kent. (*c.s.*) Sprint. (*c.s. Kent.*) *Lakes*: Skelsmerg tarn, 2 *m.* N.E. Gurnal Dubs, 3m. N. (*See Kendal.*)

Burnt Mill (Essex).—G.E.R. Stort; pike, roach, &c. (*See Stratford.*)

Burscough (Lancs.).—L. & Y.R. Eller brook. (*See Hesketh Bank.*)

Burslem (Stafford).—L. & N.W.R.; M.R.; G.N.R. Fowler brook. (*See Gainsborough.*)

Burton (Northton.)—M.R. Ise. (*See Wisbeach.*)

Burton Bradstock (Dorset), n.s. **Bridport**, 3 *m.*—On Bredy. Bredy rises at Little Bredy (n.s. **Dorchester**, 7 *m.*), runs 3 *m.* to Little Cheney, and Burton Bradstock, 5 *m.* (*See c.t. Axe.*)

Burton-on-Trent (Stafford).—M.R.; G.N.R.; L. & N.W.R.; N.S.R. Trent; roach, dace, pike, perch, chub, barbel; fishing free from Stapenhill bridge to Burton bridge. (*c.s.*) Dove, 3 m. N.E.; coarse fish, pike, trout, grayling. The Sudbury and Rolleston water in Dove, which holds grayling, trout, and coarse fish, is preserved by the Burton-on-Trent Angling Association; hon. sec., Mr. R. Clarke: s.t. 40s. J. C. Perfect & Co. issue salmon and trout licences. (*c.s. Trent.*) Rolleston brook, 4 m. N. *Lakes*: Tatenhill lake, 3 m. S.W. Rolleston Hall lake, 3 m. N. Drakelow Hall lake, 3 m. S. Six lakes in Bretby Park, 4 m. S.E. Three mill ponds at Hartshorn, 5 m. S.E. Byrkley Lodge pond, 5 m. W. Repton Park lake, 5 m. N.E. on S. side of Trent. Foremark ponds, 6 m. N.E. *Hotels*: Queen's, White Hart, Station, Midland, George, and Saracen's Head. (*See Gainsborough.*)

Burton Joyce (Notts).—M.R. Trent; pike, chub, roach, salmon. (*c.s.*) Cocker beck. (*See Gainsborough.*)

Bury (Lancs.).—M.R.; L. & N.W.R.; G.N.R. Irwell. Tottington brook. Roch, 1 m. E. Blackbrook, 3 m. S.E. Naden Water. 3 m. E. *Lakes*: Mill ponds by Elton, 1 m. E. Reservoir, 1 m. S.W. (*See Runcorn.*)

Bury St. Edmund's (Suffolk).—G.E.R. Lark; trout, roach, dace, and coarse fish. Preserved by the Lark Angling Society from Mildenhall to Bury St. Edmunds. 14m.: a.t. 5s., w.t 2s. 6d., d.t. 1s. 6d., from the gen. sec., Mr. W. Howlett, Lord Mayor's Cottage, Barton Mills, Mildenhall (*c.s.* all fish, except trout and pike, March 15 to June 15 inclusive; trout, Oct. 1 to March 31 inclusive; pike, none). Trout under ½lb. to be returned to water, also other fish under following lengths: perch, 7 inches; chub, carp, tench, bream, 12 inches; roach and dace, 6 inches. *Hotels*: White Hart, Mildenhall, and Bull, at Barton Mills, Mildenhall.

Busnbury (Stafford).—L. & N.W.R. *Lakes*: Morseley Mill pond, 1 m. N.E. (*See Gains-borough.*)

Buttermere (Cumland).—Cocker; trout. (*c.s. Derwent.*) *Lakes*: Buttermere; trout, char; boats. (*c.s. Derwent.*) Crummock water; trout, char; boats. (*c.s. Derwent.*) Bleaberry tarn, 1 m. S.W. *Inns*: Victoria, Fish. (*See Cockermouth, Keswick.*)

Buxton (Derby).—M.R.; L. & N.W.R. Wye; trout. (*c.s. Trent.*) Goy, 4 m. N.W. Dane, 4 m. S.W.; trout; private. (*See Frodsham.*) Goyt or Mersey, 4 m. N.W.; fishing good. (*See Runcorn.*) Moorstone brook, 4 m. N.W. (*See Runcorn.*) Dove, 5 m. S.E., at Glutton mill. (*c.s. Trent.*) Manifold, 6 m. S.E., at **Longnor**. Chapel-en-le-Frith reservoir, 6 m. *Hotels*: Crescent, George, Lee Wood, Shakespeare. The trout and grayling fishing in Dove Dale (easily accessible from Buxton) is very good; tickets of the Izaak Walton and Peveril of the Peak, Dove Dale, and of the Ashbourne hotel proprietors. *Tackleist*, J. Banks, 37, Spring Gardens. (*See Gainsborough.*)

Buxton (Norfolk).—G.E.R. Bure; bream, roach, perch; leave freely given. *Lake*: Scotton pond, 2 m. N.E. (*See Yarmouth.*)

Byfield (Northton.).—E. & W.J.R. On Cherwell. (*See London, M.T.*) There are two reservoirs near here.

Caerleon (Monmouth).—G.W.R. Usk; salmon, trout. Llwyd. (*See Newport.*) (*c.s.*)

Calne (Wilts).—G.W.R. (*See Bristol.*) On Marden (coarse fish). River brook. Fisher's brook. *Lake* in Bowood Park; pike, perch, carp, tench, roach; leave from Lord Lansdowne.

Calthwaite (Cumland).—L. & N.W.R.—Petterill; trout. (*c.s. Eden.*) Ive, 4 m. S.W. (*See Carlisle.*)

Calverley (York).—M.R. Aire. (*c.s. York.*) (*See Rawcliffe.*)

Cam (Glo'ster).—M.R. Cam Brook. (*See Dursley.*)

Cambourne (Cornwall).—G.W.R. Gwythian brook. Gwythian rises by **Cambourne**, runs 6 m., and is joined on left bank by Gwinear brook, which rises 2 m. S.E. of **Gwinear** Station (G.W.R.), and is 5 m. long. Gwythian runs to the sea in 2 m. (*c.s. Camel.*)

Cambridge.—G.N.R. and G.E.R. Cam; coarse fish; preserved. Below Baitsbite Locks the fishing for pike, &c., is very fair, and the farther down you go the better. Good fishing for pike in the South Level Cut two days a week. Baits from D. Banham, Jesus Sluice, or Dewsbury. There is trout fishing at Linton, 9 m. off; leave must be obtained from a Fellow of Pembroke College. (*See King's Lynn.*) *Hotels*: Castle, Hoop, Bull, Red Lion.

Campden (Gloucester).—G.W.R. (*See Shipston, Gloucester.*) Knee brook.

Cannock (Stafford).—L. & N.W.R. Saredon brook. Penk, at Penkridge, 5 m. N.W. *Lakes*: Hatherton Hall lake, 1 m. W. Biddulphs pool, 2 m. E. Marston Wood ponds, 3 m. N.W. Pottal reservoir and Pottal pools, 3 m. N. Galey reservoir, 4 m. W. Norton reservoir, 4 m. S.E. Cannock Chase reservoir, 4 m. S.E. Park pool and Keepers' pool, Teddesley Park, 5 m. N.W. Upper, middle, and lower Sherbrook pools, 6 m. N. Moseley Court pond, 6 m. S.W. (*See Gainsborough.*)

Canterbury (Kent).—L.C. & D.R. and S.E.R. *Hotels*: The Rose, Fleur de Lis, County, Fountain, Fleece, Saracen's Head, and The Falstaff. (*See Sandwich.*) On Stour; trout, pike, perch, roach, tench; preserved by the Stour Fishery Association from Shalmsford to Canterbury. Trout fishing begins April 15 and ends September 30. For trouting, only the artificial fly is allowed. No trout may be killed under 13in. long, or salmon or salmon trout under 3lb. No dogs. Each member has three tickets for friends. (*c.s.*) The Lower Stour Fishery preserves Stour from Canterbury to **Sturry**; season April 1 to September 30, fly only; s.t. 39s., m.t. (July, Aug. and Sept.) 21s. of the hon. sec., F. C. Nash, Esq., 6, Westgate, Canterbury.

Cantley (Norfolk).—G.E.R. Yare; pike, roach, bream, perch; breaming good; fishing free. *Inn*: Red House. (*See Yarmouth.*) (*c.s. Norfolk.*)

Capel (Suffolk).—G.E.R. Capel brook. (*See Manningtree.*)

Carlisle (Cumland).—L. & N.W.R. ; M.R. Eden ; salmon, trout, chub. Eden rises on Millersting Common 9 *m.* N.W. from **Hawes**, and 2 *m.* down is joined on right bank by Hell Gill beck, 2 *m.* long. Eden runs 10 *m.* to **Kirkby Stephen**. Here Bigg beck, 4 *m.* long, joins just above the town, and Birkett beck, 3 *m.* long, just below the town. Two *m.* down Eden, near Winton, Scandal beck joins on left bank. Scandal rises on Kirkby Stephen Common, and 4 *m* down, at **Ravenstonedale**, is joined on left bank by Artlegarth beck, 3 *m.* long. A branch joins Artlegarth here which drains Greenside tarn, near **Ravenstonedale**. Scandal runs to **Smardale**, 3 *m.*. **Crosby Garrett**, 1 *m.*, Soulby, 1 *m.*, and Eden, 1 *m.* 1 *m.* down Eden, Belah river joins on right bank. Belah rises on Winton fell, 6 *m.* E. across country from **Kirkby Stephen**, and 5 *m.* down is joined on left bank by Greenfell beck, which rises near Greenfell Craig. 3 *m.* E. across country from **Kirkby Stephen**, and is 4 *m.* long. 1 *m.* down Belah, Argill beck, 5 *m.* long, joins on right bank. Belah runs 4 *m.* to Eden. Eden runs 1 *m.* to **Musgrave**. Here Stainmore beck joins on right bank. Stainmore rises on Musgrave fell, and 6 *m.* down at Brough (*Hotel*, Castle) is joined on left bank by Hell Gill beck, 5 *m.* long. Stainmore joins Eden 2 *m.* down. Eden runs 2 *m.* to **Warcop**, and **Ormside** 3 *m.* Here Helm beck joins on left bank. Helm, under the name of Potts, runs 2 *m.* W. of **Crosby Garrett**, and is 9 *m.* long. 1 *m.* down Eden, on the N. side of **Ormside**, Hilton beck joins on left bank. Hilton rises in Gaskill tarn on Mirton Fell 5 *m.* N.E. across country from **Appleby**. and is 7 *m.* long, passing Hilton halfway down. Eden runs to **Appleby** 2 *m.* 1 *m.* below. Hoff beck joins on left bank. Hoff is 8 *m.* long, and runs half way down within 2 *m.* of **Ormside** on right bank. Eden runs 4 *m.* to **Kirkby Thore**, and here Trout beck joins on right bank. Trout beck rises on the slopes of Mirton Fell, runs 5 *m.* to **Long Marton**. and joins Eden 3 *m.* down. Eden runs to **Temple Sowerby** 2 *m.* Here Lyvennet joins on left bank. Lyvennet rises above Crosby Ravensworth, and 8 *m.* below is joined on left bank by Leith. Leith rises 2 *m.* N. of **Shap**, runs 6 *m.* to Melkinthorp. 1 *m.* E. of **Clifton** station, 3 *m.* to **Cliburn**, and joins Lyvennet 1 *m.* below. A little above the junction a stream joins Lyvennet on left bank, which rises 3 *m.* above Newby, runs 2 *m.* to Morland, and joins Lyvennet 1 *m.* down. Lyvennet runs 2 *m.* to Eden at **Temple Sowerby** station. 2 *m.* down Eden, 1 *m.* on N. side of **Temple Sowerby**, Eller beck joins on right bank. Eller rises 5 *m.* above **Newbiggin**, and at that place is joined on left bank by Milburn beck, 5 *m.* long. Eller runs 2 *m.* to Eden. Eden runs 1 *m.* to **Culgaith**, and 2 *m.* below is joined on left bank by Eamont river. Eamont, under the name of Goldrill beck, rises in Hayes tarn 3 *m.* above **Patterdale**, and 2 *m.* down is joined on left bank by the outflow of Brothers water a short distance up (*Inn*, Brothers Water). 1 *m.* down, the outflow of Angle tarn (3 *m.* from **Patterdale**), 1 *m.* up, joins on right bank. 1 *m.* down, Burdale beck, 3 *m.* long, joins on left bank. Goldrill runs 1 *m.* to Ullswater lake and Patterdale Hotel. Here Griesdale beck joins on left bank. Griesdale rises in Griesdale tarn, and is 4 *m.* long. 1 *m.* down, by the Ullswater Hotel on the left bank. Glenridding beck joins Ullswater lake. Glenridding rises in Red tarn, and 1 *m.*, down is joined on left bank by the outflow of Keppel Cove tarn 1 *m.* up. 1 *m.* down Glenridding is the outflow of the reservoir by the Greenside mine 1 *m.* up ; Glenridding runs 2 *m.* to Ullswater. 3 *m.* down on the left bank of the lake at Glencoin Park. Ara beck, 4 *m.* long, joins. On the opposite side of the lake at How town is Farrars *Hotel*. Ullswater lake is 7 *m.* long, the river Eamont leaving it at Pooley Bridge (*Hotel*, Sun), 2 *m.* down Eamont Dacre beck, which rises on Matterdale Common, runs 4 *m.* to **Penruddock** (1 *m.* off on N. bank), and joins Eamont 4 *m.* down. Eamont runs 4 *m.* to **Penrith**, and 1 *m.* below is joined on right bank by Lowther. Lowther rises 5 *m.* above **Shap**, and 3 *m.* down is joined on left bank by Swindale beck, 6 *m.* long. 2 *m.* below. at Bampton, Hawes beck joins on left bank. Hawes rises in Blea tarn, and 1 *m.* down is joined on right bank by the outflow of Small water, 1 *m.* up. 2 *m.* below. Rigindale beck, 3 *m.* long, joins on left bank. 1 *m.* down, the combined streams form Hawes Water lake (trout), 3 *m.* long. Halfway down the lake, Measand beck, 3 *m.* long,. joins on left bank. From the exit of the lake to Lowther at Bampton is 2 *m.* Close to the junction, Hows beck, 4 *m.* long, joins on left bank. 1 *m.* down Lowther. Ghyll beck, 3 *m.* long, joins on left bank, and a little, below, on the same side, Heltondale beck, 4 *m.* long. Lowther runs 6 *m.* to **Clifton**, joining Eamont 2 *m.* below. 3 *m.* down Eamont, by St. Ninian's church, there is a pond (Whin's pond) 1 *m.* off on left bank 3 *m.* E. of **Penrith**. Hence to Eden is 2 *m.* Eden runs 2 *m.* to **Langwathby**, 2 *m.* to **Little Salkeld**. Here Briggle beck and Hunsonby beck join on right bank. Briggle, under the name of Skirwith, beck rises by Kirkland, and 2 *m.* below, at Skirwith, is joined on left bank by Blencarn beck, 3 *m.* long, the two forming Briggle beck, which runs 3 *m.* to **Langwathby** and 2 *m.* to Eden. Hunsonby beck is 6 *m.* long. Eden runs 3 *m.* to **Lazenby**. Here Glassonby beck, 4 *m.* long, joins on right bank. 1 *m.* down Eden, at Kirkoswald, Raven beck, which rises above Renwick in two branches, and is 7 *m.* long, joins on right bank. 1 *m.* down Eden, Croglin water, which rises above Croglin, and is 10 *m.* long, joins on right bank. Eden runs 4 *m* to **Armathwaite**, **Coathill**, (1 *m.* off on left bank), 5 *m.*, **Cumwhinton** 2 *m.*, **Wetheral** 2 *m.*, Warwick 1 *m.* Here Trout beck, which rises above **How Mill**, and is 4 *m.* long, joins on right bank. 1 *m.* down Eden,. Irthing joins on right bank. Irthing rises at Irthing Head on Paddaburn Moor in three branches. 8 *m.* down, Butterburn, 6 *m.* long, joins on right bank. Irthing runs to **Gilsland** 9 *m.*, **Low Row** 5 *m.*, **Brampton** (1 *m.* off on left bank), 5 *m.* Here Kingswater joins on right bank. Kings water rises in the hills some 6 *m.* N.E. of **Gilsland**, runs 5 *m.* to within 3 *m.* N.E. of **Gilsland**, and 4 *m.* below is joined on left bank by Mill beck, 3 *m.* long; hence to Walton (n.s. **Brampton** 3 *m.*) 5 *m.*, and Irthing 1 *m.* 1 *m.* down Irthing, Cam beck joins on right bank. Cam rises 3 *m.* above Kirkcambeck, and 2 *m.* down is joined on left bank by Knossen beck 3 *m.* long. Hence to Walton (1 *m.* off on left bank) is 3 *m.*, and Irthing, at Irthington Mill, 1 *m.* N.E. of **Brampton**, 2 *m.* 3 *m.* down Irthing, Gelt joins on left bank. Gelt rises on the Geltsdale Moors, and runs 8 *m.* to the railway, 2 *m.* N.E. of **How Mill**. 1 *m.* below, the outflow, 2 *m.* long, of Talkin tarn, 3 *m.* S.E. of **Brampton**, joins on right bank Hence to Irthing is 3 *m.* Irthing joins Eden 3 *m.* down. 3 *m.* down Eden, Scotby beck joins, which rises near **Coathill**, runs 2 *m.* to **Cumwhinton**, **Scotby** 3 *m.*, and joins Eden 2 *m.* down. Eden runs to **Carlisle** 4 *m.* Petterill joins on left bank. Petterill rises by Greystoke. 1 *m.* W. of **Blencow Station**, runs 6 *m.* to Catterden Mill, 3 *m.* N.W. of **Penrith**, **Plumpton** 2 *m.*, **Calthwaite** 5 *m.*, **Southwaite** 5 *m.*, **Wreay** 4 *m.*, **Cumwhinton** (2 *m.* off on right bank), 2 *m.*, and **Carlisle** and Eden 5 *m.*

BRUNSTOCK BECK, 9 *m.* long, joins Eden on right bank.

CALDEW here joins Eden on left bank. Caldew rises in Skiddaw Forest 4 *m.* N. from **Keswick**, runs 6 *m.* to Mosedale, 5 *m.* N.W. from **Troutbeck**; thence 5 *m.* to Millhouse. Here Gillcourbon beck, 4 *m.* long, joins on right bank. Caldew (trout), runs 2 *m.* to Hesket Newmarket, and 1 *m.* down is joined on right bank by Caldbeck. Caldbeck rises on Caldbeck Moor, and 3 *m.* down is joined on left bank by Parkend beck. 4 *m.* long. Caldbeck runs 2 *m.* to Caldbeck, and joins Caldew 1 *m.* below. Caldew runs to Sebergham 2 *m.*, and 4 *m.* below is joined on right bank by Roe beck. Roe rises in Inglewood Forest, and 5 *m.* down by Highbridge is joined on right bank by Ive. Ive rises in the forest 4 *m.* S.W. of **Calthwaite**, runs 4 *m.* to Ivegill, 2 *m.* S.W. from **Southwaite**, and joins Roe 1 *m.* below. Roe runs 4 *m.* to Gategill, and joins Caldew 1 *m.* below. Caldew runs to **Dalston** 2 *m.*, and 1 *m.* below is joined on right bank by Pow beck, 4 *m.* long. Caldew runs to **Cummersdale** 1 *m.*, and reaches **Carlisle** and Eden 3 *m.* further. Eden runs 2 *m.* to Grinsdale on left bank (n.s. **Kirkandrews** 1 *m.*), Beaumont (n.s. **Kirkandrews** 1 *m.*) 2 *m.*, and 2 *m.* down is joined on left bank by Powburgh beck.

POWBURGH rises by Great Orton 5 *m.* W. of **Carlisle**, runs 3 *m.* to Monkhill Lough 1 *m.* W. of **Kirkandrews**, and joins Eden 3 *m.* down. Eden runs 2 *m.* to the Estuary. Parts of Eden are preserved by the Carlisle Angling Association; s.t. for non-residents, salmon and trout, 42s., m.t. 21s., w.t. 10s. 6d., d.t. 2s. 6d.; trout only, s.t 21s., w.t. 5s. Salmon season opens Feb. 16 to Nov. 15; trout, March 1 to Oct. 1. No Sunday fishing. Sec.: T. W. Sharp, 6, Mulcaster-crescent, Stanwix. *Tackleist*, J. Strong, Castle Street. *Hotels* : County and Station, Great Central, Bush, Victoria, Red Lion.

~~Carlton (Durham)—N.E.R. Thorpe beck; trout; preserved by the Stockton Anglers' Club of 100. (See Stockton.)~~

Carlton (Notts).—G.N.R. Trent; chub, roach, pike, perch, barbel. (*c.s.*) Crosby dyke. *Lakes*: Mons pool and Cowarth pool, 2 *m.* E. (*See Gainsborough.*)

Carnerton (Cumberland).—L. & N.W.R. Derwent; trout, salmon. (*c.s.*) (*See Cockermouth.*)

Carnforth (Lancs.)—Fs. & M R. Keer. Keer rises 4 *m.* above **Borwick**, and runs into Morcambe bay 3 *m.* below by **Carnforth**.

Carshalton (Surrey).—L.B. & S.C.R. Wandle; trout. (*See London, L.T.*)

Castle Ashby (Northton.). — L. & N.W.R. Nene; pike, perch. bream. tench, &c.; preserved for the most part by Nene Angling Society (*see Northampton*). A small Association, the Earl's Barton, has about a mile of fishing on the Nene. Sywell brook, 1 *m.* W. Ashby brook, 1 *m.* S.E. *Lakes*: Castle Ashby Park, 2 *m.* S. (Lord Northampton), jack, &c.; preserved. Sywell Mill, 3 *m.* N.W. Sywell Park, 5 *m.* N.W. *Hotel*: Station. (*See Wisbeach.*)

Castle Bromwich (Warwick).—M.R. Tame. (*c.s. Trent.*) East brook. *Lake*: Plankbrook Forge pond. 1 *m.* N. (*See Gainsborough.*)

Castle Carey (Somerset).—G.W.R. Brue; trout, roach; preserved. (*c.s. Avon.*) Evercreech brook. (*See Highbridge.*)

Castle Donnington (Leicester).—M.R. Trent, 1 *m.* N. at Shardlow; pike, perch. roach, dace, barbel, salmon; preserved: s.t. 42s., from Mr. Wood, Chapel Bar, Nottingham, or at the hotels. *Hotels* : Station, Castle Arms. and Railway. (*c.s.*) (*See Weston.*) Derwent, 3 *m.* N. (*c.s. Trent.*) Breedon brook, 3 *m.* S.W. at **Tong.** (*See Gainsborough.*)

Castleford (York).—G.N.R.; N.E.R.; L. & Y.R. Aire. (*c.s. York.*) Calder. (*c.s. York.*) (*See Rawcliffe.*)

Castlehill (Devon).—L. & S.W.R. Bray : trout. (*c.s. Taw.*) (*See Barnstaple.*)

Castle Howard (York).—N.E.R. Derwent; preserved. Cram beck. *Lakes* : Castle Howard Park lake, 3 *m.* N.W. (*c.s. York.*) (*See Wressel.*)

Castle Rising (Norfolk).—n.s. **North Wootton**, 2 *m.* Babingley river, which rises in the lake at Hillington Hall, and is 9 *m.* long.

Castleton (Derby). n.s. **Chapel-en-le-Frith,** 6 m. —L. & N.W.R. and M.R. Peaks Hole water. Now, 2 m. E.; trout, grayling. Bradwall brook, 2 m. S.E. Derwent, 4 m. E. (c.s. Trent.) (See Gainsborough.)

Castleton (Lanc.)—L. & N.W.R.; G.N.R.; M.R. Roch. Sadden brook. Lakes: Marland mere, 1 m. W. (See Runcorn.)

Castleton (York).—N.E.R. Esk; trout; preserved above the junction of Commondale beck, free for about 1½ m. below. (c.s.) Danby beck; trout; private. Commondale beck; trout; private. Tower beck. 2 m. S.; trout; preserved. Basedale beck, 2 m. W.; trout; private. Stockdale beck. 5 m. S.W; trout; private. (See Whitby.)

Castor (Northton.).—L. & N.W.R.; G.N.R. Nene: pike, perch, bream, chub. &c.; preserved by Lords Huntley and Fitzwilliam, who will give an occasional day. Billing brook. Lakes: Old Field pond, 1 m. N.E.; tench; free. Milton Park, 2 m. N.E.; preserved. (See Wisbeach.)

Catfield (Norfolk).—S.E.R. Ant. Barton Broad, 1 m. W.; fishing by payment. Wormack Broad, 2 m. S. by Ludham. Catfield Broad, 2 m. S.W. (See Yarmouth.) (c.s. Norfolk.)

Catford Bridge (Kent).—S.E.R. On Ravensbourne. (See Lewisham).

Caton (Lancs.)—M.R. Lune. (c.s.) Tarn brook. Artle river. Foxdale beck, 4 m. S.E. Udale beck, 4 m. S.E. (See Lancaster.)

Cattal (York).—N.E.R. Nidd. (c.s. York.) (See York.)

Cavendish (Suffolk).—G.E.R. Stour; pike, perch, roach, carp, dace, bream, tench. Glemsford Brook, 2 m. E.; same fish; preserved. (c.s. N. and S.) (See Manningtree.)

Cawood (York), n.s. **Ulleskelf,** 4 m.—**Selby,** 4 m.; or **Riccall,** 3 m. Ouse; coarse fish; mostly free. (c.s. York.) Wharfe, 1 m. N. (c.s. York.) (See York.)

Cawston (Norfolk).—G.E.R. Blackwater brook. Lake: Blackwater, 1½ m. N. Haveringham lake. 2 m. S. (See Yarmouth.)

Caythorpe (Lincoln).—G.N.R. Brant, 2 m. W. (See Boston.)

Cayton (York).—N.E.R. Belford, 1 m. S.; coarse fish. (See Wressel.)

Chancewater (Cornwall).—G.W.R. Sevecock water. (See Truro.)

Chapel-en-le-Frith (Derby).— M.R.; L. & N.W.R. Black brook. (See Runcorn.) Now, 4 m. N.E. (See Castleton; Gainsborough.) Lakes: Tunstead reservoir, 2 m. W. (See Runcorn.)

Chapelton (Devon).—L & S.W.R. Taw; private above; below to Barnstaple, a.t. 63s. Yarnscombe brook. Chittlehampton brook (2 m.). Swimbridge water (3 m.). (c.s.) (See Barnstaple.)

Chapeltown (Yorks).—G.C.R. Blackburn brook. New beck, 2 m. N.E. Lakes: Reservoir, 2 m. N.E. (See Goole.)

Chapple (Essex).—G.E.R. Colne. (See Colchester.)

Chard (Somerset).—L. & S.W.R. (See Seaton.)

Chard Junction (Somerset).—L. & S.W.R. On Axe. Mr. Langdon, Parrock Lodge, Chard, preserves the fishing, and sometimes gives leave. (See Seaton.) (c.s. Axe.) Hotel: Tytherleigh Arms.

Charfield (Gloucester).—M.R. Little Avon; trout and coarse fish; preserved by Mr. Long. Bleworth brook. Ozleworth brook, 2 m.; trout; preserved. (See Berkeley.) (c.s. Severn.)

Charlbury (Oxford).—G.W.R. On Evenlode; trout. (See London, U.T.)

Charmouth (Dorset).—G.W.R. On Char; trout. Char is some 7 m. long, and works two or three mills. (See c.s. Axe.) General sea fishing.

Chartham (Kent). — S.E.R. On Stour; trout. (See Sandwich.) Here begins the water belonging to the Stour Fishery Association. 3 m. of the river above belongs to C. S. Hardy, Esq., who preserves strictly. Inn: Railway Tavern. (See Canterbury.) (c.s.)

Chatburn (Lancs.).—Lanc. & York R. Ribble, 1 m. W.; trout, salmon; preserved by Clitheroe Angling Association; hon. sec., J. L. Bulcock, fishing tackle depôt, Kingstreet, Clitheroe. Grindleton beck, 1 m. W. (See Preston.)

Cheadle (Cheshire).—G.N.R. Poynton brook. Mersey, 1 m. N. (See Runcorn.)

Cheadle, n.s. **Blythe,** 3 m. (Stafford).—Tean. Blythe, 3 m. S.W. Churnet, 3 m. N.E. (c.s. Trent.) Lakes: Whympney Wood pond, 2 m. N.W. (See Gainsborough.)

Cheadle Hulme (Cheshire).—L. & N.W.R. Poynton brook. (See Runcorn.)

Checker House (Notts).—M.R. Ryton. Poulter 2 m. S. Lakes: Clumber Park, 3 m. S.W. (See Althorpe.)

Chedder (Somerset).—G.W.R. Ax. Chedder water. Lakes, decoy (See Axbridge.) (c.s. Avon.)

Cheddleton (Stafford).—L. & N.W.R. and M.R. Churnet; trout, grayling, coarse fish; fishing injured by Leek drainage. (c.s. Trent.) Endon brook, 1 m. N.W. West brook, 1 m. S.E. Lakes: Pond by Wetley, 3 m. S. (See Gainsborough.)

Chelford (Cheshire).—L. & N.W.R. Peover. Bug. Birkin, 1 m. N. Lakes: Astle Hall lake, Reed's mere, and Capesthorne Hall lake, 2 m. S.E. Over Peover Hall lake, 3 m. S.W. Wicken Hall mere, 3 m. S.E. (See Frodsham; Runcorn.)

Chellaston (Derby).—M.R. Trent, 1 m. S.W. at Swarkstone; chub, dace, roach, pike, perch, barbel, salmon; preserved on S. side up to Willington by Sir F. Burdett; a.t., coarse fish 10s. 6d., ditto and salmon 21s., from Mr. Newbold, of King's Newton; below, Sir V. H. Crewe owns 1 m., and then the King's Mill Fishery commences. (See Weston.) (c.s.) Lakes: The Moor ponds by Stanton, 3 m. S.W. (See Gainsborough.)

Chelmsford (Essex).—G.E.R. Cann. Chelmer; pike, perch, roach dace, carp, tench, and, below Boreham, bream; fishing good, leave from farmers and lords of manors. (See Maldon.) There is a large pond at the Nunnery, Boreham, 3m. from Chelmsford, containing carp, tench, and roach; permission from the land steward, on the estate. 4 *m.* from Chelmsford is Mill Pond. belonging to Col. Tufnell Tyrrel, of Boreham House; leave to fish can be obtained. Good fishing can also be had at Little Baddow, 3 *m.* from Chelmsford. on the Navigation river, on payment of 1*s.* *Hotels ·* Saracen's Head. White Hart.

Cheltenham (Gloucester).—G.W.R. Chelt; trout, coarse fish. The Chelt carries a few trout in the upper reaches only; below, it is more or less polluted. An association of 25 members, whose headquarters are at the Plough Hotel, holds the fishing rights of the Whitcomb reservoirs (stocked with trout), 30 acres. A coarse fishing club (headquarters, Royal Hotel) has several miles of water in the Avon. (*See Gloucester.*) *Tackleist,* J Ogden, 28, Winchcombe-street.

Chepstow (Monmouth).—G.W.R. Wye; trout, salmon, chub, pike, dace. Mounton brook. (*See Portskewet.*) Wye rises on the slopes of Plynlimon, 10 *m.* above **Llangurig** (M.W.R.). 4 *m.* down, Tavenig, 5 *m.* long, joins on right bank. 5 *m.* down Wye, Bidno, 6 *m.* long, joins on left bank. 1 *m.* down Wye is **Llangurig**. Wye runs 8 *m.*, and is joined on left bank by Marteg, which rises 4 *m.* above **Pont-y-dwr** (N.W.R.), runs to **St. Harmon** (N.W.R.) 2 *m.*, and Wye 4 *m.* Wye runs 3 *m.* to **Rhayader** (M.W.R.). Here a stream joins on left bank, which runs out of Glan Llyn, 1½ *m.* up. 2 *m.* down Wye. Elan joins on right bank. Elan rises in Llyn Helygen (n.s. **Llangurig**, 6 *m.* cross country), and 4 *m.* down is joined on right bank by Gwngy, which rises in a lake (Llyn Gwngy) 3 *m.* up, 1 *m.* S.W. of Llyn Helygen. 2 *m.* down Elan. Hirin joins on right bank. Hirin rises in Llyn Cerrig Llwydion Uchaf (n.s. **Rhayader**, 9 *m.*), runs in 1½ *m.* to Llyn Cerrig Llwydion Isaf, and 4 *m.* down joins Elan. 8 *m.* down Elan, Clearwen joins on right bank. Clearwen rises 6 *m.* E. of **Strata Florida** (M. & M.R.), runs 2 *m.*, and is joined on left bank by Figen, which rises in Llyn Fyrddyn-fach (n.s. **Strata Florida**, 7 *m.*), runs ½ *m.* to Llyn Fyrddyn-fawr. ½ *m.* below this lake a stream 1 *m.* long joins on right bank, rising in Llyn-du, ½ *m.* S.E. of Llyn Fyrdden-fawr. Figen runs in 1 *m.* to Llyn Figen-felan (n.s. **Strata Florida**, 8 *m.*), and 3 *m.* down joins Clearwen. 2 *m.* down Clearwen, Brwynog, which rises in Llyn Gynon (n.s. **Strata Florida**, 7 *m.*) and is 3 *m.* long, joins on right bank. Clearwen runs 3 *m.*, and is joined on right bank by Arban, 3 *m.* long (n.s. **Doldowlod**, M.W.R., 8 *m.*), 3 *m.* down Clearwen, Garw, which rises in Llyn Garw (n.s. **Doldowlod**, 9 *m.*) and is 4 *m.* long, joins on right bank. 3 *m.* down Clearwen, at Capel Naut-gwylh, is Elan, which runs 4 *m.* to Wye. Wye runs 2 *m.* to **Doldowlod**, 5 *m.* to **New Bridge** (M.W.R.). 1 *m.* below, Hirnant, 4 *m.* long, joins on right bank, and Ithon on left bank. Ithon rises in Llyn Dwr (6 *m.* S. of **Newtown** (O. & N.R.), runs 6 *m.* to Abergwenlas Inn (n.s. **Pen-y-bont**, C.W.R., 10 *m.*, or **St. Hermon**, M.W.R., 8 *m.*), Llanno 4 *m.*, Llanbister 1½ *m.* 2 *m.* down, Cam-ddwr joins on left bank. This stream rises above the pound and alehouse 5 *m.* W. from **Llangynllo** (C.W.R.), and is 5 *m.* long. Ithon runs to **Pen-y-bont** (C.W.R.), and here Arran joins on left bank. Arran rises 3½ *m.* W. of **Llangynllo**, on the road to the alehouse above mentioned, runs to **Doban** (C.W.R.) 7 *m.*, and Ithon 2 *m.* 2 *m.* down Ithon, Llandegley brook, 4 *m.* long, joins on left bank, and 5 *m.* down Ithon, at Llanbadarn, 1 *m.* from **Pen-y-Bont**, Clywedog joins on left bank. Clywedog rises in Fish pool 4 *m.* E. from **St. Harmon** (M.W.R.), and 4 *m.* down is joined on left bank by Crych brook, 5 *m.* long. 5 *m.* down Clywedog is Ithon and **Pen-y-Bont**. 1 *m.* down Ithon, Camllo, 4 *m.* long, joins on right bank, and 1 *m.* down Ithon again, Dulas joins on right bank. Dulas rises by Wherby 4 *m.* S.W. of **St. Hermon**, and 4 *m.* down, at Nantmel, is joined on the right bank by a brook 1 *m.* long, draining Llyn Gwyn (2 *m.* N.W. from **Doldowlod**, M.W.R.) Dulas joins Ithon 3 *m.* down, Ithon runs to **Llandrindod** (C.W.R.) 3 *m.*, and 2 *m.* down. at Disserth, is joined on left bank by Hawddwy, 3 *m.* long. 3 *m.* down, Ithon joins Wye by **New Bridge**. 4 *m.* down Wye, at **Builth Road** (M.W.R.), Dulas. 5 *m.* long, joins on left bank. Wye runs to **Builth** 2 *m.* Here Irfon joins on right bank. Irfon rises on the Bryn Garw range, runs 6 *m.* to Llanfihangel Abergwessin, where Gwessin, 5 *m.* long, joins on right bank. 1 *m.* down, Calant, 3 *m.* long, joins on right bank. Irfon runs to **Llanwrtyd** 4 *m.*, and 2 *m.* down by the railway is joined by Cerdin, 5 *m.* long, on left bank. 1 *m.* down, Cledan, 3 *m.* long, joins on right bank. Irfon runs 3 *m.* to **Llangammarch** (preserved by the Llangammarch Wells Angling Association). Here Dulas, 8 *m.* long, joins on right bank. 1½ *m.* down, Annell, 3 *m.* long, joins on right bank, and Camddur, 4 *m.* long, on left bank. Cammarch joins ½ *m.* down on left bank. Cammarch rises on Coraigan-duon, runs 5 *m.*, and is joined on right bank by Cnyffiad, 4 *m.* long. 3 *m.* down Cammarch Einon. 3 *m.* long, joins on right bank, and 2 *m.* down Cammarch joins Irfon. Irfon runs 2 *m.* to **Garth**. Here Dulas joins on left bank. Dulas rises 8 *m.* N. from **Garth**, and 4 *m* down is joined on left bank by Gwenwest. 4 *m.* long. Irfon runs to **Cilmeri** 4 *m.* (C.W.R.), and 2 *m.* below, close to **Builth**, is joined on right bank by Cueiddon, 2 *m.* long. 1 *m.* down Irfon, Chwefrn joins on left bank. Chwefrn rises 4 *m.* S.W. of **Doldowlod** (M.W.R.), runs 4 *m.* to Llanafan-fawr, and 5 *m.* to Irfon, which joins Wye just below at **Builth**. 2 *m.* down Wye, at Llanfaredd, Dihonw joins Wye on right bank. Dihonw rises 3 *m.* S.W. of **Garth** (C.W.R.) at Ffrwd-wen, and is 6 *m.* long. Wye runs 3 *m.* to **Aberedw** (M.W.R.). Here Edw joins on left bank. Edw rises at Rowton 2 *m.* S. of Llandegley, 3 *m.* from **Pen-y-Bont** (C.W.R.), and 3 *m.* down. at Rhos-maen, is joined on left bank by a stream 2 *m.* long, which drains Llyn Melan, 4 *m.* S.W. of **New Radnor** (L. & K.R.), at Llanfihangel-nant-Melan. Edw runs 2 *m.* to Bettws Disserth, and 2 *m.* below, at the

Hundred House, Camnant, which rises 4 m. N.E. of **Builth,** and is 4 m. long, joins on right bank. ½ m. down Edw is Cregrina, and 1 m. down, at Glan Edw. Rhulen brook, 2 m. long, which rises in the Llyn pools 5 m. N.E. from **Aberedw,** joins on right bank. Edw runs to Llanbadaen-y-Garreg 2m., and 1 m. down is joined on right bank by Baili brook, which rises by Pen-blaen, 2½ m. from **Builth,** and 3 m. down is joined on right bank by a stream 2 m long, which drains Llyn Cawr, and another tarn 3 m. N. from **Aberedw.** 1 m. down is Edw, which runs in 2 m. to **Aberedw** and Wye. Wye runs to **Erwood** (M.W.R.) 3 m. Here Llogin joins on right bank, running out of Llyn Llogin. 6 m. up, 1 m. down Wye, Bach-howey brook joins on left bank. This brook rises near Pant, 6 m. from **Aberedw,** and 5 m. down at Llanddewi-fach is joined on right bank by a stream which rises in 2 small pools on Llanbedr Hill 2½ m. E. of **Aberedw,** runs 1 m. to Llyn Llanbychllyn (n.s. **Aberedw** or **Erwood** 3 m), and 1 m. down joins Bach-howey; Wye is 3 m. down. Wye runs 1 m. and is joined on right bank by Cunrig, 5 m. long Wye runs to **Boughrood** (M.W.R.) 2 m. and **Glasbury** (H.H. & B.R.) 4½ m. Here Llyfni joins on right bank. Llyfni rises at Middlewood 2 m. E. of Llansaintffraed or **Tal-y-bont** (B. & M.T.Y.R.), and runs 2 m. to Llyn Saffada or Llangorse, 1 m. E. of **Tal-y-Llyn Junction** (M.W.R.), 3 m. down at Llandevailog, Cwm brook, 2 m· long joins on left bank, and **Trefeinon** (M.W.R.) is 1 m. on. Llyfni runs to **Talgarth** (M.W.R.) 3 m. Enig here joins Llyfni on right bank and Dulais brook on left bank. Enig is 4 m. long. and is joined close to the town by 2 short branches. Dulais is 7 m. long, and 2 m. from Talgarth is joined on left bank by Treffrwd brook, 5 m. long. Llyfni runs 2 m. to **Three Cocks Junction** (H.H. & B.R.), and 1 m. down joins Wye at **Glasbury.** Wye runs to **Hay** (H.H. & B.R.) 5 m. (where Dulas brook, 4 m. long, joins on right bank), and **Whitney** (H.H. & B.R.) 5 m. 6 m. down, at Willersley (N.S. **Bardisley** 1 m), Upcot brook joins, which rises in the lakes in Newport House Park and Upcot, by **Almeley** (H.H. & B R.), runs 1 m., and is joined on right bank near **Eardisley** (H.H. & B.E.), by Holywell brook, 2 m. long, Upcot runs to Wye 2½ m. 1 m. down Wye, by Letton, Letton Lake, which rises by **Almeley,** runs 2 m. to **Kinnersley** (H.H. & B.B.), and Wye, 5 m., joins on left bank. Wye runs to Monnington 4 m., **Credenhill** (2 m. off the river, H.H. & B.B.), 6 m. 2 m down, near Eaton Bishop, **Gage** brook joins on right bank. Gage rises by Kingston, 3 m. W. from **Tram Inn Station** (N.A. & H.R.), and is 4 m. long. Wye runs to **Hereford** 4 m. Here Withy brook, 4 m. long, joins on right bank, and Sugwas brook on left bank. Sugwas brook rises 1 m. N.W. of **Moorhampton** (H.H. & B.R.), runs 6. m. to **Credenhill** (H.H. & B.R.), and Hereford 5 m. 3 m. down Wye, Red brook, 3 m. long, joins on right bank, and 1 m. down Wye is **Holme Lacy,** and 1 m. below, Lugg joins on left bank at Mordiford. Lug rises in a pool on Pool Hill 5 m. above **Llangynllo** (C.W.R.), and 3 m. below that place is joined on right bank by Graig brook. which rises in Graig Pool 3 m. E. of **Dolaw** (C.W.R.), runs 2 m. to Bleddfa, just below which Bleddfa brook joins on left bank, which rises in a pool 2 m. S.W. of **Llangynllo,** and is 3 m. long. Craig runs to Lug 2 m. Lug runs 6 m, to **Presteign,** where Boullibrook, 3 m. long, joins on left bank. 2 m. down Lug, Summergill brook joins on right bank. Summergill rises by Llanfihangel-nant Melan, 4 m. above **New Radnor.** At **New Radnor** it is joined on left bank by Black brook, 3 m. long. Summergill runs 4 m. to Knill, 3 m. to **Presteign** (1 m. off on N. bank), and 2 m. down joins Lug. Lug runs to Kinsham 2 m., where is the water of the Lyepool Club of 10 members. Below this water to Aymestrey is the Yatton Court, preserved by T. B. Ward, Esq. Lug then runs to Mortimer's Cross; trout, grayling: in private hands, and strictly preserved; particulars of Lyepool Club water of Percy Wilkinson, Esq., Shobdon R.S.O., Hereford; **Kingsland** 2 m., and **Leominster** 4 m. Here Pinsley brook joins on right bank, Ridgemore brook and Stretford brook on left bank. Pinsley rises above the Lady pools in Shobdon marshes (Lord Bateman), 1 m. from **Pembridge,** runs 3 m. to **Kingsland,** and Lug 4 m. Ridgemore rises in a series of ponds by Croft Castle, runs to **Eye** 3 m., and **Leominster** 4 m. Stretford brook rises by Cornford 6 m. N.E. from **Leominster,** runs 3 m., and is joined on left bank by Pudleston brook, which drains the lake at Pudleston 2 m. up. Stretford runs 4 m. to **Leominster,** where Cogwell brook, which rises above Kimbolton, and is 3·m. long, joins on right bank. 2 m. down Lug. Arrow joins on right bank. Arrow rises in Mann pools, lying 1½ m. N.E. of the Llyn pools, 6 m. N.E. of **Aberedw,** runs 3 m., where it is joined by a stream 3 m. long on left bank. 3 m. down Arrow. at Newchurch, 4 m. from **Whitney,** Cwm-illa brook, 3 m. long, joins on right bank. Arrow runs 8 m. to **Kington,** where Gilwern brook joins on left bank. Gilwern rises 6 m. above **Dolhier,** where it is joined by Cynon brook, 3 m. long, on left bank, and Hales brook, 2 m. long, on right bank. Gilwern runs to **Stanner** 2 m., and **Kington** 2 m. Arrow runs to **Titley** 2 m., **Pembridge** 5 m., Eardisland 3 m. (there are coarse fish below here), Monkland 3 m. (fishing poor, but decent quarters, strictly preserved by Capt. Curtis), and Broadward Bridge, 1½ m. from **Leominster,** 2 m. Here Stretford brook joins on right bank. Stretford rises by Weobly (n.s. **Moorhampton,** 3½ m.), and 5 m. down, at Stretford, is joined on left bank by Tippets brook, which rises 2 m. S. of **Pembridge,** and is 6 m. long. Stretford joins Arrow 5 m. down. Arrow runs in 1 m. to Lug, which runs to **Ford** 1 m., and 2 m. down, at Hampton Court, is joined on left bank by Humber brook, which· rises 4 m. above Steens Bridge, 3 m. from **Leominster,** runs 4 m.

to the lake in Hampton Park, and 1 *m.* to Lug. 1 *m.* down Lug, Marston brook, which rises by Marston Chapel, 4 *m.* from **Ford**, and is 4 *m.* long, joins on left bank. Lug runs to Bodenham 1 *m.*, **Dinmore** 1 *m.*, Maiden 3 *m.* Here Derndole brook, which rises by Kings Pion and is 6 *m.* long, joins on right bank. Lug runs to **Moreton-on-Lug** 1 *m.*, and 4 *m.* down at Lug Bridge, 2 *m.* from **Hereford**, is joined on left bank by Sutton brook, which rises by Ullingswick, runs 5 *m.* to Sutton St. Nicholas (n.s. **Moreton-on-Lug**, 2¼ *m.*), and Lug 3 *m.* 4 *m.* down Lug, at Hampton Bishop, (n.s. **Holme Lacy**, 2 *m.*), Frome joins on left bank. Frome rises 8 *m.* above **Bromyard**, where it is joined on right bank by Inkstone brook, 5 *m.* long. Frome runs 3 *m.*, and is joined on left bank by Linton brook, 2 *m.* long. Frome runs to Bishops Frome 3 *m.* and Stretton Grandison 4 *m.* (n.s. **Ashperton**, 2½ *m.*). Here Leddon joins on right bank. Leddon rises by Grendon Bishop 4 *m.* W. from **Bromyard**, runs to Stoke Lacy 5 *m.* (n.s. **Bromyard**, 4 *m.*), and Frome 6 *m.* Frome runs to Yarkhill (n.s. **Stoke Edith**, 1 *m.*), and Lug 5 *m.* Lug runs to Mordiford 1 *m.* (n.s. **Holme Lacy**, 2 *m.*), and here Pentelow brook joins on left bank, rising in three lakes in Devereux Park (n.s. **Ashperton**, 4 *m.*), and is 4 *m.* long. Just below Mordiford Lug joins Wye. (The best flies for Lug and tributaries are March brown, duns of various shades, grannam, and willow fly.) Wye runs to Fownhope 3 *m.*, **Fawley** (H.R. & G.R.), to the N., 5 *m.*, and 2 *m.* down, Wriggle brook, 4 *m.* long, joins on right bank. Wye runs to Sellock Ferry 2 *m.*, and **Fawley** to the S. 2 *m.* 1 *m.* down, Sollers brook, 4 *m.* long, joins on left bank. Wye runs to **Ross** (H.R. & G.R.) 6 *m.* Here Rudhall brook joins on left bank. Rudhall rises by **Mitcheldean Road Station** (H. & G.R.), and is 8 *m.* long. Wye runs to **Kerne Bridge** (R. & M.R.) 5 *m.*, where Castle brook, rising in some ponds at Weston-under-Penyard, 2 *m.* from **Mitcheldean Road Station**, and is 5 *m.* long, joins on left bank. Wye runs to **Simmonds Gate** (R. & M.R.). Here the river makes a large horseshoe, and at the head of the curve, 2 *m.* down (n.s. **Kerne Bridge**, 2 *m.*), Garron joins on right bank. Garron rises by Orcop (n.s. **Pontrilas** (N.H. & H.R., 6 *m.*), and 6 *m.* down is joined on left bank by Llanwarne brook, which rises by Llanwarne (n.s. **Fawley**, H.R. & G.R., 5 *m.*). 3 *m.* down, the outflow of Trewarthen pool, ¼ *m.* up, joins on left bank (n.s. **Ross**, 7 *m.*). 4 *m.* down is Garron. 1 *m.* down, at Llangarron, Lammerch brook, 2 *m.* long, joins on right bank (n.s. **Ross** or **Kerne Bridge**, 5 *m.*). 5 *m.* down Garron, Luke brook, which rises by Everston, 4 *m.* from **Ross**, and is 4 *m.* long, joins on left bank (n.s. **Kerne Bridge**, 2 *m.*). Garron runs to Wye 1 *m.* Wye runs back again 2 *m.* to **Simmonds Gate**, and reaches **Monmouth** in 6 *m.* Monnow and Trothy here joins Wye. Monnow rises by Craswall Chapel, 6 *m.* S.E. from **Hay**, runs to Longtown (n.s. **Pandy**, N.A. & H.R., 5 *m.*), and here Eseley brook joins on left bank. Eseley rises on Cusop Hill, 5 *m.* S.E. from **Hay**, runs 4 *m.* to Michaelchurch Eseley, and Longtown 4 *m.* 1 *m.* down Monnow, at Clodock, 4 *m.* from **Pandy**, Olchon brook joins on right bank. Olchon rises on the N.E. slopes of the Black Mountains, 8 *m.* from **Hay**, runs 3 *m.* to Llanveyno and 3 *m.* to Clodock. Monnow runs to **Pandy** 4 *m.* Here Honddu joins on right bank. Honddu rises on the W. slope of the Black Mountains (n.s. **Glasbury**, 7 *m.*), runs 3 *m.* to Capel-y-ffin, Llanthony 4 *m.* (here tickets can be had for a length of water from the Llanthony Abbey Inn, which has two tickets attached), **Llanfihangel** (W.A. & H.R.), 6 *m.*, and **Pandy** 2 *m.* Monnow runs 4 *m.* to Langua, 1 *m.* from **Pontrilas** (N.A. & H.R.), and here Rowlston brook, 2 *m.* long, joins on left bank. 1 *m.* down Monnow, at **Pontrilas**, Dore joins on left bank. Dore rises 2 *m.* above Dorston, 5 *m.* E. from **Hay**, runs to Peterchurch 3 *m.*, and **Pontrilas** 8 *m.* Here Worm Brook joins on left bank, and Dulas brook on right bank. Worm brook rises in the ponds at Allenmore House, 1 *m.* N. from the **Tram Inn Station** (N.A. & H.R.), runs to **Devereux** (N.A. & H.R.) 4 *m.*; here a stream joins on right bank, draining a pond 2 *m.* up. 4 *m.* down is Pontrilas and Dore. Dulas brook is 5 *m.* long. Dore joins Monnow just below. Monnow runs 8 *m.* to Skenfrith (fair fishing, accommodation at the inn), where Black brook, which rises in some ponds at Black-brook House, 6 *m.* from **Pontrilas**, and is 3 *m.* long, joins on right bank. Monnow runs to Rockfield 6 *m.* and **Monmouth** 3 *m.* Here Trothy joins Wye on right bank. Trothy rises 2 *m.* above Llanfetherine, 5 *m.* N.E. from **Abergavenny**, and is here joined on right bank by Full brook, which rises 2 *m.* S.E. of **Pandy** by Great Campstone, and is 3 *m.* long. 4 *m.* down Trothy, Mynachdy brook (trout), which rises by Llanddewi Skirrid, 3 *m.* N.E. of **Abergavenny**, and 4 *m.* down by Llanvapley is joined by a brook on right bank 3 *m.* long. 1 *m.* down, Mynachdy joins Trothy. Trothy runs to Llantillio 2 *m.*, Llanfihangel Istern Llewertt 3 *m.* (n.s. **Dingestow**, 4 *m.*). Here Llumon (trout), 4 *m.* long, joins on left bank. Trothy runs 1 *m.*, and is joined on right bank by Nant-y-fuchan, 3 *m.* long (n.s. **Dingestow**). Trothy runs to **Dingestow** 2 *m.*, and **Monmouth** and Wye 5 *m.* Wye runs to **Redbrook** 2 *m.*, **Bigsweir** 5 *m.*, **Tintern** 3 *m.*, and **Chepstow** 8 *m.* The best flies for trout in Wye are Mayfly, Carshalton cocktail, March brown, coch-y-bonddhu, and duns of various shades; orle, orange palmer, spider, and rough red palmer. The Wye salmon flies are chiefly made with bittern hackle wing, with a greenish yellow (blue dun dyed yellow) hackle from head to tail and a pretty full body of orange floss silk, one golden pheasant topping over the bittern's wing; tail, sprigs of bright red parrot or ibis, mixed with a like amount of wood-duck. The same fly with a lemon-yellow body or blue dun hackle and silver tinsel is good. Then salmon-coloured bodies with the same wings and hackle varied. The Welsh fly, made with brown turkey or bittern wing, is the best general fly that can be used. Sometimes the body and hackle are varied from the real blue cock's hackle and tawny body to bright yellow or red with claret body; but the yellow brown wing remains the same. The Butcher, Priest, and Blue Doctor are now commonly used. *Hotel*: Beaufort Arms. ·

Chequerbent (Lancs.).—L. & N.W.R. Croal. *Lakes*: Hulton Park lake. 1 *m.* S.E. (*See Runcorn.*)

Cherry Tree (Lancs.).—(L. & Y.R ; L. & N.W.R. Darwen. (*See Preston.*)

Chertsey (Surrey).—L & S.W.R. (*See London. L.T.*) Thames: pike, perch, chub, roach, bream, trout. *Hotels*: Cricketers, Bridge. *Fishermen*: J. Chapman, H. Vickery, and L. Hackett; address, care of Cricketers' Hotel. Good fishing also in Abbey river, a branch which runs out of Thames at Penton Hook, and runs in at Chertsey Weir. The best fishing on the Abbey river is in the hands of the Chertsey Angling Association ; tickets 1*s.*, from the Hon. Sec., C. H. Lovett, or at the Cricketers' Hotel.

Cheshunt (Herts).—G.E.R. (*See Stratford.*) On Lea and New River. The King's Weir Fishery on the old river Lea from the end of the Government Powder Mill stream. **Waltham**, to the **Broxbourne** Fishery, is preserved. It is very good. (*See London, Waltham, and Broxbourne.*)

Chester.—L. & N.W.R.; G.W.R. ; M.R. Dee. Dee, under the name of Lliw, rises in the Merioneth hills, 8 *m.* above **Llannwchllyn**, and 4 *m.* from its source (4 *m.* above **Llannwchllyn**) is joined on left bank by Afon-yr-Wynt, 3 *m.* long. At **Llannwchllyn**, Dwfrdwy, 5 *m.* long, joins Lliw on right bank. ¼ *m.* below. Twrch, 6 *m.* long, joins Lliw on right bank. 3 *m.* up Twrch, above the railway, a stream joins on left bank, draining Llyn Ulwbran 3 *m.* S. of **Llannwchllyn**. ½ *m.* down, Lliw runs into Bala lake. ¼ *m.* down the lake, 2 *m.* from **Llannwchllyn**, Llafar, 5 *m.* long, joins on left bank, and on the opposite side of the lake, 2 *m.* from **Llannwchllyn**, Rhydwen, 4 *m.* long, runs in. Bala lake is 3 *m.* long, and at the lower end lies **Bala**, and here the river takes its proper name. At **Bala** Tryweryn joins Dee on left bank. Tryweryn rises in Llyn Tryweryn, 3 *m.* above **Arenig**, and 1 *m.* below **Arenig** is joined on right bank by a brook draining Llyn Arenig 1 *m.* up. 1 *m.* below, at Pont-a-Gelyn, Gelyn. which rises in Llyn Arenig-bach, 1½ *m.* N. of **Arenig** station, and is 3 *m.* long, joins on right bank (*see Arenig*). Tryweryn runs 3 *m.*, when Hescyn, which rises in Llyn Heccyn, and is 3 *m.* long, joins on left bank. Tryweryn runs to **Frongoch** 1 *m.*, and here two streams, each 3 *m.* long, join, one on left bank and one on right bank. Tryweryn runs to **Bala** and Dee 3 *m.* 1 *m.* down Dee, 1 *m.* N.E. of **Bala**, at Llanfer, Corgnant, 2 *m.* long, joins on left bank, and 1 *m.* further on, on same side, is Meloch, 4 *m.* long. On the opposite side of Dee, 2 *m.* from Bala, Hirnant, 5 *m.* long, joins the main stream. 2 *m.* up from the junction of Hirnant and Dee, Cymmerig, 2 *m.* long, joins Hirnant on left bank. Dee runs 2 *m.*, when Calettwr, 3 *m.* long, joins on right bank. Dee runs 1 *m.* to **Llandderfel**, and **Llandicillo** 3 *m.* Here Cendiog, 3 *m.* long, joins on right bank. ½ *m.* down Dee a stream joins on left bank, 2 *m.* long, draining Llyn Mynyllod, 3 *m.* N. of **Llandicillo**. At the same spot, but on right bank of Dee, 1 *m.* N.E. of **Llandicillo**, Llynor, 4 *m.* long. runs in. Dee runs 2 *m.* to **Cynwyd**, where begins the water preserved by Corwen Fishing Association, and here Trystion, 3 *m.* long, joins on right bank. 1 *m.* down Dee, at Llangar, Alwen joins on left bank. Alwen rises in Llyn Alwen 9 *m.* E. of **Bettws-y-Coed**. 5 *m.* down it is joined on right bank by outflow of Llyn-dau-Ychen ¼ *m.* up, 3 *m.* N. of **Cerrig-y-Druidion**, and 2 *m.* further down is joined on left bank by Brenig, which rises in Llyn Llymbran 9 *m.* S.W. from **Denbigh**, and is 6 *m.* long. Alwen runs to **Llanfihangel Glyn Myfyr**, 6 *m.* W. of **Derwen**. Here Derwydd, 3 *m.* long, joins on left bank. Alwen runs to Bettws Gwerful Goch, 3 *m.* W. of **Gwyddelwern**. 2 *m.* down Alwen, at **Maerdy**, 5 *m.* W. of **Corwen**, Geirw joins on right bank. Geirw rises 5 *m.* W. of **Cerrig-y-Druidion**, 10 *m.* N.W. of **Corwen**, runs to 1 *m.* S. of the place, and 3 *m.* down is joined on the right bank by a brook 5 *m.* long, which runs down by Llangwin, 8 *m.* N.W. from **Corwen**. 2 *m.* down Geirw, Merddwr, which rises in Llyn Grwyni, 3 *m.* N. from **Llandderfel** and is 4*m.* long, joins on right bank. 1 *m.* down, Geirw joins Alwen at **Maerdy**. Alwen runs 3 *m.*, when F'franan, 4 *m.* long, joins on right bank 1 *m.* below the Druid Inn, and 1 *m.* down, Alwen joins Dee at Llangar. ½ *m.* down Dee, Dwr, which rises above **Gwyddelwern** and is 4 *m.* long, joins on left bank. Dee runs to **Corwen** 1 *m.* Here Trewyn, 2 *m.* long, joins on left bank, and Camladd, 2 *m.* long, on right bank. Dee runs 1 *m.* to Llansantffraid, and here Llechog, 2 *m.* long, joins on right bank. Dee runs to **Carrog** 1 *m.*, where the C.F. Association ends and the Glyndwr Society begins, and here Morwynion, 7 *m.* long, joins on left bank. Dee runs to **Glyndyfrdwy** 3 *m.*, **Berwyn** and **Llantisilio** 6 *m.* ½ *m.* below, Berwyn, 4 *m.* long, joins on left bank. Dee runs to **Llangollen** 1 *m.* (and 2 *m.* above the town the G. Society's fishing ends, and the Llangollen Trout and Grayling Preservation Society begins), **Trevor** 4 *m.*, **Cefn** 2 *m.* (here ends the L.T. and G.P. Association's fishing), and 2 *m.* down is joined on left bank by a stream draining the lake at Wynnstay Park by **Ruabon** 1 *m.* up. 1½ *m.* down Dee, 2 *m.* from **Cefn** station, Ceiriog joins on right bank. Ceiriog rises in the hills 4 *m.* S. of **Carrog** (a bridle path leads to it), runs to Llanarmon 3 *m.*, Llansantffraid Glyn Ceiriog, 3 *m.* S. of **Llangollen**, 5 *m.*, and 5 *m.* down, at Castle Mill, is joined on left bank by the outflow, 1 *m.* long, of the lake in Chirk Park. Ceiriog runs to **Chirk** 2 *m.*, and 2 *m.* down is joined on right bank by

Morlas, which rises by Selattyn, 2 *m.* S.W. of **Prysgwaen**, runs by **Prysgwaen**, and joins Ceiriog 3 *m.* below. 1 *m.* down, Ceiriog joins Dee. 3 *m.* down Dee, Shell brook, which rises 2 *m.* N.W. of **Ellesmere** and is 3 *m.* long, joins on right bank. Dee runs to Overton 2 *m.* (station, **Overton-on-Dee**), runs to Bangor 5 *m.* (station, **Bangor-on-Dee**). 1 *m.* down Dee, Mill brook, 3 *m.* long, joins on right bank, and 1 *m.* below, at Pickhill Hall, 5 *m.* E. of **Wrexham**, Clywedog joins on left bank. Clywedog rises in Llyn Maur-y-Mynydd, 5 *m.* S.W. of **Brymbo**, or 7 *m.* W. of **Wrexham**, runs 3 *m.* to Miners, and 5 *m.* down, 1 *m.* S. of **Wrexham**, is joined on right bank by Saddle brook, 5 *m.* long. 1 *m.* down Clywedog, 1 *m.* S.E. of **Wrexham**, Wrexham brook, 5 *m.* long, joins on left bank. Clywedog runs to Dee 6 *m.* Dee runs 1 *m.*, when Worthenbury brook joins on right bank. Worthenbury rises in Llyn Bedydd, 2 *m.* N.E. of **Bettisfield**. 1 *m.* below, the outflow of Hanmer Hall lake, 3 *m.* N. of **Bettisfield**, joins on left bank. 2 *m.* down Worthenbury the outflow of Hanmer mere, 2½ *m.* N. of **Bettisfield**, joins on left bank. 1 *m.* down Worthenbury a stream joins on left bank, draining the lakes at Bettisfield Park, 1½ *m.* N. of **Bettisfield**. Worthenbury runs 3 *m.* to Halghton Mill and ponds, 6 *m.* N.W. from **Penn's Bank**. Here Halghton brook, which rises 2 *m.* above Penley, 4 *m.* N. of **Ellesmere**, and is 5 *m.* long, joins on left bank. 2 *m.* down Worthenbury, at Worthenbury, Sarn joins on right bank. Sarn rises in Wolvesacre Mill pond, 2 *m.* N.W. of **Whitchurch**, runs 1 *m.* to Dirtwich Mill pond, 3 *m.* N.W. of **Whitchurch**, and joins Worthenbury 7 *m.* down. Worthenbury runs 1 *m.* to Dee. Dee runs 7 *m.* to Holt (n.s. **Rossett**, 2 *m.*), and 2 *m.* down Alyn joins on left bank. Alyn rises above Llandegla (*Inn*, Crown), 7 *m.* N. of **Llangollen**, or 6 *m.* E. of **Byearth**. Here Rhys, 3 *m.* long, joins on right bank. 3 *m.* down, at Llanarmon, 5 *m.* E. of **Byearth**, or 5 *m.* S.E. of **Ruthin**, a brook 2 *m.* long joins on right bank, which drains Llyn Cyffynny, 7 *m.* S.E. of **Ruthin**, or 7 *m.* E. of **Byearth**. Alyn runs 3 *m.* to Llanferres, 6 *m.* E. of **Ruthin**, and **Rhyd-y-Mwyn** 6 *m.* Here Fechlas brook, 3 *m.* long, joins on left bank. Alyn runs to **Mold** 3 *m.*, **Llong** 3 *m.* Here Terrig joins on right bank. Terrig rises in Llyn-y-Mynydd-du, and Llyn Neyn, ½ N. of it, runs 3 *m.* to Nerquis, and Alyn and Alyn 2 *m.* Alyn runs to **Hope** 5 *m.*, and 2 *m.* below, at Gwastad Bridge, is joined on right bank by Gadyn, which brook runs down in two branches, each 3 *m.* long, to within 1 *m.* N.W. of **Brymbo**. and 3 *m.* down joins Alyn. Alyn runs to **Gresford**, 4 *m.*, **Rossett**, 2 *m.*, and Dee, 2 *m.* Poaching is carried on *ad libitum* at Rossett, and the Alyn is badly cared for. There are a few trout late in the season. Dee runs to **Radley**, 3 *m.*, and here Pulford brook, which rises 4 *m.* above Pulford, 1 *m.* N.E. of **Rossett**, and is 7 *m.* long, joins on left bank. Dee now waters Eaton Hall Park for 3 *m.*, receiving the drainings of the lakes there. Midway through the park Holywell brook joins on right bank. Holywell rises in Edge Mill ponds, 2 *m.* N. of **Malpas**, runs 3 *m.* to 1 *m.* W. of **Broxton**, and 4 *m.* down is joined on right bank by Keys brook, which rises above **Tattenhall** and is 4 *m.* long. Holywell runs to Aldford, 2 *m.*, and Dee, 1 *m.* After leaving Eaton Hall Park. Dee runs 4 *m.* to **Chester**. (*c.s.*) *Hotels*: Grosvenor, Queen.

Chesterfield (Derby).—M.R.; G.C.R. Rother. Munster brook. Hipper. Linnacre brook, 1 *m.* W. Hockley brook, 4 *m.* S.W. Doe Lea, 5 *m.* W. *Lakes*: All Pits pond by Oldfield, 2 *m.* N.E. Great dam, 4 *m.* S.W. Wingerworth Hall lakes, 4 *m.* S.W. Sutton Scarsdale Park lake, 4 *m.* S.E. Birley pond, 6 *m.* N.W. (*See Goole.*)

Chichester (Sussex).—L.B. & S.C.R. The canal; pike, perch, bream, roach; the "basin," a large pond at the end of the canal by the city, is a good spot; fishing free. There are a few small brooks in the neighbourhood holding trout, but strictly preserved. At Aldingbourne Mill pond good roach, carp, bream, and perch fishing can be had at 1s. a day. *Hotel*: Dolphin.

Chigwell-lane (Essex).—G.E. and G.N.J.R. On Roding. Fishing very poor. (*See Barking.*)

Chilcompton (Somerset).—G.W.R.; L. & S.W.R. (*See Bristol.*)

Childwall (Lancs.).—S. & C.L.R. Childwall brook. (*See Runcorn.*)

Chilham (Kent).—S.E.R. On Stour. Fishing preserved by Col. Hardy. (*See Sandwich.*) *Inn*: Alma. (*c.s.*)

Chippenham (Wilts)—G.W.R. (*See Bristol.*) On Avon and Marden; coarse fish. Above the mill there is good pike, perch, and chub fishing in the deep water: and below the mill are a few trout, and plenty of dace and roach; preserved by land and mill owners, who often give leave. (*c.s.*)

Chipping Norton (Oxon).—G.W.R. On a tributary of Evenlode. (*See London, U.T.*)

Chipping Norton Junction (Oxon).—G.W.R. On Evenlode. (*See London, U.T.*)

Chipping Ongar (Essex.).—G.E.R. (*See Maldon and Barking.*) On Roding and Cripsey brook; poor fishing.

Chirnside Bridge, n.s. **Chirnside**—N.B.R. Tweed and Whiteadder: trout and salmon. (*See Berwick.*)

Chiswick (Middx.).—L. & S.W.R. Thames. (*See London, L.T.*)

Chorley (Lancs.)—L. & Y.R.; L. & N.W.R. Black brook. Yarrow, 1 *m.* S. Roddlesworth, 2 *m.* E. Liverpool Waterworks reservoir 2 *m.* E. *Lakes*: Rivington reservoir, 2 *m.* E. (*See Liverpool, Preston,* and *Hesketh Bank.*)

Christchurch (Hants).—L. & S.W.R. Avon and Stour. Salmon, pike, perch, chub, roach, tench, dace. Very strictly preserved. *Hotel*: King's Arms, the proprietor of which has nearly 3 *m.* of the Avon and upper part of Stour free to visitors.

at the hotel, salmon and perch excepted. Avon rises in Wilts, at Bishops Gunning, 4 m. from **Devizes**, runs 5 m. to Beachingstoke (n.s. **Woodborough**, ½ m.). Here a stream joins on left bank which works two mills, 1 m. up. ½ m down Avon a stream joins on right bank, working two mills 1 m. up. 4 m. down Avon is Upavon; Enford, 4 m.; Nether Avon, 3 m. (good trouting, preserved by the farmers); Amesbury (n.s. **Porton**), 7 m. (trout and grayling strictly preserved by Sir E. Antrobus); Wilsford, 2 m.; Great Durnford, 1½ m.; Stratford, 6 m.; **Salisbury**, 2 m. Here the Wylye and Winterbourne join, one on the left bank, the other on the right bank. Wylye rises by Hill Deverill Mill, 4 m. S. of **Warminster**, and in 2 m. is joined on left bank by the outflow of the Shire Water lake 1 m. up. 2 m. on Wylye touches **Warminster**, 1 m. off; runs 3 m. to **Heytesbury**; Codford, 3½ m. Here a stream joins on the left bank, which rises beyond Chiltern St. Mary, and is 4 m. long. Wylye runs in 4 m. to **Wylye**. (1¼ m. above begins the Wilton Flyfishing Club water.) 4 m. below, Winterbourne, 5 m. long, joins on left bank. Wylye runs to **Wishford**, 1 m.; **Wilton**, 3 m. (Here ends the W.F.C. water.) Nadder here joins Wylye. Nadder rises at Nadder Head Lake, by **Shaftesbury**, and in 5 m. is joined on right bank by the outflow of five large ponds in Wardour Park. 1 m. on, a small stream, 3 m. long. joins on left bank. Nadder runs in 1½ m. to **Tisbury**. Here the outfall from the large lake at Fonthill Giffard, 1 m. up, joins on right bank. Nadder runs to **Dinton**, 6 m., **Wilton**, 7 m., and Wylye 1 m. Wylye joins the Avon at **Salisbury** in 4 m. Winterbourne rises beyond Cholerton (n.s. **Grately**), 3 m., runs through Wilbury Park to Newton Toney, 2 m., **Porton**, 4 m., Winterbourne, 1 m., **Salisbury**, 6 m. Avon now runs to Nunton, 4 m., where the Chalk Stream joins on right bank. Chalk Stream rises near Alvediston (n.s. **Tisbury**, 5 m.), runs to Broad Chalk. 5 m., Toney Stratford, 4 m., Avon, 5 m. Avon runs to **Downton**, 5 m., **Braemore**, 4 m., **Fordingbridge**, 4 m. Here a stream (trout, grayling; leave from the owner of West Park) runs down from Demerham, 4 m. long, working two mills, joins Avon on right bank. Avon runs to Ibbesley, 4 m., Ellingham, 1 m. Here Black Water, 5 m. long, joins on right bank. Avon runs to **Ringwood**, 5 m. Here two streams join on left bank, rising in the New Forest, and are 8 m. long and 6 m. long. Christchurch is 10 m. on. Here the landlord of the King's Arms preserves a good stretch of water, including the junction of the Stour. The roach run very large. Boat and man can be had. Above and adjoining the hotel water some good coarse fishing can be had at 10s. per day, including boat and man. (See c.t. Avon.) The local flies on the Avon are the March brown, grannam, sand-fly, alder, green and grey drakes, orange flies; an artificial grasshopper for grayling. (c.s.)

STOUR rises in Stour Head ponds (n.s. **Witham**), runs 6 m. to **Gillingham**. Here Shreen water joins on left bank. Shreen rises at Mere, 4 m. from **Gillingham**, and works 2 mills. ½ m. below, at Accliff Mill, Ledden joins Stour. Ledden rises 5 m. E. of **Gillingham**, and 3 m. down is joined on left bank by Fern brook, which rises in Lashmere pond, 1 m. N.W. of **Shaftesbury**, and is 4 m. long. Ledden now runs in 1 m. to Stour. Stour runs to Fifehead Magdalen 4 m., 3 m. below Cale river joins on right bank. Cale rises by **Wincanton**, runs 6 m. to **Temple Combe**, 1½ m. off, and 3 m. down is joined on left bank by Bow brook, which rises 2 m. N. of **Temple Combe**, and is 6 m. long, working some mills. Stour runs in 2 m. to **Stalbridge**, 1 m. off, where a short stream working a mill 3 m. up, joins on right bank. 1 m. down Stour Lidden river joins on right bank. Lidden rises some 8 m. S.W. of **Sturminster Newton**, in Stoke Mill. and 2 m. down is joined by a stream on left bank 3 m. long. 5 m. down Lidden a stream 6 m. long joins on left bank, which works a mill or two. 3 m. down, Lidden reaches Stour. 1 m. down Stour, Divelish river joins on right bank. Divelish rises at Fifehead Neville, 3½ m. from **Sturminster**, and is 5 m. long. 1 m. down Stour is **Sturminster**. 3 m. down Stour, at Manston, a stream joins on left bank. which rises at Melbury Abbas, 2 m. S. from **Shaftesbury**, runs 6 m. to West Orchard, where a short stream joins on right bank. Hence to Stour is 1½ m. 1 m. down Stour a stream, which rises by Fontmell Magna, 5 m. up, working some mills, joins on left bank. Stour runs in 3 m. to **Shillingston**. 5 m. down, at Stowerpaine. Iwerne river joins Stour on left bank. Iwerne rises by Iwerne Minster, and is some 5 m. long, turning a mill or two. Stour runs in 4 m. to **Blandford**, 5 m. to **Spettisbury**. Here Tarrant river joins on left bank. Tarrant rises by Tarrant Gunville, runs 4 m. to Tarrant Monkton, and Stour 5 m. Stour runs to **Bailey Gate**, 3 m., **Wimborne Minster**, 8 m. Here Allen river joins on left bank. Allen rises in St. Giles's Park, 2 m. from Cranborne (n.s. **Verwood**), and 3 m. down, after working four mills, is joined on right bank by the outflow of the large lake at More Critchell. Hence to **Wimborne** is 7 m. Three m. down Stour, Blackwater, 4 m. long, joins on right bank Stour runs in 7 m. to Holdenhurst (n.s. **Hern Bridge**, 2 m.). Here Moors river joins on left bank. Moors rises by Cranborne, runs 10 m., and is joined on right bank by a stream which rises in a lake by Queen's Wood (n.s. **Verwood**, 3½ m.) and is 7 m. long. Moors runs to **Hern Bridge**, 4 m., and Stour 1 m. 5 m. on, Stour joins Avon at **Christchurch** (preserved.) See *Bournemouth*.) (See c.s. Avon.) The sea fishing at Christchurch is good. The time to fish for mackerel with lines in the Bay is July and August, on the first of the ebb tide running over the Christchurch Reef east and west, where pollack may also be taken earlier in the season. Bass in the harbour's mouth. The Stour is now most rigidly preserved.

Church (Lancs.).—Lanc. & York R. Church brook. Hyndburn brook, 1 m. N. (See *Preston.*)

Church Fenton (York).—G.N.R.; N.E.R.; S. & K.R. Cook beck, 2 *m.* W., at Saxton. (*See York.*)

Churchill (Worcester).—G.W.R. Churchill brook, feeding numerous mill ponds. Hoo b'ook (1 *m.* S.) (*See Gloucester.*)

Church Road (Monmouth).—P.C. & N.R. Rumney; trout, salmon; preserved. (*c.s.*) (*See Cardiff, Wales.*)

Church Stretton (Salop).—S. & H.R. Cound's brook; trout; private. Quenny brook (2 *m.* S.). Heath brook (4½ *m.* E) (*See Gloucester.*)

Cirencester (Gloucester).—G.W.R.; M. & S.W.J.R. *Hotel:* King's Head. On Churn; few trout below, above more plentiful. There are many trout streams near, mostly private. At Cricklade is pike fishing. (*See London, U.T.*) In Lord Bathurst's park is a large lake; pike, perch, &c.

Clacton (Essex).—G.E.R. (*See Thorpe.*) *Hotels:* Royal, Osborne, Towers.

Clapham (York).—M.R. Wenning. (*c.s. Lune.*) Kettles beck. Fen beck. Anstwick beck. Clapham beck. Newby beck, 1 *m.* W. Keasden beck, 3 *m.* S.W. The Bentham and Clapham Angling Association preserve 6 *m.* of water: s.t. 5*s.*, d.t. 1*s.*, licence 2*s.* 6*d.* *Hotel:* Flying Horseshoe; the landlord can obtain leave. (*See Lancaster.*)

Clare (Suffolk).—G.E.R. Stour. (*c.s.* N. and S.) (*See Manningtree.*)

Claycross (Derby).—M.R. Rother. *Lakes:* Williamthorpe ponds, 2 *m.* N.E. Wingerworth Hall lakes (2), 2½ *m.* N.W. Great dam, 3½ *m.* N.W. (*See Goole.*)

Claydon (Bucks).—L. & N.W.R. Claydon brook. *Lakes:* Claydon Farm and Middle Claydon ponds (2 *m.* S.). (*See King's Lynn.*)

Claydon (Suffolk).—G.E.R. Gipping; roach, perch, pike, tench, chub; preserved from above Blakenham to Boss Hall, 5 *m.* down, by Gipping Angling Preservation Society. (*See Ipswich.*)

Claypole (Lincoln).—G.N.R. Witham. Sand beck, 3 *m.* E. (*See Boston.*)

Clayton Bridge (Lancs.)—L. & Y.R. Medlock. (*See Runcorn.*)

Cleeve (Gloucester).—M.R. Swilgare. (*See Gloucester.*)

Cleobury Mortimer (Salop).—G.W.R. Rea; trout, grayling; private. (*See Gloucester.*) (*c.s. Severn.*)

Clevedon (Somerset).—G.W.R. Kenn. 1½ *m.* off. Kenn rises in a mill pond on Bakewell Common, near **Bourton** Station (G.W.R.), runs 2 *m.* to **Nailsea** (G.W.R.), Kenn 6 *m.*, and the sea 2 *m.* By staying at the Battle Axes Inn, Wraxall, fair trout and coarse fishing can be had. The drainings of Nailsea Moor here join the sea. This water course rises by **Flax Bourton** (G.W.R.). and runs 8 *m.* to Jacklands Bridge, where the two main drains commence. called Middle Yeo and Land Yeo, which run to **Clevedon** in 6 *m.* Within easy distance is Blogdon reservoir, where the fishing is very good. *Hotel:* Walton Park.

Cliburn (Westland).—N.E.R. Leith, Lyvennet, 1 *m.* E. (*See Carlisle.*)

Clifton (Derby).—M.R. Dove; trout, grayling. (*c.s. Trent.*) Henmoor; trout, grayling, (*See Gainsborough.*)

Clifton (Lancs.)—L. & Y.R. Irwell. (*See Runcorn.*)

Clifton (Westland.).—L. & N.W.R. Lowther; salmon, trout, chub. (*c.s. Eden.*) Leith, 1 *m.* E. Eamont, 2 *m.* N.; salmon, trout, chub. (*c s. Eden.*) Ghyll beck, 6 *m.* S. Heltondale beck, 6 *m.* S. (*See Carlisle.*)

Clifton Mill (Warwick).—L. & N.W.R. Avon; chub, dace, roach, pike, perch, bream. Swift (2 *m.* W.) (*See Gloucester.*) (*c.s. Severn.*)

Clitheroe (Lancs.)—Lanc. & York R. Ribble; trout, salmon, grayling, above; chub below; preserved by the Clitheroe Angling Association; hon. sec., J. L. Bulcock, fishing tackle depot, King-street, Clitheroe. Bashall brook. Clitheroe beck. Waddington beck. 1 *m.* N. Bradford beck, 2 *m.* N. Smithies Bridge beck. Hodder, 3 *m.* W.; trout, salmon; fishing can be had by staying at the Whitewell Hotel or Red Pump Inn, Clitheroe; Three Fishes Inn, Mitton. Higher Hodder Bridge Hotel; and Aspinall's Arms, Mitton. *Lakes:* Bashall Moor pond, 5 *m.* N.W. *Hotel:* Red Pump. (*See Newton, Whitwell, Preston.*) (*c.s. Ribble.*) *Tackleist,* T. Robinson, 3, Wesleyan-road.

Cloughton (York).—N.E.R. Burniston beck; trout; preserved. Lindhead beck. (*See Scalby.*)

Clun (Salop).—(n.s. **Broome**, 8 *m.*) Clun; trout, grayling; private, but leave may often be had. Lower Redlake brook (3¼ *m.* S.); trout. *Lakes:* Acton Pool (4 *m.* W.) (*See Gloucester.*) (*c.s. Severn.*)

Clutton (Somerset).—G.W.R. (*See Bristol.*)

Coalport (Salop).—G.W.R.; L. & N.W.R. Severn; pike, roach, chub, dace, salmon. *Lakes:* Willey Park lakes (3¼ *m.* S.W.) (*See Gloucester.*) (*c.s. Severn.*)

Coalville (Leicester).—M.R. Dishley brook, 2 *m.* N. at Whitwick. Sence, 2 *m.* S. at **Hugglescote.** *Lakes:* Old reservoir, 4 *m.* N.E. (*See Gainsborough.*)

Cockerham (Lancs.)—M.R. n.s. Bay Horses, 2 *m.* Cocker. Cocker rises 3 *m.* above **Bay Horses,** runs 7 *m.* to **Cockerham,** and 2 *m.* below joins the sea.

Cockermouth (Cumland).—L. & N.W.R. *Hotel:* Globe. Derwent; salmon, trout. Derwent rises on Bowfell, and 1 *m.* down is joined on left bank by a stream which drains Sprinkling tarn 1 *m.* up; 1 *m.* down a stream joins draining Sty Head tarn 2 *m.* up. These two tarns are some 5 *m.* N.E. from **Wastdale Head Hotel.** Derwent runs 4 *m.* to **Crosthwaite,** and here Stonethwaite beck joins on right bank. Stonethwaite rises in Angle tarn, 7 *m.* E. of **Wastdale Head,** near the source of Derwent, and is 8 *m.* long.

Derwent runs 2 *m.* to Grange bridge, and runs into Derwentwater 2 *m.* below at **Borrowdale**, near **Lodore** and **Borrowdale Hotels**. Here Watendlath beck runs into the lake. This beck rises in Blea tarn, runs 2 *m.* to Watendlath tarn, and joins Derwentwater 2 *m.* below. No streams join Derwentwater on the left bank. On the right bank, 2 *m.* down, Brockle beck, 3 *m.*, joins. Hence to **Keswick** and the lake's foot is 1 *m.* Here Greta joins Derwent on right bank. Greta, under the name of Glendermakin, rises on the slopes of Bannerdale Crags, runs 4 *m.* to **Mungrisdale**. Four *m.* down Troutbeck joins on left bank, which rises 4 *m.* above **Troutbeck** station and joins Glendermakin 2 *m.* below. One *m.* down Mosdale beck, 3 *m.* long, joins on left bank. Glendermakin runs 3 *m.* to **Threlkeld**, and here St. John's beck joins on left bank. St. John's, under the name of Wyth tarn, rises in Dale head tarn, runs 4 *m.* to Wythburn; here a stream joins, draining Harrop tarn 1 *m.* up. Wyth runs 1 *m.* to Thirlmere. *Inn*: Nag's Head. This lake is 2 *m.* long, and out of it runs St. John's beck, which joins Glendermakin, or Greta, at **Threlkeld**, 5 *m.* down. One *m.* down Greta Naddle beck, 5 *m.* long, joins on left bank; and a little below Glenderaterra beck, 3 *m.* long, joins on right bank. Greta runs 3 *m.* to **Keswick**, and joins Derwent just below the lake. Derwent runs 4 *m.* to Bassenthwaite lake; Newlands beck here joins the lake on the left bank near Derwent. Newlands rises in the hills 3 *m.* S.W. of **Borrowdale Hotel**; across the hills, and 3 *m.* down, is joined on left bank by Little Dale beck, 3 *m.* long; 1 *m.* down, Rigg beck, 2 *m.* long, joins on left bank. Newlands runs 3 *m.* to 3 *m.* W. of **Keswick** at **Braithwaite**, and here Coledale beck, 3 *m.* long, joins on left bank. Two *m.* behind Coledale beck joins Newlands on left bank, and 1 *m.* down is Bassenthwaite lake. This lake is 4 *m.* long; there are no tributaries on left bank, but on right bank Dash beck, 6 *m.* long, joins 1 *m.* above the foot of the lake at **Bassenthwaite**. On leaving the lake, Derwent runs 5 *m.* to Isell bridge, 4 *m.* N.E. from **Cockermouth**, and here Isell beck, 4 *m.* long, joins on right bank; Derwent runs to **Cockermouth**, 5 *m.* Here Cocker joins on left bank. Cocker rises in two short streams which water Buttermere lake, 1½ *m.* long. At the lower end is the village of **Buttermere**. Here the outflow of Bleaberry tarn, 1 *m.* up, joins on left bank; ½ *m.* below the stream joins Crummock water, 3 *m.* long. At the lower end of the lake, by the **Scale Hill Hotel**, Mosedale beck joins Crummock. Mosedale rises in Flowtern tarn, 2 *m.* N.E. across the hills from the **Angler's Inn** at the foot of Ennerdale lake. Four miles down Mosedale a stream joins on left bank, draining Lowes water ¼ *m.* up. One *m.* below is Crummock water and the **Scales Hill Hotel**. Cocker runs 4 *m.*, where Whit beck, 4 *m.* long, joins on right bank. Cocker runs 6 *m.* to **Cockermouth** and Derwent. Derwent runs 3 *m.* to **Brigham**, and here Dovenby beck, 4 *m.* long, joins on right bank; and Ellerbeck, 3 *m.* long, on left bank. Derwent runs 3 *m.* to **Marron Junction**, and here Marron joins on left bank. Marron, under the name of Colliersgate beck, rises by **Rowrah**, and 2 *m.* below is joined on right bank by Scallow beck, 2 *m.* long; 1 *m.* below, Woodbeck, 3 *m.* long, joins on right bank. Marron runs 1 *m.* to **Wright Green**, **Ullock**, 2 *m.* Mockerkin tarn is 1 *m.* S.E. from here. Marron runs to **Branthwaite**, 2 *m.*, and joins Derwent at **Marron Junction**, 5 *m.* below. Just above the junction of the rivers, Lostrigg beck, which rises 2 *m.* W. of **Branthwaite**, and is 5 *m.* long, joins on left bank. Derwent runs 2 *m.* to **Camerton**, and joins the sea at **Workington**, 5 *m.* below.

Cockfield (Suffolk).—G.E.R. Lavenham brook. (*See Manningtree.*)

Codford (Wilts).—G.W.R. On Wylye; trout, grayling; preserved by the owner of Ashton Gifford. (*c.s. Avon.*)

Codnor Park (Derby). — M.R.; G.N.R. Erewash. *Lakes*: Golden Valley reservoir. Butterly reservoir, 3 *m.* W. (*See Gainsborough.*)

Codsall (Stafford).—G.W.R. Penk, 1 *m.* N. *Lakes*: The pool, Chillington Park, 2 *m.* N.W., good fishing. (*See Gainsborough.*)

Cogie Hill (Lancs.)—G. & K.E.R. Pilling water. (*See Pilling.*)

Colchester (Essex).—G.E.R. Colne. Crockle, 1 *m.* E. Roman River, 3 *m.* S. Colne rises 5 *m.* above **Yeldham**, runs 4 *m.* to **Hedingham**, **Halstead** 3 *m.* 2 *m.* down, Gosfield brook, 6 *m.* long, which drains the lake at Gosfield Hall, 3 *m.* S.W. of **Halstead**, joins on right bank. 1 *m.* down Colne, at **Colne**, Pebmarsh brook, 4 *m.* long, joins on left bank. Colne runs to **Chapple** 3 *m.*, and **Colchester** 10 *m.* 1 *m.* below, Crockle brook, 4 *m.* long, joins on left bank. (*See Nayland.*) *Hotels*: George, Old Red Lion Cups.

Cole (Somerset).—L. & S.W.R.; M.R. Brue; trout; preserved. Shepton brook. (*See Highbridge.*) (*c.s. Avon.*)

Coleshill (Warwick).—L. & N.W.R. Blyth; bream, roach. (*c.s. Trent*). Cole. Ulverley brook, 2 *m.* S.W. Tame, 2 *m.* N. (*c.s. Trent*). Alley brook, 2 *m.* N.E. *Lakes*: Maxtoke Park lakes, 2 *m.* W. Coleshill pool, 2 *m.* S. Chelmsley Wood ponds, 2 *m.* S.W. Packington Park lakes, 4 *m.* S.E. (*See Gainsborough.*)

Collingham (Notts)—M.R. Trent, 2 *m.* W.; pike, roach, dace, chub, grayling. (*c.s.*) *Lakes*: Collingham ponds, Cowarth pool, Mons pool, and Black pool, 1 *m.* N.W. (*See Gainsborough.*)

Collingham (York)—M.R. Wharfe. (*c.s. York.*) Collingham beck. (*See York.*)

Collins Green (Lancs.)—L. & N.W.R. Sankey brook. (*See Runcorn.*)

Colne (Essex).—G.E.R. Colne. Pebmarsh brook. (*See Colchester.*)

Colne (Lancs.)—M.R. Laneshaw. Trawden brook, 1 *m.* E. Roughlee water, 2 *m.* W., at Lawerwood. Wycoller water, 3 *m.* E. Catlow brook, 3 *m.* S. (*See Preston, Rawcliffe.*)

Coltishall (Norfolk).—G.E.R.—Bure; roach, bream, perch, pike; leave freely given. Sprixworth beck, 3 m. S. (*See Yarmouth.*)

Colwall (Worcester).—G.W.R. Leigh brook (or Cradley). Good trouting; leave from Mr. Cook, of Leigh Court. (*See Gloucester.*)

Colwich (Stafford).—L. & N.W.R. Trent; roach, chub, pike, trout; fishing very good; preserved by Mr. L. Morgan. (*c.s.*) Sherbrook brook, 3 m. W. Colton brook, 3 m. N.E. Sow, 4 m. W.; roach, pike, chub. Blyth, 5 m. E. (*c.s Trent.*) *Lakes:* Oakedge Park lakes (*See Gainsborough.*)

Colwick (Notts).—M.R. Trent; pike, perch, roach, chub, salmon. (*c.s.*) (*See Gainsborough.*)

Colyford (Devon).—L. & S.W.R. (*See Seaton.*) Axe and Coly; trout, salmon. (*c.s.*)

Colyton (Devon).—L. & S.W.R. (*See Seaton.*) Axe; trout, salmon; preserved by Sir W. E. Pole, Bart., and others. (*c.s.*) Coly; trout; good, but reserved. Shute brook; trout; preserved by Sir W. E. Pole. *Hotel:* Colcombe Castle, where fishing can be had in Sir W. Pole's water for a limited number of rods.

Combe Row (Somerset).—G.W.R. (*See Watchet.*)

Commondale (York).—N.E.R. Commondale brook; trout; preserved. (*See Whitby.*)

Condor Green (Lancs.)—L. & N.W.R. Condor. (*c.s. Lune.*) (*See Galgate.*)

Condover (Salop).—L. & N.W.R., G.W.R. Connd brook; trout; private. *Lakes:* Bomer pool; pike, perch, rudd, roach, bream; preserved, but leave may sometimes be had. (*See Gloucester.*)

Congleton (Cheshire).—L. & N.W.R. Dane; trout, dace, roach, chub; private. Biddulph brook. Dairy brook, 1 m. W. Wheelock, 2 m. S.W. Midge brook, 3 m. N. at Marton. *Lakes:* Moreton Hall, 2 m. S.W. Bag mere, 4 m. W. (*See Frodsham.*)

Congleton (Warwick).—L. & N.W.R. and G.W.R. Arrow; pike, perch, chub, roach, dace, bream, and a few trout. (*See Gloucester.*)

Congresbury (Somerset).—G.W.R. Yeo. Yeo rises by Blagdon (n.s. **Sandford**, G.W.R., 6 m.), runs to Wrington 4 m. (good trouting; preserved by C. L. F. Edwards, Esq , of The Court, Axbridge, to Iwood), and **Congresbury** 2½ m. The tide flows to this point. The sea is 6 m. The fishing (trout, eels, and flat fish) from Iwood down, is preserved by Rev. J. C. Bathurst Norman, Iwood Manor, Congresbury, who sometimes gives leave on application. (*c.s. Avon.*)

Conisborough (York).—G.C.R.; M.R. Don. (*c.s. Yorkshire.*) Dearne, 1 m. W. (*See Goole.*) Warmsworth beck or St. Catharine's Well stream, 1 m. S.W. *Lakes:* Crookhill Hall, 1 m. S.W. (*See Althorpe.*)

Coniston (Lancs). Fs. R. Yewdale beck—Torver beck, 2½ m. S. *Lakes:* Coniston: pike, perch, char, t out. (*c.s. Kent.*) Lever Water 2 m. N.W.; Gaits Water, 2 m. W; Low Tarn 2 m. N.E. The char fishing is very good in May and June. *Hotels:* Waterhead, Crown. (*See Ulverston.*)

Cononley (York).—M.R. Aire; trout, grayling, perch, chub, roach. (*c.s. York.*) (*See Gargrave, Rawcliffe.*)

Constable Burton (York).—N.E.R. Broomber beck. Betterby beck. Bedale, 2 m. N. (*See York.*)

Constantine (Cornwall).—(n.s. **Penryn**, 6 m). Constantine brook; trout. This brook rises some 3 m. above Constantine, where it is joined by a brook 3 m. long. 2 m. down, Constantine joins the estuary of Helford river (*c.s. Fowey*). 2½m. W. runs Helford river. HELFORD rises by Polgrean, runs 2½ m. to Penglase Mill (the nearest point to **Constantine**), and 1½ m. down is joined on left bank by Trecoos brook, which rises by Trecoos 1½ m. W. of **Constantine**, and is 2 m. long. ½ m. down Helford, Gweek water joins on right bank. Gweek rises 3 m. N.E. of **Helston**, and is 5 m. long. 1 m. down is the estuary. Trout in Helford above Gweek.

Cookham (Berks).—G.W.R. Thames. (*See London, M.T.*) Lord Boston preserves one of the back waters below the bridge; leave may sometimes be obtained from Mr. Hepworth, Hedsor. *Hotels:* King's Arms and Ferry. *Fishermen:* E. Godden, A. Hutch, and B. Buttery. Wye; polluted.

Cooper Bridge (York).—L. & Y.R. Calder. (*c.s. York.*) Colne polluted. (*See Rawcliffe.*)

Copgrove (York).—N.E.R. Robert beck. Tutt or Minship beck. Ure, 3 m. N. (*c.s York.*) *Lake:* Bishop Monkton pond, 3 m. N. (*See York.*)

Copmanthorpe (York).—N.E.R.; G.N.R.; S. & K. Joint R. Ouse, 2 m. W. (*c.s. York.*) *Lakes:* Angram dam, 5 m. N.W. (*See York.*)

Coppull (Lancs.). – L. & N.W.R. Yarrow. *Lakes:* Birkane ponds, 1 m. N. (*See Hesketh Bank.*)

Corby (Lincoln).—G.N.R. Glen. Edenham brook, 3 m. E. *Lakes:* Grimthorpe Park, 2 m. S.E. (*See Spalding.*)

Cornhill (Northland).—G.N. of S.R. (*See Berwick.*) Tweed and Till; trout and salmon.

Cornwood (Devon).—G.W.R. Yealm; trout; preserved. Yealm rises 4 m. above **Cornwood**, runs 1 m. to the station, and 6 m. to Yealmton (n.s. **Plympton**, 5 m.). The tide flows to 1 m. below the town, and 1 m. below, Braxton water, 5 m. long, joins on right bank. 1 m. below on right bank, Ford brook, 2 m. long, joins, and 2 m. down, at Newton Ferrers, Newton brook, 4 m. long, joins on left bank. The sea is 1 m. on. Good bass and pollack fishing in the harbour and outside.

Corpusty (Norfolk).—G.E.R. and G.N.R. Bure; trout; private. *Lakes:* Thurning Hall, 3 m, S.W. Barrington Park, 4½ m. N.E. (*See Yarmouth.*)

D

Corsham (Wilts).—G.W.R. (*See Bristol.*) Lakes: Corsham Park lake; pike, perch; preserved by Lord Methuen.

Coryton (Devon).—G.W.R. Lid; good trouting, but preserved. Lew. Maryston brook, 3 m.; trout. (*See Plymouth.*)

Cotehill (Cumland).—M.R. Scotby beck. Eden; salmon. trout. (*c.s.*) (*See Carlisle.*)

Cotham (Notts).—G.N.R. Devon. Car dyke, 1 m. N.W. Smite, 2 m. S. at Shelton. Trent. 2½ m. N W., at East Stoke (*c.s.*) Witham, 3 m. S.E., at Bennington. (*See Gainsborough.*)

Cotherstone (Yorks).—N.E.R. Tees; salmon, trout, bull trout, coarse fish; tickets from the agent of T. Hutchinson, Esq.. Eggleston; also from Lord Barnard's agent, Ruby Castle, Staindrop; also from — Silvertop, Esq., Lartington Hall, Darlington. (*c.s.*) Crook beck. Balder river; tickets from T. Hutchinson, Esq. (*c.s Tees.*) Wilden beck, 1 m. N.W. Hunder beck, 5 m. W. Hotel: Fox and Hounds. (*See Stockton.*)

Cottingham (York).—N.E.R. Hull, 2 m. E. (*See Hull.*) (*c.s. York.*)

Conghton (Warwick).—L. & N.W.R. Arrow. (*See Gloucester.*)

Counter Drain (Lincoln).—G.N.R. Glen. Counter Drain. (*See Spalding.*)

Coventry (Warwick).—L. & N.W.R. Sherborne. Low (3 m N.E.). Withybrook (3 m. N.E.).. Lakes: Coombe Abbey Lake (4 m. E.); roach, pike, perch, bream (private); Lord Craven. (*See Gloucester. Hotels: King's Head Queen's, Craven Arms.*)

Cover Bridge (Middleham, York), n.s. **Spennithorne**, 2 m.—Ure; trout, grayling, pike; preserved by landlord of Cover Bridge Inn for 3 m. Cover; trout, grayling; preserved as Ure for 2 m. (*See Leyburn, York.*)

Cowbit (Lincoln).—G.N.R. Welland; pike, perch, dace; free. (*See Spalding.*)

Cowton (York).—G.N.R. Wiske; grayling, trout, chub, pike; preserved; leave sometimes. (*c.s. York.*) (*See York.*)

Coxbench (Derby).—M.R. Holbrook brook. Lakes: Smalley Mill pond, 2 m. E. (*See Gainsborough.*)

Coxwold (York).—N.E.R. Hole beck. (*See York.*) Lakes: Moor Farm reservoirs (2), 3 m. S.E. (*See York.*)

Cradley (Worcester).—G.W.R. and L. & N.W.R. New Pool. (*See Gloucester.*)

Crakenhall (York).—N.E.R. Bedale beck (*See York.*)

Cranley (Surrey).—L.B. & S.C.R. (*See London, L.T.*) Wey.

Craven Arms (Salop).—L. & N.W.R. and G.W.R. Onny; trout, grayling; private. Quenny brook (2 m. N). Eaton brook (4 m. N.E.). Lakes: Whittleton Pool (1 m. E.). (*See Gloucester.*) (*c.s. Severn.*)

Crawley (Sussex).—L.B. & S.C.R. Mole. (*See London, L.T.*) Near here are the Buchan Hill ponds; trout; leave from Mr. P. Saillard; also Ifield Mill pond, free; Bewbush Mill pond, leave from Mr. Brown; Three Bridges pond, leave from Mrs. Montifiori; Hazelwick Mill pond. leave from Mr. Caffyn. Hotel: George.

Crayford (Kent).—S.E.R. (*See Dartford.*) Cray; trout; private.

Credenhill (Hereford).—G.W.R. Sugwas brook. Wye (2 m.); chub, pike, salmon, dace, perch. trout. (*c.s.*) (*See Chepstow.*)

Crediton (Devon). - L. & S.W.R. Creedy; trout; preserved by Gen. Sir Redvers Buller, Sir J. Davie, and Sir J. Shelley. Spreyton water; trout. Yeo, 3 m.; trout; leave from the farmers. (*See Exeter.*) Hotel: Ship.

Cressage (Salop) —G.W.R. Severn; pike, perch, chub, dace, salmon, trout. Langley brook (3 m. S.W.). Leighton brook (3 m N.E.). Lakes: Harnage Grange pond (3 m. S.W.). Acton Burnell Park lakes (5 m. S.W.). (*See Gloucester.*) (*c.s.*)

Creswell (Derby).—L. & N.W.R. Blythe. (*c.s. Trent.*) Tean brook, 2 m. E., at Upper Tean. (*See Gainsborough.*)

Crewe (Cheshire).—L. & N.W.R.; G.W.R. Inglesway brook Wistaston brook, 1 m. S W, Foul Brook, 1 m. N.E. Swill brook, 2 m. S.W., at Wistaston. Weaver, 3 m. W.: coarse fish. Lakes: Crewe Hall, 2 m. S.E. Winterley mill, 2 m. N.E. (*See Frodsham.*)

Crewkerne (Somerset).—L. & S.W.R. (*See Seaton.*) Hotel: George. Axe (3 m. off); trout. (*c.s.*) Parret (1 m. off); trout (for a few meadows), roach, dace. (*See Bridgwater.*) (*c.s. Avon.*) Leave must be obtained for both streams from the landowners and millers.

Crick (Northton.).—L. & N.W.R. Streck, 2 m. S. Lakes: Middlemore and Dunsland reservoirs (pike, &c.), 3 m. S.W. (*See Wisbeach; Bramston.*)

Croft (Durham).—N.E.R. Tees; salmon, trout, grayling, coarse fish. (*c.s.*) Clow beck; trout; private. Skerne; pike, chub, roach; preserved by the Darlington Anglers' Club (*see Pierce Bridge*) and the tenants. (*c s. Tees.*) Waterfall beck, 4 m. W. (*See Stockton.*)

Cromer (Norfolk).—G.E.R. Aldborough beck, 5 m. S.W.; private. Lake: Felbrigg Park, 3½ m. S.W. Gunton Park lake, 6 m. Hempstead Lake (private) 9 m. W. Salhouse, Wroxham, and Ranworth within easy distance by rail. (*See Yarmouth.*) Hotels: Bath, Tucker's, Royal, West Cliff.

Cromford (Derby).—M.R. Derwent; trout, grayling; preserved by Matlock and Cromford A.A., hon. sec., H. Cooper, Esq., Thorncliffe, Cromford. (*See Matlock.*) (*c.s. Trent.*) (*See Gainsborough.*)

Cropredy (Oxford).—G.W.R. Cherwell. (*See London, M.T.*) Clattercut reservoir lies near.

Crosby Ravensworth (Westland).—Lyvennet; trout.

Crosby Garrett (Westland).—M.R. Scandal beck. Potts or Helm beck, 2 m. W. Eden 3 m. N.E.; trout. (*c.s.*) (*See Carlisle.*)

Cross Keys (Monmouth).—G.W.R. Ebwy, trout, salmon. Sirhowey; trout. (c.s. Usk.) (See Newport.)

Crosthwaite (Cumberland).—Derwent; trout, salmon. (c.s.) Stonethwaite beck. Inns: Scafell, Royal Oak. (See Cockermouth.)

Croston (Lancs.).—L. & Y.R. Yarrow. Lostock, 1 m. N. Douglas, 2 m. W. (c.s. Ribble.) (See Hesketh Bank.)

Crowland (Lincoln), n.s. **Postland,** 3 m.—Welland; pike, perch, dace; free. Nen, 2 m. S.E. at Black Horse Mills. (See Spalding.)

Crowle (Lincoln).—G.N.R. Idle North Drain. The new Idle river. (See Althorpe.) Old Don river. This stream rises above **Crowle,** runs 8 m. to Luddington and Trent estuary at Adlingfleet, 6 m. below.

Crow Park (Notts.).—M.R.; G.N.R. (See Sutton).

Croxhall (Derby).—M.R. Mease. (c.s. Trent.) Pessal brook. (See Gainsborough.)

Croydon (Surrey).—L.B. & S.C.R. (See London, L.T.) Wandle; trout. Hotel: Greyhound.

Crudgington (Salop).—G.W.R. Tern; a few trout and coarse fish. Strine. Beanhill brook (2 m. S.) (See Gloucester.) (c.s. Severn.)

Crumlin (Monmouth).—G.W.R. Ebwy; trout, salmon; trout rod licences, 1s., from the post office. (c.s. Usk.) Lakes: Ponnd-y-Coed Cae (2 m.) (See Newport.)

Cuddington (Cheshire).—L. & N.W.R. Whitgate brook, 2 m. S. Lakes: Cuddington mill ponds. New Church Common ponds, 2 m. S. Petty pool in New Park, 2 m. S.E. (See Frodsham.)

Cudworth (Yorks).—M.R.; G.C.R. Dearne. (See Goole.)

Culgaith (Cumland).—M.R. Eden; trout; preserved by Yorkshire Angling Association. (c.s.) Eller beck, 1 m. S. Eamont, 4 m. W. Tees, 6 m. N.E; trout; private. (See Stockton, Carlisle.)

Culham (Oxon).—G.W.R. Thames. (See London, M.T.)

Cullingworth (Yorks).—G.N.R. Harden beck. (See Rawcliffe.)

Cullompton (Devon).—G.W.R. Culm; trout. Hotel: Railway. The Culm is the earliest river in Devon. It is mostly preserved. (See Exeter.) (c.s. Exe.) Kentisbere brook. Ashford brook. Fulford water.

Culmstock (Devon).—G.W.R. (See Exeter.) Hotels: Railway, Culm Valley. Culm; trout; the fishing good, and preserved. (c.s. Exe.)

Cummersdale (Cumland).—L. & N.W.R. Caldew; trout. Pow beck, 1 m. S. (See Carlisle.)

Cumwhinton (Cumland).—M.R. Eden, 1 m. E.; trout. (c.s.) Coatby beck. Petterill, 2 m. E. (See Carlisle.)

Cwm (Monmouth).—G.W.R. Ebwy; trout. (c s. Usk.) (See Newport.)

Cwm Afon (Monmouth).—G.W.R. Llwyd; trout. (c.s, Usk.) (See Newport.)

Cwmbran (Monmouth).—G.W.R. Llwyd. (See Newport.) (c.s. Usk.)

Dacre (York).—N.E.R. Nidd. (c.s. York.) (See York.)

Dalston (Cumland).—L. & N.W.R. Caldew; trout. Pow beck, 1 m. E. (See Carlisle.)

Dalton (Yorks).—N.E.R. Tees, 2 m. N.; salmon, trout, grayling, coarse fish. (c.s.) (See Stockton.)

Danby (York).—N.E.R. Esk; salmon, trout; preserved above by the landowners, below to Fryup Beck End by the Lealholm and Danby Anglers' Club of 20 members; s.t. 15s. A limited number of m. and w. tickets are issued at 10s. 6d. and 3s.; hon. sec., Harland Duck, Esq., Lealholm. (c.s.) (See Whitby.)

Danby Wiske (York)—N.E.R. Stelt, 3 m. W. Wiske; grayling, trout, chub, pike; preserved; leave sometimes. (c.s. York.)

Darfield (Yorks).—M.R. Dearne. Dove. Ings dyke, 1 m. E. (See Goole.)

Darley (Derby).—M.R. Derwent; trout, grayling; preserved from Rowsley to **Matlock** bridge by the Darley Dale Angling Club (hon. sec., J. H. Dawson), subscriptions 84s., s.t. 40s., d.t. 2s. 6d. for a portion of the water, fly only. (c.s. Trent.) Sydnope brook. Lakes: Mill ponds (2), 1 m. N.E. Flash dam, 3 m. N.E. (See Gainsborough.)

Darley (York).—N.E.R. Nidd. (c.s. York.) Darley beck. (See York.) Washburn, 6 m. S.W., at Blubberhouses. Spinksburn beck, 7 m. S.W. (See York.)

Darlington (Durham).—N.E.R. Tees; salmon, trout, grayling. Skerne; pike, chub, roach; preserved by Darlington Anglers' Club of 50; entrance, 10s.; s.t., 30s.; sec., Mr. A. Lascelles, Northgate, Darlington. Licenses of Mr. J. F. Smythe, Fish-tackleist, Horse-market, Darlington. (c.s. Tees.) Cocker beck. (See Stockton.)

Dartford (Kent).—S.E.R. On Darenth; trout, perch, roach, &c. The Darenth rises by Westerham, and in 6 m. runs by **Dunton Green, Sevenoaks** station, 1 m. (good trouting, preserved by Lord Stanhope); **Otford.** 2 m.; **Shoreham,** 12 m.; **Eynesford,** 4 m., passing Lullingstone. 1½ m. on is **Farningham,** and **Dartford** is 6 m. A mile below Dartford the Cray joins Darenth. Cray rises near **Orpington,** and in 1 m. runs by **St. Mary Cray; Bexley,** 4 m., passing St. Paul's Cray and Foot's Cray. From Bexley to **Crayford** is 1½ m.; whence to the junction of Cray and Darenth is 2 m. 2 m. below this junction Darenth joins Thames. Bream are in the lake of the Phœnix Paper Mills at Dartford, close to which is the Dartford Creek, conveying the Darenth water to the Thames. In the creek are large dace, flounders, pike, and occasionally salmon trout. There is a peculiar blue roach to be found in a small pond on the Dartford marshes. There are many large carp in the pond of Messrs. Pigou and Wilkes' powder mills. Hotel: Bull.

Dartmouth (Devon).—G.W.R. On Dart; salmon and trout. Dart rises in the centre of Dartmoor, and immediately divides into two parts, the East and West Dart. 5 m. brings the East Dart to Post Bridge, where fisherman's accommodation can be had at the inn, and at some lodgings in the village. 4 m. down, Wallabrook joins Dart. This stream rises in Merripit Hill, 1½ m. from Post Bridge, and has a course of 5 m. There are plenty of trout in this stream. Dart next runs in 2 m. to Dartmeet, where it is joined by the West Dart. This stream, when it leaves the parent brook, runs in a course of 5 m. to Two Bridges, where is a nice fishing inn. Two Bridges is 1½ m. from **Prince Town**, where is the Duchy Hotel, one of the best in the West. At Two Bridges Cowsic brook, 4 m. long, joins Dart. A mile below Two Bridges, Black brook joins Dart on the right. This stream rises on Mis Tor, runs by Dartmoor Prison, close to Prince Town, and joins Dart 1½ m. on. All these streams are full of small trout. A mile below, Cherry brook joins Dart on the left bank. This stream rises close to West Dart, and passes the Post Bridge Road 2 m. from Two Bridges, and the same distance from Post Bridge. The stream is 6 m. long, and fishes well. 2 m. down Dart, Swincombe brook joins on the right bank. This stream is 3 m. long, and worth fishing. 3 m. from this point the two Darts meet. Fishing can be obtained in the above rivers and their tributaries by payment (*see c.s. Dart*); tickets to be obtained at the above inns. Spring and autumn are the best seasons. The best flies are silver grey, willow bud, grouse, badger, and fernweb. From Dartmeet Bridge to New Bridge, 7 m., the river is preserved on the left bank by Dr. Blackall, of Spitchwick, and on the right by the owner of Holne Chase. A mile down from New Bridge Webbern joins Dart. This stream divides in two parts close to its junction with the Dart. The East Webbern rises near Widecombe, and has a course of 4 m. The West Webbern is 7 m. long: the fishing is free. The Dart next runs for 2 m. through the properties of Mr. Bastard, of Buckland, on the left bank, and Holne Chase, on the right, until Holne Bridge is reached. Leave is sometimes granted. Holne Bridge is 2 m. from **Ashburton.** Leaving Holne Bridge, Dart runs to **Buckfastleigh**, 3 m. Here a stream join Dart, 5 m. long, which rises 3 m. north of Ashburton, and flows through that town. ¾ m. below, a brook enters Dart on the right bank, having a course of 6 m. Hence to **Staverton** is 4 m. 3 m. below **Staverton**, a brook, 5 m. long, joins on the right bank. ½ m. below, a stream, 8 m. long, joins on the left bank. ½ m. below this again **Totnes** is reached. Hence to Dartmouth the tide flows. 5 m. below **Totnes**, on the right bank, a considerable stream joins Dart on right bank. This stream, 12 m. long, after running for 4 m., passes 1 m. south of the village of Rattery, thence to Harberton 3 m., and thence 5 m. to Ashsprington at the estuary, where all the estuary fish can be taken freely. There is excellent whiting fishing 7 m. from land. In August there is generally very fair whiting fishing just outside Dartmouth Harbour, abreast of Blackpool Beach in ten fathoms water, about 1 m. from shore. Pollack and bass are to be found near the Mewstone and Eastern Blackstone. At neap tides, in this inner ground, the bottom may be kept with leads of 1lb. and 2lb., but towards the springs 2lb., 3lb., and 4lb. must be used with as fine a line as possible. Whiting fishing not good until after midsummer. (*c.s.*) (*See Stoke Flemming* and *Slapton Ley.*) *Hotel*: Castle.

Darton (Yorks.).—L. & Y.R. Dearne. Darton brook, 1 m. S. (*See Goole.*)

Datchet (Bucks).—L. & S.W.R. Thames. Very good roach swims in the neighbourhood. (*See London, M.T.*) *Fishermen*: J. Keene and Lumsden. *Hotels*: Manor House and Royal Stag.

Dauntsey (Wilts).—G.W.R. Avon; pike, perch, roach; preserved. Thunder brook. (*See Bristol.*) (*c.s.*) *Lakes*: Dauntsey reservoir; pike, perch; leave from Col. Heneage, Dauntsey.

Daventry (Northton.).—L. & N.W.R. Streck, 4 m. E. *Lakes*: Dunsland reservoir; pike perch, &c. Middlemore reservoir, 1½ m. W.; pike, perch, &c. (*See Wisbeach.*)

Dawlish (Devon).—G.W.R. Haldon water; trout. *Hotel*: London, and others. The brook rises on the slopes of Halden, and is 6 m. long. Leave from the farmers and mill-owners. Mr. Hoare, of Luscombe, preserves some portion. Dabs, mackerel, pollack, pout, herrings, and sprats, are caught off here in moderate weather. A sand-eel seine is kept. A line thrown off the breakwater pier at the mouth of the brook, and baited with squid or cuttle, will take large bass in rough weather. The squid must be obtained from the mackerel nets. Pollack towards and close to Parson and Clerk rocks, also ¼ m. off shore, half-way W.

Deal (Kent).—S.E. & C.R. A few roach and perch in the Richboro' stream, Sandwich. There is good fishing in the evening off the pier for pollack, mackerel, &c., in autumn. (*See Margate.*)

Debenham (Suffolk), n.s. **Eye**, 9 m. N.—Deben. (*See Woodbridge.*)

Deepcar (Yorks).—G.C.R. Don. (*c.s. Yorkshire.*) Little Don. Ewdew, 2 m. S. (*See Goole.*)

Defford (Gloucester).—M.R. Avon; chub, dace, roach, pike, perch, bream; free. Bore brook. *Lakes*: Croome Park lakes (3 m. N.W.). (*See Gloucester.*) (*c.s. Severn.*)

Deighton (Yorks).—L. & N.W.R. Colne; polluted Button beck. (*See Rawcliffe.*)

Delamere (Cheshire).—L. & N.W.R.; G.W.R. Brent brook, 1 m. N.E. Ash brook, 2 m. S.E. Oulton brook, 2 m. S. *Lakes*: Flax mere, 1 m. N. Oak mere, 2 m. S.E. Fish pool, 2 m. S. (*See Frodsham.*)

Denby Dale (Yorks).—L. & Y.R. Dearne. (*See Goole.*)

Denholme (York).—G.N.R. Harden beck. *Lakes*: Denholme reservoir. (*See Rawcliffe.*)

Denston (Stafford). — L. & N.W.R.; G.N.R.; M.R. Churnet; trout, grayling; fishing spoilt by Leek drainage. (*c.s. Trent.*) (*See Gainsborough.*)

Dent (Yorks).—M.R. Dee. Deepdale beck.

Denton (Lancs.)—L. & N.W.R. Tame. *Lakes*: Godley reservoir. 2 m. E. (*See Runcorn.*)

Derby.—M.R.; L. & N.W.R. Derwent; pike, coarse fish, grayling, trout; the borough waters free to the mouth of Chaddesden brook, preserved *below* to **Borrowash** by a club. (*c.s. Trent.*) Cuttle brook. Chaddesden brook, 2 m. E. *Lakes*: Allestry Hall lake, 3 m. W. Langley Park lakes, 4 m. N.W. Kedleston Park lake, 4 m. N.W. Locko Park lake, 4 m. N.E. Radburn ponds, 4 m. W. (*See Gainsborough.*) *Hotels*: Midland, St. James.

Desborough (Northton.).—M.R. Ise. (*See Wisbeach.*)

Desford (Leicester).—M.R. Rothley brook. *Lakes*: Gabriel pool, 3 m. W. Kirkby Hall lake, 4 m. S.W., at Kirkby Mallory. (*See Gainsborough.*)

Devereux (Hereford).—G.W.R. Worm brook. (*See Chepstow.*)

Devizes (Wilts).—G.W.R. Kennet and Avon Canal; roach and tench; preserved for 4 m. each side of town; s.t. 2s. 6d., m.t. 1s. Avon, 8 m.; trout and grayling; preserved by landowners. (*See Christchurch.*) Also several brooks and Drew's pond; fishless. (*See Bristol.*) (*c.s.*) *Hotel*: Bear.

Devock Water (Cumland.).—Trout. The lake is preserved. *Inn*: The King of Prussia, 2¼ m. off. River Esk (salmon and trout) and several lakes are near. Burnmore tarn contains large trout and pike.

Dewsbury (Yorks).—G.N.R.; L. & N.W.R.; L. & Y.R. Calder. (*c.s. York.*) (*See Rawcliffe.*) *Lakes*: The Whitley reservoir (trout),

Dicconson (Lancs.).—L. & Y.R. Barsden brook. (*See Hesketh Bank.*)

Didsbury (Lancs).—M.R. Mersey. Poynton brook. (*See Runcorn.*)

Dingestow (Monmouth).—G.W.R. Trothy; trout; preserved. Nant-y-fuchan (2 m.) *c.s. Wye.*) (*See Chepstow.*)

Dinmore (Hereford).—L. & N.W.R.; G.W.R. Lugg; trout, grayling, pike, perch, chub, dace, roach; preserved by the Bodenham Club of 30 members (hon. sec., R. C. Bailey, Esq., the Pigeon House, (Bodenham), from Bodenham, through Dinmore to first iron bridge below Dinmore Station (*c.s. Wye.*) Marston brook (2 m.) (*See Chepstow.*)

Dinsdale (Durham).—N.E.R. Tees, 1 m. S. Salmon, bull trout, grayling, coarse fish; s.t., 10s. 6d.; d.t. 1s. (salmon, d.t. 2s. 6d.) at the Spa Hotel, Dinsdale. *Hotel*: Sulphur Spa (*c.s.*) (*See Stockton.*)

Dinton (Wilts.).—L. & S.W.R. Nadder; trout, roach, dace. (*See Christchurch.*) (*c.s. Avon.*)

Diss (Norfolk).—G.E.R. Waveney. (*c.s. N. and S.*) *Lakes*: Diss mere. (*See Yarmouth.*)

Ditchford (Northton.).—L. & N.W.R. Nene; pike, perch, bream, roach, tench, chub, dace; preserved by Wellingborough Nene Angling Association hence to **Wellingborough**; hon. sec., F. W. Marriott. (*See Wisbeach, Wellingborough.*)

Dodworth (Yorks).—G.C.R. Dove, 1 m. S.E. *Lakes*: Lowe Mill reservoir, 1 m. S. (*See Goole.*)

Dogdyke (Lincoln).—G.N.R. Witham. Bain. (*See Boston.*)

Doncaster (Yorks). — G.N.R.; M.R.; N.E.R.; G.C.R.; L. & Y.R. Don. (*c.s. Yorkshire.*) (*See Goole.*)

Donington (Lincoln).—G.N.R. Hammond beck, 1 m. W. (*See Boston.*)

Dorchester (Dorset).—G.W.R. and L. & S.W.R. Frome; trout; preserved for 3 m. above and 2 m. below the town by the Dorchester Fishing Club, of 24; Hon. Sec., Capt. Dymond, Brooklands, Dorchester. *Entrance*, 15l. 15s.; s.t., 10l. 10s. The rest of the stream is strictly preserved by the landowners. Daily tickets to officers on duty at Weymouth, Dorchester, or Portland are issued by the tackleists, Messrs. Jeffrey and Sons. (*c.s.*) (*See Wareham.*) *Hotels*: King's Arms and Antelope.

Dorking (Surrey).—L.B. & S.C..R and S.E.R. Mole. (*See London. L.T.*) Leave may be obtained from the millers; trout, coarse fish. Very difficult to obtain trouting, which is very good in parts. *Hotels*: Three Tuns, White Horse, Red Lion.

Dorrington (Salop).—L. & N.W.R.; G.W.R. Cound brook; trout; preserved by the owner of Underhill Hall. Row brook (2 m. E.) (*See Gloucester.*)

Doublebois (Cornwall).—G.W.R. Fowey; trout. St. Neot; trout. (*c.s.*) (*See Fowey.*)

Dove Cliff (Yorks).—G.C.R. Dove. *Lakes*: Reservoir, 1 m. W. (*See Goole.*)

Dover (Kent).—S.E. & C.R. On Dour. The trouting in Dour is good, and preserved; leave from the miller at Dovercourt. (*See Kearsney.*) There is good sea fishing from the jetty. Mullet, coal whiting, silver whiting, whiting pouts, smelts, dogfish, and rock tench. Lugworm is the best bait. The wind should be southerly or westerly. Whiting can be taken from the end of the Admiralty Pier, with a long rod, running line, and 3 hooks. Large bass and coal whiting may be taken with worms found between the rocks under the cliffs; codlings and coal whiting from the North Jetty. Mullet and flounders in the harbour.

Downderry (Cornwall).—Good pollack and other sea fishing.

Downham Market (Norfolk).—G.E.R. Ouse; coarse fish except barbel. (*c.s. N. and S.*) The tide runs to Denver Sluice, 2 m. up. *Lakes*, Stradset Hall Lake (4 m. N.E.). (*See King's Lynn.*)

Downton (Wilts.).- L. & S.W.R. Avon; trout, grayling, dace, and pike; preserved. The landlord of the Bull Inn gives leave for 2½ m. of fishing, principally pike and roach. (*See Christchurch.*) (*c.s.*)

Draycot (Somerset).—G.W.R. Stoke Decoy Lakes. (*See Axbridge.*)

Draycott (Derby).—M.R. Derwent; pike, coarse fish, grayling. *(cs. Trent.)* Trent, 3 m S.W., at **Sawley**. *(c.s.)* *(See Gainsborough.)*

Drayton (Norfolk).—G.E.R. Wensum. *(c.s. N. and S.)* Sprixham beck, 2½ m. N.E. *(See Yarmouth.)*

Driffield (York).—N.E.R. Hull. *(c.s. York.)* Very good trouting on Hull for 10 *m.*, preserved by a club of 20 members; entrance 10 guineas; s.t. 10 guineas, with six day cards for friends. The riparian owners are Lord Londesborough, Viscount Downe, Sir Tatton Sykes, and Mr. Reynard, each entitled to silver transferable tickets in proportion to the size of their estate. The season commences on the first Tuesday after the 20th of April, and ends on October 1st. Only artificial fly permitted; limited to ten brace per day, and all fish under 11in. to be returned. The best flies are small duns of different shades, and also a light sand fly. Driffield beck. *(See Hull.)*

Droitwich (Worcester).—G.W.R.; M.R. Salwarpe; trout above, coarse fish below; leave from the landowners. Body brook. Hampton brook (2 m. N.W.), Doverdale brook (2 m. W.) Henbrook (4 m. N.E.). Severn (6 m. W.); pike, perch, chub, dace, roach, trout, salmon. Dean brook (6 m. E.). *Lakes:* Westwood Park lakes (3 m. W.) *(See Gloucester.)* *(c.s. Severn.)* *Hotels:* The Worcestershire Brine Baths, Raven.

Dronfield (Derby).—M.R. Drone. *(See Goole.)*

Dudley (Worcs.). G.W.R. *Lakes:* Gades Green reservoir (2 m. S.). Old Park pond (2 m. W.). Pensnet Park lakes (3 m. S.W.). Himley Park lakes, and Common Pool (4 m. W.). *(See Gloucester.)*

Duffield (Derby).—M.R. Derwent; pike, coarse fish, grayling, trout; preserved by the Duffield Angling Club; s.t. 21s.; m.t. 7s. 6d., w.t. 5s., d.t. 2s.; hon. sec., E. Barnes, Esq., 1, Railway-terrace, Duffield. *(c.s. Trent.)* Ecclesbourne; preserved as Derwent. Holbrook brook, 1 m. E. Cutler brook, 3 m. S.W. *Lakes:* Allestry Park lake, 2 m. S. Kedleston Park lake, 3 m. S.W. *Hotel:* White Hart. *(See Gainsborough.)*

Dulverton (Somerset).—G.W.R. Exe, Haddeo (preserved), Barle, Danes brook (preserved), Brushford brook (preserved). Trout, salmon. *Hotels:* Carnarvon Arms *(see Advt.)*, Red Lion, Lamb, and Royal Oak, Winsford (4 m. fishing free to visitors). The trouting in Exe and Barle is very good. 5 to lb. Fishing in Barle for 3 m. above the town free by ticket; *below* free to visitors staying at the Lion and Lamb hotels, The fishing in Exe is free by ticket one side, preserved the other; season commences March 1. Salmon from June, sometimes later. For trout only—s.t., 21s.; m.t., 10s. 6d.; w.t., 5s.; d.t., 1s.; 10s. 6d. extra for salmon. Tickets at hotels, and from the tackleist, Heath, who will supply every information. The landlord of the Carnarvon Arms, who preserves the Exe above and below Exbridge, has the right also of fishing Lord Carnarvon's water, 5 m. (free to visitors). *(See Exeter and Tiverton.)* At Winsford, 4 m. of fishing free to Royal Oak hotel visitors. *Tackleist:* E. Heath, High-street.

Dulwich (Surrey).—There is a pond here, by the roadside, containing carp, but it belongs to Dulwich College, and it is very difficult to obtain leave. *Hotels:* Crown and Greyhound.

Dunford Bridge (Yorks).—G.C.R. Don. *(c.s. Yorkshire.)* Little Don, 2 m. S. *Lakes:* Dunford Bridge reservoir. *(See Goole.)*

Dunham (Norfolk).—G.E.R. *(See Litcham, King's Lynn).*

Dunmow (Essex)—G.E.R. On Chelmer and Roding; a few trout and other fish. *(See Maldon and Barking.)* *Inns:* Saracen's Head, Star, and White Lion. Leave from the landowners.

Dunstable (Beds).—G.N.R.; L. & N.W.R. Ousel (4 m. S.W.). *(See King's Lynn.)*

Dunster (Somerset).—G.W.R. Dunster brook; trout. Dunster rises in three branches 3 or 4 m. S. of Timberscombe, where the three streams unite, runs to **Dunster** 4 m., and joins the sea 2 m. down. Preserved *above* by Mr. Battersby, of Knowle, and *below* by Mr. Lutterell, of Dunster Castle.

Dunton Green (Kent).—S.E.R. *(See Dartford.)* On Darenth.

Dursley (Gloucester).—M.R. Cam brook. Cam rises by Oldpen in a large mill head, and 1 m. down is joined on left bank by the outfall of a lake in Ley Farm. 2 m. down is Dursley, Cam 2 m., **Dursley Junction** 2 m. Here Ham brook, 3 m. long, joins on right bank. 2 m. down Cam is Slimbridge, and 1 m. down, Slimbridge brook joins on right bank. Slimbridge rises by **Frocester**, and is 5 m. long. 2 m. below the junction is the estuary. Waterley brook. *(See Berkeley.)*

Dursley Junction (Glo'ster).—M.R. Cam brook. Ham brook. *(See Dursley.)*

Durston (Somerset).—G.W.R. *(See Bridgwater.)*

Dymock (Glos.).—G.W.R. Leadon. Preston. *(See Gloucester.)* *(c.s. Severn.)*

Earby (York).—M.R.; L. & Y.R. Elslack. *(See Rawcliffe.)*

Eardisley (Hereford).—G.W.R. Upcott brook. Holywell brook. Wye (1½ m.); salmon, chub, pike, dace, trout. *(c.s.)* *(See Chepstow.)*

Earith (Hunts).—G.E.R. Ouse; coarse fish, except barbel; good free fishing. *(c.s. N. and S.)* *(See King's Lynn).*

Earswick (York).—N.E.R. Fang Hall beck. Foss, 2 m. W., at Huntington. *(See York.)*

East Anstey (Devon).—G.W.R. Yeo. Sturcombe (4 m.). Knowstone water (4 m.). Little Dart (5m.). *(c.s. Taw.)* *(See Barnstaple.)*

East Cottingwith (York), n.s. **High Field**, 4 m.—Derwent; coarse fish; free on the E. Cottingworth side. Pocklington Canal; pike, coarse fish; preserved by the York Angling Club, d.t. 2s. 6d., from the secretary. *(c.s. York.)* *(See Wressel.)*

East Farleigh (Kent).—S.E.R. (*See Rochester* and *Yalding.*) On Medway; preserved by Maidstone Angling Society; hon. sec., F. J. Munn, 17, Bower-street, Maidstone. *Hotels*: Bull and Victory.

East Grinstead (Sussex).—L.B. & S.C.R. On Medway; trout. (*See Rochester.*) *Hotels*: Dorset Arms, Railway.

East Norton (Leicester),—G.N.R.; M.R.; L. & N.W.R. Eye brook. Chater, 3 m. N.E. *Lakes:* Withcote Hall, 4 m. N. (*See Spalding.*)

Easton Court (Hereford). — G.W.R. Teme; trout, grayling, chub, dace, pike. West brook. Cadmore brook (1 m. E.). Ledwych (1½ m. E.); trout, grayling, chub. (*See Gloucester.*) (*c.s. Severn.*)

Eastwood (Notts).—G.N.R.; M.R. Erewash. *Lakes:* Alder Car Hall lakes, 1 m. N. Loscoe dam, 2 m. N.W. (*See Gainsborough.*)

Eastwood (Yorks).—L & Y.R. Calder. (*c.s. York.*) (*See Rawcliffe.*)

Eaton (Salop).—B.C.R. Onny; trout, chub; preserved hence down to **Morderly** by Plowden Fishing Club; hon. sec., H. Manby Colegrave, Lydbury North, Salop. (*c.s. Severn.*) (*See Plowden, Gloucester.*)

Ebbw Vale (Monmouth).—G.W.R. Ebwy; trout. (*c.s. Usk.*) (*See Newport.*)

Eccles (Lancs.)—L. & N.W.R. Irwell. (*See Runcorn.*)

Ecclesfield (Yorks).—G.C.R. Blackburn brook. (*See Goole.*)

Eccleshall (Stafford), n.s. **Norton Bridge**, 3 m.—Sow; trout. Offley brook. *Lakes:* Oatland pond, 4 m. W. Cop mere, 2 m. W. (*See Gainsborough.*)

Eckington (Derby). — M.R.; G.C.R. Rother. Doe Lea. Moss brook, 2 m. N.W. *Lakes:* Quarry dam, 2 m. W. (*See Goole.*)

Edenbridge (Kent).—S.E. & C.R. (*See Rochester.*) On Eden; roach, dace, &c.; d.t. 1s., from landlord of the Star. *Hotels:* Star, Station.

Edensor (Derby), n.s. **Bakewell**, 2 m.—M.R. Derwent; trout, grayling; preserved by the Duke of Devonshire from New bridge *above* to Rowsley bridge *below*. *Hotel:* Chatsworth, where fishing can be had (*see Baslow.*) (*c.s. Trent.*) Bar brook, 2 m. N.E. Wye at **Bakewell**, 2 m. S.W. (*c.s. Trent.*) (*See Gainsborough.*)

Edwalton (Notts).—M.R. Thurbeck. *Lakes:* Roclaveston Manor, 1 m S.E. (*See Gainsboro'.*)

Edington (Somerset). —G.W.R. Brue; roach, carp, perch, pike; free. (*See Highbridge.*) (*c.s. Avon.*)

Eggesford (N. Devon).—L. & S.W.R. On Taw and Little Dart; 20 m. of good trout fishing and 2 m. salmon fishing free to hotel visitors. (*c.s.*) (*See Barnstaple.*) *Hotel:* Fox and Hounds, good accommodation. A good station for trouting.

Egginton (Derby).—G.N.R. Dove; chub, bream, barbel, pike, perch. (*c.s. Trent.*) Longford brook. Trent; 2 m. S.; grayling, pike, chub. (*c.s.*) *Lakes:* Egginton Hall lake; preserved. (*See Gainsborough.*)

Egglescliffe (Durham).—N.E.R. Tees; salmon, trout, bull trout, grayling. coarse fish; preserved above Yarm for 10 m. on the Durham side by the Stockton Angling Association of 120; sec., J. G. Featherstone, Esq., 12, Wilson-street, Thornaby. Entrance, 5s.; s.t., 13s.; hon. members' subscription, 10s. 6d. (*c.s.*) Nelly Burden's beck. Leven trout; private. (*c.s. Tees.*) Saltergill beck; trout; 2 m. E. Bassleton beck, 4 m. N.E. *Hotel:* Blue Bell; fishing from the landlord. who rents 3 or 4 m. of water. (*See Stockton.*)

Egremont (Cumland). — L. & N.W. and Fs.R. Ehen; sea trout, salmon, trout. (*c.s. West Cumland.*) Preserved by a society. S.t., 10s. 6d. Ehen, under the name of Liza, rises on the slopes of Kirkfell and runs 8 m. to Ennerdale lake. This lake is 3 m. long, and at the lower end is the **Boathouse Inn**. The river, as it leaves the lake, takes the name of Ehen. Two m. down, at Ennerdale bridge, Crossdale beck, 4 m. long, joins on right bank Ehen runs 2 m. to **Frizington**, and here Windergyll beck, which rises by **Rownah** and is 4 m. long, joins on right bank. One m. down Lingla beck, 3 m. long. joins on right bank. Ehen runs 3 m. to **Wood End**, and here Keekle joins on right bank. Keekle rises 4 m. above **Moresby Parks** station, 2 m. N.W. from **Whitehaven**, and 2 m. below is joined on left bank by Dub beck, 5 m. long. Keekle runs 2 m. to **Moor Row Junction**. and joins Ehen 1 m. below at **Woodend**. Ehen runs 2 m. to **Egremont**, and **Beckermet** or **Braystones**, 5 m. Here Kirk beck joins on left bank. Kirk beck rises on Cleator Moor, runs 3 m. to 2 m. E. of **Egremont**; thence to **Beckermet** is 5 m. Here also Black beck. 4 m. long, joins on left bank. Four m. down Ehen, a little below **Sellafield**, Calder (*c.s. West Cumland.*) river joins Ehen at the estuary. Calder rises in the hills S. of Ennerdale lake, and 4 m. down is joined on left bank by Worm beck, 5 m. long. Calder runs 5 m. to Calder bridge (*Hotel: Stanley Arms*), 2 m. S.W. of **Beckermet**, and thence to the estuary by **Sellafield**, 3 m. Here also New Mill beck, 5 m. long, joins the estuary. *Hotel:* Globe. The Ehen is much discoloured by mines, so fly fishing is poor.

Egton Bridge (York).—N.E.R. Esk; salmon, trout; preserved by the Esk Fishery Association (m.t. not extending beyond September 30, 3l. 3s. from Mr. Brown, Saw Mills, Whitby) from **Glaisdale** *above* to **Whitby** *below*. (*c.s.*) (*See Whitby.*)

Eland (York).—L. & Y.R. Calder. (*c.s. York.*) Dean. (*See Rawcliffe.*)

Ellesmere (Salop). — C.R. Shell brook, 2 m. N.W. Halghton brook, 4 m. N. (*See Chester.*) Roden, 6 m. S.E. *Lakes:* Ellesmere mere; pike, perch, roach, bream, dace; free. Black mere, 1½ m. S.E.; same fish; license required. White mere, 2 m. S.E.; same fish; leave. Kettle mere, 2 m. S.E.; same fish; leave. Newton mere, 2½ m. S.E.; same fish; leave. Colemere mere, 3 m. S.E.; same fish; leave. Cross mere, 4 m. S.E.; same fish; leave. (*See Gloucester.*) (*c.s. Severn.*)

Elslack (York).—M.R.; L. & Y.R. Elslack. *(See Rawcliffe.)*

Elstead (Sussex).—L. & S.W.R. Western Rother. *(See Littlehampton.)*

Elston (York), nearest station **Grimsargh.**—On Ribble. Good trout, mort, and **sprod** fishing. Leave must be obtained from J. Fletcher, Esq., Leytham. *(c.s.)*

Elstree (Herts). M.R. *(See London, M.T.)*. Elstree reservoir; pike, perch, roach, carp, tench. *Inn*, Fishery.

Elton (Hunts).—L. & N.W.R. Nen; pike, perch, bream, chub, tench, &c.; preserved by Lord Carysfort, who will sometimes give leave. Willow brook. *Lake*: Elton Park (Lord Carysfort). *(See Wisbeach.)*

Ely (Cambridge).—G.E.R. Ouse; coarse fish, except barbel; preserved. *(c.s. N. and S.)* *(See Cambridge).* Cam 3 m. S; same fish; preserved. Lark : 3 m. N.E.; same fish. *(See King's Lynn).* *Hotels* : Lamb, Bell.

Emsworth (Hants).—L.B. & S.C.R. Ems; trout. Ems rises above Racton, where is good trouting, but preserved; runs 2 m. to West Bourne, where fishing is free, and 2 m. on to **Emsworth.** Bass at the harbour's mouth.

Endon (Staffs.).—M.R. Endon brook. *Lakes*: Stanley Mill pond, 1 m. N. *(See Gainsborough.)*

Enesham (Warwick).—G.W.R. Avon : chub, pike, perch, bream, roach, dace. Isborne; few trout, but much polluted. *(See Gloucester.)* *(c.s. Severn.)*

Enfield Lock and Ponder's End (Middx.).—G.E.R. *(See Stratford and London.)* On New River and Lea; roach, dace, chub, barbel, jack, perch, bream. *Hotels*: Anchor and Pike, Swan and Pike, Royal Small Arms Hotel, Enfield Lock. S.t., 10s. 6d.; d.t., 1s. The Ordnance water, containing some good fish, especially chub, comprises the river between the Silent Mill stream and the southernmost boundary of the War Department's property; s.t., 21s.; d.t., 1s.; jacking to s.t. holders only. Above this is the Old King's Head water, which commences at the Tumbling Bay and ends at Chingford Marsh, rented by Mr Coventry. Chub and barbel are plentiful. S.t. 10s. 6d. Trolling begins Sept. 1st. Minnow fishing allowed to season ticket-holders only.

Ennerdale (Cumland).—*Lakes*: Ennerdale; trout. Floutern tarn, 2 m. N.E. *Inn* : Anglers. *(See Cockermouth, Keswick.)*

Entwistle (Lancs.)—L. & Y.R. Bradshaw brook. *Lakes*: Entwistle reservoir. *(See Runcorn.)*

Epsom (Surrey). L. & S.W.R. and L.B. & S.C.R. *(See London, L.T.)* There are some ponds on Epsom Common.

Escrick (York).—G.N.R. Stillingfleet beck. Ouse, 3 m. W. *(c.s. York.)* *(See York.)*

Esher (Surrey).—L. & S.W.R. Mole; pike, perch, chub, &c.; fishing free. *(See London, L.T.)* *Hotel* : Bear.

Esholt (Yorks).—M.R. Aire. *(c.s. York.)* Yeadon beck, 1 m. E. *(See Rawcliffe.)*

Esk Bridge (Cumland).—N.s. **Boot,** 3 m. Esk; trout. *(c.s. West Cumland.)* *Lakes*: Stony tarn, 2 m. N.W. *(See Ravenglass.)*

Eskdale Green (Cumland).—R. & E.R. Esk; trout. *(c.s. West Cumland.)* *Lakes* : Devoke water, 3 m. S.E.; trout; leave from the steward or at the King of Prussia. Mite; trout; 1 m. N.W. *(c.s. West Cumland.)* *Inn:* King of Prussia, Bowerhouse. *(See Ravenglass.)*

Essendine (Rutland).—G.N.R. Glen. Gwash, 1 m. S.W., at **Ryhall.** Edenham brook, 3 m. N.E. *(See Spalding.)*

Etchingham (Sussex).—S.E.R. *(See Rye.)* On Rother. *(c.s.)*

Etwall (Derby).—G.N.R. Etwall brook. Longford brook, 2 m. S.W., at Hilton. Trent, 3 m. S.E., at **Willington.** *(c.s.)* Dove, 4 m. S.W, at **Tutbury.** *(c.s. Trent.)* *(See Gainsborough.)*

Euxton (Lancs.)—L. & N.W.R.; L. & Y.R. Yarrow, 1 m. S. *(See Hesketh Bank.)*

Evercreech (Somerset).—G.W.R. Evercreech; carp, perch, roach, trout, pike. *(See Highbridge.)*

Evercreech Junction (Somerset).—G.W.R. Evercreech. *(See Highbridge.)*

Evershot (Dorset).—G.W.R. *(See Wareham and Bridgwater.)*

Evesham (Worcester). — G.W.R. On Avon; pike, perch, bream, roach, dace, chub; preserved by Evesham Fish Preservation Society for 10 m.; s.t. 1s., d.t. 3d.; with trolling, s.t. 2s. 6d.; licences from Mrs. Whitford, Bridge-street, Fish and Anchor Inn, Littleton, Evesham, Boat Inn, Offenham, Evesham. For fishing from Nortonbrook to notice board above Chadbury Weir, and from Fladbury Weir to Mr. Faulkner's water, s.t., allowing use of boats and fishing in Mr. Faulkner's water, 10s.; season begins June 16, ends March 14; no trailing from boats; hon. sec., A. H. Sharp, Esq., Evesham. *Hotels*: Crown, Northwick Arms, Cross Keys, Rose and Crown. *(c.s. Severn.)*

Ewell (Surrey).—L. & S.W.R. Hog's Mill River; trout; leave from landowners. *(See London, L.T.)*

Ewood Bridge (Lancs.)—L. & Y.R. Irwell. Swinnel brook, 1 m. S.W. *(See Runcorn.)*

Exeter (Devon.)—G.W.R. and L. & S.W.R. On Exe; salmon, trout, pike, dace, perch. Exe rises on Ashcombe Hill, in the centre of Exmoor, and runs 6 m. to Exford (trouting very good, and free, n.s. *Hotel*: White Horse, which has some private fishing.) 6 m. down stream is Winsford (n.s **Dulverton.** 6 m. *Hotel*: Royal Oak, very comfortable; good trouting early in the season free of the hotel). 2 m. below at Exton, Quarme Water joins Exe on left bank. Quarme rises 2 m. N. of Exford, and is 7 m. long. Exe flows in 6 m. to Hele Bridge, **Dulverton** being 1 m. distant on right bank. 1 m. below, Haddeo joins Exe on left bank. Haddeo rises some 2 m. E. of Exton, and in 4½ m. is joined on left bank by a stream 2 *m.* long. 1½ *m.* down, a stream joins Haddeo on left bank, which is some 3 *m.* long, running in two streams, which meet at Stert Bridge. Haddeo joins Exe 4 *m.* down. Lord Carnarvon preserves Haddeo. Exe runs in 1½ *m.* to Exe Bridge and **Dulverton** Station. Here Barle joins Exe on right bank. Barle rises in the centre of Exmoor, and runs in 3 *m.* to Simondsbath (n.s. **Dulverton,** 14 *m.*). Trout numerous but small. Leave from Mr. Viceout, of Ebington; (a good inn, but no beer or spirit licence). 3½ *m.* down at Landacre Bridge, Sheardown Water, 4 *m.* long, joins on right bank (fishing very good, and free). Barle flows in 3 *m.* to Withypool (n.s. **Dulverton,** 8 *m.* (leave from Landacre Farm). There is a decent little inn here, and the trouting very good, and free. (Exford and River Exe is 3 *m.* over the hills from here.) A stream 4 *m.* long joins Barle here on left bank. 6 *m.* down Barle, Danes brook, 6 *m.* long, joins on right bank (this brook is preserved by the owner of the property, but leave is often given). **Dulverton** (*Hotel*: Carnarvon Arms, free fishing), is 2 *m.* down Barle. 2 *m.* on, Barle joins Exe at Exbridge, where the Tiverton Association rights begin. ½ *m.* below Exe Bridge, Brushford brook, 4 *m.* long, joins on right bank; preserved. 4 *m.* down Exe, Belbrook joins on right bank (n.s. **Bampton,** 2 *m.*) Belbrook is some 7 *m.* long, and midway is joined on right bank by two short streams. The whole is in private hands. 1 *m.* down Exe, Bampton brook joins on left bank. Bampton rises above Raddington (n.s. **Venn Cross,** 2 *m.*), and 5 *m.* down is joined on right bank by a short stream rising 1 *m.* E. of **Morebath.** Bampton runs 2 *m.* to **Bampton,** and 1½ *m.* below joins Exe. This stream is free. There is a decent angling inn at the junction of Bampton with Exe. 6 *m.* down Exe a short stream joins on right bank, which rises by Culverleigh. **Tiverton** is 1 *m.* on. Here Loman joins on left bank. Loman is some 9 *m.* long, and receives a tributary 5 *m.* long at Uploman. 4 *m.* down Exe at **Bickleigh** (here the Tiverton fishing ends) there is a nice little inn—Bickleigh Bridge Inn. There are plenty of dace below the weir, but only trout and salmon above. The fishing for 1½ *m.* is private, thence to **Thorverton** is preserved by Up. Exe F. Assoc. At **Bickleigh,** Dart river joins Exe on right bank. Dart is about 9 *m.* long, and rises above Coombe Mill, 6 *m.* W. of **Tiverton.** 2 *m.* down Exe, Butterleigh brook, 4 *m.* long, joins on left bank. Exe runs in 1½ *m.* to **Silverton, Thorverton** (here the Up. Exe Society ends) 1 *m.*, **Brampford Speke** on right bank, and Stoke Cannon on left bank, 3 *m.* (Here begins Lord Iddesleigh's water, which runs to Cowley bridge.) 1 *m.* down Exe, Culm river joins on left bank. Culm rises 3 or 4 *m.* above **Hemyock,** where a stream of the same length joins on left bank. Culm runs 2½ *m.* to **Culmstock,** and 2 *m.* down Sheldon brook joins on left bank, 5 *m.* long. **Ufculm** is 1 *m.* down Culm, **Tiverton Junction** 2 *m.*, and **Cullompton** 2 *m.* Here Kentisbere brook, 4 *m.* long, joins on left bank. 1 *m.* down Culm, Ashford brook joins on right bank. Ashford rises 1 *m.* W. of Sampford Peverell (n.s. **Tiverton Junction,** 3 *m.*), and 3 *m.* down is joined on right bank by a stream which rises by Halberton (n.s. **Tiverton Junction,** 2 *m.*) 1 *m.* down Ashford, and 1 *m.* from **Cullompton,** Fulford water, 4 *m.* long, joins on right bank. 1 *m.* down, Ashford joins Culm. 2 *m.* down Culm, Langford brook, 3 *m.* long, joins on left bank. 1 *m.* down Culm is **Hele,** Stoke Cannon 5 *m.*, and Exe 1 *m.* 2 *m.* down Exe is Cowley Bridge. (Here Lord Iddesleigh's fishing ends, and hence to **Exeter** the river is in private hands, but permits for pike and roach fishing may often be obtained. Creedy joins on right bank. Creedy rises 3 or 4 *m.* above Woodfardisworthy (n.s. **Crediton,** N.D.R.), and 5 *m.* down is joined on left bank by Yeo brook, 5 *m.* long. 1 *m.* down Creedy at Sandford. Sandford brook, 3 *m.* long, joins on right bank. Crediton is 2½ *m.* down Creedy. Here Spreyton water joins Creedy on right bank. Spreyton rises by Spreyton (n.s. **Bow,** C.R., 2 *m.*), runs 6 *m.*, when it is joined at Colbrook by two short streams on either bank. Spreyton runs in 3 *m.* to **Crediton,** where a short stream joins on right bank; and 1 *m.* down, Spreyton joins Creedy. Creedy runs 2 *m.* to **St. Cyres** (N.D.R.), where Shobrook brook, 4 *m.* long, joins on left bank. From hence to the junction of Creedy with Exe is 5 *m.* **Exeter** is 1 *m.* down Exe. There are plenty of dace, &c., close to the city.

The EXETER SHIP CANAL contains roach, dace, pike, perch, carp, tench, eels, and flounders. The best part is the low half beyond Countess Weir, beginning opposite the limekilns on the broadwater. Large carp and tench have been taken here. The roach are also fine. Between Topsham Lock and the nearest drawbridge is a very good spot; 1½ *m.* farther is Turf Lock House, a very comfortable inn. *C.s.* Mar. 1 to June 15.

ALPHINGTON brook joins Exe Estuary on right bank at Alphington, 3 *m.* S. of Exeter. This brook rises by West Town, and in 2 *m.* is joined by Adder Water on left bank, which rises by Whitestone, and is 3 *m.* long. Alphington runs to Ide 1 *m.* and Alphington 1 *m.* *Tackleists*, W. Osborne, 251, High-street, and J. Webber and Sons (late E. Prickman), 51, High-street.

Exhall (Warwick).—L. & N.W.R. Sow. Breach brook. (*See Gloucester.*)

Exminster (Devon).—G.W.R. Towsington brook; few trout. This brook rises by Shillingford, and is 4 *m.* long.

Exmouth (Devon).—L. & S.W.R. Bass are caught here in summer by towing a dead sand-eel in a boat under sail. Flounders and eels, with soft crab bait, especially off Lympstone. Outside the bar, dabs may be taken with mussel bait. Pollack with sand or freshwater eel bait, off Straight Point, where pout, bream, and congers are also found. Mackerel fishing is much followed in spring, summer, and autumn under sail. (*See Ottery St. Mary.*) *Hotels*: Imperial (*see Advertisement*), Royal Beacon. Good trouting, by permission of Imperial Hotel, in the river Otter, by rail from Exmouth. *Fly-tyer*, Miss Ellis, 6, Danby-terrace.

Eye (Hereford).—L. & N.W.R.; G.W.R. Bidgmore brook. *Lakes:* Croft Castle (3 m.) (*See Chepstow.*)

Eye (Suffolk).—G.E.R. Eye brook. Waveney, 4 m. N. (*See Yarmouth.*)

Eye Green (Cambs).—G.E.R. Muscal River. Fen drains. (*See Wisbeach.*)

Eynsford (Kent).—S.E. & C.R. (*See Dartford.*) On Darenth; trout; fishing good. Mr. W. B. Leaf, who preserves 2 m. of the Darenth, occasionally has a rod to let. His address is Kilvington, Eynsford. *Hotel:* Eynsford Castle. The landlord of the Lion Hotel, at Farningham, has some fishing free to visitors.

Eynsham (Oxford).—G.W.R. Thames; chub, perch, pike. &c. *Hotels:* Red Lion and Swan. (*See London, U.T.*)

Facit (Lancs.)—L. & N.W.R.; G.N.R.; M.R. Dodd. (*See Runcorn.*)

Fairfield (Lancs.)—G.N.R.; M.R. *Lakes:* Gorton reservoir. (*See Runcorn.*)

Fairford (Glo'ster).—G.W.R. On Coln; trout. D.t. to visitors staying at the hotel, 2s. 6d. Good fishing, beginning April 1st. Fly only. Fishing good. *Hotel:* Bull. *Tacklelst;* T. Powell. (*See London, U.T., Cirencester, Bibury.*)

Fakenham (Norfolk)—G.E.R. Wensum. (c.s. N. and S.) (*See Yarmouth.*)

Falmouth (Cornwall).—G.W.R. (*See St. Mawes, Penryn, Manaccan, and St. Keverne.*) 2 m. S.W. at Budock runs Budock water, 3 m. long. (c.s. *Fowey.*) *Hotels:* Royal, Green Bank.

Fangfoss (York). — N.E.R. (*See Kexby, Sutton-on-Derwent.*) Foss beck. (*See Wressel.*)

Fareham (Hants.).—L. & S.W.R. Meon; trout, roach. Meon rises in a mill pond at East Meon (n.s. **Petersfield,** 5 m.), runs to Droxford, 7 m., Wickham, 4 m., Titchfield, 4 m., and 2 m. on joins the sea. From its source to a mile below Wickham the stream is private. Hence to Titchfield (*Hotel,* Bugle) it is preserved by E. Goble, Esq., solicitor, Fareham: s.t., 8l. 8s. Local flies are March brown, hawthorn, and May fly. Close to the shore is Brownwich Pond, preserved. A stream ran into Portsmouth Harbour here, which rises in Rudley Mill, and in 2½ m. is joined on left bank by the drainage of Creech Pond ¼ m. up. 1 m. on is Southwick, where is a large lake at the Priory. 1 m. below a stream joins on right bank, draining a pond 1 m. up. **Fareham** is 3 m. on. This stream is small and private.

Farington (Lancs.)—L. & N.W.R.; L. & Y.R. Lostock. (*See Hesketh Bank.*)

Farnborough (Hants).—L. & S.W.R. Near here is a large pond, the source of Blackwater. 3½ m. off are the Fleet Ponds. Fishing good, but reserved for the men at Aldershot. *Hotel:* Queen's. (*See London, M.T.*)

Farnham (Surrey). — L. & S.W.R. Wey; trout. 4 m. S. on Frensham Common are the Great and Little Ponds; pike, perch, tench, and carp. *Hotel:* Frensham Pond Hotel. (*See London, L.T.*).

Farningham (Kent). — S.E. & C.R. On Darenth; trout. (*See Dartford.*) Fair trouting early in the season, which commences on April 1, by staying at the Lion Hotel, for 1½ m.; fly only. The owner of Franks also preserves a portion of the water.

Farnsfield (Notts).—M.R. Rainsworth brook. *Lakes:* Inkersall dam, 3 m. N.W. (*See Althorpe*).

Farnworth (Lancs.)—L. & N.W.R.; G.N.R. Irwell. Tange. *Lakes:* Black Leech pond, 2 m. S. Lynnyshaw dam, 3 m. S. (*See Runcorn.*)

Fawley (Hants.).—1 m. off, on Fields Heath, are some small ponds, and one large one. 2 m. off runs the Dark Water. This stream rises in Flash Pond on Beaulieu Heath, runs 1 m. to another pond. Here joins on right bank the outflow from four ponds on the heath, ½ m. up. 1½ m. down the outflow of a pond joins on right bank, ½ m. up. 4 m. down is the sea.

Fawley (Hereford). — G.W.R. Wye; salmon, pike, chub, dace, trout. (c.s.) Sollers brook (1 m.). Wriggle brook (2 m.). Llanwarne brook (5 m.) (c.s.) (*See Chepstow.*)

Felixstowe (Suffolk).—G.E.R. The King's Fleet, a good piece of water, is near here, about 2 m., belonging to E. G. Pretyman, Esq., but managed by A. T. Cobbold, Esq. Spronghton, Ipswich, who gives leave on payment of a small fee (devoted to charity). (c.s. S. and E.)

Felmingham (Norfolk).—G.E.R. Gunton beck. (*See Yarmouth.*)

Felstead (Essex).—G.E.R. On Chelmer; coarse fish. (*See Maldon.*)

Feltham (Middx.).—L. & S.W.R. A branch of Colne. Some fishing can be had, at per day, from one Dawes. (*See London, L.T.*)

Felton (Northland.). - n.s. **Acklington.** Coquet; trout. *Hotels:* Northumberland Arms and Stag's Head. Fishing preserved by Northumbrian Anglers' Federation; s.t. holders can fish Lord Armstrong's water at Rothbury; bull trout and salmon in spring and autumn. *Tacklelsts,* R. and J. Mack. (*See Warkworth* and *Rothbury.*) (c.s.)

Fenniscowles (Lancs.).—L. & N.W.R.; L. & Y.R. Dorwen. Roddlesworth. (*See Preston.*)

Fenns Bank (Salop).—L. & N.W.R. Worthenbury brook, 6 m. N.W. Halghton brook, 6 m. N.W. *Lakes:* Halghton Mill ponds, 6 m. N.W. (*See Chester.*)

Fenny Compton (Warwick). — G.W.R. Ham brook (2½ m. N.), Itchene (3 m. N.), *Lakes:* Stoneton House Lake (2½ m. N.E.) (*See London, M.T.,* and *Gloucester, L.S.*)

Fenny Stratford (Bucks).—L. & N.W.R. Ousel. (*See King's Lynn.*)

Fenton (Stafford).—L. & N.W.R. Trent. (c.s.) *Lakes:* Pond by railway, 1 m. E. (*See Gainsborough.*)

Ferry (Lincoln).—G.N.R. Nen. Fen drains. (*See Wisbeach.*)

Perry Hotel (Lancs.), opposite **Bowness.**—Cunsey beck; trout. (*c.s. Kent.*) *Lakes:* Windermere; pike, perch. large trout, char. Esthwaite Water; pike, perch, trout;. 2 m. W. (*c.s. Kent.*) (*See Ulverston.*)

Filey (York).—N.E.R. Heltord, 3 m. W.; coarse fish. (*See Wressel.*)

Filleigh (Devon).—G.W.R. Bray; trout; preserved mostly by Sir T. Acland and Lord Poltimore; elsewhere free, except at Castle Hill Park (Lord Fortescue).

Filton (Glo'ster).—G.W.R. Frome. 3 m.; coarse fish. Bradley brook, 3 m.; trout, coarse fish; leave from the landowners. (*See Bristol* and *Lea Mills.*)

Finedon (Northton.).—M.R. Ise. *Lake:* Findorn Hall, 2 m. S.E. (*See Wisbeach.*)

Pingall (York).—N.E.R. Bedale, 2 m. N. (*See York.*)

Finningley (Notts).—G.N.R. Torne, 2 m. N.E. at Auckley. (*See Althorpe.*)

Fisherton de la Mere (Wilts.) n.s. **Wylye.**—G.W.R., 1½ m. Wylye; trout, grayling; preserved.

Fishponds (Glo'ster).—M.R. Frome. *Lakes:* Stoke Park. Frenchay pond on Frenchay Common; tench; leave from W. Perry, Esq., Hambrook. Duchess pond; carp, perch,. roach, dace; leave on application to Duke of Beaufort or Admiral Close, Stoke Park. (*See Bristol.*)

Fiskerton (Notts).—M.R. Trent; pike, chub, roach, dace, perch, barbel, a few trout; preserved below Greet mouth by Nottingham Piscatorial Society of 100 (sec. J. Clements,. 1, Mount Pleasant, Mount Street); the Wellington Angling Society (hon. sec,, H. Spray,. Esq., 24, Pilcher Gate) preserves the opposite side. (*c.s.*) Greet. *Hotel:* Bromley Arms. (*See Gainsborough.*)

Five Mile House or Fiskerton (Lincoln).—G.N.R. Witham. Langworth, 2 m. E. (*See Boston.*)

Flamborough (York).—N.E.R. *Hotel:* Ship. Lodgings can be had. From June to Sept. there is good fly fishing from off the rocks. Billet, pollack, coalfish, are plentiful.

Flax Bourton (Somerset).—G.W.R. (*See Clevedon.*)

Fleetwood (Lancs.)—L. & Y.R.; L. & N.W.R. Wyre. Wyre rises on Tarnbrook Fell, and 5 m. down is joined on right bank by Grizedale river, 2 m. long. 1 m. down Wyre,. Marshaw Wyre, 4 m. long; joins on left bank. Wyre runs 1 m., where Catshaw brook,. 3 m. long, joins on left bank. Wyre runs 3 m., where Damas stream, 3 m. long, joins on right bank, **Bay Horse** being 2 m. W. on right bank. Wyre runs to **Scorton** 5 m.,. and **Garstang** 3 m. Just above, Grizedale brook, 5 m. long, joins on left bank. 3 m. below **Garstang**, Calder river, 9 m. long, joins on left bank. Wyre runs 3 m. to St. Michael's-on-Wyre, where Brock river joins on left bank. Brock rises 8 m. above **Brock** Station, and 2 m. below **Brock** is joined on right bank by Blay brook, 3 m. long,. and on left bank by Woodplumpton brook; this brook, under the name of Blundel brook,. rises 4 m. above the railway, 1 m. S. of **Broughton**, and 5 m. down is joined on right bank by Barton brook. This brook, under the name of Westfield brook, rises 6 m. above **Barton**, and joins the parent brook 4 m. below, which joins Brock 3 m. down. Wyre runs 6 m. to the estuary, and here Thistleton brook, 4 m. long, joins on left bank. 6 m. down the estuary by **Poulton** a stream joins on left bank, draining Marten mere 4 m. S. of **Poulton**. Wyre runs to **Fleetwood** in 5 m.

Florden (Norfolk).—G.E.R. Lese; good fishing. (*See Yarmouth.*)

Foleshill (Warwick).—L. & N.W.R. Sow. Marches brook (*See Gloucester.*)

Ford (Hereford).—L. & N.W.R.; G.W.R. Lugg; trout, grayling, pike, perch, dace; Mr. Arkwright, of Hampton Court, preserves 5 m. from Ford to Bodenham; preserved above Ford by the Leominster Club (*see Leominster*). (*c.s. Wye.*) Humber brook (2 m.). Marston-brook (4 m.). *Lakes:* Hampton Park (2 m.). (*See Chepstow.*)

Ford (Sussex).—L.B. & S.C.R. Arun. (*See Littlehampton.*)

Ford Green (Stafford).—L. & N.W.R. Foxley brook. Trent, 1 m. E. (*c.s.*) (*See Gainsborough.*)

Fordham (Cambs.)—G.E.R. Kent (3 m. E). (*See King's Lynn.*)

Fordingbridge (Hants).—S. & D.R. On the Avon; trout, grayling, perch, &c. *Hotel:* Greyhound. Mr. Coventry's fishing is now let; elsewhere preserved by Marchioness of Anglesea. (*See Christchurch.*)

Forge Valley (York).—N.E.R. Derwent; trout, grayling, coarse fish below Ayton; preserved by Derwent Anglers' Club; d.t. 5s. and 2s. 6d. of hon. sec. S. W. Fisher, Esq., J.P., Gainsborough Private Hotel, Scarborough. (*See Hackness, Wressel.*)

Forncett (Norfolk).—G.E.R. Lese. (*See Yarmouth.*)

Foulridge (Lancs.)—L. & Y.R. *Lakes:* 3 reservoirs. (*See Preston.*)

Four Ashes (Stafford).—L. & N.W.R. Saredon brook. Penk, 1 m. W. (*See Gainsborough.*).

Fowey (Cornwall). — G.W.R. Fowey river; trout, sea trout, salmon; preserved by B. Fortescue, Esq., and Lord Robartes, who give leave; free below; autumn is the best time. (*c.s.*) Fowey rises 5 m. N. E. of Temple (n.s. **Bodmin**, 7 m.),. runs 15 m. to Doublebois, where it is joined on right bank by St. Neot river (n.s. **Liskeard**, 5 m.) St. Neot rises on Bodmin Moor, 4 m. from Temple, and 1 m. down is joined on left bank by the outflow of Dozmare pool 1½ m. up. St. Neot. runs 6 m. to St. Neot (n.s. **Liskeard**, 6 m.), and Fowey, 3 m Fowey. runs 3 m., and is joined on right bank by Temple brook. Temple rises by Temple,. runs 5 m. to Warleggon (n.s. **Bodmin Road**, 6 m.), and Fowey, 5 m. Fowey runs 4 m. to **Bodmin Road** station, where Milton brook, 7 m. long, joins on right bank. Fowey runs 4 *m.* to **Lostwithiel**, and 1 *m.* down is joined on right bank by Red brook, which rises in some ponds on Red Moor and Creek, and is 4 *m.* long. 4 *m.* down Fowey on left bank is the Leign, which rises 2 *m.* above Boconnock (n.s. **Lostwithiel**, 3 *m.*), and is 7 *m.* long, holding trout. 1 *m.* down Fowey on left bank is Penpole Creek, into which runs Trebant water, which rises 2 *m.* E. of Boconnock, and is 7 *m.* long, holding trout, fishing free. Fowey runs to **Fowey**, and the sea in 2 *m.* Into the left side of the harbour opposite the town flows Pont brook, 4 *m.* long, holding trout, fishing free. There is capital sea fishing of all kinds. *Hotels*: Fowey, St. Catharine's.

Framlingham (Suffolk).—G.E.R. Ore. Deben, 4 *m.* S.W. *Lake*: Framlingham pond. *(See Orford; Woodbridge.)*

French Drove (Cambs.)—G.E.R. Muscal river. Fen drains. *(See Wisbeach.)*

Freshford (Somerset).—G.W.R. *(See Bristol.)* Avon; roach, perch, trout, &c. Preserved by the Avon and Tributaries Angling Association (hon. sec., J. Justice, Esq., 18, Freemantle-sq., Cotham, Bristol), s.t. 2*l.*; obtainable at the New Inn. *(c.s.)* Frome; roach, trout; reserved.

Frisby (Leicester).—M.R. Wreak; roach, bream. *(c.s. Trent.)* *(See Gainsborough.)*

Frizington (Cumland).—L. & N.W. and Fs.R. Ehen. *(c.s. West Cumland.)* Windergill beck. Lingla beck, 1 *m.* W. *(See Egremont.)*

Frocester (Gloucester).—M.R. Slimbridge brook. *(See Dursley.)*

Frodingham.—G.C.R. Bottesford beck; roach, dace.

Frodsham (Cheshire).—L. & N.W.R. and G.W.R. Weaver. Weaver rises in Moss mere in Cholmondeley Park, 3 *m.* N.E. of **Malpas**, runs thence to Capel mere, also in the park, and 3 *m.* down is joined on right bank by the drainage of Cholmondeley mere ½ *m* up, 4 *m.* N.W. of **Wrenbury.** 3 *m.* down at **Wrenbury**, Marbury brook joins on right bank. Marbury rises in Bret's mere, 4 *m.* W. of **Malpas**, runs 1 *m.* to Bickley Mill pond, and just below waters Bar mere, 3 *m.* S.E. of **Malpas.** 1 *m.* down, Marbury joins the Ellesmere and Chester canal. 2 *m.* down, Oss brook joins on right bank, which rises in Oss mere, 2 *m.* N.E. of **Whitchurch**, and 1 *m.* down is joined on left bank by the outflow of Marbury mere and Marbury Mill pond, ½ *m.* up, 3 *m.* N.E. of **Whitchurch.** 2 *m.* down is Marbury, which runs 1 *m.* to Weaver. Weaver runs to **Wrenbury** 1 *m.*, and 3 *m.* down is joined on right bank by Salesbrook, which rises in Combermere mere at Combermere Abbey, 2 *m.* S. from **Wrenbury**, and is 2 *m.* long. Weaver runs 3 *m.* to **Audlem.** Here Adderley brook joins on right bank. Adderley rises in New pool at Shavington, 1 *m.* S.W. of **Adderley.** and 1 *m.* down is joined on right bank by the outflow of Adderley Hall lake, ½ *m.* up, and close to **Adderley** station. ½ *m.* down Adderley is the outflow of another pond in the park, and 2 *m.* down, a stream, 1 *m.* long, joins on right bank, draining "the mere" close by the railway station to the N. ½ *m.* down, Adderley joins Weaver. 4 *m.* below **Audlem** Birch Hall brook, which rises in Woodfall pool, 2 *m.* N.E. of **Audlem**, and is 2 *m.* long, joins on right bank. 1 *m.* down Weaver, Artle brook joins on right bank. Artle rises in two lakes in Madeley Manor Park, 1 *m.* W. of **Keel**, and 1 *m.* down waters Bowsey Mill pond, 1 *m.* N. of **Madeley.** 1 *m.* down Artle, Madeley brook, which rises in Madeley Mill pond by **Madeley**, and is 2 *m.* long, joins on left bank. Close to the junction is Wrinehill Mill pond, 2 *m.* N.W. of **Madeley.** Artle runs 2 *m.* to Howbeck bridge, 2 *m.* S.E. of **Nantwich**, and here joins Howbeck, which drains the lakes in Doddington Park, 2 *m.* up, 4 *m.* S.E. of **Nantwich** or 3 *m.* S.W. of **Basford.** Weaver runs 2 *m.* to Shrew bridge, where Baddiley brook, which rises in Baddiley mere, 2 *m.* N. of **Wrenbury**, and is 4 *m.* long, joins on left bank. Weaver runs to **Nantwich**, 1 *m.*, and 2 *m.* down is joined on right bank by Cheer brook, 3 *m.* long, 1 *m.* E. of **Nantwich.** Weaver runs to **Worleston**, 2 *m.*, and here Pool brook joins on left bank and Wistaston brook on right bank. Pool brook rises in a lake by Hurleston, 3 *m.* N.W. of **Nantwich**, and is 5 *m.* long. Wistaston rises in Betley mere, 3 *m.* N.W. of **Madeley**, runs to Little mere close by, and 1 *m.* down is joined on right bank by the outflow of Betley Hall lake, 3 *m.* S.E. of **Basford.** Wistaston runs 1 *m.* to **Basford**, Wistaston Old Hall, 1 *m.* S.W. of **Crew**, 3 *m.*, and 1 *m.* down is joined on left bank by Swill brook, which rises W. of **Basford**, and is 5 *m.* long. 1 *m.* down Wistaston, Inglesway brook joins on right bank. Inglesway rises in Balterley mere, 1 *m.* E. of **Basford**, runs 2 *m.* to Monneley mere, 1 *m.* to Crewe House lakes, **Crewe** 1 *m.*, and joins Wistaston 2 *m.* down. Wistaston joins Weaver 1 *m.* down. Weaver runs to Church Minshull, 2 *m.* S.W. of **Minshull Vernon** station (1 *m.* off on E. bank), 4 *m.*, and is here joined on left bank by Ash brook. Ash rises in Oak mere in Delamere Forest, 2 *m.* S.E. of **Delamere** station, and 4 *m.* down is joined on right bank by Oulton brook, which rises in Fish pool in Delamere Forest, 2 *m.* S. of **Delamere**, runs 1½ *m.* to Oulton Mill, ½ *m.* to Oulton Hall lake, 4 *m.* N.E. of **Beeston**, and 2 *m.* down joins Ash. At the junction a stream joins on left bank, working a large mill and pond 1 *m.* up at Little Budsworth, 5 *m.* W. of **Winsford.** 2 *m.* down Ash, Wettenhall brook, which rises in Tilston Hall lake, 1 *m.* N.E. of **Beeston**, and is 5 *m.* long, joins on right bank. Ash joins Weaver 2 *m.* down. 2 *m.* down, Weaver waters a lake at Stocks Hill, 1 *m.* S. of **Winsford** and 3 *m.* W. of **Middlewich**, runs to **Winsford**, 1 *m.*, and 2 *m.* below is joined on left bank by Whitgate brook, which rises in some ponds on Newchurch Common, 2 *m.* S. of **Cuddington**, runs 2 *m.* to Pettypool in New Park, 2 *m.* S.E. of **Cuddington**, and joins Weaver 2 *m.* down. Weaver runs 4 *m.* to **Northwich.** Here Dane joins on right bank. Dane rises on the west slope of Axe Edge, 4 *m.* S.W. of **Buxton**, and 5 *m.*

down is joined on right bank by Folly brook, 4 *m.* long, 5 *m.* N.E. of **Bosley.** Dane runs 3 *m.*, when it receives the outflow of Bosley reservoir by **Bosley.** Dane runs in 1 *m.*, 1 *m.* N. of **Rushton,** 2 *m.* to **Bosley,** and 2 *m.* down at Colley Mill is joined on right bank by Cow brook, which rises in Great Oak reservoir, 2 *m.* N. of **Rode** or 3 *m.* S. of **Macclesfield,** runs 2 *m.* to Rode reservoir by, **Rode,** and joins Dane 1 *m.* down. Dane runs 3 *m.* to **Congleton,** and here Biddulph brook, 5 *m.* long, joins on left bank. 4 *m.* down Dane, Dairy brook joins on left bank, which runs 1 *m.* W. of **Congleton,** where it waters a mill pond, and joins Dane 2 *m.* below. Dane runs 2 *m.* to within 2 *m.* E. of **Holmes Chapel,** when two streams join on either bank; the left waters Bagmere, 4 *m.* W. of **Congleton** or 3 *m.* S.E. of **Holmes Chapel,** and the other Midgebrook, on right bank, rises by Marton, 3 *m.* N. of **Congleton,** and is 5 *m.* long. Dane runs 2 *m.* to **Holmes Chapel,** and **Middlewich,** 5 *m.* Here Wheelock joins on left bank. Wheelock rises in Moreton Hall lake, 2 *m.* S.W. of **Congleton,** running to **Sandbach,** 5 *m.* 1 *m.* below, at Wheelock, Betchton brook, 6 *m.* long, and Hassall brook join on left bank. Hassall rises in Alsager pond by **Alsager,** and 2 *m.* down is joined on right bank by Lawton brook, which rises in Lawton Hall lake, 2 *m.* E. of **Alsager,** and 1 *m.* below is joined by the outflow of Lawton mere and Rode Hall lake, the one on the right bank and the other on the left bank. 2 *m.* down, Lawton joins Hassall, which joins Wheelock 2 *m.* down. Wheelock runs 2 *m.*, when Foul brook, which rises in Winterley Mill pond, 2 *m.* N.E. of **Crewe** or 2½ *m.* S. of **Sandbach,** and is 4 *m.* long, joins on left bank. Wheelock runs to Forge Mill, 1 *m.* E. of **Minshull Vernon,** and **Middlewich,** 4 *m.* Here Croco joins Wheelock on right bank Croco rises 6 *m.* above **Holmes Chapel,** and joins Wheelock 4 *m.* below. At the junction Sanderson's brook, 6 *m.* long, joins Croco on left bank. Dane runs to **Northwich** and Weaver, 6 *m* Here at the salt works, Norcot brook, Budworth brook, and Kincham brook join on right bank. Norcot is 7 *m.* long, watering the lake at Cogshall, 2 *m.* up. Budworth rises in Pickmere mere, 2 *m.* N.E. of **Northwich,** runs 1 *m.* to Budworth mere, 2 *m.* N. of **Northwich,** and joins Weaver 1 *m.* down. Kincham rises in the lake at Toft Hall, 3 *m.* E. of **Plumley,** and 2 *m.* down is joined on right bank by the outflow of Nether Tabley lake, 1 *m.* N. of **Plumley.** ¾ *m.* down, Waterless brook joins on right bank. Waterless rises above Arley, 5 *m.* N.E. of **Northwich,** and here Birch brook, 4 *m.* long, joins on right bank. This brook waters the long lake in Arley Hall Park, close to its junction with Waterless. Waterless runs 4 *m.* to Kincham. 1 *m.* down Kincham, Peover brook joins on right bank. Peover rises in a mill pond by Gawsworth, 3 *m.* S.W. of **Macclesfield,** and 1 *m.* down, at Siddington, is joined on right bank by the drainage of the lakes at Thornycroft Hall, 3 *m.* S.W. of **Macclesfield.** 1 *m.* down Peover is the draining of a small mere on the right bank, 3 *m.* S.E. of **Chelford.** 2 *m.* down Peover, a brook, 1 *m.* long, joins, which drains Reeds mere and Capesthorne Hall lake, 4 *m.* W. of **Macclesfield** or 2 *m.* S.E. of **Chelford.** Peover runs 1 *m.* to **Chelford** and Astle Hall lake, and here Bug brook joins on right bank. Bug rises in Henbury Hall lake, 3 *m.* W. of **Macclesfield,** and 1 *m.* down receives the drainage of the lake at Old Hall, 3 *m.* W. of **Macclesfield.** Bug runs to **Chelford** in 3 *m.* Peover runs 6 *m.* to Nether Peover, and here a brook, 2 *m.* long, joins on right bank, draining the lake at Over Peover Hall, 3 *m.* S.W. of **Chelford.** Peover runs 2 *m.* to **Plumley** and Kincham 1 *m.* 1 *m.* down Kincham, at **Lostock Chapel,** Crow brook, which rises above Goostrey, 3 *m.* N.E. of **Holmes Chapel,** and is 10 *m.* long, joins on left bank. Kincham runs 2 *m.* to **Northwich.** Weaver runs 5 *m.* to Acton Bridge by **Acton,** 2 *m.* to Dutton railway bridge, and here Bent brook joins on left bank. Bent rises in Flax mere, and another lake, 1 *m.* W. of **Delamere** station, and 4 *m.* down. is joined on right bank by Cuddington brook, which rises in some mill ponds at **Cuddington,** and is 8 *m.* long. Weaver runs 4 *m.* to **Frodsham.**

Froghall (Stafford). — L. & N.W.R. and G.N.R. Churnet; trout, grayling, coarse fish ; fishing spoilt by Leek drainage. (*c.s. Trent.*) *Lakes:* Dark Mill, 1 *m.* N. Consall Hall lake, 3 *m.* N.W. Ipstone lake, 3 *m.* N. (*See Gainsborough.*)

Frome (Somerset).—G.W.R. (*See Bristol.*) On Frome; fair trouting, preserved by Vallis Vale Angling Association. (*c.s. Avon.*) *Lakes* at Berkley House, Orchardleigh ; pike, tench, perch ; preserved by W. Duckworth, Esq., leave difficult. Marston Park lake; perch, carp, roach, pike ; Lord Cork ; leave from the agent.

Fulbourn (Cambs.)—G.E.R. Bottesham Load ; perch, roach, &c. (*See King's Lynn.*)

Fullbridge (Essex), n.s. **Maldon.**—Langford water; preserved by Maldon and Heybridge Angling society ; sec., Mr. T. Springett, Lion Hotel, s.t. 5s. Free fishing in canal and tidal water. *Hotel:* Lion.

Fullerton Bridge (Hants).—L. & S.W.R. On Test; trout ; preserved by the owners of Wherwell Priory. (*See Southampton.*)

Fulwood (Lancs.).—L. & N.W.R.; Lanc. & York R. Ribble. Tun brook. Mellor brook, 3 *m.* E. (*See Preston.*)

Fyling Hall (York).—N.E.R. Jugger Howe beck; trout; free. Stoupe beck, 3 *m.* long. Mill beck, 3 *m.* long. 1 *m.* N. (*See Wressel.*)

Gainsborough (Lincoln).—G.N.R. Trent; pike, perch, roach, chub. (*c.s.*) Trent rises in a reservoir by the railway, 1 *m.* N. from **Black Bull** station, runs 1 *m.* to a large reservoir 1 *m.* E. from Black Bull. 4 *m.* down, at **Milton,** Foxley brook joins on right bank. Foxley rises 1 *m.* above **Black Bull,** runs 3 *m.* to **Ford Green,** and Trent and **Milton,** 1 *m.* Trent runs to **Bucknall,** 2 *m.*, where a short stream,.

running out of a large mill head, 1 m. up, joins on left bank, and **Stoke**, 2 m. Here Fowler brook joins on right bank. Fowler rises in Bath pool, 7 m. above **Tunstall**, runs thence to **Burslem**, 1 m., **Hanley**, 2 m., and **Stoke**, 2 m. 1 m. down Trent, at **Fenton**, is the drainings on left bank of a large pond by the railway, 1 m. up. Trent runs 2 m. to Hanford, 2 m. N.W. from **Trentham**, and here Lyme joins on right bank. Lyme rises in a couple of ponds on the racecourse, 2 m. N.W. from **Newcastle**, and runs through that place and joins Trent 3 m. down. Trent runs 1 m. to Trentham Park, **Trentham** station being 1 m. off on left bank; here Northwood brook joins on right bank. Northwood rises in Keel Hall Park lakes, 2 m. S.W. from **Newcastle**, and 3 m. down waters a lake in Trentham Park; just below this lake a stream joins the outflow on the right bank, draining some ponds at Hanchurch farm, 1 m. up. ¼ m. down, Northwood joins Trent. Just below Longton brook joins Trent on left bank. Longton rises in Park Hall lake, 1 m. above **Longton**, and 2 m. down is joined on left bank by a brook 2 m. long, working several mills. Longton runs to **Trentham** station, 2 m., and Trent, 1 m. Trent now waters the large lake, 1 m. long, in Trentham Park. 1 m. down Trent, **Barlaston** being 1m. off on left bank, a brook joins on left bank draining Barlaston Park lakes, 1 m. up. Trent runs to **Stone**, 4 m. Here Filly brook, 4 m. long, joins on right bank, and Moddershall brook, which rises in Moddershall Mill ponds, 2 m. S.E. from **Stone**, and is 3 m. long, working some mills, joins on right bank. Trent runs 7 m. to **Weston**, and here Gayton brook, 4 m. long, joins on left bank. 5 m. down, at **Great Haywood**, 1 m. N.W. from **Colwich** (fishing very good; roach, pike, chub, trout; preserved below by Mr. L. Morgan), Sow joins Trent on right bank. Sow rises 6 m. above **Eccleshall**. n.s. **Norton Bridge**, 3 m. (trout), and is here joined by Offley brook on right bank. Offley rises in Blore Park, runs thence to the lake at Oatland, and 1 m. below waters Cop Mere, running thence to **Eccleshall**, 2m. 4 m. down, Meese brook joins on left bank. Meese rises in the lake in Whitmore park by **Whitmore**, runs 3 m to Hatton Mill pond, 1½ m. N. from **Standon**, runs to **Standon** 2 m., and 1 m. down is joined on right bank by Bromley brook, 3 m. long, which rises in the two large mill ponds at Bromley and in Podmore pool, 3 m. W. from **Standon**. Meese runs 2 m., when a stream joins on left bank, draining the lakes at Meese House, 2 m. S.W. from **Standon**, on the banks of Meese, and also the lakes at Swinnerton park, 3 m. W. from **Stone**. Meese runs 3 m. to **Norton Bridge**, and 1 m. down joins Sow. Sow runs 1 m. to **Great Bridgeford**, and 3 m. down is joined on right bank by Clanford brook, 6 m. long. Sow runs to **Stafford**, 1 m. 1 m. down Sow, Penk joins on right bank. Penk rises in The Pool in Chillington Park, 2 m. N.W. from **Codsall**, runs in 2 m., 1 m. N. from that place, and 4 m. down is joined on right bank by a brook, 3 m. long, rising in the large Moseley mill pond, 1 m. N.E. from **Bushbury**. 1 m. down Penk, **Four Ashes** being 1 m. off on right bank, Saredon brook joins on right bank. Saredon rises in Upper Brindley pool, 1½ m. N. from **Hednesford**, runs thence to Lower Brindley pool, and thence to Furnace pool, and ¼ m. down waters Hednesford pool. Saredon runs 2 m. to **Cannock**, and 2 m. down is joined on right bank by the outflow of the lake in Hatherton Hall, 1 m. W of **Cannock**. Saredon runs 4 m. to **Four Ashes** and Penk. 1 m. Penk runs to **Brewood** (n.s. **Four Ashes**, 2 m.), 1 m., and **Penkridge**, 5 m. Here Whiston brook joins on left bank. Whiston rises 3 m. above Wheaton Aston, and 4 m. down is joined on left bank by Eaton water, which rises by **Gnosall**, and is 7 m. long. 2 m. down, Whiston reaches **Penkridge**. Here also Galey brook, which rises in the reservoir 1 m. E. of **Galey**, and is 4 m. long, joins on right bank. Pillaton brook here joins Penk on right bank. Pillaton rises in Pottal reservoir 3 m. N. from **Cannock** or 3 m. W. from **Penkridge**, and 1 m. down receives on left bank the outflow of Pottal pools ¼ m. up. Pillaton runs to Pillaton 2 m., where the outflow of 3 ponds in Maustey Wood joins on left bank, 2 m. from **Penkridge**. 2 m. down, Pillaton joins Penk. 1 m. down Penk, a stream. 2 m. long, joins on right bank, rising in a pond by Bangley, and working two mills. ½ m. down Penk, the outflow, 1 m. long, of the Keepers' pools and Park pool in Teddesley Park (2 m. N.E. from **Penkridge**) joins on right bank. Penk runs to Sow, 6 m. Kingston brook joins Sow on left bank just below. Kingston rises in Ingestre Park pool 2 m. S.W. from **Ingestre** or **Weston-on-Trent** waters 3 other pools just below, and runs 2 m. to Kingston pool, 1 m. E. of **Stafford**, just on the banks of Sow. 1 m. down Sow on left bank is the outflow of 4 ponds lying close on the banks. 3 m. down Sow on left bank is the outflow of Tixall Park pool, 2 m. up, 4 m. E. of **Stafford**. ¼ m. down, Sherbrook brook, which rises in the upper, middle, and lower Sherbrook pools, 3½ m. W. of **Rugeley**, and is 4 m. long, joins on right bank. Sow runs to Trent 1 m. Trent runs to **Colwich**, 2 m., where the outflow of 3 ponds in Oakedge Park, ¼ m. up, joins on right bank. Trent runs to **Rugeley**, 4 m. Here Colton brook, 6 m. long, joins on left bank, and Rising brook, which rises in Balands pool, 2 m. N.E. from **Hednesford**, runs 1 m. to New Coppice pool, 2 m. S.W. from **Rugeley**, joins Trent 2 m. below on right bank. Trent runs to **Armitage**, 3 m., and here How brook runs in, which rises in the lake at Beaudesert, 4 m. S.W. from **Armitage**, and joins Trent 4 m. down. 2 m. down Trent, Blythe joins on left bank. Blythe rises 3 m. above **Blithe**, runs 2 m. to **Creswell**, **Leigh**, 4 m. and 2 m. below, is joined on right bank by a stream which drains the lake in Birchwood Park, 2 m. S.W. across country from **Leigh**. Blythe runs 4 m. to **Grindley**, and 5 m. down, **Abbots Bromley** (n.s. **Rugeley**, 4 m.) being 1 m. off on left bank, Tad brook, 5 *m.* long, joins on left bank. 3 *m.* down Blythe, Bromley brook, which rises in the lakes in Bagots Park, runs 2 *m.* to **Abbots Bromley**, and Blythe, 3 *m.*, joins on left bank. 1 *m.* down Blythe, at Hamstall Ridware, 3 *m.* N.E. from **Armitage**, Part brook, 7 *m.* long, joins on left bank. 1 *m.* down, Blythe joins Trent. 3 *m.* down Trent, at Orgreave, Bourne brook joins on right bank. Bourne, under the name of Bilston brook, rises in Coney mill pond, 3 *m.* N.W. from **Hammerwich**, and 5 *m.* down is joined on right bank by Ashmore brook, 3 *m.* long, and which runs 2 *m.* N.W. from **Lichfield**. 1 *m.* below, at Seedy mill, 2 *m.* S.E. from **Armitage**, Ben brook, 2 *m.* long, joins on left bank. Bourne runs to Trent in 4 *m.* 1 *m.* down Trent, 2 *m.* N.W. from **Alrewas**, Swarbourne brook joins on left bank. Swarbourne rises in a lake by Newborough, 4 *m.* N.E. from **Abbots Bromley**, and 4 *m.* down is joined on left bank by Lin brook, which rises in the lake in the deer park at Byrkley Lodge, 5 *m.* west from **Burton**, and is 3 *m.* long. 1 *m.* down Swarbourne, the drainage of Luce pool, 1 *m.* up, and 4 *m.* N.W. from **Walton**, joins on right bank. 3 *m.* down, Swarbourne joins Trent, which runs to **Alrewas**, 1 *m.* Here Alrewas brook, which rises in some mill ponds by **Lichfield**, and is 7 *m.* long, joins on right bank. Trent runs 2 *m.* to **Wichnor**, and here Tame joins on right bank. Tame rises in Titford reservoir at **Langley Green**, and 2 *m.* down waters the pond at **Oldbury**. Tame runs 4 *m.* to **Wednesbury**, and 1 *m.* down receives on right bank the outflow of the pond by the foundry, 1 *m.* up. 1 *m.* down Tame at **Bescott Junction** is a lake on the left bank, and here Sneyd brook and Ford brook join on left bank. Sneyd rises in Sneyd pool 1 *m.* N.W. of **Bloxwich**, runs, in 3 *m.*, 1 *m.* W. of **Walsall**, and joins Tame 3 *m.* down. Ford brook rises above **Pelsall**, runs to **Walsall** 3 *m.*, and Tame 2 *m.* Tame runs 3 *m.* to **Newton Road**, and here the outflow, of the pond at Red House Hall, 1 *m.* up, joins on left bank; there is also a considerable lake (Forge pond) on the right bank. Tame runs to **Perry Barr** 4 *m.*, and here a stream joins on left bank which rises in the lakes at Barr Park, 2 *m.* E. of **Newton Road**. Tame runs to **Aston**, near **Birmingham**, 2 *m.*, where the outflow of the lake in Aston Park joins on the right bank. Here also joins on left bank the brook which rises in Lodge pool 3 *m.* N. from **Perry Barr** station, runs 1 *m.* to Upper Witton pool, 2 *m.* N. from **Aston**, and thence in 1 *m.* to Lower Witton pool, 1 *m.* N. from **Aston**. 1 *m.* down Tame, Rea joins on right bank. Rea rises above **Lifford**, where it waters two mill dams, and 3 *m.* down is joined on left bank by Bourne brook, which rises in a pond by Frankley, 3 *m.* S.E. from **Halesowen**, and 3 *m.* down waters the large mill pond at Harborne mill, 2 *m.* N. from **Lifford**. 2 *m.* down, Bourne joins Rea. 2 *m.* down, Rea waters the lake at Cannon Hill, and the reservoir at Edgbaston on the outskirts of **Birmingham**, and running through that town joins Tame at **Aston**. Before doing so, however, it is joined by the outflow of Thimble mill pond, Smethwick reservoir, Rotten Park reservoir, and some other ponds, all lying on the W. side of **Birmingham**. Tame runs 3 *m.* to **Castle Bromwich**, and here East brook joins on left bank. East brook rises in Bracebridge pool 2 *m.* N.W. from **Sutton Coldfield**, runs 1 *m.* to Blackroot pool and 1 *m.* to **Sutton Coldfield**. Here the outflow of Long Moor mill pond, Powell's pool, and Windley pool, all within a mile of the town, joins on right bank. East brook runs to Plantsbrook forge, where it waters a lake, and 1 *m.* below reaches **Castle Bromwich**. Tame runs 6 *m.* to **Whitacre** junction, and here Blythe joins on right bank. Blythe rises in Earlswood reservoir 6 *m.* W. from **Knowle** station, or 6 *m.* S.W. of **Solihull**, runs 5 *m.* to **Solihull**, 3 *m.* to **Knowle** (1 *m.* off on right bank). **Hampton** 6 *m.* and 2 *m.* down it receives the outfall of the lakes in Packington Park on right bank. 1 *m.* down Blythe on left bank is the outflow of Coleshill pool 1 *m.* up (2 *m.* S. of **Coleshill**), and **Coleshill** is 3 *m.* down Blythe. In left bank, Cole joins on left bank. Cole rises some 2 *m.* E. of **Lifford**, and at Titterford mill pond, 4 *m.* W. of **Solihull**, is joined on right bank by Inkford brook 5 *m.* long. Cole runs 6 *m.* to **Stichford**, and 4 *m.* down, 2 *m.* S.W. of **Coleshill**, is joined on right bank by Ulverley brook, which rises in Kineton reservoir, 2 *m.* N.W. of **Solihull**, runs 3 *m.* to **Marston Green**, and Cole 2 *m.*, receiving just above the junction the outflow of the ponds in Chelmsley Wood, 2 *m.* S.W. from **Coleshill**. Cole runs to **Coleshill**, 2 *m.*, and 1 *m.* down joins Blythe, which joins Tame 1 *m* on at **Whitacre Junction**. Here Arley brook, which rises above **Arley**, runs 2 *m.* to **Shustoke**, and **Whitacre** 1 *m.*, joins Tame on right bank. Tame runs 3 *m.* to **Kingsbury**, and 8 *m.* down is joined on left bank by Langley brook, which, rising in the ponds at Langley Hall and mill, 2 *m.* E. of **Sutton Coldfield**, runs 3 *m.* to Middleton Hall and lake, and 1 *m.* down joins Tame. 1 *m.* down Tame, Gallows brook, which rises in a pond by Canwell Hall, 4 *m.* N.E. of **Sutton Coldfield**, and is 3 *m.* long, joins on left bank. Tame runs 2 *m.* to **Wilnescote**, where Bourne brook joins on left bank. Bourne rises in Bourne pool, 4 *m.* N.W. of **S. Coldfield**, runs 4 *m.* to Shenstone, where Crane brook, which rises in Biddulphs pool, 2 *m.* E. of **Cannock**, runs 1 *m.* to the large reservoir, 1 *m.* N. of **Brownhills**, and 5 *m.* down joins Bourne, which runs to Weeford, 3 *m.*, and 3 *m.* below waters the lakes at Drayton Manor, 1 *m.* below which it joins Tame, which runs 2 *m.* to **Tamworth**, and here Anker joins on right bank. Anker rises by Wolvey, 5 *m.* above **Nuneaton**, and here Griff brook joins on left bank. Griff rises by **Bedworth**, and 3 *m.* down is joined on left bank by a brook 2 *m.* long, which rises in Seds Wood pool, and other ponds in Arbury park, 1 *m.* S. of **Stockinford**. Griff runs 2 *m.* to **Nuneaton**. Anker runs 6 *m.* to **Atherstone**, and 1 *m.* down is joined on right bank by Sence. Sence rises above **Hugglescote**, and 2 *m.* below, at **Heather** is joined on right bank by Blower's brook, 3 *m.* long. Sence runs 3 *m.* to **Shakerstone**, and 2 *m.* down is joined on left bank by Bosworth brook, which runs 1 *m.* N. of **Market Bosworth**, and is 4 *m.* long. 5 *m.* down Sence, Tweed joins on left bank. Tweed rises above **Shenton**, where the outflow from the duckery in Bosworth Park, 2 *m.* up, joins on right bank. Tweed joins Sence 5 *m.* down. Sence joins Anker 1 *m.* below. Anker runs to **Polesworth** 5 *m.*, **Tamworth** and Tame, 6 *m.* 7 *m.* down Tame Freeford brook, which rises in the lakes at Swinfin and Freeford Halls, 2 *m.* S.E. of **Lichfield**, and is 4 *m.* long, joins on left bank. 4 *m.* down, Tame joins Trent. Here also Mease joins on right bank. Mease rises by **Ashby-de-la-Zouch**, runs 6 *m.* to **Snarston**, **Measham** 2 *m.*, and 1 *m.* below is joined on right bank by a brook 3 *m.* long draining the large lake in Willesley Park, 1 *m.* S.W. from **Ashby**. 1 *m.* below at Nether Seal, Seal brook joins on right bank, which rises in the large reservoir by **Overseal**, runs 1 *m.* to Barrat pool, and Mease 3 *m.* Mease runs 6 *m.* to Harleston, **Croxhall** 3 *m.*, and Trent 1 *m.* Trent runs 3 *m.* to **Walton**, and 2 *m.* down, the outflow, 2 *m.* long, of Tatenhill lake, 3 *m.* S.W. of **Burton**, joins on left bank. Trent runs to **Burton** 4 *m.*, and 3 *m.* down, Dove joins on left bank. Dove rises 6 *m.* above **Longnor**, runs 4 *m.* to **Hartington** (n.s. **Parsley Hay**, 3 *m.*). Alstonfield, 1 *m.* off, on right bank, 4 *m.*, Thorp, 5 *m.* Here Mannyfold joins on right bank. Mannyfold rises 4 *m.* above **Longnor**, and 3 *m.* down is joined on right bank by Blackbrook, 3 *m.* long. Mannyfold runs 5 *m.* to Ecton bridge, where Elkstone brook, 3 *m.* long, joins on right bank. Mannyfold runs to Wetton (1 *m.* off on left bank), 2 *m.*, and 1 *m.* below is joined on right bank by Hamps. Hamps rises 4 *m.* above Onecote, 5 *m.* E. of **Leek**, and is there joined by a brook, 2 *m.* long, draining two ponds at its head at Lower Acre 5 *m.* E. of **Leek**. Hamps runs 8 *m.* to Calton, and joins Mannyfold 4 *m.* below. Mannyfold runs to **Ilam** (n.s. **Ashbourne**, 5 *m.*), 4 *m.*, and 1 *m.* down joins Dove. Dove runs 2 *m.* to Mappleton (good trouting), and 2 *m.* to Birdsgrove, **Ashbourne** being 1 *m.* off on left bank (preserved for 4 *m.* by the Birdsgrove Fishing Club of 30 members; s.t. 4*l*. 4*s.*; sec., G. M. Bond, Esq., Alrewas House, Ashbourne), and here Bradbourne brook, 7 *m.* long, joins on left bank. 1 *m.* below, at **Clifton**, Henmoor brook joins Dove on left bank. Henmoor rises in the lake at Hopton Hall, 2 *m.* S.W. of **Wirksworth**, runs 7 *m.* to **Ashbourne**, and Dove 2 *m.* Dove runs 4 *m.* to **Norbury**, where Calwich brook, 6 *m.* long, joins on right bank. Dove runs 2 *m.* to **Rocester**, and 2 *m.* below is joined by Churnet on right bank. Churnet rises 4 *m.* above **Leek**, and 1 *m.* down is joined on right bank by the outflow of Rudyerd reservoir, 3 *m.* N.W. of **Leek**, **Horton** station, being close on the banks. 4 *m.* down Churnet, Endon brook joins on right bank. Endon rises in Stanley Mill pond, 1 *m.* above **Endon**, and 3 *m.* below is joined on right bank by a brook 4 *m.* long, which drains a pond W. of Wetley, 3 *m.* S. from **Cheddleton**. Endon joins Churnet 1 *m.* down, which runs 1 *m.* to **Cheddleton**. 2 *m.* below, West brook, 7 *m.* long, joins on left bank, 1 *m.* down Churnet is the outflow on right bank of the lake at Consell Hall, 3 *m.* N. W. from **Froghall** station. 1 *m.* down Churnet the outflow of the lake W. of Ipstone, 3 *m.* N. from **Froghall**, joins on left bank. Churnet runs to **Froghall**, 2 *m.*, and here a brook joins on left bank, which rises in Dark Mill head, 1 *m.* N. of **Froghall**. Churnet runs to **Oakamoor**, 4 *m.*, **Alton**, 2 *m.*, and 2 *m.* down is joined on left bank by Hulford brook, 3 *m.* long, which feeds the lake at Woolton Grange, half-way down, 2 *m.* N.W. from **Norbury**. Churnet runs 1 *m.* to **Denston**, **Rocester**, 2 *m.*, and 2 *m.* down joins Dove. 2 *m.* down Dove Tean brook joins on right bank. Tean rises above **Cheadle**, runs 10 *m.* to **Uttoxeter** (1 *m.* off on right bank), and joins Dove 1 *m.* below. Dove runs to Dovebridge, **Uttoxeter** being 1 *m.* off on right bank, and 2 *m.* below is joined on right bank by Stonyford brook, which rises 5 *m.* above **Uttoxeter**, and joins Dove 2 *m.* below. 3 *m.* down Dove by **Marchington** station Somershall brook, 6 *m.* long, joins on left bank, and Marchington brook, 5 *m.* long, on right bank. Dove runs to **Sudbury**, 2 *m.*, (preserved by Burton-on-Trent Angling Society), and here Sudbury brook, which rises in a large pond 3 *m.* above **Sudbury**, joins on left bank. 3 *m.* down Dove, at Scropton, Cubley brook, 9 *m.* long, joins on left bank. Dove runs to **Tutbury**, 2 *m.*, and 3 *m.* down by Rolleston is joined on right bank by Fleam or Little Dove, an offshoot of the main stream, which runs by **Tutbury** to Rolleston, where it is joined by Rolleston brook, 4 *m.* long, which feeds the lake at Rolleston Hall, 2 *m.* S.E. from **Tutbury**. Dove runs to **Egginton**, 2 *m.*, and here Longford brook joins on left bank. Longford rises in Yeldersley pond, 3 *m.* S.E. from **Ashbourne**, and 1 *m.* down waters the lakes in Shirley Park. Longford runs to Longford, 5 *m.*, and here Bradley brook joins on right bank. Bradley rises in two lakes by Bradley, 3 *m.* E. from **Ashbourne**, and joins Longford 5 *m.* down. Longford runs to Sutton, 3 *m.*, where it waters a pond, and 1 *m.* below is joined on right bank by Limbersitch brook, 5 *m.* long, 3 *m.* N. from **Tutbury**. Longford runs to Hilton, 2 *m.*, and Dove, 2 *m.*, watering the lake at Eggington Hall, close to the junction. Dove joins Trent 2 *m.* down. Trent runs 2 *m.* to **Willington**, where Etwall brook joins on left bank, and Repton brook on right bank. Etwall rises in a pond by Radburn, 3 *m* N.W. from **Mickleover**, and 1 *m.* down waters another large pond. Etwall runs 2 *m.* to **Etwall**, **Egginton** 2 *m.*, and 3 *m.* down joins Trent at **Willington**. Repton rises in two ponds by Hartshorn, 3 *m.* N.E. of **Swadlincote**, runs 1 *m.* to Screw Mill pond, 1 *m.* to Glovers Mill, 2 *m.* N.E. of **Swadlincote**, and 1 *m.* down at Repton mill, is joined on left bank by the outflow of the six ponds in Bretby Park, 3 m. N. from **Swadlincote**; 1 m. down, Repton waters the lake in Repton Park, 2 m. S.E. of **Willington**, runs 1 m. to Repton, and Trent 1 m. 2 m. down Trent, by Twyford, **Foremark** brook joins on right bank, which rises in a pond by Repton rocks, 4 m. N.E. from **Swadlincote**, and, 2 m. down, waters four ponds by Foremark. 3 m. S.E. from **Willington**, 1 m. down, Foremark joins Trent. (Trent is preserved hence to Swarkstone; s.t. 21s., from Mr. Newbold, of King's Newton.) 1 m. down Trent on right bank is the overflow of Foremark Hall pond, 3 m. S.E. from **Willington**. Trent runs to Swarkstone (n.s. **Chellaston**, 1 m.), where begins the King's Mill fishery (*see Weston*), and 1 m. down is joined on right bank by a brook draining four ponds on the moor, by Stantin, 3 m. S.W. from **Chellaston**. 1 m. down Trent, by Weston Ferry, Breedon brook joins on right bank. Breedon rises in three ponds, by Coleorton, 3 m. E. from **Ashby-de-la-Zouch**, runs to **Worthington**, 4 m., **Tong** 3 m., **Melbourne** 3 m., and here Carr brook joins on left bank. Carr rises in Dog Kennel pool, and two ponds a mile above it, 2 m. W. of **Worthington**, runs to Staunton Hall ponds, and 1 m. down is joined on left bank by the outflow from seven ponds in Calke Park, 3 m. N.W. from **Worthington**. Carr runs to **Melbourne** and Breedon, 3 m. Breedon joins Trent 1 m. down. Trent runs to King's Mills, 1 m., **Weston** being 1 m. off on left bank, and here on right bank is the lake in Donnington Park. 1 m. down, where the railway crosses, the King's Mill fishery ends, and the Shardlow fishing begins. Trent runs 2 m. to Cavendish bridge and Shardlow (n.s. **Castle Donnington**, 1 m.; salmon, pike, barbel, dace, roach, perch; fishing good; preserved; s.t. 42s., from Castle Hotel, C.D.; Mr. Wood, Chapel Bar, Nottingham, lessee of the river from Cuttle brook including Weston-on-Trent, Kings Mills, and Shardlow; salmon begins Feb. 1. Trent runs 1 m., where Derwent joins on left bank. Derwent rises in the hills some 12 m. above **Ashopton**, and 6 m. from its source is joined on left bank by Little Howden brook, 2 m. long, and on right bank by the river Westend. 5 m. down Derwent, Abbey brook, 3 m. long, joins on left bank. Derwent runs to Derwent Chapel, 3 m., and here Mill brook, 2 m. long, joins on left bank. Derwent runs 2 m. to **Ashopton** (n.s. **Sheffield**, 12 m.); here Ashop joins on right bank. Ashop rises on the N. edge of The Peak, and 2 m. down is joined on left bank by Lady Clough brook, 2 m. long, which rises on Alport moor, 5 m. S.E. of **Glossop**. 1 m. down Ashop, Fair brook, 2 m. long, joins on right bank. Ashop runs to Alport bridge 2 m., and here Alport joins on left bank. Alport rises on Alport Moor, 6 m. E. of **Glossop**, and is 7 m. long. Ashop runs 5 m. to **Ashopton**. The high road between **Glossop**, **Ashopton**, and **Sheffield** runs up the Ashop Valley. At **Ashopton**, Ladybrook brook, 2 m. long, joins on left bank. 1 m. down Derwent is Yorkshire bridge, where the Derwent Fly-fishing Club water begins, thence to Mytham bridge 3 m., and here Now joins on right bank. Now rises in the Peak, 4 m. E. of **Hayfield**, runs 2 m. to Barber Booth, 4 m. N.E. from **Chapel-en-le-Frith**, and 7 m. down at Hope, 2 m. E. of **Castleton** (n.s. **Chapel-en-le-Frith**, 6 m.) (preserved by the Peak Forest Angling Club), is joined on right bank by Peaks Hole Water, which runs through **Castleton**, and is 3 m. long. Now runs 1 m., and is joined on right bank by Bradwell brook, 2 m. long. 1 m. down, Now joins Derwent. 2 m. down Derwent, by **Hathersage** (n.s. **Dronfield**, 9 m.), Hood brook, 2 m. long, joins on left bank, 1 m. down Derwent, at Lead mill, Highlow brook, 2 m. long, joins on right bank. Derwent runs 2 m., where Burbage brook, 5 m. long, and running 6 m. W. of **Dronfield**, joins on left bank. Derwent runs to New bridge, 2 m. (here ends the Derwent F.F. Club water, and the Duke of Devonshire's and Subscription water begins); thence 3 m. to **Baslow** (n.s. **Bakewell**, 3 m.) 1 m. below, Bar brook, 6 m. long, joins Derwent on left bank; near this junction Black Leach brook, 4 m. long, joins Bar on left bank. Derwent runs 1 m. to **Edensor** (n.s. **Bakewell**, 2 m.), and **Rowsley**, 4 m. Here ends the Duke's subscription water, and Wye joins Derwent. Wye rises above **Buxton**, from whence it is preserved for four miles down by the Buxton Angling Association; from hence Wye runs 4 m. to **Miller's Dale** (private), **Monsal Dale**, 3 m. (Duke of Devonshire), **Ashford** (n.s. **Longstone**, 1 m.) (Duke of Devonshire) 3 m, **Bakewell** 2 m. (here begins the Rutland Arms water), Fillyford bridge 6 m. (here ends the Rutland Arms water), and 1 m. down Wye reaches **Rowsley** and Derwent. Derwent runs to **Darley**, 3 m. (here begins the Darley Dale Club water), and here Sydnope brook, which rises in Flash dam, 3 m. up, joins on left bank; there are also two large mill ponds up Hall Dale, 1 m. up from the station. Derwent runs to **Matlock Bath**, 3 m. (here the D.D. Club water ends and the Matlock Angling Association begins), and here Bentley Brook, 3 m. long, joins on right bank. Derwent runs to **Cromford**, 2 m. (preserved by M.A.A.). **Whatstandwell Bridge**, 3 m. (here the M.A.A. water ends), and 2 m. down is joined on right bank by a brook, 1 m. long, draining Aldderwasley ponds, 2 m. S.W. from **Whatstandwell**. Derwent runs 1 m. to **Ambergate**. Here Amber joins on left bank. Amber rises 4 m. N.E. of **Matlock**, above Ashover, and 5 m. down at Ogston Bridge, 1 m. S. of **Stretton**, is joined on left bank by Stretton brook, which rises 5 m. above **Stretton Station**, and joins Amber 1 m. down. Amber runs to **Wingfield**, 3 m, and here Normanton brook and Birches brook join on left bank and right bank. Normanton rises 5 m. above **Alfreton**, and 1 m. above that town is joined on right bank by Westwood brook, which rises 8 m. above **Westhouse**, and joins Normanton 1 m.

E

down. Normanton joins Amber 2 *m.* below **Alfreton.** Birches brook is 4 *m.* long
Amber runs 4 *m.*, when a brook joins on left bank, draining Batterley reservoir, 2 *m.* up,
1 *m.* N. of **Ripley.** Amber runs 2 *m.* to **Ambergate** and Derwent. Derwent runs to
Belper, 3 *m.*, and here Black brook, 3 *m.* long, joins on right bank. Derwent runs 3 *m.*
to **Duffield,** and here Ecclesbourn joins on right bank. Ecclesbourne rises at
Wirksworth, runs 4 *m.* to **Idridgehay, Haslewood,** 4 *m.*, and **Duffield,** and
Derwent, 2 *m.* 2 *m.* down Derwent is **Little Eaton,** and here Holbrook brook joins
on left bank. Holbrook rises above **Kilburn,** runs to **Coxbench,** 2 *m.*, and here a
brook joins on left bank, draining Smalley mill pond, 2 *m.* up. Holbrook runs to
Derwent, 2 *m.* Here also the drainage, 1 *m.* long, of Allastry Hall Park pond, joins on
right bank. 2 *m.* down Derwent, at Darley Abbey, Ferryby brook joins on left bank,
which rises above **Breadsall,** and joins Derwent 2 *m.* down. Derwent reaches **Derby**
in 2 *m.* Here Cutler brook, which rises 5 *m.* above Kedleston Park, where it waters the
large lake (n.s. **Duffield,** 3 *m.*), runs 2 *m.*, when it receives on right bank a brook
draining two ponds by Kirk Langley, 3 *m.* up, and 2 *m.* down joins Derwent on right bank.
1 *m.* down Derwent, where the angling club water begins, Chaddesden brook, which
rises in the lake at Locko Park, 2 *m.* N. from **Spondon,** and is 3 *m.* long, joins on left
bank. Derwent runs to **Spondon,** 3 *m.*, **Borrowash,** 2 *m.* (here the club water ends),
Draycott, 3 *m.*, and here the drainings of Elvaston Park lake, 1 *m.* S. of **Draycott,**
joins on right bank, and 3 *m.* below, Derwent joins Trent. Flies for the Upper Derwent,
i.e., from Frogatt bridge, are ash dun, straw dun, dotterel dun, and their spinners,
February red, little chap, red clock, furnace, corncrake, April black, wrentail,
claret and orange bumbles. Trent runs to **Sawley,** 1 *m.*, **Trent,** 1 *m.* Here
Soar joins on right bank. Soar rises in the lake in Leicester Grange, 2 *m.*
S. of **Hinckley.** 4 *m.* down, at Sharnford, a brook, 2 *m.* long, joins on right
bank, which rises in Claybrook Mill pond, 1 *m.* N. from **Ullsthorpe.** Soar runs
5 *m.*, when Normanton brook, which rises in Kirkby Hall lake, by Kirkby Mallory, 4 *m.*
S.W. from **Desford,** waters the lake in Normanton Hall, 4 *m.* N.W. from **Harborough,** joins Soar 4 *m.* down on right bank. Soar runs 2 *m.* to **Narborough.**
Here Whetstone brook, 4 *m.* long, joins on right bank. 1 *m.* down Soar, Billesdon brook
joins on right bank. Billesdon rises 8 *m.* above **Glen Magna,** 1 *m.* below is the
outflow of the lake in Wistow Hall, on the banks of the river. Billesdon runs to **Blaby,**
6 *m.*, and 1 *m.* down joins Soar, which runs to **Leicester,** 6 *m.* Here the outflow
of Braunstone Hall lake, 2 *m.* S.W. of **Leicester,** joins on left bank. Just below the
town Willow brook, 4 *m.* long, joins on right bank, 2 *m.* down Soar, at Belgrave,
Ingersby brook, 7 *m.* long, joins on right bank, and 5 *m.* down at Rothley Paper Mill,
Wreak joins on right bank. Wreak, called also Eye, in its upper parts, rises above
Wissendine, where it is joined on the left bank by the outflow of Edmunthorpe Hall
pond 2 *m.* up, and on the right bank by a stream 3 *m.* long, draining a pond at Leesthorpe;
Wreak, next waters the lake at Stapleford Park, 1 *m.* S. of **Saxby,** to which place
Wreak runs, and here Saxby brook, 7 *m.* long, joins on right bank. Wreak runs 6 *m.* to
Melton Mowbray, here Melton Brook, which rises in the lake at Goadby Marwood
2 *m.* above **Scalford,** runs thence to Melton, 4 *m.*, joins on right bank. Wreak runs
4 *m.* to **Ashfordby,** and here a stream joins on right bank draining a pond by Welby
2 *m.* up. Wreak runs to **Frisby,** 2 *m.*, and 1 *m.* below, a stream joins on right bank,
draining a pond 1 *m.* above Saxelby (n.s. **Grimston,** 1 *m.*). Wreak runs to **Brooksby,**
2 *m.* (preserved by the owner of Brooksby Hall), and 1 *m.* below at **Rearsby** station
(preserved by H. C. Woodcock, Esq.), is joined on right bank by Ox brook, which rises
in Ragdale Hall pond and is 4 *m.* long. 3 *m.* down Wreak, Queniborough brook, 9 *m.* long,
joins on left bank. 1 *m.* up from its junction with Wreak, Ashby brook, 7 *m.* long, joins
Queniborough on left bank. Wreak runs to **Syston** 1 *m.*, and here Barkby brook,
which rises in a pond by Hungerton and is 8 *m.* long, joins on left bank. 1 *m.* down,
Wreak joins Soar. 1 *m.* below, Rothley brook joins Soar on left bank. Rothley rises in
two branches above **Desford,** where it is joined on right bank by the drainage of Gabriel
pool 2 *m.* up, runs to **Ratby** 2 *m.*, **Glenfield** 2 *m.*, 1 *m.* below, the outflow of a large mill
pool 2 *m.* N.W. of **Glenfield,** joins on left bank; Rothley runs to Soar 7 *m.* Soar runs to
Mount Sorrel 3 *m.*, and **Barrow-on-Soar** 3 *m*; and here Quorndon brook (trout;
strictly preserved by the owner of Bradgate Park), which rises above Newtown Linford,
3 *m.* N.W. of **Glenfield,** and is 9 *m.* long, joins on right bank. Soar runs to **Loughborough,** 3 *m.* Here Walters brook, 5 *m.* long, joins on right bank. 1 *m.* down Soar, at
Stanford, a brook joins on right bank, which drains the lake at Stanford Hall 2 *m.* up,
3 *m.* N.E. of **Loughborough.** 2 *m.* down Soar, where the navigation joins, Dishley
brook joins on left bank. Dishley rises above Whitwick 2 *m.* N. of **Coalville,** and 6 *m.*
down is joined on right bank by Carr brook, which rises in the Old Reservoir 4 *m.* N.E. of
Swannington, and is 3 *m.* long. Dishley runs 1 *m.*, when the outflow of the lake in
Garendon Park, 2 *m.* W. of **Loughborough,** 1 *m.* up, joins on right bank. Dishley runs
to Soar 2 *m.* Soar runs 2 *m.* to Zouch Bridge and **Hathern.** Here Osgathorpe brook
joins on left bank. This brook rises in three lakes by Coleorton, 2 *m.* E. of **Ashby-de-la-
Zouch,** and 7 *m.* down is joined on left bank by Diseworth brook, which rises in Langley
Priory pond 1 *m.* E. of **Tong,** and is 4 *m.* long. Osgathorpe joins Soar, 3 *m.* below. Soar
runs to **Kegworth,** 3 *m.*, and here Kingston brook, 9 *m.* long, joins on right bank. Soar
runs 3 *m.* to **Trent.** Trent runs 2 *m.* to **Eaton Junction,** and here Erwash
joins on left bank. Erwash rises some 3 *m.* above **Pinxton,** where is the outflow of the

lake at Brookshill Hall 2 m. N. Erwash runs to **Pye Bridge**, 2 m., **Codnor Park**, 2 m., where is the outflow of the reservoir in the Golden Valley 1 m. up. Erwash runs to **Eastwood**, 3 m., and here join the drainings of the lakes at Aldercar Hall, 1 m. N., and of Loscoe dam, 2 m. N.W. Erwash runs to **Newthorp**, 3 m., 2 m. W. of which are the three reservoirs at Shipley Hall, and 1 m. further W., Mapperley reservoir. 1 m. down Erwash, Gilt brook, 3 m. long, joins on left bank, and 1 m. below is **Ilkeston**, and **Stanton**, 3 m. Here Nut brook, which rises above **West Hallam**, 2 m. N. of which is Mapperley reservoir, and is 6 m. long, joins on right bank. Erwash runs to **Sandiacre**, 2 m., and Trent, 4 m. Trent runs to **Attenborough**, 1 m., and **Beeston**, 2 m. (here begins the free water on the left bank, but the right bank is preserved). Here Tottle brook, which drains Bilborough Cut, 2 m. W. of **Radford**, and is 4 m. long, joins on left bank. 2 m. down Trent, Fairham Brook, which rises by **Widmerpool**, and is 12 m. long, joins on right bank. Trent runs to Trent-bridge (where the free water ends) at **Nottingham**, 2 m. Here Leen joins on left bank. Leen rises in the upper and lower lakes at Newstead Abbey, 2 m. N. of **Linby**, and 2 m. down waters the mill pool at Popplewick, 1 m. E. of **Linby**. Leen runs 3 m. to Forge Mill dam, **Bulwell**, 2 m., **Basford**, 2 m. Here a brook joins on right bank draining a lake by Nuthall 3 m. up, 1 m. N.E. from **Kimberley Station**. Day brook, 3 m. long, here joins Leen on left bank. Leen runs to **Radford**, 2 m., and **Nottingham**, 3 m. Trent runs to **Colwick**, on left bank, 2 m., and **Radcliffe**, on right bank, 5 m., and here Thurbeck river, which rises by **Plumtree**, waters the lake at Roclaveston Manor, 1 m. S.E. of **Edwalton**, and runs 5 m. to Trent, joins on right bank. Trent runs to **Burton Joyce**, 3 m., and here Cocker Beck joins on left bank. Cocker rises 2 m. above **Lowdham**, and joins Trent 4 m. below. Two miles down Trent, Dover beck, which rises 7 m. above **Lowdham**, and joins Trent 2 m. below joins on left bank. Trent runs to **Bleasby** on left bank, 4 m., and **Fiskerton**, 3 m. Here Greet joins on left bank. Greet rises in two ponds on Kirklington Moor, 4 m. N.W. of **Southwell**. 1 m. down it is joined on right bank by the outflow of Edingley Cotton Mill pond by **Farnsfield**, 2 m. up, and on left bank by the outflow of the lake in Kirklington Hall, 3 m. N.W. of **Southwell**. 1 m. down, Halam Beck, 3 m. long, joins Greet on right bank. Greet runs to **Southwell**, 2 m., **Rolleston**, 3 m., and Trent, at Fiskerton Mill, 1 m. Trent runs 5 m., when it divides into two parts. The right hand stream runs through **Newark** in 2 m., and joins the larger stream 2 m. below. The larger stream runs to Kelham and Muckham bridge, each 2 m. from **Newark**, and joins the right branch, 1 m. below. Just where the waters separate, Pingley Dyke, 8 m. long, joins on left bank, and at **Newark**, Devon river joins on right bank. Devon rises in Knipton reservoir, 4 m. S.E. of **Redmile**, where a brook joins on right bank, draining the lakes in Croxton Park, 2 m. up, 5 m. N.E. of **Scalford**. Devon in 1 m. waters the lake at Woolsthorpe, 3 m. S.E. of **Redmile**. Devon runs 5 m. to **Bottesford**, and 5 m. down by Shelton is joined on left bank by Smite. Smite rises by Nether Broughton (n.s. **Upper Broughton**, 1 m.) and 6 m. down is joined on left bank by Dalbybrook, which rises by **Upper Broughton**, and is 5 m. long. Smite runs to **Barnston** (1 m. off on right bank), 4 m., **Aslacton**, 4 m. Here Whipling river, which rises by **Barnston**, and is 3 m. long, joins on right bank. Smite joins Devon 5 m. down. Devon runs to **Cotham**, 2 m., and 3 m. below, at Hawton, is joined on left bank by Car Dyke. Car Dyke rises by **Bingham**, runs to Sibthorpe (n.s. **Cotham**, 3 m.), and joins Devon, 5 m. down. Devon runs to **Newark** and Trent, 2 m. Two miles below **Newark** the two branches of Trent reunite, and run to **Carlton**, on left bank, 7 m. Here Crosby Dyke, 9 m. long, joins on left bank. Just below, the outflow of Cowarth pool and Mons pool, and a pond by **Collingham** joins on right bank. Trent runs to **Sutton** (n.s. **Crow Park**, 2 m), and here Girton brook joins on right bank. Girton rises in Skelmire's pond on Thurlby Moor, 2 m. S.E. of **Swinderby**, and is 7 m. long. Where Girton joins Trent is the outflow of the Fleet and Black Pool, 1 m. up. 1 m. down Trent, Grassthorpe brook, 6 m. long, and which runs just N. of **Crow Park Station**, joins on left bank. Trent runs 8 m. to **Torksey** (where Foss Dyke Navigation, joining Trent and Witham, joins on right bank), **Marton**, 2 m., **Gainsborough**, 7 m. There are a few fish to 3 m. below **Gainsborough**.

Gainsford (Durham).—N.E.R. Tees; salmon, trout, bull trout, grayling, coarse fish tickets 2s. (c.s.) Alwent beck, 1 m. W.; trout private. Langton beck, 2 m. N. (*See Stockton*.)

Gaisgill (Westland).—Lune. Langdale beck. Ellergill beck. Rais beck. Chapel beck, 2 m. W. (*See Lancaster*.)

Galey (Stafford).—L. & N.W.R. Penk, 1 m. W. *Lakes*: Galey reservoir, 1 m. E. (*See Gainsborough*.)

Galgate (Lanc.).—L. & N.W.R. Condor. (c.s. *Lune*.) Condor rises in the lakes in Quernmore Park, 4 m. N.E. of **Lancaster**, and 3 m. down is joined on left bank by Rowton brook, 3 m. long, 4 m. S.E. of **Lancaster**. Condor runs 5 m. to **Galgate**, and 3 m. to Lune estuary at **Condor Green**.

Gamlingay (Cambs.) L. & N.W.R. *Lakes*: Gamlingay Old Park. (*See King's Lynn*.)

Ganton (York).—N.E.R. Derwent; chub, pike, grayling, trout. Helford; same fish. Ruston beck, 2 m. W. (c.s. *York*.) (*See Wressel*.)

Garforth (York).—N.E.R. Cock beck. *Lake*: Parlington Hollings lake, 1 m. N. (*See Aberford, York*.)

Gargrave (York).—M.R. Aire; trout, grayling; preserved hence *down* to Eastburn brook by Aire Fishing Club of 20 members; entrance 5*l.* 5*s.*, s.t. 6*l.* 6*s.*; season for trout from March 16 to Oct. 1, grayling from June 16 to March 14. In addition to the above 20 members, a further additional number of 40 can fish from Carlton stone bridge to Eastburn brook. s.t. 20*s.*; hon. sec., T. H. Dewhurst, Esq., Skipton. (*c.s. York.*) Eshton beck. Mill beck, 2 *m.* N.E. (*See Rawcliffe.*)

Garstang (Lancs.)—L. & N.W.R. Wyre. (*c.s. Lune.*) Grizedale brook, 1 *m.* N.E. Calder river, 1 *m.* S.E. (*See Fleetwood.*)

Gathurst (Lancs.)—L. & Y.R. Douglas. (*c.s. Ribble.*) Lakes: Roby Mill pond, 1 *m.* W. Standish Mill pond, 2 *m.* N. (*See Hesketh Bank.*)

Geddington (Northton).—M.R. Ise. (*See Wisbeach.*)

Geldiston (Norfolk).—G.E.R. Waveney. (*c.s. N. and S.*) (*See Yarmouth.*)

George Lane (Essex).—G.E.R. On Roding. Fishing very poor. (*See Barking.*)

Giggleswick (York).—M.R. Ribble; trout, salmon, pike, chub, roach. (*See Preston.*)

Gilling (York).—N.E.R. Hole beck (*See York.*)

Gillingham (Dorset).—L. & S.W.R. Stour. Shreen. Ledden. (*See Christchurch.*) Trouting good. (*c.s. Avon.*)

Gilsland (Cumland.—N.E.R. Irthing; trout. (*c.s. Eden.*) King's water, 3 *m.* N.E. Mill beck, 3 *m.* W. Butterburn, 6 *m* N.E. Hotels: Station, Bridge House. (*See Carlisle.*)

Gisburn (York).—Lanc. & York R. Ribble; trout, salmon. Stock beck. Cuddy beck, 4 *m.* W. at Bolton by Bowland. (*See Preston.*)

Glaisdale (York).—N.E.R. Esk; salmon, trout; preserved above by the Lealholm and Danby Anglers' Club; hon. sec., Mr. Harland Duck, Lealholm Lane, Grosmont (*See Lealholm*), and below by the Esk Fishery Association, to **Whitby**; sec., Mr. W. Brown, The Saw Mills, Whitby; m.t. not extending beyond Sept. 30. 3*l.* 3*s.* Between Lealholm and Glaisdale the fishing is in private hands. (*c.s.*) Glaisdale beck: trout; preserved. (*c.s. Esk.*) Stonegate beck, 1 *m.* N.W.; trout; preserved. (*See Whitby.*)

Glastonbury (Somerset).—G.W.R. Brue; roach, dace, trout; preserved above by R. N. Grenville, Butleigh Court; preserved below to **Shapwick**. Wootton brook. (*See Highbridge.*) (*c.s. Avon.*)

Glenfield (Leicester).—M.R. Rothley Brook. Quorndon brook, 3 *m.* N.W.; trout; preserved by owners of Bradgate Park. Lakes: The pool, Grooby, 2 *m.* N.W (*See Gainsborough.*)

Glen Magna (Leicester).—M.R. Billesdon brook. Lake; Wiston Hall lake. (*See Gainsborough.*)

Glossop (Derby).—G.N.R. and M.R. Shelf brook. Lady Clough brook, 5 *m.* E. Alport, 6 *m* E. Ashop. 7 *m.* S.E. (*See Runcorn; Gainsborough.*)

Gloucester.—G.W.R. Severn. Severn rises 12 *m.* above **Llanidloes**, and just above the town Brochan joins on right bank. Brochan rises 1 *m.* N. from **Llangurig**, and 4 *m.* down is joined on right bank by Dulas brook, which rises 1½ *m.* E. of **Llangurig**, and 3 *m.* down is joined on right bank by Tylwch, which rises 5 *m.* above **Tylwch**, and joins Dulas 2½ *m.* below. Dulas runs 2 *m.* to Brochan, which joins Severn ½ *m.* on. At **Llanidloes**, Clywedog joins Severn on left bank. Clywedog, which is 14 *m.* long, and is poisoned from its source, is joined 6 *m.* from its source, on right bank, by Llwyd, 4 *m.* long (n.s. **Llanidloes**, 8 *m.*). 1 *m.* down, Biga, 4 *m.* long, joins on right bank (n.s. **Llanidloes**, 7 *m.*). 1 *m.* down Clywedog, at Heblid, a stream joins on left bank, which drains Llyn Derw-llwydion 1 *m.* up (n.s. **Llanidloes**, 6 *m.*). Clywedog runs 8 *m.* to **Llanidloes** and Severn. Severn runs to **Dolwen** 4 *m.*, and here Ebyr, which rises in Llyn Ebyr 3 *m.* up, joins on left bank. 1 *m.* down Severn, at Aber Berthin, Berthin, 4 *m.* long, joins on right bank. Severn runs to **Llandinam**, 3 *m.*, and **Caersws**, 3 *m.* Here Tarannon and Garno join on left bank. Tarannon rises in Llyn Gloyw (4 *m.* W. from **Carno**), runs 8 *m.* to Trefeglwys, 3 *m.* below which, Relaf, 4 *m.* long, joins on left bank (n.s. **Caersws**, 2 *m.*). ½ *m.* down Tarannon, Ceryst joins on right bank. Ceryst rises 2 *m.* N. from **Llanidloes**, 2 *m.* N.W. 1 *m.* long. It is poisoned. 1 *m.* down Tarannon is **Caersws** and Severn. Garno rises 4 *m.* above **Carno**, under the name of Llwyd; at Carno it is joined on right bank by Pwll-Llydan, 3 *m.* long. Oledun, 3 *m.* long, also joins at this place. 1 *m.* down Garno, Cerniog, 3 *m.* long, joins on right bank. Garno runs 3 *m.*, when a stream joins 2 *m.* long, which drains Llyn Du (n.s. **Pont-y-ddolgoch**, 3 *m.*). Garno runs 1 *m.* to **Pont-y-ddolgoch**, and Severn 2 *m.* Severn runs 3 *m.*, when Tarw joins on left bank. Tarw rises in Llyn Tarw, which lies 4 *m.* N. from **Pont-y-ddolgoch**, and 1 *m.* E. from Llyn Mawr and Llyn Du, and runs 6 *m.* to Severn. 2 *m.* down Severn, at Aberhavesp (n.s. **Scafell**, 1 *m.*), a stream joins on left bank, which drains Fachwen pool 2 *m.* up. Severn runs 2 *m.*, when Hafren, 8 *m.* long, joins on right bank. Severn runs to **Newtown**, 2 *m.* 3 *m.* down Severn a stream 10 *m.* long joins on left bank, and 2 *m.* down Severn, at **Abermule**, Mule, which rises 4 *m.* above **Kerry**, and runs thence 6 *m.* to Severn, joins on right bank. Severn runs 4 *m.* to **Montgomery** station, and 1 *m.* down is joined on left bank by a stream which rises in two or three small ponds 5 *m.* up. 1 *m.* down Severn, at Glan Severn (n.s. **Montgomery**, 2 *m.*), Rhiw joins on left bank. Rhiw rises in Llyn-y-bugail 7 *m.* N. from **Carno**, runs 8 *m.* to Tre-ganol, and here Mawr joins on right bank. Mawr rises in Llyn Mawr 2½ *m.* N. from **Pont-y-ddolgoch**, and close to Llynnen Du and Tarw, runs 6 *m.* to Llanlluggan, and Rhiw 2 *m.* Rhiw runs to Manafon 2 *m.*, Berriew 6 *m.*, and Severn 1 *m.* Severn runs 1 *m.* to **Forden**, where Camlad joins on right bank. Camlad rises in a pond at Lower Bent 1¼ *m.* N. from **Lydham**, waters a pond at **Lydham**, runs to Snead 1 *m.*, Church Stoke 4 *m.* Here Caerbitra joins on left bank. Caerbitra rises 3 *m.* E. from **Kerry**, and is 8 *m.* long. Close to its junction with Camlad, Lacks brook, 4 *m.* long, joins on left bank. Camlad runs to Chirbury 4 *m.* 2½ *m.* below, Hailesford brook, which rises in Marton pool (n.s. **Forden**, 5 *m.* W.), and is 3 *m.* long, joins on right bank. Camlad runs to **Forden** and Severn in 6 *m.* Severn runs to **Welshpool** 7 *m.* Here Sylvan brook, 5 *m.* long, joins on left bank. Severn runs to **Buttington**, 2 *m.*, and 3 *m.* down, below where the railway crosses the river (**Pool Quay** being 1 *m.* off on left bank), Trewern joins on right bank. Trewern rises by **Middleton**, and is 4 *m.* long. 5 *m.* down Severn, **Criggion** being 1 *m.* off on right bank, Bete brook joins on left bank. Bete rises in a lake 3 *m.* above Guilesfield (n.s. **Pool Quay**, 3 *m.*), and 1 *m.* down is joined on right bank by a stream which crosses the turnpike-road from **Welshpool** to Guilesfield, 2 *m.* from the former place, and is 5 *m.* long. Bete runs to **Pool Quay**, 2 *m.*, and Severn, 3 *m.* ¼ *m.* down Severn, Maerdy brook, 7 *m.* long, joins on left bank, passing **Arleen** *en route.* Severn runs to **Llandrinio**, 2 *m.*, **Ferry**, 4 *m.* Here Vyrnwy joins on left bank. Vyrnwy rises on the slopes of Cefn Coch, 8 *m.* S.E. from **Bala**, runs 3 *m.* to Lake Vyrnwy. 1¼ *m.* down the lake, Ennant (trouting preserved by landlord of Lake Vyrnwy Hotel), 4 *m.* long, joins on right bank, and 1 *m.* on, Hirddu (preserved as above), 4 *m.* long, joins on right bank. 2 *m.* down the lake, Cedig, 5 *m.* long, joins on left bank (preserved as above in the lower part, and by Sir W. W. Wynne in the upper). ½ *m.* down the lake, Gwnion, 3 *m.* long, joins on left bank. ¼ *m.* below is the dam and **Lake Vyrnwy Hotel.** 1½ *m.* below the dam, Marchnant, 3 *m.* long, joins Vyrnwy river on left bank. 2 *m.* down Vyrnwy, Cowny, 5 *m.* long, joins on right bank; and 1 *m.* down Vyrnwy, Dyfnant, 3 *m.* long, joins on left bank. 3 *m.* down Vyrnwy, Llwydiarth joins on left bank. This brook rises 2 *m.* N.E. above Llanfihangel (n.s. **Llanfyllin**, 6 *m.*), and 3 *m.* down is joined on left bank by a brook 1 *m.* long, draining a pond by Llwydiarth. The brook runs to Vyrnwy in 1½ *m.* Vyrnwy runs 2 *m.*, when Cringae, 3 *m.* long, joins on right bank. 8 *m.* down Vyrnwy, Einion joins on right bank. Einion rises in Llyn-hir 9 *m.* N.E. from **Carno.** 1 *m.* down, the outflow of Llyn Grahwyddan ½ *m.* up joins on left bank (n.s. **Carno**, 10 *m.*) 3 *m.* down Einion, a brook 4 *m.* long joins on right bank. 3 *m.* down Einion, Banw joins on left bank. Banw rises on the slopes of Moel-y-Llyn 8 *m.* from **Dinas Mawddwy**, and 2 *m.* down is joined on right bank by Yoguthan, 2 *m.* long. 3 *m.* down Banw, at Garthbibio (n.s. **Dinas M.**, 12 *m.*), Twrch joins on left bank. Twrch (good trouting, but preserved for the most part by Sir W. Wynne and Mr. Price) rises on the slopes of Careg-y-fran, 2 *m.* E. from Llan-y-Mowddwy (n.s. **Dinas M.**, 4 *m.*), 4 *m.* down, Llechog, 2 *m.* long, joins on right bank. 1 *m.* down Twrch, Cathan, which rises in Llyn-y-bugail (trout; preserved, but leave may sometimes be had) 2 *m.* up, joins on right bank (n.s. **Dinas M.**, 9 *m.*, or can be fished from **Cann-Office**, 7 *m.*). Twrch runs 4 *m.* to Garthbibio and Banw. Banw runs 2 *m.* to Llangadfan and **Cann-Office** (n.s. **Dinas M.**, 12 *m.*). Here Eira joins on right bank. Eira rises 3 *m.* N.E. from **Llanbrynmair**, 7 *m.* down, Cannon, which rises in Llyn Gwyddior (perch, trout), 3 *m.* up joins on left bank (n.s. **Llynbrynmair**). Eira runs 3 *m.*, when Cledan joins on right bank. Cledan rises 5 *m.* N. from **Carno**, and is 5 *m.* long. Eira runs 2 *m.*, when Nydwydd, 2 *m.* long, joins on left bank. 1 *m.* down Eira is **Cann-Office** and Llangadfan. Banw runs 2 *m.* to Llanerfyl. 1 *m.* down, Gwylfryn, 3 *m.* long, which drains Llynn Gwylfryn 2 *m.* from **Cann-Office**, joins on left bank. Banw runs 4 *m.*, when Einion joins on right bank. Einion rises in Llyn-her (trouting preserved, but leave may be had sometimes) 4 *m.* S. from **Cann-Office**, and 1 *m.* down is joined on left bank by the outflow of Llyn Granwyddan (good trouting, but preserved; leave sometimes), ½ *m.* up. Einion runs 3 *m.* and is joined on right bank by a brook 4 *m.* long. 3 *m.* down Einion is Banw. Banw runs 2 *m.* to **Llanfair** (n.s. **Welshpool**, 8 *m.*), and 5 *m.* down, at Mathynafal Park, is joined on right bank by a stream 3 *m.* long, draining a pond at Maesmawr, 5 *m.* N.W. from **Welshpool.** Banw joins Vyrnwy 1 *m.* down. 1 *m.* down Vyrnwy, at Meifod, a brook joins on right bank, draining Llyndu 1½ *m.* up (n.s. **Llansantffraid**, 6 *m.*, or **Welshpool**, 6 *m.*). From Meiford down to **Llanymynech** the river is preserved by the landowners; leave freely given. (*See Llanymynech*). Vyrnwy runs 10 *m.* to **Llansantffraid**, where Cain (preserved) joins on left bank. Cain rises 6 *m.* above **Llanfyllin**, 1 *m.* above which place Llechwedd, 5 *m.* long, joins on right bank. Cain runs to **Llanfechan**, 5 *m.* and 1 *m.* down is joined on right bank by Brogan. 8 *m.* long. Cain runs to **Llansaintfraid** and Vyrnwy, 2 *m.* 1 *m.* down Vyrnwy, Tanat joins on left bank. Tanat, which with its tributaries—except a small portion of the Moch brook —is strictly preserved. rises 5 *m.* above **Llangynnog** (n.s. **Llanderfel**, 9 *m.*), and 4 *m.* from its source is joined on right bank by Goch, which stream is joined on right bank ¾ *m.* above the junction by a brook draining Llyn Pennan 1 *m.* up. At **Llangynnog**, Eiarth, 5 *m.* long, joins Tanat on left bank; it runs by the side of the high road to **Llanderfel.** 3 *m.* down Tanat, Hirnant, 4 *m.* long, joins on right bank. 4 *m.* down Tanat, **Llanrhaider-yn-Mochnant** being 1 *m.* off on left bank, Moch (some good, free trouting) joins on left bank. Moch rises in Llyn Llynecaws 6 *m.* N.W. from **Llanrhaider-yn-M.**, and 2 *m.* down is joined on right bank by Disgynfa, 3 *m.* long. Moch runs 6 *m.* to **Llanrhaider-yn-M.**, and 1 *m.* down joins Tanat. Tanat runs 1 *m.*, when Twrch joins on left bank. Twrch is 9 m. long, and runs 1 m. E. of **Llanrhaider-yn-M.** 1 m. down Tanát again a brook joins on left bank 5 m. long, and running 3 m. E. from **Llanrhaider.** (Good flies for all these streams are light duns, sandfly, red dipper, alder, willow, grannom, iron blue and stone fly. Also the following : *body*, hare's ear and yellow wool mixed; *legs*, freckled dun, with reddish tips. *Body*, mole's fur; *wing*, two small feathers, tipped reddish, taken from the outside of a cock sparrow's wing. *Body*, hare's ear; *legs*, feather from a partridge's back.) Tanat runs to Llangedwyn 3 m. (n.s. **Llanyblodwel** or **Llanfechan** 4 m.). *Inn:* Green; comfortable; the river is strictly preserved by Lady Wynne down to Penybont bridge, and by other owners to its mouth ; salmon, trout, pike, grayling. 3 m. down Tanat, Cynllaith joins. (Strictly preserved.) Cynllaith rises 4 m. W. from **Oswestry**, and after running 5 m. is joined at New Mill by a brook on right bank 4 m. long. 1 m. down. near Llansilin, a stream joins on left bank, draining Llyn Rhyddwyn 1 m. up (n.s. **Oswestry**, 5. m. E.). 2 m. down Cynllaith a stream joins, on right bank, the outflow of Llyn Moelin 3 m. up. Moelin lies 4 m. N. from **Llangedwyn**. 3 m. down, Cynllaith joins Tanat, which runs to **Llan-y-blodwell**, 2 m., and joins Vyrnwy 3 m. down. Vyrnwy runs 3 m. to **Llanymynech**, and 3 m. down is joined on left bank by Morda, which, after a course of 3 m., runs 3 m. W. from **Oswestry**, runs 5 m., when it passes again 1 m. S. of that town, and 5 m. down is joined on left bank by the stream 3 m. long which drains the lake at Aston 3 m. S.E. from **Oswestry**. Morda runs 6 m. to Vyrnwy, which joins Severn 5 m. down. 2 m. down Severn, Wear brook joins on left bank. Wear rises in Sandford Hall pond 3 m. above **Kinnersley**, and joins Severn 3 m. down. Severn runs to Shrawardine 5 m., where is a large lake at Shrawarding Castle (n.s. **Shrewsbury**). and 5 m. down at Mountford Bridge a stream joins on right bank, draining a lake by Onslow Hall 2 m. up (n.s. **Hanwood**, 3 m.). 1 m. down Severn, Perry joins on left bank. Perry rises by **Gobowen**, and 3 m. down, near **Whittington**, the outflow of the lakes at Halston Hall joins on left bank. Perry runs 3 m. to Rednall Mill, **Rednall** being 2 m. off on right bank. 4 m. down, at Wykey, a stream joins on right bank, draining a lake at Shelyocke (n.s. **Rednall**, 3 m. N.W.). Perry runs 5 m. to **Baschurch**, and 1 m. down is joined on left bank by War brook, which rises in Berth pool ½ m. N. from **Baschurch** Station, runs thence in ½ m. to Buch Grove pool, in ½ m. to Marton pool on left bank, and, running through Fennymere pool, joins Perry 3 m. down. Perry joins Severn 3 m. below. Severn runs 4 m. to **Leaton** Station (1 m. off on left bank), and in 7 m. reaches **Shrewsbury**. Here Raddle brook, which rises in Onslow Hall lake 3 m. N. from **Hanwood**, and is 4 m. long, joins on left bank. Just below Raddle, and on same side, **Rea** joins. Rea rises 7 m. above **Minsterley**, where it is joined on left bank by Minsterley brook, 5 m. long. Rea flows 3 m. to **Pontesbury** (1 m. off on right bank), and here Habberley brook, 6 m. long, joins on right bank. 3 m. down Rea, at **Hanwood**, Yockleton brook joins, which rises 3 m. above **Westbury**, runs 4 m. to **Yockleton**, and Rea 2 m. 2 m. down Rea, at Hooka Gate, Longden brook, 4 m. long, joins on right bank. 2 m. down Rea, at Meole Brace, Meole brook, which rises in Bomer pool 2 m. N. from **Condover**, and is 2 m. long, joins on right bank. Rea runs to **Shrewsbury** 2 m. Close by the station runs a stream draining Almond pool, Black pool, and Hencott pool, 3 m. N. from **Shrewsbury**.

LOWER SEVERN.—3 m. down Severn, Sundorn brook joins on left bank. Sundorn rises in a pond by **Yarton**, runs 4 m. to **Hadnall**, and 3 m. down waters the lakes at Sundorn Castle, joining Severn ½ m. below. Severn runs 6 m. to Atcham, where a stream joins on right bank, watering two lakes near **Berrington**, and is 2 m. long. 1 m. down Severn, Tern joins on left bank. Tern rises in Maer Hall lake 2 m. S. from **Whitmore**, runs 6 m. to **Norton**, and 3 m. down is joined on left bank by Hemp Mill brook, 3 m. long, and which waters, half-way down, Daisy lake, near Audley Cross 3 m. N.E. from **Market Drayton**. Tern runs to **Market Drayton** 2 m., where Coal brook, 6 m. long, joins on left bank, after watering some lakes by Peats Wood close to the junction. 3 m. down Tern is the outflow of the Buntingsdale Hall lake, ½ m. up. 2 m. down, Baile brook joins Tern on right bank. Baile rises in a pool at Sandford Hall 2 m. E. of **Prees**, and 5 m. down is joined on left bank by a brook which rises in Big pool, 3 m S.W. from **Adderley**. 1 m. down, the outflow of Old pool at Titley Park, ½ m. up, joins on left bank. 2 m. down, **Market Drayton** being 2 m. off on left bank, is the outflow of a pond at Stych Farm, ½ m. up. A little lower down, on the same side, a stream joins, which rises in Cloverley pond 5 m. from **Market Drayton**, runs 2 m. to Mordon Mill pond, and 2 m. down joins the main stream, which joins Baile 2 m. down. Baile joins Tern 1 m. down. Tern runs to Stoke-upon-Tern 4 m. (n.s. **Hodnet**, 1 m.). Here Saltern brook, which rises in two ponds by Wardale 4 m. S. from **Market Drayton**, runs 2 m. to the mill-pond at Rose Hill, thence 2 m. to Salter's Mill, and Stoke 1 m., joins on left bank. Tern runs to **Peplow** 3 m., just above which is the outflow of a pond on the right bank. 2 m. below **Peplow**, Alford brook, 5 m. long, joins on left bank. Tern runs 2 m. to Great Bolas, where Polford brook, 6 m. long, and which runs 2 m. S.W. of **Peplow**, joins on right bank, and Meess on left bank. Meess rises in the White Sitch lake 5 m. N.E. from **Shiffnal**, and 8 m. down runs through Aquadale Meer 2 m. from **Newport**. 2 m. down, Meess receives the outflow of Chetwynd Park pond, close to **Newport**, on left bank, and ½ m. on, Lomeo brook, 7 m long joins, on right bank. 3 m. down Meess, Ellerton brook joins on right bank. Ellerton rises in

Heywood ponds 4 *m.* S.E. from **Market Drayton**, runs 3 *m* to Ellerton Mill pond, and
1 *m.* below is joined on left bank by a brook 4 *m.* long running out of the canal reservoir
at Great Soundley, 7 *m.* S.E. from **Market Drayton**. Ellerton passes through
Showed Mill pond, and joins Meess 1 *m.* down. Meess runs 5 *m.* to Tibberton, and Tern
4 *m.* Tern runs 3 *m.* to **Crudgington**. where Strine joins on left bank. Strine rises
3 *m.* W. of **Newport**, and 4 *m.* down is joined on left bank by Brockton brook, which
rises in Wildmoor pool, runs to Minton's pool in ½ *m.*, ½ *m.* below which the outflow
of Limekiln pool joins on left bank. These lakes are close together 3 *m.* S. of **Newport**.
Brockton joins Strine 6 *m.* down. Strine runs 2 *m.* to Broad lake, where Preston brook
joins on left bank. Preston rises in a lake by **Hadley**, and is 6 *m.* long. 1 *m.* down,
Strine joins Tern at **Crudgington**. 1 *m.* down Tern, Beanhill brook, 5 *m.* long, joins
on left bank. Tern runs to **Walcott** 5 *m.*, and here Roden joins on right bank. Roden
rises in White Meer 2 *m.* from **Ellesmere**, runs ½ *m.* to Blackmere, and 1 *m.* on to
Colemere, and 1 *m.* below is joined on right bank by a brook 3 *m.* long, draining Crose
Mere 4 *m.* S.E. from **Ellesmere**. Roden runs 8 *m.* to **Wem**, and 3 *m.* down is joined
on left bank by Prees brook, which rises in **Prees** mill-pool, and is 4 *m.* long. 1 *m.* down
Roden a brook joins on left bank, draining the large lake in Hawkstone Park 5 *m.* E.
from **Wem**. Roden runs 6 *m.* to Stanton, 3 *m.* to Shawsbury (n.s. **Hadnall**, 4 *m.*) (good
trouting, especially in Mayfly season; preserved by Sir V. Corbet and Sir T. Meyrick), and
6 *m.* down joins Tern at **Walcott**. Tern runs to Severn 5 *m.* Severn runs 1 *m.* to
Wroxeter (n.s. **Berrington**, 2½ *m.*), a short distance above which Bell brook, 4 *m.* long,
joins on left bank. 2 *m.* down Severn, Cound brook joins on right hand. Cound rises
above **Church Stretton**, runs 5 *m.* to **Le Botwood**, **Dorrington**, 4 *m.*, watering the
pond at Longnor Forge midway, **Condover** 4 *m.*, **Berrington** (1 *m.* off on left bank)
3 *m.*, and 3 *m.* down is joined on right bank by Row brook 7 *m.* long. ¼ *m.* on Acton
brook joins on right bank. Acton rises in a pond at Hobsley Coppice 1 *m.* E. of
Frodesley (n.s. **Le Botwood**, 4 *m.*), and is 4 *m.* long. 1 *m.* down Cound, Langley brook
joins on right bank. Langley rises in Langley pond by Langley (n.s. **Le Botwood**,
5 *m.*). 2 *m.* down the outflow of the lakes in Acton Burnell Park (n.s. **Cressage**, 5 *m.*)
joins on left bank. 2 *m.* down the outflow of Harnage Grange Pond (n.s. **Cressage**,
3 *m.*) joins on right bank. 1 *m.* down, Langley joins Cound, which runs 1 *m.* to Severn.
Severn runs 4 *m.* to **Cressage**, and 1 *m.* down is joined on right bank by Hughley
brook, which rises 5 *m.* above Hughley (n.s. **Presthorpe**, 2 *m.*), runs 4 *m.* to **Much
Wenlock** (1½ *m.* off on right bank), and joins Severn 4 *m.* down. Severn runs to
Leighton 1 *m.*, where Leighton brook, working two or three miles, joins on left bank.
Severn runs 3 *m.* to **Buildwas**, where Farley brook joins on right bank. Farley rises
in two ponds in the Marsh 1 *m.* E. of **Much Wenlock**, and is 5 *m.* long, working four
mills. Severn runs to **Iron Bridge**, 3 *m.*, **Coalport**, 2 *m.*, **Linley**, 3 *m.* Here Linley
brook joins on right bank. Linley rises in the large lakes in Willey Park 3 *m.* W. from
Linley, and is 4 *m.* long. 4 *m.* down Severn, Worf joins on left bank. Worf rises in a
pond in the marsh 3 *m.* N. from **Shiffnal**, runs ½ *m.* to Burlington Pool, ½ *m.* to New
pool, 1¼ *m.* to Forge pool; and 3 *m.* down at the Pavilion is joined on left bank by
Norning brook, which rises in the Moat and two other ponds at Weston Park; and 4 *m.*
down is joined on right bank by Tong brook, which, rising in Cowley Wood pond and
Weston Mill pond, waters Norton Meer (n.s. **Shiffnal**, 3¼ *m.*), and joins Norning 2 *m.*
down. Worf runs 3 *m.* to Ryton, where a brook, which rises by **Shiffnal** 5 *m.* up, and works
several mills, joins on right bank. Worf runs to Stableford 4 *m.*, where Badger brook, 3 *m.*
long, joins on left bank. Badger rises in Snowdon pool 3½ S.W. from **Albrighton**. Worf
runs 4 *m.* to Worfield (n.s. **Bridgnorth**, 4 *m.*), and here Stratford brook joins, which rises
in the large lake at Patshull (n.s. **Albrighton**, 3 *m.*), and running 4 *m.*, is joined on left
bank by Claverley brook, 6 *m.* long. Stratford runs 1 *m.* to Worf, which joins Severn 4 *m.*
down. Severn runs to **Bridgnorth** 1 *m.*, and 5 *m.* down at Stermford is joined on
right bank by Mor brook. Mor rises 4 *m.* above Acton Round, 3½ *m.* S.E. of **Much
Wenlock**, where it is joined on left bank by Beggarhill brook, 3 *m.* long. Mor runs to
Morville 3 *m.*, where the outflow of three ponds, 1 to 2 *m.* to the N., joins on left bank (n.s.
Bridgnorth, 3½ *m.*). Mor (trout) joins Severn 8 *m.* down. Severn runs 2 *m.* to
Hampton, 3 *m.* to Alverley, 1 *m.* below which Borle brook joins on right bank. Borle
rises by Upton Cressett, 5 *m.* W. from **Bridgnorth**, and is 11 *m.* long. Severn runs to
upper **Harley** 2 *m.*, **Bewdley** 4 *m.* Just above, at Dowles, Dowles brook joins on
right bank. Dowles rises in a series of ponds at Kinlet, 3 *m.* S.W. from **Alveley**, runs
9 *m.* to **Wyre**, and Severn 3 *m.* Just below **Bewdley** the outflow of a large lake close
to Bewdley on the W. joins on left bank. Severn runs to **Stourport** 3 *m.*, where
Gladder brook, 4 *m.* long, joins on right bank, and Stour on left bank. Stour rises by
Halesowen in Grange Mill pond. 2 *m.* down, the outflow from Lutley Mill pond joins
on left bank. 2 *m.* down, at **Cradley**, a brook joins on right bank, running out of
Gades Green Reservoir, 2 *m.* S. of Dudley,, and feeding the New pool close to **Cradley**
on the W. Stour runs to **Stourbridge** 3 *m.*, where a brook joins on left bank, draining
Gig Mill pond and another pond close to Stourbridge on the S. 1 *m.* down Stour
a stream, 2 *m.* long, joins on right bank, draining the reservoir in Pensnett Chase
by **Brierley Hill**. 3 *m.* down Stour, at Devil's Den, Smestow joins on right
bank. Smestow rises by Tettenhall, 2 *m.* N.W. from **Wolverhampton** runs
7 *m.* to Trysull, 2 *m.* below which Wombourne brook joins on left bank, 5 *m.* long,
working several mills. 2 *m.* down Smestow, at Hollow Mill, a stream, 5 *m.* long,

joins on left bank, which rises in the ponds in the Old Park, 2 *m.* W. of **Dudley,** and works several mills. Here also joins at the same place the stream, 3 *m.* long, draining the ponds in Himley Park, and the common pool by Himley. 2 *m.* down Smestow, Philley brook, 5 *m.* long, and feeding some mills, joins on right bank. Smestow joins Stour 2 *m.* on. Stour runs to **Kidderminster,** 10 *m.* Here a brook, which rises by **Churchill,** and feeds numerous large mill ponds, joins on left bank ; it is 6 *m.* long. 2 *m.* down Stour, Hoo brook joins on left bank. Hoo rises in a large pond, 2 *m.* above Bell Broughton (n.s. **Churchill,** 3 *m.*), and is 8 *m.* long. Stour runs to **Stourport** and Severn in 3 *m.* 4 *m.* down Severn, Dick brook, rising above Heightington, 3 *m.* W. from **Stourport,** and 9 *m.* long, joins on right bank ; 1 *m.* above the junction, the outflow of Sharpley Pool, 4 *m.* S. of **Stourport,** joins Dick on right bank. Just below Weir Ferry, 1 *m.* down Severn, the outflow of Frog pool, and another pond 1 *m.* up, joins on right bank. 1 *m.* down Severn, Shrawley brook, 4 *m.* long, and which drains the lakes at Witley Court (Lord Dudley), 7 *m.* from **Stourport,** joins on right bank. 5 *m.* down Severn, at Hawford, 4 *m.* N. from **Worcester,** Salwarp joins on left bank. Salwarp rises in Fockbury mill pond, 2 *m.* N. from **Bromsgrove,** where Spadsbourne brook, 4 *m.* long, working some mills, joins on left bank. 5 *m.* down Salwarp, at Upper Warren, Hen brook, 4 *m.* long, joins on left bank. Salwarp runs to **Droitwich,** 4 *m.,* where Body brook, 3 *m.* long, joins on left bank. 2 *m.* down Salwarp, Hampton brook, 10 *m.* long joins on right bank. 1 *m.* down Salwarp, Doverdale joins on right bank. Doverdale runs 2 *m.* E. of **Thurtlebury,** and is 14 *m.* long. Salwarp joins Severn 4 *m.* down. Severn runs 5 *m.* to **Worcester.** 2 *m.* below, Teme joins on right bank. Teme rises some 15 *m.* above **Knucklas,** runs 3 *m.* to **Knighton, Bucknall,** 6 *m.,* **Leintwardine** (n.s. **Hoptonheath,** 3 *m.*). Here Clun joins on left bank. Clun rises 11 *m.* above **Clun** (n.s. **Broome,** 8 *m.*). Here Lower, 10 *m.* long, joins on left bank. Clun runs to Clunbury, 3 *m.,* and Broome, 2 *m.* Here Kempton brook, which rises in Acton pool, 4 *m.* N. from **Clun,** and is 8 *m.* long, joins on left bank. Clun runs 2 *m.* to Clungunford, **Hoptonheath,** 2 *m.* 2 *m.* down, Red Lake brook joins on right bank. Redlake rises 10 *m.* above **Bucknall,** and joins Clun 3 *m.* below. Clun runs to **Leintwardine** and Teme, 1 *m.* Teme runs 3 *m.,* when Allcox brook, 5 *m.* long, joins on right bank. 1 *m.* down Teme at Burrington the outflow of Burrington pool, 1 *m.* up, joins on right bank. Teme flows to **Bromfield,** 6 *m.* Here Onny joins on left bank. Onny rises in Marsh pool, 8 *m.* up from **Lydham,** and 4 *m.* down is joined on left bank by a brook draining Shelve pool, 2 *m.* N. (n.s. **Lydham,** 7 *m.*) 1 *m.* down Onny, Black brook, 3 *m.* long, joins on left bank. Onny runs to **Lydham,** 4 *m.,* and **Eaton,** 2 *m.* Here Eaton brook, which rises by Robin Hood's baths, 4 *m.* S.W. from **Le Botwood,** and is 10 *m.* long, joins on left bank. Onny runs to **Plowden,** 2 *m.,* and 6 *m.* down, by Strefford bridge, Quenny brook joins on left bank. Quenny rises 4 *m.* above **Marsh Brook** station, and 4 *m.* down is joined on left bank by Eaton brook, which rises by Cardington, 3 *m.* N.W. from **Longville,** runs 9 *m.* to **Harton Road,** and 4*m.* down joins Quenny, which joins Onny 1 *m.* below. Onny runs to **Craven Arms,** 1 *m.,* **Onibury,** 4 *m.,* **Bromfield** and Teme, 4 *m.* Here the outflow of the Decoy pools, lying 2 *m.* to the S.W. of **Bromfield,** joins on right bank. Teme runs 3 *m.* to **Ludlow,** and here Corve joins on left bank. Corve rises 1 *m.* S. of Burton, 1 *m.* from **Presthorpe,** and 2 *m.* down is joined on right bank by a stream rising in Letwiche mill pond 2 *m.* up (n.s. **Longville,** 2 *m.*). Corve runs 5 *m.,* when Thonglands brook, 5 *m.* long, joins on left bank. Corve runs 2 *m.,* when Tugford brook, 5 *m.* long, joins on left bank. 5 *m.* down Corve, at Culmington, Pye brook, 7 *m.* long, joins on left bank. Corve joins Teme at **Ludlow,** 8 *m.* down (Corve is preserved by private owners throughout its length). 2 *m.* down Teme the drainage of the lakes in Ludford Park, 1 *m.* S. from **Ludlow,** joins on right bank. Teme runs to **Woolferton,** 4 *m.,* and 1 *m.* down, Brimfield brook, rising in two ponds, and running by **Woolferton** Station, and 6 *m.* long, joins on right bank. 1 *m.* down Teme, at **Easton Court,** West brook, 4 *m.* long, joins on right bank. 1 *m.* down Teme, Cadmore brook, 3 *m.* long, joins on right bank. 1 *m.* down Teme, Ledwych joins on left bank. Ledwych rises 4 *m.* above Middleton, 3 *m.* N.E. from **Ludlow,** and is joined on right bank at that place by the outflow of the lakes at Downton Hall, 1 *m.* up. Dogditch brook, 5 *m.* long, joins also on the left bank. 3 *m.* down Ledwych, 2 *m.* S.E. of **Ludlow,** Cay brook, 3 *m.* long, joins on left bank. 1 *m.* down Ledwych the outflow of Wooton pool, 2 *m.* up, joins on left bank (n.s. **Ludlow** or **Tenbury,** 5 *m.*). 7 *m.* down, Ledwych joins Teme, which runs to **Tenbury,** 1 *m.* Here Kyre brook joins on right bank. Kyre rises 2 *m.* above Kyre Magna, runs through Kyre Park just below, receiving the outflow of Kyre pool ½ *m.* up. Thence to **Tenbury** is 5 *m.* 2 *m.* down Teme, Corn brook, 6 *m.* long, joins on left bank. 1 *m.* down Teme, by **Newnham Bridge,** Rea joins on left bank. Rea rises 15 *m.* above **Cleobury Mortimer,** and 5 *m.* down is joined on right bank by Cleobury brook, 3 *m.* long. Thence to **Cleobury** is 10 *m.,* **Neen Sollers** 6 *m.,* just above which Banhall brook, 3 *m.* long, joins on left bank. 1 *m.* below, Hopton brook joins on right bank. Hopton runs 3 *m.,* when Hopper brook, 2 *m.* long, joins on right bank. Thence to Rea is 4 *m.*; Rea runs to **Newnham Bridge,** 2 *m.,* where the outflow of Bickley pools, 2 *m.* up, join on right bank; thence to Teme is 1 *m.* Teme runs to Eastham, 3 *m.,* where Pipers brook (trout) joins on right bank. 6 *m.* down Teme, at Stanford Bridge, the outflow of Stanford Park lake, ½ *m.* up, joins on right bank. Teme runs 12 *m.* to Knightsford Bridge, **Knightswick** being 1 *m.* off on right bank (the landlord of the Talbot has 2 *m.* of good fishing); and here Sapey brook, 7 *m.* long, joins on right bank. Teme runs 3 *m.* to Broadwas and **Leigh Court**, 4 *m.* Here Leigh Brook joins on right bank. Leigh, under the name of Cradley, rises by **Colwall**, runs 4 *m.* to Mathon, 4 *m.* W. from **Great Malvern**, and joins Teme 10 *m.* down. Teme runs 2 *m.* to **Bransford**, and 3 *m.* down, at Powick Bridge, is joined on left bank by Laughern brook, which is 14 *m.* long, and passes close on the W. side of **Worcester**, and 2 *m.* down joins Teme, which joins Severn 2 *m.* down. Severn runs to Kempsey, 4 *m.*; **Upton-on-Severn**, 8 *m.*; **Ripple**, 4 *m.*; **Tewkesbury**, 4 *m.* Here Ripple brook, which drains the lakes in Croome Park, 3 *m.* N.W. from **Defford**, joins on left bank. Here also Avon joins on left bank. Avon rises in the reservoir by **Naseby** (n.s. **Kilworth**, 5 *m.*), and 3 *m.* down at Welford, 2 *m.* from **Kilworth**, is joined on right bank by the outflow from another reservoir 1 *m.* up. Avon runs 3 *m.* to **Kilworth** : **Stanford**, 4 *m.*; **Lilbourne**, 2 *m.* Here Yelvertoft brook, 6 *m.* long, joins on left bank. Avon runs to **Clifton**, 3 *m.*; **Rugby**, 3 *m.* Here Swift joins on right bank. Swift rises by Kimcote, 4 *m.* N.W. from **W. Kilworth**, runs 4 *m.* to **Lutterworth** (n.s. **Ullesthorpe**, 4 *m.*), and **Rugby** 8 *m.* Avon runs 10 *m.* to **Brandon**, and 9 *m* below, at **Stoneleigh** (n.s. **Kenilworth**, 3 *m.*), is joined on right bank by Sow. Sow rises 3 *m.* above **Bedworth**, runs 2 *m.* to **Exhall**, where Breach brook, 3 *m.* long, joins on right bank. Sow runs 3 *m.* to **Foleshill**, where Marches Brook, 2 *m.* long, joins on left bank. Sow runs 3 *m.* to Sow, 3 *m.* from **Coventry**, where Withy brook, 6 *m.* long, joins on left bank. 1 *m.* down Sow, Coomb brook joins, which rises in Burden pool 5 *m.* above **Brinklow**, runs thence in 3 *m.* to the lake in Coomb Park, and join Sow ¼ *m.* on. 5 *m.* down Sow, Sherburne joins on right bank. Sherburne rises 5 *m.* above **Coventry**, and joins Sow 3 *m.* below. 2 *m.* down Sow, a stream joins on right bank 6 *m.* long, rising in some ponds on Westwood Heath (n.s. **Tile Hill**, 2 *m.*, or **Kenilworth**, 3 *m.*). 1 *m.* down, Sow joins Avon, which runs 8 *m.* to **Leamington**. Here Leam joins on left bank. Leam rises 6 *m.* above **Braunston** (n.s. **Crick**, 5 *m.*) and 4 *m.* down is joined on right bank by Rains brook, 7 *m.* long, which runs 3 *m.* S. of **Rugby**. Leam runs to **Birdingbury** 5 *m.*, and 3 *m.* down, at Martin's, is joined on left bank by Ichene. Ichene rises in a lake at Stoneton House, by Wormleighton (n.s. **Fenny Compton**, 2 *m.*), and 7 *m.* down is joined on left bank by Ham brook, which runs 1 *m.* N. from **Fenny Compton** Station, and is 4 *m.* long. Itchene runs 3 *m.* to **Harbury** and 3 *m.* to **Southam**, and 8 *m.* down joins Leam, which joins Avon 12 *m.* down. Avon runs 1 *m.* to **Warwick**, and 1 *m.* down is joined by a brook on left bank, which rises in a mill pond at Chesterton, 3 *m.* W. from **Harbury**, and 7 *m.* down waters the large lake in Warwick Park on the Avon's bank. Avon runs 3 *m.* to Barford and Hampton Lacey 5 *m.* (n.s. **Stratford-on-Avon**, 5 *m.*). Here Thelesford brook, 7 *m.* long, joins on left bank A little below, running through Charlcote Park, Dene joins on left bank. Dene rises by **Kington**, and 3 *m.* down is joined on right bank by a brook which rises in 3 ponds on Pool Fields, 2 *m.* N. from **Kington**, and waters the large lakes by Coombrooke, 2 *m.* N.W. from **Kington**, and joins Dene 1 *m.* down. Dene runs 8 *m.* to Avon, which runs to **Stratford**, 7 *m.* 1 *m.* below, Stour joins on left bank. Stour rises 12 *m.* above **Shipston** (n.s. **Campden**, 7 *m.*), and 7 *m.* down, at Mitford Bridge, is joined on left bank by Compton brook, 8 *m.* long. 1 *m.* down, at Burmington, Knee brook, which rises by **Campden**, runs 5 *m.* to **Blockley** and 8 *m.* to Stour, joins on left bank. Stour runs 3 *m.* to **Shipston**, Halford 5 *m.*, 2 *m.* below which the outflow of Ealington Park lake, 1 *m.* up, joins on right bank. 9 *m.* down, Stour joins Avon. Avon runs to **Milcote** 2 *m.*, Bidford 9 *m.* (*Inns* : Pleasure Boat and White Lion; fishing very good), **Salford Priors** 2 *m.* Here Arrow joins on right bank. Arrow rises by **Alvechurch**, runs 5 *m.* to **Redditch**, just above which place a stream joins on right bank, draining the lake at Hewell Grange 2¼ *m.* N.W. from **Redditch**. 1 *m.* down Arrow a brook joins on right bank, draining the pond at Ipsley Lodge, 1 *m.* S.E. of **Redditch**. Arrow runs to **Studley**, 3 *m.*; **Congleton**, 3 *m.*; **Alcester**, 3 *m.* Here Alne joins on left bank. Alne rises above Lapworth Bridge, 4 *m.* N. from **Henley-in-Arden** (n.s. **Bearley Cross**, 5 *m.*), runs 20 *m.* to Wootton Wawen, 2 *m.* S. of **Henley**, and 2 *m.* from **Bearley Cross**. Here Alne waters a large lake, and is joined also on right bank by a brook running down from **Henley**. 2 *m.* down Alne, at Gray Mill, Edstone brook, which rises by **Hatton**, runs 6 *m.* to **Bearley Cross** and 2 *m.* to Alne, joins on left bank. Alne runs to **Alcester** 7 *m.* 2 *m.* down Arrow the outflow of the lake in Ragley Park, 1 *m.* N.W. of **Wixford**, joins on right bank. Arrow runs to **Wixford** 1 *m.*, and **Salford Priors** and Avon 3 *m.* Here Ban brook, 5 *m.* long, joins on right bank. Avon runs 3 *m.* to **Harvington**, and 2 *m.* down, by Offenham, Wickham brook joins on left bank. Wickham rises 2 *m.* above Child's Wickham (n.s. **Hinton**, 5 *m.*), runs to Badsey 4 *m.*, and Offenham 3 *m.* Avon runs to **Evesham** 2 *m.*, and here Isborne joins on left bank. Isborne rises by **Winchcombe** (n.s. **Cheltenham**, 8 *m.*, S.W.), runs 12 *m.* to **Hinton**, and **Evesham** 3 *m.* Avon runs 7 *m.* to Cropthorn, **Pershore** 5 *m.* Here Wyre joins 1 *m.* above the town on right bank. Wyre rises by **Inkberrow** (n.s. **Alcester**, 6 *m.*), runs 6 *m.* to Flyford Flavell, and 5 *m.* down is joined on left bank by Whitsun brook, which rises above Bishampton (n.s. **Pershore**, 5 *m.*), and is 6 *m.* long. Wyre runs to **Pershore** and Avon 3 *m.* 8 *m.* down Avon, by **Defford**, Bow brook joins on right bank. Bow rises 7 *m.* N.W. of **Alcester**, above **Feckenham**, and 5 *m.* down is joined on right bank by Dean brook, 3 *m.* long. Bow runs to Himbleton 1 *m.*, 5 *m.* to White Ladies' Ashton, 2 *m.* from **Spetchley, Pershore** station 4 *m.*, and 2 *m.* down is joined on right bank by Stoulton brook, which drains the lake in Spetchley Park, 6 *m.* up by **Spetchley.** Bow joins Avon 4 *m.* down at **Defford.** Avon runs 4 *m.* to **Bredon,** and Severn, at **Tewkesbury,** 4 *m.* Here Carant brook, 7 *m.* long, joins on left bank. 1 *m.* down Severn Swilgare joins on left bank. Swilgare rises at **Prestbury,** 2 *m.* N.E. from **Cheltenham,** runs 4 *m.* to **Cleve** station, and 5 *m.* down close by **Tewkesbury,** is joined on right bank by Tirle brook, 5 *m.* long. 1 *m.* down, Swilgare joins Severn. 5 *m.* down Severn by Norton, 5 *m.* from **Gloucester.** Chelt joins on left bank. Chelt rises 4 *m.* above **Cheltenham,** and runs to Norton 7 *m.*, and Severn 2 *m.* Severn runs 8 *m,* to **Gloucester,** just above which Longford brook, 8 *m.* long, joins on left bank. Close to the junction with Severn, Broadboard brook, 7 *m.* long, joins Longford on right bank. At **Gloucester,** Leadon joins Severn on right bank. Leadon rises 7 *m.* above **Ledbury,** a mile *above* which place a stream joins on left bank, 2 *m.* long, draining the Dogberry pools. 2 *m.* down Leadon the drainings of the canal reservoir ½ *m.* up join on left bank. 1 *m.* down Leadon is Dormington, and 2 *m.* **Dymock,** where Preston river joins, 9 *m.* long, on right bank. Leadon runs to Pauntley, 6 *m.*, and 3 *m.* down at **Upleadon** is joined on left bank by Clynch brook, which rises in Eastnor Castle lake, 2 *m.* E. from **Ledbury,** and is 11 *m.* long. Leadon runs to Hartpury, 3 *m.*, where Newent brook which rises above **Newent,** and is 6 *m.* long, joins on right bank. Leadon runs 5 *m.* to **Gloucester.** Here also Twiver, 6 *m.* long, joins Severn on left bank. (*See Upleadon, Newent.*) (*c.s.*) Close to the town are some pits holding perch, tench, and pike; fishing free. *Hotels* : Wellington and Bell.

Glynde (Sussex) —L.B. & S.C.R. (*See Newhaven.*)

Gnosall (Stafford).—L. & N.W.R. ; G.N.R. Eaton water (*See Gainsborough.*)

Goathland (York).—N.E.R. Murk Esk; trout; private. Eller beck; trout; private. Little beck, 1 *m.* S. Brocka beck, 2 *m.* S. Little Eller beck, 4 *m.* S.E. (*See Whitby.*)

Gobowen (Salop).—G.W.R. Perry. (*See Gloucester.*) (*c.s. Severn.*)

Godalming (Surrey).—L. & S.W.R. Wey; preserved by a society. (*See London, L.T.*) *Hotels* : King's Arms, Angel.

Goldsborough (York).—N.E.R. Nidd ; preserved for 14 *m.* by the Knaresborough Angling Club of 30 members; entrance 40*s.*; s.t. 40*s.* No w. or d.t. Hon. Secs., Mr. A. Sellers and Mr. C. F. Smith, Knaresborough. D. and w.t. for Knaresborough Joint Anglers' Club water from the sec., Mr. J. W. Bramley, Gracious-street, and from Mr. Hall, Gunsmith, Market Place, Knaresborough. (*c.s. York.*) (*See York.*)

Gomshall (Surrey).—S.E.R. (*See London, L.T.*) On Tillingbourne trout. There are some lakes at Albury Park.

Goodworth Clatford (Hants).—L. & S.W.R. On Test; trout, grayling. (*See Southampton and Andover.*) The owner of Clatford Mills has extensive rights.

Goole (Yorks). — N.E.R. : G.C.R. : L. & Y.R. Don or Dun. (*c.s. Yorkshire.*) Don rises in Dunford Bridge reservoir at **Dunford Bridge,** runs to **Hazelhead Bridge** 3 *m.*, **Penistone** 4 *m.*: here Scout dyke, 4 *m.* long, joins on left bank. Don runs to **Deep Car** 7 *m.* Here Little Don, which rises in Cloudberry Moor, 2 *m.* S. across the hills from **Dunford Bridge,** runs 4 *m.* to the post road 2 *m.* S. of **Hazelhead Bridge,** joins Don 7 *m.* down on right bank. 2 *m.* down Don from **Deep Car,** Ewden river, 8 *m.* long, joins on right bank. Don runs 1 *m.*, where Tinkers brook (running 1 *m.* N.W. of **Oughtibridge**), 3 *m.* long, joins on right bank. Don reaches **Oughtibridge,** and here joins on right bank a brook draining a pond 1 *m.* up. Don runs to **Wadesley Bridge** 2 *m.* 2 *m.* below **Wadesley Bridge** Rowel joins on right bank. Rowel rises in a large reservoir in the hills, and 1 *m.* down is joined on the left bank by a short stream draining Agden reservoir. 2 *m.* down Rowel. Uphill brook, 3 *m.* long, joins on right bank. 2 *m.* down Rowel, Storr brook, 3 *m.* long, joins on right bank. 2 *m.* down Rowel, Rivelin joins on right bank. Rivelin rises on the Hallam Moors, and 3 *m.* down forms a large reservoir 7 *m.* W. of **Sheffield.** Here a stream joins on right bank, draining another reservoir 1 *m.* up, 7 *m.* W. of **Sheffield.** Rivelin runs 5 *m.* to Rowel, which joins Don 1 *m.* below. Don runs 2 *m.* to **Sheffield.** Here Porter brook, 6 *m.* long, joins on right bank, and at the same point of junction Sheaf also joins Don. Sheaf rises 5 *m.* above **Beauchelf** Station, a mile above which place Fenny brook, 4 *m.* long, joins on left bank. Sheaf runs 1 *m.* to **Mill Houses,** where a stream joins on right bank, draining the lake at Norton Hall, 2 *m.* up. Sheaf runs 1 *m.* to **Heeley,** where Moors brook, 3 *m.* long, joins on right bank. Hence to **Sheffield** and Don is 2 *m.* Don runs to **Brightside,** 3 *m.*, and **Blackburn Junction** 1 *m.* Here Car brook, 4 *m.* long, joins on right bank, and Blackburn brook on left bank. Blackburn rises 4 *m.* above **Chapeltown,** runs 2 *m.* to **Ecclesfield,** **Grange Lane** 1 *m.*, and joins Don 2 *m.* below. Don runs to **Rotherham** 2 *m.* Here Rother joins on right bank. Rother rises 2 *m.* above **Claycross,** and 1 *m.* below is joined on left bank by Hockley brook, which rises in Great dam 4 *m.* S.W. of **Chesterfield,** or 3½ *m.* N.W. of **Claycross,** runs thence to Hockley 1 *m.*, where are two lakes at Wingerworth Hall, 2½ *m.* N.W. of **Claycross;** thence to Rother is 1 *m.* Rother runs to **Chesterfield** 4 *m.* Here Hipper joins on left bank. Hipper rises in two ponds by the Swiss Cottage on the borders of East Moor, 3 *m.* N.E. of **Rowsley,** runs 9 *m.*, where Linacre brook, which rises in a pond by Birley, 6 *m.* N.W. of **Chesterfield,**

and is 6 m. long, joins on left bank. From this junction to **Chesterfield** is 1 m. Muster brook, which rises in some ponds at Williamthorpe 2 m. N.E. of **Claycross**, and is 5 m. long, also joins on right bank. Rother runs to **Whittington** 2 m. Here **Drone** joins on left bank. Drone rises above **Dronfield**, runs 2 m. to **Unston**, and **Sheepbridge** 2 m. Here Millthorpe brook, 6 m. long, joins on right bank. Drone runs 2 m. to Rother. Rother runs 3 m. to **Staveley**. Here a brook joins on right bank, draining All Pits pond by Oldfields, 2 m. N.E. of **Chesterfield**, and another pond close to its junction with Rother. Rother runs to **Eckington** 4 m. Here Doe Lea river joins on right bank. Doe Lea rises in two ponds, Great pond and Miller's pond, 3 m. N.W. of **Teversall**, and half a mile below the last named receives the outfall of Stainsby pond ½ m. up, 4 m. N.W. of **Teversall**. Doe Lea runs 2 m., where Stockley brook, 2 m. long, rising in a pond, joins on right bank. 3 m. down Doe Lea a stream, 2 m. long, which drains the lake in the Deer Park at Sutton Scarsdale, 4 m. S.E. of **Chesterfield**, joins on left bank. 2 m. down Doe Lea a brook joins on right bank, draining Woodthorpe Mill dam 1 m. up, 2 m. S.W. of **Staveley**. Hence to Rother is 3 m. At **Eckington** a brook joins Rother on right bank, draining Quarry dam 1 m. up, and 2 m. W. of the station. Rother runs 2 m., where Moss brook, 4 m. long, joins on left bank, and 1 m. down Rother is **Killamarsh**. Here Short brook, 3 m. long, joins on left bank, and 1 m. down Rother, Pebley brook joins on right bank. Pebley rises in Barlborough Hall lake, 3 m. S.E. of **Killamarsh**, runs ½ m. to Pebley dam, and ½ m. below is joined on right bank by the outflow of Harthill reservoir and Woodhall pond immediately below. 2 m. down is the outflow of Woodhall Moor dams, close to the brook on the right bank, and 2 m. below again is Rother. Rother runs 2 m., where Pigeon Bridge brook, which rises in a pond in Sicker Wood, 3 m. E. of **Woodhouse Mill**, and is 2 m. long, joins on right bank. Half a mile down Rother, Shire brook, 4 m. long, joins on left bank. Rother runs 1 m. to **Woodhouse**, **Treeton** 2 m., **Rotherham** and Don 4 m. Don runs to **Park Gate** 3 m. Here Dalton brook, 8 m. long, joins on right bank, and Morley brook on left bank. Morley rises 2 or 3 m. above Wentworth Park, where it waters the Morley ponds, and joins Don 2 m. below. Don runs to **Kilnhurst** 2 m., **Swinton** 2 m., **Mexborough** 1 m. 3 m. below, Dearne joins on left bank. Dearne rises above **Denby Dale**, and runs thence 2 m. to **West Clayton**, and 2 m. below waters Bretton Park lake, 1 m. W. of **Haigh**; the lake is 1 m. long, and the outflow runs 1 m. to **Haigh**. Dearne now runs to **Darton** 2 m. 1 m. down, Darton brook, which rises in a pond by Gamthwaite Mill, 2 m. N. of **Penistone**, and is 6 m. long, joins on right bank. Dearne runs to **Barnsley** 4 m., **Cudworth** 4 m., **Darfield** 4 m. Here Dove joins on right bank. Dove rises in Lowe Mill reservoir, 1 m. S.E. of **Dodworth**. 1 m. down, Dove waters another large reservoir 1 m. W. of **Dove Cliff**. This latter lake receives in an arm on right bank the outflow, 1½ m. long, of Rockley dam, 1 m. N.W. of **Birdwell**. Dove runs 2 m. to **Dove Cliff, Wombwell** 3 m., and Dearne 1 m. Dearne runs 2 m., where New beck, which rises in a large reservoir lying 2 m. N.E. of **Chapeltown** and is 5 m. long, joins on right bank. 1 m. down Dearne, Ings dyke, which runs 1 m. E. of **Darfield** and is 5 m. long, joins on left bank. Dearne runs 1 m. to **Bolton-on-Dearne**, and joins Don 6 m. below. Don runs 1 m. to **Conisborough**, **Doncaster** 5 m., **Barnby** 6 m., **Stainforth** 8 m., **Thorne** 2 m. 4 m. down, Went joins on left bank. Went rises in the mill pond at **Sharlston**, and 3 m. down is joined on right bank by a stream 2 m. long, draining the upper and lower lakes at Nostell Priory by **Nostell**. Went runs to **Ackworth** 2 m., **Kirk Smeaton** 6 m., **Norton** 2 m. 3 m. down, Lake Drain joins on left bank, which rises in the lake in Stapleton Park 1 m. W. of **Womersley**, and is 5 m. long. Went runs 1 m. to **Balne**, and Don 6 m. Don runs 6 m. to **Goole**.

Goring (Oxford).—G.W.R. Thames. *Hotels*: Sloane, Miller of Mansfield. **Streatley** *Hotels*: Swan and Bull. *Fisherman*: J. Saunders. (*See London, M.T.*) Chub fishing good; other fishing uncertain.

Goring (Sussex).—L.B. & S.C.R. (*See Littlehampton*.)

Govilon (Monmouth).—L. & N.W.R. Usk; trout, salmon. (*c.s.*) Wenarth. *Lakes*: Forge Pond 2 m. (*See Newport*.)

Grampound (Cornwall).—G.W.R. Fal. Fal rises on the E. side of Castle Down (n.s. **St. Columb**, 3 m.), runs 3 m., and is joined on right bank by the outflow of a large lake on Tregoss Moor, close to the river. 1 m. down Fal a stream joins on left bank, which is 2 m. long, and a branch of which drains another pond on Tregoss Moor. Fal runs 5 m. to St. Stephen's, and 2 m. down (n.s. **Grampound Road**, G.W.R., 1¼ m.) is joined on left bank by Gwendra Water, 5 m. long, passing St. Stephen's midway. Fal runs 2 m. to **Grampound**, Tregony 2 m., and 6 m. down runs into Falmouth Harbour. (*c.s. Fowey*.)

Grampound Road (Cornwall).—G.W.R. Tresillian water; trout, grilse. Trelassick brook. (*See Truro, New Quay, Tregony, Veryan*.)

Grange (Lancs).—Fs.R. Winster 1 m. N. (*c.s. Kent*.) Winster rises 2 m. S of **Bowness**, and runs parallel with lake Windermere for 6 m. Here Awdale beck, 3 m. long, joins on left bank. Winster 3 m. down waters Helton tarn, and 5 m. below joins the sea by **Grange**. *Hotels*: Grange, Crown, Commercial.

Grange Court (Gloucester).—G.W.R. Hope brook (1½ m. (*See Westbury*.)

Grange Lane (Yorks).—G.C.R. Blackburn brook. (*See Goole*.)

Grantham (Lincoln).—G.N.R. Witham; good trouting, but strictly preserved. Old beck, 4 *m.* W., at **Sedgebrook**. Devon, 6 *m.* W., at **Bottesford**. *Lakes:* Belton Park lakes, 3 *m.* N. Denton reservoir, 3 *m.* S.W.; pike, perch, bream. Syston Park lakes, 4 *m.* W., by **Barkston**. Denton House lakes, 4 *m.* S.W. Belvoir Castle lake, 7 *m.* S.W. Knipton reservoir, 8 *m.* S.W. Croxton Park lakes, 8 *m.* S.W. (*See Boston.*) The Bottesford Angling Association (hon. sec., J. W. Cooper, Bottesford, Notts) has some 8 *m.* of water on the canal (pike, perch, roach, bream, chub, tench); tickets from Mr. Cooper, Rutland Arms Hotel, Bottesford. *Hotels:* George, Angel, and Royal.

Grant's House Station (Northland.).—(*See Berwick.*) Whitadder; trout.

Grasmere (Westland).—Rothay; trout. Easdale beck; trout. *Lakes:* Grasmere; pike, perch, few trout. (*c.s. Kent.*) Rydal Water 3 *m.* S.E.; perch, pike, few trout. The stream joining Grasmere with Rydal, gives fair trouting; tickets as for Rothay. (*See Ambleside.*) Easdale tarn 3 *m.* N.W.; good perch, trout. Codale tarn, 4 *m.* N.W.; trout, perch. *Hotels:* Rothay, Prince of Wales. (*See Ulverston.*)

Grassington (York).—M.R. Wharfe; trout, grayling; preserved by the Grassington and Burnsall Angling clubs; sec., W. Harker, Grassington, Skipton; a.t. 10*s.* (members outside 3 *m* radius 20*s.*), d t. 5*s.* (*c.s. York.*) Eller beck. Hebden beck, 2 *m.* E. *Lakes:* Priest tarn, 5 *m.* N., at Black Edge. Blea beck dams, 4 *m.* N.E. *Boarding House:* Grassington House. (*See York.*)

Grateley (Hants).—L & S.W.R. Winterbourne; trout and coarse fish. (*See Christchurch.*) (*c.s. Avon.*)

Grayrigg (Westland).—L. & N.W.R. Mint. (*c.s. Kent.*) *Lakes:* Grayrigg tarn, 3*m.* N.E. (*See Kendal.*)

Great Bridgford (Stafford).—L. & N.W.R. Sow. Chamford brook, 3 *m.* S.W. (*See Gainsborough.*)

Great Chesterford (Essex).—G.E.R. Cam; pike, roach, &c.; preserved. (*See King's Lynn.*)

Great Haywood (Stafford), n.s. **Colwich**, 1 *m.*—Trent; roach, pike, chub, trout; fishing very good; preserved below by Mr. L. Morgan, *above* by Stoke Angling Association. (*c.s.*) Sow; roach, pike, chub. Sherbrook brook, 1 *m.* S.W.; Colton brook, 3 *m.* E.; Blythe, 5 *m.* W.; preserved. *Lakes:* Tixall Park pool, 2 *m.* N.W.; Oakedge Park lakes, 2 *m.* S.E.; preserved. *Hotel:* Clifford Arms. (*See Gainsborough.*)

Great Marlow (Bucks).—G.W.R. Thames; perch, roach, trout, pike, chub. *Hotels:* Anglers, Crown, Railway, Greyhound, George and Dragon. *Fishermen:* A. Cox, and W. Coster. (*See London, M.T.*)

Great Ponton (Lincoln).—G.N.R. Witham. Stoke brook. Cringle brook, 2 *m.* S. *Lakes:* Stoke Mill pond, 1 *m.* S. Wyvill ponds, 3 *m.* W. (*See Boston.*)

Greenfield (Yorks).—L. & N.W.R. Tame. Greenfield brook. Chew brook, 2 *m.* E. (*See Runcorn.*)

Greenodd (Lancs).—Fs.R. Leven; salmon, trout. (*c.s. Kent.*) Colton beck. Crake; salmon, trout. (*c.s. Kent.*) Newland beck. (*See Ulverston.*)

Green Road (Cumland).—Fa.R. Black beck. This stream rises on Thwaites Fell, and in 4½ *m.* reaches Broadgate. From Broadgate Bridge to Hallthwaites Bridge is 1 *m.* From Hallthwaites to its junction with the Duddon Estuary is 2 *m.*

Grimoldby (Lincoln).—G.N.R. Grayfleet. (*See Saltfleet.*)

Grimsargh (Lancs.).—L. & N.W.R.; L. & Y.R. Tun brook. Ribble, 2 *m.* E. (*See Preston.*)

Grimsby (Lincoln).—G.N.R.; G.C.R. 1 *m.* N.W. runs Laceby beck. 6 *m.* long.

Grimston (Leicester).—M.R. *Lake:* Saxelby pond, 1 *m.* E. (*See Gainsborough.*)

Grimstone (Dorset).—G.W.R. Frome. Piddle. Salmon, trout. (*See Wareham.*) (*c.s.*)

Grindley (Stafford).—L. & N.W.R.; G.N.R. Blythe. (*c.s. Trent.*) Tad brook, 2 *m* S.E. (*See Gainsborough.*)

Grinstead, West (Sussex).—L.B. & S.C.R. On Adur. (*See New Shoreham.*)

Gristhorpe (York).—N.E.R. Helford; coarse fish. (*See Wressel.*)

Groombridge (Kent).—L.B. & S.C.R. (*See Rochester.*) On Medway.

Grosmont (York).—N.E.R. Esk; trout, salmon; preserved by the Esk Fishery Association above to **Glaisdale**, and below to **Whitby**; sec., Mr. W. Brown, The Saw Mills, Whitby; m.t. 3*l.* 3*s.* (*c.s*) Murk Esk; trout, salmon; preserved by Esk Fishery Association as far as Beck Hole. (*See Whitby.*)

Grove Ferry (Kent).—S.E. & C.R. On Stour; trout, perch, bream, roach, tench, jack; preserved. (*See Sandwich; Canterbury.*)

Guernsey.—Pollack (here called whiting), mackerel, turbot, &c., are taken. Best season from April to end of October. *Fisherman:* C. F. Ferguson. Terms: 10*s.* per *diem.* Sea-fishing can be had from the pier at St. Peter's Port, and at St. Sampson's, with rod and ledger lines, for pollack and sand smelts. *Hotels:* Gardner's Royal, Channel Islands, Old Government House.

Guildford (Surrey)—L. & S.W.R.; L.B. & S.C.R., and S.E. & C.R. *Hotels:* Lion, Angel. (*See London, L.T.*). Wey; pike, roach, bream; fishing free and decent, but preserved above in parts. At Clandon Park are some lakes, also on Broad Street and Whitmore Commons.

Guiseley (York).—M.R.; N.E.R. Mire beck. Yeadon beck, 1 *m.* S. Aire, 2 *m.* S. (*c.s. York.*) *Lakes:* Yeadon Moor pond, 2 *m.* E. (*See Rawcliffe.*)

Gunton (Norfolk).—G.E.R. Gunton beck. *Lakes:* 3 in Gunton Park (Lord Suffield); pike, &c. (*See Yarmouth.*)

Guyhirne (Cambs.)—G.N.R. ; G.E.R. Nen; pike, perch, bream, chub, &c. (*See Wisbeach.*)
Gwinear (Cornwall).—G.W.R. Hayle; trout. Gwinear water. (*See Hayle and Cambourne.*) (*c.s. Camel.*)

Hackness (York), n.s. **Scarboro'**, 6 *m.*—Derwent; trout and grayling; preserved from Hilla Green Bridge, 2 *m. above*, to Hertford Dale Bridge, 7 *m. below*, by the Derwent Angling Club of 40 members; entrance, 63s.; s.t., 50s.; strangers s.t., 84s.; d.t., 5s., upper water; lower water, 2s. 6d., of hon. sec., S. W. Fisher, Esq., J.P., Gainsborough private hotel, Scarborough. Trouting begins April 15, ends Sept. 30; grayling June 16 and March 14. Fly only in the upper part on d.t. in May and June, no dogs, no wading), below **Ayton** all lures. Capt. Hon. F. Johnstone preserves from Barnes Cliff above to Hilla Green Bridge; s.t. 5s., for artificial fly only, from May 1 to Aug. 1, from Mr. Little, Hackness. Lowdale beck. Troutdale beck, 1½ *m.* W. ; trout. Black beck, 2 *m.* N.W.; preserved by Mr. Bland. Deepdale beck, 3 *m.* N.W. Hipper beck, 4 *m.* N.W.; very few trout. Stockland beck, 5 *m* N.W. Jugger Howe beck, 5 *m.* N. *Hotel*: Everley Arms, having a free ticket for the D.A. Club water. (*See Wressel and Scalby.*)

Haddiscoe (Norfolk).—G.E.R. Waveney. New Cut. *Lakes*: Fritton Decoy, 1 *m.*; leave required; boats at Fritton Hall. (*See Yarmouth.*) (*c.s. Norfolk.*)

Hadfield (Derby).—M.R.; G.N.R. Etherow. Hollingworth brook. Armfield brook. Shelf brook, 1 *m.* S.W. (*See Runcorn.*)

Hadham (Essex).—G.E.R. (*See Stratford.*) On Ash ; a few trout, pike, &c.

Hadleigh (Suffolk).—G.E.R. Brett; pike, perch, roach, carp, dace. Stour, 6 *m.* S.; pike, perch, roach, carp, dace, tench. (*c.s. S. and E.*) (*See Manningtree.*)

Hadley (Salop).—L. & N.W.R. Preston brook (2 *m.* N.W.), and a lake in which the brook rises. (*See Gloucester.*)

Hadnall (Salop).—L. & N.W.R. Sundown brook. Roden (4 *m.* E.) (*See Gloucester.*) (*c.s. Severn.*)

Haigh (Yorks).—L. & Y.R. Dearne. *Lakes*: Bretton Park lake, 1 *m.* W. (*See Goole.*)

Hailsham (Sussex).—L.B. & S.C.R. Cuckware, 2 *m.* (*See Berwick.*)

Halesowen (Worcester).—G.W.R.; L. & N.W.R. Stour. Rea. *Lakes*: Grange Mill pond, Sutley Mill pond (2 *m.* W.). New pool (3 *m.* N.W.). Frankley pond, 3 *m.* S.E. (*See Gloucester; Gainsborough.*) (*c.s. Severn.*)

Halesworth (Suffolk).—G.E.R. Wissett brook; coarse fish. Blyth, 1 *m.* S.; coarse fish. (*See Southwold.*)

Halewood (Lancs).—C. Lines R.; S. & C.L.R. Ditton brook. (*See Runcorn.*)

Halifax (York).—G.N.R.; L. & Y.R.; L. & N.W.R. Calder, 2 *m.* S. (*c.s. York.*) (*See Rawcliffe.*)

Hallatrow (Somerset).—G.W.R. (*See Bristol.*) *Lakes*: Stone Easton Park lake.

Hallington (Lincoln).—G.N.R. Ludd. (*See Louth.*)

Halstead (Essex).—G.E.R. Colne; pike, perch, roach ; leave freely given by the farmers. Gosfield brook, 2 *m.* S. Pebmarsh brook, 3 *m.* E. *Lake*: Gosfield Hall lake. (*See Colchester.*)

Halton (Lancs).—M.R. Lune. (*c.s.*) Cote beck. (*See Lancaster.*)

Hammersmith (Middx.)—L. & S.W.R. Thames. (*See London, L.T.*)

Hammerton (York).—N.E.R. Nidd. (*c.s. York.*) (*See York.*)

Hammerwich (Stafford).—L. & N.W.R. Bilston brook, 3 *m.* N. Ashmore brook, 3 *m.* N.E. *Lakes*: Coney Mill pond, 3 *m.* N.W. (*See Gainsborough.*)

Hampsthwaite (York).—N.E.R. Nidd. (*c.s. York.*) Rowden beck. Kettlesing beck. (*See York.*)

Hampton (Middx).—L. & S.W.R. Thames. (*See London, L.T.*) *Inns*: Red Lion, Tagg's Island Hotel (where some private fishing can be had), and Bell. *Fishermen*: J. Langshaw and Son. E. Reddick, and G. Martin at Tagg's Island.

Hampton (Salop).—G.W.R. Severn; pike, perch, chub, dace, trout, salmon. Borle brook (2 *m.* W.). Mor brook (2¼ *m.* N.). (*See Gloucester.*) (*c.s. Severn.*)

Hampton (Warwick).—L. & N.W.R. Blythe; bream, roach. (*c.s Trent.*) *Lakes*: Packington Park, 2 *m.* (*See Gainsborough.*)

Hampton Court (Middx.)—L. & S.W.R. Thames, Mole, the Island Fishery, Home Park ponds, and Bushey Park ponds. *Hotels*: Mitre, King's Arms, Greyhound. *E. Moulsey.* Island, Castle, Thames, and Carnarvon Castle. *Fishermen*: T. Milbourne, J. Smith, G. Martin. The Home Park ponds hold pike, perch, carp, tench. Fishing free, as also in Bushey Park ponds.

Handbrough (Oxford).—G.W.R. On Evenlode and Glyme. (*See London, U.T.*) There is some good fishing in the lakes in Blenheim Park, the property of the Duke of Marlborough.

Handforth (Cheshire).—L. & N.W.R. Dean. (*See Runcorn.*)

Hanley (Stafford).—L. & N.W.R.; G.N.R. Trent. (*c.s.*) Fowler brook. (*See Gainsborough.*)

Hanwell (Middx.)—G.W.R. Brent; fishing poor and free; perch, pike, and chub. (*See London, L.T.*) At Osterley Park are two fine lakes; perch.

Hanwood (Salop).—L. & N.W.R.; G.W.R. Rea; roach, dace, chub; fishing free. Yockleton brook. Longden brook (2¼ *m.* S.). *Lakes*: Onslow Hall lake (3 *m.* N.). (*See Gloucester.*) (*c.s. Severn.*)

Harbottle (Northland.).—On Coquet; trout. (*See Warkworth.*) (*c.s.*) Near here is Harbottle Lough; trout.

Harbury (Warwick).—G.W.R. Itchene. *Lakes*: Chesterton Mill Pond (3 *m.* W.). (*See Southam, Gloucester.*)

Hardingham (Norfolk).—G.E.R. Yare. (*c.s. N. and S.*) Blackwater river. (*See Yarmouth.*)
Harleston (Norfolk).—G.E.R. Waveney, 1 m. S. (*c.s. Norfolk*) (*See Yarmouth.*)
Harling (Norfolk).—G.E.R. Thet; private. (*See King's Lynn.*) (*c.s. Norfolk.*)
Harlington (Beds).—M.R. Tod, 3 m N.W.; few coarse fish. *Lakes*: Tingrith House Lake (3 m N.W.); good fishing, strictly private. (*See King's Lynn.*)
Harlow (Essex).—G.E.R. (*See Stratford.*) On Stort; fishing on the towing path is free; leave is freely given for the back waters and mill tails; pike, perch, tench, roach, chub, grayling, rudd, carp, bream, barbel, trout. *Hotel*: Railway. (*c.s.*)
Harmston (Lincoln).—G.N.R. Witham, 2 m. W. Brant, 2 m. W. (*See Boston.*)
Harpenden (Herts).—M.R. & G.N.R. On Lea; fishing can be had from the millers and landowners, who often give permission, and sometimes let the fishing. (*See Stratford and London, M.T.*) *Hotel*: Railway.
Harringworth (Northton).—M.R. Welland. (*See Spalding.*)
Harrogate (York).—N.E.R.; G.N.R.; L. & N.W.R.; M.R.; L. & Y.R. Crimple, 4 m. S.W.; trout; preserved by the Harrogate Conservative Club (sec., Mr. Heald, Franklin Mount, Harrogate). The club also preserves 5 m. of Upper Nidd and Oak beck; entrance 40s., s.t. 20s. A limited number of m., w., and d.t. (*See York.*)
Harrold (Beds).—n.s. **Sharnbrook.** 4 m.—Ouse; coarse fish except barbel; fishing private. (*c.s. N. and S.*) (*See King's Lynn.*)
Harston (Cambs).—G.N.R. Rhee; coarse fish. Cam, 3 m; coarse fish. (*See King's Lynn.*)
Hartfield (Sussex).—L.B. & S.C.R. On Medway. (*See Rochester.*)
Hartington, (Derby).—L. & N.W.R. Dove; trout, grayling. (*c.s. Trent.*) *Hotel*: Charles Cotton (very comfortable). Mannyfold, 1 m. W; trout, grayling; preserved as Dove. Elkstone brook. 4 m. S.W., beyond Mannyfold. Hamps, 7 m. S.W., at Onecote. The station for Hartington on the Leek and Mannyfold Light Railway is Hulme End. (*See Gainsborough.*)
Hartland (Devon).—(n.s. **Bideford**, G.W.R., 15 m.) Hartland Abbey stream. Spoke's Mill (2 m.). Welcombe (4 m.). Torridge (5 m.). Marshland (6 m.). All hold trout, Marshland especially. *Hotels*: New Inn and King's Arms. Hartland Abbey stream rises 4 m. E. of Hartland, and joins the sea 3 m. down. Spoke's Mill stream rises 2 m. S. of Hartland, and is 4 m. long. Welcombe rises 4 m. S. of Hartland, runs 4 m., and is joined on right bank by a stream 3 m. long. Marshland rises 5 m. S. of Hartland, and is 4 m. long, joining the sea close to Welcombe stream. Fish of all kinds may be killed off the coast and in the fissures of the rocks at low tide. Capital bass fishing with indiarubber sand-eel at times from a boat.
Harton Road (Salop).—G.W.R. Eaton brook. Quenny brook (3 m. W.). *Lakes*: Lutwitch mill pond (2 m. N.E.). (*See Gloucester.*)
Harvington (Warwick).—G.W.R. Avon; chub, pike, perch, roach, dace, bream; preserved by Evesham Fish Preservation Society. The two stretches of the Avon known as Honey and Pike are rented by the owner of the Mill water rights. (*See Evesham.*) Wickham brook (3 m. S.). (*See Gloucester.*) (*c.s. Severn.*)
Harwich (Essex).—G.E.R. At Dovercourt runs Ramsey brook, 7 m. long.
Harwood Dale (York).—9 m. from **Scarborough.** Jugger Howe Beck and Derwent. Trout and grayling; free. (*See Hackness.*)
Haslemere (Surrey).—L. & S.W.R. (*See London, L.T.*; *Littlehampton.*) *Hotel*: White Horse.
Haslingden (Lancs.)—L. & N.W.R. Swinnel brook. Irwell, 2 m. E. at Rawtenstall. (*See Runcorn.*)
Hassocks Gate (Sussex).—L.B. & S.C.R. (*See New Shoreham.*)
Hatch (Somerset).—G.W.R. (*See Bridgwater.*)
Hatfield (Herts). — G.N.R. On Lea. The river belongs to the Marquis of Salisbury, who sometimes gives permission. In Hatfield Park is a large lake; pike and coarse fish. (*See Stratford.*)
Hathern (Leicester).—M.R. Soar; pike, perch, bream, roach, carp, tench. (*c.s. Trent.*) Osgathorpe brook. Dishley brook. 1 m. S. Kingston brook, 2 m. N.E. *Lakes*: Garenden Park lake 2 m. S. (*See Gainsborough.*)
Hathersage (Derby), n.s. **Bakewell.**—M.R. Derwent; trout, grayling; preserved by the Derwent Fly-fishing Club from Yorkshire bridge above to New bridge below, where the Duke of Devonshire's water begins (*see Baslow, Ashopton*). (*c.s. Trent.*) Hood brook; trout. Highlow brook, 1 m. S. Now, 2 m. N.W. Burbage brook, 3 m. S.E. (*See Gainsborough.*)
Hatton (Warwick).—G.W.R. Edstone brook. (*See Gloucester.*)
Haughley (Suffolk).—G.E.R. Gipping. *Lake*: Wetherden. (*See Ipswich.*)
Haverhill (Suffolk).—G.E.R. Albery brook. Stour, 2 m. E. Birdbrook, 3 m. S.E. (*c.s. S. and E.*) (*See Manningtree.*)
Haverthwaite (Lancs). F.R. Leven; salmon, trout. (*c.s. Kent.*) Rusland pool. *Lakes*: Bigland tarn 2 m. E. (*See Ulverston.*)
Hawes (York).—N.E.R.; M.R. Upper Yore; trout, grayling; preserved, with all its tributaries, from the Moor Cock Inn, 6 m. *above*, to Yore Bridge, 5 m. *below*, by the Hawes and Hign Abbotside Angling Association. Non-residents, s.t. 10s., w.t. 5s., d.t. 2s.; residents, s.t., 5s.; fishing begins March 16 and ends Oct. 1; sec., Mr. T. T. Fawcett, Hawes. (*c.s. York.*) Good trouting in Lake Semmerwater, 4 m. S.E. (Hawes Angling Association); boat can can be hired. Hearne beck. Duerley beck. Mossdale beck. Widdale beck, 1 m. W. Cotterdale beck, 2 m. N.W. Snaizholme beck, 3 m. S.W. Eden, 9 m. N.W.; trout. Hell Gill beck, 9 m. N.W. *Hotels*: Crown, White Hart, and Fountain. (*See York.*)

Hawes Junction (Yorks).—M.R.; N.E.R. Clough river. Vor Gill, 1 m. N. Cross Howbeck, 2 m. N. Wandale beck, 4 m. N.E. Backs beck, 4 m. N. Red Gill, 5 m. E. Sally beck, 5 m. N.E. Grisdale beck, 8 m. E. *Lakes*: West Bangh Fell tarns, 5 m. E. East tarns, 5 m. E. East Hough Fell tarn, 7 m. E. (*See Lancaster*.)

Hawes' Water (Westland.).—Trout and char.

Hawkshead (Lancs.).—Grisdale beck, 3 m. S. *Lakes*: Esthwale Water, 1 m. S.E.; pike, perch, trout. (*c.s. Kent.*) Grisdale tarn, 3 m. S. *Hotel*: Old Red Lion. (*See Ulverston.*)

Haxby (York).—N.E.R. Foss. (*See York.*)

Hayburn Wyke (York).—N.E.R. Hayburn beck, 3 m. long.

Hayfield (Derby).—M.R. Sett brook. Now, 4 m. E. (*See Runcorn; Gainsborough.*)

Hayle (Cornwall).—G.W.R. Hayle; trout. Hayle rises in Clowance Park (n.s. **Gwinear Road**, G.W.R., 3 m), runs 4 m., and is joined on left bank by Germoe brook, 3 m. long. Hayle runs to **St. Earth** (G.W.R.), 3 m., and Hayle 2 m. Here Gwinear water, which rises by **Gwinear** (G.W.R.), and is 5 m. long, joins on right bank. The tide flows to this point. (*c.s. Camel.*)

Hayling Island.—There is very good fishing from boats in the harbour, all sorts of fish, especially bass. A lady keeps a boarding establishment, and there are two first-rate modern hotels.

Hazelhead Bridge (Yorks.).—G.C.R. Don. (*c.s. Yorkshire.*) Little Don, 2 m. S. (*See Goole.*)

Hazlewood (Derby).—M.R. Ecclesbourne. Derwent, 2 m. S.E., at **Duffield**. (*c.s. Trent.*) (*See Gainsborough.*)

Heather (Leicester).—M.R.; L. & N.W.R Sence. Blower's brook. (*See Gainsborough.*)

Headcorn (Kent).—S.E.R. (*See Rochester.*) On Beult; trout.

Heapy (Lancs.).—L. & N.W.R.; L. & Y.R. Black brook. (*See Hesketh Bank.*)

Heathersett (Norfolk).—G.E.R. Yare, 2 m, N.E. *Lakes*: Ketteringham Hall, 1 m. S; Carlton Lodge lake, 3 m. S.E. Bracon Hall lake, 4 m. S.E. (*See Yarmouth.*)

Heatley (Cheshire).—C. Lines. Bollin; trout, roach, dace, pike. Arden brook. 1 m. S.E. Mersey, 1 m. N. (*See Runcorn.*)

Hebden (York).—L. & Y.R. Calder. (*c.s. York.*) Hebden. Calderclough beck. Horsebridge brook, 2 m. N. Wadsworth brook, 4 m. N. Gorple water, 5 m. N.W. Widdop water, 6 m. N.W. *Lakes*: Nodale dam, 4 m. N.W. (*See Rawcliffe.*)

Hedingham (Essex).—G.E.R. Colne; pike, perch, roach; permission freely given by the farmers. (*See Colchester.*)

Hednesford (Stafford).—L. & N.W.R. Saredon brook. *Lakes*: Hednesford pool. Lower Brindley pool, 1 m. N. Furnace pool, 1 m. N. Upper Brindley pool, 2 m. N. Balands pool, 2 m. N.E. (*See Gainsborough.*)

Heeley (Yorks).—G.C.R. Sheaf. Moors brook. (*See Goole.*)

Hellesdon (Norfolk). — G.E.R. Wensum. (*c.s. N. and S.*) Costessey brook. (*See Yarmouth.*)

Hellifield (Yorks).—L. & Y.R. Hellifield beck. Ribble, 1 m. S.; trout, salmon. *Hotel*: Hellifield. (*See Preston.*)

Helmedon (Northton).—L. & N.W.R. Tove. (*See King's Lynn.*)

Helm Shore (Lancs.).—G.N.R.; M.R.; L. & N.W.R. Swinnel brook. Irwell, 1 m. E. (*See Runcorn.*)

Helmsley (York).—N.E.R. Rye; trout, grayling; preserved *above* by Lord Feversham, *below* by the Ryedale Angling Club. Lord Feversham issues a ticket for the water above Rievaulx Bridge and the Seph through Bilsdale; fly and minnow only; s.t. 12s., 3 m.t. 7s., 4 w.t. 3s., w.t. 1s.; apply to Mr. Bowman, Duncombe Park Estate Office, Helmsley. (*See Kirby Moorside*). Seph, 6 m. N.W. Ladhill beck, 7 m. N.W. Blowgill beck, 10 m. N.W. Lodge beck, 10 m. N.W. Prodale beck, 13 m. N.W. Wheat beck, 13 m. N.W. *Hotels*: Royal Oak, Crown, Black Swan, Feversham Arms. (*See Wressel.*)

Helston (Cornwall).—G.W.R. Loe river and Pool; trout. Loe rises 4 m. S. of **Carn Brea Station**, runs 4 m., and is joined on left bank by a brook, 2 m. long. Loe runs 1 m. to Wendron and **Helston**, 3 m. 1 m. down, Loe forms a large lake, 2 m. long, separated from the sea by a sand bar. (*c.s. Fowey.*) (*See Constantine.*) *Hotel*: Angel.

Hemel Hempstead (Herts).—L. & N.W.R. Gade; trout; preserved by Sir A. Cooper, Mr. Halsey, Earl Brownlow; there is some free water. (*See London, M.T.*). *Inn*: King's Arms.

Hemyock (Devon).—G.W.R. Culm; trout; preserved. *Hotels*: Culm Valley, Railway. (*c.s. Exe.*) (*See Exeter.*)

Hendon (Middx.)—M.R. Brent and Welsh Harp Reservoir. *Hotel*: Old Welsh Harp. (*See London, L.T.*) Leave for the Decoy and Tenterden lake by introduction to the proprietors; chub, roach, pike, perch, carp, tench, eels.

Henfield (Sussex).—L.B. & S.C.R. On Adur; dace, &c.; some free fishing. (*See New Shoreham.*)

Hengoed (Monmouth).—L. & N.W.R. Rumney; trout, salmon; preserved. (*c.s.*) (*See Cardiff, Wales.*)

Henley (Oxford).—G.W.R. Thames. (*See London, M.T.*) Henley Fisheries Preservation Association preserve between Hurley and Shiplake Locks; hon. sec., Mr. A. E. Hobbs, 28, Hart-street, Henley. *Hotels*: Angel, Red Lion, Catherine Wheel. *Fishermen*: J. James, G. Arlett, G. and W. Vaughan. Leave to fish the two mill tails at Marsh Lock must be obtained.

Henley-in-Arden (Warwick).—G.W.R. Alne (1¼ m. E.) · *Lakes*: a large lake at Wootton Warwen (1½ m. S.) (*See Gloucester*.)

Hereford.—G.W.R.; L. & N.W.R., and M.R. Wye; salmon, pike, chub, dace, trout, perch, grayling; preserved by the Wye Fisheries Association; sec., Major H. Beresford Peirse, The Friars, Hereford. Salmon fishing begins Feb. 2, and ends Nov. 16; trout begins Feb. 15, ends Oct. 1, both inclusive. No spinning or worm fishing for trout on the salmon catches; no gaff before April 2; no boat fishing except in the Palace pool; no Sunday fishing; no person can fish without having previously obtained ticket and licences; no dogs. The following are the prices of tickets for the various waters: Belmont Fishery extends from above Wye Bridge, Hereford, to about 200 yards above the landing-place in Uff pool, in the parish of Eaton. Salmon: s.t. to one person renting the whole fishing, 6*l*.; 2 persons, 3*l*. each. The renter of the whole water may issue 1 transferable ticket; if rented by 2 people, 2 transferable tickets. In case the water is not taken up by s.t., the committee will issue m. and d.t.; salmon m.t. 10*s*. 6*d*., d.t. 5*s*. 8. and d. tickets for fish other than salmon are issued—s.t. 10*s*. 6*d*., d.t. 1*s*. The Palace pool, extending from lower side of Wye Bridge to opposite the end of the Castle Green on the south side of the Wye—salmon d.t. 5*s*. Withy brook. Sugwas brook. Red brook (2 m.). Lug (2 m.); pike, perch, a few trout and grayling, and coarse fish. Sutton brook (2 m.). Cage brook (3 m.). (*c.s.*) Salmon and trout licenees from Mr. C. Southgate, 5, St. Peter's-street, Hereford. (*See Chepstow*.) *Hotels*: Green Dragon, City Arms. *Tacklist*, T. Cooke, 21½, Maylord-street.

Hornbridge (Dorset).—L. & S.W.R. Stour. Moors; both hold pike, perch, chub, roach. Fishing reserved. (*See Christchurch*.) (*c.s. Avon*.)

Herne Bay (Kent).—S.E. & C.R. Fine rudd may be taken in the dykes near here. Good sea fishing. *Hotels*: Dolphin, Pier.

Hertford (Herts).—G.E.R.; G.N.R. (*See Stratford and London*). On Lea, Mimram, Beane, Rib, and New River. *Hotels*: Salisbury Arms, Dimsdale Arms, White Hart, Station. Trout, jack, perch, chub. Above Hertford, H. Clinton Baker, Esq., has 3 m. of good trout water (strictly preserved). The fishing in Mimram is preserved. From Luton down there is good trouting—fish running 2lb. or 3lb. Lady Cowper has the right to the junction of Mimram with Lea; this fishing is jealously guarded. The fishing on Beane is good—trout especially; but leave is difficult to obtain. ½ m. of water below Waterford Mills is preserved by the Hon. Mrs. Reginald Smith, and a day's leave is sometimes given. Apply to Mr. J. Hawkins, Keeper's Lodge, Goldings. The old river Lea is preserved by Mr. E. Oram, St. Andrews-street, Hertford, s.t. 10*s*., from the town mill tail to the engine-house in the King's Mead; trout, jack, perch, chub. The Corporation waters are preserved by the Hertford Angling Preservation Society; hon. sec., Mr. H. Smith, Station Hotel, Hertford, who issues a.t. 5*s*., d.t. 1*s*. *Tackleists*, Simson and Co., Market-place.

Hesketh Bank (Lancs.)—L. & Y.R. Douglas. Douglas rises 3 m. above **Blackrod**, where Horwich brook, which rises in some ponds at Wallsuches, 3 m. up, joins on right bank. Here also are two ponds on right bank. Douglas runs to **Adlington** 3 m., and 2 m. below is joined on left bank by Barsden brook. Barsden rises by **Hindley**, runs 2 m. to **Dicconson**, **Hilton** 2 m., and joins Douglas 3 m. down by **Standish**. ½ m. down Douglas, Idlington brook. 6 m. long. joins on right bank, 1 m. N.E. from **Standish**. Douglas runs 1 m. to **Standish**, **Boar's Head** 1 m., **Wigan** 3 m. Here Clarenden brook, 3 m. long, joins on left bank. Douglas runs 3 m. to Crook, where a stream joins on right bank, draining Standish Mill pond 2 m. up, 2 m. N. of **Gathurst**. Douglas runs to **Gathurst** 1 m. Here a stream joins on left bank. draining Roby Mill pond and another pond 1 m. up. Douglas runs 1 m. to **Apply Bridge**. Here the outflow of the lake at Wrightington Hall, 1 m. N.E., joins on right bank. Douglas runs to **Parbold** 2 m., and 2 m. down is joined on left bank by Tawd river, 1 m. N.E. from **Hoscar Moss**. Tawd rises by **Pimbo Lane**, runs to **Skelmersdale** 3 m., **Hoscar Moss** 5 m., and joins Douglas 1 m. down. 1 m. down Douglas, Henley brook, 4 m. long, joins on right bank. Douglas runs to **Rufford** 2 m. Here Eller brook joins on left bank. Eller rises 2 m. E. of **Ormskirk**, runs 5 m. to **Burscough**, and **Rufford** 3 m. 2 m. down Douglas, Yarrow river joins on right bank. Yarrow rises on **Anglezark Moor**, 4 m. E. of **Chorley**, near which place it waters the Liverpool Waterworks reservoirs. On leaving the reservoirs, which it does on the right bank, opposite Rimington, Yarrow runs 3 m. to 1 m. S. of **Chorley**, where Black brook joins on right bank. Black brook rises some 2 m. above **Heapy**, waters a pond at that place, runs 1 m. to **Chorley**, and joins Yarrow 1 m. below. Yarrow runs 2 m. to **Coppull**, waters the mill ponds at the Print Works, runs 4 m. to 1 m. S. of **Euxton**, **Croston** 6 m. 1 m. below, Lostock river joins Yarrow on right bank. Lostock rises at Whittle-le-Woods, 2 m. E. of **Leyland**, where also is a small lake, runs 4 m. to **Bamber Bridge**, where there is also a lake, **Lostock Hall** 1 m., **Farrington** 1 m., Dunkirk Hall 1 m. E. of **Midge Hall** 3 m., **Croston** 5 m. Here Wymott brook, 3 m. long, joins on right bank. Lostock joins Yarrow 1 m. down. Yarrow runs 1 m. to Douglas. Douglas runs to **Hesketh Bank** 5 m.

Hexham (Northland.).—M.R.; N.E.R. On Tyne; salmon and trout; the owner of Bean-front Castle preserves some 3 m. of water. 1 m. fair salmon fishing free in town; licence, 10*s*. October best month. (*c.s.*)

Heyford (Oxford).—G.W.R. Cherwell. (*See London, M.T.*)

Heytesbury (Wilts).—G.W.R. Wylye; trout; preserved. (*See Christchurch*.) (*c.s. Avon*.)

Heywood (Lancs.).—L. & N.W.R.; G.N.R. Roch. Naden Water, 1 m. N.W. (*See Runcorn*.)

Higham Ferrers (Northton.)—L. & N.W.R. Nene; pike, perch, bream, tench, chub. (*See Wellinborough, Wisbeach.*)

Highbridge (Somerset).—G.W.R. Brue; carp, perch, roach, trout, jack. (*See c.s. Avon.*) Brue rises E. of **Bruton**, where Cambe river, 3 m long, joins on right bank. Brue runs in 1 m. to **Cole**, where Shepton brook, 4 m. long, joins on left bank. Brue runs to **Castle Carey** 2 m., and 2 m. below is joined on right bank by Evercreech brook. Evercreech rises in a mill pond some 2 m. N. of **Evercreech**, and 1½ m. down at **Evercreech Junction** is joined on left bank by a stream rising in a mill pond at Milton Cleveland 1 m. from **Evercreech**. Evercreech joins Brue 4 m. down. Brue runs in 6 m. to Baltonbury on right bank, and **Glastonbury** 5 m. Here Wootton brook joins on right bank. Wootton rises by North Wootton (n.s **Pennard**, S.D.R., 2½ m.), and 4 m. down is joined on left bank by a stream rising W. of **Pennard Station**, and is 4 m. long. Wootton runs in 4 m. to **Glastonbury**. Brue runs in diverse channels through the moors for 4 m. to **Meare**, where Godney brook joins on right bank. Godney rises at Croscombe (n.s. **Shepton Mallet**, 2 m.), runs to **Wells** 3 m., **Polsham** 2 m., and Brue 6 m. Brue runs in 1½ m. to Westhay Bridge (n.s. **Shapwick**, 1 m.); 3 m. down on left bank is **Edington Station**, 1½ m. off the river. Brue runs in 4 m. to **Woolavington** and **Cossington Station** and **Highbridge** 1½ m. Brue joins Parret estuary 1½ m. below. *Hotel:* Coopers' Arms.

High Force Hotel (Yorkshire).—n.s. **Middleton-in-Teesdale**, 5 m. Tees; trout, salmon, and bull trout below the fall; tickets at hotel, or of Lord Barnard's agent, Raby Castle, Staindrop, and from Lord Strathmore's agent, Mr. John Brown, Bow Bank, Middleton-in-Teesdale. (*c.s.*) (*See Stockton.*)

Hightown (Lancs).—L. & Y.R.; L. & N.W.R. Alt. (*See Altcar.*)

High Wycombe (Bucks).—G.W.R.; G.C.R. Wick; trout. *Hotels:* Red Lion and White Hart. There is some free water close to the town, which is, however, very much fished. A branch runs through the lake in Lord Carington's grounds; pike, perch, roach. Leave is sometimes given. (*See London, M.T.*)

Hilgay (Norfolk).—G.E.R. Ouse; coarse fish except barbel. (*c.s. N. and S.*) Wissey or Stoke River (*c.s. N. and S.*); Sams Cut Drain; pike, perch, &c. (*See King's Lynn.*)

Hilton House (Lancs).—L. & Y.R. Barsden brook. (*See Hesketh Bank.*)

Hinckley (Leicester).—M.R.; L. & N.W.R. Soar, 3 m. S.E. (*c.s. Trent*). Anker. 4 m. S.W., at **Nuneaton** (*c.s. Trent*). Lakes: Leicester Grange lake, 2 m. S. (*See Gainsborough.*)

Hindley (Lancs).—L. & Y.R.; W.J.R. Barsden brook. (*See Hesketh Bank.*)

Hindolvestone (Norfolk).—G.E.R. Bure; trout; private. *Lake:* Melton Park, 1 m. N. (*See Yarmouth.*) (*c s. N. and S.*)

Hingham (Norfolk).—n.s. **Kimberley**, 3 m. Hackford brook. Blackwater, 3 m. N. Yare, 3 m. N. *Lakes:* Sea mere, 1 m. S.E. Heath mere, 2 m. W. (*see King's Lynn.*) Wirklewood mere, 3 m. E. Kimberley Park lake, 4 m. N.E. by Kimberley. (*See Yarmouth.*)

Hinton (Glos.).—G.W.R. Isborne; few trout, but the stream is much polluted. (*See Gloucester.*)

Hitchin (Herts).—G.N.R. Hiz. (*See King's Lynn.*) *Hotels:* Cock, Railway.

Hoddesdon (Herts). — G.E.R. (*See Stratford and London.*) On Lea, Stort, and New River. The Lea here is preserved. *Inn:* Fish and Eels. The proprietor of the Fish and Eels preserves the Dobbs Weir Fishery; s.t. 7s 6d., d.t. 1s. Fishing free from towing path only from Broxbourne fishery to Ware.

Hodnet (Salop).—G.W.R. Tern (1 m. E.); a few trout and coarse fish. Salten brook (2 m. E.). *Lakes:* Rose Hill ponds (4 m. N.E.) (*See Gloucester.*) (*c.s. Severn.*)

Hoghton (Lancs.)—L. & Y.R. Darwen, 1 m. E. (*See Preston.*)

Holbeach (Lincoln).—G.N.R. Whaplode river, 2 m. W. This watercourse rises above **Whaplode**, and is 8 m. long.

Holly Bush (Monmouth).—L. & N.W.R. Sirhowey; polluted. (*See Newport.*)

Holme (Hunts).—G.N.R. Holme brook. *Lakes:* Holme Cuttings, 1 m. S.; jack, tench; reserved. Caldecot pond, 4 m. W. (*See Wisbeach.*)

Holme (York).—L. & Y.R. Calder. (*c.s. York.*) Foulness. Foss dyke, 3 m. S.W. (*See Rawcliffe and Staddlethorpe.*)

Holme Hall (Norfolk).—G.E.R. Erneford brook. (*See King's Lynn.*)

Holme Lacy (Hereford).—G.W.R. Wye; plenty of coarse fish, and a few trout, grayling, and salmon. Lug (1 m.); pike and coarse fish. Frome (2 m.). Pentelow brook (2 m.) (*c.s.*) *Inns:* Green Dragon and Mitre. (*See Chepstow; Hereford.*)

Holmes Chapel (Cheshire).—L. & N.W.R. Dane; coarse fish, few trout; preserved by landowners. Croco. Crow brook, 3 m. N.E. *Lakes:* Bag mere, 3 m. S.E. (*See Frodsham.*)

Holmwood (Surrey).—L.B. & S.C.R. (*See London, L.T.*) Ewood Pond is 1½ m. off.

Holmfirth (York).—L. & Y.R. Holme. *Lakes:* Bilbury reservoir, 3 m. S.W. (*See Rawcliffe.*) Holmstyes reservoir, 2½ m.; trout; preserved by Huddersfield Angling Association; hon. sec., S. Hellowell, Esq. Blacksike reservoir, 3½ m.; trout; preserved as above. Bawshaw reservoir, 9½ m.; trout; preserved as above. Ramsden, Ridings Wood, and Yateholme Reservoirs (trout) preserved by Batley Angling Club; hon. sec., Mr. Isaac Wilson, Eldon Ville, Batley. (*See Huddersfield.*)

Holmsley (Hants).—L. & S.W.R. On Warburn; dace, trout, salmon peel; preserved. Warburn rises near the station, and is about 10 m. long, joining the sea at Key Haven, 6 or 7 m. S.W. of **Lymington**. Another stream rises by the "Rising Sun," by Wooton, 2½ m. from **Holmsley** station, runs 5 m. to Milford, and joins the sea 1 m. down; fishing fair. (*See Lymington.*)

F

Holsworthy (Devon).—G.W.R. Holsworthy water. Deer, trout: free. Tamar, 4 m.; trout. (c.s.) Claw, 4 m. S.E. Fox water, 4 m. *Lakes:* Tamar Lake, 7 m. (*See Bude.*) (*See Plymouth.*)

Holt (Wilts).—G.W.R. (*See Bristol.*) Avon; roach, perch, pike; leave from owners (c.s.)

Holt (Norfolk).—G.E.R. Glaven. Glaven rises in Selbrigg pond 3 m. E. of **Holt**, runs 1 m. to **Holt** Mill pond, 1 m. S.E. of **Holt**, and 1 m. down is joined on left bank by a stream draining a pond at Pond hills, 3 m. S.E. of **Holt**. Glaven runs 3 m., 2 m. S. of **Holt**, when Thornage brook, which rises in the pond at Gunthorpe Hall, 2 m. N.E. of **Thursford** and is 4 m. long, joins on left bank. Glaven runs to **Holt** 2 m., and joins the sea at Cley, 6 m. down.

Holton Holgate (Lincoln).—G.N.R. Steeping river. (*See Wainfleet.*)

Holton-le-Clay (Lincoln).—G.N.R. Tetney drain. Tetney rises above Kirmond-le-mire, 6 m. N.E. of **Market Rasen**, runs 5 m. to Thorganby, and 2 m. down is joined on left bank by the outflow of Croxby pond, ½ m. up, 9 m. E. of **Moortown** Station. Tetney runs 5 m. to Brigsley, and Waith, 1 m. S. of **Holton-le-Clay**, 3 m. 4 m. below, Tetney joins the Louth navigation.

Holton Moor (Lincoln).—G.C.R. Owersby drain. (*See Brigg.*)

Holy Stone (Northland.).—Coquet: trout. Accommodation can be had. (c.s.)

Homersfield (Suffolk).—G.E.R. Waveney. (*See Yarmouth.*) (c.s. N. and S.)

Honiton (Devon).—L. & S.W.R. Otter; trout; preserved. (c.s.) Blancombe brook. Awlescombe brook. (*See Ottery St. Mary and Seaton.*)

Honley (York).—L. & Y.R. Holme. (*See Rawcliffe.*)

Hopton Heath (Salop).—L. & N.W.R. Clun; trout, grayling; private, but leave may often be had. Redlake brook (2 m. S.); trout. (*See Leintwardine, Gloucester.*) (c.s. Severn.)

Horbury (York).—L. & Y.R. Calder. (c.s. York.) (*See Rawcliffe.*)

Horderly (Salop).—B.C.R. Onny; trout, chub, grayling; preserved by Plowden Fishing Club up to **Eaton**. (c.s. Severn.) (*See Plowden, Gloucester.*)

Horley (Surrey)—L.B. & S.C.R. Mole; few small trout above; below, pike, perch, carp, tench, bream, roach. Leave from the millers. By Horley Church is some deep water holding good fish. 2 m. below Horley Mill is a similar stretch of water. (*See London, L.T.*)

Hornby (Lancs.).—M.R. Lune. (c.s.) Wenning. (c.s. Lune.) Hindburn river. (c.s. Lune.) Roeburndale river, 2 m. E. Whitcray beck, 7 m. E. (*See Lancaster.*)

Horncastle (Lincoln).—G.N.R. Bain; trout, roach; preserved. Witham, 7 m. by rail, at **Kirkstead**. Tupholme brook, 7 m. N.W. *Lakes:* Stourton Hall, 5 m. N.W. Gautby Hall, 5 m. N.W. Beninworth pools, 8 m. N. (*See Boston.*)

Horning (Norfolk).—G.E.R. Bure; pike, perch, bream, roach. Ant. *Lake:* Dilham lake (trustees, W. H. Windham, Esq.). Salhouse Broad; Decoy Broad, permission to fish, which may be obtained of John Cator, Esq., of Woodbastwick Hall. *Hotel:* Horning Ferry. (*See Yarmouth.*)

Hornsea (York).—N.E.R. Hornsea mere; pike, perch, roach.

Hornsey (Middx.).—G.N.R. On New River. (*See London.*)

Horrabridge (Devon).—G.W.R. Walkham; trout. Tavy, 3 m.; trout. (c.s. Tamer.) (*See Plymouth.*)

Horsham (Sussex).—L.B. & S.C.R. Arun; perch, roach, jack. Chennell's brook; trout. (*See Littlehampton.*) *Hotels:* Bedford, King's Head.

Horton (Northton.).—G.N.R. *Lakes:* Rudyard reservoir. (*See Gainsborough.*)

Horton (York).—M.R. Ribble; trout; preserved from its source to Helwith Bridge, including all tributaries, by the Manchester Anglers' Association of 80 members; entrance 63s., a.t. 42s.; season begins March 6, ends Sept. 30; no Sunday fishing; no dogs; hon. sec., E. R. Austin, Esq., Ollerbarrow-rd., Hale, Cheshire. Horton beck. *Lakes:* The Tarn, 2 m. N.; trout; preserved as Ribble. (*See Preston.*)

Moscar Moss (Lancs.).—L. & Y.R. Tawd. Douglas, 1 m. N.E. (c.s. Ribble.) Henley brook, 1 m. W. (*See Hesketh Bank.*)

Hougham (Lincoln).—G.N.R. Witham. Foster beck, 1 m. W. (*See Boston.*)

Hovingham (York).—N.E.R. Marro beck. Hole beck, 1 m. N. Wath beck, 1 m. E. at **Slingsby**. Rye, at **Helmsley**; trout, grayling; preserved for 5 m. by Ryedale Angling Club of 20. There is some free water below **Hovingham**. Bulmer beck, 4 m. S. *Lakes:* Cotton Mill pond, 2 m. S.W. Park lake, 3 m. S. There are several streams round Helmsley which can be fished by ticket from Duncombe Park Estate Office. (*See Helmsley.*) Good hotel accommodation. *Hotel:* Worsley Arms. (*See Wressel.*)

Howgill (Yorks).—Lune. (c.s.) Blands Gill, 2 m. S. (*See Lancaster.*)

How Mill (Cumland).—N.E.R. Trout beck. Gelt, 2 m. N.E. (*See Carlisle.*)

Howsham (Lincoln).—G.C.R. North Kelsey beck. (*See Brigg.*)

Huddersfield (York).—L. & N.W.R. · L. & Y.R.; G.N.R.; G.C.R. Colne; polluted. Holme. (*See Rawcliffe.*) *Lakes:* Woodside reservoir, 2 m.; trout; private. Longwood Compensation reservoir, 3 m.; perch, roach, &c.; preserved by the Huddersfield Angling Association of 55; hon. sec., S. Hellowell, Esq; season, June 16 to March 16. Longwood Top reservoir, 3½ m.; pike, perch; preserved as above; season, June 16 to March 16. Longwood Bottom reservoir, 3½ m.; pike, perch; preserved as above; season, June 16 to March 16. Blackmoorfoot reservoir, 4 m.; pike, perch; preserved as above; season, June 16 to March 16. Deerhill reservoir, 6 m.; roach; preserved as above; season, June 16 to March 16. Blacksike reservoir, 8 m.; trout;

preserved as above; season, April 1 to Sept. 30. Holmstyes reservoir, 8½ m.; trout; preserved as above; season, April 1 to Sept. 30. Bawshaw reservoir, 9½ m.; trout; preserved as above; season. April 1 to Sept. 30. Ramsden, Ridings Wood, and Yateholme Reservoirs, Holmfirth (trout) preserved by Batley Angling Club; hon. sec., Isaac Wilson, Batley. *Hotel*: Imperial.

Hugglescote (Leicester).—M.R.; L. & N.W.R. Sence. (*See Gainsborough.*)

Hull (York).—N.E.R.; G.C.R.; G.N.R.; L. & N.W.R.; M.R.; L. & Y.R. Hull. (*c.s. York.*) Hull rises above **Southburn**, runs to **Driffield** 3 m. Here. Driffield beck, 3 m. long, joins on left bank. Hull runs to Wansford 3 m.. 1 m. S. of **Nafferton**, on left bank. 2 m. down Hull, Skerne beck, which rises by **Hutton Cranswick** and is 3 m. long, joins on right bank. 2 m. down Hull, Frodingham beck joins on left bank. Frodingham, under the name of Kelk beck, rises at Killam 4 m. above **Lowthorpe**, runs 5 m. to Frodingham, and joins Hull 2 m. below. 4 m. down Hull, Walton beck, which rises by Walton, 3 m. N. of **Lockington**, and is 5 m. long, joins on left bank. Hull runs 2m., where Aike beck joins on left bank. Aike rises above **Lockington**, and 2 m. below, by the station, is joined on right bank by Scoby beck, 4 m. long. 2 m. down, Aike joins Hull. Hull runs 1 m. to **Arram**, Beverley 3 m.. Cottingham (2 m. off on right bank) 6 m.. **Sutton-on-Hull** (1 m. off on left bank) 1 m., and **Hull** 3 m. The Hull affords good fishing from 4 m. above the town—trout, dace, roach, perch, pike, also bream and chub. Some grayling have been turned in. *Tackleist*, H. Booth, 21, Paragon-street.

Hungerford (Berks).—G.W.R. Kennet and Dunn; trout, grayling. *Hotels*: Three Swans and Bear. (*See London, M.T.*) The river is preserved and well-stocked with trout and grayling; s.t. 10l. 10s., m.t. 3l. 3s., w.t. 1l. 1s., d.t. 5s.; of the lessee, Capt. Morse, Riverside. and T. G. Freeman. Bridge-street. May and June reserved for a.t. holders, fly only; no Sunday fishing. There is fair roach and pike fishing in the canal, by permission of the Mayor. The Kennet Valley Fisheries issue s.t. for 7 m. of preserved water. *Tackleists*, Freeman Brothers, Bridge-street (*see Advertisement.*)

Hunslet (York).—M.R.; L. & Y.R. Aire. (*c.s. York.*) Killing beck. 2 m. E. (*See Rawcliffe.*)

Huntingdon.—G.N.R. Ouse; coarse fish except barbel. (*c.s. N. and S.*) *Hotel*: George. (*See King's Lynn; Wisbeach.*)

Hurworth (Durham).—N.E.R. Tees; salmon, trout, chub, dace. Skerne; pike, chub, roach; preserved by Darlington Anglers' Club of 50; entrance,·10s.; s.t., 25s.; sec., Mr. A. Lascelles, Northgate, Darlington. Licence distributor: Mr. J. F. Smythe, Fishtackleist, Horsemarket, Darlington. (*c.s. Tees.*) (*See Stockton.*)

Husthwaite (York).—N.E.R. Hole beck. (*See York.*)

Hutton Cranswick (York).—N.E.R. Skerne beck. Hull, 2 m. E. (*See Hull.*) (*c.s. York.*)

Huttons Ambo (York).—N.E.R. Derwent; preserved. Menethorpe beck. Howl beck, 1 m. S. Mill beck, 1 m. S. (*c.s. York.*) (*See Wressel.*)

Huyton Quarry (Lancs.)—L. & N.W.R. Ditton brook. *Lakes*: Logwood Mill, 1 m. S. (*See Runcorn.*)

Hykeham (Lincoln).—G.N.R. Witham. (*See Boston.*)

Hythe (Kent).—S.E. & C.R. In the military canal are bream, roach, perch, and a few pike. Fishing fair; m.t. 1s. *Hotel*: Swan. In summer, whiting pout are caught amongst the rocks a quarter of a mile from the toll bar on the lower Sandgate road. The fishing at sea from a boat is good. Good jack fishing at **Wye**,

Idridgehay (Derby).—M.R. Ecclesbourne. (*See Gainsborough.*)

Ilam, n.s. **Thorpe Cloud** (Derby).—L. & N.W.R. Manifold; trout, grayling. Dove, 1 m. E.; trout, grayling. At the Izaak Walton Hotel fishing for 5 m. can be had in Manifold and Dove; w.t. 7s. 6d., d.t. 2s. A portion is free to hotel visitors. (*c.s. Trent.*) Hamps. 4 m. W.; private. (*See Gainsborough.*)

Ilford (Essex).—G.E.R. On Roding. (*See Barking.*)

Ilfracombe (Devon.)—L. & S.W.R.; G.W.R. (*See Lynton.*) 3 m. off runs Braddy water, which rises by Horedown Gate, 4 m. from Ilfracombe. runs 3 m. to Berrynarbor, and the sea 2 m.; leave from Mrs. Bassett, Watermouth Castle, Ilfracombe. Good trouting in the reservoirs 1¼m.; tickets of the Clerk to District Council, Town Hall, Ilfracombe. *Hotels*: Ilfracombe and Royal Clarence. Excellent sea fishing from pier or boat; cod, conger, bass, bream.

Ilkestone (Derby).—M.R.; G.N.R. Erewash. Gilt brook, 2 m. N. Nut brook, 2 m. S. *Lakes*: Shipley Hall reservoir, 2 m. N.W. Mapperley reservoir, 3 m. N.W. (*See Gainsborough.*)

Ilkley (York).—M.R.; N.E.R. Wharfe; trout, grayling; preserved from Addingham to Ben Rhydding for 4 m. by the Ilkley Angling Club of 35 members; w.t. 21s., d.t. 5s., from Mr. H. J. Rose, Brook-street, Ilkley; hon. sec., E. Beanlands, Esq.; season—trout, from April 1 to Oct. 1; grayling June 15 to Jan. 31; coarse fish, Oct. 2 to March 15, no dogs. *Hotels*: Stoney Lea, Middleton, and New Inn. (*c.s. York.*) (*See York.*)

Ilminster (Somerset).—L. & S.W.R. Yarty. (*c.s. Axe.*) (*See Seaton.*) Isle; trout, pike, and coarse fish; leave may be obtained. (*See Bridgwater.*) (*c.s. Avon.*)

Ingatestone (Essex).—G.E.R. On Cann. (*See Maldon.*) About 2½ m. from here is the large lake of Fitzwater.

Ingestre (Stafford).—G.N.R. Trent (*c.s.*) Gayton brook. Sow at **Stafford**, 5 m. S.W. Penk at Baswich, 5 m. S.W. *Lakes*: Ingestre Park pool and Hopton pools, 2 m. S.W. Tixall Park pool, 4 m. S. (*See Gainsborough.*)

Ingham (Suffolk). — G.E.R. Lark, 3 *m.* W.; dace, &c. (*c.s. Norfolk.*) *Lakes:* Livermere Park and Ampton Park (1 *m.* E.). Culford Park (2 *m.* W.). (*See King's Lynn.*)

Ingleby (Yorks).—N.E.R.—Broughton Bridge beck. Otters Hill beck, 1 *m.* N. *See Stockton.*)

Ingleton (York).—M.R. Greta; trout; preserved by Ingleton Angling Association for 8 *m.*; sec., Mr. S. Worthington, Wheatsheaf Hotel; s.t. 7s. 6d., f.t. 3s. 6d., d.t. 1s. 6d.; season, March 1 to Oct. 1, no dogs. (*c.s. Lune.*) Doe; trout; preserved as above. *Hotels:* Wheatsheaf, and Punch Bowl, Burton-in-Lonsdale, where tickets can be had. (*See Lancaster.*)

Ingrow (York).—G.N.R.; M.R. Worth. (*See Rawcliffe.*)

Inkberrow (Worcs.).—u.s. **Alcester**, 6*m.* Wyre. (*See Gloucester.*)

Instow (Devon).—L. & S.W.R. Good sea fishing, and salmon in Torridge; preserved by a society. Tickets are to be obtained. (*See Bideford.*) (*c.s. Taw.*)

Ipswich (Suffolk.)—G.E.R. Gipping; roach, dace, chub, pike, tench, perch, carp. Flowton brook, 1 *m* S. *Lakes:* Bixley Decoy ponds, 2½ *m.* S.E.; strictly private. Gipping rises in a lake at Wetherden, 1 *m.* N. W. of **Haughley**, runs to **Haughley** 2 *m.*, **Stowmarket** 3 *m.* Here Rattlesden brook, 7 *m.* long, joins on right bank. Gipping runs to **Needham Market** 4 *m.* 1 *m.* down, the drainage of Bosmere close to the river's bank joins on left bank. Gipping runs 4 *m.* to **Claydon**, **Bramford** 3 *m.*, and **Ipswich** 4 *m.* Fishing is free from **Ipswich** *up* to Boss Hall, 2 *m.*; thence to Blakenham (close to **Claydon**) the river is preserved by the Gipping Angling Preservation Society; family tickets 21s., d.t. 1s., pike 2s 6d., of hon. sec., Mr. Charles Prentice, 19. Tower-street, Ipswich: of Mr. H. Hodgson, Butter Market; Mr. B. Bird. 129, Norwich-road, Ipswich; at the Chequers Inn and Post Office, Claydon; and P. O. Bramford, Soroughton. Flowton brook joins Orwell 1 *m.* below the town. This brook rises 5 *m.* above Burstall Bridge, 4 *m.* W. of **Ipswich**, and runs thence to Orwell 5 *m.* Good codling, whiting, and flounder fishing below Ipswich. *Hotels:* Great White Horse, Golden Lion, Crown and Anchor.

Iron Acton (Gloucester).—M.R. Frome; roach, dace, perch, trout; preserved *below* to Frampton Cotterell by the Clifton Angling Association of 50 members at 21s. a year. (*See Bristol.*)

Iron Bridge (Salop).—G.W.R. Severn: pike, perch, chub, dace, trout, salmon, &c. *Lakes:* Willey Park ponds (3 *m.* S.) (*See Gloucester.*) (*c.s. Severn.*)

Irton Road (Cumland).—B. & E.R. Mite; trout. (*c.s. West Cumberland.*) (*See Ravenglass.*)

Isfield (Sussex).—L.B. & S.C.R. On Ouse; trout, pike, perch. *See Newhaven.*) (*c.s.*)

Isle of Man.—The sea fishing is excellent for pollack, there called "killick," mackerel, cod, and codling, whiting and plaice. The chief bait for ground fish is herring; but lugs, sand-eels, small fresh-water eels, and shellfish are also found there. Whiffing with white and coloured flies and indiarubber sand-eel for pollack and mackerel is followed with success. There is also good bream fishing in and off Ramsay Bay. Double and treble gut foot links and casting lines are requisite. At sea and along the rocky coast, "bollans" (wrasse) and congers may be taken; good pollack fishing from the Queen's Pier. The small White and Black Water rivers unite their streams and fall into the sea at Douglas. There is trout fishing in this and other streams of the island. *Hotels:* Mona, Grand. There is trouting at Drindale, 10 *m.* from Douglas. For white trout the season begins on February 9th, and ends in May, to come on again in September. The rivers are nearly all free, and leave is seldom refused. Ramsay is the best head-quarters. *Hotels:* Mitre, Imperial, Prince of Wales. At Milntown, 1 *m.* from Ramsay, there is a good stream, the river Sulby (trout, small, eels, and a few salmon). The river is practically free, only a small portion of it being preserved. March and April are the best months, as sea trout are then to be had, but the ordinary brown trout fishing continues up to the end of October. Small flies and very fine gut casts are requisite. Licence, 2s. 6d. per week, 5s. per month, or 10s. 6d. for the season, to be had from Mr. W. Cubbon, tobacconist, Parliament-street. The Glen Aldyn, and Rhenabb, with those running through Ghenmoor, Ballaugh, Little London, Dhoon Glen, and Kirk Michael, are all good. 3 *m.* from Ramsey are the Ballaglass and Corm rivers, also good.

BALLASALLA (I. of M.R.).—Trout, sea trout. *Hotel:* Rushen Abbey. (*See Castletown.*) (*c.s.*)

BALLAUGH (I. of M.R.).—Glass Dhoo, 5 *m.* long; trout. Fishing dependent on rain. (*c.s.*)

CASTLETOWN.—Silver burn; trout, sea trout. This stream rises on the slopes of South Barrule, runs 5 *m.* to **Ballasalla**, here Awin Ruy. 4 *m.* long, joins on left bank. Silver burn runs 3 *m.* to the sea at **Castletown**. (*c.s.*)

COLBY (I. of M.R.).—Colby river; trout. This stream is 4 *m.* long; the lower part is preserved, but free above **Colby**. (*c.s.*)

CROSBY (I. of M.R.).—Dhoo; trout; free. (*See Douglas.*) (*c.s.*)

DOUGLAS (I. of M.R.).—Douglas river; sea trout, trout. Douglas is formed by the junction of Dhoo and Glass, a mile above the town. Dhoo rises 2 *m.* above **Crosby**, runs 3 *m.* to **Union Mills**, and 2 *m.* below is joined by Glass on left bank. Glass rises on the slopes of Ingebreek hill, and 4 *m.* down is joined on left bank by Baldwin river, 4 *m.* long. Glass runs 3 *m.* to its junction with Dhoo, thence to **Douglas**, and the—

sea is 1 *m.* The fishing of the Douglas river and the lower part of the Dhoo is preserved. but free above **Union Mills**. Glass is, we understand, free. (*c.s.*)

KIRKMICHAEL (I. of M.R.).—Wyllin burn, 4 *m.* long; trout. 4 *m.* S. is Glen Moor burn, 3 *m.* long; trout. (*c.s.*)

LAXEY.—Laxey river; trout. This stream is 5 *m.* long and 1 *m.* above its junction with the sea at Laxey, Glen river (trout), 3 *m.* long, joins on right bank. (*c.s.*)

PEEL (I. of M.R.).—Neb; trout. Neb rises above Little London, and runs 3 *m.* to Glen Helen (*Hotel*: Glen Helen); leave required for Glen Helen but free above and below. Neb runs 4 *m.* to **St. John's**. Here Foxdale river, 6 *m.* long. joins on left bank. Hence to Peel is 5 *m.* Foxdale and the Neb below the junction is spoiled by rush from the lead mines. (*c.s.*) Three *m.* S. is Meay river, 4 *m.* long; sea trout below the waterfall, trout above.

PORT SODERICK (I. of M.R.).—Sautin burn, 6 *m.* long; trout. '*c.s.*)

RAMSEY (I. of M.R.)—Sulby; salmon. sea trout, trout. Sulby rises on the W. slopes of Snaefell and runs 7 *m.* to **Sulby Glen**. **Sulby Bridge**, 3 *m.* Three *m.* down Glen Auldyn, 4 *m.* long, joins on right bank, hence to Ramsey is 1 *m.* (*c.s.*) Five *m.* S. is Cornah river, 5 *m.* long, which runs into the sea at Port Cornah. Sea trout in the lower portion and trout above. (*c.s.*)

ST. JOHN'S (I. of M.R.).—Neb; trout. Foxdale spoilt by lead mines. *Hotel*: Glen Helen. (*See Peel.*) (*c.s.*)

SULBY BRIDGE (I. of M.R.).—Sulby; trout. (*See Ramsey.*) (*c.s.*)

SULBY GLEN (I. of M.R.).—Sulby; trout. (*See Ramsey.*) Two *m.* N. is Lhen river, 6 *m.* long, joining the sea at Blue Point; trout. (*c.s.*)

UNION MILLS (I. of M.R.).—Dhoo; trout; free above. (*See Douglas*) (*c.s.*)

Isle of Wight:

ALVERSTONE (I. of W.R.).—(*See Brading*)

BLACKWATER (I. of W R.).—(*See Cowes.*)

BRADING (I. of W.R.)—On Yar; roace, dace, trout; s.t. 10*s.* 6*d.*, d.t. 1*s.*, at the Anglers' Inn, for 1 *m.* below Yarbridge Yar rises in Ford Mill (n.s. **Wroxhall**, 3 *m.*). 5 *m.* down a stream joins on right bank, which rises in French Mill 2½ *m.* up. Yar runs in 1½ *m.* to **Horringford**, 1 *m.* to **Newchurch, Alverstone** 1 *m.*, 1 *m.* to **Sandown**, and Yarbridge 2 *m.*, joining the sea 4 *m.* below. Here two streams join, each working a mill at its source. The united streams run in 1 *m.* to the sea.

COWES (I. of W.R.).—On Medina. Medina rises 3 *m.* above Gatcombe Hill and Park, 1 *m.* from **Blackwater Bridge**, runs 1 *m.* to **Shide**, 1 *m.* to **Newport**, to which the tide flows, and joins the sea at Cowes 6 *m.* below. Mullet may be caught with a small fly on the ebb tide. *Hotels*: Glo'ster and Fountain.

HORRINGFORD (I. of W.R.).—(*See Brading.*)

NEWCHURCH (I. of W R.).—(*See Brading.*)

NEWPORT (I. of W.R.).—(*See Cowes.*) - There are some large ponds near Carisbrook holding very fine trout; leave may sometimes be had.

NEWTOWN.—On Newtown River, which rises in Cambourne Mill, runs to Green Mill, and is 4 *m.* long.

RYDE (I. of W.R.)—There is very good pout and whiting fishing here. Very fair fishing from the jetty; the largest fish are under the timbers.

SANDOWN (I. of W.R.).—(*See Brading.*) Brading (1 *m.* N.); trout, roach; preserved by Lady Oglander. There is some free fishing below the bridge; dace, roach. There is a reservoir here holding roach; fishing free.

SHIDE (I. of W.R.).—(*See Cowes.*)

VENTNOR (I. of W.R.).—Fair fishing from the pier when the tide is up; there are plenty of rock tench and flounders.

WOOTON.—Wooton Brook here joins the sea; it is 5 *m.* long.

WROXHALL (I. of W.R.).—(*See Brading.*)

YARMOUTH.—On Yare, which rises in the large lake at Freshwater, 3 *m.* off. At sea is good pout and whiting fishing.

Isleworth (Middx.).—L. & S.W.R. Thames and Yedding Brook. (*See London, L.T.,* and *Richmond, Surrey.*) *Fisherman*: W. Clarke.

Islip (Oxford).—L. & N.W.R. Cherwell and Ray. Good chub. roach, perch, and pike fishing may be had in the Cherwell. Good accommodation at either of the inns or in the village. *Hotels*: The Fox and Grapes, Red Lion, Swan. (*See London, M.T.*)

Itchen Abbas (Hants).—L. & S.W.R. Itchen; trout. (*See Southampton.*)

Itchinfield (Sussex).—L.B. & S.C.R. Arun; good pike fishing. (*See Littlehampton.*)

Ivy Bridge (Devon).—G.W.R. Erme; trout numerous, but small. Erme rises on Dartmoor; runs 8 *m.* to **Ivybridge**, Ermington 3 *m.* Here Ugborough brook joins on left bank. Ugborough rises by Ugborough (n.s. **Wrangaton**, G.W.R., 2 *m.*), and 2 *m.* down is joined on right bank by Wood brook, 2 *m.* long. 2 *m.* down is the Erme. Erme runs 1 *m.*, and is joined on left bank by Shilstone brook, 5 *m.* long. 2 *m.* down Erme the tide flows, and here Modbury brook joins on left bank. Modbury rises 1 *m.* E. of Modbury (n.s. **Ivybridge**, 5 *m.*), and is 4 *m.* long. 2 *m.* down Erme is the sea. (*c.s. Avon.*) The fishing is preserved, and leave difficult to obtain. *Hotel*: London.

Ixworth (Suffolk)—n.s. **Thurston**, 4 *m.* Ixworth River. *Lakes*: Stowlangtoft Hall (2 *m.*) (*c.s. Norfolk.*) (*See King's Lynn*).

Jersey.—General Information.—There is no fresh water fishing except in a few ponds for carp, tench, eels, &c. The sea fishing is very good. The rock upon which Elizabeth Castle stands in St. Aubin's Bay is a very good spot; bass, mullet, and conger. There is shore fishing for pout, pollack, &c. The rocks about Bouley Bay, Rozel Bay, St. Brelade's, and St. Aubin's are good spots, and red mullet, soles, plaice, &c., can be taken in a trammel net. Fine freshwater eels can be also caught in St. Heller's harbour by ground-lines or a trot, baited with bits of sand-eel or soft crab found under stones. Close to all the insulated rocky shoals which environ St. Aubin's Bay, pollack may be caught, here called whiting. Les Pignonets and Grune du Port rocks near Noirmont Port are favourite spots. Apply to J. de la Mare, or P. Le Ray.

Kearsney (Kent)—L.C. & D.R. On Dour; trout. In Kearsney Abbey lake there are some trout; leave from the occupier. (*See Dover.*)

Keele (Staffs.).—N. Staff. R. Artle, 1 *m.* W. *Lakes:* Madeley Manor, 1 *m.* W. (*See Frodsham.*)

Kegworth (Leicester).—M.R. Soar; chub, roach, pike, perch, bream, carp, tench. (*c.s. Trent.*) Kingston brook. (*See Gainsborough.*)

Keighley (York).—G.N.R.—M.R. Aire; trout, grayling, perch, chub, roach; polluted below, but preserved from hence *up* to Eastburn brook by the Keighley Angling Club; hon. sec., F. L. Wood, 3, Elholme View; s.t. 10s., d.t. for both Aire and Ponden reservoir (35 acres) 1s., within a mile of the town. There is some fair free roach fishing, with an occasional trout, in the Leeds and Liverpool Canal. (*See Kildwick*). (*c.s. York.*) Worth. (*See Rawcliffe.*)

Keld (York), n.s. **Kirkby Stephen**, 12 *m* —M.R. and N.E.R. Swale; trout, grayling. (*c.s. York.*) Stonesdale beck; trout, after a flood. Whitsundale beck, 1 *m.* W.; trout. Great Sleddale beck, 2 *m.* W.; trout; free. Little Sleddale beck, 4 *m.* W.; trout; free. East Gill beck, Sleddale. *Lake:* Birkdale tarn, 3 *m.* W. *Inn:* Cat Hole, Keld, Reeth. (*See York.*)

Kelston (Somerset).—M.R. (*See Bristol.*) On Avon; roach, dace, pike, perch, trout; free; Boyd. (*c.s.*)

Kelveden (Essex).—G.E.R. Blackwater; pike, roach. (*See Maldon.*) There is a fine sheet of water in Braxted Park. *Hotels:* Star and Fleece and Railway Tavern. 4 *m.* off is Oldfield Grange pond, belonging to Mr. Felton, of Oldfield Grange, Coggeshall, who often gives permission; pike, perch, carp, tench, and roach.

Kendal (Westland).—Kent. Salmon; trout: mostly preserved. (*c.s.*) Kent rises in Kentmere reservoir, 10 *m.* N. of **Staveley**. At **Staveley** a stream joins on left bank, draining Skeggles water 4 *m.* up. Here also Gowan river joins on right bank. Gowan rises 2 *m.* N.E. of **Windermere** station, and runs 6 *m.* to Kent and **Staveley**. There is a reservoir 2 *m.* S.W. of **Staveley**. 3 *m.* down Kent a stream joins on left bank, draining Gurnal Dubs on Potter Fell, 2 *m.* up. Kent runs 1 *m.* to **Burneside**. Here Sprint (*c.s. Kent*) joins on left bank. Sprint is 13 *m.* long. 1 *m.* down Kent a stream joins on left bank, draining Skelsmergh tarn, 2 *m.* up. A little below, Sprint joins Kent on left bank. Mint (*c.s. Kent*) rises on Bannisdale Fell, and 7 *m.* down is joined on left bank by the outflow of a pond, 1 *m.* up, and a little lower down the outflow of two ponds. 1 *m.* up, join on right bank. 1 *m.* down Mint, by **Grayrigg**, the outflow of Grayrigg tarn, 3 *m.* N.E. of **Grayrigg**, joins on left bank. Mint runs 5 *m.* to **Kendal**. Kent runs 8 *m.* to the estuary. Here Gilpin joins on right bank. Gilpin rises 7m. N.W. of **Kendal**, and 7 *m.* down is joined on left bank by Underbarrow beck. which rises above Underbarrow, 4 *m.* W. of **Kendal**, and is 7 *m.* long. Gilpin runs 3 *m.* to Kent. Kent, Mint and Sprint are for the most part preserved by the Kent Angling Society (sec., F. B. Pollitt). The Kent below Kendal is preserved by the Kent Angling Association; s.t. 5s. The Levens Park fishing, just below, private. The Low Levens fishery follows on; good, but tidal; private. Stainton beck 2 *m.*; trout. Beehive beck 2 *m.* E. (*See Milnthorpe.*) *Hotels:* Railway and County, King's Arms, Commercial.

Kenilworth (Warwick).—L & N.W.R. (*See Stoneleigh.*) *Lakes:* Ponds on Westwood Heath (3 *m.* N.) (*See Gloucester.*)

Kennet (Cambs.)—G.E.R. Kent. (*See King's Lynn.*)

Kerne Bridge (Hereford).—G.W.R. Wye; chub, dace, pike, perch, salmon, trout. (*c.s.*) Castle brook. Garran (2 *m.*); trout. Luke brook (2 *m.*). Lammerch brook (5 *m.*). (*See Chepstow.*)

Keswick (Cumland).—L. & N.W.R. and M.R. Derwent; Greta: trout. salmon (late in autumn); preserved by Derwent Fishery District Board; sec., — Dodgson, Esq., solicitor, Cockermouth. Licence for Keswick portion lakes and rivers above Ouse Bridge: salmon; s.t. 15s., m.t. or shorter period 10s.; trout; s.t. 5s., m.t. 2s. 6d., d.t. 1s.; to be obtained of Mr. H. Mayson, photographer, Keswick. Licence for Cockermouth portion below Ouse Bridge: salmon s.t., 30s.; m.t., 20s.; trout w.t. 5s.; m.t., 2s. 6d.; w.t., 2s. 6d. *Permits below Marron;* s.t. 20s., m.t. 10s., w.t. 5s.; *above Marron;* s.t. 10s., m.t. 5s., w.t. 2s. 6d. Cocker; s.t. 5s., m.t. 2s. 6d., or shorter period; to be obtained from Mr. G. P. Graham, fishing tackle maker, Cockermouth, Mr. Slee, Borrowdale, Mr. Thomas Rook, Washington Street, Workington, Mr. Ees, Pell Wyke, and Mr. Robertson, Swan Hotel, Thornthwaite; coarse fishing free; licences at both hotels. Derwent; trout, salmon; preserved as above. St. John's; trout; preserved as above. Newlands beck; trout. Borrowdale beck; trout. Caldew, 4 *m.* N.; trout. *Lakes:* Thirlmere; perch, pike, trout; preserved by the Manchester Corporation, who issue tickets. Derwentwater; pike, perch, trout, salmon, vendace; good fishing in May when the Mayfly is in season. Some thousands of yearling trout were turned into the lake last season. Crummock, 9 m.; trout, char; good fly fishing; boats and men can be had at Buttermere and Scale Hill. Ennerdale; trout. Wastwater; trout. Bassenthwaite, 4 m.; pike, perch, trout, salmon; boats and men at the Swan, Thornthwaite, and the Pheasant, Peil Wyke. Large catches of perch were made last season. There are fewer pike in the lake. The trout are increasing, and, although sluggish at other times, take well during the Mayfly. Overwater; pike; leave from Miss Gough, Whitefield House, *via* Mealsgate. Sty Head tarn; trout. Sprinkling tarn; trout. Tarn-at-Leaves; trout. The above tarns are in Borrowdale. Sour Milk tarn; trout; in Buttermere. Red tarn; trout; Helvellyn. Blea tarn; trout; Wythburn. Spring and autumn are the best times. For lake fishing a good fly is *hook* No. 3 (Kendal); *body*, red worsted or mohair; *wings*, dark blue; *legs*, of a lighter shade. For sea trout a good fly is, *hook*, various sizes; *body*, moderately dark blue. with or without gold or silver tag, and ribbed or not; *hackle*, brown or black-red; *wings*, strips of green parrot, tied on as long legs underneath the shoulder. the rest mostly peacock, with a few strips of brown mallard, golden pheasant tippet, and brown turkey. Another good fly has a *body* light blue; *hackle*, brown or black red, with or without gold and silver tag and ribbing; *wings*, mallard and light turkey mixed. *Hotels*: Keswick, Queen's, Royal Oak, Lake, George, King's Arms, Derwentwater Hotel, Portniscole.

Kettering (Northton.)—M.R. Ise; trout; private. (*See Wisbeach.*) *Hotel*: Royal.

Kettlewell (York), n.s. **Bolton Abbey**, 14 m.—M.R. Wharfe. (*c.s. York.*) Skirfare, 2 m. W. Cover, 4 m. N.; trout. Cowside beck, 2 m. W. (*See York.*)

Ketton (Rutland).—G.N.R.; M R.; L. & N.W.R. Welland. Chater. (*See Spalding.*)

Kew (Surrey).—L. & S.W.R. Thames. (*See London, L.T.*)

Kexby (York), n.s. **Fangfoss**, 3 m.—N.E.R. Derwent; pike, chub, &c., free. (*c.s. York.*) (*See Wressel.*)

Keynsham (Somerset).—G.W.R. (*See Bristol.*) On Avon: chub, pike, perch, carp; free. Chew; perch, roach; leave from owners and in parts (d.t. 1s.) can be had. Siston brook; good all-round fishing. (*c.s.*)

Kibworth (Leicester).—M.R. Saddington brook, 1 m. S. Hardwick brook, 3 m. W. *Lakes*: Saddington reservoir, 3 m. S. Gumley pond and Gumley Hall ponds, 3 m. S. (*See Spalding.*)

Kidderminster (Worcester).—G.W.R. Stour; coarse fish and trout above, polluted below; private. Churchill brook, feeding numerous mill ponds. Severn, 3 m. W.; pike, perch, chub, trout; free. (*See Gloucester.*) (*c.s. Severn.*) *Hotel*: Lion.

Kilburn (Derby).—M.R. Holbrook brook. (*See Gainsborough.*)

Kildare (York-).—N.E.R. Leven; trout; private. (*c.s. Tees.*) Basedale beck, 2 m. S. (*See Stockton.*)

Kildwick (York).—M.R. Aire; trout, grayling, perch, chub, roach; preserved by Aire Fishing Club from **Gargrave** *above* to the junction of Eastburn brook at this place. (*See Gargrave.*) From Eastburn brook down, the river is preserved by the Keighley Angling Club as far as Bingley; s.t 10s., d.t. 1s.; sec., Mr. F. L. Wood, 3, Eelholme View, Keighley. (*c.s. York.*) Eastbourne. *Lakes*: Cowloughton dam; 7 m. S.W. (*See Rawcliffe.*)

Killamarsh (Derby). — M.R.; G.C.R. Rother. Short brook. *Lakes*: Woodhall Moor dams, 2 m. E. Barlborough Hall lake, 3 m. S.E. Pebley dam, 3 m. S.E. Harthill reservoir, 3 m. E. Woodhall pond. 3 m. E. (*See Goole.*)

Kilnhurst (Yorks).—G.C.R.; M.R. Don. (*See Goole.*)

Kilnsey (York), n.s. **Bolton Abbey**, 12 m.—M.R. Wharfe; trout; preserved by Kilnsey Angling Club of 35 members, from Starbotton above to Netherside, 1 m. below Kilnsey; entrance, 5l. 5s.; s.t. 94s. 6d.. d.t. 5s. (fly only, no wading), from the keepers. (*c.s. York.*) Skirfare, 1 m. N.; trout; preserved as Wharfe up to Arncliffe, where there is an hotel. *Hotel*: Tennants Arms. (*See York.*)

Kilworth (Leicester).—L. & N.W.R. Avon; dace, roach, perch. (*See Naseby* and *Welford.*) Swift (4 m. W.). (*See Gloucester.*) (*c.s. Severn.*)

Kimberley (Notts).—M.R. *Lakes*: Nuthall lake. (*See Gainsborough.*)

Kimberley (Norfolk).—G.E.R. Hackford brook. Bara, 1 m. E. Dyke beck, 2 m. S.E. Yare, 2 m. N.W. *Lake*: Kimberley Park, 1 m. Wicklewood mere, 2 m. S. Sea mere, 3 m. S.W. by Hingham. (*See Yarmouth.*)

Kimbolton (Hunts).—M.R. Kym. *Lake*: Warren fishpond. (*See King's Lynn*).

Kingsbridge (Devon).—G.W.R. Kingsbridge brook; fishless. This brook is 3 m. long, and forms in addition a long estuary, up which the tide flows to Kingsbridge. 2 m. below Kingsbridge, at Charlton, Buckland brook, 6 m. long, joins on left bank; trout; private. 1 m. down, Chillington water, which rises 3 m. N.W. of Torcross, and is 6 m. long, joins on right bank; trout. Capital sea fishing in the estuary. Good bass fishing at Saltstone Rock, half-way between Kingsbridge and Salcombe. Avon, 2 m. N.; trout, salmon Trouting commences March 1 and ends Sept. 30. (*See Loddiswell.*) *Hotel*: King's Arms. *Tackleist*, S. Perrott, 24, Fore-street.

Kingsbury (Warwick).—M.R. Tame. (*c.s. Trent.*) Langley brook, 3 m. N.W. *Lakes*: Middleton Hall lake, 3 m. N.W. (*See Gainsborough.*)

King's Cliffe (Northton.)—G.N.R. Willow brook. Welland, 3 m. N.W., at Duddington. *Lake*: Blatherwyck Park (Stafford O'Brian, Esq.), 2 m. W.; pike, carp, bream, &c.; strictly preserved. (*See Wisbeach.*)

Kingsland (Hereford).—G.W.R.　Lugg, Arrow. and Pinsley brook; trout, grayling.　(c.s. *Wye.*)　The fishing generally preserved by the landowners, but a stretch is preserved by the Eyton Club of four members.　2 m. from **Kingsland**, the river Arrow at Eardisland. There are two inns at Kingsland, and private lodgings can be had.　(*See Chepstow.*)

King's Lynn (Norfolk).—G.E.R.　Ouse; coarse fish of all kinds except barbel.　Ouse rises in the Biddlesdon Park lakes 4 m. N.W. from **Brackley**, runs to **Brackley** 4 m., Water Stratford 6 m.　2 m. below, a stream joins on the left bank, draining the lakes at Stowe 3 m. up, 4 m. N.W. from **Buckingham**.　Ouse runs to **Buckingham** 3 m. 3. m. down Ouse, near Maid's Morton Mill, Claydon river joins on right bank, rising in Cottisford pond, 5 m. S. from **Brackley**, runs 12 m. to **Claydon**, where a stream joins on right bank, draining the ponds at Claydon Farm and Middle Claydon, 2 m. S. from **Claydon**.　The stream joins Ouse 7 m. down.　4 m. down Ouse, at Beachampton, a stream joins on right bank, draining a lake at Whaddon, 3 m. N. from **Swanbourn**.　Ouse runs 4 m. to **Stony Stratford** (n.s. **Wolverton**, 2 m.).　Here a stream joins on left bank, draining the lakes in Whittlewood Forest, 4 m. N.W. from **Stony Stratford**.　2 m. down Ouse, at **Wolverton**, Tove joins on left bank.　Tove rises by **Helmedon**, runs 4 m. to **Wappenham**, and 4 m. down is joined by Blakesley brook on left bank, which rises above **Blakesley**, and is 7 m. long.　Tove runs to **Towcester** 2 m., Stoke lock 2 m. S. of **Roade**, 7 m., and Ouse 8 m.　Ouse runs to **Newport Pagnel** 9 m., and here Ousel joins on right bank.　Ousel rises by Eddlesborough 4 m. S.W. from **Dunstable**, runs 9 m. to **Leighton Buzzard**, where Battlesden brook joins on right bank.　Battlesden rises in the lakes in Woburn Abbey Park, 3 m. S.E. from **Woburn** Station, runs 5 m. to Battlesden Park and lakes, 4 m. N.E. from **Leighton Buzzard**, and joins Ousel 4 m. down.　3 m. down Ousel the outflow, 1 m. long, of Rushmore pond, 2 m. N. from **Leighton**, joins on right bank.　Ousel runs 7 m. to **Fenny Stratford**, and 6 m. down is joined on right bank by Crawley brook, which runs 3 m. N. of **Woburn** Station, and is 6 m. long. Ousel runs 3 m. to **Newport Pagnel** and Ouse.　Ouse runs to **Olney** 8 m., **Turvey** 5 m., **Harrold** (n.s. **Sharnbrook**, 4 m.), 3 m., **Sharnbrook** 5 m. (tickets), **Oakley** 5 m.　Here Ouse makes a bend of 4 m., returning to **Oakley**, runs to Clapham 2 m. (preserved by Hon. Miss Trevor, of Bromham Hall), **Bedford** 6 m.; Burford Bridge, 1 m. W. of **Blunham**. 7 m. (Mr. King, of Roxton, owns the N. side, and Mr. Elliot, of Blunham, the S.), and 3 m. down at **Tempsford** is joined on right bank by Ivel.　Ivel rises by **Baldock**, runs 5 m. to **Arlesey**, where Hiz joins on left bank.　Hiz rises by **Hitchin**, and is 9 m. long.　3 m. down Ivel, at Langford, Tod joins on left bank.　Tod rises in the lakes at Tingrith House, 3 m. N.W. from **Harlington**, runs 2 m. to Flitwick Park and lakes, 3 m. S. from **Ampthill**, runs 9 m. to **Shefford**, where Gull brook, 4 m. long, joins on left bank, and Compton brook, 6 m. long, which rises in the lakes of Wrest Park, 5 m. S.E. from **Ampthill**, on right bank.　Tod joins Ivel 3 m. down.　Ivel runs to **Biggleswade** 3 m.　2 m. down, Sutton brook, which rises in the lake in Gamlingay Old Park, close to **Gamlingay**, runs 2 m. to Potton, and Ivel, 4 m., joins on right bank.　Ivel runs to **Sandy** 2 m.; and here is Southill brook, which rises in the lake in Southill Park, near **Southill**, receives the drainings of Old Warden Park lake 2 m. down, and 3 m. further joins Ivel on left bank.　Ivel runs to **Blunham** 2 m., and Ouse 2 m.　Ouse runs to **St. Neots** 5 m., and 1 m. down is joined on right bank by Kym.　Kym rises above **Kimbolton**, where it is joined by the outflow from the fishpond at the Warren, and 9 m. down joins Ouse.　1 m. down Ouse. Gallow brook, 5 m. long, joins on right bank.　Ouse runs 4 m. to **Offord** and 4 m. to **Huntingdon** (the fishing mostly in private hands). Here Alconbury brook, 14 m. long, joins on left bank.　Ouse runs 5 m. to **St. Ives**, **Swavesey**, 3 m., **Earith**, 4 m. (and here the Bedford level or Bedford river leaves the main stream, joining again by Downham Market: **Manea** is the only station half-way down) **Stretham**, 10 m., and **Thetford** (n.s. **Stretham**, 2 m.) 2 m.　Here Cam joins on right bank.　Cam rises in the lakes at Debden, 2 m. E. of **Newport**, passes **Newport**, and runs 4 m. to **Saffron Walden**, where it runs through Audley End Park, **Great Chesterford**, 4 m., **Whittlesford**, 4 m., **Shelford**, 3 m.　Here Bourn joins on right bank.　Bourn rises 3 m. above Bartlow, runs 2 m. to **Linton**, **Pampisford**, 3 m., and **Shelford**, 4 m.　3 m. down Cam, at Trumpington, Rhee joins on left bank.　Rhee rises at Ashwell, runs 10 m. to **Meldreth** (1 m. off on right bank). Here a stream joins on left bank, draining a lake in Wimpole Park 4 m. up, 2 m. S. from **Old North Road** Station.　Rhee runs 4 m. to **Harston**, and Cam 3 m.　1 m. down Cam at Trumpington, Bourn brook joins on left bank.　This stream rises by Bourn, runs 8 m. to **Lords Bridge**, and Cam 3 m.　Cam runs to **Cambridge** 3 m. (preserved by Cambridge and Ely Angling Association, hence to below Ely), **Waterbeach** 6 m., and here Bottisham Load, which runs down from **Fulbourn** 9 m., joins on right bank.　1 m. down Cam Swaffham Load, 6 m. long, joins on right bank.　Cam runs to Upware, 2 m. (good fishing. *Inn*: Five Miles from Anywhere), and 4 m. down joins Ouse.　Ouse runs to **Ely** 8 m., 4 m. below, Lark joins on right bank.　Lark rises above **Bury St. Edmunds**, and is here joined by Linnet, which rises in the lake in Ickworth Park, 3 m. S. from **Saxham**, and is 5 m. long, and 5 m. down at West Stow is joined on right bank by a brook rising in the lake in Livermere Park, runs thence in 1 m. to the lake in Ampton Park, 1 m. W. of **Ingham**, and 3 m. down waters the lakes in Culford Park 2 m. W. of **Ingham**, and joins Lark 1 m. down.　Lark runs 3 m. to Icklingham where Cavenham brook, which rises by **Saxham**, and is 7 m. long, joins on left bank.　Lark runs 4 m. to **Mildenhall**, and 4 m. below is joined on left bank by Kent, which, rising 5 m. above **Kennet**, runs thence 4 m. to

Freckenham (n.s. **Fordham**, 3 *m.*), and 2 *m.* down joins Lark near Isleham (n.s.
Fordham, 3 *m.*). Lark joins Ouse 7 *m.* down, **Mildenhall** Station being 2 *m.* off on right
bank. Ouse runs 3 *m.* to **Littleport**. Here Mildenhall drain enters on right bank, and
Old Croft river, 14 *m.* long, joins on left bank. 3 *m.* down Ouse, at Brandon Creek bridge,
Brandon or Little Ouse joins on right bank. Little Ouse rises in the lake in Redgrave Park
by **Botesdale** (n.s. **Mellis**, 4 *m.*), runs to Hopton, 5 *m.*, Rushford, 5 *m.*, and 2 *m.* down
Ixworth river joins on left bank. Ixworth rises in the lake in Drinkstone Park,
4 *m* S.E. from **Thurston**, runs 3 *m.* to the railway 1 *m.* W. of Elmswell; 3 *m.* down at
Stowlangtoft the outflow from the lake in Stowlangtoft Hall, 1 *m.* up joins on right bank. 2
m. on is **Ixworth** (n.s. **Thurston**, 4 *m.*). The stream now runs to Pakenham, 7 *m.*, and,
just below, it waters the lake in Euston Park, and 3 *m.* down joins Ouse. Ouse runs 4 *m.* to
Thetford. Here Thet joins on right bank. Thet rises 6 *m.* above **Kelling**, and runs
in 10 *m.* to **Thetford**. Little Ouse runs 9 *m.* to **Brandon**, **Lakenheath**, 3 *m.*, and
Great Ouse. 9 *m.* Ouse runs to **Hilgay** 5 *m.*, and here Sam's Cut Drain, holding pike and
perch, and Wissey or Stoke river join on right bank. Wissey rises in Heath Mere, 5 *m.* E. from
Walton, runs 6 *m.* to **Walton**, where the outflow of Saham Mere, 1 *m.* N., joins on right
bank. Wissey runs to Hilborough, 7 *m.*, where Erne'ord Brook. which rises above **Holm-
Hall**, and is 10 *m.* long, joins on right bank. 4 *m.* down Wissey, at Ickborough, the
draining of the lakes in Buckenham House Park joins on the left bank, being 6 *m.* N.E.
from **Brandon**. 2 *m.* down Wissey, at Mundford, a stream joins on left bank, draining
Toff's Mere, 3 *m.* up, and 5 *m.* N.E. from **Brandon**. 2 *m.* down, Wissey receives the
drainings of the lake in Didlington Hall, which lies almost on the bank of the river, 5 *m.*
S.E. from **Stoke Ferry**. Wissey runs 4 *m.* to **Stoke Ferry**, where Barton brook,
draining the lake in Stradset Hall, 7 *m.* up, joins on right bank. This lake is 4 *m.* N.E. from
Downham Market. Wissey runs to **Hilgay**, and Ouse in 8 *m.* Ouse runs 1 *m.*
to Denver sluice. Here the Hundred Foot river joins the Ouse immediately below the
sluice, and contains all kinds of coarse fish except barbel. Smelts are caught in large
quantities. The part of the Ouse between Wissey and the Denver sluice is good. Ouse
runs 2 *m.* to **Downham Market**, Stow 3 *m.*, **Magdalen**, 3 *m.*, and **King's Lynn**,
8 *m.* Here Nar or Setchey joins on right bank. Nar (a good trout stream in its upper reaches,
but with pike and coarse fish below) rises by **Litcham** (n.s. **Dunham**, 3 *m.*), runs 6 *m.*
to Castle Acre, 4 *m.* N. from **Swaffham**, **Narborough**, 5 *m.*, and **King's Lynn**,
12 *m.* 4 *m.* of Nar is preserved by King's Lynn Association; trouting begins April 1 and
ends Sept. 15; grayling fishing begins Aug. 1, ends Nov. 30; pike fishing begins Aug. 1,
ends Feb. 28, except in Nar and Gaywood, where there is no close time. Close time for
other coarse fish, March 15 to June 15. Gaywood river (trout), 7 *m.* long, also joins Ouse
on right bank; preserved by the King's Lynn Angling Association; sec., Mr. J. E. Mussett;
s.t. 21s., 10s. 6d., and 5s., w.t. 2s. 6d., d.t. 1s. This association also preserves part of the
Babingley river and 7 *m.* of the Middle Level Main Drain. The Walks rivulet, and Long
pond are free. *Hotels* : Globe, East Anglian. Duke's Head. (*c.s. N. and S.*)

Kings Langley (Herts).—L. & N.W.R. (*See London, M.T.*) Gade.

King Sombourne (Hants).—L. & S.W.R. The Test; large trout. (*See Southampton.*)

Kingston (Surrey).—L. & S.W.R. Thames and Hog's Mill River. (*See London, L.T.*)
Lakes: Bushey Park, Home Park lakes. *Hotels:* Sun, Griffin. *Fishermen:* J. Johnson,
B. Pope, E. Stephens, J. Wilks, and Knight. *Tackleist,* J. R. Richardson, Bridge Foot,
Kingston.

Kington (Hereford). — G.W.R. Arrow; trout; preserved by a club below to Titley.
above by the landowners. (*c.s. Wye.*) Gilwern brook. (*See Chepstow.*)

Kington (Warwick).—G.W.R. Dene. *Lakes* : Coombroke lake (2 *m.* N.W.). Ponds in Pool
Fields (3 *m.* N.) (*See Gloucester.*)

Kinnerley (Salop).—L. & N.W.R. Wear brook. Morda (3 *m.* W.) Severn (3 *m.* S.);
chub, dace, trout. pike, salmon. Vyrnwy (4 *m.* S.W.); trout, salmon, chub, &c. *Lakes* :
Sandford Hall lake (3 *m.* N.) (*See Gloucester.*) (*c.s. Severn.*)

Kinnersley (Hereford).—G.W.R. Letton lake brook. (*See Chepstow.*)

Kintbury (Berks).—G.W.R. Kennett; pike, perch, roach, dace. (*See London, M.T.*)

Kirkandrews (Cumland).—Eden; salmon, trout. (*c.s.*) Powburgh beck, 1 *m.* W.
Lakes: Monkhill Lough, 1 *m.* W. (*See Carlisle.*)

Kirkburton (Yorks.).—L. & N.W.R. Burton brook. (*See Rawcliffe.*)

Kirkby (Lancs.).—L. & Y.R. Simonswood brook. Alt, 1 *m.* S. Flukers brook, 1 *m.* S.
(*See Altcar.*)

Kirkby Lonsdale (Westland.).—On Lune; trout. (*c.s.*) Leave can be had by ticket
for 2 *m.*; apply at Royal Hotel. Lupton beck. 2 *m.* N.W. (*See Milnthorpe.*) Leek beck,
3 *m.* S.E. *Lakes:* Tarnhouse tarn, 4 *m.* N.W.; Terrybank tarn, 4 *m.* N.W. (*See
Milnthorpe.* *Hotels:* Royal, Green Dragon, King's Arms. (*See Lancaster.*)

Kirkby Malzeard (York), n.s. **Tanfield**, 4 *m.*—Kep beck. Laver, 1 *m.* S. Stock beck.
(*See York.*)

Kirkby Moorside (York).—N.E.R. Dove, in Farndale, 1 *m.* E.; trout, grayling. Hodge
beck, in Sleightholme Dale, 1 *m.* W.; trout, grayling (*see Helmsley*). Rudland beck,
2 *m.* N. Riccal below Harome; preserved by Lord Feversham; s.t. 12s.. 3 months 7s.
4 weeks 3s., 1 week 1s.; fly and minnow only; apply to Mr. Bowman. Duncombe Park
Estate Office, Helmsley. *Hotels:* King's Head, White Horse. (*See Wressel.*)

Kirkby Stephen (York).—M.R.; N.E.R. Swale, 5 m. S.E.; trout. (c s. York.) Little-
Steddale beck, 6 m. S.E.; trout; free. Great Steddale beck, 7 m S.E.; trout; free.
Lake: Birkdale tarn 7 m. S.E. (*See York.*)

Kirkby Stephen (Westland).—M.R.; N.E.R. Eden; trout; leave from the land-
owner. (c.s.) Bigg beck. Birkett beck. Scandal beck, 2 m. Belah, 6 m. E. Greenfell beck, 3 m. E. *Hotels*: King's Arms, Black Bull. (*See Carlisle.*)

Kirkby Thore (Westland).—N.E.R. Eden; trout (c.s.) Trout beck. (*See Carlisle.*)

Kirknewton (Northland.).—The College and Bowmont here join, and form Glen. (*See
Berwick-on-Tweed.*)

Kirk Smeaton (Yorks).—G.C.R. Went. Lake Drain, 3 m. N.E., at **Womersley.**
Lake: Stapleton Park lake, 2 m. N. (*See Goole.*)

Kirkstead (Lincoln).—G.N.R. Witham. (*See Boston.*)

Kirtlington (Oxford).—G.W.R. Cherwell. (*See London, M.T.*)

Kiveton Park (Notts).—G.N.R. Oldcoates, 6 m. N.E. *Lake*: Laughton pond, 6 m. N.E.
at Roche Abbey. (*See Althorpe.*)

Knaresborough (York).—N.E.R. Nidd; trout, grayling, chub, dace; preserved for
14 m. by the Knaresborough Angling Club of 30 members: entrance 40s.; s.t. 40s.; season
begins March 16, ends September 30; secs., A. Sellers and C. F. Smith. Joint anglers' water::
Knaresborough High Bridge to field above Goldsbro' dam. D. and w. tickets from Mr.
J. W. Bramley, Gracious-street, and Mr. Hall, Gunsmith, Market Place, Knaresborough.
(c.s. York.) Crimple, 3 m. S. (*See York.*)

Knightwick (Worcester).—G.W.R. Teme; trout, grayling, chub, perch, pike. Sapey brook.
(*See Gloucester.*) (c.s. Severn.) *Hotel*: Talbot, which has 3 m. of fishing free to visitors.

Knottingley (Yorks).—G.N.R.; L. & Y.R. Aire. (c.s. York.) (*See Rawcliffe.*)

Knowle (Warwick).—G.W.R. Blyth, 2 m. E. (c.s. Trent.) *Lakes*: Earlswood reservoir,
6 m. W. (*See Gainsborough.*)

Knutsford (Cheshire).—L. & N.W.R. Birkin, 1 m. N. *Lakes*: Tatton Park lake. Mere-
Hall lake, 3 m. N.W. (*See Runcorn.*)

Lake Bank Hotel (Lancs)., (n.s. **Torver,** 3 m.).—At the foot of Coniston lake; pike,.
perch, trout. (c.s. Kent.) (*See Ulverston.*)

Lakenheath (Suffolk).—G.E.R. Little Ouse; pike and coarse fish; fishing easily obtained
(*See King's Lynn.*) (c.s. Norfolk.)

Lake Side (Lancs). Leven; salmon, trout. (c.s. Kent.) *Lakes*: Windermere; pike,
perch, char, trout. (c.s. Kent.) Bortree tarn, 2 m. W. *Hotel*: Lake side. (*See Ulverston.*).

Lamport (Northton.)—L. & N.W.R. Nen. *Lakes*: Lamport Hall, Maidwell Dale and
Maidwell Hall, 1 m. W. Faxton Hall, 2 m. E. (*See Wisbeach.*)

Lancaster.—Lune; salmon, trout. (c.s.) Condor. 4 m. N.E. (c.s. Lune.) Rowton brook,.
4 m. S.E. *Lakes*: Quernmore Park lakes, 4 m. N.E. (*See Galgate.*) Lune is formed by
the junction at **Ravenstonedale** of two becks, Greenside beck and Sanwath beck,
each 2 m. long. Half a mile down, Weasdale beck, 3 m. long, joins on left bank. Lune
runs 1 m., where Bowderdale beck, 5 m. long, joins on left bank. Lune runs to
Gaisgill, 3 m. Here Langdale beck, 5 m. long, joins on left bank, and just below the
junction on the same side Ellergill beck, 3 m. long, joins the main stream. A little
below, on right bank, Rais beck joins Lune. This stream is some 7 m. long, and 2 m.
from its source receives the drainage of Sunbiggin tarn, 2 m. W. of **Ravenstonedale.**
Station. Lune runs 1 m., where Tebay Gill, 4 m. long, and which runs on the E. of
Tebay, joins on left bank. A short way below this tributary Chapel beck, which
runs down from Orton 2 m. up, joins on right bank. One m. down Lune, Blind beck,
2 m. long, joins on right bank, and here also on the same side joins Birk beck. This
stream is 9 m. long, and 4 m. from its source on Shap Fell is joined on right bank by
Wasdale beck, 3 m. long. One m. above the junction of Birk beck with Lune, Bretherdale beck, 4 m. long, joins Birk beck on right bank. Lune runs in 1 m. to **Tebay.**
Two m. below, Barrow beck, 9 m. long, joins on right bank. Lune runs to **Howgill**
5 m. Two m. below, Blands Gill, 3 m. long, joins on left bank, and 1 m. below Blands.
Gill, Crossdale beck, 3 m. long, joins on left bank. **Sedbergh** is 2 m. S. of this
junction. Lune runs 3 m., passing 1 m. W. of **Sedbergh,** and is here joined on left bank
by the River Rawthey. Rawthey rises in West Baugh Fell tarn on Baugh Fell, and
2 m. down is joined on right bank by Red Gill, 2 m. long, which rises in four tarns
(East tarns) on East Baugh Fell. Rawthey runs 4 m., where Sally beck, 2 m. long,
joins on right bank. One m. below, Wandale beck, 2 m. long, joins on right bank, and
1 m. below again, Backs beck, 3 m. long, joins on right bank. Rawthey runs 3 m.,
where Cross How beck, 2 m. long, joins on left bank, and 1 m. down Rawthey, Vor Gill,
4 m. long, joins on left bank. 1 m. below again, 1 m. N. of **Hawes Junction.**
Clough river joins Rawthey on left bank. Clough, under the name of Grisdale
beck, rises on the slopes of Baugh Fell, and 3 m. down is joined on right
bank by the drainage (3 m. long) of a nameless tarn on East Haugh Fell, lying
within a short distance of the East tarns before mentioned. Clough runs 9 m.
to **Hawes Junction,** and 1 m. to Rawthey. Rawthey runs 3 m. to **Sedbergh.**
Here Dee joins on the left bank. Dee rises 7 m. above **Dent,** and just above that
station is joined on the left bank by Deepdale beck, 3 m. long. Dee runs to **Sedbergh,**
and Rawthey in 6 m. Rawthey joins Lune 2 m. below. Lune runs 1 m. to **Middleton,** 5 m. to **Barbon,** 1 m. off on E. bank, and here Barbon beck, 7 m. long, joins on.

left bank. Lune runs to **Kirkby Lonsdale**, 3 m. Three m. below, by Whittington, Leek beck, 9 m. long, joins on left bank. Lune runs 3 m. to **Arkholme**, and here Greeta joins on left bank. Greeta rises on Blackside Pasture. 6 m. above **Ingleton**, and here Doe river or Dale beck, 10 m. long, joins on left bank. Greeta runs to Burton-in-Lonsdale, 3 m., and joins Lune 4 m. down. Here also joins Lune, on left bank, Cant beck, 4 m. long, and on right bank Beckthwaite beck, 3 m. long. Lune runs to **Melling**, 2 m., and **Hornby**, 3 m. Here Wenning joins on left bank. Wenning is formed by the junction of five becks close to **Clapham** Station, viz.: Kettles beck (4 m. long), Fen beck (4 m. long), Austwick beck (5 m. long), Clapham beck (4 m long), and Newby beck, 3 m. long. Two m. down Wenning, Reasden beck, 6 m. long, joins on left bank. Wenning runs to **Bentham** (4 m.), Wennington (3 m.), **Hornby** (3 m.). Here Hindburn river joins Wenning on left bank. Hindburn rises on Botton Head Fell, and 2 m. down is joined on right bank by Whitcray beck, 2 m. long. Three m. below, Tatcam beck, 4 m. long, joins on right bank. Hindburn runs to Wray, 5 m. Here Roeburndale river joins on left bank. This stream rises on Mallowdale Fell, and is 12 m. long. Hindburn runs to **Hornby**, 2 m., and joins Lune 2 m. below. Lune runs to **Caton**, 6 m. Here Tarn brook, 4 m. long, joins on right bank, and on the same side Artle joins the main stream. Artle is formed by the junction of Foxdale and Udale becks, each some 4 m. long, at Crossgill: thence to **Caton** and Lune is 6 m. Lune runs to **Halton**, 3 m. Here Cote beck, 4 m. long, joins on right bank. Lune runs 3 m. to **Lancaster**.

Langdon Beck Hotel (Durham).—(n.s. **Middleton-in-Teesdale**, 8 m.) Harewood beck; trout; tickets at hotel. Langdon beck; trout; tickets at hotel. Tees, 1 m. S; trout; tickets at hotel, or of Lord Barnard's agent, Raby Castle, Staindrop. (c.s.) Maize beck, 4 m S.E.; trout; permission from Lord Hothfield, Appleby. (*See Stockton.*)

Langford (Essex).—G.E.R. On Chelmer. (*See Maldon.*)

Langley (Bucks).—G.W.R. In Black Park (Duke of Somerset), and Langley Park (Sir R. Harvey) are some large lakes; pike, perch, and chub. (*See London, M.T.*)

Langley (Cheshire).—Trout and perch fishing can be had in the Macclesfield Corporation Waterworks reservoirs; 60 tickets are issued at 21s., and 26 at 10s. 6d., d.t. 2s., half day 1s. Fishing commences on April 1st, and ends Oct. 8th.

Langley Green (Stafford).—G.W.R.; L. & N.W.R. Tame. (*c.s. Trent.*) Lake: Titford reservoir. (*See Gainsborough.*)

Langport (Somerset).—G.W.R. Parret and Yeo. (*See Bridgwater.*) (*c.s. Avon.*)

Langrick (Lincoln).—G.N.R. Witham. (*See Boston.*)

Langwith (Notts).—M.R. Poulter. Lakes: Langwith Lodge. Whaley Mill, 2 m. N. (*See Althorpe.*)

Langworth (Lincoln).—M.R. Langworth. Clay brook. Snelland brook, 1 m. N. Lake: Hackthorn Hall, 7 m. N.W. (*See Boston.*)

Langwathby (Cumland).—M.R. Eden; salmon, trout; preserved by Yorkshire Anglers' Association. (c.s.) (*See Carlisle.*)

Lanternan (Monmouth).—G.W.R. Dowlas brook 2 m. (*See Newport.*)

Lapford (Devon).—L. & S.W.R.—Taw. Lapford water. Washford brook. (c.s.) (*See Barnstaple.*)

Lartington (Yorks).—N.E.R. Scar beck. Tees, 1 m. E.; salmon, trout, bull trout, grayling. (c.s.) (*See Stockton.*)

Launceston (Cornwall).—G.W.R. Tamar; trout; preserved by Mr. Coode, Polapit Tamar, Launceston; Mr. Bradshaw, Lifton Park, Launceston; Mr. Kelly Kelly, Tavistock; these gentlemen will often give leave if properly approached. Yeolm; trout. Attery; trout; river very bushy. Cowdery water, 5 m. Inny, 4 m.; trout; preserved by C. Archer, Esq., Trelaske, Launceston, who will give a few days after April 1st. Penpont water. 4 m.; trout. (c.s. Tamar.) (*See Plymouth and St. Germans.*) Hotels: White Hart and King's Arms.

Lavenham (Suffolk).—G.E.R. Lavenham brook. Bret, 3 m. E.; pike, perch, roach, carp, tench, dace. Lakes: Lavenham Park pond, 4 m. N.E. (*See Manningtree.*)

Lazonby (Cumland).—M.R. Eden; trout. (c.s.) Glassonby beck. Raven beck, 1 m. N. Croglin water, 3 m. N. (*See Carlisle.*)

Lea (Lincoln).—G.N.R. Trent, 1 m. S.; chub, pike, perch, barbel. (c.s.) (*See Gainsborough.*) Tilt, 3 m. S.E. Lakes: Fillingham lake, 8 m. W. (*See Boston.*)

Lea Bridge (Essex).—G.E.R. (*See Stratford.*) On Lea; pike, barbel, roach, bream, carp, chub, tench; s.t. 15s., d.t. 1s. Only annual subscribers can fish for jack.

Leadenham (Lincoln).—G.N.R. Brant, 3 m. W. Sand beck, 3 m. W. Lakes: Leadenham Hall. (*See Boston.*)

Lealholm (York).—N.E.R. Esk; salmon, trout; preserved from Duck Bridge to Fryup beck by the Lealholm and Danby Anglers' Club of 20 members at 15s.; a limited number of m.t. 10s. 6d., and w.t. 3s., are issued by the hon. sec., Mr. Harland Duck, Lealholm. (c.s.) Stonedale beck, 1 m. E.; trout; preserved. Great Fryup beck, 2 m. S.W.; trout; private. (*See Whitby.*)

Leamington (Warwick).—L. & N.W.R.; G.W.R. Avon; bream, chub, dace, roach, pike, perch; preserved by an association; s.t. 10s.; day tickets 2s. 6d. and 2s. for portions of the water may be obtained of the tackleist. Leam; roach, dace, chub, pike, perch, and carp. 3 m. Corporation water; s.t. 2s. 6d., d.t. 6d. (*See Gloucester.*) (*c.s. Severn.*) Tackleist, J. Hobson, Gunmaker.

Leatherhead (Surrey).—L. & S.W.R. (*See London, L.T.*) Mole; trout, dace, and perch; retained by the landowners.

Leaton (Salop).—G.W.R. Severn (1 m. W.); chub, dace, pike, trout, salmon. *Lakes*; Almond Pool, Black Pool, and Henent Pool (2. m. S.) (*See Gloucester.*) (*c.s. Severn.*)

Le Botwood (Salop).—L. & N.W.R.; G.W.R. Cound brook; trout; private. **Row brook** (3½ m. N.E.). Acton brook (4 m. E.). Eaton brook (4 m. S.W.). (*See Gloucester.*)

Lechlade (Gloucester).—G.W.R. On Thames, Colne, and Leach; chub, trout, dace, pike, perch, and roach. Trouting on Leach very good; strictly preserved by the landowners. (*See London, U.T.*)

Ledbury (Hereford).—G.W.R. Leadon. *Lakes*: Eastnor Castle lake (2 m. E.). **Dogberry** pools (3 m.) Canal reservoir (3 m.). (*See Dymock, Gloucester.*) (*c.s. Severn.*)

Lee (Kent).—S.E.R. On Ravensbourne. (*See Lewisham.*)

Leeds (Yorks.).—G.N.R.; L. & N.W.R.; M.R.; N.E.R.; L. & Y.R.; G.C.R. Aire. (*c.s. York.*) Adel beck and dam (private). Killing beck and 2 ponds (private), 2 m. E. *Lakes*: Roundhay Park lakes, 4 m. N.E. Electric cars to gates. The Leeds and District Amalgamated Society of Anglers (hon. sec., Mr. J. N. Green, White Swan Hotel, Call Lane, Leeds) have control of the fishing on these lakes. D.t. 1s. The larger lake (Waterloo) contains pike, chub, perch, roach, tench, carp, &c., and has had a number of rainbow trout and 1200 large chub turned in; the small lake is stocked with trout, carp and roach. At Swinsty and Fewston, 16 m. out, are the Leeds Corporation reservoirs, containing trout. (*See Rawcliffe.*) (*See Clapham.*) *Tackleists*, Walbran Ltd. (*See Advt.*)

Leek (Stafford). — M.R.; L. & N.W.R.; G.N.R. Charnet; trout, grayling, coarse fish; preserved by landowners. (*c.s. Trent*). Hamps, 5 m. E., at Onecote. *Lakes*: Rudyerd reservoir, 3 m. N.W. Lower Acre ponds, 5 m. E. (*See Gainsborough.*)

Leeming (York).—N.E.R. Bedale beck. Swale, 2 m. N.E. (*c.s. York.*) (*See York.*)

Leicester.—M.R.; L. & N.W.R.; G.N.R.; G.C.R. Soar; roach, pike, perch, chub, dace, carp, tench, bream; preserved by the Leicester Angling Society, which society also preserves about 6 m. of the Grand Junction Canal (pike, perch, roach, and tench); sec., Mr. T. S. Jackson. (*c.s. Trent.*) Willow brook. Aylestone brook, 2 m. S.; preserved as Soar. Ingersby brook, 2 m. N.E. Rothley brook, 3 m. N.W., at **Glenfield**. Billesdon brook, 5 m. S. Barkby brook, 5 m. N.E. Quorndon brook, 6 m. N.W., at Bradgate Park; trout; preserved by owner. *Lakes*: Braunston Hall lake, 2 m. S.W. The Pool, 5 m. N.W., at Groby. Queenby Hall lake, 7 m. E., at Hungerton. (*See Gainsborough.*) Thornton reservoirs, 7 m. W. Wreake; Melton Mowbray, 15 m. N.E. to Syston 5 m. N; perch, roach, dace, chub, bream, pike. Queniborough brook, 6 m. N.E. Gaddesby brook, 7 m. N.E. Cropston reservoir, 5 m. N.W. Saddington reservoir, 10 m. S.E. Swithland reservoir, 6 m. *Hotels*: Grand, Wyvern Temperance, Bell, Royal, George, Stag and Pheasant, and Wellington. *Tackleists*, Clarke and Sons, Midland Gun Works, Gallowtree Gate; and Keen and Son, Church Gate.

Leigh (Lancs.).—L. & N.W.R. Glaze brook. *Lakes*: Atherton Hall lake, 1 m. N. (*See Runcorn.*)

Leigh (Stafford).—L. & N.W.R. Blythe (*c.s. Trent*). Tean brook, 2 m. N.E. *Lakes*: Birchwood Park, 2 m. S.W. (*See Gainsborough.*)

Leigh Court (Worcester).—G.W.R. Teme; trout, chub, dace, grayling, pike, perch, salmon; preserved by Mr. L. F. Higgs, of Bridge-street; below to Powick free by favour of riparian owners; from Powick to mouth by Worcester A.S. Leigh brook; trout; preserved by Mr. L. F. Higgs. (*See Gloucester.*) (*c.s. Severn.*)

Leighton Buzzard (Beds.).—L. & N.W.R. Ousel. Battledon Brook. *Lakes*: Rushmore Pond (2 m. N.), Battlesden Park Lakes (4 m. N.E.) (*See King's Lynn.*)

Leintwardine (Hereford).—(n.s. **Hopton Heath**, 2½ m.) Teme; grayling, trout; preserved by the Leintwardine Angling Club of 15 members (hon. sec., A. R. Boughton Knight, Esq. Downton Castle), elsewhere by the landowners; fishing first-class; there is 100 yards of free water below the bridge. Clun; trout, grayling; preserved as the T me. (*See Chepstow.*) (*c.s Severn.*)

Lenwade (Norfolk).—G.E.R. Wensum. (*c.s. N. and S.*) Blackwater brook. (*See Yarmouth.*)

Leominster (Hereford). - L. & N.W.R.; G.W.R. *Hotels*: Royal Oak, Talbot. Lugg; trout, grayling, pike, perch, dace. Above the town the river is preserved by the landowners, but the landlord of the Royal Oak has leave over 2 m. for visitors to the hotel. The Eaton Fishing Club of limited numbers (sec., H. Gosling, Esq., solicitor, Leominster) preserve 3½ m. below the town. (*c.s. Wye.*) Pinsley brook; trout, grayling; preserved by landowners. Ridgemore brook. Cogwell brook. Arrow (1½ m.); trout, grayling, dace, perch; preserved by Eaton Club, above by landowners, and for 3 m. by the Monkland Fishing Club; d.t. of Mr. J. Parry, Westbury. (*c.s. Wye.*) Stretford brook (1½ m.). Humber brook (3 m.). Puddleston brook (4 m.). (*See Chepstow.*)

Levisham (York).—N.E.R. Pickering beck. Levisham beck. Thornton beck. (*See Wressel.*)

Lewes (Sussex).—L.B. & S.C.R. (*See Newhaven.*) On Ouse; pike, perch, bream, roach, dace, chub, and a few trout; preserved by a society; hon. sec., C. H. Morris, Lewes; tickets: Family, 21s.; annual, 10s. 6d.; w.t., 2s. 6d.; daily, 1s. *Hotels*: White Hart, Crown, and Bear.

Lewisham (Kent).—S.E. & C.R. On Ravensbourne. This stream rises by Hayes, runs by **Bromley** 3 m., 3½ m. to **Catford Bridge**, Lewisham 1 m. 1 m. below, at **Lee**, a stream joins Ravensbourne, having a course of 6 *m.* Ravensbourne joins Thames 2 *m.* on at Greenwich.

Leyburn (York).—N.E.R. Ure; grayling, trout; leave at Cover Bridge Inn. (*c s. York.*)—Broomber beck, 1 *m.* N.W. Belleiby beck, 2 *m.* N. Cover, 3 *m.* S.E.; trout, grayling, preserved as Ure. Gill beck, 3 *m.* N.; trout; preserved; leave sometimes. Sowdenbeck, 4 *m.* S.E. Stainton Moor beck, 6 *m.* N. Swale. 7 *m.* N.; grayling, coarse fish. *Hotel*, Bolton Arms. (*c.s. York.*) (*See Middleham, York.*) *Tackleist*, Philip Wray, Town Hall.

Leyland (Lancs.)—L. & N.W.R.; L. & Y.R. Lostock, 2 *m.* E. (*See Hesketh Bank.*)

Leytonstone (Essex).—G.E.R.: M.R. On Roding. (*See Barking.*)

Lichfield (Stafford).—L. & N W.R. Alrewas brook. Blackbrook at Shentone. Ashmere brook, 2 *m.* N.W. Bilston brook, 3 *m.* N.W. Tame, 3 *m.* E. Ben brook, 4 *m.* N.W. *Lakes*: Mill ponds at Lichfield. Swinfen Hall and Freeford Hall, 2 *m.* S.E. (*See Gainsborough.*)

Lidford (Devon).—G.W.R. Lyd; trout; preserved below. Lew, 3 *m.* Tavy, 3 *m.*; trout; preserved by the Tamar and Plym Fishery Board, who issue tickets. (*c.s. Tamar.*) (*See Plymouth.*)

Lidlington (Beds.).—L. & N.W.R. Thame; coarse fish. (*See London, M.T.*)

Lifford (Warwick).—M.R. Rea. Bourne brook, 2 *m.* N. Cole, 2 *m.* E. *Lakes*: Harborne Mill, 2 *m.* N. (*See Gainsborough.*)

Lifton (Devon).—G.W.R. Lid. Thistle brook; trout. (*See Plymouth.*)

Lilbourne (Northton).—L. & N.W.R. Avon: chub, dace, roach, pike, perch, bream. Yelvertoft brook. (*See Gloucester.*) (*c.s. Severn.*)

Limpley Stoke (Wilts).—G.W.R. (*See Bristol.*) On Avon; good all-round fishing; trout, perch. roach, pike; preserved by Avon and Trib. Angling Assoc. hence to Avoncliffe; sec., J. J. Justice, Esq., Carlton Chambers, Baldwin-street, Bristol. (*c.s.*) Midford brook; trout, perch, roach, dace.

Linby (Notts).—M.R.; G.N.R. Leen. *Lakes*: Papplewick Mill ponds, 1 *m.* E. Newstead Abbey lakes, 2 *m.* N. (*See Gainsborough.*)

Lincoln.—G.N.R.; G.E.R.; M.R.; G.C.R. Witham. Foss Dyke Navigation. (*See Boston.*) Ancholme, 12 *m.* N. (*See Brigg.*) George Parkinson, 58, Cross-street, water bailiff for Witham District and for Lincoln A.A.

Linley (Salop).—G.W.R. Severn; pike, perch, chub, dace, salmon. Linley brook. *Lakes*: Willey Park ponds (3 *m.* W.). (*See Gloucester.*) (*c.s. Severn.*)

Linton (Cambs.).—G.E.R. Bourn; trout; preserved by Pembroke College; good fishing. (*See King's Lynn.*)

Liphook (Hants).—L. & S.W.R. *Lakes*: Ripley Pond 2 *m.* Packet and Worlmer ponds 3½ *m.* There is a small trout stream at Fernhurst, 3 *m.* away. (*See London, L.T.*)

Liskeard (Cornwall).—G.W.R. St. Germans river. Seaton river. Looe river, 1 *m.* Looe rises 2 *m.* above **Liskeard**, runs to that town, and 3 *m.* on runs by **Menheniot** Station, 3 *m.* off, on left bank. 2 *m.* down, a short stream joins on left bank, and 5 *m.* down is Looe. Here a stream, 8 *m.* long, joins on right bank. There are trout in the river above the tideway. Good sea fishing. Immediately outside the harbour pollack are caught whiffing. Larger pollack towards the island, dabs at the anchorage, and whiting, &c., in the offing. (*See Fowey, St. Germans,* and *Menheniot.*) *Hotel*: Webb's.

Liss (Hants).—L. & S.W.R. Western Rother: trout. (*See Littlehampton.*)

Litcham (Norfolk).—(n.s. **Dunham**, 3 *m.*). Nar. (*See King's Lynn.*) (*c.s. N and S.*)

Littleborough (Lancs.)—L. & N.W.R.; G.N.R.; M.R. Roch. *Lakes*: Hollingworth reservoir, 1 *m.* S. Spoddle Hill and another reservoir, 2 *m.* N. Blackstone reservoir, 3 *m.* N.E. Lower White Holme reservoir, 4 *m.* N.E. (*See Runcorn.*)

Little Bytham (Lincoln).—G.N.R. Glen. (*See Spalding.*)

Little Eaton (Derby).—M.R. Derwent: pike, coarse fish, grayling, trout (*c.s. Trent*). Holbrook brook. Ecclesbourne, 2 *m.* N.W. Cutler brook, 4 *m* W. *Lakes*: Allastry Hall lake, 2 *m.* S.W. Smalley Mill pond, 3 *m.* N.E. Kedleston Park lakes, 4 *m.* W. (*See Gainsborough.*)

Littlehampton (Sussex). — L.B. & S.C.R. Arun rises in Coolhurst pond in St. Leonard's Forest (pike, perch, roach; leave from C. Dickens, Esq.). Runs 1 *m.* to Hammers pond (pike, perch, roach, dace; leave from P. Sallard, Esq., Crawley) and Hawkins' pond (trout; leave from Col. Aldridge, Horsham). ¼ *m.* on is a pond on the right bank. 1 *m.* on, at Amy's Mill, a stream joins on right bank 3 *m.* long, rising in a lake 1½ *m.* N. of Hawkins' pond, and watering lakes at New Lodge and Highland Farm, near **Horsham.** Arun runs in 1 *m.* to **Horsham**, where it waters a private lake in Hill's Place, just below which Channel brook, 2 *m.* long, from Warnham Mill Pond, joins on right bank. Arun runs in 1 *m.* to **Itchinfield**, 2 *m.* to **Slinfold**, 2½ *m.* to **Rudgwick.** 2 *m.* below a stream joins on right bank, draining the lake at Loxwood, and a mill pond or two 2½ *m.* up. 2 *m.* down Arun on right bank are two lakes by Mallham, and 2 *m.* on is **Billinghurst.** 1 *m.* below, a large stream joins Arun on right bank. This stream rises in five or six large lakes in Shillinglee Park (Lord Winterton) (n.s. **Haslemere**, 4 *m.*), runs 2 *m.* to Evernoll, where more lakes on the common. and a large one in Pheasant Court. At Evernoll a stream 3 *m.* long joins on left bank, rising in some ponds at Ash Park and East End Farm, 1 *m.* W. of Shillinglee Park. (The ponds in the Wealds are innumerable, and are full of fish—carp, pike, perch. and tench.) The main stream now runs 2 *m.* to Kudford where is a lake, and 1 *m.* below is joined by the outflow of three ponds on right bank. 1 *m.* on is Wisborough Green, and Arun 1½ *m.* 5 *m.* down Arun is-

Pulborough. Here the Western Rother joins on right bank. Rother rises at Hawkley Mill, by Empshot, runs 3 m. to **Liss**; here the drainage of a pond ½ m. up joins on right bank. 2 m. down, at Sheet Mill, a stream joins on right bank, rising in Steep Mill 1 m. up. 1 m. down Rother is **Petersfield**. Here is the drainage of the large pond on Petersfield Heath. 2 m. on is the outfall of a lake at Down Park, 1 m. W. of **Rogate** Station. Rother runs 2½ m. to **Elstead**, where the effluent of three lakes lying alongside the road from the station joins on right bank. 1 m. on at Chithurst a stream joins on left bank draining some lakes in Harting Combe, Cook's Pond on Newick Common, Milland Millpool, and some other lakes, all within 2 m. of each other (n.s., **Liphook**), runs 2 m. to Hammer Pond, by Chithurst, and ½ m. to Rother. 2 m. down Rother is the drainage, 3 m. long, on right bank of a lake at Newhouse Farm, ½ m. S. of **Elstead** Station. Rother runs in 2 m. to **Midhurst** and receives the drainage of a lake on Midhurst Common. 1 m. on, on right bank, a stream joins, rising in Bex Mill, 2 m. S. of **Midhurst**, and turning another mill; and 1 m. on is the drainage from the lakes in Cowdry Park on left bank, and the lake on Ambersham Common on right bank. 1½ m. on a stream joins on left bank, rising at Cook's Mill, near Fernhurst (n.s. **Haslemere**), runs 3 m. to Lugershall, and its fine mill pond, ½ m. below which it is joined on left bank by the drainage from the ponds in Chillinghurst Park, and on the right bank by the drainage of the large lake at River Park (trout). 1 m. on, at Salmon Bridge, on the left bank, is the drainage of a pond on River Common (trout) (n.s. for these lakes, **Petworth**), 2 m. on this brook joins Rother. There are trout more or less in all these streams above this point. 1½ m. down Rother a stream joins on right bank, which rises in a pond by Grapham, runs 2 m. to Barrett's Mill and Pond, and ½ m. to Rother. 3 m. on by **Petworth** Station is the drainage of the lakes in Petworth Park (Lord Leconfield), and ½ m. on, on right bank, is the drainage of the large lakes in Burton Park (pike, perch, carp, and tench). 1 m. on, on left bank, is the drainage, 1 m. long, of a lake by Egdean, 2 m. from **Petworth**, and 3 m. on, Rother reaches **Pulborough** and the Arun. 1 m. down Arun on left bank a stream joins, 2 m. long, which waters two mills by West Chiltington, and two lakes on Chiltington Common. 3 m. down Arun a stream, 2½ m. long, joins on right bank, rising in Bignor Mill Pool, and feeding another lake half way down. 2 m. down Arun is **Amberley**; Burpham, 3½ m., and **Arundel**, 2 m.; **Ford**, 2 m. Here a stream joins on left bank, rising in Patching Pond (nearest station, **Goring**, 2 m.: **Arundel**, 4 m.); runs to **Angmering**, 2 m., where the drainage of four lakes at New Place, 1 m. up, joins on right bank; and 2½ m. on is Arun. Hence to **Littlehampton** and the sea is 3 m. Good fishing from the pier, also grey mullet and sand smelts. Open sea fishing but moderate. *Hotel:* Beach.

Littleport (Cambs.).—G.E.R. *Hotels:* Railway, Black Horse, Granby. Ouse; coarse fish, except barbel; preserved up to **Ely** by South Level Commissioners; tickets of H. Archer, Esq., solicitor, Ely; baits from E. Pettit, Sandhill Bridge. (*See Cambridge.*) (c.s. *N. and S.*) E. Pettit, Sandhill Bridge, Littleport, will afford all information and supply all requisites. The Great Ouse below the Creek is preserved by Capt. Taylor. *Hotels:* Granby, Railway Tavern, Black Horse, Globe. Brandon Creek (Capt. Luddington); *Inn,* Ship (a punt and fishing attached). A fine stretch of Ouse, 2 m. long, connecting the Commissioners' fishing with Mr. H. T. Luddington's water, which extends from Capt. Taylor's, Egremont House, to 1 m. towards Littleport, is now being preserved by Ouse and Nen Fishery District Board, who have stopped all netting. Mildenhall Drain; poor fishing. Old Croft River; poor fishing. Lark (3 m. S.); coarse fish; free. Little Ouse or Brandon (3 m. N.); preserved by W. C. Peacock, Esq., who grants a limited number of tickets. *Inn:* Ship, comfortable. (*See King's Lynn.*)

Little Ribston (York), n.s. **Wetherby**, 4 m.—Nidd. (c.s. *York.*) Crimple beck. Allerton beck, 1 m. E. (*See York.*)

Little Salkeld (Cumland).—M.R. Eden; trout. (c.s.) Briggle beck. Hunsonby beck. Blencarn beck, 3 m. S.E. (*See Carlisle.*)

Liverpool (Lancs.). — L. & N.W.R.; M.R.; L. & Y.R.; G.W.R.; C. Lines. Fishing can be had in Rivington reservoirs, belonging to the Corporation—non-ratepayers' s.t. 2l. 2s., d.t. 3s.: ratepayers—s.t. 1l. 1s., d.t. 1s. 6d., on application to the Water-Engineer, Municipal Officer. Fly only, except in Lower Rivington reservoirs, and the Lower Roddlesworth and Rake brook reservoirs. Lochleven trout season from March 15 to Sept. 30; no wading; no dogs; no Sunday fishing. The Liverpool Angling Association (C. E. Hornby, hon. sec., Club House, Stork Hotel, Queen-square) has private fishing in a lake at Knowsley (coarse fish and a few trout and grayling); entrance 2s. 6d., life 7l. 7s., s.t. 12s. 6d., d.t. for friends 2s. 6d. The Sefton and Newsham lakes in the public parks are stocked with trout and coarse fish; licences 10s. 6d. per annum for ratepayers or inhabitants of the city, 1l. 1s. for others. Meols Lake Fishery (trout, roach, perch, carp, &c.), s.t. 2s., d.t. 6d. of the tackleist. There is some free fishing also in the rivers Dee, Alyn, and Alt, all within easy access. Good fishing about **St. Helens**, under the St. Helens Angling Association; hon. sec., Mr. H. M. Greer, 7, Haydock-street, St. Helens; d.t. to members' friends 1s., at the Cotham Arms Hotel. The Association has fishing in two Corporation waters (St. Ann's dam and Leg of Mutton dam), and in the L. & N.W.R. Co.'s canal from Redgate Bridge to Carr Mill. Eccleston mere (A. Walmsley Cotham, Esq., J.P.) by permission. Fishing in Garswood New dam, (trout) strictly preserved; Stanley Mill dam, Eccleston Mill dam, Mr. Swift's dam, at d.t. 1s. Carr Mill dam (trout), near St. Helens (Sir Dd. Gamble, Bart., by permission). About

Northwich is some good general fishing; s.t. 3*s*., d.t. 6*d*.; apply to Mr. G. Scales, Wincham, Northwich. The Bolton Association has some good and extensive fishing: members only; sec., G. T. Moore, 19, Raphael-street, Bolton. The Northern Anglers' Association (sec., T. W. Redford, 57, Dorset-street, Bolton) has fishing in the Shropshire Union, Trent and Mersey, and the Lancaster canals; s.t. 2*s*. 6*d*. *Tackleist*, W. Ramsbottom, 14B, N. John-street.

Lizard, The (Cornwall).—Good bass and pollack fishing from the rocks here in summer time, with salmon rod and light artificial baits.

Llandenny (Monmouth).—G W.R. Olway; trout; preserved. Raglan brook. Pill brook. (*See Newport.*)

Llanfihangel (Monmouth).—G.W.R. Honddu; trout, preserved by the landowners. (*See Chepstow.*)

Llanfyllin (Salop) C.R. *Lake Vyrnwy*, 10 *m*. Good trouting, fish averaging ½-lb. River Vyrnwy, 3 *m*. River Cowrny, 2 *m*. River Machnant, 2 *m*.; strictly preserved by hotel proprietor. *Hotel*: Lake Vyrnwy.

Llangurig (Monmouth). — Wye; trout. (*c s.*) Bidno (1 *m*.). Tavenig (5 *m*.). *Llyns*, Helygen (6 *m*.). Gwngy (7 *m*.) (*See Chepstow.*)

Llan-y-blodwell (Salop).—Tanat; trout, grayling, chub, &c. Cynlliath (3 *m*. W.). Vyrnwy (2 *m*. S.); trout, salmon, chub, &c.; preserved by the landowners. (*See Llanymynech.*) Cain; trout, salmon (3 *m*. S.); preserved as Vyrnwy. (*See Gloucester.*) (*c.s. Severn.*)

Llanymynech (Salop). — C.R. Vyrnwy; preserved by landowners, leave freely given; trout, salmon, grayling, roach, perch, pike, chub, &c.; there is a good stretch of free water. Tanat (2 *m*. N.W.); trout, grayling, chub, pike, &c.; a portion free. Morda (1 *m*. E.); pike, chub, trout; a portion free. Severn (4 *m*. S.); trout, salmon, chub, pike, perch; free. Cain (4 *m*. W.); trout, salmon a portion free. (*See Gloucester.*) (*c.s. Severn.*) *Hotel*: Cross Keys.

Lockington (York).—N.E.R. Pike beck. Scarborough beck. Hull, 2 *m*. E. (*c.s. York.*) (*See Hull.*)

Loddiswell (Devon).—G.W.R. Avon; trout, salmon. Avon rises on Dartmoor, and 7 *m*. down is joined on right bank by Red brook, 3 *m*. long. Avon runs 2 *m*. to **Brent**, and 2 *m*. below, Black brook, 2 *m*. long, joins on left bank. Avon runs 2 *m*. to Diptford, 1 *m*. to Bickham Bridge, Newhouse 2 *m*., **Loddiswell** 4 *m*. Here Woodleigh brook, 7 *m*. long, joins on left bank. 3 *m*. down Avon is Aveton Giffard, to which the tide flows. (*c.s.*) Avon is preserved by the Avon Fishing Association hence to beyond Shipley Bridge; s.t. (limited to 30) 40*s*., m.t. 20*s*., w.t. 10*s*.; sec., C. E. Turner, Esq., solicitor, Salcombe: *rod licences* — salmon 20*s*., trout 10*s*., w.t. 5*s*., d.t. 2*s*.; from C. E. Turner, Esq. *Hotel*: Turk's Head.

Loddon (Norfolk), n.s. **Beccles**, 7 *m*., G.E.R.—Thet. Yare, 3 *m*. N.E. (*See Yarmouth.*)

Lodge Hill (Somerset.)—G.W.R. Ax. (*See Axbridge.*) (*c.s. Avon.*)

London.—On Thames and New River. New River rises by **Hertford**, and flows to **Hoddesdon**; **Broxbourne**, 2 *m*.; **Cheshunt**, 5 *m*.; **Waltham**, 1½ *m*.; **Enfield**, 6 *m*.; **Winchmore Hill**, 2½ *m*.; **Wood Green**, 6 *m*.; **Hornsey**, 1½ *m*.; **Torrington Park**, 3½ *m*. Here at Stoke Newington are the New River Company's waterworks and reservoirs, where the fishing is very good (pike, perch, &c.), but strictly forbidden.

UPPER THAMES. — Thames rises at Thames Head, near **Tetbury-road Station.** It flows through Pool Keynes, Somerford Keynes (good preserved trouting depending on the wetness or dryness of the seasons), Ashton Keynes (pike, chub, &c.), where it is joined on left bank by Swill brook, 5 *m*. long. 4 *m*. on, at Cricklade (pike fishing is very good and free. *Hotels*: White Hart and White Horse). Churn joins Thames on left bank. Churn rises by Cubberly (Glo'ster), and in 14 *m*. runs to **Cirencester,** passing Colesbourn, Rendcomb, and North Cerney, where the trouting is good and preserved. The owner of Rendcomb Park sometimes gives leave. 12 *m*. on Thames is reached, passing South Cerney midway. ½ *m*. down Thames, Dancy brook, 4 *m*. long, joins on right bank, and ½ *m*. on Ray joins on right bank. Ray rises in a mill head at Wroughton, 2½ *m*. from **Swindon,** and 6 *m*. on, a brook joins on left bank, running out of a large lake at Lydiad Tregoz, 2½ *m*. up stream. 1 *m*. down Ray **Purton** is reached, 1 *m*. from the river. Thames is 6 *m*. on. 8 *m*. down Thames Byde Mill brook joins on right bank. This brook runs out of a large lake at Warnford Place; nearest station, **Shrivenham,** and is 8 *m*. long. 1 *m*. down Thames, Cole joins on right bank (coarse fish and a few trout). Cole rises in Cole Reservoir, 2 *m*. from **Swindon,** and in 5 *m*. is joined by a stream on right bank, which has a large mill head 2 *m*. up. 4½ *m*. on a stream joins on right bank, which drains a large lake in Beckett Park, 1½ *m*. up (nearest station, **Shrivenham**). From hence to Thames is 8 *m*., passing Coleshill. 1½ *m*. down Thames, at **Lechlade,** Colne joins on left bank. The Glo'ster Colne rises in a mill pond 1½ *m*. N. of **Shipton,** runs to Withington, 3 *m*., Yanworth 4 *m*., Coln St. Dennis 3 *m*., Coln Rogers 1 *m*., **Bibury** 3 *m*., Coln St Aldwin's 1½ *m*., Hatherobs 1 *m*., Quenington 1 *m*., **Fairford** 2½ *m*., **Lechlade** 6 *m*. 1 *m*. below, Leach joins Thames on left bank. Leach rises at North Leach, and runs in 13 *m*. to East Leach Turville, 1½ *m*. to Southrop, and Thames 4 *m*., passing Little Faringdon, 1 *m*. from **Lechlade** station. 3 *m*. down Thames Kelmscott is reached, thence to Tadpole Bridge, near **Bampton,** 2½ *m*. off the river, is 7 *m*. 5 *m*. down, Charney brook joins on left bank. Charney rises in a mill pond at Black Bourton, 1 *m*. W. of Bampton, and running through that town joins Thames 5 m. down. 3 m. on, at Newbridge (some good preserved fishing below), Windrush joins Thames on left bank. Windrush rises in a mill pond at Guiting Power (Glo'ster), and runs in 7 m. to **Bourton-on-the-Water**. 1½ m. below, Dickler river joins Windrush on the left bank. Dickler rises in Donnington Mill, 2 m. N.W. of **Stow**, and is 6 m. long. 1½ m. down Windrush is Rissington, and 2 m. on a stream joins on the right bank, which rises in a mill pond at Sherborne, 2 m. up. 1½ m. down Windrush is Windrush and Barrington, Tainton 2 m., Burford 1½ m., **Witney** 11 m., Ducklington 1 m.. Standlake 4 m. (large trout), and 2 m. on the Thames. 7 m. down Thames is **Eynsham**. *Hotel*: Red Lion and Swan. 1 m. below, Evenlode river joins Thames on left bank. Evenlode rises in a lake close by **Adlestrop**. ½ m. down, at Daylesford, is a large pond. 3 m. down, at **Chipping Norton** junction, a stream joins on left bank, which rises in a mill pond by Little Rollwright, runs to Salford, 1½ m., **Chipping Norton** (1½ m. off) ½ m., Church Hill 3 m., Evenlode 2 m. Evenlode next runs in 4½ m. to **Shipton**, 1½ m. to **Ascott**. 5 m. on, at Shorthampton, a stream joins on left bank, which drains a mill pond 1 m. up. From here to **Charlbury** is 1 m. 1 m. below, the overflow from several large ponds (trout) in Cornbury Park joins Evenlode on the right bank. 5 m. on is Stonesfield, and 6 m. on, at **Hanbrough**, Glyme River joins on left bank. Glyme rises in some lakes in Heythrop Park, 2 m. above Enstone, where it is joined on right bank by a stream 3 m. long, which works some mills. Glyme flows next to Glympton 5 m., and Wootton 3 m. Here Darne River joins on the left bank. Darne rises in some pools by Sandford, runs 1 m. to Westcot Barton, and 7 m. on to Glyme. Woodstock is 2 m. on down Glyme. Here the river waters the large lakes in Blenheim Park (pike, strictly preserved), and in 2 m. reaches Evenlode, and 5 m. on Evenlode joins Thames (Lord Abingdon preserves the left bank of Thames for some distance). Hence to **Oxford** is 5 m.

MIDDLE THAMES.—At **Oxford** Cherwell joins Thames on left bank. Cherwell rises in Northampton 1 m. above Woodford (nearest station **Byfield**), and flows in 8½ m. to **Copredy**. There are eight mills. At **Cropredy** a stream joins on right bank, which rises in two reservoirs by **Cropredy**, 3 m. below which a stream joins on right bank, rising in Wormleighton reservoir (nearest station **Fenny Compton**); 3 m. down this stream the overflow from Clattercutt reservoir, 1 m. off, and 1 m. from Claydon village, joins on right bank. 2 m. down, Cropredy is reached. 4 m. down Cherwell, passing four mills, a stream joins on right bank, which rises by Farnborough in a large lake, and is 7 m. long, passing Mollington and Hanwell. 2 m. down Cherwell **Banbury** is reached, and King Sutton in 5 m., where a stream 1½ m. long joins on left bank, draining a lake at Astrop House. 1½ m. down Cherwell two streams join on right bank. The first rises in a pool by Cherrington, and working five mills, and passing Shutford half-way, reaches Broughton in 5 m. Here two streams join, one on right bank and one on left bank. The first rises by Horley, in a pool, and flowing by Drayton and Wroxton, 2 m. from Banbury, has a course of 5 m., likewise draining the lake in Wroxton Abbey. The other rises in a pool by Epwell, and is 5½ m. long, passing Tadmarton village. From Broughton to the junction at Cherwell is 8 m., passing Adderbury and working 3 mills. The second stream is the Swere, which, rising in Priory mill pool by Great Rollwright, runs in 3 m. to Swerford Park, where it waters a large lake, and 10 m. down joins Cherwell, passing South Newington and Barford, and four mills. 2 m. down Cherwell, **Aynho** is reached (Deddington is 1½ m. off), and 2 m. on a stream joins on right bank, which drains some lakes by Great Tew and Lower Warton, and, passing close to Deddington, has a course of 8 m. One m. below the junction of this stream with Cherwell, **Somerton** is reached; 4½ m. on is **Heyford**; 5½ m., **Kirtlington**; 2 m., **Woodstock Road**, and Islip, 4 m. Here Ray joins on left bank. Ray rises by **Bicester**, and is 8 m. long. At Islip a stream joins Ray on right bank, which rises in a large lake in Middleton Park, 3 m. from **Bicester**, and is 8 m. long. The Cherwell now runs in 6 m. to **Oxford**. The Thames next flows in 2 m. to Iffley. (*Inn*: Isis Tavern.), Kennington 1 m., Sandford 1 m. (*Inn*: King's Arms), and **Abingdon** 5½ m. Ock rises west of Chartrey Basset, and 6 m. below that village a stream joins on the right bank 9 m. long, which, rising in a mill pool at Letcombe Regis, and, passing Wantage and East Hanney, feeds three mills. The Ock now flows in 4 m. to **Abingdon**. 2 m. down Thames a stream joins on right bank, which is 9 m. long. It rises in some pools near Ardington and flows to **Steventon** in 4 m., thence 5 m. to Sutton Courteney-on-Thames, working six mills. **Culham** is on the opposite side of river. Thames now flows to Appleford, 2 m., Long Wittenham, 1½ m. (*inn*, The Vine Cottage); Clifton Hampden, 1 m. (*Inns*: Barley Mow and Plough; good fishing); Little Whittenham, 2½ m.; ½ m. below which Thame joins Thames on left bank. Thame (a good pike and roach river) rises some 9 m. above **Aylesbury**. 6 m. down is Coddington, and Chearsley 1 m. 1 m. below, at Notley Abbey, a stream joins on right bank, which rises in a large lake at Wotton. 1 m. down a stream joins on right bank, 1 m. long, which drains the lake in Dorton. 5 m. on Thame river is reached; 3 m. on **Thame** is reached; 5 m., **Liddington**; Wheatley, 5 m.; Addesden, 2 m.; Stadhampton, 4 m. ½ m. below, Baldon brook, 5 m. long, joins on right bank. 2 m. down Thame is Drayton, and Dorchester 2 m. further. *Hotels*: White Hart, Fleur-de-lis, and Crown.) ½ m. on Thames is reached. Shillingford is 1 m. down Thames, Bensington 1½ m. (a few trout, pike, and perch), and **Wallingford** 1½ m. Here a stream joins on right bank, which, rising in a mill pool at Blewberry, runs 3 m. to South Moreton, feeding four mills, thence

3 *m.* to **Wallingford.** 1½ *m.* below Wallingford, and close to Thames on left bank, is a large lake at Mongewell. Thames now runs in 3 *m.* to **Moulsford;** Streatley (*Private Hotel*, River View; *Inn*, Swan. *Fisherman*, Saunders), and **Goring** 3 *m.* (*Hotel*, Miller of Mansfield.) **Pangbourne** 4 *m.* Here the Pang (a fine trout stream, strictly preserved), some 12 *m.* long, joins on right bank. Thames next runs in 3 *m.* to Mapledurham and Purley (n.s. **Tilehurst.** *Hotel*: Roebuck. Caversham *Inns*: Crown and Caversham Hotel), and **Reading** 4 *m.* Kennet here joins Thames. Kennet rises a few miles north of East Kennet, runs 1 *m.* to West Overton, Tyfield 2 *m.*, **Marlborough** 2 *m.*, Ramsbury 6 *m.*, **Hungerford** 4 *m.* Here Dunn joins on right bank, 3 *m.* long, which flows out of two ponds at Froxfield. Kennet next runs to **Kintbury** 4 *m.*, and 2 *m.* below the river runs through Hampstead Park (Lord Craven), where the drainings of a series of lakes in the park, holding trout, joins on the right bank (the river, ponds, and canal, good perching, is preserved by Lord Craven); **Newbury** 2½ *m.* 1 *m* down Kennet, Lambourne river joins on left bank. Lambourne rises by Lambourne, runs to Eastbury 1½ *m.*, East Garston 1 *m.*, Great Shelford 1½ *m.*, Boxford 3 *m.*, and Kennet 5 *m.* Kennet now flows in 3 *m.* to **Thatcham, Midgham** 3 *m.*, **Aldermaston** 2 *m.* 1½ *m.* below, Emburne river joins Kennet on right bank. Emburne rises in a pond on Holt Common, and in 1½ *m.* is joined by a brook on right bank, which drains some ponds 2 *m.* up. Emburne runs in 2 *m.* to Newton (2 *m.* S. of **Newbury,** and 4 *m.* on is joined by a stream on right bank, 3½ *m.* long, rising in a mill pool at Kingsclere. Emburne now runs to **Midgham** 4 *m.*, **Aldermaston** 3 *m.*, Kennet 1½ *m.*; Kennet runs in 3 *m.* to **Theale,** and Thames 6 *m.* Thames now runs in 2½ *m.* to Sonning. (*Inns*: Bull, White Hart, and French Horn. Fishermen must be bespoken from Reading. Good for pike above. The mill tails belong to Mr. Witherington; preserved by the Reading Association from Goring to Shiplake lock); 2½ *m.* to **Shiplake,** and 1½ *m.* to Wargrave (n.s. **Shiplake** or **Twyford,** 2 *m.*). Lodden here joins Thames (good trouting, strictly preserved in the upper part, pike, perch, and coarse fishing). Lodden rises in Newram Springs, a series of ponds close to **Basingstoke,** and 7 *m.* down is joined on left bank by a stream rising in a mill pool 3 *m.* up by Bramley. 3 *m.* down Loddon. Strathfieldsay, the Duke of Wellington's place, is reached (leave must be obtained from the Duke. *Inn*: Wellington Arms. Pike, perch, &c. Nearest station, **Mortimer**), and 4 *m.* on, at Swallowfield, Blackwater joins Loddon. Blackwater rises in a large pond by **Farnborough,** and runs in 5 *m.* to **Blackwater,** where a stream joins on right bank, rising in a lake 1 *m.* up. Blackwater runs in 3 *m.* to **Sandhurst.** 5½ *m.* down Whitewater joins Blackwater on left bank. Whitewater rises in a lake by Grewell, and 1 *m.* down waters a large lake at Wanboro' Castle, by Odiham town (nearest station **Winchfield,** 2 *m.* off). 8 *m.* down, at Heckfield, a stream joins on right bank, which rises in a large lake, Fleet Pond, by the L. & S.W.R., 3½ *m.* from **Farnborough** station, and is 7½ *m.* long. Whitewater joins Blackwater in 2 *m.*, and hence to Loddon is 2 *m.* Loddon runs in 9 *m.* to **Twyford** taking up two branches down to Twyford Mill. First, the main stream out of Hants by Swallowfield, Arborfield, and Early (**Loddon Bridge**) 1 *m.* falls in. Secondly, a stream from Easthampstead Park and Wokingham, thence 3 *m.* by Hurst and Whistley to **Twyford** (all private). Thirdly, from Cæsar's Camp, Bagshot, by Easthamptead village to **Bracknell** (1 *m.*) ½ *m.* receives a small stream from Ascot Place by Warfield, and bending east by north with long curve near St. Lawrence Waltham, through Ruscombe, course about 10 *m.*, to Twyford Mill (all private). Then full river 2½ *m.* to Thames at Wargrave; preserved by Reading and Henley United Associations; good coarse fishing, and some trout and grayling. The Patrick stream runs from Thames about half-way between Shiplake and Sonning into Loddon 1½ *m.* below Twyford on left or west bank, and is preserved by R. and H. Association; s.t. 21*s.* for Loddon and Patrick stream. Henley and District Angling Association preserves the water from Shiplake to Henley (hon. sec., A. E. Hobbs, Hart-street, Henley-on-Thames); s.t., including Loddon and Patrick streams, 21*s.* Thames now runs to Wargrave; (*Inns*: St. George and the Dragon, and White Hart); 2 *m.* to **Henley,** Remenham, 1½ *m.*; Hambledon, 2 *m.* (The lock-keeper makes up a bed or two); Medmenham, 2½ *m.* (*Inn*, Ferry Hotel. *Fisherman*: R. Young). Hurley, 1½ *m.* (Above the lock on left bank is a stream under the woods holding dace.) **Great Marlow,** 3 *m.*: **Bourne End,** 4 *m.* Here Wye joins on left bank. Wye rises in a large mill pool by **West Wycombe,** runs in 2½ *m.* to **High Wycombe,** 3½ *m.* to **Loudwater,** 2 *m.* to **Woburn,** and joins Thames 2½ *m.* below. Thames runs to **Cookham** 1½ *m.*, **Maidenhead** 4 *m.*, 1½ *m.* to Bray: (*Hotel*: George. Bray mill tail is private.) Monkey Island, 2 *m.* (*Hotel*: Monkey Island. The water from just below Bray Lock to Col. Hertford's is private.) Dorney 1½ *m.*, and 4 *m.* to Clewer. Eton, and **Windsor.** Here a stream joins on left bank, 4 *m.* long, draining a large lake in Stoke Park 2 *m.* from **Slough.** 1 *m.* below Windsor a stream 4½ *m.* long joins Thames on left bank, which rises in the large lake in Black Park, and in the lake in Langley Park, 1 *m.* on, nearest station **Langley,** 1 *m.* off. Thames runs 1 *m.* to **Datchet,** 2½ *m.* to Old Windsor (nearest station **Wraysbury,** 1½ *m.* *Hotel*: Bells of Ouseley). 2½ *m.* on the Hertford Colne joins Thames. Colne (under the name of Ver) rises by Redburn (nearest station **Harpenden,** 2½ *m.*), runs to **St. Alban's** 4 *m.*, **Park-street** 2 *m.*, and 2 *m.* on is joined on left bank by a stream which rises by London Colney, and in 2 *m.* is joined by a stream on left bank, which rises in Elstree reservoir, **Elstree,** 1½ *m.* off, and runs in 3 *m.* to **Radlett,** 1 *m.* below joining the parent brook, which joins Colne 1 *m.* below. Colne runs to **Watford Junction,** 3 *m.* Here a stream 2 *m.* long

joins on left bank, running out of some ponds at Hill Field Lodge (pike, perch, carp, roach ; good fishing ; strictly preserved). 1 m. on is **Watford**, and **Rickmansworth** 4½ m. Gade river joins here on right bank. Gade rises in some ponds by Great Gaddesden, runs 3 m. to **Hemel Hempstead**, and 1 m. below, at **Box Moor**, is joined by a brook on right bank. which rises by **Berkhampstead**, and is 4 m. long. Gade runs next to **King's Langley** 4 m., and **Rickmansworth** 6 m. Here Chess joins Colne on right bank. Chess rises by Chesham (good trouting preserved by Lord Chesham) runs 5 m. to Cheneys (good trouting preserved by the Duke of Bedford to Sarratt Mill, and below by different owners. Below Sarratt are some coarse fish, and below Loudwater the stream is polluted). Chess runs to **Rickmansworth** 5 m. 6 m. down Colne, Misbourne stream joins on right bank. Misbourne passes Great Missenden (capital trouting in the lakes at Missenden Abbey), runs 2 m. to Little Missenden, and 1 m. on waters the large lake at Shardloes (Mr. Drake, from whom leave must be obtained). Amersham is 1 m. on, Chalfont St. Giles, 3 m., Chalfont St. Peter's 1½ m., and Colne 5 m. Colne, in numerous streams, runs to **Uxbridge** 1 m. **West Drayton** 3 m. Here a stream joins on left bank, rising in Ruislip reservoir (fishing strictly preserved) ; runs to **Rickmansworth**, 4 m., to Ruislip 1 m. **Uxbridge** 3 m., Hillingdon 1 m., **West Drayton** 2 m., **Colnbrook** 1¼ m. (*Hotel*: Golden Cross), **Wraysbury** 2 m., and joins Thames, with several outfalls, 1 m. on.

*LOWER THAMES—***Staines** is 1 m. down Thames, Laleham 2½ m. (*Inn*: Horseshoe.) **Chertsey** 1½ m., **Weybridge** 2 m. Bourne brook and Wey here join Thames on right bank. Bourne brook divides into two parts close to its effluence, the left stream rises in the lakes at Sunninghill Park and Silwood Park (nearest station **Ascot**), runs 1½ m. to Virginia Water and the other ponds in Windsor Park (nearest station, **Virginia Water**), 3 m. to Chertsey, and 1½ m. to the junction. The right stream rises by Chobham, runs 3 m., and is joined on left bank by a stream 2½ m. long, rising in Glover's, Gracious, and other ponds (good tench fishing), and in ½ m. waters the lake in Ottershaw Park (good tench fishing, nearest station **Woking Common**), and 4½ m. on joins Thames. The Wey rises by **Alton**, Hants, and runs 1 m. to Holybourne, Froyle 1½ m., **Farnham** 6½ m. 2 m. down, a stream 4 m. long joins on left bank, running out of a lake by Alder Holt Wood, 3 m. from **Farnham**. 2½ m. down Wey a stream joins on right bank, which rises in Ripsley pond, 2 m. W. of **Liphook**. 1 m. on a stream joins on right bank, draining a pond close to the station. 1 m. on Parket pond is reached. 1 m. down, a stream 1 m. long joins on left bank, draining Woolmer pond and two others close by. Greatham village is 1 m. off, and **Liphook** 3½ m. 1 m. on a stream joins on right bank, rising by **Haslemere**, in some ponds ; runs 4 m. to Bramshot, where it is joined by a stream 1½ m. long, draining some ponds on Greyshot Down. 2½ m. on is the main stream, which runs 2 m., when it is joined on left bank by a stream draining the lake in Headley Park. 1 m. on, the drainings of two lakes on Wishang Down (one holding trout, the other pike and perch ; leave from the owner of Greyshot Hall) joins on right bank. 1 m. on the outflow of Frensham Great pond joins on right bank. 1 m. on is Frensham (nearest station **Farnham**, 4 m.), and 1 m. on the outflow of Frensham Little Pond joins on right bank. These two ponds are 1 m. apart on Frensham Common. 1 m. on Wey is reached. 1½ m. down Wey the outflow of Abbot's Pond and two lakes on Hankley Common join on right bank. These ponds are 1 m. from Frensham Little Pond. 1½ m. down, at Elstead, a stream 2 m. long drains a pond on Thursley Common, about 1 m. from Abbot's Pond. 1 m. below Elstead the drainings of the lakes on Puttenham Common join on left bank (nearest station, **Tongham**, 3 m.). 1½ m. down Wey a stream 2 m. long joins on right bank draining Hammer's Pond on Witley Common (nearest station, **Milford**, 2½ m.). 2½ m. down Wey is **Godalming**. Here a stream joins on right bank, rising in some ponds by Witley, runs 2 m. to **Milford**, where a stream joins on right bank, draining a pond 1 m. up. ½ m. on is the draining of a lake at Bushbridge, 1 m. up. 1½ m. on is **Godalming**. 1 m. down Wey the drainage of New and Old Pond joins on left bank. 1 m. on a stream joins on right bank rising in a large lake 1 m. from **Crawleigh**, runs 4 m. to **Bramley**, where the drainage of some ponds, 1½ m. up, on Black Heath, joins on right bank. 1½ m. on is Wey which runs to **Shelford** where Tillingbourne joins on right bank, rising in a lake on Abinger Common, runs to **Gomshall**, 3 m., Shiere 1 m., where it feeds the lakes in Albury Park 1 m. on, below which it feeds some lakes, and **Shelford** is 3 m. on. Wey runs to **Guildford**, 1 m. At Stoke, 1 m. on. the drainage of a lake 1 m. up on left bank joins Wey ; 3 m. on is **Woking** ; and 2 m. on, at Ripley, two streams join on right bank and left bank. The one drains the ponds in Clandon Park, 3 m. from **Guildford**, and is 4 m. long: the other rises in some ponds close to the railway (**Pirbright**), and 2 m on is joined on left bank by the drainage of a pond on Pirbright Common 1 m. up, and ½ m. on the drainage of two other ponds, 1½ m. up, runs in on right bank. and ½ m. on is the drainage of another pond on right bank. 3 m. down a stream joins on right bank, rising in a pond on Broad Street Common, 2 m. from **Guildford**, runs 2 m. to Whitemore Common. where it waters a lake, and ½ m. on joins Whitmore pond, reaching the main brook 1 m. on. The stream next runs to **Woking**, and 2 m. on reaches Wey, which runs to Witley, 1 m.; Byfleet, 1 m.; and **Weybridge**, 4 m. here a stream joins on right bank, rising in two ponds on Horsley Common ; runs 4 m. to Wisley, where the drainage of Hut Pond (carp, pike, roach ; d.t. 1s., at the inn next the pond). and several other ponds on Witley and Ockham Common, join on right bank, and 1½ m. on, on right bank, is the overflow of a pond on Cobham Common. 2 *m.* on is **Weybridge.** Here the outfall of the lake in Oatlands Park joins Wey on right bank close to the Thames. Thames flows next to **Shepperton,** ½ *m*; Hallitord, ½ *m.* (*Hotels*: Ship, Anchor, Red Lion.); Walton-on-Thames, 1 *m.* (*Hotels*: Duke's Head, Swan.) ½ *m.* below a stream joins Thames on left bank, draining a lake at Littleton, close to Laleham. Thames runs next to **Sunbury,** ½ *m.*; **Hampton,** 2 *m.*; Moulsey and **Hampton Court,** 1 *m.* Mole here joins Thames. Mole rises in two large lakes close by the H.B.R., 1 *m.* W. of **Crawley,** and in 1 *m.* is joined by the drainings of a lake close to on the right bank. 1 *m.* on, on right bank, a stream joins 1½ *m.* long, which rises in a pond in Tilgate Forest, and in ½ *m.* joins another large pond. **Crawley** is 1 *m.* N. Mole runs in 1 *m.* to **Three Bridges; Horley,** 3 *m.*; here a stream joins on left bank, which rises by Charlwood, and in 3 *m.* is joined by a stream 2 *m.* long, draining a lake at Woolborough 1 *m.* N. of **Three Bridges.** 2½ *m.* below **Horley** a stream joins Mole on right bank, which rises in some pools by **Rowfant,** and 1 *m.* on is joined by the overflow of lakes at Bashford Castle on the right bank, and two lakes by Wakeham's Green on the left bank. **Rowfant** Station is 1 *m.* N.E. and N.W. from each of these lakes. This stream now runs to **Horley,** 3 *m.*, and Mole, 3 *m.* 1 *m.* on, a stream joins Mole, rising in the large lake in Gatton Park, by **Merstham,** and in a smaller lake ½ *m.* E. of Merstham, runs to **Red Hill,** 3½ *m.*, and Mole, 5 *m.* 2 *m.* down Mole a stream 3 *m.* long joins on left bank, draining Ewood Pond, 1½ *m.* from **Holmwood** Station. Mole runs next to **Betchworth,** 4 *m.*; **Dorking,** 1½ *m.* Here Pip brook joins on left bank, draining some ponds belonging to R. Fuller, Esq., of the Rookery, 4 *m.* on up by Wootton. Mole runs to **Box Hill,** 1½ *m.*; **Leatherhead,** 4 *m*; Cobham, 4 *m.*; **Esher,** 4½ *m.*; **Moulsey,** Thames, 2½ *m.* Thames runs to **Thames Ditton,** 1 *m.*; **Kingston,** 2 *m.* Here Hogg's Mill river joins on right bank. The stream rises by **Ewell,** and 1½ *m.* below is joined on left bank by a stream rising in some ponds on Epsom Common (nearest station, **Epsom,** and is 3 *m.* long. Hogg's Mill runs to **Malden,** 1 *m.*; **Kingston,** Thames, 2½ *m.* Thames flows to **Teddington,** 1 *m.*; here a branch of the Colne running from Harmondsworth joins on left bank. It passes Stanwell, 2 *m.* (nearest station, **Ashford,** 2 *m.*). East Bedfont, 1 *m.*, **Feltham,** 1 *m.*, and **Teddington,** 4 *m.* Thames runs to **Twickenham,** 1½ *m.*; **Richmond,** 1½ *m.*; **Isleworth,** 1 *m.* Yedding brook here joins Thames. Yedding rises some miles N. of Cranford (nearest station, **Southall,** 1½ *m.*), runs 5½ *m.* to **Twickenham,** where a branch of Colne joins it, and passing several powder and other mills, 2 *m.* on joins Thames. Thames runs next to **Brentford,** 1 *m.* Here Brent joins on left bank. Brent rises in a lake on the property of the late Lord Tenterden, runs to the decoy at **Hendon,** runs to **Welsh Harp** reservoir, 1 *m.* Here a stream joins on right bank 3 *m.* long, which holds fish—pike, perch, roach—at times. Brent runs in 1 *m.* to Kingsbury. Twyford (Middlesex), 2½ *m.* (nearest station **Willesden Junction,** 2 *m.*); Perivale, 1½ *m.* (pike, bream, and tench in a mill pond; d.t., 1*s.*) Greenford, 1 *m.*; **Hanwell,** 1½ *m.*; Thames, 3 *m.* Thames runs to **Kew,** 1 *m.*; **Mortlake,** 1½ *m.*; **Barnes,** 1 *m.*; **Chiswick,** 1 *m.*; **Hammersmith** 1 *m.*; **Putney,** 1½ *m.* Here a stream joins on right bank, rising at Lower Morden, 1 *m.* E. of **Malden,** runs in 6 *m.* to **Barnes,** and joins Thames 1½ *m.* on. Thames runs to **Wandsworth,** 1 *m.*, where Wandle joins on right bank. Wandle rises by **Croydon,** runs to Beddington, 1 *m.* (a little trouting can be had free; also at Hackbridge and the Snuff Mills); **Carshalton,** 1 *m.*; **Mitcham,** 1½ *m.*; **Merton,** 1 *m.*; Thames, 4½ *m.* From Wandsworth to Westminster Bridge is 5½ *m.*

Long Ashton (Somerset).—G.W.R. Ashton Brook; trout; preserved by Sir G. Smyth of Ashton Court. (*See Bristol.*)

Longhope (Glo'ster).—G.W.R. Hopebrook. (*See Westbury.*) Denn (1 *m.*) (*See Ockle Street.*)

Long Marton (Westland).—M.R. Trout beck. Eden, 3 *m.* W.; trout. Maize beck, 5 *m.* N.E.; trout; leave from Lord Hothfield, of Appleby, or Mr. J. Tarn, of Birkdale. *Lakes*: Great Rundale tarn, Seamore tarn, Little Rundale tarn, and another pond, 5 *m.* N.E. *Hotel*: Langdon Beck. (*See Stockton.*)

Longnor, n.s. **Buxton,** 7 *m.* (Derby).—Mannyfold; trout, grayling. Dove, 1 *m.* E.; trout, grayling. (*c.s. Trent.*) Blackbrook, 2 *m.* S. (*See Gainsborough.*)

Long Preston (Lancs.)—L. & Y.R. Ribble; trout, salmon, pike, chub, grayling, coarse fish. Long Preston beck. Wigglesworth beck. Rathmell beck, 1 *m.* N. *Lakes*: Tapa Tarn, 2 *m.* W. *Hotel*: Boar's Head, where fishing can be had in Ribble at d.t. 1*s.* (*See Preston.*)

Longridge (Lancs.)—L. & N.W.R.; L. & Y.R. Loud. Chipping beck, 4 *m.* N.E. Lees beck, 4 *m.* N.E. Hodder, 5 *m.* N.E.; trout, salmon. Dean brook, 6 *m.* N.E. *Lakes*: Moor Game Hall pond, 6 *m.* N.E. Crowshaw reservoir, 6 *m.* E. (*See Ribchester, Preston.*)

Longstone (Derby).—M.R. (*See Ashford.*)

Longton (Stafford).—L. & N.W.R.; M.R.; G.N.R. Longton brook. *Lakes*: Park Hall, 1 *m.* N.E., trout. (*See Gainsborough.*)

Longville (Salop).—G.W.R. Corve (2½ *m.* S.E.); trout, grayling. Eaton brook (3 *m.* N.W.). Thonglands brook (3½ *m.* S.E.) (*See Gloucester.*) (*c.s. Severn.*)

Longwood (York).—L. & N.W.R.; M.R.; G.N.R. Colne. *Lakes*: Longwood Top reservoir; pike, perch; preserved by Huddersfield Angling Association; hon. sec., S. Hellowell, Esq., Huddersfield. Longwood Compensation reservoir; perch, roach, &c.; preserved as above. (*See Huddersfield* and *Rawcliffe.*)

Lords Bridge (Cambs).—L. & N.W.R. Bourn; pike, roach, &c. Cam, 3 *m.*; chub, pike, dace, &c.; preserved. (*See King's Lynn.*)

Lostock Hall (Lancs.).—L. & Y.R. Lostock. Croal. (*See Runcorn* and *Hesketh Bank.*)
Lostock Chapel (Cheshire).—L. & N.W.R. Kincham brook. Crow brook. (*See Frodsham.*)
Lostwithiel (Cornwall).—G.W.R. Fowey; sea trout, salmon, brown trout; Viscount Clifden permits fair fishing from Lostwithiel up to Glyn Bridge, excluding Lanhydrock Grounds to Resprin Bridge. July, September, and October are the best months. Minnow fishing best. Red brook. Lynner (3 m.); trout. (*c.s.*) (*See Fowey.*) *Tackleist*, C. Greach, stationer.
Loudham (Notts).—M.R. Cocker beck. Dover beck. 1 m. E. Trent, 2 m. S.; pike, chub, roach. (*c.s.*) (*See Gainsborough.*)
Loudwater (Bucks.).—G.W.R. Wye. (*See London, M.T.*). Here pollutions begin.
Loughborough (Leicester).—M.R., G.C.R., and L. & N.W.R. Soar; pike, roach, perch, bream, tench; preserved by Soar Angling Society from 3 m. above to 4m below; sec. Mr. G. Ford, 62, Ratcliffe-road, Loughborough; s.t. including pike, 6s.; w.t. 2s.; d.t. (pike) 1s.; no Sunday fishing; piking begins Aug. 1, ends March 14. (*c.s. Trent.*) Walton brook. Dishley brook, 1 m. N.W. Quorndon brook, 3 m. S.: trout; preserved by owner of Bradgate Park. *Lakes*: Loughborough reservoir: trout, perch, roach, carp, and tench; preserved by L.R.A.S.; s.t. 42s; d.t. burgesses, 5s.; strangers, 7s. 6d. Garendon Park lake, 2 m. W. Stamford Hall lake, 3 m. N.E. Blackbrook reservoir, 4 m. S.W. *Hotel*: King's Head. (*See Gainsborough.*)
Loughton (Essex).—G.E.R. On Roding; fishing very poor. (*See Barking.*)
Louth (Lincoln).—G.N.R. Ludd; trout. Ludd rises above **Hallington**, runs 3 m. to **Louth**, Alvington 4 m., and joins the sea 8 m. below. Grayfleet, 1 m. S. (*See Saltfleet.*) Bain, 7 m. W. (*See Boston.*)
Lower Darwen (Lancs.).—L. & Y.R. Darwen. (*See Preston.*)
Lowestoft (Suffolk).—G.E.R. 5 m. S.W., at Rushmere Hall, runs Benacre brook (roach, dace, bream, perch), which rises in the pond in Sotterley Hall Park, 4 m. S.E. from **Beccles**, runs 4 m. to Rushmere Hall, and joins the sea at Benacre sluice 4 m. down. Waveney, 5 m. W.; bream, roach, perch, pike, tench, carp; free. *Lakes*: Oulton Broad, 2 m. N.W.; same fish; leave and boats at Wherry Hotel (*see Mutford*). Flixton Decoy, 3 m. W. Lake at The Villa. 4 m. N.W. Fritton Decoy, 6 m. N.W. *Hotels*: Royal, Harbour, and Suffolk. (*See Yarmouth.*) (*c.s. Norfolk*). *Fishing stations within two hours of the town*: Beccles, Geldeston, Bungay, Mutford, Somerleyton, Haddiscoe, Reedham, Cantley, Buckenham, Brundall, Whitlingham, Norwich, Yarmouth.
Low Row (Cumland).—N.E.R. Irthing; trout. (*c.s. Eden.*) (*See Carlisle.*)
Lowthorpe (York).—N.E.R. Kelk or Frodingham beck: pike, coarse fish. (*See Hull.*)
Lubenham (Leicester).—L. & N.W.R. Welland. *Lakes*: Gumley pond. Gumley Hall ponds, 3 m. N.W. (*See Spalding.*)
Luddenden-foot (Yorks).—L. & Y.R. Calder. (*c.s. York.*) Luddenden. *Lakes*: Cold Edge dam, 3 m. N. (*See Rawcliffe.*)
Ludlow (Salop).—L. & N.W.R.; G.W.R. Teme; trout, grayling, chub, dace, roach, perch, pike; leave from the landowners. Lord Windsor gives occasional leave for the Oakley Park water. Corve; same fish; preserved for 3 m. up, from its junction with Teme, by Lord Windsor, who often gives leave, and above by private owners. Fishmore brook. Ledwych (1¼ m E.); trout, grayling, chub, &c.; leave from the landowners. Cay brook (2 m. E.). Onny (2½ m. N.W.); trout, grayling; preserved. Dogditch brook (3 m.). *Lakes*: Ludford Park Lakes (1 m. S.). Downton Hall Lakes (4 m. N.). Wootton Pool (5 m. E.). Burrington Pool (5¼ m. S.W.). *Hotels*: Feathers, Angel, Bull, Elephant and Castle, and Rose and Crown. (*See Gloucester.*) (*c.s. Severn.*)
Luffenham (Rutland).—G.N.R.; L. & N.W.R.; M.R. Chater. Welland, 2 m. S. (*See Spalding.*)
Lulworth.—(*See Weymouth.*)
Lustleigh (S. Devon).—G.W.R. On Bovev. (*See Teignmouth.*)
Luton (Beds.).—M.R.; G.N.R. (*See Stratford.*) On Lea; the river is preserved where it runs through the lakes in Luton Park by Sir Julius Wernher. Permission is sometimes granted. *Hotels*: George, Red Lion, Midland.
Lutterworth (Leicester).—(n a. **Ullesthorpe**, 4 m.) Swift. Avon (6 m. S.E.): chub, dace, roach, pike, perch, bream. (*See Gloucester.*) (*c.s. Severn.*)
Lydham (Salop)— B.C.R. Onny; trout, grayling, chub, pike; strictly preserved. Camlad; trout, grayling, chub, &c. Black brook (4 m. N.). *Lakes*: Shelve Pool (7 m. N.) Marsh Pool (8 m. N.) (*See Gloucester.*) (*c.s. Severn.*)
Lydiate (Lancs.).—S. & C.L.E.R. Lydiate brook. Alt. 3 m. S.W. (*See Altcar.*)
Lydney (Gloucester).—G.W.R. Lydney brook. Lydney rises in the centre of the Forest of Dean, and is 9 m. long.
Lyme Regis.—5 m. from Axminster and from the Axe. The Coly and the Otter are still farther distant; but there is omnibus accommodation to Axminster, whence the Coly and the Otter are easily reached by railway. (*See Seaton* and *Ottery St. Mary.*) Bass may be caught in rough weather by throwing out a line baited with squid or cuttle from the pier, on the flowing tide. Under the same conditions a rod and floated line might be used, same bait or soft crab. Mackerel by hook and line in the season.

Lymington (Hants).—S.W.R. *Hotels*: Londesboro', Angel. On Boldre; coarse fish Boldre rises by Bolderwood Lodge, in the heart of the New Forest, 5 m. N. from **Holmsley,** and in 2 m. waters the large lake in Burley Lodge. 3 m. down, at Queen's Bower, a stream joins on left bank, which rises 2 m. W. of **Lyndhurst,** runs 2 m., when it is joined by a stream on right bank 2 m. long. ½ m. on is the Boldre. 2 m. on is **Brocken-hurst Station.** 5 m. down a stream 4 m. long joins on right bank, which drains Lachmore pond. 1½ m. from **Brockenhurst.** 1 m. on is **Lymington.** The river is preserved by E. H. Pember, Esq., Vicars Hill, Lymington, who will often give a day. 3 m. E. of Lymington is Sowley Pond; good pike and perch fishing. Bass and salmon peel sometimes at mouth of Lymington creek; flounders, plaice, and grey mullet up the channel.

Lymm (Cheshire).—L. & N.W.R. Mersey. Sow brook. *Lakes*: Lymm lake. (*See* Runcorn.)

Lyneside.—N.B.R. On Lyne; salmon, trout, salmon trout, whitings; free up to Cliff.

Lynmouth (Devon).—East and West Lyn; trout, salmon. *Hotel*: Lyndale Hotel: East Lyn rises by Oare Oak, and in 4 m. is joined by a short stream on left bank. 1 m. down Lyn, Oare water joins on right bank. Oare (preserved by Mr. Snow, of Oare) rises on Lucott Hill, 5 m. from Porlock, runs 5 m., and is joined on left bank by Badgworthy Water, 2 m. long Oare runs in 4 m. to East Lyn, which runs 2 m., when Farley water joins on left bank; Lynmouth is 2 m. on. West Lyn is some 5 m. long, and half-way down is joined on left bank by a short stream. West and East Lyn join close to the sea. S. licence, 10s. 6d.; s.t. 40s.; w.t. 5s.; d.t. 1s.; tickets and licence at the Post Office. 5 m. off at Paracombe runs Paracombe water, which joins the sea at Trentishoe in 6 m.

Macclesfield (Cheshire).—L. & N.W.R.; N.S.R.; G.C.R. Bollin. Langley reservoirs; trout; North Rode lake, d.t. 2s. 6d.; Great Central Canal, good coarse fishing, s.t. 2s., d.t. 4d.; private. Turk's Head Reservoir, 2 m. S.; d.t. 1s. Peover brook, 5 m. S.W., at Siddington. Dane, 3 m. N. *Lakes*: Great Oak reservoir, 3 m. S. Gawsworth Mill pond, 3m. S.W. Thornycroft Hall, 3 m. S.W. Henbury Hall, 3 m. W. Old Hall, 3 m. W. Reed's mere and Capesthorne Hall lake, 4 m. N.W. Wickenhall mere, 5 m. S.W., at Siddington. Astle Hall, 6 m. W., at Chelford. (*See* Frodsham; Langley: Runcorn.) *Tackleist,* J. H. Fearn, 38, Chester-gate.

Madeley (Stafford).—L. & N.W.R. Madeley brook. Artle, 1 m. N. *Lakes*: Madeley Mill. Bowsey Mill, 1 m. N. Wrinehill Mill, 2 m. N.W. Betley mere, 3 m. N.W. Little mere. 3 m. N.W. (*See Frodsham.*)

Magdalen (Norfolk).—G.E.R. Ouse; coarse fish except barbel. (c.s. N. and S.) (*See King's Lynn.*)

Magor (Monmouth).—G.W.R. Penhow brook, 7 m. long.

Maidenhead (Berks.).—G.W.R. (*See London, M.T.*) Thames; roach, trout, pike, perch, chub, barbel, dace. *Hotels*: Skindle's, Raymead, Thames. *Fishermen*: E. Andrews, C. Andrews, A. Carter, J. Carter, and J. and T. Owen.

Maiden Newton (Dorset).—G.W.R. Frome. (*See Wareham.*) (c.s.)

Maidstone (Kent).—S.E. & C.R.—Medway; chub, pike, perch, roach, bream. *Hotel*: Royal Star (the proprietor of which will gladly afford every information.) There is good free fishing from 2 m. up the river to Tonbridge. Some waters in the neighbourhood are preserved, and permission is difficult to obtain. The ponds at Leeds Castle, 5 m. off, and the "Mote" (Sir Marcus Samuels) hold pike. The fish ponds at the paper mills of Messrs. Hollingsworth on the Len are very good; but permission is rarely given. (*See Rochester.*)

Malden (Surrey).—L. & S.W.R. Hogg's Mill river. (*See London, L.T.*)

Maldon (Essex).—G.E.R. *Inn*: King's Head. On Blackwater; pike, perch, roach, dace, and a few trout. This stream rises 5 m. east of **Saffron Walden,** and, under the name of Pant, in 20 m. runs to **Braintree** within 1 m. of the town, passing the villages of Sampford, Bardfield, Shalford, and Bocking. From **Braintree** the river runs, in 8 m., to Coggeshall; **Kelvedon,** 4 m.; hence to the junction of Pods brook, on the left bank, with the Blackwater at **Witham** is 6 m. Pods brook rises 6 m. north-west of **Braintree,** and then follows the railway to **Bulford,** 3 m.; from **Bulford** to **Witham** is 8 m.; passing the village of White Notley in its course. This stream is preserved the whole way. Pike, perch, roach, dace, &c. From the junction of Pods brook with the Blackwater to **Wickham** is 2 m., to **Langford** 1 m., and **Maldon** 2m. From **Maldon** to the junction of the Chelmer, on the right bank with the Blackwater is 3 m. The Chelmer rises close to the Blackwater, and, in 4 m., runs by Thaxted, and thence to **Dunmow** 8 m. Below **Dunmow** there are a few trout, pike, perch, roach, &c.; leave must be obtained from the farmers. 4 m. on, at **Felsted,** a brook joins on the left bank, 8 m. long. From Felsted the Chelmer runs, in 14 m., to **Chelmsford.** Here the Cann joins Chelmer. This stream rises 13 m. N.W. from **Chelmsford,** and 2 m. above that town is joined by a brook which rises 5 m. east of **Chipping Ongar,** and, in 8 m., flows to **Ingatestone,** 1 m. from the town, and, flowing by Margaretting and Writtle, in 8 m. joins the Cann. The Chelmer now becomes navigable. 6 m. below **Chelmsford** a brook joins on the right bank, which rises 2 m. north-east of Billericay, and is 14 m. long. The Chelmer now runs 6 m. to **Langford,** then 1 m. to **Maldon,** and thence to its junction with the Blackwater, 2 m. Just outside the entrance of the Blackwater river, whiting, cod, ling, and dabs are caught with hook and line.

Malling (Kent).—S.E. & C.R. Lakes belonging to Miss Savage hold pike and roach. Permission of the owner.

Malpas (Cheshire).—L. & N.W.R. Holywell brook, 2 m. N.E. Weaver, 3 m. N.E. Marbury

brook, 3 m.| S.E. *Lakes*: Edge Mill pond, 2 m. N.E. Moss mere, Capel mere
(Cholmondeley Park), 3 m. N.E., Bickley Mill pond and Bar mere, 3 m. S.E. Brets mere,
4 m. W. (*See Frodsham, Chester.*)

Malton (York).—N.E.R. Derwent. Rye, 2 m. N. Settrington beck, 2 m. E. Costa beck,
2 m. N.E. *Lakes*: Welham pond, 1 m. S. Settrington lake, 3 m. S.E. Castle Howard
Park lake, 5 m. W. (c.s. *York*.) (*See Wressel.*)

Malvern (Worcester).—G.W.R. Teme (rail 5 m. to **Bransford**). (*See Bransford*).
Severn (3 m. E.); chub, dace, roach, pike, perch, salmon, trout. Leigh brook (4 m. W.);
good trouting; leave from Mr. Cook, of Leigh Court. (*See Gloucester.*) (c.s. *Severn*).
Hotels: Imperial, Abbey, Tudor House.

Manaccan (Cornwall).—(n.s. **Falmouth**). Manaccan brook, 4 m. long. (c.s. *Fowey*.)

Manchester (Lancs.).—L. & N.W.R.; M.R.; G.N.R.; G.W.R. Irwell. Irk. Medlock.
(*See Runcorn*.) All the water in Manchester is more or less polluted, and holds no fish;
but there is fair fishing (trout and perch) in the Manchester reservoir at Hadfield, 10 m.
out; s.t. 20s.; and at Poynton, also 10 m. out, in the canal, s.t. 2s., d.t. 4d. At Worsley (6 m.),
in the Worsley canal, about 12 m. of coarse fishing, s.t. 2s. 6d. 18 m. from Manchester,
at Northwich, there is some good free coarse fishing in the Weaver and Flashes; Sunday
fishing allowed. The Warrington Anglers' Club has trouting in the Gowey at Tatten-
hall-road, near Chester, also 3 m. of coarse fishing in the Bollin at Heatley; apply to
Secretary, Latchford. Cheap train tickets for anglers to all these places. *Tacklist*,
W. Chambers and Co., 35, Market-place.

Mangotsfield (Glouca.).—M.R. (*See Bristol*.) Feltham brook. Siston brook.

Manningtree (Essex).—G.E.R. Stour; pike, perch, roach, dace, carp, bream, tench,
trout, salmon, &c. Suffolk Stour rises above Great Bradley 6 m. N. from **Haverhill**,
runs 6 m. to Kedington (2 m. W. of **Haverhill**), and 2 m. below, at **Sturmer**, is joined
on right bank by Albery brook, which rises 4 m. above **Haverhill**, and joins Stour 2 m.
below. 1 m. down Stour, Birdbrook, 6 m. long, joins on right bank. Stour runs to **Stoke**
3 m., **Clare** 3 m., **Cavendish** 3 m., and 3 m. down is joined on left bank by Glemsford
brook, which rises 5 or 6 m. above Glemsford, and joins Stour 2 m. down. Stour runs
2 m. to **Melford**, and here Melford brook, 8 m. long, joins on left bank. 3 m.
down Stour, Bardfield brook, 5 m. long, joins on right bank. Stour runs 1 m. to
Sudbury, **Bures** 6 m., and 1 m. down is joined on left bank by a brook draining
Assington Mill pond 3 m. up. Stour runs to Wiston Mill 3 m., **Nayland** 1 m., and 4 m.
down is joined on left bank by Boxford river. Boxford rises 5 m. above Boxford
(n.s. **Sudbury**, 6 m.), and joins Stour 7 m. down. ½ m. down Stour, Brett joins on
left bank. Brett rises in the Brettenham Park pond 4 m. N.E. from **Lavenham**, and
5 m. down is joined on right bank by Lavenham brook. Lavenham rises above **Cookfield**,
runs 5 m. to **Lavenham**, and Brett 5 m. Brett runs 8 m. to **Hadleigh**, and 6 m. to
Stour at Higham. Stour runs 7 m. to **Manningtree**, and the estuary; 4 m. N.E. on the
other side of Stour runs Capel brook. Capel rises above **Capel**, runs 6 m. to within
2 m. of **Bentley Station**, and 2 m. below waters the large mill pond of Stutton close
to its junction with Stour, 4 m. N.E. of **Manningtree**. *Hotel*: White Hart. (c.s. *Suffolk*
and *Essex*.)

Mansfield (Notts). —M.R. Maun. Coldwell brook. Rainworth water, 3 m. S.E. at
Blidsworth. Meden, 1 m. N.W. at Pleasby. *Lakes*: King's Mill reservoir, 2 m. S.W.
Bath Wood lake, 3 m. S.W. at **Sutton**. Four ponds by Rainworth, 3 m. S.E. (*See
Althorpe.*)

Mansfield Woodhouse (Notts).—M.R. Maun, 1 m. E. Meden, 2 m. N. Vicay water,
3 m. E. *Lakes*: Park Hall, 2 m. N.E. (*See Althorpe.*)

Manton (Rutland).—M.R.; G.N.R. Gwash. Chater, 1 m. S. (*See Spalding*.)

Marazion (Cornwall).—G.W.R. Marazion water, 6 m. long.

March (Cambs.).—G.E.R.; G.N.R. Old river Nen; pike, perch, bream, &c. Innumerable
fen drains. (*See Wisbeach*.)

Marchington (Stafford). L. & N.W.R.; G.N.R.; M.R. Dove; chub, barbel, bream, pike,
trout. (c.s. *Trent*.) ' Somershall brook. Marchington brook. (*See Gainsborough*.)

Margate.—The deep-line fishing off Margate is good; the whitings run large. The bass—
called locally the salmon dace—is taken close in at high water with a spoon bait. They
are often taken off the jetty with rod and line, as also whiting and flounders, the hook
baited with a piece of oyster. Fish from a boat where the gulls hover; you will take some
fine bass with the spoon. Mullets are abundant, and cod are taken with the long line, which
the fishermen shoot at one tide and take up at another, with sometimes more than a hundred hooks thereon, baited with sprats as fresh as it is possible to obtain them. A portion of
the skate resembling sweetbread, and of which mullets are exceedingly fond, is here used
as a bait. Fishing off Ramsgate is better than that off Margate, and there is good dab-
fishing in the Downs off Deal. Bass are found in the entrance of Sandwich Haven, and on
the North Foreland ledge.

Market Bosworth (Leicester). —M.R.; L. & N.W.R. Bosworth brook, 1 m. N.; trout;
preserved by the owner of Bosworth Hall. Sence, 3 m. W. Tweed, 3 m. S.W. *Lakes*: The
Duckery, Bosworth Park, 1 m. S.; pike, &c. Gabriel pool, 3 m. N.E. (*See Gainsborough*.)

Market Deeping (Lincoln).—n.s. **Deeping St. James**. Welland; pike, perch,
chub, dace, roach; preserved by Market Deeping Angling Society hence down to Kenulphstone, 6 m.; hon. members (one friend's ticket) 10s.; ordinary members, s.t. 5s., labourers

2s. 6d. (if living *within* 10 m. of the fishing boundary); for persons *outside*, s.t. 21s., w.t.
2s. 6d., d.t. 1s.; hon. sec., S. B. Sharpe, Esq.; fishing good, especially fly fishing for dace.
Glen, 4 m. N. at Kates Bridge. (*See Boston.*)

Market Drayton (Salop).—G.W.R. Tern; a few trout, pike, roach, dace. Coal brook.
Hemp Mill brook (3 m. N.E.). Baile brook (4 m S.W.). *Lakes:* Peats Wood lake (1 m.
S.E.). Buntingsdale Hall lake (2 m. S W.). Daisy lake (3 m. N.E.). New pool, Old pool, and
Big pool 3¼ m. N.W.). Rose Hill ponds (4 m. S.). Heywood ponds (4 m. S.E.). Morden
Mill pond (4 m. W.). Wardale ponds (4 m. S.). Cloverley pond (5 m. N.W.). Canal
reservoirs, Great Saundley (7 m. S.E.). (*See Gloucester.*) (c.s. Severn.)

Market Harborough (Leicester).—M.R.; L. & N.W.R. Welland. Saddington brook,
3 m. N. Hardwick brook, 4 m. N.E. at Thorpe Langton. *Lakes:* Gumley Hall lakes, 4 m.
N.W. Saddington reservoir, 5 m. N.W. (*See Spalding.*)

Market Rasen (Lincoln).—G.C.R. Rase. Ancholme, 5 m. W. (*See Brigg.*) (*See
Holton-le-Clay.*)

Marks Tey (Essex).—G.E.R. Roman river. *Lakes:* Birch Hall lake. (*See Wyvenhoe.*)

Marlborough (Wilts.)—G.W.R.; L. & S.W.R. Kennett; trout. (*See London, M.T.*)
Hotels: Ailesbury Arms (close to the river). Castle and Ball.

Marlesford (Suffolk).—G.E.R. Ore. Alde, 3 m. N.E. (*See Orford.*)

Marple (Cheshire).—M.R. Goyt or Mersey. Etherow. 1 m. N. (*See Runcorn.*)

Marron Junction (Cumland.)—L. & N.W.R. Derwent; trout, salmon. (c.s.)
Marron. (c.s. *Derwent.*) (*See Cockermouth, Keswick.*)

Marsden (York).—L. & N.W.R. Colne; polluted. *Lakes:* Wissenden reservoir, S.
March Hill reservoir, 2 m. W. (*See Rawcliffe.*)

Marsh Brook (Salop).—L. & N.W.R. Quinny brook. Eaton brook (3 m. E.). Clun (3 m.
S.W.); trout, grayling. (*See Gloucester.*) (c.s. Severn.)

Marsh Mills (Devon).—G.W.R. Plym; trout, sea trout; preserved. Tory brook. (*See
Plymouth.*) (c.s. Tamar.)

Marston (York).—N.E.R. Nidd, 2 m. N.W. (c.s. York.) Ouse, 3 m. N., at Nun Monkton.
(c.s. York.) (*See York.*)

Marston Green (Warwick).—L. & N.W.R. Ulverley brook. Cole, 2 m. N. *Lakes:*
Chelmsley Wood ponds, 1 m. N.E. Coleshill pool. 2 m. W. (*See Gainsborough.*)

Marston Magna (Somerset).—G.W.R. (*See Bridgwater.*)

Martham (Norfolk).—G.E.R. Hundred stream or Thurne. *Lakes:* Martham Broad (Mr.
Thain, Somerton), Horsey mere, 4 m. N. (R. Rising, Esq.) (*See Yarmouth.*) *Inn:* King's
Arms. (c.s. N. and S.)

Martock (Somerset).—G.W.R. (*See Bridgwater.*) (c.s. Avon.)

Marton (York).—On Leven. Leven rises at the head of Rosedale, receives several small
streams, flows past Rosedale Abbey, Cropton, Linnington, Marten, Normanby, and Barugh
into the Rye. Leven is a very good trout stream, from Linnington Mill upward; strictly
preserved; from there downwards leave may sometimes be got; below Marton mostly free;
grayling, pike, chub, dace, and a few trout. Good inn at Marton.

Maryport (Cumland.).—On Ellen; trout.

Mary Tavy (Devon).—G.W.R. Tavy; salmon, trout. Tavy, Meavy, Plym, Cad, and
Walkham, with their several branches and tributary streams, are preserved by the Tavy,
Walkham, and Plym Fishing Association; sec., W. W. Mathews, solicitor. Tavistock;
s.t. for all the Association's water, including licence, 30s.; Meavy only, 10s.; Cad only,
s.t. 5s.; Walkham, 5s.; Tavy to junction with Walkham, 5s., d.t. 1s. Salmon, March 1 to
Nov. 1; trout, March 1 to Sept. 30. No wading, no Sunday fishing; trout less than 6 inches
to be returned. (c.s. Tamer.) (*See Plymouth.*)

Masham (York).—N.E.R. Ure; trout, grayling; by staying at the King's Head 1¼ m.
of fishing can be had. (c.s. York.) Burn. Swinney beck. Sale beck, 2 m. S.W. Grimes
Gill beck, 4 m. S W. Spuce Gill beck, 6 m. W. Beik Gill beck, 7 m. W. *Lakes:* Swinton
Park lakes, 2 m. S.W. *Hotel:* King's Head. (*See York.*)

Matlock Bath (Derby).— M.R. Derwent; trout, grayling; preserved from Cawdor
Bridge *above* **Matlock**, to the Saw Mills, **Whatstandwell**, 6 m., by the Matlock and
Cromford Angling Association; hon. sec., Henry Cooper, Esq., Derby-road, Cromford;
entrance fee 42s., s.t. 42s.; below Cromford (fly only), w.t. 10s., d.t., 2s. 6d., to staying
visitors. Trouting begins March 25, ends Sept. 30; grayling, June 15 to Jan. 31; bottom
fishing allowed from Cawdor Bridge to Masson Weir, s.t. 20s.; from Cawdor Bridge up to
above **Rowsley**, river preserved by the Darley Dale Club. Bentley brook; trout.
Amber, 6 m. E., at Ambergate Lumsdale dams; trout. *Hotels:* New Bath, Royal, and
Devonshire at Matlock Bath, and Greyhound at Cromford, where tickets can be had. (*See
Gainsborough.*)

Meare (Somerset).—G.W.R. Brue; roach, dace, carp, pike; preserved above, and below to
Shapwick. Godney brook. (*See Highbridge.*) (c.s. Avon.)

Measham (Leicester).—L. & N.W.R. Mease. (c.s. Trent.) (*See Gainsborough.*)

Melbourne (Derby).—M.R. Breedon. Carr brook. Trent, 2 m. N., at Weston Ferry (*see
Weston, Gainsborough.*) (c.s.)

Meldreth (Cambs).—G.N.R. Rhee, 1 m.; good coarse fishing. (*See King's Lynn.*)

Melford (Suffolk).—G.E.R. Stour; pike, perch, roach, tench, few carp and dace. Melford
brook. Glemsford brook :same fish as Stour. (c.s. N. and E.) (*See Manningtree.*)

Melksham (Wilts).—G.W.R. Avon; trout, perch, pike, chub, roach, dace, tench; preserved by the Avon, Brue, and Parret Fishery District from the town bridge on both banks

as far as Monkton (down stream), and then on one side only nearly to Holt station; s.t. 2s. 6d., m.t. 1s., d.t. 6d., including trout, of A. W. Jolliffe, the P.O., Melksham (c.s. Avon.) The Wilts and Berks Canal runs through Melksham (d.t. 3d.), and joins the Kennet and Avon Canal at Semington about 2 m. from here (free). There are also numerous ponds and brooks containing good fish. Hotel: King's Arms. Lodgings can always be obtained. Above bridge, and almost as far as Lacock, there is plenty of pike and coarse fishing; leave from the farmers.

Melling (Lancs).—Furn. & Mid. R. Lune. (c.s.) (See Lancaster.)

Mellis (Suffolk).—G.E.R. (See Botesdale, King's Lynn.)

Meltham (York).—G.N.R.; L. & N.W.R.; M.R.; L. & Y.R. Lakes: Reservoir, 1 m. E. (See Rawcliffe.) Deerhill reservoir, 6 m.; roach; preserved by Huddersfield Angling Association. (See Huddersfield.)

Melton (Suffolk).—G.E.R. Deben. (See Woodbridge.)

Melton Mowbray (Leicester).—M.R.; G.N.R.; L. & N.W.R. Wreak; roach, bream; polluted near the town (c.s. Trent). Melton brook. Lakes: Welby pond, 3 m. N.W. Saxelby pond, 4 m. N.W. Stapleford Park pond, 4 m. S.E. Leesthorpe pond, 4 m. S.E. Goadby Marwood lake, 6 m. N. Croxton Park lakes, 6 m. N.E. Knipton reservoir, 8 m. N., at Branston. (See Gainsborough.)

Menheniot (Cornwall).—G.W.R. St. Germans; trout. (See St. Germans.) Seaton river. (See Liskeard.) Seaton rises 4 m. N. of **Liskeard**, runs 1 m. E. of the town, and reaches **Menheniot** Station in 3 m.; thence to the sea is 6 m. (c.s. Fowey.) Loe, 3 m.; trout.

Menthorpe (York).—N.E.R. (See Breighton, Wressel.)

Merstham (Surrey).—S.E. & C.R. (See London, L.T.) The lake in Gatton Park belongs to Mr. Coleman. There is a catchwater mill pond near, and a smaller one full of perch to the west of the lake. Hotel: The Feathers.

Merton (Surrey).—L. & S.W.R. Wandle; trout. Below, the fish are nearly all destroyed. (See London, L.T.)

Messingham.—Bottesford beck; roach, dace.

Methley (Yorks).—G.N.R.; M.R.; L. & Y.R. Aire. (c.s. York.) Kollin brook. (See Rawcliffe.)

Mevagissey (Cornwall).—Excellent sea-fishing, especially in summer. There is, however, hardly any fishing from the shore. Off Chapel Point, and round the Gwineas Rocks, are good places for pollack. Shoals of large bass frequent the Gwineas during May and June. There are two small inns at Mevagissey, and lodgings can also be had. Small trout in the brook. 4 m. off, at St. Ewe, free trouting can be had in Ewe: good. (c.s. Fowey.)

Mexborough (York).—G.C.R.; M.R. Don. (c.s. Yorkshire.) Dearne, 2 m. N. (See Goole.)

Mickfield (York).—N.E.R. (See Aberford, York.)

Mickleover (Derby).—G.N.R. Lakes: Radburn pond, 3 m. N.W. (See Gainsborough.)

Middleham (York), n.s. **Leyburn**, 2 m.—Ure; trout, grayling. (c.s. York.) Cover; trout, grayling; preserved as Ure. Hotel: White Swan. (See Leyburn, York.) fishing, free for 4 m.; leave obtainable elsewhere. (See Leyburn.)

Middleton (Lancs.)—L. & N.W.R.; M.R.; G.N.R. Irk. Lune. (c.s.) Lakes: Three Pits Bridge ponds, 2 m. N.E. Heaton lake, 3 m. S.W. (See Runcorn and Lancaster.)

Middleton-in-Teesdale (Durham).—N.E.R. Tees; trout, salmon, bull trout; tickets from Lord Barnard's agent, Raby Castle, Staindrop, for the Durham side. On the Yorkshire side Lord Strathmore preserves the river to Park End, but grants tickets below. Apply to his agent, Mr. John Brown. Bow Bank, Middleton. (c.s.) Middleton beck. Lune, 1 m. S.E.; trout; private. (c.s. Tees.) Rowton beck. 3 m. N.W. Blea beck, 5 m. N.W. Howgill beck. 5 m. S.W. Wemmergill beck, 5 m. S.W. Soulgill beck, 5 m. S.W. Rowantree beck, 5 m S.W. Skyer beck, 6 m. N.W. Long Grain beck, 7 m. S.W. Arngill beck, 7 m. S.W. Oiose beck, 8 m. S.W. Maize beck, 9 m. W.; trout; leave from Lord Hothfield, of Appleby. Harewood beck, 9 m. N.W. Langdon beck, 9 m. N.W. Lakes: Fishpond, 9 m. S.W. (See Stockton.)

Middlewich (Cheshire).—L. & N.W.R. Dane; chub, dace, roach, trout; preserved Wheelock. Croco. Sanderson's brook. Weaver, 3 m. W. Lakes: Stocks Hill lake, 3 m. W. (See Frodsham.)

Midford (Somerset).—M.R. (See Bristol.) On Avon. (c.s.)

Midge Hall (Lancs.).—L. & Y.R. Lostock, 1 m. (See Hesketh Bank.)

Midgham (Berks).—G.W.R. Kennett. Embourne. (See London, M.T.)

Midhurst (Sussex).—L. & S.W.R.; L.B. & S.C.R. Western Rother: pike, bream, trout, carp, roach. Fishing free from hence to Pulborough. (See Littlehampton.)

Midsomer Norton (Somerset).—M.R. (See Bristol.)

Milborne Port (Somerset).—L & S.W.R. (See Bridgwater.)

Mildenhall (Suffolk).—G.E.R. Lark; dace, roach, rudd, carp, trout; preserved from Bury St. Edmunds to Pickwillow (22 m.) by Lark Angling Society; s.t. 2s. 6d.; non-residents' s.t. 5s., d.t. 1s. 6d., from sec., Mr. W. Howlett, Lord Mayor's C ttage, Barton Mills. Tronting opens March 16. Hotels: Bell, White Hart. (See King's Lynn and Bury St. Edmunds.)

Milford (Surrey).—L. & S.W.R. There are some lakes on Puttenham Common. (See London, L.T.)

Millcote (Warwick).—G.W.R. Avon; chub, dace, roach, pike, perch, bream. (See Gloucester.) (c.s. Severn.)

Miller's Dale (Derby).—M.R. Wye; trout, grayling; preserved by a club of limited numbers. (c.s. Trent.) (See Gainsborough.)

Mill Hill (Lancs.)—L. & Y.R.; L. & N.W.R. Darwen. (See Preston.)

Mill Houses (Yorks).—G.C.R. Sheaf. Lakes: Norton Hall, 2 m. S.E. (See Goole.)

Milnrow (York).—L. & Y.R. Beal. (See Runcorn.)

Milnthorpe (Westland).—L.&N.W.R. Bela or Beetha; trout. Beetha rises on Docker Fell, under the name of Saint Sunday Beck, and 5 m. down, 2 m. **E. of Oxenholme**, is joined on right bank by Beehive beck. Beehive rises in a pond on Hay fell. 2 m. E. of **Kendal**, and runs 3 m. to 1 m. E. of **Oxenholme**, joining Sunday 1 m. below. Beetha runs 6 m. to **Milnthorpe** station. Here Peasey beck, called Hutton in its upper waters, joins on left bank. Peasey rises in Lily Mere, 3 m. W. of **Sedbergh**, thence waters the Killington reservoir (perch, pike; leave from Lady Bentinck's agent); on Hutton common, close below. Hutton (trout; leave as above) runs 5 m. to Hutton bridge, 3 m. S.E. of **Oxenholme**, where a stream joins, draining a pond ½ m. up. 7 m. down Peasey, 2 m. N.E. of **Milnthorpe**, Lupton beck joins on left bank. Lupton rises on Killington common, and 4 m. down is joined on right bank by a stream, draining Tarnhouse tarn, 1 m. up. On the left bank of Lupton, at the same spot, is Terrybank tarn; both tarns are 4 m. N.W. of **Kirkby Lonsdale**. Lupton runs to within 2 m. N.W. of **Kirkby Lonsdale**, on left bank, and joins Peasey, 5 m. down. Peasey runs 1 m. to Beetham. The river here makes a southward loop of 4 m., running back to the town of **Milnthorpe**, and a little below joins the estuary. Hotel: Cross Keys. Preserved by the Milnthorpe Angling Association, and confined to members and their guests; entrance, 42s.; s.t. 42s.; hon. sec., F. L. O'Dwyer, Esq., Beetham, Milnthorpe. The Association also preserves St. Sunday's beck from Deepthwaite Bridge, and Peasey beck from Watn Sutton downwards, and thence, from the joining of the two streams, to Beetham Mill. Fishing, which opens Feb. 16 and ends Sept. 16, is very good in March, April, May, and August. (c.s. Kent.)

Milton (Stafford).—L. & N.W.R. Trent. (c s.) Foxley brook. (See Gainsborough.)

Milverton (Somerset).—G.W.R. Milverton brook and Norton brook. (See Bridgwater.)

Minehead (Somerset).—G.W.R. (See Lynton.)

Minety (Wilts).—G.W.R. (See Bristol.) On Bredon Pond.

Minshull Vernon (Cheshire).—L. & N.W.R. Weaver, 1 m. W. Wheelock, 1 m. E. Ash brook, 3 m. W. (See Frodsham.)

Minsterley (Salop).—L. & N.W.R.; G.W.R. Rea; trout, grayling. Minsterley brook. Habberley brook (3 m. S.E.). Lakes: Marton pool (7 m. S.W.) (See Gloucester.) (c.s. Severn.)

Mirfield (Yorks).—L. & N.W.R.; L. & Y.R. Calder. (c.s. York.) (See Rawcliffe.)

Misterton (Notts).—G.N.R. Marther drain. Trent. Idle, 6 m. W. (c.s. Trent.) (See Althorpe.)

Misterton (Somerset).—L. & S.W.R. (See Seaton.) Axe; trout. (c.s.)

Mitcham (Surrey).—L. & S.W.R. Wandle; trout. Preserved, but much polluted below. (See London, L.T.)

Mitcheldean Road (Hereford).—G.W.R. Rudhall brook. (See Chepstow.)

Mitton (York), n.s. **Walley**, 2 m.—Ribble; trout, salmon, chub. Hodder; trout. Hotels: Three Fishes and Aspinall's Arms, where fishing can be had in Ribble and Hodder. (See Preston.)

Mobberley (Cheshire).—L. & N.W.R. Mobberley brook. Ashley brook, 1 m. N. Birkin, 1 m. W. Lakes: Tatton Park lake, 2 m. S.W. (See Runcorn.)

Molland (Devon).—G.W.R. Yeo; trout; d t. 1s. Molland water. Knowstone water (3 m.) (c.s. Taw.) Hotel: Black Cock. (See Barnstaple.)

Monmouth. — G.W.R. Wye; salmon, pike, trout, grayling, chub, dace, salmon; preserved. (c.s.) Monnow; trout, grayling, chub, dace; preserved by landowners. (c.s. Wye.) Trothy trout; preserved. Particulars at the Troy Estate Offices, Monmouth; or of G. Harris, 8, Monnow-street. Short term tickets for the Crown water at Symonds Yat may be obtained of Francis Hobbs, Esq., Land Agent, Monmouth. (c.s. Wye.) Hotel: Beaufort Arms. (See Chepstow.)

Monsal Dale (Derby).—M.R. Wye; trout, grayling; leave from the Duke of Devonshire. (c.s. Trent.) (See Gainsborough.)

Moorhampton (Hereford).—G.W.R. Lugwas brook (1 m.) Stretford brook (3½ m.) (See Chepstow.)

Moor Row Junction (Cumland.).—C. & W.R. Keekle. Ehen, 1 m. S.E. (c.s. Westberland.) (See Egremont.)

Moortown (Lincoln).—G.C.R. Tetney drain, 9 m. E. Lakes: Croxby pond, 9 m. E. See Holton-le-Clay.) Some trouting can be had in the beck running near the station; it is, however, much wooded. The fishing at Riverhead is open all the year; d.t. 1s., s.t. 5s., of Mr. Scott, Skipworth Arms.

Morchard Road (Devon).—L. & S.W.R. Braddiford brook. (See Barnstaple.)

Morebath (Devon).—G.W.R. Bampton brook. (See Exeter.)

Moresby Parks (Cumland.).—C. & W.J.R. Keekle. Dubbeck, 2 m. S.E. (See Egremont.)

Moreton (Dorset).—L. & S.W.R. Frome, Piddle; trout, salmon. (See Wareham.) (c.s.)

Moreton Hampstead (Devon).—G.W.R. Hotel: White Hart. (See Teignmouth.) On Teign and Bovey; trout. The river Teign is preserved from Stepsbridge to Lees Teign 12 m. Tickets at the White Hart, the landlord of which also grants tickets for the upper part of the Bovey. (c.s.)

Moreton-on-Lug (Hereford).—L. & N.W.R.; G.W.R. Lug; trout, grayling, pike, perch, roach, dace (*c.s. Wye*); preserved above by the Bodenham Club of 30. Hon. Sec., R. C. Bailey, Esq., Pigeon House, Bodenham. (*See Dinmore.*) Derndale brook (1 m.), Sutton brook (2½ m.) (*See Chepstow.*)

Morpeth (Northumld.).—On Wansbeck: trout. There are 5 m. or 6 m. of open water below the town. Above this water the river belongs to several private persons, who, however, are liberal to stranger gentlemen. There are several feeders of the Wansbeck, where sport is good at times, and leave easily obtained.

Mortehoe (Devon).—L. & S.W.R. (*See Braunton.*)

Mortimer (Berks.).—G.W.R. Strathfieldsaye is near. (*See London, M.T.*)

Mortlake (Surrey).—L. & S.W.R. Thames. (*See London, L.T.*)

Mossbank (Lancs.).—L. & N.W.R.; L. & Y.R. Sankey brook. Newton brook, 1½ m. E. Lakes: Carr Mill dam, 1½ m. E. (*See Runcorn.*)

Mossley (Yorks.)—L. & N.W.R. Tame. Car brook. Lakes: Knoll Hill, 1 m. S.W. Lrnyshaw dam, 2 m. N. (*See Runcorn.*)

Mottisfont (Hants.).—L. & S.W.R. On Test; plenty of trout, but closely preserved. (*See Southampton.*)

Moulsford (Berks.).—G.W.R. On Thames. Jack, perch, and roach. *Inn:* Beetle and Wedge. *Fisherman:* Frank Coxe. (*See London, M.T.*)

Much Wenlock (Salop).—G.W.R. Hughley brook (1½ m. N.W.). Beggarhill brook (3 m. S.E.), Mor brook (3½ m. S.E.); trout. Severn (4 m. N.); chub, pike, dace, salmon, trout. Lakes: Marsh ponds (1½ m. E.). Willey Park ponds (3 m. E.). (*See Gloucester.*) (*c.s. Severn*).

Muker (York), n.s. **Askrigg**, 10 m.—Swale; trout, grayling. (*c.s. York.*) Muker beck: trout. Thwaite beck, 1 m.W.; trout; free. Oxnop beck, 1 m. E. Gunnerside beck, 1 m. E.; spoilt by lead mines. Summer Lodge beck, 5 m. E.; trout; preserved. (*See York.*)

Mullion (Cornwall).—(n.s. **Penryn**, 19 m.) Mullion brook. Mullion rises in Hayle Pool near Roan Major, and is 3 m. long. Good pollack, conger, &c., fishing at sea.

Muncaster (Cumland.).—R. & E.R. Esk; trout. (*c.s. West Cumberland.*) Mite; trout. (*c.s. West Cumberland.*) Sarngath beck, 2 m. S.E. (*See Ravenglass.*)

Musgrave (Westland.).—N.E.R. Eden; trout; free. (*c.s.*) Belah, Stainmore, and Argill becks, 4 m. E.; trout. (*See Carlisle.*)

Naburn (York).—G.N.R. Ouse; roach, dace, chub, bream; preserved on left bank, free on right bank. (*c.s. York.*) (*See York.*)

Nafferton (York).—N.E.R. Hull, 1 m. S., at Wansford. Skerne beck, 2 m. S. (*See Hull.*) (*c s. York.*)

Nailsea (Somerset).—G.W.R. Kenn; trout, coarse fish. *Inns:* Battle Axes Wraxall, Royal Oak. Lakes: Nailsea ponds; pike, perch, carp, roach, rudd; leave from the Supt. G.W.R., Bristol.

Nailsworth (Gloucester).—M.R. Nailsworth brook. (*See Stonehouse.*) Lakes: Longthorpe lake; pike, carp; leave from C. Playne, Esq., Thescombe House, or Hon. Mrs. Ricardo. Woodchester Park lake; pike; leave difficult to obtain.

Nantwich (Cheshire).—G.W.R.; L. & N.W.R. Weaver; coarse fish, trout. Baddiley brook, 1 m. S. Cheer brook, 1 m. E. Artle brook, 2 m. S.E., at Howbeck Bridge. Howbeck brook, 2 m. S.E. Pool brook, 3 m. N.W. Lakes: Harleston Lake, 3 m. N.W. Doddington Park, 4 m. S.E. (*See Frodsham.*)

Nantyderry (Monmouth).—G.W.R. Usk; salmon, trout. Llanarth brook, 3 m. (*See Newport.*) (*c.s.*)

Narborough (Leicester).—L. & N.W.R. Soar (*c.s. Trent*). Whetstone brook. Normanton brook, 2 m. W. Billesdon brook, 2 m. N.E. Lakes: Normanton Hall lake, 4 m. N.W. (*See Gainsborough.*)

Narborough (Norfolk).—G.E.R. Nar; excellent trouting; strictly preserved. (*See King's Lynn.*) (*c.s. N. and S.*)

Naseby (Northampton).—n.s. **Kilworth**, 5 m. Avon rises in the large reservoir W. of the town. (*See Gloucester.*)

Nassington (Northton.)—L. & N.W.R. Nen; pike, perch, bream, chub, tench, &c. (*See Wisbeach.*)

Navenby (Lincoln).—G.N.R. Brant, 2 m. W., at Skinnand. Witham, 4 m. W. at Bassingham. (*See Boston.*)

Nayland (Suffolk), n.s. **Colchester**, 6 m.—Stour; pike, perch, roach, carp, dace, bream, tench. Boxford, 3 m. N.E. (*c.s. S. and E.*) (*See Manningtree.*)

Needham Market (Suffolk).—G.E.R. Gipping; roach, perch, pike, tench. Lake: Bosmere, 1 m. S.E. (*See Ipswich.*)

Neen Sollers (Salop).—G.W.R. Rea; trout; private. Ranhall brook. Hopton brook. Hopper brook (2½ m. N.W.). (*See Gloucester.*) (*c.s. Severn.*)

Netherton (York).—L. & Y.R. Lakes: Blackmoorfoot reservoir; pike, perch; preserved by the Huddersfield Angling Association; hon. sec., S. Hellowell, Esq., Huddersfield. (*See Huddersfield.*)

Netherwastdale.—On Wastwater Lake; trout. The fishing on both lake and river free. Sport is good in May and June. There are also several small tarns in the hills but the fishing is indifferent. There are two small inns at Netherwastdale, both clean and comfortable. The **Drigg Station** (W.R.) is distant 6 m. One of the best flies is a red and orange body, gold twist, and woodcock's wing. Brown and dun flies are—

very killing. Red and black hackles ribbed are good flies; also one with black silk; body, black hackle, and crow's wing. The dotterel hackle and a fly with peacock's tail, body tipped with gold, hackle black or red, wings mallard, are also good, and so is the coch-y-bonddhu. Sprinkling tarn holds large trout. Burnmoor tarn, large pike and eels. After heavy floods good sport in the river that runs into Wastwater. (c.s. *Cumberland.*)

Newark-on-Trent (Notts.).—G.N.R.; M.R. Trent; roach, dace, perch, pike, chub, barbel, bream; preserved below by Newark and Muskham Fishery Association, d.t. from D. Slater, fishtackleist, Newark; there is some free water (c.s.). Devon; same fish. Carr dyke, 2 m S.W. at Hawton. Pingley dyke. 3 m. N.W. at Averham. Witham, 4 m. S.E. at Barnby. Crossby dyke, 5 m. N. (See *Gainsborough.*) *Tackleist*, D. Slater, Lombard-street.

Newbiggin (Lancs.), n.s. **Roose**, 3 m.—Fs.R. Newbiggin beck. This brook rises in Urswick tarn by Great Urswick, 3 m. S. of **Ulverston**, and 2 m. down receives the outflow of Mere tarn, 1½ m. up on left bank. 3 m. down is **Newbiggin**.

Newbiggin (Westland).—M.R. Eller beck. Millburn beck. Eden, 2 m. W.; trout. (c.s.) (See *Carlisle.*)

Newbridge-on-Usk (Monmouth.)—G.W.R. Usk; salmon and trout; preserved by the United Usk Fisheries Association; salmon rod licences, season 30s., 14 days 10s.; trout 2s. 6d.; salmon d.t. 20s., at the P.O. Usk; w.t. 10s., d.t. 2s. 6d., from the P.O. Usk and Newbridge Hotel; salmon and trout, s.t. from the secretary, Westgate-chambers, Newport. (See *Usk; Brecknock.*) Hotel: Newbridge. (c.s. *Usk.*) (See *Newport.*)

Newbury (Berks).—G.W.R. On Kennet and Lambourne. Hotel: Jack of Newbury. The Newbury District Angling Association preserves the Kennet hence to Aldermaston. Entrance 10s., s.t. 10s.; treasurer and sec., Mr. Wm. Scott Veitch, Jack Hotel. (See *London, M.T.*) Good general fishing in Kennet.

Newby Bridge (Lancs.).—Fs.R. Leven; salmon, trout. (c.s. *Kent.*) Lakes: Windermere, 1 m. N.; salmon, trout, char, pike, perch. (c.s. *Kent.*) Bortree tarn, 2 m. N.E. Hotel: Swan. (See *Ulverston.*)

Newby Wiske (York).—N.E.R. Wiske; grayling, trout, chub, pike; preserved; leave sometimes. Swale, 1 m. S.W. (c.s. *York.*) (See *York.*)

Newcastle-on-Tyne.—Coarse fishing free at Newton; trout, roach, dace. At Ryton, salmon, trout, roach, dace. At Prudhoe good trouting in reservoirs; s.t. 10s. 6d., d.t. 2s. 6d., from Newcastle Water Offices. The Duke of Northumberland also sometimes gives leave. At Newton and Ryton permission obtainable. *Tackleist*: H. A. Murton, 8, Grainger-street (see *Advt.*) who will gladly give information concerning the fishing in the district.

Newcastle-under-Lyme (Stafford).—L. & N.W.R.; M.R. Lyme. Fowler brook. 1 m. N.E. Trent, 2 m. S.E. (c.s.). Northwood brook, 2 m. S. Foxley brook, 5 m. N.E. Lakes: Ponds on racecourse, 2 m. N.W. Keel Hall Park lakes, 2 m. S.W. Trentham Park lakes, 4 m S.E. Whitmore Park, 4 m. S.W. (See *Gainsborough.*)

Newent (Gloucester).—G.W.R. Newent brook. (See *Gloucester.*)

Newhaven (Sussex).—L.B. & S.C.R. On Ouse. Ouse rises in two large ponds close to Slaugham village, and in 6 m. is joined by a stream on left bank, which rises in a large lake at Balcombe, 2 m. down from which a stream joins on left bank, which drains two or three ponds 1½ m. up. ¼ m. below this Ouse is reached. 4 m. down Ouse a stream joins on left bank, 4½ m. long, which rises in a lake by Horsted Keynes, 5 m. down Ouse, near Fletching, a stream 3 m. long, which runs out of some large lakes in Sheffield Park, and mill, joins on left bank (preserved by Lord Sheffield). 3 m. down, at Sharp's lock a stream, 3 m. long, joins on left bank, one branch of which flows out of a lake in Maresfield Park and the other from a large pond in the village (n.s. **Buxted**). Ouse next flows in 2 m. to **Isfield**. Here a stream joins on left bank, which rises in a lake by High Hurst Wood, 3 m. N. of **Buxted**. At **Buxted** a stream joins on left bank, 4 m. long, which drains several ponds and mill dams. Next **Uckfield** is reached in 2 m. and **Isfield** in 3½ m., 1½ m. below **Isfield**, two streams join Ouse, one on the right bank and the other on left bank. The right-hand stream rises in a lake by Chailly, flows 2 m. to Old Park, where it waters a large lake, and then 3½ m. on to the Ouse. The stream on the left bank is 2 m. long, and drains some large lakes near Mole Wood. Ouse next flows in two branches to **Barcombe** 2 m., thence to **Lewes**, 6 m. 3 m. below a stream, 5 m. long, joins on left bank. **Glynde** is in the centre of it. Thence to **Newhaven** (N.R.) is 6 m., passing Rodmill, Tarring Niville, Piddinghoe, South Heighton, and Denton, 1 m. from **Newhaven** Ouse joins the sea. (c.s.) Fair sea fishing, whiting, &c. Bass at harbour's mouth and round Beachy Head. Good fishing from the pier. (c.s.)

Newlay (Yorks).—M.R. Aire. (c.s. *York.*) Old Mill beck. (See *Rawcliffe.*)

Newmill End (Herts.).—M.R.; G.N.R. On Lea. (See *Stratford.*)

New Mills (Cheshire).—M.R.; L. & N.W.R. Goyt or Mersey. Sett brook. Lady Gate brook, 1 m. N. (See *Runcorn.*)

Newnham Bridge (Worcester).—G.W.R. Teme; trout, chub, grayling, dace, roach, pike; preserved above by the Tenbury Angling Association; below, privately. (See *Tenbury.*) Rea; trout, chub. Piper's brook (2 m. E.). Lakes: Bickley pools (2 m. N.); trout, pike, perch, roach, carp; preserved by M. Tomkinson. Stanford Park lake (7 m. S.E.). Hotel: Talbot, which has 2 rods on the Teme. (See *Gloucester.*) (c.s. *Severn.*)

New Passage (Gloucester).—G.W.R. Pilning brook. Pilning rises 5 m. N.E. of **Pilning** (G.W.R.), and runs to **New Passage** 3 m. 2 m. N. Orreston brook joins the sea; it is 4 m. long.

Newport (Essex).—G.E.R. Cam. *Lakes:* Debden Park, 2 m. E. (*See King's Lynn*).

Newport (Monmouth.).—G.W.R. Usk; salmon, trout. Usk rises in Brecon 12 m. above **Devynock**, in a small lake full of trout. 7 m. from the source, Hydfer (trout), 5 m. long. joins on right bank. 2 m. down, at Trecastle (a good inn, and fishing free *above*, but preserved below by United Usk Fisheries Association; trout rod licences 2s. 6d, of the postmaster) (*see Brecon*), a stream joins on left bank, which, dividing in two parts at Llywel, is 5 m. long. 2 m. down, Clydach (4 m. long) and Cray join Usk (n.s. **Devynock**, 2 m.), one on left bank and the other on right bank. Cray rises 3 m. above **Cray** Station, and is 7 m. long. Usk runs 2 m. to **Devynock**. Here Senni joins on right bank. Senni is 6 m. long, and receives on left bank Treweren, 4 m. long, close to the town. 2 m. down Usk, Cilleni joins on left bank. Cilleni is 9 m. long, and is joined by Llandeilor brook on right bank midway down. Usk runs 3 m. to **Aberbran**. Here Bran, 11 m. long, joins on left bank. 1 m. down Usk, at Aberyscir, Yscir joins on left bank. 4 m. above the junction Yscir divides into two parts, Yscir-fechan and Yscir-faur, each some 8 m. long. Usk runs in 3½ m. to **Brecknock** (N. & B.R.); there Honddu joins on left bank, and Tarett on right bank. Honddu rises 4 m. above Capel Dyffryn, runs 4 m. to Llanfihangel-fechan, and **Brecknock** 6 m. Tarett rises on the Beacons, and 6 m. down is joined on right bank by a brook rising in Llyn-cwm-Llwch, 4 m. up. Tarett runs 2 m. to Usk. 2½ m. down Usk, Cynrig, 5 m. long, joins on right bank, and 2 m. down Usk, at Llanhamlath (n.s. **Tal-y-llyn Junction**, N. & B.R., 2 m.). Mehascia, 5 m. long, joins on right bank. 3 m. down Usk, at Llansaintfred or **Tal-y-Bont** (B. & M.T.J.R.) (preserved by the United Usk Fisheries Association; salmon rod licences, s. 30s., 14 days 10s.; trout 2s. 6d.), Alwynd joins on right bank. This stream rises near **Torpantau** Station, and is 8 m. long. 3 m. down Usk, Dyfferyn Crawnon, 4 m. long, joins on right bank, and 2 m. down, Claisvare, 3 m. long, joins on right bank, passing Llangynidr 1 m. up from the junction (preserved by U.U.F.A. *Hotel*, Red Lion, where licences can be had, *see Brecknock*). 2 m. down Usk, Rhiangoll Cwmdu joins on left bank. Rhiangoll rises 4 m. S.W. of **Talgarth**, runs 5 m. to Llanfihangel Cwmdu, 2 m. to Tretower, and Usk 1 m. Usk runs in 2 m. to Crickhowel (n.s. **Gilwern**, 4 m.) The trouting is very good both above and below the town. The fishing for the most part belongs to private owners and the United Usk Fisheries Association; salmon and trout rod licences from Mr. Harris, chemist. March and April are best for trout; salmon fishing varies with the water. *Hotel:* Bear. 2 m. down, Grwyne (trout) joins Usk on right bank. Grwyne rises 6 m. across country from **Talgarth**, runs 13 m. to Llanbedr, 2 m. from Crickhowel, where it is joined on right bank by Grwyne-fechan, 7 m. long. 3 m. down is Usk. 1 m. down Usk, Clydach, which rises 4 m. above **Gilwern** Station and is 5 m. long, joins on right bank. Usk runs to **Govilon** 4 m., where Wenarth joins on right bank. Wenarth rises in the Forge Pond 2 m. S. of the station, and is 3 m. long. Usk runs to **Abergavenny** 2 m. Here Gavenny joins on left bank. Gavenny rises near **Llanfihangel**, and is 5 m. long. Usk runs 3 m. to **Penpergwm** 2 m., below which Llanover brook, which rises in a small lake and is 6 m. long, joins on right bank, and 1 m. down Usk, Llangattock brook, which runs 1½ m. E. of **Penpergwm** and is 3 m. long, joins on left bank. ½ m. down Usk, Llanarth brook, 4 m. long, joins on left bank. Usk runs 3 m. to **Nantyderry**, and Usk 3 m. Here Olway river runs close to the town, and joins Usk on left bank 2 m. down. Olway rises by Trellech (n.s. **Bigsweir**, 2 m. E.), and 5 m. down is joined on right bank by a brook 4 m. long. 1 m. down Olway, at **Llandenny**, Raglan brook, which rises by **Raglan** and is 4 m. long, joins on right bank. 1 m. down Olway. Pill brook, 4 m. long, joins on left bank. Olway runs 3 m. to **Usk**, and Usk river 2 m. Usk runs to Kemeys inferior 5 m. (preserved by the United Usk Fisheries Association; salmon rod licences, season 30s,. 14 days 10s.; trout, 2s. 6d. from the Post Office, Usk, and Newbridge Hotel, Newbridge-on-Usk,) and 3 m. on is joined on right bank by a brook which rises by **Panteg** and is 7 m. long. Usk runs to **Caerleon**, 1 m. Here Llwyd joins on right bank. Llwyd (poisoned) rises 2 m. above **Blaen-Afon**, runs to **Cwm Afon** 3 m., **Abersychan** 2 m., **Pontypool** 2 m., **Panteg** 2 m., **Pontrhydyran** 1 m., **Pontnewydd** 1 m., **Cwmbran** 1 m., and 3 m. down is joined on right bank by Dowlas brook, which rises 2 m. N. of **Llantarnam**, and is 4 m. long. Llwyd joins Usk 3 m. down. Usk runs 4 m. to **Newport**, to which point the tide flows (licences as above, and w.t. 10s. and d.t. 2s. 6d. for trout, from Mr. Mullock, Austin Friars.) (*See Usk*.) March and April are the best trouting months, and April to October for salmon. Flies for Usk are March brown, with more yellow in the body; blue and yellow duns coch-y-bonddhu; spider fly, *body*, dark slate blue; *hackle*, long, black; *wing*, hen pheasant's; Hoffland's Fancy and the spinners. At the end of May the "little purple" comes on (*body*, dark mole; *hackle*, dark grizzly blue; *wing*, dark starling). At the same time a large yellow dun comes on, and continues during the season (hook No. 9; *body*, yellow ribbed with gold; *hackle*, smoky, golden tipped; *wing*, light starling). This and the alder dressed buzz are the best general flies. The black gnat, stone fly, the fern fly (dark orange-red body, light blue hackle, and hen pheasant wing), and the large cinnamon, are also useful flies. The larger flies, as the cob, alder, large spinner, and large dun, must be dressed on No. 9 hooks, the others on 10, and the purple and gnats on 11 and 12. Mr. Francis recommends these salmon flies as good general Welsh patterns: 1. Gold tip, pale blue sprigs of Indian jay and flamingo, or ibis, or red macaw fibres for tail, orange wool body, brown hackle, long and full all the way up; gold tinsel sparingly, and brown mottled turkey wing;

black head. 2. Tip and tail as before; light orange silk bod\; yellow hackle long and full, gold twist sparingly, and dirty red hackle at shoulder; mottled turkey wing. 3. Tail and tip as before; dirty yellow wool body; golden olive hackle; gold twist fine, large bunch of peacock's harl for wings. 4. Gold tip, two red macaw fibres, and a gold pheasant's topping for tail; dark brown wool body; golden olive (rather inclining to orange) hackle, with black tints to the fibres, spare gold twist, turkey wing. 5. Gold pheasant tippet tail, dark brown wool body. bronzed olive hackle, with darkish dirty green tips, turkey wing, no tinsel. 6. Gold tip, fancy tail of two sprigs of blue macaw, light yellow toucan feather and small green parrot feather (this tail is not indispensable). two twists of ostrich harl (black), over yellow silk body, gold tinsel. and light smoky blue hackle with golden tips; wing, two bittern's hackles. All the hackles are dressed very full and long, and most of the bodies are fattish. Hooks. about No. 7 or No. 8, salmon size. Another good Usk fly has a bit of yellow floss silk for tail, a pale yellow or lemon body, pale blue or dun hackle, and wings of either the striped feathers under a hawk's, or snipe's, or woodcock's wing, dyed pale yellow. (*c.s.*)

EBBW rises 2 or 3 m. above **Beaufort**, and passing there runs to **Ebbw Vale** (2 m.), **Victoria** (1 m.), **Cwm** (2 m.), **Aberbeeg** (3 m.). Here Ebwg-fach, which rises above **Blaina**, runs thence to **Abertillery** (3 m.) and **Aberbeeg** (2 m.), joins on left bank. 2 m. down Ebbw by **Crumlin**, a stream joins on right bank 1¼ m. long, which drains a pond—Ponnd-y-Coed-Cae. 2 m. S.W. from **Aberbeeg**. Ebbw runs to **Newbridge** (1 m.), **Abercarne** (1 m.), **Cross Keys** (1 m.). Here Sirhowey joins on right bank. Sirhowey rises in Llyn-garn-fawr 3 m. N.W. from **Trefil**, and 2 m. down is joined on left bank by a stream draining a pond 1 m. up. 1 m. down Sirhowey, Naut-y-llecha joins on right bank, draining a pond 3 m. up. Sirhowey runs to **Tredegar** (2 m.), **Holly Bush** (5 m.). **Argoed** (3 m.), **Black Wood** (2 m.), **Tredegar Junction** (2 m.), **Ynysddu** (2 m.), and **Cross Keys** (4 m.). Ebbw runs to **Risca** (1 m.), **Tydee** (3 m.), **Bassaleg** (2 m. from **Newport**) 1½ m. Ebbw joins Usk Estuary 8 m. down. Both Ebbw and Sirhowev are poisoned. (*c.s. Usk.*) Hotel: Westgate.

Newport (Salop).—G.W.R.; L. & N.W.R. Meess (1 m. N.); tront; private. Strine (3 m. W.); private. Lorneo brook (3 m. N). Brockton brook (3 m. S.). Ellerton brook (5 m. N.W.). Lakes: Chetwynd Park pond (1 m. N.). Aquadale mere (2 m. N.E.); pike, bream; Sir J. Boughey, who sometimes gives leave. Minton's, Limekiln and Wildmoor pools (3 m. S.). (*See Gloucester.*) (*c.s. Severn.*) Hotel: Victoria.

Newport (Yorks).—N.E.R. Tees estuary. Thorpe beck; trout and coarse fish in lower part: preserved by the Stockton Anglers' Club. (*See Stockton.*)

Newport Pagnel (Bucks).—L. & N.W.R. Ouse. (*c.s. N. and S.*) Ousel. (*See King's Lynn.*)

New Quay (Cornwall).—G.W.R. Kestle water. Kestle rises 1 m. S.W. from **St. Columb** Station. runs 5 m., and is joined on left bank by Tredinick water. Tredinick rises 2 m. N. of St. Michael's (n.s. **Grampound**, G.W.R., 6 m.) 3 m. down Newlyn water, which rises on Newlyn Down. runs by Newlyn, and is 3 m. long, joins on left bank. Tredinick runs 2 m. to Kestle. 1 m. down Kestle. Stringer's water, which rises a short distance N. of Newlyn, and is 2½ m. long, joins on left bank. Kestle runs to the sea and **New Quay** in 2 m. (*c.s. Camel.*) 2 m. N. from **New Quay** runs Mellincoose water, which rises 1 m. N. from **St. Columb** Station. runs 7 m. to St. Columb Minor, where it is joined by Trewince water, 2 m. long, and runs to the sea in 1 m. 2 m. S.W. from **New Quay**, at Crantock, runs Trevowa water. 3 m. long. 4 m. W. down the coast from **New Quay** into Holywell Bay runs Holywell brook. 6 m. long. Fair sea fishing.

Newsholme (York).—L. & Y.R. Ribble; trout, salmon. Forest beck, 4 m. W. Bond beck, 5 m. N.W. (*See Preston.*)

New Shoreham (Sussex).—L.B. & S.C.R. On Adur. Adur rises in a lake by the railway 2 m. W. of **Burgess Hill**. In 2½ m. a stream ½ m. long joins on right bank, which drains a large lake. 2 m. on a stream joins on right bank, 1 m long, which drains two large ponds near Bolney village. 2 m. on a stream joins on left bank, which rises by **Hassocks Gate** Station, and is 5 m. long, supplying three mills. 1 m. down Adur, at Shermanbury. a stream joins on right bank, which rises in some lakes 9 m. off. Cowfold village is half-way up this stream. 2 m. down Adur, where the railway crosses (n.s. **Henfield**). a stream joins on left bank, which rises in some ponds at Strude Garden, 1 m. west of **Hassocks Gate** Station, and in 6 m. is joined by a stream on the left bank, 2 m. long, which rises in a large lake at Woodmancote (n.s. **Henfield**, 3 m.) 1½ m. on, this stream joins Adur. ¾ m. down, at **Henfield** a large stream joins on right bank, which rises 1 m. east of **Billing-hurst**, and after 7 m. is joined by a stream on right bank, which runs out of a large lake 1½ m. off. ¾ m. down a stream joins on left bank. which drains Knepp pond (n.s. **Grinstead**, 1½ m. off.) 2½ m. down stream, 1 m. south-west of **Partridge Green** Station, a stream joins on the right bank, which drains some ponds near Ashington, and is 3½ m. long. 1½ m. down, Adur is reached. Adur runs to **Steyning**, 5 m., where a stream joins on the right bank, which drains two ponds at Wiston, 2½ m. off; Adur runs to **Bramber** 1 m., and **Shoreham** 5 m., passing Botolphs and Combes. Bass at harbour's mouth. and a variety of sea fish outside and in the offing.

Newthorpe (Notts).—G.N.R. Erewash. Lakes: Shipley Hall reservoir, 2 m. W. Mapperly reservoir, 3 m. W. (*See Gainsborough.*)

Newton (Cheshire).—G.N.R. Lakes: Godley reservoir. (*See Runcorn.*)

Newton (Lancs). n.s. **Clitheroe**, 8 m.—Hodder; trout. Easington brook. Whitendale river, 3 m. W. Langden river, 4 m. W. Brennand river. 6 m. N.W. Hotel: Parker's Arms, where fishing in 2½ m. of Hodder for two days can be had. (*See Preston.*)

Newton Abbot (S. Devon).—G.W.R. On Teign; trout, salmon, and sea trout; preserved by the Lower Teign Fishing Association hence *up* to **Dunsford**. *Hotels:* Globe, Queen's, and Commercial. (*See Teignmouth.*) There are a few trout in the stream which joins Teign here. Fish *above* the town. *(c.s.)*

Newton Ferrers (Devon), n.s. **Steer Point** (G.W.R.).—Yealm; trout; preserved; s.t., salmon and trout 10s., trout 2s. 6d. Good bass. pollack and other sea fishing, and the accommodation is first class. *Hotel:* River Yealm (see *Advt.*). *Tackleist:* W. Hearder, Union-street, Plymouth. (*See Cornwood.*)

Newton Kyme (York).—N.E.R. Wharfe. (*c.s. York.*) (*See York.*)

Newton-le-Willows (Lancs.).—L. & N.W.R. Newton beck runs near; trout. There is good jack, roach, bream, perch, and trout fishing in Newton mere; preserved by Lord Newton.

Newton Road (Stafford).—L. & N.W.R. Tame. (*c.s. Trent.*) *Lakes:* Forge Pond. Red House Hall, 1 m. N.E Bar Park, 2 m. E. (*See Gainsborough.*)

New Walsingham (Norfolk).—G.E.R. Blakeney river. Blakeney rises 10 m. above this place, and 5 m., down is joined on right bank by a stream 4 m. long, which rises in a pond on Langham Common, 5 m. N.E. from **N. Walsingham.** Blakeney joins the sea 3 m. down.

Norbury (Derby).—M.R. Dove; trout, grayling. (*c.s. Trent.*) Calwich brook. *Lakes:* Wootton Grange ponds, 2 m. N.W. (*See Gainsborough.*)

Norham (Northland.).—(*See Berwick*)

Northallerton (York).—N.E.R. Wiske; grayling, trout, chub, pike; preserved; leave sometimes. (*c.s. York.*) Brompton beck. (*See York.*)

Northampton.—M.R.; L. & N.W.R.—Nene; pike, perch, bream, chub, king carp, &c.; preserved by Nene Angling Club from Paper Mills to Wellingborough; s.t. (whole water) 21s.; Paper Mills to Billing, 10s. 6d.; d.t. 2s., 1s. 6d., and 1s.; pike fishing, d.t. 5s.; no Sunday fishing; 2 days' piking in any one week only allowed; hon. sec, James Jackson, Esq., 6, St. Giles-street. Wootton brook, 3 m. S. Billing brook, 4 m. N.E. *Lakes:* Abington Park, 1 m. N.E. Dallington Hall, 2 m. N.W. Overstone Park, 4 m. N.E. Althorp Park, 5 m. N.W. *Fishing Stations within reach:* Roade, Wolverton, Aylesbury, Boxmore, Towcester, Wappenham, Helmdon, Banbury, Weedon, Althorp Park, Rugby, Brampton, Brixworth. Lamport, Kelmarsh, Market Harborough, Rockingham, Castle Ashby, Wellingborough, Higham Ferrers, Thrapston, Oundle, Wansford, Peterborough. Olney. Bedford. (*See Wisbeach.*) *Hotels:* Plough. Grand, George.

North Elmham (Norfolk).—G.E.R. Wensum. (*c.s. N. and S.*) *Lake:* Elmham Hall Lake. (*See Yarmouth.*)

North Tawton (Devon).—L. & S.W.R. Taw. (*c s.*) (*See Barnstaple.*) Trouting in Taw is fairly good; tickets (s. 21s., d. 2s. 6d.) at the hotel. *Hotel:* Gostwick Arms,

North Walsham (Norfolk).—G.E.R. Ant. 1 m. E. Gunton beck, 4 m. W. *Lakes:* Perch pond, Mill pond, Heath Plantation (2 m. S.). Antinham ponds (Lord Suffield), 2 m. N.W. (*See Yarmouth.*)

Northwich (Cheshire).—L. & N.W.R. and C.L.C.R. Weaver. Dane. Norcot brook. Cranage brook. Budworth brook. Wincham brook. Birch brook, 4 m. N. Waterless brook, 5 m. N.E. *Lakes:* Pickmere mere. 2 m. N.E. Budworth mere, 2 m. N. Cogshall lake, 3 m. N.W. Arley Hall, 5 m. N.E. For information apply to Mr. G. Scales, Wincham, Northwich. (*See Frodsham.*)

North Wootton (Norfolk)—(*See Castle Rising.*)

Norton (Cheshire).—L. & N.W.R.; G.W.R. Kekwick brook. (*See Runcorn.*)

Norton (Salop).—G.W.R. Tern; few trout, pike, roach, dace. (*See Gloucester.*) (*c.s. Severn.*)

Norton (Yorks).—G.N.R.; L. & Y.R. Went. Lake Drain, 2 m. N. (*See Goole.*)

Norton Bridge (Stafford).—L & N.W.R. Meese. (*c.s. Trent.*) Sow, 2 m. W. (*See Gainsborough.*)

Norton Fitzwarren (Somerset). — G.W.R. Norton brook and Tone; trout. (*See Bridgwater.*) (*c.s. Avon.*)

Norwich (Norfolk).—G.E.R. Yare; pike, perch, roach, bream, tench, carp; free. (*c.s. N. and S.*) Tasse; same fish. Wensum; same fish. (*c.s. N. and S.*) All lakes and ponds hold the same fish; leave from the owners. *Hotels:* Royal, Maid's Head, and Bell. *Fishing stations within two hours of the city:* Whitlingham, Brundall, Buckenham, Cantley, Reedham, Haddiscoe, St. Olave's, Somerleyton, Mutford, Harleston, Homersfield, Bungay, Geldeston, Beccles, Diss, Eye. Salhouse, Wroxham, North Walsham, Coltishall, Buxton, Aylsham, Acle. (*See Yarmouth.*) *Tackleist,* A. J. Rudd, 54, London-street.

Norwood (Surrey).—L.B.&S.C.R. The South Norwood Park Lake; jack, carp, perch, roach, tench. Subscription, 21s. per annum; d.t., 1s. 6d.; limited to 50 members.

Nostell (Yorks).—G.N.R. *Lakes:* Nostell Priory lakes, 1 m. N. Cold Hindley reservoir, 2 m. S.W. (*See Goole.*)

Nottingham.—M.R.; G.N.R. Trent; salmon, trout, grayling, perch, roach, pike, chub, barbel, bream; free on left bank from Trent Bridge up to **Beeston,** preserved on the right bank, s. t. 10s. (*c.s.*) Leen. Fairham brook, 3 m. S.W. Tottle brook, 4 m. W. Thurbeck, 4 m. S.E. *Lakes:* Bilborough Cut, 4 m. N.W. (*See Gainsborough.*) Trent, close to **Trent;** bream, roach, and perch. *Fishing stations within two hours:* Ambergate, Ashlockton, Attenborough. Barrow, Barnston, Bashford, Beaston Belper, Bleasby, Borrowash, Bottesford, Breadsall, Bulwell, Burton, Burton Joyce Carlton, Castle

Donnington, Chellaston, Codnor Park, Colwick (Colwick Waters—top length, tickets, 20s., from sec., Race Committee; bottom length, 20s., from Mr. Parr, Carrington-street, Clifton), Daybrook, Derby, Draycott, Duffield, East Norton, Eastwood, Eggington, Farnsfield, Fiskerton, Gotham, Grantham (in the Canal), Harby, Harringworth, Hathern, Holme Pierrepont (some of the best fishing in the district; tickets, 10s., of tackleist), Hykeham, Huckall, Ilkeston, Kegworth, Kimberley, Kirklington, Leicester, Limby, Lincoln, Long Eaton, Loughborough, Lowdham, Mansfield, Manton, Market Harborough, Melton Mowbray, Newark, Newthorpe, Pinxton, Pye Bridge, Radcliff, Rolleston, Sandiacre, Sawley, Saxby, Sileby, Southwell, Spondon, Stanton, Sutton, Syston, Trent, Weston, Wilford (Wilford Waters; tickets, 10s., from tackleist), Wissendine; close to Trent Lock is the Soar (bream, roach, perch, chub, pike). The Nottingham Anglers' Association (headquarters, Newshouse-street, James-street) preserve the Lock and the Clifton Red Hill, Carlton and Shelford waters; s.t., 7s. 6d. *Tackleist*, W. Snowden, 7, St. John-street.

Nuneaton (Warwick).—L. & N.W.R.; M.R. Anker (c.s. *Trent.*) Griff Brook. *Lakes:* Sedswood pool, 3 m. S.W. Arbury Park ponds, 4 m. S.W. (*See Gainsborough.*)

Nunnington (York).—N.E.R. Rye; trout, grayling; preserved. Riccal, 1 m. N.; trout, grayling. (*See Wressel.*)

Nun Monkton (York), n.s. **Naiston**, 2 m.—(*See York.*)

Oakamore (Stafford).—L. & N.W.R.; G.N.R. Churnet; trout, grayling, coarse fish; fishing spoilt by Leek drainage. (c.s. *Trent.*) (*See Gainsborough.*)

Oakham (Rutland).—M.R.; G.N.R. Gwash, 3 m. S. Chater, 4 m. S. *Lakes:* Burley Park, 1 m. E. Exton Park, 8 m. N.E. 1 m. distant are the Oakham Angling Society's waters (pike, perch, and roach), d.t. 1s. *Fishing within two hours:* Manton, Harringworth, Geddington, Kettering, Wissendine, Saxby, Melton Mowbray, Upper Broughton, Plumptree, Edwalton, Nottingham. (*See Spalding.*) *Tackleist*, J. E. Whitehouse, gun and cartridge works.

Oakley (Beds).—M.R. Ouse; coarse fish, except barbel; preserved hence to Passenham Bridge by the Duke of Bedford; good jacking. (c.s. *N. and S.*) (*See King's Lynn.*)

Oaks (Lancs.)—L. & Y.R. Tange. Bradshaw brook. (*See Runcorn.*)

Oakworth (York).—M.R. Worth. Oxenhope beck. *Lakes:* Keighley Moor pond, 4 m. N.W. (*See Rawcliffe.*)

Ookle Street (Gloucester).—L. & S.W.R. Denn brook, which rises 1 m. E. from **Longhope** station, and 4 m. down is joined on right bank by a brook 3 m. long. Denn runs to Severn (2 m.).

Offord (Hunts.).—G.N.R. Ouse; coarse fish, except barbel; 1 m. from here is a famous breaming station, called Barnes's Hole. (*See King's Lynn.*)

Okehampton (Devon).—L. & S.W.R. On Taw; trout. East and West Okement; trout. (c.s. *Taw.*) Marshford brook, 3 m. (*See Bideford* and *Barnstaple.*) *Hotel:* White Hart, where licences are issued, and which has fishing free to visitors.

Oldbury (Worcester).—L. & N.W.R.; G.W.R. Tame (c.s. *Trent.*) *Lakes:* Oldbury pond. (*See Gainsborough.*)

Old North Road Station (Cambs.).—L. & N.W.R. *Lakes:* Wimpole Park lakes; Lord Hardwick; good fishing, strictly preserved. (*See King's Lynn.*)

Ollerton (Notts.).—Maun. Rainworth brook. Meden, 3 m. N.W. *Lakes:* Rufford dam, 1 m. S. Thoresby Park, 3 m. N.W. (*See Althorpe.*)

Olney (Bucks).—M.R. Ouse; coarse fish, except barbel; private. (c.s. *N. and S.*) (*See King's Lynn.*)

Onibury (Salop).—L. & N.W.R. Onny; trout, grayling; preserved above. Teme (3 m. S.); trout, grayling, chub, dace. Corve (3 m. E.). *Lakes:* Decoy pool (2 m. S.) (*See Gloucester.*) (c.s. *Severn.*)

Orford (Suffolk).—Ore or Alde. Alde rises 5 m. above Bendham, 2 m. W. from **Saxmundham**, and 5 m. down is joined on right bank by Ore. Ore rises in a large pond by **Framlingham**, runs 4 m. to **Parham**, **Marlesford** 3 m., and Alde 3 m. Alde runs 2 m. to **Snape**. Here Saxmundham brook, which rises 2 m. above **Saxmundham**, runs thence 5 m. to **Snape** and Alde, joins on left bank. Alde runs 8 m. to **Aldborough**, and **Orford** 5 m. (c.s. *S. and E.*)

Ormesby (Norfolk).—G.E.R. *Lakes:* Ormesby (c.s.), Rollesby, and Filby Broad; leave required. (*See Yarmouth.*) *Inn:* Sportsman's Arms, Rollesby Bridge, where fishing can be had.

Ormside (Westland).—M.R. Eden; salmon, trout. (c.s.) Helm beck. Hilton beck. Hoff beck, 2 m. W. (*See Carlisle.*)

Ormskirk (Lancs.).—L. & Y.R.; Eller brook, 2 m. E. (*See Hesketh Bank.*)

Orpington (Kent).—S.E. & C.R. On Cray. (*See Dartford.*) *Hotel:* Maxwell Arms.

Oswestry (Salop).—G.W.R. Cynllaith. Morda (1 m. S.). Tanat (6 m. S.W., at **Llan-y-blodwell**). Vyrnwy (8 m. S., at **Llanymynech**). *Lakes:* Aston lake (3 m. S.E.). Rhyddwyn (5 m. W.). Halston Hall (5 m. N.E.). Vyrnwy at **Llanfyllin** (good trouting, fish averaging ½lb.) *Hotel:* Lake Vyrnwy. (*See Gloucester.*) (c.s. *Severn.*)

Otford (Kent).—S.E.R. Darenth; trout. (*See Dartford.*)

Otley (York).—M.R.; N.E.R. Wharfe; trout, grayling, chub, barbel; preserved by the owner, F. H. Fawkes, Esq., who has formed a small club; s.t. 21s.; apply to the Estate Agent (G. F. Weatherill), Farnley. Above Otley there is a little free fishing. Below Otley the Leeds A.S.A. preserve the Wharfe from High Mill Weir at Pool to Castley Ford on right bank, and to Lord Harewood's water at **Weeton** on left bank. Season, April 1 to

Jan. 31. (*c.s. York.*) (*See Pool.*) Hollinbeck, polluted. Mire beck, 2 *m.* S. W. Washburn, 3 *m.*
N. : trout; preserved. (*See York.*)
Otterington (York).—N.E.R. Wiske. (*c.s. York.*) Cod beck, 2 *m.* E Broad beck,
m. E. Sorrow beck, 4 *m* E (*See York.*)
Ottery Road (Devon).—L. & S.W.R. Otter and Tailwater brook. (*See Ottery St. Mary.*)
(*c.s.*)
Ottery St. Mary (Devon).—L. & S.W.R. Otter and Tailwater brook; trout, salmon. Otter
rises at Otterford on the S. slopes of the Black Down Hills (n.s. **Taunton**, 8 *m.*); 2¼ *m.* down
a stream joins on left bank, working a mill 1 *m.* up. Otter runs to Upottery 3 *m.*, and 4½ *m.*
on is joined on right bank by Pennythorn Brook, 4 *m.* long. Otter runs in 2 *m.* to **Honiton**.
(S.W.R.). Here Blanscombe Brook, 3 *m.* long, joins on left bank. 1 *m.* down, Awliscombe
brook joins on right bank, 4 *m.* long and working a mill. 2½ *m.* down Otter is **Ottery Road**
Station (S.W.R.), 1 *m.* off the river on right bank, and 3 *m.* down is **Ottery St. Mary.**
Here Tailwater Brook joins on right bank. Tailwater rises at Broadhembury (n.s. **Ottery**
Road, 4 *m.*), runs in 5½ *m.* to that station, working three mills, and **Ottery**, 3 *m.* Otter
runs in 2½ *m.* to **Tipton** (the water above here is private; from hence down to Clamour-
bridge it is preserved by Hon. Mark Rolle. A single ticket for visitors can be had at the
Imperial Hotel, Exmouth, and Rolle Hotel, Budleigh Salterton), Newton Poppleford 2 *m.*,
Otterton 3 *m.* 1 *m.* down a small stream joins on right bank, working a mill above Budleigh 1 *m.* up. The tide flows to this junction, to which fishing is free. Exmouth, Budleigh Salterton, and all the stations on the Otter are now connected by branch railway.
(*See c.s.*)
Oughtibridge (Yorks).—G.C.R. Don. (*c.s. Yorkshire.*) Tinker brook, 1 *m.* N.W. Bowel,
3 *m.* S. Uphill brook, 3 *m.* S.W. Storr brook. 3 *m.* S. *Lakes*: Reservoir, 5 *m.* W. Ogden
reservoir, 4 *m.* W. (*See Goole.*)
Oulton Broad (Suffolk).—G.E.R. Waveney, 2½ *m.* N.W.; bream, roach, perch, pike;
free. *Lakes*: Oulton Broad; same fish; boats and bait at the Wherry Hotel (*see Advt.*).
Flixton Decoy, 2½ *m.* N. Lake at the Villa, 2½ *m.* N. (*See Yarmouth.*) (*c.s. Norfolk* and
Suffolk.)
Oundle (Northton.)—L. & N.W.R. Nen pike, perch, bream, chub, tench, &c. *Lakes*:
Bigein, 1 *m.* W. Southwick lake, 3 *m.* N.W. *Inn* : Talbot. (*See Wisbeach.*)
Over Darwen (Lancs.)—L. & Y.R. Darwen. (*See Preston.*)
Over Seal (Leicester).—L. & N.W.R. Seal brook. *Lakes*: Ashby Wolds reservoir, 1 *m.* N.
Barrat pool, 1 *m* S. (*See Gainsborough.*)
Overton (Hants.). —L. & S.W.R. On Test; trout and grayling; the fishing belongs to
Capt. Brydges. (*See Southampton.*) Good accommodation.
Overton (Hunts.).—L. & N.W.R.; G.N.R. Nen; pike, perch, bream, chub. &c.,
preserved by Lord Huntley. (*See Wisbeach.*)
Oxenholme (Westland).—L & N.W.R. Beetha, 2 *m.* E. (*c.s. Kent.*) Beehive beck, 1 *m.* E.
Peasey beck. 3 *m.* S.E. (*See Milnthorpe.*)
Oxenhope (York).—M.R. Oxenhope beck. (*See Rawcliffe.*)
Oxford.—G.W.R.; L. & N.W.R.; M.R. Thames, Cherwell, and Isis. (*See London. M.T.*)
Hotels: Clarendon, Three Cups (headquarters of the Oxford A.S.), Roebuck, and Anchor.
Fishermen: J. Bossom. P. and A. Beesley, D. Talboys. *Tackleist*, J. W. Innes, 42, Queen-
street.
Padiham (Yorks.)—L. and Y.R. West Calder; polluted. Lodge river. Shaw brook,
1 *m.* S. (*See Preston.*)
Padstow (Cornwall).—L. & S.W.R. Petherick Water; trout. This stream rises 3 *m.* N.
of **St. Columb** (G.W.R.) and is 7 *m.* long. (*c.s. Camel.*) In summer there are bass,
also pollack by the rocky cliffs and round the shore of Stepper Point, round the Gull,
Newland, and Penlike Point.
Paignton (Devon).—G.W.R. Pollack at back of pier, mackerel, bass, &c.; sand-eel
seines kept.
Pampisford (Cambs).—G.E.R. Bourn; coarse fish, few trout. (*See King's Lynn.*)
Pandy (Monmouth). — G.W.R. *Hotel*: Pandy Inn. Monnow; trout, grayling; private
throughout and strictly preserved. Honddhu ; trout; strictly preserved. (*c.s. Wye.*) Full
brook, 2 *m.* Olchon brook, 4 *m.* Escley, 5 *m.*
Pangbourne (Berks).—G.W.R. (*See London, M.T.*) Thames and Pang. Few trout,
perch, pike, &c. *Inns*: George, Elephant and Castle, and Swan. *Fishermen*: G. Ashley, jun.
and W. Chidsey. Over the weir at Whitchurch is the Bridge House, very comfortable. The
Pang is full of trout, especially near Tidmarsh, but is private, and belongs to R. Hopkins,
Esq.
Pannal (York).—N.E.R. Crimple. Nor beck. (*See York.*)
Panteg (Monmouth).—G.W.R. (*See Newport.*) Llwyd. (*c.s. Usk.*)
Par (Cornwall).— G.W.R. Bream. Bream rises 2 *m.* S.W. of **Victoria** station, close
by the line, runs 3 *m.*, and is joined on right bank by Rosemellon brook, 2 *m.* long.
¼ *m.* down Bream, a stream joins on right bank, which drains a pond 1 *m.* up. 2 *m.* down
Bream Treverbyn Water, 4 *m.* long, joins on right bank. Bream runs 1 *m.* to **Bridges**,
where Luxulian Brook, 4 *m.* long, joins on left bank. Bream runs 3 *m.* to **St. Blazey**.
Par. 1 *m.*, and the sea 2 *m.* (*c.s. Fowey.*) Sand-eels at Par sands, mackerel from the bay,
pollack by Gribben Head and near the harbour, large pollack, conger, &c., in the
offing.
Parbold (Lancs.)—L. & Y.R. Douglas. (*c.s. Ribble.*) Tawd, 2 *m.* W. (*See Hesketh Bank.*)

Parham (Suffolk).—G.E.R. Ore. (*See Orford.*)

Park (Essex).—G.E.R. (*See Stratford.*) On Lea; dace, roach, chub, perch, barbel, bream, jack, carp.

Parkbridge (Lancs.)—G.C.R.; L. & N.W.R. Medlock. *Lakes:* Knoll Hill lake, 2 m. S.E. (*See Runcorn.*)

Park Gate (Yorks).—G.C.R.; M.R. Don. Dalton brook. Morley brook. *Lakes:* Morley ponds, 2 m. N.W. (*See Goole.*)

Park Street (Herts.).—G.N.R. Colne. (*See London, M.T.*)

Parsley Hay (Derby).—(*See Hartington.*)

Partington (Cheshire).—C. Lines R. Mersey. Glaze brook. 2 m. W. (*See Runcorn.*)

Partridge Green (Sussex).—L.B. & S.C.R. (*See New Shoreham.*) On Adur; trout, &c.

Pateley Bridge (York.)—N.E.R. Nidd; trout, grayling; preserved by a club. (*c.s.* York.) Greenbow beck. Ashfordside beck, 1 m. N.W. Far beck, 3 m. S.E. Skell, 3 m. N.E.; trout. Laver, 6 m. N.; trout. *Lakes:* Eavestone Park. 5 m. N.E. *Hotel:* Crown. (*See Ramsgill, York.*)

Patricroft (Lancs.).—L. & N.W.R. Irwell. Worsley brook, 1 m. W. (*See Runcorn.*)

Patterdale (Westland).—Goldrill beck. Griesdale brook. Glenridding beck. Bindale beck, 1 m. W. Bindale beck, 2 m. S.E. Ara beck, 3 m. N. Hawes beck, 5 m. S.E. Rigindale beck, 5 m. S.E. *Lakes:* Ullswater; perch, trout; free. Greenside reservoir, 2 m. Brothers water, 2 m. S.E.; trout. Hayes tarn, 2 m. S.E.; strictly preserved by Dr. Murray, of Armthwaite. Angle tarn, 2 m. S.E.; trout. Red tarn, 4 m. S.W. Griesdale tarn, 4 m. S.W. Keppel Cove tarn. 4 m. W. Blea tarn, 5 m. S.E.; trout. Small Water tarn, 6 m. S.E. *Hotels:* Patterdale, Ullswater, White Lion. (*See Carlisle*).

Peak (York).—N.E.R. Helworth beck; trout; free. Jugger How beck, 3 m. S.W.; trout; free. Bloody beck, 3 m. S.W.; trout; free. (*See Wressel.*)

Pelsall (Stafford).—L. & N.W.R. Ford brook. (*See Gainsborough.*)

Pembridge (Hereford). — G.W.R. Arrow; trout, grayling; preserved by landowners. (*c.s. Wye.*) Tinsley brook (2 m.); preserved by landowners. Tippets brook (2 m.). *Lakes* at Shobdon Park (2 m.) (*See Chepstow.*)

Pengarn (Monmouth).—L. & N.W.R.; B. & M.R. Rumney; trout, salmon; preserved. (*c.s.*) (*See Cardiff, Wales.*)

Penistone (Yorks.).—G.C.R.; L. & Y.R. Don. (*c.s. Yorkshire.*) Scout dyke. Darton brook, 2 m. W. *Lakes:* Gamthwaite Mill pond, 2 m. N. (*See Goole.*)

Penkridge (Stafford)—L. & N.W.R. Penk. Whiston brook. Galey brook. Pillaton brook. Eaton Water, 5 m. W. *Lakes:* Pottal reservoir, 3 m. W. Manstey Wood ponds, 3 m. S.E. Bangley Mill pond, 2 m. W. Keeper's pools and Park pool, Teddesley Park, 2 m. N.E. (*See Gainsborough.*)

Pennard (Somerset).—S.W. & M.R. Wootton Brook. (*See Highbridge.*)

Penpergwm (Monmouth). — G.W.R. Usk; salmon, trout; preserved by United Usk Fishery Association, trout, w.t. 10s., d.t. 2s. 6d., from station master, and Mr. Thomas, Pont Kemys Farm, Chain Bridge. Salmon and trout s.t. from the secretary, Horace Lyne, Westgate Chambers, Newport. (*See Newport. Usk, Brecknock.*) (*c.s.*)

Penrith (Cumland).—M.R.; L. & N.W.R.; N.E.R. Eamont, 1 m. S.; salmon, trout, upper portion (trout only), preserved by the Penrith Angling Association; s.t. 20s., m.t. 10s., w.t. 3s. 6d.; lower portion preserved by Yorkshire Anglers' Association. (*c.s. Eden.*) Lowther, 1 m. S.; salmon, trout, chub; preserved by Lord Lonsdale, who grants leave. (*c.s.*) Petterill, 3 m. N.W.; trout. Eden, 5 m. E.; salmon, trout, chub; preserved as Eamont. (*c.s.*) *Hotels:* Crown, George, Gloucester Arms. *Lakes:* Whins pond, 3 m. E.; pike, perch, and carp: preserved by Yorkshire Anglers. Ullswater, 5 m. S. (free). Haweswater, 10 m. S.E.; by permission of Lord Lonsdale. (*See Carlisle.*)

Penruddock (Cumland).—M.R. Dacre beck, 1 m. S. Eamont, 5 m. E.; salmon, trout, chub. (*c.s. Eden.*) (*See Carlisle.*)

Penryn (Cornwall).- G.W.R. Penryn River. Penryn river is 6 m. long, and runs into the head of Falmouth Harbour. (*c.s. Fowey.*) (*See Mullion, Ruan Minor, Helston, Constantine.*)

Pensford (Somerset).—G.W.R. (*See Bristol.*) On Chew; perch, roach, trout; preserved by Mr. Popham, of Hunstrete Park. (*c.s. Avon.*) *Lakes:* Hunstrete Park lake; preserved by Mr. Popham, who often gives leave.

Penshurst (Kent).—S.E. & C.R. (*See Rochester.*) On Eden.

Penzance (Cornwall).—G.W.R. 3 brooks join the sea here. Gulvall brook rises 1 m. above New Mill, and 2 m. down is joined by a brook 2 m. long. 1 m. down is the sea. Madron brook rises by Boskedrian, and passing Madron 1 m. from **Penzance**, is 4 m. long. Newlyn brook runs into Guavas Lake. Newlyn rises above Bosullow, and is 7 m. long. Good pollack fishing off the Scillies, reached by steamer from Penzance. The trout fishing is not very good, but the sea fishing is excellent; pollack, mackerel, whiting, cod, hake, bream, conger, &c.; good pollack fishing from the pier. All the rocky ground also affords good sport. August and September best months. Two good hotels at St. Mary's. Penzance *Hotels:* Mount's Bay, Queen's, Western, Union.

Peplow (Salop).—G.W.R. Tern; a few trout, pike, roach, dace. Polford brook (2 m. S.W.), Alford brook (3 N.E.). Meese (4 m. S.); trout. (*See Gloucester.*) (*c.s. Severn.*)

Perran (Cornwall).—G.W.R. Perran. Trewedfra water. Stithians water. Perran rises by St. Dye (N.s. **Scorrier Gate**, G.W.R. 2 m.), runs 3 m., and is joined on right bank by Gwenna brook, 3 m. long. 2 m. down by **Perran**, Trewedfra water, 4 m. long, joins on right bank. 1 m. down Perran, Stithians water joins on right bank. Stithians rises in a pond by Caverlock, 1¼ m. W. of Stithians, and is 7 m. long. The tideway is now reached. (c.s. *Fowey*.)

Perranzabuloe (Cornwall.), n.s. **Truro**, 7 m.—Towan. Towan rises by Chiverton, and 1 m. down waters a lake by **Perranzabuloe**. 2 m. down, Golla water, 3 m. long, joins on left bank. 1 m. down is the sea. (c.s. *Fowey*.)

Perry Bar (Stafford).—L. & N.W.R. Tame (c.s. *Trent*.) Lakes: Lodge pool, 3 m. N. (See *Gainsborough*.)

Pershore (Worcester).—G.W.R. Avon; pike, perch, roach, dace, chub; free. Wyre (1 m. N.). Stourton brook (3 m. N.W.). Whitsun brook (5 m. N.). (See *Gloucester*.) (c.s. *Severn*.)

Peterborough (Northton).—G.N.R.; G.E.R.; L. & N.W.R.; M.R. Nen; pike, perch, bream, chub, &c. ; poor fishing near. Old river Nen. Muscal river or Cats Water. Lakes: Milton Park. 3 m. W.; strictly preserved. Hotels: Great Northern, Angel, Golden Lion, Grand. (See *Wisbeach*.)

Petersfield (Hants).—L. & S.W.R. Western Rother; trout, perch. (See *Fareham, Littlehampton*.)

Petworth (Sussex).—L.B. & S.C.R. (See *Littlehampton*.) Pike, perch, roach, carp, and tench in Chingford lake, Burton Park. Rother: pike, perch, roach, carp, trout; preserved. Leave may be obtained. Some of the smaller streams hold trout.

Pevensey (Sussex).—L.B. & S.C.R. On Pevensey river; roach, perch, &c. This stream rises in two or three large ponds at Penshurst, and then flows in 1 m. to Ashburton, where there are some large lakes. ½ m. down, a stream joins on right bank, 2½ m. long, rising in Bucksteep Mill Pond. 1 m. down, at Boreham Bridge, a stream 5 m. long joins on the right bank. 6 m. down, **Pevensey** is reached. Here a stream joins on the right bank, which rises in five or six lakes in Hurstmonceau Park, and flows in two streams, some 6 m. long each, to **Pevensey**.

Pickering (York).—N.E.R. Pickering beck; trout, grayling; private above, preserved below by an association; sec., H. W. Hunt, White Swan Hotel, Pickering. Costa, 1 m. W.; trout, grayling; preserved by the Costa Anglers' Club of 30; sec., E. Mitchell, Esq., Gordon House, South Cliffe, Scarborough; entrance 8l. 8s., s.t. 5l. 5s.; no Sunday fishing. 20 days' fishing in the trout season; no limit for grayling fishing after Oct. 1; fishing opens April 16. Thornton beck, 3 m. E. at Thornton Dale. Hotels: Black Swan, White Swan. (See *Wressel*.)

Pickhill (York).—N.E.R. Swale, 1 m. E. (c.s. *York*.) Wiske, 1 m. E.; grayling, trout, chub, pike; preserved. (c.s. *York*.) (See *York*.)

Picton (Yorks).—N.E.R. Leven. 1 m. E.; trout; private. (c.s. *Tees*.) (See *Stockton*.)

Piddington (Northton).—M.R. Wootton brook. (See *Wisbeach*.)

Piercebridge (Durham).—N.E.R. Tees; trout, salmon, bull trout, grayling, dace, chub, pike; preserved by M. J. Wilson, Esq., Cliffe Hall, and Duchess of Hamilton Snow Hall; also by Lord Barnard, tickets from his agent, Raby Castle; s.t., 1s. (c.s.) Alwent beck. Summerhouse beck, 2 m. N. Ulnaby beck, 2 m. E. Cocker beck, 2 m. N. Aldborough beck, 3 m. S. Lakes: Forcett Park, 3 m. S. Hotel: George. Licensee of Mr. J. F. Smythe, Tackleist, Horsemarket, Darlington.

Pilling (Lancs.)—G. & K.E.R. Pilling water. Pilling rises 2 m. above **Cogie Hill**, and 3 m. down is joined on left bank by a branch 4 m. long, which rises in Pilling Moss. From the junction Pilling runs in 1 m. to **Pilling** and the sea.

Pillmore (York).—N.E.R. Sun beck. Swale, 2 m. W. (c.s. *York*.) (See *York*.)

Pilning (Gloucester).—G.W.R. Pilning Brook. (See *New Passage*.)

Pimbo Lane (Lancs.)—L. & Y.R. Tawd. (See *Hesketh Bank*.)

Pinner (Middx.).—L. & N.W.R. Ruislip reservoir is 3¼ m. off (see *London, M.T.*); pike, perch, tench; preserved. Inn: Queen's Head.

Pinchbeck (Lincoln).—G.N.R.; G.E.R. Glen. Welland, 2 m. S.E. (See *Spalding*.)

Pinxton (Derby).—M.R. Erewash. Lakes: Brookshill Hall lakes, 2 m. N. (See *Gainsborough*.)

Pleasley Road (Salop).—There is some trouting 3 m. off. Leave may sometimes be obtained from the owner of Wrentnall House.

Plowden (Salop).—B.C.R. Onny; trout, chub; strictly preserved from **Eaton** above to **Horderly** below, by Plowden Fishing Club of 19, with 14 transferable day tickets; season from April 1 to Sept. 30; hon. sec., H. Manby Colegrave, Esq., Plowden Cottage, Lydbury North. (See *Gloucester*.) (c.s. *Severn*.)

Plumley (Cheshire). — L. & N.W.R. Peover. Kincham brook, 1 m. N.W. Waterless brook, 1 m. N. Lakes: Nether Tabley, 1 m. N. Toft Hall, 3 m. E. (See *Frodsham*.)

Plumptree (Notts).—M.R. Thurbeck. Lakes: Roclaveston Manor lake, 1 m. N. (See *Gainsborough*.)

Plumpton (Cumland).—L. & N.W.R. Petterill; salmon, trout. (c.s. *Eden*.) (See *Carlisle*.)

Plymouth (Devon).—G.W.R. Plym. Tamar; trout, salmon. Hotels: Royal and Duke of Cornwall. Plym rises 8 m. N.E. of **Bickley** (G.W.R.) on Dartmoor, and 6 m. down, Meavy joins on left bank. Meavy rises 5 m. E. of **Horrabridge** (G.W.R.), runs 5 m. to Meavy, and Plym 3 m. Plym runs to **Bickley** 1 m., **Marsh Mills** (G.W.R.) 3 m., and 2 m. down is joined on left bank by Tory Brook, which rises 4 m. E. of **Bickley**, runs 6 m. to **Plympton** (G.W.R.), and Plym 1 m. This brook is poisoned with clay water. Plym runs to **Plymouth** in 2 m. Plym is all private. (c.s. *Tamar*.) The Tavy and Plym Fishery Board grant tickets for Meavy, Cad, and Tavy, to be obtained of Messrs. Hearder.

TAMAR rises 4 m. N.E. of Kilkhampton, runs 4 m., where is the Tamar Lake (good trout fishing). (See *Bude*.) 2 m. below at Morton Mill, Stratton being 4 m. off on right bank, Foxwater brook, which runs 1 m. E. of Kilkhampton, and is 4 m. long, joins on right bank; 4 m. down Tamar a brook joins on left bank, 5 m. long, Holsworthy lying 4 m. off on left bank. 8 m. down Tamar, Holsworthy water (fishing free) joins on left bank. Holsworthy rises 4 m. N. of Holsworthy town. (*Hotel*: Stanhope), at which place Deer, 4 m. long, joins on left bank (trout; free). 6 m. down, Holsworthy joins Tamar. 1 m. down Tamar, Claw river joins on left bank. Claw rises on Claw Moor, 4 m. S.E. of Holsworthy, runs 4 m. to Clawton and Tamar. 3 m. Tamar runs 2 m. to Luffincot, 3 m. to Boyeton, and 3 m. down is joined by Bear Water 6 m. long on right bank. 2 m. down Tamar at New Bridge (n.s. **Launceston,** 2 m.). Yeolm river joins on right bank. Yeolm rises by Otterham, and 2 m. down is joined by Cancer water, 2 m. long, on left bank. 4 m. down Yeolm, Warbstow being 2 m. off on right bank, Wilsey brook, 4 m. long, joins on right bank. 5 m. down Yeolm, near North Petherwin (n.s. **Launceston,** 5 m.), Cowdery water, 7 m. long, joins on left bank. 3 m. down Yeolm, Kingsford water, 5 m. long, joins on left bank. Yeolm runs to Yeolm Bridge, 2 m. (n.s. **Launceston,** 2 m.), where it runs for 2 m. through the park at Werrington House and waters the lake there, and 1 m. down joins Tamar. 1 m. down Tamar, Carey joins on left bank. Carey rises 6 m. S.E. of Holsworthy on Hallwill Moor, runs 4 m. to Ashwater, and 2 m. down is joined on right bank by a stream 3 m. long. Carey runs 1 m. to Virginstow and Tamar 6 m. 1 m. down Tamar, Attery river joins on right bank. Attery rises by Tresmeer, runs 4 m. to Egloskerry, 5 m. to **Launceston**, and Tamar 2 m. Tamar runs 2 m., and is joined on left bank by Lyd river. Lyd rises 3 m. N.E. of **Lidford**, runs 5 m. to **Coryton**, where Lew water joins on right bank. Lew rises 2 m. N. of **Bridestow**, and runs from thence in 4 m. to Lew Mill, **Lidford** being 3 m. off, and 3 m. down joins Lyd. 2 m. down Lyd, Mary Stow brook joins on left bank. Mary Stow rises 2 m. S. of **Coryton**, and is 5 m. long. 3 m. down Lyd at **Lifton**, Thistle brook joins on right bank. Thistle rises 2 m. N. of **Bridestow**, runs to Stowford 7 m. (n.s. **Lifton,** 3 m.), 2 m. down, Bradwood water joins Thistle on right bank. Bradwood rises near Germansweek, runs 3 m. to Henwood Mill, where a short stream joins on right bank, runs to Bradwood Wiger 2 m. and Thistle 3 m. 1 m. down, Thistle joins Lyd, which runs in 2 m. to Tamar, 2 m. down Tamar, a small brook 3 m. long, which runs 2 m. S. of **Lifton,** joins on left bank. 2 m. down, Tamar, Laudno water, which rises 2 m S. of **Launceston**, and is 5 m. long, joins on right bank. 1 m. down Tamar, 6 m. from **Launceston,** Inny river joins on right bank. Inny rises by Davidstow, 4 m. N.E. from Camelford (*Hotel*: King's Arms. Fishing free.), runs 4 m. to St. Clether, and 6 m. down at Two Bridges, 4 m. from **Launceston**, Penpont water, 7 m. long, joins on right bank. Inny runs 10 m. to Tamar. 4 m. down Tamar a brook 2 m. long joins on left bank, and 2 m. on another short stream working a mill joins on right bank. Tamar runs 5 m. to New Bridge, **Tavistock** being 3 m. off on left bank, Calstock 5 m. (*Hotel*: Ashburton). 1 m. down, Cleve water, 3 m. long, joins on right bank. To this point the tide flows. 7 m. down, Tavy joins Tamar. Tavy rises on Dartmoor, 3 m. E. of **Lidford**. 2 m. down, Rattle water, 2 m. long, joins on right bank. Tavy runs 5 m. to **Mary Tavy**, and 2 m. down is joined by Burn brook, which rises 2 m. N.W. of **Mary Tavy**, runs by that station, and joins Tavy 2 m. down. Tavy runs to **Tavistock**, 2 m. and 2 m. down is joined on right bank by Lumbern brook, 5 m. long. 2 m. down Tavy, Walkham river joins on left bank. Walkham rises on Cocks Hill, 5 m. E. of **Mary Tavy**, runs 4 m. to Merriville Bridge, **Tavistock** being 4 m. off on right bank; runs 2 m. to Sampford Spiney, 4 m. to **Horrabridge**, and Tavy, 1 m. To 5 m. down Tavy the tide flows (n.s. **Yelverton**, 4 m.), 3 m. down, Tavy joins Plymouth Sound (Tavy holds trout, sea trout, salmon, and is preserved by the Tavy and Plym Fishery Association, who issue tickets). The Tavy and Plym Association issue tickets for all their rivers; agent, Mr. Wm. Hearder. River Dart; salmon, trout; s.t., 20s., including salmon licence; trout, s.t. 10s., m.t. (after May 1) 5s., d.t 2s. from Hearder and Son (*see Advertisement*). Sea fishing excellent—bass, pollack, mackerel, hake, conger. Bass fishing off Rame Head from the rocks with a rod, and piano-convex minnow, or spinning sand eel, equal to salmon fishing. Fish run from 2lb. to 20lb. in weight. In the Sound, whiffing for pollack or mackerel. Bottom fishing for chad, pouting. whiting, near the Cobbler Buoy, Mallard, and inside the east and west ends of Breakwater. Large whiting, cod, conger, and hake in the offing near the Eddystone. Rod fishing for smelt, bass, mullet, and pollack, off the piers and rocks. For information as to tackle, boatmen, and baits, &c., apply to Messrs. Hearder and Son, 195, Union-street, Plymouth.

Plympton (Devon).—G.W.R. Tory brook; white with clay water now. (*See Plymouth.*) (*c.s. Tamer.*)

Polesworth (Warwick).—L. & N.W.R. Anker. (*c.s. Trent.*) (*See Gainsborough.*)

Polperro (Cornwall), n.s. **Looe,** 6 m.—On Polperro brook, 6 m. long. Good sea fishing for pollack, mackerel, whiting, conger, and bream; use pilchard bait.

Polsham (Somerset).—G.W.R. Godney brook. (*See Highbridge.*)

Pontesbury (Salop).—L. & N.W.R.; G.W.R. Rea (1 m. N.); trout, grayling. Habberley brook (1 m. E.). (*See Gloucester.*) (*c.s. Severn.*)

Pontnewydd (Monmouth.)—G.W.R. Llwyd. (*See Newport.*) (*c.s. Usk.*)

Pontrhydyran (Monmouth.)—G.W.R. Llwyd. (*See Newport.*) (*c.s. Usk.*)

Pontrilas (Hereford.) — G.W.R. Monnow; trout, grayling; preserved by tenant of Kentchurch to 3 m. below here, thence by private owners to within 1 m. of Monmouth. (*See Pandy.*) (*c.s. Wye.*) Dore. Worm brook. Dulas brook, Rowlston brook (1 m.).

Garron (6 m.); trout. Black brook (6 m.); trout; preserved. *Lakes:* Black brook House
(6 m.) (*See Chepstow.*)

Pontypool (Monmouth.)—G.W.R.; L. & N.W.R. Llwyd; trout rod licences 2s. 6d., and
w.t. 10s., and d.t. 2s. 6d., trout, from Mrs. Fox, hairdresser. *Lakes:* Troenant Reservoir
(2 m.); trout. (*See Newport, Usk.*) (*c.s. Usk.*)

Pool (York).—N.E.R. Wharfe; trout, grayling, chub, barbel; preserved by the owner
of Farnley Hall, F. H. Fawkes, Esq., who has formed a small club; at 21s., of the estate
agent; also by the Leeds A.S.A., innkeepers, and others. Lord Harewood preserves for 8 m.
below; leave may sometimes be had from his agent. Above Otley there is a little free
fishing. *Hotels:* White Hart and Fountain. (*c.s. York.*) (*See York.*)

Poole (Dorset).—L. & S.W.R.; M.R. On Rockle. *Hotel:* London. Rockle rises in a mill pool
above Morden Park 6 m. N. from **Wareham**, runs in 1 m. to the large lake in Morden Park,
and runs into the Lytchett branch of Poole Harbour 6 m. down at Kirkley Point.
On the opposite side of the harbour from the town debouches Corfe river; salmon
(s.t. 1l.), sea trout, trout. Corfe rises 1 m. W. of Corfe Castle (n.s. **Wareham**, 4½ m.),
and is here joined by Byle brook on right bank. Corfe runs into Poole Harbour 5 m.
down. Fishing may sometimes be obtained by application to one or other of the landowners. Good sea fishing between Branksea Castle and mouth of the harbour; pollack,
whiting, codling, and conger. (*c.s. Frome.*)

Pooley Bridge (Westland).—Eamont; trout. (*c.s. Eden.*) Dacre beck, 2 m. N.
Lakes: Ullswater; pike, perch, trout; leave from Lord Lonsdale's steward. *Hotels:*
Swan, Sun. (*See Carlisle.*)

Poppleton (York).—N.E.R. Ouse; chub, roach, pike; free on left bank, preserved on
right bank. (*c.s. York.*) (*See York.*)

Porlock (Somerset).—There are two streams on the east side of Porlock, belonging to Sir
C. T. D. Acland, Bart.; one rises E. of Dunkerry, runs by Holnicote to Bassington, and
joins the Horner stream (strictly preserved); the other rises near Chetsford Water, flows
by Luccott, Horner Wood, and West Luccombe to Bassington; permission of Sir C. T. D.
Acland's Agent. The trout run very small. *Hotels:* Ship, Castle, and Lorna Doone.
Some 4 m. across the hills runs Oare water, preserved by Mr. Snow, of Oare, who will
give leave. (*See Lynmouth.*)

Portishead (Somerset).—G.W.R. Here the drainings of Clapton moor, 5 m. long, joins
the sea.

Portland (Dorset).—G.W.R.; L. & S.W.R. (*See Weymouth.*)

Porton (Wilts.).—L. & S.W.R. Avon and Winterbourne; trout and coarse fish; preserved
by landowners. (*See Christchurch.*) (*c.s.*)

Portskewet (Monmouth).—L. & S.W.R. Morenton brook (1 m. N.E.). Morenton rises above
Morenton (n.s. **Chepstow**, 2 m.), and 3 m. down at St. Pierre the outflow from the lake in
St. Pierre Park (pike, tench, perch, roach, dace; leave from Mr. Lewis, St. Pierre Park)
joins on right bank. 1 m. down is the Severn estuary. 1 m. W. of **Portskewet** runs
Nedden Brook. Nedden rises in Went Wood under the name of Cas Troggy Brook, runs
5 m. to Lanvair Discoed, Caerwent 2 m., **Portskewet** 4 m.

Portsmouth (Lancs.)—L. & Y.R. Calder. (*c.s. York.*) (*See Rawcliffe.*)

Portsmouth Arms (Devon).—L. & S.W.R. On Taw; salmon and trout private. (*c.s.*)
Yarncombe brook (14 m.) (*See Barnstaple.*)

Potter Heigham (Norfolk).—M. & G.N.R. Hundred stream of Thurne, 1 m. S.; good bank
fishing. *Lakes:* Hickling, Chapman, and Whitesley Broad. (*See Yarmouth.*) *Hotel:*
Bridge; boats at Applegate's, by the bridge. (*c.s. N. and S.*)

Poulton (Lancs.)—L. & Y.R.; L. & N.W.R. *Lakes:* Marton mere, 4 m. S. (*See Fleetwood.*)

Powburn (Northland.).—(*See Wooler.*)

Powerstock (Dorset).—G.W.R. (*See Bridport.*) On Asker; trout; good fishing, preserved
by the farmers. *Inn:* Three Horseshoes.

Poynton (Cheshire).—L. & N.W.R. Poynton brook. *Lakes:* Poynton Park, 1 m. N.
(*See Runcorn.*)

Prees (Salop).—L. & N.W.R. Sandford Hall lake (2 m. E.) (*See Gloucester.*)

Prescot (Lancs.).—L. & N.W.R. Ditton brook. Alt, 3 m. W. *Lakes:* Mizzy dam.
Knowsley Park lake, 2 m. N.W. (*See Runcorn, Altcar.*)

Prestbury (Cheshire).—L. & N.W.R. Bollin; trout, roach, dace, pike; private. Dean,
2 m. N.E. (*See Runcorn.*)

Prestbury (Worcester).—M.R. Swilgare. (*See Gloucester.*)

Presthorpe (Salop). — G.W.R. Hughly brook (1 m. N.W.). Corve (2½ m. S.); trout,
grayling, &c. (*See Gloucester.*) (*c.s. Severn.*)

Preston (Lancs.)—L. & N.W.R.; L. & Y.R.; W.L.R.; G.W.R.; Js.R.; N.B.R.;
C.R. Ribble. Ribble rises some 3 m. above **Ribbles Head** (preserved by the
Manchester Anglers' Association), and is here joined by Gale Water, 3 m. long
(preserved as Ribble). 3 m. below, Cam beck, 6 m. long (preserved as Ribble), joins
Ribble on left bank. 1 m. down Ribble is a tarn immediately on left bank (trout;
preserved as Ribble). Ribble runs to **Horton** 2 m. Here Horton brook, 3 m. long,
joins on left bank. Ribble runs to Helwith Bridge 3 m. (here ends the M.A. water,
private below). 2 m. below, at Great Stainforth, 3 m. above **Settle**, Ribble is joined
on left bank by Cowside or Stainforth beck, 3 m. long. Ribble runs to **Settle** 3 m.,
Giggleswick 2 m., and 2 m. down is joined on right bank by Rathmell beck, 5 m long.
Ribble runs to **Long Preston** 1 m.; here Long Preston beck joins on left bank, and

Wigglesworth beck on right bank. Long Preston beck, under the name of Scaleber beck, rises above Scaleber Bridge 2 *m.* E. of **Settle**, and joins Ribble 4 *m* down. Wigglesworth beck is 4 *m.* long, and drains Tapa tarn by Wigglesworth 2 *m.* W. of **Long Preston**. Ribble runs to Halton Bridge 3 *m.*, and here Hellifield beck, wnich rises above **Hellifield**, and is 4 *m.* long, joins on left bank. Ribble runs to **Newsholme** 3 *m.*, and **Gisburn** 2 *m.* Here Stock beck, which rises above **Barnoldswick**, and is 5 *m.* long, joins on left bank. 3 *m.* down Ribble. at Bolton Park, **Rimington** being 3 *m.* off on left bank, Tosside beck joins on right bank. Tosside is 7 *m.* long, and 3 *m.* from its source is joined on right bank by Bond beck, 3 *m.* long. 1 *m.* down Tosside, Forest beck, 4 *m.* long, joins on left bank. 2 *m.* down Tosside, Cuddy beck, 3 *m.* long, joins on right bank. 1 *m.* below, close to the junction of Tosside with Ribble, Fell brook, 4 *m.* long, joins on right bank. Ribble runs 2 *m.*, where Swanside beck joins on left bank. Swanside beck rises above **Rimington**, and 2 *m.* below is joined on left bank by Ings beck, 4 *m.* long. 1 *m.* down is Ribble. (Here begins the water of the Clitheroe Angling Association.) 1 *m.* down Ribble, at Grindleton Mill, 1 *m.* N.W. of **Chatburn**, Grindleton beck, 3 *m.* long, joins on right bank. Ribble runs 1 *m.* to West Bradford, 2 *m.* N. from **Clitheroe**, and here Bradford beck, 3 *m.* long, joins on right bank. 1 *m.* below, Waddington beck, 3 *m.* long, joins Ribble on right bank. Ribble runs to Bungerley Bridge 1 *m.* (here ends the water of the C.A.A.), and **Clitheroe** 1 *m.* Here Bashall brook, which rises in Bashall Moor pond 5 *m.* N.W. from **Clitheroe**, and is 6 *m.* long, joins on right bank. Ribble runs 1 *m.*, where Clitheroe beck, which rises above **Clitheroe**, and is 5 *m.* long, joins on left bank. (Here begins the water of the Red Lion Inn, **Clitheroe**, Three Fishes Inn, and Aspinall's Arms, **Mitton**.) Ribble runs 1 *m.* to **Mitton**. (Clitheroe Angling Association.) Hodder here joins on right bank. Hodder rises on the slopes of Lamb Fell, and 4 *m.* down is joined on left bank by Hasgill beck, 4 *m.* long. 2 *m.* down, Bridge House beck. 5 *m.* long, joins on left bank. 2 *m.* down Hodder, Barm Gill, 3 *m.* long, joins on left bank. Hodder runs 1 *m.* to **Slaidburn** (n.s. **Chatburn**, 7 *m.* ; private above); here Dunsop river joins on right bank. Dunsop rises on Croasdale Fell, and 5 *m.* down is joined on right bank by Croasdale beck, 4 *m.* long. Just below, Eller beck joins Dunsop on right bank. Dunsop joins Hodder 1 *m.* down. Hodder runs to **Newton** (n.s. **Clitheroe**, 8 *m.*) 2 *m.*, and here Easington brook, 4 *m.* long, joins Hodder on left bank. Hodder runs 4 *m.*, where Whitendale river joins on right bank. Whitendale rises on Whitendale Fell, and 4 *m.* down is joined on right bank by Brennand river, 4 *m.* long. Whitendale joins Hodder 3 *m.* below. 1 *m.* down Hodder, Langden river, 5 *m.* long, joins on right bank. Hodder runs 2 *m.* to **Whitewell** (n.s. **Clitheroe**, 7 *m.*) 2 *m.* below, Greystoneley beck, 3 *m.* long, joins Hodder on right bank. 1 *m.* below, at Doeford Bridge (here begins the water of the Red Lion Inn, Clitheroe), Loud river joins on right bank. Loud rises 4 *m.* above Derby Arms, which is 2 *m.* N. of **Longridge**, and 3 *m.* below is joined on left bank by Chipping beck, 4 *m.* long. Loud runs 1 *m.*, where Lees beck, 4 *m.* long, joins on left bank. Loud joins Hodder 1 *m.* below. Hodder runs 2 *m.*, where Mill beck, 2 *m.* long, joins on left bank. Hodder joins Ribble 6 *m.* below. 1 *m.* down Ribble, West Calder (polluted) joins on left bank. West Calder rises on Oliveger Moor by **Holme**, 4 *m.* S.E. of **Burnley**. One portion (East Calder) runs E., and joins Aire; the other portion (West Calder) runs W., and joins Ribble. 1 *m.* from its source a brook joins West Calder on left bank, draining a pond on Castle Hill 1 *m.* up. Calder runs to **Burnley** 2 *m.*; here Don river joins on right bank. Don rises 7 *m.* above **Burnley**, and 1 *m.* above that town is joined on left bank by Swinden water, 3 *m.* long, and Bran river, 4 *m.* long. Laneshaw river here joins Calder on right bank. Laneshaw rises 5 *m.* above **Colne**, and 2 *m.* from its source, at Laneshaw Bridge, is joined on left bank by Wycoller water, 3 *m.* long. 1 *m.* below, Trawden brook, 3 *m.* long, joins Laneshaw on left bank. Laneshaw runs to **Colne** 1 *m.*, and 1 *m.* below is joined on the right bank by a brook 2 *m.* long, draining the three reservoirs by **Foulridge**. 1 *m.* down Laneshaw, Catlow brook, 4 *m.* long, joins on left bank. Laneshaw runs to **Burnley** in 5 *m.* Calder runs 2 *m.*, where Roughlee water, which rises on Pendle Hill, runs 8 *m.* to Lawerwood, 2 *m.* W. of **Colne**, thence to Calder 6 *m.*, joins on right bank. Calder runs to **Padiham** (n.s. **Burnley**), 4 *m.*, and here Lodge river joins on left bank. Lodge rises 3 *m.* above **Rose Grove**, where Tower brook, 3 *m.* long, joins on left bank. 1 *m.* down Lodge, Shaw brook, 2 *m.* long, joins on left bank. Lodge runs to Calder in 1 *m.* Calder runs to Altham 2 *m.*, and 1 *m.* down is joined on left bank by Hyndburn brook; this brook rises 2 *m.* above **Accrington**, and 2 *m.* down is joined on left bank by Church brook, 2 *m.* long. 2 *m.* below, the outflow (2 *m.* long) of Rishton reservoir by **Rishton** joins on left bank; hence to Calder is 1 *m.* Calder runs 1 *m.*, where Sabden brook, 6 *m.* long, joins on right bank. Calder runs to **Whalley** 3 *m.*, and joins Ribble 2 *m.* below. 1 *m.* down, Ribble Park brook, which rises by **Wilpshire**, and is 6 *m.* long, joins on left bank. 1 *m.* down Ribble, Dean brook, which rises in a pond at Moor Game Hall, and is 3 *m.* long, joins on right bank. 1 *m.* above this junction a stream joins Dean on right bank, draining Crowshaw reservoir 2 *m.* up, 5 *m.* N.W. from **Whalley**. Ribble runs 1 *m.*, where Starting brook, 2 *m.* long, joins on right bank. Ribble runs to **Ribchester** 2 *m.* Here Boyce's brook, 4 *m.* long, joins on right bank. Close above the junction, Dutton brook, 3 *m.* long, joins Boyce on left bank. Ribble runs 7 m. to **Fulwood**, 1 m. off on right bank; and here Tun brook, which rises above **Grimsargh**, and is 4 m. long. joins on right bank. 1 m. down Ribble, Mellor brook, 4 m. long, joins on left bank. Ribble runs to **Preston** 4 m. Here Darwen joins Ribble on left bank. Darwen rises above **Over Darwen**, runs 3 m. to **Lower Darwen**, **Mill Hill** 1 m. S. of **Blackburn**, 2 m., **Cherry Tree** 1 m., **Penniscowles** 2 m. Here Roddlesworth joins on left bank. Roddlesworth rises in the Rivington reservoirs of the Liverpool Waterworks 2 m. E. of **Chorley**, runs 3 m. to **Brinscall**, and 1 m. down by **Withnell** waters another Liverpool reservoir. 3 m. down, Roddlesworth joins Darwen. Darwen runs, in 2 m., 1 m. E. of **Hoghton**, and 7 m. down runs 2 m. N.W. of **Hoghton**, joining Ribble 2 m. below at **Preston**.

Princetown (Devon).—G.W.R. E. Dart. 6 m. W. Dart, 1½ m. Tributaries—Blackabrook, ½ m.; Cowsic, 1 m.; Cherry brook, 3 m.; Swincombe, 3 m.; besides many smaller streams near Upper parts of Plym, ½ m. Walkham, 2½ m.; preserved. Licences at the hotel; salmon and trout, s.t. 20s., w.t. 7s. 6d, d.t. 2s. 6d.; trout only s.t. 10s., d.t 2s., m.t. from May 1, 5s. The W. Dart and tributaries have been much improved by the recent restocking with trout by the Dart Conservators. *Hotel*: Duchy. (*See Dartmouth*.)

Pulborough (Sussex).—L.B. & S.C.R. Arun and Western Rother. Fishing free in Rother, hence to Midhurst. Fishing good on Arun. Pike, bream, roach, perch, carp, salmon, trout, &c. *Hotel*: Arun. (*See Littlehampton*.)

Purfleet (Essex).—L.T. & S.R. On Mardyke. This stream rises by East Horndon, and in 4 m. is joined on the right bank by a stream which rises by Little Warley. From this junction to Purfleet is 8 m.

Purton (Wilts.).—G.W.R. On Ray. (*See London, U.T.*)

Putney (Surrey).—L. & S.W.R. Thames. (*See London, L.T.*)

Puxton (Somerset).—G.W.R. *Lakes*: Puxton pond; pike, rudd, tench, carp; private. *Fish-tackleist*, O'Hundlen, Victoria-street, Bristol (*see Advt.*).

Pye Bridge (Notts).—M.R. Erewash. (*See Gainsborough*.)

Quay Haven.—(*See Milford*.)

Radcliffe (Lancs.).—L. & N.W.R.; G.N.R.; M.R. Irwell. Roch. *Lakes*: Reservoir, 1½ m. N. (*See Runcorn*.)

Radford (Notts).—M.R. Leen. *Lakes*: Bilborough cut, 2 m. W. (*See Gainsborough*.)

Radlett (Herts.).—M.R. Colne, chub, roach, pike, perch; preserved. (*See London, M.T.*)

Radstock (Somerset).—G.W.R.; S. & D.R. (*See Bristol*.)

Raglan (Monmouth.).—G.W.R. Raglan brook; trout rod licences 1s., from the post-office. (*See Newport*.)

Rainford (Lancs.).—L. & N.W.R. Sankey brook. (*See Runcorn*.)

Rainham (Essex).—G.E.R. On Ingreburn Brook. This stream rises 4 m. N.W. of **Brentwood**, and in 3 m. reaches Upminster. 3 m. on a stream joins, which runs through Berwick Pond. 1½ m. down, Rainham is reached. 1 m. on, the brook joins Thames. There are fish throughout its course. 1½ m. from Rainham runs Beam brook. This stream, under the name of Bourne brook, rises 5 m. north of **Romford**. 4 m. on is Beam Bridge, 1½ m. from **Rainham**, and 1 m. further the brook runs into Dagenham Reach; pike, perch, bream, roach; fishing here is very good; day tickets can be had. The outfall of the lake runs into Thames Estuary.

Ramsbottom (Lancs.).—M.R.; G.N.R. Irwell. (*See Runcorn*.)

Ramsey (Hunts).—G.N.R. Old river Nen; pike, perch, bream, &c. Holme brook. Winton brook. *Lake*: Ramsey mere, 3 m. N.E. (*See Wisbeach*.)

Ramsgate.—Fair sea fishing for cod and whiting. There is fresh-water fishing at Minster in the Stour. (*See Margate and Sandwich*.) Good pier fishing. *Hotel*: Royal.

Ramsgill (York). u.s. **Pateley Bridge**, 5 m.—Nidd; trout, grayling. (*c.s. York*.) Ramsgill Beck. Lul Beck. How Stone Beck 2 m. N.W.; trout; free. Burn Gill Beck, 2 m. S.E. *Hotel*: Yorke Arms. (*See York*.)

Ramskill (Notts).—G.N.R. Oldcoates dyke. Idle, 2 m. E. Rytor, 3 m. W. *Lakes*: Serlby Park, 2 m. N.W (*See Althorpe*.)

Ratby (Leicester.).—M.R. Rothley brook. *Lakes*: The Pool, Grosby, 2 m. N. (*See Gainsborough*.)

Ratcliffe (Notts).—G.N.R. Trent; pike, perch, roach, chub, salmon. (*c.s.*) Thurbeck (*See Gainsborough*.)

Ravenglass (Cumland.).—R. & E.R.; Fs.R. Esk; salmon, sea trout, trout. (*c.s. West Cumberland*.) Esk rises on Scawfell, and 4 m. down is joined on left bank by Lingrove beck, 3 m. long. Two m. down, Curcove beck, 2 m. long, joins on right bank. Esk runs 1 m. to **Esk Bridge** (n.s. **Boot**, 3 m.). One m. down Esk a stream joins on right bank, draining Stony tarn 2 m. up, 2 m. across the hills N.W. of **Esk Bridge**. Esk runs 2 m. to **Boot**. Here Whillan beck joins on right bank. Whillan rises in Burnmore tarn, 3 m. N. of **Boot**, and 2 m. down is joined on left bank by the outflow of Eel tarn, 1 m. up, 2 m. N.E. across the hills from **Boot**. Whillan runs to **Boot** and Esk, 2 m. Here also Stanley gill, 3 m. long, joins on left bank. Esk runs 1 m. to **Beckfoot**. Here joins the drainage of Blea tarn, 1 m. N.W. Esk runs 2 m. to **Eskdale Green**, and 2 m. down is joined on left bank by Linbeck gill, which drains Devoke water (trout) 2 m. up. Two m. down Esk is Muncaster Castle; to this point the tide flows. One m, below, Samgarth beck, 4 m. long, joins on left bank. The tidal water of Esk flows to **Eskmeals**, 1 m., and **Ravenglass**, 2 m. The rivers Mite and Irt here join Esk.

MITE.—(*c.s. West Cumberland.*) Rises in Eskdale fell, runs in 4 *m.* to **Irton Road**, 3 *m.* to **Muncaster**, and joins Esk at **Ravenglass** 4 *m.* below. Irt (*c.s. West Cumberland*) here joins **Esk**. IRT rises in two branches, each some 3 *m.* long, on Wastdale fell. The combined streams water Wastwater lake (trout) 1 *m.* below **Wastdale Head**. This lake is some 3 *m.* long. (*c.s. West Cumberland.*) There are no tributaries on the left bank, but on the right bank, about 1 *m.* down. Overbeck joins, which rises in Low tarn, 3 *m.* up, 2 *m.* W. across the hills from **Wastdale Head**. A short way below, Nether beck, rising in Scoal tarn, 4 *m.* up, runs into the lake. This lake is 3 *m.* across the hills from **Wastdale Head**. One *m.* below again, Greendale beck joins, which runs out of Greendale tarn, 3 *m.* up. 3 *m.* S.W. of **Wastdale Head**. Irt runs out of Lake Wastwater, and 3 *m.* down is joined on right bank by Bieng. Bleng (*c.s. West Cumberland*) rises in Copeland Forest, and is 10 *m.* long. Irt runs to **Drigg**, 5 *m.*, and joins the Esk estuary at **Ravenglass**, 3 *m.* below. *Hotels:* King's Arms, Pennington Arms. May and June are best for trout; June, July, August for sea trout; September, October. and November for salmon.

Ravenstonedale (Westland).—N.E.R. Lune. (*c.s.*) Greenside beck. Sanwath beck. Weasdale beck. (*Carlisle.*) Bowderdale beck, 2 *m.* W. *Lakes:* Greenside tarn. Scandal beck. Artlegarth beck. Sunbiggin tarn. 2 *m.* W. (*See Lancaster.*)

Rawcliffe (York).—L. & Y.R. Aire. Aire rises in Malham tarn (preserved by W. Morrison, Esq.), 7 *m.* N.E. of **Settle**. or 8 *m.* N. of **Bellbusk**. 3 *m.* below Malham, Gardale beck (trout), 3 *m.* long, joins on left bank; a portion free. Aire runs to Airton 1½ *m.* (here begins the water of the Yorkshire Anglers' Club). Aire runs 1 *m.* to Kirkby Malham (n.s. **Bellbusk**, 4 *m.*). Here Kirkgill beck, 3 *m.* long, joins on right bank. 1½ *m.* down Aire, a stream joins on left bank, draining Eshton tarn 1 *m.* up. Aire runs 1 *m.* to **Bellbusk**; here Otterburn beck joins on right bank. Otterburn rises on Otterburn Moor, 3 *m.* across the hills N.E. from **Long Preston**. 2 *m.* down, Ingle beck, 3 *m.* long, joins on left bank. Hence to **Bellbusk**. is 3 *m.* Just below **Bellbusk**, the outflow of the lake at Coniston House, ½ *m.* up, joins on right bank. Aire runs to **Gargrave**, 4 *m.* (Here begins the water of the Aire Fishing Club.) 1 *m.* below, Eshton beck joins on left bank. Eshton rises on the slopes of Malham Moor, runs 10 *m.* to Eshton (n.s. **Gargrave**, 2 *m.*), where it is joined on the left bank by Mill beck, 4 *m.* long. Eshton runs to **Gargrave**, and Aire, 2 *m.* 2 *m.* down Aire, Elslack brook joins on the right bank. Elslack rises above **Barnoldswick Junction**, runs to **Earby**, 1 *m.* Thornton, 2 *m.* **Elslack**, 1 *m.* Aire, 3 *m.* Aire runs 1 *m.* to **Skipton**, 1 *m.* off on left bank; here Eller beck, 6 *m.* long, joins on the left bank. Aire runs 3 *m.* to Cononley, **Kildwick**, 2 *m.* Here Eastbourne brook joins on right bank. (Here ends the A.F.C. water, and that of the Stockbridge and Eastbourne Club begins.) Eastbourne rises in Cowloughton dam, 6 *m.* E. of **Colne**, or 7 *m.* S.W. of **Kildwick**, and is 6 *m.* long. Aire runs to **Steeton**, 2 *m.*; here Silsden beck, 4 *m.* long, joins on left bank. Aire runs to **Keighley**, 1 *m.* off on right bank, 4 *m.* Here Worth river joins Aire on right bank. Worth rises 5 *m.* above **Oakworth** Station, and there Oxenhope beck, which rises above **Oxenhope**, and is 3 *m.* long, joins on right bank. Worth runs 2 *m*, to **Ingrow**. **Keighley**, 1 *m.* Here a beck, which rises in a pond on Keighley Moor, 5 *m.* up, joins on left bank. Worth runs to Aire, 1 *m.* 2 *m.* down Aire, Moulton beck, 3 *m.* long, joins on left bank. Aire runs to **Bingley**, 1 *m.* (Here ends the water of the Stockbridge and Eastbourne Angling Club.) Here Harden beck joins on right bank. Harden rises above **Denholme**, just below which it joins the waters of a reservoir, runs 1 *m.* to **Cullingworth**, and joins Aire, 3 *m.* down at **Bingley**. (Here begins the water of the Saltaire Club). Aire runs 3 *m.* to **Shipley**. Here Bradford beck joins on right bank. Bradford beck rises 1 *m.* N. of **Thornton**, and 2 *m.* down is joined on the right bank by Clayton beck. 1 *m.* below, a brook joins on left bank, draining a pond 1 *m.* up by Denby. 2 *m.* down is **Bradford** and **Shipley**, and Aire 4 *m.* below. Aire runs 2 *m.* to **Baildon**. 1 *m.* below, Gill beck, which waters a pond 2 *m.* up, joins Aire on left bank. Aire runs to **Esholt**, 1 *m.* 1 *m.* below, Yeadon beck, which rises in a pond in Yeadon Moor, 1 *m.* E. of **Guiseley**, and is 8 *m.* long, joins on left bank. Aire runs to **Calverley**, 4 *m.*, **Newlay**, 2 *m.* Here Old Mill beck, 5 *m.* long, joins on left bank. Aire runs to **Leeds**, 4 *m.* Here Farnley beck joins on right bank. Farnley rises 4 *m.* above **Bramley**, and runs to **Leeds**, 5 *m.* Addle beck here joins Aire on left bank. Addle beck rises in a pond at Bush's Farm, 1½ *m.* S.W. of **Arthington**. Addle runs 1 *m.* to Black Hill dam, thence to Addle dam, passing the village of Addle immediately below, and joins Aire 6 *m.* down. Aire runs 2 *m.* to **Hunslet**, and 2 *m.* down, on left bank, is joined by Killing beck, which rises in the lake in Roundhay Park, 4 *m.* N.E. of **Leeds**, and is 5 *m.* long. Aire runs to **Woodlesford**, 4 *m.*; 1 *m.* below, Rothwell beck, 5 *m.* long, joins on right bank. 1 *m.* down Aire, by **Methley**, Kollin beck, 3 *m.* long, joins on left bank. Aire runs to **Castleford**, 2 *m.* Here Calder joins on right bank. Calder rises on Cliviger Moor, 4 *m.* S.E. of **Burnley**, by **Holme**, runs thence 2 *m.* to **Portsmouth**. 2 *m.* down, a brook joins on left bank, 2 *m.* long, draining Redmires dam, 3 *m.* W. of **Todmorden**. Calder runs 2 *m.* to **Todmorden**. 1 *m.* below, the outlet of some ponds, 1 *m.* up at **Lee**, joins on right bank. These ponds are 2 *m.* S.E. of **Todmorden**. Calder runs 2 *m.* to **Eastwood** and **Hebden** 2 *m.* Here two streams join on left bank. The first up-stream, Calderclough, rises in Nodale dam, 4 *m.* N.W. of **Hebden**. The other stream is the river Hebden. Hebden rises on Widdop Moor, and 2 *m.* down it is joined on right bank by Widdop water, 2 *m.* long. 1 *m.*

down Hebden, Gorple water, 3 m. long, joins on right bank. 1 m. down Hebden, Wadsworth beck, 3 m. long, joins on left bank. 2 m. down Hebden, Horsebridge beck 3 m. long, joins on left bank. Hebden runs to **Hebden** and Calder, 2 m. 3 m. down Calder, at **Luddenden Foot**, Luddenden beck joins on left bank. Luddenden rises in the two Cold Edge dams in Saltonstall Moor, 3 m N. of **Luddenden**, and is 5 m. long. Calder runs 2 m. to **Sowerby Bridge**, and here Ribourne joins on right bank. Ribourne rises in two branches some 4 m. above **Rishworth**, runs 2 m. to Rippenden, and joins Calder at **Sowerby Bridge**, 4 m. down. Calder runs to **Elland**, 3 m. **Halifax** being 2 m. off on left bank. Here Dean, which rises in a small reservoir, 2 m. S. of **Rishworth**, and runs 5 m. to **Stainland**, and **Elland**, 3 m., joins on right bank. Calder runs 3 m. to **Brighouse** and **Cooper Bridge**, 3 m. Here Colne joins on right bank. Colne rises in Wessenden reservoir, 2 m. above **Marsden**, and here a stream joins on left bank, draining the March Hill reservoir, 2 m. up. Colne runs to **Slaithwaite**. 2 m., and here a stream joins on left bank, draining a pond on Slaithwaite Common 2 m. up. Colne runs to **Longwood**, 2 m., where the drainage of a pond and reservoir 1 m. up, joins on left bank. Colne runs to **Huddersfield**, 2 m., and here Holme joins on right bank. Holme rises in Bilbury reservoir, 3 m. above **Holmfirth**, and here a stream joins on right bank, draining Holmealey reservoir 2 m. up. Holme runs to **Honley**, 3 m. Here a stream joins on left bank, draining a reservoir, 1 m. E. of **Meltham**. Holme runs to **Huddersfield** and Colne, 3 m. Colne runs to **Deighton**, 3 m., and here Burton beck, which rises above **Kirkburton**, and runs thence 3 m. to Kirkheaton and **Deighton**, 2 m., joins on right bank. Colne runs to **Cooper Bridge**, 2 m. Calder runs to **Mirfield**, 3 m., **Dewsbury**, 3 m., **Horbury**, 5 m. 2 m. down, a stream joins on right bank, draining the large lake in Cheval Park, 2 m. up. and 2 m. S.W. of **Sandal**, or 4 m. S. of **Wakefield**. Calder runs 1 m. to **Wakefield**, and, 1 m. below, is joined on right bank by Walton beck, which rises in the reservoir at Cold Hindley by **Ryhill**, and runs to Walton, 2 m. where the outflow of Walton Park lake, 2 m. S.E. of **Sandal**, joins on right bank. Walton flows to **Sandal**, 2 m. and Calder 1 m. Calder runs to **Stanley**, 4 m. and the Aire at **Castleford**, 7 m. Aire runs to **Knottingley**, 6 m. **Temple Hurst**, 7 m. **Snaith**, 3 m. **Rawcliffe**, 4 m. and joins Ouse 3 m. below.

Rawtenstall (Lancs.).—G.N.R.: L. & N.W.R. Irwell. Lamy Water. (*See Runcorn.*)

Reading (Berks.).—G.W.R.; L. & S.W.R.; S.E. & C.R. Hotels: Great Western, Queen's, George, Vastern, and Ship. Thames and Kenner. (*See London, M.T.*) Good pike, chub, roach, and trout fishing. A society preserves the Thames from Goring Lock to Shiplake. *Fishermen*: Rush, W. Moss, and J. Keel. *Tackleists*, Perry and Cox, 88, Broad-street.

Rearsby (Leicester). — M.R. Wreak; roach, bream, chub: preserved. (*c.s. Trent.*) Ox brook. Queniborough brook, 1 m. S.W. Ashby brook, 1 m. S. (*See Gainsborough.*)

Redbridge (Hants.).—L. & S.W.R. On the Test; salmon and trout, pike, roach, dace, &c. The Test here falls into Southampton Water; strictly preserved by a society of limited numbers; a.t. 50l.; salmon fishing very good. (*See Southampton.*)

Redbrook (Monmouth.) — G.W.R. Wye: chub, dace, pike, perch, salmon. (*c.s.*) (*See Chepstow.*)

Reddish (Lancs.)—L. & N.W.R.; G.N.R.; M.R. Tame. (*See Runcorn.*)

Redditch (Worcester). — M.R. Arrow; pike, perch, chub, roach, dace, bream, few trout; preserved above. *Lakes*: Ipsley Lodge pond (1 m. S.E.) Hewell Grange lake (2½ m. N.W.) (*See Gloucester.*)

Redhill (Surrey).—L.B. & S.C.R. (*See London, L.T.*)

Redmile (Leicester).—G.N.R. Devon, 3 m. S.E. *Lakes*: Woolsthorpe Lake, 3 m. S.E. Knipton reservoir, 4 m. S.E. (*See Gainsborough.*)

Redmire (York).—N.E.R. Yore; trout, grayling; preserved by Lord Bolton. (*See York.*)

Rednall (Salop). — G.W.R. Perry (2 m. N.). *Lakes*: Shelyocke lake (3 m. S.E.) (*See Gloucester.*) (*c.s. Severn.*)

Redruth (Cornwall).—G.W.R. Tresillian. This brook rises 2 m. N. of the town, and is 4 m. long. (*c.s. Fowey.*)

Reedham (Norfolk).—G.E.R. Yare; bream (very good), roach, pike, perch. New Cut, same fish. Thet, 3 m. S.W. (*See Yarmouth.*) (*c.s. Norfolk.*)

Reepham (Norfolk).—G.E.R. Blackwater brook; trout. Wensum. 3 m. S. (*See Yarmouth.*)

Reeth (York), n.s. **Richmond**, 12 m.—Swale; trout, grayling. (*c.s. York.*) Ackle beck; trout; leave from tenants. Healaugh beck, 2 m. W.: trout. Marske beck; 4 m. N.E. trout; preserved by Major Morley, G. Brown, Esq., and J. Hutton, Esq. Throstle beck, 4 m. N.E. Straw beck, 5 m. N.W. Moorsdale beck, 5 m. N. Roe beck, 7 m. N.W. *Inn*: Buck. (*See York.*)

Retford (Notts).—G.N.R. Idle. (*c.s. Trent.*) Poulter, 4 m. S. Meden, 4 m. S. Maun, 4 m. S. *Lakes*: Babworth Hall, 1 m. W. The Idle above Retford is in private hands. Below, it is preserved for 14 m. (trout only) by the River Idle Fly Fishing Club of 30 members. Entrance, 10l. 10s.; s.t., 10l. 10s. Sec., W. E. Channon, 19, Churchgate, Retford. The Retford Angling Association rent a long stretch above Retford of the Chesterfield Canal, which is well stocked with coarse fish. Sec., J. A. Vickers, 12, Cobwell-road, Retford. Below Retford until it reaches the Trent the canal is free. (*See Althorpe.*)

Rhywderin (Monmouth)—L. & N.W.R. Rumney (2 m.); salmon, trout; preserved. (*c.s.*) (*See Cardiff, Wales.*)

Ribble Head (York).—M.R. Ribble; trout; preserved by the Manchester Anglers' Association of 80 members, from the source, including all tributaries, to Helwith Bridge; entrance 21s., s.t. 42s.; season from March 6 to Sept. 30; no Sunday fishing; hon. sec., E. R. Austin, Esq., Fernside, Ollerbarrow-road, Hale, Cheshire. Gale water; trout; preserved as Ribble. Cam beck. 2 m. S.E.; trout; preserved as Ribble. *Hotel:* Crown Inn, Horton-in-Ribbsdale. (*See Preston.*)

Ribchester (Lancs.), n.s. **Longridge**, 5 m.—Ribble. Boyce brook. Dutton brook. Starting brook, 2 m. N.E. Dean brook, 3 m. N.E. *Lakes:* Crowshaw reservoir, 4 m. N.E. Moor Game Hall pond, 5 m. N.E. The De Tabley Arms, Ribchester Bridge, is a good hotel, and gives leave to fish. Tickets are also granted to visitors at the Whitewell Hotel. See *Preston.*)

Riccall (York).—G.N.R. (*See Caword, York.*)

Richmond (Surrey).—L. & S.W.R.; N.L.R.; D. & Met. R. (*See London, L.T.*) *Hotels:* Star and Garter, Station, Greyhound, White Cross, King's Head. and Pigeons, close to the river. Thames. *Fishermen:* F. and C. Brown, Hayter, F. Redknap, H. Mansell, Job Brain, J. Brain, jun., J. Bushnall, and T. Young. From here to **Isleworth** (S.W.R.) is good fly fishing for dace. In Richmond Park the Penn ponds hold pike, perch, carp, and bream. Leave from the deputy-ranger. The upper pond holds most pike. *Tacklests,* Gaynor and Son, 4, Bridge-street (*see Advt.*).

Richmond (York).—N.E.R. Swale; above the town, trout; below, grayling, pike dace, and barbel. Sand beck, 1 m. S. Ask beck, 1 m. N. Gilling beck, 3 m. N. Colburn and Hipswell becks, 2 m. S. Clapgate beck, 4 m. W. Ravensworth beck, 5 m. N.W. Smelt mill beck, 4 m. N. Marske beck, 5 m. W. Eller or Marrick beck, 6 m. W.; all trout. Skeeby beck, 2½ m. N.E.; trout and grayling. *Lakes:* Ask Hall Park Lake, 2½ m. N. Fawcett Park, 8 m. N.; pike and perch. Calf Hole tarn, 4 m., S. Tickets can be had for the Hipswell water. Apply to the Agent, Hipswell Estate Office. (*See York.*) *Tackleist,* K. Metcalfe, Market Place (*see Advt.*),

Rickmansworth (Herts).—Met. R.; L. & N.W.R. Colne; trout, chub, dace, roach, pike, perch, trout. The True Waltonians preserve 6 m., including the Harefield fishery. Mrs. J. Hutchings, the landlady of the Railway Hotel at Rickmansworth, can obtain leave to fish a good stretch of water in the Colne, which has recently been restocked; good bottom fishing. Gade; trout. Chess; trout. (*See London, M.T.*) Ruislip reservoir is 3½ m. off; pike, perch, tench. (*See Harrow.*)

Riding Mill (Northland).—N.E.R. On South Tyne. At Minsteracres, 4 m. off, is some good fishing in two lakes. (*c.s.*)

Rillington (York).—N.E.R. Derwent, 1 m. W.; coarse fish. Seampston beck, 1 m. E. Rye, 2 m. W. Costa beck, 3 m. W. *Lakes:* Scampston Park lake, 1 m. N.E. Newton House lake, 2 m. S.E. (*c.s. York.*) (*See Wressel.*)

Rimington (York).—L. & Y.R. Swanside beck. Ings beck, 1 m. S. Ribble, 2 m. W.; trout, salmon. Tosside beck, 3 m. N.W. Fell beck, 3 m. N.W. Grindleton beck, m. S.W. (*See Preston.*)

Ringstead (Northton.)—L. & N.W.R. Nen; pike, perch, chub, bream, tench (*See Wisbeach.*)

Ringwood (Hants).—L. & S.W.R. (*See Christchurch*). Avon; salmon, pike, roach, grayling, trout, perch, dace. For salmon, best time February 1 to May 15; no salmon ever caught after June. Grilse never run far up in this river. The spring fish, although few and easy, are very heavy fish, averaging 25lb. Flies only from Feb. 2 to May 1, after that prawns or other bait. Flies: yellow and grey eagle, Popham, Jock Scott, rainbow; sizes: 7 0 for heavy water, 5 0 to 4 0 for low water. Coarse fishing in season very good; trout very few; but a few grayling, and pike splendid—best time October to March. *Hotels:* White Hart. where tickets can be had at 7s. 6d. a day, hotel visitors 5s.; Crown Hotel, where tickets can also be had. Crown has some private water (coarse fish, and a few trout and grayling); d.t. 2s. 6d. (*c.s.*)

Ripley (Derby).—M.R. Amber, 3 m. N.W. *Lakes:* Lescoe dam, 2 m. S.E. Butterley reservoir, 2 m. N. Golden Valley reservoir, 3 m. N.E. (*See Gainsborough.*)

Ripley (York).—n.s. Ripley Valley. Nidd; trout; preserved by the Knaresborough Angling Club hence down to Ribston village, 4 m. below **Knaresborough**. Pike below Goldsboro' Dam. (*c.s. York.*) Thornton beck. Oak beck, 2 m. S.E. Saltergate beck, 2 m. S.E. *Lakes:* Ripley Park lake. (*See York.*)

Ripon (York).—N.E.R. Ure; trout, grayling, pike, perch, chub; preserved for 3½ m. by Ripon Angling Club of 30, entrance 30s., s.t. 25s., w.t. 5s., d.t. 2s. 6d., of the hon. sec., W. Waldon, Esq., South Crescent, Harrogate-road; or at Station Hotel. (*c.s York.*) Laver; preserved as Ure, for members only. Skell; preserved as Laver. *Lakes:* Studley Park, 3 m. S.W.; private. Bishopmonkton pond, 3 m. S.; private. *Hotels:* Station, Unicorn, Crown. (*See York.*)

Ripple (Worcester).—M.R. Severn; salmon, pike, perch, chub, dace, roach. Ripple brook. Avon (2 m. E.); chub, dace, roach, pike, perch. (*See Gloucester.*) (*c.s. Severn.*)

Risca (Monmouth).—G.W.R. Ebwy; trout, salmon; trout rod licences 1s., from the post-office. (*c.s. Usk.*) (*See Newport.*)

Rishton (Lancs.)—L. & Y.R. Hyndburn brook, 2 m. E. *Lake:* Rishton reservoir. (*See Preston.*)

Rishworth (York).—L. & Y.R. Ribourne. *Lakes:* Reservoir, 2 m. S. (*See Rawcliffe.*)

Roade (Northton.).—L. & N.W.R. Tove, 2 m. S. (*See King's Lynn.*)

Roadwater (Somerset).—G.W.R. Washford; trout. (*See Watchet.*)

Robertsbridge (Sussex).—S.E. & C.R. (*See Rye.*) On Rother. The river is preserved by the Rother Fishery Association; sec., Thos. Daws, Esq., Soggs House, Ewhurst, Hawkhurst. Tickets at the hotel. (*c.s.*) *Hotel:* George (*see Advt.*).

Rocester (Stafford).—G N.R.; L. & N.W.R.; M.R. Dove; trout, grayling *above* the town, grayling, chub, pike, barbel, few trout *below*; preserved above for 6 *m.* by the Dove Fishing Club; s.t., 8*l.*; hon. sec., G. Percival Heywood, Esq., Doveleys, Uttoxeter. (*c.s. Trent.*) Churnet; trout, grayling; fishing ruined by pollutions from Leek and Oakamoor. (*c.s. Trent.*) (*See Gainsborough.*)

Rochdale (Lancs.).—L. & N.W.R.; M.R.; G.N.R. Roch. Dodd. Beal, 1 *m.* N.E. Saddon brook, 1 *m.* S. Naden Water, 3 *m.* N.W. *Lakes:* Bolderstone pond, 1 *m.* S. Hollingworth reservoir, 3 *m.* N.E. (*See Runcorn.*)

Rochester (Kent). — S.E. & C.R. On Medway. The river rises 2 *m.* west of **East Grinstead**, and flows in 12 *m.* to **Hartfield**, and then to **Withyham** 1 *m.* below which a stream joins on the right bank which rises at **Tunbridge Wells** and in 4 *m.* passes **Groombridge**, and joins Medway 1½ *m.* below. 2 *m.* below this junction Medway is fed by a stream 6 *m.* long on the left bank: hence to the junction of Eden with Medway at **Penshurst** is 4 *m.* The Medway is preserved for 8 *m.* from Penshurst Park to East Lock by Tonbridge Angling Society; hon. sec., F. J. Tanton, 88, Barden-road. Good coarse fishing. Accommodation at the Angel or Bull Hotel. Eden rises near Limpsfield, Surrey, and, after passing Oxted and Crowhurst, in 10 *m.* is joined by a branch which rises 3 *m.* south of Lingfield (Surrey), and has a length of 7 *m.* From this junction to **Edenbridge** is 2 *m.* From Edenbridge to **Chiddingstone** is 8 *m.*, thence to Medway is 4 *m.* The Medway runs now to **Tonbridge** in 4 *m.* 6 *m.* below, a brook joins on the left bank, having a course of 9 *m.*, passing Hadlow on its way; and 3 *m.* below this again, at **Yalding**, Teise and Beult join Medway. Teise rises near **Tunbridge Wells**, and is 26 *m.* long, passing Lamberhurst, Goudhurst, and Horsemonden. Beult rises 7 *m.* east of **Headcorn**, thence runs to **Staplehurst** 3 *m.*, and **Yalding** 10 *m.* Medway next flows to **Wateringbury** 3 *m.*, **East Farleigh** 5 *m.*, **Maidstone** 3 *m.*, **Aylesford** 4 *m.*, and **Snodland** 4 *m.*, and **Rochester** 8 *m.*, passing Lower Halling and Cuxton. *Hotels:* King's Head, Royal Victoria.

Rockingham (Northton.).—L. & N.W.R.; G.N.R. Welland. Eye brook. (*See Spalding.*)

Rode (Cheshire).—L. & N.W.R. Cow brook. Dane, 1 *m.* S. *Lakes:* Rode reservoir. Great Oak reservoir, 2 *m.* N. (*See Frodsham.*)

Rogate (Sussex).—L. & S.W.R. Western Rother. (*See Littlehampton.*)

Romaldkirk (Yorks).—N.E.R. Tees; trout, salmon, grayling, coarse fish. (*c.s.*) Reer beck. East Sikcar beck, 1 *m.* N. Wilders beck, 1 *m.* S. Balder river, 2 *m.* S. (*c.s. Tees.*) Hunder beck, 6 *m.* S.W. *Lakes:* White Hill pond, 6 *m.* N. (*See Stockton.*)

Romford (Essex).—G.E.R. (*See Rainham.*)

Romsey (Hants.).—L. & S.W.R. On the Test; grayling and trout fishing good; salmon fishing good below the town, all preserved. Mr. Vickers, Hon. Evelyn Ashley, Mrs. Vaudrey, and Col. H. C. Bruce own the principal parts of the water. *Hotel:* White Horse. (*See Stockbridge, Southampton.*)

Roose (Lancs.).—Fs.R. (*See Newbiggin.*)

Rose Grove (York).—L. & Y.R. Lodge. Tower brook. (*See Preston.*)

Ross (Hereford). — G.W.R. Wye; salmon, trout, grayling, roach, dace, and chub: a fair stretch of free fishing. (*c.s.*) Garren, Gamber (6 *m.*), and the Monnow (9 *m.*) are good trout streams. *Lake:* Trevervan pool (5 *m.*) (*See Chepstow.*) *Hotel:* Royal.

Rossington (York).—G.N.R. Torne. St. Catharine's Well stream. (*See Althorpe.*)

Rothbury (Northland.).—N.B.R. On Coquet; trout (sea trout and salmon, autumn). The Duke of Northumberland's water (12 *m.*), on the Coquet, is now leased to the Coquet Committee of the Northumbrian Anglers' Federation. Tickets for whole of waters—s.t. 21*s.*, m.t. 10*s.*, w.t. 7*s.* 6*d.*, d.t. 2*s.* 6*d.*; of the Clerk to the Committee, John A. Williamson, Solicitor, Newcastle-on-Tyne. (*See Acklington, Weldon Bridge, Felton,* and *Warkworth*). Between Thrum Mill and Tosson Ford the Federation issue a free permit. (*c.s.*) *Hotels:* County, Queen's Head, Station. *Tackleists,* J. Soulsby and W. Mavin.

Rotherham (Yorks).—M.R.; G.C.R. Don. (*c.s. Yorkshire.*) Rother (*see Goole*). Oldcoates brook, 8 *m.* E. at Maltby. (*See Runcorn.*)

Rowfant (Sussex).—L. & S.W.R. (*See London, L.T.*)

Rowrah (Cumland).—L. & N.W. and Fs.R. Colliersgate beck or Marron. (*c.s. Derwent.*) Scallow beck, 2 *m.* N. (*See Cockermouth.*) Windergyll beck. (*See Egremont.*)

Rowsley (Derby).—M.R. Derwent; trout, grayling; preserved from Cawder Bridge up to above **Rowsley** by the Duke of Devonshire (*see Baslow*), and below by the Darley Dale Club; d.t. (for portion of their water and fly only) 2*s.* 6*d.* (*see Baslow, Matlock*). Wye; trout, grayling. (*See Bakewell* and *Gainsborough.*) (*c.s. Trent.*) Hipper, 3 *m.* N.E. *Lakes:* Swiss Cottage ponds, 3 *m.* N.E. (*See Goole.*) *Hotel:* Peacock (very comfortable), where fishing can be had.

Roydon (Essex).—G.E.R. *Inns:* New Inn and Temple. (*See Stratford; Rye House.*) On Stort; pike, roach, &c.; preserved hence to Hunsdon Mill; below that by the Rye House. (*See Rye House.*)

Royton (Lancs.)—L. & Y.R. Irk. (*See Runcorn.*)

Ruan Minor (Cornwall).—(n.s. **Penryn**, 22 m.) Caerleon water joins the sea 1 m. N. Caerleon rises in Croft Pascoe Pool on Goonhilly Down, and 1 m. down is joined on right bank by a stream which drains Leech Pool 1 m. up. Caerleon runs 4 m. to the sea.

Rudgwick (Sussex).—L.B. & S.C.R. Arun. (*See Littlehampton.*)

Rufford (Lancs.).—L. & Y.R. Douglas. (*c.s. Ribble.*) Eller brook. Yarrow, 3 m. N. (*See Hesketh Bank.*)

Rugby (Warwick).—L. & N.W.R.; G.C.R. Avon; chub dace, roach, pike, perch. Swift. Rain s brook (3 m. S.). (*See Gloucester.*) (*c.s. Severn.*) *Hotel*: Royal George.

Rugeley (Stafford).—L. & N.W.R. Trent; roach, pike, chub, trout. (*c.s.*) Colton brook. Rising brook. Blythe, 3 m. N.E. (*c.s. Trent.*) *Lakes*: New Coppice pool, 2 m. S.W. Upper Middle, and Lower Sherbrook pools 3½ m. W. (*See Gainsborough.*)

Ruislip (Middx.)—Met. R. Ruislip reservoir (*see London, M.T.*); pike, perch, tench; preserved.

Runcorn (Cheshire).—L. & N.W.R. On Mersey. Mersey, under the name of Goyt, rises some 3 m. above Goyt Bridge, 4 m. N.W. from **Buxton**. Here Moorestone brook, 2 m. long, joins on right bank. Goyt runs 4 m. to **Wale** Station, where a brook joins on right bank, draining Tunstead reservoir 3 m. up, 2 m. N. from **Chapel-en-le-Frith**. There is here also a considerable reservoir on left bank. 1 m. down Goyt, Black brook joins on right bank, which rises by **Chapel-en-le-Frith**, runs 3 m. to **Bugsworth**, and joins Goyt 1 m. down. Goyt runs 3 m. to **New Mills**. Here Sett brook joins on right bank. Sett rises some 3 m. above **Hayfield**, and 2 m. below is joined on right bank by Lady Gate brook, 3 m. long. Sett runs to **New Mills** and Goyt, 1 m. Goyt runs to **Strines** Station 2 m., **Marple** 3 m. 1 m. below, Etherow joins on right bank. Etherow rises in Woodhead reservoir, 2 m. long, at **Woodhead**. Half-way down the reservoir, Witherow brook, 3 m. long, joins on right bank. Etherow runs out of Woodhead reservoir into Torside reservoir immediately below. Half a mile down Torside reservoir, Great Crowdon brook joins on right bank. This brook is 4 m. long, and 1 m. up from its junction with the reservoir it is joined on left bank by Little Crowdon brook, 3 m. long. Torside reservoir is 2 m. long, and drains into another reservoir immediately below. This reservoir is 1 m. long. Etherow from this reservoir runs 2 m. to **Hadfield**. Here Hollingworth brook, 4 m. long joins on right bank. Hollingworth is joined, 1 m. up from its junction with Etherow, by Armfield brook, 3 m. long. 1 m. down Etherow, Shelf brook, which runs down from **Glossop**, 7 m. long, joins on left bank. Etherow runs to **Broadbottom** 2 m., and joins Mersey 5 m. down at **Marple**. Mersey runs to **Stockport**, 7 m. Here Tame joins on right bank. Tame rises 7 m. above **Saddleworth** Station, and is here joined on left bank by Diggle brook, 4 m. long. Tame runs 2 m. to **Greenfield**, where Greenfield brook. 4 m. long, joins on left bank. Chew brook, 3 m. long, joins Greenfield half-way up. Tame runs 3 m. to **Mossley**, where Car brook, 3 m. long, joins on left bank. 2 m. down Tame, Swineshaw brook, 3 m. long, joins on left bank. Tame runs to **Stalybridge** 1 m., **Ashton** 1 m. 2 m. down, a brook joins on right bank, draining the Gorton reservoir by **Fairfield**, 2 m. up. Tame runs to **Deriton** 1 m. Here a brook joins on right bank, draining Godley reservoir by **Newton**, 2 m. up. Tame runs to **Reddish** 5 m., and **Stockport** 2 m. Mersey runs to **Heaton Mersey** 2 m., **Didsbury** 1 m. Here Poynton brook joins on left bank. Poynton rises 4 or 5 m. above **Poynton**, and a mile below waters the lake in Poynton Park; thence to **Cheadle-Hulme** is 4 m., **Cheadle** 2 m., and Mersey 1 m. Mersey runs 1 m, to **Northenden**, and **Stretford** 5 m., where Gore brook, 6 m. long, joins on right bank. Mersey runs to **Urmiston** 2 m., **Flixton** 3 m., **Irlam** 3 m. Here Irwell joins on right bank. Irwell rises some 3 m. above **Bacup**, runs to **Stuckstead** 2 m., **Waterfoot** 1 m., **Rawtenstall** 2 m., where Larny Water, 5 m. long, joins on right bank. Irwell runs to **Ewood Bridge** 2 m., and 1 m. below is joined on right bank by Swinnel brook, which rises by **Baxenden**, runs to **Haslingden** 2 m., **Helm Shore** 2 m., and Irwell 1 m. Irwell runs to **Stubbins** 2 m. Here a stream joins on left bank, draining a pond by Hare Hill 3 m. up, and lying 3 m. S. from **Waterford**. Irwell runs to **Ramsbottom** 1 m., **Summerseat** 2 m., **Bury** 3 m. Here Tottington brook, which works some mills and is 4 m. long, joins on right bank, and just below, on the same side, run in the drainings of some 8 ponds by Elton. 1 m. down Irwell. on right bank, on the further side of the canal, is a large reservoir, and Irwell reaches **Radcliffe** 2 m. below. Here Roch joins on left bank. Roch rises 4 m. above **Walsden**, and just below is joined on right bank by the overflow of a large pond 1 m. up. 2 m. down Roch the outflow of a pond 1 m. up joins on left bank. 1 m. down Roch a stream joins on left bank, which rises in Gadden reservoir 1 m. E. from **Walsden**, runs in 1 m. to Upper White Holme reservoir, thence to Tunnel End reservoir immediately below. At the lower end of this latter lake the Lower White Holme reservoir joins on left bank. The outflow runs 1 m. to Blackstone reservoir, thence 1 m. to Spoddle Hill and another reservoir, and joins Roch just below. Roch runs to **Littleborough** 2 m., where a stream joins on left bank, draining Hollingworth reservoir 1 m. up. 2 m. down Roch, Beal joins on left bank. Beal rises 3 or 4 m. above **Milnrood**, and joins Roch 3 m. below. Roch runs to **Rochdale** 1 m. Here Dodd joins on right bank. Dodd rises above **Shawforth**, runs 1 m. to **Facit**, **Whitworth** 1 m., **Shawclough** 2 m., **Rochdale** and Roch 2 m. Roch runs to **Castleton** 2 m., and here Saddon brook, which rises in a pond by Bolderstone, and is 3 m. long, joins on left bank. Marland mere is 1 m. W. from **Castleton**. Roch runs 3 m. to **Heywood**, 1 m. off on left bank, and here Naden Water, 5 m. long, and working some mills, joins on right bank. Roch runs 2 m. to Heap Bridge, 1 m. E. of **Bury**, and 1 m. below is joined on left bank by Black brook, 4 m. long. Roch joins Irwell 1 m. down at **Radcliffe**. Irwell runs 5 m. to **Farnworth**, and here Tange joins on right bank. Tange, under the name of Eagle, rises in Longworth reservoir, 6 m. N.W. of **Bolton-le-Moors**, and 5 m. down, at Walmsley, is joined on right bank by the outflow of Springwater reservoir, 4 m. N.E. from **Bolton**. Below this point the river takes the name of Tange, and runs 2 m. to **Oaks** Station, and 1 m. down, at Sharples, is joined on right bank by Dean brook. which rises in two reservoirs on Rivington Moor. 4 m. N.W. of **Bolton**, and is 5 m. long, watering several mill pools in its course. Tange runs 2 m. to **Bolton**, where Croal river, which rises in the lake in Hulton Park, 1 m. N. from **Atherton**, and runs to **Chequerbent** 1 m., **Lostock** 3 m., and Tange, 4 m , joins on right bank. 2 m. below **Bolton**, Bradshaw brook joins Tange on left bank. Bradshaw rises in the reservoir by **Entwistle**, runs to **Turton** 2 m., **Bromley Cross** 2 m., and joins Tange 5 m. down. Tange runs 1 m. to Irwell and **Farnworth**. Irwell runs to **Clifton** 4 m., and **Salford** and **Manchester** 6 m. Here Irk and Medlock join on left bank. Irk rises 3 or 4 m. above **Royton**, runs 3 m. to **Middleton**, where a stream joins on right bank, draining some ponds by Three Pits Bridge, 2 m. up. 3 m. down Irk the drainage of the lake at Heaton, 1 m. up and 3 m. S.W. of **Middle'on**, joins on right bank; thence to **Manchester** Irk runs 5 m. Medlock rises 6 m. above **Parkbridge**, and 2 m. below is joined on left bank by a brook 3 m. long, which drains a lake on Knoll Hill 1 m. S.W. from **Mossley**, or 2 m. S.E. of **Parkbridge**. Medlock runs to **Clayton Bridge** 2 m., and **Manchester** 2 m. Irwell runs to **Eccles** 4 m., and 3 m. down. **Patricroft** being 1½ m. off on right bank, Worsley brook joins on right bank. Worsley rises in a pond by Black Leech, and 1 m. down is joined on left bank by the outflow of Linnyshaw dam a little way up. Worsley runs to **Worsley** 3 m., and Irwell 3 m. Irwell runs 1 m., where Longford brook. 7 m. long, and, running 1 m. N. of **Urmiston**, joins on left bank. Irwell joins Mersey 3 m. down at Irlam. Mersey runs 2 m. to **Partington** on left bank, and 1 m. down, at Hollinfare, Glaze brook joins on right bank, and Wych brook on left bank. Glaze brook rises above **Leigh**, where it receives the drainage of the lake at Atherton Hall, and is about 10 m. long. Wych brook rises in three branches above **Timperley**, and runs to Mersey 5 m. Mersey runs 1 m. to **Warburton**, and 1 m. below is joined on left bank by Bollin. Bollin rises above **Macclesfield**, runs to **Presbury** 3 m., **Wilmslow** 6 m. 1 m. down, Dean joins on right bank. Dean rises above **Bollington**, runs to **Adlington** 4 m. 1 m. below, a brook joins on right bank, draining the lake at Stypherson Park, 2 m. up, 1 m. N. of **Bollington**. Dean runs to **Handforth** 4 m., and 2 m. down joins Bollin. Bollin runs to **Ashley**, 1 m. off on left bank, 7 m. 2 m. below, Birkin joins on left bank. Birkin rises 1 m. N. of **Chelford**, runs 5 m. to **Knutsford**, 1 m. off on left bank: **Mobberley**, 1 m. off on left bank, 2 m.; **Ashley**, 1 m. off on right bank, 2 m. Here Mobberley brook, which rises above **Mobberley** and is 5 m. long, and Ashley brook. 5 m. long, join on right bank; whilst the outflow, 2 m. long, of the lakes in Tatton Park by **Knutsford** joins on right bank. 1 m. down Birkin, a brook joins on right bank, which rises in Mere Hall lake, 3 m. N.W. from **Knutsford**, runs 7 m. to Rosthern mere, 2 m. W. of **Ashley**, and joins Birkin 1 m. down. Birkin runs to Bollin 1 m. 3 m. down Bollin, Arden brook, 4 m. long, joins on left bank. Bollin runs 1 m. to **Heatley**, and joins Mersey 2 m. down. 1 m. down Mersey by **Lymm**, Sow brook, which waters the lake by **Lymm**, joins on left bank. Mersey runs to **Thelwall** 3 m, and **Warrington** 4 m. Here Black brook, 7 m. long, borders the town on the E., and Sankey brook on W. Sankey rises above **Rainford**, runs to **Mossbank** 3 m., **St. Helens** 2 m. Here a brook joins on right bank, draining the lake at Eccleston Hall, 2 m. S.W. of **St. Helens**. Sankey runs to **Collins Green** 2 m., and 2 m. down is joined on left bank by Newton brook. Newton rises above Carr Mill dam. 1½ m. E. of **Mossbank**, runs to Stanley Mill pool 1 m.. 1½ m. N.E. of **St. Helens**, where it receives the outflow of the lake at Garswood. 3 m. N.E. of **St. Helens**, and runs thence to Sankey 3 m. Sankey runs to **Warrington** 6 m., and joins Mersey 2 m. down. 1 m. down Mersey, Kekwick brook, which rises above **Boston**, and is 5 m. long, joins on left bank. Mersey runs to **Runcorn** 6 m.

DITTON BROOK.—This brook joins Mersey 11 m. below the town, on right bank. Ditton, called Tarbock in its upper part, rises in Mizzy dam, 1½ m. N.W. of **Prescot**, runs to **Huyton Quarry** 2 m., and 1 m. below waters Logwood Mill dam. 2 m. below. Childwall brook. which rises above **Childwall** and is 4 m. long, joins on right bank. Ditton runs to **Halewood** 2 m., and 3 m. below joins Mersey estuary.

Rushton (Northton.)—M.R. Ise. (See *Wisbeach*.) Dane. 1 m. N.: trout, dace, chub, roach; private. (See *Frodsham*.)

Ruswarp (York).—N.E.R. Esk; salmon, sea trout, trout: preserved *above* to **Sleights** Bridge, and *below* to **Whitby**, by the Esk Fishing Association; s.t. 20s., d.t. 1s. 6d; apply to Mr. Sedman. water bailiff, Ruswarp. (c.s.) Wash beck; trout; private. Rigg Mill beck; trout; private. (See *Whitby*.)

Ryburgh (Norfolk).—G.E.R. Wensum. (See *Yarmouth*.) (c.s. N. and S.)

Rye (Sussex).—S.E. & C.R. On Rother. The stream rises near Rotherfield, in Sussex. In 5 m. it is joined by a stream on the left bank 4 m. long. 1½ m. down, near **Ticehurst Road**, a stream 6 m. long joins on the left bank. 6 m. on, at **Etchingham**, the Dudwell, 8 m. long joins on the right bank; 3 m. on, at **Robertsbridge**, a stream joins on the right bank, having its source in a large pond in Brightling Park. 6 m. on, the Kentish Ditch joins on the left bank. Some 6 m down, passing Newenden, a trout stream of 8 m. long joins on the left bank rising 3 m. N.E. of Hawkhurst. Hence to Rye is 9 m., passing Wittersham and Playden. At Rye two branches join on the right bank, the first, Tillingham water, 8 m. long, rises near Beckley, and the second, the Brede, rises near **Battle**, and has a course of 15 m., passing Whatlington, Sedlescombe, Brede, Udimore, and **Winchelsea**. Rother and tributaries Tillingham and Brede are preserved by the Rother Fishery Association; s.t. 10s., with 5 day tickets for friends. Each subscriber, for every extra 10s. he pays, gets 5 day tickets for friends; d.t., 1s.; trout licences, 1s. Trouting begins April 1st, ends Oct. 31st. The smaller tributaries mostly abound in trout. Sec., Thos. Daws, Esq., Soggs House, Ewhurst, Hawkhurst. The Rother Valley Railway, which joins S.E. & C.R., at **Robertsbridge**, is very convenient for Rother fishing stations. **Bodiam** and **Northiam** are good points. (*See c.s.*) Bass at harbour's mouth, and flat fish in the bay.

Rye House.—G.E.R. (*See Stratford.*) On Lea. *Hotels*: Rye House and King's Arms. This fishery joins on to Cook's; the proprietors have thrown open their fishery free of charge. The preserve extends up the Stort as far as Hunsdon Mill. Trout perch, barbel, roach, chub, jack. Trouting begins on May 1st. Regulations same as at Broxbourne. Boats can be had.

Ryhall (Rutland).—G.N.R. Gwash. Glen, 1 m. N.E., at **Essendine**. Welland, 3 m. S., at **Stamford**. (*See Spalding.*)

Ryhill (York).—G.C.R. *Lakes*: Cold Hindley reservoir. (*See Rawcliffe.*)

Ryther (York), n.s. **Ulleskelf**, 3 m.—Wharfe; coarse fish, mostly free. (*c.s. York.*) Ouse, 1 m. W. (*c.s. York.*) (*See York.*)

Saddleworth (Yorks.)—L. & N.W.R. Tame. Diggle brook. (*See Runcorn.*)

Saffron Walden (Essex).—G.E.R. Cam; trout; mostly preserved by Lord Braybrook, of Audley End. (*See King's Lynn.*) *Hotel*: Rose and Crown.

Salford Priors (Warwick).—G.W.R. Avon; chub, dace, roach, pike, perch. Arrow, same fish. Ban brook. (*See Gloucester.*) (*c.s. Severn.*)

Salhouse (Norfolk). — G.E.R. Bure, 1 m. N.E. *Lakes*: Salhouse Broad. 1 m. N.E.; private. Wroxham Broad, 1 m. N.; fishing on payment. (*c.s. N. and S.*) Woodbastwick Broad, 2 m. N.E.; preserved by A. Cator, Esq. Little Ranworth Broad, 3 m. E. (Misses Kerrison). Ranworth Broad, 4 m. E.; preserved by A. Cator, Esq. (*c.s. N. and S.*) Pedham mill dam, 4 m. S.E. South Walsham Broad, 5 m. E.; preserved by Major Jury. (*c.s. N. and S.*) (*See Yarmouth.*)

Salisbury (Wilts).—L. & S.W.R. Avon; trout, grayling, jack, roach. Wylye and Winter-bourne; trout, grayling, and coarse fish; preserved. (*See Christchurch.*) At Britford, 1½ m. off, the Avon is preserved for 4 m. by the owner of the Moat; Lord Radnor, of Longford Castle, preserves some part of the river below the city; 1 m. belongs to the Electric Lighting Co.; fishing now let. The owner of Stockton House preserves a length of Wylye; good grayling and trout fishing. Hampshire Avon; roach, dace, trout and grayling. Mr. Hills' fishery (Rose and Crown); trout, s.t. 21s., d.t. 2s.; hotel accommodation excellent. (*c.s.*) *Hotels*: White Hart, Angel, and Red Lion.

Saltfleet (Lincoln), n.s. **Saltfleetby**, 3 m. — Withern. Grayfleet. South ditch. Withern rises some 10 m. above **Aby**. 2 m. above **Aby**, Calceby beck, which rises in the lake in Ormesby Park, 5 m. S.W. from **Aby**, joins on right bank. Withern runs to Withern 3 m., **Theddlethorpe** 6 m., and **Saltfleet** 5 m. Here Grayfleet, which rises 1 m. S. of **Louth**, runs to **Grimoldby** 4 m., and **Saltfleet** 7 m. Here also South ditch, 6 m. long, joins on left bank.

Saltfleetby (Lincoln).—G.N.R. (*See Saltfleet.*)

Saltford (Somerset).—G.W.R. (*See Bristol.*) Avon; roach, dace, carp, pike, perch, trout; free. Boyd. (*c.s.*) Good all-round fishing.

Salton (Yorks).—N.E.R. 6 m. from Pickering, and 4 m. from the **Barton-le-Street** station. Plenty of excellent fishing can be had both in a stream that runs through the town and in the river Rye, 1 m. distant; permission easily obtainable. *Inn*: the Angler's Arms.

Sampford Courtney (Devon).—L. & S.W.R. Exbourne water. (*See Bideford.*)

Sandal (Yorks).—G.N.R.; M.R.; G.C.R. Walton beck. Calder, 1 m. N. (*c.s. York.*) *Lakes*: Walton Park lake, 2 m. S.E. Chevel Park lake, 2 m. S.W. (*See Rawcliffe.*)

Sandbach (Cheshire).—L. & N.W.R. Wheelock. Betchton brook, 1 m. S. Hassall brook, 1 m. S. Foul brook, 3 m. S. *Lakes*: Winterley Mill, 2½ m. S. (*See Frodsham.*)

Sandford (Somerset).—G.W.R. (*See Congresbury*). *Lakes*: Sandford and Banwell ponds; rudd, tench; private.

Sandhurst (Berks).—*Stations*: Wellington College or Blackwater, S.E. & C.R., Camberley, L. & S.W.R. Blackwater. (*See London, M.T.*)

Sandiacre (Derby).—M.R. Erewash. Trent, 4 m. S. (*c.s.*) (*See Gainsborough.*)

Sandside (Lancs.).—Steers pool. (*See Broughton.*)

Sandwich (Kent).—S.E. & C.R. On Stour. The Stour rises 15 m. north-west of **Ashford**. Here a stream 10m. long joins on the right bank, which rises near **Weston-hanger** station, passing the villages of Sellinge, Smeeth, and Sevington. At Smeeth, are roach, few trout, and pike. Mr. Knatchbull-Hugessen owns the water. From Ashford the Stour flows to **Wye**, 6 *m.*. thence to **Chilham**, 6 *m.*, passing Godmersham Park, (Kay, Esq.) 4 *m.* on **Chartham** is reached; hence to **Canterbury** is some 3 *m.* The Stour next runs to **Sturry**, and Fordwich is 3 *m.* (here begins the Fordwich and Grove Ferry Angling Club water); thence to **Grove Ferry** is 6 *m.* 3 *m.* below **Grove Ferry** is Sarre, where are two good inns. ¼ *m.* below, Little Stour joins the Stour. This stream rises 7 *m.* south of **Bekesbourne**. 4 *m.* below, a small stream joins on the right bank. From this point to the junction with the Stour is 6 *m.* The Stour next runs in 3 *m.* to **Minster**; thence to **Sandwich** 6 *m*; and finally to the sea, 7 *m.* Day tickets for killing coarse fish—from here to Coal Harbour, 1 *m.* above Grove Ferry—are 1*s.* each. (*c.s.*) Bass at the mouth of the haven; flounders, grey mullet, plaice, dabs, codlings, and pout more seaward.

Sandy (Beds).—G.N.R.; L. & N.W.R. Ivel: coarse fish, except barbel, trout. Southill brook. (*See King's Lynn.*)

Sawbridgworth (Herts.).—G.E.R. (*See Stratford.*) On Stort and Pincey brook. Leave may often be obtained by applying at Sawbridgworth Mill, Mr. E. B. Barnard. *Inn,* Bell and Feather.

Sawdon (York).—N.E.R. Sawdon beck. Beedale beck, 3 *m.* S.E. (*See Wressel.*)

Sawley (Yorks).—N.E.R. On Ribble; salmon, trout, mort, sprod, dace, carp, grayling. 2 *m.* from **Chatburn** station on L. & Y.R. Trout and mort fishing excellent. Earl Cowper's water is now let to Mr. Smith, of Hazeldene, Wilpshire, Blackburn, who might grant a day's fishing if properly approached.

Sawley (Derby).—M.R. Trent; roach, dace, perch, pike, chub, bream, barbel; a.t. 10*s.* for fishing above the weir; a.t. 21*s.*, d.t. 2*s.* 6*d.*, *below* the weir on the S. or Lockington side. (*c.s.*) *Hotel* : White Lion, where tickets can be had. Derwent, 1 *m.* W. (*c.s. Trent*). Soar 1 *m.* S.E. (*c.s. Trent.*) (*See Gainsborough.*)

Saxby (Leicester).—M.R.; G.N.R. Wreak (*c.s. Trent.*) Saxby brook. *Lakes* : Stapleford Park lake, 1 *m.* S. Leesthorpe pond, 5 *m.* S.W. (*See Gainsborough.*)

Saxham (Suffolk).—G.E.R. Cavenham brook. *Lakes* : Ickworth Park lake, 3 *m.* S. (*See King's Lynn.*)

Saxilby (Lincoln).—G.E.R.; G.N.R. Tilt, 2 *m.* E. (*See Boston.*)

Saxmundham (Suffolk).—G.E.R. Saxmundham brook. Alde, 2 *m.* W.; roach, &c.; fishing free. (*See Orford.*) *Hotel* : White Hart.

Scalby (Yorks).—N.E.R. Scalby beck: sea trout, trout, grayling, chub, dace. Scalby is formed by a beck which takes the flood water from the Derwent 1 *m.* below **Hackness**. From the intake to **Scalby** is 4 *m.* Here Burniston beck joins on left bank. Burniston rises 3 *m.* above **Cloughton**. Here Lindhead beck, 3 *m.* long, joins on right bank; hence to **Scalby** is 3 *m.* Scalby runs 1 *m.* to the sea. Fishing free from Scalby Mill down to the sea, elsewhere private, as is Burniston beck.

Scale Hill Hotel (Cumland).—Cocker; trout. (*c.s. Derwent.*) Mosedale beck. Whitbe:R, 4 *m.* N. *Lakes* : Crummock Water; pike, trout, char. (*c.s. Derwent.*) Lowes Water, 2 *m.* W.; trout; preserved. (*c.s. Derwent.*) (*See Cockermouth, Keswick.*)

Scalford (Leicester).—L. & N.W.R.; G.N.R. Melton brook. *Lakes* : Goadby Marwood, 2 *m.* N. Croxton Park ponds, 5 *m.* N.E. (*See Gainsborough.*)

Scarborough (Yorks).—N.E.R. Scalby beck, 2 *m.* N.; trout and bull trout in autumn; grayling; preserved by Scalby Beck Angling Club; hon. sec., Mr. A. W. Thompson, 32, St. Nicholas-street; entrance, 60*s.*; a.t. 45*s.*, d.t. (Tuesday, Thursday, and Friday only) 5*s.*; (fly only); from Mr. Rhodes, fish tackleist, North-street, Scarborough (n.s. **Scalby**). Burniston beck, 3 *m.* (n.s. **Scalby**); trout; preserved by a club; hon. sec., Mr. T. J. Hart, Rye Croft, Fulford-road, Scarborough. Derwent, 6½ *m.* W.; trout, grayling, coarse fish below; n.s. **Forge Valley**. (*See Hackness, Harwood Dale, Wressel.*) Several small streams full of little trout enter the sea to the north of Scarborough. Thorney beck and Stainton Dale beck preserved by a club; no d.t. are now issued. The sea fishing is good from boat or pier most of the year. Autumn whiting and gurnard fishing very good in the bay, and winter codling fishing from First or Second Points to the south of Scarborough, and Colam Hole (n.s. **Cloughton**) or Beast Cliff (n.s. **Stainton Dale**), to the north, very good. Mackerel whiffing in August and September, and occasionally pollack are taken close in shore; good plaice fishing from boat or pier in summer. There is a sea angling club (known as the Scarboro' Rock Fishers), which meets at the Albemarle Temperance Hotel during the rock fishing season, Sept. to March; a.t. 5*s.* of hon. sec., J. Watson, 113, Longwestgate.

Scawby (Lincoln).—G.C.R. Ancholme, 3 *m.* E. North Kelsey beck, 3 *m.* E. (*See Brigg.*)

Scholes (York).—N.E.R. Cock beck. Carr beck. (*See York.*)

Scorrier Gate (Cornwall).—G.W.R. Perran. (*See Perran.*) (*c.s. Fowey.*)

Scorton (Lancs.).—L. & N.W.R. Wyre. (*c.s. Lune.*) Grizedale brook, 1 *m.* S.E. (*See Fleetwood.*)

Scorton (York).—N.E.R. Scorton beck. Swale, 2 *m.* S. (*c.s. York.*) Howl beck. Bridgworth beck. (*See York.*)

Scotby (Cumland).—M.R.; N.E.R. Scotby beck. Eden, 2 *m.* E. at **Wetheral** ; salmon, trout. (*c.s.*) (*See Carlisle.*)

Scrooby (Notts).—G.N.R. Idle. (*c.s. Trent.*) Ryton. (*See Althorpe.*)

Scruton (York).—N.E.R. Swale; preserved. (*c.s. York.*) (*See York.*)

Seamer (York).—N.E.R. Seamer Drain; chub, grayling, trout; free. Derwent runs near; preserved. (*See Scarborough.*)

Sea Mills (Glo'ster).—G.W.R. On Trim. Trim rises 3 m. N.W. of **Pilton,** and is 5 m. long

Seaton (Devon).—L. & S.W.R. Axe; trout. salmon. Axe rises above Picket Mill (n.s. **Misterton** and **Crewkerne,** 3½ m.), runs 4 m. to Clapton Bridge (n.s. **Crewkerne,** 3 m.). Here a stream joins on left bank, which works a mill 2 m. up. Axe runs to Winsham 3 m., where a stream joins on left bank, working a mill 1 m. up. 1 m. down at Ford Abbey, a stream joins on right bank, working a mill 2 m. up. (The fishing hereabouts is very good, but preserved by the owners of Ford Abbey.) 2 m. down Axe a stream joins on right bank, which rises by **Chard,** and is 3 m. long, working three mills. 2 m. down Axe, at **Chard Junction,** a stream joins on left bank 3 m. long, working a mill. 1 m. on a stream joins on right bank, which rises at Warnbrook Mill (n.s. **Chard,** 2 m.). runs 2 m., and is joined on left bank by a stream working a mill 1 m. up; it then runs to Chardstock 1 m., and Axe 2 m. Axe runs in 3 m. to **Axminster,** and 2 m. down is joined by the Yarty on right bank. Yarty rises above Keat's Mill (n.s. **Ilminster,** 6 m.), runs 2 m., and is joined by a stream on left bank 2 m long. Yarty runs to Yarcombe (fishing begins: good accommodation) 2 m., where a small stream joins on left bank, then to Stockland 3 m. (fair accommodation), Kilmington 6 m. Here Dalwood brook (trout) joins Yarty on right bank, which rises 1 m. W. of Stockland, runs to Dalwood 3m. and Yarty 3 m. Yarty joins Axe ¼ m. down. Axe runs 3½ m. to **Colyton,** and 2 m. to **Colyford.** Here Coly joins Axe. Coly rises by Cotleigh (n.s. **Honiton,** 4 m.), runs 6 m. to **Seaton Junction,** and 2 m. to **Colyton.** Here a stream joins on right bank, which rises by Offwell (n.s. **Honiton,** 3 m.). 2 m. down a stream joins on right bank, which rises by Northleigh, and is 3 m. long. 2 m. down, **Colyton** is reached. Axe is 2 m. on. 1 m. down is **Axmouth** and **Seaton.** The best flies for Axe and tributaries are blue dun, March brown, blue upright, and red palmer. From the east end of Seaton beach a ground line, baited with squid or cuttle bait, may be thrown out in rough weather. By crossing the ferry the pier at Axmouth may be reached, whence, with a heavy floated line, bass may be angled for with soft crab or squid bait, or a large and gaudy artificial fly. Squid to be procured from the mackerel seines, or trawl boats at Beer. Many pollack are at times caught off Beer Head. Pout may also be taken. (*See Beer.*) (*c.s.*)

Seaton (Rutland).—L. & N.W.R.; G.N.R. Welland. (*See Spalding.*)

Seaton Junction (Devon).—L. & S.W.R. (*See Seaton.*) Coly; trout. *Hotel:* Shute Arms, where a limited number of tickets for Axe and Coly can be had.

Sedbergh (Yorks.).—L. & N.W.R. Rawthey river. Lune, 1 m. W. (*c.s.*) Crossdale beck, 2 m. N. Clough river, 3 m. E.; salmon. trout; free. A Conservators' licence is necessary; salmon 10s, trout 2s. 6d. (*See Lancaster.*) Hutton beck, 3 m. E. *Lakes :* Lily mere, 3 m. E. Killington reservoir, 3 m. E.; pike, perch. *Hotels :* Black Bull, White Hart. (*See Milnthorpe.*)

Sedgebrook (Lincoln).—G.N.R. Foster Beck. (*See Boston.*)

Sedgefield (*Durham*).—N.E.R. Skerne, 2 m. N.; trout, pike, chub. roach; free by permission of the farmers. Licenses of Mr. J. F. Smythe, Fishtackleist, Horsemarket, Darlington. *Lakes :* Hardwicke Hall, 1 m. N.W. (*c.s. Tees.*) (*See Stockton.*)

Seend (Wilts).—G.W.R. (*See Bristol.*)

Sefton (Lancs.).—S. & C.L.E.R. Alt. (*See Altcar.*)

Selby (York).—G.E. & G.N.J.R.; N.E.R. (*See Cawood, York.*)

Sellafield (Cumland).—L. & N.W. and Fs.R. Ehen. (*c.s. West Cumland.*) Calder. (*c.s. West Cumland.*) New Mill beck. (*See Egremont.*)

Semley (Dorset).—L. & S.W.R. (*See Shaftesbury.*)

Sessay (York).—N.E.R. Willow beck, 1 m. N. Cod beck, 2 m. W. Swale, 2 m., S.W. (*c.s. York.*) (*See York.*)

Settle (Yorks).—M.R. Ribble; trout, salmon, and coarse fish below. Cowside beck, 3 m. N. Long Preston beck, 2 m. E. *Lakes :* Malham tarn, 7 m. N.E.; preserved by W. Morrison. Esq *Hotel :* Ashfield. (*See Preston.*)

Sevenoaks (Kent).—S.E. & C.R. On Darenth; trout; preserved by Lord Stanhope. A short reach may be fished for a small fee on application to the miller at Longford Mill. (*See Dartford.*) *Hotel:* Royal Crown.

Sexhow (*Yorks*).—N.E.R. Potto beck. Leven; trout; private. (*c.s. Tees.*) Faceby beck, 1 m. E. (*See Stockton.*)

Shaftesbury (Dorset), n.s. **Semley.**—Nadder; trout, roach, dace. Fern brook. (*See Christchurch.*) (*c.s. Avon.*) *Lakes :* Lashmere pond.

Shakerstone (Leicester).—L. & N.W.R.; M.R. Sence. Bosworth brook, 2 m. S. (*See Gainsborough.*)

Shalford (Surrey).—S.E. & C.R. Wey and Tillingbourne; trout; preserved above to Chilworth by Col. Godwin-Austen, Shalford House, Guildford. (*See London, L.T.*) *Inns:* Parrot and Victoria.

Shap (Westland).—L. & N.W.R. Lowther; trout. Leath, 2 m. N. Swindale beck, 3 m. W. Hawes beck, 5 m. N.W. Hows beck, 5 m. N.W. at **Bampton** Ghyll beck, 6 m. N.E. Measand beck, 8 m. W. *Lakes :* Hawes water. 6 m. W.; trout, char, pike, perch; leave from Lord Lonsdale's steward, Lowther Castle, Penrith. *Hotels:* Shap Wells Hotel 4 m., Greyhound. (*See Carlisle.*)

Shapwick (Somerset).— G.W.R. Brue; roach, dace. carp, perch, pike; preserved above, free below. (*See High Bridge*) (*c.s. Avon.*)

Sharlston (York).—L. & Y.E. Went. *Lakes*: Sharlston Mill pond. Nostell Priory lakes, 3 m. S. (*See Goole.*)

Sharnbrook (Beds.).—M.R. (*See Harrold.*) Ouse; coarse fish, except barbel; preserved by W. Whitworth, Esq. ; there is good fishing hence to Milton, 4 m. down, and good bream fishing up to Falmarsham, 1 m. above. (*c.s. N.* and *S.*) (*See King's Lynn.*)

Shawclough (Lancs.) L. & Y.R. Dodd. Naden Water, 2 m. W. (*See Runcorn.*)

Shawforth (Lancs.).—L. & N.W.R. ; G.N.R.; M.R. Dodd. (*See Runcorn.*)

Sheepsbridge (Derby).—M.R.; G.C.R. Drone. Millthorpe brook. (*See Goole.*)

Sheffield (Yorks). — G.C.R. ; M.R.; G.N.R.; N.E.R. Don. (*c.s. Yorkshire.*) Porter brook. Sheal; coarse fish, trout; mostly free. Rowel, 2 m. N.W. Rivelin, 3 m. W. *Lakes*: two reservoirs, 7 m. W. (*See Goole, Ashopton.*)

Shefford (Beds).—M.R.; L. & N.W.R. Tod; few coarse fish. Gull brook. Campton brook, 3 m. Ivel, 3 m. (*See King's Lynn.*)

Shelford (Cambs).—G.E.R. Cam; pike, perch, dace, roach chub, &c.; preserved. Bourn; coarse fish. (*See King's Lynn.*)

Shenton (Warwick).—L. & N.W.R. Tweed. (*See Gainsborough.*)

Shepperton (Middlx.). - L.&S.W.R. Thames. (*See London, L.T.*) *Hotel*: Anchor. *Fishermen*: H. Perdue, G. Rosewell, and J. Haslett. Punts of G. J. Purdue.

Shepton Mallet (Somerset).—G.W.R. Godney Brook. (*See High Bridge.*)

Sherborne (Dorset).—L. & S.W.R. Yeo. (*See Bridgwater.*) (*c.s. Avon.*)

Sherburn (Yorks).—G.N.R.; M.R. Fine trout in the mill dam.

Shiffnall (Salop).—G.W.R Worf (2¼ m. E.); trout and coarse fish. *Lakes* : Cramp pools (2 m. N.E.). Long Castle lakes (2¼ m. E.). Forge pool (3 m. N.E.). Marsh pool, Burlington pool, New pool, Cowley Wood pool, Weston Mill pool, Norton Meer (4 m. N.E.). White Sitch lake (6 m. N.E.). (*See Gloucester.*) (*c.s. Severn.*)

Shildon (Durham).—N.E.R. Woodham beck, 1 m. S. (*See Stockton.*)

Shillingston (Dorset).—S. & D.J.R. Stour. (*See Christchurch.*) (*c.s. Avon.*)

Shingle Street-on-Sea.—Good sea fishing. Bass. whiting, &c.

Shiplake (Oxon).—G.W.R. Thames. (*See London, M.T.*) *Fisherman*: Compton.

Shipley (York).—G.N.R.; M.R.; N.E.R. Aire. (*c.s. York.*) Bradford beck. (*See Rawcliffe.*)

Shipston (Worcester).—G.W.R. Stour. Knee brook (2¼ m S.). Compton brook (3 m. S.). *Lakes*: Eatington Park lake (5¼ m. N.) (*See Gloucester.*)

Shipton (Oxon).—G.W.R. On Evenlode. (*See London U.T.*)

Shirebrook (Notts).—M.R. Meden, 1 m. S.E. (*See Althorpe.*)

Shireoaks (Notts).—G.N.R. Spont. *Lakes*: Moor Mill dam, 2 m. S.W. (*See Althorpe*)

Shoreham (Kent).—S.E. & C.R. On Darenth. (*See Dartford.*)

Shrewsbury.—G.W.R.; L. & N.W.R. Severn; chub, dace, pike, perch, roach, trout, salmon, grayling; fishing free; some sport in early spring and in autumn. Raddle brook. Rea; roach, dace, chub, pike, trout; fishing free. Meol brook (2 m. S.); roach, dace, chub; fishing free. Sundown brook (3 m. N.E.). Perry (7 m. N.W.) ; trout, pike, roach. dace. Fishing may sometimes be had also in the Condover, Stapleton, Shiraton, and Onny brooks (trout only), and the Sunderton and Betton pools. *Lakes*: Alkmond pool, Black pool, and Hencot pool (2¼ m. N.) ; pike, perch, roach, rudd. carp. bream, tench. Sundorn Castle lakes (3 m. N.E.); same fish. Onslow Hall lake (4 m. W.); same fish. Bomer pool (4 m. S.); pike, bream ; leave sometimes given. Shrawardine Castle lake (8 m. N.W.) ; same fish. (*See Gloucester.*) (*c.s.*) *Hotel*: Raven.

Shrivenham (Berks).—G.W.R. On Byde Mill brook. There is a large lake at Warnford Place (*See London, U.T.*) and in Beckett Park.

Shustoke (Warwick).—M.R. Arley brook; a few trout of fair size. (*See Gainsborough.*)

Sidmouth (Devon).—L. & S.W.R. Sid ; trout. Sid rises in two streams some 3 m. above Sidbury, and 1½ m. below it is joined on left bank by a short stream. **Sidmouth** is 2 m. down. The river is partly preserved. Mackerel, whiting, &c., are caught in the bay and offing. Pollack and pout on rocky ground towards Salterton. At Chit rock bass may sometimes be taken by throwing out a line with squid bait off the beach during a S.W. breeze. *Hotel*: Knowle.

Silecroft.—Fs.R. Whicham beck runs near. After a course of 6 m. it runs into Haverigg pool, which joins the Duddon estuary at Haverigg. *Inn:* Royal Albert.

Silverton (Devon).—G.W.R. Exe; trout, salmon, dace, pike, perch; preserved by the Up Exe Fishing Association. (*c.s.*) (*See Thorverton, Exeter.*)

Simmonds Gate (Gloucester).—G.W.R. Wye ; pike, perch, chub, dace, salmon. (*c.s.*) (*See Chepstow.*)

Sinnington (York).—N.E.R. Leven; trout; preserved by R. Lesley, Esq., of Sinnington Lodge, who sometimes gives leave. Catter beck, 1 m. W. Sutherland beck, 4 m. N. Harlof beck, 7 m. N. Northdale beck, 8 m. N. (*See Wressel.*)

Skelmersdale (Lancs.).—L. & N.W.R.: L. & Y.R. Tawd. (*See Hesketh Bank.*)

Skelwith Bridge (Westland).—Great Langdale beck. *Lakes* : Loughrigg tarn, 1 m. W. Eller water, 1 m. W. Little Langdale tarn, 3 m. W. Blea tarn, 5 m. W. Stickle tarn, 6 m. N.W.; trout. There is a comfortable inn here. (*See Ulverston.*)

Skipton (York).—M.R.; L. & Y.R. Aire; trout, grayling, pike, perch, chub, roach; preserved by Bradford Angling Association; clubhouse, County Restaurant, Bradford. (*c.s. York.*) Eller beck. Elslack, 2 m. W. on other side of Aire. (*See Rawcliffe.*)

Skipton Bridge (York), n.s. **Baldersby**, 1 m.—Swale. (c.s. *York.*) (*See York.*)
Slaidburn (York), n.s. **Chatburn**, 7 m.—Hodder; trout; private above. Dunsop river.
  Eller beck, 1 m. W. Croasdale beck, 1 m. N.W. Barn Gill, 1 m. N. Bridge House beck,
  3 m. N. Hasgill beck. 5 m. N. (*See Preston.*)
Slaithwaite (Yorks).—L. & N.W.R. Colne; polluted. *Lakes* : Slaithwaite Common pond,
  2 m. W. (*See Rawcliffe.*)
Sleights (York).—N.E.R. Esk; salmon, sea trout, trout; preserved *above* and *below* by
  Esk Fishery Association; clerk, Mr. W. Brown, The Saw Mills, Whitby; m.t. (not beyond
  Sept. 30), 3l. 3s.; (c.s.) Little beck; trout; private. (*See Whitby.*)
Slinfold (Sussex).—L.B. & S.C.R. On Arun. Good fishing. (*See Littlehampton.*)
Slingsby (York).—N.E.R. Wath beck. Rye, 2 m. N.E. (*See Wressel.*)
Slough (Bucks).—G.W.R. In Stoke Park is a large lake. (*See London, M.T.*)
Smardale (Westland).—N.E.R. Scandal beck. (*See Carlisle.*)
Snaith (Yorks).—L. & Y.R. Aire. (c.s. *York.*) (*See Rawcliffe.*)
Snape (Suffolk).—G.E.R. Alde; roach, &c.; fishing free. Saxmundham brook. *Lakes* :
  Iken Decoy, 4 m. S.E. (*See Orford.*)
Snarston (Leicester).—L. & N.W.R.; M.R. Mease. (c.s. *Trent.*) (*See Gainsborough.*)
Snelland (Lincoln).—G.N.R. Snelland brook. Langworth, 1 m. S.W. Fristhorpe brook,
  1 m. N.W. (*See Boston.*)
Snodland (Kent).—S.E. & C.R. (*See Rochester.*) On Medway.
Solihull (Warwick).—G.W.R. Blyth, 1 m. S.E.; bream, roach, &c. (c.s. *Trent.*) Cole.
  4 m. W. Inkford brook, 4 m. W. *Lakes* : Kineton reservoir, 2 m. N.W. Titterford Mill
  pond, 4 m. W. Earlswood reservoir. 6 m. S.W. (*See Gainsborough.*)
Somerleyton (Suffolk).—G.E.R. Waveney. (*See Yarmouth.*)
Somerton (Oxon).—G.W.R. Cherwell. (*See London, M.T.*)
Southall (Middlesex).—G.W.R. (*See London, L.T.*)
Southam (Warwick), n.s. **Harbury**, 3½ m.—Itchene. (*See Gloucester.*)
Southampton (Hants).—L. & S.W.R. Itchen and Test. Itchen rises by Cheriton
  (belonging to Lord Ebury, trout), runs to Titchbourne 1½ m. **Alresford** (L. & S.W.R.)
  2 m. Here is Alresford pond (Lady Rodney), and a tributary rising by Brown Candover
  mill pond. runs to Northington 1 m., Swaverton ½ m., where it waters the lake and the
  Grange (Lord Ashburton, fishing very good), and **Alresford** 3 m. Itchen runs to
  Avington 1 m. (good fishing, but preserved by Mr. Shelly, Mr. Wall, of Worthy Park,
  and Capt. Hewson); to **Itchen Abbas** (L. & S.W.R.) 2 m., Easton, Abbotts Worthy,
  and King's Worthy 1 m. (preserved by Capt. Fryer, of Worthy Kennels); and **Winchester** (L. & S.W.R.) 4 m ; Shawford 4 m. (where is fishing in the barge river) ;
  Otterbourne 4 m. (where is a small but clean inn; fishing strictly preserved by
  T. Chamberlayne. Esq., Cranbury Park ; Magdalene College. Oxford ; Sir T.
  Fairbairn, Bambridge); 1½ m. below, the outfall of Fisher's pond, Golden Common
  (good piking, belonging to Capt. W. P. Standish, J.P., Marwell Hall, Winchester), joins
  on left bank, and 1 m. on is **Bishopstoke** (L. & S.W.R.): 4 m. on, at South Stoneham
  (salmon, preserved by Sir Samuel Montagu, M.P., of South Stoneham Park), a stream
  joins on right bank, holding a few pike and salmon, preserved by C. Standish, Esq.,
  and rising in Marlbrook pond. 2 m. W. of **Bishopstoke**, and in 1½ m. receives
  the drainage of the ponds in North Stoneham Park (Squire Fleming). 1 m. from the
  station. Hence to **Southampton** is 4 m. Here on the left bank is the drainage of
  Miller's pond (good coarse fishing). In Freemantle pond and the private water in
  Bannister's Park there are a few tench, carp, perch. Pout, whiting, and eels in
  Southampton Water; and whiting, bass, grey mullet, and sand smelts from the piers
  and quays. The best flies for Itchen are Governor, Wickham's fancy, Coch-y-bonddhu,
  Hammond's favourite, Mayfly, alder.
TEST holds trout, grayling, salmon, pike, perch, roach, and rises in a pond in Ash Park,
  2 m. above **Overton** ; runs to Freefolk (trout) 2 m. ; **Whitchurch** (L. & S.W.R.) 1½ m. ;
  Tufton 1 m. One m. below a branch joins on right bank, which rises by Hurstbourne
  Tarrant, runs 4 m. to St. Mary Bourne (trout), 3 m. to Hurstbourne Priors, and Test 1 m.
  The principal owners here are Lord Portsmouth (who sometimes gives leave on a proper
  introduction), the representatives of the late Col. Hawker, Mr. Coles, Mr. Bright, and
  Mr. Tremayne. The trouting is first-rate. Four m. down Test a fine trout stream joins
  on left bank, which rises by Micheldever, runs to Bullingdon 6 m., and Test 2 m. (the
  rest of the fishing belongs to Mr. Henniker Wilson and Mr. Wickham.) Test runs to
  Chilbolton (where the freeholders have the fishery on one side from Ashbridge to
  Testcombe Bridge, fish run very large; trout and jack), Wherwell 2 m (preserved by Mr.
  Iremonger: first-rate trouting now let.) 1 m. down at **Fullerton Bridge** Anton
  joins Test on right bank: Anton rises some 3 m. N. of **Andover**, 1 m. below which,
  at Upper Clatford, Pillhill brook joins on right bank. Pillhill rises at Fifield and
  Thruxton in Mollins' pond, runs to Anton 5 m. Anton now runs 1½ m. to **Goodworth
  Clatford**, and Test 3 m. Test runs to Leckford 2 m. (preserved by the Stockbridge club).
  Stockbridge 3 m., Houghton Drayton 2 m. (preserved by the Stockbridge club : trout and
  grayling), and **King Sombourne** 1 m. Here a stream joins on right bank, which rises
  by Wallop and its mill, and joins Test 4 m. down. Test runs to **Mottisfont** 4 m., where
  a stream, 3 m. long, joins on right bank, which rises by Lockerley, feeding two mills.
  Test runs in 5 m. to **Romsey**, Nursling 4½ m. (capital pike and grayling). 1 m. on a stream
  joins on right bank, which rises in a mill pool at Landford, runs 4 m. on to Wallow Mill,

I

and 3 *m.* down is joined on right bank by a stream, 1½ *m.* long, which drains the lake in Paulton's park. Three *m.* down is Test. Test runs to **Redbridge** 2 *m.* Half a mile below a stream, 8 *m.* long, joins on right bank, which rises in a large mill pool 1½ *m.* N. of **Lyndhurst.** Half a mile below, the outflow of Shirley pond, 1 *m.* up, joins Test on left bank. Southampton is 8 *m.* on. The flies for the Test are the same as for the Avon (*see Christchurch*). but dressed smaller; in addition, the alder. willow fly. yellow Sally, and grannom. *Hotels*: Royal, Dolphin. *Tackleists,* Cox and Macpherson, 62, High-street.
Southburn (York).—N.E.R. Hull. (*See Hull.*) (*c.s.* York.)
Southend (Essex).—G.E.R.; L.T. & S.R.; M.R. (*See Burnham.*) Large flounders can be taken from the pier.
Southill (Beds).—G.N.R.; M.R. Southill brook. Ivel, 5 *m.* *Lakes*: Southill Park. Old Warden Park, 2 *m.* (*See King's Lynn.*)
South Molton (Devon).—G.W.R. Mole; trout. Bray; trout; d.t. *3s. 6d.*, at hotel. The streams have been restocked with trout by the Conservators. (*c.s.* Taw.) (*See Barnstaple.*) *Hotel*: George. where good trouting free to visitors can be had on Mole, Bray, Yeo, and Crooked Oak. Salmon, s.t. *20s.*; trout, s.t. *5s.* The fishing is free for some distance below the town. Yeo. Nadder water. Knowstone water, 3 *m.* (*see Castle Hill*).
South Molton Road (Devon).—L. & S.W.R. Taw and Mole; salmon, trout, peel. Yeo; trout. (*c.s.*) (*See Barnstaple.*) *Hotel*: Fortiscue Arms (comfortable), where fishing can be had.
Southry (Lincoln).—G.N.R. Witham. Tupholme brook. (*See Boston.*)
Southwaite (Cumland).—L. & N.W.R. Petterill; salmon, trout. (*c.s. Eden.*) Eden, 3 *m.* E. at **Armathwaite.** (*c.s.*) Ive, 2 *m.* S.W. Roe, 3 *m.* S.W. (*See Carlisle.*)
Southwell (Notts).—M.R. Greet; trout; good fishing; preserved by a society; season begins May 1. Trent, 3 *m.* S.E. at **Fiskerton.** (*See Fiskerton.*) *Hotel*: Saracen's Head. (*See Gainsborough.*)
Southwold (Suffolk).—S.R. Blyth. Blyth rises in the lakes in Heveningham Hall Park, 3 *m.* S.W. from **Halesworth,** runs 5 *m.* to **Halesworth,** 1 *m.* off on left bank, and here Wisset brook, 4 *m.* long, joins on left bank. Blyth runs to **Wenhaston,** 2 *m.*, and 5 *m.* down is joined on left bank by Stoven brook (pike, perch, roach; tickets at **Wenhaston** Station), 7 *m.* long. 2 *m.* down Blyth is **Southwold** and the sea. Smelts can be taken some distance up the river. 2 *m.* N., at Potters Bridge, runs Wrentham brook; perch, roach, bream, pike; leave from the farmers. This brook rises in Benacre Hall Park, runs 6 *m.* to Potters Bridge, and 1 *m.* below waters Easton Broad; pike, roach, perch, bream; Sir A. Gooch. 5 *m.* N. of **Southwold** is Benacre Broad; pike, roach, tench, perch; Sir A. Gooch. *Hotel*: Swan, Centre Cliff, headquarters of the Southwold Sea Anglers' Society. (*c.s. S.* and *E.*)
Sowerby Bridge (Yorks).—L. & Y.R. Calder. (*c.s.* York.) Ribourne. (*See Rawcliffe.*)
Spalding (Lincoln).—G.N.R.; G.E.R. Welland; pike, perch, chub; free. Welland rises above **Market Harborough,** and 5 *m.* below is joined on left bank by Saddington brook, which rises in the reservoir by Saddington, 3 *m.* S. from **Kibworth,** and 6 *m.* down, just below Wide bridge, 3 *m.* N. of **Market Harborough,** is joined on right bank by a brook 4 *m.* long, draining Gumley pond and two ponds in Gumley Hall Park, 3 *m.* S. of **Kibworth,** or 3 *m.* N.W. of **Lubenham.** Saddington joins Welland 3 *m.* down. ½ *m.* down Welland, Hardwick brook, which rises above Staunton Wyville, 4 *m.* E. of **Kibworth** and is 8 *m.* long, joins on left bank. Welland runs to **Ashley,** 3 *m.*, and here Medbourne brook. 6 *m.* long, joins on left bank. Welland runs 6 *m.* to **Rockingham,** where Eye brook joins on left bank. Eye rises above **East Norton,** and joins Welland 9 *m.* below. Welland runs 5 *m.* to **Seaton** on left bank, and **Harringworth** on right bank; thence to Turtle Bridge 2 *m.*, **Wakerley** 2 *m.*, Duddington 4 *m.*, **Ketton** 3 *m.*, and 1 *m.* below, Chater joins on left bank. Chater rises in Withcote Hall lake 4 *m.* N. from **East Morton,** runs 8 *m.* to **Manton,** **Luffenham** 5 *m.*, **Ketton** 3 *m.*, and joins Welland 2 *m.* down. Welland runs to **Stamford** 2 *m.*, and 1 *m.* below is joined on left bank by Gwash. Gwash rises 5 *m.* above **Manton,** and 5 *m.* below is joined on left bank by a stream which drains the lake in Burley Park by **Oakham** 4 *m.* up. 2 *m.* down Gwash by Empingham a stream joins on left bank draining the lake in Exton Park, 8 *m.* N.W. from **Stainford,** or 8 *m.* N.E. from **Oakham.** Gwash runs 4 *m.* to Great Bridge, 3 *m.* to **Ryhall,** and 3 *m.* down joins Welland. Welland runs to **Uffington** 2 *m.*, **Tallington** 2 *m.* **Market Deeping** (n.s. **St. James Deeping**) 3 *m.* (here begins the Market Deeping Angling Society's water), **St. James Deeping** 2 *m.* Here we are fairly in the fens, and Welland becomes a "drain," running to **Kenulphstone** 4 *m.* (here ends the M.D.A.S. water), **Crowland** (n.s. **Postland,** 3 *m.*) 2 *m.*, **Cowbit** 5 *m.*, **Spalding** 4 *m.* 5 *m.* down Welland, at the reservoir 1 *m.* N.E. of **Surfleet** Station, Glen joins on left bank. Glen rises above **Corby,** runs thence to **Little Bytham** 6 *m.*, **Essendine** 5 *m.*, and 4 *m.* down, at Wilsthorpe, is joined on left bank by Edenham brook. Edenham rises 8 *m.* above Edenham (n.s. **Bourn,** 2 *m.*), and 2 *m.* below, 2 *m.* W. of **Bourn,** is joined on right bank by the drainage, 2 *m.* up, of the large lake in Grimsthorpe Park, 2 *m.* S.E. of **Corby.** Edenham runs 6 *m.* to **Braceborough Spa,** and Glen 2 *m.* Glen runs 1 *m.* to Kates Bridge, 3 *m.* S. of **Bourn, Counter Drain** 6 *m.*, Money Bridge 4 *m.*, **Pinchbeck** 1 *m.*, **Surfleet** 2 *m.*, and Welland 1 *m.* Welland joins the Wash 2 *m.* down at Fossdyke Bridge. Counter Drain; pike, perch, roach, carp. North Drove; same fish. South Drove; same fish Vernatts Drain; same fish.

Sparkford (Somerset).—G.W.R. Camel Brook; trout; mostly preserved by the owner of Cadbury House. (*See Bridgwater.*)

Speech House (Gloucester).—M.R. Blackpool brook. (*See Aure.*)

Spennithorne (York).—N.E.R. Ure; trout, grayling. (*c.s. York.*) *Lakes*: Calf Hole dam, 4 *m.* N. High and Low Ponds, 3 *m.* N. (*See Cover Bridge, York.*)

Spetchley (Worcester).—M.R. Stoulton brook (1 *m.* S.). Bow brook (2 *m.* E.). *Lakes*: Spetchley Park lake. (*See Gloucester.*)

Spetisbery (Dorset).—M.R.; L. & S.W.R. (*See Christchurch.*) Stour and Tarrant; pike, perch, &c.; good fishing. (*c.s. Avon.*)

Spilsby (Lincoln).—G.N.R. Steeping river, 1 *m.* N. (*See Wainfleet.*)

Spofforth (York), n.*. **Wetherby**, 3 *m.*—Crimple. Nidd, 3 *m.* N.E. (*c.s. York.*) Wharfe, 3 *m.* S.E., at **Wetherby**. (*c.s. York.*) (*See York.*)

Spondon (Derby).—M.R. Derwent; pike, coarse fish, grayling, trout; preserved by a society at Derby. (*See Derby.*) (*c.s. Trent.*) Chaddesden brook, 1 *m.* N.W. *Lake*: Locko Park lake, 2 *m.* N. (*See Gainsborough.*)

Spratton (Northton.)—L. & N.W.R. Nen. Stowe brook Pitsford brook, 1 *m.* S. (*See Wisbeach.*)

Stackstead (Lancs.).—M.R. Irwell. (*See Runcorn.*)

Staddlethorpe (Yorks.).—N.E.R. Foulness. Foulness rises 4 *m.* above **Holme**, and 3 *m.* down is joined on right bank by Foss dyke, 5 *m.* long. Foulness runs 7 *m.* to **Staddlethorpe.**

Stafford.—L. & N.W.R.; G.N.R. Sow; perch, pike, dace, roach, chub, trout; preserved by an association; s.t. 7*s.* 6*d.*, d.t. 1*s.* Clanford Brook, 1 *m.* W. Penk, 1 *m.* S.E.; preserved as Sow. Kingston brook, 1 *m.* N.E. *Lakes*: Ingestre Park pool and Hopton pools, 4 *m.* N.E. Tixall Park pool, 4 *m.* E. *Hotels*: Swan, North Western, Vine, Alexandra, Waverley. (*See Gainsborough.*)

Staines (Middx.).—L. & S.W.R.; G.W.R. Thames. Colne. *Hotels*: Angel, Railway, Packhorse, Swan at Staines Bridge, Bridge House. *Fishermen*: G. Osman, T. Clarke, and T. Spicer. There is capital dace fishing in the Colne on Staines Moor, free in parts; elsewhere preserved by a society. The water by side of L. & S.W. Railway belongs to the company.

Stainforth (Yorks).—G.C.R.; N.E.R. Don. (*c.s. Yorkshire.*) (*See Goole.*)

Stainland (Yorks).—L. & Y.R. Dean. (*See Rawcliffe.*)

St. Alban's (Herts). — G.N.R.; M.R.; L. & N.W.R. Colne; roach, dace, perch. pike, bream, trout; preserved by landowners and millers. Ver; trout; private. *Hotels*: Peahen and George. (*See London, M.T.*)

Stalbridge (Dorset).—M.R.; L. & S.W.R. Stour; pike, perch, roach. Lidden; trout. (*See Christchurch.*) (*c.s. Avon.*)

Stalham (Norfolk). — M.R.; G.N.R. Ant; free. *Lakes*: Stalham Broad; free. (*c.s. N. and S.*) Barton Broad, 1 *m.* S.; free. (*See Yarmouth.*) *Inns*: Swan, Railway, Maid's Head, where information and fishing can be had.

Stalybridge (Cheshire).—L. & N.W.R.; M.R.; G.N.R. Tame. Swinneshaw brook, 1 *m.* N. (*See Runcorn.*)

Stamford (Lincoln).—G.N.R.; L. & N.W.R.; M.R. Welland; chub, dace, roach, pike, perch; fishing free on N. bank between Hudds Mills and Broadeng Bridge, elsewhere preserved by Stamford Angling Association; subscribers living within 10 *m.* of Stamford, entrance 2*s.* 6*d.*, s.t. 3*s.* 6*d.*, on nomination of 2 club members; two days' piking a week only permitted; no dogs; sec., H. N. Fisher, Esq. Gwash, 1 *m.* E.; trout, grayling; preserved as above; entrance, 10*s.* 6*d.*; s.t. for Gwash and Welland, 10*s.* 6*d.*; two days a week only allowed in Gwash. Glen, 4 *m.* N.E., at Langford Bridge. *Lakes*: Burghley Park, 1 *m.* S.E. Easton Heath, 3 *m.* S. (*see Wisbeach*). Exton Park, 8 *m.* N.W. *Hotel*: Stamford. *Fishing stations within reach*: Essendine, Braceborough Spa, Bourn, Counter Drain, Little Bytham, Corby, Peterborough, Ketton, Luffenham, Seaton. Rockingham, Ashley, Market Harborough, Kilworth, Stamford, Lilbourne, Clifton, Rugby, Lamport, Brixworth, Spratton. Northampton.

Stamford Bridge (York).—N.E.R. Derwent; pike, chub, dace, bream; free. Skirpen beck, 2 *m.* N. *Lakes*: 2, Buttercrambe Moor lakes. 1 *m.* N. (*cs. York.*) (*See Wressel.*)

Standish (Lancs.).—L. & N.W.R. Douglas. (*c.s. Ribble.*) Barsden brook, 2 *m.* E. Idlington brook, 2 *m.* N.E. (*See Hesketh Bank.*)

Standon (Herts).—G.E.R. (*See Stratford.*) On Rib; trout. Above here the river is preserved by Col. Tower and Miss Mellish, of Hamel's Park; below Standon trout are scarce: jack, perch, chub, dace, and roach plentiful; leave may sometimes be obtained from the farmers.

Standon (Stafford).—L. & N.W.R. Mease (*c.s. Trent.*) Bromley brook, 1 *m.* S. *Lakes*: Hatton Mill, 2 *m.* N. Mease House lakes, 2 *m.* S.W. Bromley Mill ponds, 3 *m.* W. Podmore pools, 3 *m.* W. (*See Gainsborough.*)

Stanford (Northton.).—L. & N.W.R. Avon; chub, dace &c. (*See Gloucester.*) (*c.s. Severn.*)

Stanhope (Durham).—G.N.R.; M.R. Wear; trout.

Stanley (Yorks).—G.N.R.; L. & N.W.R.; C.L.R. Calder. (*c.s. York.*) (*See Rawcliffe.*)

Stanner (Hereford).—G.W.R. Gilwern. (*See Chepstow.*)

Stanstead (Essex).—G.E.R. (*See Stratford.*) On Stort.

Stanton Gate (Notts).—M.R. Erewash. Nut brook. (*See Gainsborough*).

Staplehurst (Kent).—S.E. & C.R. (*See Rochester.*) On Beult; trout, coarse fish.

Stapleton Road (Gloucester).—G.W.R. Frome; roach, dace, pike; poor fishing, mostly free. (*See Bristol.*)

Starbolton (York), n.s. **Bolton Abbey**, 16 m.—Wharfe. (*c.s. York.*) (*See York.*)

Starcross (Devon.) — G.W.R. Kenn; trout; mostly preserved by Lord Devon. Kenn rises by Dunchideock, runs 3 m. to Kenn (n.s. **Exminster**, G.W.R., 2¼ m), Kenton (n.s. **Starcross**, 1 m.), and the Exe estuary, 1 m. At Cockwood, ¼ m. from **Starcross**, a small stream joins the Exe estuary, which runs down from Mamhead, and is 3 m. long, working a mill.

St. Austell (Cornwall).—G.W.R. St. Austell river. This stream rises 2 m. N. of the town, and 2 m. below, it is joined on right bank by Clissy Brook, which rises by **Burngullow** (G.W.R.), and is 3 m. long. The sea is 3 m. below the junction. 4 m. off at Penlewan Basin is a series of ponds holding trout; tickets by the day.

Staveley (Derby).—M.R. Rother. Doe Lea, 1 m. E *Lakes*: Pond on brook, 1 m. S. Woodthorpe Mill dam, 2 m. S.W. (*See Goole.*)

Staveley (Westland).—L. & N.W.R. Kent. (*c.s.*) Gowan. *Lakes*: Skeggles water 4 m. N. Kentmere reservoir, 10 m. N. (*See Kendal.*)

Staverton (Devon).—G.W.R. (*See Dartmouth.*) On Dart; salmon and trout; preserved by an association; s.t. 10s. (*c.s.*) Comfortable hotel and good lodgings.

St. Blazey (Cornwall).—G.W.R. Bream. (*See Par.*) (*c.s. Fowey.*)

St. Columb (Cornwall). — G.W.R. Mawgan; trout; sea trout. Kestle. Mellincose. Porthcothan, 5 m. Mawgan rises 3 m. N.E. from **St. Columb**, runs through the town, thence 4 m. to Mawgan (*Hotel*, Gilbert's, fishing preserved), hence to the sea 2 m. Above, preserved by E. Brydges Willyams, Esq.; below the village, s.t. 10s, m.t. 7s. 6d., w.t. 5s. By the sea Whitewater joins Mawgan, which rises 1½ m. N. of **St. Columb**, and is 6 m. long. (*c.s. Camel.*) 5 m. N. from **St. Columb**, at St. Ervan, runs Porthcothan brook, 5 m. long. (*See Padstow, New Quay, Grampound.*)

St. Cyres (Devon).—L. & S.W.R. Creedy; trout. Shobrook brook. (*See Exeter.*)

St. Earth (Cornwall). G.W.R. Hayle; trout. (*See Hayle.*) (*c.s. Camel.*)

Steer Point (Devon).—Yealm; trout; preserved. Good sea fishing. *Hotel* : River Yealm, at Newton Ferrers, 2m.

Steeton (York).—M.R. Aire; trout, grayling, perch, chub, roach; preserved by the Keighley Angling Club from Eastbourne brook *above* to **Bingley** below; s.t. 10s., d.t. 1s from sec., F. L. Wood, Esq., 3, Eelholme View, Keighley. (*c.s. York.*) Ponder Reservoir; preserved as Aire. (*See Kildwick.*) Silsden beck. (*See Rawcliffe.*)

Stevenage (Herts).—G.N.R. (*See Stratford ; Hertford.*) On Beane; trout; preserved.

Steventon (Berks).—G.W.R. A small affluent of Thames runs here with some mills on it. (*See London, M.T.*)

St. Ewe (Cornwall), n.s. **Burngullow**, 5 m.—On Ewe; trout; fishing free. Ewe rises 2 m. south of **Burngullow**, runs 4 m. to St. Ewe, and the sea 6 m.

Steyning (Sussex).—L.B. & S.C.R. On Adur; dace, &c. (*See New Shoreham.*)

St. Germans (Cornwall).—G.W.R. St. Germans river and Cad ; trout. St. Germans rises by St. Ive (n.s. **Liskeard**, 3 m.), runs 3 m. to Hepple Mill (n.s. **Menheniot**, 2½ m.) and **St. Germans** 8 m. 1 m. below the town, Cad joins on left bank. Cad rises 1 m. south of Alternan (n.s. **Launceston**, 8 m.) 5 m. down Trewartha water, 5 m. long, joins on right bank. Cad runs to North Hill 1 m., Callington (1½ m. off river on left bank ; fair accommodation at Golding's Hotel ; fishing from Tamar and Plym Fishery, s.t. 5s.) 9 m., Pillaton 4 m., and **St. Germans** 6 m.

St. Helens (Lancs.).—L. & N.W.R. Sankey brook ; polluted. Newton brook, 1 m. E. *Lakes*: Eccleston Mill dam, 2 m. S.W. ; preserved by St. Helens Angling Association ; d.t. to members' friends, 1s. Eccleston mere (A. Walmsley Cotham, Esq.), by permission. Stanley Mill dam, 1½ m. N.E. ; Windle Farm dam, preserved by St. H.A.A. Garswood lakes, 3 m. N.E. ; preserved by St. H.A.A. St. Ann's dam ; preserved by Corporation ; tickets to ratepayers, and special privileges to members of the S.H.A.A. Leg o' Mutton dam ; preserved as St. Ann's dam. Car Mill Lake, near St. Helens, by permission from Sir Dd. Gamble, Bart. *Hotel*: Cotham Arms, the headquarters of the S.H.A.A. For all information apply to Mr. H. M. Greer, 7, Haydock-street, St. Helens. (*See Runcorn.*)

Stilton.—Some fair pike, perch, bream, roach, carp and tench fishing can be had in the drainage of what was once Whittlesea mere.

St. Ives (Cornwall).—G.W.R. Good sea fishing from pier and boats.

St. Ives (Hunts.).—G.E.R.; G.N.R. Ouse; coarse fish, except barbel ; there is capital fishing in the neighbourhood and within 3 m. or 4 m., notably at Hartford, Houghton, Hemingford, Holywell, Overcoat Ferry and Bluntesham Staunch, where sea trout are occasionally taken. The fishing at Hemingford is very good. (*c.s. N. and S.*) *Fisherman*: Phurnall. (*See King's Lynn.*)

Stixwould (Lincoln).—G.N.R. Witham. (*See Boston.*)

St. James Deeping (Lincoln.) - G.N.R. Welland ; chub, dace, roach, pike, perch ; preserved by Market Deeping Angling Society. *Hotel*: Ship. (*See Market Deeping, Spalding.*)

St. Keverne (Cornwall).—N.s. **Falmouth**, 11 m. Two brooks join the sea here—one 1½ m. N. at Mabal Mill, and the other running through the village and joining the sea 2 m. down. (*c.s. Fowey.*)

St. Leonards (Sussex).—L.B. & S.C.R. West. A small stream by West St. Leonards station. This stream rises 1 m. N.W. of Catsfield in three small ponds; 6 m. on a stream joins on the left bank, which rises in two large lakes in Battle Abbey, **Battle.**

¼ *m.* down is the Peppering Powder Mill Head, where a streamlet joins on the left
bank, running out of a small pond 1 *m.* off, close to the railway. 1½ *m.* down, at
Crewhurst, a stream joins on the right bank, rising out of a pond ¼ *m.* off. 2 *m.* down, the
brook joins the main stream; 2 *m.* on St. Leonards is reached. *Hotel:* Alexandra.

St. Margaret's (Herts).—G.E.R (*See Stratford.*) On Lea and Stort; trout, jack,
perch, chub, &c. Here is the Amwell Magna fishery of thirty members. Hon. sec.,
Mr. W. Fred. Laurie, Stanstead Abbotts, Ware, Herts. S.t. 10*l.* 10*s.* Each member has
the privilege of introducing a companion. There is a good number of large trout.

St. Mary Cray (Kent).—S.E. & C R. (*See Dartford.*) Cray; trout; private.

St. Mawes (Cornwall), n.s. **Falmouth.**—Corymack water. This brook, some 3 *m.* long,
runs into the head of St. Mawes harbour.

St. Neots (Hunts)—G.N.R. Ouse; coarse fish, except barbel; free from Eaton Mill to
Kym mouth; elsewhere preserved by Lord Esme Gordon and others; leave not difficult.
(c.s. *N. and S.*) Kym, 1 *m.* down. Gallow brook, 3 *m.* down. (*See King's Lynn.*)

Stockbridge (Hants.).—L & S.W.R. The Test; trout; preserved by the Stockbridge Club
above and below the town; below most of the freeholders of Stockbridge have the right of
fishing in the marsh on one side of the river for ¼ *m.*; leave from one of these. The
principal proprietors below the free water are Mr Hennessy, Mrs. Vaudrey, Mr. Johnson,
and Mr. Deverell. (*See Andover, Southampton.*) *Hotel:* Grosvenor.

Stockingford (Warwick).—M.R. *Lakes*; Sedswood pool and Arbury Park ponds, 1 *m.* S.
(*See Gainsborough.*)

Stockport (Cheshire).—L. & N.W.R.; M.R.; G.N.R. Mersey. Tame. (*See Runcorn.*)

Stockton (Durham).—N.E.R. Tees; trout, salmon, bull trout, grayling, coarse fish. (*c.s.*)
Tees rises on the slopes of Cross Fell, 5 *m.* N.E. of **Culgaith**, and 5 *m.* down is joined on
right bank by Trout beck (trout), 3 *m.* long. Tees runs 7 *m.*, where Maize beck joins on
right bank. Maize (trouting, from the landlord of Langdon Beck Hotel) rises in Great
Rundale tarn, 5 *m.* N.E. of **Long Marton** (there are three other tarns close by,
Seamore tarn, Little Rundale tarn, and a nameless pond) and is 10 *m.* long. Tees
runs 4 *m.*, where Harwood beck joins it on right bank. Harewood rises on Grasshill
Common, and 4 *m.* down is joined on right bank by Langdon beck, 3 *m.* long. Just
above the junction is **Langdon Beck Hotel.** 2 *m.* below this junction Harewood
joins Tees. Tees runs 2 *m.* to **High Force Hotel** (tickets), where Skyer beck, 2 *m.*
long, joins on right bank. 1 *m.* below, Blea beck, 2 *m.* long, joins Tees on right bank.
Tees runs to Holwick, 4 *m.*, and here Rowton beck, 3 *m.* long, joins on right bank. Tees
runs to **Middleton-in-Teesdale**, 3 *m.*; here a beck 5 *m.* long joins on left bank. 1 *m.*
below **Middleton**, Lune joins on right bank. Lune rises on Burton Fell, and 5 *m.* down
is joined on right bank by Close beck, 3 *m.* long. 1 *m.* down Lune, Long Grain beck
joins on left bank. Long Grain is 6 *m.* long, and 4 *m.* above its junction with Lune is
joined on left bank by Arngill beck, which drains the Arngill fishpond, 1 *m.* up. Lune
runs 3 *m.*, where Howgill beck, 4 *m.* long, joins on left bank. Here also joins Wemmergill beck, 3 *m.* long. 1 *m.* down Lune, Soulgill beck, 3 *m.* long, joins on right bank;
and Rowantree beck, 2 *m.* long, joins Soulgill 1 *m.* above its junction with Lune. Lune
runs 5 *m.* to **Mickleton.** and Tees and **Middleton**, 1 *m.* 2 *m.* down Tees, a little above
Romaldkirk, East Silcar beck joins on left bank. This beck rises on Middleton
Common, and 4 *m.* down is joined on left bank by a beck 3 *m.* long running out of a pond
on White Hill. Thence to Tees is 5 *m.* Tees runs 1 *m.* to **Romaldkirk**, where Beer
beck, 2 *m.* long, joins on right bank. 2 *m.* below, Wilden beck, 3 *m.* long, joins Tees on
right bank, and, just below, Balder river joins on right bank. Balder rises on Hunder-
thwaite Moor in two branches, each some 3 *m.* long. 4 *m.* down, Hunder beck, 4 *m.*
long, joins on right bank. Balder runs to Tees in 6 *m.* 1 *m.* down Tees, by **Cotherstone**, Crook beck, 3 *m.* long, joins on right bank. Tees runs 2 *m.* to where the
railway crosses the river 1 *m.* E. of **Lartington**, and here Scur beck, 4 *m.* long, and
passing through **Lartington**, joins on right bank. 1 *m.* down Tees, by **Barnard
Castle**, Harmire beck, 3 *m.* long, joins on left bank, and Deepdale beck on right bank.
Deepdale rises on Bowes Moor, and is 12 *m* long. 1 *m.* below **Barnard Castle**,
Thorsgill beck, 3 *m.* long, joins on right bank, and 2 *m.* further down Tees, Greta joins
on right bank. Greta rises in Stainmore forest, by the railway, and follows the line
the whole way to **Bowes**, 9 *m.* Here the stream leaves the line, and 3 *m.* below **Bowes**
is joined on right bank by Eller beck, 5 *m.* long. 2 *m.* down Greta, Garnathwaite beck,
4 *m.* long, joins on right bank, and 1 *m.* below, Gill beck, 3 *m.* long, joins on the same
side. Greta runs to Brignall, 2 *m.*, and 2 *m.* down is joined on left bank by Tutta beck,
4 *m.* long. 1 *m.* below this junction, Greta joins Tees. Tees runs 2 *m.* to Whorlton,
where Whorlton beck, 3 *m.* long, joins on left bank. Tees runs 4 *m.* to **Whiston**,
and 1 *m.* down, where the railway crosses the river, is joined on left bank by Alwent
beck. Alwent, under the name of Langley beck, rises above Paddock Wood, 5 *m.* N.
from **Barnard Castle**, runs 5 *m.* to Staindrop, where the outflow of the lakes in Raby
Park, 1 *m.* up, joins on left bank. 1 *m.* below, Sudburn beck joins on right bank;
Sudburn rises on Hawksley Hill, 4 *m.* N. from **Barnard Castle**, and is 7 *m.* long.
Alwent runs to Tees in 3 *m.* Tees runs 1 *m.* to **Gainsford** and **Piercebridge**, 4 *m.*
here Dyance beck joins on left bank. Dyance, under the name of Langton, rises 2 *m.*
above Langton, which is 2 *m.* N. of **Gainsford**, and 3 *m.* below is joined on left bank
by Summerhouse beck, 4 *m.* long. From this junction to Tees at **Piercebridge** is 2 *m.*
2 *m.* down Tees, by High Constable, Ulnaby beck, 3 *m.* long, joins on left bank. Tees

runs to **Croft**, 6 *m.*; here Clow beck joins on right bank and Skerne river on left. Clow beck, under the name of Nor beck, rises above Barningham, 8 *m.* S.E, of **Barnard Castle**, runs 5 *m.* to Great Hutton. 4 *m.* S. of **Winston**, where it takes the name of Hutton beck; thence 3 *m.* to Caldwell, where it takes the name of Caldwell beck; thence 4 *m.* to Aldborough, 3 *m.* S of **Piercebridge**, where the stream takes that name. Here the outflow of the lake in Forcett Park, 2 *m.* up, joins on right bank. 3 *m.* down, Waterfall beck, which rises by Barton and is 3 *m.* long, joins on right bank. Hence to Tees at **Croft** is 5 *m.* Skerne rises by **Thirndon**, runs 3 *m.* to **Hurworth**, runs in 6 *m.* to 2 *m.* N. of **Sedgefield**, and 2 *m* down is joined on left bank by the outflow of Hardwicke Hall lake, 1 *m.* N.W. of **Sedgefield**. 1 *m.* down Skerne is **Bradbury**, and 2 *m.* down it is joined on right bank by Woodham burn. Woodham rises 1 *m.* S. of **Shildon**, and is 7 *m.* long. Skerne runs 5 *m.* to **Aycliffe**, and **Darlington**, 9 *m.*, and here Cocker beck joins on right bank. Cocker rises above Denton, 2 *m.* N. of **Piercebridge**, and thence to **Darlington** is 7 *m.* Skerne runs to **Croft** and Tees, 4 *m.* Below **Croft**, Tees makes a series of big loops, running in 2 *m.* to within 2 *m.* N. of **Dalton**, and then back again to Hurworth, 1 *m.* E. of **Croft**, there looping again to 1 *m.* S., and back again to Neasham, 2 *m.* E. of **Croft**; then S.E. again for 4 *m.* to 3 *m.* E. of **Dalton**, and then back again due N. in 5 *m.* to Middleton-over-Row, 1 *m.* S. of **Dinsdale**. Tees runs hence 5 *m.*, where Saltergill beck, 3 *m.* long, joins on right bank; hence to **Egglescliffe** is 3 *m.* Here Nelly Burdon's beck, 4 *m.* long, joins on the left bank, and Leven river on the right bank. Leven rises 3 *m.* above **Kildale**, and 2 *m.* down, 1 *m.* N.W. of **Battersby**, is joined on left bank by Otter Hills beck, 3 *m.* long. Leven runs 2 *m.* to **Ayton** and **Stokesley**, 3 *m.* Here Broughton Bridge beck joins on left bank. Broughton Bridge beck rises 4 *m.* above **Ingleby**, and joins Leven 5 *m.* down, receiving on its way near the railway stat on Broughton beck, 3 *m.* long. Two other streams join Leven here, West beck, 4 *m.* long, on left bank, and Tame river, 6 *m.* long, on right bank. From this point Leven becomes very sinuous in its course, so much so that the distances given will be approximate only. From the junction of Tame with Leven the latter runs 3 *m.* where Faceby beck, 4 *m.* long, and Carlton beck, 3 *m.* long, both becks joining close to the Leven, join Leven on left bank. Leven runs 3 *m.* to Rudly (n.s. **Sexhow**, 1 *m.* off). Here Potto beck, 8 *m.* long, joins on left bank, running close by **Sexhow** station. Leven runs 4 *m.* to Crathorne (n.s. **Picton**, 1 *m.* off on left bank). Leven runs 3 *m.* to Middleton, and joins Tees 5 *m.* below at **Egglescliffe**. Tees runs 4 *m.* when Bassleton beck, 3 *m* long, joins on right bank. Tees runs to **Stockton** in 4 *m.*

STAINSBY BECK, 7 *m.* long, joins the old river 2 *m.* S.E. of **Stockton**.

~~THORPE BECK joins the estuary at Newport. Thorpe rises by Carlton, runs 3 m. to Thorpe Thewles, Billingham, 4 m., and Newport and Tees 3 m.; tweet.~~ The Stockton Anglers' Club of 120 (secretary, R. Readman, Esq., 18, Vane-street) preserve some 10 *m.* of the Tees; entrance 5*s.*, s.t. 13*s.*, visitor's d.t. 1*s.*; tickets at the hotels. *Hotels:* Blue Bell, and the Ship at Worsall.

Stogumber (Somerset.)—G.W.R. Williton brook; trout. (*See Williton.*)
Stoke (Suffolk.)—G.E.R. Stour. Birdsbrook, 2½ *m.* S.W. Albery brook, 3 *m.* W. (*c.s. S. and E.*) (*See Manningtree.*)
Stoke Edith (Hereford). G.W.R. Frome (1 *m.*) (*See Chepstow.*)
Stoke Ferry (Norfolk). — G.E.R. Wissey. (*c.s. N. and S.*) Barton brook. *Lakes:* Didlington Hall Lake, 5 *m.* S.E. (*See King's Lynn.*)
Stoke Fleming (Devon).—n.s. **Dartmouth**, 2 *m.* Blackpool Water. This stream is some 4 *m.* long, and divides into two branches a mile above its mouth.
Stoke-on-Trent (Stafford).—L. & N.W.R.; M.R. Trent. (*c.s.*) Fowler brook. (*See Gainsborough.*)
Stokesley (York).—N.E.R. Leven: trout; private. (*c.s. Tees*). Broughton Bridge beck. Tame, 1 *m.* W. (*c.s. Tees.*) Broughton beck, 1 *m.* S.E. West beck, 2 *m.* S. (*See Stockton.*) Raisdale beck, 4 *m.* S. Bilsdale beck, 4 *m.* S. Seph, 6 *m.* S.E. (*See Wressel.*)
Stone (Stafford).—L. & N.W.R. Trent. (*c.s.*) Filly brook. Moddershall brook. *Lakes:* Moddershall Mill. Swinnerton Park, 3 *m.* W. Trentham Park, 4 *m.* N. (*See Gainsborough.*)
Stonehouse (Gloucester).—G.W.R.; M.R. Frome. Frome rises in Miserden Park (n.s. **Stroud**, 8 *m.*), runs to Sapperton 6 *m.*, **Brimscombe** 4 *m.*, and **Stroud** 3 *m.* Here Slean brook, Painswick brook, and Nailsworth brook join Frome. Slean brook is 3 *m.* long, and, working 7 mills, joins on right bank. Painswick brook rises by Cranham (n.s. **Worton**, 4 *m.*) in two branches, each working a mill, runs 1½ *m.*, where a stream, 1 *m.* long, working a mill, joins on left bank. Painswick is 1 *m.* down., ½ *m.* below which a stream, 2 *m.* long and working 4 mills, joins on right bank. **Stroud** is 3 *m.* on. Nailsworth brook joins Frome on left bank. This stream rises by Cherrington in a pond, and runs 4 *m.* to **Nailsworth**. 1 *m.* down, a short stream joins on left bank, which rises in some large ponds 2 *m.* up. Nailsworth runs to **Woodchester** 1 *m.*, and Frome 2 *m.* Frome runs to **Stonehouse** 3 *m.*, and 6 *m.* down joins the Severn estuary.
Stoneleigh (Warwick).—n.s. **Kenilworth**, 3 *m.* Avon; chub, dace, roach, pike, perch, bream. Sow. (*See Gloucester.*) (*c.s. Severn.*)
Stoney Stratford (Bucks).—n.s. **Wolverton**, 2 *m.* Ouse; coarse fish, except barbel; mostly private. (*c.s. N. and S.*) *Lakes:* Whittlewood Forest ponds, 4 *m.* N.W. (*See King's Lynn.*)

Stourbridge (Worcester).—G.W.R. Stour. (*See Gloucester.*) (*c.s. Severn.*)

Stourport (Worcester).—G.W.R. Severn; salmon, trout, grayling, chub, dace, pike, perch, &c. Gladder brook. Stour. Dick brook (3 m. S.W.). Shrawley brook (7 m. S.W.). *Lakes*: Sharpley pool (4 m. S.). Frog pool (5 m. S.). Witley Court ponds (7 m. S.W.); pike, perch, roach, &c. (*See Gloucester.*) (*c.s.*)

Stow (Gloucester).—G.W.R. 2 m. off is Donnington Mill Pool and Dickler River; trout. (*See London, U.T.*)

Stowmarket (Suffolk).—G.E.R. Gipping; roach, perch, pike, tench. Rattlesden brook. (*See Ipswich.*)

Stow Park (Lincoln).—G.N.R.; G.E.R. Trent, 2 m. W.; chub, pike, perch. (*c.s.*) (*See Gainsborough.*) Tilt, 3 m. S.E., at Tilt Bridge. (*See Boston.*)

Stratford (Essex).—G.E.R. *Hotel*: White Hart. On Lea. The Lea rises 6 m. N.W. of **Luton** (M.R.; G.N.R.), 1½ m. below which town it flows through Luton Park where it waters a large lake. Leave is sometimes given on proper application. ½ m. below the outfall **New Mill End Station** is reached. The Lea runs next to **Harpenden** 3 m.; to **Wheathampstead** 2 m. 3 m. below, Lea runs through Brocket Hall, making a large lake. **Hatfield** is 2 m. on, thence to **Hertford** is 6 m. A little above Hertford the Mimram joins Lea on the left bank. This stream rises 5 m. N.W. of Codicote, passing in its way through a large lake in Kimpton Hoo Park, and then runs 3 m. to **Welwyn**; thence to its junction with Lea is 6 m. At **Hertford**, Beame river joins Lea on the left bank. This stream rises 3 m. N. of **Stevenage**. 7 m. below, a brook joins on the left bank, which has a course of 10 m., and flows by Walkern and Aston. 1 m. below the junction Watton is reached. Here the Beame runs through Woodhall Park, forming a large lake. Hence to Hertford is 5 m. Just below **Hertford** the Rib river joins Lea. This stream rises by Buckland, and flows 4 m. to **Buntingford**. In 2 m. the stream runs to **Westmill**; 2½ m. down, at **Braughing**, Quin river joins Rib on left bank. This stream has a course of 10 m., passing the villages of Great and Little Hormead about the centre of the river. 1½ m. down the united stream, **How Street** station is reached. Hence to **Hertford** is 10 m. The Lea now flows in 2 m. to **Ware**; 1½ m. below, Ash joins on the left bank. This brook rises by Furneaux Pelham, and, in a course of 10 m., flows to **Hadham Cross**, thence in 1½ m. to **Widford**, and then 3½ m. to the Lea. From this junction to **St. Margaret's** is 1 m. 2 m. below Stort joins Lea on left bank. This stream rises by Measden, and runs 12 m. to **Stansted**, passing on its way Clavering, Bearden, and Manewden. From Stansted to **Bishop Stortford** (fishing preserved, and very good) is 3 m.; thence to **Sawbridgeworth** is 5 m. 1½ m. below, Pincey brook joins Stort on left bank. This stream is 11 m. long, rising by **Takeley**. 1 m. down from the junction of Pincey with Stort **Harlow** is reached, and, 2¼ m. further on, **Burnt Mill**. 1 m. above this place a stream joins on the right bank, which feeds a large lake in New Place. From Burnt Mill to **Roydon** is 3 m. Here a stream joins on the right bank, which runs out of a large lake at Hunsdon Grange and two other ponds on the right of the road. From **Roydon** to Hunsdon fishing is private; and from Hunsdon to the junction of Stort and Lea at **Hoddesdon** belongs to Rye House fishery. (*See Rye House.*) From Hoddesdon to **Broxbourne** is 2¼ m., **Cheshunt** 3¼ m., **Waltham** 1½ m. 1 m. below, Cobbin's brook, which rises near Epping, and has a course of 7 m., joins Lea on left bank. 4 m. on **Enfield** is reached; **Park Station** 3 m.; **Tottenham**, 2 m.; **Lea Bridge**, 2½ m., and Stratford, 3 m. 4 m. down, Lea joins Thames. The fishing at Stratford is poor; a few bream and roach, barbel and flounders.

Stratford-on-Avon (Warwick).—L. & N.W.R.; G.W.R.; G.C.R. Avon; pike, bream, roach, perch, chub, dace, carp. *Hotels*: Shakespeare, and others. The Avon is preserved by the corporation; s.t. (including pike), 10s.; m.t. 2s. 6d.; w.t. 2s.; d.t. 1s.; excluding pike, s.t. 5s.; m.t. 2s. 6d.; w.t. 2s.; d.t. 6d. Tickets at the hotels. Stour (1 m.). Dene (5 m. N.E.). Thelesford brook (7 m. N.E.). (*See Gloucester.*) (*c.s. Severn.*)

Strensall (York).—N.E.R. Foss. Foss Navigation cut, 1 m. N.E. Whitecar beck, 1 m. N.E. (*See York.*)

Stretham (Cambs).—G.E.R. Ouse; coarse fish, except barbel. (*c.s. N. and S.*) (*See Thetford, King's Lynn.*)

Stretton (Derby).—M.R. Stretton brook. Amber, 1 m. Westwood brook, 2 m. S.E. at Morton. (*See Gainsborough.*)

Strines (Derby).—M.R.; G.C.R. Goyt or Mersey. (*See Runcorn.*)

Stroud (Gloucester).—G.W.R. Frome; a few trout and coarse fish. Slean brook. Painswick brook. Nailsworth brook. (*See Stonehouse.*) Pike and coarse fishing in the canal.

Stubbins (Lancs.).—L. & Y.R. Irwell. (*See Runcorn.*)

Studley (Warwick).—L. & N.W.R. Arrow; pike, perch, chub, dace, bream, few trout. (*See Gloucester.*)

Sturmer (Essex).—G.E.R. Stour. Albery brook. Birdbrook, 1 m. S. (*c.s. S. and E.*) (*See Manningtree.*)

Sturminster Newton (Dorset).—S. & D.J.R. Stour; chub, dace, pike, perch; free, good fishing. (*c.s.*) Divelish. (*c.s. Avon.*) Lidden; trout. (*c.s. Avon.*) (*See Christchurch.*) *Hotel*: River Arms; comfortable.

Sturry (Kent).—S.E. & C.R. On Stour. (*See Sandwich.*) 2 m. of the river belong to Mr. W. Cannon (preserved also by Stour Fishery Protection Association). (*See Canterbury.*) (*c.s.*)

Statton (York).—N.E.R. Cock beck. Wharfe, 1 m. N. (c.s. York.) (See York.)

Sudbury (Derby).—G.N.R.; N.S.R. Dove; coarse fish, trout, grayling; preserved by Burton-on-Trent Angling Association, hon. sec., R. Clarke, Esq., Burton-on-Trent; at 40s.; salmon and trout rod licenees from Messrs. J. C. Perfect & Co., Burton-on-Trent. (c.s. Trent.) Cubley brook, 2 m. E. Lakes: pond at Aldermoor, 3 m. N.; Foston Hall lake, 3 m. E. (See Gainsborough.)

Sudbury (Suffolk).—G.E.R. Stour; pike, perch, roach, carp, dace, bream, tench (c.s. Suffolk and Essex). Bardfield brook, 1 m. N.W. Melford brook, 4 m. N.W. Glemsford brook. 4 m. N.; same fish as Stour. Boxford, 6 m. N.E. The Stour (and its tributaries) from the source to the sea is under the control of the Suffolk and Essex Fishery District Board. A. Townsend Cobbold, Esq., is the clerk. The river is free throughout. (See Manningtree).

Summerseat (Lancs.).—L. & Y.R. Irwell. (See Runcorn.)

Sunbury (Middx.).—L. & S.W.R. Thames. (See London, L.T.) Hotels: Magpie, Flower-pot, and Weir. Fishermen: A. Stroud and Clarke Brothers.

Surfleet (Lincoln).—G.N.R. Welland. Glen. (See Spalding.)

Sutton (Notts).—M.R. Maun. Lakes: Bath Wood. King's Mill reservoir, 1 m. N.E. (See Althorpe.)

Sutton Bingham (Somerset).—L. & S.W.R. (See Bridgwater.)

Sutton Coldfield (Warwick).—L. & N.W.R.; M.R.; roach, pike, perch, tench, carp, and bream. Lakes: Bracebridge pool, 2 m. N.W. Blackroot pool, 1 m. N.W. Long Moor Mill pond. Powells pool. Windley pool, 1 m. S.W. (Fishing to be had on the spot at these pools; d.t. and ½ d.t. at reasonable rates.) Langley Hall ponds, 2 m E. Canwell Hall pond, 4 m. N.E. Hill Hook pool, 3 m. Penn's pool, 3 m. (See Gainsborough.)

Sutton-on-Derwent (York), n.s. **Fangfoss**, 5 m.—Derwent; pike, chub, &c.; free. Foss beck, 3 m. S. (See Wressel.)

Sutton-on-Hull (York).—N.E.R. Hull, 1 m. S.W. (See Hull.) (c.s. York.)

Sutton-on-Trent (Notts.), n.s. **Crow Park**, 2 m.—M.R.; G.N.R. Trent; pike, roach, dace, chub, grayling. (c.s.) Girton brook. Grassthorpe brook, 2 m. N. Lakes: The Fleet, 2 m. E. Blackpool, Nuns pool, and Cowarth pool, 3 m. S.E. Collingham ponds, 4 m. S.E. (See Gainsborough.)

Swadlincote (Derby).—M.R. Repton brook, 2 m. N.E. Lakes: Glover mill, 2 m. N.E. Hartshorn ponds and Screw Mill pond, 3 m. N.E. Bretby Park ponds, 3 m. N. Repton rocks pond, 4 m. N.E. (See Gainsborough.)

Swaffham (Norfolk).—G.E.R. Nar, 4 m. N., at Castle Acre; good trouting; strictly preserved. (See King's Lynn.)

Swainthorpe (Norfolk).—G.E.R. Tese. Yare, 3 m. N. Lakes: Bracon Hall and Carlton Lodge, 2 m. W. (See Yarmouth.)

Swanage (Dorset).—L. & S.W.R. Round Peveril Ledge and Durlestone Head is good pollack fishing to St. Alban's Head; also bass. Eels for bait procurable in the brook.

Swanbourn (Bucks).—L. & N.W.R. Lakes: Whaddon, 3 m. N. (See King's Lynn.)

Swannington (Leicester).—M.R. Dishley brook, 2 m. N.E. Seuce, 2 m. S. Lakes: Coleorton pools, 2 m. N.W. Old reservoir, 4 m. N.E. (See Gainsborough.)

Swavesey (Cambs.).—G.E.R. Ouse; coarse fish, except barbel; good fishing. (See Cambridge). (c.s. N. and S.) Inn, Boat, New Staunch, Over. (See King's Lynn.)

Swimbridge (Devon).—G.W.R. Swimbridge water. (See Barnstaple.)

Swinderby (Lincoln).—M.R. Girton brook. Lakes: Skelmires pond, 2 m. S.E. (See Gainsborough.)

Swindon (Wilts).—G.W.R. On Ray and Coate; coarse fish and a few trout. (See London, U.T.) In Coate Reservoir, (pike, roach, tench), the source of Coate, 2 m. off, good fishing from May 1 to Feb. 28. S.t., 2l. 2s.; d.t., 1s. 6d. Hotel: Goddard Arms.

Swinehead (Lincoln).—G.N.R. Hammond Beck. (See Boston.)

Swinton (Yorks).—G.C.R. M.R. Don. (c.s. Yorkshire.) (See Goole.)

Syston (Leicester).—M.R. Wreak; roach, bream, pike, perch, chub, dace: preserved by the landowners. (See Leicester.) (c.s. Trent.) Barkby brook. Soar, 1 m. W.; preserved as above. The casual fishing is, we believe, free. (See Leicester.) (c.s. Trent.) (See Gainsborough.)

Tadcaster (York).—N.E.R. Wharfe; salmon, coarse fish; preserved by Tadcaster Angling Club and by Leeds and District A.S.A. to Ulleskelf Bridge. (c.s. York.) Cock beck, 1 m. S. Foss, 3 m. N., at Wighill. Catterstone beck, 2 m. N.E. Hotel: Britannia, where d.t., 6d.; for the Leeds A.S.A. water may be obtained. (See York.)

Takeley (Essex).—G.E.R. (See Barking and Stratford.) On Roding and Pincey brook.

Tallington (Lincoln).—G.N.R. Welland: pike, perch, dace; private. (See Spalding.)

Tamworth (Stafford).—L. & N.W.R.; M.R. Tame; much polluted. (c.s Trent.) Anker; few chub, dace, &c. (c.s. Trent.) Bourne brook; trout, grayling; preserved by landowners. Lakes: Drayton Park, 2 m. S. Middleton Park. 4 m. S. Canwell Hall, 4 m. S.W. Swinfen Hall, 5 m. N.W. Freeford Hall, 6 m. N.W. (See Gainsborough.) Hotel: Castle.

Tanfield (York).—N.E.R. Yore; trout, grayling; preserved on N. bank by Tanfield Angling Club of 30 at 4l. 4s., and 5l. 5s. entrance fee; hon. sec., F. M. Walbran, 3Ra, Wellington-street, Leeds. The club also have a stretch of 3½ m. on S. bank; no day tickets. Adjoining the club water, Sir Reginald Graham preserves and grants leave sometimes. (c.s. York). Hotel: Bruce Arms. (See York.)

Taplow (Bucks).—G.W.R. Thames. (*See London, M.T., Maidenhead.*)

Tarsett (Northland.).—On North Tyne; trout; the river is, we believe, preserved by a society who will give leave. The fishing is first-rate. (*c.s.*)

Tattenhall (Cheshire).—L. & N.W.R. Keys brook. (*See Chester.*)

Tattershall (Lincoln).—G.N.R. Bain. Witham, 1 m. W. (*See Boston.*)

Taunton (Somerset). — G.W.R. Tone; trout, dace, roach, perch, tench, and pike. Kingston brook; trout. Black brook; trout. (*See Bridgwater.*) Tone is preserved from. Bishops Hull to Bradford Weir by an association: trouting poor. The best is at Bradford, 4 m. up. The association also preserves the Hillfarrance stream, which at times yields good fish. Below the town are many weirs where large trout are constantly taken, also many coarse fish. The pike fishing is good below the town. Leave from the millers and the land owners. Small perch, roach, tench, and eels, in the Bridgwater canal. (*c.s. Avon.*). Otter rises 8 m. off. (*c.s.*) (*See Ottery St. Mary.*) *Tackleist*, G. Hinton, Fore-st. (*see Advt.*)

Tavistock (Devon).—G.W.R.; L. & S.W.R. Tavy; trout, salmon peel, salmon; preserved by Tavy, Walkham, and Plym Fishing Association; s.t. 30s., d.t. 1s. Lumburn brook (2 m.); trout, peel; preserved as above. Tamar (3 m.); trout, salmon, peel. Walkham (3 m.); trout, peel, salmon; preserved as above. Plym, 5 m.; trout, peel, salmon; preserved as above. Meavy, 5 m.; trout, peel, salmon; preserved as above. (*c.s. Tamar.*) (*See Plymouth.*) *Hotel*: Bedford.

Tebay (Westland).—L. & N.W.R. Lune; trout, salmon; trouting free. (*c.s.*) Birk beck. Tebay gill, 1 m. E. Blind beck, 1 m. N. Bretherdale beck, 2 m. N.W. Barrow beck, 2 m. S; trout. Wasdale beck, 6 m. N.W. Barrow beck and Howgill are good streams. (*See Lancaster* and *Borrowbridge.*)

Tedingham Bridge (Yorks.)—By rail to West Hesterton Station. On Derwent; pike, roach, grayling, and chub. Free.

Teddington (Middlx.).—L. & S.W.R. Thames, and a branch of Colne. (*See London, L.T.*) *Inns*: Anglers, The Cottage, and Royal Oak. *Fishermen*: W. and S. and P. McBride. Above the lock and at the weir is some good pike and perch fishing.

Teigngrace (Devon).—G.W.R. On Teign. (*c.s.*) (*See Teignmouth.*)

Teignmouth (Devon).—G.W.R. On Teign. Teign rises in the heart of Dartmoor. In 5 m. it is joined by a small stream, and 4 m. on is joined by the South Teign on the right bank, which has a course of 5 m. 1 m. down, a stream, 7 m. long, joins on the left hand. This stream rises in Rayburrow pool, and passes the villages of Throwleigh and Gidleigh, the latter 1 m. from the junction with Teign. 1 m. on Chagford is reached. *Hotels*: Moor Park, Three Crowns, Globe, Monte Rosa Boarding House. Trout are plentiful from the source down. The Upper Teign Association preserves the water from Chagford Bridge to Steps Bridge, 12 m.; fishing begins March 3, ends Sept. 30. ; s.t. 21s. ; d.t. 2s. 6d., from the hon. sec., C. G. Hayter-Hames, Esq., or of Mr. Perrott, Chagford; d.t. also to be had from Webber and Sons, High-street Exeter; White Hart and White Horse Hotels, Moretonhampstead ; Moor Park Hotel, Chagford; Royal Oak, Dunsford; Sandy Park Inn and Druid Arms, Drewsteignton. No dogs. No wading. No Sunday fishing, and nothing but fly allowed before June. The nearest station is **Moretonhampstead**, 5 m. for the upper part of the water, and **Christow**, 2m. from Stepsbridge, for the lower portion. 3 m. down, by the village of Drewsteignton. a stream, 4 m. long, joins on the left bank; 2 m. on, Wood brook joins on the left bank. 3½ m. down—at the village of Dunsford, 4 m. from Moreton—a brook, 4 m. long, joins on the right bank, and 1 m. on another 4 m. long. 2 m. on, Cherry brook, 4 m. long, joins on the left, 2 m. on a stream joins on the right bank. This stream rises 2 m. east of **Moreton**, and is 6 m. long. **Lustleigh** is 1½ m. west of the middle part of this stream. ½ m. down Teign a small stream runs close by the village of **Trusham**, 1 m. from the junction. 2 m. down a stream joins on the left bank, which passes by **Chudleigh** (*Hotel*: Clifford Arms), and joins Teign 1 m. from the town. All these streams contain more or less trout. 2½ m. down Teign, Bovey joins. This stream rises 5 m. west of **Moreton**, close to the Prince Town road, and 7 m. down is joined by Hele Brook on the right bank. This stream rises on the slopes of Hamildown, and is 3 m. long. (The fishing, which is very good, is reserved by the farmers, but leave may often be obtained.) Bovey next flows past North Bovey (where lodgings can be had, and there is also a good boarding house close to the water: the fishing is preserved by Hon. W. F. D. Smith, M.P.) 2½ m. on is Lustleigh Cleve. ½ m. below, Beckey joins on the right bank. This stream, with a course of 4 m., rises 2 m. east of Widecombe on the moor. ½ m. down Bovey, Wrey joins on the left bank, which rises near Moreton, runs 4 m. to **Lustleigh**, and joins Bovey 1 m. on. The river now runs in 2 m. to **Bovey Tracey**, and joins Teign 4 m. down. 1 m. down Teign, at **Teigngrace**, a stream 4 m. long joins on the right bank; and ½ m. further on a stream, 3 m. long, joins on the left bank. 1 m. on is **Newton Abbot**; the tide flows to this point. The Lower Teign Fishing Association preserves the rivers from Steps Bridge and Bovey to **Newton Abbot**. Trout, peel, salmon. S.t. 21s., m.t. 10s., w.t. 7s. 6d.; fishing begins March 3, and ends (trout) Sept. 30, (salmon) Oct. 31 ; no Sunday fishing or dogs; sec., H. G. Michelmore, Esq., Devonia, Newton Abbot. No wading below New Bridge, and nothing but fly allowed above until June; no wading in Bovey at any time, and the artificial minnow allowed only from June 1: no gaff can be used before May 1. At Newton, Lemon, 8 m. long, which holds a few trout, joins on the right bank. Tickets for both associations from the secretaries and all hotels and inns near the-river, and the tackle shops at Exeter, Newton, and Teignmouth. At Teignmouth bass may be taken about the bar, at the harbour entrance. Dabs outside on sandy ground; also mackerel, pollack, and whiting, the latter in the autumn near the coast, but in early summer far in the offing. Yachts can be hired here. Bass fishing best at spring tides; Ferry Point is the best position. Sand-eel seines kept here. *Hotels:* Royal, Queen's, London.

Templecombe (Somerset). — L. & S.W.R. On Cale and Bow brook; rudd and perch, where ponds have been made; leave from the owners. (*See Christchurch.*)

Temple Hurst (York). — G.N.R. Aire. (*c.s.* York.) (*See Rawcliffe.*)

Temple Sowerby (Westland). — N.E.R. Eden; salmon, trout; preserved by Yorkshire Anglers' Association. (*c.s.*) Eller beck, 1 *m.* W. Lyvennet; trout; preserved as Eden. (*See Carlisle.*)

Tempsford (Beds). — G.N.R. Ouse; coarse fish, except barbel. (*c.s.* N. *and* S.) Ivel; same fish. (*See King's Lynn.*)

Tenbury (Worcester). — G.W.R. *Hotel:* Swan. Teme; trout, grayling, chub, perch, pike, roach, dace; preserved by the Tenbury Angling Association from Tenbury Bridge to Rochford Ford; tickets (limited) free to Swan hotel visitors. Below Newnham the river is strictly private. Ledwych; trout, grayling (preserved). (*See Gloucester.*) (*c.s.* Severn.)

Teversall (Notts). — M.R. Meden. Doe Lea, 3 *m.* N.W. *Lakes:* Car ponds, 3 *m.* N.W. Great pond. 3 *m.* N.W. Millers pond, 3 *m.* N.W. Stainsby pond, 4 *m.* N.W. (*See Althorpe, Goole.*)

Tewkesbury (Gloucester). — M.R. Severn; chub, dace, roach, pike, perch, salmon. Avon; chub, dace, roach, pike, perch, bream; preserved by a society; tickets at the Record Office. Ripple brook. Carant brook. Tirle brook. Swilgate (1 *m.*). *Hotels:* Swan, Bell, and Black Bear. (*See Gloucester.*) (*c.s.*)

Thame (Oxon.). — G.W.R. Thame. (*See London,* M.T.) *Hotel:* Spread Eagle.

Thames Ditton (Surrey). — L. & S.W.R. Thames. (*See London,* L.T.) *Hotel:* Swan. *Fishermen:* C., W., E., and A. Tagg, H. Hammerton.

Thatcham (Berks.). — G.W.R. Kennett; pike, perch. chub, dace, trout; preserved by the Newbury Angling Society. (*See London,* M.T.; *Newbury.*)

Theale (Berks.). — G.W.R. Kennett. (*See London,* M.T.)

Theddlethorpe (Lincoln). — G.N.R. Withern. (*See Saltfleet.*)

Thelwall (Cheshire). — L. & N.W.R. Mersey. (*See Runcorn.*)

Thetford (Cambs). — n.s. **Stretham**, 2 *m.* Ouse; coarse fish, except barbel. (*c.s.* N. *and* S.) Cam: same fish. (*See King's Lynn.*)

Thetford (Norfolk). — G.E.R. Little Ouse; pike and coarse fish; private above; permission frequently given; free below. Thet; pike, coarse fish; private. *Hotels:* Bell, Anchor, Temperance. (*See King's Lynn.*)

Thirsk (York). — N.E.R. Cod beck; trout. grayling; preserved by Col. Mott, of Kilvington Hall, from Braywith Bridge to Spittal beck, from Spittal beck to Swale preserved by the Thirsk Angling Club of limited numbers; hon. sec., J. R. Stockdale, Esq., Market Place. Ellers beck, 2 *m.* N. Fisher beck, 2 *m.* S.E. Wiske. 4 *m.* N.W.; grayling, trout, dace, chub, pike; preserved. (*c.s.* York.) Willow beck, 4 *m.* S.E. Swale, 4 *m.* W. at Skipton. (*c.s.* York.) Hood beck, 4 *m.* S.E. Tickets for Swale and the Cod beck may be obtained at the principal hotels at Topcliffe. (*See York.*)

Thorington (Essex). — G.E.R. 1 *m.* S.W. from the station is a large mill head at Thorington Mill.

Thorabury (Gloucester). — M.R. Bradley brook. 1 *m.* N. runs Moreton brook, 5 *m.* long. (*See Bristol.*)

Thorne (Yorks). — G.C.R.; N.E.R. Don. (*c.s.* Yorkshire.) Went, 4 *m.* N. (*See Goole.*)

Thornton (Yorks). — M.R.; L. & Y.R. Elslack. Bradford beck. Clayton beck. (*See Rawcliffe.*) Ulceby beck. (*See Ulceby.*)

Thornton Dale (York). — N.E.R. Thornton beck; trout; preserved by Rev. J. E. Hill. Pickering beck, 3 *m.* W. Derwent, 3 *m.* S. (*See Wressel.*)

Thorpe (Essex). — G.E.R. Holland brook. This brook rises 7 *m.* above **Thorpe**, and joins the sea 6 *m.* down, 2 *m.* E. of **Clacton.**

Thorpe (Northton). — L. & N.W.R. Nen: pike, perch, bream, chub, tench. (*See Wisbeach.*) Steeping river. (*See Wainfleet.*)

Thorpe Arch (York). — N.E.R. Wharfe. (*c.s.* York.) (*See York.*)

~~**Thorpe Thewles** (Durham). — N.E.R. Thorpe beck; trout; preserved by the Stockton Anglers' Club. (*See Stockton.*)~~

Thorverton (Devon). — G.W.R. Exe; trout, salmon, dace; preserved hence up to within 1½ *m.* of **Bickleigh** by the Up Exe Fishing Association; hon. sec., J. R. Cummings, Esq., Thorverton; a.t., salmon and trout, 3*l.* 3*s*; trout only, s.t., 31*s.* 6*d.*; half season, from May 2, 21*s.*; m.t.. 15*s.*; w.t., 7*s.* 6*d.*; worm fishing after June 1; season from March 1 to Aug. 31 for trout; salmon, October 19; no wading until June 1. Trout licence. s. 5*s.*, w. 2*s.* 6*d.*, d. 1*s.*, from Exe Conservators necessary. (*c.s.*) (*See Exeter.*) Lord Iddesleigh preserves the water down to Cowley Bridge; limited number of salmon tickets at 6*l.* 6*s.*; pike: s.t. 21*s.*; d.t. to June 1, 5*s.*; for rest of season, 2*s.* 6*d.*; no restrictions on rod and line fishing, which begins March 1, ends Aug. 31.

Thrapston. (Northton.) — L. & N.W.R.; M.R. Nen: pike, perch, chub, tench, roach and bream. Harper's brook, 1 *m.* N. (*See Wisbeach.*) *Tackleist,* A. Bargh, Bridge-street.

Three Bridges (Sussex). — L.B. & S.C.R. Mole. (*See London,* L.T.)

Threlkeld (Cumland).—L. & N.W.R. Greta or Glendermakin; trout, salmon. (c.s. *Derwent.*) St. John's beck; trout. (c.s. *Derwent.*) Naddle beck, 1 m. W. Glenderaterra beck, 2 m. W. *Lakes:* Thirlmere, 5 m. S.; perch, pike, trout; preserved by the Manchester Corporation, who issue tickets. Harrop tarn, 9 m. S. (*See Cockermouth, Keswick.*)

Thursford (Norfolk).—G.E.R. *Lakes:* Gunthorpe Hall, 2 m. N.E.

Thurston (Suffolk).—G.E.R. (*See Ixworth.*) *Lakes:* Drinkstone Park, 4 m. S.E. (*See King's Lynn.*)

Thurtlebury (Worcester).—G.W.R. Dovedale brook (2 m. E.). Severn (3 m. W.); chub, dace, roach, pike, perch, trout, salmon. (*See Gloucester.*) (c s. *Severn.*)

Ticehurst (Sussex).—S.E. & C.R. (*See Rye.*) On Rother. (c.s.)

Tickhill (York), n.s. **Bawtry**, 4 m.—Torne, 1 m. S. *Lakes:* Sandback Park, 2 m. S. (*See Althorpe.*)

Tiddington (Oxon.).—G.W.R. Thame. (*See London, M.T.*)

Timperley (Cheshire).—L. & N.W.R.; G.N.R.; M.R. Wych brook. (*See Runcorn.*)

Tintern (Monmouth).— G.W.R. Wye; chub, dace, pike, salmon. (c.s.) (*See Chepstow.*) The Crown have several large, well-stocked trout ponds in the Anjidy Valley; s.t. 3l. 3s., of Francis Hobbs, Esq., Crown Office, Monmouth. *Hotel:* Beaufort Arms.

Tipton (Devon).—L. & S.W.R. Otter; trout. (*See Ottery St. Mary.*)

Tisbury (Wilts).—L. & S.W.R. Nadder; trout, roach, dace. Chalk Stream. (*See Christchurch.*) (c.s. *Avon.*)

Titley (Hereford).—G.W.R. Arrow; trout, grayling, dace; preserved by a club of limited numbers above. (c.s. *Wye.*) (*See Chepstow.*)

Tiverton (Devon).— G.W.R. Exe, Lowman, and Dart; trout, salmon. Preserved from Bickleigh Bridge, 4 m. below Tiverton, to about 4 m. above the town, by the riparian owners and the Tiverton Angling Association. S.t. (residents within 5 m. only), 30s. Fishing very good. There is some fishing in and close to the town, limited to working men, at a nominal price. Wading is necessary. The Exe is a very early river. (*See Exeter.*) *Hotels:* Palmerston and Angel.

Tiverton Junction (Devon). — G.W.R. Culm; trout; s.t., 21s.; w.t., 4s., d.t., 2s. Ashford brook. *Inn:* Railway; good fisherman's accommodation. (*See Exeter.*)

Todmorden (Lancs.).—L. & Y.R. Calder. (c.s. *York.*) *Lakes:* Lee ponds, 2 m. S.E. at Lee. Redmires dam, 3 m. W. (*See Rawcliffe.*)

Toller (Dorset).—G.W.R. On Frome. (*See Wareham and Bridport.*) (c.s.)

Tollerton (York).—N.E.R. Kyle. Ouse at **Aldwick**, 4 m. W., and Linton lock, 3 m. S., and 7 m. N.E. at Stillington. (c.s. *York.*) (*See York.*)

Tonbridge (Kent.)—S.E. & C.R. On Medway; roach, bream, chub, perch, pike, carp, tench, eels. Tonbridge A. A. (hon. sec., F J. Tanton, 89, Burden-road) preserve about 8 m. of the Medway and tributary streams from Ensfield Bridge, near Penshurst, to East Lock, near East Peckham. Here the Maidstone Club water begins. *Hotels:* Bull, Rose and Crown, Castle, Angel.

Tong (Leicester).—M.R. Breedon. (*See Gainsborough.*)

Tongham (Surrey).—L. & S.W.R. (*See London, L.T.*)

Topcliffe (York).—N.E.R. Swale. (c.s. *York.*) Cod beck. (*See York.*)

Topsham (Devon).—L. & S.W.R. Clist. Greendale brook. Clist rises some 2 m. N. of Clist Hydon (n.s. **Hele**, 3 m.), runs to **Broad Clist**, 6 m. 2 m. down, close to the **Broad Clist** Station, South brook joins on left bank. South brook rises by **Whimple**, and 1½ m. down is joined by a small stream on left bank. 1½ m. down, a stream running by Rockbere joins South brook on left bank. **Broad Clist** Station is 1¼ m. on. 1 m. down Clist, at Honiton Clist, Halbrook Brook joins on left bank. Halbrook rises above Faringdon Mill, by Aylsbere, and is 3 m. long. Clist runs 3 m. to St. Mary's Clist (plenty of dace below the mill and in its vicinity, very few trout so low down), where Greendale brook (4 m. long) joins on left bank. Clist now runs to **Topsham**, 2 m., and just beyond joins Exe Estuary. (*See c.s. Exe.*)

Torcross (Devon.)—(n.s. **Kingsbridge, Dartmouth**, thence by coach.) *Hotel:* Torcross Hotel. Good fishing, pike, perch, rudd in a large lake belonging to the hotel; boats. The sea fishing is very good.

Torksey (Lincoln).—M.R. Trent; pike, roach, chub. (c.s.) Foss Dyke navigation. (*See Gainsborough.*)

Torquay.—G.W.R. Angling from the pier for pollack, small mackerel, dabs, pout, sand smelts, and by throw-out lines for conger after sunset. The offing fishing for whiting has of late been poor until much after midsummer. Dabs and mackerel in the bay. Pollack fishing by trailing or whiffing; often good from Arbrick Rock, near Corbyn Head, and by Livermead Head; also at the back of Paignton old pier to middle of July; also from back of Torquay pier, past London Bridge to Shag, Thatcher, Orestone, and Flat Rocks. In Thatcher Gut, good drift-line fishing for pollack, with some bass and large mackerel. Sand eels for bait often obtainable at Paignton, where seine nets are kept for their capture. Worms from the peat at Tor Abbey sands; pilchards and squid from seineboats at Brixham. At Thatcher Gut, moor twenty yards inside the rock, at two hours flood of spring tide until one hour ebb; at neaps (not so good) from three hours flood to high water. Capital trouting can be had in Tottiford and Kennick reservoirs, near Lustleigh; for particulars apply to F. S. Hex. Esq., Town Clerk, Torquay. Yachts and boats, Brown Brothers. (*See Babbacombe, Teignmouth, Paignton, Brixham, Dartmouth, and Bovey.*) Indiarubber spinning baits useful.

Torrington (Devon).—L. & S.W.R. On Torridge; salmon peel, trout, and dace.. Langtree brook. Woolly brook; trout. *Hotel:* The Globe. Lodgings can be bad. Apply, with stamped envelope, to Mrs. E. Skemp, fishing-tackle maker (*see Advertisement*). The Taw is 8 m. distant. The time for salmon is either late or early. Plenty of peel after summer flood. Visitors to the Globe can fish in 8 m. of preserved water. There are 2 m. of fishing free to persons living or lodging in Torrington. (*See c.s. Taw.*) (*See Bideford.*) Permission also frcm Hon. Mark Rolle and Lord Clinton, but application must be made before the end of April.

Torrington Park (Herts).—G.N.R. New River. (*See London.*)

Torver (Lancs.). Fs.R.—Torver beck. *Lakes:* Coniston, 1 m E.; pike, perch, trout. (*c.s. Kent.*) Goat's Water. 3 m. N.E. Beacon tarn. 5 m. S.. (*See Ulverston.*)

Totnes (Devon).—G.W.R. (*See Dartmouth.*) *Hotels:* Seymour, Seven Stars, Commercial, and Castle. On Dart; trout and salmon; fishing from the Conservators from here up stream to Dartmoor. Licences at the Seymour. Fishing with Association ticket up to Buckfastleigh, except about 3 m., for which tickets must be had from Mr. Robert Nichols, Furseleigh, and on the Dartington estate, preserved by A. Champernowne, Esq., Dartington Hall. *Tackleist,* J. Selwood.

Tottenham (Middlx.).—G.E.R. (*See Stratford.*) On Lea; dace, roach, chub, barbel, jack, &c.; d.t. 6d. *Inn:* Ferry Boat House.

Towcester (Northton.)—L. & N.W.R. Yore. Blakesley brook (2 m.). (*See King's Lynn.*)

Tram Inn (Hereford.)—G.W.R. Worm brook (1 m.). Gage brook (3 m.). *Lakes:* Allenmore House ponds (1 m.) (*See Chepstow.*)

Tredegar (Monmouth).—G.W.R.; L. & N.W.R. Sirhowey; polluted. Nant-y-llecha (2 m.).. (*See Newport.*)

Tredegar Junction (Monmouth).—Sirhowey; polluted. (*See Newport.*)

Treeton (Derby).—M.R. Rother. (*See Goole.*)

Tregony (Cornwall).—(n.s. **Grampound Road,** 5 m.) On Fal; trout. (*See Grampound.*) 2 m. off runs Polglaze brook, 4 m. long; trout. (*c.s. Fowey.*)

Trent (Derby).—M.R. Trent; roach, dace, perch. pike. chub, bream. (*c.s.*) Soar; same fish. (*c.s. Trent.*) Derwent, 3 m. N.W.; same fish. (*c.s. Trent.*) Erewash, 3 m. N.E. (*See Gainsborough.*)

Trentham (Stafford).—L. & N.W.R. Trent. (*c.s.*) Northwood brook. Longton brook, Lyme, 2 m. N. *Lakes:* Trentham Park. Handchurch Farm, 1 m. W. (*See Gainsborough.*)

Trevil (Monmouth).—L. & N.W.R. Sirhowey (3 m.). *Lakes:* Llyn-garu-fawr (3 m.). (*See Newport.*)

Trimdon (Durham).—N.E.R. Skerne; pike, chub, roach. (*c.s. Tees.*) (*See Stockton.*)

Troutbeck (Cumland).—L. & N.W.R. Troutbeck; trout. Glendermakin, 2 m. W.; trout, salmon. Mosedale beck, 3 m. W. (*See Cockermouth, Keswick.*) Caldew, 5 m. N.W.; trout. (*See Carlisle.*)

Trowbridge (Wilts).—G.W.R. (*See Bristol.*) Biss; coarse fish, few trout; polluted below the town; leave freely given. Avon (1½ m. N.); pike, perch, roach, dace, chub, carp, tench, trout at the weirs· the river is free for 4 m. (*c.s.*) Whaddon brook. 2½ m.; trout, coarse fish. Frome (3 m. W.); trout; mostly preserved by W. H. Laverton, Esq., Westbury, but portions are open. In the canal, 1 m. off, are jack and perch. *Lakes:* Edington ponds; roach, tench. *Hotels:* George, Woolpack.

Truro (Cornwall).—G.W.R. St. Allen river; trouting good. Tregarthen water. St. Allen rises by St. Allen, and 5 m. down is joined by Boswallock water, 3 m. long, on right bank. 2 m. down, St. Allen reaches **Truro.** Here Tregarthen water, 4 m. long, joins on right bank (the brook holds good fish, but is much wooded.) 1 m. down St. Allen, Sevecock water joins on right bank. Sevecock rises 1 m. N. from **Chacewater Station,** runs 5 m. to **Truro,** and 2 m. down joins St. Allen. 1 m. down, Tresillian water, holding trout and grilse, joins on left bank; fishing very good. Tresillian rises by St. Enoder (n.s. **Grampound Road,** 6 m.). and 5 m. down, at Ladock (n.s. **Grampound Road,** 1½ m.), is joined by Trelassick Brook, 3 m. long, on right bank. Tresillian runs 3 m. to Probus (n.s. **Grampound Road,** 3 m.), and 1 m. down is joined on right bank by Kestle water, which rises 2 m. S. of St. Michael's (n.s. **Grampound Road,** 5 m.): in 3 m. passes 1 m. W. of Ladock, and 3 m. down joins Tresillian. 2 m. down Tresillian, Woodland Brook (plenty of small trout), which rises by St. Erme (n.s. **Truro,** 4 m.), and is 5 m. long, joins on right bank. 3 m. down, Tresillian joins St. Allen and the estuary. The fishing in Tresillian is mostly free. In these brooks trout run 6 to the pound. The best flies—hare's-ear, March brown. red palmer, black gnat, and coachman. The natural fernweb in May and June is most killing. The sea fishing is very good. (*See Perranzabuloe.*)

Tunbridge Wells (Kent).—L.B. & S.C.R.; S.E. & C.R. (*See Rochester.*) There is a mill-pond at Broomhill, 1 m. from here, where, by paying a shilling, angling may be had. There are some ponds at the High Rocks, where trout fishing can be had at the rate of 6d. per day. Good fishing at **Ashurst,** 5½ m.. and Medway Valley to **Tonbridge,** 4 m. off; farmers grant leave if properly approached. *Hotels:* Royal Mount Ephraim, Castle, facing the common and railway at Ashurst.

Tunstall (Stafford).—L. & N.W.R.; M.R. Fowler brook. *Lakes:* Bath pool, 2 m. N.W. (*See Gainsborough.*) Good trouting in Tunstall and Waskerley reservoirs.

Turton (Lancs.).—L. & Y.R. Bradshaw brook. (*See Runcorn.*)

Turvey (Beds).—M.R. Ouse; coarse fish, except barbel; fishing private. (*c.s. N. and S.*) (*See King's Lynn.*)

Tutbury (Stafford).—L. & N.W.R.; G.N.R.; M.R. Dove: chub. bream, barbel, pike, trout. (*c.s. Trent.*) Cubley brook, 2 *m.* W. Longford brook, 2 *m.* E. Rolleston brook, 2 *m.* S.E. Limbersitch brook, 3 *m.* N. *Lakes*: Rolleston Hall lake, 2 *m.* S.E Foston Hall lake, 3 *m.* N.W. (*See Gainsborough.*)

Tuxford (Notts).—G.N.R. Maun, 3 *m.* N.W. Bevercotes beck, 3 *m.* N.W. Idle, 4 *m.* N.W. (*c.s. Trent.*) Poulter, 4 *m.* N.W. Meden, 4 *m.* N.W. *Lakes*: Haughton Decoy and the lower ponds, 3 *m.* N.W. (*See Althorpe.*)

Twerton (Somerset).—G.W.R. (*See Bristol.*) On Avon; roach, chub, dace, pike, perch, carp; fishing free. (*c.s.*) Newton brook, 1 *m*; trout; preserved by W. Gore Langton, Esq., Newton St. Lo.

Twickenham (Middlx.). L. & S.W.R. Thames and Yedding Brook. (*See London, L.T.*) *Hotels*: Queen's Head, Two Sawyers, Island (closed Sept. to May), and White Swan. *Fishermen*: G. R. and J. Coxon, C. W. Brown, H. Harper, N. Humphreys, G. Lee, C. Lee, A. Turner, J. and R. Spong, R. Moffat, G. Chamberlain, H. Spiers. The river Crane in Isleworth and district is preserved by the Crane Fly Fishers Club.

Twyford (Berks.).—G.W.R. (*See London, M.T.*) Loddon. Trout, pike, large chub, barbel, &c.; preserved.

Tydd St. Mary's (Lincoln) —G.N.R. Nen. Muscal river. Fen drains. (*See Wisbeach.*)

Tydu (Monmouth) —G.W.R. Ebbw; polluted. (*c.s. Usk.*) (*See Newport.*)

Tytherington (Gloucester).—M.R. Laden. (*See Bristol.*)

Uckfield (Sussex).—L.B. & S.C.R. Ouse; trout, perch, jack. (*See Newhaven.*) (*c.s.*) *Hotel*: Bridge.

Uffculme (Devon) —G.W.R. Culm; trout. Sheldon brook. There is a bit of open water here. The rest, *up* to **Culmstock**, and *down* to **Cullompton**, is private. (*See Exeter.*)

Uffington (Lincoln).—G.N.R. Welland; pike, perch, dace; private. (*See Spalding.*)

Ulceby (Lincoln).—G.C.R. Ulceby beck. Ulceby rises in the lakes at Newsham Abbey by **Brocklesby**, runs to **Ulceby** 1 *m.*, **Thornton** 3 *m.*, and joins Humber 4 *m.* below.

Ulleskelf (York.)—G.N.R.; S. & K.J.R.: N.E.R. (*See Cawood, York.*) Wharfe. (*c.s. York.*) Foss, 1 *m.* N. Cock beck, 3*m.* W. (*See York.*)

Ullesthorpe (Leicester).—L. & N.W.R.: M.R. Swift, 3 *m.* S.E at **Lutterworth**. Soar, 5 *m.* N.W. at Sharnford. (*c.s. Trent.*) *Lakes*: Claybrook Mill, 1 *m.* N. (*See Gainsborough, Gloucester, Lutterworth.*)

Ullock (Cumland).—L. & N.W. and Fs.R. Marron. (*c.s. Derwent.*) *Lakes*: Mockerkin tarn, 1 *m.* S.E. (*See Cockermouth.*)

Ulverston (Lancs.).—Fs.R. Leven; salmon, trout. (*c.s. Kent.*) Leven flows out of Windermere, which lake is formed principally by the rivers Rothay and Brathay which join 1 *m.* below **Ambleside** and fall immediately into the lake. Rothay rises 4 *m.* or 5 *m.* above **Grasmere.** Just above the village Easdale beck joins on right bank. Easdale rises in Codale tarn, runs 1 *m.* to Easdale tarn, and joins Rothay 2 *m.* down. Rothay runs to Grasmere lake, 1 *m.* This lake is about 1 *m.* long. The effluent (fair trouting, but preserved), runs 1 *m.* to Rydal Water, 1 *m.* long. At the lower end of the lake at Rydal, Rydal beck, 4 *m.* long, joins on left bank. **Ambleside** is 2 *m.* on. Here Scandal Beck, 4 *m.* long, joins on left (bank. Brathay river joins on right bank. Brathay rises on Langdale fell, some 7¹ *m.* above **Skelwith Bridge.** 1 *m.* down a stream joins on left bank, draining Blea tarn, 1 *m.* up. Brathay now waters Little Langdale tarn, and 3 *m.* down joins Elter water lake on right bank. On the left bank of Elter water, Great Langdale beck joins. Great Langdale beck rises on the slopes of Great Langdale, fell, and 3 *m.* down is joined on right bank by the outflow of Stickle tarn (trout), 1 *m.* up. The beck now runs 4 *m.* to Elter water; at the lower end of the lake on right bank, near **Skelwith Bridge,** the outflow of Loughrigg tarn, 1 *m.* up, joins. From **Skelwith** to **Ambleside** is 3 *m.* Windermere (pike, perch, trout). the largest English lake, is some 10 *m.* long. Going down the left bank for 4 *m.* is Trout beck, 7 *m.* long, and 2 *m.* from **Windermere** station. 2 *m.* down the lake is **Bowness** (n.s., **Windermere,** 2 *m.*). Hence to **Lakeside** station, at the foot of the lake, is 6 *m.* Returning to **Ambleside,** on the right bank of the lake, a stream joins just opposite the Low Wood Hotel, draining Blelham tarn, 1 *m.* up. 5 *m.* below is the **Ferry Hotel,** opposite **Bowness,** and 2 *m.* below is Cunsey beck, draining Esthwaite water. The head feeder of this lake rises near the head of Coniston lake, and runs 3 *m.* to **Hawkshead,** 1 *m.* down wa'ering Eastwaite. This lake is 2 *m.* long, and its effluent, Cunsey beck, runs to Windermere, 2 *m.* It is 5 *m.* or thereabouts, to **Lakeside Station** at the foot of the lake. where the Leven leaves it. Two *m.* N.W. from **Lakeside** over the hills is High tarn. Leven runs 1 *m.* to **Newby Bridge.** Here a stream joins on right bank, draining Bortree tarn 1 *m.* up. Leven runs to **Haverthwaite,** 2 *m.*, and 1 *m.* below, a stream joins on left bank, draining Bigland tarn 2 *m.* up. 2 *m.* below. Rusland pool joins on right bank. Rusland, under the name of Grisdale beck, rises above Grisdale, where it receives the drainage of Grisdale tarn 1 *m.* up, some 3 *m.* across the hills S. of **Hawkshead,** and runs to Satterthwaite 2 *m.* 3 *m.* down, at Rusland, Ashes beck, 4 *m.* long, joins on left bank. Rusland runs 5 *m.* to Leven. 1 *m.* down Leven, Colton beck, 5 *m.* long, joins on right bank just above **Greenodd.** Here, also, Crake joins on the same side. Crake is the effluent of Coniston Lake. Yewdale beck is the principal feeder of the lake, which has no streams entering on the left bank. Yewdale rises in the hills 4 m. N. of **Coniston**, and half-way down takes the draining of Low tarn 1 m. up. Church beck here also falls into the lake. This stream drains Lever water, and is 3 m. long. **Torver** is 3 m. below **Coniston**. Here Torver beck, 4 m. long, runs into Coniston Lake, draining Goat's water 3 m. up, which is 6 m. long. **Lake Bank Hotel** is at the lower end of the lake 3 m. from **Torver**, and here the stream, flowing out of Beacon tarn, 2 m. up, joins on right bank. Crake runs to **Greenodd** and Leven in 7 m. Newland beck here joins Leven on right bank. This beck is 5 m. long, and runs within a m. N.E. of **Ulverston**. *Lakes:* Ulswick tarn 3 m. S. Mere tarn 5 m. S. (*See Newbiggin.*) *Hotels:* County, Sun, Queen's.

Umberleigh (Devon).—L. & S.W.R. Taw. (*c.s.*) Hon. Mark Rolle issues 25 tickets for his water; preserved by private owners elsewhere. (*See Barnstaple.*)

Unston (Derby).—M.R. Drone. (*See Goole.*)

Upleadon (Gloucester).—(n s. **Gloucester**, 9 m.) Leadon. Clynch brook. (*See Gloucester.*) (*c.s. Severn.*)

Upper Arley (Stafford).—G.W.R.; L. & N.W.R. Severn; salmon, trout, grayling, chub, dace, pike, &c. Dowles brook (3 m. S.) (*See Gloucester.*) (*c.s. Severn.*)

Upper Broughton (Notts).—M.R. Dalby brook. Smite. 1 m E. (*See Gainsborough.*)

Uppingham (Rutland).—L. & N.W.R. Eye brook, 2 m. W. Welland, 3 m. S.E., at **Seaton**. Chater, 3 m. N. Gwash, 4 m. N., at **Manton**. (*See Spalding.*) *Tacklei st,* T. L. Andrews, High-street.

Upton-on-Severn (Worcester).—M.R. Severn; chub, dace, roach, pike, perch, salmon. (*See Gloucester.*) (*c.s.*)

Urmiston (Lancs.).—C. Lines. Mersey. Longford brook. 1 m. N. (*See Runcorn.*)

Usk (Monmouth).—G.W.R. *Hotel:* Three Salmons. Usk; salmon, trout; preserved by the United Usk Fishery Association, sec., H. S. Lyne, Esq.. Westgate Chambers, Newport, Mon. Olway; trout; preserved. (*See Newport.*) (*c.s.*) Salmon rod licences, season. 30s., 14 days 10s., trout 2s. 6d., from Mrs. Creese, Post-office, Usk, and postmistress, Llanvihangel-Gobion. The Association Fisheries are divided into the Upper and Lower Waters. The Upper Water consists of the Association Fisheries from the mouth of the Llanover Brook downwards to the upper boundary of the Lan Fishery; including, speaking generally, the Pant-y-Goitre Fishery, and part of the Kemeys Fishery, but excluding the Llanvair Glebe and Pant Fisheries. The Lower Water consists of the Association Fisheries between the lower boundary of the Upper Water and Redland pool, but does not include the Lan Fishery. The Clytha, Forge Mill, Brynderwen, Lan, and some other smaller Fisheries are not at present in the occupation of the Association. The fishing from off Trostrey Weir is exclusively reserved for Classes A, B, and C. All applications for season tickets must be made to the secretary; trout, w.t. 10s. and d.t. 2s. 6d., may be obtained of Mrs. Creese. Post-office. Usk: of Messrs. Mullock and Sons. Ltd., stationers, Newport; of Newbridge Hotel. Newbridge-on-Usk; of Mr. Fox. hairdresser, Pontypool; Mr. Thomas, Pont Kemey's Farm. Chain Bridge; and at the Post-office, Llanvihangel-Gobion; and station master, Penpergwm. S.t., trout, 21s. for the Upper Fishery, and 21s. for the Lower Fishery. Transferable season trout tickets, to be called house tickets, and available on both waters, 3l. each, to persons residing in the district, to be used only by the holder and one friend staying in his house. such friend not being resident in the county. S.t. holders may obtain house tickets for friends at 40s. for one and 60s. for two. Twelve non-transferable season salmon tickets at 50l. each for the Lower Fishery and twelve for the Upper at 26l. will be issued to members of the association. Three non - transferable salmon day tickets, available on beats upper, middle, and lower respectively on the Lower Fishery (Class C), at 20s. a day, will be placed with Mrs. Creese, Post-office, and one salmon day ticket at 20s. for the Upper Fishery will be placed with Mrs. James, Llanvihangel-Gobion. Any person may engage one of such tickets for any day or days not already fully occupied, *on payment of the price of the ticket.* Provided that no person can engage tickets for more than three consecutive days before five o clock in the evening of the last of such days ; and no person can engage a ticket for more than twenty-one days before the date for which it is required. Season tickets (Class D) may be granted to angle for salmon between the top of the Withey Bed (Catch No. 42) below Trostrey and the County Bridge at Usk (the field belonging to Col. M'Donnell, and any private gardens excepted), at 20s. for the season to bona fide residents in the Usk and Ebbw Fishery District, within the county of Monmouth ; and for trout, between the stable of the Old Mill at Trostrey and Pont Sampit (with the same exceptions), at 5s. for the season. Such tickets can be obtained of Mrs. Creese. Post-office, Usk, and of Mr. Fox, hairdresser, Pontypool. All salmon tickets include the right of angling for other fish during the trout season. If any gentleman who has hitherto held a salmon s.t., or to whom one has been offered, neglects to apply for a fresh one before Jan. 1st in each season, and to pay for it before Feb. 10, it cannot be reserved for him. No night line or night lobworm fishing allowed ; no fishing for salmon (except below the bridge at Newbridge) except with artificial fly, and no spinning or bait fishing on salmon catches. No gaff before May 1 or after Oct. 1. Trout angling commences on Feb. 15, and ends on Sept. 1, inclusive. Artificial fly *only* till June 1. Trout tickets not available to holders of more than one trout licence. Salmon angling commences on March 2, and ends on Nov. 1, inclusive. No dogs or Sunday fishing.

Uttoxeter (Stafford).—L. & N.W.R.; G.N.R.; M.R. Stonyford brook. Dove; chub, barbel, bream, pike, trout, grayling; d.t. can be had. *(c.s. Trent.)* Tean brook, 1 *m.* N. Blythe, 4 *m.* S.W. *(c.s. Trent.)* *(See Gainsborough.)*

Uxbridge (Middx.).—G.W.R. *Inn* : Queen's Head. *(See London, M.T.)* Colne; trout, pike, perch, roach. On Uxbridge Moor the fishing is free and fair, many trout being caught in the season. In the Grand Junction Canal are many coarse fish, especially tench. 3 *m.* is preserved by the Anglers' Association.

Venn Cross (Somerset).—G.W.R. Bampton brook. *(See Exeter.)*

Verwood (Wilts).—S. & D.R. Allen and Moors. *(See Christchurch.)* *(c.s. Avon.)*

Veryan (Cornwall).—n.s. **Grampound Road**, 9 *m.* 1 *m.* W. runs Crugsillack water, 3 *m.* long. *(c.s. Fowey.)*

Victoria (Cornwall).—G.W.R. Withiel water. *(See Wade Bridge.)* *(c.s. Camel.)* Bream. *(See Par.)* *(c.s. Fowey.)*

Victoria (Monmouth).—G.W.R. Ebbw; polluted. *(c.s. Usk.)* *(See Newport.)*

Virginia Water (Berks).—L. & S.W.R. *(See London, L.T.)*

Wade Bridge (Cornwall).—G.W.R. Camel; trout, sea trout, salmon. Kestle water. Manscorve brook. Combe water. Camel rises 4 *m.* above Camelford (*Hotel*, King's Arms); fishing good; begins, *trout*, March 16 and ends Sept. 30; *salmon*, May 1st and ends Nov. 30: use small flies, and the fern-web the end of June; and 3 *m.* below that town is joined on left bank by Gaspard brook. Gaspard rises in Gaspard' Pool in Crowdey Marsh, 3 *m.* E. of Camelford, runs 4 *m.*, and is joined on left bank by a brook 2 *m.* long : 2 *m.* down Gaspard joins Camel. 6 *m.* down Camel, De Lauk river joins on left bank. De Lauk rises 4 *m.* S.E. of Camelford, and is 10 *m.* long. ½ *m.* down Camel, Bisland water, 3 *m.* long, joins on left bank. Camel runs in 6 *m.* to **Bodmin**, 1½*m.* off the river. Here a stream 2 *m.* long joins on left bank. ½ *m.* down Camel, Kirland water, 2 *m.* long joins on left bank. ½ *m.* down Camel, Lanivet water, 4 *m.* long, joins on left bank. 1 *m.* down, Withiel water joins, which rises by **Victoria**, runs 3 *m.* to Withiel, and is joined on left bank by a small stream, 2 *m.* long, working a mill. 2½ *m.* down, Tremore water, 3 *m.* long, joins on right bank. Camel is 1 *m.* on. 3 *m.* down Camel, near **Wade Bridge**, Kestle water joins on right bank. Kestle rises by the famous Delabole Slate Quarries, 3 *m.* W. of Camelford, runs 3 *m.* to St. Teath, and Camel, and Egloshayley, 8 *m.*; Camel runs to **Wade Bridge** 1 *m.* Here Manscorve brook, 3 *m.* long, joins on left bank. The tide flows to **Wade Bridge.** Two miles down Camel, Combe water joins on right bank. Combe rises 3 *m.* above St. Kew, and is 8 *m.* long. *(c.s.)* *(See Padstow.)* Good bass and pollack fishing. The best flies for salmon and peal are blue doctor, goldfinch, and Dromore. The best trout fishing is above Helland Bridge. Conservators' licences, salmon and trout, s.t., 12*s.*, f.t. 5*s.*, d.t. 1*s.* (trout and char only, 4*s.*, 2*s.* 6*d.*, and 1*s.*), from G. Lisker-Ellis, Esq., Wadebridge.

Wadesley Bridge (Yorks.).—G.C.R. Don. *(c.s. Yorkshire.)* Rowel, 1 *m.* S. *(See Goole.)*

Wadhurst (Sussex).—S.E. & C.R. Trout.

Wainfleet (Lincoln).—G.N.R. Steeping river. Steeping rises 5 *m.* above **Spilsby** (1 *m.* off on left bank), runs thence to **Halton Holegate** 4 *m.*, **Thorpe** 4 *m.*, **Wainfleet** 2 *m.*, and joins the sea 4 *m.* below.

Wakefield (Yorks).—G.N.R.; M.R.; L. & Y.R.; L. & N.W.R.; G.C.R. Calder *(c.s. York.)* Walton beck, 1 *m.* E. *Lakes* : Chevel Park lake, 4 *m.* S. *(See Rawcliffe.)*

Wakerley (Northton.)—L. & N.W.R. Welland. *(See Spalding.)*

Walcott (Salop).—L. & N.W.R.; G.W.R. Tern; a few trout, pike, roach, dace. Roden; a few trout and coarse fish. Bell brook (3 *m.* S.) *(See Gloucester.)* *(c.s. Severn.)*

Wallingford (Berks).—G.W.R. Thames. *(See London, M.T.)* *Hotels* : The Lamb, Town Arms, George, Feathers. *Fishermen* : J. Whiteman, W. Moody.

Wallingford Road (Berks).—G.W.R. *(See London, M.T.)*

Wallington (Surrey).—L.B. & S.C.R. On Wandle. *(See London, L.T.)*

Walsall (Stafford).—L. & N.W.R.; M.R. Ford brook. Sneyd brook, 1 *m.* N.W. *Lake* : Hatherton lake; pike. *(See Gainsborough.)*

Walsden (Lancs.).—G.N.R.; M.R. Roch. *Lakes* : Gadden reservoir, 1 *m.* E. Upper White Holme reservoir, 2 *m.* S.E. Tunnel End reservoir. 3 *m.* S.E. Lower White Holme reservoir, 4 *m.* S.E. Blackstone reservoir, 5 *m.* S.E. Spoddle Hill and another reservoir, 4 *m.* S. *(See Runcorn.)*

Waltham (Essex).—G.E.R. *(See Stratford and London.)* *Inns* : King's Arms and Britannia. On Lea, Cobbin's Brook, and New River ; roach, chub, perch, pike. The Abbey stream (chub and roach) is preserved. Jack fishing ends Feb. 28. Fishing is good, especially in the mill stream above the town and the back stream below it. The King's Arms fishery comes next. In the barge cut is good tench fishing. free: also good fishing in the smaller Lea by the Britannia Hotel, free. Next comes Capt. Saunders's water; subs. 2*l.* 2*s.*: very good fishing. The Fisheries Society have taken the water recently rented by the Gresham Anglers, and it is now open to all holders of a privilege ticket either from the Central Committee of London Anglers, the West Central, or Central Associates.

Walton-on-Trent (Stafford).—L. & N.W.R.; M.R. Trent; pike, perch, roach, dace, chub, barbel, trout. *(c.s.)* *Lake* : Luce pool, 4 *m.* N.W. *(See Gainsborough.)*

Wandsworth (Surrey).—L. & S.W.R. *(See London, L.T.).* Thames and Wandle.

Wansford (Northton.)—L. & N.W.R. Nen; pike, perch, chub, bream, &c.; good fishing, preserved by Lord Westmorland and J. M. Vipan, Esq., who sometimes give a day. Wittering brook, 1 m. E. (*See Wisbeach.*)

Wanstead (Essex).—G.E.R. *Lakes:* Long pond; preserved. Perch pond; pike, perch, tench, eels. Leg of Mutton Pond; same fish; preserved by a club. Basin; tench, carp, roach, pike, eels; preserved by the Wanstead Golf Club.

Wappenham (Northton.)—L. & N.W. R. Tove. Blakesley brook (4 m.). (*See King's Lynn.*)

Warburton (Cheshire)—L. & N.W.R. Mersey. Bollin, 1 m. S.; trout, roach, dace, pike. (*See Runcorn.*)

Warcop (Westland).—N.E.R. Eden; salmon, trout; preserved to Appleby. (*c.s.*) (*See Carlisle.*)

Ware (Herts).—G.E.R. (*See Stratford.*) On Lea. The Amwell Magna fishing (strictly preserved) begins here. (*See St. Margaret's*). At the Red House, half-way to Hertford, the proprietor of this fishery has thrown open a portion of the water above Ware to the public. The fishing is, however, very uncertain. A good spot for tench is the Old Basin Lock, near the gasworks, Hertford. The New River rises near here. The pool at its source, and some portion of the stream belong to the Amwell Magna Fishery. Mr. Sewell, Hard Mead Lock, will give all information required. (*See London.*)

Wareham (Dorset).—L. & S.W. R. Frome and Piddle; salmon, sea trout, trout. Frome rises in a pond on Rampisham Down, 4 m. N.W. from **Toller**, runs to **Toller**, thence in 2 m. to **Maiden Newton**. Here a stream joins on left bank, which rises by Rampisham (n.s. **Evershot**, 1½ m.), runs to Wraxhall ½ m., below which a short stream joins on left bank, draining a pond 1 m. up; hence to **Maiden Newton** is 2 m. Frome runs in 4 m. to **Grimston**, and **Dorchester** 5 m. Here Crane river (trout) joins on left bank. Crane rises by Minterne Magna (n.s. **Evershot**, 5 m.), and 1 m. down receives the drainings of a pond on the left bank. 1 m. down, at Cerne Abbas, the outflow from a pond ¼ m. up joins on right bank. Godmanstone is 3 m. down, and **Dorchester** 4 m. Frome runs in various streams to **Moreton** 7 m. 1 m. down, a stream 5 m. long, working three mills, joins on right bank. Frome runs to **Wool** 3 m. 3 m. down, a stream joins on right bank, which drains two ponds on Povington Heath 3 m. up, and 1 m. down Frome, a stream joins on right bank, which drains a pond on Grange Heath 2 m. up, and also works a mill. **Wareham** is 2 m. down Frome, and 2 m. down the river runs into Poole Harbour. (*c.s.*)

PIDDLE rises in a mill pond 1 m. N. of Piddletrenthide (n.s. **Grimston**, 7 m.), runs 6 m. to Piddletown (n.s. **Moreton**, 6 m.). Here a stream joins on left bank 6 m. long, working some mills. Piddle runs in 2 m. to Affpiddle (n.s. **Moreton**, 4 m.). 4 m. down at Upper Hyde (n.s. **Wool**, 3 m.) a stream joins on left bank, which rises in the lakes in Milton Abbey Park (n.s. **Blandford**, 7 m.), runs 3½ m. to Milborne St. Andrews, Ben Regis (n.s. **Wareham**, 6 m.) 4 m., and Piddle 2 m. Piddle runs to **Wareham** 4 m. Here a stream 3 m. long joins on left bank, which drains the decoy pond on Decoy Heath. 1½ m. on the estuary is reached. (*See c.s. Frome.*) *Hotel:* Red Lion.

Warwick.—G.W.R. Avon; chub, dace, roach, pike, perch; fishing fair, but leave must be had. *Lakes:* Warwick Park lake (1 m. S.) (*See Gloucester.*) (*c.s. Severn.*) *Hotel:* Woolpack.

Warkworth (Northland.).—N.E.R. On Coquet; trout, sea and bull trout. *Hotels:* Sun and Hermitage. Felton is another point to fish Coquet, which is in the hands of the Northumbrian Anglers' Federation. The accommodation is good. At Weldon Bridge is a comfortable inn and good fishing. The Brinkburn Priory water is preserved, but leave can be obtained. At Rothbury there are several inns; lodgings may be had in the village. At Thropton (1½ m. from Rothbury) Wrigh joins Coquet. Wrigh is preserved in parts. The quarters are bad. At Allerdene, ¾ m. from Thropton, lodgings can be had. At Holystone, 7 m. from Rothbury, there is an inn. At Harbottle, 9 m. from Rothbury, lodgings and furnished houses can be had. At Alwinton, 2 m. from Harbottle, there is an inn, and beyond this nothing but sheep farmers. There are two or three nice burns here. Trout fishing begins on March 4th, and ends Oct. 1st; bull trout from Feb. 1 to Oct. 31. No fishing is allowed after the first hour after sunset, or before the first hour before sunrise. No gaffs are allowed. (*See Wooler.*) (*See c.s.*).

Warminster (Wilts).—G.W.R. On Wylye; trout; preserved. (*See Christchurch.*) (*c.s. Avon.*)

Warmley (Gloucs.).—M.R. (*See Bristol.*) Boyd; trout; preserved by landowners. Siston brook; trout; leave from landowners. *Lakes:* Wick Court. Warmley tower; perch, carp, pike; preserved.

Warrington (Lancs.)—L. & N.W.R.; M.R.; G.N.R. Mersey. Blackbrook. Sankey brook. (*See Runcorn.*)

Washford (Somerset).—G.W.R. Washford; trout. (*See Watchet.*)

Washingbrough (Lincoln).—G.N.R. Witham. Washingbrough brook, 1 m. S. (*See Boston.*)

Wastdale Head (Cumland).—Irt; salmon, trout. (*c.s. West Cumberland.*) Overbeck, 2 m. S. Netherbeck, 2½ m. S. Derwent, 5 m. E. : trout; *c.s. Lakes:* Wastwater; trout, char. (*c.s. West Cumberland.*) Mosedale and Lingwell brooks run into the head of Wastwater lake. The Irt is the outlet of the lake and runs through Netherwastdale, Santon Bridge, and Holmrook to the sea. Styhead tarn, 3 m. N.E. Burnmoor tarn, 2 m. S.W. Low tarn, 2 m. W. Scoat tarn, 3 m. N.W. Greendale tarn, 3 m. S.W. *Hotels:* Wastwater, Wastdale Head, Strands Inn. Netherwastdale Bridge Inn, Santon Bridge, Lutwidge Arms, Holmrook. (*See Ravenglass, Cockermouth, Keswick.*)

Watchet (Somerset).—G.W.R. Washford stream; trout; preserved by a society. Season tickets only, from March 1 to Sept. 1. Washford rises by Luxborough, runs 5 m. to **Roadwater**, when a stream joins on the right bank, running down from **Combe Row** 3 m. up. Washford runs to **Washford** 3 m., and **Watchet** 3 m.

Waterbeach (Cambs)—G.E.R. Cam; pike, perch, chub, roach, &c. Bottisham Load; pike, perch, roach. Swaffham Load. (*See Cambridge.*) *Inn*: House of Lords. (*See King's Lynn.*)

Waterfoot (Lancs.).—L. & Y.R. Irwell. *Lakes*: Hare Hill, 3 m. S. (*See Runcorn.*)

Wateringbury (Kent).—S.E.&C.R. (*See Rochester* and *Yalding.*) On Medway; good fishing; pike, perch, chub, bream; preserved by the Maidstone and Medway Angling Society; sec., F. J. Munn, 17, Bower Street, Maidstone; d., w., and m.t. *Hotels*: King's Head, Railway, Anchor and Hope. There are some mill ponds here belonging to Mr. Fremlin, and some large lakes belonging to Lord Falmouth.

Watford (Herts.).—L. & N.W.R. (*See London, M.T.*). Colne; chub, dace, roach, pike, perch, trout. Colne is preserved, except a small piece at the back of the High-street. The canal and part of Colne is preserved by the Watford Piscatorn; hon. sec., A. Masser, Norcombe, Vicarage-road, Watford. *Hotels*: Clarendon, Rose and Crown, Malden.

Watford Junction (Herts).—L. & N.W.R. Colne. (*See London, M.T.*)

Watton (Norfolk).—G.E.R. Wissey. (*c.s. N. and S.*) *Lakes*: Saham Mere, 1 m. N. Heath Mere, 5 m. E. (*See King's Lynn.*)

Wednesbury (Stafford).—G.W.R.; L. & N.W.R.: M.R. Tame. (*c.s. Trent.*) *Lakes*: Wood Green pools; pike, roach. Foundry pond, 2 m. S.E. (*See Gainsborough.*)

Weedon (Northton.).—L. & N.W.R. Nen; pike, perch, bream, &c.; fishing poor. Streck. Fawsley brook, 1 m. W. Horsestone brook, 4 m. S.E. *Lakes*: Fawsley Park. (*See Daventry; Wisbeach.*)

Weeton (York.).—N.E.R. (*See York.*) Wharfe. (*c.s. York.*)

Weldon (Northton.)—M.R. Harper's brook, 2 m. S. *Lakes*: Dene Park, 2 m. N.E. (*See Wisbeach.*)

Weldon Bridge (Northland.).—Stations: **Acklington**, N.E.R., 7 m.: **Brinkburn**, N.B.R., 4 m.; and **Morpeth**, N.E.R., 9½ m.—On Coquet; trout (sea trout and salmon, autumn). The Duke of Northumberland's water (12 m.) on Coquet, is now leased to the Coquet Committee of the Northumbrian Anglers' Federation; s.t. 21s., m.t 10s., w.t. 7s. 6d., d.t. 2s. 6d., of the Clerk to the Committee, John A. Williamson, Solicitor, Newcastle-on-Tyne. *Hotel*: Anglers' Arms (*see Advertisement*), which has some 4 m. of fishing free to visitors. (*c.s.*) (*See Warkworth, Rothbury, Brinkburn, Felton,* and *Acklington.*)

Welford (Northton).—n.s. **Kilworth**, 2 m. Avon and large reservoir. At Naseby Wooleys, 4 m. off, there is good trouting in the lakes and streams; strictly private. (*See Gloucester.*)

Wellingborough (Northton.).—L. & N.W.R.; M.R. Nene; pike, perch, bream, tench, chub, roach. dace; strictly preserved by Wellingborough Nene Angling Club from Doddington Boundary to Ditchford; hon. sec., F. W. Marriott. Ise. (*See Wisbeach.*)

Wellington (Somerset).—G.W.R. Tone; trout, dace. Fishing preserved to Bradford by Mr. Sandford, of Ninehead Court; above Mr. Sandford's water by the various landowners. (*c.s. Avon.*) (*See Bridgwater.*)

Wellow (Somerset).—M.R.; L. & S.W.R. (*See Bristol.*)

Wells (Somerset).—G.W.R. Godney brook. (*See Highbridge* and *Axbridge.*) *Hotel*: Swan.

Wells-next-the-Sea (Norfolk).—G.E.R. Blakeney, 3 m. S.W. at Wighton. *Lakes*: Holkham lake, 3 m. W.

Welsh Harp (Middx.).—M.R. (*See London, L.T.*) Brent and Reservoir. 5 m. from Marble Arch. *Hotel*: Old Welsh Harp. Boats, bait, &c. Pike, perch, roach, bream, carp, tench; d.t., pike, 2s. 6d.; bottom fishing, 1s.; punts, 2s. 6d; s.t., 1l. 1s.

Welwyn (Herts).—G.N.R. (*See Stratford* and *Hertford.*) On Mimram; trout, coarse fish; preserved.

Wem (Salop).—L. & N.W.R. Roden; coarse fish above, good trouting and coarse fishing below, preserved by Lord Hill. Prees brook (3 m. N.E.). *Lakes*: Hawkstone Park lake (5 m. E.). (*See Gloucester.*) (*c.s. Severn.*)

Wenhaston (Suffolk).—G.E.R. Blyth. (*See Southwold.*)

Wensley (York.).—N.E.R. Broomber beck, 2 m. N. (*See York.*) Ure. (*c.s York.*) (*See York.*)

Westbury (Salop).—L. & N.W.R.; G.W.R. Yockleton brook. (*See Gloucester.*)

Westbury-on-Severn (Gloucester).—(n.s. **Grange Court**, 1½ m.) Hope brook, which rises 2 m. above **Longhope**, runs thence 5 m. to Westbury and Severn Estuary 1 m. **Westbury** (Wilts).—G.W.R. (*See Bristol.*)

West Clayton (Yorks).—L. & Y.R. Dearne. (*See Goole.*)

West Derby (Lancs).—S. & C.L.E.R. Alt, 1 m. N.E. (*See Altcar.*)

West Drayton (Middx.).—G.W.R. (*See London, M.T.*) Colne; trout, pike, perch, bream, dace, roach, tench, chub. Preserved for 2 m. by Thorney Weir Fishing Club; sec., F. H. Shimmell. who resides at the clubhouse; s.t., 4l. 4s., limited to 75 members; no day tickets except to members' visitors and residents at Thorney "Weir Cottage" Hotel (*see Advertisement*) at 2s. 6d. Subscriptions commence in March. Trouting begins April 1, ends September 30. Pike fishing begins August 1, ends Feb. 28. Perch fishing begins June 16, ends Feb. 28. Below and above the Thorney Weir water the river is private. The Iver river is preserved.

Westenhanger (Kent).—S.E. & C.R. On Stour. (*See Sandwich.*) (*c.s.*)

K

West Hallam (Derby).—G.N.R.; Nut brook. *Lakes:* Mapperley reservoir, 2 m. N. Shipley Hall reservoir, 3 m. N. Locko Park lake, 3 m. S.W. Smalley Mill Pond, 3 m. N.W. (*See Gainsborough.*)

West Hesterton (York).—N.E.R. (*See Yedingham Bridge.*)

Westhouses (Derby).—M.R. Westwood brook. Normanton brook, 1 m. S. Amber, 2 m. S.W. (*See Gainsborough.*)

Westmill (Herts.).—G.E.R. (*See Stratford.*) On Rib; trout; preserved.

Weston (Somerset).—M.R. (*See Bristol.*) Avon; roach, chub, pike, perch, carp; free. (*c.s.*) Newton brook, 1 m., trout; preserved by W. Gore-Langton, Esq.

Weston Junction (Somerset).—G.W.R. (*See Axbridge.*)

Weston-on-Trent (Derby). — M.R. Trent; chub, dace, roach, pike, perch, barbel, salmon; preserved from Weston to the iron bridge below Kings Mills by Mr. T. Wood, 9, Chapel Bar, Nottingham; from the iron bridge to bottom of the Shardlow waters by the Wellington Club. Accommodation can be had in the village. (*c.s.*) Gayton brook. Sow at **Stafford**, 5 m. S.W. Penk at Baswich, 5 m. S.W. *Lakes:* Ingestre Park pool and Hopton pools 2 m. S.W. (*See Gainsborough.*)

West Pennard (Somerset).—S. & D.R. Good roach fishing in a large pond by station; leave from the station master.

West Rounton (York).—N.E.R. Wiske; grayling, trout, chub, pike; preserved, leave sometimes. (*c.s. York.*) (*See York.*)

West Wycombe (Bucks.).—G.W.R. Wye; trout. (*See London, M.T.*)

Wetheral (Cumland.).—N.E.R. Eden; trout; preserved. (*c.s.*) Trout beck, 2 m. N. Irthing, 3 m. N. (*c.s. Eden.*) Scotby beck, 2 m. W. at **Scotby**. *Hotel:* Crown. (*See Carlisle.*)

Wetherby (York).—N.E.R. Wharfe. (*c.s. York.*) Crimple, 2 m. N.W., at Spofforth, Midd, 4 m. N., at **Little Ribston**. (*c.s. York.*) (*See York.*)

Weybridge (Surrey).—L. & S.W.R. (*See London, L.T.*) Thames, Wey, and Bourne brook; pike, trout, bream, perch, and barbel. *Hotels:* Lincoln Arms (facing confluence of Thames and Wey), Ship, Old Crown, and King's Arms. *Fishermen:* H. Curr and A. Poulter. Wey contains pike, perch, carp, tench, bream. There is good fishing in the lake in Oatlands Park; carp, roach, bream: private.

Weymouth.—G.W.R.; L. & S.W.R.; S. & D.R.; L. & N.W.R. There is good sea-fishing under the Breakwater at Portland for pollack, whiting, mackerel, and rockfish. The best time to fish is when the flood-tide is making. Bass may also be taken with a fly. Lulworth is also a good place. Pollack, bream, and mackerel may be angled for from the pier at the opening of the breakwater with ragworm or soft crab. Myriads of sand smelts are found here on the ebb tide; bait, half an inch of ragworm on No. 9 hooks. Bass are also met with at the Fleet Bridge. Mackerel fishing best from a small yacht, several for hire. Ground fishing for pout or whiting from open boats. Pollack by trailing at the Mixon shoal by the beacon buoy, bass in harbour's mouth and back of Weymouth jetty. Pollack also on north shore. Sand eels sometimes procurable on the beach; ragworms from the backwater; mackerel under sail. *Hotels:* Imperial. Burdon.

Whale (Cheshire).—L. & N.W.R. Goyt or Mersey. Black brook, 1 m. N. *Lakes:* Whale reservoir. (*See Runcorn.*)

Whalley (Lancs.).—L. & Y.R. W. Calder; polluted. (*c.s. Ribble.*) Ribble, 2 m. W.; trout, salmon. (*c.s.*) Hodder, 2 m. W.; trout, salmon. (*c.s. Ribble.*) Sabden brook, 2 m. E. Park brook, 3 m. S.W. Dean brook, 4 m. W. *Lakes:* Crowshaw reservoir, 5 m. N.W. (*See Preston.*)

Whaplode (Lincoln).—G.N.R. Whaplode river. (*See Holbeach.*)

Wharram (York).—N.E.R. Menethorpe beck. *Lakes:* Birdsall pond, 1 m. W. (*See Wressel.*)

Whatstandwell Bridge (Derby).—M.R. Derwent; grayling, trout, and coarse fish; preserved *above* by the Matlock and Cromford A.A. Hon. Sec., Henry Cooper, Esq., Derby-road, Cromford. (*See Matlock.*) (*c.s. Trent.*) *Hotel:* Derwent, good; tickets at hotel. Amber; grayling, trout, coarse fish. (*See Ambergate.*) *Lakes:* Alderwasley ponds, 2 m. S.W.; preserved by Mr. Hurt. (*See Gainsborough.*)

Wheathampstead (Herts).—G.N.R. (*See Stratford.*) On Lea.

Whimple (Devon).—L. & S.W.R. South brook. (*See Topsham.*)

Whissendine (Rutland).—M.R. Wreak or Eye. (*c.s. Trent.*) *Lakes:* Stapleford Park lake, 2 m. N.W. Edmonthorpe Hall lake, 2 m. E. Leesthorpe pond, 3 m. S.W. (*See Gainsborough.*)

Whitacre Junction (Warwick).—M.R. Tame. (*c.s. Trent.*) Blythe. (*c.s. Trent.*) Arley brook. Cole, 2 m. S.W. at **Coleshill**. (*See Gainsborough.*)

Whitby (York).—N.E.R. Esk; salmon, sea trout, trout; preserved by Esk Fishery Association from Whitby to beyond Glaisdale. (*c.s.*) Esk rises at Esklets on Westerdale Moor, 6m. above **Castleton**. (a little free fishing), and 2 m down is joined on left bank by Stockdale beck, 2 m. long. Three m. down Esk, lower beck, 3 m. long. joins on right bank, and a little below Basedale beck, 6m. long, joins Esk on left bank. Two m. down Esk is **Castleton**. Here Danby beck, 5 m. long. joins on right bank. Here also Commondale beck, called in its upper part Sleddale beck, which rises 4 m. above **Commondale** and runs thence 4 m. to Esk, joins left bank. Esk runs to **Danby** 2 m., and 3 m. down is joined on right bank by Great Fryup beck, 4 m. long. Esk runs to **Lealholme** Bridge 2 m.

Two *m.* below Stonegate beck, 4 *m.* long, joins Esk on left bank, and 1 *m.* below' at **Glaisdale**, Glaisdale beck, 4 *m.* long, joins on right bank. Esk runs 2 *m.* to **Egton**, and **Grosmont** 2 *m.* Here Murk Esk joins on right bank. Murk Esk, under the name of Wheeldale beck, rises on Glaisdale Moor. Six *m.* down it is joined on right bank by Rutmoor beck. 5 *m.* long. Murk Esk runs 3 *m.* to **Goathland**, 1 *m.* off on right bank, and 1 *m.* below Eller beck joins on right bank. Eller beck rises 5 *m.* above **Goathland**. and 1 *m.* from its source is joined by Little Eller beck, 2 *m.* long. on right bank. Two *m.* down, Brooks beck, 3 *m.* long, joins on right bank. One *m.* below, Little beck, 3 *m.* long, joins on right bank. One *m.* down is **Goathland**. Eller beck runs thence to Murk Esk 3 *m.* Murk Esk runs to the main stream 3 *m.* Esk runs 4 *m.* to **Sleights**, and 1 *m.* down is joined on right bank by Little beck (called at lower end Iburndale beck). 8 *m.* long. Esk runs to **Ruswarp** 2 *m.* Here Wash beck, 3 *m.* long, and Rigg Mill beck, 4 *m.* long, join on right bank. **Whitby** is 3 *m.* down Esk. Good trailing or whiffing for pollack through the Sledway and over the rough ground off Whitby Rock. on which is a bell buoy; also at Upgang Rock, bearing N.W. ½ W., a mile distant, on which are only 4ft. or 5ft. water, this ledge stretching out from the shore. Whiting, cod, flat fish, in the bay and offing, and angling from the pier for small pollack (called leets), and for young coalfish, known as billet. Esk Fishery Association grants m.t.. 63*s.*. up to Sept. 30. For tickets and licences, apply to Mr. W. Brown, The Saw Mills, Whitby. (*See* Scarborough: *Lealholme Bridge*) (*c.s.*)

Whitchurch (Hants).—L. & S.W.B. (*See* Stockbridge.) The Test; trout; strictly preserved. The principal proprietors of the fishing are Sir William Portal, of Malshanger, Lord Portsmouth, and Mr. H. Hawker. Above the town a club of limited non-resident members preserves the river between Laverstock and Hurstbourne, 3 *m.*: no tickets are granted. The fish are here very numerous, but not so large as farther down. There is a nice hotel, the White Hart, here, where every information may be obtained

Whitchurch (Salop).—L. & N.W.R. Oss brook, 2 *m.* N.E. Sarn, 2 *m.* N.W. *Lakes*: Blakemere, 1 *m.* N.E. Brown Moss Lakes, 1½ *m.* S.E. Oss mere, 2 *m.* N.E. Wolveracre Mill pond, 2 *m.* N.W. Quoisley Big and Little meres, 3 *m.* N. Combermere mere, 3 *m.* N.E. Marbury mere and Marbury Mill pond, 3 *m.* N.E. Dittwitch Mill pond, 3 *m.* N.W. (*See* Frodsham, *Chester.*)

Whitehaven (Cumland.).—L. & N. W.R.; Fs.R.; M.R.; N.E.R. Keekle, 2 *m.* N.W. *Hotels*: Grand, Globe, Golden Lion. (*See* Egremont.)

Whitewell (Lancs.). n.s. **Clitheroe**, 7 *m.*—Hodder; trout, salmon, sea trout. (*c.s.* *Ribble.*) Langden river, 2 *m.* N. Mill beck. 2 *m.* S.E. Greystoneley beck, 2 *m.* S.W. Whitendale river, 3 *m.* N. Loud river, 3 *m.* S. Brennand river, 6 *m.* N. *Hotel*: Whitewell. (*See* Preston.)

Whitmore (Stafford).—L. & N.W.R Meese. (*c.s.* *Trent.*) Tern, 2½ *m.* S.W.; pike. roach, dace, trout. (*c.s.* *Severn.*) *Lakes*: Whitmore Park lake. Maer Hall lake, 2 *m.* S. (*See* Gainsborough; *Gloucester.*)

Whitny (Hereford.) - M., & N. & B.R. Wye; pike, perch, dace, chub, salmon. (*c.s.*) Arrow (4 *m.*); trout, grayling, dace. Cwm Illa brook (4 *m.*) (*c.s.*) (*See* Chepstow.)

Whitstable (Kent).—S.E. & C.R. Fine rudd can be caught in the dykes here. Good sea fishing. *Hotel*: Bear and Key.

Whittington (Derby).—M.R. Rother. Drone. (*See* Goole.)

Whittington (Salop).—G.W.R. Perry. *Lakes* Halston Hall lake (2 *m.* E.). (*See* Gloucester.) (*c.s.* *Severn.*)

Whittlesford (Cambs.).—G.E.R. Cam; pike, roach, perch, dace, &c.; some fishing can be had up to Duxford Mill, on left bank, from the hotel; otherwise preserved. *Hotel*, Red Lion. (*See* King's Lynn.)

Whitwell (Derby).—M.R. Poulter. *Lakes*: Welbeck Park, 3 *m.* S.E. (*See* Althorpe.)

Whitworth (Lancs.).—L. & N.W.B. Dodd. (*See* Runcorn.)

Wickham (Essex). - G.E.R. On Blackwater. (*See* Maldon.)

Wickham Market (Suffolk). G.E.R. Deben. Potford brook, 1 *m.* N.W. *Lake*: Ash Abbey Decoy, 2 *m.* S.E. (*See* Woodbridge.)

Wickwar (Gloucester).—M.R. Little Avon; trout and coarse fish. Laden. Tortworth brook. (*See* Berkeley and *Bristol.*) (*c.s.* *Severn.*)

Widford (Herts.).—G.E.R. (*See* Stratford.) On Ash.

Widmerpool (Notts).—M.R. Fairham brook. (*See* Gainsborough.)

Wigan (Lancs.).—L. & N.W.R.; C.L.R.; L. & Y.B.; W.J.R. Douglas. (*c.s.* *Ribble.*) Clarenden brook. (*See* Hesketh Bank.)

Willington (Derby).—L. & N.W.R.; M.R. Trent; chub, roach, pike, perch, trout, salmon; preserved; a.t. (except salmon), 10*s.* 6*d.*, from Mr. W. K. Newbold, of King's Newton; fishing fair. (*c.s.*) Etwall brook. Foremark brook (preserved by Trout Fish-culture Co.), 3 *m.* S.E. *Lakes*: Foremark Mill pond, 3 *m.* S.E.; preserved by T.F.C.C. Repton Park lake, 3 *m.* S.E. Foremark Hall pond, 3 *m.* S.E. (*See* Gainsborough.)

Willesden Junction (Middx.).—L. & N.W.R. Brent. (*See* London, L.T.)

Williton (Somerset).—G.W.R. A stream joins the sea 2 *m.* below here, which rises 2 or 3 *m.* S. of **Stogumber**, and runs 4 *m.* to Williton; it holds trout; leave from the landowners.

Wilmslow (Cheshire).—L. & N.W.R. Bollin; trout, roach, dace, pike. Dean, 1 *m.* W. (*See* Runcorn.)

Wilnecoote (Warwick).—M.R. Tame; chub, dace, &c.; rather polluted. (*c.s. Trent.*)
Bourne brook; trout, grayling; preserved by landowners. *Lakes*: Drayton park, 2 m. W.
(*See Gainsborough.*)

Wilpshire (York).—L. & Y. R. Park brook. (*See Preston.*)

Wilstrop (Yor.k).—N.E.R. Nidd. (*c.s. York.*) (*See York.*)

Wilton (Wilts).—G.W.R.; L. & S.W.R. Wylye; trout, grayling, coarse fish; private below,
and preserved hence *up* to 1½ m. above **Wylye** by Wilton Fly-fishing Club of 25 members, entrance 20*l.*, a.t. 20*l.*; season—trout, May 1 to Aug. 31; grayling, July 30 to Nov. 30;
artificial fly only; no wading Nadder; trout, roach, dace. (*See Christchurch.*) (*c.s. Avon.*)

Wilton (York).—N.E.R. Thornton beck, 1 m. S.E. (*See Wressel.*)

Wimbledon (Surrey).—L. & S.W.R. In Wimbledon Park is a lake containing pike, carp,
&c.; a.t. 21*s.*

Wimborne (Dorset).—S. & D.R. Stour; pike, perch, trout. Allen; trout. Blackwater,
trout. (*See Christchurch.*) (*c.s. Avon.*)

Wincanton (Somerset).—S. & D.R. On Cale. (*See Christchurch.*)

Winchelsea (Sussex). - S.E. & C.R. On Brede. (*See Rye.*) (*c.s. Rother.*) At Pickham Mill,
near Guestling, 4 m. off, is a large waterhead.

Winchester (Hants.)—L. & S.W.R. (*See Southampton.*) Itchen; trout above the town,
and below, trout, grayling. The fishing above the town is strictly preserved. The
reach between the city mills, known as the Weirs, free; below the town it is also
strictly preserved, but for ¾ m. on the Old Barge and Mill rivers, tickets may be
obtained of Chalkley, fish-tackleist; a.t., 5*l.* 5*s.*: w.t., 12*s.* 6*d.*; d.t., 3*s.* 6*d.* Between
St. Cross and Bishopstoke the river is let by the various proprietors, with exclusive
rights: in the lower reaches there are plenty of grayling as well as trout. *Hotels*:
Royal (*see Advertisement*), George, and Black Swan.

Winchfield (Hants.)—L. & S.W.R. On Whitewater; trout. (*See London, M.T.*) The
Fleet ponds are near, but are reserved for the use of the men quartered at Aldershot.

Winchmore Hill (Middx.).—G.N.R. On New River. (*See London.*)

Windermere (Westland).—Trout beck, 2 m. N.; trout. (*c.s. Kent*). Gowan, 2 m. N.E.
(*See Kendal.*) Lake Windermere. 1 m. W.; pike, perch, char, large trout. (*c.s. Kent.*)
Hotel: Windermere. (*See Ulverston.*)

Windsor (Berks.).—G.W.R.; L. & S.W.R. (*See London, M.T.*) Thames; chub, dace,
roach, pike, perch, bream, barbel. *Hotels*: Castle, White Hart, Bridge House, Crown
and Cushion, Three Tuns, Swan. *Fishermen*: Pace, J. Bunce, R. and J. Grey, Lumsden
and Keene at Datchet. In the Virginia Water, Windsor Park, fishing is good; leave
difficult to obtain. Apply to the Deputy Ranger.

Wingfield (Derby).—M.R. Amber. Normanton brook. Birches brook. (*See Gainsborough.*)

Winscombe (Somerset).—G.W.R. Loxton brook. (*See Axbridge.*)

Winsford (Cheshire).—L. & N.W.R. Weaver. Ash, 3 m. S.W. Whitegate brook,
3 m. N.W. *Lakes*: Stocks Hill, 1 m. S. Little Budsworth, 5 m. W. (*See Frodsham.*)
Hotel: Royal Oak.

Winston (Durham).—N.E.R. Tees; trout, salmon, bull trout, grayling, coarse fish.
(*c.s.*) Alwent beck, 1 m. E.: trout, private. Sudburn or Hutton beck, 2 m. N. Clow
beck, 4 m. S. *Lakes*: Raby Park. (*See Stockton.*)

Wirksworth (Derby).—M.R. Ecclesbourne. Derwent, 2 m. N. at **Cromford**. (*c.s.
Trent.*) Dove, 9 m. S.W. at **Ashbourne**. (*c.s. Trent.*) *Lakes*: Hopton Hall lake,
2 m. S.W. (*See Gainsborough.*)

Wisbeach (Cambs.).—G.E.R. and G.N.R. Nen; pike, perch, bream, roach. Nen
rises above **Weedon**, and at Dodford Mill, 1 m. above that place, is joined on
right bank by Fawsley brook, 4 m. long, draining the lake in Fawsley Park,
4 m. S.W. from **Weedon**. Here Streck joins on left bank. This stream rises in
Dunsland reservoir (pike) by **Daventry**, and 1 m. down is joined on right bank
by a brook draining Middlemore reservoir 1 m. up, 1½ m. N. from **Daventry**.
Streck runs 2 m. S. from **Crick**, and joins Nen 7 m. down. 3 m. down Nen, at
Nether Heyford, Horsestone brook, 6 m. long, joins on right bank, and 5 m. down,
at Upton Mill, Wootton brook, which rises by **Piddington**, runs 4 m. to Wootton,
3 m. S. from **Northampton**, and thence to Nen 4 m. joins on right bank. Nen
runs to **Northampton** 3 m. Here a branch of Nen joins on left bank; it rises
in the lakes at Maidwell Dale and Maidwell Hall, 1 m. N. from **Lamport**. There
the outfall from the lakes at Lamport Hall join on left bank. Nen runs to **Brixworth** 3 m.; here Calendar brook, 6 m. long, joins on right bank. 2m. down, at
Spratton, Stowe brook, 8 m. long, joins on right bank, and 1 m. down, Pitsford brook
joins on left bank. Pitsford rises in Faxton Hall ponds 2 m. E. from **Lamport**, and is
8 m. long. Nen runs 2 m. to **Brampton**, and here Moulton brook, 3 m. long, joins on
left bank. 2 m. down, Althorp brook, which rises in the lakes in Althorp Park, by
Althorp Park Station, and is 5 m. long, joins on right bank. The two Nens meet
4 m. down at **Northampton**. Just above the junction the outfall from Dollington Hall
lake, 2 m. N.W. from the town, joins on right bank. (Nen is preserved by Nen Angling
Society to Doddington Mill.) Nen runs 3 m. to Weston Mill, where the drainage of
Abington Park lake (1 m. N.E. from **Northampton**), 1 m. up, joins on left bank. 1 m.
down Nen, at Houghton Mill, Billing brook, which rises in the lake at Overstone Park,
4 m. N.E. from **Northampton**, and is 4 m long, joins on left bank. 1 m. down Nen,

by **Billing** Station, the outflow of another lake in Overstone Park joins on left bank. 2 m. down Nen, at Whiston Mill (the guinea subscription water ends here), Sywell brook joins on left bank, which rises in Sywell Park pond 5 m. W. from **Wellingborough**, runs 2 m. to Sywell Mill pond, and joins Nen 3 m. down. Nen runs to **Castle Ashby** 1 m., and 2 m. down, at Doddington Mill (here ends the Nen Angling Club fishery), Ashby brook joins on right bank, which rises in the lakes in Castle Ashby Park, 2 m. S. from **Castle Ashby** Station, and runs 3 m. to Nen. Nen runs to **Wellingborough** 2 m., and here Ise joins on left bank. Ise rises above **Kilmarsh**, where it waters a lake, runs 2 m. to Arthingworth, near **Kilmarsh** Station, 4 m. to **Desborough**, **Rushton** 3 m., **Geddington** 3 m., **Kettering** 4 m., **Burton** 3 m., **Pinedon** 1 m. 1 m. down, at Harrowden Mill, the outflow of the lake at Finedorn Hall, 1 m. up, joins on left bank. 1 m. down, a stream, 2 m. long, joins on right bank, rising in Dickins' Mill pond 1 m. N. from **Wellingborough**. Ise runs 2 m. to **Wellingborough** and Nen. Nen runs to **Ditchford** 2 m. (here the water of the Wellingborough and Higham Ferrars Angling Association begins), **Higham Ferrers** 3 m., Stanwick 1 m. (here the fishing of W. and H.F.A.A. ends), **Ringstead** 3 m., **Shrapston** 4 m. 1 m. down, Harper's brook, which rises above Stanion 2 m. S. from **Weldon** and is 9 m. long, joins on left bank. Nen runs to **Thorpe** 2 m., **Oundle** 6 m. Nen here makes a loop of 2½ m. (Baron Rothschild) to the other side of the town, and runs to Perio Mill 3 m. Here the drainings of the pond at Southwick, 3 m. N.W. from **Oundle**, join on left bank. Nen runs 4 m. to **Elton**, where is the lake in Elton Park (Lord Carysfort). Here Willow brook joins on left bank. Willow rises in the lakes in Dene Park, 2 m. N.E. from **Weldon**, runs 3 m. to Blatherwycke Park and lake (Stafford O'Brian, Esq.), 2 m. W. from **King's Cliff**, runs to **King's Cliff** 2 m., and Nen 5 m. Nen runs to **Nassingham** 3 m., **Wansford** 2 m., (Lord Westmorland and Mr. J. M. Vivian). 1 m. below, Wittering brook, which rises in the lake at Easton, 3 m. S. from **Stamford**, and is 5 m. long, joins on left bank. Nen runs to **Castor** 2 m. (Lords Huntley and Fitzwilliam), and here Billing brook, 5 m. long, joins on right bank. Nen runs to **Overton** 4 m. (Lord Huntley), and 1 m. down the outflow of the lakes in Milton Park, 3 m. W. from **Peterborough**, joins on left bank. Nen runs 2 m. to **Peterborough**. Hence the river runs in various branches and cuts. The main stream runs in a straight line through the fens to **Guyhirne**, 12 m., and thence to **Wisbeach** 7 m. The right branch, called the Old River Nen, runs round by **Ramsey**, where Holme brook joins it. Holme rises in a pond by Caldecot, 4 m. W. from **Holme**, and is 7 m. long. Here also Wiston brook, which rises above King's Ripton, 4 m. N.E. from **Huntingdon** and is 10 m. long joins on right bank. 2 m. below **Ramsey**, on the right bank, is Ramsey mere, thence to **March** is 10 m. 6 m. down, Old Welney river, 8 m. long, joins on right bank. 3 m. down, at Outwell, Nen joins the Wisbeach Canal, which runs to **Wisbeach**, 6 m. A third branch, from **Peterborough**, is the Muscal river or Cats Water, anciently a branch of Nen. This runs 7 m. to 1 m. E. of **Eye Green**, thence 9 m. to **French Drove**, and 2 m. below joins North Level Main Drain, which joins Nen 10 m. down at **Tydd St. Mary's**. From **Wisbeach** Nen flows to **Ferry** Station 3 m., **Tydd St. Mary's** 3 m., **Sutton Bridge** 2 m., 1m. below which Nen joins the Wash. The fen district is so cut up and intersected by watercourses of all kinds and sizes that it would be impossible to describe them in detail. They all contain fish more or less, and are mostly free. It is very difficult to approach many of the best.

Wishford (Wilts).—G.W.R. Wylye; trout, grayling; preserved by Wilton Fly-fishing Club (*see Wilton*). (*See Christchurch.*) (*c.s. Avon.*)

Witham (Somerset).—G.W.R. Stour, Frome, and *lakes* in New Hitchlings and Witham Park. Stour Head lakes (three); pike, tench, rudd, trout, perch; leave from the owner of Stour Head House (Sir H. H. A. Hoare). (*See Christchurch: Bristol.*) (*c.s. Avon.*)

Witham (Essex).—G.E.R. (*See Maldon.*) Blackwater and Pods brook; pike (good), perch, roach, dace, eels, carp, tench, and a few trout. Almost the whole of the fishing is preserved. *Inns*: White Hart, Spread Eagle, Albert, and Railway Tavern. 3 m. from the station is Rivenhall Place Pond, belonging to Sir H. Ewart, of Felix Hall, Kelvedon, from whom leave must be obtained; pike, perch, roach, dace. 4 m. off is Terling River, belonging to Lord Rayleigh; pike and dace 3½ m. from the station is Braxted Park lake, N. T. Lawrence, Esq.; pike, perch, carp, dace, roach.

Withingham (Norfolk).—G.E.R. Yare. (*See Yarmouth.*) (*c.s. N. and S.*)

Withnell (Lancs.).—L. & Y.R.; L. & N.W.R. Roddlesworth. *Lakes*: Liverpool Waterworks Lake. (*See Liverpool, Preston.*)

Withyham (Sussex).—L.B. & S.C.R. On Medway. (*See Rochester.*)

Witley (Surrey). L. & S.W.R. (*See London, L.T.*)

Witney (Oxon.).—G.W.R. On Windrush; large trout; leave must be obtained from the proprietors; there is a good rise of May-fly. (*See London, U.T.*)

Wiveliscoombe (Somerset).—G.W.R. Tone. Milverton Brook. Norton brook; trout. (*See Bridgwater.*) (*c.s. Avon.*)

Wixford (Warwick).—M.R.; G.W.R. Arrow; pike, perch, roach, dace, bream, chub, few trout; good fishing from the Fish Hotel for 2½ m.; s.t. 5s.; d.t., 6d. *Lakes*: Ragley Park lake (1 m. N.W.). (*See Gloucester.*)

Woburn (Beds).—L. & N.W.R., Crawley brook. 3 m. N. *Lakes*: Woburn Abbey lake (3 m. S.E.); good fishing, preserved by the Duke of Bedford. (*See King's Lynn.*)

Woburn (Bucks).—G.W.R. Wye; polluted. (*See London, M.T.*)

Woking (Surrey).—L. & S.W.R. (*See London, L.T.*) Basingstoke canal; roach, perch, pike, mostly free.

Wollaton.—On Nottingham and Grantham canal; fishing good; pike, perch, roach, bream, and tench.

Wolsingham (Durham).—G.N.R. Wear; trout.

Wolverhampton (Stafford).—L. & N.W.R. Smeetow (2 m. W.). (*See Gloucester.*) Hotel: Star and Garter. *Tackleist*, T. Shakespeare, 9, Market-street.

Wolverton (Bucks).—L. & N.W.R. (*See Stoney Stratford.*) Ouse; coarse fish; mostly private. (*c.s. N. and S.*) Tove. (*See King's Lynn.*)

Wombwell (Yorks).—G.C.R. Dove. New beck, 1 m. S.E. Dearne, 2 m. E. (*See Goole.*)

Womersley (Yorks).—G.N.R.; L. & Y.R. Lake drain. Went, 2 m. S. *Lakes:* Stapleton Park lake, 1 m. W. (*See Goole.*)

Woodborough (Wilts).—G.W.R. Avon; trout, grayling, chub, roach, pike; preserved by landowners. (*See Christchurch.*) (*c.s.*)

Woodbridge (Suffolk).—G.E.R. Deben; roach, pike, tench, perch; preserved by landowners. Deben rises above **Debenham**, runs 9 m. to Kettleburgh, 4 m. S.E. from **Framlingham**, and 5 m. down is joined on right bank by Potford brook, 4 m. long. Deben runs 2 m. to **Wickham Market**, and 2 m. down waters the decoy at Ash Abbey close by the railway. Deben runs to **Melton** 4 m., and **Woodbridge** 1 m. 1 m. down, Fyn joins on right bank. Fyn rises 4 m. above **Bealings**, where it waters Playford mere, and 1 m. below is joined on left bank by Otley brook, 7 m. long. 2 m. down, Fyn joins Deben estuary. *Hotels*: Bull, Crown.

KIRTON brook runs 4 m. S. from **Woodbridge** at Brightwell-cum-Foxhall. Kirton rises in Bixley decoy ponds on Black Heath, 2½ m. S.E., from **Ipswich**, runs 3 m. to Brightwell, and 4 m. below joins Deben estuary.

Woodbury Road (Devon).—L. & S.W.R. Woodbury brook. This brook rises E. of Woodbury, and runs 3 m. to the Exe Estuary close to the station.

Woodchester (Gloucester).—M.R. Nailsworth brook. Frome (2 m.) (*See Stonehouse.*)

Woodend (Cumland).—L. & N.W. and Fs.R. Ehen. (*c.s. West Cumberland.*) Keekle. (*See Egremont.*)

Woodford (Essex).—G.E.R. (*See Barking.*) On Roding; few dace and perch.

Wood Green (Middlx.).—G.N.R. On New River. (*See London.*)

Woodhall Spa (Lincoln).—G.N.R. Witham, 1 m. S.W., at **Kirkstead.** Bain, 3 m. E. Haltham Beck, 3 m. E. (*See Boston.*)

Woodhead (Derby).—G.C.R. Etherow. Witherow brook Great and Little Crowdon brooks, 1 m. W. *Lakes*: Woodhead reservoir. Torside reservoir. (*See Runcorn.*)

Woodhouse (Derby).—G.C.R. Shire brook. 1 m. S. Rother, 1 m. E. (*See Goole.*)

Woodhouse Mill (Derby).—M.R. Rother. Pigeon Bridge brook, 2 m. S.E. Shire brook, 2 m. S.W. *Lakes*: Sickers Wood pond, 3 m. E. (*See Goole.*)

Woodland.—Fs.R. Steerspool. (*See Broughton.*)

Woodlesford (Yorks).—M.R.; L. & Y.R. Aire. (*c.s. York.*) Rothwell beck, 1 m. S. (*See Rawcliffe.*)

Woodstock Road (Oxford).—G.W.R. Cherwell. (*See London, M.T.*)

Woofferton (Salop). — G.W.R., L. & N.W.R. Teme; trout, grayling, chub, dace, roach, pike, perch; strictly preserved above, but open below to the members of the Tenbury Angling Club. (*See Tenbury.*) Brimfield brook; trout. *Hotel*: Salwey Arms; the proprietor of which can obtain fishing in the preserved waters of the Teme above Tenbury. (*See Gloucester.*) (*c.s. Severn.*)

Wookey (Somerset).—G.W.R. Ax. (*See Axbridge.*) (*c.s. Avon.*)

Wool (Dorset).—S. & D.R. Frome. Piddle; trout, salmon. (*See Wareham.*) (*c.s.*)

Woolaston (Gloucester).—L. & S.W.R. Cone brook. Cone rises by Hewelsfield, and is 5 m. long.

Woolavington (Somerset).—G.W.R. Brue; roach, perch, carp, pike; free. (*See Highbridge.*) (*c.s. Avon.*)

Wooler (Northland.).—N.E.R. The fishing is good. Till and Glen join below Wooler, running through Millfield Plain into Tweed, and are under the Scotch or Tweed Act, and open for sea trout angling from February to December. If there is a flood to bring the fish over the caulds and dams, whitling, &c., will be met with early in the summer; in the latter end of the season large fish are numerous. There are good pike in the deep waters, and some few perch about Etal. Trouting in the Wooler, Bowmont, and Bremish streams, in the neighbourhood. The Till is free in all but a few places. At the mouth of Till and about Etal the fishing is good, but leave must be obtained from the landed proprietors. Bowmont is preserved. There is some good trout fishing about Canna Mill, and up to Yetholm. College is now preserved, except on the Heathpool ground. Wooler waters may be fished up to Langlee Ford. A small portion is preserved, but leave may be obtained. In summer the water is very low, and there are few pools. From its junction with the Till, upwards of 1½ m., the lower part of the Glen is preserved by Sir H. St. Paul, who kindly grants leave. Mr. Culley preserves the Coupland Castle water, the best part of the Glen, for about 2½ m., and Hon. F. W. Lambton owns the Lanton water, and gives leave for a day or two. Above and up to Langlee Ford, and foot of Cheviots, it is better fishing. At Chaton, 5 m. off, there is some good open water on Till, on the Duke of Northumberland's ground. Nearest part of Coquet is at Weldon Bridge. By driving to Powburn (or, better, Branton), some part of the Bremish can be fished. Begin at Ingram, and fish up. Some miles below, Bremish becomes Till. The wading in Till is dangerous. The Bowmont and College may also be fished from Wooler. Red Lion Hotel and Tankerville Arms are very good inns. For fishing the lower part of Till accommodation can be had at the Blue Bell, Crookham. The water is very heavy, except a few short streams about Ford Islands belonging to the Dowager Marchioness of Waterford, who kindly grants leave to any gentleman leaving his card. Below Milfield (belonging to A. Grey, Esq., who gives leave also) there are some nice streams. Sir H. St. Paul is the owner on one side, and sometimes give leave, and Hon. F. W. Lambton the owner of the other. Here Lord Tankerville's water commences, and he has kindly opened it for the benefit of the inhabitants of Wooler from March 1 to September 30.

Wooton (Gloucester).—(*See Stonehouse.*)

Wootton Bassett (Wilts).—G.W.R. (*See Bristol.*) On Thunder Brook.

Worcester.—G.W.R. Severn; pike, twaite, chub, dace, roach, salmon, trout, &c. Laughern brook. Teme (2 *m.* S.); chub, dace, roach, pike, grayling, trout, salmon; preserved on left bank from Powick Old Bridge to Severn by Mr. Willis Bund, and let to a club; a club also fishes the right bank; above the bridge Mr. Bund preserves privately. Above the mills the water is private. Salwarp (4 *m.* N.); trout and coarse fish. (*See Gloucester.*) (*c.s.*) There is fair fishing in Leigh brook, which can be reached from the n.s. **Bransford-road** Station; let to a club. The brook is private elsewhere, but the farmers will generally give leave. *Hotels*: Star, Unicorn, Great Western, Holt Fleet Hotel at Holt Weir.

Workington (Cumland).—L. & N.W.R.; **Fs.R.** Derwent; trout, salmon. (*c.s.*) *Hotel*: Green Dragon. (*See Cockermouth.*)

Worksop (Notts).—G.N.R. Ryton. Spont, 2 *m.* N.W. Poulter, 5 *m.* S. *Lakes*: Manor Park, 2 *m.* S.W. Carlton lake, 3 *m.* N.W. Carburton, 5 *m.* S. Clumber Park, 5 *m.* S.E. Welbeck Park, 5 *m.* S.W. Langold lake, 5 *m.* N. (*See Althorpe.*)

Worle (Somerset).—G.W.R. *Lakes*: Worle pond; rudd, tench, carp; d.t. 1s., including boat from Mr. Barrett, mineral water merchant, Worle.

Worleston (Cheshire).—L. & N.W.R. Weaver. Pool brook. Wistaston brook. (*See Frodsham.*)

Wormald Green (York.) N.E.R. Robert beck. *Lakes*: Bishop Monkton pond, 3 *m.* N.E. (*See York.*)

Worstead (Norfolk).—G.E.R. Ant, 1 *m.* N.E. Stake beck, 2 *m.* W. *Lakes*: Worstead Hall lake. Westwick Park lake, 1 *m.* W. Scottow pond, 2 *m.* W. Dilham lake, 2 *m.* E. Dilham Broad, 2 *m.* S.E. (*See Yarmouth.*)

Worthington (Leicester).—M.R. Breedon. Carr brook, 2 *m.* W. *Lakes*: Dog Kennel pool and two other ponds, 2 *m.* W. Stanton Hall ponds, 2 *m.* N.W. Calke Park ponds, 3 *m.* N.W. (*See Gainsborough.*)

Wranagton (Devon).—G.W.R. (*See Ivy Bridge.*)

Wraysbury (Bucks.).—L. & S.W.R. (*See London, M.T. and L.T.*) Thames, Colne, and Fleet. Trout, jack, barbel, chub, roach, and perch. *Inn*: George. *Fishermen*: W. and H. Haines. The Colne is preserved by the City of London Piscatorial Society. Fishing good. Chub, dace, roach, pike. The Fleet holds roach, dace, chub, and barbel; fishing free.

Wreay (Cumland).—L. & N.W.R. Petterill; trout. Scotby beck, 2 *m.* E. (*See Carlisle.*)

Wrenbury (Cheshire).—L. & N.W.R. Weaver. Marbury brook. Sales brook, 2 *m.* S. Baddiley brook, 2 *m.* N. *Lakes*: Combermere mere, 2 *m.* S.; pike, perch, roach; leave sometimes from the steward. Baddiley mere, 2 *m.* N. Cholmondeley mere, 4 *m.* N.W. (*See Frodsham.*)

Wressel (York).—N.E.R. Derwent. Derwent rises on Wykeham High Moor, 8 *m.* above **Hackness**, and 3 *m.* down is joined on the left bank by Jugger Howe beck. This brook rises by Biller Howe, 3 *m.* S.W. of **Fyling Hall**. 8 *m.* down, Helwath beck, 3 *m.* long, joins on left bank (this stream rises 1 *m.* S.W. of **Peak**), and Bloody beck, 2 *m.* long on right bank. 4 *m.* down, Jugger Howe beck joins Derwent. 3 *m.* down Derwent, 2 *m.* from **Hackness**, Black beck joins on right bank. This stream, under the name of Grain beck, rises on Alleston Moor, and 6 *m.* down is joined on left bank by Stockland beck. 3 *m.* long. 1 *m.* down, Hipper beck, 3 *m.* long, joins Black beck on left bank. 1 *m.* down Black beck, Deepdale beck, 2 *m.* long, joins on right bank. 1 *m.* down, Black beck joins Derwent, 1 *m.* down at Hilla Green Bridge (preserved above for some distance by Capt. Johnstone, but free above and below to Preston Ings by the Derwent Angling Club). Troutsdale beck, 4 *m.* long, joins Derwent on right bank. Derwent runs to **Hackness**, 1 *m.*, and here Lowdales beck, 3 *m.* long, joines on left bank. Derwent runs to **Ayton** and **Forge Valley**, 5 *m.*, 3 *m.* to Preston Ings, where the water of the Derwent Angling Club ends, and **Ganton**, 3 *m.* 1 *m.* *above* this station, Helford river joins on left bank. Helford rises by **Gristhorpe**, 1 station from **Filey**, runs 3 *m.* to **Cayton** (1 *m.* off on right bank), and joins Derwent 4 *m.* below. 2 *m.* below **Ganton**, Ruston beck joins on right bank. Ruston, under the name of Beedale beck, rises 3 *m.* above **Wykeham**, at which village it is joined on the right bank by Sawdon beck, which rises by **Sawdon**, and is 3 *m.* long. Ruston runs to Derwent in 3 *m.* Derwent runs 1 *m.*, where Brompton beck, which rises above Brompton, 2 *m.* S.W.

of **Wykeham**, and is 4 *m.* long, joins on right bank. Derwent runs to **Yedingham.** (n.s. **Kesterton**, 1 *m.*), and 1 *m.* down by Newstead Grange is joined on left bank by Scampston beck. This brook rises in a pond by Wintringham. 2 *m.* E. of **Rillington**, runs to Scampton Park, where it waters the lake (n.s. **Rillington**, 1 *m.*), and joins Derwent 2 *m.* down. 1 *m.* down Derwent, Thornton beck joins on right bank. Thornton rises on Allerston Moor, 2 *m.* E. of **Levisham**, runs 5 *m.* to **Wilton** (1 *m.* off on left bank), 2 *m.* to **Thornton Dale**, and joins Derwent 4 *m.* down. Derwent runs to Ryemouth, 3 *m.*, **Rillington** Station being 1 *m.* off on left bank. Here Rye joins on right bank. Rye rises on the slopes of the Cleveland Hills, 14 *m.* above **Helmsley**, and 3 *m.* down is joined on left bank by Prodale beck, 3 *m.* long. 1½ *m.* down, Wheat beck, 3 *m.* long, joins Rye on right bank. 2 *m.* down, Blow Gill beck, 3 *m.* long, joins on left bank. 3 *m.* down Rye at Hawnly, Ladhill beck, 4 *m.* long, joins on left bank. 1 *m.* down Rye, Seph joins on left bank. Seph is formed by the junction of **Raisdale** and Bilsdale becks, each some 3 *m.* long, both rising some 6 *m.* S.E. of **Stokesley**. 3 *m.* down Seph, Ledge beck, 4 *m.* long, joins on left bank. Seph runs to Rye, 6 *m.* Rye runs to **Rievaulx**, 3 *m.*, **Helmsley**, 5 *m.* (preserved *above* by Lord Feversham, below to Nunnington Bridge by the Rydale Angling Club), **Nunnington**, 4 *m.* 3 *m.* below, Riccal joins on left bank. Riccal rises on Helmsley Moor, 6 *m.* N. of **Helmsley**, and joins Rye 7 *m.* below. Half a mile below the junction of Rye and Riccal, Dove joins on left bank. Dove rises on Farndale Moor, 12 *m.* above **Kirkby Moorside**, and 2 *m.* below that place is joined on right bank by Hodge Beck, which rises in two branches on Bunsdale Moor, 10 *m.* above **Kirkby Moorside**, and joins Dove 2 *m.* below. Dove joins Rye 4 *m.* down by Salton. 1 *m.* down Rye, Hole beck joins on right bank. Hole rises above **Gilling**, runs 1 *m.* N. of **Hovingham** at Stonegrave, and 2 *m.* below is joined on right bank by Marro beck, which rises above Cotton Mill Pond, 2 *m.* above **Hovingham**, through which village it runs and joins Hole 2 *m.* below. Hole runs 2 *m.* to Rye. Just above the junction, Wath beck joins Hole on right bank. Wath rises in the lakes in the park. 3 *m.* S. of **Hovingham**, runs to **Hovingham**, 1 *m.* off on left bank. 2 *m.*, **Slingsby**, 2 *m.*, and joins Rye 2 *m.* below. 2 *m.* down Rye, Severn joins on left bank. Severn rises on Rosedale Common, 12 *m.* above **Swinington**. 4 *m.* down at Rosedale Abbey, Northdale beck, 3 *m.* long, joins on left bank. 3 *m.* down, Harloft beck, 4 *m.* long, joins on left bank. 3 *m.* down, Sutherland beck, 3 *m.* long, joins on left bank. Severn runs to **Swinington**, 4 *m.* 1 *m.*, below, Catter beck joins on right bank. Catter, named Rudland in its upper course, rises on Spaunton Moor, 5 *m.* N. of **Kirkby Moorside**, and runs in 5 *m.* within a mile of that town the *other* side of Dove, and joins Severn 2 *m.* below. Severn runs to Normanby, 2 *m.*, and joins Rye 4 *m.* down at Brawby. 6 *m.* down Rye at Howe Bridge, 3 *m.* N.E. of **Malton**, Costa beck joins on left bank. Costa rises near Middleton, 4 *m.* N.W. of **Pickering** (preserved by Costa Anglers' Club). and 5 *m.* down, Pickering beck joins on left bank. Pickering beck rises 3 *m.* above **Levisham** Station, and 2 *m.* below that place is joined on left bank by Levisham beck, which runs through **Levisham**, and is 4 *m.* long. Pickering beck runs to **Pickering**, 5 *m.*, and joins Costa at Kirkby Misperton, 3 *m.* down. Costa joins Rye 4 *m.* below. Rye joins Derwent 1 *m.* down. 1 *m.* down Derwent, Settrington beck, which rises in Settrington Lake, 3 *m.* S.E. of **Malton**, and is 4 *m.* long, joins on left bank. Derwent runs to **Malton**, 2 *m.* 2 *m.* down is the outflow of Welham pond, ½ *m.* up on left bank. Derwent runs 2 *m.* to **Hutton Ambro**. Here Menethorpe beck, which rises in a pond at Birdsall Ings, 1 *m.* W. of **Wharram**, and is 5 *m.* long, join on left bank. 1 *m.* down Derwent, Howl beck and Mile beck, each 3 *m.* long, joins on left bank, both streams uniting just above their junction with Derwent. Derwent runs 3 *m.* to **Castle Howard**. Here Oram beck, which rises in the great lake in Castle Howard Park, 3 *m.* up, joins on right bank. Derwent runs to Howsham Bridge 3 *m.* Here Spittle beck joins on right bank. Spittle, under the name of Bulmer beck, rises above Dalby 4 *m.* S. of **Hovingham**, runs 4 *m.* to Bulmer. **Barton Mill** 3 *m.*, and joins Derwent 3 *m.* down. 1 *m.* down, White Carr beck and Loppington beck, each 3 *m.* long, join Derwent on left bank at the same spot. Derwent runs 1 *m.* to Scrayingham, where Swallowpits beck, 3 *m.* long, joins on left bank. Derwent runs 2 *m.*, where Skirpen beck, 6 *m.* long, joins on left bank Derwent runs to **Stamford Bridge** 2 *m.* Here the outfall of two ponds on Buttercrambe Moor, 1 *m.* up, joins on right bank. Derwent runs to **Kexby** 3 *m.* (n.s. **Fangfoss**, 3 *m.*), **Sutton-on-Derwent** (n.s. **Fangfoss**, 5 *m.*). and 2 *m.* down, at Ings Bridge, Foss beck, which rises in three different branches joining 2 *m.* above **Fangfoss**, and is 7 *m.* long, joins on left bank. Derwent runs to **East Cottingwith** (n.s. **Bubwith**, 4 *m.*), and 4 *m.* down reaches **Bubwith**. Derwent runs 2 *m.* to **Breighton** (n.s. **Menthorpe**, 1 *m.*), and **Wrestel** 2 *m.* Derwent joins Ouse 2 *m.* down.

Wright Green (Cumland).—Marron. (*c.s. Derwent.*) Woodbeck, 1 *m.* S. (*See Cockermouth.*)

Wroxham (Norfolk).—G.E.R. Bure; roach, bream, pike, perch, tench; fishing from boats only generally permitted. Spixworth beck, 3 *m.* S.W. Ant, 6 *m.* E. *Lakes*: Brickfield Broad, right bank and Belaugh Broad, left bank (E. S. Trafford, Esq.). Bridge Broad, right bank; fishing from King's Head Hotel. Knapes water left bank. Wroxham Broad, right bank; fishing, 2*s.* 6*d.* per boat by ticket, from J. Major or T. Ellis. (*c.s. N. and S.*) Hoveton Hall lake, 1 *m.* N. Hoveton Great Broad, left bank, 2 *m.* S.E. (J. H. Hackblock, Esq.); private. (*c.s. N. and S.*) Salhouse Broad, right bank, 2 *m.* S.E. (John Cator, Esq.); private. Little Hoveton Broad, 2 *m.* N.E. Burnt Fen Broad, 3 *m.* E. King's water, 3 *m.* E. Beeston Hall lake, 4 *m.* N.E. Oliver Broad, 6 *m.* N.E.; private (*See Yarmouth.*) *Hotels*: King's Head, Horse Shoes.

Wye (Kent).—S.E.& C.R. On Stour; jack, roach, &c.; the fishing free, but, owing to the weeds, not good until late in the season. 3 *m.* below Wye the river belongs to J. S. W. Erle Drax, Esq, of Olanteigh Towers, Wye. The lake in Eastwell Park holds good pike. (*c.s.*) (*See Sandwich.*) *Inns*: Victoria, King's Head.

Wykeham (York).—N.E.R. Beedale beck. Sawdon beck. Brompton beck, 2 *m.* S.W. at Brompton. Derwent, 3 *m.* S. (*See Wressel.*)

Wylye (Wilts).—G.W.R. Wylye; trout, grayling; preserved by Wilton Fly-fishing Club (*see Wilton.*) *See Christchurch.*) (*c.s. Avon.*)

Wymondham (Norfolk).—G.E.R. Bass. Tiffey. Dyke beck. 2 *m.* Hackford brook, 2½ *m.* N.W., at Crownthorpe. Yare, 6 *m.* N., at Marlingford. *Lakes*: Kimberley Park lake, 3 *m.* N.W. Wicklewood mere. 4 *m.* W. Ketteringham Hall lakes 4 *m.* E. Sea mere, 5 *m.* W., by Hingham. (*See Yarmouth.*)

Wyre (Worcester).—G.W.R. Dowles brook; trout, Severn (3 *m.* E.): salmon, trout, grayling, chub, dace, pike, perch, &c. (*See Gloucester.*) (*c.s. Severn.*)

Wyvenhoe (Essex).—G.E.R. Roman river. This stream joins Colne estuary on right bank opposite Wyvenhoe. It rises by **Marks**, and 3 *m.* down is joined on right bank by a short stream draining the lake at Birch Hall, 4 *m.* S.E. of **Marks.** 4 *m.* down, Roman river is joined on right bank by Layer brook, 9 *m.* long. The main stream runs 4 *m.* to **Wyvenhoe.** 1 *m.* E. are 3 ponds at Villa Farm.

Yalding (Kent).—S.E.&C.R. (*See Rochester.*) On Medway; pike, perch, roach, bream, &c.; preserved from Allington Lock, below Maidstone to East Lock, near Tonbridge, by the Maidstone Angling and Medway Preservation Society; hon. sec., Frank J. Munn, 17, Bower-street, Maidstone; d., w., and m.t. Teise; coarse fish Beult; coarse fish, trout; mostly private. *Hotel*: George.

Yarmouth (Norfolk).—G.E.R. Waveney; pike, perch, bream, roach. Yare; same fish. Bure; same fish. *Lakes*: Fritton Decoy, 6 *m.* S.W. Waveney rises above **Diss**, where is Diss mere, and 4 *m.* down is joined on right bank by Eye brook, which rises 8 *m.* above **Eye**, and joins Waveney 6 *m.* down by Oakley Park. Waveney runs 7 *m.* to **Harleston**, 1 *m.* off on left bank, **Homersfield** 5 *m.*, **Bungay** 6 *m.* Here the river makes a loop of 3 *m.*, running again through the town, and 2 *m.* down is joined on left bank by a brook draining the lakes at Ditchingham Hall, 2½ *m.* N. of **Bungay.** Waveney runs 2 *m.* to **Geldeston, Beccles** 2 *m.* 9 *m.* down, 2½ *m.* N.W. from **Mutford**, a cutting on right bank joins the river with Oulton Broad, which runs to **Lowestoft** through Lake Lothing. **Mutford** being at the junction of Oulton with Lothing. ½ *m.* down Waveney the outflow, 1 *m.* long, of Flixton Decoy, and the lake at the Villa, 2½ *m.* N. from **Mutford**, joins on right bank. Waveney runs to **Somerleyton** 2 *m.*, **Haddiscoe** 2 *m.*, just below which place the outflow of Fritton Decoy, 1 *m.* up, joins on right bank. Here also is the New Cut, 3 *m.* long, joining Yare with Waveney. Waveney runs to **Belton** 3 *m.* (1 *m.* off on right bank), and 2 *m.* down joins Breydon water. Here Yare joins on left bank.

YARE rises above **Hardingham**, and here Blackwater river, 6 *m.* long, joins on right bank. 7 *m.* down Yare, by Barford, Bass river joins on right bank. Bass rises 4 *m.* above **Wymondham**, where it is joined by Tiffey river, 4 *m.* long; 2 *m.* down, Dyke beck, 3 *m.* long, joins on left bank. 1 *m.* down, Bass waters the lake in Kimberley Park (n.s. **Kimberley**, 1 *m.*), and here Hackford brook joins on left bank. Hackford rises in Sea mere, 1 *m.* S.E. from **Hingham** (n.s. **Kimberley**, 3 *m.*), and 2 *m.* down, at Hackford, waters Wicklewood mere, 2 *m.* S. from **Kimberley**, and 3 *m.* down joins Kimberley Park pond. Bass runs 4 *m.* to Yare. 10 *m.* down Yare, ½ *m.* below Cringleford, 3 *m.* S.W. from **Norwich**, a brook, 3 *m.* long, joins on right bank, draining the lakes at Ketteringham Hall 1 *m.* S. from **Hethersett**, and the lakes at Bracon Hall and Carlton Lodge, 2 *m.* W. of **Swainthorpe.** Yare runs 3 *m.* to **Norwich**, and here Taes joins on right bank. Taes rises above **Forncett**, runs 3 *m.* to **Flordon, Swainthorpe** 4 *m.*, and Yare and **Norwich** 5 *m.* Yare runs 2 *m.* to the other side of the city, and here Wensum joins on left bank. Wensum rises above **Fakenham**, runs 3 *m.* to **Ryburgh, North Elmham** 7 *m.*, **Lenwade** 10 *m.*, and here Blackwater brook joins, which rises in Black lake, 1½ *m.* N. from **Cawston**, runs thence to **Reepham** 2 *m.*, and **Lenwade** and Wensum 3 *m.* 1 *m.* down Wensum a brook joins on left bank, 5 *m.* long, draining the lake at Haveringland 2 *m.* S. from **Cawston.** Wensum runs 1 *m.* to **Attlebridge**, 8 *m.* to **Drayton**, and **Hellesdon** 2 *m.*, and here Costessey brook joins on right bank. This brook rises by **Yaxham**, runs 7 *m.* to Honingham, where is a large pond at the Hop Grounds 4 *m.* S. from **Attlebridge**, and runs 5 *m.* to Wensum, which runs to **Norwich** and Yare 5 *m* Yare runs to **Whitlingham** 3 *m.*, **Brundall** 4 *m.* (here is Surlingham Broad on right bank). 1 *m.* down a brook joins on left bank, draining the lakes in Plumpstead Hall 2 *m.* N. of **Brundall.** ½ *m.* down Yare on left bank is Strumpshaw Broad, and just below, Rockland Broad on right bank. ½ *m.* down Yare is **Buckenham**, and 1 *m.* down the outflow of Buckenham Broad and Hasingham Broad joins on left bank. Yare runs 2 *m.* to **Cantley**, and 2 *m.* below is joined on right bank by Chet, which rises in the lake at Brook Hall, 8 *m.* S.E. of **Norwich**, runs to **Loddon** (n.s. **Beccles**, 7 *m.*) 5 *m.*, and Yare 4 *m.* Yare runs to **Reedham** 2 *m.*, where the New Cut, joining Yare and Waveney, enters Yare, and 4 *m.*

down runs into Breydon water at **Berney Arms** Station. Breydon water is salt, and is 4 m. long, **Yarmouth** being at the lower end.

BURE joins the sea at **Yarmouth**. Bure rises in Melton Park lake, 1 m. N. from **Kindolveston**, runs 4 m. to Thurning, where it waters the lake in Thurning Hall, thence 3 m. to **Corpusty**, and 4 m. below at Blicking Mill a stream joins on left bank, watering two ponds by Apple Tree Plantation ½ m. up, 4 m. N.W. from **Aylsham**. 1 m. down Bure, Aldborough beck joins on left bank. Aldborough rises in the lake in Felbrigg Park, 5 m. S.W. from **Cromer**, runs 4 m. to Aldborough and its mill pond, 5 m. N. from **Aylsham**, and 1 m. down is joined on right bank by a brook, 3 m. long, draining the lake in Barningham Park by Town Barningham, 4½ m. N.E. from **Corpusty**. Aldborough joins Bure 2 m. below. ½ m. down Bure is the outflow, on right bank, of the lake at Blickling, ½ m. up, 2 m. N.W. from **Aylsham**, and 2 m. down, Bure reaches **Aylsham**, 5 m. down Bure, just above **Buxton**, Gunton beck and Stake beck join on left bank. Gunton beck rises in the lakes and ponds in Gunton Park (Lord Suffield) by **Gunton**, runs 2 m. to **Felmingham**, and 4 m. down joins Bure. Stake beck rises in the Perch pond and mill pond in Heath Plantation, 2 m. S. of **North Walsham**, runs 2 m. to Scottow pond, 2 m. W. of **Worstead**, and Bure at **Buxton** 1 m. Bure runs 3 m. to **Coltishall**, and 3 m. down, 2 m. S.W. from **Wroxham**, Spixworth beck, which rises by Horsham St. Faith. 2½ m. N.E. from **Drayton** and is 6 m. long, joins on right bank. 1 m. down Bure is Brickfield Broad on right bank, and on left bank Belaugh Broad : a little further down, is Little Belaugh Broad on right bank. ½ m. down on right bank is Bridge Broad, then on left bank two backwaters from the river and Knapes water. These broads are all close to **Wroxham**. Opposite Knapes water on right bank is the top of Wroxham Broad, 1 m. long, and Hoveton Great Broad on left bank. Next to Wroxham is Salhouse Broad, 1 m. N.E. of **Salhouse**. ½ m. down Bure is Decoy or Woodbastwick Broad on right bank, 2 m. N.E. of **Salhouse**. On the opposite or left bank is Little Hoveton Broad, 2 m. E. of **Wroxham**. Here Hoveton brook, which rises in the Hoveton Hall lake 1 m. N. of **Wroxham**, runs 2 m. to Burnt Fen Broad and King's water, 3 m. E. of **Wroxham**, and waters Hoveton Broad, joins on left bank; accommodation can be had at New Inn and Horning Ferry, close by these broads. Bure runs 2 m., when the outflow of Little Broad, ½ m. up, 3 m. E. of **Salhouse**, joins on right bank. ½ m. down Bure on right bank is Ransworth Broad, 1 m. long, 4 m. E. of **Salhouse**. 2 m. down Bure, at Horning Hall, Ant joins on left bank. Ant rises in the Antingham ponds, 2 m. N.W. from **North Walsham**, and 4 m. down runs 1 m. E. of that town, and 4 m. below, at **Horning**, waters Dilham lake. 2 m. down, an arm, Dilham Broad, runs up on the right bank to Dilham, and this is watered by a brook which drains Worstead House lake by **Worstead** 2 m. up. Ant runs to Stalham Broad by **Stalham** 2 m., and 1 m. below waters Barton Broad, ½ m. long, 1 m. W. of **Catfield**. The drainings, 1 m. long, of Beeston Hall lake, 4 m. N.E. of **Wroxham**, join the right arm of Barton Broad. 1½ m. down Ant is a broad on left bank 1 m. S.W. from **Catfield**, and here also the drainings of Oliver Broad, 1 m. up, join on right bank. Oliver is 5 m. N.E. from **Wroxham**. ½ m. below on left bank of Ant is a pond, and 3 m. down Ant, joins Bure. ½ m. down Bure, Fleet dyke joins on right bank. This rises in Pedham Mill dam, 4 m. S.E. from **Salhouse**, runs 2 m. to Walsham Broad. 5 m. E. of **Salhouse**, and 1 m. down joins Bure. 2 m. down Bure, the Hundred stream or Thurne joins on left bank. This runs down from above Martham Broad by **Martham**, and here the drainings of Horsey mere, 1 m. up, join on right bank. Horsey is 4 m. N. from **Martham**. 1 m. below, Hundred stream joins on right bank Hickling, Chapman, and Whitesley Broad, and these are practically one large lake, 3 m. long. **Potter Higham** lying half-way down it. 3 m. down Hundred stream, on right bank, is Womack Broad by Ludham, 2 m. S. of **Catfield**. 1 m. down. at Thurne (*Inn*, Red Lion), is the Bure, which runs to **Acle** 4 m. Here Muck Fleet joins on the left bank. This waterway is 4 m. long, and runs out of Ormsby, Rollesby, and Filby Broad, one large lake, 4 m. long, near **Ormesby**. 1 m. down Bure, Tunstall dyke joins on right bank, draining Acle Decoy, ½ m. S. of **Acle**. Bure runs 9 m. to **Yarmouth**. Leave to fish in most of the broads must be obtained, but the rivers are free. The broads and rivers hold pike, perch, tench, bream, roach, rudd, and carp. Good sea fishing from the pier and from the beach with throw-out lines : whiting fishing good from September to November. *Hotels* : Angel, Bath House. Bridge, Crown and Anchor, Norfolk, Royal, Queen's, Victoria. (*c.s. Norfolk.*) *Fishing stations within two hours of the town* : St. Olave's, Beccles, Geldeston, Bungay, Reedham, Cantley, Buckenham, Brundall, Acle, Ormesby, Martham, Potter Higham, Stalham, North Walsham. *Tackleist*, A. J. Rudd.

Yarnton (Oxford).—G.W.R. (*See London, U T.*)

Yarton (Salop).—L. & N.W.R. Sundown brook. *Lakes* : Yarton pool. (*See Gloucester.*)

Yate (Gloucester).—M.R. (*See Bristol; Frome.*) On Boyd, 7 m. *Lakes* : Doddington Park lake, 6 m.; carp, perch; leave from Sir G. Codrington. Badminton Park lake, 8 m.; carp; Duke of Beaufort; leave from Mr. Thompson, the steward, at Badminton. There is good roach and perch fishing at Nibley Mills on Frome. (*See Bristol; Iron Acton.*)

Yaxham (Norfolk).—G.E.R. Costessey brook. (*See Yarmouth.*)

Yealmpton (Devon).—G.W.R. Yealm: trout: preserved. Good bass, pollack, and other sea fishing. 4 m. off. at Newton Ferrers, is a good hotel—the River Yealm. *Tackleist* : W. Hearder, Union-street, Plymouth (*see Advertisement*). (*See Cornwood.*)

Yedingham (York), n.s. **Hesterton**, 1 *m.* Derwent; grayling, chub, pike, coarse fish; free. (*See Wressel.*).

Yeldham (Essex).—G.E.R. Colne; pike, perch, roach; permission freely given by the farmers. (*See Colchester.*)

Yeovil (Somerset).—L. & S.W.R.; G.W.R. Yeo; coarse fish and a few trout. *Hotel:* Mermaid. (*See Bridgwater.*) (*c.s. Avon.*)

Yeovil Junction (Somerset).—L. & S.W.R. Yeo. (*See Bridgwater.*) (*c.s. Avon.*)

Yetminster (Dorset).—G.W.R. (*See Bridgwater.*)

Ynysddu (Monmouth).—S.B. Sirhowey; trout. (*See Newport.*)

Yockleton (Salop).—L. & N.W.R.; G.W.R. Yockleton brook. Rea (2½ *m.* S.); trout, grayling. (*See Gloucester*). (*c.s. Severn.*)

York.—G.E. & G.N. Joint R.; G.N.R.; N.E.R.; L. & N.W.R.; M.R.; G.C.R.; L. & Y.R.; N.B.R. Ouse. (*c.s. York.*) Foss. Tang Hall beck. Osbaldwick beck. Ouse is formed by the junction of Swale and Ure 2 *m.* below **Burroughbridge.** Swale rises on Birkdale Common, 5 *m.* S.E. of **Kirkby Stephen.** 2 *m.* down, Little Steddale beck (trout; free), 3 *m.* long, joins on right bank. 1 *m.* below, 7 *m.* S.E. of **Kirkby Stephen,** the outfall of Birkdale tarn, ½ *m.* up, joins on left bank. 1 *m.* down Swale, Great Steddale beck (trout; free), 2 *m.* long, joins on right bank. 1 *m.* down Swale, Whitsundale beck (trout), 5 *m.* long, joins on left bank. 1 *m.* down Swale, at **Keld**, Stonesdale beck, 3 *m.* long, joins on left bank. Swale runs 3 *m.* to **Muker.** Here Muker beck (trout) joins on right bank. Muker rises in Stockdale, and 2 *m.* down is joined at Thwaite on right bank by Thwaite beck (trout), 2 *m.* long. Hence to **Muker** is 1 *m.* 1 *m.* down Swale, Oxnop beck, 2 *m.* long, joins on right bank. Swale runs 1 *m.* to Gunnerside (*inn*, King's Head). 1 *m.* down Swale, Gunnerside beck (spoilt by lead mines), 4 *m.* long, joins on left bank. 2 *m.* down Swale, Summerlodge or Crackpot beck (trout), which rises in Summerlodge tarn, 3 *m.* N. of **Askrigg**, and is 3 *m.* long, joins on right bank. 3 *m.* down Swale, Healaugh beck, 5 *m.* long, joins on left bank. Swale runs 2 *m.* to **Reeth.** Here Arkle beck joins on left bank. Arkle beck (injured by lead mines) rises in Arkengarthdale Moor, and 5 *m.* down is joined on right bank by Roe beck, 2 *m.* long. 2 *m.* down Arkle, Straw beck, 3 *m.* long, joins on left bank. Arkle runs to Swale 5 *m.* Swale runs 4 *m.*, when Gill beck (trout) joins on right bank. Gill rises in Preston Moor, 4 *m.* N.W. of **Leyburn.** 6 *m.* down, Stainton Moor beck, 3 *m.* long, joins on left bank. 1 *m.* below is Swale. 1 *m.* down Swale, by Marske, Marske beck (trout) joins on left bank. Marske, under the name of Arndale, rises on Hexwith Moor, 6 *m.* N. across the hills from **Reeth.** 3 *m.* down, Moresdale beck, 2 *m.* long, joins on right bank, 5 *m.* N. from **Reeth.** 3 *m.* down, Throstle beck, 3 *m.* long, joins on left bank. Marske runs 3 *m.* to Swale. 1 *m.* down Swale, Clapgate beck, 2 *m.* long, joins on left bank. Swale runs to **Richmond**, 5 *m.* 1 *m.* down, Sand beck, 4 *m.* long, joins on right bank. 2 *m.* down Swale, Colburn beck, 6 *m.* long, joins on right bank. Swale runs 1 *m.* to Brompton-on-Swale and **Catterick** Bridge, close to the Catterick station. Here Skeeby beck joins on left bank. Skeeby, under the name of Dalton beck, rises on Hornbriggs, runs to Ravensworth 4 *m.*, 3 *m.* to Hartforth, where Smelt Mill beck, 3 *m.* long, joins on right bank. Skeeby beck runs to Gilling 1 *m.*, 3 *m.* N. of **Richmond.** 1 *m.* below, Aske beck joins on right bank. Aske rises in Richmond Moor, runs 3 *m.* to Aske Hall, where it waters Aske Hall lake, 1 *m.* N. of **Richmond,** and joins Skeeby 1 *m.* below. Skeeby runs 4 *m.* to Swale. Swale runs 3 *m.* to **Catterick.** Here Brough beck joins on right bank. Brough beck, under the name of Scotton beck, rises in Calfhole tarn on Barden Moor, 4 *m.* N. of **Spennithorne**, or 4 *m.* S.W. of **Richmond,** and 8 *m.* down, 1 *m.* above **Catterick**, is joined on the right bank by Tunstall beck, 4 *m.* long. 1 *m.* below the junction is **Catterick** and Swale. Swale runs to Langton 5 *m.* Here Scorton beck joins on the left bank. Scorton, called Fivehill beck, in its upper course rises above Middleton Tyas, runs thence to **Scorton** Station 3 *m.* Here Howl beck, 4 *m.* long, joins on the left bank, and Bridgeworth beck, which rises above Moulton and is 3 *m.* long, joins on right bank. Scorton runs to **Scorton** 1 *m.*, and joins Swale 5 *m.* below. A little below Langton, the Stell, 5 *m.* long, joins on left bank. Swale runs to **Scruton** on right bank, and **Ainderby** on left bank. 2 *m.* down, Bedale beck joins on right bank. Bedale, under the name of Garriston, rises in the high and low ponds on Barden Moor, 3 *m.* N. of **Spennithorne**, runs to Garriston 2 *m.* N. of **Constable Burton**, and thence 2 *m.* to Hunton, 2 *m.* N. of **Fingall**, and 3 *m.* below is joined on right bank by Newton beck. Newton, under the name of Broomber beck, rises in Broomber Rigg, 2 *m.* N. of **Wensley**, runs 4 *m.* to within 1 *m.* N. of **Leyburn**, and 3 *m.* below, at **Constable Burton**, is joined on left bank by Bellerby beck, which rises above **Bellerby** 2 *m.* N. of **Leyburn**. and is 4 *m.* long. Newton runs 1 *m.* to **Fingall**, and joins Bedale 2 *m.* down. Bedale runs to **Crakehall** 1 *m.*, **Bedale** 2 *m.*, **Leeming** 3 *m.*, and joins Swale 2 *m.* below. Swale runs to Maunby (n.s. **Newby Wiske**) 1 *m.*, and 2 *m.* below, by Scarborough House, **Pickhill** being 1 *m.* off on right bank, Wiske river joins Swale on left bank. Wiske rises on Whorlton Moor 6 *m.* above **West Rounton**, runs 6 *m.* to **Cowton. Danby Wiske** 4 *m.*, **Northallerton** 4 *m.*, and here Brompton beck joins on left bank. Brompton rises some 4 *m.* above **Brompton**, and at that place is joined on left bank by Winton beck, 4 *m.* long. Brompton runs to **Northallerton** 2 *m.*, and joins Wiske 1 *m.* below. Wiske runs 3 *m.* to **Newby Wiske**, and Swale 4 *m.* Swale runs 3 *m.* to **Skipton Bridge** (n.s. **Baddersby**, being 1 *m.* off on left bank, 4 *m.*), **Topcliffe** (n.s.

Sessay) 3 m., Here Cod beck joins on left bank. Codbeck rises above Toxton 3 m. E. of **Brompton.** Here Howl beck, 3 m. long, joins on left bank. 6 m. down Cod near Braywith Hall, 2 m. E. of **Otterington,** Broad beck joins on left bank. Broad beck rises above Over Silton, and 5 m. down is joined on left bank by Sorrow beck, 4 m. long. 2 m. below Broad beck joins Cod. Cod runs 2 m. to **N. Kilvington.** Here Spittle-beck, 4 m. long, joins on left bank. Cod runs to **Thirsk,** 3 m. 4 m. down by Dalton, 1 m. W. of **Sessay** station, Fisher beck, 3 m. long, joins on left bank, and Willow beck, also on the same side. Willow beck, under the name of Lunshaw beck, rises 2 m. above Boltby, 5 m. N.E. of **Thirsk,** and 5 m. down at Balk, 4 m. S.E. of **Thirsk,** Hood beck, 4 m. long, joins on left bank. 5 m. below, Willow beck joins Cod. Cod now runs 2 m. to Swale. Swale runs to **Brafferton** 5 m. Here Sun beck joins on left bank. Sun beck, under the name of Hole beck, rises above **Gilling,** runs 2 m. to **Ampleforth,** where the outflow of the lake in Gilling park joins on left bank. 2 m. down Sun is the outflow of the lakes of Park House, 2 m. up on the left bank. Sun runs to **Coxwold** 3 m., **Husthwaite** 2 m. Hole, now taking the name of Hole beck, runs 5 m. to **Pillmoor** and 3 m. to **Brafferton** and Swale. Swale runs 4 m. to Myton-on-Swale, and here Ure joins on right bank. Ure rises on Abbotside Common, and runs 4 m. to Moorcock Inn, **Hawes,** (here begins the water of the Hawes Angling Association.) 4 m. down Ure, Cotterdale beck, 5. m. long, joins on right bank, ¼ m. down Widdale beck joins on right bank. Widdale rises at Old Widdale Head, 4 m. N. of **Ribble Head.** Lake Semmerwater (Hawes Angling Association, sec., T. T. Fawcett, Hawes), 4 m. S.E., across the hills from **Hawes.** 2 m. down Widdale, Snaizholme beck, which rises in Snaizholme Head, and is 3 m. long, joins on right bank. Widdale runs to Ure 2 m. ½ m. down Ure close to **Hawes,** Hearne beck, 5 m. long, joins on left bank. Ure runs to **Hawes,** 1 m. Here Duerley beck, 5 m. long, joins on right bank. Ure runs to **Askrigg** 1 m., Bainbridge Bridge 5 m. (here ends the water of the Hawes Association). Here Bain river joins on right bank. Bain, under the name of Cragdale water, rises in Middletongue tarn 10 m. across the hills from **Askrigg,** 1 m. below a stream joins on right bank, draining Cray tarn 10 m, S. of **Askrigg.** 3 m. down Bain, Raydale beck, which rises in Outershaw tarn, and is 4 m. long, joins Bain on left bank. Just below, Bardale beck, 4 m. long, joins on left bank. Bain runs ½ m. to Semmerwater. The outflow from this lake, taking the name of Bain, runs 3 m. to Ure. Just opposite the junction of Bain with Ure, Sargill beck, 5 m. long, joins on left bank. 1 m. down Ure by **Askrigg,** Cogill beck, 4 m. long, joins on left bank. Ure runs to **Aysgarth,** 4 m. (the river is private below). 2 m. down, Bishopdale beck, 8 m. long, joins on the right bank. ¼ m. up Bishopdale from its junction with the Ure, Walden beck, 7 m. long, joins Bishopdale on right bank. 1 m. down Ure at **Redmire,** Beldon beck joins on left bank. Beldon rises on Carperby Moor, and 3 m. below is joined on right bank by the outflow of Locker tarn, ¼ m. up. This lake is 1 m. N. of **Carperby.** Beldon runs 2 m. to Ure. A little way below, Apedale beck, 4 m. long, joins on left bank. Ure runs 3 m. to **Wensley, Leyburn,** 1 m., **Middleham,** 2 m. 1 m. below **Middleham** the Cover joins the Ure just below Ellshaw Bridge on right bank. Cover rises on Cover Head Moor. 4 m. N. of **Kettlewell,** and is 16 m. long. 2 m. down Ure, Sowden beck, 4 m. long, joins on right bank. Ure runs 9 m. to **Masham,** where Burn joins on right bank. Burn rises in Thorny Grane Moor, and 3 m. below is joined on left bank by Birkgull beck, 3 m. long. 1 m. down Burn, Sprucegill beck, 4 m. long, joins on right bank. 2 m. down Burn, Grimesgill beck, 5 m. long, joins on right bank. 2 m. down Burn, Sale beck, 3 m. long, joins on right bank. 1 m. below, the outflow of the lakes in Swinton Park, ¼ m. up, joins on right bank. Burn runs 2 m. to **Masham,** and here receives on the left bank Swinney beck, 5 m. long. Burn joins Ure just below. Ure runs to Hackfall, 3 m., where the Tanfield Club water begins, **W. Tanfield,** 3 m., Hutton Mill, 5 m., where the Ripon Angling Club water begins, **Ripon,** 3 m. Here Laver joins on the right bank. Laver rises on Dallowgill Moor, 6 m. N. of **Pateley Bridge,** 5 m. down, Stock beck, 3 m. long, joins on left bank. Laver runs 2 m. to Laverton. **Kirby Malzeard** being 1 m. off on the left bank. 6 m. below, Kexbeck, which rises 3 m. above **Kirby Malzeard,** joins Laver 4 m. below, joins on left bank. Laver runs 3 m. to **Ripon.** Here Skell joins on right bank. Skell rises in Dallow Moor 3 m. N.E. of **Pateley Bridge.** 6 m. down, by Grantley Hall, the outflow of Eavestone lake, 5 m. N.E. of **Pateley Bridge,** joins on the right bank. 3 m. down, Skell waters the lakes in Studley Park and Hill House, and joins Laver at **Ripon** 3 m. below. Ure runs to Hewick bridge (here ends the water of the R.A.C.). 3 m. down Ure the outflow of a pond by Bishop Monkham, ½ m. up, joins on right bank. ¼ m. down Robert beck joins on right bank. This stream rises 6 m. above **Wormold Green,** runs to **Copgrove** 4 m., and 3 m. down joins Ure. Ure runs 4 m. to **Boroughbridge.** Here Tutt or Minskip beck, which rises above **Copgrove,** and is 6 m. long, joins on right bank, and 2 m. below Ure joins Swale, forming Ouse. (The fishing on Ouse—all coarse fishing—is mostly free.) Ouse runs 3 m. to **Aldwark** (n.s. **Tollerton,** 4 m.), Linton Lock, 4 m. (n.s. **Tollerton,** 3 m.). Here Kyle joins on right bank. Kyle rises 7 m. above **Alne** station, and there is joined on left bank by Hawkhill beck, 5 m. long; 1 m. below this junction, just above **Alne,** Derings beck, 3 m. long, joins on right bank. Kyle runs to **Alne,** 1 m., **Tollerton,** 1 m., and joins Ouse 4 m. below. Ouse runs 2 m. to **Nunmonkton,** and here Nidd joins on right bank. Nidd rises on the slopes of Great Whernside 9 m. above

Ramsgill, 7 *m.* down How Stone beck, 5 *m.* long, joins on right bank. Nidd runs 3 *m.* to **Ramsgill**. Ramsgill beck, 4 *m.* long, here joins on right bank, and Lat beck, 3 *m.* long, on left bank. Nidd runs 3 *m.*. where Burn Gill, 3 *m* long, joins on right bank. 2 *m.* down Nidd, Ashfordside beck, 5 *m.* long, joins on right bank. Nidd runs to **Pateley Bridge** 1 *m.* Just below here Greenhow beck, 5 *m.* long, joins on right bank. Nidd runs 2 *m.*, where Ear beck, 3 *m.* long, joins on left bank. Nidd runs 2 *m.* to **Dacre**, and **Darley** 2 *m.* Here Darley beck, 3 *m.* long, joins on right bank. Nidd runs to **Hampsthwaite** 4 *m.* Here Kettlesing beck, 3 *m.* long, joins on right bank. 1 *m.* down Nidd, Rowden beck, which runs through **Hampsthwaite** and is 3 *m.* long, joins on right bank. Nidd runs to **Ripley** 1 *m.* (here begins the waters of the Knaresborough Club). Here Thornton beck joins on left bank. Thornton is 7 *m.* long, and at **Ripley** waters the lakes in Ripley Park. 2 *m.* down Nidd, Oak beck joins on the right bank. Oak rises in the forest of Knaresborough by John of Gaunt's Castle, 2 *m.* E. of Fewston, which is 7 *m.* S. of **Darley**. 8 *m.* down, at Knox Mill, Saltergate beck, 3 *m.* long, joins on left bank. 1 *m.* down, Oak joins Nidd. Nidd runs 4 *m.* to **Knaresborough**, 5 *m.* to **Goldsborough**, and 5 *m.* below, by **Little Ribston** (here ends the water of the Knaresborough Club), is joined on right bank by Crimple beck. Crimple rises at Crimple Head 4 *m.* S.W. of **Harrogate**, runs 4 *m.* to **Pannal**, where Nor beck, 4 *m.* long, joins on right bank. Crimple runs to **Spofforth** 6 *m.*, 3 *m.* N.W. of **Wetherby**, thence to Nidd is 4 *m.* 1 *m.* below, Allerton beck, which rises in the lakes in Allerton Park 2 *m.* N. of **Allerton**, and is 5 *m.* long, joins on left bank. Nidd runs 3 *m.* to **Cattal**, 3 *m.* to **Hammerton** and **Wilstrop**, and 4 *m.* down joins Ouse at **Nun Monkton**. Ouse runs 3 *m.* to Nether Poppleton, 1 *m.* N. of **Poppleton**, and **York** 4 *m.* Here Foss river joins on left bank. Foss rises in two reservoirs at Moss Farm, 3 *m.* S.E. of **Coxwold**, runs 5 *m.* to Stillington (n.s. **Tollerton**, 7 *m.*), and 4 *m.* down, where the Foss Navigation Cut joins, is joined on right bank by White Car beck, 4 *m.* long. Foss runs to **Strensall** 2 *m.*, **Haxby** 3 *m.*, and **York** 5 *m.* Here Tang Hall beck joins Foss on left bank. Tang Hall rises above **Barswick** Station, and runs thence to Foss in 4 *m.* Just above the junction, Osbaldwick beck, 4 *m.* long, joins Tang Hall. Ouse runs to **Naburn** 4 *m.*, and 5 *m.* down is joined on left bank by Stillingfleet beck. This brook rises some 4 *m.* above **Escrick**, runs to Stillingfleet 2 *m.*, and joins Ouse 1 *m.* below. 1 *m.* below, just above **Cawood**, Wharfe joins Ouse on right bank. Wharfe is formed by the junction of Outershaw beck and Green Field beck, both some 3 *m.* long, and both rise on the slopes of Cam Fell, 8 *m.* across the hills E. from **Ribble Head**. Wharfe runs 6 *m.* to **Buckden**, **Starbolton** 2 *m.*, **Kettlewell** 2 *m.*, and 2 *m.* below is joined on right bank by Skirfare. Skirfare rises on Ber Gill, 5 *m.* N.E. across the hills from **Horton**, and 2 *m.* down, at Halton Gill, is joined on right bank by Foxup beck, 2 *m.* long. 2 *m.* down, Hesleden beck, 3 *m.* long, joins on right bank. The head of this beck is 4 *m.* N.E. of **Horton**. Skirfare runs 1 *m.* to Litton, and Arncliffe 4 *m.* Here Cowside beck, 5 *m.* long, joins on right bank. Skirfare runs 5 *m.* to Wharfe. 1 *m.* down Wharfe is Kilnsey and **Grassington**, 5 *m.* (Here begins the water of the Burnsall Angling Club.) Here Eller beck, 5 *m.* long, joins on right bank. Wharfe runs 2 *m.* to Hebden, where Hebden beck, 5 *m.* long, joins on left bank. Wharfe runs to **Burnsall** 1 *m.*, and 1 *m.* down Dibb river joins on left bank. Dibb, under the name of Blea beck, rises on Coniston Moor, and 2 *m.* down waters Priest tarn, 5 *m.* N. of **Grassington**, at Black Edge. 2 *m.* down it waters Blea beck dams, 4 *m.* N.E. of **Grassington**. 1 *m.* down, Gate Up Gill, 3 *m.* long, joins on left bank. 1 *m.* down, Guinaith beck, 2 *m.* long, joins on left bank. Hence to Wharfe is 4 *m.* Wharfe runs 2 *m.* to Appletreewick. Here Skyreholm beck, which rises in New dam 3 *m.* N. of Appletreewick, and is 4 *m.* long, joins on left bank. 1 *m.* down Wharfe, Gill beck, 2 *m.* long, joins on right bank. ¼ *m.* below is Barden Bridge, where ends the water of the Burnsall Angling Club. ¼ *m.* below, Barden beck, 4 *m.* long, joins Wharfe on left bank. Wharfe runs 3 *m.* to **Bolton Abbey**, and 1 *m.* below is joined on left bank by Kex beck, 3 *m.* long. Wharfe runs 2 *m.* to **Addingham**, **Ilkley** 3 *m.*, **Ben Rhydding** 1 *m.*, **Burley** 4 *m.*, **Otley** 2 *m.* Hollin beck here joins on right bank. Hollin rises on Ilkley Moor, and 3 *m.* down is joined on right bank by Mire beck, which rises by **Guiseley**, runs 2 *m.* to Menston, and joins Hollin 1 *m.* below. Hollin joins Wharfe 1 *m.* down. Wharfe runs 2 *m.*, where Washburn river joins on left bank Washburn rises in Tarn Gill 6 *m.* N.E. of **Burnsall**, and 3 *m.* down is joined on right bank by Harden beck, 2 *m.* long. 2 *m.* down Washburn, Akeds beck, 2 *m.* long, joins on right bank, which rises in Akeds dam, 6 *m.* N.E. of **Bolton Abbey**. Washburn runs 3 *m.* to Blubberhouses, 6 *m.* S.W. from **Darley**, and 1 *m.* down is joined on right bank by Gill beck, 3 *m.* long. 1 *m.* down Washburn, Spinksburn beck, 2 *m.* long, joins on left bank. Washburn runs 7 *m.* to Wharfe, which runs to **Pool** 1 *m.* 1 *m.* below, Riffa beck, 4 *m.* long, joins on left bank. Wharfe runs to **Arthington** 1 *m.*, **Weeton** 3 *m.*, Harewood Bridge 3 *m.*, and 1 *m.* down is joined on right bank by Harewood beck. Harewood, under the name of Sturdy, rises on Wike Ridge 4 *m.* W. of **Bardsey**, and 2 *m.* down is joined on left bank by Eccup beck, which rises in the reservoir at Alwordley, runs 3 *m.* to Harewood Park, where it waters the lakes, and joins Wharfe 3 *m.* down. Wharfe runs 5 *m.* to **Collingham**. Here Collingham beck joins on right bank. Collingham rises 3 *m.*

above **Bardsey**, and joins Wharfe 3 m. down. Wharfe runs to **Wetherby** 2 m., **Thorpe Arch** 3 m., **Newton Kyme** 3 m., **Tadcaster** 2 m. 1 m. below, Cock beck joins on right bank. Cock beck rises above **Scholes**, and 4 m. down is joined on left bank by Carr beck, which rises by **Scholes** and is 3 m. long. 1 m. down, Cock waters the lake in Parlington Hollins, 1 m. N. of **Garforth**, runs to Aberford, 3 m. N. of **Garforth**, 3 m., **Stutton** 7 m., and joins Wharfe 2 m. down. Wharfe runs 3 m. to **Ulleskelf**, and 2 m. below is joined on left bank by the Foss. This stream rises 1 m. N. of Wighill, which is 3 m. N of **Tadcaster**, and 3 m. down, at Wood House. **Tadcaster** being 2 m. S.W., is joined on left bank by Catterton beck, which rises in the dam by Angram, 5 m. N.W. of **Copmanthorpe**, and is 3 m. long. Foss runs to **Bolton Percy** 4 m., and joins Wharfe 1 m. below. Wharfe runs to **Ryther** (n.s. **Ulleskelf**) 2 m., and 1 m. down joins Ouse 1 m. above **Cawood** (n.s. **Ulleskelf**, 4 m.). *Tackleist*, H. T. Lloyd, Sportsman's Depot, Davy Gate.

IRELAND.

General Information.—There is a heavy penalty for fishing with rod for salmon without a licence, and a licence can be obtained in the towns of any fishing tackle maker, and in remote parts the postmaster, or some other person, is appointed to sell licences, which are now available for the whole island. Sea fishing generally good; many places are excellent.

Abbey Feale.—W.L & W.R. On Feale; salmon, sea trout, and trout. Good accommodation at Mr. Leahy's and Mr. Elligott's. **Listowel.**

Achill, Island of.—Good white and brown trout fishing can be had in two lakes, one of them, Keel Long, being 3 m. in extent, and close to hotel. Keel Strand and the Cathedral rocks. Sea fishing very good. *Hotel*: Slievemore (*see Advertisement*), the proprietor of which will afford every information.

Annstown (near Waterford).—Good pike fishing. Leave may be obtained from Mr. Power, of Tramore. *Tackleist*: E. Wardell, Main-street, Tramore.

Antrim.—G.N.R. On Lough Neagh; trout. Boat and man, 5s. per diem. Toom Bridge, at the west end of the lake, is the favourite angling station. *Inn*: the O'Neill Arms. With regard to the feeders of the lake, the Blackwater, Ballindery, and Mainewater are good streams. The Mainewater runs through **Randalstown** (C.R.)

Ardara (Donegal).—A village on the Owenea and Owendeskar. The Owendeskar belongs to the Nesbitt Arms Hotel, and is reserved to visitors. Salmon, sea trout, and brown trout are plentiful. The flies are—an orange tip, mallard tail, fiery brown merging into light green body, red and black hackle, mallard wing, and macaw feelers; also small fiery brown bodies, with a sprig of mallard for tail with a turn of tinsel, wing mallard, with dark red, black, or coch-y-bonddhu hackle; a black fly with orange, silk tip, a turn or two of silver twist, no tail, black hackle, and mallard wing, twist or not, a little fiery brown at the shoulder may be added; another, a hare's ear and fiery brown mixed body, gold tinsel at tail, dark hackle (black or brown), a mallard's wing. When the river is in spate the flies may be dressed on No. 8 hook; when the river is low, on No. 9. In low water little can be done. 2 m. off there are several small lochs full of large brown trout. The "Midge" loch contains some very large trout, which may be taken trolling. The nearest loch is Loch Arv-y-Neil, which is full of nice trout. The flies for these lochs are the same as for the river, only smaller. Hare's ear and fiery brown with red hackle and mallard or any dark feather for wing is a good fly. Accommodation may be obtained at the Nesbitt Arms. The Owenea flows 1 m. off. The town of Donegal is 14 m. distant, and Glenties 6 m.

Ardee (n.s. **Dunleer**, 6 m.)—Dee; salmon, trout; fishing good and free for some miles above the town, and for 6 m. below to White Mills, where is the Half-crown Salmon Fishery; d.t., 2s. 6d.

Armagh.—G.N.R. Callan; free. Blackwater free good fishing. *Season*, March 16 to Oct. 19.

Athboy (Meath).—M.G.W.R.: G.S. & W.R. Good fishing here.

Athlone—M.G.W.R.; G.S. & W.R. Shannon and Lough Rea; good trout and salmon fishing free. (*See Carrick*.) *Hotel*: Prince of Wales. Boats, &c., can be obtained from Brown, Strand, Athlone. who is also a good fisherman.

Ballina (Mayo).—M.G.W.R. Salmon fishing on the Moy opens on Feb. 1. *Hotels*: Moy, Imperial (*see Advertisement*). Boat and men 6s. per day. There are two large lakes. Loughs Conn and Cullen. containing salmon, brown trout, pike, and perch, distant 3 m. from Ballina; free fishing. Salmon fishing ends Sept. 16; brown trout fishing October 15. Thomas Clarke supplies boats and men, terms as above stated. The Moy is a beautiful river, and salmon fishing on it very good; all sea and brown trout may be retained. On the loughs all fish taken may be retained by the angler. *Fishermen*: Jem and Pat Hearns (*see Advertisement*), H. Hearn, and John Devers. The Ardnaree fishing (on the Moy) extends 2½ m.; above the weirs at Ballina it belongs to Mr. J. C. Wilson, who issues d.t., 7s. 6d. All fish killed belong to the angler. There are 20 m. of angling water, besides several lakes. Ballina is a centre from which many *radii* run. There are Lough Talt, Lough Easky, Higgin's Lake, Lough Oh, Carrakeribly Lake, Cara Lake, and many others, all open.

Ballinahinch (Galway).—Ballinahinch river, 3 m.; lakes from 50 to 100; salmon, sea-trout, brown trout. The principal lakes are Loch Inagh, Derryclare, Ballinahinch, Glendalough, in all of which there are first-rate salmon stands and very good sea-trout fishing. The Ballynahinch Fishery is let in stands at from 50l. to 300l. each per season. and all stands this season are already taken up. The spring salmon fishing is excellent, and fish run very early. The season opens the 1st of February, ends September 30th. The sea-trout fishing is very good. There are several fishings in Connemara. At present they are all in private hands and of limited extent; but some fishing may be had at Doohulla, though salmon are rarely taken. The Erriff was advertised for sale as a whole, but it is very much dependent upon high water; sometimes very good. *Salmon*—Flies tied on hooks No. 6—7; Jock Scott, blue doctor, silver grey, Popham, grey monkey, black jay, claret, &c. *Sea Trout*—Any small size flies of ordinary patterns. Best months, April and May for spring salmon; June and July, grilse; and for salmon and sea trout, August and September. *Hotels*: Recess, and Zetland Hotel, Cashel, the proprietor of which has leased the Gowla salmon and sea trout fishery and Athry lakes for hotel visitors; w.t. 50s., d.t. 10s.; boats free. (*See Advertisement.*)

Ballincollig (Cork).—M.R. On South Bride; trout; free. (*See Cork.*)

Ballinderry (Tyrone).—n.s. **Cookstown**. Trout, salmon; free. *Season*, March 1 to Oct. 31.

Ballineen (Cork).—C.B. & S.C.R. On Bandon; salmon and trout, the latter free.

Ballinrobe.—M.G.W.R. On river Robe. From town to L. Mask are trout 1lb. to 3½lb.; not much use to fish for them except with a dry fly. Above town, about Robeen, Hollymount and up to Crossboyne trout are more numerous, but are much smaller. Pike are abundant everywhere along the Robe; perch are small. L. Mask, 2 m.; trout, perch, pike, char. Trout up to 3½lb. take fly; larger up to 14lb. only to be got by trolling. Flies, on No. 6 Pennell sneck scale—Zulu, Pennell's lake flies, black and claret hackles and red hackle, green drake from May to end of season, black hackle with orange body (black and yellow caterpillar), best on wet days. In trolling, gilt Devon or gilt and brown phantom; sometimes blue and silver phantom is good; natural bait is good. L. Carra, 2 m.; trout, pike, and perch. Trout will not rise freely; best for pike. The Cut at Carna Gower, 3 m., gives good trout, but is difficult to fish except early in season, when water is high. The small river at Cross, 4 m., holds salmon and small trout, which come into condition early in the season. *Hotels*: Valkenburg's (*see Advertisement*) and others.

Ballisadare.—M.G.W.R. Mr. Cooper gives leave to fish Lough Arrow; salmon, sea-trout, and brown trout. The Ballisadare salmon fishing is very good, but generally let.

Ballycastle (Antrim).—Tolerable lodgings may be had here. Trout and salmon. Boats. and boatmen can be had.

Ballymena.—B. & N.C.R. Good fishing can be had here, with good hotel accommodation. *Season*, March 16 to Oct. 19.

Ballyroney.—G.N.R. Bann; free fishing. *Season*, March 1 to Oct. 31.

Ballyshannon.—G.N.R. On Erne; salmon and trout. Fly fishing only is allowed, and the river is divided up into eight beats. There are 4 m. of fishable water (Bally-shannon to Belleek). Salmon w.t. 4l.; trout w.t. 1l., of Erne Fisheries Co., Ballyshannon. The Erne above Belleek, belonging to the Marquis of Ely, is in the hands of the Erne Fisheries Co. The brown trout fishing is excellent, especially in the months of May and June, and the fish run large. Dry fly prove exceptionally killing, and the night rise during the summer months affords excellent sport. The salmon and grilse fishing in the Erne is so good that a rod on the river is greatly sought after. Good salmon flies are: 1, green parson; 2, golden olive; 3, fiery brown; 4, black and claret; 5, Rogan's Fancy; 6, Ballyshannon; 7, olive and claret; 8, pink and orange. There is also pike, bream, and perch fishing. There are two capital hotels in Ballyshannon, and one at Belleek, at the opposite end of the river. The local tackleists are Messrs. M. Rogan and Sons, (*see Advt.*), Bridge End House, and Wm. Lynn, Knathy, Ballyshannon. 4 m. from Belleek and Bundoran is Lough Melvin, which affords salmon and trout fishing, trouting being particularly good. Lough Melvin opens on Feb. 1, and closes Sept. 30. The western portion of the lake, which is distant but 2¼ m. from Bundoran, is free for both trout and salmon fishing for about 2½ m. E. The lake abounds with the famous gillaroo trout and brown trout and great lake trout (*Salmo ferox*). Salmon fishing very good in the months of March, April, and May, and good grilse fishing in June and July. The preserved portion of the lake is owned by the Marquis of Ely, Mr. J. Johnston, and Mr. H. Stubbs; the charge for fishing the preserved portion, which is known as the Garrison End, and also the middle portions of the lake, is 3s. 6d. a day, or 18s. per week. Tickets of Mr. J. Hamilton, Garrison, or Major White, Ballyshannon. The Garrison end of the lake is the chief salmon water of Lough Melvin. Scott's Hotel, Garrison, which is almost on the lake shore, is the only hotel close to the lake that is entirely devoted to the comforts of anglers; proprietor, Mr. A. Scott, who has excellent boats and experienced boatmen. Good accommodation in Bundoran at the Great Northern, Hamilton's, Sweeny's, and Graydon's Hotels; also at several farm houses on the shores of the lake. The Bunduff river, 3½ m. from Bundoran, opens March 1, and closes Sept. 30; best months for salmon, June, July, and August; permission from Capt. C. R. Barton, Waterfoot, Pettigo, co. Donegal; and from Mrs. Colonel Dickson, Tullaghan House, *via* Bundoran; and from Mr. McYntire, Bunduff Bridge, Tullaghan. Fair trout fishing always to be had on this river. 1¼ m. from Bundoran is the river Bundrowes, which flows from Lough Melvin, and is a salmon and trout river. Season opens Feb. 1, and closes Sept. 18; w.t. 3l., d.t. 12s. 6d., to be obtained of R. Hamilton, Esq., Bundoran, co. Donegal, or the proprietors of the fishery, C. J. Singleton, Esq., Bundrowes (who owns the river from Mullinabeck Bridge to the sea), and Colonel Vernon, of Lareen House, Kinlough, co. Leitrim. There is a good train service from Dublin to Belleek, Ballyshannon, and Bundoran, on the Great Northern Railway. Much depends on the flies and the manner in which they are tied, different coloured hackles being more killing according to the season. Erne requires a smaller fly for brown trout than Lough Melvin. There are three kinds of trout in Lough Melvin, and the fishing is good until the end of May. The parson is a good Erne fly. F. Francis recommends the following: Hook No. 7; tail two twists gold, small topping and two or three sprigs gold pheasant tippets, black harl, three twists; body, golden olive silk, changing into pigs' down of the same shade, then into orange and fiery brown towards the shoulder; golden olive hackle three parts down the body, with full claret hackle over; wing, two golden pheasant saddle feathers, over this three or four toppings with sprigs of green parrot, gold pheasant tippet, pintail, turkey, and wood duck, with a kingfisher's or blue chatterer's feather at each jowl, and blue macaw's feeler head, black harl, gold tinsel according. Other parsons are dressed larger, with six, seven, or eight toppings in the wing, with cock of the rock *ad lib.*, and with jay's hackle and purple cock instead of pintail, and even small toppings on the breast. This last one is good in heavy water. Another fly: Hook No. 5; silver twist and puce silk tag, golden pheasant topping and tippet sprigs for tail; ostrich harl over; apple-green silk body tipped with black twist and silver greenish yellow hackle all the way down; gold pheasant tippet feather, tied hackle fashion, and jay's hackle over; black harl head, and mixed wing of gold pheasant saddle feather, ditto tail and tippet, gallina and bustard and red and blue macaw, two or three sprigs of each. Another: Hook No. 5; blue silk and silver tag, golden pheasant topping and tippet sprigs for tail; black harl over; body about a third of an inch of velvet silk, the rest orange; golden olive hackle all the way down; jay's hackle over silver tinsel; wing mixed of gold pheasant tail and tippet, gallina, and one topping and red macaw feeler, black harl head. Another of a smaller size: silver and puce silk tag, topping and tippet tail: black head: orange silk body, with claret hackle all down, silver tinsel wing as before with blue feelers. A yellow body and hackle may also be fitted to the same fly. Add to these for bright weather and low water later in the season a fly with dark orange body (spare), fine silver; a cock of the rock feather for tail; two cock of the rock for inner wing; gold pheasant tail and dark Argus over that; dark mallard over all, and blue chatterer on each side of the cheek; golden olive hackle with claret hackle at shoulder; and blue macaw feeler. Also three, bodies of dark blue, and a red tail joint; yellow and claret joint, or claret and yellow joint respectively; silver tinsel tips; ostrich head; blue, claret, and golden olive hackles respectively; jay at shoulder of each, fineish silver twist; wing same for each, two toppings, pintail, green parrot, and gold pheasant tail; blue macaw's feelers. The brown trout fishing is good; the white trout are not plentiful, but the grilse fishing is fair. Fair brown trout fishing can be had free in the many mountain lakes of the surrounding country. The fish commence running up in May. The trout fishing in Lough Erne is first-rate, the Mayfly being exceptionally good. There are very large pike in it, and salmon, besides perch and bream. (*See Ardara* and *Bundoran.*) (*See c.s.*)

Baltimore.—On the Ilen; salmon, sea trout, &c. The river runs into the sea here. The sea fishing is good; pollack abundant. The river fishing is better at Skibbereen.

Banbridge.—G.N.R. Bann; fair fishing. *Season*, March 1 to Oct. 31.

Bandon.—C.B. & S.C.R. On Bandon; salmon, brown and white trout; preserved by a club. Comfortable quarters can be had either here or at Ballyneen or Dunmanway.

Bangor.—On the Owenmore, which is much fished. Good rough lodging can be obtained at the inn. Post each way daily. Bangor is 6 m. from Corick Bridge. (*See Corick Bridge.*) The Owenmore is, we believe, let in its upper portion. The generous proprietor reserves a small tract of the lower water for himself. A day, however, may sometimes be obtained. The Owenduff is about 6 m. off. We believe the upper portion may be fished by taking a monthly ticket at about 25l. The fishing is very good. Three m. distant is the Munhin, which rises in Corranmore lake and runs to the sea. It is a very good salmon and white trout river.

Bannagher (more correctly spelt Banagher).—By train G.S. & W.R., and steamers from here up and down the Shannon daily from May till October. Trout and salmon fishing May, June, and July; perch and pike very good in August and September. Small but good inns and boats in Banagher. (*See Meelick.*)

Bantry.—C.B. & S.C.R. Salmon, white and brown trout, and sea fishing. Vickery's hotel comfortable. The sea fishing for bass, hake, bream, mullet, pollack, conger, and mackerel is excellent. There is fair salmon and white trout fishing to be had in the rivers that fall into the sea between this and Glengariffe; but care should be taken to ask permission personally, when it would generally be granted. There are a number of brown trout lakes within driving distance, in some of which the fishing is very good, but the fish do not run large.

Belderg.—On the coast. The mountain streams are full of small trout, and the sea fishing is excellent. There is a fair inn here, with a post-car attached. (*See Glenamoy.*)

Belfast.—Messrs. Braddell and Son, fish-tackleists, of Belfast, will give every information as to fishing in the north of Ireland (*see Advt.*). They have some good fishing to let; apply to them. Good trouting can be had on the waters preserved by the Belfast Anglers' Association; hon. sec., F. J. Kennedy, 4, Clarence-place, Belfast: entrance fee 21s. (officers of army and navy not on retired list exempt) s.t. 42s. The Association also have special rates for travelling to almost every fishing station in Ulster. Good trouting in the Water Commissioners' lakes; tickets at the W.C. office. Good sea fishing in Belfast Lough. *Fishing stations within two hours*: Antrim, Armagh, Ballinderry, Ballymena, Ballynahinch, Co. Down, Ballyroney, Banbridge, Castledawson, Coleraine, Comber, Crossgar, Crumlin, Cullybackey, Downpatrick, Dromore, Dunadry, Glarryford, Glenarm, Glenavy, Glenwherry, Kellswater, Kilkeel, Lagan, Moy, Newcastle, Randalstown, Toomebridge.

Belleek (Fermanagh). - G.N.R. On Erne; salmon and trout; fishing to be had by ticket. There is capital pike fishing in Lough Erne and river. Johnstone's Hotel, Belleek, is good, and preserved trout and pike fishing can be had free by those staying in the house. The May-fly season is a grand time.

Bird Hill.—(*See Nenagh.*)

Blackwater Bridge.—(*See Waterville.*)

Blarney (Cork).—G.S. & W.R. On Blarney; fair brown trout fishing free.

Boyle (Roscommon).—M.G.W.R. A capital trout stream runs through the place. It is preserved, but leave can be obtained. There is capital trout fishing to be had in Lough Arrow and the Sligo lakes. There are many other good lakes in the neighbourhood—all free.

Buncrana.—Rail from Derry, 1 hour. On Crana and Mill river; salmon, white and brown trout; d.t. for salmon on Crana river, 5s.; Mill river free. 9 m. by mail car is Clonmeny; first-rate white trout fishing, a few salmon; good accommodation. Minteagh and Mindoran lakes hold trout and char.

Bundoran (Donegal).—G.N.R. The river Bundrowes runs close by here (salmon and trout), rising in Lake Melvin, 2½ m. off, celebrated for its salmon, large lake trout, gillaroo, and brown trout. Angling on lake and river opens Feb. 1; closes—river, Sept. 18: lake, Sept. 30. Mr. Malling, the proprietor of the Marine and Family Hotel, Bundoran, keeps boats on the lake in connection with the hotel, also post-cars. Accommodation for fishing the lake can be had either at Scott's (Garrison), Murphy's (Rossinver), or Moor's, near Kinlough, or Coulter's, Derryhirk House, on the shores of the lough. Lord Ely, Mr. Stubbs, and Mr. Johnstone charge 3s. 6d. per day or 18s. per week for fishing, and 15s. a day for Lough Na-Vagh. Bunduff river distant from Bundoran on the Sligo mail road about 3½ m. Angling for salmon can be had from May until September. Mr. Barrington and Mr. C. J Singleton own the Bundrowes fishing, the latter from Mullinabeck Bridge to the sea; and Capt. Barton, Waterfoot, Pettigo, co. Donegal, gives leave for the Bunduff river. (*c.s. Ballyshannon.*) *Tackleist*, Mr. Rogan, Ballyshannon (*see Advertisement*).

Bunmahon.—8 m. from Waterford. Trout and pike. Permission required.

Bushmills (Antrim).—On Bush: salmon. From Salmon Leap to the sea, 2½ m., the fishing is preserved by the owner, though a rod—one of two—is sometimes let; apply to R. M. Douglas, Esq., Portballantrae, Bushmills.

Buttevant.—G.S. & W.R. There is a capital inn here. Good pike fishing near.

Cahir (Tipperary).—W.L. & W.R. The Glengall Arms is comfortable. Salmon and trout on the Suir ; strictly preserved by the proprietors.

Cahirciveen (co. Kerry).—(*See Waterville.*) The lakes and river of Carhan to the east of the village are good after a fresh. (*See Valencia.*) The Feartagh, Kearan, and Einegh run near. Salmon, sea trout, and brown trout. These are late rivers, and useless before July. August is the best month. Leslie's Hotel is good. The fishery is free. The following are good flies: No. 1. Tip, fine gold tinsel. Tail, mallard and ruff. Tag, golden yellow pig's wool. Body, fiery brown mohair ribbed with silver. Legs, blue and scarlet hackle rolled up together. Shoulder, golden yellow pig's wool. Wing, rich mixed, with crimson horns. No. 2. Tip and tag as above. Tail topping and kingfisher. Body, purple silk, ribbed with silver. Hackle, black. Shoulder, claret hackle. Wing, mallard. Horns, blue macaw, long. Either of these, if tied on a small grilse hook, will rarely be found to fail. There are three small lakes, one at Raheal, and the others at Kells, both full of brown trout. A boat is absolutely necessary. Lough Curraine lies near. Salmon are early with troll, and rise freely in June.

Caragh Lake (Co. Kerry).—This picturesque lake, within half a mile of G.S. & W. Railway Station of same name, is about 6 m. long, and affords excellent salmon and trout fishing (free). The Southern Hotel, under the same management as the G.S. & W.R. Co's. hotels at Killarney, Kenmare, Parknasilla, and Waterville, already so favourably known to sportsmen, is situated on the shore of the lake. The Lower Caragh river is carefully preserved by the Company for the use of their guests at a moderate charge. A hatchery for salmon and Leven trout is also working successfully in hotel grounds. Numerous mountain lakes in the vicinity are well stocked with fish.

Carrick.—M.G.W.R On Shannon, salmon, trout, and pike. The Shannon rises on the slope of Kulkeagh Mountain, and the stream then flows into Lough Allen, a basin 8 m. long by 3 m. broad. Several small streams join the lake. At Battle Bridge streams from two loughs (Lough Key and another) join the main river. 2 m. from here is the town of Carrick. Fishing of all kinds may be had here. 2 m. below Carrick the river widens out into Corry Lough, and a short distance below lies Jamestown. Fishing free. Below Jamestown the river widens out into Loughs Tap, Boedarrig, Boeffin, and Sconnell. In these loughs the trout run from 1lb. to 7lb. Boedarrig is the best. Below the town of Ruskey, 2¼ m., the river enters Lough Forbes. Below this Richmond is reached, and 7 m. on Lanesborough below which is Lough Ree. The trouting in the May-fly season here is first-rate. The town of Athlone lies 2 m. from its southern point. At Shannon Bridge, 12 m. below Athlone, the Suck joins Shannon. The fishing is good. This river runs down from beyond Ballinasloe. At Shannon Harbour the Brusna joins Shannon, and then Lough Derg is reached. The fishing in the May-fly season is here first-rate. Killaloe is the best station for this lake. Castle Connell is the next station on the Shannon, and the fishing is here preserved. Limerick is the next station, and is distant 12 m. from Lough Derg.

Carrick (Donegal).—Glen and Ownwee rivers; salmon, white and brown trout. *Hotel*: Glencolumbkille (*see Advertisement*), where guests have fishing on the two rivers and several lakes, which for years have been carefully preserved. The Glen and Ownwee run into Teelin Bay, where the sport is good The sea fishing generally is excellent.

Carrickfergus.—M. & N.C.R. 9 m. from Belfast. The reservoirs (over 300 acres) of the Belfast Water Commissioners are situate at Woodburn, 3 m. off, and hold, in large numbers, brown trout, averaging three-quarters of a pound. Loch Leven, Fontinalis, and Rainbow trout have also been turned in at various times. The best flies are hare's ear, cow-dung, coachman, and Wickham's fancy. In the Copeland Reservoir the white sea trout may be taken on a bright day with the Alexandra. Annual license 10s., at the Water Office, Royal Avenue, Belfast.

Carrick-on-Suir (Waterford).—W.L. & W.R. 12 m. above Waterford. On Suir; pike, trout, salmon. Fish above the town. The fishing on Suir is free on the north bank for 12 m. and on the south bank for 7 m. Within a short drive are several loughs, and the trout streams, Cloda, Glen, and Coolnamuck, all free. 8 m. off, on the Comeragh mountains, are several lakes giving good trouting, such as Lough Coumshuigaun, Crolty's Lough, Lough Coumdualla, Lough Mor, and the Stillogues. The Stillogues give good fishing by day, trout running herring size. The best fishing is in Coumshuigaun at night, fish running up to 5lb. and 6lb. Coumshuigaun is 2 m. from the Stillogues; July, August, and September are the best months, and a clear, cloudless day with wind is necessary.

Castlebar.—M.G.W.R. Loughs Conn and Cullen; pike, trout. Lough Beltra, 6 m. good fishing.

Castle Bellingham (Louth).—G.N.R. On Glyde; salmon and trout.

Castle Blayney.—G.N.R. On Castle Blayney lake; pike, perch, &c.; strictly preserved

Castle Cauldwell (Fermanagh).—G.N.R. On Erne; salmon and trout.

Castle Connell (Limerick).—G.S. & W.R. On Shannon; salmon, trout, pike, perch, &c. *Hotel*: The Shannon; good. Rods are sometimes to let for a time. Apply to J. Enright and Son, fishing rod and tackle makers, Castle Connell (*see Advertisement*). The following tributaries of the Shannon are within easy distance: Glen, Abington, Newport, Coole, Mulcaire, and Blackwater rivers. (*See Carrick* and *Limerick*.)

Castle Dawson.—M. & N.C.R. On the Moyola, which enters Lough Neagh about 3 m down; good trout fishing in spring, especially after a flood; heavy lake trout in autumn. *Hotel*: Garvin's; fairly good Trouting free, except through castle grounds.

Castle Island.—G.S. & W.R. On the Maine, Feale, and Smerleagh; first-rate trouting, salmon, and sea trout.

Castle Martyr (Cork).—On Dour; trout.

Castle Pollard.—M.G.W.R. 2 m. off is Lough Dereveragh; large brown trout. The drake season is the best time. The Imry is a good stream; also lakes Glove Sheelan and Lane. *Hotel*: Pollard Arms; comfortable. Visitors at this hotel have plenty of free fishing. Cars to and from all lakes and rivers free of charge. (*See Mullingar.*)

Castle Townsend.—(*See Skibbereen.*)

Cliffden (Galway).—There is a nice little river here, but the salmon can get no higher than the falls close by the town. About 2 m. from Clifden is Lake Ballinaboy: a salmon and sea trout, but they rise very badly. A good fly for brown trout is hare's ear and yellow or fiery brown, with red or black hackle, and starling's wing. For white trout, orange tip, black and blue mohair mixed, black hackle, fine silver twist, and mixed wing of gold pheasant breast, plover, green parrot, mallard, gallina, and pintail, with a sprig or two of gold pheasant tippet, and blue macaw feelers. Another: Body, blue mohair, orange tip, red hackle, tails, wing, &c., as above. Another: Body, black and red, or orange tip, tails, wings, &c., as above. (*See Roundstone.*) The Doohulla white trout fishery is near here. The Doohulla fishery is 7 *m.* from Clifden and 5 *m.* from Round-stone. The fishery comprises a river and many lakes well stocked with white, brown trout, and salmon. *Hotel*: Railway.

Clonbur, 8 *m.* from **Ballinrobe** Station.—L. Mask, 3 *m.*, and L. Corrib 2 *m.* L. Mask: good trouting, free. (*See Ballinrobe.*) L. Nafooey, 8 *m.*: trout and abundance of pike. *Hotel*: Mount Gable (*see Advertisement*). Good trout and salmon fishing in L. Corrib, preserved by an association.

Clonmel (Waterford).—W.L. & W.R. Suir; capital piking can be had on Anner.

Coleraine (co. Derry).—M. & N.C.R. On Bann; salmon and trout. *Hotels*: Clothworkers' Arms and Corporation Arms. The fishing up to the salmon leap is free. Above it is preserved. Tickets may be had at a moderate cost. The Bann below the salmon leap is very broad, and can only be fished from a boat. The Bann is a late river, little can be done before July; August is better; and September best.

Comber.—B. & C.D.R. Fair, free trouting after rain.

Cong (Galway).—On Lough Corrib; salmon and trout. *Hotel*, Carlisle Arms. A very good station. Trolling with natural bait is best. Lough Mask can also be fished from here.

Connemara.—The Gowla fishery is preserved. *Hotel*: Cashel.

Cookstown (Tyrone).—B. & N.C.R. (*See Ballinderry.*)

Coomclogherane Lake (co. Kerry).—About 2 *m.* north of Keenkeen Lake, and about 1¼ *m.* from the road. The ground round it is very boggy, and the trout very plentiful.

Corick Bridge.—There is a tolerable inn here. The white trout fishing in August and September is first-rate.

Cork.—On Lee. (*See Macroom.*) The Lee, from Gougane Barra Lake (its source, where there is excellent trout fishing) flows through Inchageelah Lakes. Capital accommodation at The Hydro, St. Ann's Hill, Cork (3 *m.* of fair, brown trout fishing in preserved waters); Brophy's Hotel, Inchageelah; also at Williams' Hotel, **Macroom,** where the Laney, Fooherish, and Sullane, &c., join the Lee. Railway to Macroom, from which place cars can be had to any district. The Lee is considered the earliest salmon river in Ireland. The following are some of the tributaries: South Bride (the Macroom rail runs nearly parallel with it), the Blarney, Shournach, Glashagorruv, Dripsey, Glanmire, Carrigaline, or Yellow River, Midleton, &c., &c. Those flowing into the tidal water hold white or sea trout, and in the fresh water portions brown trout. Trout fishing is entirely free. Within easy reach of Cork, *viâ* rail 17 *m.*, is the Bandon river, which flows into Kinsale harbour; white and brown trout; four days a week free to anglers taking out a license in the district. Also further west, the Arrigadeen, which flows into Courtmacsherry Bay. The North Bride, a tributary of the Blackwater, is about 9 *m.* from Cork, and is a fine brown trout river; so is the Clyda. Stations, Glenville and Rathcormac, with an excellent inn at Rathcormac and Conna. There is good trouting in the Fenisk, which joins Blackwater above Villiers Town. March, April, and May are the best months for salmon. Full particulars may be obtained from W. Haynes and Son, 63, Patrick-street (*see Advertisement*). Most of the fishing is within easy distance of Cork, either by rail or car. Sea-fishing very good. (*See c.s. Cork.*)

Crookstown (Cork)—On South Bride; free trouting.

Crookstown Road (Cork).—C. & M.R. On South Bride; trout; free. (*See Cork.*)

Crossgar (Co. Down).—B. & C.D.R. Ballynahinch river; trout, salmon. *Season*, March 1 to Oct. 31. Preserved by Belfast Anglers' Association; hon. sec. F. J. Kennedy Esq., 4, Clarence-place, Belfast.

Crosshaven (Cork).—There are two good hotels here. The Minane at Ringabella and the Carrigaline can be reached from here. Good sea fishing close at hand, especially pollack.

Crumlin.—G.N.R. Some trouting in the brook here; free.

Cullybackey.—M. & N.C.R. Maine; good fishing; free. *Season*, March 1 to Oct. 31.

Curragh, The.—In the canal there is fair perch and pike fishing.

Cushendall.—n.s. **Larne.** Fair brook fishing; free.

Dervock.—M. & N.C.R. Bush; trout, salmon; preserved. *Season*, March 16 to Oct. 19.

Dingle.—The Connor Hill lakes lie near here. Lough-a-doon, the Pedlar's Lake, the White Lake, Mount Eagle Lake, &c., and several trout streams. *Hotel*: Benner's; accommodation good.

Donass.—On Shannon; salmon and trout; leave to fish here is difficult to obtain. The stands are always let at a high figure.

Donegal.—Lough Eske is 3 *m.* off. In August char may be caught. The trout run from ½lb. to 8lb. The fishing of the river is in the hands of Mrs. White; w.t. 15*s.*, d.t. 3*s.* The flies are small fiery browns and blacks, ribbed with silver and hare's ear, &c., with mallard or teal wing. We believe a boat may be had on the loch. A few salmon and plenty of white trout may be taken about July. The river is small and shallow, and holds a few salmon and white trout. *Hotel*: Arran Arms, very comfortable.

Donemanagh, n.s **Strabane,** 6 *m.*—On Dinnet; excellent brown trout fishing in spring; white trout and an occasional salmon in autumn. Comfortable lodgings. There are some lakes near in which large trout may be caught, and which can be fished from the shore.

Doonisky (Cork).—C. & M.R. On Lee; salmon and trout. (*See Cork.*)

Downpatrick.—B. & C.D.R. Annacloy; fair fishing. *Season*, March 16 to Oct. 19.

Dromore.—(*See Kenmare.*) On the Blackwater. The river is let to a club. The best flies are fiery browns, orange silk, and black hackles, and a crimson silk body, with a blue and fiery brown hackle brought up to shoulder with jay at throat, mixed wings.

Dublin.—There is fairly good trout fishing in Dodder, Tolka, Liffey, Rye, Ward, Swords, Delvin, Nanny, Rathmines reservoir, Shankill, and Crooked river, all within fairly easy reach, and mostly free, or by leave from the landowners. which is freely given. Good trouting in the Mattock, a tributary of the Boyne, 30 *m.* by rail from Dublin to Drogheda station, thence 2 *m.* by road ; fish run about 3lb. The Wicklow rivers (full of trout) are practically free, but the fish run small. *Tackleists*, C. Weekes and Co., 26 and 27, Essex Quay.

Dunadry.—M. & N.C.R. Clady; trout. *Season*, March 16 to Oct. 19.

Dungiven.—M. & N.C.R. On Roe; salmon, white and brown trout. April and May for brown trout, August and September for white trout, September and October for salmon. (*See Limavady.*)

Dungloe (Donegal). — On Rosses fishery, situated between the Gweedore and Gweebara rivers, and is 2½ *m.* from Derry, Letterkenny, and Burtonport light railway. There are over 100 lakes holding white and brown trout. Loughs Meenmore, Tully, and Dungloe, all within 1½ *m.* of the hotels, give good white trouting; w.t., including Crolly river and Loughanure, 25*s.* ; boat and man 3*s.* 6*d.*; there are 15 boats on the different loughs. Anglers can also fish Loughanure and Crolly river; salmon and white trout. July 1 to Oct. 20 best time for white or sea trout fishing. *Private Hotel* : Hanlan's. *Hotels* : Sweeney's, Boyle's. In all these lochs olive duns' hare's ears mixed with claret or fiery brown, with small red and black hackles, starling or mallard wings, will kill. Licences of Mr. S. Hanlan, manager of the fishery, who will give every information. (*See Gweedore.*)

Dunkettle (Cork).—G.S. & W.R. 3 *m.* from **Cork.** (*See Cork.*) On Glanmire; trout.

Dunmanway.—C.B. & S.C.R. Bandon; trout fishing free. (*See Bandon.*) Good accommodation.

Dunmore.—Near **Waterford.** Excellent sea fishing. Car from Waterford. Boats and lines at Dunmore. All information to be obtained from E. Wardell, Fishing Tackle Maker. 117, Quay, Waterford.

Enfield.—M.G.W.R. Blackwater; trout, pike; trouting good and free. Enfield is 24 *m.* from Dublin.

Farranfore.—G.S. & W.R. About 8 *m.* from Killarney. First-rate trout fishing.

Fermoy.—G.S. & W.R. On Blackwater Leave may possibly be obtained on application to the proprietors. The water between Lismore, Fermoy, and Killavullin affords probably the best spring salmon angling in the kingdom. There is good free trout fishing on the Funcheon. North Bride, Anbeg, and Araglin, which flow into the Blackwater; trouting free. *Hotel* : Royal.

Foxford (Mayo).—M.G.W.R. On Moy; salmon and trout. *Hotel* : Foxford Hotel. Loughs Conn and Callow lie near. The landlord of the hotel has a considerable fishery.

Galway.—M.G.W.R. *Hotels* : Mack's Royal Hotel, and Railway Hotel (*see Advertisement*). The river is full of salmon and sea-trout; the fishing is almost in the town, and the catch has averaged well during the past five years. The rod fishing opens Feb. 1, but the best time for spring fishing is from March 15 to May 15. The month of June is the best for peal fishing, as many as twenty peal being killed by one rod in a day. July, August, and September are good also, '' provided there is water in the river.'' but not quite so good as June. The white trout begin to run about July 18; August and September are [the two best months for white trout fishing. Good pike fishing in the neighbourhood. For lough trout the month of May is the best for fly fishing on Lough Corrib, which lies n-ar; June, July, and August are the best for trolling. The principal flies for the Galway river are—black and yellow goldfinch, black and orange body, olive hackle, jay shoulder ; crimson and orange body, claret hackle, jay shoulder ; green and orange body, jay shoulder, or orange hackle—blue and orange body, blue hackle breasted with jay. Flies for sea trout fishing are—blue body, blue hackle. jay's wing; claret body, claret hackle breasted with jay; blue and claret mixed rough body, claret hackle; black body. yellow tip, black hackle, and silver grey. The best quarters for fishing the lakes from is Oughterard. Some rods are constantly to be let on the Galway river. Apply to Mr. W. N. Milne, Superintendent of the Galway Fishery. The pollack fishing on coast to N.W. of Galway is excellent. Take plenty of indiarubber baits, white flies, double and treble gut collars. On shallow ground use 15-fathom lines without lead.

Garrison (n.s. **Belleek**).—On Lough Melvin. The best time to fish the lake for gillaroo with artificial fly is February, March, and early April. In the Bundrowes good sport can be had with natural fly during May and June, using cowdung or cricket on the finest tackle. They also then take boiled shrimp well. In August use the natural daddy longlegs in the lake. In September there are great numbers in the Drowes, belonging to Lord Massey. between the lake and Mullinabeck. (*See Bundoran.*) 10 *m.* south is Lough Glencar. Good salmon, white and brown trout, pike; closely preserved. Fishing on Melvin is, w.t. 18*s.*, d.t. 3*s.* 6*d.*; apply to landlord of the hotel. A good trout fly for the lough is hen pheasant wing, light red ginger hackle, with a pale yellow silk body and silver twist. The best part of the lough is where the two rivers run into it. Leave required. The following are good salmon flies: One lap of gold at tail, tag of orange silk; tail, small topping, two turns of ostrich harl, about a third of an inch of greenish-yellow pig's wool merging into dark fiery brown, then into black and fiery brown at the shoulder; claret hackle running two-thirds down the body with jay over it, gold twist; wing, golden pheasant tippet, covered by mallard; feelers, blue macaw, and a black ostrich head. Another is, one lap of silver twist, orange silk tag, small topping for tail; mulberry pig's wool body, dressed medium; mulberry hackle, jay over all; same wing and head as the first fly. Again: Two laps of silver twist, dark orange tag, tail of mallard, and three or four fibres of gold pheasant tippet; body, black pig's wool, rather spare, with a dark fiery brown ring half-way up it, and then black again, a small bit of fiery brown at shoulder to stick out for legs; jay's hackle, gold-pheasant tippet, and mallard's wing; black head. Lough Melvin is good in spring. The Garrison Hotel (Mr. A. Scott) is comfortable. 5 m. from here is Lough-na-Bagh. The trout average 2½lb. Leave from Mr. Maude, at 15s. per day. Next come Loughs Dernacorbut and MacNean. The trout are herring size, but very numerous. Loughs Meeny-mean and Glen Orawan are full of fish averaging ½lb. Lough Anany contains very large perch and small trout.

Glaeryford.—M. & N.C.R. Maine; salmon, trout; free. *Season,* March 1 to Oct. 31.

Glandore.—(*See Skibbereen.*) There are in the immediate neighbourhood fourteen trout lakes, two pike lakes, and three salmon and white trout rivers. First-rate sea fishing. The accommodation is limited, but at the inn the quarters are cheap and comfortable; there is also a boarding house. There is good trout fishing in the Shepperton lakes, half way to Skibbereen. White trout may be caught in streams near, after a flood.

Glenamoy.—7 m. from **Belderg.** A bed or two may be had here; accommodation very bad. This is one of the best white-trout fishings in Ireland. (*See Belderg.*)

Glenarm.—M. & N.C.R. Fair trouting; partly reserved.

Glenavy.—G.N.R. Good trouting in the brook after rain

Glenbeg.—(*See Killorglin.*)

Glencar.—There is good spring salmon fishing in the beginning of the year on the upper Cara river. The river flows into Cara lake, on which there is also very fair salmon fishing early and late in the year. free. Trout are numerous, not very large. There are several brown trout lakes in the mountains accessible from the hotel. Coose lake is close to the hotel; good trouting; Cloon lake, 6m.; excellent salmon and trout fishing.

Glengariffe.—C.B. & S.C.R. On Glengariffe; salmon. Visitors at Roche's Hotel can fish here. (*See Cork.*) Near here are Loughs Bue and Bordlin. Bue is on the top of "Priest's-leap Mountain." It is easy of access from the hotel. Brown trout running herring size. The river that runs out of it is also good. Bordlin Lake, on the top of Bordlin Mountain, is within two or three hundred yards of the road leading from Bantry to Killgarran. There are plenty of trout. Several trout streams and an immense number of mountain lakes in the vicinity. Brown trout very plentiful. Comhola river 3 m. (one of the best *late* salmon and white trout rivers in the South; Mr. Roche preserves 2 m. for his visitors); Ballylicky 6 m. (salmon and white trout; leave freely given); both by good carriage road. Salmon, white trout, and brown trout. Sea-fishing is very good, especially in September.

Glenties.—On the Owenea. (*See Adara.*)

Goresbridge (Carlow).—G.S. & W.R. On Barrow; salmon, trout, and coarse fish.

Gortin (n.s. **Newtown Stewart**).—G.N.S.R. 5 m. On Owenkillea; salmon and white trout. Fishing good late in the season; rain absolutely necessary. 4 m. off is Glenelly river; good brown trout fishing in spring, salmon and white trout in autumn. Good accommodation.

Gweedore (Donegal). — There is a capital hotel here, and fishing for salmon, sea, and brown trout. Gentlemen staying at the Gweedore Hotel may fish in the rivers and lakes belonging to Capt. Hill, as follows: The lakes, and that part of Clady river which is in the landlord's hands may be fished without any charge by gentlemen staying at the hotel, provided they take out their salmon licence from Mr. Robertson, manager, or pay 1l. towards the preservation of the waters. Boats are kept. Gentlemen fishing the river Clady between the hotel and Bunbeg, and in the Gweedore river, must attend to the rules made by the lessees of the fishery. There are numerous good lakes full of small trout open to the public in the Rosses district. which can be fished with ease either from the Gweedore Hotel or Mr. Sweeney's hotel at Dungloe. The Gweedore river, better known by the gillies as Crolly river, is about 1½ m. from Gweedore hotel; salmon and sea trout. Loughanure lake is strictly preserved. (*See Dungloe.*)

Headford (Galway).—(n.s. **Galway,** 10 m.) Lough Corrib; salmon, pike, trout.

Headfort.—G.S. & W.R. The Quagmire river runs under the line. Good for brown trout.

Inchageelah.—There are some good lakes here (Lough Allua containing salmon, char, &c.), and a good hotel. Boats can be had. (*See Macroom.*) The Owvane rises on the Kerry side of Gougane Barra (excellent trouting), and flows into Bally Licky Bay, Bantry. Sheby Lake and Cool Mountain river may also be fished from here.

Inchilea.—Gougane and Inchageelah lakes, &c., also the rivers, the Foarish, the Glasha Gorruv, the Toon, the Laney, the Lullane, the Douglas, the Bride, the Bunyea, may be fished from here.

Innishannon (Cork).—O.B. & S.O.R. Bandon; salmon, trout; preserved by a club.

Jamestown.—On Shannon. (*See Carrick.*)

Jamney.—(*See Rosnakill.*)

Kells.—B. & N.O.R. Good trouting and some salmon; free. *Season*, March 16 to Oct. 19.

Keenkeen Lake (co. Kerry).—The trout are a good size and plentiful. The river that runs from it into the Slahenny is full of trout. The lake is 1½ *m.* from the main road.

Kenmare.—The lesser Blackwater runs 8 *m.* from here, also Sheen 1 *m.*; salmon and trout. Preserved by private persons. Good accommodation at the Southern Hotel. The river rises in Loch Brinn (full of trout), owned by Mr. Mahony, of Dromore Castle. About 2 *m.* off runs the Roughty, rising in Glen Flesk. The salmon and trout fishing in it is free. All the pools and streams can be fished from the bank Good trouting in the Clones Lakes, Glenmore, and Gleninchiquin. On the top of Little Mangerton mountain is Red Trout Lake, containing fine fish. Good in May. Also Humphrey's Lake and Coolnood Lake. The owner of the Falls preserves the Sheen. Cameenbrick and Dromorthy Lakes are good in July and August. Salmon, sea trout, trout, and sea fishing good, especially pollack.

Kilgarvan.—(*See Kenmare.*)

Kilkeel (Down).—Good trouting.

Killaloe (Clare).—W.L. & W.R. On the Shannon; salmon and trout; trouting free. Loch Derg lies above the town; trout, pike, perch, salmon; fishing very good, and free, especially in the Mayfly time; boat and two men 10s. 2 *m.* of the Clare side of the river is leased by O. Dell Vinter, Esq., and the subletting of this fishery is in the hands of the proprietor of Grace's Hotel, which is close to the river and Lough Derg (*see Advertisement*). The best trout flies are an orange body, a little tinsel, a rail's wing, partridge hackle. A green body, red hackle, and starling's wing. A grouse hackle, with orange body. A yellow body, ribbed with gold, and rail's wing. **Limerick** is distant 12 *m.* The Gillaro trout is found in Derg. There are plenty of pike and perch. (*See Carrick.*) Peal fishing in the river is very good about June, but reserved. The trouting very good. In the rapids below the weir is some of the best public trouting in Ireland. Mostly fished from a boat. (*See Nenagh.*) There is ½ *m.* of water free for salmon, on which a fish may be killed in high water. The natural fly, the green drake, is almost exclusively used for the lake; the stone fly is very successful on the river in May, June, and July.

Killarney.—G.S. & W.R. Salmon and trout. The trout run herring size, although large fish are occasionally creeled. The usual charge for a paddle boat and man is 7s. per day. The river Flesk runs near; the fishing is occasionally very good, and open; sport is also good in the Finnow, which flows from Lough Guittane and joins the Flesk at Minish, 4 *m.* from Killarney. The Victoria Bay, opposite hotel, is good during May and June, where there is always a good rise of green drake or May fly; Mahoneys Bay also good, and lower part of Fossa shore to the outlet of the River Laune. A little way up Tomies shore is unequalled for trout fishing, owing to the uniform depth and rocky ground known as The Bank. The edge of Bank is good for salmon; and The Ledges, Brown Island, Killeen, Innisfallen, back of Ross Island, Cow Island, Muckross shore, and Glena Bay are all good salmon grounds. Fair trout fishing can be had round these islands and by the mouth of River Flesk, and towards Billerough shore and Abbey Hall. There is also some good trout fishing in the middle lake by Devil's Island, Jackybys Bay, and Dundag Bay, also along by the mouth of Toro Waterfall. This lake is very good for spring salmon in February, March, and April. The upper lake is also good for salmon in the early months, as both it and the middle lake are clean when the lower lake is dirty from the heavy floods of the Flesk. Good bags of trout may be had in Newfoundland Bay, mouth of Derrycunniny river, also the mouth of Gaerahameen. This river flows from the Black Valley, where is fair trouting. The best flies for these lakes are the orange grouse, the March brown, the hare's ear, the claret and the olive, and the ribbed alder. The best salmon flies are orange jay, black and brown, jointed brown ant, blue jay, orange grouse with jay and blue at shoulder, jointed blue and grey, orange and green jay, and plain ant. About 4 *m.* of the best part of the River Flesk, which is a very free rising river for salmon, is preserved by the Earl of Kenmare. 4 *m.* from Killarney is Lough Guittane, partly preserved by the Earl of Kenmare and Lord Ardilaun. The best flies are Zulu, black and orange, red spinner, red palmer, special partridge, hare's ear; the cochybondhu and alder are good in bright weather. The Laune joins the lakes with the sea. Rod fishing commences on Feb. 1, and ends Oct. 31. Netting opens Jan. 17, and closes July 31; best time in March. Little or no fly fishing is done in the early months, trolling with spoon bait or phantom affording the best sport. The natural graveling is also much used, and is especially good in cold weather. There is a good spot for salmon near Brickeen bridge, and another near "Prince of Wales's Island"; but the first-named is the best ground. There are eels, perch, and flounders in the lake. (*See Cahirciveen; Farranfore; Killorglin.*) Near Kenmare is Lough Loosecannagh, holding great numbers of trout. There are some trout in Lacka Lake 4 *m.* N.E. of Killarney. Waterville opens Jan. 1, and closes July 15; rod fishing Feb. 1 to Oct. 15. *Tacklist*, T. Courtney, Killarney (*see Advertisement*), from whom licences can be obtained.

Killeagh (Cork).—G.S. & W.R. 18 *m* from **Cork.** On Killeagh; trout.

Killibegs (Donegal).—D.R. There is good boat fishing in the harbour, and one or two nice little trout streams near, on which leave may be obtained. The hotel is good.

Killorglin.—*Hotel*: Railway. On Laune. Salmon fishing is very good in August and September after netting has ceased. White trout commence running about the middle of May, from 1½lb. to 3lb. weight. The proprietor of the Railway Hotel gives permission to visitors to fish the salmon pools on the Laune, also the Upper and Lower Caragh river, and Lakes Caragh, Acoose, Yganavan. and Cloone. (*See Glencar.*) Trains run every day from Killarney. The River Maine, on which there is very fair autumn salmon fishing, and good trout fishing earlier in the year, is within an hour and a quarter's drive. 7¼ m. off is the Wales Inn at Glenbeagh, where leave can be obtained to fish two capital burns near the house, one for white trout and the other for brown.

Killumney (Cork).—C. & M.D.R. On South Bride; trout; free. (*See Cork.*)

Killurin.—G.S. & W.R. On Slaney.

Kilmurry (Mayo).—On Owenmore and Mannion; salmon and trout.

Kilrea (Derry).—M. & N.C.R. On Bann; salmon, trout; preserved by a club; salmon, trout, perch, bream. Fishing from the bank, s.t. 1s. (trout only). Trout or salmon fishing from a boat, with single rod and line. between Portna Navigation Weir and the Navigation Weir at Movanagher, and between the Agivey Bridge and the Cutts, near Coleraine; s.t. 7l. 7s., w.t. 1l. 1s.; between Agivey Bridge and the Cutts, near Coleraine—s.t. 4l. 4s., w.t. 12s. 6d.; of James Robb, Carnroe, Kilrea; Mr. Gracey, Kilrea; Andrew King, Toomebridge; man and boat 5s. a day. The trouting is good, fish running from 1lb. to 7lb. each. Dan O'Fee, Basharkin, sells the best flies. The club waters at Carnroe, between Movanagher and Agivey Bridge, Coleraine, are strictly preserved, and leave is difficult to obtain. *Hotel*: Mercer's (*see Advertisement*); whose visitors can fish in the club waters between Movanagher and Kilrea.

Kilshelan.—W.L. & W.R. Suir; salmon and trout. Count de la Poer grants leave for the asking. Fishing very good.

Kinsale.—C.B. & S.C.R. Sea fishing very good. Mackerel can be taken with hook and line in great numbers in summer, and all this coast abounds in pollack.

Lanesborough.—On Shannon. (*See Carrick.*)

Larne.—M. & N.C.R. (*See Cushendall.*)

Laytown.—G.N.R. 27 m. from Dublin. Nanny; sea trout, pike, B. trout. Nanny rises by Navan. The sea trout fishing is very good. Between the railway bridge and the sea are three or four pools full of fish on the ebb tide. They will only take worm or imitation sand eel. From Julianstown to Duleek are plenty of pike.

Leenane (Connemara).—Erriff; salmon, sea and brown trout; preserved by a club. Bundorragha, 2 m.; salmon, sea trout. *Loughs*: Dhulough, 3 m. (watered by Bundarra); salmon, sea trout. Fee, 4 m. Muck, 4 m. Tawnyard (head of Erriff fishery), 5 m.; salmon, sea trout; at 10s. 6d., with boat. Kylemore, 5 m.; salmon, sea trout; leave from the Duke of Manchester and Lord Ardilaun. Nafooey, 6 m.; gillaroo, brown trout, pike. Very good sea fishing; mackerel, whiting, sole, pollack, plaice, &c. July, August, and September are the best months for salmon and trout. *Hotel*: Leenane, where tickets can be had, and free fishing in Loch Nafooey, Rivers Maam and Leenane, and two lakes on the road to Kylemore. Spring salmon fishing opens in February. Fishing may now be had from Dhulough House; proprietor, R. H. McKrown, Leenane.

Letterfrack (Connemara).—Dawross river. *Loughs*: Pollacapul. Kylemore; salmon, sea and brown trout; preserved by M. Henry, Esq.; leave may be obtained. Best months, July, August, and September. Two fair hotels and lodgings.

Limavady.—M. & N.C.R. On Roe; excellent salmon and white trout fishing both above and below the town. Late in the season the salmon fishing near **Dungiven** is better than here.

Limerick.—(*See Killaloe*). On Shannon; good salmon and trout fishing. At Castle Connell there is splendid salmon fishing, though all let on lease. Cruiser Royal Hotel, in Limerick, is one of the best, and can always provide its visitors with good free fishing; apply to proprietor, James Flynn. (*See Carrick.*) From the Lax Weir upward some 5 m. or 6 m. is free. There is good salmon fishing in the Maigne 4 m. off. Good fishing can also be had at Castle Connell by month or season. Apply to landlord. *Tackleist*, A. Nestor, George-street.

Lismore.—G.S. & W.R. On the Blackwater. Leave from the lessees, but all fish must be given up. March and April, and again in June and July, are the best months.

Listowel.—W.L. & W.R. (*See Abbeyfeale.*)

Londonderry.—Two miles off is the Faughan; salmon, white, and brown trout. For brown trout, go six miles up the river to Clady, and fish *up*.

Longford.—M.G.W.R. Stokestown can be reached from here: Kilglass lakes can be fished; pike, perch, and trout. Midway between here and Stokestown is a weir on the Shannon, at Tormandary. Capital trouting. Rough accommodation in the village.

Louisburgh (Lough na Nattora).—n.s. **Westport**. Louisburgh river; trout, salmon, sea trout; leave must be obtained from Marquis of Sligo. Fishing from June 1 to Nov. 1. Carrownisky 5 m.; salmon, sea trout, brown trout. Fishing begins July 1, ends Nov. 1. There are two good lakes 6 m. off—one especially, Nahaltora, but there are no boats.

Maam.—Lough Corrib; pike. trout. &c.: fishing free. *Inn* very comfortable.

Macroom (Cork).—C. & M.R. 2 *m.* off is the Lee; salmon, trout, &c. *(See Cork.)* The Victoria Hotel, Macroom *(see Advt.)*, is close to the fishery. Within ⅓ *m.* of the hotel are three tributaries of the Lee, the Salane (good salmon and trout), the Foarish and Laney (trout). The Toon, the Glashagorror, and lakes Inchageelah 6 *m.* off, Gougaen-Burra, the source of Lee, 15 *m.* off, well stocked with trout. The upper waters near Inchageelah are well stocked. The Macroom Railway runs parallel with the river Bride, a large trout stream tributary to the Lee, and holding the very finest brown trout in county Cork. Macroom is 24 *m.* from Cork. Cars may be had at the Hotel.

Mallow (Cork).—On Blackwater; salmon and trout. Leave may sometimes be obtained on application to the proprietors. In some of the streams of the Upper Blackwater, from Banteer and beyond Millstreet, fishing is free. There is good trouting on the Clyda Leer and other small streams in the neighbourhood. Mr. Harold, fishing tackle maker, Mallow, has often fishing to let; he will give all information.

Meelick.—A few miles below Bannagher. There is fair sport about June with the peal. Above Bannagher is Shannon Bridge, but there is no trout fishing, and very little salmon fishing; boats are necessary. There is a clean little inn here. *(See Carrick.)*

Milford (Donegal).—Near Derry. Close by is Lough Fern; the fishing is very good both for salmon and trout, and free. The best season from March 20 to end of June. The best flies for Lough Fern are fiery browns, clarets, and olives, and the following: tip, silver tinsel; tag, golden yellow pigs' wool, ribbed with silver; red hackle, jay at the shoulder; wing, jungle cock, two toppings, and fibres of bustard; long crimson horns; head, yellow pigs' wool. Lough Keel, 3 *m.*: brown trout; best months May and June. There are several trout lakes in the vicinity. and sea trouting in Mulroy Bay. *Hotel*: McDevitt's, Milford. *(See Advertisement.)* *(See Rathmelton.)*

Mount Shannon.—A few miles above Killaloe; reached by steamer from Killaloe. Best place for Mayfly (May and June) in Lough Derg.

Moy (Tyrone).—Blackwater; good fishing. *Season*, March 16 to Oct. 19.

Moy Valley (Kildare).—On M.G.W.R. Blackwater; trout. pike; trouting good and free from here to Kilmacow, the fishing of which is free. Trout small, but tolerably plentiful.

Mullinavat.—G.S. & W.R. 5 *m.* from Waterford. A good trout stream runs from here to Kilmacow, the fishing of which is free. Trout small, but tolerably plentiful.

Mullingar.—M.G.W.R. The station for Belvidere and Lough Owel, the famous West-meath lakes. Lake Deravaragh lies near. The trout run large, and during the May-fly season great numbers may be caught with the natural fly. Good sport can be had in Belvidere Lake, 2½ *m.* on the Castletown-station road. The river Inny and Brosna are good streams. *Hotel*: Greville Arms, where boats can be had.

Naas (Kildare).—G.S. & W.R. On Liffey; trout.

Nenagh (Tipperary).—G.S. & W.R. 5 *m.* off is the Shannon and Lough Derg, at Dromineer, where are two small hotels. This is a good point for the first of the May fly fishing. There are several fishermen here. At Mount Shannon, 7 *m.* off by water, is a capital country hotel, recently enlarged and improved. Mount Shannon can be reached also from Bird Hill, 15 *m.* off. Artificial fly has not been much tried on the lake, unless with cross-line. Derg holds, besides plenty of large trout, pike, perch, and rudd; the last can be caught in large quantities with artificial fly in the shallows. The best places for pike are in Coos, Rosamore, and Scaup bays, which can be best fished from Mount Shannon, where good fishermen and boats can be had.

Newcastle.—B. & C.D.R. Good trouting; good sea fishing. Good hotel.

Newport (Mayo).—M.G.W.R. On Newport, Burrishole, and Owengarve; salmon and sea trout; salmon fishing worthless; white trout fishing very fair. There are two or three lakes near, where the trout fishing is fair. At the head of the river is Lough Beltra. There are two pools by the town. Small black or dark blue silk bodies, with red or orange tips, silver twist, black hackles, and starling wing, are good for white trout; lemon and hare's ear, silver twist, red hackle, and mallard wing for salmon. There are salmon and sea trout on the lake, but only one boat, belonging to a private person. The fishing on Furnace Lake, about 2 *m.* from Newport, is good: the landlady can give permission. Lough Fyough is above Lough Furnace, but is, we believe, private property.

Newtownstewart.—G.N.R. Three hours from Belfast (Belfast and Liverpool route); one hour from Londonderry *(vid Belfast and Heysham)*. Rivers Mourne, Strule, Derg, and Glenelly; all strictly preserved; salmon s.t. 4*l.*; w.t. 10*s.*; d.t. 2*s.* 6*d.*; brown trout, s.t. 5*s.*; permits can be obtained in the village. Splendid salmon and trout fishing. Season opens April 1, ends October 10. The brown trout fishing is excellent, especially in the months of April and May. The first run of salmon and sea trout takes place towards the end of June. July is considered best month for salmon fishing; September and October are also very good. Salmon up to 10lb. are plentiful, and very game. This is perhaps the very best and cheapest station in the North of Ireland for a salmon fisher, and he has his choice of four rivers, all within easy reach, and which contain pools that remain fishable even under abnormal conditions. *Hotels*: Abercorn *(see Advertisement)*, Castle *(see Advertisement)*, Maturin Baird Arms.

Oughterard.—There is very good fishing here in the hands of the Lough Corrib Fisheries Association. The secretary, S. B. Doig, Esq., J.P., will give all information. *(See Galway).*

Pettigo (Donegal).—On LoughErne; good trout and pike and perch fishing on the lough, and splendid trout and bream fishing on several lakes in the vicinity; free. The best months for Lough Erne are March to June; for the smaller lakes, which teem with trout, May to September. Sport excellent. Hotel accommodation good at Arthur McHugh's, Middlebrook, who finds boats.

Port Rush.—M & N.C.R. Sea fishing excellent.

Port Stewart.—M. & N.C.R. Excellent sea fishing.

Portumna (Galway).—At the head of Lough Derg; salmon, trout, perch, pike; reached by steamer from Banagher or Athlone. Excellent salmon fishing by boat in late autumn; very good perch and pike in early autumn; phantoms and spoons for baits; flies, small Shannon pattern.

Queenstown (Cork).—At Rostelian Castle, Ringabella, there is a good trout lake, and also ponds and streams at Inch, near Aghada. Excellent sea fishing both inside and outside this harbour. Pollack at the Harbour Rock, and Turbis Bank, and along the line of the rocky cliffs of both sides of the entrance, and at the Cow, Calf, or Stag Rocks, a little without the point on the east side. Round and at the points of Haulbowline and Spike Island bass and pollack are met with; and in the offing plenty of hake, whiting, and ground fish. (*See Cork* and *Crosshaven.*)

Randalstown (Antrim).—M. & N.C.R. On Maine; salmon and trout preserved. Lough Neagh is 2 m. off. April, September, and October are best for salmon in Maine. (*See Antrim.*)

Rathmelton (Donegal).—On the Lennon; salmon, trout. The salmon fishing in the reserved part of the river is capital in early spring, and in July, August, and September both on the upper and lower river, particularly between Lough Fern and Rathmelton, where the spring fishing is good. Lough Fern is entirely dependent on the rainfall. If the freshes come at suitable times, the salmon fishing in the lake is good in April, May, June, July, and August. June is generally the worst month. The *two best spring flies* for salmon here by far are (1) grey *body*; *hackle* claret, with a little jay; mallard's *wing*. (2) *Body* orange, with blue tip; claret and little jay *hackle*; *wing*, mallard's wing, with dash of golden pheasant. Trout fishing in river not very good, but good in lake April to end of August. Best *general* fly, orange body, black or red hackle. Good accommodation at the Stewart Arms Hotel. There are many open lakes near; the two best are Loughs Fern (3 m.) and Garten. (*See Milford.*) Garten Lough is 9 m. distant, and holds trout. A good summer trout fly for the Lennon and Lough Fern is a small-sized fly, with a rough fluffy body of dirty yellow and a brown wing; also the brown Palmer. The Lennon is a narrow, sluggish river.

Rosnakill (Donegal).—On Mulroy Bay. Sea trout may be caught here in the bay; Rowros Ferry, near the village of Carrigart, and Morass Ferry, near Rosnakill, are the best spots. The following are good flies: Hook, No. 4 or 5; green peacock tag; tail, 3 fibres guinea-fowl; body, pale silk ribbed with fine silver; hackle, claret; wing, landrail. Hook, No. 4 or 5; body, dark blue silk ribbed with gold; tail, 3 fibres mallard; hackle, claret; wing, duck underwing and brown turkey mixed. Hook, No. 4; body, half black wool and half green peacock ribbed with gold; hackle, black; wing, starling or jay. Lake Kindrum (trout) lies near here. Jamney is the nearest post-town. The fishing is very good. Good flies are grouse hackles over orange silk; golden olive mohair bodies, and dark olive, with the hackle lapped half way up the body. The cowdung, hare's ear, and red hackle and black hackle over claret. Lord Leitrim preserves one side of the lake, and Colonel Barton the other. The fishing is free to visitors staying either at the Rosapenna or the Portsalon Hotel (*see Advt.*).

Rossbeigh (Kerry).—*Hotel*: Headley Arms, very comfortable. On Cara and Cara Lake; salmon, white and brown trout. The landlady rents the lower part of Cara for her guests. The best places for white trout are below, and on two hundred yards above the bridge. The salmon flies are all small. Blue, orange, and grey are the usual bodies, a bunch of mallard and a pair of blue macaw horns for wings, blue, orange, and fiery brown hackles, bodies very spare and hackles short. The "Claverhouse" is a good fly. *Tag*, silver tinsel; *tail*, one topping; *body*, lower half golden olive silk, upper bright blue with silver twist; *hackle*, blue on body, being brown at shoulder; *wing*, bunch of mallard with one topping; *head*, peacock's herl; *hook*, No. 11. Sea-trout fly, "Quin's Fancy," *Tail*, two fibres mallard; *butt*, bright green peacock; *body*, orange silk with fine silver twist; *hackle*, bright brown on body, darker at shoulder; *wing*, mallard; *head*, green peacock; dressed very small. This is a good fly all over the South of Ireland. In lake Coomasaharn, out of which runs the river Beigh, are small brown trout, white trout and salmon, and char. The best side of the lake is the west. There is no boat. In Lough Coomeeneragh or "Eragh," the brown trout run large, but are bad risers. There are several other good lakes near. The salmon fishing in Lough Cara is poor, but the trouting, five or six to the pound, is good. All these waters are free except the Beigh, which is let. There is good salmon fishing in the Laune in August and September. (*See Killorglin.*) There are two free boats belonging to the hotel on Cara Lake. Boatman 2s. 6d. a day, and whisky and bread 1s. a head. The hotel is 1¼ m. from the sea; good fishing.

Ruskey.—On Shannon. (*See Carrick.*)

Shannon Bridge.—(*See Meelick.*) At the fords above Derryholmes there are a few good trout. There is fair salmon fishing. Up Shannon, towards the Seven Churches, good pike and perch fishing can be had. (*See Carrick.*)

Skibbereen (Cork).—C.B. & S.C.R. On Ilen: salmon, sea-trout, and trout. Free from the weir (1 *m.* north of Skibbereen) to a mile below the town, the tide flowing as far as the weir. There are two or three hotels, and private lodgings can also be obtained. The river near the town affords the best sport. A peculiar fish called Coolhahan abounds in the tideway. Purples, fiery browns with gold; in spring, olive, and gold, are the best flies, tied on Parkin's five, six, and seven round bend. The numerous lakes round Skibbereen—viz., Ballyally, 4 *m.*, Loughine, 2½ *m.* (sea-trout; splendid sea fishing close adjoining). Drimminidhy, 10 *m.*, Shepperton, 4 *m.*, and Lissard (all free)—afford good trout fishing in April and May. After dark in June, July, and August, the lakes afford rare sport; and also in the river after dark to midnight at Poulnarab, the Swimming Hole, Soldier's Hole, Downing's Reach, Burnt Mill, &c., fair white trout fishing prevails. The best salmon months are July, August, September, and October, when the fishing closes. Sea-fishing can be had at Glandore (8 *m.*) and Castle Townsend. A boat, with four men, is about 6*s.* per day, and there are plenty of public cars to be had at reasonable cost. (*See Baltimore.*) Half-way to Glandore are the Shepperton lakes (brown trout, running herring size). Lough Ballyally, 4 *m.*, contains large fish. Just beyond this lake is Toe Bay, where sea-fishing can be had from the rocks or boat. There are two streams to the west which after a flood hold salmon and white trout, and for which leave might be obtained.

Sligo.—M.G.W.R. The fishing in the lake is very good; permission, we believe, can be obtained.

Stranorlar.—D.R. On the River Finn, in which there is very good salmon and trout fishing. This river joins the Mourne at Strabane, from which point the two combined form the Foyle. The fishing of the Finn is open to the public in the neighbourhood of Stranorlar, where there is comfortable hotel accommodation. There are several good-sized lakes convenient to the town, where excellent trout fishing can be had.

Thomastown (Kilkenny).—G.S. & W.R. Nore; trout, salmon. The owner of Brown's Barn preserves some 4 *m.*

Toombeola (Galway).—Good sea fishing. (*See Ballinahinch.*)

Toome Bridge.—Bann; trouting good from May. There is also some good pike and perch fishing, large numbers having been taken recently with live bait and spoon. *Hotel*: O'Neill Arms; very comfortable. Boat and boatmen 5*s.* a day. The best flies are coachman, pheasant and orange, partridge and orange, wren and olive, and the Fenian. Very good natural fly fishing under the fall. P. and J. McKinless, George Gribben, and W. J. McIlroy are all good boatmen. Post town and telegraph office, Toome. Toome Bridge is 30 *m.* from Belfast (M. & N.C.R.)

Tramore.—There is a capital lake here for large trout, Ballyscanlon, belonging to Mr. Power, who freely gives leave. Sea fishing in the bay; bass at the mouth of Rinshack harbour.

Tullamore.—In Pallas lake is good fishing—perch, tench, &c.; the tench are very large and the perch often reach 5lb.

Valencia, Island of.—About 2½ *m.* from Cahirciveen. There is first-class sea fishing here, and fresh-water fishing in the autumn in the Inny (leased by the hotel proprietor), after a fresh. There is a good hotel (the Royal) (*see Advertisement*), and lodgings are to be had on moderate terms. Pollack, gurnet, and bass are numerous in the harbour. Boats can be hired on moderate terms. Capital bathing and boating on the island, and the scenery is some of the finest in Ireland.

Waterford.—(*See Carrick.*)

Waterville (Co. Kerry).—10 *m.* from Cahirciveen, on the G.S. & W. Railway. Salmon fishing commences on Feb. 1, and white trout are plentiful during June, July, August, and September. Waterville is beautifully situated between Ballinskelligs Bay on the west and Lough Currane on the east. The lake is about 4 *m.* long by 2 *m.* broad, and is a veritable angler's paradise. The fishing is free to hotel visitors, accommodation good, and the requirements of sportsmen well attended to. Bay View (*see Advertisement*) and Butler Arms hotels are in the village. The Cummeragh river, together with the following lakes, Nabrackdarrig. Cloonaghlin, Eilaineane, and Loughnahiska, are open only to Bay View Hotel visitors, and are all well preserved, but Derriana and Namona open to all visitors for a small payment. Both the Bay View and the Butler Arms have fishing in the River Inny, and the Butler Arms has also fishing in Loughna Mona lake. The best flies for Lough Currane are dark claret or brown-red mohair, dark red hackle, dark woodcock or mallard wings, and a turn of gold twist. *Flydresser*: Tim McCarthy. Ballinskelligs Bay affords good sea fishing. For further information refer to hotel advertisements.

Westport (Mayo).—M.G.W.R. There are small brown trout in the neighbouring lakes and rivers for which leave is freely given, except the river and lake in Lord Sligo's demesne. 8 *m.* off is Erriff; salmon, sea trout; tickets can be had.

Wexford.—G.S. & W.R. On the Slaney; salmon and sea-trout.

Wicklow.—D.W. & W.R. There are some salmon, and plenty of white trout in Vartrey; fishing free. There are a quantity of wide and deep drains, called "sconces," where there is capital roach fishing, with some trout.

SCOTLAND.

Aberdeen.—(*See Alford Bridge, Newburgh,* and *Aboyne.*) Dee and Don; salmon, trout. 1*l.* 10*s.* per rod is charged for liberty to fish in the tidal waters. At Murtle, salmon, sea and brown trout fishing can be had in Dee for over 2 *m,* by staying at the Deeside Hydropathic Establishment, (*see Advertisement*). The Grandholm water on Don, 4 *m.* long, is in the hands of the Earl of Suffolk, who lets a limited number of rods for the spring and summer fishing. Inschgarth fishing on Dee let for season. Tickets may be had on the Ellon Castle water at 3*s.* per day, or 7*s.* 6*d.* per week (hotel visitors only) ; apply to Mr. Edward Reid, New Inn, Ellon. The Ugie Fishery (lessee, J. W. Forbes, Esq.) includes the Pitfour water from the junction of the North and South Ugie, at about 6 *m.* from the sea, and the Balmoor fishings near the sea (finnock and sea trout, spring and autumn). Season opens Feb. 25 and closes Oct. 31. Balmoor to the sea, s.t. 40*s.*, m.t. 25*s.*, w.t. 10*s.* ; s.t. for whole of river 5*l.* 5*s.*, of the tackleists. *Tackleists,* W. Brown & Co., 64, George-street.

Aberfeldy.—(*See Weem.*) By staying at the Breadalbane Arms or Palace Hotel, a good stretch of the Tay can be fished free ; salmon, trout ; also Loch-na-Craig ; trouting is very good. Fishing can be had in the above water of Tay, at 5*s.* for two months, from the secretary of the Aberfeldy Angling Club, who preserve. (*See Kinloch Rannoch.*)

Aberfoyle (Stirling).—N.B.R. Forth ; salmon, trout, grayling. *Lochs* : Ard and Chon ; trout and pike ; boat and man, 7*s.* per diem. *Hotel* : the Bailie Nicol Jarvie.

Aberlour (n. s. **Craigellachie,** 3 *m.*).—Spey ; salmon, sea trout, trout. *Hotel* : Aberlour, where fishing can be had by week ; number limited, 7 rods.

Abington.—C.R. On Clyde ; trout and grayling.

Aboyne.—On Dee. Rods are occasionally to be let. Farland burn, free. *Hotel* : Huntly Arms, where 5 *m.* of salmon fishing in Dee can be had in July and August.

Achiltubuie (Ross).—Salmon, ferox, trout. By staying at the Achiltubuie Hotel, fishing can be had.

Alford Bridge.—26½ *m.* from Aberdeen. On Don ; salmon and trout. *Hotels* : Forbes Arms and Haughton Arms ; permission at the hotels. Fishing begins on April 1st. 2 *m.* north, in the parish of Tullynessle, are some good trout burns, one especially, which divides the lands of Knockespoch from those of Lord Forbes. Leochel burn, which joins the Don 1 *m.* up, is a good trouting stream.

Altnaharra Hotel (Sutherland).—Loch Naver ; tolerably good trout, two to the pound(fly) ; good salmon fishing in February, March, and April, and half of May, and occasionally in June and July ; two boats at the hotel, two rods to a boat. Mudale Water runs into the head of Loch Naver. Trout plenty, and fine. Loch Meadie (boats) is the source of Mudale Water, 6 *m.* from Altnaharra. Lots of free rising trout of three to the pound : larger ones by trolling. A small loch, lying to the east of the road, through Strath Bugastie, about 4 *m.* from the inn, gives very good fishing on a rough day. Loch Coulside (boats), 5 *m.* from Altnaharra, on the road to Tongue, is very good, fish average two and a half to the pound. Wading is bad. Loch Halam (boat), 2 *m.* or 3 *m.* N.E. of the southern end of Loch Coulside, is swarming with trout of about two to the pound. There are plenty of fish nearly a pound weight. Loch Brach Buie (boat), a very small loch, with a tiny island in it, about 2 *m.* E. by S. of shepherd's house, at the north end of Loch Coulside. Trout average nearly a pound. Loch Tarvie, 2 *m.* ; large trout (boats). Loch Stauk, 3 *m.* (boats). Very large ferox can be caught in Loch Loyal (boats), 6 *m.* off. Occasionally salmon are taken.

Amulree.—There is a good inn here. Loch Freuchie lies near. (*See Dunkeld* ; *Corriemuchloch.*)

Arbroath (Forfar).—C. & N.B.R. Elliott ; trout ; fishing for visitors in 2 to 3 *m.* Lunan ; trout ; fishing for 5 *m.* There are two hotels.

Ardentinny.—On Loch Long. The Finnart runs into Loch Long here ; sea trout, trout. The fishing is preserved by Mr. T. Douglas.

Ardeonaig.—On Loch Tay. (*See Kenmore.*)

Ardgay (Ross).—By staying at the Balnagown Arms some salmon fishing can be had in the Carron at 5*s.* per day, and the fish may be retained. The fishing is good when there is plenty of water, and the quarters are very comfortable.

Ardlui (Dumbarton).—Loch Lomond ; fishing free. *Hotel* : Ardlui.

Ardrossan.—(*See Brodick, Corrie,* and *Lamlash.*)

Aultnacealgach Hotel. By Lairg (Sutherland).—28 *m.* from Lairg. This inn makes up 24 beds ; capital trouting. Loch Boralan, at the hotel door ; trout (three to the pound) and char ; boat. Loch Urigill, 1 *m.* on the other side of Boralan ; trout, char. Loch Cama, 4 *m.* ; trout (three to the pound), ferox. Loch Veyatie, 4½ *m.* ; trout, char, ferox ; good sport in a breeze. There are some good trouting streams in the neighbourhood, such as the Aultnacealgach and Ledbeg ; fish well with water in August and September. The landlord of the hotel has 10 boats on the lochs. Fishing free.

Aviemore (Inverness).—Fishing can be had by staying at the Aviemore Station Hotel.

Aylort Inn.—The inn is 27½ *m.* from Fort William. On Loch Eilt and river Aylort ; salmon and trout. The fishing is in the hands of the proprietor, A. W. Nicholson, Esq., who generally lets it for the season.

Ayr.—(*See Loch Doon.*)

Ballantrae (Ayr).—n.s. **Girvan**, 13 *m.* Stinchar: trout, sea-trout, salmon; Lord Stair lets the first mile up from the sea; above it is preserved by different owners, who will give leave. Mr. Hunter. of Glenagass Castle, preserves a good loch, and gives occasional leave. There are many good lochs 12 to 18 *m.* inland. Sea fishing good.

Ballater.—On Dee; salmon and trout. The proprietor of the Invercauld Arms, Braemar, lets the fishing; the water is let by the rod.

Ballindalloch (Banff).—By staying at the Dalnashaugh Hotel, fishing can be had in Avon.

Balmacarra.—Some sea fishing may be got here. There is trouting in two lochs near the inn, which is a very comfortable one.

Banavie.—N.B.R. *Hotel*: Banavie Hotel. On Caledonian Canal and river Lochy. July is the best month. This river is, with the exception of one small beat, taken up. The Spean runs 5 *m.* off. Spean rises in two lochs, full of trout. and, after a course of 8 *m.*, falls into Loch Laggan. (*See Loch Laggan.*) At Roy Bridge river Roy joins Spean. Salmon and trout. Roy rises in a good loch 12 *m.* off. There are no feeders of any consequence. The fishing is now taken up. At Spean Bridge, 3 *m.* from Roy Bridge (quarters: Spean Bridge Inn), there is a good burn, holding occasionally salmon and sea trout. The Spean is all taken up from the falls (2 *m.* above Roy Bridge) to the Lochy, which it joins some 4 *m.* on. Trouting in Loch Lochy free to visitors at the hotel.

Banff.—Capital pollack fishing just outside the harbour with indiarubber bait whiffing. Salmon and trout fishing can be had in Deveron, free near the mouth, elsewhere by permission. Also free fishing in the burn of Boyne and burn of King Edward, 6 *m.* by rail. 4 *m.* of Deveron free to visitors at Fife Arms Hotel, Braemar.

Beattock.—2 *m.* off is Moffat. (*See Moffat.*) *Hotel*: Beattock.

Beauly.—On Beauly; salmon, sea trout, trout; preserved by Lord Lovat. *Hotels*: Lovat Arms; Glen Affaric (has fishing rights in Cannich and Glass rivers); Priory (which has fishing in Beauly). Spring and autumn fishing good.

Ban Wyvis Hotel.—Salmon fishing in the Blackwater.

Birnam (N.B.).—On Tay. By staying at the Birnam Hotel 6 *m.* of salmon fishing can be had in Tay, and trout fishing in Bran, which joins Tay here. Bran runs out of Loch Freuchie nearly 12 *m.* S.W. of Dunkeld. There are plenty of fish; May and June are the best months. (*See Amulree* and *Corriemuchloch.*)

Blairgowrie.—On Ericht. There are several lochs near. The Ericht. Ardle, Shee, and Blackwater (free) are all accessible from here, and afford good trouting. There are some good pike in Marlu Loch. Fishing free on Lunan and Loch Stormont.

Bonar Bridge (Sutherland).—G.N. of S.R.; H.R. *Hotel*: Balnagown Arms. where trouting can be had in the Carron.

Bowland Bridge.—N.B.R. On Gala and Caddow; trout.

Braemar.—On Dee; trout and salmon. By staying at the Fife Arms salmon fishing can be had in over seven miles of water. Particulars on application.

Brawl Castle.—On Thurso: salmon, sea trout, brown trout. Rods from 15*l.* to 60*l.* per month. Apply to Mrs. Janet, Dunbar, Brawl Castle. Fishing very good. (*c.s.*).

Brechin (Forfar)—C.B. & N.B.R. Eunice; trout; permission required. South Esk, 4 *m.*; salmon, trout. *Loch*: Lee; trout, char; leave from the owner of Invermack Forest. *Hotel*: Crown

Bridgend (Islay).—By staying at the Bridgend Hotel fishing can be had in Lochs Gorm and Finlaggan.

Bridge of Allan (Stirling).—C.R. Visitors to Royal Hotel can obtain some trout and salmon fishing.

Bridge of Turk.—Lochs Ard, Chon, and Dronkie lie near. Dronkie is full of trout, and can be fished easily from the side.

Brodick (Isle of Arran).—There is a very fine hotel where the steamer touches. The river fishing is worthless. (*See Lamlash*).

Bute, Island of.—About 2 *m.* from Rothsay is Loch Greenan, containing large trout and braise. Opposite Rothsay on the mainland is the Ardine—sea trout and brown trout; and the Ruel (strictly preserved), further on towards the Kyles of Bute, contains the same fish. Pollack, lythe, cod, and other sea fish.

Cairndow.—10 *m.* from Inverary, near the head of Loch Fyne. *Hotel*: Cairndow, where fishing can be obtained in river Kinglass and Loch Restal. Close at hand a stream runs into the loch; in June sea trout and salmon enter this stream. There is capital herring, mackerel, lythe, and cod fishing in the loch. The fishing is free.

Callander (Perth).—On the Teith: salmon and trout. In Loch Vennachar (1 *m.* from Hydro, 2 *m.* from town) the trout fishing is very good; from ½lb. to 2lb. The loch can be fished from the bank, but the best sport is from the boat, preferably on the north side. Boats and men are always available. Loch Lubnaig (salmon and trout) is within half hour's drive; boats and men available. Both these lochs are free. Loch Voil, which swarms with trout, is a short journey by rail to Balquhidder station. It is a private loch, with only one boat, which can be had by arrangement. In Loch Achray (about 6 *m.* on Trossachs road) the trout run large, but are somewhat shy. Trolling is best. Pike of large size are to be had. Visitors to the Hydropathic (*see Advertisement*) have about 5 *m.* of free fishing on both sides of the Teith and part of the Leny. Large yellow and sea.

trout, also salmon, are numerous. *Hotels*: Hydropathic (most comfortable, and recommended), Ancaster Arms (with free fishing). Dreadnought (ditto). *Tackleists*: D. and J. Stewart, who issue tickets for the south bank of the Teith (*see Advertisement*).

Campbeltown (Argyll).—There is trouting in several small lochs near the town, and sea fishing (whiting, haddock, &c.) in the harbour and Firth of Clyde.

Canonbie (Dumfries).—Visitors at the Cross Keys Inn (very good) can have salmon, sea and brown trout fishing on the Esk and its tributaries by paying 5s. per diem for salmon and 2s. 6d. for trout. The salmon fishing is not good till October, and sea trout till July.

Carsphairn, Dalry (Galloway).—Good fishing in the river Dench when there is water enough, but always sport to be had in the "Lane" hard by. *Hotel*: Salutation (*see Advertisement*), which is very comfortable.

Castle-Douglas (Kirkcudbright).—Urr, trout; free. Dee, 5 m.; pike, salmon, trout; poor fishing.

Clovenford.—Below Peebles. On Tweed: salmon and trout. The fishing is good.

Coll, Island of (Southern Hebrides).—There are twelve well-stocked lochs, and the trout fishing, which is very good, is free to visitors to the Aringour Hotel (*see Advertisement*). The accommodation is good and the hotel is within 200 yards of pier and post office. Good sea fishing for lythe and saithe.

Colonsay Island.—*Hotel*: Scalasaig. Visitors to the hotel have good trouting free in two of the lochs. Sea fishing good; boats.

Corrie (Isle of Arran).—(*See Lamlash.*)

Corriemuckloch.—Loch Freuchie lies near. (*See Dunkeld.*) There is a nice inn at Amulree, 2 m. off. Close to the old inn of Corriemuckloch is a small loch holding large trout. It is at present let with the shooting.

Craigellachie. — G.N.S.R. Spey; salmon, sea trout, trout; salmon preserved, but trouting can be obtained on application to owners or lessees (*see Aberlour*). Free fishing on Levet burn; salmon, trout. *Hotel*: Craigellachie, which has 2 m. of Spey free to visitors.

Creetown (Kirkcudbright).—*Hotel*: Barholm Arms. On Cree, Beg, Fleet, Minnich, Moneypool, and Feery. The fishing on the Cree is in the hands of the Earl of Galloway, who occasionally gives leave. Tickets for Fleet from Mr. Murray Stewart, of Cally, Gatehouse. Trout, salmon, sea trout. *Loch*: Skerrow, let with shooting.

Crianlarich.—Coaches pass daily during the season, going to all parts of the country. On Loch Dochart; trout, perch, and sometimes salmon. The fishing in Loch Dochart is not very good, but sometimes very heavy baskets are made during the floods; late in the season salmon find their way into the lake and up the river running into it. The fishing in the river Dochart is sometimes good. (*See Luib.*) There are two good burns joining Loch Dochart, both full of fish; the angler cannot mistake them by walking down the road. There are two lochs, Marrigan and Essent, belonging to — Place, Esq., some 3 m. over the hills on the other side of the river, both very full of fish. A day may sometimes be obtained. About 6 m. behind the village, to the south-west, is a mountain tarn, holding some large fish, and another on a mountain range close to the village, to the westward. The one on the west of the village is a little pool containing some splendid trout. By taking the road to Inveroran, at the head of Loch Lomond, the river Falloch is soon reached, where fair fishing can be enjoyed. (*See Inveroran.*) The Dochart is really the head waters of the Tay. *Hotel*: Crianlarich

Crieff (Perth).—On Earn; salmon and trout. At St. Fillans, 12 m. off, fair trouting can be had. *Hotels*: Drummond Arms and Stewart Arms, where fishing can be had; Sept. 3l. 10s. per week; good salmon fishing in October at 4l. per week; rods limited. The Drummond Castle lengths can be fished at 5s. a day for September, and 10s. in October Good trouting in Allmond, 6 m. off; also in Barbhie, Brau, and Lednock.

Dalguise.—On Tay; salmon and trout; all strictly preserved.

Dalmally.—Rivers Orchy and Awe. Salmon, trout, ferox, pike, perch. *Hotels*: Dalmally and Loch Awe Hotels (*see Advts.*). very good. Boats can be had. In the bay, on the south side of Kilchurn Castle, there is good pike fishing Orchy joins Awe 2 m. from the hotel; good salmon fishing preserved by the hotel. The fishing is very fair early in the season. There are several small rivers and burns near, all full of trout, though small. There are two or three lakes some short distance in the hills-full of trout. About two hours and a half walk from the inn are two lochs, the largest of which (Loch Ancruich) contains large trout. (*See Inveroran*; *Loch Awe*.)

Dalmellington. — Loch Doon lies near; plenty of small brown trout; fishing free. The Cross Keys Inn is good, and the proprietor has boats on the loch, which is 4 m. off.

Dalwhinnie (Perth).—*Hotel*: Locberict Hotel, Dalwhinnie (*see Advt.*); good. On Loch Ericht; fair trouting. June, July, or August and September, are the best months. Large ferox are constantly taken. The best part of the loch for trolling is from the Forester's Lodge, near the middle of the loch, to the west end, and as near the shore as can be done with safety to the tackle. The best flies are red, yellow or orange, green and black bodies. The red, yellow and orange should have a red hackle and the green a black; the red is the best. The wings are woodcock, jay, or teal; the body should be ribbed with gold. Boats at the hotel free of charge. About 6 m. down the loch on the north side is the shooting lodge, and 9 *m.* further down on the same side is a keeper's house, where a bed may be got; the house is called Benalder. Remember to take your provisions with you. Good sport can be had in the river Ericht, which runs out of the loch into Loch Rannoch. It is about 8 *m.* long; the fish are neither so large nor so good as in the loch. (*See Tigh-na-linn.*) Truim runs close by the hotel; trout and grilse in autumn. Cuisch burn is good fishing, and Loch Cuiach is open to visitors.

Dinnet, Dee Side (Aberdeen). — Dee; salmon, trout pike, perch. *Hotels*: Ritchie's Commercial.

Dornoch (Sutherland).—G.N. of S.R.; H.R. Trouting free in Lochs Launsie, Lea, and Tarvie. There are two good hotels.

Dromore (Kirkcudbright).—C.R. Fleet; salmon, and trout The owner of Rusko owns a portion of the water.

Drumbeg Inn (Sutherland).—About 16 *m.* from Loch Inver, or it can be reached from Scourie by taking a boat (fare 10*s.*) from Badcall Bay. Loch Drumbeg, in front of house, is very good; fish average over ½lb. Most other lochs near (there are hundreds) hold small fish. A stream which runs through Glen Leraig, out of Loch Leod into Nedd Bay, gives sea trout and grilse after rain. Another burn, running out of Loch Poule, about 3 *m.* west of the inn, also gives sea trout when there is water enough. Fishing free. Large *dark* flies best. Good sea fishing and bathing; boats. Telegraph office. Daily mail car from Lochinver.

Dufftown (Banff).—G.N. of S.R. Fiddich; trout: free. Dullan; trout; free. Spey, 4 *m.* Tickets can be obtained at the hotels, of which there are two.

Dumfries.—G. & S.W.R.; C.E. Nith, Cairn, and Cargen; salmon, sea trout, trout, grayling, pike, &c., preserved by Dumfries and Maxwelltown Angling Association; s.t. 6*s.* 6*d.*, d.t, 1*s.*; juveniles 2*s.*, boys 1*s.*; treasurer, D. M'Millan, tackle manufacturer, 6. Friars' Vennel, Dumfries (*see Advertisement*), who will give every information. There is some free fishing.

Dunblane (Perth). Allan; trout; free. *Hotel* : Stirling Arms.

Dunkeld.—On Tay. By staying at the Birnam Hotel the angler can fish for salmon in 1¼ *m.* of the river; but it is mostly preserved. The river Bran joins Tay at this place. It runs out of Loch Freuchie nearly 12 *m.* south-west of Dunkeld. There are plenty of fish. May and June are the best months. (*See Amulree* and *Corriemuckloch.*)

Dunoon (Argyll).—Fair fishing in Meikle and Little Eohaig, and in Loch Loskin.

Dunphail (Moray).—H.R. On Findhorn and Divie; salmon, trout.

Dunrossness (Shetland).—(*See Lerwick.*)

Duns (Berwick).—N.B.R. Whitadder; trout; preserved for 8 *m.* by Mr. Turnbull, of Abbey St. Bathans, who will give leave for a portion of his water; apply, with stamped envelope, to Mr. J. Shiel, Abbey St. Bathans, Grant's House, N.B.; season from April 1 to Sept. 30. There is some free water. The following streams are within easy reach: Fasney, Bothwell, Dye, Blacksmill, Watchburn, and Monynut.

Durness (Sutherland).—*Hotel :* Durness. The river Dionard or Grudie is reserved; the salmon and sea-trout fishing on it is good with plenty of water. (*See Rhiconich Inn.*) The Kyle of Durness, also in the landlord's hands, during the greatest drought, affords excellent sea-trout fishing. The deep-sea fishing towards Cape Wrath is particularly good; very large lythe.

Earlstone (Roxburgh).—N.B.R. On Leader; trout.

Ecclefechan (Dumfries).—C.R. On the Annan; salmon and trout; the river is closely preserved from here to the sea. and it is not easy to obtain permission. At a short distance is the Kirtle water; trout.

Edinburgh.—In the immediate neighbourhood there are many natural ponds, almost all of which contain trout; but some are preserved. 8 *m* off is Compensation Pond, in the Pentland Hills; the fishing is poor, but the trout run large; very small flies should be used. The top of the pond is best. The Esk (Midlothian) Angling Improvement Association of 30 members preserves 3 *m.* of the Esk next the sea; sec., J. Sutherland St. Clair, Esq., Musselburgh; s.t. 21*s.*, and short period tickets, 2*s.* 6*d.*, are issued for the tidal water only; excellent sea trouting in spring or autumn. The Association having well-stocked their water, yellow trouting with natural minnow affords very good sport.

Edzell (Forfar.). N.B.—By staying at the Panmure Arms trout fishing can be had free.

Ellon (Aberdeen).—G.N.S.R. Ythan; salmon and trout. 4 *m.* are here preserved by the owner of Ellon Castle. Visitors staying at the New Inn may fish this water at 3*s.* per day or 7*s.* 6*d.* per week.

Etal.—On Till; salmon, trout, perch, and pike; the mill-pool is a good spot. About Etal is deep water, good for pike and perch. The same flies as for Tweed kill in Till, only dressed smaller. In the lower 6 *m.* of Till in early spring and autumn use two full-sized trout flies as droppers and a tail fly; wing, grey drake; tail, American wood duck, brown mallard, or silver pheasant; body, black or blue mohair, amber or golden-coloured mohair below; tipping for tail, legs either blue jay wing or black or red hackles. The local flies are Tweed white tip, Doctor (blue and silver and black). Virgin, &c. Accommodation can be had at the Blue Bell, Crookham, or at Black Bull, Etal. All fishing round Etal is strictly preserved, but Mr. G. Grey, Millfield, gives liberty to anyone by card.

Ettrick (Selkirk).—Fishing free. *Hotel :* Tushielaw.

Fearnan.—On Loch Tay; salmon, trout; free. *Hotel*: Tighanloan.

Fetlar Island (Shetland)—(*See Lerwick*.)

Findhorn.—Several miles of excellent fishing can be obtained, free to visitors at the hotel. The trout run large.

Fochabers.—On the Spey. The Duke of Richmond reserves the right of salmon fishing; permission for a few days may, however sometimes be obtained by application to his Grace or his Commissioner. The best pools are close to the mouth of the river. The Gordon Arms is very comfortable, and near the river.

Forfar (Forfar).—3 *m.* off is Rescobie; pike and perch.

Forgandenny (Perth).—C.R. May and Earn; salmon, trout.

Forres (Elgin).—G.N. of S.R.; H.R. *Hotels*: Hydropathic, Royal Station, Commercial. Findhorn; salmon, trout. Tickets for a length on the lower Findhorn from Messrs. Stewart & Son. Lithen, 2½ *m.*; trout; open to respectable anglers.

Forsinard (Sutherland).—H.R. On Halladale; salmon, trout. *Hotel*: Forsinard, where fishing can be had. March, April, and May are the best months. There are many lochs near, mostly free. *Lochs*: Baden, Na-Sealg, and Coorach, abounding in trout. Loch an Ruar, 3 *m.* S.; trouting good; free to hotel visitors; boats; June, July, August, and September are best. Loch Araich-lin; small trout, char; preserved by shooting tenant; good fishing. Loch Jubilee, 2 *m.* N.W.: Loch Leven trout. Loch Coolie, 2¼ *m.* S.W.: large trout; preserved by shooting tenant. Loch Leven, 2 *m.*; small trout; free. Loch Leir, 3 *m.* E.; large trout; free. Loch Sletil, near Loch Leir; preserved. Lochan Dubh, 3 *m.*; trout; free. Loch Clachengeal, 4 *m.*; trout; free. Loch Tallechirl, 4½ *m.* Loch Leam-na-Claven, 5½ *m.*; good trouting, char; preserved by the Baddan-loch shooting tenant. Loch Coire-nam-Meann, 6 *m.*, near Loch Olaven; trout, char; good fishing.

Fort Augustus (Inverness).—*Hotels*: Lovat Arms and the Douglas Hotel. Oich; salmon, trout; private. Also in Loch Ness and Loch Oich; salmon, trout, pike, perch; free. Season opens Feb. 11.

Forteviot (Perth).—C.R. May and Earn; salmon and trout.

Fortingall.—On the Lyon. (*See Kenmore*.)

Fortrose (Ross).—H.R. Good sea fishing and trouting in Avoch and Rosemarkie burns. The hotel is comfortable.

Fort William.—There is fair trouting in the Nevis, with an occasional sea-trout; free. Loch Ondavra, 6 *m.* in the hills south west of the town, contains lots of trout, five to the pound; free. (*See Loch Laggan; Aylort Inn.*) Good sea and loch (trout) fishing free to visitors of West End Hotel.

Foyers Hotel (Inverness).—On Foyers; trout. Anglers staying at the hotel can obtain trout fishing in the river, and salmon and trout in Loch Ness, free. The nets having been taken off the river, the fishing should be much improved, especially in the summer and autumn. Also trouting in Lochs Farraline and Garth, now joined in one, and known as Loch Mhor, also Loch Bran. Sport is very good, takes of 6 or 7 brace of ½lb. fish being common; best months, April, May, and June. Address Foyer's Hotel, Loch Ness, by Inverness. A railway to Fort Augustus is now opened.

Gair Loch (Ross).—*Hotel*: Gairloch. There are two streams in the immediate neighbourhood: the one close by the inn runs through three lochs, two of which, Loch Tollie and Loche Bodachean are stocked with Loch Leven trout, and strictly reserved to hotel visitors; the one down the road on the left-hand side runs through six lochs, being joined by two streams on the right, both running out of lochs. The Ewe river runs some 4 *m.* off. This stream rises on Ben Lair in a chain of five lochs, all close to the road, of which Loch Clair is the largest. At the further end of the loch a stream joins Clair, running out of a hill loch. Nearest station, **Kinlochewe Inn.** Close to the inn a considerable burn joins Ewe, which runs into and forms Loch Maree 1 *m.* below the inn. This loch runs within 4 *m.* of Shieldag Inn, and most of the large burns joining the loch run out of hill lochs. The course of the river from Loch Maree to the sea is about 6 *m.*, and Poolewe river and Poolewe Hotel is close to its mouth. There is one burn joining Ewe in this part of its course on the left hand, running out of a hill loch. Steamers from Glasgow stop at stated intervals; or by rail, *via* Inverness and Achnasheen, thence by coach or motor.

Gatehouse.—n.s. **Kirkcudbright**, 8 *m.* *Hotel*: Murray Arms. Trout fishing can be had by permission in Lochs Whinyeon (boats belonging to hotel) and Grannoch (private). Loch Skerrow is in private hands. Salmon, grilse, and sea trout in the river Fleet; s.t. 10s., w.t. 5s., d.t. 2s.,; as far as Stroquhain pool; the fishing above the pool is reserved; to be obtained from Mr. Murray Stewart, at the Cally Estate Office, Gatehouse. Visitors at the hotel have free fishing in Fleet and Loch Whinyeon.

Girvan (Ayr).—G. & S.W.R. Girvan water; salmon, sea and brown trout: m.t. 10s., w.t. 5s., d.t. 1s. 6d.; Sept. 1 to end of season. d.t. 2s. 6d., from the Girvan Angling Club. Season opens Feb. 24, ends Oct. 31; but owing to pollution the fishing is very poor. Girvan rises in Loch Girvan, Ayrshire, and is 25 *m.* long. Leave may sometimes be had on the upper waters; 3 *m.* from Girvan is a small reservoir holding large trout, leave may sometimes be obtained; fishing poor. Good sea-fishing for lythe, &c. *Hotel*, King's Arms (comfortable), where all information can be had. (*See Ballantrae*.)

Glasgow.—(*See Brodrick, Corrie,* and *Lamlash.*)

Glenelg (Inverness).—n.s. **Strome Ferry,** 12 *m.* By staying at the Glenelg Hotel, trout and salmon fishing can be obtained in the neighbourhood free. Good fishing in Lochs Duich and Ourn.

Grantown (Moray).—G.N. of S.E., H.B. Spey; salmon, trout; permits are granted to fish in the following lochs and rivers on application to the Strathspey Estate Office: Milton burn, Glenbeg burn, Arraboard burn, Altmore burn, 5 *m.* S.W., Dava burn, 6 *m.* N., Advie burn, 7 *m.* E., Tulchan burn, Dorback burn, Aultcharn burn, 3 *m.* S.E., Dillifure burn, rivers Dulnain, Nithy, and Spey. Permission from the shooting tenants is required to fish Lochs Vaa, Loch-na-dorb, Loch-an-Eilan, Loch-an-Gearn, Loch Marten, Loch Brusach. There are three good hotels.

Grantully (Perth) by **Strathay.**—On Tay; salmon (strictly preserved by Lady Stewart, of Grantully Castle). Loch Derculich has good trouting; leave from Derculich House. *Hotel :* Grantully.

Guardbridge (Fife).—N.B.B. On Eden and Moultrie; sea trout and trout.

Haddington (Haddington).—Tyne; trout; free.

Hebrides.—Sea fishing generally good all round these islands.

> BENBECULA.—Between N. and S. Uist. There are numerous lochs, giving good sea and brown trout fishing. May to September is the best time. *Hotel :* Creagorry, very comfortable, where leave to fish all the streams and lochs can be had. Creagorry is reached by mail boat from Oban to Lochboisdale, thence 20 *m.* drive. Excellent brown and sea trout fishing May to August. Boats (free) on lochs.

> COLONSAY.—*Hotel :* Scalasaig. Good trouting to visitors at hotel. Two boats on the lochs.

> HARRIS.—At Tarbert there is a good hotel. Good sea fishing for lythe and saythe. Lochs Lacisdale (3), 2 *m.* off, hold salmon, sea and brown trout; fishing free of the hotel. 10 *m.* off is Loch Scourst; leave must be obtained. July is best for sea trout, and September for salmon. All plain, large loch flies kill. On Scourst a good fly is : *wing,* brown mallard; *body,* dark red ; *hackle,* black ; *tail,* golden pheasant's crest. The same fly may be varied with a green body and silver tinsel, or dark mottled turkey hen or grouse wing with the same bodies. *Hook,* small grilse size, if there is wind. There is capital sea and brown trout fishing in other lochs, but they are mostly let with the shooting. Right of fishing (brown trout) and shooting, however, on a loch in the island of Scalpay, 5 *m.* distant, free to visitors at the hotel, where for convenience of visitors a case of flies, &c., is always kept.

> LEWIS.—At Loch Tarbert, in the S., there is fishing attached to the hotel, which is good. Leave may sometimes be obtained from Lady Matheson's factor for the preserved water. Good salmon, white and brown trout fishing in River and Loch Creed, preserved by Lady Matheson; fishing in Blackwater is preserved; d.t. 15*s.*, m.t. 15*l.*, for the river, and d.t. 10*s.*, m.t. 10*l.*, for the lochs; salmon fishing very good; apply to the landlord, Prince Arthur Hotel, Garynahine, Stornoway. There are numberless lochs holding brown trout. Very good flies for brown trout on the river Creed are silver dun, cowdung, and red spinner.

> NORTH UIST.—Abounds in lochs and seapools (numbering hundreds), well stocked with salmon, sea, and brown trout. 120,000 salmon ova put in hatcheries three years ago for distribution amongst the principal lochs, which are fished alternately by shooting tenants and visitors at hotel. There are twenty boats on the lochs. First run of salmon and sea trout begins end of February and closes end of October; best months : March to May, and August to October. Brown trout fishing good from April to July. *Hotel :* Lochmaddy. Route: Rail to Oban, Mallaig, or Kyle of Lochalsh, thence steamer.

> SOUTH UIST.—To the S. of the island is Loch Boisdale; salmon, sea and brown trout, *Hotel :* Loch Boisdale; the fishing in several lochs is attached. There is little sea-fishing. In the island are a great number of lochs and streams well stocked with brown trout; many of them also abound in sea trout. Howmore river is famous for sea trout, but reserved. Hotel and telegraph office at Loch Boisdale Pier, reached by steamer from Oban. Fishing in south end of island is attached to hotel. Loch Bee, in the north of the island, is an excellent trout loch, the right to fish which is accorded to guests at Creagorry Hotel.

Helensburg (Dumbarton).—N.B.R. Leven; trout; free. Luss; trout, Fruin; trout. Season tickets for these can be had from Sir James Colquhoun, Bart., of Luss, at 21*s.*

Helmsdale (Sutherland).—On Helmsdale; salmon and trout; a limited number of rods are let by the month; trouting very poor.

Huntley.—On Deveron and Bogie; salmon and trout. A great part of the fishing here is open. *Hotel :* the Gordon Arms. The fishing is fair. In the Kirkney, 4 *m.* from Huntley, and an affluent of the Bogie, there is good fishing, but the trout run small.

Inchnadamph (Sutherland).—Loch Assynt. Salmon fishing (fair) in autumn on the upper end of Loch Assynt and in the Loannan water, which runs into it out of Loch Awe. Very good trouting sometimes in the Loannan and the Tralligill. Loch Awe gives capital trouting. Loch Assynt holds numbers of small trout, and a fair stock of *Salmo feros.* Near here is the celebrated Gillaroo loch and others. *Hotel :* Inchnadamph. Fishing free.

Innerleithen (Peebles).—Teviot; trout; free. *Loch:* St. Mary's; perch, pike, trout; free. The fishing is free in the Tweed and its tributaries, Gala Water included, Yarrow and tributaries yield the best trout.

Inveraray.—(Argyll). Rivers Aray, Douglas, and Garron; salmon, sea and brown trout. Dhuloch, a tidal water. *Hotel:* Argyll Arms (*see Advertisement*), where fishing for salmon and trout can be had in a tidal water, the Dhu loch and rivers Aray and Douglas. Good sea fishing.

Invergarry (Inverness).—On Caledonian Canal and Loch Oich and River Garry. *Hotel:* Invergarry (*see Advertisement*). The Garry rises in a loch S.W. of Loch Quoich, and runs into that loch at its west end. Capital trouting. The river leaves Loch Quoich at its east end, and in 2 *m.* is joined by a considerable burn on its right bank; 1 *m.* on, the river expands into a loch, and in 2½ *m.* from this loch it passes **Tomdown Inn.** The Garry next joins Loch Garry, 2 *m.* on. 3 *m.* from Loch Garry a burn joins on the right bank, running out of a small hill loch 5 *m.* in the hills, and 1½ *m.* on is another, running out of a loch on the left-hand side 3 *m.* off. 2 *m.* on, Garry falls into Oich. A road runs on the left bank of Garry as far as Loch Quoich.

Invergordon (H.R.).—The Alness, 4 *m.* W., yields good fishing in the early part of the season; salmon, white and brown trout. Yellow-bodied flies, such as the "full stone," are very good. Preserved principally by Sir G. Smith.

Invermoriston Hotel (Inverness).—Visitors can fish in Loch Ness; salmon, trout, free.

Inverness.—G.N. of S.R., H.R. Ness; salmon, trout. The lower beats are open to residents in Inverness on every eighth lawful day. *Hotels:* Palace, Station, Royal, Caledonian, Glenalby. Free fishing in Farigaig, and by visitors to Foyers Hotel in Loch Fariline.

Inveroran.—On Loch Tulla, and but 2 *m.* from the river Orchy, although 3 *m.* from the obtainable fishing; salmon, trout; fly only. The salmon fishing in the Orchy is good in the autumn, but, given good water, July is the best month. There are few trout in the river, and those large. The fishing extends to the lower fall, below which the Dalmally fishing begins. (*See Dalmally.*) There are salmon and trout in Loch Tulla: a boat can be had. A fair stream runs into Tulla by the keeper's house, running out of Loch Dochar, full of trout. Another stream falls into Loch Tulla at the opposite end; both this stream and the loch out of which it runs contain great quantities of small trout. Close by the inn is a good burn, running out of a small pond containing some large trout. A little way below Orchy Bridge the Auch Burn, full of fish, joins Orchy. Loch na Baw, 6 *m.* from Inveroran, on the Moor of Rannoch, contains any quantity of trout five to the pound. There are numberless other lochs and streams about. *Hotel:* Inveroran, very good, and the fishing in lake and 7 *m.* of Orchy free to any visitor from April 1 to Oct. 31.

Invershin (Sutherland).—H.R. Plenty of loch fishing in the neighbourhood; sea trout and sea fish in the Kyles of Sutherland. Boats free of charge. *Hotel:* Inveran (*see Advertisement*), where salmon fishing can be had by the mouth.

Inversnaid.—Loch Lomond; salmon, trout, perch, pike; fishing free. *Hotel:* Inversnaid.

Inverurie.—On Don and Ury: salmon and trout. By staying at the Kintore Arms Hotel the visitor can fish in these two rivers.

Isla, Island of.—Loch Guram, 9 *m.* from Bridgend, the principal town, is famous for its trouting.

Jedburgh (Roxburgh). Teviot; preserved by Lord Lothian. Good fishing can be had in the neighbourhood.

Kelso.—On Tweed: salmon and trout. The best salmon fishings on the Tweed are Mertown, Rutherford, Ednam House, Carham, Floors Castle, Hindersyde, Makerston, Sprouston, Birgham, Cornhill, Lees, and Wark. The trout fishing on Floors Castle, Makerston, Birgham, Rutherford, Carham, and Wark are all preserved, and permission can only be had from the gentlemen who rent the fishings. The trout fishings on Hindersyde and Sprouston are free. For information apply to Mr. J. Wright, Sprouston, Kelso, N.B.

Kenmore.—On Loch Tay; salmon and trout. The river Lyon and Loch Lyon are within reach by taking a conveyance; the loch is preserved, and the salmon fishing on the river. The fishing is excellent. The best flies are woodcock or jay's wing, with orange, bright red, and green bodies; hackle, red for orange and red bodies, and black for green; the hook dubbed with a little gold tinsel. Large trout may be caught trolling. Another good fly is black body and hackle, with light jay or teal drake wing. There are no inns nearer than Kenmore or Fortingall. The river Tay flows out of Loch Tay here. Trout, salmon, and perch. The first 3 *m.* of the loch next Kenmore are strictly preserved for salmon by Lord Breadalbane, but visitors to the Breadalbane Hotel are privileged to fish at a charge of 30*s.* per day. Fishing in the open water on Loch Tay may be obtained by staying at the Kenmore and Killin Hotels, and the Bridge of Lochay Inn, and Ardeonaig Inn. The number of boats is limited, as follows: Killin Hotel, 12 boats; Kenmore Hotel, 6 boats; the inns of Ardeonaig, 2; Ben Lawers, 2; and Bridge of Lochay, 3. Anglers residing in the hotels pay 1*l.* per salmon caught per week, with a limit of 5*l.* Resident in the country, 1*l.* When the applications for boats exceed the number available, two anglers may occupy the same boat, using one rod each, at 15*s.* each. Anglers retain all fish. Boatmen 3*s.* 8*d.* per day each, lunch being optional. Anglers will be entitled to the boats according to priority of

M

application for them; but no angler can retain a boat for more than one week or ix fishing days at a time if there are other applicants. If a boat is disengaged, it may be again secured for another week. No more than two rods are allowed in each boat, Visitors are only entitled to use the boat or boats attached to the inn or hotel where they are residing. The best flies for trout fishing on Loch Tay are, corncrake wing, orange body, and gold tinsel; grey wing, with red or orange bodies; the Zulu, also red hackle, with silver tinsel. Trout fishing free of charge, boatman's wages excepted. Trolling allowed for trout.

Kilkerran (Ayr).—G. & S.W.R. Girvan; trout, salmon; preserved for 5 m. by the lessee of Kilkerran Lodge.

Killin (Perth).—C.R. Dochart or Tay; salmon, trout; salmon fishing reserved, but leave for visitors to the Killin Hotel is obtained by the landlord. Lyon; salmon, trout; salmon reserved, but trouting can be had on application. *Loch*, Tay; salmon, trout; free to visitors at the hotel, which has twelve boats on the lake; two rods are allowed to each boat at 20s. per salmon caught; reserved water 30s. a day; fish retained; boatmen, 3s. 8d. a day and lunch. Larigeelie; trout; free. *Hotel*: Killin. (*See Kenmore*; *Luib*.)

Kilmalcolm (Renfrew).—*Hotel*: Kilmalcolm Hydropathic. Some fishing can be had near.

Kilmelford (Argyll).—Near Oban. *Hotel*: Cuilfail, Pass of Melfort. Capital trouting on several different lochs. Boats on all the lochs. Good sea fishing close at hand on Loch Melfort. Season, April 1 till end of September.

Kilmun.—On Holy Loch and Frith of Clyde. The Echaig (strictly preserved), running out of Loch Eck, falls into the sea here; salmon, sea trout, and, in the loch, lake trout, powan, and goldie.

Kingussie (Inverness).—There is very poor trout fishing in the district, and but little salmon fishing. 4 m. off is Spey, which can be fished by persons staying in the hotel. Fishing poor. (*See Loch Laggan.*)

Kinloch Rannoch (Perth), n.s. **Struan**, 13 m. — *Hotels*: Dunalastair, and Bun Rannoch, where good trout fishing can be had in Tummel and Loch Rannoch free. During June and July trout rise freely to the same flies as in Loch Ericht. (*See Dalwhinnie.*) Visitors at the hotels at Kinloch Rannoch can have boats and fish the whole loch There are dozens of lochs in the neighbourhood. Of these, Loch Lydoch is the best. The river Gauer runs out of this loch, and joins Rannoch after a course of 8 m.; it is a good fishing stream. Midway between Lydoch and Rannoch the river expands into a loch, called Aich, full of fish; a boat is necessary on account of the weeds; in spring and autumn heavy fish lie in the river. Loch Lydoch is full of fish. There is no road whatever over the Moor of Rannoch, where these small lochs are. Visitors at the hotels can fish 3 m. of the Tummel. It is well to take a guide on the moor. Certain lochs and streams can only be fished by permission from Sir Niel Menzies. There are ferox in Rannoch; the west end is best for trout; between the old tower and Sir Niel Menzies', 9 m. from the inn, is the best end. Boatman 4s. per diem; lunch, &c., 1s. 6d. to 2s. The best flies are mallard wings, red, green, and yellow bodies. The red and yellow should have a red hackle, and the green a black. The coch-y-bonddhu is also a good fly. Half-way between Rannoch and Pitlochry is Loch Tummel; large trout and pike.

Kinross.—Loch Leven is 17 m. from Perth; trout; preserved by a company. *Hotels*: Harris's, Gray's, Bridgend, Kirklands. Charge for a boat, 2s. 6d. per hour. The best months for fishing are May, June, July, and August. *Manager*, Miss Whyte.

Kirkcudbright.—Dee; good salmon fishing, but permission must be got from lessee of fishing. Above the mills at Tongland the water is in private hands. Leave sometimes given.

Kirkwall (Orkney).—Loch Ham lies 5 m. S.E. from here; the fish are small, but plentiful. Loch Kirbister, 6 m. S.W., holds plenty of small brown trout. At the Stroma burn, 2½ m. from Kirkwall, there is excellent free brown trout fishing; there are also the Lake of St. Mary's Holm and Græmshall, both 6 m. south-east from here. Scapa Bay and Burn, 2 m. Lakes of Wasdale, Stennis (10 m. W.), and Harray, 10 m., and about 3 m. from Stromness. All free. Yellow, sea, and brown trout In Hoy and Rowsay there is very good sea-trout and lake fishing, but preserved. In Birsay parish are Lakes Boardhouse and Swanney, both containing good trout. Lythe and saithe are also plentiful. The best fishing is to be had in Lakes Stenness and Harray, joined by Bridge of Brogar. Comfortable hotel at head of Lake Harray. Lakes Birsay (20 m. from Kirkwall and 14 from Stromness), Hundland, and Swanney provide good sport (brown trout). They are strictly preserved by the Barony Hotel (on the shores of Lake Birsay) which is very comfortable.

Kirriemuir "Thrinus" (Forfar).—C R. *Hotel*: Airlie Arms. Trouting free in Orammil, Carraty, Kinnel and Lidnethie burn; also in Loch Wharnal.

Kylesku Ferry Inn.—Very small clean house 12 m. from Scourie, on the road to Loch Inver. Can be reached either from Scourie or Inch-na-Damff. From here can be fished the Duartmore river (fairly good for salmon, grilse, and sea trout), the Maldie burn and two burns running into Glens Dhu and Coul respectively. These last all give grilse and sea trout after rain. Very good trout fishing can be had on Loch Brach More, at the head of Stack Corrie. The sea fishing in the Kyle itself is first-rate for lithe, saithe, mackerel, &c. The landlord will provide a boat. Fishing free.

Lairg (Sutherland).—*Hotel*: the Sutherland, comfortable and moderate. On Loch Shin; good trouting, three to the pound, at the Lairg end of the lake, and two to the pound by Overskeck. (*See Overskeck*.) *Salmo ferox* abound. Boat and man, 5s. 6d. per day. In Loch Beannoch, 4 m. from Lairg, the trout run from ¼lb. to 3lb. Lochs Craggie and Doohulla are preserved by Major Matheson, who gives an occasional day. The upper part of the river Shin is let with the shooting, but on payment of 10s per day leave may be obtained, during July, from the landlord of the hotel. (*See Rhiconich Inn*.) There is very good ferox fishing in Loch Greamb, at the head of Loch Shin, 3 m. from Overskeck; we believe a boat must be taken from Lairg.

Lamington.—On Clyde; trout and grayling.

Lamlash (Isle of Arran).—Steamboats start from Glasgow three times a day, and once a day from Ardrossan. There are several small hotels here. There is scarcely any river fishing, but very fair sea fishing; large lythe are frequently taken at the back of the island. From nine to ten in the evening sport can be had with the coal-fish, angling with a white moth. Indiarubber red and grey spinning eels recommended. The burns contain a few small trout; the Duke of Hamilton preserves the best streams. (*See Brodick* and *Corrie*.)

Lanark (Lanark).—Clyde, trout. *Hotel:* Clydesdale.

Langholm (Dumfries).—N.B.R. The Esk, Liddle, and their tributaries are preserved by the Esk and Liddle Fisheries Association, who issue various tickets for different parts of the rivers. Nos. 1 and 2 give fishing rights in parts of Esk, Liddle, and all other of the Association waters; s.t. 4l., w.t. 20s., d.t. 5s. No. 3 takes parts of the Esk and Liddle; s.t. 1l. 10s., d.t. 2s. No. 4 takes Liddle; s.t. 1l., d.t. 2s. No. 5 is the Canonbie ticket for portions of Esk and Liddle; s.t. 25s., d.t. 2s. 6d. No. 6, Langholm ticket, for parts of Esk, Ewes, Wauchope, and Tarras waters; s.t. 20s., d.t. 2s. No. 7, the Westerkirk ticket, for parts of Esk; s.t. 7s. 6d., d.t. 1s. 6d. No. 8, Eskdalemuir ticket. Esk; s.t. 10s. d.t. 1s. 6d. No. 9, Ewes ticket, for Ewes (except Castleholm) and tributaries; s.t. 10s. d.t. 1s. 6d. No. 10, Newcastleton ticket, for parts of Liddle; s.t. 10s., d.t. 1s. 6d. Nos. 1, 2, will be granted on and after Feb. 15, but for fly only, and below Canonbie Glebe Lands until March 15. The remaining tickets on and after March 15, and then only for fly till June 1, excepting in Esk and Liddle, when the limit is May 1. No fishing allowed after 10 p.m., except in the months of June, July, and August, when the hour is 12 p.m. for the Esk and Liddle, and 11 p.m. for the remaining waters. No hook of the Stewart tackle or any compound tackle of a size larger than No. 5 of Adlington and Hutchinson's make. No bait or minnow fishing before May 1 or after Sept. 15 in Esk and Liddle, except in the Willow and Caldron pools, which are available for bait or minnow until Nov. 1, or before June 1 or after Sept. 1 in the other waters of the Association. No gaff until after April 1; fly-fishing the whole season. The Association's waters—excepting the Esk and Liddle, which are open till Nov. 1—shall be closed for rod fishing on Oct. 1. Salmon fishing best in autumn; June and July for sea trout. Comfortable accommodation at any of the hotels at Langholm, Longtown, the Eskdale Temperance Hotel, at the hotel at Crosskeys, Canonbie; or at Bentpath, Westerkirk, which is very convenient for the upper reaches of the Esk; sec., R. M'George, Esq., Langholm. Any of the tickets may be had from the secretary, and Nos. 1 and 2 from Messrs. Beaty, drapers, Longtown; or at the police stations at Canonbie, Newcastleton, and Eskdalemuir. Sea trout and brown trout are numerous. The Upper Esk tributaries, viz., Moodlaw, and the Rae burns, are well stocked with trout.

Latheron (Caithness).—Fishing, by staying at the Latheronwell and Dunbeath Hotels.

Lauder.—On Leader. Trout. There is a comfortable inn here, and fishing free.

Lawes.—On Loch Tay. (*See Kenmore*.)

Lerwick (Shetland).—*Hotels*: Queen's, Royal, Grand. Black Loch and Sandy Loch, 2 m. W. from Lerwick, past village of Sound; trout plentiful, but small. Loch Tingwall, 6 m. from Lerwick, 2 m. from Scalloway; fish plentiful, from ½lb. to 1lb.; preserved by Mr. Goed, Queen's Hotel. Adjoining is Loch Asta; fish plentiful, fully larger than above; preserved as Tingwell. Loch of Strand, 6 m. from Lerwick; excellent sea trout, running to 15lb.; plenty of brown trout in burn running into it; preserved as above. Mr. Goed, of "Queen's," Lerwick, keeps a private hotel here for anglers. Girlsta Loch, 2½ m. from this hotel. Loch Broo and Loch Ustaness, and other five small lochs about 3½ m. from it, where good fishing is to be had. At Dale's Voe, 3 m. N. of Lerwick, sea trout and brown trout may be taken. A boat frequently sails from Lerwick to Ollaberry on the east coast of the north mainland. Good fishing in Eela Water, North Mavin, near Ollaberry, and in many other lochs in the neighbourhood. Lodgings may be had at Mr. Sinclair's, at Ollaberry. In Pundswater, beyond Eela Water, the fish run larger. There are many other lochs in Shetland where excellent fishing is to be had, but accommodation is very limited. It is always necessary to take plenty of provisions with you. Loch Spiggey, 20 m. S. from Lerwick; fish plentiful and large. Very good fishing in Fetlar. Vidlin Loch and burn, good sea and yellow trout, but are let. Kirkhouse Loch and North Loch have brown trout. In the island of Unst, to which there is communication by steamer three times a week in summer and twice

M 2

in winter, there is splendid fishing and shooting, and the accommodation for tourists is now good, especially at Baltasound. where there is a a first-class hotel within 1 m. of Loch Cliff, the best fishing loch in the island.

Loch Awe (Argyllshire).—Salmon, sea trout, brown trout, perch, pike, ferox; fishing free. *Hotel*: Loch Awe (*see Advertisement*). Orchy river runs in at **Dalmally**; salmon, trout; fishing at hotel (*see Dalmally*). Awe river flows out of the loch; salmon; private, except some good sections available for visitors staying at the Loch Awe Hotel, and 2 m. at the lower end on the left bank, fishable by staying at the Taynuilt Hotel, **Taynuilt** (*see Taynuilt*). Some of the best trouting is in Cladich and Ardbricknish bays, and thence to **Portsonachan** Hotel (*see Advertisement*), 3 m., the fishing is very good. Hence to **Portinisherrach** is 8 m., and after passing Crow Island the fishing is good. From **Portinisherrach** to Ford the S.W. end of the loch is 8 m., all good fishing ground. At **Ford** is a comfortable inn. In a small loch almost opposite is good pike and perch fishing. The other side of the loch is also good in parts. Opposite Port Sonachan is **Tayoreggan** Hotel. where boats can be had; boat and man 6s. a day. The fishing round the islands is generally good. The best salmon flies are: 1, the black dragon—wings, feather from raven; body, black mohair, black hackle; tip, golden pheasant crest feather. 2, the black dog—wings, blue heron feather mixed with red turkey; body, lead-coloured mohair trimmed with gold twist, and large black hackle; shoulder, dark green mohair. It would be well to divide the wings with gold twist, and let it show about the head. The loch trout flies are as follows: 1, wings from pheasant's tail; body, ginger hackle over orange mohair. 2, the green drake fly. 3, wings, mottled feathers of bustard; body, upper part, blue dubbing, lower, orange ditto, a light brown hackle carried well down the bend of the hook; tinsel and a tail tuft should be used, the latter from tippet of the golden pheasant. The salmon flies for the Awe are nearly all "wasp" bodies, with light or dark turkey wings, pale light blue rough bodies, with heron wings, or sometimes a smooth green body, with mallard wings. Light and dark March brown, alder fly, cowdung, dark spinner, Professor dark and light; and No. 1, speckled teal wing, light red spinner; No. 2, yellow silk body, red hackles run down the body, cock pheasant wing, and two fibres for tail from cock pheasant wing; No. 3, pale green silk body ribbed with gold, black hackle legs, wings dark mallard, peacock harl and red macaw, tail, strands black hackle: No. 4, dark blue silk body, black legs, sea-swallow wing, tail two or three fibres dark mallard—known in Westmorland as "Broughton's point." Trout flies: 1, yellow and woodcock—a large cowdung; 2, red and teal—Soldier palmer, with teal wings; 3, green and teal—green crewel body, silver thread, black hackle, and teal wings. The best bait for pike fishing in Loch Awe is the natural minnow of medium size. There are plenty of eels to be caught by night lines, and there are some large perch in the bays near at hand.

Loch Doon (Ayr).—Capital sport. The loch can be reached from Ayr.

Loch Dow (Inverness).—A peculiar deformed trout is sometimes caught in this lake.

Lochearnhead (Perth).—*Lakes :* Loch Earn; trout and char; free. *Hotel :* Lochearnhead.

Lochgoilhead.—There is some good trouting in the Restel Loch and Loch Awe.

Lochinver (Sutherland).—*Hotel :* Culag. On Inver and Kirkaig (3 m.); salmon and trout. There are many lochs within 6 m. full of trout, all free. The hotel-keeper grants permission to fish for salmon in the Kirkaig and Inver at 12s. 6d. per day (limited to two rods each). In some of the lakes there are ferox, especially in Loch Assynt, Fewin Beanach, and Badnine. Boats can be obtained at 2s. 6d. a day. The motor car runs daily between this and Lairg. and steamers from Glasgow and Oban frequently. The Kirkaig flows through Lochs Boarlan, Urigill, Cama. Veyattie, and Fewin. They all contain trout, some large Loch Beannoch, 5 m., is also a free rising loch, having two boats. Sutherland flies should be full-bodied worsted or pig's wool. Red, blue, purple, green, or black, with plenty of gold and silver tinsel with or without red tag. Loch Culag holds salmon and grilse. There is a boat: fishing 5s. a day. Inver runs out of Loch Assynt 6 m. off. The entire Kirkaig goes with the hotel. The sea fishing is very good.

Loch Katrine.—There is some fishing to be had on this loch. Loch Chon, and several hill lochs, which is free to visitors to the Stronachlachar Hotel.

Loch Laggan.—Trout and ferox; free. There is a nice little hotel here, distant from **Kingussie**, 18 m. **Tulloch**, station on West Highland Railway, 14 m. from which there are two coaches daily. The fishing is excellent, averaging three to the pound; plenty of ferox. Boats at the inn. Good trouting in the river Pattach, which joins the loch close by the inn. This river runs out of two hill lochs, full of fish. Off the islands large fish can be taken, also in the bays on the north side, especially in a large bay about 4 m. down, where a large burn runs into the loch. Great numbers may be taken in the bay belonging to Cluny Macpherson. This is close to the hotel. The river Spean runs out of the loch; capital sport, though the fish run smaller than in the loch. There are salmon below the falls. which is 2 m. above Roy Bridge, 18 m. from Laggan, strictly preserved. Good sport in Loch Treag. not far off ; we believe it is free. A good fly for the loch is a bright scarlet body with a teal or grouse wing. (*See Banavie.*)

Loch Lomond.—The streams running through the Luss property are preserved by the owners, who issue tickets at 2l. for the season. The Duke of Montrose gives free permission to fish the streams on his property, except the river Endrick, where it runs through his park, where special permission is required

Lochmaben (Dumfries).—8 m. north of **Dumfries**, and 4 m. west of **Lockerbie** (Cal. R.). There are nine lochs near. The Castle Loch is the largest, and one of a series of four, full of vendace, pike, perch, roach, bream, eels, and a few trout. The river fishings within easy walking distance are the Ae, Kinnel, Dryfe, and Annan. The first three are tributary to the last. The Annan contains salmon, sea trout, hirling, grilse, and yellow trout. The fishing opens on March 10, and closes November 1. May, June, July, and August are the best months, and September and October for salmon. Leave to fish is sometimes given. There are three fair inns here. and plenty of lodgings. The Milk, Ae, and Dryfe are nearly all free.

Lochmaddy Hotel (North Uist, N.B.).—Salmon and sea and brown trout fishing free (*see Advertisement*).

Loch Mhor.—18 m. from Inverness and 4 m. from Inverfarigaig and Foyers Piers, Loch Ness. The loch is 4 m. long by ½ m. broad, and contains trout averaging 1lb. *Hotel:* Loch Mhor.

Lochsunart (Argyll).—By staying at the Salen Hotel salmon and trout fishing can be had in Lochshiel.

Lockerbie (Dumfries).—Annan; Milk; Dryfe. C.R.;(*See Lochmaben* and *Langholm*). *Hotels:* Blue Bell, King's Arms. Good fishing, salmon, sea trout, brown trout; in Annan Towns water, 2 m., s.t. 10s.; Milk, preserved by Sir R. Jardine; and other streams. The principal flies for the months of April, May, and June are chaffinch with hare ear or red hackle, lark with mouse-coloured body, thrush with hare ear or dark hackle, or yellow body, woodcock and red hackle, landrail with dark hackle and silver tinsel lip, teal with red or dark hackle, red and black spiders, grey spider from partridge breast. The natural Mayfly is also very deadly, and can be gathered in great numbers on the sides of the river. For the following months, when sea trout and herlings are run, jay and teal with yellow or blue silk body (the latter preferred), and dark hackle and tinsel, landrail and teal, yellow body and dark hackle and clear tinsel.

Logierat. — On Tay; salmon and trout. Tummel here joins Tay. Fishing strictly preserved.

Longformacus.—Some 7 m. from Dunse. On Dye, Watch and Blacksmill Burns. Whitadder runs near. Trouting good.

Luib.—On the Dochart, 6 m. from Kilin. *Hotel:* Luib (*see Advertisement*); good salmon fishing in August and September. The trout are numerous, and run a fair size. The water is very deep and sluggish below Luib, but above and as far as Loch Dochart there are some capital streams and pools. From Loch Dochart to within 2 m. of Killin the fishing is preserved by the hotel for its visitors. Rob Roy's burn joins the river 3 m. above Luib, and here capital sport can be had. (*See Kilin.*) (*See Crianlarich.*)

Luss.—N.B.B. Loch Lomond and Clyde; salmon, sea and brown trout, pike, perch. Fishing free. The brown trouting early in the season before the sea fish enter the loch is very good.

Mainland Island consists of **Kirkwall** and East Mainland, and **Stromness** and West Mainland. *Hotels:* Castle and Kirkwall, at Kirkwall. A few sea trout may be killed where the tide runs through Aer into the Peerie Sea, also in Scapa Bay. At Wideford, 3 m. from Kirkwall, is good for sea trout, also at Sabay, 6 m., and Tankerness Hall, 6 m. Plenty of lythe and saithe.

Meikleour.—The Isla here joins Tay; trout, salmon, pike, and perch, all preserved. The Isla in its upper waters above Airlie Castle contains plenty of small trout; fishing free. May and June are the best months. A small red palmer, or reddish hackle with a teal drake wing, is a good fly. The fishing in the Melgum is very good. The Isla from its junction with the water of Dean, a few miles below Airlie Castle is very sluggish, and is full of pike, large trout, and perch. The water of Dean rises in the loch of Forfar, and contains capital trout. The fishing on the Tay is strictly preserved.

Melrose (Roxburgh).—On Tweed; salmon, trout. By staying at the Waverley Hydropathic Establishment trouting can be had free.

Melvich Hotel (Sutherland).—n.s. **Thurso** or Forsinard. Good trouting in several lochs; free. Boats kept. Good sea fishing.

Moffat.—The Moffat, Evan, and Annan run near. The Well Burn, Granton Burn, Hartfell Burn, Lochan Burn, Garpel Burn, Cloffin Burn, Cornal Burn, Blackshope Burn, Selcoth Burn, Corriefron Burn, the Tail Burn. Also, at medium distances, the Daar, the Dryfe (8 m.), the Clyde, the Ettrick (8 m.), the Fruid (8 m.), the Kinnel (4 m.), Wamphray Water. Also Loch Skene (11½ m.), the Loch of the Lowes (14 m.), St. Mary's Loch, the Megget, and the Yarrow: they are unpreserved. (*See St. Mary's Loch.*) *Hotel:* Annandale Arms. The Daar and Head of Clyde are easy of access.

Montrose (Forfar).—North Esk holds salmon and trout: preserved by Earl of Dalhousie. Tickets to fish lower reaches from Messrs. Johnstone, Montrose, who will give every information. Lunan gives some trouting. *Hotel:* Panmure Arms, Edsell.

Mound (Sutherland). On Fleet; trout and salmon, and good sea fishing.

Mull (Island of).—Tobermory is the capital of the island. and here good accommodation both at the Mishnish Hotel (fishing in the Bellart and in Loch Freesa) and in lodgings can be obtained. Excepting the Aros and the stream connecting Loch Baa with the sea, the rivers are mere burns. 3 *m.* from Tobermory are the Micknish lakes; good trouting; leave easily obtained. 4½ *m.* from Tobermory is Loch Freesa, the outlet of which is the Aros river. Forsa holds salmon, white and brown trout; the fishing belongs to Capt. Campbell and Mrs. Forsyth, who often give leave. Accommodation can be had at a shepherd's house on the shore. For the river, leave must also be had. On the N.W. of the island is **Bunessan**, reached by steamer from Oban three days a week and calling at Tobermory. The landlord of the Bunessan Hotel has the fishing in Loch Assopol (white and yellow trout, salmon) and Loch Potee; fishing free to visitors at hotel: July, August, and September for white trout, October for salmon (*see Advertisement*). Loch Baa is closed. Salen Asor Hotel has the fishing rights in the Forsa river, and in Loch Sconban and other lakes; August and September are the best months. There are many other lakes, mostly free.

Newburgh (Aberdeen).—12 *m.* from **Aberdeen**. Ythan : salmon, sea trout, bull and lake trout, brown trout, pike, flounders. Ythan rises on the E. slopes of Bisset hills, and is 35 *m.* long. The principal owners are Earl of Aberdeen, Sir M. Duff Gordon, Bt., Lady Gordon-Cathcart, Col. Turner, Col Wolrige Gordon, Mr. Udny, Mr. Gordon, and Miss Buchan. The principal tributaries are the burns of Foveran, Tarty, Forvey, March, Brony, Ebue (fishing free, sea trout), Michael Muir, Kelly, Schivas, Chapelton, Burn, Grains, Little Water (fishing free, sea trout), Petty, Farden, Tifty, Pitdoulsie, Garries. *Hotel* : Udny Arms, where capital sea trouting, &c., can be had.

New Galloway (Kirkcudbright). — *Hotel* : Kenmure Arms. *Lochs* : Dee, Skerrow, Harrow, and Lochinvaty, Huie, Barscoble, The Lowes, and Dee; trout. Ken and Lochs Ken, Dee, and Strom; salmon, trout, pike, and perch. There is a long stretch of fishing attached to the Kenmure Arms. (*See Parton.*)

Newtonmore (Inverness).—H.R. On Spey and Calder. Salmon and trout. *Hotels* : Bolavil Arms and Newtonmore Hotel.

Oban (Argyll).—C.R. The following lochs in the district are stocked with trout—viz., Loch-an-Glennaberrach, Pennyfuir Loch, and Balnagown Loch, Lismore. Lismore Loch, which is strictly preserved, is considered one of the best in Argyllshire: the trout average ¾lb., and it is not unusual to get one 2lb. Loch Nell and River Nell are 4 *m.* off, and are good for sea trout in the autumn, with an occasional salmon, also brown trout; fishing on application to proprietor, Cleigh Inn, near Oban, at moderate rates. Loch Scammadale. 8 *m.* off; salmon, sea and brown trout; preserved, but leave occasionally got from various proprietors. The Oban Angling Association preserves some trouting; tickets by week or month. Other minor lochs in district, but mostly preserved. At Easdale is the Inshaig Hotel, which has fishing on Loch Sicl. (*See Kilmelford.*)

Ollabury.—In North Mavine. (*See Lerwick.*)

Orkney (Islands).—There are twenty-eight inhabited islands. Sea trout are to be found wherever a drop of fresh water runs into the sea. The fishing is poor now, though it is about to be preserved by fishery districts. Worm is the best bait, used by sinking and drawing. Wading trousers are desirable. The sea-trout fishing in the sea belongs to the landowners whose land adjoins the shore. Trout fishing is best in September and October. By fishing with a worm, however, from the rocks which abut on the tidal flows, or by wading into bays, such as Scapa and others, and throwing well out, you may occasionally take a happening fish. Lythe and saithe abound. (*See Kirkwall; Stromness; Mainland Island.*)

Overskeok Hotel (Sutherland).—About 16 *m.* from Lairg, on the side of Loch Shin. Seven boats are kept on Shin, two on Loch Merkland, one on Merkland river, and one on Loch Griam. It is the best station on the loch both for fly and troll. Loch flies for Sutherlandshire are large as a rule (No. 6 hooks), and are best when tied very bright, scarlet being the favourite colour. Lochs Griam, Merkland, and Fiag can also be fished from here; they are very good. Loch Griam is reported to be one of the best lochs in Scotland for ferox. The large burn which runs out of Loch Fiag gives pretty good fishing in its upper portions. Fishing free.

Oykel Bridge Inn (Ross).—On rivers Oykel and Cassley. These rivers are now let by the month; for particulars of the Oykel, apply to Mr. D. Marhay, Oykel Bridge. Day tickets for Carron.

Parton (Kirkcudbright).—At and around New Galloway some good fishing can be had; salmon, trout, sea trout, pike, perch. &c. The proprietors are exceedingly liberal in granting leave. There is a boarding house here, the Spalding. (*See New Galloway.*)

Peebles.—On Tweed; salmon and trout; the fishing is good, and free. This is a good head-quarters, as there is a railway both up and down the river. *Hotel* : Tontine very comfortable. (*See Clovenford.*)

Perth.—Salmon are plentiful in Tay. Late in the season, when the nets are off, salmon can be taken in the tideway. Whitling are numerous between Thistle Bridge and for some distance below Perth, and will take a fly freely. (*See Stanley.*) From Almond Mouth, some 2 *m.* above the town to Aberfeldy, the fishing is strictly preserved. Many beats from Perth to Isla mouth are leased by Mr. Malloch, fishtackleist, Perth, who often lets. Spring and Autumn fishing is good (*see Advertisement*).

Phinstown (Orkney).—(*See Stromness.*)

Pitlochrie (Perth).—H.R. On Tummel; salmon and trout; by staying at the Loch Tummel Hotel the angler can fish in more than 1 *m.* of the river. Loch Tummel is free; boats from hotel. The end of May is the best time. Loch Broom lies 6 *m*. off; the fishing is first-rate. Leave to fish is not easily obtained. (*See Kinloch Rannoch*.)

Pointstown (Orkney).—(*See Stromness*.)

Porlewe (Ross).—Ewe; trout, sea trout. Lochs Ewe, Maree. *Hotel:* Porlewe, where fishing can be obtained.

Port Askaig (Islay).—By staying at the Port Askaig Hotel trouting can be had in Loch Finlaggan.

Portinisherrach (Argyll).—Loch Awe; trout, perch, pike, sea trout, salmon; fishing free. *Hotel:* Portinisherrach, very comfortable, where boats can be had. (*See Loch Awe*.)

Portpatrick (Wigtown).—Good trouting. *Hotel:* Portpatrick.

Portree (Skye).—Good trouting in Loch Fada; two hours walk towards Storr rocks. Wading necessary. Flies of the local tackleist. Lythe fishing in the harbour. Charge for boat and two men, 2s. an hour. Visitors at Sligachan Inn can fish the river Sligachan. Loch and sea fishing can also be had.

Port Sonachan (Argyll).—By rail to Loch Awe Station, then by steamer "Caledonia." Loch Awe; trout, salmon, sea trout, perch. pike; fishing free. *Hotel:* Port Sonachan (*see Advertisement*); very comfortable. Boats can be had. Fifteen hill lochs, which have been stocked with rainbow, brown, and American trout, are free to Hotel visitors only. For best flies, &c.. see Loch Awe.

Reay Inn, N.B.—Good trout and sea fishing.

Rhiconich Inn (Sutherland).—14 *m*. from Durness. Very comfortable angler's quarters. Mr. Wallace gives permission to fish salmon in Loch Garbetbeg; with a north-west or a south-east wind sport is almost certain; sea trout are plentiful. Numberless unnamed lochs all round will give any amount of trout fishing. This place can be reached by mail car from Lairg, a distance of 42 *m*.. usually occupying six hours. Excellent sea fishing by hiring local boat and man, charges moderate. Best time August and September.

Riccarton Station.—N.B.R. On Tyne. The Tyne consists of two rivers, the North and the South, which meet in a good salmon stream at Howford, about one mile above Hexham. The North Tyne and the Liddel rise within a few hundred yards of each other near Thurlowshope. not far from **Riccarton Station**, and flow down opposite sides of the watershed. A few miles below its source the North Tyne joins a mountain burn, the Keilder, at Keilder Castle, and receives a considerable tributary, the river Reed, at Reedsmouth, below Bellingham. Just below Reedsmouth is the Hargrove stream, the best salmon stream in Northumberland, belonging to the Duke of that ilk. Except near Keilder and in some of the mountain burns flowing into the Tyne, where the trout are preserved, there is now no trout fishing in the Tyne worth following.

Rowardennan (Stirling).—Loch Lomond; fair fishing. *Hotel:* Rowardennan.

St. Boswell's (Roxburgh).—N.B.R. Tweed: salmon, sea trout, brown trout. *Hotel:* Buccleuch Arms. There are 3 *m*. free trouting water; fishing variable.

St. Fillans (Loch Earn).—Visitors staying at the Drummond Arms Hotel or St. Fillans can have fair trout fishing free in the loch and river; there are plenty of boats, and the hotel comfortable. Loch Boltachair holds many small trout.

St. Mary's Loch (Selkirk).—Good quarters. The nearest station is Moffatt. Fair trout and pike fishing in the loch, Meggat waters (by ticket), and the river Yarrow. The loch belongs to Napier Weemys and Duke of Buccleuch, who permit visitors to fish from the shore. The Loch of Lowes is connected with St. Mary's Loch by a short stream; this is the better loch for pike and perch. Cramult burn is good, but is preserved; so is Chapehope burn (free). There are several other burns abounding in trout, running into St. Mary's Loch and Loch of Lowes: boats for hire on the lochs. The best time is the end of April. The address of the inn is St. Mary's Cottage, Yarrow, Selkirk.

Scalloway (Shetland).—(*See Lerwick*.) Lythe and saithe fishing, good.

Scourie (Sutherland).—Reached from Lairg by mail car. Sea fishing very good Trout fishing in Gorom Loch and Trout Loch (fair). Sea trout fishing in Baddinamoult Loch after rain. Salmon sometimes caught by fly and troll in the salt water off the mouth of the Laxford. Free

Selkirk (Selkirk).—Yarrow; trout: fishing free above Yarrow ford. Loch, St. Mary's: perch. pike, trout; free. *Hotel:* Fleece. which has free fishing.

Shetlands.—The Shetlands are the most northerly group of isles in the British dominions. About thirty of the islands are inhabited. Its lochs and brooks are numerous, and, as the freshwater fishing is almost neglected by the inhabitants. the angler may make certain in many of them of good sport. Some of the lochs. such as Loch Brouster in Walls. Lochs Kettlesta in Hamnavoe. and Ulsta in Yell. Loch Cliff in Unst, Loch Fladabister in Cunningsburgh. Loch Spiggie in Dunrossness (*Hotel:* Spiggie). Lochs Setter and Velzie in Fetlar, &c., &c.. give very good sport, but as they are at a distance from the capital town, Lerwick. although in some instances accommodation of a sort may be obtained, yet frequently the angler must rough it Near Lerwick the hotel accommodation is excellent. and the fishing near it is plentiful and easily accessible. Loch Brough and Loch Setter are in Bressay, an island lying opposite Lerwick, and Loch Girlsta is in Tingwall. the nearest parish. The proprietor of the Queen's Hotel, Lerwick, strictly preserves the lochs of Asta and Strand in Tingwall for visitors to the hotel, and capital sport is generally to be had. He has also provided a boat at Loch Asta. Good sea-trout fishing in the sea; and at Lerwick and other places good sport may be had with other fish both with fly and line.

Shiel Bridge (by Loch Moidart, N.B.).—On *Loch* and River Shiel : salmon, grilse, and sea trout. Fishing on Shiel opens Feb. 11, and closes Oct. 31; but the best time is from June 10 to first week in August. Favourite flies : Shiel wasp; dark turkey wing, with yellow body and black hackle; teal wing, yellow body, black hackle: turkey wing, black body, silver tinsel with blue hackle: Thunder and Lightning, Black Doctor, Blue Doctor, Silver Doctor, Jock Scott, Childers. The charge is 5l. per week. The loch fishing is good for salmon, grilse, sea and brown trout, from June to the end of September. The lower end is best, and is fished with fly and minnow, ordinary sea-trout fly being best killer; grouse wing and claret body; teal wing, yellow body, and black hackle, and Zulu with silver tinsel. Most suitable bait for trolling is Brown's Aberdeen, blue and gold, blue and silver phantoms, Nos. 3, 4, and 5; and Devon minnow, 3 and 4, and steel traces.

Skye, Island of.—Speaking generally the trout and salmon fishing is preserved, but some good free fishing is to be had from the proprietors of the following hotels : Broadford (in Broadford river and lochs, 2½ m. from hotel, stocked with rainbow and Lochleven trout) (Sligachan river). Also from Sligachan Inn and King's Arms Hotel, Kyleakin There is also some fishing attached to the Portrel Hotels, Royal and Caledonian (Uig, Kyleakin, and Isleornsay, Ardavassar, Dunvegan). Camasenary and Loch Cornisk are let with the shootings. The accommodation is good. Good sea fishing all round Skye.

Sprouston.—On Tweed. The Earl of Home preserves the greater part of the Carham water above this place.

Stanley.—On Tay. Some of the best salmon pools are near here, such as Cat's Hole and Hell's Hole, but all strictly preserved. A good fly is the following : Body, from the head to a third up the hook, black or dark blue—above that to the finish, yellow; a heron's hackle dyed bright blue tied about half-way up, and another red or yellow, tied and wound round the head with silver tinsel about the body; wings, peacock's tail feathers put on full and rather straggling. Also the black dog : Body, black, with blue at the head and red at the tail, tinsel, gold, or silver: wing, mottled grey turkey; hackle, black. The size of the hook is very large, but diminishes as you advance up stream. For grilse the best fly is the wasp, and next—body, black and red, yellow near the tail, and ribbed with red gold tinsel; wing, brown or dark grey turkey wing with small mottled spots.

Stow (Midlothian).—**Edinburgh** is 26 m. distant by rail. There is a good hotel standing on the banks of the Gala. The fishing is free for 5 m. below Stow, and 4 m. above. The railway runs along the banks of the river. The trout below Stow average five to the pound, above, six to the pound. 6 m. off is the Leader. Some open water also in Earnscleuch burn. (*See Lauder.*)

Strathcarron (Ross).—H.K. On Carron: salmon. Some 2½ m. are preserved by the lessees of New Kelso Lodge.

Strathpeffer. Blackwater, Conon. - *Hotels* : Ben Wyvis and Spa (*see Advertisement*). Some good salmon and loch fishing attached to the hotels. The Spa has fishing on the Conon, and Lochs Luichert and Garve.

Strome Ferry (Ross).—*Hotel* : Station, which has free trout fishing on six lochs for visitors staying at the hotel. Weekly terms, 52s. 6d. Nearest point for Glenshiel, Loch Duich, and Balmacara. Good salt-water fishing in Loch Carron.

Stromness (Orkney).—Good brown trout fishing in Loch Stennis, and sea trout at the Bridge of Waith, and below it to the sea. Boats can be had at the bridge. Loch Harray lies beyond Loch Stennis; it is 6 m. from Stromness and 3 m. from Phinstown, where there is a little inn; excellent brown trout fishing and a few sea trout. July, August, and September are considered the best months. Fishing on Lochs Twatt (11 m.). Stennis, and Harray; leave required for Loch Swanney (14 m.). Loch Stennis, flies : mallards with claret and red body, grouse ditto, teal red and green body (all of medium size and dark wings); also March brown with red and claret body; Zulu, hackle (dark and red), Alexandra, and Heckam. Loch Birsay is 10 m. from Stromness. *Hotels*: Barony and Smithfield, the proprietors of which have fishing in Lochs Birsay, Twatt, Himland, and Swanney. The sea fishing for lythe and saithe is very good.

Tarbet.—On Loch Lomond. Salmon, sea and brown trout, perch, pike. The Loch Lomond Angling Improvement Association (sec., Henry Lamond, 163, West George Street, Glasgow) are lessees of the salmon and sea trout fishing in the loch, and have greatly improved the fishing. Boats and men at the Tarbet hotel.

Tarff (Kirkcudbright).—G. & S.W.R. On Tarff.

Taycreggan (Argyll).—Loch Awe; trout, perch, pike, sea trout, salmon; fishing free. *Hotel*: Taycreggan, where boats can be had. Lochs Nant, Avich, and ten other lochs free to hotel visitors. (*See Loch Awe.*)

Taynuilt (Argyllshire).—C.R. On Awe; salmon, sea trout, trout. *Hotel*: Taynuilt, good; 1½ m. of water attached to hotel; fly only allowed; the fishing is very good from April to October. Loch Etive is close by, and sea trout are caught with fly or minnow from June. The fishing is divided into 5 beats, 3 of which are available to hotel visitors.

Thornhill (Dumfries).—The Nith, and its tributaries below the bridge, also the waters of Ae and its tributaries, are preserved by the Mid-Nithsdale Angling Association; sec., John McKerlie. Trout, s.t. 6s., m.t., 4s., w.t. 2s., d.t. 1s. Salmon, s.t. 10s., w.t. 4s. *Hotels*: Buccleuch, George, and Temperance.

Thurso (Caithness).—(*See Brawl Castle.*) On Thurso; salmon, sea trout, &c. The river rises in three small lochs in the hills, and, after a short course, runs through Loch More. These lochs are very much out of the way. Below Loch More another stream joins Thurso, which takes its rise in three lochs (Loch Stemster, Loch Rangay, and Loch Ruard) not very far apart. At Brawl Castle a stream joins on the left which rises in Loch Calder.

Tobermory (Mull).—By staying at the Mishnish Royal Hotel, fishing can be had in Bellart, and in Loch Freesa, 4½ *m.* (good brown trouting).

Tomintoul by Grantown.—Sea trout, grilse, and salmon fishing can be had by staying at the Richmond Hotel (*see Advertisement*).

Tongue Hotel (Sutherland).—*Lochs:* Coalside, Brach Buie, Hallow (a boat), Slam, Na Hakel, Craggie, and Loyal; trouting fair, fish about three to the pound; many large lake trout; boat belongs to inn; leave must be obtained from the Duke's factor, Mr. Crawford. Many other small lochs with burns. The salmon fishing in the Borgie is taken up. Good salmon and sea trout fishing on Kyle of Tongue. (*See Aultnahara.*) The best killing fly in the lochs are a magenta-coloured body, ribbed with silver and a red tag, black hackle and grouse wing, the Soldier Palmer, and a large yellow fly.

Torphins (Aberdeen).—C.R., N.B.R., Deeside R. Dee; salmon, trout. Beltie burn; trout; free.

Trossachs Hotel.—There are three or four streams in the neighbourhood, free. *Lakes:* Katrine; trout; boats at hotel. Achray; trout, salmon; boats. Vennachar; trout and occasional salmon; boats can be arranged for. Drunkie; fine trout (preserved). The Tinker; lots of trout, four to pound; free.

Tummel Bridge—On the Tummel (early river); trout. *Hotel:* Tummel Bridge, by Pitlochry. Here the fishing is fairly good; but the trouting is better some 20 *m.* up where the moor of Rannoch begins. Loch Tummel lies 2 *m.* down stream, and contains some goodly pike and trout; by fishing very late in the evening some good trout may be taken. The best flies are the coachman and a fly with a teal drake's wing, black hackle and red wool body.

Tyndrum (Perth).—Fillan; Orchy. Lochs Na Baa, Dochart. *Hotel:* Royal, where fishing can be had.

Ullapool (Ross).—On Loch Broom; salmon; 3 *m.* of river fishing can be had from the Caledonian (*see Advertisement*), and Royal Hotels, also seven large lochs (boats on each), containing excellent brown and rainbow trout up to 4lb. Good sea fishing. Mail coach daily to and from Garve station; steamers weekly from Glasgow, Oban, Mallaig and Kyle.

Weem (Perth).—On Tay. Pretty good fishing in the neighbourhood.

Wick (Caithness).—G.N. of S.R., H.R. *Hotels:* Station, Caledonian. Fishing by permission can sometimes be obtained in Lochs Hempriggs and Wester; Ruttar and Corsetack are free.

Wigtown.—Bladenoch. Salmon, trout.

Winton.—Humbie; trout; free.

WALES.

Aber (Carnarvon).—L. & N.W.R. Aber; trout. Aber rises in Llyn-an-afon, and 3 *m.* down is joined on left bank by Aber-fawr, 3 *m.* long. Aber runs to **Aber** and the sea in 2 *m.* *Hotel:* Bulkeley Arms.

Aberaeron (Cardigan).—n.s. **Lampeter**, 14 *m.* Aaron; trout, salmon. (*c.s.*). Mude, 3 *m.* Oilcennin brook, 4 *m.* Aaron rises in Llyn Eiddwen, 7 *m.* N.W. from **Tregaron**, and 2 *m.* down is joined on right bank by a brook which drains Llyn Fanod, 2 *m.* up, 6 *m.* N.W. from **Tregaron.** Aaron runs 4 *m.* to Llangeitho, 4 *m.* W. from **Tregaron**, and here Telyn, 3 *m.* long, joins on right bank. 2 *m.* down Aaron, at Capel Bettws Lleici, 4 *m.* W. from **Pont Llanio**, Gwenffrwd, 3 *m.* long, joins on right bank. 3 *m.* down Aaron, Meurig joins on left bank, which rises 3 *m.* N. of **Derry Ormond**, and is 3 *m.* long. 2 *m.* down Aaron (n.s. **Derry Ormond**, 4 *m.*), Rhewfallen, 4 *m.* long, joins on right bank, and 1 *m.* down Aaron, Nant-y-fergy, 2 *m.* long, joins on right bank. 1 *m.* down Aaron, Gelli, which runs 6 *m.* N.W. from **Lampeter** and is 3 *m.* long, joins on left bank. ½ *m.* down Aaron, Gerwen, which rises above Llanfihangel Ystrad, 7 *m.* from **Lampeter**, and is 2 *m.* long, joins on left bank. 2 *m.* down Aaron, Cilcennin brook, 2 *m.* long, joins on right bank, 4 *m.* above **Aberaeron.** Aaron runs 2 *m.*, when Mude, 6 *m.* long, joins on left bank. Aaron runs to Aberaeron and the sea 3 *m.* ARTH runs 1½ *m.* N.E. of **Aberaeron** at Aber Arth. Arth rises in Llyn March, 6 *m.* S.E. of **Llanrhystyd.** This llyn is 1 *m.* S.W. of Llyn Fanod. Arth runs 5 *m.*, when Bran, 2 *m.* long, joins on left bank. Arth runs 5 *m.* to Aber Arth and the sea.

Aberafon (Glamorgan).—G.W.R. Afon (trout) rises by Blaen Afon, and 4 *m.* down, where the road from **Cymmer** (2½ *m.* off on left bank) crosses it. Cerwg, 5 *m.* long, joins on right bank. 5 *m.* down Afon (n.s. **Aberafon**, 4 *m.*) a stream 4 *m.* long joins on right bank. Afon runs 5 *m.* to **Aberafon**, and 1 *m.* below is joined on left bank by Gwinan, 5 *m.* long. (*c.s. Usk.*)

Aberaman (Glamorgan).—G.W.R. Cynon. Aman. (*See Cardiff.*)

Aber Angell (Montgomery).—L. & N.W.R. Dovey: salmon trout. Angell. (*c.s.*) Hir, 1 *m.* E. , Mynach, 1 *m.* N.E. Angell-Tafolog, 3 *m.* W. Dulas, 4 *m.* E. (trout). (*c.s. Dovey.*) Llefeni, 4 *m.* E. *Lakes:* Llyn Llecoediog, 1 *m.* E. (*See Machynlleth.*)

Aberbran (Brecon).—(*Brecon.*) N. & B.R. Usk; trout, salmon; preserved by a society. Bran; trout. Yscir; trout. (*See Brecon and Newport.*) (*c.s.*)

Aberdaron (Carnarvon). n.s. **Pwlhelli**, 18 *m.*—Daron runs down in two branches joining at **Aberdaron**—Afon-fawr 5 *m.* long, and Afon-fach 3 *m.* long.

Aberdare Junction (Glamorgan). G.W.R.; T.V.R. Taff; salmon, trout. (*c.s.*) Cynon. Gelli (2 *m.*). (*See Cardiff.*)

Aberdene (Glamorgan).—G.W.R. Cynon. Rhondda Fychan (4 *m.*). (*See Cardiff.*)

Aberdovey (Merioneth).—G.W.R. Good bass fishing, with a large fly of mixed crimson and white feathers. The following fishing stations are within two hours' journey:— Towyn, Llwyngwiel, Arthog, Dolgelley, Brynglas, Dolgoch, Abergynolwyn, Glandovey, Machynlleth, Cammaes Road, Llanflhangel. *Hotel:* Trefeddian, where fishing can be had.

Aberdylias (Glamorgan).—G.W.R. Neath. Dylias. (*See Neath.*)

Aberedw (Radnor).—C.R. Wye; chub, dace, trout, salmon. Edw; good trouting; permission freely given. Bach-howey brook (1 *m.*); trout. *Lakes:* Cawr (3 *m.*). Llanbychllyn and two other lakes (3 *m.*). Llyn pools (5 *m.*). Mann pools (6½ *m.*). (*c.s.*) (*See Chepstow.*)

Aberffraw (Anglesey).—n.s. **Bodorgan**, 3 *m.* Coron lake, 1½ *m.* Ffraw; trout. Ffraw, under the name of Gwna, rises 4 *m.* above **Bodorgan**, and just below **Bodorgan** it waters Llyn Coron. The stream now takes the name of Ffraw, and ½ *m.* below the lake is joined on the left bank by Fraich Wen, which runs close to **Bodorgan** on the E. side, and is 1½ *m.* long. 1 *m.* down Ffraw a stream joins on the right bank, which rises near **Gwalchnai**, and is 3 *m.* long. Ffraw runs to **Aberffraw** and the sea in 1½ *m.*, Fraich Wen 1½ *m.* E., Lake Coron 1½ *m.* N.E. (trout), Maelog 3 *m.* N.W., also Orygyll river, which rises above Bryngwrau, and flows to the sea close to Maelog. *Hotel:* Maelog Lake (*see Advt*). Sea fishing very good, particularly for pollack and sea bream. Near Carreg-y-Trai (stone of the ebb), pollack between 5lb. and 11lb. often taken; variety of other fish. Trailing for pollack with the patent wire lines gives very good sport, the fish biting freely, especially in clear water. In August and September bass are caught from the rocks on the flowing tide; use a trolling or salmon rod with Nottingham reel and plenty of line; best bait, soft crab, procured from boatmen: mussels are also good bait, and are easily obtained. At the estuary of Malldraeth Bay bass are caught from boats by trailing the Sarcelle bait: also mackerel, cod, and gurnets. Mr. R. D. Williams, Penrhyn, Aberffraw, Tycroes, who is agent here for the British Sea Anglers' Society, will be pleased to give any information. *Hotel:* Prince Llewellyn.

Abergele (Denbigh).—L. & N.W.R. Gele. (*See Rhyl, Llanfair, Talhaiarn.*)

Abergwili (Carmarthen).—L. & N.W.R. Towy; salmon, sewin, trout; fishing free. Gwili; trout, sewin, salmon; fishing free. (*c.s.*) (*See Carmarthen.*)

Abergwynolwyn (Merioneth).—G.W.R. Dysynni; trout; fishing free. (*c.s. Dovey.*) Gwynolwyn. (*See Towyn.*)

Abermule (Montgomery).—C.R. Severn; trout, salmon, chub, &c. Mule. (*c.s. Severn.*) (*See Gloucester.*)

Aberystwyth (Cardigan).—G.W.R.; L. & N.W.R. On Ystwyth; more or less polluted. Rheidol, now polluted; salmon, trout. Melynddwr. 6 *m.* E. *Lakes:* Glan Rheidol, 7 *m.* E. Ystwyth rises 5 *m.* S.W. from **Llangurig**, and 1 *m.* down is joined on right bank by Dillon, 4 *m.* long (n.s. **Llangurig**, 5 *m.*). 4 *m.* down Ystwyth, Tilwyn, 2 *m.* long, joins on left bank, and 1 *m.* down. Eglwysnewydd Gai, 2 *m.* long, joins on left bank (n.s. **Traws Coed**, 7 *m.*). 2 *m.* down Ystwyth a stream joins on right bank, draining a llyn 2½ *m.* up, by Llantrisant (n.s. **Traws Coed**, 5 *m.*). Ystwyth runs to **Traws Coed** 6 *m.*, and 2 *m.* down is joined on right bank by Magwyr, 3 *m.* long. Ystwyth runs 2 *m.* to **Llan Llar**, just above which Creiddyn brook, 4 *m.* long, joins on right bank. 3 *m.* down Ystwyth, Mad, 3 *m.* long. joins on left bank. 2 *m.* down Ystwyth is **Llanrhystyd Road**, and 1½ *m.* down Eos, 4 *m.* long, joins on right bank. Ystwyth runs to Aberystwyth and sea in 1½ *m.*

RHEIDOL rises on one of the spurs of Plymlimmon, 8 *m.* S.E. of **Machynlleth**, and 3 *m.* down is joined on left bank by a stream draining Llyn Llygad, 1 *m.* up under the brow of Plymlimmon, 9 *m.* N. from **the Devil's Bridge**. ½ *m.* down, Llygnant, 8 *m* long, joins on right bank. 10 *m.* N from **Devil's Bridge**. 1 *m.* down Rheidol, Llechweddmaur, 5 *m.* long, joins on right bank 9 *m.* from **Devil's Bridge**. 2 *m.* down Rheidol, Rhyddlan, 4 *m.* long. joins on right bank 7 *m.* from **Devil's Bridge**. Rheidol runs 5 *m.* to Pont Erwyd, where Castell (polluted), 4 *m.* long, joins on left bank. Rheidol runs 3 *m.* to **Devil's Bridge**, and here Myherin joins on left bank. Myherin rises in the two lakes Jenan, 6 *m.* N.E. from the **Devil's Bridge**, runs 4 *m.*, when Rhyddnant, which rises in Llyn Rhyddnant 5 *m.* N.E. of **Devil's Bridge** and is 3 *m.* long, joins on left bank. Myherin runs 3 *m.* to **Devil's Bridge**. Here also a stream joins on right bank, draining a small lake 2 *m* up; also the drainings of Llyn Lon, 1 *m.* W. of **Devil's Bridge**, join on right bank. Rheidol runs 8 *m.* to near Capel Bangor, where Melynddwr, 7 *m.* long, joins on right bank. Just above this junction the outflow of a lake at Glan Rheidol, ½ *m.* up, joins on right bank. Rheidol runs to **Aberystwyth** and sea 6 *m.*; a few bass are taken between this and Borth with a fly, also mackerel and gurnet. *Hotel*: Queen's. There are three small lakes up in the mountains, 2 *m.* from the Dyffryn Castle Hotel, which lies 14 *m.* from Aberystwyth. Permission may be had from Mr. Evans, 3, Commercial-street, Newport, Mon. The fish run very large. Also the lakes which supply Aberystwith with water: fishing free. (*See Pen-y-Bont.*) Lead poisoning has practically ruined the fishing in Ystwyth and Rheidol, but the tributaries joining the Rheidol above Pont Eruyd contain trout, which, however, are mere fingerlings. Along the road from Aberystwyth, 1½ *m.* before Pont Eruyd, there are two lakes (one very small), which contain trout, and belong to Capt. Bray, of Aberystwyth. Permission to fish them can be obtained from the owner, or by staying at the hotel at Pont Eruyd. There are two small lakes about 2 *m.* N. of these, Craig-y-Nau-ddu and Pont Syfydrin; the former contains trout, the latter eels only.

Afon-wen (Merioneth).—L. & N.W.R. Wen. Wen rises 4 *m.* above **Llangybi** station, runs 1 *m.* to **Chwilog** and the sea at **Afon-wen**, 1 *m.*

Amlwch.—(*See Penrhoslligwy.*)

Arenig (Merioneth).—G.W.R. Tryweryn; trout; preserved from its source to the junction of Gelyn 2 *m.* below **Arenig**; d.t. 1s. 6d., from the hotel; visitors free. (*c.s. Dee.*) Gelyn. 2 *m.* N.E. trout; preserved as Tryweryn. Lliw, 4 *m* N. Clettwr, 7, *m.* N. Conway, 8 *m.* N. at Yspythy Evan. (*c.s.*) (*See Conway.*) *Lakes*: Arenig-bach, 1½ *m.* N. Arenig, 2 *m.* S.E. Tryweryn, 3 *m.* W. Lliw, 6 *m.* N.W. *Hotel*: Rhydy Fen.

Arleen (Montgomery).—O.R. Maerdy brook. Bete brook (1 *m.* S.). Severn (2 *m.* E.); chub, dace, trout, salmon. (*See Gloucester.*) (*c.s. Severn.*)

Arthog, near Dolgelly (Merioneth).—L. & N.W.R.; C.R.; G.W.R. Mawddach; Wnion; trout, sewin, salmon, red-fin; tickets at hotel. (*c.s. Dovey.*) Creignant. *Lakes*: Creigennan, 1 *m.* S.E.; trout: preserved by landlord; boats. Llyn-y-Wylfa, 2 *m.* N.E. Cyri, 1 *m.* S. *Hotel*: Arthog Hall, very comfortable (*see Advertisement*). (*See Barmouth.*)

Bala (Merioneth).—G.W.R. Dee; trout, salmon, grayling; s.t. 42s., w.t. 5s., d.t. 2s. 6d.; tickets at the hotels. (*c.s.*) Tryweryn; trout; s.t. 21s., w.t. 5s., d.t. 1s. 6d.; detached portions free. The river opens on Feb. 14, and closes Oct. 15. No worm fishing before April 1 and after Sept. 1. (*c.s. Dee.*) Llechweddhen and Tynycarnel preserves on Tryweryn; s.t 42s., m.t., 21s., w.t. 7s., d.t 2s. 6d. Corgnant, 1 *m.* N.E. Hirnant, 1 *m.* E.; trout. Cymmerig, 1 *m* S.E. Meloch, 2 *m.* N.E. *Lake*: Bala or Tegid, 4 *m.* long (a small portion of upper part reserved); pike, perch, roach, trout: boats at the hotels. June, July, and August are the best months. At Llanuwchllyn, trout fishing in Twrch, Dee, Lliw, Llafar, and Arran Lake. The streams and Arran Lake are preserved by Sir W. W. Wynn, Bart., from whom permission must be obtained. Hotel quite close to fishing. (*c.s. Dee.*) *Hotels*: Royal (*see Advertisement*), White Lion Plascoch, Bull. *Tackleist*, M. Roberts (*see Advertisement*). (*See Arenig, Chester.*)

Bangor (Carnarvon).—L. & N.W.R. Bangor brook, 7 *m.* long; few trout; free.

OGWEN, 2 *m.* E.; salmon, trout; preserved by Lord Penrhyn for 2 *m.* next the sea, free above. Ogwen rises in Llyn Lloer, 6 *m.* N.W. from **Capel Curig**. runs 1 *m.* to Llyn Ogwen (capital trouting). 5 *m.* N.W. of **Capel Curig**, or 5 *m.* S.E. of **Bethesda**. 1 *m.* down the lake, near the lower end, a stream joins on left bank, draining Llyn Bochlwyd 1 *m.* up, 6 *m.* W. of **Capel Curig**. A trifle further on a stream joins on left bank, which, rising in Llyn-y-Cwm, 8 *m.* W. of **Capel Curig** or 8 *m.* S.E. of **Bethesda**, runs 1 *m.* to Llyn Idwell (good trouting, boat), 7 *m.* W. of **Capel Curig** or 7 *m.* S.E. of **Bethesda**, and ½ *m.* to Llyn Ogwen. 3 *m.* down Ogwen, 3 *m.* S.E. of **Bethesda**, Berthan, 2 *m.* long, joins on right bank, and 2 *m.* below, ½ *m.* above **Bethesda**, Casey joins on right bank. Casey rises in Llyn Casey 5 *m.* S.E. of **Bethesda**, and 4 *m.* down, 1 *m.* S.E. of **Bethesda**, is joined on left bank by Llafer, 3 *m.* long. Casey runs to Ogwen in 1 *m.* Ogwen runs to **Bethesda** ½ *m.* Here Ffridd-las, 2 *m.* long, joins on right bank, and March on left bank. March rises in March-llyn-mawr, 3 *m.* across the hills, N.E. from **Llanberris**, runs 3 *m.* to the Penrhyn slate quarries and St. Ann's Chapel, and 1 *m.* below is joined on left bank by a stream which rises in March-llyn-bach, lying ½ *m.* N.W. of March-llyn-mawr, 3 *m.* N.E. of **Llanberris**. This stream is 4 *m.* long. Ogwen runs 5 *m.* to the sea. *Hotel*: British. (*See Beaumaris.*)

Bargoed (Glamorgan).—L. & N.W.R.; B. & M.R. Rumney; trout, salmon; preserved. Crinlach. (*See Cardiff.*) (*c.s.*)

Barmouth (Merioneth).—G.W.R. Mawddach; salmon, trout. Mawddach rises in Llyn Crych-y-wayen, 4 *m.* N. across the hills for **Drws-y-nant**, and, 3 *m.* down, is joined on left bank by Geirw, 2 *m.* long, and a nameless brook on right bank. 3 *m.* down Mawddach, 3 *m.* N. from **Tyn-y-groes**. Gain joins on right bank. Gain is some 7 *m.* long, and, 3 *m.* from its source, is joined on right bank by a short stream draining Llyn Gelli-gain, 3 *m.* S.E. from **Trawsfynydd**. 2 *m.* down Mawddach, at Pont-ar-Eden, 1 *m.* N. from **Tyn-y-groes**, Eden joins on right bank. Eden rises in Llyn Pryvyd (good trout), 9 *m.* N. from **Tyn-y-groes**, or 7 *m.* N.E. from **Llanbedr** up the Artro Valley, past Llyn Cwm Bychan, and 1 *m.* N.E. of that lake runs ½ *m.* to Llyn Twrgla, and 1 *m.* down is joined on left bank by a stream, 1 *m.* long, draining Llyn Graigddrwg, 1 *m.* E. of Llyn Ciddew-Mawr, and 4 *m.* E. of **Talsarnan**, or 5 *m.* N.E. of **Harlech**. 5 *m.* down Eden, at Pont Llyn-y-Cafn, 4 *m.* N. from **Tyn-y-groes**, Ddu, which rises in Llyn Ddu (many small trout), and is 3 *m.* long, joins on right bank. Llyn Ddu lies 7 *m.* N.W. from **Tyn-y-groes**. Eden joins Mawddach 3 *m.* down. Camlan joins Mawddach ½ *m.* below on right bank. Camlan rises in Llyn-y-bi, 5 *m.* N.W. from

Tyn-y-groes. 2 *m.* down (1 *m.* below the slate quarries), a stream, 1 *m.* long, joins on left bank, draining Llyn-y-Fran. 4 *m.* N.W. from **Tyn-y-groes.** 2 *m.* down Camlan a stream, 1 *m.* long, joins on left bank, draining Llyn Pen-y-ganllwyd, 3 *m.* N. from **Tyn-y-groes.** 1 *m.* below Camlan joins Mawddach, which runs 1 *m.* to **Tyn-y-groes** (n.s. **Dolgelly**), 4 *m.* 2 *m.* down Mawddach, two streams, 4 *m.* and 3 *m.* long, join on left bank. 3 *m.* below, **Dolgelly** being 1 *m.* off on left bank, Wnion joins on left bank. Wnion rises 4 *m.* above **Drws-y-nant**, just below which place, on left bank, the Harnog and Cwm-ochr, each 3 *m.* long, join Wnion at the same spot. 1 *m.* down Wnion, Ciddow, 3 *m.* long, joins on right bank, and, ½ *m.* down, Fidw, 3 *m.* long, joins on right bank. Wnion runs 2 *m.* to **Pont Newydd**, and, 2 *m.* down, is joined on left bank by Ddybin, 4 *m.* long. Wnion runs to **Dolgelly** 2 *m.* Here a stream joins on left bank, which drains Llyn Aras 3 *m.* up. Wnion joins Mawddach 2 *m.* down. Mawddach runs 2 *m.* to **Penmaenpool**, and here Mynach, which rises in Llyn Cwm-mynach an.' is 4 *m.* long, joins on right bank. 1 *m.* down Mawddach Gadr joins on left bank. Gadr rises in Llyn Gadr, 4 *m.* S.W. from **Dolgelly**, runs ½ *m.* to Llyn Gafr, and, 1 *m.* below, where the main road crosses, is joined on right bank by the drainage of Llyn Gwernan, ½ *m.* up, 2 *m.* S.W. of **Dolgelly**. Gadr runs to Mawddach 2 *m.* Mawddach runs 1 *m.*, when Llechan, 4 *m.* long, joins on right bank. 1 *m.* down Mawddach, a stream joins on left bank, draining Llyn-y-Wylfa 2 *m.* up, 2 *m.* N.E. from **Arthog.** ½ *m.* down Mawddach, on the right bank, Goetref, 4 *m.* long, joins on right bank. 1 *m.* down Mawddach. close to **Barmouth**, Creigennan joins on left bank. Creigennan rises in Llyn Cyri, and, 2 *m.* down, close to **Arthog.** is joined on right bank by the drainage of Llyn Creigennan, 1 *m.* up. The brook joins Mawddach 1 *m.* down, which runs to Barmouth and the sea 1 *m.* on. (*c.s. Dovey.*) **Egryn**, 2 *m.* N., 3 *m.* long, joins the sea below Egryn Abbey: good sea fishing, skate, haddock, whiting, whiting pout, and a few bass and dog fish. *Hotel:* Marine. *Fishing stations within reach:* Arthog, Penmaenpool, Dolgelly, Dyffryn, Llanbedr, Harlech, Talsarnan, Penrhyndendraeth, Portmadoc, Llwyngwril, Towyn, Aberdovey, Machynlleth.

Beaumaris (Anglesea).—n.s. **Bangor.** 6 *m.* Llandigfan brook, 3 *m.* S.W. *Lakes*: Bodgolched, 1½ *m.* N.W. Llyn-y-pare, 1½ *m.* S.W. Llyn-y-gors, 2 *m.* S.W. Llwydiarth, 4 *m.* N.W. (*See Llangeinwen.*) Opposite the town and all along the Straits you may get plenty of small codlings, flatfish, &c. The best baits are mussels, black bait, and soft crabs. There is fair bass fishing between the Menai and Tubular Bridges, also at Puffin Island for pollack; sand-eels at the Dutchman Sands. There is good rod-fishing off shore along the north and west coast of Anglesea, epecially at the Skerries, where, with a white fly, the black and white pollack may be taken. August and September are the best months for bass fishing here.

Beddgelert (Carnarvon).—N.W.N.G.R. Glaslyn; trout, sewin, salmon; s.t. 21*s.*, m.t. 15*s.*, d.t. 2*s.* (*c.s. Dovey.*) Colwyn. Nant-mor, 3 *m.* S.E. Croesor, 4 *m.* S.E. Dwyfach, 5 *m.* W.; trout. (*c.s.*) (*See Criccieth.*) *Lakes* (all private, except Dinas and Gwynant). Llyn-y-Ddinas, 2 *m.* N.E.; salmon, trout; boats. (*c.s. Dovey.*) Y-Arddu, 3 *m.* S.E. Lynnian Cerig-y-Mellt, 3 *m.* S.E. Hafod-y-Llyn, 3 *m.* S. Gwynant, 4 *m.* N.E; trout, sewin, salmon; boats. (*c.s. Dovey.*) Llagi, 4½ *m.* E. Y-Adar, 5 *m.* E. Biswail, 5 *m.* E. Edno, 6 *m.* N.E.; large trout. Llynian Cwm, 6 *m.* N.E.; large trout. *Hotels:* Royal Goat (fishing free to visitors), Saracen's Head, Prince Llewelyn. (*See Portmadoc.*)

Begelly (Pembroke).—G.W.R. Kilrelgy brook, 5 *m.* long, runs 1 *m.* E. Carn (3 *m.*). Langdon brook (3 *m.*). (*See Loveston.*)

Berwyn for Llantisilio (Denbigh).—G.W.R. Dee; chub, grayling, trout, pike, salmon; preserved by Glvndwr Society from **Carrog** above to **Llangollen** below. (*See Llangollen.*) (*c.s.*) Berwyn. (*See Chester.*)

Bethesda (Carnarvon).—n.s. **Bangor**, 5 *m.* Ogwen; trout, salmon, sea trout. Casey. Ffridd-las. March. Llafer, 1 *m.* S.E. Berthan, 3 *m.* S.E. *Lakes*: Ogwen, 5 *m.* S.E.; trout; free; boats. Casey, 5 *m.* S.E. Ffynnon Llyffaint, 5 *m.* S.E. Melynllyn, 6 *m.* E. Dulyn, 6 *m.* E. Idwell; trout; boats; free; 7 *m.* S.E. Llyn-y-Cwm, 8 *m.* S.E. *Hotel*, Douglas Arms. (*See Bangor; Conway.*)

Bettws Garmon (Carnarvon).—N.W.N.G.R. Gwrfai; salmon, trout; free. (*c.s. Seiont.*) (*See Llanwnda.*)

Bettws-y-Coed (Carnarvon).—L. & N.W.R. Conway; trout, salmon, sewin; tickets for the Gwydyr fishery can be had of Mr. Parry, chemist, who also supplies the necessary licences (*for terms see Llanrwst*). (*c.s.*) Llugwy; trout, salmon; *salmon fishing* begins May 1; tickets to fish the S. bank of Llugwy from Pont-y-pair to the junction with Conway, May 1 to Nov. 14, 2*l.*; m.t. 10*s.*, w.t. 3*s.*, d.t. 1*s.*; *trout fishing* from March 1 to Oct. 1 *above* Pont-y-pair, s.t. 2*s.* 6*d.*, w.t. 1*s.* (*c.s. Conway.*) Lledr, 1 *m.* S.; trout, salmon; *salmon fishing* same as for Llugwy; no Sunday fishing; no dogs; tickets of Mr. Parry. (*c.s. Conway.*) Machno, 3 *m.* S. Hwch, 4 *m.* S.E. Eidda, 5 *m.* S.E. Cadnant, 6 *m.* S.E. Merddwr, 6 *m.* S.E. Laethog, 10 *m.* S.E. Pentrevodas river. 6 *m.*, trout. *Lakes*: Elsi, 1 *m.* S.W.; trout; boats. Pen-craig, 3 *m.* N.W. Capel Curig, 6 *m.* Siabod, 6 *m.* Conway; trout; 9 *m.* S.; preserved. (*c.s.*) Alwen, 9 *m.* E.; boats. Llyn-y-Cwrt. 10 *m.* S.E. *Hotels*: Royal Oak, Waterloo, Gwydyr, and Glanaber. (*See Conway; Chester.*)

Bishopston (Glamorgan).—n s. **Mumbles Road**, 3 *m.* Kittle brook, 5 *m.* long.

Black Mill (Glamorgan). G.W.R. On Ogmore. (*See Bridgend.*) (*c.s.*)

Bodfari (Denbigh).—L. & N.W.R. Wheeler. Clwyd, 1 *m*. W.; salmon, trout. (*c.s.*) (*See Rhyl.*)

Bodorgan Anglesea).—L. & N.W.R. Ffraw or Gwna; trout. Faich-wen. Cefni, 2 *m*. S.E.; salmon, trout. (*c.s. Seiont.*) Cefni rises 2 *m*. above **Llangwyllog**, runs 5 *m*. to **Llangefni**. 1 *m*. down, Llanfinnan brook, 6 *m*. long, joins on left bank. Cefni runs to the sea in 5 *m*. *Lakes*: Coron; trout. Bodric or Maelog, 4 *m*. N.W. (*See Aberffraw.*) *Hotel*: Bodorgan Arms.

Boughrood (Brecon).—C.R. Wye: trout, salmon, chub, dace. Cunrig (2 *m*.) (*c.s.*) (*See Chepstow, England.*)

Branwydd Arms (Carmarthen).—Gwili; trout, sewin, salmon; free fishing. (*c.s.* Towey.) (*See Carmarthen.*) Cynnen (2 *m*.) (*See Laugharne.*)

Brawdy (Pembroke).—n.s. **Haverfordwest**, 10 *m*. Brawdy brook, 7 *m*. long.

Brecknock (Brecon).—M. R.; B. M. and N. &. B.R. Usk: trout, salmon. Honddu; trout. Tarrell; trout. Cynrig (2 *m*.). Brau, Yskir. (*See Newport.*) (*c.s.*) Usk is preserved by the United Usk Fishery Association from **Defynock**, except a portion. The Castle Hotel Company will supply information. Salmon and trout rod licences 20*s*. and 1*s*., from Mrs. Hughes, stationer. Residents within 1 *m*. of Brecon Town Hall can fish—salmon and trout s.t. 10*s*., trout s.t. 5*s*.—from notice board in Venny Wood to the bottom of Defauden meadow; tickets for fishing in any of the Association waters in Brecknockshire are issued at—salmon and trout s.t. 40*s*., w.t. 10*s*, d.t. 5*s*.; below Aberbran Bridge 20*s*.; tickets from Mrs. Hughes, stationer, Castle Hotel, Brecon, and at Post-office, Sennybridge; salmon fishing begins March 2, ends Nov. 1; trouting begins March 2, ends Sept. 1; no gaff before May 1; no dogs; no Sunday fishing. 5 *m*. from Brecon is Llangorse lake, containing several kinds of fish, principally pike and perch; boats can be hired, and the fishing is good; all bait must be taken to the lake. Excellent roach and gudgeon fishing to be obtained in the canal. *Fisherman:* Pritchard. A large fly is good for big pike here. (*See Usk.*)

Bridgend (Glamorgan).—G.W.R. Ogmore and Ewenny; trout, sewin, salmon. Ogmore rises by **Black Mill** station, runs 9 *m*. to **Tondu**, 1 *m*. below which, at St. Bride's, Llynvi joins on right bank. Llynvi rises by **Cymmer**, runs 2 *m*. to **Maesteg**, 2 *m*. to **Llangonoyd**, 4 *m*. to **Tondu**, and Ogmore 1 *m*. Ogmore runs 4 *m*. to **Bridgend**, and 3 *m*. below, at Ogmore Castle, is joined on left bank by Ewenny river. Ewenny rises above **Pencoed**, runs 5 *m*. to **Bridgend** (1½ *m*. off), and 3 *m*. down joins Ogmore. The sea is reached in 2 *m*. *Tackleist*, R. H. Dyer, 19 and 20, Queen-street.

Brymbo (Denbigh).—L. & N.W.R. Eadyn, 1 *m*. N.W. Alyn, 1 *m*. N.; trout. (*c.s. Dee.*) Clywedog, 5 *m*. S.W. *Lakes*: Mawr-y-Mynydd, 5 *m*. S.W. (*See Chester.*)

Bryn-Amman (Carmarthen).—G.W.R.; L. & N.W.R. Amman; trout. (*See Llwchur.*) (*c.s. Towy.*)

Bryn Glas (Merioneth).—G.W.R.; L. & N.W.R. Fefinder. Dysynni, 2 *m*. W.; sewin, trout, salmon. (*c.s. Dovey.*) (*See Towyn.*)

Brynkir (Carnarvon).—L. & N.W.R. Dwyfach; trout, sewin, salmon. (*c.s.*) Dwyfawr, 2 *m*. E.; trout, sewin, salmon. (*c.s.*) Istrallyn, 2 *m*. E. (*See Criccieth.*)

Builth (Brecon). — C.R. Wye; chub, dace, pike, roach, salmon, trout, grayling. Irfon; chub, dace, trout, grayling. salmon. Chwefru. Cneiddon (1 *m*.). Dihonw (2 *m*.), preserved. Baili brook (2¼ *m*.). Camnant (4 *m*.). Edw (trout), 2¼ *m*.; d.t. 2*s*. 6*d*. *Hotel*: Lion. (*c.s.*) (*See Chepstow, England.*)

Builth Road (Radnor).—C.R. Wye; salmon, trout, chub, dace, pike. Dulas. (*c.s.*) (*See Chepstow, England.*)

Buttington (Montgomery).—C.R. Severn; trout, salmon, chub, dace. Trewern (1 *m*. N.E.). (*See Gloucester.*) (*See Severn.*)

Cadoxton (Glamorgan).—n.s. **Cardiff**, 7 *m*. The Cadoxton stream (trout) rises by Michaelston (strictly preserved), 3½ *m*. from **Cardiff**, runs 3 *m*. to Cadoxton, and joins the sea 4 *m*. below; leave is sometimes given by the owner at Dynas Powis.

Caerphilly (Glamorgan).—R.R. Glydyr. Ceffyl. Rumney (1 *m*.); trout, salmon. (*c.s.*) (*See Cardiff.*)

Caersws (Montgomery).—C.R. Severn; trout, salmon, chub, &c. Tarannon. Garno, Relof (2 *m*.). Taru (3 *m*.). (*c.s. Severn.*) (*See Gloucester.*)

Caerwys (Flint).—L. & N.W.R. Wheeler. Helyg, 3 *m*. N. *Lakes*: Helyg, 3 *m*. N. (*See Rhyl.*)

Cann-Office (nr. Welshpool) (Montgomery).—n.s. **Llanfair Caer**, 7 *m*. Banw; trout, salmon. Twrch (2 *m*. N.W.); good trouting; tickets to visitors at the hotel. Nant yr Eira (1 *m*. E.). Vyrnwy (4 *m*. N.); preserved by Sir W. W. Wynn. *Lakes*: Llyn Coch Hwyad (8 *m*. W.) Llyn Gwyddior (7 *m*. S.W.); preserved by Sir W. W. Wynn; leave occasionally. By staying at the Cann-Office Hotel (very comfortable) 12 *m*. of fishing can be had, commencing March 1. (*See Gloucester; Welshpool.*) (*c.s. Severn.*)

Capel Curig (Carnarvon). — n.s. **Betts-y-Coed**, 5 *m*. Llugwy: trout; preserved by Lord Denbeigh from Bettws-y-Coed to Pew-y-Gwryd. (*c.s. Conway.*) Gwryd; trout. Ogwen, 6 *m*. N.W.; trout; free. *Lakes*: Mymbyr (2); trout; boats. Coryn, 1 *m*. N.E. Bychan, 2 *m*. N.E. Cwlyd, 2 *m*. N.; trout. Crafnant, 3 *m* N.; trout; boat. Bodgynwydd, 3 *m*. E.N.E. Geirionydd, 3 *m*. N.E.; polluted. Goddion-duon, 4 *m*. N.E. Eigian, 4 *m*. N. Dyweinydd, 4 *m*. S.; trout; preserved by H. Brandreth, Esq. Ogwen, 5 *m*. N.W ; trout; free; boats. Llugwy, 5 *m*. N.W.; trout. Idwal, 6 *m*. W.; trout; free; boat. Bochlwyd, 6 *m*. W.; trout. Melynllyn, 6 *m*. N.N.E. Llover, 6 *m*. N.W. Dulyn, 6 *m*. N.N.E. Ffynnon

Llyffaint, 6 m. N.W. Idwell, 7 m. W. Llyn-y-Cwm, 8 m. W. *Hotels*: Royal, Cobden's.
(*See Conway.*)

Cardiff (Glamorgan).—G.W.R. *Hotels*: Park, Angel, Alexandra (headquarters
Cardiff Piscatorial Society). On Ely, Taff, and Rhymney. Ely rises 8 m. N. of
Llantrissant, and 5 m. down is joined by a stream on left bank 3 m. long.
Llantrissant town is 1 m. E. of the junction. 9 m. down Ely, Dowlas brook, 6 m. long,
joins left bank. 2¼ m. down Ely is Llantrissant station, and ½ m. lower a brook 3 m. long
joins on right bank. Ely runs 4 m., and is joined on right bank by a stream which
drains the lake in Hensol Park 1 m. up. 2 m. further down Ely is **Peterston**, and here
a stream joins on right bank, which drains 4 ponds (these minor rivulets are not suitable
for angling, and only contain trout in flood time) by Welsh St. Donats 4 m. up. Ely
runs 4 m. to **St. Fagans**, **Ely Bridge** (G.W.R.), and **Llandaff** (1 m. away) 2 m.,
and joins the sea at Penarth 2 m. from Cardiff. (*c.s.*) Taff and Ely are preserved by Taff
and Ely Fishing Association: s.t. 30s., d.t. 3s. 6d., roach s.t. 7s. 6d. of hon. sec., A. Waldron,
17, Church-street. The Reservoir, between the East and West Bute Docks, contains
some tolerably fine roach. The best point is at the entrance of the feeder, or opposite,
below the upper reservoir, which contains a few fish. Penarth Harbour, just opposite
Cardiff, ten minutes by boat, contains abundance of fine mullet and small bass at times.
Bait with ragworm (here called mudworm). (*See Cadoxton.*) The lake in Roath Park
(trout) is open to ratepayers only at 5s. the season. Cardiff Waterworks reservoirs
contain fine trout, and at Llanishen and in the Taff Vawr Valley are open to ratepayers
at 21s. per season. Artificial bait only. *Tackleist*: S. Chambers. Castle-street, Cardiff,
who will always supply additional information.

TAFF.—Trout (a few only), roach. Taff rises 5 m. above **Dolygaer**, runs thence 2 m. to
Ponticill, **Pant** 1 m., **Cefn** 3 m. Here Taff Vawr joins on right bank. This stream
rises on the slopes of Bryndu, and 5 m. down is joined at Pont-ar-daf on right bank by
a stream 1 m. long which runs out of Llyn-y-Gader. Taff Vawr runs to **Cefn** 4 m. Taff
runs to **Merthyr** 1 m., **Troedyrhiw** 2 m., **Quakers' Yard** 4 m. Here Bargawd
Taff, 6 m. long, joins on right bank. Taff runs to **Aberdare Junction** 1 m. Here
Cynon rises 4 m. above **Hirwain**, runs thence to **Llyndeged** 2 m., **Aberdare** 2¼ m. 2 m. down, at **Aberaman**, Aman, 3 m. long,
joins on right bank. Cynon runs to **Mountain Ash** 2 m., and Aberdare Junction and
Taff 4 m. Taff runs 2 m., and is joined on right bank by Gelli, 6 m. long. Taff runs to
Pontypridd 2 m. Here Rhondda joins on right bank. Rhondda rises 2 m. above
Treherbert, runs 4 m. thence to **Ystradfodwg** and **Pont** 5 m. Here Rhondda
Fychan joins on left bank. This stream, after running 3 m., passes 4 m. S.W.
from **Aberdare**, runs to **Pont** 6 m. Rhondda runs to **Pontypridd** and Taff 3 m.
Taff runs to **Treforest** 1 m., **Walnuttree** 5 m., **Llandaff** 4 m., and Cardiff 3 m.

RUMNEY (trout, salmon, sewin) rises 4 m. above **Rhymney**, runs thence to **Pontlottyn**
2 m., **Tir Phil** 3 m., **Bargoed** 3 m. Here Crinlach, which rises by **Fochriw**,
runs 3 m. to **Darran**, and Rumney, 3 m., joins on left bank. Rumney runs to
Pengarn 2 m., **Hengoed** 2 m., **Bedwas** 6 m. Here Ceffyl, 6 m. long, and Glydyr,
4 m. long, joins on right bank. **Caerphilly** is midway up on both these streams, and
1 m. from Rumney, which runs to **Church Road** 4 m., **Rhywderin** (2 m. off) 4 m.,
and Rumney (n.s. **Cardiff**, 2 m.) 6 m. Here a brook joins on right bank 6 m. long. 1 m.
down is Usk Estuary. (*c.s.*) Rumney and Taff are preserved for some distance above
the town; leave is sometimes granted. Inquire at the local tackle shops.

Cardigan—n.s. **Crymmich.**—Teifi; salmon, trout. Teifi rises in Llyn Teifi 3 m. from
Strata Florida, and 2 m. down is joined on left bank by Egnant, which rises in Llyn
Ifer, which lies ¼ m. E. of Llyn Teify, runs thence to Llyn Egnant ½ m. Close to the
lower end of the Llyn a stream joins on right bank, draining Llyn Gron a short way up.
1 m. down Egnant a stream joins on right bank, draining Llyn-y-gorlan 1 m. up. This
Llyn lies W. of, but close to, Llyn Gron. All of them are within 4 m. of **Strata
Florida** (trouting very good at times). 2 m. down Egnant, Mwyro, 3 m. long, joins on
left bank. 2 m. from **Strata Florida**, and 1 m. down, Egnant joins Teifi. Teifi runs
1 m. to **Strata Florida**, and here Glasffrwd, 4 m. long, joins on left bank, and Rhuest,
3 m. long, on right bank. Teifi runs 1 m. to the railway station, where Marchnant
joins on right bank. Marchnant 4 m. from its source is joined on left bank by
Gwyddyl, 2 m. long 2 m. down, Marchnant joins Teifi. 3 m. down Teifi, Tflur, which
rises 2 m. S. from **Strata Florida**, and is 4 m. long, joins on left bank. Teifi runs
3 m. when the outflow of Maes Llyn, ½ m. up, joins on left bank (n.s. **Tregaron**, 2 m).
½ m. down Teifi, Camddwr. 6 m. long, joins on right bank. Close to the junction,
Fulbrook, 2 m. long, joins on left bank. Teifi runs 2 m. to **Tregaron**, where Nant-y-
groes joins on left bank. This stream rises in Llyn Crugnant. 4 m. S. from **Strata
Florida**. 7 m. down, Berwyn, 4 m. long, joins on left bank. **Tregaron** and Teifi are
2 m. down Teifi runs 2 m. to **Pont Llanio**, where Carfan, 2 m. long, joins on left
bank. 3 m. down Teifi, Brenig, which rises 5 m. above Llanddewi Brefi (n.s. **Pont
Llanio**, 2 m.), and runs thence to Teifi 2 m., joins on left bank. Teifi runs to Llanfair
Clydogan (n.s. **Derry Ormond**, 2 m.). Clywedog, 5 m. long, here joins on left bank.
Teifi runs 2 m., when Cynon, 3 m. long, joins on left bank (n.s. **Lampeter**, 2¼ m.). 1 m.
down Teifi, Goy, 2 m. long, joins on left bank, and 2 m. down again is **Lampeter**. Here
Dulas, which rises 4 m. above **Derry Ormond**, and joins Teifi 4 m. down, joins on
right bank. 1 m. down Teifi a stream 5 m. long joins on right bank. 4 m. down Teifi

Granell. 8 *m.* long, joins on right bank (n.s **Llan-y-Byther** 3 *m.*). Teifi runs 2 *m.* to Pencarreg, near which, close by the railway, is Llyn Pencarreg (n.s. **Llan-y-Byther,** 2 *m.*), where a stream 3 *m.* long joins on left bank Teifi runs 3 *m.*, and is joined on left bank by Ceiliog, 3 *m.* long (n.s. **Maes-y-Crugian,** 3 *m.*). 1 *m.* down Teifi, Cathal, 7 *m.* long, joins on right bank (n.s. **Llan-y-Byther,** 2 *m.*). Teifi runs 3 *m.* to **Maes-y-Crugian,** and 2 *m.* down is joined on right bank by Cletwr. 6 *m.* from its source Cletwr is joined on left bank by Cletwr fach, 4 *m.* long. 2 *m.* down, Geyron, 2 *m.* long, joins on left bank; and 1 *m.* down Cletwr, Cinen, 4 *m.* long, joins on left bank. Cletwr runs to Teifi 2 *m.* 3 *m.* down Teifi, just above **Llandyssil,** Cerdin joins on right bank. Cerdin rises by Capel Cynon, runs 7 *m.*, when Ythan, 4 *m.* long, joins on right bank. 1 *m.* down Cerdin is Teifi and **Llandyssil.** Just below Llandyssil, Twelli joins on left bank. Twelli rises 3 *m.* above **Pen Caber,** and 3 *m.* down is joined on left bank by Gweddel, 4 *m.* long. 1 *m.* down Twelli is Teifi. Teifi runs 3 *m.* to Llangeller, and 2 *m.* down is joined on left bank by Bydrel, 6 *m.* long (n.s. **Llandyssil,** 5 *m.*). Teifi runs ½ *m.*, when Gernos, 5 *m.* long, joins on right bank. Teifi runs 3 *m.* to **Newcastle Emlyn** (n.s. **Llandyssil,** 8 *m.*)., and 2 *m.* down is joined on right bank by Ceri. 2 *m.* from its source, Bedw, 4 *m.* long, joins Ceri on left bank. Ceri runs 4 *m.*, when Dulas joins on right bank, 4 *m.* long. Ceri runs 5 *m.* to Teifi. 4 *m.* down Teifi a stream 5 *m.* long joins on right bank. 2 *m.* down Teifi, Cych joins. Cych rises some 6 *m.* S. of **Newcastle Emlyn,** and 3 *m.* down is joined on right bank by Bowy. 2 *m.* long. 1 *m.* down Cych, Mamog, 3 *m.* long, joins on right bank. 1 *m.* down Cych a stream 3 *m.* long joins on left bank. 1 *m.* down Cych, Connud, which rises by Capel Coleman, 8 *m.* S. of **Cardigan,** and is 5 *m.* long, joins on left bank. Cych joins Teifi 3 *m.* down. Teifi runs to Manordivey, 4 *m.* S.E. of **Cardigan,** where Iefed, 2 *m.* long, joins on right bank. Teifi runs 1 *m.* to Llechrhyd, 3 *m.* from **Cardigan,** where a stream, which rises by Tremain 5 *m.* N.E. of **Cardigan,** and is 5 *m.* long, joins on right bank; and another, 3 *m.* long, on left bank. Teifi runs 2 *m.* to Cilgerran, 3 *m.* S.E. of **Cardigan,** where a brook 3 *m.* long joins on left bank. Teifi runs to **Cardigan** 3 *m.* Here Ffrwyd, which rises above Bridell, and is 6 *m.* long, joins on left bank; and Llwyn-Llwyd, 5 *m.* long, on right bank. 3 *m.* down, Teifi joins Cardigan Bay. (*c.s.*)

Carew (Pembroke).—n.s. **Pembroke.** 4 *m.* Carew brook, which rises by **Saunders-foot,** and is 4 *m.* long.

Carmarthen.—L. & N.W.R. *Hotel:* Boar's Head. Towey; salmon, sewin, pike, trout; free fishing. Towey rises in Llyn Ddu (n.s. **Strata Florida,** 5 *m.* S.E.). 2 *m.* down a stream joins on left bank, which drains Llyn Gorast 1 *m.* up (n.s. **Strata Florida,** 4 *m.*). Towey runs 10 *m.* and is joined on right bank by Camddwr, which rises 6 *m.* E. from **Tregaron,** reached by the road up Nant Berwyn, and is 9 *m.* long. Towey runs 4 *m.* and is joined on right bank by Docthiam, which rises in Llyn Berwyn 5 *m.* E. from **Tregaron** (reached by the road up Nant Berwyn), runs 4 *m.*, when Docthiam fach, 3 *m.* long, joins on left bank. 5 *m.* down, Pysgotwr joins on right bank. Pysgotwr rises 4 *m.* E. from Llanddewi Brefi (n.s. **Pont Llanio,** 2 *m.*), and 4 *m.* down is joined on right bank by Pysgotwr fach, 3 *m.* long. 2 *m.* down, Pysgotwr joins Docthiam, which joins Towey 2 *m.* down. 2 *m.* down Towey (n.s. **Cynghordy,** 6 *m.*), Gwenfirwd, 5 *m.* long, joins on right bank. 4 *m.* down Towey, at Aber Rhaiadr (n.s. **Cynghordy,** 3 *m.*) (fishing free), Rhaiadr. 3 *m.* long, joins on right bank. 3 *m.* down Towey, at Abergwenlas (n.s. **Llandovery,** 4 *m.*), Gwenlas (fishing free), 5 *m.* long, joins on right bank, passing Oilewin 1 *m.* up from the junction. ½ *m.* down Towey, Dunant. 3 *m.* long, joins on right bank. Towey runs to **Llandovery** 3 *m.*, and 1 *m.* down is joined on left bank by Bran. Bran rises 4 *m.* above **Cynghordy,** and 3 *m.* below that station is joined on left bank by Crychan, 6 *m.* long. 4 *m.* down Bran, at **Llandovery,** Gwdderig, 10 *m.* long, joins on left bank. 3 *m.* up Gwdderig from **Llandovery,** Gwenst, 3 *m.* long, joins on right bank. Bran joins Towey 2 *m.* below. Towey runs 3 *m.* to **Llanwrda,** where Ynys (6 *m.* long) and Dulas (8 *m.*) join on right bank. 3 *m.* down Towey, at **Llangadock,** Marles, 5 *m.* long, joins on left bank, and Sefin and Sawdde on left bank. Sefin rises 2 *m.* above Myddfai (n.s. **Llangadock,** 6 *m.*), and 2 *m.* below the village is joined on left bank by Llechdawdd, 4 *m.* long. 2 *m.* down Sefin, Sefin Isaf, 5 *m.* long, joins on right bank. Sefin runs to Towey and **Llangadock** 3 *m.* Sawdde rises in Llyn-y-fan-fach (plenty of small trout), which lies 2 *m.* W. of Llyn-y-fan-fawr (n.s. **Pen-y-wyllt,** 7 *m.*). 3 *m.* down by Llanddansain, Buartharch, 2 *m.* long, joins on left bank. 2 *m.* down Sawdde, Dyfnant, 3 *m.* long, joins on right bank. 1 *m.* down Sawdde, Sawdde fechan joins on left bank. After running 4 *m.*, this brook is joined by the Clydach, 5 *m.* long, on left bank, the united stream running 1 *m.* to Sawdde, which runs to Towey and **Llangadock** 5 *m.* Towey runs to **Glanrhyd** 2 *m.*, and **Talley Road** 2 *m.* Here Dulas joins on right bank. Dulas rises by Talley and 4 *m.* down is joined on right bank by Tallaris, which rises in Llyn Taliaris 3½ *m.* from **Talley Road,** and is 2 *m.* long. Dulas joins Towey 2 *m.* down. Towey runs 2 *m.* to **Llandilo** (fishing in Towey is free hence to its source, but preserved below by Earl Cawdor), where Cennen joins on left bank. Cennen rises 5 *m.* above **Derwydd Road,** and runs thence to **Llandilo** in 4 *m* 3 *m.* down Towey (n.s. **Golden Grove,** 1 *m.*), Cyfyng, 5 *m.* long, joins on right bank. Towey runs to **Golden Grove** 1 *m.*, and **Llanarthney** 3 *m.* Fishing free below; preserved by Earl Cawdor above. Here Dulas joins on right bank. Dulas 5 *m.* from its source is joined on right bank by Sannan, which rises 2 *m.* above Llanfynydd, and joins Dulas 4 *m.* down. Dulas runs to **Llanarthney** 3 *m.* Towey runs

3 m. to **Nantgaredig**, when Cothi joins on right bank. Cothi rises 6 m. S.E. of **Pont Llanio**, and 9 m. down is joined on right bank by Mancoed, 3 m. long. 3 m. down Cothi, Twrch joins on right bank. Twrch rises 6 m. S.E. of **Pont Llanio**, close to Cothi, runs to Llan-y-Crwys 6 m., and 1 m. down is joined on left bank by Cwmpedol, 3 m. long, **Lampeter** being 5 m. off. 3 m. down, Twrch joins Cothi. 4 m. down Cothi, Bannell, 7 m. long, joins on left bank (n.s. **Llanwrda**, 7 m.), and ½ m. down, Vellinddwr, which divides into two parts at Llansawyl, 1½ m. up from Cothi, each some 6 m. long, joins on right bank (n.s. **Llanwrda**, 7 m.). 2 m. down Cothi, 1½ m. from Llansawyl, the outflow of two lakes by Talley, ½ m. up, joins on left bank (n s. **Talley Road**, 6 m.) Cothi flows to Abergorlech 4 m. (*Hotel:* The Cottage, n.s. **Talley Road**, 10 m.). Here Gorlech, 4 m. long, joins on right bank. 4 m. down Cothi, Clydach. 6 m. long (sewin and trout plentiful) joins on right bank. 1 m. down Cothi, near Brechfa, Marles joins on right bank; this stream divides into two parts, each 5 m. long, 1 m. up, at Brechfa (*Hotel:* Forest Arms, n.s. **Nantgaredig**, 8 m.). Cothi joins Towy, 8 m. down. at **Nantgaredig.** 5 m. down Towy, at **Abergwili**, Gwili joins Towy. Gwili rises 6 m. above **Llanpumpsaint**, where it is joined on right bank by a short stream, runs thence to **Cynwyl** 4 m., where Duad joins on right bank: this stream is 6 m. long, and 1 m. up from the junction, at Cynwyl Elfed, is joined on left bank by a stream 4 m. long. Gwili runs to **Branwydd Arms** 3 m., and **Abergwili** 3 m. Towy runs to **Carmarthen** 2 m. 2 m. down, Pibwr, which rises 1½ m. S. of **Nantgaredig** and is 6 m. long joins on left bank. To 3 m. down Towy the tide flows. The best flies are blue duns and yellow March brown. (*See Kidwelly.*)

Carnarvon.—L. & N.W.R. Seiont; salmon, trout, sewin. (*c.s.*) Seiont rises in two small lakelets in Cwm-glas. under the crest of Snowdon, and runs to **Llanberis**, 3 m. Here Seiont enters the Llanberis lakes Llyn Peris and Llyn Padarn. Llyn Peris, which is 1 m. long, belongs to the Snowdon Railway Company, and is reserved by the company for visitors to their hotels, the Victoria, at the lower end, and the Padarn Villa. Here joins on left bank Llwch. Llwch rises in Llyn-dur-Arddu, 4 m. S.E. of **Llanberis**, and 3 m. down is joined on left bank by the drainage of Llyn Dwythwch ½ m. up, 2 m. S.W. of **Llanberis** station. 1 m. down, Llwch joins the lake. Seiont runs in ½ m. to Llyn Padarn, 2 m. long. Seiont runs to Carnarvon in 8 m. Braint, 4 m. N.W.; salmon, trout. (*See Llangeinwen.*) *Hotels:* Snowdon Ranger, Royal Victoria, and Padarn Villa, Llanberis. Fair sea fishing. good bass at times.

Carno (Montgomery).—C.R. Garno or Llwyd. Pwll-llydau. Cledau. Cerniog (1 m.). Tarrannon (4 m.); trout. *Lakes:* Gloyw (4 m.). Bugail (7 m. N.). Hir (9 m. N.E.); good trouting; preserved, but leave may sometimes be had. Grahwyddan (10 m.); good trouting; preserved, but leave may be had sometimes. (*See Gloucester.*) (*c.s. Severn.*)

Carrog (Merioneth).—G.W.R. Dee; trout, grayling, salmon (*c.s.*); preserved *above* for 12 m. by the River Dee Fishery (*see Corwen*); s.t. 30s.. w.t. 6s., d.t. 2s., at the hotel; *below* here begins the fishery of the Glyndwr Society (*for terms see Llangollen*); tickets at the railway station. Morwynion. Llechog, 1 m. W. Ceiriog, 2 m. S.; trout. (*c.s. Dee.*) *Hotel:* Grouse. (*See Chester.*)

Castle Martin (Pembroke).—n.s. **Pembroke,** 5 m. Castle Martin brook, which rises in the lakes at Orielton 3 m. from **Pembroke.** runs 3 m. to Castle Martin and the sea 3 m.

Cefn (Denbigh).—G.W.R. Dee; salmon. chub, trout, grayling, pike; preserved between Newbridge and Llangollen by Llangollen Trout and Grayling Preserve. (*c.s.*) (*See Llangollen.*) Ceiriog, 2 m. S.E. (*c.s. Dee.*) (*See Chester.*)

Cefn (Glamorgan).—L. & N.W.R. Taff; trout, salmon. Taff Vawr; trout salmon. (*c.s.*) Kenfig. *Lakes:* Llyn-y-Gader (5 m.) (*See Cardiff, Pyle.*)

Cemmaes (Montgomery).—L. & N.W.R. Dovey; trout, sewin. salmon in autumn. (*c.s.*) (*See Machynlleth.*)

Cemmaes Junction (Montgomery).—L. & N.W.R. Dovey; salmon, trout. (*c.s.*) Twymyn: trout. (*See Machynlleth.*)

Cerrig-y-Druidion (Merioneth).—n.s. **Corwen**, 10 m. Geirw, 1 m. S.; trout. (*c.s. Dee.*) *Lakes:* Dau-y-Cheu, 3 m. N. (*See Chester; Corwen.*)

Cheriton (Glamorgan).—n.s. **Pen-clawd**, 7 m. Bwry brook, 6 m. long.

Cheriton (Pembroke).—G.W.R. n.s. **Pembroke**, 3 m. Stackpole brook rises near here, and 1 m. down is joined by a stream, which runs down 3 m. from Merion Court. Below the junction, Stackpole waters the lakes in Stackpole Park, and joins the sea at Broad Haven 2 m. down.

Chirk (Denbigh).—G.W.R. Ceiriog. (*c.s. Dee.*) *Lakes:* Chirk Park, 1 m. N.W. (*See Chester.*)

Chwilog (Carnarvon).—L. & N.W.R. Wen. (*See Afon Wen.*)

Clarbeston (Pembroke).—G.W.R. Lyfynfy. Eastern Cleddau (3 m.) (*c.s.*) (*See Haverfordwest.*)

Clogne (Pembroke).—G.W.R. Taf; trout. (*See Laugharne.*) (*c.s. Towey.*)

Colbren (Brecon).—N. & B.R.R. Llech (1 m.). Tawe (2 m.). (*See Swansea.*)

Colwyn (Carnarvon).—L. & N.W.R. Nant-y-Groes, 3 m. long. Nant-Ffynnon runs 1 m. E., 3 m. long.

Conway (Carnarvon).—L. & N.W.R. Conway; salmon, trout. (*c.s.*) Conway rises in Llyn Conway (trout), 8 m. N.E. of **Ffestiniog**, or 9 m. S. of **Bettws-y-Coed.** 4 m. down, Scrw joins on right bank. Scrw rises in Llyn Scrw, 7 m. W. of **Ffestiniog,** or

6 *m.* across country N.W. from **Arenig**, and is 7 *m.* long. Conway runs 4 *m.* to Yspytty Evan, 8 *m.* N. of **Arenig**, or 8 *m.* S.E. of **Bettws-y-Coed.** 1 *m.* below, Clettwr, 3 *m.* long, joins on right bank. 1 *m.* down, Merddwr joins on right bank. Merddwr rises 5 *m.* above Pentre Voelas, 7 *m.* S.E. from **Bettws-y-Coed.** 2 *m.* from its source, Laethog, 2 *m.* long, joins on right bank. 1 *m.* down Merddwr the outflow of Llyn-y-Curt, 1 *m.* up, joins on right bank. 2 *m.* down is Pentre Voelas, and 1 *m.* below, Codnant, 3 *m.* long, joins on right bank. ¼ *m.* below, Merddwr joins Conway. 1 *m.* down Conway, Eidda, 2 *m.* long, joins on left bank. 1 *m.* down Conway, Hwch, 3 *m.* long, joins on right bank. 2 *m.* down, Machno joins on left bank. Machno rises in L'lyn-y-firth-graig, 3 *m.* across the hills W. from **Manod**, and is 8 *m.* long. 1 *m.* down Conway, at Pont-ar-Lledr, Lledr joins on left bank. Lledr rises on the slopes of Moel Lledr, 7 *m.* above **Dolwyddelan**, and a little below is joined on right bank by the outflow of Llyn Dannogen 1 *m.* up. This lake is 3 *m.* across the hills N. of **Grisian**. 3 *m.* down Lledr is the outfall of the lakes Dyweunydd (2), 5 *m.* W. of **Dolwyddelan**, or 2 *m.* across the hills S.E. from **Pen-y-Gwryd**. Lledr runs 3 *m.*, where Ystumian, which rises in Llyn-y-Foel 3 *m.* N E. of **Dolwyadelan** and is 5 *m.* long, joins on left bank. Lledr runs to **Dolwyddelan** 1 *m.*, **Pont-y-Pant** 2 *m.*, and 3 *m.* down joins Conway. Conway runs to **Bettws-y-Coed** 2 *m.*, and here Llugwy joins on left bank. Llugwy rises in Llyn Llugwy 5 *m.* N.W. from **Capel Curig**, runs 6 *m.* to **Capel Curig**, and here Gwryd joins on right bank. Gwryd rises in Llyn-y-Cwm-Ffynnon, 1 *m.* above **Pen-y-Gwryd**, and 3 *m.* below waters the Mymbyr lakes at **Capel Curig**. Llugwy runs 3 *m.*, where the drainage of Llyn Goddion-duon, 1 *m.* up. 4 *m.* N.E. of **Capel Curig**, joins on left bank. 2 *m.* down Llugwy the drainage of Llyn Pen-craig, 1 *m.* up, 3 *m.* S.W. of **Llanrwst**, or 3 *m.* N.W. of **Bettws-y-Coed**, joins on left bank. 2 *m.* down Llugwy, 1 *m.* from **Bettws-y-Coed**, the outflow of Llyn Helsi (trout), 1 *m.* S.W. of **Bettws**, joins on right bank. Llugwy runs 1 *m.* to **Bettws-y-Coed**, and joins Conway 1 *m.* down. 1 *m.* below the junction the outflow of Llyn-y-Parc, 2 *m.* S. of **Llanrwst**, or 2 *m.* N. of **Bettws**, joins on left bank. Conway runs to **Lanrwst** 3 *m.*, and **Trefriw** 2 *m.* Here Crafnant joins on left bank. Crafnant rises in Llyn Crafnant 3 *m.* across the hills N.E. from **Capel Curig**, or 3 *m.* S.W. of **Trefriw**, and 1 *m.* below is joined on right bank by a stream which rises in Llyn Bodgynwydd 3 *m.* across the hills E.N.E. of **Capel Curig**, or 3 *m.* S. W. of **Llanrwst**. 1 *m.* down the outflow of Llyn Bychan, 1 *m.* up, joins on left bank. This loch is ½ *m.* W. of the Llyn Bodgynwydd. ½ *m.* below, the stream waters Llyn Geirionydd, and 1 *m.* below joins Crafnant, which runs to **Trifriw** in 2 *m.* Conway runs 2 *m.*, where Ddu, which rises in Llyn Cwlyd 2 *m.* N. of **Capel Curig**, and is 5 *m.* long, joins on left bank. 1 *m.* down Conway, Porth-lwyd joins on left bank. This stream rises in Ffynnon Llyffaint 5 *m.* S.E. of **Bethesda** up the Llafer valley, or 6 *m.* N.W. of **Capel Curig**, the latter lying 1 *m.* due N. from Llyn Llugwy. The stream runs 3 *m.* to Llyn Eigian, which lies 4 *m.* due N. from **Capel Curig**, passing the left-hand side of Llyn Cwlyd. Porth-lwyd runs 6 *m.* to Conway. 1 *m.* down Conway, Tal-y-Bont joins on left bank. Tal-y-Bont rises in Llyn Melynllyn, and 1 *m.* down is joined on left bank by the outflow of Llyn Dulyn ½ *m.* up. These two lakes are within ½ *m.* of each other, lying N. and S., and 6 *m.* E. of **Bethesda** up the Cassey valley, or 6 *m.* across country N.N.E. from **Capel Curig**. Tal-y-Bont runs 6 *m.* to Conway. At this point, but on Conway's right bank, the outflow of Llyn Syberi, 1 *m.* up, joins. 1 *m.* down Conway, Ro, 5 *m.* long, joins on left bank. Conway runs 2 *m.* to **Tal-y-Cafn**, and 1 *m.* below is joined on right bank by Hiraethlyn, 5 *m.* long. Conway runs to **Glan Conway** and the estuary in 5 *m.* (*c.s.*)

RHIW, 5 *m.* long.

LLWYNOG, 2¼ *m.* W., 4 *m.* long.

Good local flies for the rivers and streams are March brown, alder, stonefly. For the lakes—*Body*, orange mohair; *legs*, yellow; *wings*, red feather from pheasant's tail. *Body*, peacock's herl; *legs*, black; *wings*, moorhen. *Body*, peacock's herl; *legs*, black; *wings*, dark mallard.

Corwen (Merioneth).—L. & N.W.R. G.W.R. Dee; trout, salmon, grayling; preserved with part of Alwen by River Dee Fishery (*see Advts.*) for 12 *m.* (sec., W. J. Stansfield, Esq., Corwen); s.t. 30s., w.t. 6s., d.t. 2s., Feb. 14 to Sept. 14, grayling, s.t. 5s., Oct. 14 to Feb. 1, fly only, no minnow or worm till April 1: tickets at the Owen Glyndwr Hotel, and from Mr. Stansfield, Meirion House, Corwen; no dogs or Sunday fishing. A rod is sometimes to be let on the Rug estate water between Corwen and Cynwyd bridges. (*c.s.*) (*See Cerrig-y-Druidion; Maerdy.*) Treweryn; trout. (*c.s. Dee.*) Camladd. Llechog, 1 *m.* E. Dwr, 1 *m.* N.W. Alwen. 2 *m.* W.; trout; preserved. (*c.s. Dee.*) Morwynion, 2 *m.* E. Ffrauon, 3 *m.* W. Trystion, 3 *m.* S.W. Geirw, 5 *m.* W.; trout; free. (*c.s. Dee.*) Llynor, 5 *m.* S.W. *Lakes*: Gloya, 2 *m.* N. *Hotels*: Owen Glyndwr, Eagles. (*See Chester.*)

Cowbridge (Glamorgan).—G.W.R. Cowbridge river or Thaw; trout. Cowbridge rises by Llansannor, 1½ *m.* W. of **Ystradowen**, runs 3 *m.* to **Cowbridge**, 4 *m.* to St. Mary Church on right bank, 5 *m.* to Bourton Bridge. Here Fonmon brook joins on left bank, which rises some 7 *m.* above Penmark, where a short stream joins on the right bank, and joins Cowbridge 3 *m.* below. 2 *m.* down, Cowbridge joins the sea at Aberthaw. The trouting is very good, and is preserved for about 4 *m.* from Cowbridge down by Mrs. F. E. Stacey, of Landough Castle; leave is sometimes given.

Cray (Brecon).—N. & B.R. Cray; trout. (*See Newport.*)

N

Creggion (Montgomery).—Severn (1 m.); chub, dace, trout, salmon. (*See Gloucester.*) (*c.s.*)

Criocieth (Carnarvon).—C.R. Dwyfawr and Dwyfach; trout, sewin, salmon. Dwyfawr rises in the hills some 5 m. across country west of **Beddgellert**, and runs in 7 m. to Dolbenmaen (n.s. **Brynkir**, 2 m.). Here Istrallyn joins on left bank. Istrallyn rises in Llyn Cwm Istrallyn, 4 m. N. from **Portmadoc**, and, 2 m. down, is joined on left bank by a stream 2 m. long draining Llyn Du, 3 m. N. from **Portmadoc**, 2 m. below Istrallyn joins Dwyfawr, which runs 6 m., when Dwyfach joins on right bank. Dwyfach rises above **Pant Glass**, runs to **Brynkir** 3 m., **Ynys** 2 m., **Llangybi** (1 m. off on right bank) 2 m., and joins Dwyfawr 2 m. below. The united streams run to the sea in 1 m. (*c.s.*)

Crinant (Glamorgan).—Dylias. (*See Neath.*)

Cronware (Pembroke).—n.s. **Whitland**, 5 m. Garnas brook rises 1 m. above here, and joins the sea 3 m. down.

Cross Inn (Carmarthen).—T.V.R. Amman. Llwchwr (1 m.). Llan-dybie brook (1 m.). Lash (1 m.). (*See Llwchwr.*) (*c.s. Towy.*)

Crymmych Arms (Pembroke).—G.W.R. Taf; trout. (*See Laugharne.*) (*c.s. Towey.*) Neave. Biron. Duad, 2 m. (*See Newport.*)

Crynanich (Pembroke).—G.W.R. Eastern Cleddau (3 m.). (*See Haverfordwest.*) (*c.s.*)

Cymmer (Glamorgan).—T.V.R. On Llynvi; trout. (*c.s. Ogmire.*) (*See Bridgend.*) Afon (2¼ m.); trout. (*c.s. Usk.*) Cerwg (2½ m.). (*See Aberafon.*)

Cynghordy (Carmarthen).—L. & N.W.R. Bran. Towy (3 m.); trout; fishing free. (*c.s.*) Rhaiadr (3 m.). Crychan (3 m.). Gwenfirwd (6 m.). (*See Carmarthen.*)

Cynwyd (Merioneth).—L. & N.W.R.; G.W.R. Dee; trout, grayling, salmon preserved by Corwen Fishing Association (*see Corwen*) (*c.s.*); tickets at the Lion and Prince of Wales. Trystion. Alwen, 2 m. N.; trout; preserved. (*c.s. Dee.*) Frannon, 2 m. N. *Inns*: The Blue Lion and Prince of Wales. (*See Chester.*)

Cynwyl (Carmarthen). — G.W.R. A good hotel. Gwili; trout, sewin, salmon; free fishing. (*c.s. Towey.*) Duad. Cywyn (7 m.); trout, sewin. (*See Carmarthen, Laugharne.*)

Darran (Glamorg.)—B. & M.R. Crinlach. Rumney (3 m.); trout, salmon. (*See Cardiff.*) (*c.s.*)

Denbigh.—L. & N.W.R.; G.W.R. Lliwen, 1 m. S. Clwyd, 3 m. E.; trout. Dennant, 7 m. W. Aled, 9 m. W. (*c.s. Clwyd.*) Brenig, 9 m. S.W. *Lakes*: Llynbran, 9 m. S.W. Aled, 11 m. S.W. (*c.s. Clwyd.*) Noel-frech, 11 m. S.W. Oreiniog, 11 m. W. (*See Chester, Rhyl, Llanfair, Talhaiarn.*)

Derry Ormond (Cardigan).—M. & M.R. Dulas. Teifi (2 m.); salmon, trout. (*c.s.*) Clywedog (2 m.) (*See Cardigan.*) Meurig, 3 m. N. Aeron, 4 m. N.W. (*c.s.*). Rhewfallen, 4 m. N.W. Nant-y-fergy, 5 m. N.W. (*See Aberaeron.*)

Derwern (Denbigh.)—L. & N.W.R. Clwyd; trout. (*c.s.*) (*See Rhyl, Llanfihangel-glyn-Myfyr.*)

Derwydd Road (Carmarthen).—G.W.R.; L. & N.W.R. Llan-dybie brook. Cennen. (*c.s. Towy.*) (*See Llwchwr, Carmarthen.*)

Devil's Bridge (Cardigan).—n.s. **Aberystwyth**, 12 m., reached by Vale of Rheidol Light Railway Rheidol; polluted, except in upper waters, 4 m. off. Myherin; trout. Rhyddnant, 2 m. E.; trout. Castell, 3 m. N. Rhyddlan, 7 m. N. Llech weddmawr, 9 m. N. Lygnant, 10 m. N. *Lakes*: Lon, 1 m. W. Rhyddnant, 5 m. N.E. 2 Jenan, 6 m. N.E. Llygad, 9 m. N. Good trouting can be had in Bray's Pool at a small charge per diem. (*See Aberystwyth.*) *Hotel*: Hafod Arms.

Devynock (Brecon).—N. & B.R. Usk;⅔ trout, salmon; preserved for about 4 m. by the United Usk Fishing Association; s.t. 40s., w.t. 10s., d.t. 5s., and rod licences 20s. and 1s., from Post-office, Sennybridge. Senni and Treweren; trout. Clydack and Cray, 2 m.; trout. Cilieni; trout, 2 m. *Hote*: Castle, Sennybridge. (*See Usk, Brecon, and Newport.*) (*c.s.*)

Diffwys (Merioneth).—C.R.—Bywydd. *Lakes*: Dubach, ½ m. E.; large trout; very shy Bywydd. (*See Penrhyndendraeth.*)

Dinas Mawddwy (Merioneth).—Mwy.R. *Hotel*: Peniarth Arms (*see Advertisement*). Dovey; sewin, trout, salmon; fishing very good for 6 m. above to 3 m. below; preserved by proprietor Peniarth Arms. (*c.s.*) Ceryst or Arris trout. Cowarch, 1 m. N. Cleivion, 1 m. S.; preserved by proprietor Peniarth Arms. Clywedog, 3 m. W. (*c.s. Severn.*) Pamrhyd, 5 m. N.E. Twrch, 6 m. N.E.; good trouting; preserved mostly by Sir W. W. Wynn and Mr. Price. Banw, 8 m. E.; trout, chub, salmon. (*c.s. Severn.*) Cathan, 9 m. E. *Lakes*: Llyn Figan and Llyn Fach, 4 m. N. Llyn Coch Hwyed, 6 m. S.E.; trout. Bugail, 9 m. E.; good trouting, but preserved; leave may sometimes be had. (*See Machynlleth, Can-Office, Gloucester.*)

Doban (Radnor).—L. & N.W.R. Aran. *Lakes*: Graig pool (3 m.) (*See Chepstow, England.*)

Doldowlod (Radnor).—C.R. Wye; trout. (*c.s.*) Elan (2 m.); trout. Chwefru (4 m.). Clearwen (5 m.). Garw (7 m.). Arban (8 m.). *Lakes*: Gwyn (2 m.). Garw (9 m.). (*See Chepstow, England.*)

Dolgelly (Merioneth).—G.W.R. & Cambrian. Wnion; trout, sewin; preserved by landowners. Mawddach, 1 m. N.W.; trout, sewin, few salmon. Sewin fishing good in early autumn if plenty of rain. (*c.s. Dovey.*) *Lakes*: Gwernan, 2 m. S.W.; trout, perch. Cynwch, 2 m. N.; perch. Aran, 3 m. S. Origenan, 4 m. S.E. Gader, 4 m. S.W. Gafr, 4 m. S.W.; good trouting. Talyllyn, 8 m. S.; just restocked with Loch Leven. (*See Towyn, Barmouth, Tyn-y-groes.*)

Dolgoch (Merioneth). — G.W.R. Fafinder. Dysyni, 2 m. N.W.; trout, salmon. (*See Towyn.*) (*c.s. Dovey.*)

Dolhier (Radnor).—G.W.R. Gilwern. Cynon brook. Hales brook. (*See Chepstow, England.*)

Dolwen (Montgomery).—C.R. Severn; trout, chub, salmon. Ebyr. Berthyn (1 *m.*). Lakes: Ebyr (3 *m.*). (*c.s. Severn.*) (*See Gloucester.*)

Dolwyddelan (Carnarvon).—L. & N.W.R. Lledr; trout, sewin, salmon; tickets at hotels (*for terms for salmon see* **Bettws**); trouting from March 1 to Oct. 1; preserved by the Dolwyddelan Angling Association; sec., Mr. W. Roberts, for the river, its tributaries, and lakes, *except* the Dyweunydd lakes. Mr. Ellis Pierce, bookseller, supplies Gwydyr Estate tickets. Autumn is the best time for salmon and sewin. (*c.s. Conway.*) Ystumian, 1 *m.* N.; trout. Lakes: Llyn-y-Foel, 3 *m.* N.E.; Dyweunydd (2), 3 *m.* W.; trout; preserved; tickets of H. D. Brandreth, Esq. Hotels: Gwydyr Arms, Elen's Castle. (*See Conway.*)

Dolygear (Brecon).—B. & M.R. Taff; trout, salmon. (*c.s.*) (*See Cardiff.*)

Drws-y-nant (Montgomery).—L. & N.W.R. Wnion; trout, sewin; preserved by land-owners. Harrog. Cwm-ocht. Ciddow, 1 *m.* W. Fiddow, 1½ *m.* W. Dovey, 3 *m.* W. (*c.s.*) Mawddach, 4 *m.* N.; trout, sewin, salmon; d.t. 2*s.* 6*d.*, m.t. 10*s.* 6*d.* (*c.s. Dovey.*) Lakes: Dyfi, 3 *m.* W. Crych-y-wayen, 4 *m.* N. (*See Machynlleth, Barmouth.*)

Dyffryn (Merioneth).—Ysgethin; trout, free. Ysgethin rises in Llyn Dulyn (good fish-ing), runs 1 *m.* to Llyn Bodlyn (trout, char; free), and, 2 *m.* down, is joined on left bank by a short stream draining Llyn Irddyn (good fishing). Dyffryn and the sea are 4 *m.* down.

Ely (Glamorgan).—G.W.R. Ely; trout, sewin. (*See Cardiff.*) (*c.s. Taff*); fishing preserved below, and above by Taff and Ely Fishing Association; hon. sec., A. Waldron, Esq., Cardiff; s.t. 30*s.*, d.t. 2*s.* 6*d.* Trout small, but numerous.

Erwood (Radnor).—C.R. Wye; salmon, trout, chub, dace, pike, &c. (*c.s.*) Llogin. Bachhowey brook (1 *m.*). Cunrig (2 *m.*). Lakes: Llanbychllyn and 2 other lakes (3 *m.*), Llogin (6 *m.*). (*See Chepstow, England.*)

Eyearth (Denbigh).—L. & N.W.R. Clwyd; trout. (*c.s.*) Llanfair brook. (*See Rhyl.*) Alyn, 5 *m.* E., at Llanarnon; trout. (*c.s. Dee.*) Rhys, 6 *m.* E. at Llandegla. Lakes: Cyffynny, 7 *m.* E. (*See Chester.*)

Ferry (Montgomery).—By.R. Severn; chub, dace, trout, salmon. Vyrnwy; trout, salmon, chub. (*See Gloucester.*) (*c.s. Severn.*)

Ferry Side (Carmarthen).—G.W.R. Good trouting on Gwendraeth, Fawr and Fach 3 *m.* off. Cywyn, from Blackbridge to Banc-y-feln village is a good stream, holding salmon and sewin. and there are numerous brooks in the neighbourhood holding plenty of trout. Hotel: White Lion. The landlord will give any information.

Ffestiniog (Merioneth).—G.W.R. and C.R. Rhaiadr; trout; s.t. 20*s.*, d.t. 2*s.* 6*d.* Dwyryd, 1 *m.* W.; trout, sewin; free. Yspytty, 1 *m.* N. Manod, 1 *m.* N. Conway, 8 *m.* N.E.; trout. (*c.s.*) Lakes: Craig-y-tan, 2 *m.* S.E. Y-Morwynion, 2½ *m.* E.; trout. Dubach, 3 *m.* E. Y-bryn-du, 4 *m.* N.E. Y-Gamallt, 4 *m.* N.E. Dywarchen, 4 *m.* E. Y-gors, 4½ *m.* N.E. Y-frithgraig, 5 *m.* N.E. Cors-y-barcut, 5 *m.* S.E. Llyn Scrw, 7 *m.* E. (*See Penrhyndeudraeth; Conway.*)

Ffos-rhiw (Glamorgan).—B. & M.R. Crinlach. (*See Cardiff.*)

Fishguard (Pembroke).—n.s. **Rosebush**, 9 *m.* Gwaen. Gwaen rises 2 *m.* from **Rosebush**, runs 5 *m.* to Llan-y-chllwydog, 4 *m.* from **Rosebush**, where Walen, 4 *m.* long, joins on left bank. Gwaen runs 5 *m.* to **Fishguard** and the sea. 1 *m.* W. from **Fishguard** runs a brook 3 *m.* long. Western Cleddau (2 *m.* S.) (*c.s. Cleddau.*)

Flint.—L. & N.W.R. Flint brook, 5 *m.* long. Northop brook, 2 *m.* S.E., 4 *m.* long.

Forden Montgomery).—C.R. Severn; trout, salmon, chub, dace, &c. Camlad; trout, grayling. Hallesford brook (4 *m.* E.). Lakes: Marton pool (5 *m.* N.E.). (*c.s. Severn.*) (*See Gloucester.*)

Frongoch (Merioneth).—G.W.R. Tryweryn; trout. (*c.s. Dee.*) Hescyn, 1 *m.* N.W. Lakes: Hescyn, 4 *m.* N. (*See Chester.*)

Garnant (Carmarthen).—G.W.R. Amman; trout. Garnant. Pedol (*See Llwchwr.*) (*c.s. Towy.*)

Garth (Brecon).—L. & N.W.R. Irfon; chub, dace, trout, salmon; trouting poor, but fair salmon fishing after floods in autumn; tickets from the Dolecoed Hotel, Llanwrtyd. Dulas; good trouting. Dihonw (3 *m.*). Gwenwest (4 *m.*). Hotel: Garth. (*c.s. Wye.*) (*See Chepstow, England.*)

Gilan Dyfi (Montgomery).—L. & N.W.R. Dovey; salmon, trout. (*c.s.*) Lymant. Einon. (*See Machynlleth.*)

Gilwern, near Abergavenny.—L. & N.W.R. Usk; trout, salmon; preserved by the United Usk Fishing Association; salmon and trout rod licences 20*s.* and 1*s.*, at the post-office. (*See Brecknock, Usk, Newport.*)

Glais (Glamorgan).—G.W.R.; L. & N.W.R. Tawe. Clydach. (*See Swansea.*)

Glan Conway (Carnarvon).—L. & N.W.R. Conway; salmon, trout. (*c.s.*) (*See Conway.*) Cymeran. This stream, 5 *m.* long, joins the estuary here.

Glanrhyd (Carmarthen).—L. & N.W.R. Towy (*c.s.*); salmon, trout; fishing free. (*See Carmarthen.*)

Glasbury (Brecknock).—G.W.R. Honddu (7 *m.*); trout. (*See Chepstow.*)

Glasbury (Radnor).—G.W.R. Wye; chub, dace, trout, salmon; preserved by land-owners. Llyfni. (*c.s.*) (*See Chepstow, England.*)

Glyndyfrdwy (Merioneth). — G.W.R. Dee; grayling, trout, salmon; preserved by Glyndwr Society from **Carrog** above to. **Llangollen** below; 9 *m.* of splendid fishing; tickets at the hotel, of the station master, or at the Medical Hall, Bridge-street

Llangollen. Spring and early summer best for trout (s.t. 42*s.*, m.t. 21*s.*, w.t. 10*s.*, d.t. 2*s.* 6*d.*). Late autumn very good for grayling and for salmon if plenty of rain. (*See Llangollen.*) (*See Chester.*) *Hotel*: Berwyn Arms.

Glyn Neath (Glamorgan).—G.W.R. Neath Nedd (3 *m.*). Llia (8 *m.*). (*See Neath*)

Golden Grove (Carmarthen).—L. & N.W.R. Towy; salmon, trout, sewin; preserved by Earl Cawdor; licenses, salmon and sewin, 21*s.*, trout 2*s.* 6*d.*, of W. Morgan Griffiths, solicitor, Carmarthen. (*c.s.*) Cyfyng (1 *m.*) (*See Carmarthen*)

Gors (Glamorgan).—Lliw. (*See Llwchwr.*)

Gresford (Denbigh).—G.W.R. Alyn; trout. (*c.s. Dee.*) (*See Chester.*)

Groes-lon (Carnarvon).—L. & N.W.R. Llifon, which rises 3 *m.* above here and joins the sea 3 *m.* below.

Gwalchmai, n.s. **Bodorgan.**—Good trout fishing in Lakes Frogwyd and Hendre, the latter having been lately stocked with trout and roach by the hotel proprietor, who has exclusive rights; fair river trouting; licence, 5*s.*

Gwyddelwern (Merioneth).—L. & N.W.R.; G.W.R. Dwr. Alwen, 3 *m.* W.; trout. (*c.s. Dee.*) *Lakes*: Gloya, 1 *m.* S. (*See Chester.*)

Gwys (Glamorgan).—G.W.R. Twrch. Gwyog. Tawe (3 *m.*). (*See Swansea.*)

Harlech (Merioneth).—L. & N.W.R. Ciddew, 8 *m.* N.E. *Lakes*: Hafod-y-Llyn, 2 *m.* S.E. Graigddrwy, 5 *m.* N.E. Dywarchen, 8 *m.* N.E. Ciddew-fach, 8 *m.* N.E. Ciddew-mawr, 8 *m.* N.E. Du, 8 *m.* N.E. (*See Barmouth.*) *Fishing stations within reach*: Talsarnan, Penrhyndeudraeth, Mynford, Portmadoc, Criccieth, Llanbedr, Dyffryn, Barmouth.

Haverfordwest (Pembroke)—G.W.R. Western Cleddau; salmon, trout. (*c.s.*) This stream rises 2 *m.* S. of **Fishguard** (n.s. **Rose Bush**, 9 *m.*), and 4 *m.* down is joined on left bank by a stream 5 *m.* long. 1 *m.* down Cleddau, Hoig joins on right bank, which rises 2 *m.* S.W. of Mathry, 6 *m.* from Fishguard, and is 6 *m.* long. 5 *m.* down, by Ford, Martel brook, which rises by **Rose Bush** station, runs 3 *m.* to Puncheston, Little Newcastle 3 *m.*, and Cleddau 3 *m.*, joins on left bank. Cleddau runs 3 *m.* to Trefgarn (n.s. **Haverfordwest**, 6 *m.*); and here Wallis brook, 4 *m.* long, joins on left bank. 6 *m.* down Cleddau, Pelcombe brook, 5 *m.* long, joins on right bank. **Haverfordwest** is 1 *m.* down Cleddau. Here Captlett brook, 8 *m.* long, joins on left bank, and Denant brook, 7 *m.* long, on right bank. 5 *m.* down Cleddau, Milling brook, which rises 3 *m.* E. of **Haverfordwest**, and is 5 *m.* long, joins on left bank. 1 *m.* down, Eastern Cleddau joins on left bank. This stream rises 3 *m.* S.W. from **Crynanich**, and 5 *m.* down is joined on right bank by Corwyn, 4 *m.* long (n.s. **Maeneloehog**, 4 *m.* S.W.) Cleddau runs 5 *m.*, and is joined on right bank by Llandilo brook, which rises E. of **Maeneloehog**, runs 5 *m.* to Llan-y-Cefn, and Cleddau 1 *m.* Cleddau is joined 1 *m.* down, at Egremont, by Gilfach brook, which rises 1 *m.* W. of **Maeneloehog**, and is 5 *m.* long. 1 *m.* down Cleddau (n.s. **Clarbeston**, 5 *m.*) Syfynfy joins on right bank. Syfynfy rises near **Rose Bush** station, runs 3 *m.* to **Maeneloehog** (2 *m.* off), 4 *m.* to Llys-y-Fran, 3 *m.* to **Clarbeston**, and 3 *m.* to Cleddau. Cleddau runs to Robeston Wathen (n.s. **Narbeth**, 2 *m.*) 3 *m.* and 6 *m.* down the two Cleddaus join and debouch into the harbour. (*See Brawdy, St. David's, Solva.*)

Hay (Brecon). — G.W.R. Wye; salmon, trout, grayling, pike, perch, chub, dace. Below **Hay** the fishing in Wye is private. Dulas brook. Eseley brook (5 *m.*). Dore (5 *m.*). Monnow (6 *m.*); trout, but rather closely preserved. Olchon brook (8 *m.*) *Hotel*: Rose and Crown, where fishing can be had in Wye. Llangorse lake can be fished from here by taking train to **Tal-y-llin**. (*c.s.*) (*See Chepstow, England.*)

Hirwain (Glamorgan).—G.W.R. Cynon. Hepste (3 *m.*). (*See Cardiff, Neath.*)

Holt (Denbigh).—n.s. **Broxton** or **Gresford**, 4 *m.* Dee; salmon, pike, chub. (*c.s.*) Alyn, 2 *m.* N.W.; trout. (*c.s. Dee.*) (*See Chester.*)

Holyhead.—Good trouting can be had by staying at the Maelog Lake Hotel, Ty Croes, near Holyhead. Llynen, Maelog, Coron, and Trogwyd are within easy reach: trouting good. Crygyll river, close to hotel, holds sea trout in spring; good pollack fishing.

Hope (Flint).—L. & N.W.R. Alyn; trout. (*c.s. Dee.*) (*See Chester.*)

Istrad-y-Fodwg (Glamorgan).—T.V.R. Rhondda; trout, salmon. (*c.s. Taff.*) (*See Cardiff.*)

Johnston (Pembroke).—G.W.R. Rosemarket brook (1 *m.*). Rickeston brook (4 *m.*). (*See New Milford.*)

Kerry (Montgomery).—C.B. Mule. Caerbitra (4 *m.* E.). (*See Gloucester.*)

Kidwelly (Carmarthen).—G.W.R. Gwendraeth fach; trout, sewin. *Hotel*: Pelican. Gwendraeth fach rises by Llanddeirac (n.s. **Nantgaredig**, 4 *m.*, or **Carmarthen**, 5½ *m.*), runs 5 *m.* to Llangyndryrn, 4 *m.* to Llandyfaelog, and **Kidwelly** 4 *m.* The stream is free up to Gelli-deg; above, permission must be had; trouting fair. Gwendraeth fawr runs 2 *m.*, E. from Kidwelly (trout, sewin). This stream rises in Llyn Llerh-wen (n.s. **Llan-dybie**, 5 *m.* E.), and is 12 *m.* long (*c.s. Towy*); trouting fair. Good general flies are blue upright and yellow March brown.

Killay (Glamorgan).—L. & N.W.R. (*See Penmaen.*) Penmaen brook (3 *m.*).

Knighton (Radnor).—L. & N.W.R. Teme; trout. (*See Gloucester.*) (*c.s. Severn.*) Lug, 4 *m.*; trout: preserved as Teme, s.t. 42*s.* (*See Chepstow.*) (*c.s. Wye.*) Good hotel accommodation.

Knucklas (Radnor).—G.W.R. Teme; trout; private. Lug (4 *m.* S.W.); trout, grayling. (*See Gloucester.*) (*c.s. Severn.*)

Lake Vyrnwy Hotel (Montgomery), *via* Llanfyllin.—n.s. **Llanfyllin**, 10 *m.*, or **Penybontfawr**, 8 *m.* Vyrnwy; trout, including rainbow: preserved by the owner of hotel. Cowny, 2 *m.* ; preserved as above. Hirddu, 3 *m.* N.W. ; trout; preserved as above. Gwnion 1 *m.* E. ; trout; preserved as above. Cedig, 1½ *m.* E.; trout; preserved as above in its lower half, and in its upper half by Sir W. W. Wynne. Eunant, 4½ *m.* N.W.; trout; preserved as above. Goch, 3 *m.* N.E. ; trout (*see Llangynnog*). Cowny 3½ *m.* S. Dyfnant, 4½ *m.* S. *Lakes*: Lake Vyrnwy; trout; capital fishing; free to hotel visitors; boats and one man 5*s.* per day. The best flies are dressed with tinsel; also the following are good: Zulu, teal and red, teal and black, black gnat, claret and grouse, coch-y-bonddhu, March brown with gold, black palmer and alder. Llyn Pennan, 3 *m.* N. (*See Llangynnog, Gloucester.*)

Lampeter (Cardigan).—G.W.R. Teifi; salmon, trout, grayling. (*c.s.*) Dulas: trout. Granell (3 *m.*); trout. Pencarreg lake (3 *m.*); perch. Aeron, 6 *m.* N.W.; salmon. sewin, trout (*c.s.*). Cothi, 8 *m.* S.E.; salmon, sewin, trout. *Hotel*: Lion Royal where salmon and trout fishing can be had free in Teifi and Dulas from March 1 to Oct. 31; for further information apply to the proprietor, or Mr. D. Roberts, 3, Bridge-street, who supplies all necessary tackle, &c. *Hotels*: Royal Oak, Castle. (*See Cardigan, Carmarthen, Llanarth, Llandissilio-Gogo, Aberaeron.*)

Lamphey (Pembroke).—G.W.R Pennar. (*See Pembroke.*)

Landore (Glamorgan).—Tawe. Ffyndrod. (*See Swansea.*)

Laugharne (Carmarthen).—n.s. **St. Clare**, 5 *m.* Taf; salmon, trout. Taf rises by **Crymmych Arms** (G.W.R.), runs 2 *m.* to **Clogne**, **Llanfirnach** 2 *m.*, **Rhydowen** 3 *m.* Here Gravil, 4 *m.* long, joins on right bank. Taf runs 2 *m.* to **Llanglydwen**, **Login** 3 *m.* 7 *m.* down Taf, Marlas joins on right bank. Marlas rises 1 *m.* N. of **Narberth**. 2 *m.* down, Gwaithnoak, 2 *m.* long, joins on right bank Marlas runs to Taf 5 *m.* ½ *m.* down Taf, Llease, which rises by Henllan Amgoed and is 5 *m.* long, joins on left bank. Taf runs 1 *m.* to **Whitland**, where Whitland joins on left bank. Whitland rises 4 *m.* above Llanboidy (n.s. **Login**, 4 *m.*), and joins Taf 6 *m.* down at **Whitland**. 3 *m.* down Taf, Feni, 5 *m.* long, joins on left bank. 3 *m.* down Taf, at Llanddowror (n.s. **St. Clears**, 3 *m.*), Coger, 5 *m.* long, joins on right bank. Taf runs 2 *m.* to St. Clare. Here Gynin joins on left bank. Gynin rises on Llanwinio Common. 2¼ *m.* S.E. from **Llanfirnach**, and 5 *m.* down is joined on left bank by Llechwydd, which rises 5 *m.* S.E. from **Llanfirnach**, and 2 *m.* down is joined on right bank by Asen, 3 *m.* long (n.s. **Llanfirnach**, 4 *m.*). Llechwydd runs to Gynin 4 *m.* Gynin runs 6 *m.* to St. Clare, and here Dewi joins on right bank. Dewi rises 4 *m.* above Trelech-ar-bettws, runs 5 *m.* to Mydrim, and **St. Clare** and Gynin 4 *m.* The united streams join Taf just below. Taf runs to Llanfihangel-Abercywyn, 3 *m.*, and here Cywyn joins on right bank. Cywyn rises 7 *m.* N.W. from **Cynwil**, and 10 *m.* down is joined on left bank by Cynnen, which rises by Llannewydd (n.s. **Branwydd Arms**, 2 *m.*), and is 6 *m* long. Cywyn runs to Taf in 8 *m.* 2 *m.* down Taf is **Laugharne**. (*c.s* Towy.) The best trout flies are coch-y-bonddhu, duns of various shades, red and black ants, black gnat, cowdung, bracken clock, and black foxtail

Llanarth (Cardigan).—n.s. **Lampeter**, 13 *m.* Gilfach, which rises 3 *m.* above Llanarth, and 2 *m.* down is joined on right bank by a brook 4 *m.* long. Gilfach runs to Llanina and sea 1 *m.* 1 *m.* N.E. runs Drowy, 4 *m.* long.

Llanarthney (Carmarthen).—L. & N.W.R. *Hotel*: Golden Grove Arms. Towy; salmon, sewin, trout, pike; preserved by Earl Cawdor to Llandilo above, free below. Licences of W. Morgan Griffiths, solicitor, Carmarthen. (*c.s.*) Dulas. Sannan (3 *m.*). (*See Carmarthen.*)

Llanbedr (Merioneth).—C.R. Artro; trout, sewin, salmon; preserved by a club; d., w., and m.t. Artro rises in Llyn Dywarchen, 8 *m.* N.E. from **Harlech**, or 3 *m.* across the hills a little S. of E. of **Talarnan** passing Llyn Caerwych (good trout). Artro, in 1 *m.*, waters Llyn Eiddew-fach (trout), and, 1 *m.* below, is joined on left bank by Eiddew, which rises in Llyn Fedw (trout), a small lake on the slopes of Y-Graigddrwg, and, 1 *m.* below, waters Llyn Eiddew-mawr (trout). (The lakes mentioned above, together with Llyn Graigddrw *see Barmouth*), are all within 1 *m.* of each other, and can be reached from **Harlech** or **Talarnan**. Ciddew joins Artro 1 *m.* down. 1 *m.* below, Bychan joins on left bank. Bychan rises in Llyn-y-morwynion, 6 *m.* N.E. of **Llanbedr**, and, 1 *m.* down, waters Llyn Cwm-bychan, 5 *m.* N.E. of **Llanbedr** (trout, sewin, salmon), and, ½ *m.* down, joins Artro. 1 *m.* down, a stream joins on left bank, draining Llyn Gloywlyn (good trouting: alder and oak flies good), 1 *m.* up, 5 *m.* N.E. of **Llanbedr**. 3 *m.* down Artro, Nantcol (good trouting free, with sewin after a flood) joins on left bank. Nantcol rises in Llyn Howel (trout), and, 1 *m.* below, is joined on right bank by the outflow of Llyn Cwm-hosan, ½ *m.* up. 1 *m.* down Nantcol the drainings of Llyn-y-ferfeddew (trout), 1 *m.* up, join on left bank. (These lakes, together with Llyn-y-bi (trout) (*see Barmouth*), lie close together 6 *m.* E. of **Llanbedr**). Nantcol runs 4 *m.* to Artro, which runs to **Llanbedr** in 2 *m.* Just below, a stream joins Artro on right bank, draining Hafod-y-Llyn 2 *m.* up, 2 *m.* N.E. of **Llanbedr**, or 2 *m.* S.E. of **Harlech**. 1 *m.* down, Artro joins the sea (*c.s. Dovey*). In the tidal waters is good bass fishing. *Lakes*: Pryvyd, 7 *m.* N.E.; good trouting. Twrgla, 7 *m.* N.E. (*See Barmouth.*) A good sewin fly is a moderate-sized one with red body and pheasant wing, with gold tinsel, and the same with mallard wing. Trout flies: March brown, coch-y-bonddu, coachman, orange dun, alder and oak flies. (*c.s. Dovey.*) *Hotel*: Victoria.

Llanberis (Carnarvon).—L. & N.W.R.　Seiont; trout, salmon, sewin; fishing free. (c.s.)
Llwch, 2 m. N.W.; trout.　March, 3 m. N.E.　*Lakes*: Llanberis lakes: salmon, trout,
char; the upper lake is preserved by the proprietors of the Victoria and Padarn Villa
Hotels for their visitors, the lower lake free. (c.s. *Seiont.*)　Dwythwch, 2 m. S.W.　Cwm-
Glas lakes, 3 m. S.E.　March-llyn-mawr and March-llyn-bach, 3 m. N.E.　Dur-Arddu,
4 m. S.E.　*Hotels*: Victoria, Padarn Villa. (*See Carnarvon, Pen-y-Gwryd.*)

Llanbrynmair (Montgomery). — C.R.　On Twymyn; trout, sewin, salmon.; fair
trouting.　Two streams join here from the N. and E. holding good trout.　The N. stream,
Ial (2 m. off), is better.　The rivers and lakes in this district are nearly all preserved
by Sir W. Wynn.　Eira (3 m. N.)　Gannon (4 m.).　*Lakes*: Gwyddwr (4 m.). perch,
trout.　*Hotel*: Wynnstay Arms. (*See Machynlleth, Gloucester.*)

Llandaff (Glamorgan).—G.W.R.　Taff and Ely; trout, sewin; preserved by the Taff
and Ely Fishing Association (hon. sec., A. Waldron, Esq., Cardiff), who issue s., w.,
and d.t. (*See Cardiff, Ely.*) (c.s.)

Llandderfel (Merioneth).—G.W.R.　Dee; trout, salmon. (c.s.)　Calettwr, 1 m. S.W.
Lakes: Grwyni, 3 m. N. (*See Chester.*)

Llandicilio (Merioneth).—G.W.R.　Dee; trout, salmon. (c.s.).　Cendiog. Llynor, 1 m.
N.E.　*Lakes*: Mynyllod, 3 m. N. (Sec *Chester.*)

Llandilo (Carmarthen).—L. & N.W.R.　*Hotel*: Cawdor Arms.　Towy; salmon, trout,
sewin; free above, but preserved below by Earl Cawdor.　Licences of W. Morgan-
Griffiths, solicitor, Carmarthen. Cennen. (c.s. *Towy.*) (*See Carmarthen.*)

Llandinam (Montgomery). — C.R.　Severn; trout, salmon, chub, &c. (c.s. *Severn.*)
(*See Gloucester.*)

Llandissilio-Gogo (Cardigan).—n.s. **Lampeter**, 20 m.　Dissilio, 6 m. long.　1 m. W.
runs Tydi, 6 m. long.

Llandovery Carmarthen).—L. & N.W.R.　Towy; salmon, sewin, trout; fishing free
4 m. from the town. (c.s.) Bran. Gwedderig. Dunant (4 m.). Pedwan (4 m.). Gwenlas
(4 m.). (*See Carmarthen, Llandilo.*)　*Hotel*: Castle.

Llandrindod (Radnor.) — L. & N.W.R.　Ithon.　Hawddwy (2 m.). (c.s. *Wye.*) (*See
Chepstow, England.*)

Llandrinio (Montgomery).—By. R.　Severn; chub, dace, trout, salmon.　Maerdy brook
(2 m. S.W.) (*See Gloucester.*) (c.s. *Severn.*)

Llandudno (Carnarvon).—L. & N.W.R.; G.W.R.　There is good fishing for codlings,
congers, &c., under the Great Orme's Head.　Boats can be obtained from the neighbouring
town of Conway. *Fishing stations within reach*: Conway, Glan Conway, Tal-y-Cafn,
Llanfairfechan, Aber, Llanrwst, Trefriw, Bangor, Bettws-y-Coed, Pont-y-Pant, Dolwyd-
delen, Festiniog, Carnarvon, Bodorgan, Ty-Croes.

Llandulas (Carnarvon).—L. & N.W.R.　Glan E'afon.　This stream is 7 m. long, and
half-way down, at Coed Coch, receives the outlet of the lake there.　This lake is 3¼ m.
from **Llandulas**.

Llan-dybie (Carmarthen).—G.W.R.; L. & N.W.R.　Llan-dybie brook.　Llwchwr, 3 m.
Gwendraeth Faur, 5 m. W.　*Lake*: Llerhwen 5 m. W. (*See Llwchwr, Kidwelly.*) (c.s *Towy.*)

Llandyssil (Cardigan).—G.W.R.　Teifi; salmon, trout (large). (c.s.)　Cerdin. Twelli;
trout (good).　Ythan (1 m.).　Cletwr (2 m.); trout (good).　Bydrel, 5 m.)　*Hotel*: Porth;
5 m. fishing in Teifi free to hotel visitors; elsewhere permission from the owners.
(*See Cardigan.*)

Llanelly (Carmarthen). — G.W.R.　Llihedi and Dann; salmon, trout; fishing free.
Llihedi is 7 m. long. Dann runs 1 m. E. from the town, and is 6 m. long.

Llanerchymedd (Anglesea).—L. & N.W.R.　Alaw. (*See Penrhoslligwy, Valley Station.*)

Llanfaethlu (Anglesea).—n.s. **Valley Station**, 7 m. S.　*Lakes*: Ceryglwyd.

Llanfair,(Anglesea).—L. & N.W.R.　Braint; salmon, trout. (c.s. *Seiont.*) (*See Llangeinwen.*)

Llanfair (Montgomery).—*Hotel*: Wynnstay Arms.　Banw; trout; leave can be obtained.
Rhiw (3 m. S.E.).　*Lakes*: Maesmawr pond (5 m. N.E.) (*See Gloucester.*) (c.s. *Severn.*)

Llanfairfechan (Carnarvon).—L. & N.W.R.　On Du, 3 m. long.

Llanfair-Talhaiarn (Denbigh).—n.s. **Abergele**, 6 m.; **St. Asaph**, 11 m.; **Denbigh**, 11 m.　Elwy; trout, sewin, salmon; preserved for 2 m. by landlord of hotel,
elsewhere by Manchester and Liverpool Association. (c.s.)　Melan, 2 m. S.W. Aled,
2 m. E. (c.s. *Clwyd.*)　*Hotel*: Black Lion. (*See Rhyl.*)

Llanfairynghornwy (Anglesea).—n.s. **Rhos-goch**, 7 m. E.　Hygeinan, 3 m. long,
runs 1 m. E.　*Lakes*: Hygeinan 2 m. S.E

Llanfechan (Montgomery).—C.R.　Cain; trout, salmon; preserved.　Brogan.　Tanat
(4 m. N.); trout, grayling, chub, pike; preserved. (*See Gloucester.*) (c.s *Severn.*)

Llanfechell (Anglesea).—n.s. **Rhosgoch**, 3 m. S.E.　Cemmaes.　This brook rises in
Llyn Felin-nant, 1 m. W. of **Rhosgoch**, and 4 m. down is joined on left bank by a brook
which rises in two lakes by Llanllwin, runs 2 m. to **Llanfechell**, and 1 m. down
joins Cemmaes, which runs 2 m. to the sea.

Llanfihangel-Glyn-Myfyr (Merioneth) - n.s. **Derwen**, 6 m.—Alwen; trout. (c.s.
Dee.)　Derwydd. (*See Chester.*)

Llanfirnach (Pembroke).—G.W.R.　Taf; trout, salmon. (c.s. *Towy.*)　Gynin (2¼ m.);
trout, sewin.　Asen (4 m.).　Llechwydd (5 m.) (*See Laugharne.*)

Llanfyllin (Montgomery). — C.R.　Cain; salmon, trout; preserved.　Llechwydd.　Tanat
(5 m. N.); trout, pike, chub; preserved. (c.s. *Severn.*) (*See Lake Vyrnwy Hotel;
Llangynog; Llanrhaiadr-yn-Mochnant; Gloucester.*)

Llangadock (Carmarthen).—G.W.R.; L. & N.W.R. Towy; salmon, sewin, trout; preserved. (c.s.) Brane; sewin, trout; free. Marles. Sefin. Sawdde; trout; mostly preserved by landowners. Sefin Isaf (3 m.). Llechdawdd (4 m.). Sawdde fechan (5 m.). Dyfnant (6 m.). Clydach (6 m.). Buartharch (8 m.). (*See Carmarthen.*) *Lake*: Van; trout; free; good fishing. *Hotels*: Glansevin Arms and Red Lion.

Llangammarch Wells (Brecon).—L. & N.W.R. Irfon; trout, dace, salmon; preserved by the two Hotels, Cammarch (*see Advertisement*) and Pump House and Lake Hotel (*see Advertisement*); season begins Feb. 14, ends Sept. 15; only fly allowed until July 1. Dulas; small trout; preserved as Irfon for 5 m. at the lower end, above private. Annell. Camddwr. Cammarch (1 m.). Einon (2 m.); private. Cledau (1 m.). Cnyffiad (3 m.); private. (*See Chepstow. England.*)

Llangefni (Anglesea).—L. & N.W.R. Cefni. (c.s. Seiont.) (*See Bodorgan.*)

Llangeinwen (Anglesea).—n.s. **Carnarvon**, 4 m. Braint; salmon, trout. (c.s. Seiont.) Braint rises in Llyn Llwydiarth, 5 m. N.W. of **Beaumaris**, runs 6 m. to **Llanfair**, and 8 m. to **Llangeinwen** and the sea.. Just before joining the sea a stream joins on right bank draining Llyn Gorsddu 1 m. up, 1 m. S.W. from **Llangeinwen.**

Llangenych (Carmarthen).—G.W.R. Llwchwr (injured by mines). Trasarch. (*See Llwchwr.*) (c.s. Towey.)

Llangian (Carnarvon).—n.s. **Pwllheli**, 7 m. Soch. Soch rises 2 m. above Meyllteyrn, and 3 m. down, at Bouwnog is joined on left bank by Cofan, 3 m. long. 1 m. down Soch, at Llandegwning, Bodlas, 4 m. long, joins on left bank. Soch runs to Llanengan 3 m., **Llangian** 1 m., and the sea 2 m.

Llanglydwen (Carmarthen).—G.W.R. Taf; trout. salmon. (*See Laugharne.*) (c.s. Towy.)

Llangollen (Denbigh).—G.W.R. Dee; trout, grayling, salmon, pike, chub; preserved by Glyndwr Society from **Carrog** above to Llangollen; salmon and trout s.t. 4l. 4s., m.t. 42s.. d.t. 5s. 6d.; trout, s.t. 42s., m.t. 21s., w.t. 10s., d.t. 2s. 6d.; tickets from Mr. E. D. Jones, Medical Hall, Llangollen; only licensed fishermen may be employed; a coracle is 2s. 6d. a day to all except season ticket holders, who pay 21s. extra for use of private coracle. and a coracle man's wages 5s.; no dogs or Sunday fishing. Season begins March 1 and ends Oct. 14 for trout, and Nov. 1 for salmon. There are 2 m of free water by the town. The Llangollen Trout and Grayling Society (hon. sec., T. R. J. Parry) preserve the Dee from Llangollen to Newbridge by **Cefn**, s.t. 20s., d.t. 1s. Deep wading is necessary ; March and April, or late in the season, is best. Duns, March brown, and gravel-bed are good flies. (c.s.) Ceiriog, 3 m. S. (c.s. Dee.) Alyn, 7 m. N., at Llandegla; trout. (c.s. Dee.) Rhys, 7 m. N. at Llandegla. *Hotel*: Bridge End. (*See Chester.*)

Llangonoyd (Glamorgan).—G.W.R. On Llynvi; trout. (*See Bridgend.*)

Llangurig (Montgomery).—C.R. Brochan (1 m.). Dulas (1½ m.). (*See Gloucester.*)

Llangwyllog (Anglesea).—L. & N.W.R. Cefni. (c.s. Seiont.) (*See Bodorgan.*)

Llangybi (Carnarvon).—C.R. Wen. Dwyfach, 1 m. E.; trout, sewin, salmon. (c.s.) (*See Criccieth, Afon Wen.*)

Llangynllo (Radnor).—L. & N.W.R. Lug. Bledla brook (2½ m.). Graig brook (3 m.). Arau (3½ m.). Cam-ddwr (5 m.). (c.s. Wye.) (*See Chepstow, England.*)

Llangynnog (Montgomery).—n.s. **Llanfyllin**, 8½ m. *Hotel*: New Inn. Tanat; trout; free fishing for 3 m. above and 1 m. below. Eiarth. Goch (2 m.). Hirnant (2½ m. S.) *Lakes*: Pennant (3 m. S.W.); fishing free. (*See Gloucester.*) c.s. Severn.) (*See Lake Vyrnwy Hotel.*)

Llanidloes (Montgomery).—C.R. Severn; trout, chub, salmon. Brochan; trout. Clywedog (poisoned). Dulas (1 m.). Ceryst (2 m. N.) (poisoned). Biga (7 m.). Llwyd (8 m.). *Lakes* ; Ebyr (3½ m. N.E.). Derw-llwydion (6 m.). (*See Gloucester.*) (c.s.)

Llanpumpsaint (Carmarthen).—G.W.R. Gwili ; trout, sewin, salmon; free below, preserved above. (c.s. Towy.) (*See Carmarthen.*)

Llanrhaiadr (Denbigh).—L. & N.W.R. Clywd; trout, salmon. (c.s.) Llewesog. (*See Rhyl.*)

Llanrhaiadr-yn-Mochnant (Montgomery). — n.s. **Llanfyllin**, 7 m. Moch; trout; free. Tanat (1 m.); trout, grayling, chub, &c. Twrch (1 m.). Disgynfa (5 m. N.W.) *Lakes*: Moelin (5 m. N E.). Llynecaws (6 m. N.W.). (*See Gloucester.*) (c.s. Severn.)

Llanrhystyd (Cardigan).—n.s. **Llanrhystyd Road**, 6 m. On Wyrai. (c.s. Teifi.) Wyrai rises 2 m. above Llanfihangel Lledrod 3 m. S.W. from **Traws Coed** Station, runs 4 m. to Llangwyryion. and 4 m. to **Llanrhystyd**. Here Mabus joins on left bank. Mabus rises 1 m. S.W. from Llangwyryion, and 2 m. down is joined on left bank by Tryal, 2 m. long. Mabus runs to **Llanrhystyd** in 3 m. Carrog. also 5 m. long, here joins Wyrai on right bank. 1 m. below **Llanrhystyd** Wyrai joins the sea. Arth, 6 m. S. *Lakes*: Llyn March. 6 m E. (*See Aberaaron.*)

Llanrwst (Denbigh).—L. & N.W.R. Conway; salmon, trout, sewin; for *salmon fishing* in the Gwydyr Fishery (the Conway from Coed, leaving Gwalch Plantation, to Llanrwst Bridge); May 1 to 30, w.t. 4s., d.t. 1s.; July 1 to 31, w.t. 6s., d.t. 1s. 6d.; Sept. 1 to 30, w.t. 8s, d.t. 2s.; Oct. 1 to Nov. 14 (all inclusive), w.t. 15s. The Conway, with above excepted: July 1 to Aug. 31, m.t. 25s., w.t. 10s., d.t. 2s. 6d.; Sept. 1 to 30, 2l., 14 days 25s., w.t. 12s.; Oct. 1 to Nov. 14 (all inclusive), the period 4l. 10s.. 14 days 2l., w.t. 25s. (holders of tickets cannot fish below the upper boundary of Pant-y-coarw Farm); from Messrs. Griffith Owen and Son, fishing tackle dealers, Greenwich House. Trouting March 1 to April 30; s.t. 10s., w.t. 2s. 6d., d.t. 1s. Crafnant Lake, s.t. 2s., d.t. 6d. Best time for salmon from Aug. 1. Flies : Conway patterns and Ballyshannon, Wilkinson's patterns. Dyffryn-gallt, 3 *m.* N.E. Derfyn, 4 *m.* E. Tickets at hotels (*for terms see Bettws-y-Coed*). Llugwy, 4 *m.* S.; trout, salmon, preserved by Lord Denbigh (*c.s. Conway*); Hwch, 5 *m.* S.E. Lledr, 6 *m.* S.; trout, salmon (*c.s. Conway*); tickets at hotels (*for terms see Bettws*). Cledwen or Elwy, 6 *m.* E. (*c.s.*) **Lakes**: Chwyth Llyn, 3 *m.* N.E. Crafnant, 4 *m.* W.; trout; boats. Aled, 8 *m.* S.E. (*c.s. Clwyd*). Noel-frech, 8 *m.* S.E. Cowlyd, 6 *m.* W. Elsi, 5 *m.* Hotels: Eagles and Victoria. (*See Conway; Rhyl.*)

Llanrhystyd Road (Cardigan).—G.W.R. (*See Llansantffraid; Llanrhystyd.*)

Llansaintffraid (Montgomery).—C.R. Vernwy; trout, salmon, chub, pike, perch, roach, dace; preserved by landowners below, free above. (*See Llanymynech.*) Cain; trout, salmon; preserved. Tanat; trout, grayling, chub, pike; preserved. *Lakes*: Du (6 *m.* S.E.) (*See Gloucester.*) (*c.s. Severn.*) Hotel: Sun.

Llansantffraid (Cardigan).—n.s. **Llanrhystyd Road**, 8 *m.* On Peris, 6 *m.* long. **Lanon**, 4 *m.* long, runs ½ *m.* S.

Llantisilio, station **Berwyn** (Merioneth).—Dee; trout, grayling, pike, chub, salmon. (*c.s.*) Berwyn. (*See Chester.*)

Llantrissant (Glamorgan).—G.W.R. Ely; trout; free. Dowlas brook; trout. (*e.s. Taff.*) (*See Cardiff.*)

Llanwchllyn (Merioneth).—G.W.R. Dee or Lliw; trout; preserved by Sir W. W. Wynn. (*c.s.*) Dwfrdwy. Twrch; trout; preserved by Sir W. W. W. (*c.s. Dee.*) Llafar, 2 *m.* N.E.; trout; preserved by Sir W. W. W. Rhydwen, 2 *m.* E. Afon-y-Wynt, 4 *m.* N.W. Ennant, 7 *m.* N.W. Lakes: Bala or Tegid, 1 *m.* N.E.; trout, pike, perch; free. (*c.s. Dee.*) (*See Chester.*) Hotel: Goat (*see Advertisement*).

Llanwndla (Carnarvon).—L. & N.W.R. Gwrfai; salmon, trout. (*c.s. Seiont.*) Gwrfai rises in Llyn-y-Gader by **Rhyddu**, and 1 *m* down is joined on right bank by a stream which rises in Llyn Glas, runs ½ *m.* to Llyn Goch. ½ *m.* down, a stream joins on left bank, draining Llyn-y-Nadraedd ½ *m.* up (these lakelets are close together under the brow of Snowdon). On the right bank the outflow of Llyn Ffynnon-y-Gwas joins ½ *m.* up. These four lakes are 3 *m.* E. of **Snowdon Ranger**. ¾ *m.* down, Gwrfai runs into Llyn Cwellyn. ½ *m.* down the lake is **Snowdon Ranger** on right bank. Llyn Cwellyn is 1 *m.* long. Gwrfai when it leaves the lake runs 2 *m.* to **Bettws Garmon**, 5 *m.* to **Llanwndla**. Here Venno, 3 *m.* long, joins on right bank. Gwrfai runs to the sea in 3 *m.*

Llanwrda (Carmarthen).—L. & N.W.R. Towy; trout, salmon, sewin; fishing free. (*c.s.*) Ynys. Dulas. (*See Carmarthen.*)

Llanwrtyd (Brecon).—L. & N.W.R. Irfon; trout, chub, dace. Cerdyn (2 *m.*). Cledau (3 *m.*); preserved. Cilent (4 *m.*). Gwessyn (6 *m.*). Lakes: Berwyn, and others. Hotels: Dolcoed House, where fishing can be had in Irfon for some miles; Neuadd Arms, and Bellevue. The best trouting is above. Birmingham Waterworks reservoirs (excellent fishing), 10 *m.* (*See Chepstow, England.*)

Llanybyther (Carmarthen).—G.W.R. Teifi; salmon, trout. (*c.s.*) Granell (3 *m.*) Lakes: Pencarreg (2 *m.*). (*See Cardigan.*)

Llong (Flint).—L. & N.W.R. Alyn; trout. (*c.s. Dee.*) Terrig. (*See Chester.*)

Llwchwr (Glamorgan).—G.W.R. Llwchwr. Lliw. Llwchwr rises some 3 *m.* E. of **Llandybie**, and 4 *m.* down is joined on right bank by Llan-dybie brook, which, after running 4 *m.*, passes 1 *m.* W. of **Derwydd Road**, runs thence to **Llan-dybie** 2 *m.*, and joins Llwchwr 2 *m.* down, 1 *m.* from **Cross Inn**. Here also Lash, 3 *m.* long, joins on right bank. Llwchwr runs 2 *m.* to **Pantyffynon Junction**, where Amman joins on left bank, and Alwyd, 4 *m.* long, on right bank. Amman rises 3 *m.* above **Bryn-Amman**, runs thence to **Garnant** 2 *m.* Here Garnant, 3 *m.* long, joins on left bank, and Pedol, 3 *m.* long, on right bank. Amman runs to **Cross Inn**, 4 *m.*, and **Pantyffynon** 1 *m.* Llwchwr runs to **Pontardulais** 8 *m.*; here Dulas, 5 *m.* long, joins on left bank. 1 *m.* down Llwchwr, Gwili joins on right bank. Gwili rises some 4 *m.* W. of **Pantyffynon**, and is 10 *m.* long (injured in its lower part by mines). 1½ *m.* down Llwchwr, at **Llangenych**, Trasarch, 5 *m.* long, joins on right bank. Llwchwr runs 2 *m.* to **Llwchwr**. (*c.s. Towy.*) (The river is mostly injured by mines). Lliw rises 8 *m.* above **Gors**, runs thence to **Llwchwr** 3 *m.*, where it joins the estuary. At Llwchwr the lesser Lliw, 6 *m.* long, joins on left bank.

Llwyngwril (Carnarvon).—C.R. Llwyd; trout. This stream is 4 *m.* long.

Llyndeged (Glamorgan).—G.W.R. Cynon. (*See Cardiff.*)

Login (Carmarthen).—G.W.R. Taf; trout, salmon. (*c.s. Towy.*) Eglwys (4 *m.*). (*See Laugharne.*)

Loveston (Pembroke), n.s. **Templeton**, 3 *m.*—Carn. Carn rises 1½ *m.* W. from **Templeton** station, runs 3 *m.* to Loveston, and 1 *m.* down, 3 *m.* from **Begelly**, is joined on left bank by Langden brook, 3 *m.* long. Carn runs 2½ *m.* to Milford Haven.

Machynlleth (Montgomery). — C.R. Dovey; salmon, sewin, trout. (*c.s.*) Dovey rises in Llyn Dyfi, 3 *m.* E. from **Drws-y-nant** station, and 4 *m.* down, at Llan-y-Mowddwy, 5 *m.* N.E. from **Dinas Mawddwy**, is joined on right bank by Pamrhyd, 2 *m.* long. 4 *m.* down Dovey, 1 *m.* above **Dinas Mawddwy**, Cowarch, 3 *m.* long, joins on right bank. Dovey runs 1 *m.* to **Dinas Mawddwy**. Here Geryst, which rises in Llynnen Figan and Fach, and is 4 *m.* long, joins on right bank. 1 *m.* down Dovey, by Mallwyd (salmon, sewin, trout; Hotel: Peniarth Arms (*see Advertisement*), where extensive fishing can be had). Cleivion joins on left bank. Cleivion rises in the hills 6 *m.* W. of Mallwyd, and 2 *m.* down is joined on right bank by

Clywedog, 4 *m.* long. 1 *m.* down Cleivion, at Pont-ar-bwlffa, Tafolog, 3 *m.* long, joins on left bank. ½ *m.* up Tafolog from its junction with Cleivion a stream joins on right bank, which drains Llyn-coch-hwyad 2 *m.* up. This lake lies 5 *m.* W. of Mallwyd and 6 *m.* S.W. of **Dinas.** Cleivion runs in 2 *m.* to Mallwyd and Dovey. Dovey runs to **Aber Angell,** 3 *m.*, and here Angell joins on right bank. Angell, after running 3 *m.*, is joined on right bank by Hir, 2 *m.* long, and on same bank by a stream draining Llyn Llecoediog ½ *m.* up. ½ *m.* down Angell, Mynach, 3 *m.* long, joins on left bank, and ½ *m.* down is Dovey. Dovey runs to **Cemmaes,** 3 *m.*, and **Cemmaes Junction,** 2 *m.* Here Twymyn joins on left bank. Twymyn rises 5 *m.* above **Llanbrynmair,** and 2 *m.* below that place, by the station, is joined on right bank by Tal, 5 *m.* long. Just above the junction a stream joins on right bank 5 *m.* long. Twymyn runs to Dovey, 5 *m.* 2 *m.* down Dovey, opposite Llanwein, Gwidol, 3 *m.* long, joins on right bank; and 2 *m.* below, 1 *m.* above **Machynlleth** station, Diflas joins on left bank. Diflas rises in Llyn Bugeilyn (good trouting) 8 *m.* S.W. from **Machynlleth.** 2 *m.* down, a stream joins on right bank, draining Glaslyn, 2 *m.* up, 8 *m.* S.W. from **Machynlleth,** and 1 *m.* N. of Llyn Bugeilyn. 2 *m.* down Dyfias a stream joins on left bank, 4 *m.* long. Dyflas runs 4 *m.* to Pont-felin-gerig, 1 *m.* W. from **Machynlleth,** and here Crial, 7 *m.* long, joins on right bank. Dovey is ½ *m.* down. ½ *m.* down Dovey Dulas (good trouting, sewin, and mort up to weir) joins on right bank. (*c.s. Dovey.*) Dulas rises above Aber-llefeni, 4 *m.* E. of **Aber Angell,** and here Llefeni, 3 *m.* long, joins Dulas on right bank. 2 *m.* down, Corys, 3 *m.* long, joins on right bank. **Tal-y-Llyn** lies 2 *m.* E. of the head of this stream. Dulas runs 5 *m.* to Dovey. Dovey runs ½ *m.* to **Machynlleth** and **Gilan Dyfi** at the estuary, 6 *m.* Here Llymant, which rises in Llyn-pen-Rhaidr (trout, perch; preserved by Sir Pryse Pryse, of Gorgerddan, who sometimes gives leave), 7 *m.* S. from **Machynlleth,** runs 4 *m.* to 2 *m.* S. of that town, joins Dovey 3 *m.* down at **Gilan Dyfi.** Here also Einon, 5 *m.* long, joins Dovey on left bank. There are several good salmon pools in Dovey; s.t. 100*s.*; April 1 to Sept. 16, 80*s.*, m.t. 45*s.*, fortnight 30*s.*, w.t. 20*s.*, d.t. 5*s.* Rheidol, 8 *m.* S.E. (*See Aberystwyth.*)

Maenclochog (Pembroke).—G.W.R. Llandilo brook. Gilfach brook (1 *m.*). Syfynfy (2 *m.*). Corwyn (4 *m.*). Crynanich (4 *m.*). (*See Haverfordwest.*)

Maentwrog (Merioneth).—n.s. **Tan-y-Bwlch,** 1 *m.*, **Maentwrog Road,** 2½ *m.* Dwyryd; trout, sewin, salmon; free to hotel guests above, preserved below; s.t. 10*s.*, m.t. 5*s.*, w.t. 2*s.* 6*d.* Prysor, 1 *m.* S. (*c.s. Dovey.*) *Lakes*: Garnedd, 1 *m.* N.; free of hotel. Hafod-y-Llyn, 1 *m.* N.W.; free. Llenyrch, 2 *m.* S.; free; Tecwyn-uchaf, 2 *m.* S.W.; free of hotel. Y-Oerfa, 2 *m.* E.; free. *Hotels*: Oakley Arms and Grapes, where fishing can be had. (*See Penrhyndeudraeth.*)

Maerdy (Merioneth).—n.s. **Corwen,** 5 *m*, Alwen; trout. (*c.s. Dee.*) Geirw, 1 *m.* S. (*c.s. Dee.*) (*See Chester.*)

Maesteg (Glamorgan).—G.W.R. On Llynvi; trout. (*See Bridgend.*)

Maesycrugiau (Cardigan).—M. & M.R. Teifi; salmon, trout. (*c.s.*) Ceilliog (3 *m.*). Cathal (2 *m.*). Cletwr (2 *m.*. trout, good). Cinen (4 *m.*). (*See Cardigan.*)

Manod (Merioneth). — Bywydd. Dwyryd, 1 *m.* S.W.; trout; free. Manod, 1 *m* S. Machno, 3 *m.* W. *Lakes*: Llyn Manod, 1 *m.* E. Llyn-y-frith-graig, 3 *m.* W. Danogen, 3 *m.* N.W. (*See Penrhyndeudraeth; Conway.*)

Manorbeer (Pembroke).—G.W.R. Pennar. (*See Pembroke.*)

Merthyr (Glamorgan).—T.V.R. Taff; salmon, trout. (*c.s.*) (*See Cardiff.*)

Middletown (Montgomery).—L. & N.W. & G.W.R. Trewern. Severn (3 *m.* W.); trout, salmon, chub, dace, &c. (*See Gloucester.*) (*c.s. Severn.*)

Milford (Pembroke).—G.W.R. Mullock brook (6½ *m.*). (*See St. Ishmael s.*) Milford Haven contains a great variety of sea fish, and the brooks trout. Thorn Island, Rat Island, and Sheep Island, and the Harbour rock, with many other places, are all good for pollack, and bass are also frequently met with. Sand-eels might be taken with a seine net at Angle Bay. At the insulated rocks outside the haven, very large pollack in the tide-races towards the Smalls Light; a steam yacht desirable for this distant fishing. The strongest tackle requisite. Spinning indiarubber eels strongly recommended.

Mold (Flint).—L. & N.W.R. Alyn trout. (*c.s. Dee.*) Terrig, 3 *m.* S.E. *Lakes*: Llyn-y-Mynydd-du, 5 *m.* S. Llyn Neyn, 5 *m.* S. (*See Chester.*)

Montgomery.—C.R. Severn (2 *m.*); trout, salmon, chub, &c. Camlad (2 *m.* N.); trout, grayling, chub. Lacks brook (2 *m.* S.E.). Caebitra (4 *m.* S.E.). Rhiw (4½ *m.* N.W.); good trouting. (*See Gloucester.*) (*c.s.*)

Morriston (Glamorgan).—Tawe. (*See Swansea.*)

Mostyn (Flint).—L. & N.W.R. 1 *m.* N. runs Afon-y-Garth, 3 *m.* long.

Mountain Ash (Glamorgan).—G.W.R. Cynon. (*See Cardiff.*)

Mumbles Road (Glamorgan).—G.W.R (*See Bishopston.*) Kittle brook (3 *m.*)

Nantclwyd (Denbigh).—L. & N.W.R. Clwyd; trout. (*c.s.*) Clywedog, 3 *m.* N.W. (*See Rhyl.*)

Nantgaredig (Carmarthen).—L. & N.W.R. Towy; salmon, trout, sewin; fishing private. Cothi; salmon, trout, sewin. (*c.s.*) Pibw, 1½ *m.* Gwendraeth fach, 4 *m.* 7 *m.* distant some trout and sewin fishing is to be had by staying at the inn at Brechfa. (*See Carmarthen; Kidwelly.*)

Nanttle (Carnarvon).—L. & N.W.R. Llyfni; trout, sewin. (*c.s. Seiont.*) *Lakes*: Nanttle (2); trout, sewin; fishing poor. (*c.s. Seiont.*) Ffynnonaw, 2 *m.* N.E. Cwm Silyn (2), 2 *m.* S. (*See Pen-y-groes.*)

Narberth (Pembroke).—G.W.R. Marlas (1 *m.*). Gwaithnoak (2 *m.*). Eastern Cleddau (2 *m.*). Taf (5 *m.*); salmon, trout. (*c.s. Towy.*) (*See Laugharne; Haverfordwest.*)
Neath (Glamorgan).—G W.R. Neath. Neath rises 4 *m.* above Ystradyfellte (n.s. **Glyn Neath,** 7 *m.*), and 4 *m.* down is joined on right bank by Llia 3 *m* long (n.s. **Glyn Neath,** 8 *m.*). 1 *m.* down is Ystrad; and 3 *m.* below, Hepste joins on left bank. Hepste, after running 6 *m.*, passes 1 *m.* N.W. of Penderyn (n.s. **Hirwain,** 2 *m.*), and 1 *m.* down joins Neath. 2 m. down Neath, Nedd, 8 *m.* long, joins on right bank (n.s. **Glyn Neath,** 3 *m.*). Neath runs 3 *m.* to **Glyn Neath,** 3 m. to **Resolyen,** 4 *m.* to **Aberdylias.** Here Dylias, which rises by **Crinant,** and is 5 *m.* long, joins on right bank. Neath runs to **Neath** 2 *m.*; and 1 *m.* down, Clydach, which rises 2 *m.* E. of **Pont-ar-dawe** station, and is 5 *m.* long, joins on right bank. Neath flows to the sea in 3 *m.*
Nevin (Carnarvon).—n.s. **Pwllheli,** 8 *m.* Geirch, 2 *m.* W., 5 *m.* long.
New Bridge (Radnor).—C.R. Wye; salmon, trout, chub, dace, pike, roach. Ithon, trout. Hernant (1 *m.*). (*c.s.*) (*See Chepstow, England.*).
Newcastle Emlyn (Cardigan).—n.s. **Llandyssil,** 8 *m.* Teifi; salmon, trout. Ceri (2 *m.*). Gernos (3 *m.*). Cych (6 *m.*). (*c.s. Teifi.*) (*See Cardigan.*)
New Milford (Pembroke).—G.W.R. Rosemarket brook. This stream rises 1 *m.* W. of **Johnston,** runs to **Rosemarket** 3 *m.*, and **New Milford** 3 *m.*
Newport (Pembroke).—n.s. **Crymmych Arms,** 10 *m.* Neave. This stream rises by **Crymmych Arms,** runs 7 *m.*, when Biron 4 *m.* long, joins on left bank. 2 *m.* down Neave, Duad, 4 *m.* long, joins on right bank. Neave runs to Nevern, 2 *m.*, and **Newport,** 2 *m.* Here Clydach, 4 *m.* long, joins on left bank. To ½ *m* below this the tide flows.
New Radnor (Radnor).—G.W.R. Summergill brook. Black brook. *Lakes*: Melan (4 *m.*). (*See Chepstow, England.*)
Newtown (Montgomery).—C.R. Severn; trout, salmon, chub, &c. Hafren (3 *m.* E.). *Lakes*: Fachwen Pool (3 *m.* N.W.) Dwr (6 *m.*). (*c.s*) (*See Gloucester* and *Chepstow, England.*)
Pant (Glamorgan).—B. & M.R. Taff; trout, salmon. (*c.s.*) (*See Cardiff.*)
Pant Glass (Carnarvon).—Dwyfach; trout, sewin, salmon. (*c.s.*) (*See Criccieth.*)
Pantydwr (Radnor).—C.R. Marteg; trout. (*See Chepstow, England.*)
Pantyffnon (Carmarthen).—G W.R. Llwchwr. Amman. Alwyd. Gwili (4 *m.*). (*See Llwch*[10]*r.*) (*c.s. Towy.*)
Pembroke.—G.W.R. Pennar. Pennar rises by **Manorbeer** station, runs 3 *m.* to **Lamphey,** and Pembroke 2 *m.* Stackpool brook (3 *m.*). (*See Cheriton.*) Castle Martin brook (3 *m.*) (*See Castle Martin.*) Carew brook (4 *m.*) (*See Carew.*) *Lake:* Orielton lakes (3 *m.*)
Pen Caber (Cardigan).—G.W.R. Twelli; trout (good) (*See Cardigan.*)
Penclawdd (Glamorgan).—G.W.R. (*See Cheriton.*)
Pencoed (Glamorgan).—G.W.R. On Evenny; trout. (*See Bridgend.*) (*c.s. Ogmore.*
Penmaen (Glamorgan).—n.s. **Killay,** 6 *m.* Penmaen brook. This stream rises on Fairwood Moor, 3 *m.* W. from **Killay,** and 3 *m.* down, near Penmaen, is joined by a brook on right bank 3 *m.* long. The sea is 1 *m.* down.
Penmaenpool (Merioneth).—L. & N.W.R.; G.W.R. Mawddach; trout, sewin, few salmon; d.t. 2*s.* 6*d.*, m.t. 10*s.* 6*d.* (*c.s. Dovey.*) Mynach. Gadr, 1 *m.* S. Llechan, 2 *m.* W. *Lakes*: Cwm-mynach, 4 *m.* N. (*See Barmouth.*)
Penrhoslligwy (Anglesea).—n.s. **Llanerchymedd,** 5 *m.* S.W. Lligwy. This stream rises in Llyn-llwyn-Crwn, 1½ *m.* S. across the hills from **Penrhoslligwy,** and is 3 *m.* long. Dulas runs 2 *m.* N. Dulas rises in Paint pools 1 *m.* S. of **Amlwch,** and 1½ *m.* down waters Llyn Meliw. Dulas runs to Wern, 2½ *m.* N.E. of **Llanerchymedd,** 4 *m.*, and 3 *m.* down joins the estuary.
Penrhyndeudraeth (Merioneth). — C.R. Dwyryd; trout, sewin, salmon. Dwyryd rises in a small nameless pool 3 *m.* above **Tan-y-Grisiau,** and, 1 *m.* from its source, is joined on right bank by a stream, 1 *m.* long, draining the reservoir 3 *m.* N. from **Tan-y-Grisiau.** At **Tan-y-Grisiau,** Orthan joins on right bank. Orthan rises in Llyn Coch, 2 *m.* N.W. of **Tan-y-Grisiau** (there are three small nameless lakes ½ *m.* N. of Coch). ½ *m.* down is a lakelet close to the right bank, and a stream on left bank draining a nameless lakelet close to the S.W. arm of Llyn Conglog. 1 *m.* below, a stream joins on left bank, draining Llyn Conglog ½ *m.* up. (There are three lakelets immediately to N. of Conglog, and Llyn Clogwyn lies close to the junction with Orthan; all these lakes are within 3 *m.* of **Tan-y-Grisiau.**) Orthan runs ½ *m.* to Llyn-Cwm-Orthan, and, 1 *m.* down, joins Dwyryd at **Tan-y-Grisiau.** Here, also, Ddu joins on right bank. Ddu rises in the reservoir by the railway, and, 1 *m.* down, is joined on left bank by a stream draining Llyn Trwstyllon 1 *m.* up, 2 *m.* S.W. of **Tan-y-Grisiau.** Ddu joins Dwyryd ½ *m.* down. 1 *m.* down Dwyryd, Bywydd joins on left bank. Bywydd rises in Llyn Bywydd, 1 *m.* N.E. of **Diffwys,** runs by that station, and, 1 *m.* below, at **Manod,** is joined on left bank by a stream, 2 *m.* long, draining Llyn Dubach, ½ *m.* E. of **Diffwys.** 1 *m.* down, Bywydd joins Dwyryd. 1 *m.* down Dwyryd, at **Rhyd-y-sarn,** 1 *m.* W. of **Ffestiniog,** Yspytty joins on left bank. Yspytty rises in Llyn-y-bryn-du. (Llyn-y-gors is ½ *m.* N.E. and Llyn-y-frithgraig 1 *m.* N.E. of this lake.) 1 *m.* below, the drainage of Llynian-y-gamallt, ½ *m.* long, joins on left bank. 3 *m.* down Yspytty, at Pont-y-pant, the drainage, 2 *m.* long, of Llyn-y-Morwynion, 2½ *m.* E. of **Ffestiniog,** joins on left bank. 1 *m.* down Yspytty, Manod, which rises in Llyn Manod, 1 *m.* E. of **Manod,** and is 3 *m.* long, joins on right bank. ½ *m.* down, Yspytty joins Dwyryd. At Tal-y-bont, 1 *m.* W. of **Ffestiniog,** Rhaiadr joins Dwyryd on left bank. Rhaiadr

rises in Llyn Dywarchen, 4 *m.* E. of **Ffestiniog**, and, 2 *m.* down, is joined on right bank by a stream, ½ *m.* long, draining Llyn Dubach, 3 *m.* E. of **Ffestiniog** and ½ *m.* E. of Llyn-y-Morwynion. 2 *m.* down Rhaiadr, a stream, 1 *m.* long, joins on left bank, draining Llyn-craig-y-tan. 2 *m.* S.E. of **Ffestiniog**. Rhaiadr runs 2 *m.* to Dwyryd, passing **Ffestiniog** midway. ½ *m.* down Dwyryd, a stream joins on left bank, 3 *m.* long, running out of Llyn-y-oerfa, 2 *m.* E. of **Maentwrog Road** station. Dwyryd runs 1 *m.* to **Maentwrog** (station, **Tan-y-Bwlch**), and here a stream joins on right bank draining Llynnen Garnedd, 1 *m.* N., and Hafod-y-Llyn, 1 *m.* N.W. from **Maentwrog.** ½ *m.* below **Maentwrog.** Prysor joins on left bank. Prysor rises in Llyn Cors-y-barcut, 5 *m.* S.E. from **Ffestiniog**, and, 1 *m.* down, is joined on right bank by a stream which rises in Llynen Conglog fach and fawr, and, ½ *m.* below these lakes, is joined on right bank by a stream, 1 *m.* long, draining Llyn Dubach. These lakes are 5 *m.* N.E. of **Trawsfynydd.** 2 *m.* down Prysor, a short stream joins Llyn-y-Garn to the main river. This lake is ½ *m.* S. of Llyn Conglog fach. Prysor runs 3 *m.*, when a stream ½ *m.* long, draining Llyn Rhythlyn, 3 *m.* N.E. of **Trawsfynydd,** joins on right bank. ½ *m.* down Prysor, Hafar, 3 *m.* long, rising in Llyn-y-graig-wen, 4 *m.* N.E. of **Trawsfynydd,** joins on right bank. Prysor runs 2 *m.* to **Trawsfynydd,** and, 2 *m.* below, is joined on right bank by a brook 3 *m.* long. Prysor runs 9 *m.*, when a brook 1 *m.* long, draining Llyn Llenyrch, 2 *m.* S. of **Maentwrog,** joins on left bank. Prysor joins Dwyryd 1 *m.* below. Dwyryd runs to **Penrhyndeudraeth** and the estuary in 3 *m.* ½ *m.* to the S. of Dwyryd a stream joins the estuary, which drains Llyn Tecwyn-uchaf, 2 *m.* S.W. of **Maentwrog.**

Penwyllt (Brecon).—N. & B.R. Tawe. Byfre. Haffys. Giaidd (6 *m.*). (*See Swansea.*) Sawdde (7 *m.*). *Lakes*: Fan-fawr (5 *m.*). Fan-fach (7 *m.*); many small trout. (*See Carmarthen.*)

Penybont (Radnor).—L. & N.W.R. Ithon; trout. Arran. Clywedog (1 *m.*); trout. Camllo (1 *m.*). Dulas (2 *m.*). Llandegley brook (2 *m.*). Edw (3 *m.*); good trouting, permission freely given. Crych brook (5 *m.*). *Hotel*: Severn Arms, (*see Advt.*) where fishing in 4 *m.* of Ithon can be had. (*c.s. Wye.*) (*See Chepstow, England.*)

Pen-y-Groes (Carmarthen).—L. & N.W.R. Llyfni; trout. Llyfni rises in Llyn-y-dywarchen, 1 *m.* N.W. of **Rhyddu**, and, 3 *m.* down, runs into the Nanttle Lakes at **Nanttle.** Half-way down the upper lake, a stream joins on right bank, which drains Llyn ffynnonaw 1½ *m.* up. ½ *m.* down the lower lake, a stream joins on left bank, draining Llynian Cwm-silyn 1½ *m.* up. From where Llyfni leaves the lower lake to **Pen-y-Groes** is 2 *m.*, and, 1 *m.* below, Dulyn, which rises in Llyn Cwm-dulyn, 3 *m.* S.E. of **Pen-y-Groes,** and is 3 *m.* long, joins on left bank. Hence to the sea is 3 *m.* (*c.s. Seiont.*)

Pen-y-Gwryd (Carnarvon), n.s. **Llanberis** or **Bettws-y-Coed.**—Gwryd; trout. Gwryd runs to Llyn Mymbyr, near Capel Curig. Glaslyn, 1 *m.* S.; trout, sewin, salmon. (*c.s. Dovey.*) *Lakes*: Llyn-y-Cwm Ffynnon; trout; boats. Tyrn, 1½ *m.* S.W.; trout. Llynian-dywannedd, 2 *m.* S.E.; trout. Llydaw, 2 *m.* S.W.; trout. Glaslyn, 3 *m.* S.W.; trout. Gwynant, 3 *m.* S.; boat. (*c.s. Dovey.*) Edno, 7 *m.* S.; large trout. *Hotel*: Pen-y-Gwryd (*see Advt.*). The proprietor, who is himself an angler, will be pleased to give every information. (*See Portmadoc.*)

Peterston (Glamorgan).—G.W.R. Ely: trout: preserved by Taff and Ely Association; hon. sec., A. Waldron, Esq., Cardiff; s.t. 30*s.*, d.t. 2*s.* 6*d.* (*c.s. Taff.*) (*See Cardiff.*)

Pont (Glamorgan). — G.W.R.: L. & N.W.R. Rhondda; trout, salmon. (*c.s. Taff.*) Rhondda Fychan. (*See Cardiff.*)

Pontardawe (Glamorgan).—G.W.R.; L. & N.W.R. Clydach. (*See Neath.*) Tawe. (*See Swansea.*)

Pontardulais (Glamorgan).—G.W.R. Llwchwr (injured by mines). Dulas; trout. Gwili (1 *m.*) (injured by mines in its lower parts). (*See Llwchwr.*) (*c.s. Towy.*)

Pontdolgoch (Montgomery).—C.R. Garno. Mawr (2½ *m.*). Tarw (4 *m.*). *Lakes*: Du (3 *m.*). Mawr (3 *m.*); good trouting. Tarw (4 *m.*). (*See Gloucester.*) (*c.s. Severn.*)

Pontestiocill (Brecon).—B. & M.R. Taff; trout, salmon. (*c.s.*) (*See Cardiff.*)

Pont Llanio (Cardigan).—Teifi: salmon, trout. (*c.s.*) Carfan. Brenig (2 *m.*) (*see Cardigan*). Aaron, 4 *m.* W. (*c.s.*) Gwrnffrwd, 4 *m.* W. (*see Aberaeron.*) Pysgotwr (6 *m.*). Cothi; trout (6 *m.*) (*c.s. Towy.*) Twrch (6*m.*). (*See Carmarthen.*)

Pontlottyn (Glamorgan).—L. & N.W.R. Rumney; trout, salmon; preserved. (*See Cardiff.*) (*c.s.*)

Pont Newydd (Merioneth).—L. & N.W.R. Wnion; trout, sewin; preserved by landowners. (*See Barmouth.*)

Pont-y-Pant (Carnarvon).—L. & N.W.R. Ledr; trout, salmon, sewin tickets at hotel (*for terms see* **Bettws-y-Coed**). (*c.s. Conway.*) Ystumian, 1 *m.* W.; trout. Conway, 3 *m.* E.; trout, salmon, sewin; tickets at hotel (*for terms see* **Llanrwst**). (*c.s.*) (*See Conway.*)

Pontypridd (Glamorgan).—T.V.R. Taff; salmon, trout. Rhondda; salmon, trout. (*c.s.*) (*See Cardiff.*)

Pool Quay (Montgomery).—C.R. Bete brook. Severn (1 *m.*); chub, dace, trout, salmon. Trewern (1 *m.*). (*See Gloucester.*) (*c.s. Severn.*)

Portmadoc (Carnarvon).—C.R. Glasslyn; trout, sewin, salmon. Glasslyn rises in Llyn Glaslyn. 3 *m.* S.W. of **Pen-y-Gwryd,** runs in ½ *m.* to Llyn Llydaw, 2 *m.* S.W. of **Pen-y-Gwryd,** and, 1 *m.* down, is joined on left bank by a short stream draining Llyn Teyrn, 1½ *m.* S.W. from **Pen-y-Gwryd.** Glasslyn runs 2 *m.* to Llyn Gwynant, 3 *m.* S.

of **Pen-y-Gwryd**, or 4 *m.* N.E. of **Beddgellert**. and, 2 *m.* below (including the lake), is joined on left bank by a stream which rises in Llyn Edno, 7 *m.* S. of **Pen-y-Gwryd**. or 6 *m.* N.E. of **Beddgellert**, and, 1 *m.* below, is joined on left bank by the drainage of Llynian Cwm, four small lakes 1 *m.* up, and 6 *m.* N.E. of **Beddgellert**. Glasslyn is 2 *m.* down. Glasslyn runs 1 *m.* to Llyn-y-Ddinas (trout, salmon) 2 *m.* N.E. from **Beddgellert**, which place it reaches in 3 *m.*, including the lake. Here Colwyn, 4 *m.* long, joins on right bank. Glasslyn runs 4 *m.*, where Nant-y-Mor joins on left bank. This stream rises in Llyn-y-Adar, 5 *m.* E. of **Beddgellert** or 3 *m.* N.W. across the hills from **Tan-y-Grisian**, runs ½ *m.* to Llyn Llagi, and, 2 *m.* down, is joined on left bank by a stream draining Llyn Biswail, ¼ *m.* S.W. of Llyn-y-Adar. Nant-y-Mor runs 1 *m.*, when the outflow of Llyn-y-Arddu, ¼ *m.* up, joins on right bank. There are two other small lakes. Llynian Cerig-y-Mellt lying ½ *m.* N.E. of this lake, the three being within 3 *m.* of **Beddgellert**. Nant-y-Mor runs 2 *m.*, when the outflow of a lake at Hafod-y-Llyn ¼ *m.* up, joins on right bank. This lake is 3 *m.* S. of **Beddgellert**. Glasslyn runs 1 *m.*, when Croesor joins on left bank. Croesor rises in Llyn diffwys, runs 1 *m.* to Llyn Cwm-y-foel, and, 1 *m.* below, is joined on left bank by a stream 1 *m.* long, draining the twin Llyn diffwys. These three lakes are close together, and are 3 *m.* in the hills up the Orthan valley from **Grisian**. 4 *m.* down Croesor, Dulif, 3 *m.* long, joins on right bank. Glasslyn is 1 *m.* below, which runs to **Portmadoc** in 4 *m.* (*c.s. Dovey.*) *Lakes* : Llyn Du, 3 *m.* N. Llyn Cwm Istrallyn, 4 *m.* N. *Fishing stations within reach* : Criccieth, Afon Wen, Pwllheli, Penrhyndeudraeth, Talsarnan, Llanbedr, Dyffryn, Barmouth, Llwyngwril, Towyn, Aberdovey, Glandovey, Machynlleth, Penrhyndeudraeth, Tan-y-bwlch, Tan-y-Grisian, Duffws, Beddgellert. The best flies are the peahen, coch-y-bonddhu, cowdung, hawthorn, black gnat, woodcock, cinnamon, coachman, red spinner, sandfly, and blue dun. Also, body, orange mohair; legs, yellow hackle; wings, red feather from a pheasant's tail, dressed smallish. Body, peacock's tail: legs. black; wings, moorhen, dressed large. Body, claret; legs, black; wings, mallard. Body, orange; legs, partridge hackle. Body, yellow, with gold tip; legs, yellow; wings, mallard. Coch-y-bonddu, wrentail, and spider are good flies. June and July are the best months. At Portmadoc the best fishing is 3 or 4 *m.* above the embankment. A good-sized cinnabar-moth (peacock harl body; wings, parrot and dusky black mixed, dressed buzz), and the common blue butterfly, or a fly with a body blood red, and wings mallard. A dun daddy-longlegs is also a good fly.

Presteign (Radnor).—G.W.R. Lug; trout, grayling. Boulti brook. Hindwell brook (1 *m.*) (*c.s. Wye.*) Lug is preserved by various owners *above*, and by Mr. Evelyn, of Corton, for 6 *m. down* (ten members at 15*l.*; apply to F. L. Evelyn, Esq., Kinsham Presteign), and then by various landowners to **Kingsland**. (*See Chepstow, England.*)

Prysgwaen (Denbigh).—G.W.R. Morlas. Ceiriog, 1 *m.* N. (*c.s. Dee.*) (*See Chester.*)

Pyle (Glamorgan) – G.W.R. Kenfig. Kenfig rises 4 *m.* N. from **Cefn** (B.R.), runs thence to **Pyle** 1 *m.* and sea 4 *m.*

Pwllheli (Carnarvon).—C.R. Erch; trout, sewin. Erch rises 1 *m* above Pont-y-gydros, 5 *m.* N. by road from **Pwllheli**. Here a stream joins on left bank, draining a lake ½ *m.* up. Erch runs 3 *m.* to Pont-y-rhyd-goch, 4 *m.* N. from **Pwllheli**, and, 1 *m.* below, Ceilog, 4 *m.* long, joins on left bank. Erch runs to **Pwllheli** in 5 *m.* Here Western Erch joins on right bank. Western Erch rises 4 *m.* above Llanor, 2 *m.* N.W. of **Pwllheli**, and here it is joined on left bank by a brook 3 *m.* long. W. Erch runs 3 *m.*, when a brook, 4 *m.* long, joins on left bank. running close to the N. of the town A little below, Geirch. 6 *m.* long, joins on right bank. W. Erch joins Erch at **Pwllheli** 1 *m.* down. *Hotel* : Crown. (*c.s. Dwyfach.*) (*See Llangrain; Nevin.*)

Quakers' Yard (Glamorgan).—G.W.R. Taff; salmon, trout (*c.s.*) Bargawd Taff. (*See Cardiff.*)

Resolyen (Glamorgan).—G.W.R. Neath. (*See Neath.*)

Rhayader (Radnor).—C.R. (*c.s.*) Wye: trout, chub, dace, salmon. Elan; trout (1½ *m.*) Marteg; trout (3 *m.*). Claerwen. trout, 6 *m.* Hirin (7 *m.*). *Lakes* : Gwngy, trout; Cerrig Llwydion Isaf, trout (8½ *m.*). Cerrig Llwydion Uchaf, trout (9 *m.*). Llyn Carw, trout (8¼ *m.*) Llyn Gynon trout (11 *m.*). *Hotel* : Lion Royal. 4 *m.* off are the reservoirs of the Birmingham Water Works (Cabancoch, Penygareg, Graiggoch, and Dolymynach), which afford very good fishing. For tickets, apply to John Jones, Esq., Penralley Estate Offices, Rhayader. (*See Chepstow, England.*)

Rhewl (Denbigh).—L. & N.W.R. Clywd; trout, salmon. (*c.s.*) Clywedog. (*See Rhyl.*)

Rhosgoch (Anglesea).—L. & N.W.R. (*See Llanfairynghornwy; Llanfechell.*) *Lakes* : Felin-nant, 1 *m.* W.

Rhyddlan (Flint).—L. & N.W.R. Clwyd; salmon, trout. (*c.s.*) Helyg, 1 *m.* N.W. (*See Rhyl.*)

Rhyddu (Carnarvon).—Gwrfai; trout. (*c.s. Seiont.*) Llyfni; trout; 1 *m.* N.W. (*c.s. Seiont.*) *Lakes* : Llyn-y-Gader. (*See Llanwndla.*) Y-dywarehen, 1 *m.* N.W. (*See Pen-y-groes*)

Rhydowen (Pembroke). — G.W.R. Taf; trout, salmon. (*c.s. Towey.*) Gravil. (*See Laugharne.*)

Rhydymwyn (Flint).—L. & N.W.R. Alyn; trout. (*c s. Dee.*) Fechlas brook. (*See Chester.*)

Rhydyronen (Merioneth).—G.W.R. ; L. & N.W.R. Fefinder. Dysynni, 1 *m.* N.W.; trout, salmon, sewin. (*c.s. Dovey.*) (*See Towyn.*)

Rhyl (Flint).—L. & N.W.R.: G.W.R. Clwyd. Clwyd rises 4 *m.* N.W. of **Derwen**, runs 7 *m.* to that place, and 1 *m.* below is joined on left bank by a brook 2 *m.* long. Clwyd runs to **Nantclwyd** 1 *m.*, and **Byearth** 3 *m.* Here Llanfan brook, 4 *m.* long. joins on right bank. Clwyd runs to **Ruthin** 2 *m.*, **Rhewl** 3 *m.*, **Llanrhaiadr** station 2 *m.*, and 2 *m.* below Clywedog joins on left bank. Clywedog rises above Clocaenog 3 *m.* N.W. of **Nantclwyd**, and 3 *m.* below, 2½ *m.* W. of **Ruthin**, is joined on left bank by Cyffylliog brook. Cyffylliog rises some 3 *m.* above Cyffylliog, and is there joined on right bank by two brooks—Mislyg, 4 *m.* long, and Ladur, 3 *m.* long. Cyffylliog joins Clywedog 2 *m.* down. Clywedog runs to **Rhewl** 3 *m.*, and 3 *m.* below, close by **Llanrhaiadr** station, is joined on left bank by Llewesog, 5 *m.* long. 2 *m.* down, Clywedog joins Clwyd. 1 *m.* down Olwyd, where the high road to **Denbigh** (2 *m.* off on left bank) crosses the river, Lliwen joins on left bank. Lliwen rises 8 *m.* above **Denbigh**, runs 1 *m.* S of that town, and joins Clwyd 2 *m.* below. 3 *m.* down Clwyd, **Bodfari** being 1 *m.* off right bank, Wheeler joins on right bank. Wheeler rises above **Caerwys** station, runs thence to **Bodfari** 3 *m.*, and Clwyd 1 *m.* 3 *m.* down Clwyd, at Pont Llanerch, **Trefnant** station being 1 *m.* off on right bank, Bach. 3 *m.* long, joins on right bank. Clwyd runs to **St. Asaph** 3 *m.* 2 *m.* below, Elwy joins on left bank. Elwy, under the name of Cledwen, rises some 3 *m.* above Gwytherm. 6 *m.* E. from **Llanrwst**, runs thence to Llangerniw, 8 *m.* N.E. from **Llanrwst**, 6 *m.* Here the river takes the name of Elwy, and is joined on left bank by Dyffryn-gallt. This stream rises in Llyn Chwyth Llyn 3 *m.* N.E. of **Llanrwst**, and 3 *m.* down is joined on right bank by Derfyn, 4 *m.* long, which is struck by the road to **Llanrwst** half-way down, 4 *m.* E. of **Llanrwst**. Dyffryn runs 2 *m.* to Llangerniw. 2 *m.* below, Fawnog, which rises in Llyn Fawnog 5 *m.* E. of **Tal-y-Cafn**, and is 3 *m.* long, joins on left bank. Elwy runs 3 *m.*, where it is joined on right bank by Melan. 6 *m.* long. Elwy runs 2 *m.* to **Llanfair Talhaiarn**, and 2 *m.* below is joined on right bank by Aled. Aled rises in Llyn Aled 8 *m.* across country S.E. of **Llanrwst**, or 11 *m.* by road S.W. of **Denbigh**. 1 *m.* down, a stream joins on right bank, draining Llyn Nivel-frech 1 *m.* up. 5 *m.* down Aled, 1 *m.* above Llansannan, 9 *m.* W. of **Denbigh**, Hyrdd, 4 *m.* long, joins on right bank. Aled runs to Llansannan 1 *m.*, and here a stream joins on left bank, draining Llyn Creiniog 1 *m.* S.W. 2 *m.* down Aled, Dennant, 5 *m.* long. and running 2 *m.* E. of Llansannan, joins on right bank. Aled joins Elwy 4 *m.* down. Elwy runs 7 *m.*, where Merchion, which runs by Henllan 3 *m.* S.W. of **Trefnant** and is 4 *m.* long, joins on right bank. Elwy runs 2 *m.* to Pont-yr-allt-goch, 1 *m.* from **Trefnant**, and **St. Asaph** 2 *m.* 2 *m.* below, Elwy joins Clwyd. Clwyd runs to **Rhyddlan** 1 *m.* and 1 *m.* below Helyg joins on right bank. Helyg rises in Llyn Helyg, 5 *m.* E. of **St. Asaph**, or 3 *m.* N. of **Caerwys**, runs to Diserth 5 *m.*, and **Rhyddlan** and Clwyd 3 *m.* 1 *m.* down Clwd, Gele joins on left bank. Gele rises 3 *m.* above **Abergele**, and joins Clwyd 4 *m.* below. Clwyd joins the sea 3 *m.* down at **Rhyl.** Sea fishing poor. *Hotel:* Westminster.

Rhymney (Glamorgan). — L. & N.W.R. Rumney; trout, salmon; preserved. (*See Cardiff.*) (*c.s.*)

Rose Bush (Pembroke).—G.W.R. Martel brook. Syfynfy. (*See Haverfordwest.*) Gwaen (2 *m.*). (*c s. Cleddau.*) (*See Fishguard.*)

Rosemarket (Pembroke).—G.W.R. Rosemarket brook. (*See New Milford.*)

Rossit (Denbigh).—G.W.R. Alyn; trout. (*c.s. Dee.*) (*See Chester, Holt.*) Pulford brook, 1 *m.* N.E.

Ruabon (Denbigh).—G.W.R. Dee, 1 *m.* S.; salmon. trout, chub, pike. (*c.s.*) *Lakes*: Wynnstay Park, ½ *m.* S.E. (*See Chester.*)

Ruthin (Denbigh.)—L. & N.W.R. Clwyd; trout, salmon. (*c.s.*) Clywedog, 2½ *m.* W. Cyffylliog brook, 2¼ *m.* W. (*See Rhyl.*) Alyn, 5 *m.* S.E., at Llanarnon; trout. (*c.s. Dee.*) *Lakes*: Cyffynny, 7 *m.* S.E. (*See Chester.*)

St. Asaph (Flint).—L. & N.W.R. Clwyd; salmon, trout; preserved for some distance. (*r.s.*) Elwy; salmon. trout. (*c.s.*) Helyg, 5 *m.* E. *Lakes*: Junction pond. Helyg, 5 *m.* E. *Hotel*: Plough. (*See Rhyl; Llanfair-Talhaiarn.*)

St. Clear's (Carmarthen).—G.W.R. Taf; trout, salmon. (*c.s. Towey.*) Gynin: trout, sewin. Dewi; trout. Cojer (3 *m.*). Cywyn (3 *m.*). (*See Laugharne.*) *Hotel*: Globe. where fishing can be had.

St. David's (Pembroke).—n.s. **Haverfordwest**, 18 *m.*. Allan (6 *m.* long); trout; fishing free and poor, and sea fishing poor.

St. Fagan's (Glamorgan).—G.W.R. Ely; trout; preserved by Taff and Ely Fishing Association, hon. sec., A. Waldron, Esq., Cardiff; s.t. 30s., d.t. 2s. 6d. (*c.s. Taff.*) (*See Cardiff.*)

St. Ishmael's (Pembroke).—n.s. **Milford**, 5 *m.* 1¼ *m.* E. runs Mullock brook (trout). 6 *m.* long, joining the sea at Dale Road.

St. Harmon (Radnor).—C.R. (*c.s.*) Marteg; trout. Wye; trout (4 *m.*). Dulas (4 *m.*). Ithon; trout (8 *m.*). *Lakes*: Fish pool (4 *m.*) (*See Chepstow, England.*)

St. Mark's (Flint).—L. & N.W.R. Wepre brook, 1 *m.* S.E. This stream is 6 *m.* long.

Saundersfoot (Pembroke).—G.W.R. Carew brook. (*See Carew.*)

Scafell (Montgomery).—C.R. Severn. Hafren. *Lakes*: Fachwen pool (2 *m.*). (*c.s. Severn.*) (*See Gloucester.*)

Selattyn.—Near here is a large lake with plenty of fish. The lake lies to the south of the river Dee, which runs near the village. (*c.s.*)

Snowdon Ranger (Carnarvon).—Gwrfai, 1 *m.* N.W.; trout, salmon. (*c.s. Seiont.*)

Lakes: Cwellyn; trout, char; free to hotel visitors: Llyn-y-dywarchan, 2 *m.* S.W.; private. Glas, 3 *m.* E.; private. Goch, 3 *m.* E.; private. Llyn-y-nadroed, 3 *m.* E.; private. Ffynnon-y-gwas, 3 *m.* E.; private. Llyn-y-gader, 2 *m.* S. free. *Hotel*: Snowdon Ranger. (*See Llanwonda.*)

Solva (Pembroke).—n.s. **Haverfordwest,** 14 *m.*. Solva brook, 9 *m.* long.

Strata Florida (Cardigan).—M. & M.R. Teifi; salmon, trout. Glasffrwd. Rhuest. Marchnant (1 *m.*). Egnant (2 *m.*). Mwyro (2 *m.*). Fflur (2 *m.*). Gwyddyl (3 *m.*). (*c.s. Teifi.*) (*See Cardigan.*) Towy (5 *m.*) (*See Carmarthen.*) (*c.s.*) Clearwen (6 *m.*). Figen (7 *m.*). Brwynog (7 *m.*) (*See Chepstow.*) *Lakes*: Teifi (3 *m.*), trout. Ifer (3 *m.*), trout. Egnant (3 *m.*), trout. Gron (3 *m.*), trout. y-Gorlan (3 *m.*), trout. Crugnant (4 *m.*), trout. (The fishing in the above lakes is sometimes very good: they belong to the Crown and Lord Lisborn.) Gorast (4 *m.*). Fyrddyn-fach (7 *m.*). Du (7 *m.*). Gynon (7 *m.*), trout. Fyrddyn-fawr (7½ *m.*). Figen-felan (8 *m.*).

Swansea (Glamorgan).—G.W.R.; L. & N.W.R. Tawe. Tawe rises 6 *m.* above **Penwyllt,** and 2 *m.* down is joined on right bank by a stream which drains Llyn Fan-fawr (n.s. **Penwyllt,** 5 *m.*). 2 *m.* down Tawe, near **Penwyllt,** Byfre, 4 *m.* long, joins on left bank. ⅓ *m.* down Tawe, Haffys, 3 *m.* long, joins on right bank. 3 *m.* down Tawe, Llech, which rises 3 *m.* N.E. of **Colbren,** runs within 1 *m.* N. of the station, joins Tawe 1 *m.* down. Tawe runs 4 *m.*, and is joined on right bank by Giaidd. Giaidd rises in Cefn rhudd (it can be reached from **Penwyllt** in 6 *m.* by taking the Haffys valley and crossing due W. from the head of the stream), and 6 *m.* down is joined on left bank by Cyw, 3 *m.* long (n.s. **Ystalyfera,** 5 *m.*). 2 *m.* down is Tawe, which runs to **Ystalyfera,** 3 *m.* Here Twrch joins on right bank. Twrch rises 7 *m.* above **Gwys,** and at that place is joined on left bank by Gwyog, 6 *m.* long. Twrch joins Tawe 3 *m.* down. Tawe runs to **Ynys-y-geion** 2 *m.*, **Pontardawe** 3 *m.*, **Glais** 3 *m.* Here Clydach, 4 *m.* long, joins on right bank. Tawe runs to **Morriston** 3 *m.* and **Landore** 2 *m.* Here Ffyndrod, 3 *m.* long, joins on left bank. Tawe runs to **Swansea** and the sea in 3 *m.*

Talgarth (Brecon).—C.R. Llyfni. Enig. Dulais brook. Rhiangoll; trout. Treffrwd (2 *m.*). (*See Chepstow.*) Grwyne; trout (6 *m.*)

Tally Road (Carmarthen).—L. & N.W.R. Towy; salmon, sewin, trout; fishing free. (*c.s.*) Dulas. Taliaris (3 *m.*). *Lakes*: Taliaris (3½ *m.*). (*See Carmarthen.*) Tally lakes (6 *m.*) Cothi (10 *m.*). Gorlech (10 *m.*).

Talsarn (Carnarvon).—Ayron; trout, salmon, sewin. *Hotel*: Vale of Ayron, where fishing can be had.

Talsarnau (Merioneth).—C.R. Caerwych. Caerwych rises in Llyn Caerwych, 3 *m.* E. (good trout) and, 2 *m.* down, is joined on left bank by a stream, 1 *m.* long, draining Llyn-y-Fedw, 3 *m.* S.E. of **Talsarnau.** Caerwych runs to the estuary in 2 *m.* Close to its debouchure a stream joins on right bank, draining Llyn Tecwyn isaf, 2 *m.* N.E. Llyn Dywarehen, 3 *m.* E. Llyn Eiddew fach, 3 *m.* E.; good trout. Llyn Eiddew-mawr, 3 *m.* E.; trout. Llyn Fedw, 3 *m.* E.: trout. Llyn Graigddrwg, 4 *m.* E. (*See Barmouth.*)

Talybont (Brecon).—B. & M.R. Usk; salmon, trout; preserved; salmon and trout rod licences 20s. and 1s., from the railway station. Alwynd. Dyfferyn (3 *m.*). Hogwy (4½ *m.*). (*See Usk, Newport.*) (*c.s.*) *Lakes*: Llyfni (2 *m.*). Llangorse lake (4 *m.*); pike, perch, &c. (*See Chepstow, England.*)

Talycafn (Carnarvon).—L. & N.W.R. Conway; salmon, trout. (*c.s.*) Hiraethlyn, 1 *m.* E. Ro, 2 *m.* S.W., at Llanbedr. Dalyn, 3 *m.* S.W. Porth-lwyd, 4 *m.* S.W. Fawnog, 5 *m.* E. *Lakes*: Siberi, 1 *m.* S. Fawnog, 5 *m.* E. (*See Conway; Rhyl.*)

Talyllin (Corris, R.S.O.) (Merioneth), n.s. **Abergwynolwyn,** 3½ *m.* Dysynni; trout; fishing by season or weekly tickets, to be had at the hotel. *Lakes*: Talyllin; trouting good; boats at hotel. Llyn Cau, 3 *m.* N.; good trouting. Llyn Trigraienyn, 4 *m.* N.E. *Hotel*: Tyn-y-Cornel. (*See Towyn.*) (*c.s. Dovey.*)

Talyllin Junction (Brecon).—Usk (2 *m.*); salmon, trout. Mehascia (2 *m.*) (*See Newport.*) (*c.s.*) *Lakes*: Llyfni. Llangorse (1 *m.*); pike, perch, &c. (*See Chepstow, England.*)

Tan-y-Bwlch (Merioneth).—F.R. (*See Maentwrog.*) *Hotel*: Tan-y-Bwlch.

Tan-y-Grisiau (Merioneth).—F.R. Dwyryd; trout; free. Orthan. Ddu. Bywydd, 1 *m.* E. *Lakes*: Llyn-cwm-orthan, 1 *m.* N.W. Reservoir, 1 *m.* S.W. Cooh, 2 *m.* N.W. Trwstyllon, 2 *m.* S.W. Reservoir, 3 *m.* N. Conglog, 3 *m.* N.W. Clogwyn, 3 *m.* N.W. Y-Adar, 3 *m.* N.W. Llagi, 3½ *m.* N.W. Biswail, 3 *m.* N.W. Llynnian-diffwys, 3 *m.* N.W. Cwm-y-foel, 3 *m.* N.W. (*See Portmadoc, Penrhyndeudraeth.*)

Templeton (Pembroke).).—G.W.R. Carn (1½ *m.*) (*See Loveston.*)

Tenby.—(*See Llandilo.*)

Tenby (Pembroke).—G.W.R. Good sea fishing from the pier; whiting, pollack, bass, codlings. Pollack and bass also near Caldy and the Woodhouse rocks. Splendid mackerel fishing in the season. *Hotel*: Royal Gate House.

Three Cocks Junction (Brecon).—Mid. & Camb. Rys. Llyfni. Wye (1 *m.*) (*c.s.*) *Hotel*: Three Cocks. Wye is preserved, but the landlord can occasionally get leave for his guests. (*See Chepstow, England.*)

Tirphil (Glamorgan).—L. & N.W.R. Rumney; trout, salmon; preserved. (*See Cardiff.*) (*c.s.*)

Tondu (Glamorgan).—G.W.R. Ogmore and Llynvi; trout. (*c.s.*) (*See Bridgend.*)

Torpanlau (Brecon).—B. & M.R. Alwynd. (*See Newport.*)

Towyn (Merioneth).—G.W.R.; L. & N.W.R. Dysynni, 2 *m.* N.; salmon, sewin, trout; d.t. 1s. Dysynni rises in Llyn Cau, on the S. slopes of Cader Idris, 3 *m.* N. from

Talyllyn, and 1 *m.* down, at Minffordd Inn (fair quarters), is joined on left bank by a stream 3 *m.* long rising in Llyn Trigraienyn, 4 *m.* S.E. of **Dolgelly**, and 4 *m.* N.E. of **Talyllyn**. Dysynni runs 1 *m.* to Llyn Talyllyn, 1 *m.* long, at the lower end of which is Tyn-y-Cornel and **Talyllyn**. Dysynni runs 3 *m.* to **Abergwynolwyn**, where Gwynolwyn, 3 *m.* long, joins on left bank. 2 *m.* down Dysynni a brook joins on right bank, 4 *m.* long. Dysynni runs to Pont-y-Garth, 2 *m.*, 2 *m.* N.W. from **Dolgooh**, runs 4 *m.* to Pont-Dysynni, 1 *m.* N.W. of **Rhydyronen**; here Fefindre joins on left bank. Fefindre rises 1 *m.* above **Dolgoch**, runs 2 *m.* to **Brynglas** and Dysynni. 2 *m.* Dysynni runs to **Towyn**, 1 *m.*, and sea, 1 *m.* The river is divided into two fishing estates—the lower or Ynys-y-Maengwyn fishery, the upper or Peniarth fishery. Tickets can be had on Feb. 2 of Mr. D. Jones, 9, College Green, Towyn. (*c.s. Dovey.*)

Trawes Coed (Cardigan).—G.W.R. Wyrai, 3 *m.* S.W. (*c.s. Teifi.*) (*See Llanrhystyd.*)
Trawsfynydd (Merioneth).—G.W.R. Prysor. (*c.s. Dovey.*) Harfar, 2 *m.* E. *Lakes:* Rhythlyn, 3 *m.* N.E. Gelli-gain, 3 *m.* S.E. Y-graig-wen, 4 *m.* N.E. Conglog fach and fawr, 5 *m.* N.E. Dubach, 5 *m.* N.E. Y-Garn, 5 *m.* N.E. (*See Penrhyndeudraeth: Barmouth.*)
Trefeinon (Brecon).—C.R. Llyfni. Cwm brook (1 *m.*) (*See Chepstow, England.*)
Treforest (Glamorgan).—T.V.R. Taff; salmon, trout. (*c.s.*) (*See Cardiff.*)
Trefnant (Denbigh).—L. & N.W.R. Clwyd, 7 *m.* E.; salmon, trout. (*c.s.*) Bach, 1 *m.* E. Elwy, 1 *m.* W.; salmon, trout. (*c.s.*) Merchion, 3 *m.* S.W. (*See Rhyl.*)
Trefriw (Carnarvon).—n.s. **Llanrwst**, 1 *m.* Conway; salmon, sewin, trout; tickets at hotel for the Gwydyr fishery (*for terms see* **Llanrwst**). (*c.s.*) Crafnant; trout. Ddu, 2 *m.* W.; trout. Porth-lwyd, 5 *m.* N.; trout. *Lakes:* Crafnant, 3 *m.* S.W : trout: boats. Geirionydd, 2 *m.* S.W.; now being restocked. *Hotels:* Belle Vue (*See Advt.*) Ship. (*See Conway.*)
Tregaron (Cardigan). — M. & M.R. Teifi; trout, salmon. *Hotel:* Talbot. Teifi is preserved, but the landlord can sometimes obtain leave for the Garth Game Farm waters near Pont Llanio. April, May, and June are the best months. (*c.s.*) Nant-y-Groes. Camddwr (2 *m.*). Fulbrook (2 *m.*). Berwyn (2 *m.*). Docthian (5 *m.*). Aaron, 4 *m.* W. Telwyn, 4 *m.* W. *Lakes:* Maes Llyn (2 *m.*). Berwyn (5 *m.*); good trouting, although the tributaries suffer greatly from netting. Fanod, 6 *m.* N.W. Eiddwen, 7 *m.* N.W. (*See Cardigan, Carmarthen, Aberaeron.*). (*c.s. Teifi.*)
Treherbert (Glamorgan).—T.V.R. Rhondda; trout. (*See Cardiff.*) (*c.s. Taff.*)
Trevor (Denbigh).—G.W.R. Dee; trout, grayling, salmon, chub, pike. (*c.s.*) (*See Chester.*)
Troedyrhiw (Glamorgan).—T.V.R. Taff; salmon, trout. (*c.s.*) (*See Cardiff.*)
Ty-Croes (Anglesea).—(*See Aberffraw.*) Crigyll; trout, sea trout; preserved by the landlord of the hotel. Crigyll rises in a lake by Gwalchmai, 5 *m.* N.E. from **Ty-Croes**. 2 *m.* down, at Llanbeulan, a short stream joins on right bank, draining Llyn Strydan 4 *m.* N.E. of **Ty-Croes**. Crigyll runs 3 *m.* to **Ty-Croes**. 1 *m.* down is Llyn Maelog, which is watered by a stream running through Ty-Croes and out into Crigyll; good trouting early in the season. After leaving the lake, Crigyll runs ½ *m.*, where Caradog, 9 *m.* long, joins on right bank. Just below the junction is the estuary. At Llangefin a lot of salmon run up during the autumn floods. The lake owned by the Valley Hotel contains plenty of perch, eels, and S. fontinalis. On the coast, bass, bream, and pollack can be had, either from the rocks or boats.
Tylwch (Montgomery).—C.R. Tylwch. Dulas (2½ *m.*) (*c.s. Severn.*) (*See Gloucester.*)
Tyn-y-Croes (Merioneth).—n.s. **Dolgelly**, 4 *m.* Mawddach; trout, sewin; d.t. 2*s.* 6*d.*, m.t. 10*s.* 6*d.*, at hotel. (*c.s. Dovey.*) Camlan, ½ *m.*; good trouting. Eden, 1 *m.* N. Gain, 3 *m.* N. Ddu, 4 *m.* N. Wnion, 4 *m.* S. Geirw, 6 *m.* N.E. *Lakes:* Pen-y-ganllwyd, 3 *m.* N. Llyn-y-Frau, 4 *m.* N.W. Llyn-y-bi, 5 *m.* N.W. Ddu, 7 *m.* N.W.; many small trout. Pryvyd, 9 *m.* N.; good trouting. Twrgla, 9 *m.* N. *Hotel:* Tyn-y-groes. (*See Barmouth.*)
Valley Station (Anglesea).—L. & N.W.R. Alaw, 3 *m.* N.E.; trout. Alaw rises 1 *m.* W. of **Llanerchymedd**, runs 9 *m.* to Llantrisaint. Llanfaban 2 *m.*, and 1 *m.* below is joined on left bank by a stream 3 *m.* long, which drains Llyn Llywean 5 *m.* N.E. from **Valley Station**. 1 *m.* down Alaw a stream, 7 *m.* long, joins on right bank. Just below, Alaw meets the estuary. *Lakes:* Treflas, 2 *m.* S.E. Penryn-Ceryg-gwylanod, 3 *m.* S.E. Treffwll, 3 *m.* S.E. (*See Llanfaethlu.*)
Walnutt Tree (Glamorgan).—T.V.R. Taff; salmon, trout. (*c.s.*) (*See Cardiff.*)
Walwyns Castle (Pembroke).—n.s. **Johnston**, 4 *m.* Rickeston brook (trout), which joins Milford Haven 4 *m.* down.
Welshpool (Montgomery).—C.R. Severn; trout, salmon, chub, dace. Sylvan brook. *Lakes:* Maesmawr pond (5 *m.* N.W.). Llyn Du (6 *m.* N.W.) (*See Llanfair, Can-Office, Gloucester.*) (*c.s. Severn.*)
Whitland (Carmarthen).—G.W.R. Taf; trout, salmon. (*c.s. Towy.*) Whitland, fishing free. Lease (1 *m.*). Marlas (1½ *m.*). Feni (3 *m.*, free trouting). Garnas brook (5 *m.*) (*See Laugharne, Cronware.*) *Hotel:* Yelverton Arms.
Wrexham (Denbigh).—G.W.R.; L. & N.W.R. Wrexham brook. Clywedog, 1 *m.* S.E. Dee, 5 *m.* S.E.; salmon, pike, chub. (*c.s.*) *Lakes:* Mawr-y-Mynydd, 7 *m.* W. (*See Chester.*)
Ynys (Carnarvon).—C.R. Dwyfach; trout, sewin, salmon. (*c.s.*) (*See Criccieth.*)
Ynys-y-geinon (Glamorgan).—G.W.R.; L. & N.W.R. Tawe. (*See Swansea.*)
Ystalyfera (Glamorgan).—G.W.R.; L. & N.W.R. Tawe. Twrch. (*See Swansea.*)
Ystrad (Glamorgan).—G.W.R. Cowbridge river or Thaw; trout. (*See Cowbridge.*)

A LIST OF FISHING STATIONS ABROAD.

AFRICA.

Cape Colony.—Good trouting, both as regards size and number, can be had in the Eerste and Lourens rivers. No licence is required; but the consent of the riparian owner, also a certificate of registration obtainable at the office of the resident magistrate of the district, must be sought. In Cape Town there is an association—the Western Province Anglers' Association. Very good sea-fishing in Table Bay. Nearly all the Cape fish take pieces of fish, mackerel being preferred. A very convenient bait for the smaller fish is got in the harbour of Simon's Bay, as well as, in a different form, in many parts of False Bay. It is found by means of three large hooks tied back to back and leaded, which are then gently dragged along the bottom; they soon stick in a lump of the bait, called "red bait," and composed of a number of cells, in appearance like transparent india-rubber, of a light colour, and not difficult to cut; the bait is inside these cells. The snook (*Thrysitis atun*, Cuv. and Val.), which appears in vast multitudes at the commencement of summer, and continues till long into autumn, is something of the shape of the pike, and even more ravenous. They attack anything moving; thus they are easily caught with a piece of prepared shark skin, cut in eight or nine strips four inches long and one-eighth of an inch broad. At one end they are tied and wound on a thin piece of lead, having a small hole for the brass wire which is attached to the hook to pass through. The strips of skin, when in their place, fall over the hook, which is generally made of brass, the shank being quite straight, about three inches long, and the bend of the same shape as a common scythe, the barb also being filed off. On the head of the shark-skin arrangement a lead rests, the brass wires also passing through it. This lead is of the shape of a sugar loaf and about three inches long by one in diameter at the thickest part, tapering to half that thickness. The best fishing at the Cape is fishing with a twenty-feet long salmon rod, from the rocks at Kalk Bay, the fashionable watering-place of Cape Town. The fish caught are red and white steenbrass up to 45lb., kabel-jauws up to 35lb., and sharks. The best time for this fishing is from September to March—in fact, during the snook season.

Diamond Fields.—The Vaal and Modder Rivers afford excellent sport. Principal fish, the "*barba*," a kind of silurus, which attains an immense size, and the yellow fish, which also runs large. The barba feeds principally by night, but may occasionally be caught by day, fishing on the bottom, and baiting with small fish. The yellow fish will take both worms and paste freely, fly occasionally, and is a game fish; the larger ones would probably take an artificial minnow. Both the barba and yellow fish are good eating, though the latter is rather bony. Tackle should be taken out from England, including strong gimp for the barba, and plenty of sound gut for the yellow fish.

Mogador.—Here and at the other ports along the coasts there is good sea-fishing when the surf permits. The numerous rivers of Morocco mostly contain the shebbel, or Barbary salmon, and also many tortoises, which the angler will find troublesome.

Natal.—There is very good sport to be obtained in the large Natal rivers, such as the Umgeni and Umkomanzi. Both these take their rise in the great Drakensberg Range, and after a course of between 150 and 200 miles debouch into the Indian Ocean; the former above, the latter below Durban. The Umgeni is a slow river compared to the Umkomanzi; good fishing both above and below the Falls. The Umkomanzi (Upper) is a fine rapid stream, with here and there long level reaches; a sandy and pebbly bottom (no mud). The fish consist of chiefly one or two sorts of barbel, roach, perch, and others. The fishing season is from September to the middle of April, during the summer or rainy season; the best time from early morning to 11 a.m., and again before sundown. After a good freshet, when the water is slightly discoloured, fish bite freely. Use ground bait, strong line with gimp hook. The rod must be strong, as the banks in many places are high and precipitous, affording no place to play and land a fish; so you must lift them out at once. Be careful not to fish too deep, because of the rocky bottom. The fish will not rise to flies. The mouths of small streams and gluits debouching into the Umkomanzi, are favourite fishing spots. The Incwardini, a small and very winding river, flowing into the Umkomanzi, about thirty-six miles above Pietermaritzburg, has small but very sweet fish, averaging from ⅓lb. to ½lb. Fishing can be got here when they will not bite in the larger rivers; fishing can also be got close to town in the Umsumduse. Houses there are none in this part, but any settler will be only too glad to entertain yourself and horse for the night.

Transvaal.—The Transvaal Trout Acclimatisation Society have made further distributions of trout fry, 500 *Salmo irideus*, in a large spring-fed dam at Roodepoort, near Klip River Station, by permission of Mr. Cullinan, and also 500 rainbows. in a dam on the Geldenhuys estate, near Sans Souci, Johannesburg. The Umgeni, in Natal, is fishing well, trout averaging 1lb. apiece; coachman a good fly. Dry fly fishing for yellow fish gives good sport. The Umsoli, a tributary of the Komati, about 20 *m.* from Barberton, and a little less from Steynsdorp Fish during the summer months, when the rains begin and the fish run up; a good fly is the silver sedge.

AMERICA.

General Information.—The flies should not be too large, and the gaudy Irish are best Red and orange and green bodies are the most killing, both with trout and salmon. These are good: a blood-red body, ditto hackle, white wing, and gold twist; this, in different sizes, kills salmon, white trout, and brown trout. The other is, for salmon, a bright green body, ribbed with gold, dun hackle, teal and golden pheasant topping mixed for wing. The same fly answers for trout, taking off the wing, and leaving it a palmer. Of trolling tackle take some of extra large size. The best time to fish for salmon in the Canadian rivers is June—Halifax and Nova Scotia being somewhat earlier. The fishing in Halifax, Nova Scotia, and Prince Edward's Island is remarkably good; the Gold River is one of the best. The Ristigouche, at the head of the Bay of Chaleurs, is also good. In the country about the head waters of the St. John's River trout run large. The best fishing is in the St. Anne's. The trout run larger in it than in any other stream in Canada. There is an Indian village named Bawdon, about forty miles north of Montreal. The Indians will conduct you to a series of lakes full of brown trout, and the large *Salmo ferox*. At Platsburg (the Saranac river there empties itself into the Champlain Lake) ascend the Saranac some thirty miles, or go back about forty miles from the Champlain, to a lake called Chateaugay, you will find a district of from fifty to sixty square miles, reaching down to Lake George; it is full of rivers and lakes. Independent of the lakes there is admirable trolling in the St. Lawrence, from Montreal to Lake Ontario, especially about the Thousand Islands, for bass, pike, and muskelunge, and also in the great lakes, where the latter fish run to an enormous size. The bass at times takes a red or yellow fly readily. The best bass fishing is about the Thousand Islands. St. Paul's or Bradore, on the Esquimaux river, is a good locality.

There is ready access from Montreal to the Memphramagog Lake, which contains plenty of the large lake trout. The river that runs out of this lake is admirable about the middle of June. The fishing in Florida is good, but there is little variety The black bass is the best, and will take a fly well, they run to 15lb. and 20lb. The devil fish is found in nearly all the bays of the Gulf of Mexico. There is good sport spearing them from a canoe. The flies best suited to the Godabout and most of the small rapid rivers to the north of the Gulf of St. Lawrence are plain, but largish brown, black, and grey hackles. There is fair trout fishing in Maine.

Salmon are plentiful in the rivers in the North of California, and the sea-fishing good. Through Idaho Territory flows Salmon River, containing a great abundance of salmon, which may be fished to advantage near a small mining town called Florence. Plenty of trout and red fish may also be caught. There is capital fishing in the Adirondacks. Lake Pleasant, Cedar lakes, Morse lake, are amongst the best, but there are great numbers. At Lake Pleasant is an hotel; the landlord will supply guides and all necessaries.

The islands along the coast of the United States, such as West Island, Cuttyhunk, and the large group of the Elizabeth Islands, chief among which is Pasque Island, a few miles from New Bedford (eastward and joining Martha's Vineyard), have club-houses on them, and afford the finest salt-water angling. The principal game fishes are the striped bass, weakfish, and bluefish, besides porgies, tautog, sea bass, flukes, and flounders.

A set of clothing for winter and summer is necessary. For the latter, stout twilled unbleached linen is good; for the former, velveteens and corduroys are good, not forgetting waterproof and a good pilot coat for boat work. In camping out, all unnecessary incumbrances should be avoided; and, in packing, it is as well to class things under different heads, such as "Daily wanted," "Occasionally wanted," "Necessary, but seldom wanted." These should occupy different boxes. Hammocks are indispensable; rugs are better than blankets. All the cooking utensils should have long handles.

An expedition to the wilds is expensive. If alone you require two Indians. It is almost impossible for two men to fish from the same canoe. It is necessary to take tea, rice, bacon, biscuits, and flour. In engaging Indians go to the village and call on the chief make him a little present, and tell him what men you want, and promise to give him another present if they behave well. Trouting is free generally, salmon fishing mostly taken up.

CANADA.

General Information.—The Saguenay River contains plenty of salmon and sea trout. The salmon ascend the Ste. Marguerite, the Little Saguenay (or Beaver), the St. John, and they remain some time just above tide water, and rise well. The sea trout do not enter the smaller rivers until late in the autumn, with the exception of the Ste. Marguerite. The sea trout take the scarlet ibis and red palmer well. It is said the Saguenay is more free of "fly" than any other stream in Canada. In proceeding from the Saguenay along the northern shore we pass the Escoumins, Portneuf, Betsiamites, Outardes, Manacouagan, Goodabout, Truty, St. Margaret, Moisie, Mingan, and Esquimaux, all containing salmon. There are a very few streams in Upper Canada where fly-fishing is to be had, owing to the drift wood. Lower Canada is far better. The lakes near Quebec and the rivers in the eastern townships afford good trouting. The fishing is best early in spring and late in autumn, unless you are impervious to black flies. The best place for taking muskelunge is the river Severn, which flows into the Georgian Bay, and in one or two small lakes in the Indian territory to the east of the river. They take the spoon well. There are fair quarters at the village of Orelia on the Severn at a place called Welshpool or Sparrow Lake. There is good black bass fishing here, the muskelunge ground being about five miles lower down the river. There are many trout at Sault St. Marie. Ordinary Scotch flies kill well; "Jock Scott," silver doctor, dusty miller, and the butcher are good. Local flies are plain ones, tied with dark turkey or mallard wings, with a bit of blue in the shoulders; bodies and hackle varied according to size and colour of the water. Grey, black, and claret all kill in turn. Generally speaking, there is no free fishing in Canada. The fisheries are held by the lessees of the Crown or the riparian owners. Rivers are often to be rented, or rods to let for a time. The principal rivers on the south side of the Gulf of St Lawrence are the York, Cascapedias (2), Metapedias, Restigouche, Miramichi, Nepisiguit; on the north side, Marguerite (rented), Godabout, Moysie, Romaine, Natysquan, and Mingan. Those on the south side are most accessible. To reach the north rivers arrangements must be made to hire from Gaspe or Rimounski. In the Jupiter river Anticosti Island is excellent salmon fishing. For all the rivers two canoemen for each rod, and a cook for the whole party, are necessary. Good men are obtainable at most of the stations, and by many, Indians are preferred. Tents are necessary. Pork, molasses, tea, and flour are essentials. Preserved soups and vegetables are very portable. All pots and pans should have long handles; and don't forget an axe and an auger. The Government overseers are very civil and obliging, and are ever willing to afford the stranger every possible information. The first fish that ascend the Miramichi in the spring are the gaspereaux, or alewives; they come up in immense shoals about the middle of May, poking along close to the banks. After depositing their spawn these fish return to the sea in the month of June. Immediately after the gaspereaux the sea trout run. Salmon commence to come into the river about June 1, and continue till August. July is the best month for fly-fishing. Small-sized flies kill best on all the New Brunswick waters. The following are good:—1. One turn gold tinsel; one ditto orange floss silk; tail, golden pheasant top; body, very dark claret pig's wool, ribbed with gold tinsel; hackle, two small bright claret hackles; wing, dark brown mallard or turkey, mixed with a little wood duck, and two sprigs blue and red macaw; head, black ostrich. 2. One turn silver tinsel; two ditto black ostrich; tail, mixed wood duck, mallard, and flamingo; body, light grey pig's wool, ribbed with silver tinsel; hackle, two dark grey mottled cock's hackles; shoulder, one turn bright red hackle; wing, mixed wood duck, mallard, and guinea fowl, with two sprigs blue and red macaw; head, ostrich.

Some sixty miles from Fredericton the road crosses from the right to the left bank of the S.W. Miramichi. The main river here is too wide and sluggish; but further on the road crosses two tributaries, the Renous and Dungarvon—capital salmon streams. A few miles above the town of Newcastle the road crosses the north-west branch of the Miramichi, a large and deep river, rich in fish. Shad, too, are abundant; also trout. Further on is the town of Chatham. Twenty miles beyond Chatham is a wayside inn, situate on a noted trout stream. The best pools are eight or ten miles down stream. There is no road, and not water enough to float a canoe. Flies cannot stand the full blaze of the sun, neither do they like a breeze of wind; therefore, the more open and exposed the situation, the better for a fisherman's camp. A veil fastened round the crown of a broad-brimmed hat, and round the neck, with elastic bands, and kept clear of the face by means of hoops like a crinoline, is an assistance. Of unguents several are used, the cleanest being the least effective, the dirtiest the most so. Mixtures of penny-royal and almond oil, and of oil of tar and turpentine in equal parts, are of some use; but creosote mixed with grease is the best. Carbolised oil is also good. It is a rare occurrence to raise a salmon in the Tabucintac, but the trout fishing is as near perfection as possible. Another twenty-mile stage, and you reach the Nepisiguit. At its mouth is the little town of Bathurst; remain at the hotel kept by a Mr. Welberg. The Nepisiguit is probably one of the most accessible rivers in North America. Twenty miles from the sea salmon are stopped in their ascent by the falls. The angling of the whole river is divided into four sections. The lower section of the Nepisiguit extends some six or eight miles from the mouth, and includes the "rough waters"—a series of beautiful ledgy pools. In the early part of the season—viz., the last of June and first of July—this section is the best on the river. Next comes the

"Pabineau." This section comprises the Pabineau Falls. The next section is the "Chain of Rocks;" this is very good at a certain pitch of water, and generally near the end of the season. The Grand Falls is a lovely spot. There is some cramped casting on the river; but no long casts to speak of. The extreme clearness of the water necessitates fine tackle and small flies, particularly at the falls. The Frenchmen on the river are capital fellows. Their tariff is a dollar and a quarter a day, and they furnish their own canoes. The best part of the Nepisiguit is now in private hands. July is the best month for the Nepisiguit; the flies should be small and dark. The following fly is killing: Body, black mohair, ribbed with fine gold twist, black hackle, very dark mallard wing, a narrow tip of orange silk, small golden pheasant's crest for tail. A rich claret body, with dark mixed wing and tail, claret hackle, and a few fibres of jay at the shoulder, is also good. Small grey-bodied flies ribbed with silver, grey legs, and a mixed wing of wood-duck and golden pheasant, kills well. A good grilse fly is of a primrose body with black head, and tip and wing of golden pheasant tippet. These flies kill anywhere in New Brunswick. Two little rivers run into Bathurst Bay and are both on the fence list. One of them, the Tête-à-gouche is dammed two miles from the mouth; but a ladder has been constructed. When there is enough water, it sometimes affords good sport. From Bathurst northwards to Restigouche, the Intercolonial Railway follows the shore of the Bay of Chaleurs, crossing numbers of little rivers of more or less interest to the trout-fisher, but only two salmon streams, Jacquet and Charlo. Both have been shamefully over-fished. Sixty miles from Bathurst, we come to the head of the Bay of Chaleurs, to the little town of Dalhousie. As we run up on the New Brunswick side of the Restigouche we see opposite to us the mouth of Escuminac, where there is capital sea-trout fishing, and a few miles farther on reach Cambelton, where the real river commences. For twenty miles above Cambelton the main stream is rather large to be fished comfortably. The first good pool is at the mouth of Upsalguitch, and for thirty or forty miles above that again there is plenty of nice fishing water, about the best of which is at the mouth of Patapediac. In choosing men to accompany them anglers cannot do better than select noted spearers; these men are necessarily splendid canoers, and well acquainted with the haunts of the fish. Both lumbermen and Indians can always be hired with their canoes for one dollar per diem, or rather less if engaged by the month. Prefer the latter; they talk less and do more. The Upsalguitch, a tributary of the Restigouche, is itself a large river, and full of likely pools. The fish are smaller than in the main river or any of the other tributaries, but take the fly freely. It is at present rented by an American gentlemen. At the head of this stream a portage of two miles enables the voyager to put his canoe on the Nepisiguit, from whence he can either go down that river to the sea, or by another short portage go on to Tobique river, and from thence to St. John. So also at the head of the main Restigouche there is another short portage to the St. John. The water of the Restigouche being very clear, and the casting heavy, the fisherman must combine a powerful rod with tolerably fine tackle. The flies are a trifle larger than those used on Nepisiguit* and Miramichi. The angling privileges of the following salmon rivers are in the hands of the Department of Marine and Fisheries, Ottawa. Written offers should be addressed to the Commissioner of Fisheries, who will doubtless be good enough to give any information that may be required. North Shore—Kegashka, Watsheeshoo, Washeecootai, Romaine, Musquarro, Pashasheeboo, Corneille, Agwanus, Magpie, Trout, St. Marguerite, Pentecost, Mistassini, Becscie; Baie des Chaleurs—Little Cascapedia, Nouvelle, Escumenac; Malhaie (near Perce); South Shore—Magdalen, Montlouis; New Brunswick—Tobique, Nashwaak, Jacquet, Charlo; Anticosti Island—Jupiter, Salmon. Rent per annum, which is payable in advance, should be stated. Leases run for from one to five years. Lessees must employ guardians at private cost.

Bathurst.—Inter-Colonial Railway. On Nepisiguit. Salmon. There are twenty miles of salmon water, divided into several sections. The lowest near Bathurst is Rough Waters. The fishing is all taken up, but fishing can often be leased on application to the Bathurst Fishing Club.

Bytown.—Hire a canoe and fish in the Rideau Canal. There is admirable trolling for pike and muskelunge.

Halifax.—The Sackville river flows into the head of the basin. It is a fine salmon and trout stream. About fifteen miles away are some beautiful lakes. You can easily arrange to lodge at a farmhouse in the neighbourhood. The trout-fishing is first-rate. There is salmon fishing in the neighbourhood. Sea fishing very good.

Lennoxville.—Some 95 miles from Montreal on the Grand Trunk line. There is good trouting in the Massawippi and St. Francis rivers, which join here.

Metapediac (New Brunswick).—Inter-Colonial Railway. On Metapediac. Salmon, trout. There is a good hotel here, where capital sport can be had for a dollar a day. The Metapediac has a course of sixty miles from a large lake in Rimouski, Lower Canada. About thirty miles from the head of Chaleurs Bay is the Cascapedia, a large

---

* This is a good change: 1 turn silver tinsel, 1 ditto orange floss silk, 2 ditto black ostrich; tail 1 golden topping; body, black floss silk ribbed with silver tinsel; hackle, two bright orange cock's hackles, with two turns black at shoulder; wing, wild gobbler with a little wood duck and Argus pheasant mixed, and two or three sprigs orange macaw; head black ostrich.

stream holding very large fish. The whole district of Gaspé is intersected by streams full of salmon and sea trout; amongst the largest are the Bonaventure, the Malbaie, and the Magdalene.

Mill Village (Nova Scotia).—There is a good hotel here, and fair free fishing also at Greenfield, where lodgings can be had at a farm. A guide is necessary.

Quebec.—Near here is the Jacques-Cartier, a fair river. when in condition; the salmon run large. A good plan is to take a boat down the St. Lawrence, fishing the rivers that run into it. The first river is the Malbay; the fishing is nothing particular. The next stream is the Saguenay. It is remarkable for its depth. Good sport is to be had in all the tributaries of this stream. The Esconmagh is a most excellent river for salmon and white trout. White trout fishing in Canada is confined to the mouths of the streams in the ebb and flow of the tide. The best fishing is about five miles up, in a large pool under a fall. The Port Neuf is the next river. It is a good-looking stream, but not worth much. There is a good pool about a mile up the river. About thirty miles farther down are the Bustard and Mainscougan rivers. The fishing is very good. In all the lakes in the neighbourhood large ferox can be taken trolling.

Red Rock (Ontario).—C.P.R. Lake Superior and river Nipigon. This river connects Lake Nipigon with Superior, and is 45 m. long. There is a Hudson's Bay Post on the N. end of Lake Nipigon. The fishing is considered the best in Canada. Permits for the season free to British subjects, and 21s. to foreigners. Use large flies.

Sherbrooke.—On the Grand Trunk line. Some sixteen miles off lies Memphremagog Lake. Trout and muskelunge. There are good hotels on various points, and the lake steamer runs constantly. The upper end of the lake is best.

CENTRAL AMERICA.

General Information.—All along the coast of Nicaragua and Mosquito territory there is an abundance of the sea fish common to the West Indies and the tropical waters of the Atlantic. The various turtles are taken in great quantities, especially on the small bays in the neighbourhood. In the shallow water which breaks over the dangerous sand-bar at the entrance of Greytown harbour are swarms of sharks. Within the lagoon are plenty of the American crocodile (*Molinia Americana*). All along the St. Juan River, and in the large freshwater lakes of Nicaragua and Managua, there is found a small species of freshwater turtle, of which both flesh and eggs are eaten. The most notable, however, is the manatee (*Manatus Australis*), which, when dried and salted, is a standard article of food among the Indians. In the great lakes is also found a large freshwater shark, said to be as dangerous and voracious as its salt-water cousin. Amongst the freshwater fish the best, both in lake and river, are the guapote, mojarro, and savallo. They are all good eating, grow to a good size, and take a fly or bait with readiness.

MEXICO.

General Information.—Capital trout fishing. Devon flies take well; and a light 10ft. rod and fine casts are all that one requires. The Mexican railway companies issue round return trip tickets from Mexico City at a cheap rate. *Hotel:* Maelos. Very good tarpon fishing at Tampico. The season commences about December 25, and lasts until the end of April. Hotel accommodation is only moderate. The British Vice-Consul would afford information.

NEWFOUNDLAND.

General Information.—The salmon fishing is very poor; sea-trout fishing *very good* when the fish are running. It is no use for sea trout before the end of July. The salmon take the fly very badly. On the west side of Hall's Bay debouches Indian Brook, a capital salmon and sea trout stream. Sea fishing in abundance, often quite inshore.

Trinity.—Some 60 m. from St. John's. There is good trouting here, fish running large.

UNITED STATES.

General Information.—The sea fishing is very good and varied along both Atlantic and Pacific coasts. At Eagle Lake, Texas, there is capital black bass, perch, and catfish fishing. The lake is within 1 m. of the railway station, and boats can be hired.

Florida.—In the South, Lake Kissimmee; headquarters at Kissimmee. Several small lakes in the central part in the Apopka, Oakland, and Wekiva neighbourhood, fished from Orlando: in the N.W., Griffin Lake, Lady Lake, Lake Eustace, and Orange Lake. Black bass, pike, and perch are of excellent quality. There are four good methods of fishing for the black bass—skittering or bobbing, still-fishing, trolling, and casting. Skittering is the most deadly if the fish are on the feed, but there must be a good ripple on the water. 14ft. rod, 2½ yards of strong coarse line, and a spoon bait, with one largish hook, to the shank of which attach a piece of deer's-tail two to four inches long. provide the necessary tackle

Gallatin (Montana).—Northern Pacific Railway. Capital accommodation at Missouri Forks Hotel. Fishing is excellent, so is the trouting.

Monterey (California).—S.P.R. 140 m. from Frisco. Vast quantities of salmon can be taken in the sea with a spoon or other trolling bait.

St. Paul's (Minnesota).—Near here is Lake Minnetonka. Here is Lake Park Hotel, very comfortable, where boats and fishermen can be had. Fishing very good; no trout, but plenty of bass, pike, muskelonge.

WEST INDIES.

Bermuda.—The lagoons and inside the coral reefs are alive with strange fish, from the shark down to the beautifully tinted sergeant-major.

ASIA.

ASIA MINOR.

Sabanga.—There is a large lake here full of pike, siluris, &c. The accommodation is bad.

INDIA.

General Information.—There is excellent mahseer fishing in the Punjáb, in the North-west Provinces and in Central India, in all rivers running through hilly or mountainous country. As a rule, all rivers rising in the Himalayas hold mahseer, as well as the rivers rising in the elevated plateau of Central India: but these rivers are only fishable as long as their course is through hilly and rocky country. It is little use fishing in the plains. Fishermen are recommended to take with them two greenheart salmon rods, spliced (Castle Connell rods are the best), as in hot climates the ferrules of brazed rods are apt to become loose and to fall off, with reels holding from 150 to 200 yards plaited hemp or silk line; a 12ft. or 14ft. trout rod, reel, and line; several hanks of good fresh salmon gut (avoid gimp); a stock of gaudy salmon flies, not too large (about No. 5 Limerick); a large stock of golden spoons, gilt on both sides; phantoms, &c.; swivels, treble gut, spinning traces, triangles, split rings, &c.; and a good big gaff (not forgetting cobbler's wax).

Assam, Upper.—Some capital mahseer fishing can be obtained in this district, especially in the neighbourhood of Debong.

Burmah.—A fly and trolling rod would be the best to take. As for tackle, take a few bright-coloured flies. Some bottom fishing may be had on the lake at Rangoon, for which a boat is necessary. Up the river to Thayetmyo very large cat-fish may be taken; they are very strong and give tolerable sport, but are filthy fish in their feeding. Any large coarse bait will take them. There is fly-fishing on the river that leads to Tonghoo, and fish have been taken at a place called Shaygeno; this stream, unlike the muddy Irrawaddy, is clear in parts. Take plenty of gut of different strengths, a few bright spinning baits, plenty of hooks of all sizes, casting lines of course, and some small bright trout flies. Cobbler's wax, too, is unknown in these parts, and should be carried in a tin box, because of the heat.

Hurdwar.—On the Ganges, where it leaves the Dhoon, good fishing up as far as Bikkikate, about 20 miles from where the Ganges leaves the Himalayas, where the best fishing is to be had. Fish run very large. There is a species of pike or fresh-water shark, and sometimes a mahseer, to be killed in the Ganges and Jumna canals.

Jhelum.—In the north the Jhelum affords splendid mahseer fishing at Tangrote (about 25 miles above the town of Jhelum, which is reached by rail), where it is joined by the Poonch river. There is a good bungalow at Tangrote for the accommodation of travellers, and supplies are plentiful. It is best to fish from a boat, several of which, with boatmen who understand their work, can be hired on the spot. The most deadly bait is a large golden spoon, fishing very deep. One should use very strong tackle, as the fish run very large (up to 50lb.), and are very game. An 18ft. salmon rod, with 200 yards of line and the strongest and newest treble gut spinning tackle, are recommended. Best months—March and April, September and October.

Madras.—In the moat round Fort St George, there are some large fish, which take a salmon fly well. Use treble gut, as they will bite through single.

Nowgong Cantonment (Bundelcund), reached by road from Cawnpore or Futtehpore on the E.I. Railway There is very good mahseer fishing in the Dessaun, 5 miles from Nowgong. In October and early in November, also in March, April, and May. A kind of rout rises well to the fly. The mahseer in this river do not rise so readily to a fly or minnow as to a small pellet of paste about the size of a pea, thrown like a fly in the rough water. A very small triangle should be used instead of a single hook, as the paste is not so easily flipped off in throwing, and a triangle will hold a lively fish better than a small single hook. The Betwa near **Jhansi**, the Kane above **Banda**, and the Sone in Rewah, are all first-class rivers for mahseer, with the chance of a shot at a crocodile or tiger. The large artificial lakes of Bundelcund—whose swampy margins are frequented by thousands of snipe in the winter months—are well stocked with coarse fish, roho (a species of carp) running up to 30lb. or 40lb., and a kind of pike also growing to a great size. Roho take a small pellet of paste (the water having previously been baited) on a small hook with fine tackle, and the pike are killed with frogs or live bait. Fishing with a cast of small trout flies of an evening, one may kill great numbers of small fish, not unlike sprats, called "chilwa."

Nowshera.—By rail to Goojerat. Drive 20 miles to Bhimber, then two marches (about 25 miles) on the Cashmere road to Nowshera, on the Tawi river, where there is a travellers' rest-house. There is good mahseer fishing for about 25 miles up the Tawi to **Rajaori**, and for some distance down, as far as its junction with the Chenáb. There are rest-houses at **Chungus** (about 12 miles) and Rajaori, and supplies are plentiful. Best months—March, April, and May, August, September, and October. This is not a snow river, and the best fishing is to be had in August and September between the showers. Three marches will take one from Nowshera to Chowmook or to Kotli on the Punch.

Punch.—From Tangrote one may have splendid sport for about 50 miles up the Punch river as far as the city of Punch. There are travellers' rest-houses at about every 10 or 12 miles, and supplies are plentiful; but, as the road does not always follow the river, it is advisable to take tents. There are rest-houses for travellers at Chowmook, Kotli, and Sairee, all close to the river, and there is a good bungalow at Punch. Starting from Tangrote in March or April, one can fish up the Punch river till the beginning of June, the large fish running up as the season advances. Fish deep in rough water, and keep out of sight, as the water is remarkably bright, except when snow-broth is coming down, and the fish wary. After fishing up to Punch one can cross over into Cashmere, distant five or six marches, where good fishing can be had in the Jehlam. Some heavy mahseer are to be killed at **Sopur**, spinning a natural bait, and fishing deep just below the bridge. Higher up the river, above where it runs into the Walloor Lake, some fine fish (something like trout, or at least spotted like them), up to 8lb. or 10lb., can be killed spinning a small artificial minnow or phantom from a boat. One should let out a lot of line and get the boatman to paddle slowly up stream. June is the best month; but, as mosquitos are troublesome at night, muslin mosquito curtains should be taken. Some nice mahseer are to be killed in the **Sind** river just above its junction with the Jehlam at **Shadipoor**. All up the Jehlam as far as Islamabad numbers of small so-called trout can be killed with a mulberry, and occasionally a good one with a minnow, especially between the bridges at **Srinagar**. At **Islamabad** some capital fishing may be had, the so-called trout rising readily to a trout fly or to a mulberry, or to a small pellet of paste used as a fly. At the end of August or beginning of September one should commence to fish down from Punch, finishing up at Tangrote in October. There is heavy rain in August and September, and the best fishing is to be had after a spate. There is no snow-broth at this season. To fish the Punch and tributaries use an 18ft. salmon rod and 150 yards of line; gaudy salmon flies (about No. 5 Limerick) and golden spoons. The fish run large, and are very game, especially those of from 10lb. to 20lb. Fish up to about 15lb. take a salmon fly readily, but the most deadly bait for the large fish is a golden spoon gilt on both sides. Use treble gut for spinning, but single gut for fly fishing.

Rajaori.—On the Towhi. There are plenty of mahseer here, but they run small.

Ropur.—On the Sutlej. At the foot of the hills good mahseer fishing, the fish running very large.

Sialkote.—In November there is good fishing to be had in the Chenáb where it is joined by the Tawi about 15 miles above the cantonment of Sialkote which is reached by rail to Wazeerabad, and thence by stage carriage.

Solun.—On the high road from Kalka to Simla there is good mahseer fishing in the Giri river, a tributary of the Jumna, near Solun.

Tangrote.—First rate mahseer fishing, the fish running very large. (*See Thelum.*)

CEYLON.

General Information.—Experiments in trout acclimatisation began in the eighties, but were temporarily abandoned. In 1890 and 1891 trout were imported, and on their proving successful a fishing club was formed which has annually imported ova ever since. Fish are plentiful in three or four rivers and several lakes. Recently rainbow trout have been introduced, and breed naturally. Tickets for the week, month, or season are issued, and can be obtained of G. M. Fowler, Esq., Government Agent W.P., Ceylon.

JAPAN.

General Information.—The streams of the interior contain a trout-like fish, which the Japanese, who are expert anglers, catch with native-made flies; but it is impossible to get leave. Around the coast, however, there is plenty of good salt-water fishing obtainable at any time. Bonita and albacore afford capital sport, and a large mackerel-shaped fish about six feet in length, takes live bait readily, and is strong enough to pull an unwary hand out of the boat. The best tackle to take will be large and small spoons, rigged with strong swivels and gimp nozzling, and an assortment of sea-hooks. Lines of native manufacture fully equal if they are not superior to any that are made at home, can be procured in the Japanese shops.

MAURITIUS.

General Information.—All round the island rivers flow to the sea from the elevated interior, which is very rainy. In these rivers there are large eels, and a fish called a carp by the Mauritians. There is also in the Grand River and Black River a freshwater mullet, called a "sheet." Both the carp and the sheet take a fly. A more deadly way of catching them is with a large live grasshopper, and in this way fish of 2lb. and 3lb. are caught. Large-sized gaudy flies are the most killing. Into many tanks and ponds in the island have been introduced from China the gourami, a game fish. They grow up to 20lb., and are usually caught with wasp grubs. The carp, so called by the Mauritians, is a grey perch. It is a very game fish, fond of the most rapid eddies, and rises boldly to a fly. Carp are never caught above any of the falls unless there are side channels at an easy gradient, as for instance on Grande Rivière, Nord-ouest, at the falls from the reservoir, and those below Beau Basin. At Grande Rivière, Sud-est, a fall occurs within a half-a-mile of the mouth of the river; no carp can be caught on the river above that; while below—the river so far is tidal, and must be fished from a boat, the banks being precipitous—are a great number of carp, particularly under the falls, and at the foot of the projecting cliff, in which is the cave with the statue of Notre Dame de la Misericorde at the entrance. Carp are caught with a live prawn among the breakers on the bar at the mouth of the Rivière des Aiguilles, and not ten yards inside, in the short space of tidal water, are caught with a fly. With regard to flies; on Tamarind River—the best river—an imitation of a large yellow-bodied grasshopper, common in that part, is killing; also of young wasps; earlier still after rain an imitation wasp grub of dirty yellow chenille, or a strip of wash leather on a slip of cork. On Grande Rivière, Nord-ouest, a small green grasshopper kills well, as also the green and yellow cabbage grub. On this river on hot clear days fish are taken with a small lizard an inch long, cut out of indiarubber. It is just the colour of the common lizard there when it comes out of the egg. Where the Reduit and Rouge Rivers run in is a good spot. All the rivers on the south coast are good, especially the Rivière des Aiguilles, where fish run larger than elsewhere. The deep and sequestered pool under the waterfall on the little river Bain des Negresses is said to hold some peculiarly large ones, but the pool is most difficult of access, owing to a belt of swamp and luxuriant tropical jungle. There is a rock overhanging the pool, some sixty or seventy feet perpendicularly above it, and from it a line may be dropped. There is a fair river at Flacq, on the north-east of the island, and more easily fished than most of the others. The sheet are principally found on the upper waters of the rivers; Grande Rivière, Sud-est, where there are no carp being the best. The immense eels that affect the rocky pools, half filled with boulders beneath the waterfalls, are difficult to catch. Even when hooked, if they once succeed in getting hold of the boulders that form the bottom and sides of the pools there is no chance of getting them out. A live duckling, with a couple of strong hooks on gimp secured beneath its wings, is the best bait, as the eel will take that about dawn or twilight and may then be run ashore before he has time to recover from his surprise. These eels are four to six feet long, and as large round as a man's thigh, so a stout stick or an axe will be wanted to quiet them.

EUROPE.

AUSTRIA.

General Information.—The streams of Transylvania hold trout in some quantity. The rivers of Lower Hungary, especially the Theiss, hold schile, pike, carp, sterl, dick, hawsen, &c.
Achenwald.—By staying at the inn some fishing can be had in Ache. Lake Achensee (pike and perch), and a considerable part of the river, is preserved.
Aussee (Styria).—Trout and grayling. (See Ischl.)
Borssek (Bavaria).—Good trouting four hours off; permission from landlord of hotel.
Bosnia and **Herzegovina.**—Trout are found in the mountain streams and in both the Pliva lakes, near Jajce. are of good size. Grayling abound in the small rivers, and the larger rivers contain huchen. Chiefly trout in the upper part of the Vrbas and Bosna, and in the Lasva. in the neighbourhood of Jajce. Good specimens of huchen are found in the Unna, and they are plentiful in the Vrbas, particularly from Dolnje Vakuf downwards. Huchen angling is good in the Drina, which also contains plenty of grayling. In Herzegovina are the Narenta, with its tributaries, the Rama, and the Buna, all well supplied with trout. Another river is the Trebinjcica, which contains rainbow. Permission to fish is easily obtainable, as the fishing is practically free. A

licence (costing 10*d*., from the officials of the district) is necessary. At Bosna springs is a fine fish-breeding establishment. Best times of year are spring and autumn. Trout-fishing ends October, but huchen-fishing may be enjoyed up to end of November if weather is favourable. Good centres are Trebinje (good hotel) for Trebinjcica; Mostar (very good hotel) for Narenta and Buna; Jablanica (Narenta and Rama), Konjica (Narenta), first-rate fishing above and below the town. Some distance from Konjica is the Borki lake (full of trout), and there is good accommodation in the neighbourhood. Good fishing at Bad Ilidze, at Visigrad, river Drina, at Travnik, the Lasva, and at Dolnje Vakuf, which is a good centre for fishing the Upper Vrbas and its tributaries. Jajce (good hotel) is conveniently situated for many excellent waters, including Vrbas and the Pliva river and lake; Banjaluka for the Vrbas and the Vrbanja; Novi, the point of departure for the district of the Upper Unna (rich in huchen, also trout above Bihac). The Unna can also be fished from Krupa as well as the Krusnica.

Bregenz.—On Lake Constance. (See Switzerland, Constance.)

Bruck (Styria).—On Lamnitzbach; trout. Murz.

Bruneck.—On Ahrenbach. Trout, grayling.

Buda Pesth.—Similar fishing as at Pressburg. The Margaretherr Insel (Margaret Island) a short distance from the capital—steamboats every half-hour—contains two restaurants, and capital bank fishing; no charge for angling. Platten See (*Balatan Lake*) is near Pesth. Large pike, perch, wels, burbot, pike-perch, bream, and schneider (or cutter fish). The latter has a knife-like edge along the belly; they are herring-size. From Pesth go to Siofok, per railway; put up at Mr. Karlberger's hotel, who will give free permission to fish the lake. Off the jetty is capital perch fishing. The bait, a portion of a raw cray fish (the universal bait for large fish). A steamboat crosses the lake daily in three-quarters of an hour to Fuered, a mineral water bathing place. Boats to be had here, but none at Siofok.

Fuered (Hungary).—On Platten See. Station Szantod, on the Stuhlweissemburg Railway from Vienna. This lake contains many varieties of fish. The autumn is the best time. Mayer's hotel is the best. Boats can be hired.

Gmunden.—On Traun. There is a lake here. The Sonne is a good inn. The grayling fishing from hence to Ischl is good: above here it is preserved.

Golling, near **Salzburg.**—Two good trout streams; tickets to be obtained at Hotel. Bahnhof.

Gross Reifling (Styria).—On Salza. Trout, grayling.

Hallstadt.—See Ischl.

Innsbruck (Tyrol).—At Mittenwald, on the Bavarian frontier, the Isar contains trout and grayling; leave is easily procurable. Three hours' drive from Mittenwald is Partenkirchen, two hours distant from which is Eib See, containing coarse fish. The fishing is let to a professional. An hour from Mittenwald, at the village of Krün, is a small lake, containing trout. Walchensee, some three hours from Mittenwald, is a post station on the lake of the same name, which contains fine trout, as does Kochel See, a lake half an hour's walk from one end of Walchensee. These lakes are rented by various people, who doubtless would give leave. Boats can be had. Walchensee is the only station on that lake, but on Kochel See there are two, Kochel and another place. Close to Leefeld, a small village two-and-a-half hours from Innsbruck, is a small lake containing trout.

Ischl.—On Traun. The landlord of the Kaiserin Elizabeth has large fishery rights as far as Hallstadt. Large ferox in Hallstatter See by trolling. Below the falls there are plenty of Hüchen. Permission must be obtained. (See Gmunden.) The Grundlsee is twenty-four miles from here. A conveyance runs from Ischl to Aussee, three miles from the lake, and on the borders of the lake is a very comfortable hotel, the Erzherzog Johann. The fern fly. Hoffland's fancy, and the coch-y-bonddhu are good flies on Traun, and wading is necessary. On Grundlsee the trolling with artificial bait is good, but they must be large. It is a good plan to troll up the Grundlsee to the Töplitzsee which is joined to the former by the Traun. There is good fly-fishing in Töplitzsee, especially by two waterfalls. For this lake use Hoffland's fancy, dressed large, and No. 2 body, crimson mohair ribbed with gold; hackle, red; wing, the starling or mallard; hook, No. 6 or 7 Limerick. (See St. Gilgen.) The water near Goisern, an hour's distance from the Hallstadter See, on the Ischl road, is very good. A couple of hours on the road to Saltzburg brings you to the Wolfganger See. There are two stations here. St. Gilgen, on the Saltzburg road, and St. Wolfgang, a village on the opposite side, where there is a small but clean and comfortable inn. The lake contains very large trout, pike, char, chub, and other white fish. From St. Wolfgang you can fish the Schwarz See, a lake about an hour and a half up the Schafberg mountain. The trout rise freely. A couple of hours' drive from St. Wolfgang is Fuschel See, containing plenty of char and white fish, and a few big trout. There are two stations here, Fuschel, at the mouth of the lake, and Hof, near its head. Permission to fish in Wolfganger See and Fuschel See is obtainable at the inns. Eight miles from Hof, over the hills to the left of the Saltzburg-road, is Hinter See, containing good trout, which rise well. The fishery is rented by the head forester of the district. Hof is two hours from Saltzburg.

Jenbach (Tyrol).—On the Innsbruck line. Achen See lies near. We understand that it is let to a professional fisherman in which case permission is easy. Trout very large.

Kochel.—See Innsbruck.

Kufstein.—On the Innsbruck line. Two hours' walk from here is a lake by the village of Barnstat.

Lambach.—Half-way between Lintz and Gmunden on Alm and Traun, great quantities of grayling. Leave can be obtained.

Leutaschthal, near **Innsbruck** (Tyrol).—Fair trout stream, with some large fish; leave to be obtained from owner at Obere Leutasch.

Lienz.—On Isel. Trout, grayling.

Meran (Tyrol).—The rivers Etoch and Passer are accessible from here, but they are too near their mountain sources to be good for angling.

Palfau (Styria).—On Salza. Trout, grayling. Between here and Wildalpen is a fair hotel (Kaiser Gams), where free fishing can be had.

Pressburg (Hungary).—On the Danube. Excellent fishing for all kinds of large fish off the promontories within a short distance of the town. A spinning bait most useful for pike-perch, which are caught here occasionally of 30lb. in weight. Wels are fished for with live baits, near the bottom, and are taken up to 300lb. in weight, and more; they are also fished for with a live duck as bait. The Neutra, a branch of the Danube, is a more sluggish stream, and abounds with wels, barbel, and perch; also a fish of the shad species, called zaerthe. Anglers' licence is five gulden, or ten shillings per annum

Reutte.—An hour's walk from here, at the village of Heiterwang, are three lakes—the Heiterwang See, a quarter of an hour's walk from the village, the Plan See, and the Bach See, the source of the Arch. The fishing belongs to a peasant of Heiterwang. All fish caught must be given up alive, or paid for at the market price. Fridays and Saturdays only can the boats be obtained, unless a high price be paid. The fish are rhenken, running up to 6lb., char and trout. The little stream by the village is a good spot. There is a clean little inn here, the Grosses Wirthshaus. It is necessary to order meat some time in advance. There is a lake near Ehrwald, a village three hours distant from Heiterwang, containing plenty of trout; the master of the inn here has the right of fishing. Near Lermoos are two lakes, one close to the Innsbruck road, and another, Weisze See, near the village of Biberweir; this last lake contains plenty of char, though no trout. The master of the Post Inn at Lermoos holds the fishery rights, as also of a small stream holding a few trout. There are two small lakes, with a boat on them, close to the Innsbruck road, two hours from Lermoos, which contain trout. The master of the inn of the village of Nassereit has the fishery rights. At Weissenbach, one station on from Heiterwang, is the Lech, containing a few trout and grayling; the fishing free. Some hours up the river, in Lechthal, the trouting is much better. One hour's drive from Weissenbach is the village of Nesselwangle, the commune of which holds the fishery rights of the Holden See, containing large pike and white fish; there is no doubt leave would readily be granted; the accommodation here is good. At the village of Tannheim, some distance from Nesselwangle, are lakes Vils-Alper See and Trau-Alper See, containing trout char, coregoni, and plenty of perch; the latter lake lies an hour's climb above the former. The fisherman who owns the fishing readily gives leave; accommodation very bad. Schattwald is the next village; accommodation good. The Vils runs close by, containing plenty of trout. The parish priest owns the fishery, and grants leave. Three hours' drive brings you to Immenstadt, on the Munich and Constance line.

Schmecks or **Füred** (Hungary).—Fair fishing. (See Füred.)

St. Gilgen.—Good fishing, trout and grayling, three miles from Ischl. Good trolling.

Salzburg.—See Ischl.

Schüttenhofen.—On Wottawa; trout; a good station.

Taufers.—On Ahrenbach. Trout, grayling.

Vienna.—Excellent fishing for salmo hucho, wels, pike, perch, barbel, &c., in the Danube, close to the town. The fishers here use brass wire lines, and throw them with a heavy lead attached into the rapid stream, and now and then haul up a monster wels.

Walchensee.—See Innsbruck.

Weichselboden (Styria).—On Salza. Trout. Preserved by Count Meran, who often gives leave. Fishing very good.

Wildalpen (Styria).—On Salza. Trout, grayling. Preserved by the monastery at Admont, but leave is only occasionally granted. Fishing very fair. *Hotel:* Zisler's.

Windisch Matrei.—*Hotel:* Hotel Zum Rauter. Isel. The landlord rents the fishing. Good trouting can be had in the Deferegger-Bach, which flows into Isel at In der Huben; the fishing begins at Hopfgarten. Fishing is also good higher up at St. Veit.

Wolfsberg (Lavantthal).—*Hotel:* Pfundner. On Lavant; trout and grayling; preserved, but leave can be had on payment. There is a papier maché mill some 2 m. above. which at times injures the fishing below. Above, the fishing is much better. The Arlingbach, a tributary of Lavant, holds fine fish, but is much overgrown.

BELGIUM AND LUXEMBOURG.

General Information.—There is fair trout and grayling fishing in the Semois and Boeq. The Ourthe, near Houffalize contains trout and grayling, and large chub, and is good for general fishing. A few salmon trout are netted occasionally near Tilff. The Hoyoux, which joins the Meuse at Huy, is full of large trout, but is very strictly preserved. Fair general sport can be had in the Amblève. Aywaille is a good spot. In the Molignée the trout are plentiful, but small; this river joins the Meuse at Moulin. At Targnon on Amblève, and in a tributary near. fair trouting can be had. Targnon is near Spa. Hamoix, on the Huy-road. is a good fishing quarter on the opposite side of the Ourthe. Fair accommodation can be had. There is good fishing in the Lesse near Chanly, which can be reached from Grupont on the Great Luxemborg line.

Ardenne.—At the Hotel Château Royal l'Ardenne, a good headquarters, permission can be obtained at the hotel.

Bouillon.—On Semois; trout. Leave easily obtainable.

Chiny.—On Semois; trout.

Comblain la Tour.—On the Ourthe and Amblève. Trout, roach, chub, and few salmon late in the season.

Diekirch (Luxembourg).—On the Sûre, which contains coarse fish in great abundance. The landlord of the Grand Hotel des Ardennes (*see Advt.*) preserves the Upper Sûre for several miles, in which there is good trout and chub fishing, while barbel are plentiful in places. (Michelau is a good place, and very picturesque.) Visitors to the hotel have also free fishing in several other rivers and streams rented by the landlord, the Weisser Ernz affording excellent grayling and trout fishing. Season opens April 1. Fishing licence 3 fr. per annum.

Dinant.—The Bocq runs six miles from here, close by the village of Spontin. The river rises between the villages of Sey and Mohiville, and joins the Meuse at Yvoir; trout are plentiful. The red and black hackles are good flies. Leave can be obtained for some portion of the water from the owner of the Hotel de la Tête D'Or; also from the burgomaster of the village of Purnode. At the former place the Meuse contains plenty of the coarser kind of fish and abounds in the queer fish called Hotische or Hoteux. It has no longer any salmon, and few trout. The Salm gives fair trout fishing. Station. Vielsalm. The Lesse joins Meuse about one and a half miles above the town. The fishing is very good. Rochefort is the best place to stop at. The railway runs through the place.

Ettelbruck (Ardennes).—Sura; trout; river much fished. Hotel accommodation fair.

Herbeumont (Ardennes).—N.s. **Beatrix.** On Semois; trout, chub. *Hotel :* Ardennes, where fishing can be had.

Huy.—Hotel de l'Aigle Noir. Some good trouting can be had in the neighbourhood.

Laroche (Ardennes).—Ourthe; pike, chub, dace, trout. Any amount of coarse fish, but the trouting has greatly fallen off.

Liege.—On Ourthe. Roach, chub, and gudgeon.

Marloie.—On Ourthe. Fair fishing.

Namur.—On the Meuse. Chub. A *few* trout, barbel, perch, and pike. Above Namur the river is clear and rapid, but below slow and dirty.

Orval (Ardennes).—n.s. **Florenville,** 6 *m.* Marche; trout; preserved; by staying at the inn (comfortable) d. and w.t. can be had.

Ostend.—Very fine smelts can be caught in the harbour from the quays; also flounders. &c.

Remouchamps.—From Liège by Ravage and Aywaille. On Amblève. Fishing free, except for a Government licence, which costs 2fr. Trouting fair (an occasional salmon); also dace and chub. *Hotel :* Hotel de la Grotte.

Rochefort (Ardennes).—On L'Homme and Lesse. Trout and grayling. Good fishing but all preserved. A day or two may sometimes be had. Apply to landlord of Hotel Biron. Three miles below Rochefort a good stream joins Lesse. The Semois runs near here.

Spa.—Hotel D'York and others. On Wayai. Some little fishing can be had 2 *m.* down the river. There are no fish by Spa.

Val de Poix.—6 *m.* W. of St. Hubert. On a tributary of L'Homme.

DANUBIAN PRINCIPALITIES.

Bucharest.—Coarse fishing in a stream near, free.

Cervanoda.—See Kustendjee.

Kustendjee.—On the Black Sea. There is a rail from here to Cervanoda. Good accommodation at either place. Fair fishing in the Danube, consisting of the shaden, reaching 350lb.; the deek, 400lb.; the shill, 40lb.; the forgoache, 50lb.; the hoochan, 70lb.; the stirl, 20lb.; also sturgeon; pike, trout, carp, &c. There is a large lake an hour's walk from here containing many heavy fish, especially the *Lucio perca.*

Roumania (GENERAL INFORMATION).—There is splendid pike, perch, and coarse fishing in the lakes and the tributaries of the Danube in the Debrogea. Arrange to go with local fishermen. From Braila or Galatz the angler can obtain permission from the domain authorities, and go with the boat from the Quay, which is to a great extent a guarantee that he *will* be brought back again.

Sulina.—Pike and coarse fishing. There is a fish something like a dace, and running up to 2lb., which takes a fly, fishing near the pier.

ICELAND—DENMARK.

Reykjavik.—There are eight salmon rivers within from one hour to six days' journey. Salmon fishing is mostly very poor, owing to the persistent use of nets in every spot where the riparian farmers can set one with effect. Very fair sport is to be had, however, by renting a river or buying the nets off a portion of one. The eight rivers are (1) the Elliðáar, one hour from Reykjavik. Herra Thomsen, its owner, resides at Reykjavik, and lets the fishing to anglers at 10s. 6d. per day. (2) The Laxá, in Kjós, one day's ride from the capital. The whole river is to be rented for from 60l. to 100l. Application to be made to the priest at Reynivellir. Excellent accommodation at that place. (3) The

Minni Laxá and (4) Stærra Laxá, distant two days' journey. Quarters at Gröf farm and Hruni parsonage. (5) The Leirárvogar Laxá, distant two days' ride. The nets could be bought off this river for about 20*l.*; it is believed the fishing would then be very good. Quarters at Llerá farm. (6) and (7) Grimsá and Nordrá, two tributaries to the Western Hvítá; three days' ride, or one day by boat, from Reykjavík. Good quarters at Hvítárvellir and Thverá farms. (8) The Laxá falling into the Straumfjardar Ós; one and a half days by boat, and six days' ride, from Reykjavík. Quarters at Miklaholt parsonage. Good trout fishing in Thingvalla lake, one day's ride, and in its outlet (Sog). The trout run up to 7lb. Quarters at the farms. There is also good trout fishing in nearly all the rivers that do not drain glaciers. There are now two good hotels at Reykjavík—the Hotel Iceland, newly built, and the Alexandra, formerly the Merchants' Club-house. As travelling is mainly on pony-back, take an English saddle well stuffed, also a portable tent, waterproof rug, and a pair of thick Canadian blankets to sleep in, preserved soups and meats, cheese, ham, biscuits, oatmeal for porridge, and some such cooking apparatus as the "Rob Roy"—that is, heated with spirit, fuel being very scarce. Clothing should consist of a couple of suits of warm thick material, a stout mackintosh, and a pair of strong fisherman's boots coming well up the thigh for riding in, as rivers have constantly to be forded. In the north there are now seven rivers in which salmon may be caught. (1) The Laxá from Mývatn, very good. Nearest port, Húsavík, where steamers call about six times during the summer. Accommodation fair. Apply to the factor. Mr. T. Gudjohnson The nearest salmon fishing is some 5 *m.* off at Laxármyri, a large and comfortable farmhouse. The farmer readily gives permission to fish, the angler to retain the trout, but give up the salmon. Quarters *are not now* obtainable at Laxármyri, but there is an inn at Húsavík. Another good fishing station on this river is at Grenjadarstadir, a very good farm, and the home of a clergyman—about 12 *m.* from Húsavík. (2) Ós Laxá, a few hours' ride from Skagaströnd, a port also called at by steamers. (3) The Laxá from the Laxárvatn, one day's ride from Skagaströnd. Quarters at Hjaltabakki parsonage; priest speaks English. (4) Vatnsdalsá, a good river, but, it is believed, the best stretches of water are rented. (5) Víðidalsá, two days' ride from Skagaströnd. Quarters at Borg; farmer speaks English. (6) Midfjardrá, three days' ride from Skagaströnd. Quarters at Reykir farm and Melstadr parsonage. (7) The Laxá, falling into the Hvammsfjördr; one day's ride from Stykkishólmr, a small port called at by steamers. Several very fair farms in the valley, at one of which a room could be had. Excellent trout fishing to be had in the lakes on the Arnarvatnsheidi, in Svínavatn, near Stóradalr; also in the upper waters of the Laxá from Mývatn. The best way to the lake is up the Laxárdalr; Grenjadarstadir should be made a half-way house. There are a vast number of char in Mývatn, but they refuse to take the fly. There is, however, excellent trout fishing in the Laxá, about 2 miles from its outlet from the lake. Good quarters are obtainable at Skútustadir, a parsonage at the south end of the lake; and also at Hopstadir, a farm lying nearer the river. On the road to the Dettifoss from Húsavík is the Botnsvatn (bottom water); good trouting. No fishing in lake Hoskuldsvatn. Ordinary salmon flies, especially the silver doctor, snowfly, Childers, "Butcher," and "Jock-Scott," for salmon, and for trout small gaudy grilse flies with red woollen or tinsel bodies, bound with gold or silver twist, golden pheasant tails, and brownish wings, have been found the most killing. July and August are the best months in Iceland, but when it is purposed to rent a river or buy the nets off a portion of one, the angler should visit the island not later than the middle of June, that all obstacles may be removed and the first run of fish allowed to enter the river. If this is not done, the angler would, in a dry summer, wait a long time before he got any fishing, as most of the rivers frequently fall very low in the months first named. A good deal of fishing is preserved by the Icelandic Angling Club. Guides, whose payment, including food, is 5 or 6 kroners a day, are easily obtainable at Reykjavick. The charge for ponies is 2 kroners (2*s.* 3*d.*) a day, hire of saddle and bridle 25 ore (3½*d.*), and for baggage ponies the hire of pack saddles and boxes is about 7*d.* a day. The fishing near here is mostly in the hands of merchants, but there is fair trout and char to be had at a small charge on the upper waters of the Ellada, about 6 *m.* from Reykjavick, from a merchant farmer named Benedict Levenson. The good fishing is on the Sog, which runs out of Lake Thingvelle (near Thingvalla), and, after a course of 30 *m.* flowing through two small lakes, joins the Hvita, runs to the sea at Eyrabakki. Sog leaves Thingvellei Lake (char fishing good in July and August), about 65 *m.* from Reykjavick, rushes through a precipitous chasm, and widens out into a lake called Ulfyötsvater. Here are plenty of trout, running from 1lb. to 3lb. (boat required). The charge for fishing here (including boat) is 3 kroners the first day, and 1 for each succeeding day. Sog flows into Lake Alftavater, below which there are plenty of sea trout, and occasionally grilse. In Iceland char are much more plentiful than trout, the proportion being about six to one. The former run large, and, although not giving the same play, provide excellent sport. The acting British Consul, Mr. Paterson, is most kind and helpful to anglers experiencing difficulties, and these are certainly not conspicuous by their absence.

FRANCE.

General Information.—All the streams in the South are netted, and occasionally dynamited. The Bavera, 14 *m.* from Moulinet to Italian frontier, passing Sispel, the Tivée and Vesabic, are fairly good rivers, as also are the Ciaus and the Esteron. Fair rivers are the Loup, Cagnes, and the Siagne. Close time for most streams, April 19 to June 20. Flies, which should be tied small, are March brown, coachman, palmers, duns, black gnats, red ant, coch-y-bonddhu. Besides trout, barbel, tench, eels, and dace, chad have been caught in the Var. The trout fishing in the department Morbihan does not open until June 1. This rule applies only to the canals and navigable streams. Near Brooms, in the Côtes du Nord, there are some streams. Fishing poor. The lake at Jugon contains pike and perch. Any person may fish with rod and line only in any public water, that is, in all navigable rivers, canals, and their cuts or affluents, the maintenance of which in good condition is chargeable to the state, and into which a fishing boat can at all times enter. No one, however, must use night lines, trimmers, bankrunners, or any instrument stuck in the bank. This does not apply to ponds or lakes which belong to the riparian proprietors. In all other rivers and streams the right of fishing belongs to the riparian proprietors. No fishing after dark is permitted. Every department makes its own byelaws, and settles its own closing time; and as these generally vary, it is well to ascertain the particulars, as sometimes the fishing on one bank of a river is closed, and the other side open. All information can be obtained at the prefecture of the principal town of each department. The French Government maps are good. For Normandy comfortable quarters can be had at Havre, with the Montivilliers and Epouville fishing a day or two at Cany, also at Pont Andemer and Pont l'Evêque. Some sport is to be had with trout, many of them large, at all the above places. There is no salmon fishing worthy the name in Normandy. Brittany will afford good sport among trout, and a salmon here and there; also capital sea-fishing, both from boats and from rocks on parts of the coast. The streams are generally preserved; it is probable that permission may be obtained by proper application. For Brittany, as stations choose Pont Scorff, Quimperlé, and Pont Aven; very good sea-fishing is also to be had near the latter place. Anyone has a right to fish from a public path. Plenty of pollack along the rocky coasts of, Normandy and Brittany, and bass in all the estuaries.

Abbeville.—Five kilomètres off, in the valley of the Somme, are some ponds which hold pike, perch, tench, roach, bream, etc.

Aix-les-Bains (Savoy).—*Hotels:* De l'Europe, d'Albion, and others. On Lake Bourget; ferox, pike, perch, dace, chub, bream, but the lake is very deep. Baits are easily procured. The best way of fishing is with a natural bait trailing from a boat, with 50 or 60 yards of line out. Large dace may be caught with fly all along the deep, wooded side of the lake, and there are some splendid perch round the shallow weedy bays. Two small streams run into the lake here, holding small chub and dace, and in the autumn a few trout.

Amélie-les-Bains (Pyrenees).—Four kilomètres distant there is a small stream (tributary of the Tech), which is full of trout. Artificial fly, and other lures.

Amiens.—There is a good deal of coarse fishing in the neighbourhood, in the river Somme, and various marshes, large peat pits, etc.

Annecy (Savoy).—Hotel d'Angleterre. On Lake Annecy; ferox, pike, perch, chub, char. Fishing fair.

Arcachon.—There is a little fishing, but poor, in the lakes along the coast N. and S. of this place.

Auvergne.—In the departments of Cantal and Puy-de-Dôme are many small streams which afford free trout fishing from February to November. The Dare and the Sioule are also free, but the Allier is let. The best stations for the Dare are Olliergues, Giraux, Compièn, Ambert, Arlam, Pont-de-Dare; for the Sioule. Pontgileaud and Chateauneuf-les-bains. In Cantal the best trouting rivers are the Truyère and Cère.

Aveyron Department. — Perhaps no other Department of France is so richly endowed in rivers and streams and the opportunities they afford for good fishing as Aveyron. There are 7040 kilomètres of rivers and streams formerly all holding fish: the Lot with its many tributaries, the Truyère, Dourdon of Bozouls or Conques, the Tarn, and its important tributary the Aveyron, &c. Although the rivers have been somewhat depleted by wholesale poaching, much good has been done to repress this, and by the restocking of the waters under their control, by the "Société des Pêcheurs à la Ligne" at Decazeville, au association formed in 1899, and which has now a membership of about eighty. The annual subscription is 6 francs. Another association, the "Société de Pisciculture et de Pêcheurs a la Ligne," formed in 1903, and of which the annual subscription is 2 francs, also intend to devote a part of their funds to the restocking of the Aveyron. Rodez should form a good centre.

Avranches (Manche, Normandy).—The Léez and Celune fall into the Bay of Mont St. Michel here. The fishing close to the town is not good for much, but by going a few miles up either river good sport can be had. On the Léez, Tirpied (six miles from Avranches), Brieey (ten), and Cuves (twelve), are the places to put up at, though the accommodation is very rough. On the Celune, Ducey (seven), and Les Biards (thirteen); accommodation very bad at the latter place, but the fishing good. The diligences run close to all these places. Leave is easily obtained. Salmon may sometimes be taken.

Bagnolles de l'Orne.—Hotel de Bagnolles. Some fishing can be had here.

Bagnolles-les-Eaux (Orne).—On Vée. Hotels St. Lucile and St. Marguerite. The lake here contains plenty of coarse fish.

Barfleur.—Salmon of 6lb. to 7lb. weight are to be caught in La Saire River, which runs into the sea at Reville, a village by the side of St. Vaast la Hougue. Trout, however are much more numerous.

Bar-sur-Aube (Paris and Mulhouse Railway).—Fair trouting in the Aube; free. Fishing is also good at Longchamps and Rennepont.

Baud.—35 kilomètres from Lorient; 30 from Vannes, and 24 from Pontivy. Good coarse fishing in the Nantes-Brest Canal, and trouting in the Evel, Auray, and Claye rivers A boat may be had at the Hotel du Commerce.

Bayonne.—The rivers Nive, Nivelle, and Bidassoa contain salmon, trout, &c.: some portions are preserved by clubs, others by private owners who reserve the right of fishing. At Campo (15 m. off), where good trouting in the Nive and other streams may be had, is an inn, the Hotel St. Martin.

Beaurainville.—On Canche; trout. Fishing generally poor, except in May fly season. Yearly ticket 10*fr.*, from the Mayor.

Belle-Isle-en-Terre (Brittany).—(*See Paimpol.*)

Bergues.—Some six miles from Dunkerque. Large pike are to be caught in the fosse. Permission must be obtained from the officer in command.

Besançon.—Barbel and other coarse fish, very scarce owing to netting. There is good accommodation. Go to Pontardier and Metiers-Travers in Switzerland for trouting. Metiers-Travers is on the Reux. By descending the river you get to Boudri.

Beussent.—Branch line from Montreuil. On Course, a tributary of Canche; trout, mostly preserved, but there is free fishing at Inxent. A few trout at La Paix Faite, half-an-hour's walk from Montreuil.

Biarritz.—At Cambo some good trouting can be had, also dace. The Nivelle holds good trout.

Blangy-sur-Ternoise.—Two hours by rail from Boulogne. On Ternoise; trout; s. t. 10*fr.*, from the Mayor. Sport very good in parts.

Boulogne-sur-Mer.—On Liane. Trout fishing higher up at Hesdigneul, Carly, and Questrecques; mostly preserved by Boulogne "Société des Pêcheurs à la Ligne." The subscription is moderate; no short period tickets. Sea trout are often caught at the weirs. Near Montreuil there is good fishing in the Canche. especially in the upper part of it at Parenty, Beussent, and Inxent. The best of the above places is Beussent, where the stream is very open all the way up to Parenty. At Bermeulles, about one mile from Beussent, accommodation if required may be had at a farmhouse, though they are all within a drive from Boulogne. 23 m. off is Fauquembergues. There is fair trouting from 6 m. above, to Lumbers, 9 m. below. At Lique, 17 m. from Boulogne, there is fair trouting. Some good pollack fishing near here; fish large; use a spinning eel.

Brest.—An excursion may be made from here to Landéoc, where there is a good salmon and trout stream (the Buis, which falls into the Aulne at Logonna Quimerch). This stream may be followed up to Braspars, a small village with poor accommodation, and thence to Huelgoët, which stands on a lake, where there is a capital inn. Good fishing may be had at Pontargonet, and in the stream that supplies the lake. From Huelgoët a mail road leads to Morlaix. From Huelgoët go to Commanna, where the trout fishing is very good, but the accommodation poor. Good sea fishing.

Brevieres (Tarentaise).—On Isére; plenty of trout. Accommodation (Aub. du Soleil Lévant) wretched.

Brimeux.—Second station above Montreuil. On Canche; trout, and very occasional salmon. Heavy trout sometimes caught during the May-Fly. Annual ticket 10 *fr.*. from the Mayor.

Caen (Normandy).—On Orne. Plenty of bream, roach, and a small white fish, locally called dárd; also trout in the tributaries of the Orne. There is fishing, also, in the Caen Canal from Caen to the sea, and in Orne from the dam to the estuary. Up the river above the dam, and in the neighbouring streams (Avon, Grand Nae, La Laije) fishing is free from the public banks from January 15 to April 15. For other parts. leave of the riparian owners must be obtained—some give permission, others refuse. *Hotel*: Hotel d'Angleterre.

Calais.—Coarse fishing (pike, perch. tench, roach, bream) in neighbouring canals. Best places are Eclude, Carrée, and Banc Valois (rail and tram), Les Attaques, Pont d'Ardres and Nortkeique (rail). Three-quarters of an hour by rail is the river Aa, at Gravelines: Lake of Ardres, 1 hour. Trouting in river Hemm a good deal preserved, but there is some free and generally poor fishing at Bonningues, Tournehem, and Zouafques, 1 to 1½ hours from Calais on Auvin Railway; also Recques, about 3 m. from Zouafques, or from Andruicy on St. Omer line. Sea-fishing from piers free; codling, whiting, flatfish, &c., August to December; fishing poor.

Cannes (A. M.).—Siane runs 3 m. off: dace, chub, grey mullet, eels, and a few trout. *Hotels*: Beau Site, and many others. Fishing is sometimes moderately good, especially some four miles up the stream just below Oribeau. Some fair trouting can be had twelve miles off across the hills near Grasse. At times mullet, mackerel, wrasse, and other sea fish can be taken between Cannes and the Isle Marguerite.

Cany (Normandy.)—There is fair trouting here; also at Villefleurs, three kilomètres off.

Cazeres.—On Garonne. Plenty of chub, and a very few trout.

Cette.—Pretty good fishing in the marine canals that intersect the town. Plenty of sea-bream (*dorade*, locally).

Chambéry.—There are two clubs here which rent water—"La Mirandelle" (360 members) and the "Franc Pêcheurs" (240 members). The subscription is merely nominal. Besides coarse fish, Lake of Bourget holds trout. Within easy distance are several fishable rivers

Champagnole.—There is a good club here which has fishing; subscription 3 *fr.* per annum. The streams in the neighbourhood abound in trout.

Chausey, Iles.—Very good sea fishing; many large pollack, and grey and red mullet abundant.

Cherbourg.—On the Divette. Grey mullet and small bass are to be taken by angling near the dock gates and pier head; atherine or sand smelt, at the influx of the river Divette, on the east side of the floating basin. The townspeople fish with throw-out lines, and angle also with rods from the outer part of the quay walls, taking with the lines numbers of flounders, from 6in. to 9in. long. There are several rocky shoals in and outside the harbour, where pollack are taken. Trout abundant in the Divette, Saire, and Diélette, but some distance away. No permit is required. Divette also contains plenty of coarse fish.

Clermont—Royat.—Auvergne is furrowed with streams containing fish, *e.g.*, the Tirrekains (trout), Monne, Cousu, Allier. Rod fishing is free and opens in April; early fishing is best. Royat is a very good station because of the numerous fishable waters in the vicinity.

Cong.—Tolerable fishing in the lake. There is little or no chance on the river.

Corps (Dauphiné).—On Drac and Souloise. Drac holds few fish, and is much discoloured. Souloise joins Drac here. Trouting good from a mile below the mill to its source (some subterranean pools 8 *m.* up). There is good trouting at St. Firmin, 16 *m.* from Corps. (*See St. Firmin.*)

Crieuil.—(*See Trevort.*)

Dax (Landes).—On Adour; pike roach dace, chub, perch.

Decaseville.—There is a society here, which preserves a portion of the Lot.

Dieppe.—Several trout streams near. Fishing opens April 1, ends October 15; d.t. (3 *frs.* and upwards), of M. Coudray, Grande Rue. 4 *m.* off, at Arguee, is a mile of water, fishable by ticket from the Grand Hotel, Dieppe. 3 *m.* off, at Martin-Eglise, fishing in Aulne may be had from the village innkeeper. From the quays there is good rod fishing for grey mullet, baiting with ragworm.

Dijon.—On Ouche; a few trout. Accommodation good. There are several good places within a circuit of twelve miles. The middle of May the best time.

Dinan (Brittany).—Rance; carp, dace, pike. Some trouting can be had at Guenroc (good accommodation), 15 *m.* up the river. Some trout can be had also at St. André des Eaux, on Rance, 12 *m.* off; also at Hinglé, 6 *m.* off. The river can be fished to where it joins the canal, from which point there is the towing path into Dinan. At Bobatail, 5 *m.* from Dinan, are some lakes holding pike, but preserved. There is a fair trout stream 12 *m.* W. of Dinan, and a lake, which is preserved. At all the locks in the canal stray trout are to be found. Minnow fishing is best, owing to the rivers being overgrown. No fishing is allowed for a month before the harvest, because of the crops. In South Brittany is excellent trouting, particularly at Carbaix. Good accommodation.

Dinard.—There is no freshwater fishing here, but plenty of sea fish of all kinds.

D'Ivourne.—(*See Geneva, Switzerland.*)

Dôle (near Dijon).—Some dace and chub can be had here.

Dunkerque.—The canals are full of roach, perch, and eels. There are carp and pike in the fosse of the fortifications. Large pike are caught at Bergues.

Eaux Chaudes.—Difficult fishing, owing to rocks and trees. Trout small.

Embrun (Dauphine).—Some distance beyond here there are good streams in the valleys of L'Argentière and Val Louise.

Evreux.—There is some good trouting for some distance above the town. Leave must be obtained.

Eu (Normandy).—Good trouting (dry fly) in Bresle, which falls into the sea near here; mostly preserved. Enquire of the Mayor at Longroy and at Blangy-sur-Bresle.

Fauquembergues.—On Aa; river Lys also near; trout; mostly preserved, but leave is obtainable. *Hotels*: Hotel de France, and Univers.

Foix.—On Ariège. A few good trout.

Gabas.—Last village before the Spanish frontier, beyond Eaux Chaudes. Trout both above and below, but best about two miles above, at the foot of the Pic d'Aule. The Lac d'Aule, near the eternal snows, contains fine trout of most superior quality, but very capricious in rising or taking any bait. Small flies best.

Gérardmer.—A club preserves the Lake of Gérardmer and the feeders, which are full of fish (trout, perch, pike, &c.). Day tickets (1 *fr*), may be obtained.

Givet.—On Meuse. There is capital pike fishing here.

Gouarec (Brittany).—The best trout fishing in Brittany, formed by the junction of the Blavet, Salon, and some streams. Quarters are bad.

Granville.—Small grey mullets are to be caught off the quays, using the tail of a rockworm, and sand eels on long-lines shot at low water on the sands.

Grenoble.—The lakes generally contain fish (occasional trout), and the rivers Romanche, Drac, Isère, and Bourne give fair trouting. Thirty kilomètres off, good fishing is to be had in waters preserved by a society. Apply to the Mayor of Voreppe. *Hotel*: Hotel Primat.

Guingamp (Brittany).—*Hotels:* Lion d'Or, la Gare, Tour d'Avergne. Rivers Trieux, Jaudy, Guindry, and Leff (which joins Trieux between Pontrieux and Paimpol). All afford good sport. At St. Nicholas du Palem 15 *m.* (Blavet 2 *m.* off), is good fishing, and the Hotel Johannin is comfortable. March, April, and May are the best months. (*See Paimpol.*)

Havre.—There is good smelt fishing off the wooden piers on the beach of Ste. Adresse, a suburb of Havre, also a few small shad and gobies. The baits are the squid, calmer, and other species of cuttle-fish; the large sand-worms, and the centipede-like red or green worms found in the harbour mud or under rocks in muddy ground at low water; also shrimps, which are freely taken by small whiting, &c., early in the season, and the mussel. Open a good lot half an hour before you reach your fishing ground, let them dry a bit, and put them on very carefully; they are a most killing bait. The sand-smelt is taken in the harbour, and in large numbers along the beach, by fine tackle, with three or four hooks baited with bits of fresh-skinned shrimps. There are some deep weedy ponds three miles from here, where fair sport with roach and rudd may be had. Near here flows the Lézarde; trout. This river, flowing through the villages of Rolleville and Epouville, and the town of Montivilliers, falls into the Seine two miles below Harfleur, a little above which town it is joined by a smaller and shallower stream coming down through the adjacent valley of Gournay. From Montivilliers up to Rolleville is the best fishing part. Besides trout in this part of the river there are a few little eels and lampreys. Montivilliers is one hour by road from Havre. Leave used to be readily obtainable on polite application to the various millers. Flies for the Lézarde should be small and tackle very fine. The season is from Feb. 1 to Oct. 31. The stream in the valley of Gournay contains a few good fish, and may be fished either near the metal-rolling works (distant about a mile and a half from the Harfleur Railway Station), application being made to the manager (*directeur*), or, if unsuccessful here, at the Corderie, half a mile further up, where the *directeur* readily gives leave. Good sport may be obtained in the following trip: Rail to Yvetôt, half-way between Havre and Rouen, diligence thence to Cany, from which town down to Villefleurs and beyond, even down to the sea at Veulettes, you may fish many miles of a large and well-stocked stream, abounding in trout of superior size and flavour, particularly near Villefleurs. But be careful to ask permission (which will scarcely ever be refused) whenever it is desirable to enter the premises of mills, farms, &c., or to go on any path which is not evidently public. Flies here may be somewhat larger than for the Lézarde. Crossing the Seine by the Honfleur steamer (passage thirty-five minutes), and proceeding by rail to the neighbouring station of Pont l'Evêque, there is fair fishing up several miles of a good large stream, where nobody will make any difficulty. Very large trout, but not very numerous, may be found in the Bisle, at and above Pont-Audemer, accessible by a little steamer from Havre, or by *voiture publique* from Honfleur. Any hotel keeper at Pont Audemer will give information as to the best waters, and persons from whom to obtain permission.

Hennebont (Brittany).—On Blavet; trout, dace, and occasionally salmon and sea trout. The water between here and Lochriste is the best. Use large and bright flies. One side of the river is preserved, the other free. No difficulty will be found in a gentleman obtaining leave on giving up every alternate salmon he catches.

Hesdin.—Canche; trout; preserved by a local association, but leave probably obtainable. (*See Montreuil.*)

Hyères.—The little river Gapeau, flowing into the sea a few miles below Hyères, holds an abundance of good chub, roach, gudgeon, &c. The fishing is free. Begin at a point about two miles from the town, and fish downwards. At the mouth of the Gapeau grey mullet may be taken with the ragworm occasionally. At the peninsula of Giens, opposite Hyères, there is good fishing from the rocks in deep water for sea-bream, wrasse, &c. The ragworm is the best bait. There are good points for fishing on both sides of the peninsula. Wherever you see deep water, you may be sure that fish abound. The local fishermen will often try to persuade you to go out in the roads in one of their boats. This appears to be a delusion. The landlord of the humble inn at Giens will at any time be able to find a boy, who for a few *sous* will get you a good stock of bait (ragworm, small prawns, &c.). The prawn is the most killing bait. Some trout are reported between Hyères and Cannes.

Inxent.—On Course; trout: fishing free, but poor.

Josselin (Brittany).—On Oust: trout. The fishing is fair. The Croix d'Or is a good inn.

Jura.—No permit required, except in Champagnole and neighbourhood. All the mountain streams, such as Ani, Valouse, Valouson, Seille, &c., are full of trout. Coarse fish also in Seille from Bletterans.

La Roche-Posay.—A good deal of trouting to be had in the departments of Vienne, Indre, Creuse, and Hte. Vienne, some of the rivers of which hold heavy trout and occasional salmon. There is a small inn here. Fishing is better higher up at Le Blanc and Argenton.

Lamalou.—The river Orb, which passes through here, and its tributaries, Jaur and Mare, are full of fish (trout, barbel, roach, &c.). No permit necessary. Best months are July to October. St. Pons, St. Gervais, and Truscas are good trouting stations.

Lamballe (Brittany).—The river here is devoid of fish.

Landivisiau (Brittany).—On Elorn. Large trout and salmon. Penser also an excellent stream. The accommodation at the Hôtel du Commerce is good.

Lanleff (Brittany).—On Leff. Trout.

Lannion (Brittany).—Fair fishing can be had in the neighbourhood. (*See Paimpol: Tréguier.*) Salmon may be taken in the Guer. Sea trout are plentiful below the town, and above brown trout are numerous.

Lanslebourg.—On the top of Mont Cenis Pass is a lake containing trout. Leave to fish must be obtained from the monks at the hospice.

Laruns.—On the road to Eaux Bonnes. Trout.

Le Faouet (Brittany).—*Hotel*: Lion d'Or. There are five rivers within easy reach, all full of trout. Above Le Faouet to the north is the Ellé, a heavy river, containing good trout and lots of dace. The Laita is heavily wooded, and contains fine trout and dace. At the valley of St. Barbe there is good fishing for small trout. Below Le Faouet the Ellé is deep and still. At the junction of the Laita is a good spot. (*See Quimperlé.*)

Le Lauzet (Savoy).—Hotel de l'Europe; poor. There is a lake near here full of trout.

Le Puy.—12 or 15 kilomètres from here, ascending the Loire, and at the same distance from Langeac, ascending the Allier, trout are met with, and in greater number the more one journeys towards the rivers' source. In Allier there are salmon occasionally. Below Le Puy and Langeac trout are fairly numerous; but small barbel, dace, roach, &c., predominate. No permit required for rod fishing. Artificial fly is particularly killing, but on account of the rapidity of the streams only wet fly fishing can be indulged in. Mons. Bizalior, the general secretary of the Syndicat d'Initiative of Velay is an enthusiastic angler, and would no doubt be delighted to render assistance to a brother piscator. His address is 10, Place du Breuil, Le Puy.

Louvie.—Between Pau and the mountains. A few trout.

Luz (Hautes Pyrenees).—There are many lakes within reach holding good trout, especially Lac Bleu. Small trout abound in the mountain streams.

Marenla.—On Canche; trout; annual ticket 10 *fr.* from the mayor.

Marquise.—On Selacque. There are a few trout, and fishing is free, but almost ruined by poaching.

Marseilles.—Good sea-fishing from the piers or boats. Suitable tackle may be hired, and various baits bought, at a kind of open-air shop nearly opposite the Bourse.

Melrand (Brittany).—At the junction of the Blavet and Sar, one of the best fishing stations in Brittany. About ten miles south of Pontivy.

Mesidon (near Caen, Normandy).—On the Dives. About two miles of water is let by the season. Fair fishing both below and above it.

Mezieres.—On Meuse; trout, &c. Fishing good between Boulzicourt and St. Pierre; leave obtainable; apply to M. Grandjean, grocer, Place Ducale, Charleville.

Mont Dore les Bains.—*Hotel*: Sarciron Rainaldy. Chaubourg on Dordogne. Trout

Montherme (near Mezières).—Fishing in the Meuse; no permit required. Close time April 15 to June 15. Good spots are from the Hotel de la Paix to Mahanté Mill.

Montreuil.—On the Canche. There are trout here, and a few salmon, and good sport may sometimes be had as far as Hesdin. 6 *m.* below Hesdin, Contes joins Canche (trout), and 5 *m.* further down, at Beaurainville, another good stream joins.

Montvilliers (Normandy).—On Lézarde; trout; fishing indifferent. Some trouble in getting leave from the millers.

Morlaix (Brittany).—The river Guer at Lannion gives good sport. (*See Brest.*)

Mortain.—By train from Vire, Avranches, St. Hilaire, and Granville. A little trout fishing in the Cance, 4 *m.* below the town, off the high road to St. Hilaire on the left. The fishing is open for the most part. The coch-y-bonddhu is the favourite fly, and May-fly in its season. Showy flies useless in general. *Hotel*: De la Poste, good and reasonable. Good lodgings may be had for 15f. per month, including linen and attendance. The only trout in the two tumbling streams close to the town are fat little things, rarely more than five inches long.

Murat (Cantal).—Fair trouting here.

Nice.—Some fair grayling fishing can be had at St. Martin Lantosque, where are two fair hotels. Some 12 *m.* off, near the Chapel of Madona di Fenestra, is a lake holding good trout.

Nielles-les-Bléquin.—St. Omer line, 1¼ hours from Boulogne. On Bléquin, trout; mostly free hence down to Lumbres, where Bléquin joins Aa.

Ouve-Wirquin.—On Aa. Trout. Yearly ticket 4*s.*, from the mayor.

Paimpol (Brittany).—Good sea-fishing round the coast. *Hotel*: Guicquel. The principal rivers are the Leff, the Trieux, the Jaudy, the Guindy, and the Guer, all containing trout; and the best localities for sport are Pontrieux, Guingamp, Roche-Derrion, Lannion, and Belle-Isle-en-Terre. Salmon may be caught at Lannion and Pontrieux. At Tréguier there is good fishing in the tidal river.

Pont Audemer.—Near Honfleur. Trout (some heavy) in Rille; leave necessary.

Pont l'Evêque.—River Tonques; trout. Leave used to be obtainable.

Pamiers.—On Ariege; trout. Poor fishing. Fishing may be got a few miles higher up.

Pau.—Good general fishing, with worm, gentle, and fly, in the Gave. Plenty of chub everywhere, gudgeon, and a good many trout, which take fly and natural minnow well. The neighbouring village of Coarraze is a good station for trout and general fishing. Many large trout lie under the railway bridge, also below the canal company's weir a little higher up. Cheap and pretty comfortable quarters.

Plestein (Brittany).—The Douron runs near; salmon and trout. Accommodation bad.

Floërmel (Brittany).—*Hotel*: Hotel de France, good. On the Lake Etang-du-Duc. Pike and eels in the lake, but the banks are very weedy. The millpool in the stream contains some good trout.

Pont-Aven.—*Hotels:* Julia's, Gloussec. The river Aven runs through the town, and is tidal to within 200 yards of the hotels. Large baskets of fish frequently taken in a day, especially in March, when salmon and sea trout are fairly abundant. From here up to Rosporden there are about 17 kilometres of fishable water.

Pontgrand (Brittany).—A secluded village. There is a nice trout stream here, much wooded. The fish average two to the pound.

Pontivy (Brittany).—The Blavet runs near. It is used as a canal. There are many over-shots where good trout may be taken. *Hotel:* Hotel Grosset. The trout fishing, in the department of Morbihan, is prohibited until June 1. This applies, however, only to the canals and navigable streams. (*See Melrand.*)

Pontrieux (Brittany).—(*See Paimpol.*)

Pont-Scorff (Brittany).—On Scorff; good trouting; salmon sometimes.

Quimper (Finisterre).—On Odet and Steir; sea-trout and trout. Mackerel's guts are very good bait for sea-trout here. The flies must be small. Red hackles, red and black palmers, coch-y-bonddhu, and dotterel hackle for March and April. Later come in wren's tail, alder fly, and March brown; and a fly, body, peacock's harl, ribbed with gold; hackle, red; wing, woodcock.

Quimperle.—On Ellé; salmon, trout, dace, &c. The fishing, which is leased by a local lawyer, who grants permission freely, is very good, the Ellé being considered one of the best salmon streams in Brittany. For flies use red, yellow, and brown bodies.

Quintin (Brittany).—There is a tolerable trout stream here, and the quarters are good.

Roche-Derrien (Brittany). (*See Paimpol.*)

Rodez.—The Lot, Aveyron, Tarn, Truyère, and other streams, are within reach. Near the end of 1903 a piscicultural society of about 64 members was formed, with an annual subscription of 2 *fr.*, and much has already been done to improve the fishing and dis-courage the wholesale poaching previously so rife.

Rosporden (Brittany).—There is a fine lake here, but the banks are very much over grown.

Rostrenan (Brittany).—The lakes of Glomel lie near; also the canal connecting Brest and Nantes. There are good pike in both. *Hotel:* Les Trois Pilliers.

Royat-les-Bains.—(*See Clermont.*) - Use fine gut and small flies—partridge hackle, black and grey spider, duns, red spinner, alder, and red tag. There are trout in a great many small streams in the surrounding hills, but poaching is very rife.

Sixt.—*Hotel:* Du Fer à Cheval. Good sporting quarters. Plenty of trout.

St. Brieuc (Brittany).—*Hotel:* La Croix Blanche. A few trout may be taken in the river.

St. Caradec (Brittany).—A village near Londéac. There is a fair stream here containing trout.

St. Firmin (Dauphine).—On Severesse; trout. Fair anglers' accommodation. 4 *m.* down from St. Firmin Severesse joins Drac. Fishing poor, but it is best above St. Firmin, 6 *m.* up to Roux, and beyond to La Chapelle. There is only a cabaret at Roux; at La Chapelle fair anglers' accommodation at the hotel. General flies are hare's ear and yellow, dark and light coch-y-bonddhu, black hackle, and plain body, or ribbed with silver, and red spinner. The head waters of Drac are well worth fishing.

St. Germain-en-Laye.—There is little fishing here. It is 20 *m.* from Paris.

St. Girons (Ariège).—River Ariège and its tributaries at Foix and Tarascon; river Salat and tributaries at Castillon, Leix, &c. Trout plentiful. Fishing from February to October. No permit required. The waters are very clear, so that anglers should show themselves as little as possible.

St. Jouan de l'Isle (Brittany).—On Rance; trout fishing fair. Accommodation poor.

St. Malo.—There is fair sea-fishing off here; pollack round all the shoals; mackerel, conger, bass at the mouth of Rance; pout, plaice, bream in the offing.

St. Martory - On Garonne; abundance of chub, barbel, &c., and a few trout.

St. Nicolas.—Accommodation fair. The Blavet stream, 3 kilometres off, is one of the best in Brittany There is another stream nearer, and these two join at Goarec, 11 kilometres due South. 4 *m.* E. of Goarec is the Daoulas.

St. Omar.—Good fly fishing. The Hotel de la Poste is the best inn. The Aa is two miles off, and the Lye nine miles. They contain very fine trout.

St. Pol-de-Leon (Brittany).—The Dourdoof runs near; sea-trout and yellow trout. The river is preserved, but leave can be obtained.

St. Valery-en-Caux.—A trip may be made from here, through the little watering place of Veulettes, fishing up the river past Villefleurs to Cany. Trout plentiful but small.

St. Valery-sur-Somme.—There is but little fishing for coarse fish. At Eu, near here, there are a few trout.

St. Vaast-la-Hougue.—La Saire; small salmon and trout.

Thonon-les-Bains.—Lake Léman contains trout, l'ombre chevalier, perch, &c., also few pike and carp. Rod fishing from February to November. Near Thonon are several rivers or streams, such as Drance, Oncion, Foxon, in which trout are plentiful. The rivers are preserved by the Piscicultural Society (s.t., 2 *fr.*). In the neighbourhood are also some ponds holding pike and carp.

Toulouse.—On the Garonne; chub, barbel, and chondrostomes (*sièges*), with gudgeon, and a few perch, carp, pike, and eels. The *Ramier du Bazacle*, a large island just below the weir is the best station; leave may be obtained from the proprietors of the *Moulin du Bazacle.* The *sièges* are caught in tolerable numbers in the rapid currents, from the shore, or better from boats, with soaked wheat, sometimes with redworm, or the chrysalis of the silkworm, which may be bought very cheaply late in the summer. *Sidges* and chub often take fly freely, morning and evening. Large barbel are sometimes caught ledger-fishing. On the weir is a capital station when the water is low enough to allow of walking thereon. The little river Lers is full of small chub and gudgeon. Fishing may be begun from the bridge on the Las Bordes road, some two and a half miles from Toulouse, and fished up stream, unless the water is high. Small redworm pays best here. The Touch, another small stream, a little farther from Toulouse, is about the same fishing. The mouth of the Ariege, distant about eleven miles up the Garonne, is a good general fishing place; others are: *up stream*, Pontet, Dinsaguel (Garonne), Venerque (Ariège); *down stream*, Blagnac and St. Joey. Barbel and roach; no permit necessary; winter months best.

Tours.—On the Loire. The Cher and canal are within an easy walk and at no great distance are the Indre and Vienne, and the little streams, the Bresne, Romer, and Cisse, which latter joins Loire at Vouvray. Loire contains salmon, pike, barbel, dace, &c. In the smaller streams and ponds are carp, eels, and perch. The most likely places for pike are on the Loire at Noisay or Vernan (between this place and Amboise), or below Tours, at the junction of the Cher and Vienne respectively. The fishing in the neighbourhood of Tours is not so good. On the Cher, Chenonceaux, Azay-sur-Cher, and St. Avertin, offer the best chance. On the Indre, Montbazon is a likely spot. Minnows, gudgeon, or small dace and perch can generally be obtained at the market every morning.

Treguier (Brittany).—Between here and Lannion is the Guindry. Salmon and trout.

Treport.—Sea-trout, trout, roach &c. Within a quarter of a mile is a lock, with two heavy falls—a good spot. Fair trout fishing can be had at Crieuil, also in a stream some two leagues off. A few trout and some large roach can be caught in the canal leading to Eu, one leagu off. The fishing at Gameches, four leagues off, is fair, but the river is much netted from here to Eu; as the water is let leave must be obtained. By paying, good pike fishing can be had in Lake L'Hable, at Cayeux-on-the-Sea, two and a half hours' drive off. Also bream, tench, roach, and eels in this lake. Above Eu the river is let, we believe to an Englishman, for a league.

Vichy.—Good trouting in the valley of the Lichon and Allier, free.

Vire.—Fishing protected among the numerous woollen mills. The best water is by Graverie, five kilomètres on the high road to Thorigny. Here the Vire and Viraine have united, and form a large open river. Good trout, but dace without end in the holes. There is a tidy village fishing inn at Graverie; or board and lodging may be had at the Hôtel St. Pierre, in Vire. The Vire, above the town and the mills, runs through a perfect jungle.

Wallen-Eperlecques.—Coarse fishing in canal, 1½ hours by rail.

Yvetot. — Near here is Cany; trout fair, but, we believe, preserved. Lower down is Vittefleurs and Veulettes, the latter on sea, partly preserved. Sea trout run up occasionally.

GERMANY.

Ahrweiler.—On Ahr; trout.

Altenahr.—On Ahr; trout, grayling, chub, dace, &c. Permission from the Burgomaster. *Hotel:* Rheinischerhof. The Ahr joins Rhine between Remagen and Sinzig. Ten miles from Altenahr is Neuenahr. Fishing is poor. Twenty-five miles off is a large lake full of good perch.

Bad Boll (Black Forest).—Ener. Preserved for guests (d.t. 3s.) by proprietor of Bad Boll Hotel, Bonndorf. Good flies are red tag, whirling dun, wickham, and blue upright.

Baden-Baden.—Fair trout and grayling fishing in the Moeng, some little way off. The river is preserved, we believe. At Gernsbach trouting can be had in the Murg. Tickets for Murg to be obtained at a shop in the Colonnade by personal application; d.t., 5 marks; w.t., 20 marks; m.t., 70 marks; s.t., 80 marks. Another ticket, 2m. 60pf., must be obtained from the police. The fishing, about 10 m. long, runs from close above Gernsbach to above Forbach, passing Oberstroth, Hilbertsan, Wissenbach, Langenbrand, and Gansbach (inn: Gasthaus-zum-Waldhorn, clean and cheap). The upper part is the better trout and grayling water, and the lower for chub, &c. At Forbach is a decent inn, the Lion. Some distance farther up is Schonmünsach. The Post is a good inn. The Schönmunz joins Murg a few hundred yards above, and is a good trout stream. There are a few small trout and dace in the stream running through Baden.

Berchtesgaden (Bavaria).—There is good fishing in the river, from this place to the König See. Leave must be obtained. The landlord of the Watzmann Hotel will give an introduction. At the lower end of the König See is a rustic inn. Good trouting can be had at Reichenhall. Hofland's Fancy is a good fly here.

Berlin.—The Spree. No angling near, being so much netted. The river is a filthy ditch.

Bertrich.—On Moselle. There is a decent trout stream here.

Biberich (Baden).—Fifteen miles above Offenburg. On Kinzig. Trout, grayling, chub, dace. The landlord of the principal inn has the right of fishing, which is very fair.

Blankenheim.—On Ahr; trout: fishing good, but preserved.

Bonn.—Trout, grayling, and chub. Fair general fishing in the Rhine, chub dace, bleak,

P 2

&c. There are many barbel, and a few pike and large perch. Chub may be taken freely with Dutch cheese, also with a parboiled paste composed of flour, milk, and eggs. The Sieg, flowing into the Rhine, 2½ m. below Bonn, on the opposite bank, contains various coarse fish. Near Bonn is Königswinter, at the foot of the Severn Mountains, and nearly opposite Königswinter is Rolandseck, both fair spots for a little sport. The Ahr joins the Rhine at Remagen, some miles above Bonn. Half way up the Kreuzberg, a hill just outside Bonn, is a pond containing abundance of very fine carp, leave for which may sometimes be obtained. A small stream flows into the Rhine some 3 m. below Bonn, on the same side. By fishing up 1½ m. excellent sport may be obtained, either with redworm or grasshopper, among chub, &c., with the chance of a trout.

Bruckhaus (Baden).—On the Schluecht. Hotel Bad Bruckhaus near Rhine and Wutach. Seven miles excellent trouting, partly *unnetted*; fishing free to guests for Schluecht and Rhine. Station, Waldshut.

Coblentz.—There is a lake near here containing very large pike and perch; fishing free; you must pay for the fish at the market price. Plenty of general fishing both in Rhine and Moselle.

Daren.—(*See Aix-la-Chapelle.*)

Darmstadt.—Not far off are the Maine and Rhine. Pike and other fish can be caught in the Grosse, Woog, Amosen, Teich, &c., near the town.

Donaueschingen (Baden).—Brigach; chub, grayling, trout. Breg, 3 m. off, at Votterdingen; trout; fishing fair; the landlord of the hotel can get leave. *Lakes*: In Prince Furstenberg's park is a large lake holding good trout. *Hotel*, Schütze.

Donauwerth (Bavaria).—On Danube. (*See Munich.*)

Dresden.—The Elbe; pike, perch, and the usual fish. Annual licence 6s. per annum, within 4 m. of the town; beyond that is free. At Pirna, half an hour off by rail, there is some fair trout fishing; also at Schandau, two hours' distant, a little fishing can be had in the Elbe, below the town. Quantities of small fish may be caught at the junction of the Weiseritz, 1 m. down. There is good trouting in the Polenzthal Valley, 2 m. walk from Rathen, one station beyond Schandau.

Dusseldorf.—On Rhine. There are a *few* salmon and trout, with plenty of chub, and other fish. In May, a fish called May-fish runs up the river; they will not take a fly.

Ems.—On Lahn; trouting poor, but plenty of chub and coarse fish.

Forcheim.—Between Miremberg and Bamberg. At Muggendorf, on Wiesent, good trout and grayling fishing can be had. Leave can be obtained.

Frankfort-on-Main.—Plenty of coarse fish and chub above the town; preserved by an association, who issue daily tickets for a small fee. Plenty of barbel here. Some good trouting at Heigenbrücken and Lohn two hours off by rail.

Freiburg (Baden).—*Hotel*: Zähringer Hof. On Dreisam: trout and grayling. 10 m. N. at Waldkirchen there is good trouting in Els; apply to the landlord of the post-house. At **Ochs** (*Hotel*: Wilden Mann) some trouting can be had by leave from the proprietor. At **Feldburg**, 24 m. off, the hotel on the spot rents the fishing of Feldsee; trout run large.

Frendenstadt (Black Forest).—*Hotel*: Schwarzwald. Good trouting.

Füssen (Bavaria).—On Lech; huchen. There are several lakes near here; Hupfen See and Banwald See, and some smaller tarns near Hohen-Schwangau. The two lakes first-mentioned contain pike and a few trout and coarse fish; leave can be obtained easily. The small lakes are strictly preserved by the king. There are some small lakes near Rosskaupten two hours from Füssen. An hour's ride from Füssen is Reutte, in Tyrol, on Lech, containing trout and grayling. The fishing is free and not very good. There are two lakes near Reutte, the one nearest the town contains plenty of carp. Near Reutte is the Arch Stream rising in some lakes, and contains trout and grayling. The master of the Crown Inn will give leave to fish it. (*See Ischl.*)

Hachenburg.—Six hours from Cologne *via* Au. By staying at the Krone Hotel fair trouting can be had.

Hanau-on-the-Main.—Ten miles by train from Frankfort. The Kinzig river runs near the town, and is full of pike, chub, &c. Half an hour's ride from Hanau is a submerged valley. When the Main becomes flooded, the water and fish enter the valley, the latter being left behind in the old peat holes when the waters have receded. Very large pike and perch are then to be had. The landlord of the inn near there charges ninepence for every pound weight of fish you take away. Wines and restauration good, and moderate charges.

Hansach (Baden).—Kinzig; grayling, chub, trout, &c. *Hotel*, Railway; the landlord can obtain some fishing for a few days.

Heidelberg (Baden).—On Neckar; barbel, chub, dace, roach, perch, May-fish; fishing very poor. D.t. 3d. Ordinary English flies answer here. The May-fish is the shad. Good trout fishing 8 m. from Heidelberg by payment of 9d. for every pound weight of fish you catch and take away with you. Very large trout at the Wolf's Spring, 2 m. off; bottom fishing for chub near the barge wharf is best. (*See Neckar-Steinach.*)

Hesse Cassel.—There is a fair trout stream near.

Hof (Bavaria).—(*See Ischl.*)

Homburg (Baden).—Gutach; trout, grayling; preserved for 2 m. by the landlord of the Bear Hotel; fishing fair; wading necessary. The brooks Essbach and Ober Eslenbach, near the town, are small, and contain a fair stock of chub. They are preserved by the 'landlord of the hotel Victoria, who has some trouting also. Nidd runs 4 m. from here. Tickets, 4d. per day, can be obtained from the burgermeister. Plenty of chub and white fish, also pike.

Immenstadt (Bavaria).—On the Munich and Constance line. (*See Reutte.*) In the Alp See there are plenty of pike, but no trout. There are one or two lakes near Martinzell, on the Munich line, an hour from here.

Katzenellenbogen.—On Dörsbach. Good and cheap accommodation at Bremser's Hotel, where leave can be obtained, but the trout must be given up. A small amount is charged for the necessary licence.

Kissingen (Bavaria).—*Hotel*: Kurhaus. Saale; pike, barbel, chub, &c.; a small fee required for permission. There is good trouting at Neustadt (10 m. off).

Klagenfurt.—On Worthersee; pike, roach, &c. The Glanfurt holds roach, but leave must be obtained. *Hotel*: Kaiser v. Oesterreich.

Konigsberg (Prussia).—No one allowed to angle in the river Pregel, as it is farmed by the fishermen. Thirty marks, or 30s. penalty. The Castle lake, near the town, is about 4 m. long, and the residents on the banks are allowed to fish from their lawns. The lake contains very large carp and perch. There are restaurants on the banks, and guests are allowed to angle from their gardens.

Kreuznach.—On Frahe; chub, perch, &c. Fishing indifferent.

Kyllburg.—On Kyll, which contains trout and grayling. The Eifeler Hof is a good hotel, and has for visitors 7 m. of free water, well stocked with trout, a few grayling and plenty of chub, and large bleak. The river is best fished from Densborn *down* past Zendscheit and St. Thomas.

Langen-Schwalbach.—Aar. A long stretch of the river may be fished by visitors to the Hôtel Metropole. Wet fly does very well, and dry fly is useful in summer. Fish run up to 1lb. Good flies are red palmer, March brown, red ant, red and blue uprights, Wickham, and governor', the latter with red hackle and no wing in the daytime, and white wing in the evening.

Ligneuville (*via* Spa and Stavelot).—On Amblève. Spring fishing is uncertain; May would be a better month. Fish run four to the lb. Flies are March brown, red spinner, and red palmer. Doumoulin's is a very comfortable and reasonable hotel.

Lorch.—There is some trout fishing in the Whispen, a small stream which runs into the Rhine here. It is, however, strictly preserved.

Mannheim (Baden).—Good pike and coarse fishing in the Rhine and Neckar. For Rhine a yearly ticket is to be obtained from the police at the Kaufhaus, also permission from a Herr Meyer, who rents fishing (his address can be obtained from any fishmonger). For Neckar, ticket, 3 marks, must be obtained from Schloss. Fair fishing; very good chub fishing near railway bridge; also good fishing in docks, but is preserved by a society of 10 members at 80 marks each. At Mannheim is an English fishing tackle maker, W. Collingwood, opposite station; very obliging, and knows the river well.

Martinszell (Bavaria).—(*See Immenstadt.*)

Mendorf.—There is a brook between here and Schlangenbad holding trout; you cannot fish with a fly. The landlord of the Crown will give leave. Mendorf is distant from Wiesbaden a quarter of an hour by rail.

Mentz.—In the Nendorf brook there is good trout fishing.

Munden (Hanover).—There are three rivers here, the Fulda, Verra, and Weser. Only coarse fish, barbel, chub, &c. There is splendid pike fishing in a large pool, formerly the bed of the Fulda.

Munich (Bavaria).—In the Iser and Amsser fair grayling and huchen fishing can be had; leave not very difficult to procure. The best fishing is in the Danube, between Donauwerth and Regensburg, and in the Inn, between Passau and Rosenheim; leave on Inn is procurable for a small sum. There is a comfortable inn at Newhaus, an hour from Passau. Göging and Braunau, higher up the river, are good stations. Accommodation bad.

Mürlenbach.—On Kyll: trout and grayling. Visitors staying at Krumpen's Hotel (Gasthof-zur Post) can fish for a mile or so above the village, but this water is poorly stocked; fishing much better below, belonging to the burgomaster and brewer, who might possibly grant leave.

Murnau (Bavaria).—There are two lakes here, Staffel See (*Hotel:* Staffelsee) and Rieg See, containing trout. We believe the landlord of the principal hotel can obtain leave. By taking a cross road Saulgrub can be reached. Accommodation indifferent. The Ammer runs near, containing trout. The fishing between Saulgrub and Unter Ammergau is very good, but it is doubtful whether fishing can be had at this latter place. At the village of Baiersoyen, three-quarters of an hour from Saulgrub, on the road to Scongau, is a small lake containing trout, and within an hour of Baiersoyen, at Wildsteig, is another lake.

Neustadt.—(*See Kissingen.*)

Neckar-Steinach (10 m. from Heidelberg).—Fair trouting; tickets from the inn. keeper.

Nieder Andorfer (Bavaria).—On the Innsbruck line. Two hours-and a half off is **Walch-See**, containing good trout.

Oderbruck.—Oder. In the pools are large trout.

Offenburg (Baden).—Kinzig; chub, grayling, pike, perch, trout; roach; preserved by the municipality: s.t. (only) 14 marks. The mill stream is preserved by the miller: payment required. *Hotel*, Fortuna.

Passau.—On Inn. (*See Munich.*)

Pirna (Saxony).—Half an hour by rail from Dresden. (*See Dresden.*)

Prague.—On Moldau. There are plenty of fish here, and trout in its tributaries.

Prenzlau (Brandenburg).—*Hotel:* De Prusse. On Uckerlake. Good fishing.

Ravensburg (Württemberg).—(*See Constance.*)

Regensburg.—On Danube. (*See Munich.*)

Reichenhall.—(*See Berchtesgaden.*)

Remagen.—(*See Altenahr.*)

Rosenheim (Bavaria).—On Inn. A small river here joins Inn, which contains grayling.

Schandau (Saxony).—(*See Dresden.*)

Schlangenbad (Nassau).—(*See Mendorf.*)

Schwalbach (Nassau).—The landlord of the Hotel Metropole rents 25 *m.* of a fine stream, which he preserves for his visitors; as does also the landlord of the Hotel Nassau.

Schwarzburg (Thüringen Wald).—Splendid trout fishing in Schwartza, also grayling; permission to fish is given by landlord of hotel Weisser Hirsch, Schwarzburg, to visitors staying at hotel; speaks English, and very obliging.

Senierke.—On Bode; good trouting; permission easily obtainable.

Siegburg.—A village ten miles from Bonn, on the river Sieg; good fishing. (*See Bonn.*)

Stettin.—The Oder; wels, pike, perch, bream, pike-perch, and roach. Fishing free, except for pike, 6s. annually. Best fishing in the Haff, or lake, between Stettin and the Baltic. There are several lakes between Stettin and Berlin, the proprietors of which generally give leave to angle.

Tels.—On Iser. Plenty of coarse fish, and some trout.

Triberg (Baden).—Gutach; trout. Some little fishing is attached to two or three of the hotels here. The town waters are let at 10 marks per season.

Vienenburg. — On Ecker; good trouting, belonging to Count Stolberg; permission impossible. Leave is sometimes given, however, by Herr von König for his fishing at Torfhaus, near Vienenburg.

Volmar-en-Sea.—Pike, perch, &c.

Walporzheim.—Ahr; trout, chub, &c.; fishing poor below, but fair above. Accommodation can be had at the Hotel St. Peter.

Weimar.—River Ilm. 8 or 10 *m.* of the best water, limited to four rods at a time, artificial fly only; fish under ½lb. to be returned in the upper water, and under 1lb. in the lower. All fish to be given up alive, or may be purchased at 1s. 6d. per pound. Charge for fishing, 5s. per day, or 1l. per week. Catches of over 20lb. not unusual. First-class accommodation at the Hotel Erbprinz, the proprietor of which will be pleased to give every information.

Weinheim (Baden).—Good trout fishing; permission can be obtained at the various inns (Pfälzerhof, &c.), where there is a "Forellenfang"; accommodation fair.

Wiesbaden.—(*See Mendorf.*)

Wildbad (Württemberg).—On Ens: trout and grayling. Sport is good, and the Hotel de Russie very comfortable Licence costs 12s. a week; fly only is allowed.

Wolfach (Baden).—Kinzig; grayling, trout, chub, &c.; preserved partly by the landlord of the hotel. Wolf; same fish. *Hotel*, Salmen.

HOLLAND.

General Information.—Excellent sport among pike, perch, carp, roach, and bream in nearly all of the numerous canals. A licence for fishing with any tackle or net, 7 florins 7 cents. Anyone taking out a licence may fish, provided he has leave over the requisite water. As a rule, permission is freely accorded. Pike fishing may be had on the Maas, near Grave, which is reached by steamer from Rotterdam or Bois le Duc; at Nijmegen, about 9 *m.* from Arnheim: and at Ouderkerk, on the Eisel, 6 *m.* from Rotterdam, between Rotterdam and Gouda. To Ouderkerk a boat runs twice a day from Rotterdam. There is some jack fishing to be had in the river at Loo, the station for which is Appeldorn. The fishing belongs to the crown, but leave may be obtained through one of the innkeepers without much difficulty. North Brabant, in the rivers Tongreep and Dommel, which run east and west of the village of Valkenswaard, a few pike are to be had, but they are not very large. The rivers in North Brabant are muddy and sluggish; they seem well stocked.

with eels. There are no trout, but plenty of roach and dace. Smelts can be taken from many of the quays and piers, and flat-fish and eels are numerous.

Delft.—Plenty of small coarse fish in the canals.

Maastricht.—On Maas; coarse fish, including pike, bream, roach, chub, &c.

Rotterdam.—Coarse fish, eels, and plenty of fine carp in the canals.

ITALY.

General Information.—Bass, grey mullet, and varieties of the bream are caught at most Italian ports.

Ancona.—On Lago Maggiore. There is good trolling here.

Baveno.—On Lago Maggiore; ferox, pike, and perch. The lake is very deep.

Breno. (*See Iseo.*)

Cadenabbia.—Lake Como. Some dace-like fish, about ½lb. a piece, can be killed with fly here; also large trout trolling.

Capri.—*Hotel:* Quisisana. Good fishing.

Como.—On Lake Como; trout, pike.

Desenzano.—Six hours from Milan. On Lake of Garda. There is fair trout trolling in summer. A fish called *cavedoni* rise freely to the fly, but run small.

Florence.—There is tench fishing in Lake Bientina and also in the Arno.

Genoa.—Grey mullet can be caught at the entrance of the Bisagno stream almost close to the city walls; also bass, bream, and red mullet.

Iseo.—On Lago d'Iseo; tench, chub, pike, and a few large trout. The tench and chub are fond of polenta and silkworm grub, and may be taken from the shore. At Breno the Oglio runs into the lake. Lake trout constantly ascend the stream from the lake.

Ivrea.—There are four small lakes near here, also the river Dora, containing trout and perch. The Hôtel Scudo di Francia is comfortable. The town is situated at the entrance the Val d'Aosta.

La Thuile de Ste. Foi.—In the Val de Tignes. *Hotel:* Des Voyageurs. There is good trouting in the Isére and Lac de Tignes.

Les Tavernettes.—Mont Cenis. *Hotel:* Posthouse of the Mont Cenis. There is a lake near here, belonging to the monks at the Hospice, containing fine trout; leave must be obtained.

Rimasco.—On Val Sermenta. There is a tolerable inn here. Trouting very fair.

Sardinia, Island of.—Trout reported in all the streams. Fair hotel at **Cagliari.**

Spezia.—There are trout in a stream about 6 *m.* E. Good hotels.

Varallo.—This is a good head-quarters to fish the streams on the Italian side of Monte Rosa, all of which contain trout. It is next to useless to fish when the snow is melting.

NORWAY AND SWEDEN.

General Information.—*Salmon and Sea Trout.*—It may be said that all the salmon rivers of any value or *accessibility* are already leased. Now and then one gets into the market from its owner being prevented from going out, but generally the chance is eagerly embraced by personal friends, although Mr. Henry Mohn, engineer, Bergen, sometimes has salmon (and trout) rivers to let. There are, however, many short, shallow, and comparatively worthless rivers advertised every year. These are mostly in the hands of Norwegian speculators or middlemen. The greatest caution is necessary before signing the contract and paying the rent (which is always paid in advance). References to former tenants should be insisted on, as well as accurate information respecting nets, traps, and other fishing rights. *Trout and Char.*—The trouting tourist, in looking at his map, sees a country studded with innumerable lakes and laced over with a network of streams. All of these contain trout, some of them char, and some of them grayling. Almost all these thousands of lakes and streams are open to him, *except, of course, those up which salmon and sea trout run*, and even these, above the falls, may be fished by asking permission from the farmers. It must, however, be borne in mind, that the angler has no *right* to fish or to trespass on the limited crop of grass, and care should be taken not to do more damage than is unavoidable. It is well to employ a son of the farmer as gillie or boatman if possible. Boats may generally be obtained, and should be subjected to a good overhaul before pushing off, as those little in use are often unseaworthy. If a man goes to Norway to fish, he must make that his *one* object. We should recommend him to take a district (such as Telemarken, Sœtersdal, or Jotunheim), and work it thoroughly. The best sport is not obtained in turbulent water, however likely looking, but in the more evenly flowing streams connecting lakes. The rivers on the east of the great watershed of the Dovrefjeld and Fillefjeld are better in this respect than those on the west. The smaller rivers are better than the very large ones, and this holds good also with respect to the lakes. In these the best places are at the inlet and outfall, and about any islands or banks, just where the shore disappears at a depth of four or five feet. On a lee shore during windy weather large trout will often take close to the bank. Before many years pass over, it will be necessary to lease trout fishing; indeed, many lakes are at the present moment rented, although permission to fish is seldom withheld. *Tackle.*—The salmon fisher knows all about tackle when he ascertains upon what kind of water he is to be located. The ordinary patterns, in different sizes to suit the rapid changes in the height of the river, are all that will be required ; 120 to 150 yards of running line, treble and single gut for heavy and fine water. Dependable tackle cannot easily be obtained in Norway. For trout, Scotch lake flies, larger or smaller according to amount of wind, will kill on the lakes. Red-bodied flies with mallard wings are best for rivers; all the principal makers know the tackle required. Mr. Cummins, of Bishop Auckland, in his catalogue, gives a list of flies which he found killers during a trouting tour in Norway, and Messrs. Hardy Brothers will also advise from personal experience. A supply of spoons, phantoms, and Devon minnows for lake spinning should be taken. The gut should be strong, and the line 60 yards. A 14ft. double-handed trout rod, with extra tops, and tops for spinning, would be best if only one rod be taken. An 11ft. rod and finer tackle all round would be occasionally useful. The net should be a folding one, and large and capable of being fastened to the pannier strap. A rod box. made with straps at each end to sling it under the shafts of the carriole, is a great protection to the rods. The rivers are mostly unsuitable for wading. Good waterproof boots, and gaiters to guard against the heavy dew, will be found better than waders. A good macintosh, reaching down to the gaiters, is indispensable, and a sou'-wester would be found a comfort. Should the traveller drink whisky, he had better bring his supply from England, as no spirits can be obtained in Norway, except at Christiania, Bergen, and Trondjem, and such large towns. *Steamers, &c.*—Wilson's line of steamers from Hull and London to Bergen and Christiania is deservedly popular, and much used by sportsmen. Berths should be secured as early as possible. The Halvorsen line from Newcastle to Bergen is supposed to be quicker. but these steamers are not so comfortable as the Wilson boats (*see* advertisements in the *Field* and other papers every week during the season). The sea voyage is so short, about thirty hours from land to land, that few tourists travel *via* Calais and Denmark. Fares about the same by the Wilson and Halvorsen lines, 6*l.* return, inclusive of victualling. There are local steamers on every fjord, and on most of the larger lakes. Information in the "Norges Communications," a kind of Bradshaw, to be obtained at Bennett's shops at Bergen or Christiania, or at Beyer's in the main street (Strandgaden), Bergen. The land travelling is by carriole, stolkjærre for two persons, or open carriage for three or more. The less luggage taken the better. *Guide Books, Maps, &c.*—Baedecker's "Norway and Sweden" contains all the requisite information for travelling, as well as numerous maps. After fixing on a district for fishing operations, it would be well to order the sheets of the Ordnance Survey through Stanford's, of Long Acre, W.C., or they might be selected at Bennett's or Beyer's at Christiania or Bergen. Information as to money, luggage, language, posting, &c., is given in the various guide books.

In Norway the occupier of land has *primâ facie* an exclusive right to all fisheries upon it ; and, except on public or waste lands, no one else can claim any right to use a rod, even on waters in which there are no salmon or sea trout. Where, as is commonly the case, strangers are freely allowed to fish for trout, char, or grayling, they do so by the permission of the occupier express or implied. Strangers should be careful not to trespass, and should always apply for permission at the nearest house, even when they believe that they are upon waste lands over which the public have rights of common. The most important rivers in the province of Tromsö are the Reisen, Skibbotten, Maal, Skö, Salang, and Lokhelle; the others, though numerous, are for the most part short, and so rapid that fish cannot run up any great distance from the sea. The larger rivers were once full of salmon and sea trout, but the stock of fish has been seriously diminished. Beginning from the frontier of Finmarken, and following the coast line of Tromsö Amt southwards to the borders of Nordland, the names of the rivers succeed each other in their natural order.

BADDERN R., 9½ m.—Rising in the Baddern Vand, a lake, 1 m. long full of non-migratory fish. the river of the same name falls into the Kvænangen Fjord. At but a short distance from the sea fish are stopped by a waterfall, immediately below which a good number of salmon are taken every year.

RUOSSA JOK, 6 m.—A small stream, draining half.a-dozen lakes of no great size, and falling into the Kvænangen Fjord.

NIEMENAIKA R., 14 m.—Issuing from the Sioka Lake, on the borders of Finmarken, the Niemenaika falls into the Kvænangen Fjord.

OLMA R., OR ABBO JOK, 10½ m.—From Lake Abbo, 3½ m. long, to its mouth in the Kvænangen Fjord, the Olma is 7 m. long.

NAVET R., 21 m.—From its source in the glaciers of Bezegel Haldi to the Kvænangen Fjord the Navet is a broad and quiet stream, with but three rapids. Close to its mouth salmon, which are there pretty numerous, are stopped by a waterfall. There are trout in the upper part of the river.

OKSFJORDS OR STORSKOGS R., 17½ *m.*—From its rise in Rokkilgaissak, between the valleys of the Navet and Reisen, the Orksfjords River flows northwards through Storskogsdalen, and 14 *m.* from its source falls into the Oksfjords Lake, 3½ *m.*, long. The lower end of this lake is not more than half a mile from the sea. The river is full of fish.

REISEN R., 70 *m.*—Next to the Maal, the Reisen is the largest river in the province. It rises close to the frontier of Finmarken, in a lake of the same name, and reaches the sea at the head of the Reisen Fjord. Above Elvevold, 3½ *m.* from the head of the fjord, there are heavy rapids; thence the river is navigable to a point a little above Sappen, the last farm in the valley, and distant by water more than 35 *m.* from the sea. Salmon run up the Reisen for more than 63 *m.*, and there are in the valley about forty landowners entitled to fishing rights. Half a mile from its mouth the Reisen is joined by the Samuel River, a large tributary, in which a strong current and frequent changes in the course of the stream render navigation difficult. Salmon, however, pass some way up it, and it also holds trout.

ROTSUND R., 14 *m.*—From its source in the mountains above Djævledal, the Rotsund is for some way a wild torrent, but in its lower course through Rotsunddal, its fall is less considerable, and at last is a broad and steady stream.

NORMANDVIK R., 5 *m.*; VINTERDALS R., 7 *m.*; NJAAMEL R., 9½ glacier *m.*—Three streams rising among the snow mountains north of the Kaafjord, and falling into the Lyngenfjord. The first-named holds trout; the others contain no fish.

KAAFJORDS R., OR GUOLAS JOK, 10½ *m.*—From Guolasjavre, a lake 4 *m.* round, the Kaafjords River has a rapid fall until within 4 *m.* of its mouth at the head of the Kaafjord, it reaches the more level part of the valley.

SKARDALS R., 3½ *m.*—Rising in the Beolajavre, a lake 1 *m.* long, the Skarsdals River falls into the Kaafjord.

MANDALS R., 17½ *m.*—On this river, running into the Kaafjord, a certain number of salmon are taken below a waterfall which stops their further ascent.

SKIBBOTTEN R., 35 *m.*—Skibbotten River is formed by the junction of two smaller rivers, which both rise in Russian Finland. The Skipajok, Ortasjok, or Didnojok—for in different portions of its course it is known by all three names—is the more northerly of the two, and is a mere torrent with frequent waterfalls, while the Kjærring River or Galgojok flows through a chain of lakes differing but little in their level until between Galko Lake and its junction with the Didnojok it forms a succession of heavy rapids. Two miles lower down, the river now known as Skibbotten passes Hélligskoven, a "fjeldstue" or mountain station for the convenience of travellers. Immediately below the station the river flows through a small lake, called Bassejavre, between which and the sea, a distance of 18 miles, there are several rapids, and the river is seldom fordable until where close to its mouth it becomes much wider, and has formed extensive sandbanks. This was at one time a good salmon stream, but of late years, owing to constant netting, salmon and sea trout have almost disappeared. Skibbotten, however, is full of large trout.

The Gakkojok, a tributary of the Didnojok, is celebrated for the number of small trout, all of them of excellent flavour and readily caught.

KIT R, 8½ *m.*—This short stream rises in 4 small lakes between the Markusfjeld, Moskovarre, and Mandfjeld, and falls into the head of the Lyngenfjord, close to the mouth of the Lyngdals River.

LYNGDALS, OR SIGNALDALS, OR STORFJORDS R., OR OMASI JOK, 28 *m.*—From its source in two neighbouring lakes, Cassa and Guovda, the latter and larger, 3½ *m.* long, the Lyngdal runs S.S.E. for about 7 *m.*, until, after receiving a tributary from the Kolta Lake, it skirts the southern end of the Markusfjeld, and then flows N.W. into the head of Lyngenfjord. Less than two miles above its mouth it is joined by the Martindals River, 4½ *m.* in length, and erroneously laid down on Munch's map, and described by Broch as a separate river. In the lower part of its course the Lyngdal frequently undermines and washes away part of its banks, which are steep and of loose material. This is a great hindrance to navigation, though boats can still be used to a certain extent.

LYNGDALS R., 9½ *m.*—A small river, also falling into Lyngenfjord, but on its western shore, about 10 *m.* S. of Lyngen Church. It is a rapid glacier river, with a large volume of water. A good many salmon are taken near its mouth.

POL R., 3½ *m.*—Quite a small stream, falling into Lyngenfjord just north of the Lyngdals River. There are a couple of mills close to its mouth.

ROTTENVIK R., 3½ *m.*—Another glacier stream falling into the Lyngenfjord, 2 *m.* N. of the church. 1½ *m.* above the mouth of the river there is a waterfall.

STOR R., I VARTO, 3½ *m.*—Rising in a small lake called Langvand, this stream falls into the Lyngenfjord on its west shore. It is famous for the number of trout.

JÆGERVANDS R., ½ *m.*—A short length of river between the Jæger vand, a large lake, and the eastern shore of the Ulfsfjord. Salmon are numerous.

STORSTENNÆS R., 3½ *m.*—A fair-sized mountain stream rising in a small lake under the east face of Isskarstind, and falling into Kjosen, an arm of the Ulfsfjord. Full of fish.

TYTTEBÆR R., 5 *m.*—This stream rises close to the sources of the Fastdal River, but flows S.W. into Kjosen. Its mouth lies 3½ *m.* E.S.E. of the mouth of the Storstennæs.

KJOS OR JER R., 3½ *m.*—Rising in two tarns in Goalsevarre Kjedel, this stream falls into the head of Kjosen.

JÆGTEVIKS R., 1½ *m.*—Rising in the Langvand, a mountain tarn, this river, after flowing through the Jægtevand, a lake a mile long, falls into Kjosen, 3½ *m.* W. of the mouth of the Fornæs River.

STOR R., 3½ *m.*—Another small stream, rising about a mile W. of the Langvand; it also falls into Kjosen, 1½ *m.* N.W. of the mouth of the Jægteviks River.

LERBUGT R., 4½ *m.*—Flowing out of the Troldvande, two tarns not far from the Langvand, the Lerbugt flows south into the Sörfjord, a branch of the Ulfsfjord. The river has no great fall, and is well supplied with water.

LAX OR SÖRFJORDS R., 13 *m.*—From its source between Riismaaltind and Pigtind, this river at first flows W. until within 2½ *m.* of the Balsfjord, whence there is a track; it turns N.E. through a cultivated valley, and falls into the Sörfjord near its head.

SKOGNÆS R., 4½ *m.*—A mountain stream falling into the Sörfjord on its western shore.

SOMMERBUGT R., 2½ *m.*—Another small stream, also falling into the Sörfjord a mile south of Sörfjords Church.

LAVANGS R., 7 *m.*—Rising on the south-west side, and skirting the west and north sides of Sjurnæs Fjeld, the Lavang falls into the Sörfjord a mile north of the church. Less than 2 *m.* from its mouth the Lavang receives a tributary, according to the Amt map, from Nakkejavre, a lake 1 *m.* long. In the Beskrivelse, however, this lake is said to be drained by the Nak, a tributary of the Bredvik River, and to be full of fish.

BREDVIKS R., 15 *m.*—Rising in Bjorneskarret, this river, owing to its slight fall, follows a tortuous course to the Ulfsfjord. A mile above its mouth it is joined from the south by the Nak, a tributary more than 7 *m.* long. The valley of the Bredvik is wide and open, and both main river and tributary are well stocked with fish—the former with salmon and trout, the latter with trout, char, and a few salmon.

OLDERVIKS R., 7 *m.*—This river falls into the Ulfsfjord on its western shore, almost opposite the mouth of the Jægervands River. It is a good-sized stream, and full of fish.

TROMSDALS R., 3½ *m.*—Another small mountain stream falling into the sound opposite the town of Tromsö.

STORSTENSBUGTS R., 5 *m.*—A small stream falling into the head of the Ramsfjord.

ANDERSDALS R., 8 *m.*—Rising in a small tarn under Svartnæstind, this stream flows north, and falls into the Balsfjord immediately south of the entrance to the Ramsfjord.

NORDKJOS, OR STOR R., 14 *m.*—Flowing out of Tabmokvand, a hill lake 1 *m.* long, this river falls into Nordkjosen at the head of the Balsfjord. At first but small, 7 *m.* from its source it has become a broad, deep, and still river. It is a good trout stream, and some salmon are taken near its mouth. Boats can ascend the river for about a mile, and there is a road to Overgaard 6 *m.* up the valley, whence again a track leads north-east, through Martinsdal, to the head of the Lyngenfjord, 7 *m.* off.

HOLE R., 3½ *m.*—Rising in the Storvand, a narrow lake 2 *m.* in length, the Hole River within a mile from its mouth is joined by the Tver, 4 *m.* long, from the west, and by the Markenæs, a tributary of like length, from the east. The Hole falls into Sorkjosen at the head of the Balsfjord. Both the main river and its tributaries are mere mountain streams, and, except in time of flood, of inconsiderable size.

SAG R., 11½ *m.*—Issuing from the Tagvand, a small lake among the Maartinder, this river, known as the Tommer in the upper part of its course, after a rapid descent of 6 *m.*, falls into the Sagelvand, a lake 2½ *m.* long, whence it emerges as a broad and shallow stream, and, after a further course of 3½ *m.*, enters the head of the Balsfjord. There is a waterfall close to the mouth of the river, which is said to contain a good stock of fish, probably trout and char only.

HOLMENÆS R., 1½ *m.*—A short stream, carrying off the waters of the Jasopvand, a lake 3 *m.* long and 1 *m.* broad; it falls into the Balsfjord, 3½ *m.* S.E. of the church.

BAKKEBYE R., 4½ *m.*; SAND R., 7 *m.*; SKUTVIG R., 4½ *m.*—These and a number of other still smaller streams, rapid in the upper part of their course, but more tranquil as they approach the sea, serve to drain the peninsula between the Malangsfjord and the Balsfjord. They are said all of them to hold fish, probably trout, or trout and char only. On the Sand River there is a waterfall close to its mouth.

LAKS R., 4½ *m.*—From the Fiskelösvande two lakes, respectively 1½ *m.* and 3½ *m.* long, the Laks River runs to the Aursfjord, a branch of Malangenfjord. Below a waterfall, 200ft. in height, the stream is rapid, and there is good salmon fishing. Trout are plentiful above the fall.

MAAR R., 9½ *m.*—Shortly after its issue from among the Maartinder this river becomes a quiet stream, flowing between high banks. There is a waterfall a short distance from the sea, below which the river is broad and shallow. The Maar falls into the Aursfjord, a branch of the Malangsfjord, and is reported to be a goodt rout stream.

MAAL R., 112 *m.*—Great Rosta Lake, 24 *m.* long, and for the greater part of its extent situate upon Swedish territory, is drained by two rivers, one a tributary of the Tornea, which falls into the Gulf of Bothnia, the other the Rosta River, which, after flowing for about 7 *m.*, enters Little Rosta Lake, 6 *m.* long. Soon after leaving this lake the river, now broad and quiet, receives two tributaries, the Tamok and the Divi, one on either bank, and thenceforward is known as the Maal. Below the junction of the three streams the river has but a slight fall, and its waters from time to time separate and form several channels, until at Fossli, 21 *m.* from the sea, they plunge over the Maalsfoss, a waterfall of between 30 and 40 feet in height. Less than a mile below Fossli the Maal is joined by the Bardo, its most important tributary. As there is but one short rapid between this junction and the sea, boats can come right up to the falls, while coasting vessels can reach Brandskognæs, 17 *m.* from the mouth of the river. The Bardo rises in the Altevand, a lake 28 *m.* long, and has a course of 44 *m.* to Fossmo, where there is also a waterfall. The two falls lie about a mile apart, and at about a like distance from the junction of the rivers. They stop the further ascent of salmon, and, owing to the deadness of the water lower down, it is only for a short distance immediately below them that salmon can be taken with a rod. On the Maal, salmon have been almost exterminated. The river and its tributaries have now for some time been under the care of a fishery association. Above the Fossli Fall the Maal contains a few trout and grayling. The Bardo and its tributaries, on the other hand, were at one time full of trout and char, but of late years their numbers have been recklessly thinned. 7 *m.* from its western end there are narrows upon Alte Lake. These are not more than 70 yards across, and through them runs a stream, against which boats must be towed. Roads run up the main valley as far as Kongsli on the Little Rosta Lake, and up Bardodal as far as Stromsli, 12 *m.* below the Alte Lake. The farmers are many of them well-to-do, and at their houses accommodation may be had far superior to that in any other valley in Tromsö Amt. Maalsnæs, at the mouth of the Maal, is a place of call for the main line steamers between Trondhjem and the north, and also for the s.s. Tromsö, a local steamer trading to and from the town of the same name. The Maal Valley may also be reached from Söveien i Salangen, another place of call for the s.s. Tromsö. There is now a good road from Söveien through Bardodal, to the Maal Valley, a distance of about 35 *m.*

TORN R., 1¼ *m.*—From a lake of the same name, 2¼ *m.* long, the Torn River flows west into the Rogsfjord; though short, it is deep and broad, and has so strong a stream that it is only with difficulty that a boat can be rowed against it. The Rogsfjord is in reality brackish water, separated from Malangsfjord by the narrows of the Rogsfjord Strommen, through which sea water enters the Rogsfjord at high tide.

FINJORDS R., 1¾ *m.*—Rising in the Finfjordsvand, a lake nearly 4 *m.* long, this river also falls into the head of the Rogsfjord. Ojord, on the eastern shore of the Gisund, is by water less than 3½ *m.* distant from Klöven, where all coasting steamers call.

TOMMER R., 9 *m.*—Rising at the foot of Hjerttind, the Tommer river falls into the Reisenvand, a lake so little above sea level that the influence of the tides is felt even some little way up the river. There are salmon in this stream, but it is only during autumn floods that it is worth fishing. By water Reisen lake is 4¼ *m.* distant from Klöven.

SKÖ R., 15 *m.*—Within a short distance from the point where it issues from a lake of the same name, the Skö is joined by a tributary called the Gumpe, and, after a further course of 7 *m.,* falls into the Reisenfjord, less than 3 *m.* S.W. of the outlet of the Reisen Lake. Salmon ascend the Skö as far as the lake. The best pools are in the first 2½ *m.* of the river below the Fos, but there are some good ones above; 5 *m.* from the mouth of the river is a long extent of still water which affords excellent sport.

LYSBOTTEN R., 12 *m.*—This and the two following rivers are in the island of Senjen. Two short links of river connect greater Lysbotten Lake with the lesser, and that again with the sea. As the lakes drained by this outlet are many, and some of them large, it would seem that the stream ought to hold salmon.

GRÆSMYR R., 8 *m.*—Græsmyr Lake, 1 *m.* in length, receives at its upper end the Skar and Mosk Rivers, and is drained by the Græsmyr River, which, after a course of about 2 *m.* falls into the Gisund half-way between the steamboat stations Klöven and Gibostad.

LAX OR LOKHELLE R., 17¼ *m.*—This river, or rather chain of lakes, is navigable by boats for a distance from its mouth upwards of about 7 *m.,* and salmon can ascend still further. There are a few salmon casts in the short lengths of stream connecting the different lakes, but the greater part of the fishing is in the lakes themselves.

ESPENÆS R., 4½ *m.*; BRODSTAD R., 7 *m.*; LOKSE R., 7 *m.*—Three small streams, falling into the sea between the Reisen and Salangen Fjords. The first-named would appear to be a mere mountain torrent; the second and third may possibly hold a few salmon near their mouths, and yield trout fishing higher up.

SALANGS R., 30 *m.*—Rising on the borders of Sweden, the Salangs River runs north, until 5 *m.* from its mouth it turns westwards, and flowing through the Ovre and the Nedrevande, two lakes, each of them a little less than 2 *m.* in length, falls into the Sagfjord, near Söveein i Salangen, one of the s.s. Tromsö's calling places. Though the Salang is very rapid, salmon can ascend as far as a waterfall called Kistefoss, 7 *m.* from the sea, and 3½ *m.* above the upper of the two lakes. Boats can be towed from the lower into the upper lake; the rapid between the lower lake and the sea is quite impassable. There are about eleven landowners entitled to rights of fishery on the Salangs River. The best netting station is at Strokenæs, at the bottom of the rapid between the lakes, where almost every fish might be netted. Apart from the lakes, the only rod fishing for salmon is upon the 3½ *m.* of water between the upper lake and the Kistefoss. From Sandvik, a farm on the south shore of the upper lake, there is a good road into the valley of the Bardo, and along that river to its junction with the Maal. There is also a road up the Salang Valley to Moholt, 21 *m.* from the sea. A fishery association for the preservation of salmon in the Salang River was constituted on Feb. 18, 1876.

SAG R., 8 m.—The Sag River takes its rise in two small hill lakes of the same name, and falls into the Sagfjord 1 m. W. of the mouth of the Salang. It is a mere torrent.

SPANDALS R., 14 m.—From its sources close to the boundary of Norlands Amt the Spandals River flows northward into the head of Lavangen Fjord. It is an impetuous and turbid stream. It holds few fish.

FJORDBOTTENS R., 4½ m.—A small stream falling into the head of Gratanjen Fjord.

STOR R., 5 m.—Rising in Ovrevand, and flowing through Mellemvand and Nedrevand, three small lakes, the Stör River falls into the head of Gratangen Fjord, close to the mouth of Fjordbotten River. Fish can run up for a distance of nearly 2 m., until just below Nedrevand they are stopped by a waterfall 200ft. in height. A good many salmon are taken in the pool below the fall, above it trout are plentiful.

LABERG R., 6 m.—Rising in a lake of the same name, the Laberg falls into Gratangen Fjord, about 5 m. W. of the mouth of the Stor River.

FOLVIK R., 3½ m.—An impetuous mountain stream falling into Gratangen Fjord. 2½ m. W. of the mouth of the Laberg River. It does not hold many fish.

SKODBERG R., 11½ m.—Two short links of river 1½ m. in length, connecting the Skodberg Lake with the Salt Lake, and the latter with the Gravfjord. As the lakes are but little above sea level, the river has no great fall, and is said to be full of fish.

The salmon fishing in Sweden is not so much sought after as that in Norway. In the rivers flowing into the Baltic and the Gulf of Bothnia salmon do not take the fly well. Still most of the rivers contain salmon where they can get up; and hold trout, char, and grayling above the falls and in the lakes. Coarse fish are also to be found in some lakes and rivers; large pike and perch are often taken when spinning.

In Sweden the inns are decent, and food more plentiful than in Norway. There are salmon in all the rivers, though in some, as the Dal and Umea, they are stopped by falls within a few miles of the sea. In the Dal, below the falls at Elfcarleby, some good fish may be taken spinning. The principal fish of the country is the grayling, which may be caught anywhere. The best rivers for fishing that run into Lake Wenern are the By, the Tryka, the Nors, the Klar, and the Let, all with an extensive lake system. There is also the large Dalslands Canal. In Wenern, besides the ordinary fish, is a large salmon, rather pale in flesh. No large rivers run into Lake Wettern, but the Rivers Götha and Mataia run out of it, with five or six lakes connected with the latter. Permission to fish must be obtained from the landowners. Both salmon and trout fishing have very much fallen off of late years. Except in out-of-the-way places, better sport can be obtained in Ireland or Scotland.

Aalesund.—On an island at the mouth of the long Stor Fjord, into which run several small rivers, of which the Valdal at Sylte, near the top, is the chief. It is leased, and fishes late; others are the Stordal, Strande, Simelve, and Nordal.

Alten.—Very fine river, draining 2700 square miles; there are over 30 miles of salmon water. It is leased, and the bag by rod is the heaviest in the country.

Asmica (Sweden).—On Bze Elfven. This stream runs from this town to Lake Wenern. There are pike in the river, and lake trout and *Lucio perca.*

Bergen.—There is no fishing to be obtained in the immediate neighbourhood, but daily steamers run to the Hardanger, Sogne, and Nord fjords (which see), and the railway runs twice a day to Vossevangen. On this line the Dale river is passed. This fishing is much spoiled by the cloth factory, still heavy fish are often killed. The next river is the Vosse, draining 550 square miles. It fishes best early, and holds large fish. All the water, from the fjord at Bolslad to the Evanger lake and that at Evanger, together with some pools above, have long been leased by Englishmen. Some intermediate water, and the portion at Bulkan, are in the hands of Bergen middlemen; reports of this perplexing. In the Evanger lake char are numerous, but small and poor. For the upper water, *see Vosserangen.*

Carlstad (Sweden).—(*See Gothenburg.*) On Lake Wenern. The Clar here joins Wenern. This river rises far up on the Norwegian fells. A little distance to N.E. of Carlstad lies Christineham, a capital station. The fish in Wenern consists of lake-trout, which run to spinning bait, silfver-lax (a species of trout), which rise freely to a fly, the brown trout run to a fair size in the lake, also burbot, pike, perch, *Lucio perca,* tench, bream, roach, and grayling are plentiful in the Clar.

Christiania.—(*See Lœzjo Yarn Vœrk.*)

Christiansand.—*Hotel,* Ernst's. At the mouth of the Torrisdal, a river with catchment basin of 1500 square miles, and of the Topdal fjord. 11 m. of salmon water on the Torrisdal to Helvedes Fos, generally rented by gentlemen of the town; leave sometimes given; all boating. Trout numerous, but small near the fos. Good trouting for many miles up the river, there called Otteraaen, to Saetendal. Within drive of the town, Christiansand, are some lakes holding very pretty trout. The Topdal falls into the head of the fjord of the same name, 10 m. to the north. There is only a short though good stretch of salmon water to Boen Fos, formerly leased to Englishmen. For some years the owner declined to re-let. The Mandal, 25 m. to the west, with a basin of 700 square miles, is said to be the most productive river in Norway, with very handsome fish; but it is most severely netted, and little but small fish are now bagged. One stretch has long been owned or leased by an Englishman. It is to be hoped the nets may be hired off some day, as has been done with the Lyngdal and the Quinna, 25 and 35 m. respectively to the west.

Disæt.—On Rena: trout. This place is two stations below Lake Storsöen. The fishing is very good; so also is it at Lonsæt, the next station above. At the northern end of the lake the fishing is also first-rate. This district is but two days from Christiania, and the accommodation is very decent and the charges moderate.

Drontheim or Trondhjem.—Many large and productive rivers fall into this fjord, but hundreds of nets on it, and on the lower reaches of the rivers have immensely injured them. The three best—Orkla, Gula, and Stjordal—have all long stretches, 30 to 60 m., of salmon water, leased in various sections. On the Nid, between the town and Lerfos, are some 5 m. of salmon water, for which leave can generally be obtained. Up the fjord to the north are the Levanger, Vaerdal, Lexdal, and Stenkjaer; the last, and probably others, are let.

Falkenberg (Sweden).—There is some capital salmon fishing here, but preserved.

Flekkefjord.—10 m. east is the Quinna, with 5 m. of fine salmon water to a fos, leased at the highest rent paid in the country. Within reach of the village are several lakes with very fair trouting. To the west of the town is the Sire. Extensive well-planned ladders have been erected on two fosses, which salmon freely use; but fish have not increased much. Probably the angling is to let; it was in the hands of a syndicate. The deep 17-mile long Siredal Vand (lake) above holds very large trout, chiefly at the upper end, Toustad, where is a fine trout stream with pretty fish.

Forde.—On the Sond fjord, at the mouth of the river running through Jölster Vand. Salmon and sea trout can go up 3½ m. to a fos. Formerly netted, and leave to fish portions obtainable. Some years back it was taken on short lease, and was said to have fished fairly, but neither the angler nor his friends retook it. It is now in Bergen hands, some of whose tenants seem to have been fairly satisfied. Sivertsen's Hotel, on north bank, very good. For Jölster Vand and upper water, *see Nedre Vosenden.*

Gottenborg (Sweden).—Salmon, trout, grayling. The Gotha runs out of Lake Wenern. The lake is fed by twenty four streams. The town of Wenersburg lies at the southern extremity of Wenern, and Carlstad on the north (*see Carlstad*), Mariestad and Lidkoping on the East, and Arnal on the west. At either of these towns good and cheap accommodation can be had. Lake Wettern is connected with Wenern by a canal thirty miles long. There is a very good trout stream about 20 m. (English) away, holding very large trout. (*See Kongelf.*)

Gouverod.—(*See Laurvek.*)

Guldholmen.—Near Tana mouth. A steamer calls once a fortnight. The best plan to fish Tana is to take boats up to Gallaghov Guaika, 10 m. above the Polmac. Tents will be required, and plenty of provisions. At Polmac lives one Shanker, a merchant, where boats and accommodation can be had, but he is fearfully exorbitant in his charges. Here the Polmac river joins Tana. This stream rises in a large lake, full of fish. The sea-trout fishing is capital in the salt water at the mouth of the river.

Hardanger Fjord.—EIDE.—Excellent hotel, kept by Mæland, who owns the small river, which contains sea trout and occasionally a few small salmon. The water is so trapped that the only chance of sport is during a flood. The Graven lake near here is not worth fishing, but between Graven and Ulvik the mountain road passes the Espeland lake, said to hold trout of great size, though, as far as our experience goes, 1lb. or 1½lb. would be the average.

EIDFJORD.—On the river Eidfjord, which runs into the Hardanger Fjord some little way S. of Bergen. The river has a fishable length of about two miles. It is not a good river, and very rapid, but famous for the size of its sea trout. Very deep and careful wading is necessary. The best cast is known as the Long Hole. There is an inn at Eidfjord kept by the brothers Neisheim; the accommodation is good. The salmon river is no doubt let. The best time is from the middle of July to the end of August.

Hoaas.—(*See Klethammer.*)

Jotunheim.—This district should be thoroughly worked by the energetic trout fisher. It is reached from the Gudbrandsdal high road on the way from Christiania to Romsdal, or from the Valders route over the Fillefjeld by ascending from Fagerlund. Skogstad, or Nystnen, where a guide and the necessary pony or packhorse may be hired. The same may be done at Aardal in the Sogne fjord. This district is very rich in lakes and streams, and tolerable accommodation can be obtained at the Tourist Club buildings and small hotels known to the guide.

Jerkin.—Through the valley runs a good stream, containing plenty of trout and grayling

Kaufford.—There is a stream here containing salmon. From the fosse to the sea, some few hundred yards, the fish rise to the fly.

Kile.—(*See Volden.*)

Klethammer.—A post station on the banks of the Undal. Above the station the brown-trout fishing is excellent, also below, as far as the hamlet of Romfog; thence to the sea, 20 m., the salmon fishing is excellent. The best fishing ground commences 2 m. below the post station. Snova, to about 2 m. below the post station Hoaas a distance of 2 m.

Only a good fisherman is likely to have much sport. Good accommodation can be had at Snova and Heaas, and also at a large farmhouse between the two. White bread, &c., can be obtained at Undalsoran, at the river's mouth, and Christiansand is only a day's journey.

Kongelf (Sweden).—12 *m.* from Gottenborg. A steamer runs daily between these two places in the summer. There is a comfortable little inn here, and trout, perch, and pike fishing: some salmon also. May is the best month. The same trout flies are used as in Scotland, only larger; and Scotch lake trout flies are admirable on the Gütha.

Lesjo Yarn Vork.—On the post-road between Christiania and Molde, near the head of the Romsdal Valley. The station is clean, and the charges moderate. The distance is some 2½ days from Christiania. There is abundance of trout in a lake near the inn door. The best fishing is in a lake—Aur-Soen, some twenty miles north.

Laurvik.—The Lauven flows by the town. Salmon run large. There are few good casts. Leave to fish is rather difficult to obtain. Three miles from Laurvek is the fishing lodge of Strobro, belonging to Capt. Maynard. Here there is an admirable cast, but a boat is desirable. There is little good water below, but half a mile higher up, near a bridge, there are two or three excellent casts. The best fishing is in the upper parts of the river, at Gouverod, in Laurdal and Cara Foss. The cast here is of limited extent, but very good. The fishing season in the Lauven begins early. June and July are the best months. There are but few sea trout in the Lauven, but in a stream which falls into the fjord, near Lauvek, at the iron works, they are numerous.

Lillehammer.—The river Laager contains very large trout. (*See Christiania.*)

Lönsaet.—(*See General Information; Diset.*) Lönsaet is at the southern extremity of the Storsöen lake, and is easily reached from Christiania. The route is as follows: Christiania to Eidsvold, by rail, 42 *m.*; thence to Stor Hamai, on the Miösen, by steamer. 42 *m.*; thence by rail to Grunsaet, 25 *m.*; and thence by carriole to Lönsaet, 30 *m.* All along this route the stations are the very cleanest and most comfortable in Norway. There is good trout and grayling fishing here. In Klar Elv, running out of Faemund Sö, there is good trouting.

Molde.—The Romsdal river, the Rauma, is a fine salmon river, and belongs to Englishmen. There is a small lake on the other side of the fjord opposite Noss where we have caught trout up to 3lb. It is about 1000ft. above the fjord. A boat can be had. The great salmon rivers, the Eikisdals, the Sundals, the Surendals, and others, are well known to the salmon fisherman, but do not affect the angling tourist.

Namsas.—At the mouth of the Namsen river, with catchment basin of 2500 square miles. Salmon go up to Fiskum Fos, over 50 miles, divided into five or six beats; all leased. Bags on each beat vary from 1000lb. to 2500lb.; all harling; fish large. The Björa, a tributary, has two beats, both leased. To the north is the Vefsen. The portion below the fos has long been leased. A ladder has been erected, and salmon were caught above in 1891; that portion was then to let. Further north are the Fasten and the Rydsaa, both fair salmon rivers; leased.

Nedre Vassenden, at the end of the Jölster lake. There is good trouting in both the lake and river. A good place to stop at.

Nord Fjord.—The rivers here have very small catchment basins, the largest not more than 260 square miles, but, being more or less glacier fed, hold out well. The Eid, which runs out of Horningdal lake, is in Bergen hands, and fishes indifferently—water, it is said, being too clear. The Gloppen, falling into the fjord at Sandene, is leased to an Englishman, who has erected a ladder past the lower fos. It is a pretty river, rather late, salmon small. The Olden, the Loen, and the Stryen run from the Justedal glaciers. Olden fishes well, and has long been leased. Loen is very poor, and is probably unlet. Stryen holds large salmon and sea trout. The best pools have long been in English hands: some portion is now in Bergen hands. The lower pools are good for sea trout, but only very late—August, September.

Quickjook (Sweden).—A village in Lapland. Lodgings can be obtained at the house of the pastor. The fishing is good both in the lake and two rivers; pike, trout, and grayling. The best time to go is in the autumn, arriving at the end of August. Quickjook is some three weeks from London. Sulitelma lies some thirty miles off.

Romfog.—(*See Klethammer.*)

Saltdal (near Bodo).—Beautiful-looking river and valley, long tried by Englishmen. It and its neighbour Beiern are the "altogether latest" rivers in Norway; in Bergen hands.

Sarna (Sweden).—On Ostre Dal; trout, grayling, pike, perch fishing very good, and free. The accommodation is clean and good.

Snova.—(*See Klethammer.*)

Sogne Fjord.—VADHEIM.—Most of the fjord steamers call here. Here commences the route north to the Romsdal. At

SANDE, the first station, there is good trout fishing and accommodation.

LYSTER FJORD, a branch of the Sogne fjord. Most of the streams are from glaciers, and unsuitable for fly work. At Skjolden and Fortun sea trout, and large ones, may sometimes be taken in a spate by spinning; the natives then kill hundreds with their favourite bait a bunch of worms.

AARDALS.—A mile only of likely-looking water, good for sea trout late in season, in Bergen hands. Aaroen, short, wild glacier stream; leased. Salmon said to be the largest and finest in Norway.

AURLAND.—There are very few true salmon in this river, though the natives apply the term "Lax" to the very large sea trout which abound here. These run to 15lb. or 16lb. and over, and afford capital sport. The fishing is let.

GUDVANGEN.—A small salmon and sea-trout river, too clear to be of much account. The fishing, such as it is, is let.

LŒRDAL.—This is one of the very best salmon rivers in Norway. The trout fishing on the river above is good. At Husum and at Hœg good quarters and excellent trout fishing may be obtained. These two stations are on the Valders route to Christiania (*see Valders*).

Sond Fjord.—DALE. pleasant station, with small river with a few grilse; good trouting above the fos. Gaula. owned and leased by Englishman, who has erected a salmon ladder. Fishing best in the tidal water. For Forde river, *see Forde*.

Stavanger.—There are many small rivers in the neighbourhood, but most of those containing salmon are let. At Sand, on the new route to the Hardanger, is the famous Suledals Elv, let on a forty-years' lease. Half-way to Bergen is the Etne, a small salmon river with 100 square miles of basin; formerly leased to Englishmen, now to a Bergen merchant, who fishes, and also lets it. Having no very high ground for source, it fishes early, and needs rain later, but is liked, and sometimes re-taken by the same rods.

Strand.—First-rate fishing is to be had here.

Telemarken.—A district unsurpassed for its trout-fishing capabilities. It lies in the centre of southern Norway, and may be reached from Odde in Hardanger on the west, or Kongsberg on the east. It is traversed by good roads, and the accommodation is first-rate. Dalen on the Bandags Vand, and Botten are good central stations to work from.

Tromso.—Near here good sport can be had in the Mols Elv and Reisen.

Undalsoren.—(*See Klethammer.*)

Valders.—This is the route over the Fillefjeld from the Sogne fjord at Lœrdal to the Mjösen lake at Gjövik, or the Randsfjord at Odnœs, from both of which places Christiania can be reached in a day. All along the route comfortable station houses will be found, and at many places tolerable trout fishing can be obtained. Fagernœs is a good example; the hotel is good, the landlord speaks English, and ten brace of trout (the largest we caught was 3½lb.) may reward a day's fishing in the river. The lake here is no good. At Tomlevold there is another good hotel; the trout run very large, coming up from the Randsfjord. but the river is much trapped.

Veblungsnæs.—On Rauma. Route, from Bergen to Molde by steamer, thence by steamer to Veblungsnæs.

Vigland.—Ten miles from Christiansand. On the Torrisdal; salmon, &c. Fishing now let. Lodgings can be had generally at the different saw mills. A boat is necessary. There are plenty of sea trout. The pool below the foss is a good one; so is the Bay pool, which is two pools down, and the Farm pool, which is next below to the Bay pool. The fishing extends to some 1½ m. downwards from the foss. There is another good cast by the ferry, 1 m. lower.

Vik-Eidfjord.—By steamer from Bergen in one day. Good trout and occasional salmon. *Hotel*: Naeshim's very comfortable.

Volden.—On the Stor Fjord. There are many small rivers near here and Kile, where sport can be had; and plenty of farmhouses on this fjord, where lodgings can be had. (*See Aalesund.*)

Vossevangen.—This favourite spot has long since lost its reputation as a fishing station. It contains some half a dozen hotels, Fleischer's being one of the largest and best hotels in Norway. The lake is nearly depleted of fish. The road to Gudvangen passes some beautiful water, but the sport to be had is poor. The best places are—
TVINDE.—Just before this station the river often fishes well. Large trout run up from the Löne Vand in wet weather. Near
VINJE, the next station, the Mörkadals river and lake afford good sport. The key of the boat may be obtained from the landlord, one Knut Vinje, whose hotel is homely but comfortable.
OPHEIM lake may be fished, and boats had at the hotel here. Trout small.

RUSSIA.

General Information.—There is capital salmon fishing on the Siberian coast. Nicolaivesk, the seaport of the Amoor, is a good spot.

Finland.—You can get to Uleaborg by steamer from Stockholm, changing at Abo, or can take the steamer from Stockholm to Tornea, and from thence travel by road to Uleaborg. A Foreign Office passport is requisite, and must be viséd by the Russian consul here or at Stockholm. As to money, take gold in preference to circular notes, though the latter will pass. Fishing and shooting are free, and a fair amount can be had. Grayling, trout, and salmon are abundant in all the rivers from Uleaborg to Tornea, but salmon only take the fly at some distance up the rivers. Plenty of good grayling may be taken close to the Uleaborg town with a red palmer fly in July. Of course you must rough it, but not very much, as good quarters are to be had in all towns and villages. A good travelling map can be bought in Stockholm, Tornea, or Uleaborg. Very little luggage should be taken; but warm flannels are almost a necessity, as the nights are sometimes cold. Start as early as possible. Living is very cheap in Finland. The portion of Murray's "Handbook for Russia" that is devoted to Finland has special reference to angling, giving a long account of trout fishing in the Vuoska, near Imatra (June to September best months). There appears to be good salmon fishing at Anjala, but permission is necessary; also in the Vuoska in June and July, when the fish run from Ladoga; also near Tornea, and in all the streams running there into the Gulf of Bothnia; in the Kumo river, at Kuopio; near Nyslott, in Lake Peruwessi; at Joensu, in Lake Enowesi; near Jyvaskyla, at the Haapakoski Falls; at Tammerfors; and throughout the waters of the Kumo lake system. The salmon run up the rivers shortly after the ice breaks up. This is generally about the middle or end of May, according to the season. Salmon in Finnish and other rivers running into the Baltic do not take the fly. The fishing at Imatra is in the hands of a club, but with an introduction to a member leave to fish could probably be got. Land at Abo, and work up the coast by road as far as Tornea, giving the innumerable rivers that would be crossed on this route a trial. A small town is generally to be found at the mouth of each river of any size, and the accommodation in Finnish towns is generally good, whereas at country stations it is wretched, food (*i.e.*, edible) being almost unobtainable.

St. Petersburg.—Three hours from here is splendid trouting, preserved by a club of limited numbers. At Serriskaia, 40 miles off, on the Warsaw Railway, runs a free stream holding plenty of small grayling. Fish below the village. Opposite Schlüsselberg, where the Neva leaves the lake, fine grayling are often taken.

SPAIN AND PORTUGAL.

General Information.—One of the best rivers is the Ason, falling into the Bay of Biscay near Larédo, about forty miles from Santander, between that place and Bilbao. The best place for fishing the river is Marron, a league up stream. There is no inn, but lodgings can be had at the farmers'. The river is good up to Ramales, where there is an indifferent inn. The fish are salmon, sea trout, and trout. The salmon fishing is let to a company, who sometimes give leave. The Pas, near Santander, contains salmon. There is another river near Puente d'Eume, in Galicia, between La Coruna and Ferrol, containing salmon, sea and yellow trout. The accommodation at Puente d'Eume is very indifferent. Another river, running into the sea near Santa Marta, between La Barquera and Cariflo, contains fish, but the accommodation at Barquera is bad. Nearly all the rivers of the provinces of Santander, Asturias, and Galicia contain heavy trout, and in fair quantities. The fly fisher can by moving his quarters fish from March till September, fishing Galicia in March and April; May and the first half of June in Santander; the latter half of June, July, and August in the rivers and lakes of the northern and mountainous portion of Asturias. The Ulla with its tributaries the Furclos, Mera, the Deza the Tambre with its principal tributary streams, and the Miño are the best trouting waters in Galicia. Finest of yellow duns, red palmer, and orange hackle are the best flies, but bait fishing with worms or minnows provides good sport early morning, and after sundown on cold days. The river Sil (afterwards the Miño) in Galicia contains trout as large as almost any river in the world. Although the Sil, however, contains heavy fish, it is fearfully poached and dynamited. There are several rivers in the provinces of Orense, Lugo, and Finistèrre where, with decent weather, an angler may take ten brace of fish a day; probable weight about 12lb. In the Deva, which divides Asturias and Santander, very good fishing can be had in the month of May; also in the river of Pesques, which runs parallel with the Deva, about three miles distant from the latter. In the Nalon, in Asturias, good sport is to be had in May, and better still in the river Eo, which divides Asturias and Galicia, near a village called St. Tiveo de Abres, some five leagues up the river. At Taverga, in Asturias, near the mountains that divide that province from Leon, very good fishing is to be had in June and July; and near Galiencia, where there are some large lakes 3000ft. above the level of the sea, splendid fishing is to be had, the fish averaging 1¼lb. At La Perruca, where there is a fair inn, the river Lena is joined by the Naredo, and near Mieres by the Nalon—excellent trouting streams, affording capital sport. Fish silvery with delicate mauve tinge. Many of the Asturian streams, however, are far too inaccessible to be fished.

Astorga.—River Esla; literally alive with trout. San Roman is the best place to stay at, but the accommodation is very rough. Use March browns for still days, and orange hackle for bright, breezy weather.

Avila (Spain).—*Inn*: Dos de Mayo, kept by an Englishman. Good trouting.

Balearic Islands.—Palma (capital of Majorca). Plenty of sea-fishing. Grey mullet abundant, and numerous other kinds. Fishing both from the rocks behind the pier and from boats in or near the harbour. Water very clear.

Barcelona.—Moderately good sea-fishing from the piers.

Burguete.—There are several streams in the neighbourhood. One mile below Ronces-valles there is a clean hotel.

Cangas de Tineo.—A large village in the midst of the Sierra de Ronadeiro. Accommodation primitive, but scrupulously clean. All the rivers and streams round about are full of trout, and some of them contain salmon.

Cuenca.—Some trouting can be had here.

Fonsagrada.—Navia and its tributaries.

Juy.—On Miño; salmon and trout.

Lugo.—Miño. Here there are no fish, but some distance S. of Lugo, near Orense, the river contains plenty of trout.

Mondonendo.—Numerous trout streams amongst the neighbouring mountains.

Orense.—On Miño; salmon and trout.

Ovar (Portugal).—Twenty miles by rail from Oporto. An hour's ride from here brings you to Oliviera d'Azemeis, where fair quarters can be had. The Karina is five miles from here. Trout, barbel, &c., plentiful.

Oviedo.—Hotel Trannoy; comfortable and inexpensive. Streams near provide only fair sport.

Pamplona.—Arga, Erro, Trati, and another stream, are within easy walking distance; excellent trout fishing early in the year, but as season advances there is very little water. *Inn*: La Perla.

Ponferrada.—In the midst of trouting waters. The Sil, Esla, Orbigo, Cua, Tera, Tuerta, and Cobrera are very good. On bright days it is practically useless fishing between 10 a.m. and 4 p.m., as fish do not rise; but between 4 and 6.30 they move freely. Use smallest and brightest coloured flies (small orange hackle or a coch-y-bondhu). Fishing very good at junction of Sil and Baeza. The whole district lying between Ponferrada, Astorga, Puebla de Sanóbria, Puente de Domingo, and Villafranca is an ideal place for the fisher, as numberless rivers and streams flow down from the surrounding mountains. *Inn*: Los Astorganos. 12 *m* from Villafranca, at Santiago de Penalva, river Oza affords good sport, and the river Cua at its confluence with the Sil, 3 or 4 *m*. up the hills is Lake Corudedo which teems with fish.

Potes (Spain).—Good fishing.

Rivadavia.—On Avia: salmon. There is a fair hotel here.

San Sebastian.—Large mullet and other fish may be taken from the public promenade along the quay, and numerous varieties of small fish from boats in the roads.

Santiago de Compostella.—There are some good trouting waters here.

Valencia.—A little freshwater fishing in the river Guadalaviar. Sea-fishing at the Grao or harbour, distant three miles from the town.

Vera.—Bidassoa river. Near the sandy mouth there are no fish on account of the netting, but farther up the valley, at Yanzi, there are a few small trout. Fair accommodation at the Casino. At Yanzi there is a coaching inn on the roadside, which is scrupulously clean. At Sumbilla, a tiny village, the river consists of alternate shallows and rapids.

Vigo.—Trout in streams in the neighbourhood. *Hotel*: Continental.

Zaragossa.—On Ebro

SWITZERLAND.

General Information.—Fair trout fishing is to be found in the Grisons and in the Braie in the Canton of Fribourg, and in the principality of Lichtenstein, on the north frontier of the Grisons, at Balzars. The flies used are ordinary English ones. A very good fly for Switzerland is a pale yellow silk body, no hackle, and wings the tip of two ginger hackles with a fibre or two worked down for legs; also bluebottle, soldier palmer, coch-y-bonddhu, red and grey spinners, black gnat, cowdung, white moth. There are trout and coarse fish in the Vaudois and Stockalper canals, which join Lake Léman at the eastern end; fishing free, but cantonal licence required. Plenty of trout in the Golzern Zee, in the Maderaner Thal.

Amsteg.—Trout in River Reuss; fishing licence necessary, cost 15 francs; no day or week ticket. The same rule applies to the Golzern See, in Maderaner Thal.

Andelfingen (Zurich).—On Thur. Fair fishing. Accommodation bad along the stream, except at Winterthur.

Andermatt. — *Hotels*: Bellevue and Danioth's. There is some good trouting in the Oberalp See, about 5 *m.* off, also some fish in the river.

Appenzell.—Good trouting in Sitter, especially early in the season. For some parts of the stream an angling licence of 20fr. is imposed.

Bâle.—There is very fair trout and grayling fishing in the Birs, some 3 *m.* from Bâle By application to the proprietor of the Three Kings leave may be obtained to fish the upper stream of the Wiesen. The middle of August is the best time.

Q

Berne.—On Aare. Between this and Thur there is good fishing. Good fish can be taken below the weirs. *Hotel:* Bernerhof.

Bienne.—At Soncebez is the Birs River.

Brunnen.—(*See Glarus.*) Trout in streams, but fishing licence necessary; cost 10 francs.

Constance.—The Hôtel Brochet is good and reasonable. In fishing the lake it is as well to make a bargain for a boat for the day, six francs is quite sufficient. The fish are silber, lachs, lachs forelle (the first a fish peculiar to the lake and running from 10lb. to 15lb., and the other, *Salmo ferox*). *Salmo hucho* (for which fishing Bregenz, at the Austrian end of the lake, is the best locality), the grayling (also found principally at Bregenz), char, gwyniad, rutten, waller (which reach 20lb. and feed on the bottom), *Lucio perca*, pike, carp, tench, bream, chub, roach, rudd, dace, and carp bream. The lower lake is best for pike. On a fine summer evening the half-mile below the bridge abounds with fish of all sorts. Half an hour's pull down the Rhine there are some stakes in mid-stream: this is a good place for chub and grayling. At Mülheim, two hours' drive from Constance, there is a trout-stream: the fish are small; there is another at Ravensburg, half-an-hour by train from Frederickshaven.

Coppet.—A station near Montreux on Versoix. Good trouting.

Cortaillod (Neuchatel).—The Areuse here runs into the Lake of Neuchatel. The river rises at St. Sulpice, and passes the towns of Fleurier, Couvet, and Travers, where good fishing quarters can be had. The fishing is fair.

Couvet.—(*See Cortaillaud.*)

Davos Platz. — A health resort in the Grisons. There are two lakes—one, Davoser See, 2 *m.*, the other 4 *m.* off—and a stream by the village. Trout and ferox. Flies must be larger than at home. A *small* grasshopper is a good bait. The fishing begins in January, and ends on Sept. 25. No fishing allowed in June, July, and part of August in the river. Deep trolling is best on the lakes. *Hotel:* Fluela Post, and many others.

Fleurier.—(*See Cortaillaud.*)

Fribourg.—Twenty miles off is the Lac Noir; pike, perch, tench, dace, and small trout in the stream. There is a first-class hotel on the bank, and an omnibus meets the train at Fribourg. The fishing is good; boats can be had.

Geneva.—On the Rhone. During summer there is no fishing to be had below the Arve mouth, owing to the melting snow from the mountains. Above the junction, however, a few trout may always be got by fishing very early or late. Commence at a mill on the north bank, about a quarter of a mile above the junction, and fish as far as the water is clear and deep, which it is for some fifty yards below the big rock opposite the junction. Deep wading is absolutely necessary. You will here pick up a few brace of trout, some of them up to 2lb. or even more, possibly a stray grayling or two, and a kind of dace which sometimes rises greedily. For flies, coachman, coch-y-bonddu, and black palmer, in the order named; but by far the best is a March brown tied with a long body, Mayfly fashion. The fishing cannot be said to commence until the Arve clears. Go by rail to the first station from Geneva on the French line, and commence fishing at an island, and fish down to La Plaine station, or even below it if you have time, returning to Geneva by the evening train. Fish of from 10lb. to 20lb. may be taken, all with fly. Wading here, as elsewhere, is absolutely necessary. In addition to the above-mentioned flies (several sizes larger), a red palmer is good, and for a big fish the following: tail, a bit of scarlet ibis, a third of an inch long; body, hare's lug and olive ribbed with narrow gold twist, a big bunchy sooty olive hackle all the way up, very small dark mallard wing, and two or three horns of either red macaw or dyed swan; medium salmon size. The best place for trouting is about 10 *m.* above Bellegarde, but the poaching is awful. At La Plaine, Loudon joins Rhone (trout and grayling), much poached. Large trout are to be taken in the lake of Geneva by trolling with minnow, under sail if possible. Fish very deep, with at least six yards of gut and sixty or seventy yards of line out, and very late in the evening or at night. Perch and small dace may be caught in large quantities also in the shallower parts of the lake. Of the various streams in the neighbourhood the Versoix is the best, and is about twenty minutes from Geneva by train. The Versoix rises at D'Ivourne, on the French frontier, where there is a good inn, but the fishing is preserved, we believe. The Swiss portion of the stream is free, and falls into the Lake of Geneva, at the village of Versoix.

Glarus.—On Linth. The fishing is nearly ruined by mill refuse.

Interlaken.—There are trout in both lakes, and grayling in the river.

Kandersteg.—Some good trouting can be had in a small lake near here in the meadows between the Gemmi Hotel and Victoria Hotel on the left-hand side of the road going towards the Gemmi Pass.

Laufenburg.—*Hotel:* Post. There is a large salmon fishery here. Apply to landlord.

Lausanne.—(*See Orbe.*) The Aubonne is a fair stream; trout and grayling. The best way to fish it is to take the train to Allaman and fish down to the lake, or *vice versâ.* The Versoix is also good, one hour and a half by train from Lausanne. Both rivers are open. Wading is necessary. There is good trolling in the Lac de Bret, 10 *m.* off; leave must be obtained. Fair trouting in Orbe, 1½ hours by rail.

Lucerne.—There is fair trolling in the lake; pike, perch, and trout. In the river any quantity of chub may be taken. and occasionally some fine trout and grayling. The flies for the lake should be large but sombre. The river flies are the yellows, and a fly with a green body, red hackle, and red partridge tail wing.

Meiringen.—On Konder. Trout may be taken with a sunk grasshopper in the eddies. (*Hotel,* Sauvage.) There is a small trout stream 3 *m.* off. There are a few trout in Aar; all fishing free.

Montreux.—Trouting in the Stockalper Canal, half hour off by rail; Grand Hotel, **Territet.** Best flies are March brown (different sizes), small coch-y-bonddhu, August dun, bluebottle, willow fly. Season begins March 15, ends Sept. 30.

Morgenthal.—On Aar; trout and grayling. The fishing is fair. There is a little stream joining Aar here in which good sport can be had. The innkeeper gives leave.

Mulheim.—(*See Constance.*)

Neuchatel.—On the lake of Neuchatel; plenty of large trout, pike, perch, &c. Bottom fishing can be had at the Pierre à Mazel, a small rock about 100 yards from the port of Neuchatel. Very large perch can be killed here

Orbe.—About 12 *m.* from Lausanne. The Hôtel des Deux Poissons is good. Fair grayling fishing. At Vallorbe, 14 *m.* up stream. there are a few trout.

Poschiavo.—*Hotel*: Croce Bianca. On Lake Poschiavo; large trout.

St. Blaise.—On the Thiele. There are fish in the river, but they rise very badly.

St. Gothard.—There are trout in the Lake of St. Gothard, but few in the river.

St. Moritz. (Upper Engadine).—Four hours by mountain railway from Chur. There are several large hotels. There are three lakes connected by the Inn, all containing trout. The upper lake, Silser See, is the best, distant six miles. *Hotels:* Edelweiss and Alfeurose.

St. Ursanne (on the Doubs).—Good trouting. *Hotel :* Denis Lune.

Schaffhausen. — On Rhine; salmon are sometimes taken trolling, a few trout are caught occasionally, and there are plenty of pike, chub, and perch. The Schweizerhof is a good hotel, and grants leave to fish. The Laufen Hotel, opposite the Schweizerhof Hotel, is very good. Salmon fishing below the fall; permission freely granted. The best method is to trail an artificial bait from the ferry canoe. A mackintosh necessary in any weather. There are fine trout, perch, chub, and a fish called nose, from the length of his prominent upper jaw—a species of grayling; they are abundant.

Sils-Maria (Engadine).—There are two lakes here and plenty of trout. The hotel is comfortable. Sils Lake is better than Silva Plana Lake. June and July are the best months; September is a fence month.

Stachelberg, Baths of.—(*See Glarus.*)

Tavannes (Berne).—On river Birs. There is a good inn (Bahnhof) here.

Thun.—(*See Berne.*) There is good spinning in the lake, and fly-fishing for trout and grayling in the river. The red grouse and black palmer tied rough are good flies, mounted on No. 7 or No. 8 hooks. Salmon may also be killed. The Thunerhof and the Belle Vue are good hotels.

Thusis (Via-Mala.)—On Rhine. There is fly-fishing here, and also in a stream a mile off. The Via-Mala Hotel is good.

Travers. (*See Cortaillaud.*)

Uster (Zurich).—There is fishing in the stream connecting Pfaff Lake with the Griffensee.

Vallorbe.—There is good trouting in Lac de Joux. and in the river Orbe. Good accommodation at Vallorbe (Grand Hotel), and at Le Pont (Grand Hotel du Lac de Joux).

Vevey.—On Lake of Geneva; trout, perch, pike, &c. There is fair trout fishing on the river Veveyse, which runs into the lake here.

Visp.—At Neubrücke; trouting can be had in the Rhone.

Winterthur. (Zurich). (*See Andelfingen.*)

Zell.—There is a lake here, and the fishing is good.

AUSTRALASIA.

General Information.—There are plenty of various kinds of fish in all the rivers and water holes. The Murray cod is a large fish, running up to 100lb. They are very good eating. The bream are something like the English bream, but much better eating. They afford capital sport. At Seymour, 500 miles above the junction of the Goulburn with the Murray, the fishing is very good. Large-sized Limerick hooks are the best to take out, which answer well for yellow perch, bream, cod, and large eels. In the upper part of the Hunter, dapping for perch with a grasshopper is good. Quantities of little fish the size of bleak, may be taken with an artificial fly. In almost every one of the rivers on the Australian continent which flow southward and eastward, from the great chain of hills which run more or less parallel to the coast, very good sport may be had with the artificial fly from October to April. The fish is the Australian grayling (*Noto-thymallus australis*, M'Coy), which swarms in all the running streams wherever there are rocks and gravel—certainly from the Glenelg, on the borders of South Australia, around the coast as far east and north as the Hunter in New South Wales. It breeds in the winter months on the long flat banks of sand and gravel, and in summer is found in the shallow broken water, in localities precisely similar to those in which one would look for a grayling in an English river. In weight the Australian grayling averages from ¼lb. to 1lb. when in season. They will take almost any fly which kills grayling in England, showing a preference for the duns, the black and red ant, and the midge. The hooks should be of the smallest size (No. 12 or 13), and the tackle of the finest possible description. At Anderson's Creek, on the Yarra, about thirty miles above Melbourne, is a good spot. In the Gippsland rivers the sport is better, and the fish larger. The upper waters of the Mitchell, the Macalister, the Dargo, &c., swarm with grayling. In the pools a fish called here the "perch" (a species of the genus *Lates*), going up to 8lb. or 10lb. in weight, with large golden scales, and excellent eating, is found. A small frog, trolled as if for a pike, is a good bait for him. The English salmon and trout are now fully established in the colony. In a few years Tasmania promises to afford the finest angling in the world, if the colonists will only take care of the fish.

Launceston (Tasmania).—Sport is very good in the Great Lakes, and the fish run large. Mr. Richard F. Irvine, one of the commissioners of fisheries, will be pleased to give information as to fishing in the Great Lakes, and in other parts of the island.

Melbourne.—A good many species and varieties of fish are to be found in bays and rivers, within easy distances, and at certain seasons. In the former the pilchard has been taken. A variety of mackerel, too, affords good sport. Another fish is often taken in the upper parts of the bay—the snapper. It makes its appearance twice during the year. March and September, and is sometimes taken off the piers up to 25lb. by means of strong hand lines. Another fish frequently taken in the bay, and by the same means, is known as the pike. In form it much resembles the river pike; but it differs materially from those in colour, being a sort of silvery-grey on the back, and glistening white on the sides and belly. Some of them are nearly a yard in length, but seldom exceed 5lb. or 6lb. in weight. The pike has a pretty close resemblance to another fish sometimes, though not often, taken in the bay, known as the baracouta, a very voracious creature, who will strike at a piece of white or red rag, or even a bit of wood. They are most readily taken with a line or lines let over a ship's or a boat's stern when scudding under a stiff breeze. In New Zealand it abounds to an extraordinary degree. Another fish very abundant at times here is known as colonial salmon, and which, when they come close in shore, afford capital sport.

Queensland.—Good sea fishing on the coast. The schnapper, weighing from 5lb. to 20lb., is caught by line in fairly deep water off the islets and rocky promontories. Flat Rock, near the south entrance of Moreton Bay, is a very prolific spot. During the winter months the sea mullet pass northwards along the coasts in vast shoals, and are netted in great quantities in the various bays. Whiting are plentiful on the sandbanks, and the garfish is also netted on the shoals of the bay waters. Rock cod and flathead are met with, and the gigantic variety of the former (the groper) is found in the bays and tidal waters. The rivers and creeks inland are well stocked with bream and perch, and Murray cod are taken in the western waters.

Tasmania.—The following are some of the fish to be caught here:—*Trumpeter*: Weight, 1lb. to 40lb. or more. Recherche Bay, some sixty miles from Hobart Town, is the great ground. When on the feed they are a very resolute, bold-biting fish. They move in shoals. Try and keep them round you with plenty of burly, and be careful not to let one break away after being hooked, or the whole lot will most probably bolt.—*Bass or Bastard Trumpeter*: This fish sometimes takes a small hook when rod-fishing for mullet. Weight, ¼lb. to 7lb.—*Ling*: Very rare. Weight, 1lb. to 8lb.—*Perch*: Very similar in shape to the English fresh-water of same name; weight, 2oz. to 8oz.; are black-red and silver; black the best, ¼lb. to 8lb.; these fish give good sport. The white are caught near the city, the black farther down. Adventure Bay, thirty miles distant, is a good spot.—*Bream*: 6oz. to 3lb. Much like the British bream in shape, usually caught in brackish water, or just above it; fine eating, and good sport. Bait, a shrimp is the best; mussel next.—*Trevally*: Weight, ¼lb. to 6lb.—*Mullet*: Tasmanian herring. Weight, 3oz. to 1lb.—*Salmon*: A coarse fish, weighing from ¼lb. to 12lb. It must be cooked very fresh, or is unsafe.—*Flathead*: White and firm eating. Requires careful handling, as it possesses two little poisonous spikes on either side of his flat head. Weight, 2oz. to 4lb.—*Rock Cod*: Rather delicate, but a little soft. Late in the afternoon or evening is the great time to catch them. Weight, 3lb. to 10lb. —*Barracouta* (3lb. to 10lb.), *Kingfish* (4lb. to 15lb.): Saltwater pikes, shaped like a jack, with abundance of teeth. Very abundant. Tow a piece of red wood with one or two hooks attached, barbs filed off, and they seize it on the top of the water. As soon as you have got him aboard you can easily shake the hook clear. *Kingfish* are always caught at night, near the bottom, and a hook without barb should be used with them. There are also *whiting*, scarce; *sprats*, not looked after; *skate*, and a few other coarse fish; amongst these are *horse mackerel*, *parrot fish*, and *leather jackets*, both the latter with rat-like teeth, and the last are very troublesome, cutting off your bait without your being able to feel them

—*Conger Eels:* Very large; from 10lb. to an enormous size.—*Guard Fish, Flounders, and Soles:* The latter scarce, but inferior to the flounder, which is remarkably good. The last three are seine fish only. The mode of fishing is generally with a hand line from a boat, two or three hooks are best on small outriggers (about four to six near Hobart Town) for perch, flathead, and trevally; rock cod require a larger hook. As you go down to the ocean you use larger up to No. 5, according to circumstances. A sinker is used at the bottom, with the lowest hook just off the ground. With anything like a Dartmouth rig (the snood and hooks below the sinker) you would constantly lose your bait before you got your line or snood up from the bottom. For real trumpeter try by letting down a sinker, hollow at bottom to contain fat, and not dropping the killick until you find coral or weed; rock or sand will not do. Rod fishing from wharves, rocks, &c., is good amusement at times with small fish, with no float, a small sinker, and two or three No. 5 Limerick hooks. Mullet give the largest amount of sport. You usually vary the contents of your basket with a mixture of flathead, trevally, and perch; very rarely indeed by a bastard trumpeter and rock cod later in the day or evening. The fresh-water herring—often called the fresh-water mullet, or cucumber fish—is a very delicate fish; it is from 5in. to 9in. in length, and will very frequently take a fly. When bottom fishing from a boat, it is generally in very strong running water; consequently, you require a large cork float balanced by a ledger lead or similar, or your hook would not get down till it had swum past you. Plumb the depth, and fish a very little off the bottom; a No. 6, 7, or 8 Limerick hook, partly concealed by a turn round of red hackle, and a gentle on the point. Throw up stream, and watch the float as it swims past; strike very quickly, but not too strongly. You often hook a fish just at the end of the swim, as you pull up for a fresh cast. There is a pretty little (native) fish called trout, spotted, but with no scales, which is very plentiful in most fresh-water creeks. It is about 3in. or so long, and can be caught in large quantities by using a fine line, and the two top joints of your rod; bait, a gentle.

NEW ZEALAND.

General Directions.—New Zealand, by persevering acclimatisation of the Salmonidæ, has now become one of the trouting paradises of the world. The smaller trout, up to 3lb. or 4lb., take artificial flies freely; but the heavy fish. which run to 20lb., and are common at 10lb., are chiefly taken by spinning, or the so-called whitebait, used alive, and during the night. In the North Island there is excellent trouting. the Government having stocked almost every little stream. Licences, s. 20s., m. 5s., w. 2s. 6d., are issued by the acclimatisation societies, and by the Government Tourist Department, Brandon-street, Wellington. The officials are extremely courteous, and would gladly afford any further information required, although their "Itinerary of Travel," which gives a list of fishable streams, with their locality, means of access, and accommodation to be had, is almost all that the angler should desire. The season is from Oct. 1 to April 15, and a licence entitles the holder to fish in any part of the colony, under the easiest of conditions. Accommodation, which is good in the towns, can be had at from 8s. to 12s. 6d. a day. The fishing is practically free. A 12ft. fly rod and an ordinary spinning rod are recommended. The tackle makers in the colony will provide flies suitable for the different localities, but it is best to take out waders and gut collars. Some of the English tackle makers keep New Zealand flies in stock. A book likely to prove of service is Captain Hamilton's "Trout Fishing and Sport in Maoriland," published at the Government Printing Office, Wellington, New Zealand.

NORTH ISLAND.

Okoroire.—Best reached from Auckland (Auckland to Rotorua line), thence by coach. Trout fishing in Waikato and tributaries. Plenty of rainbow trout. *Hotels:* Hot Springs and Ateamuri.

Rotorua.—Terminus of Auckland-Rotorua Railway. Reached from Wellington as follows:—Rail to Wanganui; steamer up the Wanganui River (a beautiful trip) as far as Pipiriki, where there is a very fair hotel, 10s. a day (engage room beforehand). Coach runs from Pipiriki two or three times a week right through the thermal district of the North Island to Rotorua. Several hotels in Rotorua, but the best hotel is at Whakarewarewa, two miles from Rotorua (Geyser Hotel, 10s.). Near Rotorua are the following streams, well stocked with trout: Utuhina, Ngongotaha, Ohau, Waikorowhiti, Paurenga, Umurua, and Kaituna. Fish caught up to 10lb., rod and line. Baits generally phantom whitebait and artificial English flies. Local Anglers' Club in Rotorua, which is very ready to give information. Fishing licences from Mr. A. Williams. The Government Tourist Agent, Rotorua, will afford anglers every information. Visitors are recommended to stay in Whakarewarewa, not in Rotorua itself.

Napier (Hawke's Bay).—Rail from Wellington. Masonic, Criterion and Pohui hotels, 10s. a day each. There is good fishing about Napier in the Pohui, Waipunga, and Rangitaiki rivers.

Pahiatua.—On the Wellington-Napier line, 107 miles from Wellington. A good deal of fishing (rainbow trout) in the Makairo river, within an easy walk of the township. Hotels, 8s. to 10s., fair, and clean, with good plain food, but not luxurious.

Masterton. — Wellington - Napier line. Several fair hotels; good fishing in the Ruamahunga. The Acclimatisation Society's ponds are here.

Wellington.—Royal Oak, 12s. 6d., best hotel in New Zealand. Several other fair hotels, and some good boarding-houses. There is trout fishing in the Hutt Valley and in the mountain streams near. Detailed information of the Government Tourist Department, in Wellington.

SOUTH ISLAND.

Nelson.—Steamer from Wellington almost daily; direct or via Picton. Average trip, 15 hours. No good hotel; much best stay at Warwick House. Another large boarding-house is Lightband's. There are a good many trout streams in the neighbourhood. Also reached by steamer from Wellington to Picton, and by coach overland from Blenheim, which is reached by railway from Picton. Sea route cheapest; coaching in New Zealand costs 6d. to 8d. a mile.

Christchurch.—By steamer from Wellington. Visitors from Australia can take a boat at Melbourne which will land them at Christchurch or Dunedin, and thence by rail. *Hotels*: Coker's, and Warners. There are a good many trout streams near Christchurch (the Heathcote, Avon, and Styx are all within easy distance), and in places easily accessible from it by rail. Some very good fishing at Ashburton (rail from Christchurch) in the river of that name. There are boarding-houses in the place.

Southern Lakes (Manapouri, Wakatipu, Wanaka, &c.).—Reached from Dunedin by rail, and then coach. There is trout fishing in some, at any rate, of these lakes. It is the Southern trout which run large. There are hotels at the towns on the lakes, especially at Queenstown.

Timaru.—By rail from Christchurch or Dunedin. *Hotels*: Empire and Grosvenor, good accommodation, and reasonable charges. Some of the best trouting in the Colony may be had in the neighbourhood; Opihi River especially good. Mr. Jasker, a local angler, will supply all information.

ADDENDA.

—

ENGLAND.

Chollerford (Northland).—N.B.R. Visitors staying at the Inn may fish a good stretch of water on payment of a small fee.

Haydon Bridge (Northland).—N.E.R. Tyne. The Haydon Bridge Angling Club preserve 2 m. of water.

Helmsley (York)—The prices of tickets for the Rye from Rievaulx Bridge to Shaken Bridge, the Seph in Bilsdale, the Riocal below Harome, and the Dove in Farndale between Lowna and Church Houses are as follows: s.t. 20s., m.t. 10s., w.t. 5s. The Hodge in Sleightholme Dale and Bransdale and the Dove above Church Houses are now reserved.

Hexham (Northland).—N.B.R. Very good fishing preserved down to Hexham Bridge on north side by riparian owners; on south side on the Lyne Green by the Hexham Local Authority, who grant permits.

Kielder (Northland).—N.B.R. Kielder, Lewis, and Oakenshaw burns are all within easy distance and hold numerous, although small, trout.

Plashetts (Northland).—N.B.R. Lewis and Oakenshaw burns hold small trout. Good accommodation at the Black Cock Inn, Falstone.

Prudhoe (Northland).—N.B.R. The water from 1 m. above is preserved by the Newcastle Angling Club. At Whittle Dene are the reservoirs of the Newcastle and Gateshead Water Company; s.t. 10s. 6d., d.t. 2s. 6d., to be obtained of H. A. Murton, Tackleist, 8, Grainger Street, Newcastle. (*See Advertisement.*)

Richmond (Yorks).—Skeeby beck, and about 2½ m. of Swale, preserved by L. Jaques, Esq.; d.t. 1s., w.t. 2s. 6d., of the water bailiff, Mr. Raine, Easby. For leave to fish the Marquis of Zetland's Wycliffe water apply to his agent, Aske Estate Office, Richmond.

Woodburn (Northland).—N.B R. Ride; trout. Ride here is preserved by the Newcastle Angling Association, and above Reedsmouth by the Tyne Angling Association. The Elsdon burn joins Ride above Woodburn. Visitors staying at the Elsdon Inn may get an occasional day's fishing. The proprietor of the Ridesdale Arms has some good water up to Rochester.

NOTABLE FISH.

Date.	Fish.	Weight.		REMARKS.
		lbs.	oz.	

NOTABLE FISH.

ate.	Fish.	Weight.		Remarks.
		lbs.	oz.	

NOTABLE FISH.

Date.	Fish.	Weight.		REMARKS.
		lbs.	oz.	

NOTABLE FISH.

ate.	Fish.	Weight.		Remarks.
		lbs.	oz.	

DIARY.

NOTABLE FISH.

Date	Fish.	Weight.		REMARKS.
		lbs.	oz.	

Date						
—	No.	lbs.	oz.	No.	lbs.	oz.
Salmon						
Grilse						
Sea Trout...						
Ferox						
Brown Trout						
Grayling ...						
Chub						
Dace						
Roach						
Pike						
Perch						
Bream						
Barbel						
Carp						
Tench						
Total						
Largest fish killed ...						
Remarks ...						

DIARY.

No	lbs.	oz.	No.	lbs.	oz.	No.	lbs.	oz.	No.	lbs.	oz.

DATE .

	No.	lbs.	oz.	No.	lbs.	oz.	No.	lbs.	oz.	No.
Salmon										
Grilse.........										
Sea Trout...										
Ferox										
Brown Trout										
Grayling ...										
Chub										
Dace										
Roach										
Pike										
Perch.........										
Bream										
Barbel										
Carp										
Tench										
TOTAL										
Largest fish killed ...										

REMARKS ..

DIARY.

TOTAL.

No	lbs.	oz.	No.	lbs.	oz.	No.	lbs.	oz.	No.	lbs.	oz.

DATE									AN
	No.	lbs.	oz.	No.	lbs.	oz.	No.	lbs.	oz.	No.

	No.	lbs.	oz.	No.	lbs.	oz.	No.	lbs.	oz.	No.
Salmon										
Grilse.........										
Sea Trout...										
Ferox										
Brown Trout										
Grayling ...										
Chub										
Dace										
Roach										
Pike										
Perch.........										
Bream										
Barbel										
Carp										
Tench										
TOTAL										
Largest fish killed ...										

No.	lbs.	oz.	No.	lbs.	oz.	No.	lbs.	oz.	No.	lbs.	oz.

DATE										'A'
	No.	lbs.	oz.	No.	lbs.	oz.	No.	lbs.	oz.	No.
Salmon										
Grilse.........										
Sea Trout...										
Ferox										
Brown Trout										
Grayling ...										
Chub										
Dace										
Roach										
Pike										
Perch.........										
Bream										
Barbel										
Carp										
Tench										
TOTAL										
Largest fish killed ...										
Remarks ..										

DIARY.   TOTAL.

o.	lbs.	oz.	No.	lbs.	oz.	No.	lbs.	oz.	No.	lbs.	oz.

DATE ....:...

	No.	lbs.	oz.	No.	lbs.	oz.	No.	lbs.	oz.	No.
Salmon										
Grilse.........										
Sea Trout...										
Ferox										
Brown Trout										
Grayling ...										
Chub										
Dace										
Roach										
Pike										
Perch.........										
Bream										
Barbel										
Carp										
Tench										
TOTAL										
Largest fish killed ...										
REMARKS ...										

No.	lbs.	oz.	No.	lbs.	oz.	No.	lbs.	oz.	No.	lbs.	oz.

DATE ......

	No.	lbs.	oz.	No.	lbs.	oz.	No.	lbs.	oz.	No.
Salmon										
Grilse.........										
Sea Trout...										
Ferox										
Brown Trout										
Grayling ...										
Chub										
Dace										
Roach										
Pike										
Perch.........										
Bream										
Barbel										
Carp										
Tench										
TOTAL										
Largest fish killed ...										

REMARKS ..

. . . DIARY.

									TOTAL.		
No	lbs.	oz.	No.	lbs.	oz.	No.	lbs.	oz.	No.	lbs.	oz.

DATE ......

	No.	lbs.	oz.	No.	lbs.	oz.	No.	lbs.	oz.	No.
Salmon										
Grilse.........										
Sea Trout...										
Ferox										
Brown Trout										
Grayling ...										
Chub										
Dace										
Roach										
Pike										
Perch.........										
Bream										
Barbel										
Carp										
Tench										
TOTAL										
Largest fish killed ...										

DIARY.

TOTAL.

No	lbs.	oz.	No.	lbs.	oz.	No.	lbs.	oz.	No.	lbs.	oz.

DATE ......

	No.	lbs.	oz.	No.	lbs.	oz.	No.	lbs.	oz.	No.	l
Salmon											
Grilse.........											
Sea Trout...											
Ferox											
Brown Trout											
Grayling ..											
Chub											
Dace											
Roach											
Pike											
Perch.........											
Bream											
Barbel ..											
Carp ..											
Tench .											
TOTAL .											
Largest fish killed ...											
ks ..											

No.	lbs.	oz.	No.	lbs.	oz.	No.	lbs.	oz.	No.	lbs.	oz.

DATE ......

	No.	lbs.	oz.	No.	lbs.	oz.	No.	lbs.	oz.	No.	l
Salmon											
Grilse.........											
Sea Trout...											
Ferox											
Brown Trout											
Grayling ..											
Chub											
Dace ...											
Roach											
Pike											
Perch.........											
Bream											
Barbel											
Carp ..											
Tench											
TOTAL											
Largest fish killed ...											
REMARKS ...											

No	lbs.	oz.	No.	lbs.	oz.	No.	lbs.	oz.	No.	lbs.	oz.

DATE	No.	lbs.	oz.	No.	lbs.	oz.	No.	lbs.	oz.	No.
Salmon										
Grilse.........										
Sea Trout...										
Ferox										
Brown Trout										
Grayling ...										
Chub										
Dace										
Roach										
Pike										
Perch.........										
Bream										
Barbel										
Carp										
Tench										
TOTAL										
Largest fish killed ...										
REMARKS ...										

DIARY.

o.	lbs.	oz.	No.	lbs.	oz.	No.	lbs.	oz.	No.	lbs.	oz.

	No.	lbs.	oz.	No.	lbs.	oz.	No.	lbs.	oz.	No.
DATE										AN
Salmon										
Grilse.........										
Sea Trout...										
Ferox										
Brown Trout										
Grayling ...										
Chub										
Dace										
Roach										
Pike										
Perch.........										
Bream .										
Barbel										
Carp										
Tench										
TOTAL										
Largest fish killed ...										
REMARKS ...										

TOTAL.

o	lbs.	oz.	No.	lbs.	oz.	No.	lbs.	oz.	No.	lbs.	oz.

	No.	lbs.	oz.	No.	lbs.	oz.	No.	lbs.	oz.	No.
DATE										
Salmon										
Grilse.........										
Sea Trout...										
Ferox										
Brown Trout										
Grayling ...										
Chub										
Dace										
Roach										
Pike										
Perch.........										
Bream										
Barbel										
Carp										
Tench										
TOTAL										
Largest fish killed ...										
REMARKS ...										

No.	lbs.	oz.	Ne.	lbs.	oz.	No.	lbs.	oz.

MEMORANDA.

DIARY.

MEMORANDA.

Date.

ANGLER'S
MEMORANDA.

DIARY.

MEMORANDA.

Date.

MEMORANDA.

ate.

W. J. CUMMINS

Will send his Magnificent Catalogue and Angler's Guide **FREE** to any Address.

This publication has been highly praised and recommended by all the principal sporting papers of the World.

The XV. Edition.

SALMON, SEA TROUT, TROUT, PIKE, AND SEA RODS.

Special Salmon and Trout Flies for Ireland, including Lough Conn, Connemara District, Killarney, the Rosses Fishery, &c. Selected List of over Seventy Patterns for the Trout Rivers of the United Kingdom. Special Patterns for the Scotch Lochs. Special Flies and Tackle for Norway (*see* page 216).

W. J. CUMMINS,

North of England Rod Works, Bishop Auckland.

Established 50 Years.

London Agents—

THE WILKINSON SWORD CO., LTD., 27, Pall Mall.

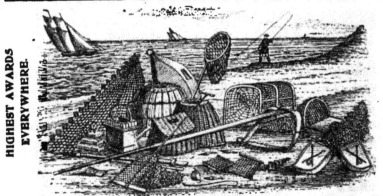

BOOKS PUBLISHED BY HORACE COX.

A POCKET BOOK FOR ANGLERS AND RAMBLERS.

In crown 12mo., buckram, 2s. 6d. ; paper covers, 1s. 6d.

A MIXED BAG.

A MEDLEY OF ANGLING STORIES AND SKETCHES.

By "RED SPINNER,"

Author of "Near and Far," "By Stream and Sea," "Travel and Trout,"
"Waterside Sketches," "Notable Shipwrecks," "The Thames from Oxford to
the Pool," &c.

NEW AND CHEAP EDITION.

With numerous Illustrations, price 3s. 6d. net, by post 3s. 10d.

PRACTICAL LETTERS TO SEA FISHERS.

By JOHN BICKERDYKE,

Author of "Angling in Salt Water," "Sea Fishing" (Badminton Library), "The
Book of the All-Round Angler," "Days of my Life on Waters Fresh and Salt,"
&c., &c.

*Drawings of Sea Fishes by the late Dr. DAY, and Tackle by W. S. TOMKIN. The
Figure Subjects from Photographs by the Author.*

CONTENTS.

BOOK I. WEATHER, TIDES, BOATS; AND LIFE SAVING AT SEA. I.—Introduction. II.—Favourable Conditions. III.—Boat Sailing. IV.—Overboard.

BOOK II. TACKLE AND TACKLE MAKING. V.—Knots, Whippings, Hooks, &c. VI.—The Sea Rod. VII.—Reels and Reel Lines. VIII.—Hand Lines and Spreaders.

BOOK III. BAITS. IX.—Natural Baits and How to Find them. X.—Artificial Baits. XI.—Baits Cast with the Fly Rod. XII.—Advantages of Ground-Bait in Sea Fishing.

BOOK IV. THE BEST METHODS OF SEA FISHING. XIII.—Bottom Fishing from the Shore. XIV.—Mid-water and Surface Fishing from the Shore. XV.—Bottom Fishing from Boats. XVI.—Fishing with Drift Lines from a Moored Boat. XVII.—Fishing from a Boat in Motion. XVIII.—Fly Fishing in the Sea. XIX.—Deep Sea Fishing. XX.—Prawning and Shrimping.

BOOK V. THE SPORTSMAN'S SEA FISH. XXI.—Bass (*Labrax lupus*). XXII.—The Mullets. XXIII.—Sea Trout and Salmon. XXIV.—Pollack and Coal-Fish. XXV.—The Cod. XXVI.—Mackerel. XXVII.—Whiting, Whiting Pout, and Haddock. XXVIII.—Flat Fish. XXIX.—The Conger and Bream. XXX.—Sharks and Dog Fish. XXXI.—Some other Sea Fish. XXXII.—Ocean Fish.

BOOK VI. IMPROVEMENTS IN RODS, REELS, LEADS, &C. XXXIII.—Modern Improvements in Tackle Suitable for Sea Fishing.

London : Windsor House, Bream's Buildings, E.C.